D1561497

The Jesus Handbook

The Jesus Handbook

EDITED BY JENS SCHRÖTER
AND CHRISTINE JACOBI

Translated by Robert L. Brawley

WILLIAM B. EERDMANS PUBLISHING COMPANY
GRAND RAPIDS, MICHIGAN

Originally published in German by Mohr Siebeck GmbH & Co. KG Tübingen
under the title *Jesus Handbuch*, © 2017 Mohr Siebeck Tübingen

Wm. B. Eerdmans Publishing Co.
4035 Park East Court SE, Grand Rapids, Michigan 49546
www.eerdmans.com

© 2022 William B. Eerdmans Publishing Co.
Published 2022 by permission of Mohr Siebeck Tübingen

28 27 26 25 24 23 22   1 2 3 4 5 6 7

ISBN 978-0-8028-7692-8

Library of Congress Cataloging-in-Publication Data

Names: Schröter, Jens, 1961– editor. | Jacobi, Christine, 1979– editor. | Brawley,
    Robert L. (Robert Lawson), translator.
Title: The Jesus handbook / edited by Jens Schröter and Christine Jacobi ; trans-
    lated by Robert L. Brawley.
Other titles: Jesus Handbuch. English.
Description: Grand Rapids, Michigan : William B. Eerdmans Publishing Com-
    pany, [2022] | "Originally published in German by Mohr Siebeck GmbH & Co.
    KG Tübingen under the title Jesus Handbuch, © 2017 Mohr Siebeck Tübingen."
    | Includes bibliographical references and index. | Summary: "An international
    collection of scholarship on Jesus of Nazareth, his world, the outcomes of his
    life, and the quest to locate him in historical context"—Provided by publisher.
Identifiers: LCCN 2022011169 | ISBN 9780802876928
Subjects: LCSH: Jesus Christ—Teachings. | Jesus Christ—Person and offices. |
    Jesus Christ—History of doctrines. | BISAC: RELIGION / Biblical Studies /
    New Testament / Jesus, the Gospels & Acts | RELIGION / Biblical Reference /
    Dictionaries & Encyclopedias
Classification: LCC BS2415 .J48913 2022 | DDC 232.9/54—dc23/eng/20220615
LC record available at https://lccn.loc.gov/2022011169

Contents

Foreword

The Jesus Handbook is perhaps the best guide we now have to the current state of the academic quest for the historical Jesus. It dispels the thought, which one occasionally encounters, that the field has grown stale, that all the feasible options are already on the table, and that one's time is better spent elsewhere. The following chapters—which are of almost consistently high quality—demonstrate that scholarly work on Jesus continues to make authentic progress.

While it may at times seem to some as though the field moves in circles, that is misperception: the apparent circles are rather spirals, and they move us in new directions. To cite an illustration: Ruben Zimmermann's chapter on Jesus's parables (D.IV.3.3) reveals the extent to which the old standards—the works of C. H. Dodd, Joachim Jeremias, and John Dominic Crossan—have given way to new, profitable discussions of narratological methods of interpretation, of parabolic forms remembered by the Gospel of John, and of the continuity (or lack of continuity) between Jewish parables and parables in the Jesus tradition.

To offer another illustration: several chapters engage the current controversy over the utility of the so-called criteria of authenticity and also discuss the ongoing disputes about the closely associated topic of memory (note, for instance, the contributions of Jens Schröter and Chris Keith in B.XI and B.IX, respectively). It is to my mind a plus that some—not all—contributors to this handbook manage, while largely eschewing the criteria, to put to good use ideas about social memory as they seek to recover the past.

In addition to exhibiting ways in which the field has advanced in recent years, *The Jesus Handbook* also serves to bring to an English-speaking audience the work of front-rank scholars whose books and articles have heretofore appeared exclusively or almost exclusively in another language. Christine Jacobi, for example, has written a significant German monograph on the vexed problem of the relationship between Paul and the historical Jesus: *Jesusüberlieferung bei Paulus? Analogien zwischen den echten Paulusbriefen und den synoptischen Evangelien* (BZNW 213 [Berlin: de Gruyter, 2015]). The long-standing puzzle, which is at the center of reconstructions of early Christian theology, has in large measure involved evaluating parallels between the authentic Paulines and passages in the Synoptic Gospels. Jacobi's contribution tackles this old issue with recent work on memory in mind, and this enables her to make a number of fresh observations and proposals. For those who cannot read German, her entry in the present volume, on the New Testament letters as a source for Jesus (C.II.1.3), offers a glimpse of her approach. Similarly, while Knut Backhaus's important, provocative book on John the Baptist and his followers—*Die "Jünger-kreise" des Täufers Johannes: Eine Studie zu den religionsgeschichtlichen Ursprüngen des Christentums*, PaThSt 19 [Paderborn: F. Schöningh, 1991])—has not found an English translator, the present volume (D.III.1.1) makes some of his ideas available beyond the German-speaking sphere.

A further virtue of the present work is that its introductions and contributions to contemporary disputes and areas of interest do not blind its authors to the great importance and continuing influence of earlier work. Indeed, the conviction that we cannot understand where we are without understanding where we have been characterizes the whole. The entirety of section B contextualizes current work by putting it into a very large history. That history stretches from antiquity to the present and includes developments in philosophy and critical historiography in the eighteenth and nineteenth centuries (B.III and B.IV), David Friedrich Strauss's ideas about myth (B.V), the emergence of the two-document hypothesis (B.V), the writings of Johannes Weiss and Albert Schweitzer on Jesus and eschatology (B.VI), and the work of scholarly contrarians (such as Martin Kähler, Rudolf Bultmann, and Luke Timothy Johnson) who have issued serious reservations about the theological value of the quest (B.VII)—all subjects one can learn about in this handbook.

One is equally pleased by the attention paid to the reception of Jesus and the so-called history of his effects. Particularly helpful are the articles at the end of the book that explore visual representations of Jesus in the first five centuries (E.VII) and that trace the dialogue between the Sermon on the Mount and evolving Christian ethics (E.VIII).

Yet one more strength of *The Jesus Handbook* is that it does not peddle a single point of view. Its contributors represent not just several religious traditions but also have different ideas as to how to retrieve the historical Jesus and more than one idea about the identity of the man so retrieved. These pages do not hide the disparity that has marked and continues to mark the field; they do not pretend to display a unanimity that does not exist. They thus inhibit easy appeal to any alleged consensus. There is no agreement about the existence and nature of Q. There is no agreement about the nature of Jesus's eschatology. And there is no agreement about his self-conception. Perhaps there never will be.

This is not an indictment of the field, even if some have imagined otherwise. People disagreed about Jesus, we should recall, from the very beginning. Even those who knew him face-to-face came to diverse opinions. Was he a prophet like John the Baptist? Was he Elijah or Jeremiah come again? Was he the one to redeem Israel? Was he a confederate of Beelzebul? Such diversity should not surprise. It is rather to be expected, given the rule that every historical figure of any significance provokes a spectrum of appraisals, positive and negative. Jesus is not the exception.

In short, *The Jesus Handbook* is an up-to-date, expertly informed, and uniformly informative orientation to a fascinating and ever-growing field of discourse. We should be grateful to the translator for bringing it into English.

Dale C. Allison Jr.

Preface

The Jesus Handbook stands in a long tradition of interpretations of the way of life, activity, and fate of Jesus of Nazareth in the history of Christianity. It is based on the multiple ways that were developed in the history of Christianity to approach the person of Jesus as the center of Christian faith. Furthermore, the handbook presents the person of Jesus in his historical context on the basis of historical-critical theology in the current state of international research. Thereby, multiple perspectives, which do not lead to a uniform image of Jesus, are considered. Indeed, distinctive points of view and varying accents are to be recognized. In this respect, *The Jesus Handbook* corresponds with the conception and implementation of the hermeneutical conclusion that there is no one "correct" or "true" approach to Jesus, but various interpretations of his person and meaning can stand alongside each other.

The handbook is divided into five main parts. A basic introduction (part A) is followed by four sections, the middle parts of which (parts C and D) present the historical material, which is foundational for today's preoccupation with Jesus, and highlight the related way of life and activity of Jesus from distinct points of view. These sections are framed by an account of the history of research on Jesus (part B) and aspects of the early history of reception of Jesus (part E). As this structure indicates, in this handbook the historical-critical approach to Jesus is set in a hermeneutical horizon. This considers the long preoccupation with Jesus in the history of Christianity that has taken place under distinctive epistemological presuppositions, and permits identifying at least to some extent that the effects that developed from his person have to be included in such a consideration. Not least of all, in this way older paradigms of research are set in relationship with current approaches that take into consideration the history of reception, which increased attention in recent scholarship.

This concept is presented in the introduction as well as in the introductory overviews to the individual sections with a view toward their particular focus. These introductions can be read, therefore, as a "common thread" running through the book; they facilitate the reading of the handbook under an overarching hermeneutical perspective.

Needless to say, the *Jesus Handbook* can and should also adduce information about individual issues and contents of Jesus research, about historical backgrounds, archaeological details, and much more. It is, therefore, so designed that all individual contributions can be read separately in order to take cognizance of prevailing themes and the current state of research. In this way the *Jesus Handbook* offers insight into the contemporary developments and findings of Jesus research and likewise organizes them in a paradigm that considers historiographical and hermeneutical insights.

We would like to express our gratitude and great appreciation to Lena Nogossek for her hard work on the handbook. She was involved in the planning of the concept from the very beginning, she did an excellent job in preparing the manuscript, and she made its completion a matter of her heart. Without her tireless and engaged, relentless, and patient work on the manuscript all the way to the last details of the index, this book would never have come about. Therefore, she is due our first, grand, and heartfelt thanks.

From the very beginning, it was the purpose to produce a book that presents the debate about Jesus on the current state of international research. Therefore, we want to thank our colleagues who have contributed to this handbook. All of them got involved in the concept with their specific knowledge and competence. Their collaboration made it possible for an idea to become a book.

Further, gratitude is extended to the collaborators in Berlin who have served to bring this handbook to fruition. Collaborators at the professorial chair for Exegesis and Theology of the New Testament and New Testament Apocrypha copyedited the manuscript multiple times, tracked down inconsistencies, and helped resolve problems of detail, which surface in the development of such a complex undertaking. To be mentioned are Konrad Schwarz, Clarissa Paul, Florian Lengle, and Katharina Simunovic.

Albrecht Beutel, editor of the Handbuch Series at Mohr Siebeck, and Henning Ziebritzki, business manager of the press, agreed after a short consideration with the idea of a Jesus handbook, which for them at first glance seemed to be something odd (does a "Jesus handbook" belong in a series of "theological handbooks"?), and then supported the undertaking wholeheartedly—not least of all Albrecht Beutel, with his own important contribution to the handbook, and Henning Ziebritzki, in his professional, friendly, and judicious way, which we have experienced from him for a long time and which shapes the press that he has managed. In the production department of this press, Ilse König supervised the handbook. She is also to be gratefully thanked for her expeditious and reliable cooperation.

Christine Jacobi and Jens Schröter
Berlin, May 2017

Translator's Preface

To speak of a specific translator disguises the multifaceted contributors to the production of this English version of *Jesus Handbuch*. Each of the forty-eight authors corrected and revised an original draft of her or his article(s). Jens Schröter exercised constant oversight. In addition, other bilingual specialists were consulted. Among them, two should be singled out. Dr. Christine Schnusenberg of Chicago made significant contributions to the English version of Martin Ohst's article "The Earthly Jesus in the Piety and Theology of Antiquity, the Middle Ages, and the Reformation." She also helped in the negotiation of rough spots here and there. Hermut Löhr's assistant Carla Weitensteiner worked on the revision of his two articles, "Jesus's Communal Meals" and "Jesus's Last Supper." Trevor Thompson of Eerdmans Publishing Company invited me to undertake this project and gave solid support along the way. Tom Raabe gave careful attention to the accuracy and style of the entire manuscript. I express my gratitude for all who joined in this mutual task.

As in all compositions, whether it is my original work or a translation, the work is always a process of discovery. Even though I published two articles on the historical Jesus in the 1990s, the state of research in the twenty-first century reflected in the articles of this handbook made my daily task of translation over the past two years and seven months a venture in new discoveries. I am persuaded that such new discoveries await many readers in the English-speaking world who use this translation.

Robert L. Brawley

Abbreviations

AAWGPH	Abhandlungen der Akademie der Wissenchaften in Göttingen, Philologisch-Historische Klasse
ABD	*Anchor Bible Dictionary* (ed. Freedman)
ABRL	Anchor Bible Reference Library
ADPV	Abhandlungen des Deutschen Palästina-Vereins
AGJU	Arbeiten zur Geschichte des antiken Judentums und des Urchristentums
AJEC	Ancient Judaism and Early Christianity
AKThG	Arbeiten zur Kirchen- und Theologiegeschichte
AnBib	Analecta Biblica
ANRW	*Aufstieg und Niedergang der römischen Welt*
ASNU	Acta Seminarii Neotestamentici Upsaliensis
ATANT	Abhandlungen zur Theologie des Alten und Neuen Testaments
BAR	*Biblical Archaeology Review*
BBB	Bonner biblische Beiträge
BE	Biblische Enzyklopädie
BETL	Bibliotheca Ephemeridum Theologicarum Lovaniensium
BEvT	Beiträge zur evangelischen Theologie
BFCT	Beiträge zur Förderung christlicher Theologie
BG	Berlin Gnostic Papyrus
BGBE	Beiträge zur Geschichte der biblischen Exegese
BHT	Beiträge zur historischen Theologie
Bib	*Biblica*
BibInt	*Biblical Interpretation*
BibInt	Biblical Interpretation Series
BK	*Bibel und Kirche*
BR	*Biblical Research*
BThS	Biblisch-theologische Studien
BTSP	Biblischtheologische Schwerpunkte
BTZ	*Berliner Theologische Zeitschrift*

BU	Biblische Untersuchungen
BWA(N)T	Beiträge zur Wissenschaft vom Alten (und Neuen) Testament
BZ	*Biblische Zeitschrift*
BzA	Beiträge zur Altertumskunde
BZNW	Beihefte zur Zeitschrift für die neutestamentliche Wissenschaft
CBQ	*Catholic Biblical Quarterly*
CIIP	Corpus Inscriptionum Iudaeae et Palaestinae
ConBNT	Coniectanea Biblica: New Testament Series
CP	*Classical Philology*
CRINT	Compendium Rerum Iudaicarum ad Novum Testamentum
DiKi	Dialog der Kirchen
DNP	*Der neue Pauly: Enzyklopädie der Antike* (ed. Cancik and Schneider)
DSD	*Dead Sea Discoveries*
EBR	*Encyclopedia of the Bible and Its Reception* (ed. Klauck et al.)
ECC	Eerdmans Critical Commentary
EHS	Europäische Hochschulschriften
EKKNT	Evangelisch-katholischer Kommentar zum Neuen Testament
EPRO	Etudes préliminaires aux religions orientales dans l'empire romain
EThSt	Erfurter theologische Studien
ETL	*Ephemerides Theologicae Lovanienses*
EuA	*Erbe und Auftrag*
EvQ	*Evangelical Quarterly*
EvT	*Evangelische Theologie*
ExpTim	*Expository Times*
FAT	Forschungen zum Alten Testament
FB	Forschung zur Bibel
FGLP	Forschungen zur Geschichte und Lehre des Protestantismus
FRLANT	Forschungen zur Religion und Literatur des Alten und Neuen Testaments
FTS	Frankfurter Theologische Studien
GCS	Die griechischen christlichen Schriftsteller der ersten [drei] Jahrhunderte
GNS	Good News Studies
GNT	Grundrisse zum Neuen Testament
GTA	Göttinger theologischer Arbeiten
HBO	Hallesche Beiträge zur Orientwissenschaft
HBS	Herders biblische Studien
Historia	*Historia: Zeitschrift für alte Geschichte*
HNT	Handbuch zum Neuen Testament
HThKNT	Herders Theologischer Kommentar zum Neuen Testament

HThKNTSup	Supplements to Herders Theologischer Kommentar zum Neuen Testament
HTR	*Harvard Theological Review*
HTS	*Harvard Theological Studies*
HUT	Hermeneutische Untersuchungen zur Theologie
IEJ	*Israel Exploration Journal*
IG	*Inscriptiones Graecae. Editio Minor*
IKaZ	*Internationale katholische Zeitschrift*
Int	*Interpretation*
IRT	Issues in Religion and Theology
ISACR	Interdisciplinary Studies in Ancient Culture and Religion
JBL	*Journal of Biblical Literature*
JBQ	*Jewish Bible Quarterly*
JBT	Jahrbuch für biblische Theologie
JECS	*Journal of Early Christian Studies*
JJS	*Journal of Jewish Studies*
JQR	*Jewish Quarterly Review*
JR	*Journal of Religion*
JSHJ	*Journal for the Study of the Historical Jesus*
JSJ	*Journal for the Study of Judaism in the Persian, Hellenistic, and Roman Periods*
JSJS	Supplements to the Journal for the Study of Judaism
JSNT	*Journal for the Study of the New Testament*
JSNTSup	Journal for the Study of the New Testament Supplement Series
JSOTSup	Journal for the Study of the Old Testament Supplement Series
JSS	*Journal of Semitic Studies*
JTS	*Journal of Theological Studies*
JudChr	Judaica et Christiana
KAV	Kommentar zu den Apostolischen Vätern
KBANT	Kommentare und Beiträge zum Alten und Neuen Testament
KEK	Kritisch-exegetischer Kommentar über das Neue Testament (Meyer-Kommentar)
KIG	Die Kirche in ihrer Geschichte
KStTh	Kohlhammer Studienbücher Theologie
LASBF	*Liber Annuus Studii Biblici Franciscani*
LASR	Luthers Schriftprinzip in seiner Bedeutung für die Ökumene
LD	Lectio Divina
LNTS	Library of New Testament Studies
MJT	Marburger Jahrbuch Theologie
MMNTS	McMaster New Testament Studies

MThA	Münsteraner theologische Abhandlungen
MThSt	Marburger theologische Studien
MTZ	*Münchener theologische Zeitschrift*
NEchtB	Neue Echter Bibel
Neot	*Neotestamentica*
NHC	Nag Hammadi codices
NHMS	Nag Hammadi and Manichaean Studies
NIGTC	New International Greek Testament Commentary
NovT	*Novum Testamentum*
NovTSup	Supplements to Novum Testamentum
NTAbh	Neutestamentliche Abhandlungen
NTD	Das Neue Testament Deutsch
NTOA	Novum Testamentum et Orbis Antiquus
NTS	*New Testament Studies*
NTTS	New Testament Tools and Studies
ÖBS	Österreichische biblische Studien
OCA	*Orientalia Christiana Analecta*
OECT	Oxford Early Christian Texts
ORA	Orientalische Religionen in der Antike
OTS	Old Testament Studies
PaThSt	Paderborn theologische Studien
PG	Patrologia Graeca
PGM	*Papyri Graecae Magicae*
P. Oxy.	Papyrus Oxyrhynchus
P. Ryl.	Papyrus Rylands
PTHe	Praktische Theologie heute
QD	Quaestiones Disputatae
RAC	*Reallexikon für Antike und Christentum* (ed. Klauser et al.)
RB	*Revue biblique*
RGG	*Religion in Geschichte und Gegenwart*
RHR	*Revue de l'histoire des religions*
RNT	Regensburger Neues Testament
SANT	Studien zum Alten und Neuen Testament
SBAB	Stuttgarter biblische Aufsatzbände
SBB	Stuttgarter biblische Beiträge
SBEC	Studies in the Bible and Early Christianity
SBL	Society of Biblical Literature
SBLEJL	Society of Biblical Literature Early Judaism and Its Literature
SBLMS	Society of Biblical Literature Monograph Series
SBLSP	*Society of Biblical Literature Seminar Papers*

SBLSS	Society of Biblical Literature Symposium Series
SBS	Stuttgarter Bibelstudien
SBT	Studies in Biblical Theology
SBTS	Sources for Biblical and Theological Study
SemeiaSt	Semeia Studies
SESJ	Suomen Eksegeettisen Seuran Julkaisuja
SGTK	Studien zur Geschichte des Mönchtums
SHT	Studies in Historical Theology
SIJD	Schriften des Institutum Judaicum Delitzschianum
SJ	Studia Judaica
SJLA	Studies in Judaism in Late Antiquity
SMHR	Spätmittelalter, Humanismus, Reformation
SNT	Studien zum Neuen Testament
SNTSMS	Society for New Testament Studies Monograph Series
SNTSU	Studien zum Neuen Testament und seiner Umwelt
SPA	Studien der Patristischen Arbeitsgemeinschaft
SpKA	Spalding Kritische Ausgabe
STAC	Studien und Texte zu Antike und Christentum
STDJ	Studies on the Texts of the Desert of Judah
StSam	Studia Samaritana
STW	Suhrkamp Taschenbuch Wissenschaft
SUNT	Studien zur Umwelt des Neuen Testaments
SuR	Spätmittelalter und Reformation
SVigChr	Supplements to Vigiliae Christianae
TANZ	Texte und Arbeiten zum neutestamentlichen Zeitalter
TB	Theologische Bücherei: Neudrucke und Berichte aus dem 20. Jahrhundert
TBei	*Theologische Beiträge*
TdT	Themen der Theologie
TEH	Theologische Existenz heute
ThBer	*Theologische Berichte*
THKNT	Theologischer Handkommentar zum Neuen Testament
TQ	*Theologische Quartalschrift*
TRE	*Theologische Realenzyklopädie* (ed. Krause and Müller)
TRu	*Theologische Rundschau*
TSAJ	Texte und Studien zum antiken Judentum
TSK	*Theologische Studien und Kritiken*
TThSt	Trierer theologische Studien
TTZ	*Trierer theologische Zeitschrift*
TU	Texte und Untersuchungen

TynBul	*Tyndale Bulletin*
UNT	Untersuchungen zum Neuen Testament
UTB	Uni Taschenbücher
VF	*Verkündigung und Forschung*
VT	*Vetus Testamentum*
WA	Weimarer Ausgabe (Luther's works)
WD	*Wort und Dienst*
WdF	Wege der Forschung
WMANT	Wissenschaftliche Monographien zum Alten und Neuen Testament
WUNT	Wissenschaftliche Untersuchungen zum Neuen Testament
ZAW	*Zeitschrift für die alttestamentliche Wissenschaft*
ZDMG	*Zeitschrift der deutschen morgenländischen Gesellschaft*
ZDT	*Zeitschrift für dialektische Theologie*
ZNT	*Zeitschrift für Neues Testament*
ZNW	*Zeitschrift für die neutestamentliche Wissenschaft und die Kunde der älteren Kirche*
ZPE	*Zeitschrift für Papyrologie und Epigraphik*
ZTK	*Zeitschrift für Theologie und Kirche*

A. Introduction

I. About This Handbook

In the series of handbooks of important figures in the history of Christianity, *The Jesus Handbook* has a special place. This is primarily because Jesus of Nazareth cannot be viewed in the history of Christianity in the same way as Paul, Augustine, Martin Luther, Karl Barth, or other important figures to whom handbooks are dedicated. With Jesus of Nazareth, the focus of this handbook is on the person who is in the center of Christian faith and whose work and fate in Christian theology and piety have been interpreted in many and diverse ways from the very beginning. The origin of Christian faith is the confession that Jesus is the Christ, the Lord, and the Son of God. This confession, which is based on the conviction that Jesus was raised from the dead and exalted to God, at the same time forms the basis for interpretations of his earthly ministry and his fate. Christian testimonies depict Jesus's way of life accordingly under the presupposition that it, including his suffering and death, was determined by God and was destined to be pursued precisely in this way. Another difference from other handbooks is that, because Jesus did not leave behind any literary attestations, reconstructions of his ministry and fate are exclusively based on testimonies *about* him.

For *The Jesus Handbook*, this means that although its structure does not deviate fundamentally from those of the other handbooks in this series, it has its own characteristics. A review of the history of research on Jesus (part B) is followed by an overview of the historical material (part C), whereas the next part is devoted to the contents of Jesus's life and ministry (part D). The final part deals with early traces of the reception of Jesus's work (part E). The usual division of the handbooks, that is, "Orientation," "Person," "Work and Activity," has accordingly been modified.

Thus, a separate section is devoted to the hermeneutical and methodological implications of the quest for the life, activity, and meaning of Jesus Christ (part B). In this the historiographical character of the handbook is articulated, in which the hermeneutical premises of Jesus research will be pointed out. For this

1

purpose, it is necessary to take into consideration the epistemological, hermeneutical, and intellectual constellations within which this question was dealt with in different epochs. The first part of the handbook is concerned accordingly with the history of research on Jesus from perceptions of his person in antiquity up until present-day discussions about "the remembered Jesus." Thereby, it shall be demonstrated that contemporary Jesus research is based on the methodological presuppositions of critical historiography, which are at the same time the basis for the relationship of history and faith in the modern era.

The historical material is presented in the next part (C). It will become clear that the interpretation of the remains of the past that are still accessible in the present is never a "neutral" endeavor. Instead, the historical material relevant for a reconstruction of the activity and fate of Jesus has been and always will be apprehended and interpreted under specific conditions. In the respective part of the handbook, the diverse sources for current Jesus research will be presented.

Based on this, part D deals with facets of the "biography" of Jesus insofar as they can be ascertained from the sources. Those stages of his biography about which hardly any traditions or only legendary traditions exist—such as his birth and the time before his public activity—can be dealt with only indirectly by illuminating the relevant historical context for the time and region of Jesus. With regard to Jesus's activity in Galilee and the surrounding regions as well as in Jerusalem and nearby places—including his trial and crucifixion—the character of early Christian texts that has been mentioned above must be taken into consideration.

Finally, part E deals with early traces of the impact and reception of Jesus. It will become clear that already in earliest Christianity basic interpretations of his person were formulated on the basis of Easter faith with the help of specific designations (the so-called christological titles) and confessions. Furthermore, effects of Jesus on the formation of early Christian communities will be highlighted. Finally, interpretations in early extracanonical texts as well as in visual representations will be dealt with.

According to the character of a handbook as the work of numerous authors, no unified portrait of Jesus emerges. Rather, depending on the assessment of the possibility of drawing conclusions about Jesus's activity from the available material, different points of view will be emphasized. On the one hand, this reflects the wide range of current Jesus research; on the other hand, it becomes clear that the interpretation of historical material provides a spectrum of *possible* interpretations. Against this background, *The Jesus Handbook* wants to provide interpretations of the sources that are based on historical-critical research, and at the same time is aware of the provisional character and limits of historical interpretations.

The authors who have contributed to the handbook are, therefore, committed to the methodological principles of historical-critical Jesus research independently from their religious and confessional affiliation. Contributors include Jewish and Christian authors; among the latter are colleagues with a Roman Catholic as well as a Protestant background. This highlights that historical-critical Jesus research is not tied to religious or confessional requirements but is characterized by common methodological and hermeneutical premises.

The view regarding early Christian sources and the person of Jesus that is presupposed throughout the handbook differs from approaches that do not share the presuppositions of critical historiography—or share them only with reservation—and instead confer on biblical texts a special status as inspired Scripture. More recently, such a view has been prominently presented in the trilogy on Jesus of Nazareth by Joseph Ratzinger. Ratzinger recognizes that the historical-critical method is important for the quest of Jesus but sees its limits in that it cannot infer the meaning of the biblical texts for today. In principle, one can agree with this assessment. Indeed, it cannot be regarded as the task of historical-critical interpretation to shed light on the relevance of historical material for the present. However, Ratzinger relativizes the historical-critical method by "canonical exegesis," the doctrine of the fourfold sense of Scripture and the inspiration of Scripture. Thereby he discards the critical potential of historical-critical interpretation of the Bible. This procedure differs fundamentally from one that interprets the biblical text in common with all other historical material in accordance with historical criticism and establishes its significance for the present by means of hermeneutical reflections and in light of its reception history. The latter approach has to be reflected with regard to its epistemological and hermeneutical premises in order to highlight its contours. This should become somewhat clearer in the following sections.

II. The Earthly Jesus and the Christ of Confession: Contours of the Jesus Quest

The Jesus quest has been expressed since its beginnings as a contrast between two perspectives that can already be found in the New Testament and have impacted the quest of Jesus in variable constellations until today. To put it somewhat simply, the question is whether the person of Jesus and his earthly activity are interpreted from the perspective of Christian faith or not. The distinction between the two is not to be equated with the contrast between the earthly Jesus and the Christ of faith, since the earthly Jesus has a constitutive meaning for the Christ of faith. The key point is instead whether the confession that Jesus is the Christ and Son of God and the resulting dynamic of divine and human nature of Jesus Christ are taken into account or whether the meaning of Jesus is limited to his earthly activity.

In early Christian sources, the conviction that Jesus participates in the divine realm in the same way as in earthly reality is expressed in various ways. Some texts emphasize the importance of Jesus Christ as the Son of God who was sent by God into the world, crucified, raised, and exalted to the right hand of God. Others pay more attention to his earthly activity. The Gospels portray his appearance in Galilee and surrounding regions as well as events in Jerusalem and its environs that finally led to his arrest and crucifixion. Accordingly, the question about the relationship between Jesus's earthly activity and his divine origin is posed by early Christian writings with all clarity—and answered in a certain way. First and above all, what was provocative about this was the assertion that in spite of and precisely in view of his disgraceful death on the cross, he appeared on earth with divine authority, and in his activity God's authority could be recognized. The irritation triggered by this conviction is reflected, for example, in the question about who Jesus really was, since he performed with power hitherto unknown (cf. Mark 1:27). It also led to misunderstandings about his—from a Christian viewpoint—"true," namely, "divine," origin, for example, when his Galilean origin is referred to as something that would contradict the claim that he is the Messiah (John 7:41–42). Early Christian writings also report that Jesus's mighty deeds were attributed by his opponents to "Beelzebul," the ruler of the demons (Mark 3:22), and his death on the cross was regarded as proof that he could not be of divine origin (Justin, *Dial.* 32.1; 89.2; Origen, *Cels.* 1.54; 2.31). In view of the ambiguity of the activity of the earthly Jesus, early Christian texts accentuate that a special cognition process is necessary to recognize the risen and exalted Christ in the earthly Jesus, and vice versa. The encounter of the risen Christ with the disciples from Emmaus (Luke 24:13–35) traces the way from a pre-Easter view of Jesus to a view determined by faith in the risen and exalted one. The Gospel of John repeatedly emphasizes that the way of the earthly Jesus can be properly understood only from a post-Easter perspective (John 2:22; 12:16; 14:25–26; 20:9).

The confession of Jesus Christ—who participates at the same time in the divine and earthly reality; who is God's preexistent Son and the "reflection" of God, the divine "logos" or the "image" of God (Heb. 1:2–3; John 1:1–2; Col. 1:15); who at the same time died for the sins of humanity; who was in the likeness of God and humbled himself to the point of death (Phil. 2:6–8)—is therefore controversial from the time of its inception. In the changing historical, cultural, and epistemological premises, it is, therefore, again and again in need of justification.

The two perspectives on Jesus—with or without Christian confession—have not only been set over against one another in modern times but can also be found in interpretations of the activity of Jesus since their beginnings. In early Christianity the perception of Jesus as a mere human being was brought forward primarily by critics of Christianity, whereas the Christian sources themselves provide a guide for understanding the relationship between the earthly Jesus and the risen Christ; that is, they see in him the one who as an earthly human being came on the scene on behalf of and in the authority of God. This constellation changed in later times.

III. The Jesus Quest in the Age of Critical Historiography

In modern times the relationship of the divine and human nature of Jesus Christ has been questioned under the influence of Enlightenment philosophy and critical historiography. The critique was now formulated by Christian scholars themselves, who, under condition of an independent, critical mind-set, subjected the Christian confession to the standards of critical reason. Consequently, the authors of the Gospels were considered "merely human historians" (Gotthold Ephraim Lessing). The confession of Jesus as the risen redeemer who was exalted to God was regarded as irreconcilable with his earthly activity and ethical teaching, by which he wanted to call people to repent (Hermann Samuel Reimarus). As a consequence, there arose the quest of the "historical Jesus," who had to be distinguished from the "Christ of faith" or the "kerygmatic Christ." At times, the historical Jesus was even polemically contrasted with the kerygmatic Christ. This juxtaposition has been formative for Jesus research since then. It occurs again and again in varying configurations, whereby the emphasis can be placed on either the historical findings or the Christian confession. Jesus research of the modern era can be described as the attempt to relate the earthly "historical" dimension of Jesus's activity under the epistemological presuppositions of critical theology to the confession of him as the earthly representative of God. The Christian confession can be considered as a "myth" imprinted on the historical material (David Friedrich Strauss), so that it would be possible to know something about the earthly Jesus only by disregarding this confession (a position often taken since Reimarus). This confession, however, can also be considered as the only reasonable access to Jesus, since the meaning of the "historic biblical Christ" (Martin Kähler) can only be grasped through the Christian confession, not without it or in contrast to it. Current Jesus research stands in this tension between historical discovery and its interpretation on the basis of the Christian confession or without it.

On this basis, critical historiography that arose in the nineteenth century led to an intensive pursuit of Jesus's activity as a Jewish Galilean. Alongside the methodological presupposition of the critical analysis of historical material, the solution to the "Synoptic problem" widely (although not unanimously) accepted today became a basic tool in historical-critical Jesus research. According to this solution, Mark's Gospel is the oldest one, and Matthew and Luke supposedly composed their gospels independently of each other by using, in addition to Mark, a second source, often called the "sayings source" or "sayings gospel" (or simply "Q" for German *Quelle*) because it supposedly contains mainly sayings and parables of Jesus. The Gospel of John, by contrast, was regarded as largely irrelevant for the quest of the historical Jesus. This point of view has stood the test, with certain clarifications and modifications, up until present research on Jesus. It is also often presumed in the portrayals of Jesus in the "third quest for the historical Jesus." Another characteristic of current Jesus research is that the material basis was significantly expanded by including Christian and non-Christian texts besides the New Testament Gospels as well as nonliterary evidence, for example, archaeological and numismatic findings. The historiographical character of Jesus research thereby made it necessary to reflect on the epistemological and hermeneutical presuppositions of historical-critical reconstructions of Jesus. This aspect has increasingly come into view in recent years. For this, the designations "remembered Jesus" and "memory of Jesus" have been coined. They are employed in Jesus research (and beyond) in different ways, which will be explained in more detail later in this handbook. The aim of this introduction, however, is to expound the significance of this approach for Jesus research.

IV. The "Remembered Jesus"—on the Relevance of a Paradigm of Current Jesus Research

While the aim of critical theology was to confront the Christian confession with critical reason or the historical-critical analysis of the sources, the concept of "memory" draws attention to the fact that critical reason and critical historiography themselves are based on epistemological premises, which are committed to Enlightenment philosophy and the access to the past based on them.

With the concept of "memory of Jesus," historiographical insights are taken up, according to which history originates by means of selective, interpretive appropriation of the past. The interpretation of the historical material, therefore, always has a provisional, revisable character. In contrast to a historicist understanding of history as series of past events, the interpretive appropriation of the historical material from the perspective of the actual present is emphasized. This facet of the consideration of history is directly connected to the development of critical historiography in the eighteenth and nineteenth centuries. For instance, it can be detected in Friedrich Schiller's inaugural lecture of 1789 entitled "Was heißt und zu welchem Ende studiert man Universalgeschichte?" ("What Does

Universal History Mean and to What End Do We Study It?"). Schiller emphasizes that while the "philosophical mind" is able to create a totality of world history from the fragments of tradition, the "common learning" only serves to "satisfy its pedantic thirst for fame" and is not in any position for creating larger coherencies. In his lectures on the task of historical work, which he gave between 1857 and 1882–1883 in Jena and Berlin, Johann Gustav Droysen declared the creation of historical correlations from historical material as the task of the historian. The reflection on the correspondence of critical evaluation of historical material and the interpretation of it by which the historian creates a historical narrative as representation of the past has thus been an indispensable part of historical-critical historiography since its foundation in the eighteenth and nineteenth centuries. The historical-critical analysis does not look for the "real historical fact" but instead presents the material from which the historian creates a picture of the past from his or her point of view (Droysen).

In recent times these methodological considerations have been taken up again. It has been emphasized that the remains of the past have a "veto power" to the extent that they permit only certain interpretations (Reinhart Koselleck), and as dead material (papyrus, stone, coins, etc.) they become "living sources" only by means of the interpretive, creative activity of the historian (Johannes Fried). We can conclude from these insights that history is not simply identical to the past but arises by means of the interpretive appropriation of the historical material from the perspective of the actual present.

The concept of memory, based on historical methodology as just outlined, does not refer to individual processes of memory, conceived of in physiological thought, but to "collective memory," through which persons and events of the past are integrated into the history and thereby become meaningful for the actual present. "Memory" understood in this way points to the fact that the past is always explored with a particular agenda and is made productive for the interpretation of one's own present. Thereby, unimportant things can be forgotten, while what is significant and constitutive for the self-perception of a community becomes a formative tradition that is recorded in texts, represented in rituals, and integrated into history in various forms of "memorials." Examples of this can be found in the history of Israel as well as in other ancient and modern societies. The memory of Jesus—recorded in narratives, represented in the performance of Christian rituals such as the Eucharist, brought to view in visual portrayals—can be conceived of from this perspective as well.

The approach characterized by the concept of memory is thus a historiographic-hermeneutical intensification of historical-critical Jesus research. It presupposes the historical-critical evaluation of the sources and is aware that it is bound to the traces of the past. Moreover, it shows that representation of Jesus takes place likewise in responsibility toward the past and the present and is based on the foundational tradition of early Christianity. With regard to the preoccupation with Jesus, this means that historical-critical portraits of him based on the selection and interpretation of the historical material must for their part be reflected on historically and hermeneutically.

This glance at these developments shows that Jesus research is closely related to the respective constellations of theology and history of thought, and has itself a significant influence on them. *The Jesus Handbook* stands in this complex history of the preoccupation with Jesus of Nazareth. It reflects the history of reception of the person of Jesus in various phases of the history of Christianity and is concerned with the facets of his activity and fate, as they can be ascertained from the sources that have been preserved. In particular, the handbook perceives of itself in the context of historical-critical research as it has evolved since the eighteenth century, first in Europe and then also in North America. The perspectives on the person of Jesus developed here exhibit a multifaceted spectrum. Nevertheless, they can be subsumed under a common paradigm. The basic characteristic of this is to interpret the historical testimonies about Jesus by means of historical criticism and to offer the results to scholarly discourse. Consequently, Jesus research characterized in this way with respect to its hermeneutical and methodological premises is committed to critical historiography that for its part received essential impulses from biblical studies. The specific challenge of Jesus research thereby is to make comprehensible the relationship between the "historical Jesus" (that is, portrayals of the activity and fate of Jesus on the basis of historical-critical evaluation of sources) and the confession of Jesus Christ, the Son of God and exalted Lord.

V. Historical Material as a Foundation for the Reconstruction of the Deeds and Fate of Jesus

Jesus himself left behind no written testimonies. His activity and fate therefore can be reconstructed only from sources *about* him. Alongside the early Christian sources, also to be counted are the few non-Christian witnesses that mention Jesus. Also considered are materials that shed light on Jesus's historical context. In addition to Jewish writings from the Hellenistic-Roman period, this includes archaeological, epigraphic, and numismatic evidence. The historical circumstances in a broader sense are the political, religious, and social constellations of the Mediterranean world of Hellenistic-Roman times, and in a narrower sense the history of Judaism of this period. In particular, the historical situation of Galilee as the area of Jesus's activity especially comes into focus, as does that of Judea and Jerusalem. Jesus's activity must be sketched into the historical constellations of these regions. In *The Jesus Handbook*, the historical testimonies of these regions are dealt with in particular to illuminate the historical context of Jesus's ministry. Thereby, current archaeological research as well as the political and religious situation of the regions are taken into account.

The Synoptic Gospels are regarded on good grounds as the most important testimonies for a reconstruction of the activity and fate of Jesus. Nevertheless, research on these writings has made it increasingly clear that they are primarily literary witnesses that portray Jesus's earthly way of life on the basis of Easter faith. Thus, in recounting the way of the earthly Jesus, they claim to present the abiding significance of the risen, living Christ. Their portrayals of Jesus are therefore oriented on the "vestiges of the past"—on historical information about places of Jesus's activity, characteristic features of his appearance, people in his environment, and so forth. This information was partly available to them in tradition shaped by (generic) forms that was adapted according to the linguistic style of the gospel writers and incorporated into their respective narratives. In this way, they have portrayed Jesus as the one who appeared on earth with the authority of God and established God's kingdom on earth. At the same time, they sketched his activities in the context of Judaism in the Hellenistic-Roman era—more precisely, in the Jewish world of Galilee and Judea in the first decades of the first century.

Insofar as the Gospels contain historical information and traditions, they can be considered as sources for the "historical Jesus." At the same time, they are part of the reception history of Jesus, since they presuppose the interpretation of his activity on the basis of Easter faith and present their narratives on this basis. This double character is particularly reflected in historical-critical research on the Synoptic Gospels. The view still held in the nineteenth century that these writings (especially the Gospel of Mark as the oldest gospel) could be interpreted as historical biographies of Jesus was replaced by the insight that they are theological narratives that reworked older traditions from a compositional and theological point of view and integrated them into their respective narratives. These distinct perspectives on the Synoptic Gospels and the assessment of their historicity and their use in historical-critical reconstructions of Jesus's activity will be discussed in detail in parts B and C of the handbook. The Synoptic Gospels will be surveyed—in common with further New Testament writings and other writings outside the New Testament—primarily with respect to what extent they can be adduced as sources for the life and work of Jesus.

This provides the foundation for the third and most extensive part of the handbook, which deals with individual contents of the life and work of Jesus from a historical-critical perspective. For this, as mentioned above, the political, social, and religious contours of the time and region of his appearance, archaeological knowledge about the places of his activity, aspects of his provenance and religious influence, characteristics of his public activity, his relationship with various social and religious groups in his environment, and finally his arrest and execution by the collaboration of Jewish authorities and Roman officials in Jerusalem need to be considered. In the contributions of this part, it becomes clear that the precise placement of Jesus in his political, social, cultural, and religious context plays a central role in current Jesus research. This is an essential distinction from the previous phase of research. Whereas the so-called new quest of the historical Jesus, which emerged around the middle of the twentieth century as a reaction to Rudolf Bultmann's dictum that the quest of the historical Jesus could not be answered historically and was theologically unproductive, was interested above all in the theological question about the relationship of Jesus's activity with the origin of Christian faith, the "third quest for the historical Jesus" that arose in the 1980s understands the quest of Jesus primarily as a historiographical task. The historical contextualization of the life and activity of Jesus therefore leads to a fruitful dialogue with adjacent disciplines and an extensive consideration of nonbiblical materials. This interdisciplinary orientation of current Jesus research is also reflected in *The Jesus Handbook*.

VI. Early Impacts of Jesus

A historical-critical reconstruction of the activity and fate of Jesus cannot disregard the early evidence of his impacts. These are first of all manifested in the confession of his resurrection and in narratives of appearances of the risen One that have led to the formation of early testimonies of faith. The wide range of receptions of Jesus's activity and fate was also reflected in extracanonical texts and early visual portrayals. Part E therefore pursues the traces of Jesus's activity into the fourth century. These include the formation of specific social structures; the emergence of convictions and beliefs that are based on the person of Jesus and his special relationship to God; the development of Christian ethics as well as the production of texts, among them also those that did not make it into the canon of the New Testament; and iconographic artifacts. Whereas the historical traces of Jesus's activity are sometimes abandoned and his meaning is expressed within new historical and epistemological paradigms, these witnesses can nevertheless be understood as the impacts and effects of his person. The distinction between a "historical reconstruction" and a subsequent "effect" of Jesus is thus supplemented by means of the perception of multiple processes of reception. These also place the earliest witnesses in the hermeneutical paradigm of a "reception history of Jesus" and highlight that each reconstruction of the historical person of Jesus is an interpretation of the historical material under the conditions of its time, and for its part stands in a history of interpretation of the oldest testimonies.

In the contributions of *The Jesus Handbook*, the respective themes on the current state of Jesus research are presented. Individual aspects can be combined to form an overall picture of Jesus—or multiple images of Jesus. However, these images of the historical person of Jesus are not to be equated with the reality behind the text, because they rest on a process of critical evaluation of sources that is due to the conditions and possibilities of cognition of our own time. Moreover, an overall picture that includes the individual aspects of Jesus's activity is based on "historical imagination" (Collingwood), since history is not found in the sources themselves but is instead developed by means of a narrative that is oriented on the sources, and represents the remains of the past in the present. These representations are determined by current knowledge of sources and epistemological interests and can be corrected or superseded—for example, by new discoveries of sources or by changing social and political constellations. Viewed in this way, there is no categorical difference between portrayals of Jesus in the Gospels, which express the meaning of Jesus in the horizon of their time and at the same time are tied to the traces of the past, and the approaches to Jesus that are presented in this handbook under premises of other epistemological presuppositions.

VII. Literature for Basic Orientation

Baumotte, Manfred, and Stephan Wehowsky, eds. 1984. *Die Frage nach dem historischen Jesus. Texte aus drei Jahrhunderten, Reader Theologie. Basiswissen—Querschnitte—Perspektiven*. Gütersloh. Relevant texts on historical-critical Jesus research from Reimarus to the 1980s, with brief introductions.

Bock, Darrell L., and Robert Webb, eds. 2009. *Key Events in the Life of the Historical Jesus: A Collaborative Exploration of Context and Coherence*. WUNT 247. Tübingen. Historical and sociological analyses of twelve "key events" in the life of the historical Jesus, from the baptism by John to the empty tomb and the appearances, with an introductory and an appraisal chapter.

Charlesworth, James H., ed. 2006. *Jesus and Archaeology*. Grand Rapids. Contributions on the significance of archaeology for Jesus research.

Chilton, Bruce, and Craig A. Evans, eds. 1994. *Studying the Historical Jesus: Evaluations of the State of Current Research*. NTTS 19. Leiden. Collection of contributions on diverse aspects of Jesus research and Jesus tradition from English-speaking scholarship.

Fiensy, David A., and James R. Strange, eds. 2014–2015. *Galilee in the Late Second Temple and Mishnaic Periods*. Vol. 1, *Life, Culture, and Society*. Vol. 2, *The Archaeological Record from Cities, Towns, and Villages*. Minneapolis. Presentation of current historical, sociological, economical, and archaeological research on Galilee by numerous experts in the respective fields.

Holmén, Tom, and Stanley E. Porter, eds. 2011. *Handbook for the Study of the Historical Jesus*. Vols. 1–4. Leiden and Boston.   Collection of contributions on methodological, historical, and reception history of Jesus research of varying quality.

Journal for the Study of the Historical Jesus. Leiden (since 2003). Second series since 2009.   Published three times annually with international contribution to Jesus research.

Jüdische Schriften aus hellenistisch-römischer Zeit. Gütersloh (since 1973).   German translations of relevant literature with introductions.

Kelber, Werner H., and Samuel Byrskog, eds. 2009. *Jesus in Memory: Traditions in Oral and Scribal Perspectives*. Waco, TX.   Contributions on the "memory approach" in Jesus research in connection to and discussion with Birger Gerhardsson, Helmut Ristow, and Karl Matthiae, eds. [2]1961. *Der historische Jesus und der kerygmatische Christus: Beiträge zum Christusverständnis in Forschung und Verkündigung*. Berlin. Significant contributions from the discussion on the "new quest of Jesus" around the middle of the twentieth century.

Schröter, Jens, and Ralph Brucker, eds. 2002. *Der historische Jesus: Tendenzen und Perspektiven der gegenwärtigen Forschung*. BZNW 114. Berlin.   Collection of contributions on Jesus research from the beginning of the twenty-first century.

Zager, Werner, ed. 2014. *Jesusforschung in vier Jahrhunderten. Texte von den Anfängen historischer Kritik bis zur "dritten Frage" nach dem historischen Jesus*. de Gruyter Texte. Berlin and Boston.   Collection of significant contributions on Jesus research up until the beginning of the twenty-first century, with introductions.

Jens Schröter and Christine Jacobi

B. History of Historical-Critical Research on Jesus

I. Introduction

1. At the beginning of the *Jesus Handbook* an overview on interpretations of the person of Jesus in the history of Christianity is provided. The survey begins with evidence about the earthly Jesus in antiquity, the Middle Ages, and the Reformation era, followed by a look at historical-critical Jesus research, which constitutes the main focus of contemporary scholarly discussions. The problem of the relationship between the earthly Jesus and the exalted Christ, which became dominant in Enlightenment theology, is not yet at the center of the pre-critical preoccupations with Jesus. Theologians of the earlier centuries by contrast regarded the human being Jesus of Nazareth as the mediator of divine salvation, as a teacher, and as an example of moral-religious life. Thus, in these times Jesus became the paradigm of a life in the grace of God, who is to be followed in faith. In addition, in the Middle Ages piety focused on the passion, and sacraments played a prominent role. Jesus's way of suffering became an example of a life in humility and self-denial to the point of monastic asceticism and self-flagellation. At the center of the "Jesus mysticism" of Bernard of Clairvaux stands immersion in the sacrifice of Jesus on the cross, which leads to the orientation of one's own life toward the Son of God who became a human being for our redemption. In the Reformation era, for example for Martin Luther, the presence of Jesus Christ in the proclamation of the gospel and in the Last Supper came to the fore.

2. The Enlightenment theology of the eighteenth century provided new accents. Critical reasoning called metaphysics and normative traditions into question and determined the autonomy of human reason as a critical benchmark. A decisive criticism of the Bible as a document of revelation was connected with the English deism that developed from this trajectory. The Bible's authority was called into question by the discovery of its historical contingency as well as its errors and contradictions. As a consequence, doctrines such as Jesus's vicarious atoning death as well as his resurrection and exaltation were critically examined and even questioned. Instead, Jesus came into view as a Jewish teacher who pro-

claimed the love of human beings for each other and called for repentance and a return to God. The orientation toward Jesus as an example was therefore directed toward Jesus as a human being and his religion, that is, toward Jewish faith in God and Jewish ethics of Jesus's time. In this process the premises for historical-critical exegesis were established, which broke up the canon into its individual writings, each of which had to be interpreted out of their own time and place.

3. Historical-critical Jesus research is set up on these premises. Important groundwork was established by means of critical historiography that was developing in the nineteenth century. On the one hand, historical research was now based on the critical evaluation of the available remains from the past. On the other hand, it became clear that the sources, critically examined by the historian, have to be integrated into a coherent historical narrative. The combination of these two aspects, which was discussed already in the eighteenth century as the interrelationship between historiography and novel, was now brought into connection with the critical scrutiny of the sources. As a scientific basis, Johann Gustav Droysen developed the discipline of "historiography" as the combination of theoretical reflection of historical research with critical work on the sources. The consequence resulting from this, not least of all for Jesus research, is that a metaphysical, divine agency that guarantees the coherence of history was replaced by the historian as the subject responsible for the historical narrative based on remains of the past. This is connected with the insight already expressed by Droysen, that the goal of historical research cannot be the "historical fact itself." Rather the task is to compile the results of critical work on the sources into a narrative that is based on current knowledge about the remains of the past and makes the past accessible for the present.

4. At its beginning, Jesus research adopted these hermeneutical insights of critical historiography only with hesitation. Instead, Jesus research was intensively concerned with clarification of the relationship between the "historical Jesus" and the "Christ of faith"—an issue that is due to its specific subject matter and the discourses that resulted from it. This already comes about with the concept of "myth" introduced into Jesus research by David Friedrich Strauss and the intense controversy arising from this. By employing the concept of "myth" Strauss wanted to demonstrate that neither the supernatural view of Jesus as a divine human being, who was empowered to perform things that cannot be explained by human reason, nor the attempt to interpret his works on a rational basis (in particular his miracles) can do justice to the character of the Gospels. Strauss defined myth as "unintentional poetic saga," that is, as a manner of presentation by which the Gospel writers depicted the activities of Jesus employing self-evident explanatory motifs and concepts of their time of which they themselves were unaware. For Strauss, it is therefore impossible to distinguish the past itself from its "mythical" interpretations.

Strauss's view called the foundation for a historical description of the life of Jesus radically into question. In return, an intensive effort developed to determine the oldest sources about Jesus. This resulted in the theory that the Gospel of Mark was the oldest narrative about Jesus in addition to a second source, already mentioned by Papias and called Jesus's "logia" by Schleiermacher. This model, developed in direct opposition to Strauss by Christian Hermann Weisse and further elaborated by Heinrich Julius Holtzmann, was later called the "two source theory." This model, although with modifications and further specifications, is today the most widely recognized theory about the relationship of the Synoptic Gospels to each other. It is also crucial for the question concerning the oldest sources of the activity of Jesus. Because of the widespread influence of this theory, the Gospel of Mark forms the basis for many portrayals of Jesus in the nineteenth century, which have the character of novels, rather than historical descriptions. The Logia source (today usually called "sayings source Q"), which is not preserved itself, but on the basis of Markan priority can be inferred as a second early source of Jesus traditions was frequently adduced for the reconstruction of the earliest layer of the sayings of Jesus.

5. Critical research on Jesus continued intensive engagement with the question posed by Strauss's pointed position about the relationship of the "historical Jesus" and the "Christ of faith." On the one hand, it was argued that early Christian texts, which first of all intended to be testimonies of faith and not historical reports, do not permit a reconstruction of the "historical Jesus." Such attempts were instead considered historically unproductive and theologically irrelevant. Advocates of this view include scholars such as Martin Kähler, Rudolf Bultmann, and Luke Timothy Johnson. Even if the character of early Christian texts is aptly described by these scholars, their radical rejection of attempts to reconstruct a portrait of Jesus on their basis is hardly persuasive. An important argument that is often used against this view is that the Gospels and also other early Christian texts explicitly relate the origin of Christian faith to Jesus's earthly activity. Although the earthly Jesus is presented from the point of view of faith in him as God's Son, who acted in the Spirit and the authority of God, this does not mean that for historical-critical interpretation of the Bible the earthly activity of Jesus would be unimportant or negligible. Rather, the testimonies about the earthly Jesus must be examined with historical-critical scrutiny and put into relationship with the confession of the risen and exalted Christ. Research on the "historical Jesus" therefore belongs to the basic foundations of engagement with Christianity, its beginnings, and essential contours—independently from a judgment about the reliability of the Gospels and the relationship between attestations of faith and historical accounts that is found in them. Not least, reflection on the activity and fate of Jesus and the central contents of his teaching—even, or in

particular, if it is undertaken with critical intent—serves as an important correction of Christian doctrines and church praxis.

Accordingly, in the era of historical-critical study of the Bible Jesus research has to a substantial extent concentrated on the relationship of the "historical Jesus" and the "Christ of faith" (or "kerygmatic Christ"). Thereby, from time to time radical solutions have been advocated that resolve matters in favor of one pole over against the other. Some profile historical evidence against Christian confession, whereas others aim at presenting the testimony of faith as making a historical foundation superfluous. Both positions, however, neglect that the dynamic indicated by the designations "historical Jesus" and "Christ of faith" does not permit one side to override the other. Rather, the tension between these two concepts serves to make Jesus research productive. This tension is grounded in the fact that the activity and fate of Jesus, the Galilean Jew from Nazareth, were already attributed by his earliest followers to God, who acted through him for the salvation of humanity. The tension between historical event and theological interpretation, therefore, remains a lasting task of historical-critical Jesus research.

6. The insights of hermeneutics in historiography, referred to above, have been considered important in recent Jesus research. By coining the concept of the "remembered Jesus" scholars have pointed out that portrayals of the "historical Jesus" as the person to whom the Gospel writers refer, are based on critical evaluation of the available sources as well as on epistemological premises and judgments of the historians. Thereby, by taking up Droysen's insights as well as recent approaches on hermeneutics of historiography, the correlation of critical evaluation of the sources and historical narrative was emphasized. At the same time, it was pointed out that portrayals of the "historical Jesus" cannot be equated with the person behind the earliest sources itself. Even if the goal of historical reconstruction is to to make the past accessible, from a hermeneutical and epistemological perspective it has to be taken into account that these reconstructions never get back behind the texts. Instead, they are always mediations of present and past, whose significance lies precisely in their perspectivity, relativity, and selectivity.

7. Against this backdrop, the common division of historical-critical Jesus research into three phases—the liberal Life-of-Jesus research of the nineteenth century, the "new quest of the historical Jesus," inaugurated by Ernst Käsemann's well-known lecture "Das Problem des historischen Jesus" ("The Problem of the Historical Jesus") from 1953, as well as the "third quest for the historical Jesus," introduced in the eighties and nineties of the twentieth century—turns out to conceal that modern Jesus research is characterized by issues and problems that appear throughout in various constellations and with different emphases. Among these are the question of what can be discovered about Jesus by means of historical criticism; the determination of the relationship of the historical evidence about

Jesus and the affirmation of his resurrection and exaltation; and finally, the question regarding the significance of the historical in theology in general. The substantial impact of these aspects in Jesus research is a consequence of the developments in the intellectual history of Europe in modern times. This makes clear that Jesus research is always carried out in the context of philosophical, historiographical, and hermeneutical thinking and in close communication with these intellectual disciplines. Moreover, it demonstrates that with the dismissal of the doctrine of inspiration and the canonical criticism associated with it, the question regarding the origins of Christian faith, which needs to be investigated by means of historical criticism—and along with this, the question of the historical Jesus—has attained a fundamental significance for Christian theology. This holds in any case for those strands of Christian theology that perceive themselves to be committed to historical-critical biblical scholarship. It can only be mentioned in passing here that Jesus can be approached in other contexts on an entirely different basis as well.

Jens Schröter and Christine Jacobi

II. The Earthly Jesus in the Piety and Theology of Antiquity, the Middle Ages, and the Reformation

The following survey runs through inventories of phenomena that prepared the way for debates about the "historical Jesus" in recent Protestant theology.

For the selection of materials I am prompted by Karlmann Beyschlag's ([2/1]1988–2000, 2/2:100–114) typological construct of a "Western Christology of Humility." From earliest times on in Western Christianity, what is operative is not only the incarnation but also the personal historical *existence* of Christ as a formative motivation both of piety and theology in a way that has no counterpart in the East (Holl 1904; Elert 1957).

1. Antiquity

In 1 Pet. 2:21–24 (associated with Rome?), perhaps the fragment of an ancient hymn is quoted (Bultmann 1967c). In conjunction with citations from Isa. 53, it presents the Jesus who suffers on the cross as an example (ὑπογραμμός, 2:21) of Christian behavior. Faith recognizes and examines Jesus as simply the authentic embodiment of a prescribed way of life precisely at the center of his redemptive work. First Clement, associated with the city of Rome, attests the same confluence of thoughts: "The scepter of the majesty of God, even our Lord Jesus Christ, came not in the pomp of arrogance or of pride, though he might have done so, but in lowliness of mind, according as the Holy Spirit spoke concerning him [Isa. 53:1–3 follows]" (1 Clem. 16:2). The parenesis corresponds precisely with this basic principle: "For Christ is with them who are lowly of mind, not with those who exalt themselves over the flock" (1 Clem. 16:1). "See, dearly beloved, who the example is that has been given unto us; for, if the Lord was thus humble, what should we do, who through him have been brought under the yoke of his grace?" (1 Clem. 16:17). Soteriological and ethical perspectives flow into each other in the concept of humility (Dihle 1957). It captures in totality the mentality and nature of the redeemer and thereby likewise specifies for those who are redeemed the guideline for their self-understanding and personal behavior.

As the humble redeemer, Jesus Christ is simultaneously the prevailing salvific will of God and the prototype and example of human existence in which God's will attains its form: "Now the will of God is that which Christ did and taught. It is humility in conduct [*humilitas in conversatione*], stability in faith, modesty in words, justice in deeds, mercy in works, strictness in morals, unwillingness to do wrong, and willingness to endure wrong; it is to preserve peace with our brethren, to love God with our whole heart, to have affection for him as our Father, to fear him as our God, to prefer nothing above Christ because he preferred nothing above us" (Cyprian, *Dom. or.* 15). In particular, martyrs are exposed to sharing God's will in Christ (see Cyprian, *Fort.* 11). Their triumph with the exalted one is promised in solidarity with the suffering Christ: "to accompany Him when He shall come to receive vengeance from His enemies, to stand at His side when He shall sit to judge, to become co-heir of Christ, to be made equal to the angels; with the patriarchs, with the apostles and the prophets, to rejoice in the possession of the heavenly kingdom" (Cyprian, *Fort.* 13). A superlative form of Christian discipleship is given and assigned to ascetics, women as well as men: they are the brighter shining part of Christ's flock, the "*inlustrior portio gregis Christi*" (Cyprian, *Hab. virg.* 3). The framework of obedience and perfection, understood as requirements for the participation in salvation, is solidly established: "Use those things which God has willed you to possess. Use them, certainly, but for the sake of *salvation*; use them, but for good purposes; use them, but for those things which God has commanded, and which the Lord has set forth. Let the poor feel that you are wealthy; let the needy feel that you are rich. Lend your estate to God; give food to Christ. Move *him* by the prayers of many to grant you to carry out the glory of virginity, and to succeed in coming to the Lord's rewards" (Cyprian, *Hab. virg.* 11).

According to Ambrose, humility is precisely the possession of salvation vouchsafed in the human Jesus Christ and at the same time his ethical-religious demand (Ambrose, *Exp. Ps. 118*, 20.3):

The one who sits on the right hand of God humbled himself on our behalf, and thus he says to us: "Learn from me, for I am meek and lowly in heart" [Matt. 11:29]. He did not say: Learn from me, for I am mighty, but that he is lowly in heart, so that you might imitate him, so that you can say to him: Lord, I have heard your voice and have fulfilled your command. You have said, that we should learn humility from you, we have not learned from your word alone, but also from your manner of life. I have done what you have commanded: Behold here my humility. (*Exp. Ps. 118*, 20.20)

Only in humility can a human being invoke God after the example of Christ as well as of the apostles and martyrs—certainly not as an accomplishment, but entirely on the basis of the confession not to be able to produce any accomplishment, even in spite of all possible effort (cf. *Exp. Ps. 118*, 20.16 and 20.7, with the series of examples that follow). Precisely in this Christ is the sublime example of humility, that he thus lived not for himself but for the many (*Exp. Ps. 118*, 20.28)! Like Cyprian before him, Ambrose emphasizes the special possibilities that asceticism offers in this regard.

His younger contemporary Jerome highlighted this relatively preferred priority considerably more clearly and at the same time brought about a further and more deeply effective motif of restlessness to Western Christianity. Both clergy and monks are obliged to follow "the naked cross naked," that is, to follow the naked Christ—following Christ is concretized and, at the same time, limited as a professional requirement. Jesus's word to the rich young man also holds for the clergy along with the following promise: "Transform the word into deed, and in that you follow the naked cross naked will you all the quicker and easier climb the ladder to heaven [Gen. 28:12]" (Jerome, *Epist.* 58.2.1). But above all here, ascetics, male and female, are in mind. Their way of life is the apostolic way, with which another signal aspect of the medieval history of religiosity is reminiscent: "Would you be perfect and stand on the pinnacle of grandeur? Do what the apostles did: Sell everything that you have and give it to the poor, and go and follow the Redeemer, and then you will follow completely nothing other than the naked, singular virtue"—so the pastor advised a wealthy widow (Jerome, *Epist.* 120.1.12). The requirement of self-denial is bolstered by the promise of exuberant restitution: "If you have wealth, sell it and give it to the poor. When you no longer have anything, then you are set free from a heavy burden: Follow the naked Christ naked! This is hard, demanding, and difficult. But the reward is great!" (Jerome, *Epist.* 125.20).

Augustine's discussions on the salvific significance of the human Jesus are linked with those of his teacher Ambrose and his contemporary Jerome. However, his considerations exceed theirs significantly: Augustine poses the problem whether human beings are in themselves able to embrace and appropriate the humility of Jesus Christ. For his work of redemption and salvation, it was absolutely necessary that Jesus Christ was completely and entirely God and equally a complete, entire individual human being.

But Augustine can also sketch the incarnation in a quite different series of thoughts, which he can spin out from the concept of grace:

> In this the grace of God is supremely manifest, commended in grand and visible fashion; for what had the human nature in the man Christ merited, that it, and no other, should be assumed into the unity of the Person of the only Son of God? What good will, what zealous strivings, what good works preceded this assumption by which that particular man deserved to become one Person with God? Was he a man before the union, and was this singular grace given him as to one particularly deserving before God? Of course not! For, from the moment he began to be a man, that man began to be nothing other than God's Son, the only Son, and this because the Word of God assuming him became flesh, yet still assuredly remained God. Just as every man is a personal unity—that is, a unity of rational soul and flesh—so also is Christ a personal unity: Word and man. (*Enchir.* 11.36)

Thus, in the recourse to its author, faith becomes aware that the salvation of the sinner does not depend on meritorious acts of man's own willpower, but solely on its ground in the divine decree of election and reprobation (cf. *Enchir.* 24.94).

Sin as transsubjective human condemnation is not merely punitive detention (*reatus*)—indeed, certainly not in the first place. Rather, it is also and especially an abnormal religio-ethical attitude that stands in opposition to God's will, so that it cannot exist together with reconciliation/redemption. Thus, reconciliation/redemption does not merely imply the appropriation of the benefit of the reconciling work of Jesus Christ for human beings, but simultaneously also implies the extermination of the abnormal attitude and the implanting of its positive counterpart. The pride (*superbia*) of the sinner must make way for the humility (*humilitas*) of the righteous One. And precisely here the human Jesus is again of decisive significance: "It was necessary . . . that man's pride might be exposed and healed through God's humility. Thus, it might be shown man how far he had departed from God, when by the incarnate God he is recalled to God; that man in his contumacy might be furnished an example of obedience by the God-Man; that the fount of grace might be opened up" (*Enchir.* 28.108). Thus the human Jesus is not only the reconciliation of divine wrath as the quintessential sacrifice, but he is simultaneously also the model of that very ethical-religious way of life that befits one who is elect/redeemed.

The human Jesus is thus teacher and at the same time so much more: "'Because Christ has suffered for us, leaving us an example,' as says the Apostle Peter, 'that we should follow his steps' [1 Pet. 2:21]. Him each one follows in that wherein he imitates him: not so far forth as he is the only Son of God, by Whom all things were made; but so far forth as, the *Son of Man*, he set forth in himself, what behooved for us to imitate" (Augustine, *Virginit.* 27).

Now from the beginning of their physical life and before the awakening of their conscience, all people are entangled in Adam's sin of pride. So, a fundamental qualitative difference exists between the teacher/example and the disciples/imitators, which is marked by the key concepts *humilitas* and *superbia*, and this very difference must be overcome so that an altogether new formation of human beings can begin by means of example and teaching.

Systematically, the concept of *gratia* has its place here. It obliterates the sin of pride in human beings and disposes them to surrender themselves to the deconstruction and new construction of themselves. For its part, grace is completely inaccessible intuitively and functions in human beings at a level of their personhood that no possible empirical knowledge can touch. Nevertheless, grace is symbolized in the sacraments, especially baptism and the Eucharist.

The sacraments both signify and uphold the mystery of grace. In their performance the remembered historical Jesus Christ is only involved as their remote cause. The God-man operates on the surface level in that by teaching and example he makes sinners aware of their need of redemption, and in that he guides them to appraise correctly the potential life that is given by grace and to make use of it. Augustine expresses this with the conceptual pair "*sacramentum et exemplum*" (*Trin.* 4.3.6): in his sacrifice on the cross Christ reconciles God and humanity and models in a mysterious way what happens in the inner person when grace is at work in him or her. Christ gives himself to the outer human being as an example to follow and to imitate, because here one is able to perceive what external embodiment the renewal of the inner person requires and grants.

This double relationship can also be rotated vertically, and it can take the shape of a schema of purification and ascent. Christ's human nature leads to beholding his divine nature by the way of faith. In connection with John 1:1–2, Augustine explains:

> But he would have been declaring the divinity of the Word to us in vain, if he had kept quiet about the humanity of the Word. In order, I mean, for me to see that, he deals with me down here; in order to purify my gaze for contemplating that, he himself comes to the aid of my weakness. By receiving from human nature the same human nature, he became man [*sacramento incarnationis*]. He came with the packhorse of the flesh to the one who was lying wounded on

the road [Luke 10:30–37], in order to give shape to our little faith and nurture it, and to clear our intellects from mist, so that they might see what he never lost as a result of what he took on. (*Serm.* 341.3.3)

And as a key for this schema of ascent, in which Christ's humanity functions as the way to participate in his divinity, Augustine cites John 14:6 again and again (references in Scheel 1901, 370–75).

2. *The Middle Ages/Humanism*

In the early Middle Ages the image of the ruler of the world (*pantokrator*) prevailed in the image of Christ in the West, and the human Jesus came preponderantly into consideration as a teacher. In addition to literary sources (cf. Hauck [6]1952, 1:192–200, 2:793–805), art history attests this (cf. Bäbler and Rehm 2001; Angenendt 1997, 143–47). Gregory the Great kept certain basic principles of Augustine up to date—in a simplified way that rendered them understandable for his contemporaries (Greschat 2005, 175–78).

An important strand of the memory of the human Jesus was expanded by the combination of the memory of the passion and sacramental devotion in the course of implementing the realistic concept of the sacrifice of the Mass, which was effectively expressed in countless miracle legends (Browe 1938).

The perception of the earthly Jesus as the source and norm of a way of life that guaranteed salvation was one of the factors that led to the "Gregorian reformation of the church" (Tellenbach 1988).

In aggressively devout arousals, early Christian and ancient church formulas and thought patterns about the earthly Jesus as the model of humility and the catchword of following the naked Christ naked woke up to new life—under newly fashioned conditions and, for that reason, also in new shapes of contemplation and realization.

Peter Damian wrote an extensive letter of admonition to the monks on Monte Cassino because they had given up the custom of flagellating themselves on Fridays with their upper body naked: the personal, existential participation in the suffering of Christ confers an entitlement to participation in his glory. Only those who are not ashamed of humiliation and allow themselves to be led by him will find grace in the face of the terrible judge at his return in glory. And precisely in this lay the salvific benefit of the way of Christ: "Say now, why did Christ suffer? In order to wash away his own guilt and in order to obliterate his own transgressions? No, listen to what Peter says about him [1 Pet. 2:22]! Why did he suffer? Then Peter himself answers [1 Pet. 2:21]. Christ thus suffered as the first; the first apostles followed after him in whose footsteps we also should follow [*vestigia imitari*], as one of them says [1 Cor. 11:1, Vulgate: *imitators . . . estote*]. Why then did Christ, as we read, suffer, except for us to take him as an example?" (Peter Damian, *Letter* 161).

The model of a life of voluntary poverty, which is guided by the example of Jesus and the apostles, penetrated across ascetic circles and their distinctive ways of life. It was employed against "secular" clerics—where it could promote their ambitions in ecclesiastical politics, even by popes and bishops. Laity did this in response to calls of repentance from itinerant preachers (Walter 1903–1906). These also spread the idea of the crusades among the populace (Peter von Amiens: Hagenmeyer 1879), who were suddenly aware of a new potential for authentic Christian existence beyond roles traditionally ascribed to them and stipulations established by their customary secular ways of life—especially women felt challenged by the gospel of apostolic poverty. In the middle of the period, such movements were fenced in by patterns of monastic lifestyle—if they refused the submission to such subsumptions, they were declared to be heretical.

The movement of voluntary poverty also became a gateway for missionaries of dualistic sects, from the activities of which influences of Catharism arose, the most serious heretical challenge to the Catholic Church before the Reformation. This was because its protagonists portrayed themselves as authentically poor apostolic disciples of Jesus in contrast to the allegedly secular church. The community of decidedly impoverished Catholic preachers of repentance, founded in Lyon by the wealthy merchant (Petrus) Waldes, wanted to cut the ground from under the Cathars. However, owing to conflicts about the right to preach, the community itself was declared heretical. A clever, somewhat cynical contemporary depicted them in this way: "They have no permanent accommodations and they roam about two by two, barefoot and in wool garments. They have no possessions and hold all things in common like the apostles, and follow the naked Christ naked" (Gonnet 1958, 123).

Francis of Assisi established the most influential synthesis of the voluntary poverty movement and the clerical church (Selge 1966, 1970). For the highly gifted promoter of himself, who was revered as a "second Christ" (receiving the stigmata), the poor Jesus and the eucharistic Christ of the salvific institution coalesced into an inseparable unity. The movement of ascetics and preachers who affiliated with Francis became established as a new facet of Western asceticism—in the midst of conflicts ("poverty controversies"), the historical mental, social, spiritual, and legal consequences of which can hardly be exaggerated (Miethke 1999, 2000).

Likewise, the activity of the Franciscans in confessional pastoral care and popular preaching was epoch making. Here the God-man Jesus Christ becomes thematic from three points of view: he is the essential enabler who opens up the possibility of salvation for sinners; the course of his life leads sinful human beings to activate the possibilities for salvation that are granted to them by grace; finally, the emotion of compassion with Jesus, who suffered and was crucified, contributes to breaking up the pride of sinners and advances in them the virtue of humility that is indispensable for salvation. In this endeavor, the popular preaching of the late Middle Ages intensively emphasizes the agonies of innocent martyrs in order to accentuate the hearers' consciousness of the religio-moral distinction of themselves from their forebears, that is, the unbelieving Jews, and thereby to heat up enmity against the Jews (Kirn 2001).

Structurally analogous figures of thought also characterize Jesus mysticism, which, beyond the cloisters, also exerted influence in the world of the educated laity. Bernard of Clairvaux, a contemporary of the religious awakening of the twelfth century, was also instrumental in shaping the style of Jesus mysticism.

Following Augustine, Bernard understood Christian existence as the ascending return of the soul to its divine origin. Already on the way, it can anticipate its goal: in the blessed sacrifice of the self, the consciousness of the self dissolves, because it touches its divine ground.

The image of the human Jesus Christ that Bernard depicts is focused by the functions of his humanity for human beings on this path. The sacrifice of the God-man on the cross is the transcendent-historical enabling condition for the ascent. Human beings have to renew the construal of their lives and their ways of life, and they can do this only with the help of Jesus. Being remembered and imagined vividly, he turns to human beings in the ascent, that is, in a thoroughly transitional phase, and to that effect, the one who became flesh points beyond himself to his pure divine nature, or God himself, as the ultimate goal (Bernard, *Serm. Cant.* 20.6–8).

The vicarious atonement as well as the guidance and advancement of the religio-moral ascent point to the selfless humility and love of the God-man, and for this, humanity owes active thanksgiving (*Serm. Cant.* 11.8—one is reminded of Zinzendorf's life-changing experience in Düsseldorf at the beginning of his grand tour; Ritschl [1880–1886] 1966, 3:201). The meditative memory of Jesus's earthly path is thus the means to the goal of the religio-ethical formation of virtue, whereas the essential matter of yearning and hope is the divine nature of Christ, namely, God himself (cf. Bernard, *Serm. Cant.* 10.8, with a characteristic reference to John 6:64).

An offshoot of this Jesus mysticism in the late Middle Ages is the rising pious counseling literature. In his "Vita Jesu Christi," Ludolf von Sachsen (d. 1378) explains individual episodes, among which there are many apocryphal elaborations, with extensive recourse to orthodox interpretive tradition: it can be deduced from Jesus how, in passing the tests of character and in the decisive access to possibilities of meritorious conduct, a truly Christian, salvific meritorious life can be shaped. Ignatius of Loyola received crucial impulses from these kinds of sources (Boehmer 1914, 299–308).

The four tractates of *De imitatione Christi* by Thomas à Kempis (d. 1479) are considerably shorter. They offer support by means of analysis of the self and nurture of the self. Time and again "Christ" himself seeks dialogue with the reader's soul and gives it encouragement, counsel, and comfort for a focused way of life in which worldly trifles are held at a distance. The preparation for encountering Christ in eucharistic communion occupies a special place.

The continuities with this in Erasmus of Rotterdam's "Enchiridion ['handbook' or 'dagger'] for the Christian Knight" (1503) are striking. The Christian's whole life is a battle of the spirit against the flesh. In this battle Christ is the commander in chief who, as the creator and redeemer, has a claim for the fidelity of his servants. As an example and encouraging advisor, he nurtures and directs the salvific exercise of his followers' freedom. Christ is qualitatively superior to all philosophical masters, because in him teaching and the way of life agree completely.

Especially the biblical humanism advocated by Erasmus had effects in all the struggling and competing churches that emerged after the disruption of the Reformation. Humanist theological thought proved its critical impact in smaller religious communities (Socinian, Arminian): in a critical recourse to biblical sources, the two-nature Christology and the doctrine of atonement were separated from Jesus's life and his original gospel; eventually the historical Jesus was positioned against the Christ of dogma.

The apology of Hugo Grotius represents an early stage of this process: "And hence it is we conclude that this religion exceeds all others in this particular also, that the author of it performed himself what he commanded, and was possessed of what he promised" (Grotius, *Veritate* 2.20). Grotius referred to Jesus's perfect religious ethic and his resurrection, the latter of which verifies his promise of eternal life, and Grotius drew furthermore a decisive argument for the credibility and reliability of Christ's doctrine from his miracles (cf. *Veritate* 2.4).

3. *Reformation*

Also, the new approach in the understanding of the historical human Jesus took root in Augustinian-Bernardian Christ meditation and yet reorganized this entire conceptual and cognitive context by means of a novel understanding of God's essence and will as well as God's action in Jesus Christ (Ohst 2012).

According to Luther, Jesus as a historical human being makes the knowledge of God available, especially by his suffering. From this the knowledge of God mounts up (WA 2:136–42). The inner awareness of God, however, is not a blissful loss of self but a reconstitution of the human self by personal faith in forgiveness and reconciliation. This happens because Jesus Christ in his once-for-all historical, salvific action is made present by means of the Word:

> Here it is beautifully shown how we are saved, namely, through Christ as the archetype and exemplar, to whose image all who are saved are conformed. For God the Father made Christ to be the sign and archetype, in order that those who adhere to him by faith might be transformed in the same image and thus be drawn away from the images of the world. . . . This gathering together of the children of God is similar to what happens when the government arranges a spectacle to which the citizens flock. They leave their work and their homes and fix their attention on it alone. Thus, the gospel as though a spectacle exhibited to the whole world attracts all people by the knowledge and contemplation of himself and draws them away from all the things to which they have clung in the world. This is the meaning of the statement that they are transformed and become like him. . . . For God does not compel people to salvation by force and fear, but by this pleasing spectacle of his mercy and love, he moves and draws through love all whom he will save. (WA 57:124–25; cf. Osthövener 2004, 41–58; U. Barth 2010)

The salvific work of Jesus Christ is no longer a remote cause for possibilities that can be realized or missed here and now. Christ addresses every believer in the same way as his first disciples, via his biblical Word: "Now when you open up, read, or hear the book of the gospel, how Christ here or there comes or someone is brought to him, then you should thereby learn the preaching or the gospel through which he comes to you or you are brought to him. For to preach the gospel is nothing other than for Christ to come to us or to bring us to him" (WA 10.1/1: 13–14).

Also, Luther's understanding of the Lord's Supper attests to this focus on the efficacious self-actualization of Christ in the Word (crucially and constructively foundational; WA 6:507–26). Christ abides with the very one with whom he becomes concurrent in the Word; not externally, but rather this comes to one in personal solidarity at the ultimate depths, for which Luther also adduces in a boldly coined way the ancient figurative world of nuptial mysticism (K. Bornkamm 1998, 183–85): Christ did not ransom us "in order to instruct us simply how to live well. Rather he did so in order that he himself might live and rule in us and be our Lord, who is active in all our works, which are brought about through faith in him" (WA 7:726–27). In this solidarity the Christian also attains participation in Christ's suffering: "St. Paul also calls the suffering of all Christians the suffering of Christ. For just as faith, the name, the word, and work of

Christ are mine by reason of my belief in him, so his suffering is also mine; for I also suffer for his sake" (WA 12:279).

The Jesus Christ who is actualized in the Word regarding his historical salvific way on earth is the risen One. He acts in divine power on the human conscience, which becomes aware of him in its own hopelessness of salvation and desolation, and experiences its reconstitution in and with him in faith. So, the distinction between *exemplum* and *sacramentum* becomes a dialectic between law and gospel, which structures Jesus Christ's action of actualizing himself in the Word. The experience of the law is the indispensable prerequisite for Christ to establish his salvific work in the conscience by bringing about faith.

The problem that Luther's redefinitions present and intensify can be stated as follows: How can it be intellectually plausible that an encounter produced in words with Jesus Christ, who was once a historical human being, time and again becomes a redemptive and liberating encounter of the conscience with God for human beings who are in completely different historical locations? And how is it possible if the previous intellectual and institutional constructs for the resolution of this problem are repudiated, because in the end they all boil down to cooperation of human choice and free will with sacramentally mediated acts of divine mercy?

Luther's own solution comes, firstly, by way of a completely new definition of the biblical Word as the self-actualization of Jesus Christ, as the exalted historical Jesus who becomes the contemporary of the one to whom he bestows faith (Ohst 2010). Secondly, Luther reaches this aim by reframing the two-nature doctrine in the course of the controversy about the Last Supper. Through the reciprocal communication of the properties of Christ's divine and human nature, the human historical Christ is set free from his attachment to time and place (J. Baur 1993, 117–44).

Luther's bold, provocative thinking, which not merely strained the established boundaries of the two-nature doctrine to the breaking point but also questioned the foundations of classical metaphysics, found resonance especially in Württemberg. The main course of Lutheran theology followed Melanchthon, who combined Luther's motives with elements of Augustinian and humanistic thought. How difficult it was to secure Luther's accomplishments under these conditions is attested, for example, by the relentless battle of Lutheran theologians with Socinian humanistic and Tridentine Catholic claims for Jesus Christ as a new lawgiver (Gerhard 1863–1875, 3:171–79). This was not an obstinate insistence on mere formulas. Rather, it was important to retain a fundamental insight of Luther's theology, namely, the understanding of the historical Jesus Christ as the gospel that in his verbal self-actualization through Scripture is appropriated for faith.

Gerhard, Johann. 1863–1875. *Loci Theologici (1610–1622)*. Edited by E. Preuß. Berlin.

Ohst, Martin. 2014. "Urheber und Zielbild wahren Menschseins: Jesus Christus in der Kirchengeschichte." In *Jesus Christus*, edited by Jens Schröter, 119–79. TdT 9. Tübingen.

Pfannmüller, Gustav. ²1939. *Jesus im Urteil der Jahrhunderte*. Berlin.

Preuss, Hans. 1915. *Das Bild Christi im Wandel der Zeiten*. Leipzig.

Richstaetter, Carl. 1949. *Christusfrömmigkeit in ihrer historischen Entwicklung*. Cologne.

Ruh, Kurt. 1990–1999. *Geschichte der abendländischen Mystik*. 4 vols. Munich.

Martin Ohst

III. The Eighteenth Century as the Context for the Origin of Critical Theology

1. Critical Philosophy

In the eighteenth century, *criticism* as the method of logical-rational analysis of all fields of knowledge and behavior developed into a leading motif of the epoch. The distinguished *Encyclopédie ou dictionnaire raisonné*, organized by Jean Le Rond d'Alembert and Denis Diderot ([1782] 1993, 10:13), ascribed to critical methodology the task of bringing its subjects before the "tribunal of truth." Shortly thereafter, Immanuel Kant broke open the frontiers of the method as the epitome of his century: "Our epoch is the very epoch of criticism, to which everything must be subjected" (1976).

The leitmotif of criticism put in question every assertion attached to a metaphysical, supernaturalistic understanding of reality, and at the same time problematized the legitimizing appeal to political, ethical, religious, theological, and philosophical norms with respect to the binding nature of authoritative traditions. Even if the developments of a critical convention of understanding differed considerably with respect to substance, they agreed altogether on the postulate of a tradition-critical *autonomie* of human reason. According to the universal claim that they asserted, it was only consistent that critical reasoning would ultimately become reflexive and thereby would also catch sight of its own stipulations, boundaries, and perils.

The history of the modern philosophical rationalism that posited the intellectual sovereignty of reason began with René Descartes in his *Meditationes de prima philosophia* (1641). In order to attain an assured ground for knowledge of truth resistant to error, he chose the approach of radical methodological doubt. He finally found irrefutable certainty only in the knowledge of doubt concerning himself: *Cogito ergo sum*. By way of contrast, English Enlightenment philosophy (F. Bacon, J. Locke, and D. Hume) was governed by empiricism and the perceptions of the senses. In distinction from Descartes's pioneering line of thinking, in this case all scientific knowledge—and, in addition, the entire way of life—should not be established by means of proof of rational cognitive faculties but should be deduced from sensory experience. Kant demonstrated, however, an uncritical use of reason in these two main streams of philosophy of the epoch. Rationalism leaves out of consideration that concepts, inasmuch as in their usage they go beyond the realm of possible sensory experience, lose their epistemological capacity, and empiricism overlooks that experience can in no way be constituted without additional categories of understanding. Thus, for him metaphysics was possible only by an encompassing critical orientation—just as science is possible on the basis of sources and, in addition, the scope and limits of rational cognition.

Criticism, however, did not mean fundamental hostility to tradition and authority. Rather, in keeping with its origin in philological text criticism, it was to be carried out in the ambivalence of dismissing and retaining on the basis of critical verification. The resulting specific philosophical procedure, which, averse to any methodological compulsion, raised up one's own critical judgment on only a decisive instance, can be defined formally as eclecticism. In this the maxim of the Enlightenment was fulfilled—"always think for yourself" (Kant 1958, 283). In the eighteenth century, the distinctive propensity for encyclopedic assurance agreed with this to the extent that it is not subject to the domination of an a priori system. Rather, it preferred to present the knowledge of the time in an additional empirical way. The popular designation of the epoch as "the philosophical century" aimed at the "revolution of the way of thinking" (Kant 1956, 698) taking place in the period by which philosophical concepts should become practical, that is, they should become creatively formative for all aspects of life. A standard theme of the Enlightenment was the question of the practical relevance of theoretical insights for life, but also for institutions, phenomena, and implementation—in short, the question of "applicability" (Spalding 2002).

2. Critical Philosophy of Religion

The beginnings of a critical philosophy of religion that was independent from Christian theology were associated with the emergence of the Western European Enlightenment. This was at the same time impacted by the formation of various types of deistic concepts of religion in England. And this provided a crucial frame of reference for discursive German Enlightenment theology to explain itself.

In his magnum opus, *De veritate* (1624), the first advocate of English Deism, Edward Herbert of Cherbury, attempted to filter out from historically developed forms of religion a natural primordial religion. For this he asserted the validity of five constitutive truths: God actually exists; worship is due God; this is accomplished primarily in virtue and practical piety; transgressions necessitate repentance, and amends should be made; God punishes and rewards in time and eternity. Herbert called this sufficient catalogue of religious truths "catholic," because in this he saw the description of the rational kernel of every positive religion. He thought he could unmask everything else as doctrinal and cultic forms that obfuscated the rational truth of religion as tools for priestly exercise of power.

From the beginning of the eighteenth century, rationalistic biblical criticism increasingly acquired interest in English Deism as well as in the rational moral purgation of ecclesiastical belief. By means of identifying parallels and influences from outside the Bible, critics then attempted to peel back the Bible to its rational kernel. The critical exegetical work of the deists (J. Towland, A. Collins, Th. Woolston, and M. Tindal) aimed at a destruction of evidence of New Testament divination and accounts of miracles as well as at a moral critique of biblical personages and issues that were in part frivolously excessive.

In France, English Deism was especially taken over as an ammunition depot in the battle for criticism of religion. The biblical criticism worked out by Voltaire purposely targeted Christian claims of revelation. In this he subjected the basic document of Christianity to an examination process according to historical, geographical, moral, and logical criteria. He wished not only to treat the Bible as an altogether quite normal book but also to demonstrate the incoherencies and absurdities contained in it, and in addition, by history-of-religions comparisons, to show its derivative nature. Whereas for Voltaire the existing Christian doctrine and tradition presented a paragon of human irrationality, he also had emphatically distanced himself from the emergent atheism of his time. As for the historical Jesus, he held this "poor man, who preached to the poor," this "Socrates of Galilee," in high esteem. At the same time, of course, this depended on rescuing Jesus from the aberrations of a religion that he neither desired nor founded in such a way that one finally would stop making out of him what he never claimed to be and never was—the Son of God.

3. Critical Theology

The classical theology of the Enlightenment, especially that which was carried out in Germany, participated in the developing awareness of truth in its epoch. Biblical tradition, the body of doctrine, and religious traditions were questioned with critical intentionality regarding their rational content as well as their relevance for practical living. By means of historical-critical exegesis and critically oriented writing on the history of doctrine, an attempt was made to distill the rational kernel of theological-ecclesiastical tradition and use it in a new, up-to-date arrangement. This critical inspection of the system of doctrine that had been handed down provoked a fundamental transformation of Christian thinking that remains decisive for the modern history of theology.

In addition, the revision of the religious program of individualization nurtured from roots in the Reformation, which was instigated by neology (cf. Beutel 2017), led to a critical examination of all traditional claims to authority. This meant not only problematizing confessional statements (already initiated in Pietism) but also revising the normative understanding attributed to Scripture, which had been handed down. It was irreversibly left behind along with the recognition of the canon as verbally inspired. For the most part, a reliable surety of authority attributed to the Bible consisted only of the life and death of Jesus, which was evaluated as exemplary, but which for the neologists no longer appeared necessarily without analogy in history. The decisive criterion for a tradition-critical examination was religious and moral plausibility, and the Archimedean fulcrum of Christian doctrine oriented toward practical ethics was provided for by the newly conceived category of the "essence of Christianity" (cf. Beutel 2013, 172). This allowed all traditional claims of authority to be relativized as historically contingent.

The eighteenth-century rationalist neologian Johann Friedrich Wilhelm Jerusalem pointed to Jesus as the greatest person sent by God, as an example and teacher who conformed to God and through whose blessed life forgiving care was validated by God in his resurrection. Accordingly, the self-sacrifice of Jesus seemed to him to be the highest expression of his moral perfection, and consequently a complete disempowerment of soteriology. In this way, in addition to hereditary sin, the conventional two-nature doctrine and the doctrine of the Trinity turned out to be dispensable. Further, the divine Sonship of Jesus was defused by adoptionism, and likewise the concept of a Holy Spirit by modalism (cf. Beutel [2]2009, 118–21). Above all, theological rationalists rejected the doctrine of the vicarious atonement of Jesus's death as contradictory to all rules of logic. So, for instance, Johann Konrad Dippel advanced the opinion that God did not have to be reconciled with human beings; rather, humans had to be reconciled with their own sinless original archetype (Dippel 1729). The theory of deception advocated by Hermann Samuel Reimarus was even more radical: whereas Jesus proclaimed a natural, rational, ethical religion, but died disillusioned in his expectation of the coming of the kingdom of God, the disciples and apostles stole his corpse, invented his resurrection, and thus falsified the earthly activities of

Jesus to the point of a religion of redemption (Beutel ²2009, 155–57). Gotthold Ephraim Lessing, who readily disguised his own opinion behind Reimarus's fragments, which he edited, reasoned analogously. The doctrine of the divinity and resurrection of Jesus, he thought, originated in the course of the formation of ecclesiastical doctrine, whereby in reality Jesus, as a teacher enlightened by God, whose message was encapsulated by the saying in John, "little children, love one another," is to be observed and revered (cf. Beutel ²2009, 181–86).

With his magnum opus, *Der Thätige Gehorsam Jesu Christi untersucht* (1768), Johann Gottlieb Toellner, who taught in Frankfurt on the Oder, rendered the most significant contribution to Enlightenment theology on the doctrine of atonement. Beginning with the orthodox satisfaction theory, which for the substitutionary satisfaction distinguished between Jesus's obedience by means of active fulfillment of the law and the passive obedience accomplished in his sacrificial death, Toellner wished to unveil the unbiblical nature of this primary doctrine. What was enlightening in this was his interest to assert the *vere homo* of God's Son unequivocally. On the basis of an extensive exegesis of corresponding biblical passages seconded by means of systematic theological considerations, Toellner showed that the reconciliation achieved by the work of Jesus is based only on his passive obedience demonstrated in his suffering and death. By contrast, his active obedience is not a component of but simply a concomitant part of the satisfaction. Because with respect to his human nature he has to be thought of as a freely acting subject and as such must be responsible like every person for active obedience toward God's command, in no case can a character of satisfaction be attributed to it. Shortly thereafter the philosopher Johann August Eberhard in Halle drew from this approach to a Christology of an example the radicalizing consequence that punishment understood as a means of disciplining could only be administered to the subject of the divine discipline, but in no case could it be transferred to a third party. With this, the concept of Jesus's substitutionary punishment had become completely invalid. Eberhard declared the New Testament's figuration of an atonement sacrifice to be an accommodation to the Jewish conceptual world. For him, Jesus's actual act of redemption lay in his liberating people from a false perception of God and in assuring anyone who is eager to improve of the forgiving care of God (cf. Beutel ²2009, 260–62).

The interest in a recovery of the *simplicitas evangelii* characterized a fundamental consensus that was pietistic and theological in the Enlightenment sense. This consensus found its classical expression in the *Lineamenta institutionum fidei christianae historico-criticarum* (1793), by the Halle theologian Heinrich Philipp Konrad Henke. With it he sought to liberate the traditional body of doctrine from a threefold superstition. He declared materially repugnant the following: "Christolatry," that is, to transfer to Jesus the worship that is due to

God alone; "bibliolatry," that is, the glorification of the canon with its historical origin to the status of Holy Scripture stripped of any critical judgment; and "ono-matolatry," that is, the inflexible adherence to obsolete doctrinal concepts, which have long since become misunderstood or useless. In the material development of his purpose, Henke set every theme of ecclesiastical doctrine over against biblical statements with a critical intention. Overall Henke sought to refine the Christian religion of revelation to a rational religion inspired by the spirit of Jesus, so that the ecclesiastical "religion of Christ," distorted by manifold meta-physical intrusions, would be restored to the simple, original *religio Christi*.

4. Historical-Critical Exegesis

At the beginning of the sixteenth century, classical philology was not the least thing to benefit from the scientific-friendly climate that humanism and the Ref-ormation had engendered. In biblical scholarship the controversial theological encrustations that the age of orthodoxy bred had once again severely restricted exegetical freedom. Radically altering the Roman Catholic concept of tradition, the old Protestantism identified the text of the Bible with the word of God, which it viewed as fully inspired and therefore exempt from any critical processing. The first direct impulses for historical-critical biblical research appeared pri-marily outside Germany. While it broke away from the custody of ecclesiastical-dogmatic power to make policy, it rose to the position of a trendsetter of an enlightened, competent, modern theology. In this process historical-critical exegesis did not represent, for instance, only a gradual refinement of method. Rather, it came about as a consequence of nothing less than an antimetaphysical paradigm shift (cf. Ebeling ³1967).

The swiftly invigorating cognitive process of the natural sciences as well as geographical and historical discoveries began to shake the literal credibility of Holy Scripture. At the same time, the widely waged Deism debate undermined claims of biblical revelation. In his *Leviathan* (1651), Thomas Hobbes postulated that the time of origin of biblical books could be deduced only from the books themselves, but in no way from doctrinal tradition. Shortly thereafter, Baruch Spinoza's *Tractatus theologico-politicus* (1670) contested the Mosaic authorship of the Pentateuch and, in view of different logical and style-critical problems, formulated the methodological principle that Old Testament research would have to be oriented on the stipulations of natural reason alone. The trendsetting biblical criticism that the French Oratorian Richard Simon propounded in his *Histoire cri-tique du Vieux Testament* (1678) was motivated by theological controversy. Against the Protestant principle of *sola Scriptura*, he insisted on the knowledge that the biblical text was unreliably transmitted, and in addition could not be understood on its own but first had to be reconstructed by textual and literary work.

In the epoch of the Enlightenment, the struggle for a possible original biblical text showed up as an essential element of New Testament exegesis. The Greek edition of the *Novum Instrumentum* (1516), which Erasmus had compiled relatively casually according to manuscripts that were largely inferior, was considered from the beginning of the seventeenth century the divinely inspired, unimpeachable *textus receptus*. That did not prevent the advancement of text criticism, but still held it back noticeably. Simon sought to produce an improved textual basis by employing all manuscripts available to him. In Germany, after Johann Albrecht Bengel and especially Johann Jakob Wettstein had accomplished essential preliminary work, Johann Jakob Griesbach, who taught in Halle and Jena, undertook the systematically source-critical *Novum Testamentum Graece* (1774–1777), which definitively set the *textus receptus* free from taboos.

Parallel to this, a gradual transition to a consistent historical interpretation of the New Testament canon took place. As early as 1572, Joachim Camerarius put forth the methodological postulate that the New Testament authors were to be explained from their time, and in cases of doubt, no longer from the authoritative exegetical tradition, but were to be given over to consideration of the world of classical language and texts. The *Annotationes in Novum Testamentum*, by Hugo Grotius (1641–1650), stood on this track. It demonstrated the analytical power of a contemporary historical explanation of the world of New Testament language and perception by copiously extending literary sources beyond Christianity. On the basis of the convergence of impulses from Deism, Spinoza, and rationalistic orthodoxy, Jean-Alphonse Turretini (1728) postulated that methodologically the exposition of biblical and nonbiblical texts should be put on equal footing and be subjected to the standards of reason alone. On the basis of the insight into the historical dissimilarity of the two Testaments, Johann August Ernesti argued for an independent historical investigation of the New Testament that could not be limited by any ecclesiastical or dogmatic premises (Ernesti 1761). In this sense the systematic distinction of biblical and dogmatic theology that Johann Philipp Gabler (1787) called for indicated only one emphasis of the general consciousness of the problem for Enlightenment theology. Additional prominent proponents of New Testament exegesis were Johann David Michaelis, whose *Einleitung in die göttlichen Schriften des neuen Bundes* (1750, [4]1788) provided an initial spark for historical genres, and Griesbach (1776), who posed the pivotal question of the historical problem of the Synoptics. Shortly thereafter Georg Lorenz Bauer, who taught in Altdorf and Heidelberg, introduced an important wider perspective on the history of religions with his groundbreaking work *Hebräische Mythologie des alten und neuen Testaments, mit Parallelen aus der Mythologie anderer Völker* . . . (1802).

By means of the "fundamental decision for the historical-critical method in diverse situations," Enlightenment Protestantism not only "secured and strengthened the Reformation decision of the sixteenth century" (Ebeling ³1967, 41) but also simultaneously created a foundation for modern biblical exegetical scholarship, which to be sure was pregnant with development, although the direction of its goal was irreversible.

Baird, William. 1992. *History of New Testament Research*. Vol. 1, *From Deism to Tübingen*. Minneapolis.

Beutel, Albrecht. ²2009. *Kirchengeschichte im Zeitalter der Aufklärung. Ein Kompendium*. UTB 3180. Göttingen.

Encyclopédie ou dictionnaire raisonné. (1782) 1993. Organized by Jean Le Rond d'Alembert and Denis Diderot. Edited by Fortuné Barthélemy de Félice. Paris.

Haakonssen, Knud, ed. 1996. *Enlightenment and Religion: Rational Dissent in Eighteenth-Century Britain*. Cambridge.

Kant, Immanuel. 1976. *Kritik der reinen Vernunft*. Edited by Raymund Schmidt. S. 7 (= A XI). Hamburg.

Reventlow, Henning Graf, Walter Sparn, and John Woodbridge, eds. 1988. *Historische Kritik und biblischer Kanon in der deutschen Aufklärung*. Wiesbaden.

Scholder, Klaus. 1966. *Ursprünge und Probleme der Bibelkritik im 17. Jahrhundert: Ein Beitrag zur Entstehung der historisch-kritischen Theologie*. FGLP 10.33. Munich.

Albrecht Beutel

IV. Critical Historiography of the Late Eighteenth and Nineteenth Centuries and Its Implications for Jesus Research

1. Critical Historiography of the Late Eighteenth and Nineteenth Centuries: Periodization and Characterization

The epoch of critical historiography of the late eighteenth through the nineteenth century was not homogenous. Diverse, even tensive, currents overlap each other. Moreover, contemporary research still strives to adequately delimit periods and their characterization in terms of content. Among other things, the chronology of scholarship becomes complicated because only in the course of achievements of research in the twentieth century did the terminology "Enlightenment history" and "liminal period" for eras, together with their contents, break off from what was initially comprehensively conceived as "historicism" (a good overview is found in the chart in Metzger 2011, 123).

1.1. *"Enlightenment History," "Pragmatism," "Saddle Period"*

The terminological designation "Enlightenment history" (*Aufklärungshistorie*), to be differentiated from "historicism" (*Historismus*), is in fact already found in Friedrich Meinecke ([4]1965, 11, 193–242). But undeniably the credit goes to Reinhart Koselleck for sharpening their content in the 1970s, subsequently also Horst-Walter Blanke. Koselleck (1975, 1979a, 1979b) perceived a time of epochal upheaval in the decades between 1750 and 1830 in which new terms and concepts were coined, which remain effective and valid even today. Among these belongs the establishment of "history" as a collective singular in general as well as other catchwords such as "progress," "evolution," and many more. On the basis of their epochal significance, Koselleck titled this era a historiographical "saddle period."

Overlapping this chronologically is the term "pragmatism" (from Fichte, 1762–1814), already in use in that period, which above all can be characterized as representational, universal, and didactic. According to a *pragmatic* way of writing history, historical events should be depicted as psychologically and intentionally understandable developments, so that the supratemporal validity of universal principles can be demonstrated and these principles can be instructive and beneficial for the life of readers.

Since Koselleck's work, Johann Martin Chladenius (1710–1759) counts as a prominent landmark of the "saddle period"—although he is usually not yet ranked as a pragmatic historian in the narrow sense of the word (primary works: *Einleitung zur Auslegung vernünftiger Reden und Schriften*, 1742; *Allgemeine Geschichtswissenschaft*, 1752). After the phase of the skeptic Pyrrhonism, and evoked by the rapid success of the natural sciences (Bacon, 1561–1626) and the logical systems of philosophy (Descartes, 1596–1650), it was his preeminent achievement to have prepared the way for a new foundation for hermeneutics by developing a detailed "art of understanding as a science." In this respect, indisputably Chladenius's most noteworthy achievement is his elaboration of the "Sehe-Punct" (point of view). By this Chladenius understood the individual, inescapable, dependent perspective of status, location, frame of mind, learning, morality, interests, and so forth of every recipient (Chladenius [1742] 1969, 187–88; cf. also Szondi 1975, 27–97; Grondin [3]2012, 80–86).

While Chladenius, by emphasizing the biased, individual viewpoint of every historian, took a major step toward a perspectival hermeneutic of history in the Göttingen School, the question of the form of speech of historical depictions was more strongly reflected by Johann Christoph Gatterer (1727–1799), August Ludwig von Schlözer (1735–1809), and finally also by Friedrich Schiller (1759–1805). Gatterer merited credit for founding the Historische Akademie or the Historische Institut at the University of Göttingen (1764–1766), the first "faculty" of historiography at a German university, and thus made an important contribution institutionally to the development of professional writing of history. In his *Vorrede von der Evidenz in der Geschichtskunde* (1767), he strived toward the combination of historical "demonstration" on the one hand and the "art" (!) of historical narratives on the other. The former was intended for the "critical reader" and was in need of support by fundamental studies of documents, monuments, *unbegeisterten* (dispassionate) authors, eyewitnesses as well as "source-sensible authors" (who, for their part, "created their reports" from documents and monuments). The latter, by contrast, was intended for the "sentient reader," who was to lead to an increase of virtue and "sentiments" by introducing acting characters—also with verbatim dialogue (Gatterer speaks about "roles")—by means of vivid, picturesque descriptions of scenes and other literary artistry. The relationship of these two poles to each other remains for him, however, unexplained. Also, in Schiller's historical works (which not infrequently begin with an introduction to theories of history, as, for instance, in *Verbrecher aus verlorener Ehre*, 1786, or in *Abfall der vereinigten Niederlande*, 1788), no contradiction exists between theoretical claims of a "cold" historian and "cold" readers and the affirmation of thorough source studies on the one hand, and the resolution of historical narratives in figurative speech, descriptions of the internal perspective of personages, integration of emotive details and descriptive adjectives on the other hand. Schiller also saw that in this vein the entire work of history moved in proximity toward the novel—concretely in *Abfall der vereinigten Niederlande*—and he insisted therefore that this was a "historically faithfully composed" work of history and not a "novel" (F. Schiller 1788, unnumbered last page of his preface).

Especially Daniel Fulda (1996) and Johannes Süssmann (2000) worked out the interconnection of writing history and historical novels from the last decade of the eighteenth century. On this epoch, see also Stefan Jordan's summary (2009, 44–45, 51): "As a matter of fact the claim to cast a preferably unadulterated glance at historical reality stands in an unresolved relationship of tension with the emotionally laden, by no means value-free manner of depiction."

Regarding the techniques of writing works of history, from then on part of the awareness of source criticism was the required disclosure of the historical constructions by inserting footnotes. By this means the reliability of the depiction could be made comprehensible by making the sources transparent; on the other hand, the performance of the historiographer in the construct became clear. Once again, in the belles lettres this technique was taken over for the simulation of reliability (Eckstein 2001).

1.2. *"Liminal Period"*

For the period between 1800 and 1850, Jordan identified specific characteristics of content in texts dealing with theoretical historiography that could not be included in either historical pragmatism or in what was later called "classical historicism" from circa 1850 (Jordan 1999b; 2001). This led to a further refinement of historical subperiods for the large period of the late eighteenth through the nineteenth century in the historical scholarship since the late 1990s. Jordan designated the newly demarcated periods with the term "liminal period" and characterized them by four tendencies:

1. Universalization and taking on a purpose of its own, thereby also renouncing a didactic function of history for ethics, society, politics, and so forth (here "pragmatism" becomes a term of opposition!);
2. Embracing empiricism, that is, the strong, indeed total emphasis on the significance of sources for the tasks of history, and with this the renunciation of pragmatic assumptions of timeless ideals;
3. Emphasizing objectivity, meaning, in opposition to the historian Johann Gustav Droysen (1808–1886; see 1.3), not yet an awareness of *interpretation* as one of the historian's methodological moves; and
4. Personalization, that is, the emphasis on the individuality of the historian, to be sure not yet in the sense of one who "reconstructs" history, but as an individual mediator whose *Absicht* (purpose) determines the *Ansicht* (viewpoint) (Leopold von Ranke, 1795–1886; see 1.3).

To be sure, Jordan's "liminal period" has not yet become a consensus in didactic historiography. His own overview, *Theorien und Methoden der Geschichtswissenschaft* (2009), does not adopt it, although Franziska Metzger's textbook *Geschichtsschreibung und Geschichtsdenken im 19. und 20. Jahrhundert* (2011), which appeared just marginally later, does. Nevertheless, the term "liminal period" makes possible a meaningful refinement of periodization for a better comprehension of the currents of theoretical historiography of the time.

1.3. *"Historicism"*

Although the term *Historismus* is attested as early as the late eighteenth century in Friedrich Schlegel (1772–1829) and Novalis (1772–1801), its utilization as a special concept for an epoch is strongly associated with Meinecke and his two-volume *Entstehung des Historismus* (1936). With this work Meinecke reacted to the *Historismuskrise* (historiographical crisis) mostly associated with Ernst Troeltsch (1865–1923) (first in *Die Krisis des Historismus*, 1922). Troeltsch (1977, 192) had dealt with historicism as "the fundamental historization of all our thinking about human beings, their culture, and their values." After forerunners like Karl Marx (1818–1883) and Friedrich Nietzsche (1844–1900), he made the concept of historicism a conceptual problem for a fundamentally relativistic historical consciousness and a crisis-prone understanding of reality. (On the side of the history of theology, almost simultaneously with its efforts to understand the mediation of "God's word" independently from historical-secular assimilation arose the dialectic theology or the theology of the Word of God; cf. Karl Barth's *Römerbrief*, [1919] 1922; Friedrich Gogarten's essay "Zwischen den Zeiten," 1920; and the journal with the same title, 1923–1933). Indeed, Meinecke then took over Troeltsch's central categories of "individuality" and "evolution" but considered historicism not as a *fundamentally* relativizing principle of historical consciousness but as a paradigm of the breakthrough of modern—specifically German!—idealistically influenced understanding of history, as it is initially found in Johann Gottfried Herder (1744–1803), Johann Wolfgang von Goethe (1749–1832), and Wilhelm von Humboldt (1767–1835), but came to full flower in the nineteenth century with Ranke, Droysen, and Theodor Mommsen (1817–1903). With this restriction of the concept of historicism to a limited epoch and the "most German achievement of the German spirit," its profoundly threatening stigma in Nietzsche was suspended and was supplanted by a positive evaluation—albeit painted with nationalistic colors. At the same time, it was limited to a historiographical epoch in Germany with the emphasis on the last two-thirds of the nineteenth century.

According to Meinecke's concept, Ranke is not considered an exponent of a relativism of history and values but rather is often mentioned as a proto-example of an epistemological "positivistic" understanding of history. Thus Ranke is frequently cited with the statement that the historian wishes "simply to say, how it really was" (Ranke 1824, sec. VI). For Ranke, an "objective" depiction of a historical event is in fact an ideal; nevertheless, it would be a misunderstanding to interpret this statement in a "positivistic" sense. For Ranke, it is not a program but a restriction and a delimitation of Enlightenment pragmatism's didactic-ethical evaluation of history. Just a few pages earlier in the same work he emphasizes the concern of an epistemology of history: "The intent of a historian depends on his viewpoint" (Ranke 1824, sec. III, 1.2). And as for the written historical account, it can be clearly seen in Ranke, who in his early years had been strongly influenced by Goethe, how the advanced source-critical claims of early historiography were productively combined with the aesthetic quality of historiography after the "evidence" in Gatterer (Fulda 1996, 296–410).

In contrast to Ranke, Droysen commented extensively and systematically on the theory of history. His *Grundriss der Historik* (first lecture 1857; first publication 1868) had the greatest impact on the theory of history within the late nineteenth century. In it Droysen stipulated not only source criticism but also a multilevel "interpretation" as an independent hermeneutical act and an explicit task of the historian. Droysen, who was still influenced by Georg Wilhelm Friedrich Hegel's ("Prussia's Herald and the harbinger of Lesser Germany's ideal" [Gall 1992, 43], 1770–1831) philosophy of the Spirit and his corresponding teleological theory of history, was completely aware that the object of historical research was not "the past" as such, "but that from the past that does not pass away in the here and now." For Droysen, the past is "ideationally" contained in the present; hence through historical research "the past does not [come] to light, but that which from it does not pass away," the "geistiges Bild" (spirit-image) of the things of the past in the commemorative present (Droysen [8]1977, 326–27). Hence, Droysen's epistemologically reflective emphasis on the dependence of the present on knowledge of the past can be understood as the further development of Chladenius's insights through the school of Hegel.

Independently from these two prominent historians of the nineteenth century, for one thing, the increasingly important study of sources and source criticism are significant for this epoch. Collections of sources and textual tools as well as critical editions of texts were edited, not infrequently in an immense scope. In Germany, the best known and the largest is the *Monumenta Germaniae Historica*, which was a collection of medieval sources founded in 1819 that continues still today. Another example is the *Corpus Inscriptionum Latinarum* (from 1866). Theological counterparts are the Patrologia Latina (from 1844), the Patrologia Graeca (from 1857), the Corpus Scriptorium Ecclesiasticorum Latinorum (from 1866), and also—somewhat later—the Weimarer Ausgabe of Luther's works (from 1883).

In terms of content, likewise intensified from the second half of the nineteenth century, the preoccupation with the "great men" of history—rulers, generals, and artists—is to be noted. This is concretized in numerous biographies, for example, Karl Heinrich Siegfried Rödenbeck, *Tagebuch oder Geschichtskalender aus Friedrichs des Grossen Regentenleben* (1840–1842); Martin Hertz, *Karl Lachmann* (1851); Rudolf Köpke, *Ludwig Tieck* (1855); Rudolf Köpke and Ernst Dümmler, *Kaiser Otto der Grosse* (1876); Philipp Spitta, *Johann Sebastian Bach* (1873–1880); Johann Gustav Droysen, *Geschichte Alexanders des Grossen* (1877); and so forth.

1.4. "Positivism?"

The term "historical positivism" should be handled with great caution for this epoch. To be sure, as a philosophical or social-scientific-political category, this term goes back to Auguste Comte (1798–1857; *Cours de philosophie positive*, 1830–1842; *Discours sur l'esprit positif*, 1842; *Système de politique positive*, 1851–1854). But with it he designated the last and highest level of the evolution of the intellectual development of humanity by way of rejecting metaphysical models of scholarship. By this he meant to surpass and contrast the "theological or fictitious" and "metaphysical or abstract" stages. Its aim was not only to accumulate encyclopedic knowledge, but, by virtue of the immutability of natural physical laws, to make social developments predictable and more maneuverable. To be sure, the debate about positivism penetrated into historiography from the time of the 1850s (e.g., by Henry T. Buckle or in the methodological controversy about Karl Lamprecht in the 1890s). In Germany, however, different from in England and America, it ran into the hermeneutics of Wilhelm Dilthey (1833–1911) as well as Droysen's historiography with its hermeneutical distinction of historiographical "understanding" in contrast to philosophical-theological "development" and "perception" as well as the disapproval of mathematical-physical "explanation" (Droysen [8]1977, 330, 339, and passim; on Buckle, 41–62).

2. *Effects on Jesus Research*

Hermann Samuel Reimarus's (1694–1768) *Fragmente*, which Gotthold Ephraim Lessing (1729–1781) published between 1774 and 1778, were a thunderbolt that allowed Erasmus's humanistic motto *Ad fontes!* to be radically applied also to the Bible. The criticism of biblical miracle stories, which in Europe had substantially been triggered as a new theme by the chaos brought on by the Thirty Years' War (famously by Spinoza, 1632–1677), was brought by Reimarus to a new pinnacle. In contrast to Spinoza, however, Reimarus now criticized the Bible as "forgery," "dissimulation," "fraud," and so forth. Even though Reimarus wrote his *Apologie* precisely in the time (ca. 1735–1768) in which Chladenius's primary works appeared, the latter's hermeneutical insights or the relevance of his *Sehe-Punct* (point of view) was not reflected. The fact that for Reimarus the entirety of Christian faith depended on the "factum of the resurrection" demonstrates his apologetic (and also biographical) perspective, but not his historiographical conceptualization. Hence, Peter Stemmer (1983, 152) has quite correctly summed up that Reimarus understood biblical exegesis above all as *fundamental theological* activity (see also Verweyen 2005, 304–6).

Therefore, the attainments of critical, professional historiography did not precipitate in Jesus research *with* but *after* Reimarus, initially in the study of source criticism, philological criticism, as well as in precursors of form criticism. This went hand in hand with the emancipation of New Testament scholarship as a separate, historical discipline, working independently from dogmatics. With this self-understanding, New Testament scholarship made significant progress, especially in text criticism as well as on the "Synoptic problem."

Exegesis ("biblical theology") as a purely historical discipline—that is, separate from dogmatics perceived as speculative—is often associated with Johann Philipp Gabler's (1753–1826) lecture in Altdorf, "De iusto discrimine theologiae biblicae et dogmaticae regundisque recte utriusque finibus" ("On the Proper Distinction between Biblical and Dogmatic Theology and the Proper Definition of Their Goals"). The limitation of "biblical theology" to a historical discipline served here to methodologically facilitate better control of interpretations and practices. Above all for Gabler, it should be converted to a philological-semantic method. Further ongoing impulses for the development of New Testament scholarship as an independent, historical discipline arose also from Ferdinand Christian Baur (1792–1860) and the early "Tübingen School" (Bauspiess et al. 2014).

General interest in the study of historical sources was paralleled in New Testament scholarship by the rapid advances in study of the historical environment and culture of Palestine, in Hellenism, in the period of Roman emperors, as well as in text criticism. The discovery of more and more manuscripts of New Testament texts facilitated the development of their genealogical relationship and evaluation, for example, in the display of a *tabula genealogica* by Johann Albrecht Bengel (1687–1752). By means of consistent use of new criteria for assessing New Testament manuscripts, Karl Lachmann's (1793–1851) edition of the New Testament (1831) brought about the downfall of what until then had been the favored *textus receptus*. The increasing sensitivity in source criticism, which was also increasingly applied to the Bible, led to the standardization of the now classic "introductory questions" and to a new book genre, the introduction to the Old or New Testament. Especially to be mentioned here are the works of Johann David Michaelis (1750), Johann Gottfried Eichhorn (to the Old Testament, 1780–1793; to the New Testament, 1804–1827), Wilhelm Martin Leberecht de Wette (1817, 1826), and Heinrich Julius Holtzmann (1885). Even today the achievements of these early authors with respect to text criticism and knowledge of sources are still truly amazing! Eichhorn had studied in Göttingen and was trained by Schlözer (Eichhorn himself later became Gabler's teacher in Jena). Although he wrote more on the Old Testament than on the New Testament, according to the universal historical objective of Enlightenment history (see his *Weltgeschichte*, 1799–1814), he integrated his history of Jesus in this great canopy. Also, his theory of a "proto-gospel" is easily integrated into the background of fascination with the ideal beginning (see significantly, among others, Diderot and Herder; cf. on the latter, Alkier 1993, 122–36, 257–58). In the comparison between Michaelis (1750) and Eichhorn's first volume of his introduction, progress in the historiographical working technique can be clearly gathered in the utilization of "secondary literature": Eichhorn, writing thirty years after Michaelis, set up footnotes for excursuses and source attestations and thus made the main text more readable. In structure and the type of questions, his *Einleitung* already bears the imprint of present-day New Testament introductions (as, for instance, Schnelle, recently [9]2017, or Pokorný and Heckel 2007).

Rather quickly after the "historical-critical method" had made its advent into biblical scholarship, it was already severely criticized. A prototypical example of the intrusion of novelistic paradigms in works of writing history is Karl H. G. Venturini's (1768–1849) four-volume *Natürliche Geschichte des großen Propheten von Nazareth* (1800–1802), which was exceptionally successful at that time. From today's viewpoint, this work may be aesthetically lacking in taste, but in regard to the history of Jesus exegesis, it deserves attention nevertheless. Venturini envisioned himself as a working critical scholar and historian, rejected "novel" as a label for his work, and pushed back against anticipated reproaches that he had mixed in too many novelistic features in his book (1800, 17). He described his *Natürliche Geschichte* as "a half poetic, half historical construct" and justified this mixed approach by reasoning that the evangelists had proceeded in like manner with their material, and in any case, historical-critical investigations achieved only obscure results (Venturini [2]1806, v–viii). In the extremely comprehensive bibliography of literature on Jesus from the second edition of Karl Hase's *Leben Jesu*, Venturini is included in the same category with Reimarus (!), under the subtitle "Kritische Richtung" (Hase [2]1835, 33–34). Later novelistic portraits of the "life of Jesus" are available by Joseph H. Ingraham (English 1855, German 1858) and Ernest Renan (French and German, 1863), among others.

In spite of Venturini's objection, the results of source criticism in scholarship on Jesus led to increasingly strong and better-supported skepticism against the historical reliability of the accounts of Jesus in the Gospels. Sure enough, the life of Jesus had been portrayed for centuries by harmonizing the gospel accounts, by retelling the story poetically, or by emphasizing its morally instructive value. On the other hand, the writings of Heinrich Eberhard Gottlob Paulus (1828) and Hase (1829) are among the first rationalistic-critical works on the life of Jesus. Paulus, a Tübingen student of Gottlob Christian Storr (1746–1805), who was supernaturalistically minded, had displayed vast knowledge of sources in his three-volume *Kommentar über die drey ersten Evangelien* (1800–1802; later expanded to five volumes, 1830–1833) and demonstrated how he considered the *historical* task primarily as a *philological* task. His *Life of Jesus* seeks to be a "historical narrative in popular terms." Indeed, it is thoroughly rationalistic, but at the same time surprisingly edifying and apologetic. Hase's presentations, by contrast, are more deliberative with respect to "secondary literature" and more reflective of the theory of historiography. His Jesus acts as a person of idealistic will and consummate divine life.

But before the great period of books on the "life of Jesus" flourished, theology was stirred up by a publication on Jesus that aimed at portraying the religion of Christ without recourse to historically verifiable findings. This publication contrived thereby to silence Paulus's rationalism: David Friedrich Strauss's (1808–1874) *Leben Jesu* (1835–1836). In his historical idealism derived from Hegel, Strauss considered himself the antipode to the historical-apologetic mind-set of Reimarus. He perceived the relevance of the portraits of Jesus in the gospel in "myth," that is, in the "vivification of the idea of humankind in itself," and claimed this as the "only way to authentic spirit-life for humanity" (Strauss 2012 [1835–1836], 2:735).

Strauss's work became enormously influential on Jesus exegesis, albeit almost exclusively *ex negativo* at the start. Instantly it gave rise to numerous publications on the "life of Jesus," mostly in a defensive style. Most of these are forgotten today (Neander 1837; J. Kuhn 1838, among many others). (Generally, in spite of the insights of professional historiography and the advances in exegesis, naïve harmonistic and edifying portraits of Jesus were composed throughout the entire century; see, for example, Bucher 1859; Baltzer 1860.) Indirectly, however, the reception of Strauss's work furthered responsible scholarly debate on the foundations of the history of Jesus and, with this, of Christianity as *historical*. Certainly, the most significant publication of this branch that has retained its influence for today is *Die evangelische Geschichte* of Christian Hermann Weisse (1838), a philosopher but, according to his own declaration, "not a theologian" and—like Strauss—a Hegelian. He wished to reclaim the historical dimension of the life of Jesus while being aware of the uncertainty of "historical constructions" in general, and the unhistorical "admixtures" in the Gospels in particular. However, in contrast to Strauss, he was persuaded along with Schleiermacher that a historical outline of the life of Jesus was theologically necessary, since in it—this time clearly differently from Schleiermacher—the "idea of the archetypal personality [dwelt] with its complete immediacy" (Weisse 1838, vol. 2, 500–542; citation 501). The result of his source-critical studies was the first postulate of a "collection of sayings" of Jesus (today: "sayings source") as the foundation of the Gospels of Matthew and Luke, that is, as a second source alongside Mark. Again, this was an asset for the idealistic thinking about origins of the time (see C.II.1.1).

Finally, Holtzmann made a resounding contribution to the gradual establishment of Markan priority and the two-source theory with his influential study *Die synoptischen Evangelien* (1863). What is noteworthy in his reasoning is that he still grounded the necessity of *historical* Jesus scholarship, on the one hand, in a hostile stance against edifying ecclesiastical dogmatism, and on the other hand, against dissolving/dissipating biblical history into myth as in Strauss (1863, 1–9).

The differentiation in sources carried out by Holtzmann (the Gospel of Mark versus "Proto-Mark" or "source A"; the Gospel of Matthew versus "Proto-Matthew" or "source Λ") made the configuration of a comprehensive portrait of the life of Jesus increasingly problematic. The numerous books on the life of Jesus, which were still written, can indeed be classified easily in the historicist interest in the "great personalities" of history, but they hardly capture the state of research of source criticism of the time. Where Holtzmann himself made a "contribution to research on the life of Jesus" he was aware—along with Schweitzer (1906)—that the subjectivity of the scholar could "not be turned off absolutely," and every account of Jesus contained "unconsciously a part of [the] theology [of its author], sometimes even [the author's] individuality altogether" (Holtzmann 1907, v). Droysen had also arrived in exegesis.

Lastly, a bleak aspect of the research on the Gospels and Jesus of the nineteenth century cannot be concealed. It strikes today's readers in a shameful way how often and with what ease Christianity was contrasted over against Judaism in opposition or supersession, Jesus's message of "freedom" and "love" over against "obdurate," "legalistic," "narrow-minded" Judaism, almost as a matter of course. Multiple causes promoted such a distortion; for one, the painfully ambivalent perception of Judaism in modern Europe in general (Reinke 2007; Litt 2009) intensified from the 1870s and 1880s, along with Hegel's idealism of Prussian progress and finally the German (pre)nationalist mentality within the entire century—right up until Meinecke—which as a whole cannot be abstracted from historical research of this epoch (Metzger 2011, 156–85). At the same time, this tendency was not limited to Germany. Also, for Renan in France, "Judaism" is depicted with unmentionable strings of negative attributes, and by contrast Jesus was made a hero as the bringer of "definitive, universal, and eternal religion"; not so completely extreme nevertheless analogous patterns of thought are found also in America in Thomas Jefferson (1743–1826).

Brown, Colin. 1985. *Jesus in European Protestant Thought, 1778–1860*. SHT 1. Durham, NC.

Jordan, Stefan. 2009. *Theorien und Methoden der Geschichtswissenschaft: Orientierung Geschichte*. UTB 3104. Paderborn.

Metzger, Franziska. 2011. *Geschichtsschreibung und Geschichtsdenken im 19. und 20. Jahrhundert*. UTB 3555. Bern, Stuttgart, and Vienna.

Reventlow, Henning Graf. 2001. *Epochen der Bibelauslegung*. Vol. 4, *Von der Aufklärung bis zum 20. Jahrhundert*. Munich.

Schweitzer, Albert. ⁹1984. *Geschichte der Leben-Jesu-Forschung*. UTB 1302. Tübingen.

Eckart David Schmidt

V. The Concept of Myth in Historical Jesus Research and the Rise of the Two-Document Hypothesis

The quest of the historical Jesus and the origins of the "Synoptic problem" can be traced at least in part to an essay by the rationalist Reimarus, "Von dem Zwecke Jesu und seiner Jünger" ("On the Intention of Jesus and His Disciples"), published after Reimarus's death by Lessing in 1778. Refusing to harmonize the accounts of Jesus in the canonical Gospels, Reimarus pointed to numerous contradictions among the Gospels, taking these to be indications of fraud. He argued that Jesus had been a teacher of simple morality and a failed apocalypticist. The self-contradictory accounts in the Gospels were due to the disciples, motivated by financial gain and political advantage, who concocted fantastic stories about Jesus, whom they now depicted as a suffering and resurrected savior of humankind. Reimarus's essay demanded a response, since he had exposed serious contradictions in the Gospels that both threatened confidence in the Gospels as records of the historical Jesus and potentially undermined the Gospels as the foundation of theological dogmas.

The response to Reimarus was swift and came from many directions, with conservative opponents maintaining supernaturalism and defending the historical reliability of the Gospels. Others—Griesbach (1789–1790), Lessing (1784), Eichhorn (1794), and Schleiermacher (1832), for example—proposed literary hypotheses in order to account for the disagreements among the Synoptics. Lessing, Eichhorn, and Schleiermacher posited one or more lost Aramaic *Urgospels* lying behind the Gospels, while Griesbach (followed by Schleiermacher) proposed a compositional and editorial genealogy that derived Luke from Matthew, and Mark from Matthew and Luke. The differences among the Gospels were thus due either to the vagaries of translation from an Aramaic original or to the deliberate editorial decisions of the evangelists. Thus was inaugurated an important initial phase of the "Synoptic problem"—the investigation of the literary and historical relationship among the first three canonical Gospels—and the modern quest of the historical Jesus.

The solutions to the "Synoptic problem" proposed during the early nineteenth century addressed only one part of Reimarus's critique of the Gospels, but not the rationalist critique, which had dismissed the miraculous stories of healings, nature miracles, and resurrections as incredible. Paulus (1828), for example, dismissed what were reported as miracles simply as faulty perceptions or coincidences: a storm subsided just as Jesus spoke; persons reported as resurrected had simply been asleep or unconscious; and the "multiplication of the loaves" was in fact a matter of Jesus inspiring wealthy pilgrims passing the crowd gathered around Jesus to share their food.

1. Strauss and the Concept of Myth

Strauss's *Das Leben Jesu: Kritisch bearbeitet* (*The Life of Jesus, Critically Examined*, 1835–1836; ET 1972) took a strikingly different view. He allowed that the sayings of Jesus transmitted by the Synoptics were "most important and efficacious" and "not at all impugned" (Strauss, letter of July 12, 1835, in Harris 1973, 61). But with regard to the miracles, Strauss rejected both rationalistic explanations and naïve supernaturalism. Developing Eichhorn's proposed "mythic method of interpretation" (1790), which recognized the mythic substructure of certain biblical stories, Strauss argued that the miracle stories and most other narratives in the Gospels were not the result of fraud but arose from the mythic content of the Gospels, expressing the early community's way of understanding Jesus within the framework of contemporary messianic expectations. Whereas Eichhorn and others had perceived the mythic basis only for isolated stories in the New Testament, Strauss saw the entire story of Jesus pervaded by myth: from the birth stories, the temptations, the miracle stories, and transfiguration to the passion and resurrection accounts. Taken literally, these reports were hopelessly contradictory and quite incredible. The truth of Christianity, however, was not based on the historicity of the Gospels, nor undermined by inconsistencies and contradictions. Taken together, these narratives embodied the myth of the God-man. Far from being fraudulent or fanciful, the myth of the God-man was at the heart of the Christian message. Interpreted philosophically by means of Hegel's philosophy of history, it expressed in mythic form the notion of the "development of human subjectivity with the emergence of finite spirit's consciousness of its participation in the self-realization of Absolute Spirit, or God, in and through the world" (Breckman 1999, 34).

Some theologians embraced the politically and theologically conservative "Old Hegelian" interpretation of Hegel's philosophy of history and held that Jesus was the historical actualization of the God-man. Strauss, however, first identified himself with the "Young Hegelians," who valorized reason and freedom as the guiding forces in history and were critical of religious beliefs as irrational. For Strauss it was the *idea* of the God-man, not Jesus as a historical person, that conveyed the notion of the embodiment of Absolute Reason in humanity. Jesus was the occasion of the entrance of this idea into human history, but he was not its embodiment.

> This is the key to the whole of Christology, that, as subject of the predicate which the church assigns to Christ, we place, instead of an individual, an idea; but an idea which has an existence in reality, not in the mind only, like that of Kant. In an individual, a God-man (Gottmenschen), the properties and functions which the church ascribes to Christ contradict themselves; in the idea of the species (Gattung), they perfectly agree. Humanity is the union of

the two natures—God become man, the infinite manifesting itself in the finite, and the finite spirit remembering its infinitude. . . . By faith in this Christ, especially in his death and resurrection, humanity is justified before God; that is, by the kindling within him of the idea of Humanity, the individual man participates in the divinely human life of the species. (Strauss 1835–1836, 2:§150, pp. 739–40; 1972, §151, p. 780)

Strauss was as remorseless as Reimarus in laying out the contradictions and incredibility of biblical stories, if interpreted literally. But unlike Reimarus, Strauss did not trace these contradictions to fraud, and he rejected rationalist explanations such as those of Paulus. The fictions of biblical literature were the result of unconscious mythmaking, and these myths should be read within a philosophical framework. Strauss's mythic approach was so comprehensive that it undermined any attempt to produce a life of Jesus. Although he claimed that his work only built on what others had already achieved, it should not surprise that the radical nature of his claims met with fierce opposition and Strauss lost his teaching position at Tübingen.

In Strauss's view, the Synoptics were composed in the second century and were the result of a very long period of oral transmission, during which time mythic interpretation occurred. The result was an account of Jesus that, "though unhistorical in its form, is nevertheless a faithful representation of the idea of the Christ" (1972, §10, p. 62)—fictitious stories that, by virtue of their mythic content, conveyed the essential truth of Christianity.

2. Reactions against Strauss and the Development of Markan Priority

Only three years after the appearance of Strauss's first volume, Weisse published *Die evangelische Geschichte: Kritisch und philosophisch bearbeitet (The Gospel History Critically and Philosophically Examined*, 1838), with a title that deliberately evoked Strauss. Weisse, a professor of philosophy at Leipzig, had initially regarded himself as a Hegelian and embraced Hegel's notion of the self-realization of absolute subjectivity in human history. But he argued that this self-realization of the Absolute occurred historically in Jesus (1838, 2:512), and, against Hegel's supposed pantheism, he asserted a principle of theistic personality (Breckman 1999, 51). This in turn implied that the historical Jesus would be critical to Weisse in a way that it was not for Strauss.

Weisse agreed in large measure with Strauss that the miracle stories were not historical but arose from the imaginations of Jesus's early followers. But he disagreed strongly with Strauss's late dating of the Synoptics and with his embrace of the Griesbach hypothesis, which held that Matthew was the main source of Luke, and Mark used both Matthew and Luke (Strauss 1972, 71). Strauss had even characterized Mark as having "almost an apocryphal appearance" (Strauss 1972, 389). Weisse, by contrast, found credible Papias's report that Mark embodied the memories of Peter, and, although he did not think that Mark was completely reliable, he argued that Mark's rough style and frequent Semitisms pointed to an early date of composition. Thus he proposed a theory of Markan priority. From Schleiermacher he adopted the idea of a sayings collection, but while Schleiermacher had argued that this collection and a narrative source were used by Matthew alone, Weisse argued that Matthew *and Luke* used Mark and the *Spruchsammlung* (Weisse 1838, 1:83–84). Thus, Weisse inverted Strauss's literary theory, treating Mark as the earliest gospel and arguing that Mark, along with the sayings collection, reflected generally reliable historical tradition (Baird 1992, 307; Schröter 2013, 15).

3. Historical Jesus Studies, 1830–1870

As Reicke has pointed out, the period between 1830 and 1870 witnessed an erratic oscillation between the Griesbach hypothesis, which placed Mark last, and the Markan hypothesis, which placed it first. Deductive approaches that began with philosophical assumptions derived from Hegel sometimes saw the Griesbach hypothesis as a literary ally (Strauss), but Markan priority was advocated by Weisse (Reicke 1987, 8). In 1841–1842 Bruno Bauer, one of the "Young Hegelians," rejected Strauss's mythic interpretation as un-Hegelian and Weisse's hypothesis of a sayings collection, but endorsed Markan priority (Bauer 1841–1842). Yet he also rejected the idea that Mark was based on reliable historical tradition: it was instead only a reflection of Mark's self-consciousness. And since Bauer had come to regard religion as a form of alienation, Mark's self-consciousness was an example of religion's projection of transcendent powers governing the self and sanctioning false material interests. Only a few years later, Marx, once a student, then a critic, of Bauer, would declare that "for Germany, the criticism of religion is essentially completed; and the criticism of religion is the prerequisite of every criticism" (Marx and Engels, 1844, 71).

Bauer's historical skepticism and radical use of the Markan hypothesis provoked yet another counterreaction in the revival of the Griesbach hypothesis by Ferdinand Christian Baur in Tübingen (1847). Baur in fact agreed that the consciousness of the evangelist was the starting point of criticism, but he employed it in what he called "tendency criticism," a forerunner of redaction criticism that allowed him to identify the intentions distinctive of each literary document and, in his later work, to distinguish early tradition from the evangelists' "tendencies."

Still under the spell of grand theories of doctrinal development, Baur saw in the Griesbach hypothesis of a progression from Matthew to Luke to Mark an instance of the dialectical relation of Matthew's Petrine Judaism meeting Luke's Hellenistic Paulinism, and the two being synthesized by Mark.

Although Baur (1847, 535–39) treated Mark as devoid of independent historical material, he did not follow Strauss's skepticism about the historical value of the Synoptics, still less Bruno Bauer's absolute rejection of historical tradition. In spite of his second-century dating of the Synoptics, Baur (1853, 22–23; ET 1878–1879, 1:23) insisted that the person of Jesus as founder was critical to understanding the essence and content of Christianity. And when late in his career he departed from the appeal to speculative philosophy for constructing the essence of Christianity, Baur then appealed to its moral teaching, regarding Jesus as having introduced a "new principle": "that form of action in accordance with which we do to others what we wish that others should do to us. The morally good is thus that which is equally right and good for all, or which can be the object of action for all alike. . . . Thus do the absolute contents of the Christian principle find their expression in the moral consciousness. What gives a man his highest moral value is simply the purity of a disposition which is genuinely moral, and rises above all that is finite, particular, and merely subjective" (1853, 31; ET 1878–1879, 1:33).

Baur died in 1860 and so never produced a life of Jesus. Moreover, the Griesbach hypothesis was in decline: most of Baur's students—the "Tübingen School"—had moved from theology to philosophy, abandoned quasi-Hegelian frameworks, or defected from adherence to the Griesbach hypothesis to Markan priority. By 1863 the Markan hypothesis was again dominant and would remain so, due to the critiques of the Griesbach hypothesis by Bernhard Weiss (1861) and Holtzmann's *Die synoptischen Evangelien* (1863). While Holtzmann (1863, 3) was extremely critical of Baur's use of the Griesbach hypothesis, he praised Baur for departing from Strauss's attribution of the content of the Synoptics to "the myth-making fantasies of the early church."

4. The Emergence of the Liberal Lives of Jesus

There had been yet more important shifts. The influence of Hegel had waned considerably, partly on account of the influence of Feuerbach's (1841) critique of Hegel and partly because Baur could not accept the atheism Strauss, Feuerbach, and Bauer saw as the logical consequence of Hegelianism (Harris 1975, 167). What replaced speculative philosophy was a return to rationalism, not in the sense of Paulus's critique of the miracles, but the rationalism of Kant, which privileged ethics as the enduring core of religion. But Holtzmann also stressed Jesus's *personality* as a key focus of study and proposed a model of psychological development (adapted from Keim 1861).

Although Holtzmann is sometimes remembered as the founder of the Markan hypothesis, he did not conclude that Mark was the earliest gospel. Instead, the foundation of a life of Jesus was a hypothetical *Urmarkus* that he called "A," which consisted of Mark supplemented by the words of John the Baptist (Matt. 3:7–12; Luke 3:7–9, 16–17), the long form of the temptation story, a version of the Sermon on the Mount (Luke 6:20–49), the story of the centurion's serving boy (Matt. 8:5–13; Luke 7:1–10), an expanded version of the Beelzebul accusation, the story of the adulterous woman from John (John 7:53–8:11), and Matthew's great commissioning (Matt. 28:9–10, 16–20). Canonical Mark had abbreviated "A" while Matthew and Luke used it as a source, combining it with a logia source.

Holtzmann's life of Jesus, though it stressed Jesus as an ethical model, ignored the logia source and focused on "A" as holding the key to Jesus's personality and psychological development. The beginning of this development was Jesus's initial self-realization as the Messiah at the baptism, when he experienced a "great enlightenment regarding his divine vocation" (1863, 476) and moved to its final phase when Jesus was acclaimed by his disciples as the Messiah and when Jesus came to realize that death "was the only possible [fate] and the only one of which he was worthy" (1863, 485) (see Kloppenborg 2006). According to Holtzmann's "life of Jesus," he was possessed of "the clarity and harmony of what constitutes a vigorous person: the convergence of understanding, emotion, perception, presentiment, genuine simplicity, and innocence" (1863, 496)—a description that served well the theological goals of liberal theology, with its strong antidogmatic and romantic inclinations.

Holtzmann's life of Jesus became the model for the next forty years of "liberal lives of Jesus," most of which stressed Jesus's notion of the kingdom of God as a spiritual kingdom of repentance and the conviction, based on Holtzmann's reading of Mark, that Jesus's messianic consciousness developed, precipitated by his baptism, and then by a "Galilean crisis" in which Jesus came to face the failure of his mission. Franz Rosenzweig's (2000, 12–13) observations on the liberal lives of Jesus in general could well be applied specifically to Holtzmann:

> Precisely romanticism's insight that only living "individuality" was called to rule the world, and not teaching—even if it taught the Truth itself—made the view of Jesus as the Teacher appear obsolete even before it could be fully developed. According to this new picture, a "teacher" could not be the one with whose appearance "the time" was supposed to be "fulfilled." Schleiermacher found the problem-solving formulation, that "the emergence of a revelation in an individual person" was to be regarded as "prepared in human nature and

as the highest development of its spiritual force." Thus, not the "teacher" but rather the "personality" was the human essence of Jesus, from which Christianity sprang, today as well as once eighteen hundred years ago. "Personality" was inhabited by a being that eluded history's deadening power. According to this thought, so it seemed, one could —indeed one had to—grasp the existence of Jesus, once one was determined to avoid dogma.

5. *The Nineteenth Century in Retrospect*

Nineteenth-century scholarship on the historical Jesus is thus characterized by major oscillations in approach. In the wake of Reimarus's radical critique of the Gospels as a reliable basis for reconstructions of the historical Jesus and Christian dogma, one (extremely varied) stream of scholarship located the importance of gospel research in the philosophical ideas: Strauss's "Hegelianism" and focus on myth as a kind of prephilosophical idea; Weisse's insistence on personalism in contrast to the pantheism of Hegel; Baur's notion of the dialectical unfolding of theology in history; and Bauer's attention to the philosophy of consciousness and religion as a false consciousness. Although these philosophical approaches also assumed different solutions to the "Synoptic problem," it is not clear that Strauss's views needed the Griesbach hypothesis (Tuckett 1979, 32) nor that Bauer's critique of consciousness required the Markan hypothesis.

The Griesbach hypothesis was more integral to Baur's view of the history of theology, but when Baur late in his career turned his attention to the historical Jesus, the Griesbach hypothesis and his second-century dating of the Gospels arguably posed a difficulty for his views, because of the century-long hiatus between Jesus in the 30s and the composition of Matthew in the period 130–134 CE, at the time of the crushing of the Bar Kokhba revolt (F. C. Baur 1847, 609).

A second stream of scholarship, also heterogeneous in its results, focused on a recovery of the historical Jesus from the Gospels. Since the rationalist critique of miracles, few were prepared to defend supernaturalism, but this meant that the core of Jesus's importance lay elsewhere. Reimarus's life of Jesus rejected most of the contents of the Gospels as unreliable and arrived at a Jesus who taught a simple piety formed about the expectation of the realization of the kingdom of God on earth. Baur (ET 1878–1879, 1:26–43) focused on the moral teachings of Jesus and his opposition to "Pharisaism," putting special emphasis on Matthew's Sermon on the Mount. But, as noted above, the late dating of his main source for Jesus's moral teachings raised potential problems for his reconstruction. It was Holtzmann's synoptic theory, which placed the sayings collection and especially "A" as the earliest sources, that allowed for the compelling reconstruction of the historical Jesus that was so attractive to nineteenth-century romanticism and its focus on the heroic personality, "full of unspoiled naïveté but at the same time full of dignity and wisdom, the ideal image of bourgeois nostalgia," as Georgi puts it (1992, 78). This would last at least until Wernle (1899) argued that a distinction between "A" and Mark was unnecessary, and Wrede (1901; ET 1971) cast profound doubts on the reliability of Mark's narrative, at which point the marriage of lives of Jesus and the two-document hypothesis began to crumble.

With the collapse of confidence in Mark as a historically reliable basis for a life of Jesus, in particular Holtzmann's theory of Jesus's psychological development, there was a short-lived attempt to base the recovery of Jesus's consciousness on Q (Harnack 1907; ET 1908). But within a few years, form criticism privileged the oral phase of transmission and stressed the creativity of the early community's transmission of Jesus materials (Bultmann [1913] 1994). This meant in turn that the historical Jesus tended to recede behind the creativity of oral performances.

Arnal, William E. 2005. *The Symbolic Jesus: Historical Scholarship, Judaism, and the Construction of Contemporary Identity*. London.

Baird, William. 1992. *History of New Testament Research*. Vol. 1, *From Deism to Tübingen*. Minneapolis.

Harris, Horton. 1975. *The Tübingen School*. Oxford.

Moxnes, Halvor. 2012. *Jesus and the Rise of Nationalism: A New Quest for the Nineteenth-Century Historical Jesus*. London.

Rosenzweig, Franz. 2000. "Atheistic Theology (1914)." In *Philosophical and Theological Writings*, edited by Paul W. Franks and Michael L. Morgan, 10–24. Indianapolis.

Schweitzer, Albert. ⁹1984. *Geschichte der Leben-Jesu-Forschung*. UTB 1302. Tübingen. ET: 2001. *The Quest of the Historical Jesus*. Edited by John Bowden. Minneapolis.

John S. Kloppenborg

VI. The "Kingdom of God" as an Eschatological Concept: Johannes Weiss and Albert Schweitzer

1. Introduction

In any narrative of the study of Jesus's use of the phrase "the kingdom of God," Johannes Weiss and Albert Schweitzer play a central role, the former sometimes seen as a herald of the latter's so-called consistent eschatological view (Lundström 1963; Perrin 1963; Willis 1987a; Morgan 1989). Such a perception of the relationship of the two was encouraged by Schweitzer himself (2000, 198–201, 312), who, in his *Quest of the Historical Jesus*, presents his own work as carrying to its corrective and "logical" conclusion the work of Weiss.

Contrary to Schweitzer's beguiling narrative, one should see these two figures, of very different temperament and disposition, side by side rather than as moments on the way to the presentation of a historical truth (Willis 1987a). As will be seen, in their understanding of the term "the kingdom of God" and, by extension, the idea of Jesus's eschatology, they had much in common, both in the positions they opposed and in the overall interpretation they advocated, though they wrote about it in books of contrasting lengths (compare Schweitzer 2000 with Weiss 1892). Other sources for Schweitzer's view are, *inter alia*, Schweitzer 1925 and 1995. Weiss wrote an extended version of *Predigt* in Weiss ²1900, and other relevant material can be found in Weiss 1901. Where they differed was the degree to which, and the manner in which, they saw the kingdom as the guiding light of Jesus's ministry, in the relationship they thought existed between Jesus and the coming of the kingdom, and in the style they wrote. To some, such differences are small, concealing more important similarities. To others, such differences are more important (Willis 1987a; Morgan 1989). Certainly New Testament scholars, while fascinated by Schweitzer's work, not least because of its vivid style, the image of Jesus that emerges from it (Rowland 1989, 225), and the fame of its author, have tended to see Weiss's work as more reliable and sober (Morgan 1989), and more innovative.

2. Weiss's and Schweitzer's Kingdom

In different ways Weiss's and Schweitzer's interest in Jesus's understanding of the phrase the "kingdom of God" arises from a dissatisfaction with contemporaneous German and, especially, liberal understanding of that phrase. Grounded in large part upon Albrecht Ritschl's view that the kingdom was an ethical entity, "arising out of the redemption of Christ, . . . the moral organization of human society inspired by love," and "the common end of God and Christians and community" (Perrin 1963, 15), liberal theologians tended to play down the futurist eschatological dimension of the phrase as used by Jesus, preferring to see the latter's usage as primarily communitarian, ethical, and this-worldly. Weiss, in the introduction to the first edition of his *Predigt* (1892, 57–60), while acknowledging that the term "the kingdom of God" proved useful to those theologians wanting to bring together dogmatics and ethics, wondered whether its dominant dogmatic understanding faithfully reflected Jesus's original use of the concept. It was this belief in the disjunction between dogmatics and history in the understanding of Jesus's use of the term that drove him to the writing of *Predigt* (Lannert 1989, 108–17, noting intimations of his view in earlier publications, e.g., J. Weiss 1888). Schweitzer never voices such a straightforward motivation for his work (in fact, he claims that his own distinctive reading of Jesus's view of the kingdom came to him in a moment of semirevelation while reading Matt. 10 on troop maneuvers; see Schweitzer 1949, 6–8), though the quest for historical truthfulness is a part of his well-honed rhetoric, and he is clear that the picture he paints of Jesus is historically correct, though theologically painful (Schweitzer 2000, 478–89). His dissatisfaction with the liberal understanding of the term lay also in a strong sense that such an interpretation produced a morally reduced and pale portrait of Jesus (Schweitzer 2000, 482–83). Weiss, by contrast, extolled Ritschl's vision of the kingdom of God (he was Ritschl's son-in-law and delayed publication of *Predigt* until three years after Ritschl died; see Willis 1987a, 2n8), in spite of its lack of biblical warrant (Weiss 1892, 59; Morgan 1989, 101). But however they conceived the results of their work, hermeneutical or otherwise, Weiss and Schweitzer were clear that the liberal interpretation of Jesus's kingdom was historically unsustainable.

3. Weiss's and Schweitzer's Interpretation

For Weiss and Schweitzer the key to understanding Jesus's use of the term "kingdom of God" lay in their reading of Judaism. While in the first version of his *Predigt* Weiss gave mild expression to this view, in his second edition, of 1900, which supplemented and filled out the first edition, he paid more attention to the matter (^{2}1900, 1–35). Here he argued that there were two concepts of the term in Judaism, one in which man was at the center and in which God's sovereignty on earth was emphasized, and another in which God was at the center and the disjunction between the world and God was emphasized. It was this latter view that had come to dominate and led to an emphasis on the need for God to come and renew the world in the future through a divine mighty act (see Isa. 40:10; Zech. 14:9, 16–21; etc.). Although the term "kingdom of God" was rare in Judaism, where it was witnessed, such as in the Kaddish prayer, or the Assumption of Moses, it referred to this specific hope. It was Weiss's (^{2}1900, 30–35) conviction that a more realistic view of Jesus's use of the term would emerge from such a contextual reading. In mapping out the context of Jesus's use of the term, Schweitzer was less interested in the history of the term itself and more in a tale of the development of eschatological thought among the Jews from the early classical prophets like Amos, through Isaiah and others (a this-worldly and messianic view), to Daniel (an otherworldly, supramessianic view), and finally to 4 Ezra and 2 Baruch, who in conceiving of the end time in terms of two consecutive kingdoms, one temporary and one eternal to replace it, combine the developing prophetic and Danielic view into one, and it is their work, the product of a scribal class, that most influences Jesus (Schweitzer 2000, 246–47), and whose contents provided Schweitzer with the means toward reconstructing Jesus's eschatologically dominated life. That is why he could write, using a well-known German Protestant coinage, that Jesus's attitudes reflected "late Judaism" (Schweitzer 1995, 117).

It was not so much in the contents of their discussion of the Jewish background to the term that Weiss and Schweitzer wrote distinctively. Their views on this matter reflected earlier work, which had been encouraged by the publication of a number of recently discovered pseudepigraphical works like 1 Enoch, the Assumption of Moses, and 2 Baruch (see Morgan 1989, 94–95). It was rather in their view, expressed differently, that Jesus's use of the term "kingdom of God" ·should be understood in continuity with such views, rather than in contrast to them, that they looked eccentric, a point neatly captured in Bousset's response to Weiss, published in 1893, which was entitled *Jesu Predigt in ihrem Gegensatz zum Judentum: Ein religionsgeschichtlicher Vergleich* (Carleton Paget 2014).

For Weiss and Schweitzer the Gospels formed the central element of their studies. Both agree that the Gospel of John is not historical (Weiss 1892, 60; Schweitzer 2000, 74–75), and Weiss ([2]1900, 60) is clear that too much scholarship on the kingdom has accepted John's realized vision of eschatology. Weiss (1892, 60–64) also questions Matthew's reliability (it is a late, ecclesial gospel) and thinks that Mark also presents problems. He is especially skeptical about using the parables as a way into understanding the idea of the kingdom. Such a reserved position on questions of historicity means that Weiss treats each saying on a case-by-case basis. Schweitzer takes a less circumspect view. For him Mark and Matthew in particular, precisely because of the disordered nature of their structures, are reliable witnesses. It is up to the imaginative critic to see how those texts can be rearranged (Schweitzer 2000, 296–302) to prove their historical character. It is precisely his eschatological reading that will serve to supplant Wrede's skeptical reading (Schweitzer 2000, 315).

Both scholars see Jesus's association with John the Baptist as central to understanding his preaching on the kingdom (Weiss 1892, 115, 128; Schweitzer 1925, 127). His baptism gave him a sense of his calling, probably of his messianic character (Schweitzer 2000, 316), placing him in the stream of eschatological expectation, for John clearly expects the imminent arrival of the kingdom. Weiss perhaps emphasizes the continuities with John more than Schweitzer does (compare Weiss 1892, 82, with Schweitzer 1925, 151), but in broad terms, their emphases are similar.

That imminence of the kingdom is important for both scholars and gives voice to a distinctive element of Jesus's message (Weiss 1892, 65–67, 129). Arising from this discussion, Weiss confronts those places in the Gospels where the presence of the kingdom seems to be implied (67–74). He rejects such interpretations of these sayings, noting that a passage like Luke 17:20 evidences a moment of "sublime prophetic enthusiasm, when an awareness of Jesus's victory comes over him," inspired by his exorcisms, which are seen as signs that Satan's power is being broken (1892, 78; [2]1900, 176), or moments when the sense of imminence is so great that it can be described as present in the same way that an approaching storm can be described as present. While Schweitzer (2000, 199) also rejects a view of the kingdom as present in Jesus's ministry, he does not discuss the set of synoptic sayings that imply a view of the kingdom as present, even though he reports Weiss's own interpretation of these in his discussion of *Die Predigt*.

Weiss's rejection of an understanding of a Jesus who preaches a present kingdom is the other side of his sense of the kingdom as an entity that will come in the future and will do so as something new, transcendent, and transformative ([2]1900, 92–96, 107–9), in opposition to the kingdom of Satan, sentiments that he sees as dominating the extant evidence (1892, 79). The kingdom is neither a phenomenon that is in the process of development nor something that will be built by men, but something that will be brought about by God in the future, as indicated, *inter alia*, by the second request of the Lord's Prayer, "Thy kingdom come," and by Mark 14:25, where Jesus indicates that he does not yet experience any of the present rule in the kingdom (1892, 84). Schweitzer agrees that the kingdom will be a new, transformative reality, brought about by God, but he sees a greater role for the repentance and the prayers of people in the process (see 1925, 122 and 144; 1995, 143). In this context special importance needs to be attributed both to his interpretation of the mission of the Twelve as reported in Matt. 10, where their activity is seen as literally wringing down the tribulations associated with the end, and to his interpretation of Matt. 11:12 (2000, 326).

This sense of the kingdom as brought about exclusively by God, which is dominant in Schweitzer's work, in spite of his comments about the role of penitence, referred to above, leads Weiss to emphasize the nonpolitical character of the kingdom. It is an otherworldly entity, which cannot be brought about by violent activity (Weiss 1892, 102, and his interpretation of Matt. 11:12 [in contrast to Schweitzer's, on which, see above]). "To hope for the Kingdom of God in the transcendental sense that Jesus understood it and to undertake revolution are as different as fire and water" (102–3). Weiss does not reject the idea that there will be a constitution in the new kingdom, or that it will involve the overthrow of the Romans. He simply wishes to make plain that it will occur as an act of God, not as the result of human activity. Although Schweitzer, like Weiss, does not expatiate on the political aspect of the kingdom, and is also clear on its totally otherworldly quality (see below on ethics), the politics of Jesus as such does not enter his discussion; that is, he seems less sensitive to the matter (Lannert 1989, 187–91, for an interesting contextual reading of this aspect of Weiss's work).

Consistent with a sense of the otherworldly character of the kingdom, both authors are unwilling to say precisely what that new kingdom will consist in. Weiss and Schweitzer reduce their commentary to vague statements about the defeat of Satan and God's enemies more generally (Weiss 1892, 102; Morgan 1989, 99). For Weiss, the absence of any detailed account of the transformed reality that will be the kingdom is an indication of the fact that Jesus's audience already knew what that reality would be.

Because the kingdom is otherworldly, distinct and different from human experience, the ethics of the kingdom cannot be described. Schweitzer (1925, 102–3; 2000, 332), sounding like Nietzsche, talks about ethics as beyond good and evil; for Jesus views the new kingdom as a transformed reality in which sin is no longer a possibility (1925, 102). Weiss ([2]1900, 126) takes a not dissimilar position, talking about the impossibility of sin in the new kingdom. It follows for both that Jesus's ethical pronouncements relate to forms of behavior that allow for entrance into the kingdom, what Schweitzer famously described as an "Interimsethik" (1925, 96; see also 1995, 106–7), but Weiss calls "the ethics of preparation" (1892, 105–13). Such an ethic, however, is not to be understood as a continuation of societal or secular norms. For both Weiss and Schweitzer, though expressed differently, it is precisely the influence of eschatology upon Jesus's ethics that gives it an otherworldly hue ("His expectation of the supernatural kingdom of God . . . puts Jesus in a position to disregard everything that ethics can achieve in this world. Their sole function is to make individual men [*sic*] face the need to reflect on the nature of the true good" [Schweitzer 1995, 121; compare with Weiss 1892, 114]). Such sentiments, according to Schweitzer, lead to a new inwardness, which brings Jesus into conflict with the Pharisees and others who insist upon the lasting value of the external law. While Weiss suggests that Jesus's ethic cannot act as a template for modern secular society, whether in relation to money, the state, or the family (1892, 109), he is clear in the second edition of *Predigt*, responding to critics of the first, that not all of Jesus's ethics need be connected with his eschatology and that there are principles and ideals that have their origins elsewhere, here noting in particular, and in contrast to Schweitzer, Jesus's opposition to the law ([2]1900, 136–38). But Weiss's emphasis is clearly on the interconnection of ethics and eschatology.

But what then of Jesus's role in all of this? Here there are striking similarities and dissimilarities between Weiss and Schweitzer. Both assume that Jesus has a messianic consciousness, but that just as the kingdom is seen as an exclusively future reality, so is the realization of his messianic status something to be realized in the future, even if it can be anticipated in the present. At that point he will appear as the Son of Man, God's glorified regent, who will adopt a position of kingly rule in the new kingdom (as Weiss puts it, "Son of man is more a claim than a self-designation" [1892, 119, 127]). For Weiss, who draws upon Daniel and 1 Enoch for his interpretation of the Son of Man, the term is a conscious rejection of a narrowly Davidic concept of the term "Messiah," in favor of a messianic ideal "that is purely religious and thoroughly transcendental" (1892, 117; see 116 for his interpretation of Mark 12:35–37). Schweitzer (2000, 258–59) is clear also in his interpretation of Mark 12:35–37 of the transcendent nature of the coming Messiah/Son of Man in keeping with the supernatural nature of the Messiah of late Judaism (Schweitzer 1995, 126). Both are skeptical of using statements where the title "Son of Man" is applied to Jesus in the present, seeing these either as misattributions or uses of the term as a designation for "man" or "I." For Schweitzer, it is important that Jesus's understanding of his messianic identity remains a secret. That some do learn this point, for example, Peter and the disciples and the high priest, is explained by Schweitzer through complex narrative reconstructions (note his claim that the story of the transfiguration should be placed before Caesarea Philippi at Schweitzer 2000, 345) and by the betrayal of Judas. As Schweitzer writes, "He was condemned as Messiah even though he had never appeared in that role" (1925, 218). For Weiss, secrecy is not an issue in his account of the ministry, reflecting his greater skepticism about using the Gospels as a means of writing an interconnected narrative of Jesus.

This sense of Jesus as possessing a complex messianic self-consciousness in which future transformation into the Son of Man is central unites Weiss and Schweitzer, even if the ways in which they work out this position differ, and the precise sequence of events they associate with the end in which Jesus participates also differs. Where they could be said to differ more is in the way they perceive Jesus's death and the events leading up to it.

Even here, however, there are similarities. Both agree that Jesus becomes concerned at the delay in the arrival of the parousia and connect this to Matt. 10 and the story of the sending out of the disciples on a mission. The use of this chapter is far more literal in Schweitzer's work—the disciples have been sent out with the intent of bringing down the kingdom, and it is assumed that they will not return to Jesus before the tribulation connected with the arrival of that kingdom has been brought about (Schweitzer 2000, 327–28). For Weiss, on the other hand, the mission of the disciples is not attached to any perceived timetable of Jesus, though Weiss sees elements of urgency in the mission strategy (J. Weiss 1892, 86) and perceives its motivation (see above) as different from that conceived by Schweitzer. Their return does not cause a crisis for Weiss's Jesus in the way it does for Schweitzer's (Weiss, unlike Schweitzer, attaches no significance to Matt. 10:23), but both agree that delay in the coming of the kingdom—for Schweitzer's

Jesus caused by a particular event (the unexpected return of the disciples from their mission journey), for Weiss by reference to the more general phrase "the pressure of certain circumstances" (1892, 86)—leads to reflection on Jesus's ongoing role in the coming of the kingdom. Weiss proposes that Jesus came to see the delay as attributable to the failure of the people to repent, Jesus concluding that the guilt of the people stood in the way of the kingdom and that its removal could only come through his death conceived as a ransom for such guilt (Mark 10:45; 1892, 88). Schweitzer's view is different. For him the delay leads Jesus to focus on the absence of the messianic woes, which for him are predicted by Matt. 10 and which the disciples' mission was meant to precipitate. These he had expected would afflict both his disciples and himself, but they had not come. So Jesus resolves to absorb the woes himself by bringing about his death, a conclusion Schweitzer has arrived at by reading Isa. 52–53 (2000, 347–49), although he was to change his mind about whether he understood Jesus to believe his death to be expiatory or something else (1995, 147, for this). It is at this point in Schweitzer's account that eschatology, understood as a dogma that Jesus is following, most acutely becomes history (2000, 315 and 346) and that Schweitzer shows how the interaction concerning a knowledge of late Jewish eschatology can unravel a mystery at the center of Jesus's life, namely, his death.

But we can exaggerate the difference between Schweitzer's and Weiss's Jesus. After all, for Weiss Jesus's death is a means to bringing about the kingdom, albeit expressed in less direct language. But Weiss does not choose to concentrate on this aspect of his account as Schweitzer does. For Schweitzer, the coming together of passion language and eschatology is fundamental to his portrait of Jesus, and indeed to his vigorous presentation of Jesus's heroic will. For Weiss, such heightened language is absent and Jesus emerges as a more sober and rational figure. As he writes: "His greatness consisted in the fact that he followed the traditional scheme but with modesty, reserve and sobriety" (1892, 104), although Schweitzer would respond that his Jesus is a profound rationalist, whose decisions are determined by the logic of late-Jewish eschatology (2000, 249).

4. Some Closing Thoughts

There is a sense in which, on many of the significant points of their accounts of the kingdom of God, Weiss and Schweitzer agree. Jesus's whole ministry is dominated by an expectation of the arrival of the kingdom, a kingdom entirely in the future, transformative and new, which will be brought about by God, not men, whose entry will be determined by an otherworldly, nonsocietal ethic, and whose appearance will see Jesus transfigured into the transcendent Son of Man.

Such an interpretation arises out of an understanding of Jesus's own Jewish context, where such expectations were a reality. In much of this Schweitzer's work can appear derivative of Weiss's.

The manner and tone in which they go about proving this case differ. Weiss's work is much more exegetical, dealing with individual gospel sayings in a piecemeal way, proceeding on a thematic basis rather than according to some narrative, ending his account with a numbered list of conclusions. Schweitzer's work is more vividly written, sustained by a narrative in which Jesus plays out the logic of a constructed dogmatic history, based on an eschatological worldview, enabling Schweitzer to create a believable story from the *disiecta membra* of Matthew and Mark (Schweitzer 2000, 315, criticizes Weiss for failing to give an account of Jesus's life that shows how all of it is influenced by an eschatological vision, a criticism that takes insufficient account of Weiss's commitment to a vision of Jesus's ministry as eschatological). Emerging from this is a more arresting and troublesome portrait of a Jesus who seeks to bring about the coming of the kingdom by a death that takes the place of the eschatological woes, and appears to end in failure.

While both are agreed that their readings of Jesus's understanding of the kingdom of God run counter to prevailing views among the scholarly establishment, and this is the starting point of the first edition of Weiss's *Predigt* (but not of the second), this has led to contrasting concluding reflections. Weiss, who, as an enthusiastic member of the Religionsgeschichtliche Schule, is no less clear than Schweitzer about the difference between Jesus/earliest Christianity and the present (as Lannert shows [1989, 235–47] in relation to *Predigt* and later works). He appears simply to accept the difference between what the historical Jesus meant by the term "kingdom of God" and what we can mean by it in the present, assuming that it is the inevitable result of the ways in which ideas change across history and upholding the Ritschlian understanding (J. Weiss 1892, 131–36; and J. Weiss 1901, where his account of the development of the term is more descriptive than programmatic, although by showing the fact that the term has changed its meaning over time he in part justifies a nonbiblical usage; see Lannert 1989, 246–47). Schweitzer (2000, 478–87) accentuates the hermeneutical difficulties, the difference between liberalism's modernized Jesus and his own "historical" account, but seeks to overcome these by focusing upon the eternal importance of Jesus's will, whose essential characteristics are seen in his now-defunct eschatological vision. Schweitzer in this respect is more like Weiss's pupil, Bultmann, than Bultmann is like Weiss.

The books, then, in which Weiss's and Schweitzer's views of the kingdom are contained are different works motivated by different aims. While Weiss's *Predigt* was opposed by the German theological establishment, a majority were clear about its qualities as a work of scholarship, and it elicited a significant debate among scholars (see Lannert 1989, 209–14). On the other hand, Schweitzer's more extravagant claims, especially as these appeared in *Messiasgeheimnis* (1925) and *Quest* (2000), were not only opposed by German scholars but scorned for their easygoing attitude to scholarly norms, not least the exegesis of the Gospels. Schweitzer's work received a better reception in Britain, not least because of its theological implications (M. Chapman 2001, 76–80), and this may account for its ongoing influence, which has been greater than Weiss's.

What is clear is that Weiss's and Schweitzer's differently conceived and argued works constituted considerable challenges to prevailing understandings of the kingdom of God among New Testament scholars and theologians at the beginning of the twentieth century, though it would be wrong to see them as arising from nowhere. The impulses stemming from their work, whether these relate to the eschatological orientation of Jesus's ministry or the latter's relationship to the Jewish environment into which he was born, continue to influence those working on the historical Jesus, whether in agreement or opposition; and their theological and hermeneutical challenges, more acutely articulated by Schweitzer than by Weiss, persist.

Schweitzer, Albert. 1925. *The Mystery of the Kingdom of God*. London. ET of the second half of 1913. *Das Abendmahl im Zusammenhang mit dem Leben Jesu und der Geschichte des Urchristentums*. Originally entitled *Das Messianitäts- und Leidensgeheimnis*. Tübingen.
———. 1949. *Out of My Life and Thought*. London.
———. 1995. *Reich Gottes und Christentum*. Munich.
———. 2000. *The Quest of the Historical Jesus*. London. ET of the 2nd ed. of 1913. *Die Leben-Jesu-Forschung*. Tübingen.
Weiss, Johannes. 1888. *Der Barnabasbrief, kritisch untersucht*. Berlin.
———. 1901. *Idee des Reiches Gottes in der Theologie*. Giessen.
———. ³1964. *Die Predigt Jesu vom Reiche Gottes*. Göttingen.
———. 1985. *The Preaching of Jesus about the Kingdom of God*. Translated by Richard Hiers and David Holland. Atlanta. ET of 1892. *Die Predigt Jesus vom Reiche Gottes*. 1st ed. Göttingen.

James Carleton Paget

VII. Historical Jesus and Kerygmatic Christ

1. Preliminary Remarks

The voices that are presented in the following history of research are woven into the history of theology of the last 150 years. In such a broad overview, it is possible to be merely exemplary and eclectic. These voices are often closely correlated with predecessors, contemporaries, and fellow travelers, and they are each intertwined with temporal developments in the history of theology. They are considerably differentiated in their presuppositions and also in their individual profiles (on the older history of research, see comprehensively Wengst 2013).

All such differences notwithstanding, the following elements link them together:

a. A critical stance or one that consults alternatives with respect to the quest for the "historical Jesus" is not primarily a manifestation of historical skepticism and, *eo ipso*, a rejection of critical methods of biblical scholarship as such, even if as a result of special developments in this field, especially in the wake of scholarship on the liberal lives of Jesus, historical skepticism appears on the scene.

b. Dealing with biblical texts as "Scripture" presents a core issue for various voices. Claims are made in distinct ways that early Christian texts are not used (only) as "sources" or as "documents" that have evolved, but rather that in their linguistic, formal character as well as in the purpose of their content they require ways of exposition and appropriation that transcend historical research.

c. In the isolated question about "who (the historical) Jesus was," processes of the reductionism of "truth" are perceived or feared. Of course, primarily Christology and soteriology are impacted. Similarly, the relationship with the "church" or contemporary believers is to be taken into consideration, for whom, especially in preaching, Christ is asserted as a present reality and not simply relegated to the past tense.

2. *Martin Kähler*

The Halle theologian Martin Kähler took a provocative theological stance in contemporary research on the life of Jesus in a lecture in Wuppertal in 1891 entitled "Der sogenannte historische Jesus und der geschichtliche, biblische Christus" ([3]1961; 1st ed. 1892; considerably enlarged 2nd ed., 1896, includes rejoinders to critics). This lecture crystallized pertinent questions in diverse ways that endure to this day. Although Kähler emphasizes the limited foundation of assured data with respect to the biography of Jesus, for him it is not a matter of historical skepticism alone; and, although he decidedly develops the "human inventive artifice" (16) of the contemporary liberal lives of Jesus research, his objective is not primarily the destruction of criticism. Kähler was not a biblicist, nor did he reject historical biblical scholarship as such (Schniewind 1952, 169, 171). He especially distanced himself from the doctrine of verbal inspiration. As the occupant of a chair for systematic theology and New Testament, however, he considered it his responsibility to establish an independent form of a theology that does not find its foundation in the fragility of historicity.

Only a few theses and observations on Kähler's famous text need to be emphasized. Kähler appeals to the "genuine Christ," who for him is the "proclaimed Christ." This entity threatens to be concealed by the "historical Jesus" that the liberal lives of Jesus reconstruct. According to Kähler, the advocates of the liberal lives of Jesus operate as quasi-"dogmatic theologians in the suspicious sense of the word" ([3]1961, 28). By contrast, the New Testament presentation takes the character and the claim of the question of the "real" Jesus seriously, which are developed completely from the Easter event and are constantly transparent concerning this (17, 78, and elsewhere). Kähler joins the special quality of the "real" Christ with talk of a "supra-history," in which "the universal merges with what is historical in an efficacious present" (19 note a). In this construction Kähler appears as a positive theologian in intensive debate both with German idealism and with contemporary concepts of *Heilsgeschichte* (on Kähler's development, see Link 1975).

The central theological thesis is: "The risen Lord is not the historical Jesus *behind* the Gospels but the Christ of apostolic preaching of the entire New Testament" (Kähler [3]1961, 41; cf. 44). Kähler speaks of an "image of Christ" in the Gospels that encounters human beings, in order that they might agree to it. In the Gospels "we" "meet Jesus . . . whom our eye of faith and our prayer finds at the right hand of God" (34). According to the Bible and according to church history, the essential and decisive "effect" of the "efficacious" Jesus exists, therefore, in the "faith of his disciples." Kähler conceives of "faith" as the "conviction that in Christ one possesses the conqueror of guilt, sin, the tempter, and death" (38–39). The intensive discussion of Kähler's lecture that soon ensued shows in retrospect how inadequate the advocates of the liberal lives of Jesus were in their discussions with systematic theologians. Especially Willibald Beyschlag insisted on a hastily generalized connection of history and faith in the case of the oldest Jesus tradition (cf. Wengst 2013, 89–112). Kähler's careful distinction of contexts of views, discoveries, and substantiation, which he distinguishes in his magnum opus *Die Wissenschaft der christlichen Lehre von dem evangelischen Grundartikel aus* (1883), demonstrates an analytical level that has rarely been realized in the wider history of a theological debate about research on Jesus. Certainly, it ought not to be overlooked that Kähler's program of a "supra-history" is due to philosophical and theological presuppositions that have not been taken over intact into the academic landscape of the twentieth century. This problem has at times been underrated in recent programmatic voices, which, in the mode of a wake-up call, wish to affiliate with Kähler. Kähler's "supra-history" presents a decidedly tension-filled construct. Kähler's goal on the one hand is to define the "supra-history" as independent of what is historically contingent, but on the other hand not to lose history as such out of sight. For him "history" is defined and motivated by Christology respectively by a theological concept of revelation.

The Protestant point of departure is unmistakable in Kähler's concentration on preaching. Simultaneously the talk about the *"preaching that established the church"* (³1961, 103) or the "faith" toward which it points presents an equivocation in Kähler's approach. What Kähler postulates as continuity between foundation and efficacy pertaining to the Gospels but also to the wider writings of the New Testament and especially to the Old Testament (which for Kähler are closely connected and integrated) cannot be demonstrated uniformly, or more precisely, can be demonstrated only conditionally. For example, the primary purpose of Mark, the oldest gospel, can hardly be "preaching." As a narrative, Mark readily presupposes "preaching" by Jesus Christ, the Son of God (Mark 1:1, text critically uncertain), and reflects this in the plot, the metaphorical world, and above all the speeches of the protagonist. Moreover, Paul's letters cannot be construed as "preaching." They offer an epistolary meta-reflection on the "gospel."

As Kähler explains later, with his lecture he sought a "way out . . . that at the same time agrees and disagrees with each side of the debate" and thereby eliminates "a cause of uncertainty in the health of Christian conviction" (100–101). This orientation begs for attention; especially Kähler thinks of himself as an advocate of "every" person who encounters the narratives of the Gospels, including people who are uninitiated with respect to history or theology.

3. On Rudolf Bultmann's Approach

Rudolf Bultmann's numerous contributions to the quest for the "historical" or "historic" Jesus begin differently from Kähler's systematic theological incentives. They are based on (among other things) research on the history of religions (H. Gunkel; W. Bousset), on the new onset of consistent eschatological interpretation (J. Weiss), and from the early 1920s on the stimulus of the emergent dialectical theology (on the embedment in the classic history of research, see Kümmel 1958, 259–515). They are themselves so dense and complex that they can hardly be outlined exhaustively, and can be described only in a few rough contours related to their influence and reception in later research on Jesus.

Bultmann's study *Die Geschichte der synoptischen Tradition*, appearing in 1921 and considerably expanded in the second edition of 1931, turned out to be exceedingly influential. Even before Karl Ludwig Schmidt, Julius Wellhausen (1905) had been able to show that the evangelists selected their materials with doctrinal purposes and located them in a context. With respect to historical inquiry about a chronology and topology of Jesus's activity, Mark especially, as the oldest gospel, proved to be awkward or unproductive. Bultmann took up the new method of form criticism innovatively, whereby—differently from Martin Dibelius (1919)—he proceeded not by synthesizing but by analyzing.

He closely linked form-critical investigation of synoptic materials with critical analysis of the transmission of tradition. Thereby, the question of the "historical" contours of the oldest Jesus tradition and the generative contribution of the post-Easter "Palestinian" and "Hellenistic" community were to be more astutely understood. Bultmann's critical judgments on the transmission of the logia tradition, the *apophthegmata* and the narrative material of the synoptic tradition formed in multiple ways the critical springboard for further analyses—even in later phases of Jesus research, in which the nexus of form criticism postulated by Bultmann proved to be faulty with respect to issues of transmission history or the *Sitz im Leben*.

In later interpretations of Bultmann, his position is often virtually reduced to the famous first sentence of his *Theologie des Neuen Testament* (1953)—that is, that Jesus belongs "to the presuppositions of the theology of the New Testament" and is "not part of this theology itself." Accordingly, the "historical" or "historic" Jesus in later theology would supposedly be significant only in focusing on a sheer "that" of his existence, but not with reference to the *what* or the *how* of his appearance and his proclamation. Especially the eschatological qualification, which according to Bultmann defines the core of the "kerygma" and presents the condition for the possibility of a conceptual reflective theology, would then still not be available for Jesus the Jew to grasp qualitatively. Rather, it would be grasped for the first time on the soil of the post-Easter community, above all, the "Hellenistic" community. According to Bultmann, this community prepares the ground for the two great theologians in the New Testament canon, namely, Paul and John.

Nevertheless, it is easy to overlook that for Bultmann the point definitely was not only to hold on to a "historical" connection between the historical Jesus and post-Easter Christology and theology as such, but also to examine it in more detail in order to understand it better and to make it theologically productive. His talk about "historical presuppositions" (⁹1984, 2) does not mean negation or failure. In this regard, until recent publications, Albert Schweitzer has often been likewise misunderstood. What Schweitzer contended in his *Geschichte der Leben-Jesu-Forschung* (⁹1984) is that the quest for the historical Jesus is in no way to be suspended or terminated. Rather, as a consequence he wanted all the more to enhance his own contribution that at the core was eschatologically determined. So, under altered terms of a much wider-reaching detachment from liberal theology, this holds likewise for Bultmann. Alongside numerous hermeneutically oriented publications, he has published works that deal with the question of the historic or "historical Jesus" (cf., among others, [8]1980a–c, 1–25, 85–113, 188–213). Above all, he also produced his own book on Jesus.

This work, which appeared in 1926, has not without reason been regarded as a Jesus book of dialectical theology (H. Weinel, among others). Here, under new designations, Bultmann fundamentally backs away from the categories of "personality," "consciousness" or religious "experience," and "development," as numerous liberal "lives of Jesus" had shaped them. Simultaneously Bultmann's "Jesus" in the *tua res agitur* of existential interpretation—which aims at the encounter with the living Christ in the decisive self-reflexive situation of one's own existence (cf. Bultmann 1988, 7–12)—is distanced from a concept of history that was in the custody of the historicism of the nineteenth century (on the genesis of Bultmann's "Jesus" and on the much-debated question of the meaning of the dialogue with M. Heidegger, cf. Körtner 2002, 23–60).

With respect to historical questions as such—in significant distinction from the advocates of the "new quest" for the historical Jesus from the 1950s—Bultmann has absolutely no difficulty in locating Jesus not as a "Christian" but rather as a Jew in the context of the Judaism of his time (1988, 20–22).

The depiction of Jesus's proclamation in three concentric circles is inspired by Adolf von Harnack (1900), although Bultmann changes the sequence of the circles by moving the section about God's will/Jesus's ethics from third to second place. In the outer circle Bultmann subsumes Jesus's talk about the kingdom of God primarily under the pressing decisive situation of the human being "now." The "ultimate decision" that encounters human beings does not imply "detachment from the world" in the sense that in life human beings do not have to allow themselves to be determined by the will of God even in a positive sense. Jesus's ethic is put in the middle circle in wide-reaching harmony with the Jewish point of view and, for example, also with the concept of eschatological reward as an ethics of obedience. To be sure, Jesus radicalized the concept of such obedience. According to Bultmann, he presented an anthropology of decision in a way that transcended common notions of a "humanistic ideal of humanity" (Bultmann 1988, 57). In the inner circle stands Jesus's concept of God. Also, here the connection with early Jewish concepts is emphasized, which is not a matter of the *aseity* of God but rather the remote God and the God of the future, whose presence exposes human beings as sinners. By contrast, for Jesus forgiveness means that the human being "should once again become a new being by the grace of God" (137). This concentric, three-step design that is not worked out *en détail* here is also reproduced in the presentation of Jesus's "eschatological proclamation" in Bultmann's *Theologie des Neuen Testaments* ([9]1984, 2–26). Finally, Bultmann also places the question of the self-consciousness of Jesus here, which is nonmessianic.

Although Bultmann also grants to the historic or "historical" Jesus a fundamental function for the presentation of the theology of the New Testament, it is still no coincidence that in the 1950s the so-called new quest for the historical Jesus triggered by Ernst Käsemann was not able to make a seamless connection with Bultmann's concept (cf. Bultmann, *Das Verhältnis der urchristlichen Christusbotschaft zum historischen Jesus*, in Bultmann 1967b, 445–69).

There is no space here for a detailed discussion and evaluation. After the 1970s, newly outlined debates with these various impulses of Bultmann justifiably emphasized, among other things, that Jesus's proclamation is in fact connected with wide-reaching biblical and particular concepts of ancient Judaism on the one hand. On the other hand, in a way that is historically and theologically problematic, it was simultaneously connected with the notion, supposedly derived from ancient Judaism, of the "legalism of human beings" understood in an existential, generalizing way. Thus, the proclamation of Jesus vaults over or, to be precise, is turned against Judaism and against the Old Testament.

4. Luke Timothy Johnson

Under quite different indicators of a North American context, Luke Timothy Johnson reacts to the "new quest for the historical Jesus" in his monograph *The Real Jesus*, published in 1996.

It is strange that Johnson does not refer more clearly to Kähler, with whom he shares central concerns and concepts. As it was for Kähler, the issue for Johnson is neither historical skepticism nor a denial of historical research as such; like Kähler, he is concerned with the destabilization of believers/"laity." Like Kähler, he takes aim at a "real" Jesus, who cannot be reached by pure historical investigation. The rhetorical tenor is reminiscent (again implicitly) of Karl Barth's "for me *critics* have to be the ones who are historically critical!" ([2]1922, xii). Certainly, the frame of reference for the history of philosophy and theology has become completely different; and especially Johnson focuses on the message/"preaching" that presents "the real Jesus" in a way that is incompatible with this frame of reference.

Johnson's work is provoked first of all by the way decisions are made in the sessions of the Jesus Seminar, which in his view also operates with dubious methodologies. Others perceive these matters quite differently (e.g., J. D. Crossan, M. Borg, B. Thiering, A. N. Wilson, S. Mitchell, J. P. Meier, J. S. Spong). The differences in individual approaches notwithstanding, Johnson perceives in them as an aggregate the danger of publicly promoting an obvious destructive misunderstanding of historical or exegetical work.

Reminiscent of critical debates on the life of Jesus at the beginning of the twentieth century, Johnson insists that the task of history is not to be confused with the task of theology and that "faith" is not to be grounded in history. Rather, it encompasses its own "reality." Likewise, the conflicts that characterized the turn of the century seem to be repeated when criticism concerning adumbrations of eschatology on Jesus and Q is practiced in research (by, among others, B. L. Mack and M. Borg). It is reminiscent of older, well-known reactions to Bultmann's program of demythologizing when Johnson claims an exceptional position regarding the reality of Christ's resurrection that evades historical access to it and is immunized against historical questions.

New methodological horizons come into play when Johnson brings in theorems from sociology of knowledge and constructivism, in order to present historical knowledge as simply one possible access to "reality," to which a religious construct is in no way inferior (cf. L. Johnson 1996, 81–104, 141–66). For this religious construct of reality, Johnson interrogates New Testament texts, which present Christ as "one who lives" and will be experienced in the fellowship of believers.

Even though the tools of historical research have been relativized in their "degree of reality," Johnson wishes to turn the weapons of his opponents back on them in order finally to open up a religious or "spiritual" space to the character of the "real Jesus." Among other possibilities, Johnson searches for this space by arguing against favoring apocryphal sources and various postulates of tradition criticism in the Jesus Seminar. He seeks to attain this space primarily at the level of a consistent synchronic reading of texts of the *canonical* Gospels (for substantiation, see 146–51). Clearly here an approach is worked out that has in mind a wide-reaching thematic unity of the writings that became canonical (cf. Johnson's critique of W. Bauer's *Rechtgläubigkeit und Ketzerei im ältesten Christentum* at 95–96). This likewise works out a conscious distinction that impacts publications from the Jesus Seminar, which in his eyes frequently argue *e silentio* (with the thesis of "suppressed evidence") and burst open an illegitimate chasm between the historical Jesus and later Christianity. Johnson ascribes Jesus's "personal identity" in the canonical Gospels to a narrative interpretive pattern of the obedient suffering "servant." In keeping with the perspective of the homogeneity of the canon and the reliability of "memory," the cases where the Gospels and the Pauline Epistles overlap (in number and content rather minimal) are also significant for Johnson with respect to their information about Jesus. He detects in Paul a substantial "pattern" that is homogeneous with the picture of the Gospels (cf. 117–22).

Johnson's book raises the question more generally whether the old perils of a theological purification and autoimmunity or a priority of distinct concepts of truth in the face of independent research on biblical texts in all their dimensions are to be avoided in toto, which reverting to the objectives behind Kähler's agenda would imply.

5. Review and Prospects

An evaluation of these quite different approaches cannot take place here and also cannot be undertaken under uniform criteria.

First, under the perspective of New Testament research that is lodged in international scholarship, it holds in general that it is not feasible to desire to inhibit or resist scholarly interrogation as such. For good reasons theology does not refer to and does not correspond to data from the past alone to make its results absolute, and quite properly it questions methodologies. But it is problematic even in theological studies to define certain areas of scholarly research per se and from the *outset* as futile (as Wengst 2013 does). With respect to the quest for the "historical Jesus," it is also the fundamental task of New Testament scholarship to plumb the depths of *all* pathways to knowledge and not to renounce particular possibilities of knowing a priori. A scholarly theology that demands this, even if it might point out appropriately that "truth" does not coincide with an *adaequatio intellectus ad rem* and with a *quid erat sive fuit?*, would stand on clay feet.

The critical evidence found in diverse forms indicates that early Christian writings did not aim at being historical reporting. Rather, that they aimed at making the "living" Christ and his significance their subject for believers/the believing "community" and for the world is to some extent valid. Certainly, at this point a distinction has to be made between individual early Christian writings and their genres (see above on Kähler). Above all, as the history of such attempts in the area of New Testament hermeneutics shows, such a "claim" for texts does not immediately turn into a methodological procedure that meets the scientific desiderata of replication, controlled conditions, and building an interdisciplinary consensus.

With respect to anxieties about "alien" or "atheistic" methods in exposition of the New Testament, or demands for research grounded on the faith of exegetes (cf. classically Schlatter 1905), it is valid to assert that on the whole, theology, as with other intellectual disciplines, is necessarily constituted by hypothetical quests, and not only in the field of historical investigations. Therefore, theology cannot renounce interdisciplinary methodological connections in general. Besides, within historiography the narrowly conducted question of the nineteenth century about "what was" has been negotiated in various ways, and precisely from a constructivist perspective can no longer be posited absolutely.

In the quest for Jesus, it can lead to aporias if synchronic and diachronic methods of interpreting texts are contrasted as exclusive alternatives (cf. differently Johnson; Wengst). Indeed, the history of research on the historical Jesus simply presents the field of advances in diachronic inquiry par excellence. Recent research has pursued a way out of this dilemma with the paradigm of "Jesus as remembered." With regard to exaggerated diachronic criticism and the use of all kinds of *argumenta e silentio* in past and present research, the principle must be stated: *Abusus non tollit usum.* This also applies to forms of epochal self-staging as such, which often affected the quest for the historical Jesus.

The positions that have been only broadly and selectively outlined here, which with respect to historical Jesus research are variously and cumbersomely handled, when taken together lead to a basic question, which remains open: To what extent are New Testament scholarship and scholarly theology as a whole assigned functions and tasks that are not only descriptive and analytical but also all the more pragmatic and decisively affirmative?

Bultmann, Rudolf K. ⁹1984. *Theologie des Neuen Testaments.* Tübingen.

———. 1988. *Jesus* (1926). UTB 1272. Tübingen.

Johnson, Luke Timothy. 1996. *The Real Jesus: The Misguided Quest for the Historical Jesus and the Truth of the Traditional Gospels.* San Francisco.

Kähler, Martin. ³1961. *Der sogenannte historische Jesus und der geschichtliche, biblische Christus.* Edited by Ernst Wolf. TB 2. Munich.

Körtner, Ulrich H. J., ed. 2002. *Jesus im 21. Jahrhundert, Bultmanns Jesusbuch und die heutige Jesusforschung.* Neukirchen-Vluyn.

Link, Hans-Georg. 1975. *Geschichte Jesu und Bild Christi: Die Entwicklung der Christologie Martin Kählers in Auseinandersetzung mit der Leben-Jesu-Theologie und der Ritschl-Schule.* Neukirchen-Vluyn.

Wengst, Klaus. 2013. *Der wirkliche Jesus? Eine Streitschrift über die historisch wenig ergiebige und theologisch sinnlose Suche nach dem "historischen" Jesus.* Stuttgart.

Reinhard von Bendemann

VIII. The Literary Designs of the Gospels and Their Relationship to the Historical Jesus

The question of the literary designs of the Gospels and their relationship to the historical Jesus presupposes a source-critical decision about the dependence that exists among the Gospels. There has existed a consensus in German exegesis since the end of the nineteenth century that the Gospel of Mark was written first, and the writers of the Gospels of Matthew and Luke used it extensively and combined it with tradition from a second source, the so-called sayings source. During the twentieth century, it was established that the outline of the sayings source can be discerned but its wording can be constructed only hypothetically. At the same time, a discussion was developing about the relationship of the Gospel of John to the other three gospels. The result of this discussion is that the Fourth Gospel presupposes at least the Gospels of Mark and Luke.

Consequently, the question of the *literary designs* of the Gospels and their relationship to the *historical Jesus* above all concerns a topic in research on Mark, which will be dealt with from two angles. The first has to do with concepts of scholars about the literary nature of the Gospels, and the second has to do with how these concepts lead to judgments regarding historical questions, especially to those pertaining to the historical Jesus.

1. William Wrede

Wrede himself was quite aware that his book *Das Messiasgeheimnis in den Evangelien: Zugleich ein Beitrag zum Verständnis des Markusevangeliums* would arouse great commotion (⁴1969, iv). Wrede put himself in conflict with his predecessors and contemporaries. For them, following Heinrich Julius Holtzmann, Mark was in essence the reproduction of the history of Jesus (Kümmel 1958, 186–91, 220–21). By contrast, Wrede regarded Mark as "the concept of a later narrator of the life of Jesus" (⁴1969, 2). Therefore, one should examine "the reports on the basis of their own intension" (3) before raising the question of the history of Jesus. We should ask "What the narrator wanted to say to his readers in his time" (3). Mark is a narrative about Jesus (3), a "historical story" (114).

Wrede presumed that in order to understand Mark as literature, one would have to refrain from understanding the text as history: "If we wish . . . to find a paltry vestige of history, we are obliged first to prune Mark's report according to our own discretion, so that it becomes tolerable for us, but in itself remains incomprehensible. If we give up history, and so leave the report complete as it is, in the supernatural view of the author, which indeed amounts to what is historically impossible—a direct way of understanding the whole" (31–32). Thus, we should ask "how Mark understood things" (14).

It is well known that Wrede proceeded with a historical-critical approach in order to show that the messianic secret is a theological concept. Wrede thought that no motif could be found in the story of Jesus "that plausibly and satisfactorily explained for us the conscious veiling of himself as Mark depicted it. . . . I go further and claim that *a historical motif actually is not possible at all*; positively: *The idea of the Messianic secret is a theological concept*" (65–66, emphasis added). Further: "I have called Mark's thought theological in order thereby to express that it did not possess the character of a historical . . . concept" (71). Thus, it is not permissible to search for historical contexts or links in the Gospel of Mark. Anyone who contemplates that does not understand Mark's authorial style (132).

The messianic secret is the theme that holds the narrative together. "What Jesus wanted, did not happen; he wants the secret, and he only becomes better known" (126). Mark narrates a life full of messianic manifestations, and "the more the individual item was connected with the focus of the whole affair, namely messiahship, the more worthwhile it was to be reported" (125). According to Wrede, the expressing of the great truth and the prohibition of its expression stand side by side as a necessity (128). The messianic secret underlines the glory of Jesus; he wished to remain hidden but quickly became well-known (127). Historically these inconsistencies could not have existed; they are nevertheless possible in the story (128).

How Mark's conception, which according to Wrede is already part of the historical development of Christian doctrine, employs the messianic secret in order to merge the partly nonmessianic Jesus tradition with the post-Easter messianic tradition that was passed on to him is well-known (cf. Breytenbach 1984, §7.4.3). We have limited ourselves here to Wrede's concept of the text. It ought to be apparent: had scholarship taken Wrede's proposition seriously, that we consider Mark to be an author, and that history and narrative should be distinguished, then we could have avoided many dead ends (Wendland [2.3]1912, 269; Hengel and Schwemer 2007, esp. 216–24). In the course of investigation of the Gospel of Mark, as Norman Perrin put it, the Wrede Street became the Main Street. Alas, first it came to a considerable detour.

2. Form and Redaction Criticism

Form criticism moved the focus from the text as a whole to individual episodes. This way of proceeding assumed that independent pericopes in oral tradition had been assembled into a compilation. The question that remains is: How much does this affect the quest for the historical Jesus?

Karl Ludwig Schmidt takes as his starting point a much-discussed problem of research on the life of Jesus: "In what locations and how long did Jesus carry out his public activity?" ([1919] 1969, v). In Mark the sequence of stories is uncertain (76, 103–4, 171–72, 208–9, 245–46), such that Mark places no value on chronology and topography nor on the psychological connection of the individual stories. Mark exhibits no outline of Jesus's story. There are only small units that are placed in a secondary framework (317).

In 1930 Julius Schniewind formulated a programmatic statement: "Our Gospels intend . . . to be understood as kerygma for a specific state of affairs and purpose; what matters is to work out the situation in which their (charismatic) kerygma is to be understood" (1939, 153). For Willi Marxsen, a related intention comes into view when he asks, "How do the evangelists depict what happened? How this actually was, is of interest only insofar as the question is related to the situation of the original community in which the Gospels originated" ([2]1959, 12–13; cf. 141). For Schniewind and Marxsen, the Gospels are evidence of the productive potential of the original Christian kerygma in view of a particular situation in the community (Schniewind 1930, 153; Marxsen [2]1959, 146). However, Marxsen deviates from Schniewind's intent when he contrasts kerygma with history. Schniewind writes, "If contemporary research derives many dominical sayings in the synoptics from the Palestinian community, then it presupposes the consciousness that the exalted one speaks right there in his community. But then it begs to be explained why for 'what the Spirit says to the churches' one searches for what are authoritative sayings of the earthly Jesus and not some '*bat qol*' of the exalted one" (1930, 159–60). In Marxsen's reception, Schniewind's differentiation goes by the wayside. Schniewind assumes the basic identity between the earthly Jesus and the exalted Lord, but also retains the distinctiveness of the earthly one (183–84). In Marxsen's view, this difference threatens to be annulled. In the categorization of Mark, he pits kerygma and history against each other: "The entire work is characterized and qualified as εὐαγγέλιον. It is *one* Gospel. But that means from the beginning on: The work is to be read as proclamation, as such it is an address, but not a 'report about Jesus.' The fact that here something of a report also surfaces is in terms of this issue almost accidental. It is in any case only raw material" ([2]1959, 87). Although Marxsen presumes the Pauline concept of the gospel as proclamation of the exalted one who was crucified, he argues, for example, that Mark 1:14–15 does not indicate the beginning of the proclamation of the earthly Jesus but of the risen one (89). For Marxsen, the earthly and the exalted one are so identical that he allows the earthly Jesus and his era to merge with the exalted one and his present age: "Christ himself is the gospel, and simultaneously the gospel makes present the one who has come and the one who is coming" (99). Only on the basis of this "suspension of time" and the reduction of Christology to the presence of the exalted one in the community is Marxsen able to discard the narrative form of the gospel and say that Mark is a *proclamation* of the exalted one to the Markan community and that in all statements of the "earthly one" in actuality the exalted one addresses the community directly (92).

In the second half of the twentieth century, this thesis from Marxsen set the trend for the redaction criticism of the oldest gospel. But it did not withstand an examination of the text. Two important aspects of criticism deserve to be repeated here (cf. Breytenbach 1984, §8.3). (1) By introducing the messianic secret, Mark shows that a clear break exists between the pre-Easter and post-Easter situation of the disciples. Not until after Easter are they able to understand and to broadcast who Jesus was. If the disciples are consistently identified with the Markan community without considering this pre- and post-, then the differentiation that Mark creates between the time before and after the resurrection is negated. But Mark holds on to the notion that before Easter the disciples did not understand and were not allowed to spread Jesus's divine Sonship any further. (How can this be reinterpreted as consistent with the post-Easter presence, without dismantling the messianic secret?) To this aspect of differentiating within the messianic secret it should be added that Mark consciously puts John the Baptizer and Jesus in a succession and that statements such as Mark 2:20; 13:33–37; and 14:8–9, 25 unequivocally set the time of being with Jesus off from the time of his corporeal absence (Conzelmann 1974a, 63; Toit 2006). Mark does not allow the time of Jesus to collapse upon itself. Rather, he holds fast to the difference of the times and understands his own present as the time of mission (Mark 13:9–10) between the advent of the kingdom of God in the arrival of Jesus (Mark 1:14–15) and the time of its coming in power at his parousia (Mark 9:1; on this, Breytenbach 1984, §9.2). The Gospel of Mark looks at Jesus's earthly activity from the point of view of the resurrection, but not such that the pre-Easter Jesus and his disciples are so related to the present of the community that they stop belonging to their past. (2) The second aspect is that Mark takes up stories about the earthly Jesus one by one and puts them in chronological order, that (as Schniewind emphasized) he allows the *earthly Jesus* to address the disciples, and not the *exalted one* to address the community. If the community is addressed in its concrete situation, Mark lets the earthly Jesus announce it before his death. All this belongs to his retrospective tendency. Hence, the stories cannot refer to the present time of the community in such a way that the orientation to the past that occurs in the evangelist's retrospective manner of depiction is nullified. If the Gospel of Mark intended to be a proclamation, this does not become clear on the basis of the form of the gospel, because the evangelist unequivocally did not choose the form of direct address in preaching, but rather the form of narration of past events (Breytenbach 1984, §3.3 and §2.1.3.4).

Even before Marxsen, Ernst Käsemann drew attention to the historical significance of the narrative character of the Gospels. In his well-known critique of Bultmann's position under the title "Das Problem des historischen Jesus" (1954), Käsemann points out that the access to the past is constantly mediated in the form of narratives: "So regarding past history we are dependent on narration, when we wish to obtain information from the past. All history becomes available to us only through tradition and becomes understandable through interpretation." Thus, Käsemann holds it to be significant that the Gospels embed the Christian message in the narration of the life of the earthly Jesus (1954, 125–53).

For those who hold the resurrection in veneration, revelation is inseparably connected with his "earthly corporeality" (202). With this Käsemann argued that the quest for the historical Jesus has to begin with the cohesion and tension between Jesus's proclamation and that of his followers (213). As a tool to distinguish Jesus's message from the message of the early church, he wielded the (in)famous criterion of dissimilarity (205; further Theissen and Winter 1997) as a means of creating distance between the literary features of the Gospels and the earthly Jesus. In his reply to Bultmann's rejoinder, Käsemann noted appropriately that the true point of contention was in the understanding of history (1964b, 52; further Breytenbach 2013, n. 3). Käsemann's reaction directs the query to Bultmann, that if early Christianity was not interested in the life of the earthly Jesus, why did it nevertheless wrap the "kerygma" in narratives about Jesus, and this even up to the time of the composition of the Gospel of John (1964b, 47)? The proclamation of the Gospels was defined by the past, not by the present. This is not a matter of ways of preaching, as Bultmann maintained, but rather a question of "reports" about the past in spite of the insufficiency of their historicity. For this reason, Käsemann drafted the task, in view of something like the high Christology of the Philippians hymn, as explaining the fact that early Christian proclamation nevertheless assumes the form of a report: "They [connect] historical dispositions with the kerygma and employ a historicizing form of presentation" (54). "How could it come in the framework of the kerygma from the doxology of the one who is the object of the proclamation once again to the narrative of the proclaimer?" (66). One does not have to agree with Käsemann's position to concur with his thesis that post-Easter theology is constantly measured by its recourse to the earthly Jesus. In that respect, "the *pre* of Christ before the Christians is shown to be the *extra nos* of the message. . . . The past gave the present the criteria for testing the spirits" (67). The fact that Jesus existed made it possible for the evangelists to remember him and to take up his story in the Gospels. However, Käsemann's hypothesis remains valid, namely, that the narrative form of the Gospels is relevant for the historical quest for Jesus.

With respect to redaction-critical approaches, like that of Marxsen, Jürgen Roloff (1969, 78) is skeptical about the methodological and factual legitimacy of considering Mark as an unmediated continuation of a kerygmatic structure that is already laid out in the tradition. The intention to present the story of Jesus as an "event of the past" lies behind the literary phenomenon of the gospel. Roloff established this thesis by reference to narrative techniques and principles of creativity that Mark used in his depiction (cf. the critical evaluation in Breytenbach 1984, §3). By intercalating the traditional pericopes, Mark had assembled them in such a way "that the reader had the impression of a plot" (Roloff 1969, 79). Similarly, the taking up of the schematic features of the activities of Jesus reveals

Mark's historical interests (79). In spite of this, Roloff did not use the fundamental geographical concept to create a narrative tendency (81). By contrast, he did take the basic idea of three groups with whom Jesus was involved—the people, the opponents, and the disciples—as the starting point for the invention of a narrative trend (82–83). The subject matter of the disciples and the opponents, which flows into the passion narrative, is a clear narrative tendency, and so the evangelist did create continuous lines of action (87–88). The thematic presentation of the disciples, which is connected with what is a mystery for the disciples (82, 84), enabled Mark to portray the companionship of the disciples with Jesus before Easter as an event of the past (90). Thus, Mark was able to sketch the disciples as constant companions of Jesus in the pre-Easter situation and simultaneously show that the disciples did not understand Jesus's instructions until after Easter. For someone who reads after Easter, this mystery no longer applies, because the temporal limitation of Mark 9:9 has been superseded (91). Nevertheless, Roloff does not distinguish between what the story of Jesus was and what Mark's story of Jesus was. But he did succeed in demonstrating that Mark depicts the relationship between the Markan Jesus and the disciples as they appear in the gospel as an event of the past, so that without further ado it is not possible to proceed, as Marxsen does, for example, from the simultaneity of the characters in Mark associated with the exalted one on the one hand and the community on the other. Roloff's consideration of the themes in Mark and his debate with kerygma theology remain substantial (Breytenbach 1984, §3). Mark certainly has an interest in telling about Jesus. Whether what he narrates stands in a close connection with the history of the earthly Jesus must, nevertheless, be demonstrated in terms of the critical history of tradition and not by literary means.

3. Narrative Study of the Gospel

Norman Perrin (1971, 1972, 1976b) has extensively addressed methods of investigating Mark, and in this there is a perceptible development in Perrin's conception. According to him, a critical method is needed "that would . . . do justice to the full range of the Evangelist's literary activity" (1976b, 120). Because Mark is an author, literary scholarship should be consulted for this (1972, 9–10; 1976b, 120n22). "If the evangelists are authors, then they must be studied as authors, and they must be studied as other authors are studied" (1972, 10). This means that as a composition the gospel must be studied in totality by literary criticism (1976b, 15, 20; 1971, 176), because "any literary criticism has to be geared specifically to the nature of the texts with which it is concerned" (1972, 10). Taking into account the historical-critical method, Perrin made a suggestion for comprehensive literary critical study of the Gospel of Mark (1971, 147) and opened access to narrative research, but it did not catch on until the end of the 1970s. The emergence of narrative research, however, made the question of the relation of the Gospel of Mark to Jesus of Nazareth completely disappear from view for a generation.

Is this justified? No one who understood Wrede's book would again attempt to identify Mark's narrative with the history of Jesus (but cf. Hengel and Schwemer 2007, 244–60), and hardly anyone would want to deny that pre-Easter individual traditions were subsequently impacted, reshaped, and in certain cases invented by Easter faith. Could anyone assume that after individual pre-Markan traditions were placed in a comprehensive narrative framework they would still follow the same purpose as in oral tradition? Since the literary context of the individual traditions taken over in Mark is now the "situation" in which they were used, the setting and purpose of Mark can be deduced only from the text itself. It was nothing less than problematic for redaction-critical research on Mark that expositors hastily moved away from the level of intratextual communication between characters in the narrative and wished to reinterpret the narrative step-by-step from a presumed situation of the Markan community. Hence, narrative criticism attempted justifiably to explain first on the level of intratextual communication what the narrator wished to say in the narrative. As a result, some then asked which understanding of the situation of the community intended as addressees is to be deduced. At the end of the twentieth century, the additional question, whether the narrative of the Gospel of Mark as a whole could be utilized for the quest for the historical Jesus, was hardly posed any longer. Nevertheless, the result of this epoch of research, that the first evangelist chose a *narrative* form for his entire text, could be significant for the quest for Jesus of Nazareth.

4. Narrative, Memory, and History

The Gospel of Mark is an "episodic narrative" that is retrospective and prospective (Breytenbach 1985). But if one asks what is the purpose of Mark as a whole, then the problem of narrative, kerygma, and history arises. History, kerygma, and narrative do not stand in opposition to each other (Vorster 1983). As early as the 1980s, it was pointed out that the then still-newer approaches of analytic philosophy of history and the related discussion of narrative theory (Danto 1968; on this, Schiffer 1980) allow for the assumption that it would be of vital interest for research on the Synoptic Gospels to engage in that discussion. In particular this was relevant for the problem of "Mark's narrative—the history of Jesus—interpretation of the life of Jesus" (Breytenbach 1984, 83). This, however, to express it in Perrin's words, still means that "The Wredestrasse becomes the Hauptstrasse"

(1966). Mark is a narrative, an episodic narrative, and it must be dealt with as a narrative. Therefore, I suggest that we have two points of view to take over from our predecessors when we pose the question concerning a possible historical assessment of the narrative. First, with Käsemann, we should point out that in this narrative there exists a tension between the earthly Jesus, with whom the narrative deals, and the position of the narrator, who presents him as the Son of God. Second, with Lategan (1984, 2004), we should choose the way that is sketched out by the implied author and the implied reader. All information for this is to be deduced from the narrative. Once we take on the role of the intended readers, our thinking should be enhanced by the connections and references to the world outside the text. With this, an interesting question arises: Can we conclude from the text of the Gospel of Mark that has been passed on to us whether we are dealing with a narrative that still contains sufficient testimony by those who remembered the teaching and deeds of Jesus? But even if Mark's story contains individual memories that are trustworthy, that does not mean that as a whole it can be viewed as a *historical* rather than a fictional narrative about Jesus. Here a detour from the Wredestrasse leads to a dead-end street (Breytenbach 2013).

The Gospel of Mark is the first transmitted attestation to the fact that an early Christian author communicated the collective memory about Jesus to a later community in a written narrative. Even if committing the text to writing in contrast to continued oral performance has to reckon with limitations, Mark nevertheless attests the well-maintained communal memory of Jesus by a significant group from the second half of the first century CE. The transfer of this secondary memory of a collective body from oral to written form highlights two major changes that the historian ought not to neglect: episodes that are coincidentally repeated are brought over into the narrative sequence (Breytenbach 1985), and this secondary memory is preserved so that it becomes a document (Ricoeur 1998, 119). Further, only if it withstands critical scrutiny can it be utilized for historiography. Thus, we must remember that the Gospel of Mark does not contain primary memory, the record of individual witnesses of events of lived experience. Rather, it comprises a structured, *secondary* memory of the community, which in this form of oral stories then makes the transfer to literature. The degree to which this has to do with structured communal memory is seen quite well in that actions of Jesus are narrated in the literary form of *chreiai* and miracle stories, and the passion narrative becomes shaped partially on patterns of psalms of suffering. Historically speaking, Jesus hardly acted according to the pattern of a *chreia* or in imitation of the Psalms.

What importance do these preserved secondary communal memories have for historiography? At this point a differentiation should be made between the memories, which are contained in the framework of the scenario of individual episodes, and the macronarrative. By and large, Mark is to be viewed as a fictive and not as a historical narrative. In this narrative, which in the course of the second century CE obtained the title *According to Mark*, the "good news" that comes from God is narrated (Mark 1:14). This good news deals with God's Son Jesus Christ (1:1), and the beginning of the good news coincides with what was written by the prophet Isaiah. By means of the voice of God from heaven that has been ripped open at his baptism, Jesus is presented to the readers (1:11) and to the inner circle of his disciples (9:7) as the beloved Son of God. Jesus begins his proclamation of the good news of the coming kingdom of God after God had delivered up John the Baptizer and the time determined by God was fulfilled (1:14–15). Jesus, the main character himself, links his efficacy to the death, which, he explains, is the divine will that he must suffer much, be rejected and killed, and after three days be raised (8:31). The divine rule, which he proclaimed, will come at the end (only the Father knows the point in time), when Jesus as the Son of Man returns (13:30–32). Further, he will punish those who rejected him and his message, and those who have opposed the adversary and have not been led astray will be saved. The setting of the time of the end, the role of some main features in the plot, like the Scripture, the returning Son of Man, and demons, as well as the purpose of Mark's Gospel are essentially grounded in the mental construct of the narrator, which is that the sequence of events and the end are determined by God, as it is written (cf. 14:21).

But is the past in this way preserved in the form of individual memories? So, are the sequence of events and the teaching of Jesus presented in Mark in such a way that they call to mind the memories of individuals who shared time and space with Jesus? The broader narrative framework between Isaiah and the return of the Son of Man does not display the character of the primary memory, not if "memory" is understood as the individual recall of what is past (so, e.g., Ricoeur; cf. Breytenbach 2013). The macronarrative of Mark can therefore hardly be distinguished from imagination, fantasy, or fiction. Rather it is, in Wrede's words, "supernatural." It is the explanation implied by the author why things happen in a certain way, and his theological understanding of the reason why humans act in a certain way. The macronarrative of Mark cannot, therefore, substitute that which once was but now has passed. Rather, it presents itself as a reflection of the hidden mystery of the Messiah and as a prediction of the future, which the narrator expects.

The Gospel of Mark is accordingly not a "historical narrative," which as an entire narrative opens up access to Jesus of Nazareth to the historian. With respect to the overall plot, the model author did not reassemble the events in the life of Jesus and his teaching in any manner as a course of action that rests on individual memory. Rather, it has to do with the portrayal of the mystery of the kingdom of God (cf. 4:11). The picture that is sketched of the hidden Son of God in the framework of an eschatological drama, who proclaims the gospel in Galilee and goes to Jerusalem and to whom things happened as they had to happen (cf. 8:31), can hardly be viewed as a story that can stand in for the remembered individual person or events. Rather, the past is explained by means of a construct of reality in which God is the main actor and the events come about in agreement with what "is written." The Markan narrative is an episodic narrative, and, according to the narrator, the coherence of the overall plot is in the last analysis grounded in divine action.

Nevertheless, individual aspects of the plot of this, in large measure, *theological* episodic narrative can be utilized for a *historical* construction if necessary caution is taken. As has already been mentioned, no one in Mark's narrative really understands who Jesus actually is. The closest followers do not understand his mission; Judas betrays him; Peter denies him; and at the end they all run away. Further, even the women search for his dead body even though he repeatedly foretold his resurrection (Toit 2006). Why were the disciples put into this role? Is it not much more likely that the past here is so brought to the present because Jesus of Nazareth was not understood? Similar questions can be raised with a view of other narrative characters. Why is Jesus's family presented in the narrative in such a negative way? Why are the Herodians involved in the Galilean conspiracy to kill Jesus (3:6), and why does the Markan Jesus issue a warning against the influence of Herod (8:15)? Why are there episodes in which Mark appears to refer to Peter's autobiographical memory (e.g., 14:54, 66–72)? I do not maintain that these questions that arise from the development of the plot can be answered altogether by recourse to the time of Jesus. In particular, some are connected with conditions at the time of the composition of Mark. Others, however, such as the unbelief of the disciples and Peter's denial, are best explained by their reference to the narrated time. Does the narrator here reflect actual knowledge about Jesus's past? A further example is this: in light of 12:35–37, it is clear that the implied author wishes to convey to his audience, to overcome the notion of the scribes, that the Christ would have to come from a family of Davidic descent, because this was disputed in the collective memory (Breytenbach 1997). The fact that both Matthew and Luke transform the story of Jesus in such a way as to confirm the Davidic ancestry should serve as a warning against neglecting historical-*critical* exegesis. Recourse to narrativity does not relieve the historian from a critical outlook with respect to the sources, and thereby the stories of eyewitnesses also constitute no exception!

Consequently, from the "framework" of Mark's narrative, which Schmidt had rejected as historically insignificant, it is possible to infer that after the arrest of John the Baptizer, Jesus proclaims the good news about the advent of the kingdom of God in cities such as Capernaum, Bethsaida, and Gennesaret (1:21; 2:1;

9:33; 6:45; 8:22; 6:53), and that Jesus recruited followers from these cities as well as Magdala (15:40, 47; 16:1). In the course of events, he also appears to have stayed in the house of Simon (Peter) and Andrew in Capernaum (1:29; 2:1; 7:17; 9:33; 10:10) and also traveled to the surrounding villages (6:6, 56; 8:27) and to marketplaces (6:56) in order to proclaim his message. As A. Alt (1953, 438, 450–51) noticed long ago, with the exception of Jerusalem, Jesus never enters a city. He visited only the villages around Caesarea Philippi (8:27) and the territory of Tyre and Sidon as well as the wider regions of the Decapolis (7:31; see also, Breytenbach 1999). The fact that the narrator configures the scenery of individual episodes in a specific way implies, to a high degree of probability, that he is reproducing the common memory about the villages and addressees of the teaching of Jesus in a new form. Presumably this common memory will have also contained reminiscences from the time of Jesus's activity.

5. Conclusion

Because the common memory became a document by means of the process of writing, today we—as late readers who are not addressed—can read the narrative framework of Mark and, historical-critical scrutiny presupposed, utilize the implied information for a historical reconstruction. If we take Wrede's way when we read Mark as a narrative and then read the text in the true sense of the word as a narrative, it becomes clear that it supplies the implied audience with valuable individual pieces of information about the person of Jesus. But the way in which the events are tied together in a plot (*emplotment*) does not allow Mark to be considered a historical narrative. By reading the Markan narrative against the background of the historical geography and archaeology of Galilee, considering the information provided by Josephus, we can extract important aspects about how the community behind the Gospel of Mark remembered Jesus of Nazareth and how this memory impacted their identity. However, we cannot consider this collective memory as the result of the "impression" that Jesus left behind without subjecting it to historical-critical scrutiny. Because of the transition from individual to collective memory, we are unable to hear what the women and men disciples heard, and we are unable to picture what they saw. We have to be content with the narrative reconfiguration of secondary collective memory.

Breytenbach, Cilliers. 2013. "From Mark's Son of God to Jesus of Nazareth—Un cul-de-sac?" In *The Quest for the Real Jesus: Radboud Prestige Lectures by Prof. Dr. Michael Wolter*, edited by Jan van der Watt, 19–56. BibInt 120. Leiden.

Perrin, Norman. 1966. "The Wredestrasse Becomes the Hauptstrasse: Reflections on the Reprinting of the Dodd Festschrift; A Review Article." *JR* 46 (2): 296–300.

Schröter, Jens. 2007b. *Von Jesus zum Neuen Testament: Studien zur urchristlichen Theologiegeschichte und zur Entstehung des neutestamentlichen Kanons.* WUNT 204. Tübingen.

Wrede, William. 1901; ⁴1969. *Das Messiasgeheimnis in den Evangelien: Zugleich ein Beitrag zum Verständnis des Markusevangeliums.* Göttingen. ET 1971.

Cilliers Breytenbach

IX. The Gospels as "Kerygmatic Narratives" of Jesus and the "Criteria" in Historical Jesus Research

Criteria for recovering "authentic" Jesus material from the Gospels converged into a formal methodology in historical Jesus studies in the mid-twentieth century. The foundation of this stage of Jesus research was form criticism's conception of the written Gospels as kerygmatic narratives. Under this conception, the written Gospels were enshrinements of the preached theology (or kerygma) of later Christians. Their overall interpretations of Jesus were thus taken to reflect not the time of Jesus but the time in which those later Christians proclaimed him. In their proclamations, they were assumed to have employed individual units of Jesus tradition such as sayings or stories. From this perspective, then, the narrative interpretations of Jesus in the written Gospels were imposed upon the tradition and not part of its earliest stages. After this form-critical theory of the development of the gospel tradition confirmed anew Albert Schweitzer's earlier condemnation of the nineteenth-century quest to write a modern biography of Jesus (the *Leben Jesu* movement), interest in the quest for the historical Jesus waned in German scholarship. In the wake of this lethargy, and while accepting form criticism's conception of the gospel tradition, several post-Bultmannian scholars used the concept of "authentic Jesus material" and criteria for recovering such material in order to inject new energy into the quest. The works of three scholars in particular provide excellent examples of this period of historical Jesus scholarship: Ernst Käsemann, Günther Bornkamm, and Ferdinand Hahn.

1. Ernst Käsemann

Käsemann was a student of Rudolf Bultmann and is the most important scholar for understanding the formal development of criteria of authenticity. Although

Käsemann was not the first to employ various criteria in historical Jesus research, just as he was not the first to affirm the largely mythical nature of the Gospels, it was his 1953 lecture "The Problem of the Historical Jesus" that called in a programmatic manner for criteria for determining "authentic Jesus material" (Käsemann 1964a, 35). In this essay, he clearly identifies the need that his proposal addresses when he claims that "apart from the parables, we possess absolutely no kind of formal criteria by which we can identify the authentic Jesus material" (35; see also 36–37). One must note two distinctive aspects of Käsemann's call for criteria of authenticity. The first important matter is Käsemann's default setting concerning the Gospels: "We can no longer assume the general reliability of the Synoptic tradition about Jesus" (34). His call for criteria that demonstrate authenticity thus places the burden of proof upon the scholar who would affirm the historicity of an aspect of the Jesus tradition. This position reverses the burden of proof expressed in, for example, David Friedrich Strauss's *Leben Jesu*, whose second edition in the 1830s developed criteria for determining the unhistorical nature of aspects of the Jesus tradition. The second important matter is Käsemann's distinct understanding of "authenticity." For Käsemann, this term stands in a contrastive relationship with the interpretations of the written Gospels. Similar to his default setting concerning the historical nature of the Gospels, his concept of "authenticity" is directly indebted to form criticism.

Fundamental for Käsemann is his belief that Bultmann and the form critics had successfully demonstrated that the Gospels were primarily kerygmatic narratives. The interpretive frameworks of the Gospels reflected the *Sitze im Leben* of early Christians, and it was through these frameworks that they articulated the significance of Jesus in their contemporary preaching. Thus, their current realities "almost entirely swallowed up his earthly history," and this happened from "the very earliest days" (23). Käsemann has no desire to cast aside this tenet of form criticism and states, "Anyone who tries to upset this verdict is seeking to rob us of the fruit and the meaning of all our research of the last two centuries" (23). He personally advocated for early Christian eschatology (or, in the case of Luke, the failure of the eschatological moment to actualize) as the determinative interpretive framework for each gospel author's image of Jesus.

Form criticism had therefore, like Albert Schweitzer before, demonstrated the futility of the nineteenth-century *Leben Jesu* movement that sought to write a modern biography of Jesus consisting of "objective facts" or "bare facts" (19). The kerygma itself shows that the early church had no use for such bare facts. This reality renders a quest for the historical Jesus, so defined, stillborn: "We can only gain access to this Jesus through the medium of the primitive Christian gospel and the primary effect of this gospel is not to open up the way for us but to bar it" (23).

Furthermore, for Käsemann, it would not matter if one could get to objective facts about Jesus. Throughout his essay, he expresses disdain for defining the historical task as recovery and arrangement of *bruta facta* in a cause-and-effect fashion. He refers frequently to the end product as *Historie*, in contrast to *Geschichte*, and finds it, for all intents and purposes, useless: "History [*Alle Historie*] is only accessible to us through tradition and only comprehensible to us through interpretation. . . . Mere history [*Historie*] is petrified history [*erstarrte Geschichte*], whose historical significance cannot be brought to light simply by verifying the facts and handing them on" (18, 24). He thus claims, "If we desire to obtain knowledge of past history [*verganger Geschichte*], we have to fall back on what has been narrated" (18). Importantly, therefore, when gazing in the direction of the nineteenth-century quest, Käsemann privileges the importance of inherited interpretive categories in the work of critically reconstructing history, and thus the kerygma as the only path—albeit a difficult one—to the historical Jesus.

Unfortunately, from his perspective, on account of the difficult nature of this path, some scholars had been "compelled to give up the attempt to construct a life of Jesus out of the Synoptic Gospels" (23). In contrast, Käsemann states that he is "not prepared to concede that, in the face of these facts, defeatism and scepticism must have the last word and lead us on to a complete disengagement of interest from the earthly Jesus" (45–46). He forwards at least two reasons for renewing the quest for the historical Jesus, both of which are based upon the kerygma itself.

First, although the early church thoroughly projected its theological categories onto the earthly Jesus, this very projection onto the *earthly* Jesus reveals the church's staunch assertion of the importance of the historical life of Jesus and its unwillingness to locate its theological center solely on the near side of Easter (24–25, 45–46). In this way, "the New Testament itself justifies us to this extent in asking the question" (24–25).

Second, despite the high degree to which the kerygma is "not authentic but was minted by the faith of the primitive Christian community," as claimed the form critics (15), it nevertheless contains some "authentic Jesus material" (35–36). Käsemann is careful with his language in this regard. He considers the kerygma to be inauthentic "for the most part" (15) and the life of the historical Jesus "almost" (23, 30, 46) swallowed up—but not entirely swallowed up. In the midst of the kerygma was "authentic Jesus material" that had been "buried" under (25), "embedded" within (15, 34), or "interwoven" with (27) the mythical and was thus "overlaid by it" (15). His metaphors for the coexistence of the authentic and inauthentic are important because they reveal the important assumption that they were mixed in the Gospels in a manner akin to different fabrics in a layered tapestry that, with some effort, could be identified and separated. This conception of the Gospels has been foundational for two generations of historical Jesus scholars, including Käsemann's immediate contemporaries, who repeat the same metaphors.

Käsemann thus sets as a goal the separation of the authentic, genuine Jesus material from the kerygmatic narratives of the Gospels. He portrays this task as the work of true "radical criticism" (35), breaking with the new orthodoxy of dismissing the historical reliability of the Synoptic Gospels altogether. Käsemann, however, also sees his approach as an extension of form criticism, insofar as it accepts form criticism's understanding of the nature of the gospel tradition and then proceeds to build upon it. He states explicitly that his procedure begins "with the work of the Form-Critics as a basis" and, in line with the method, pursues the "genuineness" not of the interpretive frameworks of the Gospels but of the "individual unit of material" (34). He thus assigns form criticism a precise role: "It can eliminate as unauthentic anything which must be ruled out of court because of its *Sitz-im-Leben*" (35). In other words, the individual units of material that are even capable of being tested for authenticity are those that form criticism has left "unimpeached" (15). This formulation is crucial for understanding Käsemann's view of how the criteria of authenticity enable an approach to the historical Jesus because it fundamentally defines "authenticity"—or even the possibility of it—in contrast to the interpretive categories of the written Gospels, which emerged directly from the early Christian *Sitze im Leben*.

In order to test individual units of tradition, Käsemann affirms what has now become known as the criterion of dissimilarity or double dissimilarity. He asserts that an element of the written Gospels is authentic Jesus material "when there are no grounds either for deriving a tradition from Judaism or for ascribing it to primitive Christianity" (37). Bultmann had already articulated a version of this criterion in his *History of the Synoptic Tradition*, though he applied it to recovering the earliest stage of the similitude form. In a qualification, Käsemann combines the criterion of dissimilarity with what has now become known as the criterion of embarrassment: "especially when Jewish Christianity has mitigated or modified the received tradition, as having found it too bold for its taste" (37). Thus, Käsemann regards as authentic anything that could not have emerged from earliest Christianity or Second Temple Judaism, as well as anything that the early church had covered up due to shame or discomfort.

Käsemann affirms this method as the only means by which "we have more or less safe ground under our feet" (37). On these grounds, he went on to affirm a handful of gospel texts as authentic Jesus material. Examples include passages that portray Jesus as usurping Moses (especially the first three antitheses of the Beatitudes, Matt. 5:21, 27, 32), an original version of the saying about the Lord of the Sabbath (Mark 2:28), Jesus's disregard for purity laws, the saying about the binding of the strong man (Mark 3:27), and Jesus's baptism by John the Baptist.

2. Günther Bornkamm

Like Käsemann, Bornkamm was a student of Bultmann and strongly influenced by Bultmann's conception of the Gospels as kerygmatic narratives. Bornkamm published his landmark *Jesus von Nazareth* in 1956, just three years after Käsemann delivered his famous lecture. In this and other publications, he expresses a variety of opinions that are similar to Käsemann's.

For Bornkamm, too, form criticism had delivered several firm results. First, the gospel tradition itself was transmitted via individual sayings and pericopes, and thus any critical inquiry into the history of its transmission must work at this level, not at the level of the interpretive frameworks of the written Gospels (G. Bornkamm 1960, 25, 218). Second, and related, the written Gospels are products of the preaching of the early church and grew directly from that preaching (17, 218–19). Indeed, "the tradition about Jesus is servant to the faith and . . . has been from the beginning" (219). Third, and as a direct result of the second point, the writing of a modern biography of Jesus in the style of the *Leben Jesu* studies is virtually impossible. Bornkamm laments "cause and effect" approaches to Jesus's life that focus upon "inner development and personality" (19; see also 1969, 74) and repeats the claim that the early church was uninterested in such "mere history [*bloße Historie*]" (1960, 25). He states strongly: "We possess no single word of Jesus and no single story of Jesus, no matter how incontestably genuine they may be, which do not contain at the same time the confession of the believing congregation or at least are embedded therein. This makes the search after the bare facts of history difficult and to a large extent futile" (1960, 14; see also 1969, 74–75).

Bornkamm, too, however, is unwilling to wave the white flag on the quest for the historical Jesus. Only the *Leben Jesu*–style search for Jesus need be abandoned—"Let it be noted that what can and should be laid to rest is not the quest of the historical Jesus as such" (1969, 76). He affirms the fundamental significance of the early church's attribution of its post-Easter theology to the pre-Easter Jesus in the kerygma as justification for inquiry into the historical Jesus (1960, 22–23, 174, 188) and thus also foregrounds the kerygma in the quest. Bornkamm thus states that the task of the historian is "to seek the history *in* the Kerygma" (21).

As with Käsemann, however, this claim refers not to the narrative interpretations of the Gospels themselves but to the individual pericopes that constitute the overarching narratives (21). For Bornkamm, too, articulates a quest that begins only once form criticism has finished its work. In reference to form criticism's laws for the transmission of the tradition, he says, "Observing these laws is an excellent aid in distinguishing the essential from the non-essential in any passage" (20). It is on this basis that "the critical exegete and the historian is obliged, in questions concerning the history of tradition, to speak often of 'authentic' or 'inauthentic' words of Jesus and thus to distinguish words of the historical Jesus from the 'creations by the Church'" (20). He repeats metaphors that express the assumption that authentic and inauthentic tradition are mixed in a manner that permits their identification and separation—the authentic traditions are "interwoven" with (14, 49, 93, 155), "overlaid" by (91), and "embedded" within (14) the kerygma. Bornkamm also refers to authentic tradition as a historical kernel within the kerygma (154, 173, 204).

In order to excavate those historical kernels from their kerygmatic contexts, Bornkamm articulates versions of the criterion of dissimilarity and the criterion of embarrassment. With regard to the first, he claims that Mark 13 and its parallels contain (1) tradition that came from late Jewish apocalypticism, (2) tradition that came from later Christianity, and (3) "genuine sayings of Jesus . . . interwoven with both" (93). This statement is one of the clearest expressions of the theory of the Gospels as a mixed-tradition entity that the criterion of (double) dissimilarity requires. On the basis of this criterion, Bornkamm affirms the authenticity of Jesus's claim about not drinking wine until the arrival of the kingdom of God in Mark 14:25, since it does not appear in the Lord's Supper tradition in 1 Cor. 11:23–25 (160). With regard to the criterion of embarrassment, Bornkamm affirms the authenticity of, for example, Jesus's baptism by John the Baptist (48–49) and Judas's inclusion in the Twelve (150). Bornkamm also appeals to versions of what have become known as the criterion of Semitic influence, the criterion of contrary-to-tradition, and the criterion of multiple forms. The first assumes that tradition that reflects an Aramaic context has a greater chance of authenticity. The second functions like a microcosm of the logic of the criteria approach altogether but applied at the level of the narrative itself, affirming that tradition that runs contrary to the interpretative agenda of the written Gospels is authentic. The third assumes that particular teachings or sayings of Jesus that appear consistently in different layers of the Jesus tradition, and different genres within those layers, have a greater chance of authenticity. In earlier editions, Bornkamm uses the criterion of Semitic influence to affirm the authenticity of Jesus's distinctive "Amen" in the Gospels as untranslated from Aramaic (99). He also uses the criterion in reverse, rejecting the authenticity of Matt. 19:28 since "the unusual term *paliggenesia* . . . cannot be translated back into the Aramaic" (210n13). (Bornkamm removed both claims from later editions of *Jesus of Nazareth*.) He uses the criterion of contrary-to-tradition in order to affirm the authenticity of Pilate's pronouncement of Jesus's death sentence, since, for him, the gospel authors work to exculpate Pilate (164). He uses the criterion of multiple forms to affirm the dawn of the kingdom of God, whose nature is hidden-yet-significant, as a key feature of the teaching of the historical Jesus (64–95).

Significantly, Bornkamm also reveals an interesting development from Käsemann by affirming that purportedly "inauthentic" tradition still can have value for the historian. He says, "It is not apparent why a word or a story which was first formulated by the Church should not in content possess historical genuineness" (11). In this light, "We should not, therefore, dismiss as mere fancy or invention what criticism might term 'inauthentic' and 'creations by the Church'" (20–21). Bornkamm thus expresses a more nuanced view of the relationship between interpretive categories and historical accuracy, thereby opening the discussion about historical aspects in the Gospels to a broader set of data than only tradition pronounced as authentic. As an example, Bornkamm affirms that Jesus did expect conflict and death in Jerusalem, even though he does not place confidence in his individual passion predictions (154–55). One must underscore that this approach runs directly counter to the search for "authentic" tradition, which severs the connections between the units of tradition and the early church. In a subsequent publication, he even posits that the historical Jesus "imposed and forced" himself upon later Christians' presentation of him in legendary terms (1969, 76). In this very qualified sense, Bornkamm can state that he is not really concerned at all with "stocktaking . . . what is genuine or spurious, authentic or secondary," though, in the same breath, he says, "No one who participates or is interested in historical research is spared any of these questions in his daily work" (1969, 77).

Although this aspect of Bornkamm's thought indicates that he envisioned more than one path to the historical Jesus, his general conception of "authenticity" nevertheless gives expression to the same conviction as Käsemann's, the conviction that scholars can recover a historical Jesus behind, and thus outside of, the interpretive frameworks of the written Gospels. Bornkamm believes himself capable of getting "behind" the tradition and to "the thing itself" (1960, 9). He refers to the Jesus recovered out of the faith convictions of the early Christians as "facts which are prior to any pious interpretation and which manifest themselves as undistorted and primary" (53; cf. also 56).

3. Ferdinand Hahn

Hahn was a student of both Käsemann and Bornkamm. Their influence is apparent in Hahn's publications, especially an essay based on lectures given in 1960 and 1961 (Hahn 1969b) and his famous monograph, *The Titles of Jesus in Christology* (1969a).

Hahn affirms the form-critical claim that the kerygma was a product of early Christian *Sitze im Leben* and has no biographical interest in Jesus (1969b, 41–45).

He likewise expresses the now familiar dual conviction that the nineteenth-century *Leben Jesu*–style quest for the historical Jesus had failed but the quest itself had not failed. In affirming Dibelius's statement that there was never a purely historical Jesus, he asks, "Does this mean that we can no longer in any way penetrate behind the preaching of the early community and must give up every quest of the prior history of Jesus?" and answers, "Certainly not!" (43).

In a manner similar to that of his teachers, Hahn affirms that scholars can pursue history *in* the kerygma: "In every individual part of the tradition we sense that a real history stands behind this proclamation of the early community. But this fact is expressed precisely *in* the proclamation" (43; see also 35). Once again, however, and as this quotation reveals, scholars must quest for history at the level of individual pericopes that constitute the kerygmatic narratives of the written Gospels, not at the level of the narrative itself. He states that critical scholars must "penetrate through" or "penetrate behind" the kerygmatic narratives in order to find history (20, 43, respectively). Hahn thus conceptualizes the task of the historical Jesus scholar as filtering authentic aspects of the kerygma out of inauthentic aspects: "To work in a historical-critical fashion means to distinguish everything within the unified, complete vision of the Gospels . . . from the things which we can still determine about the concrete history of Jesus, the way his ministry originally appeared, and the parts of his proclamation which are undoubtedly genuine" (18).

Appealing to Bornkamm, Hahn affirms the utility of the criterion of dissimilarity in order to accomplish this task: "All the elements which are clearly part of the post-resurrection experiences of the community must be set to one side, together with all statements which can be proven to have been taken over from Jewish concepts" (45). He refers to the traditions left over as an "initial base" (45). As an example, he affirms that the distinction between Jesus and the Son of Man in texts such as Mark 8:38 par. Luke 12:8–10 must be "a genuine word of Jesus" because later Christians conflated the two figures, as does the Matthean parallel in Matt. 10:32–33 (1969a, 29; see further 32–34). Hahn also employs the criterion of Semitic influence in order to recover "Aramaic original" sayings of Jesus from the Gospels' Greek (1969b, 40), including using it in reverse to deny authenticity to words that cannot be retroverted to Aramaic (1969a, 40–41).

Also similar to Bornkamm, Hahn is not interested in discarding inauthentic tradition entirely. For example, although he accepts that the speeches of Jesus in John's Gospel "yield no information" for the preaching of the historical Jesus, he nevertheless sees them as part of a reception history that reflected "the reality of the history of Jesus" (1969b, 32). He thus claims that a distinction between "original and secondary" sayings of Jesus has "nothing at all to say about the true worth of the biblical sayings of Jesus" (33). He even claims that scholars must reckon with the fact that the early church was as indebted to what it inherited from the past of Jesus as it was to its charismatic present: "Perhaps the first church was impelled not only by the working of the Spirit but first and foremost by the example of the earthly Jesus" (1969a, 30). Hahn is therefore careful, especially in his *Titles of Jesus in Christology*, to observe links between Jesus and the early church (for example, 75).

Importantly, however, for Hahn, this continuity exists only between the early church and the "earthly" Jesus. He distinguishes between this Jesus and the "historical" Jesus, as he also distinguishes between the quests for these respective Jesuses (1969b, 45). The quest for the earthly Jesus can presuppose continuity with the kerygma, whereas the quest for the historical Jesus must accept "those premises which are determinative for the modern idea of history" (45). As is the case also with his *Doktorvater*, then, it is clear that his overall conception of how one reaches the authentic, historical Jesus is by discarding the kerygmatic narratives of the Gospels in order to attain an uninterpreted historical Jesus. He states this matter explicitly: "When I speak of the historical Jesus I go behind all the statements of the community, limit myself to the facts of his earthly life, his ministry and proclamation, and attempt to gain a picture which is free from all post-resurrection conceptions, in order to grasp the history of Jesus on its own terms" (45).

4. Summary

The works of Käsemann, Bornkamm, and Hahn illustrate how criteria for recovering "authentic" Jesus tradition were developed directly upon the foundation of the form-critical theory of the written Gospels as kerygmatic narratives. The starting point for each scholar is form criticism's demonstration that the Gospels grew out of the community theologies of the early church, as well as its insistence on working with the gospel tradition at the level of the individual pericope. The shadow of form criticism, as well as the shadow of the failure of the nineteenth-century quest to write a modern biography of Jesus, thus looms over the developmental stages of the criteria of authenticity.

Those same shadows induced many of the contemporaries and predecessors of Käsemann, Bornkamm, and Hahn to abandon the quest for the historical Jesus. In contrast to this trend, these three scholars insisted that the quest itself had not failed; only an earlier stage of it had failed. Each of these scholars, in related ways, used criteria such as dissimilarity, embarrassment, and Semitic influence to pronounce some sayings and deeds of Jesus in the Gospels as "genuine" or "authentic" in contrast to the kerygmatic narratives of the Gospels in which those traditions were embedded.

Criteria of authenticity proved incredibly attractive for Jesus research down through the so-called third quest for the historical Jesus from the 1980s to the first decade in the new century. Scholars often presented them simply as the main way to carry out the quest. Nevertheless, the criteria bequeathed an interpretive or, better, epistemological problem to subsequent Jesus-questers that has perhaps only recently come fully to light as scholars become increasingly skeptical that historians can get "behind" the Gospels to an uninterpreted Jesus. This problem emerges from how "authentic Jesus material" is defined in this model. Especially in light of their criticisms of the nineteenth-century questers, Käsemann and his contemporaries did not consider "authentic" material to be *bruta facta* in the sense of biographical details of Jesus. But it also was not simply the earliest stage of the tradition. Käsemann thought he was going beyond Bultmann, who had contented himself with "the earliest stratum of primitive Christian proclamation" (1964a, 15–16). Bornkamm likewise stated that one cannot be satisfied with "mere tradition" but must "seek behind it to the thing itself" (1960, 9). Hahn could speak of authentic tradition as the very words of Jesus himself, "unchanged" (1969b, 42). It is clear that these scholars believed the "authentic" Jesus to consist of the very words, actions, and person of Jesus of Nazareth himself.

The question this state of affairs raises is whether one can really attain the words, actions, and person of Jesus himself apart from the interpretations of his earliest followers, who retained and passed on those interpretations, a concern that Bornkamm and Hahn apparently already felt in light of their efforts to reserve a very carefully nuanced role for "inauthentic" tradition in their work. Nevertheless, the "authentic" Jesus of Käsemann, Bornkamm, and Hahn, while perhaps not consisting merely of the raw biographical facts prized by the *Leben Jesu* studies, was a Jesus who had not (yet) been interpreted by his earliest followers. This reality proves intriguing in light of their criticisms of the nineteenth-century questers for abandoning the kerygma in a search for brute facts. As mentioned above, looking backward to the nineteenth century, they tout the kerygma as the only path to the historical Jesus. Looking forward from the mid-twentieth century, however, they immediately break apart the kerygma and abandon the interpretive frameworks it exhibits en route to the historical Jesus. The kerygma is the path to the historical Jesus, but only because of what can be recovered out of its mythological interpretations. Stated otherwise, relying "on what has been narrated" (Käsemann 1964a, 18) is precisely what these scholars, at the end of the day, did not do when searching for "authentic" tradition, since they fundamentally disregarded the narrations of the Gospel authors. A certain irony therefore accompanies this model for historical Jesus research. Although each of these scholars acknowledged that there was no such thing as an uninterpreted Jesus, they developed and forwarded a methodology that explicitly assumed that it can recover precisely that.

Contemporary research has witnessed numerous criticisms of the criteria of authenticity, some of which address specifically these issues (see esp. Keith and Le Donne 2012, 25–48). Other scholars continue to advocate for the criteria of authenticity as a legitimate method in Jesus studies. The debate itself reveals the effect that the criteria approach to the "authentic" Jesus has had upon historical Jesus research over roughly a century and a half.

Bornkamm, Günther. 1960. *Jesus of Nazareth*. Translated by Irene and Fraser Mc-Luskey with James M. Robinson from ³1959. New York.

———. 1969. "The Significance of the Historical Jesus for Faith." In *What Can We Know about Jesus? Essays on the New Quest*, by Ferdinand Hahn, Wenzel Lohff, and Günther Bornkamm, translated by Grover Foley, 69–86. Edinburgh.

Hahn, Ferdinand. 1969a. *The Titles of Jesus in Christology: Their History in Early Christianity*. Translated by Harold Knight and George Ogg. Cambridge.

———. 1969b. "The Quest of the Historical Jesus and the Special Character of the Sources Available to Us." In *What Can We Know about Jesus? Essays on the New Quest*, by Ferdinand Hahn, Wenzel Lohff, and Günther Bornkamm, translated by Grover Foley, 9–48. Edinburgh.

Käsemann, Ernst. 1964a. "The Problem of the Historical Jesus." In *Essays on New Testament Themes*, translated by W. J. Montague from ²1960, 15–47. SBT 41. London.

———. 1964b. "Sackgassen im Streit um den historischen Jesus." In *Exegetische Versuche und Besinnungen*, by Ernst Käsemann, 2:31–68. Göttingen.

Keith, Chris, and Anthony Le Donne, eds. 2012. *Jesus, Criteria, and the Demise of Authenticity*, 25–48. London and New York.

Chris Keith

X. The "Third Quest for the Historical Jesus"

1. Introduction

The "third quest for the historical Jesus" refers to the phase of research on Jesus that began around 1980 and became established in Jesus research in English, especially in the USA, but then on a global scale as the paradigmatic norm of scholarly research on Jesus.

In comparison with the phases of previous research on Jesus ("new/second quest"), the "third quest" is distinguished primarily by a change in direction of the quest. In particular, the issue is the degree to which Jesus was shaped by his historical context (cf., for instance, the title *Jesus and the Constraints of History*

[Harvey 1982]). On the basis of this question, interest inevitably shifted to understanding Jesus *within* his historical context, that is, first of all, in the framework of Palestinian Judaism. The leitmotif of the third quest is consequently the construal of the context. In this respect it is fundamentally distinguished from the previous phase of Jesus research initiated by Ernst Käsemann. There the question was the uniqueness of Jesus in comparison with Judaism and Christianity. For this the criterion of double dissimilarity was utilized as a tool to eliminate tradition considered to be irrelevant for constructing the historical Jesus. By contrast, the scholarship on Jesus of the third quest understands Jesus precisely in continuity with Second Temple Judaism.

This new direction in the quest implies that the context of Jesus's living environment does not serve simply as a foil for the presentation of Jesus's proclamation. Rather, it is a decisive and indispensable source that informs who Jesus was (for example, Crossan 1991, 1–224; cf. du Toit 2001, 88–91). The result of this from a methodological standpoint is a substantial enhancement of those disciplines that deal with the environment of Jesus, such as archaeology, research on the cultural and sociological history of Galilee, sociological investigations of the structures of society in Jesus's time, and historical or cultural studies and history-of-religion studies on Second Temple Judaism in general. These were considered the necessary methodological instruments for the most probable, thorough construct of Jesus's historical context, which, again, has the function of enabling a rendering of a plausible picture of Jesus as an ancient Jew.

2. Developments

In the meantime, the third quest is forty years old and manifests many elements of development as a research paradigm in the sense of Thomas Kuhn. A revolutionary phase beginning in the 1980s was followed by a consolidation toward a standard for research, whereas particular new developments in the twenty-first century already signal the first signs of disintegration in the sense of Thomas Kuhn's anomalies.

2.1. Seminal Stimuli

First, it needs to be put on record that the third quest was prepared for by a quite different image of ancient Judaism that in general arose in the '60s and '70s. Apart from this general development in research on Judaism, three scholars, as early as the '70s, launched forays that decisively prepared for and shaped the third quest.

First to be mentioned is Geza Vermes, who in 1973 published *Jesus the Jew: A Historian's Reading of the Gospels*. This book constituted at that time a veritable foreign body in the landscape of scholarship. Vermes demanded embedding Jesus and his proclamation in current Judaism and explaining the *type* of Jew Jesus had been. He interpreted Jesus as a Galilean charismatic and miracle worker of the same stripe as the Jewish thaumaturge Hanina ben Dosa, a "holy man" or ḥasid. Vermes's book became a kind of programmatic publication. It framed the program of the third quest not only in locating Jesus specifically as a Jew within Judaism but also in describing Jesus's social role. Hence, he focused his discussion not on Jesus's proclamation but on his deeds.

Morton Smith, in his provocative book *Jesus the Magician* (1978), critiqued the established scholarship on Jesus for one-sidedly privileging the picture of Jesus as a teacher who preached, and urged that the one-sided devaluation of the miracle tradition in favor of the transmission of the word had to be reversed. Further, Jesus's deeds, which according to Smith identify him as a magician, had to be restored to the center of attention. In a similar manner as Vermes, he also inquired about Jesus's social role. Smith's challenge to dedicate more attention to the miracle tradition as a potential source for the quest for the historical Jesus was taken up positively, especially in the USA, and consequently shaped the nascent third quest decisively.

A third seminal impulse is Gerd Theissen's *Soziologie der Jesusbewegeung* (1977). It was quickly translated into English in 1978 (*Sociology of Early Palestinian Christianity*) and made a major impact, especially in the USA. Theissen utilized methods from sociology in order to subject the Jesus tradition (especially the sayings source) to a sociological analysis. He coined the sociohistorical category "itinerant radicalism," in order to designate the social role or position of the "Jesus movement" as an inner-Jewish reform movement, which according to him was characterized by an ethos of homelessness and defenselessness, of living without family and possessions. With this study Theissen paved the way especially for sociological, sociohistorical, and cultural anthropological methods of analysis and categories in Jesus research. Consequently, he also indirectly became a forerunner of ideological criticism, especially of feminist approaches. His itinerant radicalism hypothesis had an effect in a particular strain of the third quest in the transformed shape of the Cynic hypothesis.

2.2. *The Beginnings*

Although Vermes's *Jesus the Jew* or Theissen's *Sociology of Early Palestinian Christianity* in a certain sense could be evaluated as the initial spark of a new type of Jesus research, the beginnings of the third quest are generally located in the '80s. The Bampton Lectures (Harvey 1982), delivered in 1980 by the British New Testament scholar Anthony E. Harvey (published as *Jesus and the Constraints of History*), are regarded as the starting shot. With this he posed the question of Jesus's historical contingency. In the narrow sense of being constrained by linguistic conventions, John Riches addressed the same question in his book *Jesus and the Transformation of Judaism* (1980). With this the program of the so-called third quest took shape. In the following, the beginnings of the third quest are delineated by reference to four monographs, which depict important stages in establishing the third quest. Further, they can be considered representative of distinct positions or methodological approaches in the third quest, which, as "classics," have exerted a formative impact on Jesus scholarship (cf. on this, du Toit 2001, 83–98).

2.2.1. Marcus J. Borg: *Conflict, Holiness, and Politics in the Teachings of Jesus* (1983)

Marcus Borg's 1983 revision of his Oxford dissertation can be counted as the first monograph on Jesus in which exemplary characteristics of a new type of Jesus research or the third quest became conspicuous. As is typical for the third quest, Borg enters Jesus into the sociological relationships of Palestine of his time (27–72). It was a time of social conflict between poor and rich, between Jews and Romans. According to Borg, in face of the gentile pollution of Israel, Palestinian Jews rallied under the banners of Torah and temple, and regarded the preservation of Israel's holiness to be a divine obligation. In this respect holiness, understood as cultic purity, was the fundamental category of value that determined Israel's identity, such that all conflicts that affected their cultic purity were always political.

Borg locates Jesus in this context (73–200). The stories in the Gospels about table fellowship, Sabbath conflicts, and purity as well as controversies about the tithe and the temple show that Jesus put radically in question holiness as the fundamental social value. Borg formulated the thesis that Jesus participated in an inner-Jewish conflict over the correct understanding of traditional values. Within the framework of this conflict, he countered the catchphrase "Be holy as God is holy" (Lev. 19:2) with the appeal "Be compassionate as God is compassionate" (cf. Luke 6:36), and he promoted compassion as an alternative paradigm for a fundamental reform of Israel.

According to Borg's interpretation, Jesus was a charismatic, a "holy man" in Vermes's terms, which enabled him to perform as both a prophet and a sage. As a prophet he called Israel to turn toward God's inclusive mercy instead of the exclusive categories of holiness and purity; as a teacher of wisdom he criticized and undermined conventional wisdom, which maintains the social order; and as the founder of a reform movement he radically called the norms of his contemporaries in question with a view toward Israel's renewal (cf. 229–47).

Further, an essential part of Borg's construct of the historical Jesus is that he rejects the concept of Jesus as an eschatological prophet (248–63; cf. also Borg 1986). For that reason, Borg argues that the majority of statements about the kingdom of God in the Jesus tradition have no eschatological reference. Rather, they are related to the present (mystic) experience of the numinous presence of God or the solidarity of those who have experienced this presence of God. He considers the unambiguous eschatological statements of Jesus about the *basileia* inauthentic, that is, as products of early Christianity. Borg became one of the most influential advocates of the third quest, who argued that Jesus's proclamation was not to be understood as eschatological.

2.2.2. Ed Parish Sanders: *Jesus and Judaism* (1985)

One of the most powerful portrayals of Jesus in the third quest comes from Ed Parish Sanders. Sanders also locates Jesus's activity or proclamation in Second Temple Judaism. He puts forth the thesis that the undisputed facts of Jesus's life require locating him between John the Baptizer, an eschatological prophet who called for repentance, and early Christianity, a messianic movement that expected an imminent end (8–13, 323–24, 334–35). Therefore, he puts Jesus's activity and proclamation in the framework of contemporary Jewish restoration eschatology (77–119) and construes him as a prophet of the eschatological restoration of Israel. According to Sanders, Jesus considered himself to be God's final messenger before the coming of God's kingdom and consequently expected that through an eschatological mighty act God would create a new order. Within the framework of God's coming dominion, he expected a new temple and the restoration of the twelve tribes of Israel (228–37). The fact that Jesus nurtured aspirations for a leading role for himself and his disciples in God's kingdom points to his highly developed self-consciousness: he likely considered himself to be God's viceroy in the coming kingdom (306–8, 321–24).

The thesis that Jesus as the advocate of a Jewish eschatology of restoration was firmly anchored in Jewish religion stands at the heart of Sanders's study. An analysis of the tradition about Jesus and the law shows that Jesus respected the law in its full amplitude (except for Matt. 8:21–22 and par.). The tradition about Jesus's ethical instruction shows that Jesus demanded high ethical standards for his adherents, which in principle conformed with the law (252–302). Nevertheless, Jesus's expectation of the destruction of the temple and his readiness to grant unrepentant sinners access to God's kingdom show that he did not hold the Mosaic order as absolutely binding. Rather, he expected that in the new age God would surpass this (245–89). Above all, his parables about a merciful God and Jesus's own unconditional acceptance of sinners suggest that God will evenhandedly allow both good and evil into the kingdom of God (e.g., Matt. 22:10).

Thus, like Borg, Sanders portrays Jesus within the Palestinian Judaism ("common Judaism"/"covenantal Judaism") of his time. But differently than Borg, Sanders locates Jesus's proclamation in the framework of the eschatological expectations of Second Temple Judaism. Further, it is noteworthy that Sanders not only allows the historical contingency of Jesus to come to bear (the principle of context) but also insists that Jesus, in the sense of plausible cause and effect, must be viewed in continuity with early Christianity.

2.2.3. Richard A. Horsley: *Jesus and the Spiral of Violence: Popular Jewish Resistance in Roman Palestine* (1987)

Richard A. Horsley also insists that an adequate understanding of Jesus can only be attained if he is located in the heart of the concrete social situation of first-century Palestinian Judaism. By means of a sociological analysis of the Jesus tradition and other contemporary sources, he designates Jesus as a prophet who propagated a social revolution among the peasant population of Palestine.

An "imperial situation" existed in Palestine (1–120), according to which Palestine was subject to the control of the Roman Empire ("subject country"), which by military might and with the help of collaborators in the population ("retainer agents") dominated, exploited, and oppressed the land. The situation is characterized by oppression and conflict between the dominant and economically powerful urban elite (Jewish aristocrats, Herodians, and Roman officials) and the economically oppressed people of the land ("rural peasantry"), who became increasingly poor on account of accumulating debt. Unavoidably, a spiral of violence was part of this "imperial situation"—structural violence and institutionalized injustice led to protest and resistance, which in turn led to intensified oppression and finally resulted in a social revolt.

According to Horsley, precisely in view of the imperial situation, apocalyptic traditions have the function to awaken the memory of God's actions of liberation as well as the expectation of restoration of society according to God's will, and apart from that to delegitimate and demonize the ruling order (121–46). Jesus is to be located in this context (147–67). Jesus harkened back to the contemporary apocalyptic for his proclamation of the kingdom of God, and he was convinced that God was at hand to put an end to the dominating demonic social powers, so that a renewal of individual and social life would be possible. What is more, Horsley interprets the "kingdom of God" as a political metaphor, which is related to the concrete historical reality (157); Jesus harbors the expectation that God would renew Israel, in that he approves those who are just and judges those who are unjust; that is, already here and now God effects a transformation of the present historical reality. Consequently, Jesus was a prophet in the sense of the prophets of Israel, who, in the face of judgment, calls for repentance (172–77, 193–98) and commits himself to the renewal of political and social structures of local communities of "traditional peasants" (209–45). In this Horsley opposes Theissen's theory of itinerant radicalism. Jesus's proclamation aimed to make God's dominion evident in the rural villages, and further to mediate it by means of healings, exorcisms, forgiveness of sin, table fellowship, and the symbolic restoration of Israel in the form of the call of the Twelve (167–206). Jesus's ethical challenges with respect to canceling debts, the abandoning of possessions, the loaning of assets without consideration of repayment, the avoidance of lawsuits, and so forth are by implication not valued as ethical norms for itinerant charismatics. Rather, they are concrete guiding principles for life in the villages of Palestinian peasants. Likewise, the command to love the enemy aims not at radical pacifism but at solidarity among village inhabitants in view of structural oppression (246–84). Because of the sociopolitical impact of his proclamation, Jesus turned out to be in conflict primarily with the priestly aristocracy and their institutions that preserved power, such as the temple. According to Horsley, Jesus was engaged in expectation of an imminent political inversion brought about by God (285–318). This conflict with the political institutions of his time then also led to Jesus's death on a cross (160–64).

Thus, like Borg and Sanders, Horsley aims to locate Jesus in the Judaism of his time, but in his case it has to do with the sociohistorical location of Jesus within the social structures of the time ("imperial situation"). Different from Borg, but like Sanders, he does not deny that Jesus made use of apocalyptic traditions, but different from Sanders, he interprets this in the first instance sociopolitically, so that the traditions of the time of the end are radically "socialized."

2.2.4. John Dominic Crossan: *The Historical Jesus: The Life of a Mediterranean Peasant* (1991)

John D. Crossan's *The Historical Jesus* ought to be deemed a final classic monograph of the early years of the third quest. Similar to Horsley, Crossan—utilizing sociohistorical and cultural anthropological approaches—locates Jesus in the society of his time, which he describes as a hierarchically structured agrarian society that was situated in a typical "colonial condition." The patriarchal structure of Mediterranean society is fundamental for Crossan. It was structured by patron-client relationships; honor and shame were held as its "core values"; and the access to power, goods, and privileges was mediated only by "brokers" (1–84). According to Crossan, the severe structural inequality of the "colonial condition" inevitably aroused the social resistance of the peasants, which precipitated protest movements in Palestine of a wide variety (from prophetic and messianic movements to brigands and violent protests) (89–224). Among these should also be counted charismatics ("holy men"), who challenged the religio-political establishment and offered an alternative access to divine reality (137–38), as well as the Mediterranean protest movement of the Cynics, which opposed the basic values of honor and shame as well as the social hierarchies in Greco-Roman culture and aimed at social "egalitarianism" (72–90). Crossan's primary thesis is that Jesus is to be understood within the framework of these two forms of social protests. He was a Jewish Cynic hailing from Palestinian peasants who acted as a healer and exorcist, that is, as a magician (or "holy man") (303–53).

According to Crossan, Jesus began his career first as a disciple of the Baptizer but quickly broke with his ascetic praxis and apocalyptic proclamation (227–64). This break with the Baptizer corresponded with Jesus's understanding of the kingdom of God as a noneschatological kingdom shaped by wisdom, of which a large amount of Jesus's sayings and parables testifies, and which (in contrast to apocalyptic traditions!) should be considered the earliest stratum of tradition. The kingdom of God was a radical, egalitarian way of life in present reality, which superseded social and religious discrimination and therefore took them as irrelevant (265–302). Jesus's proclamation that aimed at radical equality corresponded with his vagabond lifestyle, comparable with the Cynics, which he linked to open table fellowship, that is, a way of life, that rejected the basic social values of patronage and honor/shame (261–64, 332–48, 421–22).

Crossan's portrait of Jesus is completed by the fact that Jesus is construed as a healer and exorcist. With this he challenged the religious monopoly of the official religion of his time, because he mediated forgiveness of sins and healing, bypassing the official authorized institutions (priesthood, temple cult) (303–38, 344, 346–47). According to Crossan, Jesus's radical itinerancy functions to avoid any form of brokerage, that is, to guard against the emergence of new dependencies. Inasmuch as he and his disciples were constantly on the move, they had to go to people, and conversely the people did not need to come to them as inferior supplicants (345–48). According to Crossan, the praxis of open table commensality and freely available healing in connection with radical itinerancy positioned Jesus in a functional opposition to the temple cult in Jerusalem. Therefore, Crossan advocated the point of view that Jesus was arrested in the wake of sayings and actions that criticized the temple, and after a hasty and unspectacular trial, was crucified by Pilate (354–94).

Like Horsley, what is at stake for Crossan is the sociohistorical location of Jesus in the social structures of the time ("colonial condition"); like Borg, he judges that the apocalyptic Jesus tradition about the time of the end is inauthentic. Rather, it arose later in early Christianity, so that in contrast with Sanders, Crossan sets Jesus apart from the apocalyptic movement of the Baptizer and the earliest Christians.

2.3. Consolidation

Around the beginning of the '90s, the third quest transitioned into a typical phase of *normal* research (in the sense of Thomas Kuhn). Although in the following years numerous monographs on Jesus were published (Schüssler Fiorenza 1994; J. Becker 1996; Wright 1996; Johnson 1996; Allison 1998; Witherington 1999; Chilton 2000; Dunn 2003a; Schröter 2006b; Casey 2010; among many others), the pictures of Jesus drawn in them fit more or less in the discourse staked out by Borg, Sanders, Horsley, and Crossan, often in direct debates with their theses. In addition, numerous special studies appeared concerning the world in which Jesus lived, such as archaeological and other studies on the cultural and sociological history of Galilee (e.g., Reed 2000; Freyne 1998; Meyers 1999; Horsley 1996) and sociological and sociohistorical investigations on the social structures of Jesus's time (e.g., Horsley 1989; Stegemann and Stegemann 1995; Hanson and Oakman 1998; Malina 2001), all of which contribute to understanding Jesus from his historical context, and therefore answer the central question of the third quest more precisely.

The convergence of the third quest into a paradigm for research becomes especially clear in endeavors to reflect on the diversification of methodologies (cf., e.g., Theissen and Winter 2002; Porter 2000; Holmén and Porter 2011, 1–851), to document the status of research in representations of the history of research (Borg 1994; Chilton and Evans 1994; Witherington 1995) and in textbooks (e.g., Theissen and Merz 1998; W. Stegemann 2010), as well as to put it on record in popular academic presentations (Borg 1987; E. Sanders 1993; Crossan 1994b, 1998).

Nothing demonstrates the consolidation of the third quest so unambiguously as John P. Meier's massive work in (at least) five volumes, *A Marginal Jew* (Meier 1991–2016). Meier, in the framework of the guidelines of the Anchor Bible

Reference Library, offers a current portrayal of Jesus in discussion with a wide and representative sector from current scholarly discourse and a comprehensive documentation of the status of research of the third quest. This holds likewise for the comprehensive *Handbook for the Study of the Historical Jesus* in four volumes by Tom Holmén and Stanley Porter (2011), which, with almost four thousand pages, depicts current discourse within the third quest.

2.4. New Developments

In the third quest—*thereby* continuing earlier Jesus research and in particular form criticism—a particular segment of the Jesus tradition, which on the basis of the criteria of authenticity is considered authentic Jesus tradition, is contextualized in the framework of Second Temple Palestinian Judaism. Around the turn of the millennium, voices were first raised that put the model of authenticity in question (cf. du Toit 2002b, 118–25; Allison 2011; Keith and Le Donne 2012) and urged that it be replaced with an approach that would adequately take into account the characteristic features of *cultural memory* in the context of oral culture (cf. Kelber 1995; Schröter 1997; Dunn 2003a; Kirk and Thatcher 2005; Allison 2010; cf. on this du Toit 2013, 113–18). Potentially this opens the way to a new phase of research on Jesus, which could supersede the third quest as the standard paradigm (see B.XI).

3. Characteristic Features

Several common features of the numerous works that have been published as part of the third quest can be identified.

3.1. The Principle of Contextual Continuity

The primary interest of the third quest is to locate Jesus *within* his historical context. For this, it is presupposed that human beings are integrated into a network of diachronic and synchronic continuities that bind them to their environment. With respect to the historical Jesus, this means that Jesus's activity was conditioned by the cultural, social, and linguistic conventions of his time. Consequently, these have high value as sources in constructing a profile of what kind of person Jesus might have been.

3.1.1. Jesus in the Context of Judaism

The primary context in which Jesus or the Jesus tradition is to be located is the Palestinian Judaism of Jesus's time. The task of Jesus research is thus to understand Jesus's person and activity as part of Second Temple Judaism, that is, to interpret him as an ancient Palestinian Jew. The central question then is what kind of *Jew* Jesus was. The response of the third quest to this question is exceedingly multifaceted. Nevertheless, the studies concerned with this question can be divided into two categories (du Toit 2001, 108, 118–22).

On the one hand there are attempts to situate Jesus with regard to the *history of religions* within the context of Palestinian Judaism of the first century CE. Here the main focus is on the question of how Jesus or his proclamation relates in the Jewish society of this time to themes such as Torah, temple, purity, holiness, Israel, messiah, Israel's future, and so forth, or how he relates to contemporary religious movements of his time (such as the Pharisees or apocalyptic currents), and how his violent death could be explained in such a context (important advocates of such approaches are, e.g., E. Sanders, J. Becker, Dunn, and Meier, also in a certain respect Borg).

The other approach is to situate Jesus in a sociohistorical manner in the Palestinian Judaism of the first century. Here the question is Jesus's role in the concrete social situation of his time, that is, his place within the social structures of contemporary Judaism and his effect on these structures and the social conditions of his age. Above all, two sociohistorical models have been established. On the one hand, Jesus is interpreted in the framework of *ancient patriarchalism*, which constitutes the *social* context of his activity (e.g., Theissen, Schüssler Fiorenza, Crossan, W. Stegemann), and on the other hand, Jesus is interpreted in the framework of Mediterranean *sociopolitical structures* ("agrarian society"), which were characterized by oppression and the economic needs of the underclasses ("colonial condition"/"imperial situation") (advocates are, above all, Horsley, Crossan, Kaylor, with some reservations, also Freyne and Borg). As a rule, sociohistorical approaches interpret Jesus as the founder of an inner-Jewish renewal movement, whereby its relationship with society was variously determined. On the one hand, it is understood as a *utopian society*, which served as an *alternative* model to the existing society with its established oppressive structures (Theissen's groundbreaking itinerant radicalism; further, e.g., Schüssler Fiorenza and Crossan). On the other hand, the renewal movement relates to a society that is urgently in need of reform (e.g., the Galilean peasants) and aims at reforming society itself and its institutions (e.g., Horsley, Kaylor, with reservations, also Borg).

3.1.2. Aspects of the Life of Jesus as the Context of His Proclamation

Whereas the previous phase of research on Jesus was characterized by a concentration on the sayings tradition to construct a picture of the historical Jesus, the third quest does not hold the sayings tradition alone as an adequate foundation on which to construct the historical Jesus. Rather, it is distinguished by the fact that the proclamation of Jesus is not interpreted in isolation but in continuity with other aspects of Jesus's life.

This applies in the first place to the miracle tradition (or healings and exorcisms). It is generally accepted that healings and exorcisms make up an integral part of the activity of Jesus in Galilee. Consequently, a historically adequate picture of Jesus can be drawn only if his healing activity and its meaning in their social context are taken into account and are related to his proclamation (cf. comprehensively Meier 1994, 509–1038; further E. Sanders 1985a, 157–73; Crossan 1991, 303–53; J. Becker 1996, 211–33). Related to this is a widespread interest to locate Jesus's miracle working in the context of ancient religions or to explain it sociologically. Thus, following Vermes, Jesus is widely associated with the social category "holy man" (e.g., Borg, E. Sanders) and is sometimes defined as a magician (M. Smith, Crossan) or even as a shaman (P. Craffert, J. Pilch).

A further characteristic feature of the third quest is its interest in interpreting Jesus's proclamation within the context of specific biographical "facts." This concerns uncontested historical aspects of Jesus's life (Sanders's "historical facts") such as Jesus's baptism by John the Baptizer, the crucifixion by the Romans, the participation of the Jewish ruling class in the death of Jesus, and so forth. These facts, especially the conditions of Jesus's violent death (cf., e.g., Horsley 1994; E. Sanders 1985a, 18–22; McKnight 2005), thus constitute fixed points in Jesus's life that present historians with the task of correlating other aspects of Jesus's life with them, especially his proclamation (but also his healing practices and social behavior). In this manner they serve historians as beacons when formulating a historically plausible hypothesis on the life of Jesus.

3.1.3. Causal Continuity in History (*Wirkungsgeschichtliche Kontinuität*)

In parts of the third quest the principle of contextual continuity (in the sense of a plausible explanation of cause and effect) is extended to the origins of Christianity. A historically plausible picture of Jesus requires that the origins of Christianity as well as the central features of early Christianity (e.g., the eschatological profile) can be made plausible as *consequences* of Jesus's activity (e.g., E. Sanders, J. Becker, Theissen, Meier, and many others).

3.2. Methodology

Since the principle of contextuality is the central motif of the third quest, the task of research on the historical Jesus consists in *contextualizing* the Jesus tradition in a plausible historical construct of the Second Temple Judaism or Palestinian Judaism or the society of first-century Galilee in such a way that Jesus's activity can achieve its particular profile or significance from the particular context. The first part of the task, that is, the construction of the historical context of Jesus in the framework of Second Temple Judaism, is achieved by the utilization of diverse specialized disciplines, such as archaeology, sociology, and cultural anthropology, and has the purpose of reconstructing the social history of Galilee or Palestine at the time of Jesus as well as the cultural and religious history of Second Temple Judaism.

When contextualizing the Jesus tradition, it is decisive which segment of the Jesus tradition is being utilized for constructing the historical Jesus. In this regard, the third quest continues the paradigm in use since the beginning of the twentieth century, according to which authentic Jesus tradition is ascertained by so-called criteria of authenticity, or alternatively inauthentic tradition is filtered out (cf. Meier 1991, 167–95; Theissen and Winter 2002; Porter 2000; cf. on this, du Toit 2013, 101–6).

However, because of the central principle of contextuality, the main criterion of earlier Jesus research, that is, the criterion of double dissimilarity, has been abandoned. It has been replaced by a procedure according to which Jesus tradition that can plausibly be traced back to first-century Palestinian Judaism should be considered as authentic Jesus tradition. Consequently, contextual continuity with respect to Palestinian Judaism holds as a necessary requirement in order for tradition to be classified as historically authentic. One part of the third quest uses the criterion of plausible causal continuity (Theissen's "plausibility of historical effects"). According to this criterion, Jesus tradition could be considered authentic when it enables us to explain certain historical consequences of the life of Jesus (cf. esp. Theissen and Winter 2002, 176–217; Theissen and Merz 1998, 116–22). For this Theissen coined the conceptual pair "plausibility of historical context" and "plausibility of historical effects" (Theissen and Winter 2002, 191–97). However, in some quarters of the third quest the criterion of dissimilarity to early Christianity is quite rigorously retained (so, e.g., Borg, Crossan, B. Mack, R. Funk, and the Jesus Seminar).

The criterion of dissimilarity acquired a new function in the third quest: since it is presupposed that each individual is embedded in a network of diachronic and synchronic *continuities* and *discontinuities*, and is both tied to the environment and separate from it (individual profile), the requirement of contextual correspondence with ancient Judaism is complemented with the requirement to look for the individual profile of Jesus *within* his Jewish context, that is, to search for that particular combination of contextual elements that constitutes Jesus's (contextual) individuality (Theissen and Winter 2002, 191–97; J. Becker 1996, 4–5, 17–18).

4. Controversies and Debates

In spite of its character as a research paradigm, the third quest is not homogeneous. From the beginning it was characterized by some, in part vehement, debates about fundamental issues. So, an especially acrimonious controversy (cf., e.g., Crossan, Johnson, and Kelber 1999) raged about the contested theses of the Jesus Seminar, which was founded in 1979 by Robert W. Funk and J. D. Crossan and managed to draw quite a lot of attention in the mass media (e.g., Funk 1997, 1998; cf. also W. Stegemann 2010, 119–20).

Below some characteristic controversies of the third quest are briefly presented (on controversies about sociohistorical interpretations see above, B.X.3.1.1).

4.1. Eschatological or Noneschatological Proclamation?

One of the most intense debates in the third quest concerns the eschatological profile of Jesus's proclamation. It divided scholars like no other issue (cf. on this, du Toit 2001, 110–13). Whereas Jesus research since the beginning of the twentieth century was convinced that Jesus's proclamation was thoroughly shaped by futuristic eschatology, a number of third-quest researchers denounced this consensus (e.g., Borg, Crossan, the Jesus Seminar, further Horsley, and many others). Because this issue has to do with the frames of reference of Jesus's proclamation, it is of fundamental significance—it determines the course for understanding the proclamation of Jesus.

The dissent rests on different judgments about the authenticity of Jesus's sayings about the coming of the Son of Man on the one hand, and on the other hand, whether the generally recognized authentic statements of Jesus about the kingdom of God refer to a present and this-worldly renewal of society (or alternatively of humanity) or reflect an imminent eschatological expectation (cf., e.g., Borg 1986 and Allison 1994).

4.2. Prophet or a Teacher of Wisdom?

A further debate of the third quest is closely related to the problem of the (non)-eschatological character of Jesus's message. Whereas some scholars hold to the old consensus that Jesus was preeminently an *eschatological* prophet, others, who contest the eschatological character of Jesus's proclamation, champion the view that Jesus was primarily a sage who created (unconventional) wisdom sayings (aphorisms) and taught subversive wisdom (e.g., Crossan, Mack, and Schüssler Fiorenza). It is characteristic for this point of view that sapiential instruction and apocalyptic or eschatological proclamation are commonly considered to be incompatible (but cf., e.g., M. Ebner 1998, who advocates a mediating position).

4.3. Jesus as a Cynic?

A particular strain of the third quest postulated the more specific thesis that Jesus should be understood not merely as a teacher of wisdom but as a Cynic sage (cf. on this, du Toit 2001, 117–18). The Cynic hypothesis was propagated in the 1980s especially by Gerald Downing (1984, 1988; further Mack 1988) and found currency through Crossan's monograph on Jesus. The Cynic hypothesis is highly controversial—especially contested is the relevance as well as the applicability of the materials drawn upon for comparison, and further whether one could at all have reckoned with Cynic presence in Galilee (cf., e.g., Tuckett 1989; Betz 1994).

4.4. Wisdom Traditions as the Oldest Stratum of the Tradition?

All the debates mentioned above have their origin in a hypothesis current in some quarters of the third quest, that the oldest stratum of the Jesus tradition exhibits the character of wisdom, whereas interest in eschatological themes surfaces only in later strata. This is construed as evidence for a noneschatological, sapiential character of Jesus's proclamation (e.g., Borg, Crossan, Mack, and many others; cf. on this, du Toit 2001, 113–17). This hypothesis is supported on the one hand by John Kloppenborg's study *The Formation of Q* (1987), which reckons with a collection of *wisdom* sayings as the earliest literary stratum of the sayings source, and rests on the other hand on the privileging of certain noncanonical sources or supposedly earlier strata in such sources (cf. esp. Crossan 1985, 1988, 1991), especially the Gospel of Thomas (Crossan 1991; Patterson 1993; but cf. Schröter 1997). Thus, in this strain of the third quest, the putative age of the tradition (as a rule together with independent multiple attestation) becomes the decisive criterion of historical authenticity (so esp. Crossan 1991, xi–xxxvi). Contradiction followed suit: in a large part of research the (traditional) eschatological character of the (earliest) Jesus tradition is maintained (cf., e.g., E. Sanders, Horsley, Meier, Allison, Dunn, and many others), whereas the correlation of the putative age and authenticity of the tradition has been sharply criticized (e.g., Kelber, Schröter).

Theissen, Gerd, and Annette Merz. 1998. *The Historical Jesus: A Comprehensive Guide*. London.
Theissen, Gerd, and Dagmar Winter. 2002. *The Quest of the Plausible Jesus: The Question of Criteria*. Louisville.
Toit, David S. du. 2001. "Redefining Jesus: Current Trends in Jesus Research." In *Jesus, Mark, and Q. The Teaching of Jesus and Its Earliest Records*, edited by Michael Labahn and Andreas Schmidt, 82–124. JSNTSup 214. Sheffield.
———. 2013. "Die methodischen Grundlagen der Jesusforschung: Entstehung, Struktur, Wandlungen, Perspektiven." *MTZ* 64: 98–123.

David du Toit

XI. The "Remembered Jesus": Memory as a Historiographical-Hermeneutical Paradigm of Research on Jesus

In historical-critical scholarship on Jesus since the second half of the twentieth century, the category "memory" has played a role in discussions about an adequate historical and methodological access to Jesus's activity and teaching. However, the term and the concept it designates are used in diverse ways. At times this permits discussion about the "memory of Jesus" and criticisms that have been advanced against it to become confusing. Therefore, in order to demonstrate the methodological and hermeneutical relevance of the model of the "memory of Jesus," what needs to be explained first is which methodological approaches have been and are identified with this term, and how this approach is to be utilized in a productive way. Along the way it should become clear that the benefit of the concept of "memory" in research on Jesus consists of a paradigm that integrates historical-critical research and historiographical as well as hermeneutical reflection.

Roughly, two models of understanding the activity and fate of Jesus by means of the concept of memory can be distinguished. In the first model the term is used to describe the preservation and transmission of the teaching of Jesus by his early followers. In this sense Birger Gerhardsson introduced the concept into Jesus research in his monumental study *Memory and Manuscript* (1961 [³1998]). In this work, Gerhardsson engaged in a critical discussion with the form-critical model of the transmission of the Jesus tradition. According to the latter, the Jesus tradition was essentially shaped by post-Easter communities, which allowed only limited access to pre-Easter Jesus traditions. In contrast with the assumption of a collective, anonymous community milieu in which the Jesus tradition was formed by the post-Easter kerygma, Gerhardsson aimed to show that it is much more likely that the origin and early formation of the Jesus tradition go back to the memorizing and transmitting of the teaching of Jesus by his disciples. Accordingly, the Jesus tradition preserved in the Gospels can be traced back to the time before Easter and even to Jesus himself by an analysis of the memorizing processes. Thereby, Jesus's teaching activity is to be considered in the context of Hellenistic-Jewish memorization techniques and its modes of transmission. Moreover, rabbinic teaching models would present an especially close analogy. Accordingly, in a way comparable to the Torah, Jesus's teaching would have been oral at a first stage, but then also preserved in writing and passed on, interpreted anew again and again, and in this way became relevant for later situations.

With this approach (in continuity with his teacher Harald Riesenfeld) Gerhardsson posed the question about the origin and transmission of the Jesus tradition on a viable historical and sociological basis. He took up the criticism that has often been brought forward against the form-critical assumption that the Jesus tradition would not allow inferences about its origin and transmission in the pre-Easter period. Heinz Schürmann (1968, 1994) had also criticized this view in an important article, pointing to the "pre-Easter beginnings of the sayings tradition" in the circle of Jesus's disciples. Representatives of the form-critical model, instead, interpreted the Gospels as anonymous "folk literature" and regarded the traditions taken over in them as shaped by the liturgical practice or preaching of early Christianity. Accordingly, these traditions "are transmitted and shaped not by an individual person but by a crowd (people, fellowship, community)" (K. Schmidt 1923, 117–18; cf. also the reference to André Jolles, "simple forms," in Bultmann [10]1995). As will be demonstrated, this model of an anonymous collective tradition has also played a role in its own way within a certain use of the memory approach. By contrast, Gerhardsson and scholars who followed his view saw a serious insufficiency in this form-critical approach which they wanted to remedy by using "memory" as a model that is oriented toward concrete historical persons as the bearers of tradition. Thereby—as also in form criticism—processes of oral transmission play an important role in describing the preservation and shaping of the Jesus tradition. Creative new interpretations of Jesus's teaching thereby are not denied, but understood within a model of their reliable, uninterrupted transmission.

Gerhardsson's approach was carried forward by his student Samuel Byrskog (2000) and in his own way by Rainer Riesner (1981 [³1988]). What is at stake for both is interpreting the origin and passing on of the Jesus tradition in the context of Jewish and Hellenistic models of transmission. Accordingly, the origin of the

Jesus tradition is to be sought with Jesus himself, whose teaching his disciples—first of all the circle of the Twelve, but also others in his environment—compiled, interpreted, and passed on. As for Gerhardsson, for Byrskog and Riesner, the assumption of a teacher-student relationship between Jesus and his disciples as well as a relationship of personal continuity from Jesus by way of his disciples to the Gospels plays an important role. In addition, Byrskog points to the formation of the Jesus tradition, e.g. in *chreiai*. This genre, which in ancient rhetoric was widespread and taught in school exercises, was particularly suitable for the preservation and passing on of Jesus's activity and teaching (Byrskog 2011). The advantage of this elaboration of Gerhardsson's approach is that it not only takes over models from the Jewish or Greco-Roman environment but analyzes the transmission of the Jesus tradition on the basis of the gospel texts themselves. According to Byrskog and Riesner, the Gospels provide ample evidence for assuming a continuity of tradition between Jesus's activity and its presentation in the narratives.

Because of the orientation toward personal transmission of tradition, for this model the recourse to eyewitnesses is crucial. Byrskog points to the fundamental significance eyewitnesses would have possessed in the ancient historiography. According to both Riesner (2011, 425–26) and Byrskog, especially Peter and the circle of the Twelve play a central role as tradents of the Jesus tradition. An intensification of the concentration on eyewitnesses is found in Richard Bauckham (2006a), who traces the Gospels directly back to eyewitness memory. Among them he includes leading guarantors of the tradition, such as Peter, whose memories are preserved in the Gospel of Mark, and the "beloved disciple" in the Gospel of John, as well as persons healed by Jesus, such as Bartimaeus, or Anna and Simeon from Luke's infancy story, or Nathanael from the Gospel of John. For Bauckham the category "testimony" is important, because he regards testimony perpetuated by eyewitnesses about Jesus's activity to be reliable. On the basis of such an approach, empirical studies on the functions and mechanisms of human memory have been adduced in order to trace the path of the Jesus tradition from the beginnings to the testimonies becoming texts in the Gospels (McIver 2011).

The concept of memory understood in this way can be related to the approach of James Dunn (2003b). Dunn assumes that the "*impact*" of Jesus was preserved in the early Jesus tradition, which therefore makes it possible to infer retrospectively the content and form of Jesus's activity from the Jesus tradition preserved in the Gospels. Thereby, Dunn traces the multiplicity of synoptic traditions back to oral transmission processes which are characterized by a fluidity which then also influenced their written forms. Different from the previously mentioned authors, however, Dunn does not trace back the Jesus tradition to eyewitnesses.

Instead, comparable to the form-critical approach and in taking up the view of Kenneth Bailey (1995), Dunn understood the Jesus tradition as "informal controlled tradition."

The concept of memory in the views described so far is thus related to recollections of persons from Jesus's environment. In this way the processes shall be included that grasp how the Jesus tradition in early Christianity was preserved and transmitted. The aim is to demonstrate a continuity of the transmission processes, which enables essential contents of the Gospels to be traced back to Jesus himself. Oral forms of transmission can thereby be applied to for both the stability and the variability of the tradition. The concept of memory in this understanding forms an alternative to the form-critical view of the Gospels and the traditions taken up in them as anonymous folk literature or "lower forms of literature" shaped by myth and the worship of the post-Easter community. By way of contrast, the memory approach as described above is oriented toward concrete historical persons, who were responsible for passing on Jesus's teaching as well as the processes of the formation and transmission of the content of Jesus's activity. Consequently, the rooting of the Gospels in anonymous collective milieus is put in question, a critique of the form-critical approach brought forward from different perspectives.

However, there are serious objections to the memory approach described above. Even if the question of dating is left aside, it is questionable whether the Jesus tradition can actually be explained on analogy to rabbinic or Hellenistic techniques of memory and transmission of tradition or whether the textual evidence suggests another approach. Even though Jesus is often addressed as "teacher" (ῥαββί or διδάσκαλος) and his followers are called "pupils" (μαθηταί), the evidence for a "school milieu," in which Jesus's teaching has been recorded and passed on, is meager. Moreover, the significance of eyewitnesses in the transmission processes is overestimated. To be sure, it is quite likely that persons such as Peter and the closest circle of Jesus's disciples played a central role in the origin of the Jesus tradition in early Christianity. Nevertheless, it is highly doubtful that this should be understood as a faithful preservation of Jesus's teaching, which would allow to reconstruct Jesus's own teaching from the Gospels. This is already unlikely regarding the relationship between oral proclamation and the written narratives about Jesus in the Gospels. That it is possible to recover situations of Jesus's activity and the use of preliterary traditions appears improbable in view of variation in wording and situations in oral tradition. Furthermore, the attempt of James Dunn to describe the relationship of consistency and variation of the Jesus tradition at the oral stage on the basis of an essay by Kenneth Bailey must be considered unsuccessful. Different from what Bailey had claimed, in the oral tradition that he cited as examples, no direct stable "kernel" can be demonstrated, which in the process of transmission would have been varied. Instead, in narrating the events on an oral level, also the basic structure of particular versions varies (cf. Weeden 2009; Kloppenborg 2012). This accords with investigations of the processes of oral transmission, which have emphasized that in oral transmission an "original" is not modified again and again, but each presentation is itself an "original."

This characteristic of processes of oral transmission is also to be presupposed for the beginnings of the Jesus tradition, as can be clearly recognized in the Synoptic Gospels—and in its own way also in Paul and in extracanonical texts. Accordingly, Jesus was confronted with different circles of hearers, and he formulated his teaching in correspondence with particular situations. For instance, the parables about something that has been lost in Luke 15:4–7 and Matt. 18:12–14 are applied to different rhetorical contexts (discussion with Pharisees and scribes or community parenesis). Similarly, each of the two versions of the parable of the great banquet (Luke 14:15–24 par. Matt. 22:1–14) has its own clue (a challenge to invite the needy and marginalized, and an interpretation of the destruction of Jerusalem as God's reaction to Israel's rejection of the call to repentance). Likewise, invitations to discipleship and debates with opponents point to distinct preliterary contexts. Thus, the Synoptic Gospels have recourse to a multiplicity of contexts in which the Jesus traditions were used and shaped. This makes access to "authentic" situations and "original" versions of particular traditions virtually impossible. Instead, the traditions, both oral and written, have obviously been used in different contexts from early on. In their Jesus narratives, the Gospels have shaped them in specific wordings and integrated them within their literary compositions. Therefore, both the form-critical attempt to reconstruct a preliterary usage of these traditions by determining their *Sitz im Leben* and the attempt to recover the preliterary meaning of traditions about Jesus by means of the concept of memory must be regarded as unconvincing.

A fundamental problem of the understanding of memory outlined so far lies in attempts to demonstrate continuity between narratives about Jesus in the Gospels and the historical situations of Jesus's activity. Jesus's teaching and activity were undoubtedly retold out of the respective situation of the eyewitnesses and actual hearers, presumably first in Aramaic, then later in Greek; they were conveyed in particular literary forms (e.g., *chreiai*, parables, healing stories); they were interpreted by means of Old Testament citations and motifs; they were incorporated in narrative contexts; they were redacted linguistically and integrated into the comprehensive narratives of the Gospels in particular ways. These multiple processes of transmission, translation, and interpretation can hardly be comprehended by means of an approach that aims at reconstructing these processes and tracing them back to their origins.

In sum, the approach to understand the "Jesus memory" as an access to the earliest stages of the Jesus tradition, aims at reconstructing earlier traditions and eventually Jesus's activities from the stories of the Gospels. It is, however, questionable whether this way is plausible in methodological and hermeneutical regard. This should by no means put in question that important impulses for the origin of the Jesus traditions emanated from his own activity. This does also not imply a return to the form-critical model of an anonymous post-Easter kerygmatic tradition shaped by the early community. That several traditions originated from Jesus's activity and teaching, however, does not mean that these traditions can be reconstructed from the available sources. This is already unlikely with regard to the wide variability of the Jesus tradition of the first and second centuries which does not support the idea of a verbatim preservation of Jesus's teaching in its original contexts. Instead, it supports the impression of new interpretation, adaptation to new situations, and free shaping of their verbal presentation. From these multiple traditions, contours of remembrances of Jesus in early Christianity can be discerned. These contours, however, cannot be traced back to Jesus's teaching and the historical situations of his activity behind the earliest texts. Rather, they present sketches of Jesus's activity which have to be analyzed by way of historical-critical methods, but are not to be equated with the historical events themselves.

The historiographical-hermeneutical insight that facts and events cannot be separated from their interpretation thus speaks against inferring the historical reality behind the text from the memories of Jesus in early Christianity. Instead, from the very occurrence of the events, they are inseparably interconnected with their interpretations—in most cases by way of a verbal or textual presentation. In this way, namely, as interpreted events, they are further perceived and passed on. The quest of Jesus's teaching and activity cannot, therefore, be pursued in such a way that the available sources are traced back to the earlier stages of the traditions and eventually to their origin with Jesus himself. Instead, this quest is to be formulated as the search for an image of Jesus in his historical context, based on memories preserved in the earliest sources. This leads to the second way of using the concept of memory.

In a way that is to be distinguished from the approach outlined above, the concept of memory is understood as a cultural-hermeneutical category which provides access to the past from the perspective of the present. In this way the concept was introduced to Jesus research in the 1990s following Jan Assmann's approach (Schröter 1997). The fundamental distinction from the view mentioned above is that, according to this understanding, "memory" is understood neither as a description of the process of the transmission of the Jesus tradition nor as the basis for a reconstruction of the historical Jesus. According to this understanding, the memory approach does not provide the basis for a reconstruction of individual words, sayings clusters, or contents of Jesus's activity. This does not deny that particular contents of the Jesus tradition can be traced back to the activity of Jesus. However, the decision about this is not directly connected with the memory approach. Instead, "memory" in this perspective is part of a historiographical-hermeneutical approach, which understands the access to the events and persons of the past within a paradigm that is oriented toward the interpretation of the present.

In this way, the concept of memory was already utilized by Jan Assmann (1992). He emphasizes that communities are related to the past in the sense of a "foundational" history in which persons and events acquire a fundamental significance for the self-understanding of a community. Thereby, it is not the factuality of the events of the past that is of primary importance, but their meaning for the constitution and identity of a given community. For this view, Assmann refers to Maurice Halbwachs, who in his studies on collective memory had emphasized that the appropriation of the past in human memory contains not only an individual, but also a collective dimension. Assmann further develops this view by emphasizing that particular events of the past should be understood as "foundational myths" which contribute to the formation of the identity of particular communities.

With regard to the Jesus tradition this approach can be applied in such a way that the processes of shaping and passing on of Jesus's teaching and activities are perceived as "memories of Jesus"—as modes of tradition in which early Christian communities affirmed their own identity by recourse to the activity of Jesus. This also explains the "transparent" ways in which the Gospels plotted Jesus's activity so that it became relevant for their particular situations. For instance, the "parable theory" in Mark 4, which calls for the appropriate hearing and observance of Jesus's teaching, as well as the call to take up the cross and follow Jesus in Mark 8:34–9:1 are conceived of as reflections of historical situations in which confessing Jesus had become a posture with consequences that tied up with perils; the exposition of Torah in Matt. 5:21–48 as well as the orientation toward Jewish praxis of piety in Matt. 6:1–18 reflect a situation in which Christian communities began to form their own identity for which the preservation of the Jewish legacy remained important; and the warning often encountered in the Gospel of Luke against pride and foolhardy dealings with earthly possessions mirrors social differences in Christian communities, which the author of Luke viewed as incompatible with the ethos grounded in Jesus's activity.

Texts like the ones mentioned here as examples are evidence of the literary composition of the Gospels for reception of Jesus's activity, which is brought to bear in each given situation in their own form. In this respect the Gospels, each in its own way, "represent" the earthly Jesus, with whom a direct encounter is no longer possible. We cannot adequately comprehend the character of these "representations" by limiting it to the narrative world of the Gospels. This character consists in the connection of the Gospels' own present with the time of Jesus's teaching, activity, and fate, which by the time of the origin of the Gospels already belonged to the past. In other words, the Gospels illuminate their own present by reflecting about Jesus's activity, which thereby perceives a foundational meaning for the situation of the Christian communities. In this way events from the past that are regarded as meaningful for the present are turned into "history." In that the Gospels interpret their own time in light of the foundational past, they also claim to provide a report about the past itself. Therefore, they put Jesus's activity in a temporal and geographical frame, mention persons in his environment—for instance, his family, male and female disciples, opponents, political rulers, and so forth—and make clear how from the events concerning Jesus's activity a community has arisen, which after the events of the passion and Easter understands itself against the background of Jesus's activity and teaching. In connection with and in continuation of Assmann's approach, the concept of memory is therefore to be reflected upon historiographical-methodologically and to be combined with more recent historiographical-hermeneutical insights, the foundations for which were already established in the nineteenth century.

This understanding of the "memory of Jesus" is differentiated from the first-mentioned approach in that it does not move the question of the origin and transmission of the Jesus tradition into the center, but rather the question of the appropriation of the past from the perspective of the present. "Memory" is, therefore, not understood in terms of individual recollections nor is it tied to processes of preservation or forgetfulness of individuals. Rather, it is aimed at processes through which traditions are formed in communities, which preserve the past that is relevant for the community's own self-understanding—traditions that again and again are made relevant for the present by means of texts, rituals, celebrations, or memorial sites. Thereby, early Christianity draws on Jewish history, traditions and writings—for instance, in the formation of the ritual of a common meal, in which Jesus's last supper in Jerusalem is made relevant for the present in the context of Jewish traditions, or in the interpretation of the activities of Jesus by means of Israel's Scriptures, which already began before these traditions were written down. To the "memory of Jesus" understood in this way also belongs the consideration that Jesus's activity was transmitted in particular forms such as *chreiai*, parables, and healing stories and finally was incorporated into larger narrative contexts in which the historical contexts of his appearance come to light. The Jesus tradition prior to the written form and the Gospels is therefore to be construed as texts that are tied to Jesus's activity and teaching and "represent" the person and activity of Jesus in such a way that they become relevant for the communities that are related to him.

At the same time, outlines of what is taken as probable for the "historical Jesus" from a historical-critical perspective can be derived from these texts. But the "historical Jesus" is itself a kind of the memory of Jesus—namely a form that makes those traditions and events the foundation of a portrait of Jesus, that on the basis of a historical-critical analysis appears to be plausible. These portraits of Jesus, which are created with the methods of critical historiography, can be brought into scholarly historiographical discourse in which they can be tested, modified, or also falsified. However, these portraits of the "historical" Jesus cannot be equated with the past behind early Christian sources because they are themselves the result of processes of selection, interpretation and composition of a historical narrative. Moreover, the traditions and historical information that are employed for such portraits could have been and can be compiled in different ways because the texts and traditions permit various possibilities of portraying Jesus's activities and teaching. The portraits of Jesus depicted on the basis of historical criticism are thus a specific form of the "memory of Jesus": they are designed on the basis of the knowledge of sources at a specific time and by a specific author, and they represent Jesus's person and teaching on the basis of critical historiography as it was developed in modern times.

This approach to memory is, therefore, skeptical about a view that searches for the "historical" or "real" Jesus "behind" the texts. The criteria of the quest for the historical Jesus developed for such an undertaking in Jesus research can be useful for a historical-critical analysis of sources. They should not, however, give the impression that they can be used to reconstruct the "real" Jesus "behind" the texts. These "criteria"—which ultimately are nothing else than rules that are commonly used in critical analysis of historical sources—can rather guide historical-critical Jesus research and contribute to the plausibility of portrayals of Jesus.

This does, of course, not deny that early Christian texts refer to a historical reality behind them. However, that reality is always available only as *interpreted* reality. The distinction of this understanding of memory from the concept explained above is, therefore, in the end the respective historiographical and hermeneutical paradigm. The latter model understands early Christian as well as historical-critical portrayals of Jesus as texts that in their own way represent the activity and fate of Jesus and thereby make the person of Jesus meaningful in their own present.

The concept of "Jesus memory" thus takes up the hermeneutical insight that the historical-critical evaluation of sources must result in a historical narrative. This requires "historical imagination" in order to create historical relationships between the sources, and in this way to allow the past to become relevant in the present. In this process the sources that are bound to traces of the past are distinguished from those that prove to be legendary presentations of Jesus's character—for instance, the so-called childhood gospels or modern adaptations of the Jesus figure, e.g. in novels and movies. The latter are not committed to a historical representation of Jesus's activity but instead develop a contemporary access to him that is detached from historical research. The concept of the "Jesus memory," by contrast, does not clash with a historical-critical reconstruction of Jesus's activity. It does not aim at replacing historical-critical analysis, but instead intends to reflect on its epistemological presuppositions . This will be made clear by way of example in what follows.

The beginnings of the activity of Jesus in the context of John the Baptizer, including his baptism by John, form a solid element of the memory of Jesus that stands up well to historical scrutiny. In order to understand the significance of Jesus's baptism by John, this event must be integrated in the context of Jesus's activity. Thereby, the activity of the Baptizer has to be regarded as the prelude to Jesus's public activity, which in turn has consequences for the view of the person and message of John in early Christian sources. Early Christian memory explains John's appearance by referring to the return of Elijah announced in Jewish Scriptures, understands him as the forerunner of Jesus, directs his activity toward that of Jesus, and makes him the first and decisive witness to Jesus's endowment with the Spirit and his declaration as Son of God. Historical-critical research questions such a view and points to differences between early Christian presentations of John and a historical plausible portrait of his person and activity. Either way an image of the past is constructed that is not to be equated with the past itself. For historical-critical research, John appears as a Jewish prophet and preacher of repentance, to whose circle Jesus may have belonged for some time. From John, Jesus has probably conceived baptism as a symbolic seal of repentance and the washing away of sins. Later, Jesus separated from John in order to begin his own activity. Probably, much of this corresponds to the actual events, even if the portrait of John in early Christian tradition is shaped in a particular way, as for instance a comparison with Josephus's description of John (*Jewish Antiquities* 18.116–119) shows. Moreover, the relationship of John and Jesus in the Gospels as well as in historical-critical presentations is sketched out in different ways (in the latter, sometimes to the point of asserting a sharp distinction between the two, which is hardly plausible). In any way, the beginnings of Jesus's public activity appear in a specific way by their conjunction with the activity of John. Other beginnings would also have been conceivable: at his birth, with events from his youth, with his proclamation of the dawning of the kingdom of God, or at the calling of disciples. The fact that the historical identifiable beginnings are connected with John points therefore to a specific form of the memory of Jesus.

The meaningful appearance of Jesus is related to the context of the activity of John, who for his part is depicted as a Jewish preacher of repentance and who is interpreted with citations from Scripture (Isa. 40:3, as well as the mixed citation from Exod. 23:20/Mal. 3:1; cf. Mark 1:2 par.; Q 7:27). The legendary stories about Jesus's birth and the traditions in the Infancy Gospels confirm this in their own way. These texts show that the beginnings of the memory of Jesus in Christian tradition were sketched in a way that illustrates the uniqueness of his humanity and his exclusive relation to God.

An interpretation of the beginnings of Jesus's appearance from the perspective of the memory approach thus highlights that both early Christian texts and contemporary portrayals of Jesus are based on the fact that the activity of John was considered significant for a description of Jesus's activity and therefore was closely associated with it. How this relationship is to be described in more detail depends on the presuppositions with which the traditions about John and Jesus are interpreted. Historical-critical analysis will depict John and Jesus in the context of ancient Judaism of Galilee and seek to understand their relationship on this basis. The methodological presuppositions of such an approach are different from those of the Gospel writers, who depict John on the basis of Christian faith and integrate him in the story of Jesus without historical-critical differentiation. A historical-critical portrait of John and Jesus is, in any case, referred to the available sources as well as to information about their historical context to formulate a plausible hypothesis about their relationship. Thereby, the sources exclude certain interpretations, but nevertheless permit several *possible* explanations of the person of John, his activity and his relationship to Jesus within a spectrum of historical descriptions of the beginnings of Jesus's activity.

A further significant example is the references to the theme of purity in early Christianity. According to Mark and Matthew, Jesus dealt with this question, even if the respective emphasis is different. According to Mark, Jesus resolves the question of clean and unclean foods in that he declares all foods clean (Mark 7:19), whereas Matthew emphasizes the ethical dimension of the theme of purity—impurity comes from the mouth of humans and hence in the end from the heart (Matt. 15:18–20). For Paul, the question of purity is a problem within the community, which he tries to resolve by interpreting purity and impurity as a question of individual judgment (Rom. 14:14). Paul designates this as a conviction acquired "in the Lord Jesus," and relativizes the observation of purity laws within the community of believers by subordinating them to the love command. Finally, in the Acts of the Apostles in a programmatic vision it is explained to Peter that God has declared unclean food to be clean (Acts 10:14), which by way of what follows is related to the fact that God welcomes all people (10:34–35).

Behind these different references to the theme of purity stands the central conviction for early Christian faith that the appearance of Jesus significantly influenced Jewish discourses about purity and impurity. Mark and Matthew connect this theme in their own ways directly with the activity of Jesus. It could, however, also be related to the welcoming of non-Jews in the Christian community (Acts) or to interactions within the Christian community in which different opinions about clean and unclean are acceptable (Paul). In Jesus's activity, there are features that could have influenced these different receptions—such as his attitude toward the sick, his disposition toward the Sabbath command, perhaps also his attitude toward non-Jews. Whether a programmatic statement of Jesus concerning purity rules can be discerned, and if so, what it aimed at, or conversely, whether the significance of this question in early Christianity led to anchoring it in the Jesus tradition, can hardly be determined in view of the evidence in the sources. What is decisive, however, is that Jesus's activity was understood as a leading to a new view of the relationship of purity and impurity. In such a way, it was integrated in the memory of Jesus.

As these examples—which can be extended to the early Jesus tradition as a whole—show, the historiographical-hermeneutical paradigm of the memory of Jesus is based on the insight that the reconstruction of the past is tied to traces that can be extracted from the early sources. These traces set up the framework within which a historical-critical depiction of Jesus has to be sketched; at the same time, they indicate the intellectual and ethical responsibility of Christian faith towards its origins. The concept of "Jesus memory" assumes that outlines of the activity and teaching of Jesus can be depicted on the basis of the historical-critical evaluation of sources. Nevertheless, these outlines are themselves a specific mode of the memory of Jesus and not a path to the past "behind" the texts. In fact, the "historical Jesus" appears from this perspective as a form of the memory of Jesus on a historical-critical foundation that is not to be equated with the "real Jesus" behind the earliest texts. The paradigm of the memory of Jesus is therefore finally based on the insight that the indispensable foundation of Christian faith is the activity of Jesus lying behind the early Christian sources. This activity nevertheless is, however, accessible only by way of presenting the past from the perspective of the present. Comprehended in this way, the "remembered Jesus" can be understood as a hermeneutical reflection on the differentiation of the "historical Jesus" and the "Christ of faith."

Early Christianity 6 (3). 2015. *Jesus and Memory: The Memory Approach in Current Jesus Research* (with contributions by Alan Kirk, Eric Eve, David du Toit, and Chris Keith).

Eve, Eric. 2013. *Behind the Gospels: Understanding the Oral Tradition*. London.

Keith, Chris, and Anthony Le Donne, eds. 2012. *Jesus, Criteria, and the Demise of Authenticity*. London and New York.

Kirk, Alan, and Tom Thatcher, eds. 2005. *Memory, Tradition, and Text: Uses of the Past in Early Christianity*. SemeiaSt 52. Atlanta.

Stuckenbruck, Loren T., Stephen C. Barton, and Benjamin G. Wold, eds. 2007. *Memory in the Bible and Antiquity*. WUNT 212. Tübingen.

Jens Schröter

C. The Historical Material

I. Introduction

1. The second part of this handbook deals with the material evidence that in historical-critical Jesus research forms the basis for the reconstruction of Jesus's provenance, activity, and fate. The scope of the material to be taken up has been considerably expanded in recent research on Jesus. Whereas the "new quest of the historical Jesus" focused primarily on the Synoptic Gospels, in contemporary discussions the Gospel of John and further writings of the New Testament, noncanonical texts from early Christianity, Jewish writings from Greco-Roman times, as well as nonliterary remains—archaeological, numismatic, and epigraphic evidence—are considered as well. The expansion of the historical sources manifests the conviction that on the basis of the available material it is possible to reconstruct a plausible historical picture of Jesus's activity and fate. Thereby, the placing of his activity in Galilean and Judean Judaism in the first century constitutes a main focus in recent Jesus research. Archaeological and epigraphic evidence provides a more precise picture of the political, religious, and cultural situation of the time and regions of Jesus's activity. Hence, the historical material can be used to reconstruct an image of the historical context in which the New Testament Gospels place Jesus's activity.

Compared to the previous phase of Jesus research, this approach sets new accents. It has often been emphasized in Jesus research of the twentieth century that the literary sources about Jesus (in the first place the Synoptic Gospels) have to be regarded as post-Easter testimonies, which would testify to faith in Jesus as the Son of God but would hardly allow a comprehensive historical reconstruction of his activity and fate. Current Jesus research, by contrast, has developed a distinct historiographical focus. It does not start with the distinction of the pre-Easter Jesus from post-Easter testimonies of faith but aims at a historical reconstruction of Jesus's activity from the available evidence. Thereby, the necessity to reflect on the relationship of interpretations of Jesus in early Christian sources and the historical reality to which they refer is not called into question. It is, however, integrated into a paradigm that reflects on the character of historical-critical reconstructions from a historiographical-hermeneutical perspective. Reflecting on the relationship of event and interpretation is important for historical research in general, but also with respect to Jesus in particular. Jesus's activity and fate are available only *in their interpretations*, never independently from them. This leads to the question whether early Christian portrayals of Jesus allow at all for conclusions about his way of life, activity, and fate—and if so, in what way. With this, however, the historical foundation of Christian faith itself is up for discussion: Is Christian faith based on the activity and fate of Jesus or on the early Christian *interpretations* of his person?

This tension, which has been a characteristic of historical-critical Jesus research from its beginning, was often depicted as the juxtaposition of "historical Jesus" and "kerygmatic Christ" (or "Christ of faith")." Recent research, however, has called attention to the fact that *every* depiction of the past is at the same time an interpretation of the events to which it refers. Therefore, a historical-critical interpretation of the available material does not lead to the historical reality behind the sources but rather represents a possible reconstruction of the past by way of a historical narrative. Even if it is the aim of historical-critical research to push back to past events themselves—historical depictions, including depictions of Jesus, often are written with precisely this aspiration—there is no doubt that it actually provides interpretations of remains of the past from the perspective of the present. Engagement with historical material gains its significance precisely against this background—as a connection of the present and the past, which makes the person of Jesus accessible on the basis of a critical interpretation of the available evidence.

2. The presentation of the historical material in this part of *The Jesus Handbook* distinguishes between literary and nonliterary evidence. The former can be further divided into Christian and non-Christian texts. Among Christian writings, the New Testament texts are of special significance. However, in a historically oriented approach, their character as testimonies of faith or canonical documents is not the primary focus. Instead, they are scrutinized for their contribution to a historical reconstruction of Jesus's activity and fate. In other words, it will be asked whether these texts contain traditions or information that can be used for a reconstruction of Jesus's activity in its historical context.

Extracanonical writings can also contain historically relevant tradition and information. The past decades have seen intense discussion about the significance of noncanonical, "apocryphal" texts for the quest of the historical Jesus. On the one hand, this has occurred because the spectrum of early Christian writings has been extensively expanded by important discoveries not only of texts such as the Nag Hammadi Codices but also of many other texts, many only in fragmentary form. On the other hand, it has been appropriately claimed that a reconstruction of the history of early Christianity should not be oriented primarily, or even exclusively, toward those writings and theological perceptions that have prevailed in the Christian tradition. Instead, for a reconstruction of the history of ancient Christianity—and also for the quest of the historical Jesus— early Christian texts must be taken into consideration independently of their (later) status as canonical or apocryphal.

In the last decades, the historical value of noncanonical traditions about Jesus has been valued very highly in some areas of North American Jesus research. Sometimes the tendency was clearly recognizable to counter the primacy of the New Testament texts with the claim that noncanonical sources for reconstructing early Christian tradition and the historical Jesus are at least of equal, if not greater, significance. This approach, however, was not successful, since, compared to the New Testament, most noncanonical texts prove to belong to a later stage of the history of the Jesus tradition. Regardless of this general observation, the distinction of Jesus traditions that became canonical from those that did not must not form the starting point or even the benchmark for the historical assessment of these documents. For historical Jesus research, this means that also noncanonical texts, such as the Gospel of Thomas or sayings of Jesus in other texts or fragments outside the New Testament, are to be examined with regard to their contribution to a historical portrait of Jesus. The depictions of Jesus in canonical and apocryphal texts are thereby to be assessed as particular receptions of Jesus, which provide insights into developments in ancient Christianity. Therefore, some of these texts will be addressed in part E of this handbook as early receptions of Jesus's activity.

According to the historiographical-hermeneutical considerations noted at the beginning of this introduction, traditions encountered in early Christian texts offer no direct access to Jesus's person and activity. This is also true for the sayings of Jesus, which in the "new quest of the historical Jesus" as well as in certain circles of more recent Q research were accorded priority in the reconstruction of the historical Jesus. The comparison of different literary concepts for the sayings and parables, such as in the Synoptic Gospels and the Gospel of Thomas, however, shows that these traditions were received in different ways and integrated into particular portrayals of Jesus. The same applies to healing stories or conflict scenarios. What certain traditions "originally" looked like is thereby inaccessible, as are their original use and function in Jesus's activity. This is not least due to the fact that the Jesus traditions first circulated in oral form. The concept of an "original" version of these traditions, which in the course of its transmission would have been altered, is therefore inappropriate. The traditions were transmitted in different contexts before they became part of the Jesus narratives in which they now occur.

The few non-Christian documents about Jesus contain no information that would expand or amend the Christian sources. Nevertheless, they provide interesting glimpses into how Jesus was perceived from a non-Christian perspective (Greco-Roman or Jewish) in the late first and early second century.

The nonliterary evidence is of an indirect kind. It contributes to our knowledge of the social and religious conditions at the time of Jesus, such as what the dwellings of ordinary people in Capernaum looked like, how fishing worked on the Sea of Galilee, which cities were constructed and which coins were minted by Herod Antipas, or what the Jerusalem temple complex looked like in Jesus's time. The nonliterary material is thus to be taken into account for analyzing living conditions in Galilee and Judea at the time of Jesus as well as for reconstructing Judaism in Hellenistic-Roman times, and the social and political conditions of the Mediterranean world as a whole.

3. On this basis, a critical evaluation of early Christian traditions about Jesus can ascertain contours of his teaching, activity, and self-understanding, which were then picked up from a post-Easter perspective and used for different portrayals of Jesus. Thereby, the Synoptic Gospels in particular prove to be texts that present the early Christian confession of Jesus as the Christ and Son of God in the form of narratives about his earthly activity. They provide historical information about places of his activity, people who encountered him (disciples, opponents, etc.), and the political and social conditions of his time. In this way they put the activity of Jesus in a concrete time and a concrete place, and therefore, they can be used for a historical-critical reconstruction of Jesus. At the same time, their depictions of Jesus are "transparent" stories that highlight the significance of Jesus for their own time.

An approach that is appropriate to the sources must therefore take into account the relationship between the traces of the past dealt with in the Gospels and such tendencies that testify to the interests of their authors. For instance, Jesus's debates with Jewish groups, which are reported in all four canonical Gospels, can be taken as plausible characteristics of his activity independently from the historicity of individual episodes, since they can be reconciled with our knowledge of Judaism of the time and region. Other writings transform such debates to later constellations of Judaism and Christianity or to debates within Christianity, which are further removed from the time of Jesus. Examples of this would be the Gospel of Peter, the Gospel of Thomas, or P. Oxy. 840.

4. Reconstructions of Jesus's activity constantly move in a circle between an overall pattern of Jesus and his time and the assessment of individual traditions. How a parable, a healing story, or a controversy about the observance of Jewish purity regulations is integrated into the overall profile of Jesus's activity depends on which picture is assumed for Jesus and his historical context and how the

respective tradition can be integrated into this framework. The overall picture can thereby change according to the assessment of, for example, the political, religious, and social situations of Galilee at the time of Jesus, or of Judaism at the relevant time, as well as the appraisal of individual traditions. The "criteria" developed in Jesus research in the twentieth century get their meaning in this process of interpreting the historical material. However, they can hardly prove the authenticity of a parable, a saying of Jesus, or a healing story.

The material for reconstructing Jesus's activity presented in more detail in what follows is to be understood as functioning within the process of historical interpretation outlined above. This evidence is the basis for a plausible historical-critical reconstruction of Jesus's activity and fate.

Jens Schröter and Christine Jacobi

II. Literary Evidence

1. Christian Texts

1.1. The Synoptic Gospels, the Sayings Source Q, and the Historical Jesus

The Synoptic Gospels and the sayings source Q represent by far the largest and most important source of materials pertaining to the historical Jesus. Other major sources include the Gospel of Thomas and the Gospel of Peter, to the extent that these contain sayings and stories that are judged to be early and independent of the Synoptic Gospels. In addition, there are a few agrapha (Resch [2]1906) and the two sayings of Jesus cited by Paul (1 Cor. 7:10–11; 9:14). Since the nineteenth century the consensus has been that the sayings and stories of Jesus found in the Fourth Gospel have been so thoroughly transformed in the interests of the Johannine group that they cannot serve as primary evidence for the words and deeds of the historical Jesus.

1.1.1. Assessing the Synoptic Gospels and Q

From the beginning of the twentieth century it has been recognized that Mark's narrative framework is an editorial construction and therefore not a reliable index to the chronology of Jesus's activities. Mark or his sources have arranged stories and sayings pragmatically, grouping together materials of similar types in chapters 2:1–3:6 (controversy stories), 4:1–34 (parables), 4:34–6:12 (wonders), and 11:1–12:44 (controversies) under a rough topographical schema. Nor can the arrangement of sayings in the hypothetical sayings source Q be used to reconstruct a life of Jesus, since the arrangement of sayings and stories is mainly thematic, with only vague topographical or temporal connectives. Thus the Synoptic Gospels and Q constitute a large set of isolated individual sayings and stories for which the original settings in the life of Jesus can no longer be ascertained. These include materials of various types: sayings (aphorisms, maxims, parables, prophetic pronouncements, and apocalyptic sayings); *chreia* (pronouncement stories); reports of wonders (healings, exorcisms, and nature wonders); a few other anecdotes and reports (the birth and childhood stories, Jesus's baptism, temptation, and transfiguration); and a narrative of the arrest and execution of Jesus with appended reports of resurrection appearances (only the Gospel of Peter narrates the resurrection itself). Of the 522 items compiled by Crossan (1991, 434–50) in documents of the early Jesus movement from the first to the mid-second century, the large majority are attested in some form in the Synoptic Gospels and Q.

In many instances—180 of the 522 in Crossan's list—the same or similar saying or anecdote appears in multiple independent sources. For example, an aphorism about seeking and finding appears in Q 11:9–11 (Matt. 7:7–8; Luke 11:9–11; Gos. Thom. 2, 92; Mark 11:24; James 1:5; 4:3; John 14:13; 15:7). The parable of the mustard seed appears three times, in Mark 4:31–32, Q 13:18–19, and Gos. Thom. 20. This makes comparisons of their "reception" in particular gospels possible. Also, the same or similar motif appears in a variety of types of sayings and stories (e.g., Jesus's association with τελῶναι), probably indicating that, because it is widespread, it is founded on good historical tradition. Yet, even when the same maxim is transmitted verbatim and attested in multiple sources, it is often used to completely different effect. For example, the "measure for measure" saying appears independently three times, in Mark 4:24, Q 6:38 (Luke 6:38; Matt. 7:2), and 1 Clem. 13:2. In each case the maxim is interpreted quite differently (Kloppenborg 2012). The warning about a housebreaker (Gos. Thom. 21, 103; Q 12:39) appears in Thomas as a warning to guard oneself against the world, while in Q and its successors (Matt. 24:43; Luke 12:39) it illustrates the impossibility of knowing the time of the coming of the Son of Man. Thus one might conclude that both sayings come from Jesus, but it remains unclear how they might have originally been intended.

The wide variety of "receptions" of material about Jesus is due at least to two factors. First, from the perspective of cognitive neuroscience, the human memory system is reconstructive rather than wholly recollective. It has the ability to remember the "gist" of an event or saying but also tends to alter, supplement, and forget details, and to adapt the memory to the context of postevent situations

(Schacter 1995; Allison 2010, 1–30; Crook 2013). Second, social memory as the collective memorialization of events is able to preserve the "gist" of memories over long periods, but it is also capable of confabulating memories, schematizing them to facilitate transmission, and adapting memories in the light of the values and interests of the present (B. Schwartz 2005, 2009). This implies that some of what is reported of Jesus preserves the basic contours of his activities and sayings, but in many if not most cases it is impossible to know exactly what Jesus said or did, or how what was said was originally intended. And we must reckon with the presence of rumors, which through sheer dint of repetition became stable elements of the tradition (Botha 1993; Kawan 2005). This implies that rather than aspiring to a single convincing reconstruction of *the* historical Jesus, we can only expect a series of somewhat divergent "receptions" of the figure of Jesus in a variety of gospel sources.

1.1.2. Common Traditions

There are some remarkable convergences in the reception of sayings and stories in multiple sources. In such instances, this agreement likely represents reliable reports about Jesus. Instances include the widespread association of Jesus with John the Baptist (Q 3:7–9, 16–17; 7:18–35; 16:16; Mark 1:2–13; John 1:19–34; Gos. Thom. 46; Gos. Heb. 2; and Gos. Naz. 2). John is depicted as predicting the advent of a "coming" (Q 3:16; John 1:27) or a "stronger one" (Mark 1:7); Jesus experiences temptation by the devil in both Q (4:1–13) and Mark (Mark 1:12–13). The facts that Jesus either called or attracted disciples, and that these were expected to recognize Jesus's authority or identity, are presupposed widely (Mark 1:16–20; 3:7–12; 8:27–38; 10:25–31; Q 6:20a, 46; 9:57–60; 10:21–22, 23–24; 12:2–12; 14:26–27; Gos. Thom. 1–2, 13, 38, 52; John 1:19–51; 20:24–29), even though discipleship is conceived somewhat differently in each of these documents. Likewise, reports related to Jesus's sending out of disciples appear in Q 10:2–11:16 and Mark 6:6–13; and whether or not Gos. Thom. 14:4 and 73 depend on the Synoptics or not, Thomas nonetheless represents Jesus's sending out disciples (Schröter 1996). And both Q and Mark portray Jesus as critical of Pharisees (Mark 8:15; Q 11:39–52). Jesus is regarded as a wonder worker both by Q (7:1–10, 22; 11:14) and by Mark, though this does not guarantee the historicity of any single story. Some of these multiply attested reports likely reflect good historical traditions; others, like the story of Jesus's temptation, are likely legendary creations.

There is little doubt that Jesus was associated with a proclamation of the βασιλεία τοῦ θεοῦ. In Mark this proclamation is called an εὐαγγέλιον and is connected with a call to repentance (Mark 1:14–15). In Mark the kingdom has spatial features such that one can "see," "be near," "enter," and "be in" it (9:1, 47; 10:15, 23–25; 12:34; 14:25). It is also a μυστήριον that can be given to those worthy of it, and is expected to grow quickly (4:26, 30) and be more available to children (10:14–15) than to the rich (10:23–25). Yet it has clear futuristic, indeed imminent, dimensions (9:1).

Q also features both the noun βασιλεία and the verb εὐαγγελίζομαι. The proclamation of the βασιλεία is framed as a series of macarisms that pronounce divine favor on the poor, hungry, those in mourning, and those persecuted (6:20; 7:22), but also with healing (10:9). The kingdom is to be sought (12:31) and, although it is also said to be coming (10:9; 11:2, 20), its coming is not accompanied by signs (Q 17:20–21), as is the coming of the Markan Son of Man. Like the Markan kingdom, it is expected to grow (or arrive?) quickly (Q 13:18–21), but it is also capable of suffering violence (Q 16:16), perhaps an allusion to the killing of John the Baptist. While Q, like Mark, connects the kingdom with reversals in status, repentance is not directly connected with announcement of the kingdom, as it is in Mark. For Q, repentance is treated as moral reform (3:7–9) and as the recognition of divine power (Q 10:13–15; 11:32).

Although both Mark and Q mention various wonders, there are important differences in nuance. Mark has numerous healings and exorcisms, the former attracting great attention of crowds and the latter underscoring Jesus's ἐξουσία (Mark 1:27) and featuring the demons' disclosures of Jesus's identity as the Son of God (Mark 1:24, 34; 3:11). By contrast, Q has only two wonders, a healing (Q 7:1–10) and an exorcism (11:14), although Q also mentions that wonders are occurring in conjunction with Jesus's activities (7:22). Q's interest in Jesus's wonders lies in the pronouncements and controversies that these wonders occasion: in the healing of a centurion's serving boy, Q's interest is in the centurion's recognition of Jesus's ἐξουσία and in the polemical statement "I have not found such faithfulness in Israel" (7:9). The function of the list of wonders in Q 7:22, "Go tell John what you hear and see: blind recover sight and lame walk; lepers are cleansed and the deaf hear, and the dead are raised and the poor are proclaimed good news," is evidently to provide an affirmative answer to the question, "Are you the Coming One or should we expect another?" The exorcism in Q 11:14 is narrated to provide an occasion for the accusation that Jesus has colluded with Beelzebul, which in turn provokes Jesus's reply and counterattack (11:15–26).

In general, while Mark and Q share a number of sayings, Q's versions are inevitably longer and more detailed: Mark 1:7–8 par. Q 3:7–9, 16–17; Mark 1:12–13 par. Q 4:1–13; Mark 4:30–32 par. Q 13:18–19, 20–21; Mark 6:7–13 par. Q 10:3–16; Mark 3:22–26 par. Q 11:14–26; Mark 8:11–12 par. Q 11:16, 29–35; Mark 12:38–40 par. Q 11:39–52; Mark 8:34–37 par. Q 14:26–27 + 17:33; and Mark 8:38 par. Q 12:2–12. The only discourse longer in Mark than it is in Q is Mark's mini-apocalypse

(Mark 13:1–36), which finds a partial parallel in Q 17:20–37. The accumulation of sayings into longer speech-units is likely a result of the transmission of Jesus's sayings rather than a recollection of Jesus as a speech-maker. Although many of the individual sayings are perhaps authentic, their "original" discursive context is now lost.

1.1.3. Mark's Jesus

In addition to the elements that Mark shares with Q, Mark has many distinctive emphases, most of which are likely literary constructions rather than historical memories. Mark's narrative structure emphasizes the identity of Jesus as the Son of God and Messiah. Not only do both titles appear in the incipit, but Jesus's identity as "Son of God" structures his gospel, being announced at the baptism (1:9–11), at the transfiguration (9:2–8), and at Jesus's death (15:39). Peter's confession of Jesus as the Christ (Messiah, 8:29), the high priest's failure to recognize this (14:61), and the centurion's acclamation (15:39) form contrasting literary panels, stressing the centrality of Christology in Mark's Gospel. Exorcisms are also used as vehicles of christological disclosures, since the demons are said to know Jesus's identity. Mark features fantastic wonders—the stilling of the storm, walking on the water, and the multiplication of the loaves— which he employs to highlight Jesus's power and the disciples' utter failure to perceive Jesus's identity; this is also a literary device rather than a historical memory (Tyson 1961). The second part of the gospel is structured around disclosures of the necessity of Jesus's death (8:31; 9:31; 10:32–34, 45). Although Jesus's declarations are unambiguously clear, Mark again depicts the disciples as oblivious or resistant to these statements. These are likely post hoc rationalizations of the fact that Jesus was executed. The conflicts of Jesus with scribes (1:22; 2:6, 16; 3:22; 7:1, 5; 9:14; 10:33; 11:18, 27; 12:28, 35, 38–40; 14:1, 43, 53; 15:1, 31) and the high priests and elders (8:31; 10:33; 11:18, 27; 14:1, 10, 43, 53, 55; 15:1, 3, 10, 11, 31) also serve in a broader narrative to account for Jesus's death. Mark turns the parable of the tenants (12:1–11)—itself a thinly veiled allegory of Jesus's ministry—into a recognition scene, where opponents recognize themselves in Jesus's parable and react by deciding to have him arrested (12:12).

Mark espouses a strongly apocalyptic eschatology, holding that the coming of the Son of Man will occur during the lifetime of some of Jesus's immediate followers (9:1; 13:30), and his mini-apocalypse exhibits the conventional tropes of associating the approaching end with empirically visible calamities (wars and famines). Even though Jesus denies knowledge of the exact time (13:32), all indications in Mark are that he expects that it will be imminent.

1.1.4. The Sayings Source Q

In comparison to Mark, Q offers both stronger examples of a sectarian or countercultural ethic and much stronger prophetic attacks on Jesus's detractors or those who fail to pay attention to his preaching (Robinson, Hoffmann, and Kloppenborg 2000). The macarisms, a form used to pronounce divine favor, appear frequently in Q (6:20–23; 7:23; 10:23–24; 11:27–28; 12:43). Macarisms never appear in Mark, but their use is expanded in Matthew (5:5, 7–10; 16:17), Luke (12:37–38; 14:14–15; cf. Acts 20:35), John (13:17; 20:29), James (1:2, 25), and Thomas (7, 18, 19, 49, 54, 58, 68, 69, 103). Woes, originally prophetic pronouncements of doom, are found only twice in Mark (13:17; 14:21) but are frequent in Q (6:24–26, 17:1; 11:39–52), and their use is expanded by Matthew, who takes over Q's woes and adds more (23:15, 16); they also appear in the Gospel of Thomas (102, 112).

Q espouses a countercultural ethic of nonretaliation and giving without expectation of return (6:27–28, 29–30), grounded in the notion of reciprocity articulated in the "golden rule" (6:31), which "functions as a 'starting mechanism' that stimulates the kind of interaction necessary to bring into existence the envisioned social relations" (Kirk 2003, 686). Likewise, the exhortation to show mercy and not to judge (Q 6:36–37) receives its motivation from an appeal to the ordinary *quid pro quo* practice of lenders measuring back what they measured out (6:38): to engage in merciful and nonjudgmental activities will, by the logic of the marketplace, redound to the honor of those who exercise social and economic power (Kloppenborg 2010). Q also encourages emulation of God's indiscriminate patronage and generosity (6:36; 11:9–13) and reliance on divine surveillance and care in its exhortations to fearless speech (12:2–7) and to a simple, unattached life (12:22–31, 33–34; 16:13). Although some—perhaps all— of these sayings reflect Jesus's own practices and attitudes, Q has undoubtedly edited and reshaped them into more complex speeches.

While prophetic threats appear in Mark (8:38; 12:38–40), they are really warnings. By contrast, prophetic threats in Q call down a terrible judgment on those who are oblivious to the presence of the kingdom (10:13–15; 11:24–26, 31–32, 39–52; 13:34–35; 17:1–2, 23–30, 34–35). Several of Q's parables end with graphic scenarios of the destruction or exclusion of the impious or unfaithful from the kingdom (12:42–46; 14:16–24; 19:12–27; A. Jacobson 1982).

In contrast to Mark's Jesus, Q's Jesus shows much more reserve toward apocalyptic, espousing the notion of the coming of the Son of Man but refusing requests for "signs" (11:29–30; 17:20–21) and depicting the coming as utterly unforeseeable and as occurring, not in the midst of wars and other disasters, but in the perfectly normal conditions of life (17:23–30, 34–35). The significant differences between Mark and Q on eschatology, and the lack of apocalyptic eschatology in the Gospel of Thomas, perhaps indicate that Jesus's eschatology was more ambiguous than is sometimes thought (e.g., Allison 1998).

Q is a significant source of aphorisms, *chreiai*, and parables, for the most part presented in larger discursive units rather than as stand-alone witticisms (Kloppenborg 1995). What is noticeably lacking in Q, but present in Mark (and John), are controversies about the Sabbath and the interpretation of the Torah (unless Luke 10:24–28 and 14:5 are from Q: see Lambrecht 1995; Neirynck 1991; Tuckett 1988).

The Gospels of Matthew and Luke, literarily dependent on Mark and Q, also supplement their sources with additional sayings, parables, and anecdotes. Some of these might reflect historical tradition about Jesus, in particular parables such as Matt. 13:24–30, 44, 45–46, 47–48; 20:1–15; Luke 10:30–35; and 15:11–32. In other cases, Matthew and Luke seem to have included legendary accretions such as the birth stories and resurrection appearances.

While the Gospel of Thomas, the Synoptic Gospels, and Q represent the most plentiful sources of material related to Jesus, each document has its own editorial interests. These interests may account for the inclusion and exclusion of individual sayings and stories, and for the particular ways in which sayings and stories are presented. Materials that are attested in multiple independent documents have a strong likelihood of reflecting historical tradition about Jesus, but even in these cases, it is important to take into account the editorial interests of the documents in which they now appear. Singly attested sayings and stories, the *Sondergut* of Matthew and Luke, the distinctive sayings of the Gospel of Thomas, and sayings in the agrapha cannot be excluded automatically as nonauthentic unless their content is clearly a matter of editorial invention. The Synoptic Gospels and Q, rather than indicating a single and unambiguous portrait of the historical Jesus, represent multiple, somewhat divergent accounts, whose disagreements resist a clear resolution.

Arnal, William E. 2011. "The Synoptic Problem and the Historical Jesus." In *New Studies in the Synoptic Problem: Oxford Conference, April 2008; Essays in Honour of Christopher M. Tuckett*, edited by Paul Foster, Andrew F. Gregory, John S. Kloppenborg, and Jozef Verheyden, 371–432. BETL 239. Leuven.

Crossan, John Dominic. 1991. *The Historical Jesus: The Life of a Mediterranean Jewish Peasant*. San Francisco.

Kloppenborg, John S. 2001. "Discursive Practices in the Sayings Gospel Q and the Quest of the Historical Jesus." In *The Sayings Source Q and the Historical Jesus*, edited by Andreas Lindemann, 149–90. BETL 158. Leuven.

Schröter, Jens. 1998. "Markus, Q und der historische Jesus: Methodologische und exegetische Erwägungen zu den Anfängen der Rezeption der Verkündigung Jesu." *ZNW* 89: 173–200.

———. 2003. "Die Bedeutung der Q-Überlieferungen für die Interpretation der frühen Jesustradition." *ZNW* 94: 38–67.

Tuckett, Christopher M. 2002. "Q and the Historical Jesus." In *Der historische Jesus: Tendenzen und Perspektiven der gegenwärtigen Forschung*, edited by Jens Schröter and Ralph Brucker, 213–41. BZNW 114. Berlin.

John S. Kloppenborg

1.2. The Gospel of John

Alongside the Synoptic Gospels and the traditions used in them, the Gospel of John comes into consideration as a historical source for Jesus only on a secondary level, because its presentation is programmatically developed from a post-Easter perspective. Its picture of Jesus reflects the perception of the divine majesty of Christ that was gradually acquired in the post-Easter period (John 1:1, 18; 20:28). Therefore, in the entire gospel, Jesus is the preexistent, incarnate, and exalted one. This image reshapes the presentation of his earthly activity and his passion, such that historically valid tradition can be ascertained only in particular passages and in critical comparison with the synoptic tradition. Of course, based on the traditional attribution to John the son of Zebedee, the Gospel of John could appear to many interpreters as historically superior. Moreover, its possible sources could offer historical information. Hence, the issue of the author, questions about possible sources, and above all the assessment of the relationship with the Synoptics play an essential role in determining the value of John for research on the Jesus of history.

1.2.1. Attestation, Authorship, Provenance, and Sources of the Gospel of John

Irenaeus (*Haer.* 3.1.1) attributes the Gospel "according to John" to John the apostle, the son of Zebedee, who is said to have composed the work at an advanced age as the last one of the four Gospels in Ephesus. According to John 21:22–23, the author is the figure mentioned in 13:23 (but not until then) as "the disciple whom Jesus loved" who "competes" with Peter in all the scenes in which he appears (John 20:2–10; 19:35; cf. 18:15–16). Only if this figure is also recognized earlier, in the reference to the unnamed first disciples in John 1:35–42, could the identification with the son of Zebedee be suggested on the basis of a knowledge of Mark 1:16–19. The name John occurs only in the secondary title of the gospel, and the sons of Zebedee are mentioned only in John 21:2. Therefore, the "apostolic" authorization, which the Gospel of John appears to imply as the report of an eyewitness, is not directly claimed in the text but only subsequently deduced. If the notice of Papias (Eusebius, *Hist. eccl.* 3.39.4) is taken seriously, which distinguishes two characters named "John," the apostle John and the "elder (πρεσβύτερος) John," and if it is taken into account that a πρεσβύτερος appears as the author of 2 and 3 John, then this one could be the transmitter of the tradition in the Johannine circle, so that the ascription to the apostle could go back to an early mistaken identity or confusion of the two (Hengel 1993).

The traditional ascription of the Gospel of John to a Palestinian eyewitness of Jesus's activity, which continues to resonate in conservative authors (Bauckham 2006a, 358–83; Ratzinger 2007, 266–67), is untenable both on linguistic grounds and in view of the subject matter and the theological design of John (Frey 2015, 93–97). On the other hand, on the basis of the early traces of its influence, the traditional view about the composition or alternatively the redaction of John in Ephesus or Asia is plausible, and likewise that John was composed as the last of the four Gospels, which is most commonly assumed to have occurred around 100–110 (Schnelle [5]2016). Among other reasons, John's high Christology (Jesus as "God": 1:1, 18; 20:28), the critical interpretation of synoptic material (Frey 2013b, 265–81), and the undifferentiated talk about "the Jews," which betrays developments after 70 CE as well as a perspective from the diaspora, speak in favor of this date.

From the beginning of the twentieth century, scholars have searched for sources of the Gospel of John. Julius Wellhausen (1908) favored a continuous basic document (similar to Mark), and Rudolf Bultmann (1948) preferred four sources (a logos hymn, a miracle or "*semeia* source," a source of revelation discourses, a passion narrative) for the evangelist's work (which was said to have been edited and corrected by an "ecclesiastical redaction"). With the exception of the source of revelatory discourses, these were accepted by many, although at no time was there a consensus about the existence of a text and the profile of the sources. Georg Richter (1977) renewed the thesis of a basic document (now considered Jewish-Christian), and Robert T. Fortna (1970, 1988) enlarged the *semeia* source to his "gospel of signs." Recently the optimism of a literary reconstruction has sharply dwindled, because the language of the Gospel of John (and of the letters) is too homogeneous to support distinguishing sources, and without parallel texts the line of argument often remains circular (Hengel 1993; Frey 1997, 429–45; 2013a). The conjecture of a coherent miracle source is untenable (van Belle 1994); only individual traditions can be ascertained (Labahn 1999); and also only isolated dominical sayings can be traced back in a limited way (Theobald 2002). To assume an independent passion narrative is superfluous as soon as awareness of the Gospel of Mark is taken into account (M. Lang 1999).

With the exception of a few interpreters who continue to follow old hypotheses of pre-Johannine sources (J. Becker 2001; Theobald 2009) or develop new bold theories (Siegert 2007; Wahlde 2010), the conviction is now widespread that the Gospel of John is a carefully organized work, which eclectically integrates synoptic traditions and its own community traditions (John 20:30, partly with parallels in 1 John), which are transformed linguistically and theologically (Hengel 1993; Schnelle [4]2008; Frey 2013a). In the end, it was edited (posthumously?) by disciples of the author with the addition of John 21 (differently Thyen 2005).

1.2.2. The Relationship among the Synoptics in Scholarship:
Supplementation, Embellishment, Replacement?

The question of the relationship between John and the Synoptics has a central impact for the assessment of the historical questions. The differences were already perceived in antiquity, not least of all by pagan critics such as Celsus, Porphyrius, and the emperor Julian the Apostate (on this, Merkel 1971, 8–31; Cook 2000). But the early criticism of Papias regarding the structure of Mark (in Eusebius, *Hist. eccl.* 3.39.15) can show the opinion that for him, who had known "John the Elder," the Gospel of John had preserved a better arrangement than Mark. According to Clement (in Eusebius, *Hist. eccl.* 6.14.7), John, at the request of the other apostles, recorded the "spiritual" things about Jesus in addition to the "material" facts of the Synoptics. Because of its Christology, the Gospel of John was readily preferred theologically. Historical differences were observed but generally glossed over by harmonizing. Augustine's *De consensu evangelistarum* led the way for harmonizing to win the day for centuries (Frey 2013b, 244–46).

Not until the consideration of the evangelists as "simply human authors" (Lessing 1784) and the critical rejection of harmonizing (Herder 1880, 416) did the discussion start up anew. Due to his preference for Johannine Christology, Schleiermacher also was disposed to argue for the historical priority of John; by contrast, David Friedrich Strauss (1835–1836) wished to demonstrate the stronger mythical character of John, and Ferdinand Christian Baur (1847, 1864; on this, Frey 2014) interpreted John idealistically as an unfolding of the idea of the logos. At the end of the nineteenth century, a consensus had become established in critical scholarship that the Gospel of John was not the report of an apostolic eyewitness but a late theological allegory. Its intention was no longer viewed as the *supplement* (Clement of Alexandria) of the Synoptics, but as *surpassing* (Baur) or even *replacing* (Windisch 1926) them. So, the historical alternative was unavoidably put in place: the portrait of the historical Jesus was to be ascertained only under the condition of abandoning the Gospel of John (Frey 1997, 30–39).

When liberal presentations of Jesus still integrated elements from the Gospel of John, they did so only in order to purge the image of Jesus from objectionable synoptic elements to make it more tolerable intellectually and philosophically.

Whereas around 1900 John's knowledge of the Synoptics was widely acknowledged, in the mid-twentieth century the thesis of John's *independence* became dominant, partly in association with the assumption of distinct nonsynoptic sources. Percival Gardner-Smith (1938; see on this, Verheyden 1992) and the influence of Rudolf Bultmann and Charles Harold Dodd established the view that the Gospel of John originated in a particular religious milieu (Noack 1954), and synoptic elements were not integrated before the stage of the late redaction. Only a minority of scholars retained the notion that John knew Mark (and possibly also Luke) (Barrett 1956; Kümmel 1963). Whereas Bultmann was not interested in historical inquiry, Dodd (1963, 423–32) reconstructed pre-Johannine traditions in which he wished to detect Semitisms, topographical clues, contact with Jewish tradition, and distinct passion traditions. His impulses, however, were sparsely carried further, because since the 1980s new synchronic and narratological approaches emerged, which were less interested in historical inquiry. The view of John's independence (J. Becker 2001; D. Smith [2]2001, 195–241) was further pushed back by striking criticism regarding the classical source hypotheses as opposed to assuming knowledge of and selective reference to Mark and possibly also of Luke (Neirynck 1977; Schnelle 1992; Hengel 1993; M. Lang 1999) or even all three Synoptics (Thyen 2005). Finally—alongside very conservative attempts to defend the apostolicity and historicity of John (Carson 1981; Blomberg 2001; Bauckham 2006a, 2007; see on this, Frey 2013a, 8–12)—interest has arisen in a revision of the critical consensus that had effectively been suppressed out of Jesus research, especially in the project *John, Jesus, and History* initiated by Paul Anderson and Tom Thatcher (Anderson 2006; Anderson, Just, and Thatcher 2007; 2016; Anderson, Just, and Thatcher 2009). Yet, Anderson's postulate of "interfluentiality" (2006, 40–41), which avoids a clear literary determination of the relationship of John and the Synoptics and wishes to take up a "bi-optical" perspective on Jesus, runs the danger of abandoning critical insights in favor of an eclecticism and historically uncritical optimism.

1.2.3. Selective Reception and Critical Interpretation:
The Relationship to the Synoptic Tradition and the Historical Assessment

Genre. Like the Synoptics, John is a narrative gospel (a *vita Jesu*) that narrates the path of Jesus, from his encounter with the Baptizer to the Easter appearances. But compared with the Synoptics, it is more strongly discursively, dialogically, and dramatically shaped. There is much to be said for the view that John did not "create" the form of a gospel independently alongside Mark, but modified and further developed Mark's genre by prefixing the prologue in John 1:1–18, the dramatic elaboration of Jesus's conflict with "the Jews" up until chapter 12, and the discursive expansion of the departing setting in John 13–17 (Schnelle [5]2016, 20)

Subject matter. The Gospel of John shares with the Synoptics multiple narrative and sayings traditions. Mark attests most of them; some have parallels in Q or in Luke. However, many other substantive synoptic materials are absent. Instead, John presents a lot of "special" materials in narratives and sayings. Even though a variety of explanations for this complex evidence are conceivable, the analogy of the sequence of pericopes of the feeding of the five thousand, the walking on the water, the crossing of the sea, the demand for a sign, and Peter's confession in John 6, as is the case in Mark 6–8, indicates knowledge of Mark on the part of the evangelist (and not only the traditions in Mark or a later redaction).

Chronology and topography. Whereas in Mark Jesus goes up to Jerusalem for Passover only once (likewise in Luke and Matthew), John mentions three Passover feasts (John 2:13; 6:4; 11:55). Hence, in Mark the time of Jesus's activity is maximally one year, whereas according to John it is two to three years. Attempts to rectify the difference by rearranging the text (of John 5 and 6) are not convincing. The difference in chronology is matched by a difference in topography, as Jesus "shuttles" multiple times between Galilee and Judea. John's material, therefore, is clearly related less to Galilee and more strongly to Judea and Jerusalem.

Chronology of the passion. According to Mark, Jesus died on Friday the fifteenth of Nisan, the feast day of Passover after the celebration of the Passover meal on the previous evening. According to John, he died on Friday the fourteenth of Nisan, the day of preparation for the feast, for which the accusers did not want to defile themselves in the residence of Pilate (John 18:28). Hence, Jesus's last supper in John is not a Passover meal. Rather, Jesus dies at about the time the Passover lambs were slaughtered in the environs of the temple for the evening meal in people's homes. The difference is also not to be bypassed by the hypothetical assumption of a different calendar, such as the Qumran lunisolar calendar (so Jaubert 1957). The result of this difference would also be a different year for the death of Jesus. The Johannine date of Jesus's death would later provide evidence for the conflict in Asia Minor with Rome about the date of Easter in the late second century.

Jesus's messianic identity and proclamation. Whereas in Mark Jesus's messianic identity remains hidden (commands to silence), and he reveals himself for the first time in his trial (Mark 14:61–62), in John his christological majesty is explicit from the beginning; there is no "messianic secret" (although there is a misunderstanding of the disciples). Jesus reveals his "glory" (John 2:11). Whereas the center of the synoptic proclamation is the kingdom of God, in John, Jesus proclaims himself and his grandeur as Messiah, Son, and "God." Here, the greater historical plausibility is on the side of the synoptic tradition.

Dramatization. The Gospel of John presents the cleansing of the temple at the beginning in 2:13–22 as the prelude to the conflict with "the Jews," whereas Mark narrates it as the cause of his arrest at the end of his activity (Mark 11:15–17). By contrast, in John the cause of his death sentence is his supreme sign, the raising of Lazarus (John 11), in which Jesus appears as the divine giver of life. Here historical plausibility is on the side of Mark. In contrast, the transposition in John is to be explained for dramaturgical reasons.

Language and diction. The most significant difference from the Synoptics is in Jesus's language. In John, Jesus does not speak primarily in the forms of the synoptic tradition—in sayings, parables, short apothegms, and so forth—but in long, to some extent repetitive or progressively convoluted speeches, which build up longer metaphorical networks and culminate in clear "I am" sayings. In the Synoptics, only Matt. 11:26–27 comes close to the Johannine diction. Also, in spite of some Semitic names, the language of John is further removed from an Aramaic substratum of the oldest synoptic tradition. But what is decisive is the observation that Jesus's language in John matches the language of the Baptizer and other characters, the language of the narrator, and also the language of 1 John. It is the language and terminology of the evangelists or, alternatively, of the community that impact the way John's Jesus speaks. Hence, it is clear: the Johannine sayings of Jesus do not reflect the diction of the earthly Jesus. Rather, the diction has gone through an extensive transformation, for example, from talk about the "kingdom of God" (still in John 3:3, 5; but then the talk is only about the kingship of Jesus, so, e.g., John 18:36) to talk about "eternal life" (John 3:15–16) as the dominant concept of salvation now, and so on (Frey 2013b, 277–81; 2016). The conclusion is clear: Jesus's sayings in John (including the "I am" sayings and the τετέλεσται on the cross, John 19:30) are not "genuine" sayings of the earthly Jesus, but the result of a transformation in light of the post-Easter "anamnesis" of the story of Jesus (cf. John 2:22; 12:16), which in the Johannine tradition was legitimated as the work of the Spirit, who enables the disciples to "remember" (John 14:25–26).

Critical reinterpretation. The transformation of older tradition implies a critical reinterpretation of the synoptic tradition in light of Johannine Christology. John 12:27–28, 14:31, and 18:10 present a reception of Mark's Gethsemane pericope (Mark 14:32–42), which shows that a prayer of Jesus about being spared from suffering and death was unacceptable for John (Frey 2013b, 265–71). Also, the cry of being forsaken by God on the cross (Mark 15:34) had to give way in John to the declaration of fulfillment (John 19:30). Numerous narrative features, such as the Johannine image of the Baptizer (John 1:19–34; 3:27–36), reveal traces of this transformation motivated by Christology and literary dramatization.

Conclusion. Substantial characteristics of John's portrait of Jesus and his proclamation, of the Baptizer (Frey 2013b, 271–77), the disciples, and the "Jews" (Frey 2013c), do not present a historically accurate image of the time and story of Jesus of Nazareth, but a reinterpretation based on older tradition.

1.2.4. The Gospel of John as a Historical Source

Nevertheless, there are indications that the evangelist is familiar with details of Palestinian Judaism and conceivably he himself comes from there (Hengel 1993, 278–81). He provides Aramaic names and terms ("Rabbi" is used eight times, and in John 20:16 the enhanced form "Rabbouni"), which he sometimes translates into Greek (so twice "messiah" in 1:41; 4:25; Cephas in 1:42; Thomas in 11:16 and 20:24; Gabbatha in 19:13; Golgotha in 19:17), precisely reduces to their component parts (Simon son of John in 1:42; 21:15; cf. Barjona, Matt. 16:17; Judas son of Simon Iscariot, John 6:71; 13:2, 26), or also interprets theologically (Siloam in 9:7). Traditions about locations in Jerusalem are especially dense (8:20: the treasury; 10:23: Solomon's portico; 18:13, 24: residences of Annas and Caiaphas; 19:17, 20: Golgotha, close to the city [wall]); another tradition from the South is 1:28: "Bethany on the other side of the Jordan" as the place of the baptism of the Baptizer in east Jordan (cf. 10:40; 3:23: Aenon near Salim with much water). Knowledge of Jewish festivals, customs, and laws further supports Palestinian local color and the credibility of the author (2:6: stone jars; 4:9: Jews and Samaritans; 7:22–23: circumcision law breaks the Sabbath law; 7:37: the last day of Sukkoth; 8:17: two witnesses; 10:22: winter; 12:13: palm branches; 18:28 and 19:31: day of preparation).

For individual aspects of the *contemporary history of ancient Judaism,* the Gospel of John is to be taken seriously as a historical source (so Hengel 1999). Thus, Sychar as a main city of the Samaritans is attested for the first time in 4:5, and 10:22 is the first reference to the celebration of Hanukkah with the Greek name τὰ ἐγκαίνια. John is the only New Testament author who mentions the city of Tiberias, newly founded by Antipas (6:1, 23–24; 21:1). The notice in 5:1–2 regarding the pool of Bethesda with its five porticos was verified as surprising knowledge of the place by the excavation of the site with a double pool and an Asclepius cult from the time after 135 CE, which evidently went back to an earlier tradition of healing. With the mention of the high priests Annas and Caiaphas, in which the latter is the one in office (11:49) and Annas is introduced as his father-in-law and the eminent advisor behind the scenes (cf. 18:13–26), John offers an accurate picture of the influence of the family clan of Annas and the complex texture of power between the priestly aristocracy and the Roman prefect.

In view of the *history of the early Christian communities*, John 4 (alongside Acts 8:4–25) could attest an early Samaritan mission (Zangenberg 1998); at least the issue of the Samaritans (with all the Johannine transformation) points back to a Palestinian sphere. Also, Jesus's discussions with the "Jews" not only reflect conflicts of the time of composition but also take up discourses about Jesus's messianism and eschatological expectations (Elijah, a prophet who worked miracles, Messiah; cf. John 1:19–21), which go back into the early history of the Jesus movement (Bauckham 2006b). Especially the term ἀποσυνάγωγος, which is attested for the first time in John, points to events of the separation or exclusion of Jesus's adherents from synagogue communities, which still left an imprint on the memory in the Johannine circle, even if the separation had occurred before the composition of the Gospel of John. The background of this, however, is not to be located in a centralized decree of rabbis in Yavneh or its expansion in the "benediction against the heretics" in the Eighteen Benedictions (so Martyn 1968; Wengst 1981), but rather in local processes of separation in the diaspora after 70 CE (Frey 2013c).

Also, with regard to *individual aspects of the history of Jesus*, the Gospel of John provides historical details that should be taken seriously. As a case in point, the provenance of Peter and Andrew (and Philip) from Bethsaida is attested only by John (1:44) and is credible; also, Cana plays an important role as the home of Nathanael (21:2) and the place of two deeds of Jesus. The significance of this location does not go back only to the evangelist, although the origin of this tradition can hardly be illumined further. John 1:35 plausibly suggests that a part of the circle of disciples of Jesus was made up of followers of the Baptizer, so that a certain competition between the circles of the Baptizer and Jesus (3:26, 30) and (in contrast to Mark) an overlapping activity (3:23), including a practice of baptism by Jesus himself (3:22, 26), are suggested (Frey 2019). John 2:20 presents a rather exact specification of forty-six years for the time from the beginning of the Herodian construction of the temple (19 BCE) until the time of the appearance of Jesus (27 CE), which is in keeping with Luke 3:23. Given that the chronology of both Mark and John can be constructed, the longer time of the activity of Jesus with perhaps more pilgrimages to festivals is definitely a possibility. The greatest difficulty to be adjudicated is the matter of the date of Jesus's death. Historically one can argue either for Mark or John: Is it conceivable that the Sanhedrin met on Passover evening and the crucifixion was carried out on the high holy day (Mark), or not? Did the Synoptics (Mark or his source) make Jesus's last supper a Passover meal, or did John undergird his Passover lamb typology (cf. John 1:29, 36) by changing the chronology? Here historians remain in largely irreconcilable aporias.

In spite of these numerous details (often discussed rather on the margins), it is still to be maintained that the Gospel of John serves only secondarily as a historical source of Jesus's activity and thereby as a subject for research on the historical Jesus. In John programmatic elements of the time of the earthly Jesus, elements of the past history of the community or communities, and questions and insights from the context of the author and the addressees are blended together in an idiosyncratic, homogenous language. To a large extent, his "sandwich" cannot be resolved in order to isolate historically valid information, especially when external parallels are missing. Jesus's teaching and discourses, significant aspects of his activity (healings and the exorcisms that are missing in John), and the historical main features of his passion are therefore primarily to be compiled from the Synoptics.

Anderson, Paul N. 2006. *The Fourth Gospel and the Quest for Jesus: Modern Foundations Reconsidered*. London and New York.

Frey, Jörg. 2013a. "Wege und Perspektiven der Interpretation des Johannesevangeliums." In *Die Herrlichkeit des Gekreuzigten: Studien zu den Johanneischen Schriften I*, edited by Juliane Schlegel, 3–41. WUNT 307. Tübingen.

―――. 2013b. "Das vierte Evangelium auf dem Hintergrund der älteren Evangelientradition: Zum Problem; Johannes und die Synoptiker." In *Die Herrlichkeit des Gekreuzigten: Studien zu den Johanneischen Schriften I*, edited by Juliane Schlegel, 239–94. WUNT 307. Tübingen.

―――. 2018. *Theology and History in the Fourth Gospel: Narration and Interpretation*. Waco, TX.

―――. 2019. "Baptism in the Fourth Gospel, and Jesus and John as Baptizers: Historical and Theological Reflections on John 3:22–30." In *Expressions of the Johannine Kerygma in John 2:23–5:18*, edited by R. Alan Culpepper and Jörg Frey, 87–115. Historical, Literary, and Theological Readings from the Colloquium Ioanneum 2017 in Jerusalem. WUNT 423. Tübingen.

Gardner-Smith, Percival. 1938. *Saint John and the Synoptic Gospels*. Cambridge.

Hengel, Martin. 1993. *Die johanneische Frage: Ein Lösungsversuch, mit einem Beitrag zur Apokalypse von Jörg Frey*. WUNT 67. Tübingen.

Schnelle, Udo. [5]2016. *Das Evangelium nach Johannes*. THKNT 4. Leipzig.

Jörg Frey

1.3. Other Writings of the New Testament

The value as sources of all those New Testament writings that, in distinction from the Gospels, pursue no biographical interest in Jesus and do not center on his earthly activity is only indirectly extrapolated and is controversially assessed. The historical question concerning the significance that the Jesus tradition possessed in early Christianity is correlated with this. Also, the response to it varies. The search for traces of Jesus tradition outside the Gospels is due to recent biblical criticism, which puts the relationship between the historical Jesus and his christological interpretation into the discussion. The fact that the activity of the earthly Jesus in these other New Testament writings is much more strongly interwoven with the development of the christological-soteriological significance and its transmission than it is in the Gospels constitutes a fundamental problem.

1.3.1. The Acts of the Apostles

In accordance with the presentation in Acts, which, as part of Luke's two-volume work, possesses close ties to the Third Gospel and is therefore especially instructive with respect to the connection of pre-Easter Jesus tradition with its post-Easter reception, early Christianity refers conspicuously seldom to the teaching and deeds of the earthly Jesus. In the speeches of Peter and Paul, which are shaped by the author of Acts and which reflect the expansion of the church in the Roman Empire and bring it to a pivotal turning point, the basic data of Jesus's activity are picked up for missionary and apologetic purposes. At the most extensive, even if also only summarily, the speech of Peter in the house of the centurion Cornelius (Acts 10:34–43) goes into the events of the activity and fate of Jesus (baptism by John, Jesus's ministry in Galilee and Jerusalem, healings, his passion, and his death on the cross, and in addition his resurrection brought about by God and his appearances; in addition to this, the kingdom of God is the theme of apostolic preaching; cf. Acts 8:12; 14:22). Moreover, it is characteristic for Luke's dealing with the synoptic tradition that in his post-Easter historical presentation he takes up somewhat fewer topics, which Mark and Matthew include in Jesus's earthly activity. Luke has Peter recognize in a vision that the food regulations are relativized (cf. Acts 10:9–48; 11:1–18), whereas Mark and Matthew make the problem of defilement by foods a theme of Jesus's earthly activity. Similarly, the testimony of false witnesses against Jesus that he would destroy the temple (cf. Mark 14:58) becomes part of the accusation against Stephen in Acts, by which Luke makes his martyrdom parallel Jesus's trial (Acts 6:14). This shows that references to the activity of the earthly Jesus in Acts do not possess any special value for information that goes beyond the synoptic tradition. Rather, in the framework of Luke's historical narrative, the few appeals to known material from the Synoptic Gospels serve to legitimate the apostles as witnesses of Jesus's appearance and his resurrection (cf. Acts 10:39–42; cf. also 13:31); to drive the plot forward, which prompts the faith or rejection of hearers (cf. Acts 10:44; 13:42–44); and finally to interpret the entire story of Jesus as fulfillment of Scripture (cf. Acts 13:17–23, 32–41).

Hence, with respect to Jesus's activity, the depiction of Acts as a whole presents no new material. It is also striking that retrospective dependence on the tradition of the sayings of the earthly Jesus for decisions that change the direction of early Christianity is lacking (cf. Barrett 1985). Although the composition of the two Lukan volumes by the same author presupposes comprehensive knowledge of the tradition of Jesus's sayings, in Acts decisions such as the acceptance of the gentiles into the people of God are not initiated by the memory of Jesus. Rather, they are unleashed by the work of the *Spirit* in Peter and Paul, and are substantiated by *Scripture* rather than by the Jesus tradition (cf. Acts 15:15–18, 28; Strange 2000, 69; Barrett 1985, 706).

Nevertheless, at the beginning of Acts, up to Jesus's exaltation, the *risen One* takes over the function of the Spirit as the driving force behind the events. With respect to the composition, Luke appeals to the words of the risen One as what controls the program that underlies central events. Thus, the risen Jesus outlines the geographical course of the mission and calls the disciples to be witnesses in Jerusalem, Judea, Samaria, and to the end of the earth (Acts 1:8). He proves thereby to be the authentic initiator of the extension of the church, which will be narrated in what follows. The previously enacted proclamations of the risen One in Acts 1:4–5 indeed possess parallels in the Gospel of Luke, but they also are not related to the Jesus tradition in the narrower sense. In the proclamation of the baptism of the Spirit, which will surpass the baptism of John, the risen One reformulates a saying of John the Baptizer that is a synoptic tradition (Acts 1:5; cf. Mark 1:8; cf. also Matt. 3:11; Luke 3:16), which is narratively redeployed in what follows and later taken up once more in Peter's speech in a virtually verbatim repetition of Acts 1:5 as the memory of a ῥῆμα τοῦ κυρίου (Acts 11:16). Thus, Luke also traces the gift of the Spirit to Cornelius and other God-fearers back to the Kyrios and creates reflective benchmarks in his narrative. In addition, the risen Jesus alludes to a citation of himself in his saying in Luke 24:49 (ἣν ἠκούσατέ μου), which he likewise had already spoken as the risen One. Here also no tradition of the earthly Jesus is taken over. Rather the passages just mentioned are created by Luke at the beginning of his story of the extension of the Christian community in order to lock it together with the conclusion of the Gospel of Luke.

A further example of the independence of the Jesus tradition in Luke in comparison with the presentation of the narrative in Acts is the instructions for mission that the pre-Easter Jesus issued for the sending out of the seventy-two (Luke 10:1–12). In the early Christian mission that Acts depicts, these instructions are not simply relocated but are partly overlooked and partly replaced by new revelations. A special case is established in the context of the self-sufficiency of Paul in his mission. It conflicts with the instructions to the preachers sent out in Luke 10:7 (cf. also 1 Cor. 9:14), and in Acts it is justified by the saying of Jesus that occurs only there, and which for its part is nowhere else attested in the Gospels: "It is more blessed to give than to receive" (Acts 20:35; cf. also the parallel in Did. 1:5). Paul cites this in a speech internal to the community. Numerous interpreters see in the dominical adage, which is otherwise known in Hellenistic literature, a secondary ascription to Jesus taken over by Luke (Horrell 1997, 598–99). Altogether the evidence shows that the Gospels did not secure and record Jesus's tradition for immediate use in post-Easter times. And also conversely, such traditions were not binding for the first Christians for the formation of congregations and for decisions by church leaders.

1.3.2. New Testament Letters

Similar to Acts, the letters of the New Testament primarily pursue other goals than the preservation and mediation of Jesus tradition. They each expound the faith convictions of early Christianity in communications for diverse contexts for the common life and Christian identity in the post-Easter era. For this they refer to key data of the story of Jesus from his preexistence and incarnation to his exaltation by way of suffering, death on the cross, and resurrection (cf. Phil. 2:6–11; 1 Cor. 15:3b–5; Rom. 4:25; 8:34; cf. also 2 Pet. 1:16–18). As implicit elements of this so-called Jesus story (a narrative concentration of salvific events), the incidents during the public activity of Jesus in Galilee and Jerusalem are not specifically addressed in the letters but worked out in the line of thought (cf. Reinmuth 1995; Wedderburn 1989). The statement in Gal. 4:4 about the sending of the Son of God "born of a woman" and "under the law" is paradigmatic for this form of reprocessing. The biographical detail in the letter as a whole does not aim at the mediation of Jesus tradition but anticipates the liberation of "those under the law" who have come to Christ, and thus has a soteriological tagline that culminates the line of thought (cf. Gal. 4:5; Scholtissek 2000, 201). Apart from the exception of cases such as mentioning the birth of Jesus "under the law," the implication of his circumcision, and his arrest in the night of the last supper (Rom. 15:8; 1 Cor. 11:23–25; cf. 1 Thess. 2:14–15), biographical details of Jesus's activity play an even more minor role than in Acts. Along with other things, this speaks against the claim that James and 1 Peter were composed by eyewitnesses (on advocates of 1 Peter as an eyewitness, cf. however Achtemeier 1996, 9-10). The echoes of Jesus tradition that appear in both letters must be interpreted not as the earliest attestations of Jesus tradition but rather as the reception of early Christian (Jesus) tradition or the tradition of the Gospels (cf. Best 1970).

Nevertheless, the letters of the New Testament process themes of Jesus's activity and its significance for early Christianity. Some of these themes can be verified as plausible for the historical profile of Jesus by means of the criterion of multiple attestation (see B.IX; B.X). Among these are Jesus's proclamation of the βασιλεία (Rom. 14:17 and passim; James 2:5) and his call to repentance, the appeal to Abba (Gal. 4:6; Rom. 8:15), features of Jesus's ethics (e.g., dealings with possessions: James 2:1–13; 5:1–6; dealings with enemies: Rom. 12:14–21), as well as echoes of the attitude of Jesus to halakic questions such as the purity of foods (cf. Rom. 14:14). References to Jesus's person and christological interpretations of his self-understanding (humility, suffering, pro-existence, Jesus as an agent of the kingdom of God and Son of God) as well as the crucifixion (and resurrection) are the starting points for considerable theological lines of reasoning in the letters. Specific motifs of the Jesus tradition, especially Jesus's suffering and preexistence, function also as a christological rationale of early Christian parenesis (cf. Phil. 2:6–8; 1 Pet. 2:21; 3:13–18; 4:1). Specifically, they are also adduced for Paul's legitimation of his apostolicity as a μιμητὴς Χριστοῦ (cf. 1 Cor. 11:1; 1 Thess. 1:6; 2 Cor. 13:4). The aspects of the person and activity of Jesus mentioned here, however, are not made the subject of discussion themselves but rather flow into instructions for the community for specific situations and proposals for a new "Christian" identity. Clear demarcation between biographical and post-Easter interpretations is often impossible, as in the case of Gal. 4:4. To be sure, occasionally the aspects mentioned here have been adduced to enhance a critical overall picture of Jesus's person and activity (cf. Scholtissek 2000; see also, works by Reinmuth, Wolter, and Becker). However, in recent discussion, in contrast to traces of the sayings tradition, they play a reduced role for the quest of the historical Jesus.

In parenetic passages, especially in 1 Thessalonians, 1 Corinthians, and Romans, also in 1 Peter and James, themes, motifs, and lexical combinations are encountered that are also familiar from the synoptic *sayings tradition* and are transmitted in the Gospels in Jesus's mouth. For this reason, in the second half of the last century, New Testament letters came into focus for scholarship on Jesus with attention turning to the questions about ways of passing on the Jesus tradition and its traces in various sources outside the Synoptics. The hope was to gain access to preserved Jesus tradition outside the Gospels, which was not influenced by what was presumed to be a later, narrative processing (see Koester, Allison, and Dunn). Thus, the quest for Jesus tradition was not limited to the writings that became canonical but also reached out to noncanonical texts, which, like New Testament letters, could have potentially transmitted Jesus tradition (see C.II.1.4). So, too, like these, parallels in the Epistles have also been discussed between the options of "dependence on or independence from" the synoptic Jesus tradition.

Traditional materials received attention in 1 Thessalonians, 1 Corinthians, Romans, 1 and 2 Peter, and James, which lexically or semantically were analogous to traditions in the Synoptic Gospels under Jesus's authority, that is, were transmitted as his *sayings*. They include both general ethical and halakic themes (prohibition of divorce: 1 Cor. 7:10–11; dealings with enemies, renunciation of vengeance, and not judging: Rom. 12:14; James 5:9; criticism of wealth: James 2:5; 5:1–2; purity: Rom. 14:14; prohibition of swearing; also humility, devoutness, mercy, doing God's will, and striving for perfection) as well as traditions that are thematically specific to the Jesus movement or alternatively to early Christian contexts (Jesus's interpretive words at the Last Supper: 1 Cor. 11:23–25; livelihood for mission: 1 Cor. 9:14 and 1 Tim. 5:18; imminent expectation: 1 Thess. 5:2; 2 Pet. 3:10; Rev. 3:3; 16:15; significance of faith: 1 Cor. 13:2; suffering for the sake of righteousness: 1 Pet. 3:14). Since such parallel traditions in New Testament Epistles—except for a few exceptions in 1 Corinthians—are never characterized as citations of Jesus or as dominical sayings and, in addition to agreements with their synoptic parallels, also manifest distinctive differences, the opinions of researchers on the actual number and the character of the parallels as echoes or allusions vary widely. As the relationships between synoptic sayings of Jesus and the analogies in New Testament Epistles are interpreted, a choice is made on underlying global theses about the beginning and the continuity of the early Christian process of passing on tradition.

Two positions that are still quite influential today can be mentioned here. Since the time of Birger Gerhardsson (1961, 1979), Scandinavian research has focused its investigation on the relationship between magisterial authorities and their disciples and on techniques of memorizing, which were practiced in the Israelite-Jewish or Greco-Roman environment of early Christianity and could have provided the first Christian structures for dealing with Jesus tradition. Beginning with models in early Judaism or a pagan environment, this line of research envisages a comparable controlled process of tradition based on authorized carriers of tradition (cf. Riesner [3]1988; Byrskog 1994, 2000, 2011). The historical Jesus allegedly functioned as the head of a school or as a teacher who initiated the process of memorization himself (cf. Riesner [3]1988), and for this reason essential parts of the tradition ultimately go back to him. By way of contrast, in the second half of the twentieth century, Dale C. Allison and Helmut Koester delineated a process of transmission in hypothetical preliminary stages alongside literary dependence of New Testament writings. The so-called Jesus tradition in Paul was to be traced back either to relatively established Jesus tradition that circulated or to presynoptic sources, such as "Q" or fixed written catechetical collections of sayings (Allison 1982, 1985; H. Koester 1990; cf. also Best 1970). In an analogous way, the finding of Jesus tradition in the Catholic Letters was explained, facilitated by knowledge of Q or editorial adaptations of Q (QM^t). This applies especially to James and 1 Peter, both of which offer a conspicuously high proportion of Sermon on the Mount traditions (Hartin 1991; Davids 1982). In the framework of the theory described here, the "Jesus tradition" contained in the Epistles is construed as a possible older form of tradition and as a side current dependent on the (pre)synoptic tradition, the main current of which entered the Synoptic Gospels. By means of critical comparison of textual evidence and knowledge of processes of memorization and transmission, an older form of the parallel tradition might be inferred and possibly a sayings tradition of the historical Jesus might be detected.

In contrast to a unilinear determination of the relationship of the Gospels to the Epistles, currently a paradigm shift stands out in research both on Paul and on James (cf. Konradt 2004; Jacobi 2015), which goes back to a wider contextualization of the evidence. For one thing, as of now, *non-Christian*, especially early Jewish, analogies for the formation of tradition are also taken into account. For another, New Testament Epistles are compared with *each other*. It is apparent that often closer points of contact exist both with traditions of Israelite-Jewish provenance and among the parenetic passages of Paul's epistles, 1 and 2 Peter, and James than with the Synoptic Gospels. Such parallels include single words but also offer larger semantic connections. The evidence indicates first that early Christian parenesis was formed not in one dimension on the basis of the Jesus tradition but substantively on the basis of Israelite-Jewish ethos (cf. Schröter 2007b, 97). The striking analogies between the Jesus tradition of the Gospels and some passages in New Testament Epistles could be attributed to the fact that both spheres of writing have access to the same topoi of early Christian ethics, which were already in place and had been formed on the basis of sayings of Scripture and early Jewish wisdom. Such traditions in the Gospels could have been connected with genuine Jesus tradition, whereas in New Testament Epistles they were connected with community instructions and teaching. In some cases, it is likewise conceivable that alongside other spheres of tradition Jesus tradition also influenced the formation of early Christian parenesis and so was further transmitted indirectly. In any case, relationships between synoptic Jesus tradition and echoes in the *Corpus Paulinum*, James, and 1 Peter are rather of a mediated and indirect sort, and they cannot be explained as directly dependent on the Jesus tradition that came into the Gospels. Rather, what needs to be taken into account are flexible and uncontrolled events that took place in the transmission of tradition, involving early Christian tradition that was mutually interactive with the Jesus tradition, and so each was indirectly influenced by a "transmission process open to both sides" (Konradt 2004, 192). This has consequences for the assessment of the significance and authority of the Jesus tradition in early Christianity (cf. Jacobi 2015).

1.3.3. Discussion of Two Cases in Point

Two examples from the *Corpus Paulinum* and James illustrate the relationships of the history of tradition and the history of transmission.

1. Romans 12:14–21, an ethical catalogue about the renunciation of vengeance and blessing of enemies, has a rather prominent synoptic analogy in the command to love enemies and to renounce vengeance in the Sermon on the Mount in Matt. 5:38–48 or the Sermon on the Plain in Luke 6:27–36, and for this reason it is not infrequently assumed that Rom. 12:14–21 is Jesus tradition (among others who so assume, Dunn 1990; D. Wenham 1994). At the same time, Rom. 12:14–21 clearly demonstrates close lexical and semantic contact with instructions to communities in Asia Minor in the pseudepigraphical 1 Peter (1 Pet. 3:8–19; cf. also 1 Thess. 5:12–22). First, in 1 Pet. 3:9a the admonition to renounce repaying evil with evil is almost identically expressed in Rom. 12:17 (namely, as a prohibition)—and in both cases it is not traced back to Jesus. Second, the phrasing in both has a remarkable parallel in non-Christian literature. Quite similarly, in the Jewish short story "Joseph and Aseneth," which comes from the Egyptian diaspora, Levi urges his brothers Simeon and Benjamin not to take revenge against the son of Pharaoh (Jos. Asen. 23:9; 29:3). Finally, in the third place, in both Rom. 12 and 1 Pet. 3 the ethical instructions are based on citations from Scripture instead of on the authority of Jesus. Against this background, the admonition to renounce vengeance in Rom. 12:17 and 1 Pet. 3:9 appears as further processing of early Jewish wisdom based on exposition of Scripture. In the context of 1 Peter, such processing is illustrated by the example of pro-existence and the meekness of Christ in his suffering, and in the context of Romans, by God's dealings in Jesus Christ, with which God proves his love toward enemies archetypically (Rom. 5:8–10). Thereby, the wisdom-ethical tradition in Romans and 1 Peter dovetails with the salvific event in Christ. In contrast to its early Jewish parallels, the tradition obtains its specific innovative reorientation from this once-for-all salvific event. The new orientation finds expression in the requirement to bless as a radical contrasting behavior demanded of those who believe in Christ. By means of the content of the tradition oriented toward the Christ event, renunciation of vengeance and blessing adversaries are connected with the authority of Christ and have no further need of a concrete location in the activity of the earthly Jesus.

147

2. Similarly, indirect connections exist between James 4:10 and the synoptic parallels in Matt. 23:12, Luke 14:11, and Luke 18:14. Behind the sapiential exhortation to humility in James 4:10, which also is attested in ancient early Judaism and produces a cause-and-effect connection between humility and exaltation, the taking up of a saying of Jesus is frequently presumed (Hartin, Mussner). At the same time, the formulation in James 4:10 in the passive imperative ταπεινώθητε and the antonym ὑψώσει, in which God is the subject, demonstrates a greater affinity with 1 Pet. 5:6, with which it also exhibits the same variations from the synoptic formulation. In addition, both epistolary variants in the tradition are embedded in a comparable context, in which there is also a quotation from Prov. 3:34 and a warning against the διάβολος. Thus, it appears plausible that James 4:10 and 1 Pet. 5:6 do not appeal independently from each other to a saying of Jesus as it is transmitted in the Gospels of Matthew and Luke. Rather, they refer to an early Christian tradition available to them that was developed from Prov. 3:34, which could have been influenced by the Jesus tradition (cf. Konradt 2004, 193).

1.3.4. Dominical Sayings in New Testament Epistles

Among the Epistles, only the undisputed Pauline Epistles adduce *explicit* sayings traditions of Jesus, albeit reproduced as instructions of the Kyrios acting in the *present* (1 Cor. 7:10–11; 9:14; cf. also 11:23–25; 1 Thess. 4:15). This indeed—and not their historical origin from the earthly Jesus—is the justification for the instructions to be binding in principle for the communities. In the line of thought as a whole, the dominical sayings in 1 Cor. 7:10–11 and 9:14 are at the same time limited in their significance and sphere of validity. For Paul, the prohibition of divorce in 1 Cor. 7:10–11 is a regulation that in any case concerns only the lifestyle of "marriage" that is subordinate with respect to an ascetic life "for Christ." By contrast, Paul construes the classical scriptural attestation for marriage as an act of God's creation (Gen. 2:24) as "becoming one" with the Kyrios (1 Cor. 6:16–17). Similarly, Paul makes use of refusing the right to livelihood in 1 Cor. 9:14 in order to meet the obligation to proclaim the gospel. In this way, the entire christological context of his remarks surpasses the individual dominical saying.

To be sure, the parenthesis in 1 Cor. 7:11a limiting the prohibition against divorce is somewhat different. Here the instructions are for the given case in which a woman does separate from her husband. The syntactical insertion has often been interpreted as a Pauline undermining of Jesus's absolute prohibition of divorce, by which the apostle gives consideration for divorce practices in the Greco-Roman environment—and simultaneously openly subverts the authority of the dominical saying. The stipulation to remain unmarried in 1 Cor. 7:11a or the reconciliation of the separated wife with her husband, however, corresponds to the saying of Jesus transmitted in the Synoptics about the connection between remarriage and adultery (cf. the double tradition in Mark 10:11–12; Matt. 5:32 par.). The notion presupposed there of marriage, that what God has joined is not to be separated by humans, could also stand in the background of the parenthesis in 1 Cor. 7:11a, and could have motivated the exhortation to the separated wife. In this case, there could be an indication in 1 Cor. 7:10–11 of a more comprehensive knowledge of Jesus traditions.

In the Pauline citation of the Lord's Supper tradition in 1 Cor. 11:23–25, some special features are encountered. "On the night when he was betrayed" appears only here in the tradition of Jesus's Last Supper, along with the quotation of the interpretive words at the center of Paul's argument. This is because in the tradition itself the Kyrios or the salvific event in Christ becomes the theme. Moreover, only here is there a biographical feature about Jesus's life that presumably is already a part of the tradition. Thus, the fact that a specific incident in Jesus's life frames the tradition of the saying and plays a substantial role for the exposition is unique among all receptions of Jesus tradition in New Testament Epistles. At the same time, the significance of the tradition is not highlighted in such a way that it would be presented as a genuine historical memory of eyewitnesses. Birger Gerhardsson's deduction ([3]1998, 290) that the introductory terms of the tradition "received" and "handed on" (1 Cor. 11:23a) by analogy to Pharisaic-rabbinic tradition would designate the tradition that Paul knew as firmly established, a *corpus* endowed with special validity, probably goes too far. For one thing, it is the interpretation of the meal scene as a symbol for salvation in Jesus's activity and death that enables the tradition to become meaningful for the Corinthians in the first place. Thus, a post-Easter interpretive process is presupposed, which formed the tradition and enabled it to become the foundation of a ritual visualization of the Kyrios. For another thing, Paul designates himself as a direct recipient of the tradition "from the Kyrios" and circumvents a human chain of tradents, which Pharisaic-rabbinic cultural tradition implies with the terms for transmitting tradition. Paul presents himself as mediator of the words of the living Kyrios to the community; the relationship among the apostle, the Kyrios, and the congregation is a dynamic one.

1.3.5. Conclusion

Nowhere does an author appeal to the earthly Jesus as the historical origin of tradition. *Direct* citations of the earthly Jesus are not found, and biographical situations that motivate what Jesus says are not invoked except for 1 Cor. 11:23. Therefore, material in the rest of the writings in the New Testament that can be established as evidence for the "historical Jesus" and that goes beyond the evidence of the Gospels cannot be substantiated. For the quest of the historical Jesus, the evidence means first of all that parallels outside the so-called synoptic Jesus tradition cannot be adduced uncritically as early, independent attestations of a reliably transmitted Jesus tradition. The Epistles do not make it possible to discern any process of passing on tradition in the sense of an ancient school, which makes use of only isolated traditional terminology and is silent in the overwhelming majority of cases about the provenance of the tradition. It is to be assumed that in the modern sense no "interest in historical preservation" of the tradition of the sayings of Jesus existed.

Thus, New Testament writings outside of the Gospels deal with Jesus tradition variably; nevertheless, they go about it so surprisingly consistently that instead of a Jesus tradition remembered and guided by care for preserving authenticity, they make the continuing activity of the living, exalted Kyrios the criterion of a Christian construct of reality. This can be observed especially in the undisputed Pauline Epistles, but also in Acts, and in a certain way this Christocentric hermeneutic supplants a reception of Jesus guided by tradition (cf. Barrett 1985, 706; Jacobi 2015, 295–98). At the same time, this must not be interpreted as a break from and discontinuity with the pre-Easter Jesus. Rather, it can be interpreted as a continuation of his claim for himself to be God's exclusive representative (cf. Wolter 2011, 449–55; see D.III.3.8). The points of contact with the pre-Easter Jesus are then certainly not to be sought on the level of individual traditions of sayings but on the level of more comprehensive convictions. A form of appropriation of Jesus tradition, which is found primarily in the undisputed Pauline Epistles and in 1 Peter, is in keeping with this. It can be described as a far-reaching mimetic and ritual reception of Jesus's activity and person that transcends the medium of language and works efficaciously by means of a prototype. In Acts, in a comparable way, the healing work of Jesus can be seen as continuing in the healings of Peter and Paul (Acts 3:1–11; 9:32–35, 36–43; and passim; cf. Neirynck 1979). The elevated significance of scriptural attestations steps up to this unique character of early Christian reception of Jesus tradition. Scriptural attestations in New Testament Epistles and Acts (cf. Acts 15:16–17; 28:26–27)—at times in place of a fitting synoptic saying of Jesus—serve as the justification for the mission practice and ethics of the first Christians. A special type of reception of Jesus tradition developed further with the formation of early Christian prophecy for which the Revelation to John can perhaps be counted as late evidence of the "unfettered" dealings with the authority of the Kyrios (cf. synoptic tradition in the mouth of the exalted Kyrios in Rev. 2:7 and passim; 3:3; 16:15; 22:7; cf. also 1 Thess. 4:15; Vos 1965).

Various hypotheses such as that Jesus tradition in early Christianity was transmitted and preserved especially for private devotion and individual ethics (prayer attitude, trust in God as "Father," love of neighbor), whereas in the development of the church it could contribute little (Barrett 1985, 708), finally remain speculative. What New Testament writings outside the Gospels taken as a whole can contribute to the question of Jesus tradition is limited essentially to the *verification* of parallel tradition transmitted under the application of the criterion of multiple attestation. The picture that results from this is nevertheless first of all significant only with respect to tradition held in common that is already available but still says nothing about the provenance of it from the historical Jesus. Thus, how the evidence in New Testament writings outside of the Gospels is interpreted continues to be influenced by the profile of the historical Jesus presupposed in each case and by the assessment of the authenticity of the sayings of Jesus in the Gospels. Exegetes who, for example, take Mark 10:45 as authentic can also see a (Petrine) reminiscence of Jesus tradition in 1 Pet. 1:18 (cf. the discussion in Best 1970, 99–100). Thus, the more reliable the tradition of the Gospels is evaluated, the more echoes are found in the Epistles. In this regard, the detachment of the interrogation of the Synoptic Gospels and the comparison of the reception of "Jesus tradition" in New Testament Epistles among each other can demonstrate that so-called Jesus tradition in early Christianity definitely circulated over a long time in an "aggregate phase" that was not fixed (cf. Wolter 2013), and presumably forms of the tradition that were not transmitted under the authority of the earthly Jesus existed outside of the four Gospels.

Byrskog, Samuel. 2011. "The Transmission of the Jesus Tradition." In *Handbook for the Study of the Historical Jesus*, vol. 2, *The Study of Jesus*, edited by Tom Holmén and Stanley E. Porter, 1465–94. Leiden.

Dunn, James D. G. 1990. "Paul's Knowledge of the Jesus Tradition: The Evidence of Romans." In *Christus bezeugen: FS Wolfgang Trilling*, edited by Karl Kertelge, Traugott Holtz, and Claus-Peter März, 193–207. Freiburg, Basel, and Vienna.

Jacobi, Christine. 2015. *Jesusüberlieferung bei Paulus? Analogien zwischen den echten Paulusbriefen und den synoptischen Evangelien*. BZNW 213. Berlin.

Strange, William A. 2000. "The Jesus-Tradition in Acts." *NTS* 46: 59–74.

Wachob, Wesley Hiram, and Luke Timothy Johnson. 1999. "The Sayings of Jesus in the Letter of James." In *Authenticating the Words of Jesus*, edited by Bruce Chilton and Craig A. Evans, 431–50. NTTS 28/1. Leiden, Boston, and Cologne.

Wenham, David. 1994. *Paul—Follower of Jesus or Founder of Christianity?* Grand Rapids.

Wolter, Michael. 2013. "Jesus bei Paulus." In *The Rise and Expansion of Christianity in the First Three Centuries of the Common Era*, edited by Clare K. Rothschild and Jens Schröter, 205–32. WUNT 301. Tübingen.

Christine Jacobi

1.4. Christian Texts, Namely, Noncanonical Writings, as Sources for the Historical Jesus?

Over the past two centuries there has been a wealth of scholarly controversy over the figure of Jesus, but until quite recently, one general presupposition had been shared by almost all parties in the discussion. That presupposition was that the canonical Gospels of Matthew, Mark, Luke, and John contained the raw material from which one could construct a picture of Jesus. Some have preferred Mark as a foundation (e.g., Manson 1967, 26–27), others have preferred the "Q" source (e.g., Harnack 1907), and many have adopted a more complex approach to the sources, taking material from all four Gospels. Almost all assumed, however, that somewhere amidst the four New Testament Gospels alone the true Jesus lurked (E. Sanders 1993, 64–65). In recent times this assumption has been questioned. Some have taken other early Christian gospels, and other sayings contained within other works, to be *independent* of the canonical Gospels, that is, to offer additional or alternative routes back to the historical Jesus, routes not influenced by Matthew, Mark, Luke, and John. The words "additional or alternative" are important here, reflecting two different ways in which the noncanonical gospels have been viewed in a positive light. For some, the apocryphal gospels can serve to supplement the canonical Gospels (hence "additional"), either by supplying fresh material that was previously unknown (e.g., Jeremias ³1963) or by providing additional testimony to existing sayings (Crossan 1991), which can then be seen as satisfying the criterion of "multiple attestation" (see B.IX). For others, the portrayal of Jesus in the New Testament is in need of modification or even significant correction, and the apocryphal literature is useful for this.

The most significant archaeological discovery in this respect was that of the Gospel of Thomas. Found in three Greek fragments from the Oxyrhynchus rubbish dump in Egypt (published 1897–1904), and in one complete Coptic manuscript from Nag Hammadi (published 1959), Thomas consists of 114 sayings and dialogues that purport to record the words of Jesus as transcribed by the apostle Thomas. Of these sayings, roughly half overlap with the Synoptic Gospels and roughly half have little if any connection to canonical sayings. Some took

(a) the genre of Thomas as a list, (b) the different order of the synoptic sayings in Thomas, and (c) the differences in wording in the sayings shared between Thomas and the Synoptics to indicate that Thomas was independent of the Synoptics, and so a further source of sayings of Jesus in addition to Mark, Q, M, and L (e.g., Patterson 1993). One reason why some of the synoptic sayings of Jesus in the Gospel of Thomas were thought to have the ring of truth about them was that Thomas's versions are sometimes shorter and more straightforward than their canonical parallels, and for some scholars brevity and simplicity were marks of authentic sayings of Jesus. The parable of the wicked tenants in Thomas, for example, has an elegant tricolon of three emissaries, servant 1, servant 2, Son (Gos. Thom. 65), in contrast to Mark's more messy servant 1, servant 2, "many others," then the Son (Mark 12:1-11). This theory of Thomas's independence, then, opened the door for Thomas to become not only an extra source for the multiple attestation of sayings elsewhere but also a source for altogether new sayings. For some, this has shifted the picture of the historical Jesus away from the majority view of Jesus as an eschatological prophet and toward an understanding of Jesus more as a sage; less a Jewish prophet of judgment and redemption, and more a teacher of universal wisdom (S. Davies 2005).

This was not the only view, however. Scholarly opinion on the historical value of Thomas varied enormously in the first generation of research on the complete text of Thomas. Some have talked of the "continental divide" between Europe, where the attitude to Thomas was largely skeptical, and the United States, where there was greater acceptance of the historical usefulness of Thomas. (This is a very broad generalization, of course.) For a number of years there was scholarly gridlock on the question of whether Thomas was independent of the canonical Gospels, or whether it was influenced by them. Opinion has recently swung, for some decisively, in the direction of seeing Thomas as extensively shaped by the Synoptic Gospels, and its historical value as negligible (e.g., Goodacre 2012; Denzey Lewis 2014; Meier 2016)—that is, its historical value for our understanding of Jesus in his original context. Thomas still of course has value for our understanding of the reception of Jesus in the second century when it was composed (see E.VI).

Some scholars have also claimed to find independent historical material in other gospels as well. In 1948, Joachim Jeremias published the first edition of his *Unbekannte Jesusworte* (ET: *Unknown Sayings of Jesus*), which advanced claims for the authenticity of a number of agrapha (sayings of Jesus "not written down" in the canonical Gospels); subsequent editions of the book grew considerably to accommodate fresh discoveries. He saw, for example, the debate over purity between Jesus and a priest in P. Oxy. 840 as reflecting an episode in the life of Jesus. In a different vein, Morton Smith (1973) argued that the Secret Gospel of Mark accurately reflects historical elements of Jesus's teaching about messiahship and the kingdom of God.

Helmut Koester (^{2}1992) has argued that a number of apocryphal gospels are independent of their canonical counterparts, and so potentially have historical value.

In addition to "apocryphal gospels," brief attention should be given to other apocryphal material, because some scholars have also seen authentic sayings preserved in other types of literature. Some have seen in the apocryphal Acts of Peter a reminiscence of Jesus's words, "They that are with me have not understood me" (Acts Pet. 10). Alternatively, the Acts of Thomas has been taken to contain reference to a parable of Jesus about a cosmic vine planted in the depths and extending up to heaven (Acts Thom. 146).

It is not just in "heretical" apocryphal material that this additional material exists, however. The church fathers also refer to a number of additional sayings of Jesus. Perhaps the most widely attested is one recorded by Clement of Alexandria, Origen, Cyril of Jerusalem, and many others: "Be skillful bankers"—sometimes with an additional statement explaining the ethical point: accepting what is pure and genuine but rejecting what is evil and counterfeit. Perhaps the most widely accepted apocryphal saying of Jesus is one recorded both in Origen and Didymus the Blind on the one hand, and in the Gospel of Thomas and the Gospel of the Savior (or Unknown Berlin Gospel) on the other: "He who is near me is near the fire; he who is far from me is far from the kingdom" (e.g., Gos. Thom. 82).

Furthermore, one small source of agrapha is variant readings in New Testament manuscripts. The fifth-century manuscript Codex Bezae, for example, inserts between Luke 6:4 and 6:5 this episode: "On that day, Jesus saw a man working on the Sabbath and said to him, 'Man, if you know what you are doing, you are blessed. But if you do not know, you are accursed, and a transgressor of the Law.'" This is another example of a saying Jeremias considers genuine, although its survival in only one among thousands of New Testament manuscripts arouses suspicion.

Despite the claims of some, arguments for the authenticity of these episodes and sayings have only been made by a very small number of scholars. Unlike the canonical Gospels, many of the apocryphal gospels, including the Gospel of Thomas, do not convey a plausible setting in first-century Judaism. Many of the agrapha are not embedded in larger literary contexts that enable us to adjudicate their plausibility. Many of the sources are individual quotations (e.g., "Be skillful bankers"), manuscript fragments (e.g., the Egerton Gospel), and texts that only survive in translation (e.g., the Gospel of Judas). In sum, with very few exceptions, they play little or no role in modern scholarly literature on the historical Jesus, though, as already noted, they are each interesting chapters in the history of the later reception of Jesus.

Frey, Jörg, and Jens Schröter, eds. 2010. *Jesus in apokryphen Evangelienüberlieferungen*. WUNT 254. Tübingen.

Gathercole, S. J. 2012. *The Composition of the Gospel of Thomas: Original Language and Influences.* Cambridge.

Goodacre, Mark S. 2012. *Thomas and the Gospels: The Case for Thomas's Familiarity with the Synoptics.* Grand Rapids.

Hedrick, Charles W. 1988. *The Historical Jesus and the Rejected Gospels.* Semeia 44. Atlanta.

Labahn, Michael. 2011. "The Non-Synoptic Jesus." In *Handbook for the Study of the Historical Jesus*, vol. 3, *The Historical Jesus*, edited by Tom Holmén and Stanley E. Porter, 1933–96. Leiden and Boston.

Nicklas, Tobias. 2011. "Traditions about Jesus in Apocryphal Gospels (with the Exception of the Gospel of Thomas)." In *Handbook for the Study of the Historical Jesus*, vol. 3, *The Historical Jesus*, edited by Tom Holmén and Stanley E. Porter, 2081–2118. Leiden.

Stroker, William D. 1989. *Extracanonical Sayings of Jesus.* Atlanta.

Simon Gathercole

2. Non-Christian Texts

2.1. Greek, Roman, and Syriac Sources for Jesus

From the morning in Jerusalem when Pontius Pilate tried Jesus, his followers became aware of the image they had with Greek and Roman officials. Paul sought the understanding of jailers and governors, and the author of Acts regularly portrayed officials' perceptions of the first generation. Justin Martyr (*1 Apol.* 35, 48) and Tertullian (*Apol.* 5, 21) were sure that Pilate had sent a report of Jesus's trial to the emperor Tiberius, and we hear of various Acts of Pilate, anti- and pro-Christian, in circulation from about the third century. When the dust of antiquity had settled, however, authentic references to Jesus in classical texts of the first two centuries were found to be few. This chapter surveys their contents, contexts, and possible significance, along with a Syriac text that understands Jesus in light of the classical tradition. A separate chapter deals with passages in the works of Flavius Josephus (C.II.2.2).

2.1.1. Mara bar Sarapion

A seventh-century parchment codex contains a collection of philosophical and medical texts in Syriac. This codex was spirited from its desert-convent home to the British Museum in the 1840s (Add. 14,658). For historical Jesus research, the greatest interest attaches to one of its smaller texts: the letter by one Mara son of Sarapion, who writes to encourage his son Sarapion—living elsewhere with a tutor—in a life of philosophical virtue. Convinced that even persecuted wise men have the last word against unjust oppressors, Mara provides a surprising list of examples (trans. W. Cureton):

> For what advantage did the Athenians gain by the murder of Socrates, the recompense of which they received in famine and pestilence? Or the people of Samos by the burning of Pythagoras, because in one hour their country was entirely covered with sand? Or the Jews by [the death of] their wise king, because from that same time their kingdom was taken away? For with justice did God make recompense to the wisdom of these three: for the Athenians died of famine; and the Samians were overwhelmed by the sea without remedy; and the Jews, desolate and driven from their own kingdom, are scattered through every country. Socrates is not dead, because of Plato; neither Pythagoras, because of the statue of Juno; nor the Wise King, because of the laws which he promulgated.

Although Jesus is not named, it is hard to find another possibility for a man killed by "the Jews" and avenged by God through the removal of the Jews from their land, in keeping with the classic Christian interpretation. The letter promises no independent access to Jesus's life, then, but it could be in contention for the earliest non-Christian reference to Jesus—depending on its date, literary character, and situation.

Mara's clues about his environment in the letter are, alas, obscure enough to suit several periods. A member of the elite from Samosata in Commagene, he regrets a recent loss of independence under a monarch. Now in custody with associates from Samosata, he hopes that the Romans will allow them to return. The background most often proposed is Vespasian's reduction of Commagene to provincial status in 72 CE. But the kingdom had already been provincialized in 17 CE by Tiberius, before Caligula restored native rule for a generation. A temporary defection to Parthia in the early 160s, reversed by Lucius Verus, is another possible context. The first English editor (W. Cureton) published Mara's letter with other works from the 160s, and an 1897 analysis highlighted mismatches between Mara's clues and the situation in 72 (F. Schulthess). Many scholars prefer that date, nevertheless, though K. McVey has dated the letter to the fourth century, viewing it as a literary exercise in which a Christian student impersonates an earlier pagan, and M. Speidel argues that the script and literary character date it to the second or third century.

Was Mara a Christian? From his preoccupation with the philosophical life (not Christian faith), failure to name Jesus, use of nonstandard titles for Christ

("Wise King"), and claim that Christ lives on *through his new laws* (not as risen Lord), scholars have inferred that he was not. But this may be too simple a conclusion, given the letter's conspicuous agreement with a distinctively Christian position on the Jews. Surviving evidence reveals considerable diversity in Christian interpretations of Jesus. Irenaeus and Eusebius deplored groups that placed Christ on the same level as other teachers such as the great physician Galen, and one such "heresy" had links with Samosata (Eusebius, *Hist. eccl.* 5.28; Irenaeus, *Haer.* 1.26.5 on Carpocratians). Further, we must reckon with the different degrees of commitment and knowledge presupposed by texts such as Luke-Acts, Hebrews, or Pliny's letter to Trajan. People were constantly moving in and out of various Christ-following groups, holding any number of ideas about their Teacher and Lord.

The many plausible explanations of this letter thus prevent us from being sure that it is non-Christian, let alone the earliest outside evidence of Jesus.

2.1.2. Suetonius

C. Suetonius Tranquillus (ca. 70–130/135 CE), a well-connected member of Rome's equestrian order, was a prolific man of letters. He entered the service of the emperors Trajan and Hadrian through the support of a senator friend, the younger Pliny, whose social circle included Tacitus (below). Suetonius's only surviving work of many is his *Lives of the Caesars*, biographies of twelve rulers beginning with the founder of the dynasty, Julius Caesar, and concluding with the Flavians. In keeping with rhetoric's prescriptions, Suetonius emphasized the rulers' origins and ends, giving each a summary moral-political assessment. He was also a notorious gossip, including juicy details about dead emperors whenever possible. When he was not recounting such tidbits or strange occurrences, he would often rattle off a list of measures taken by his imperial subject with little by way of context, date, or explanation.

In a paragraph on Nero's correction of abuses and new measures (*Nero* 16.2), thus, Suetonius mentions in rapid succession that young emperor's limits on expenditures, restriction on meat sold in taverns, punishment of the Christians for a novel and dangerous superstition, banishment of pantomime actors, and restraints on chariot racers who tended to consider themselves above the law. We wish we knew more, especially about the Christians. Fortunately, Tacitus (see below) elaborates.

Of more direct interest for Jesus research is Suetonius's *Life of Claudius* (emperor 41–54 CE). Its middle content is like that of Nero's *Life*, with a long paragraph listing Claudius's beneficial measures, engineered by the wives and freedmen who supposedly dominated this ruler. We read about Claudius's revival of old Roman customs and rites, his summary punishment of those who feigned Roman citizenship, his adjustments to the status of various provinces, and social privileges he granted German envoys in Rome. In the middle of all this, Suetonius mentions that Claudius "drove out from Rome the Jews/Judaeans who were relentlessly fomenting disturbance, with Chrestus as instigator (*Iudaeos impulsore Chresto assidue tumultuantis Roma expulit*)." At only seven Latin words, this sentence is even more cryptic than those around it. It has become an object of scholarly fascination.

Suetonius's main point lies in just five words: Claudius expelled Judeans because of their ongoing disturbances. If that had been everything, scholars would mainly be discussing the connection between this expulsion and Acts 18:2 ("Claudius having ordered all the Judaeans out of Rome"), as well as a measure mentioned by Cassius Dio (60.6.6) forbidding Judeans from assembling—Dio claims they were too numerous for expulsion—because they were attracting Romans to foreign ways.

But the phrase *impulsore Chresto* has greatly complicated matters and beguiled historians. Scholars agree on other grounds that Roman Christianity began in the city's synagogues under Claudius. The name Chrestus is tantalizingly close to Christus, especially since we know that the two were frequently confused. In speech, moreover, the Greek *ι* in *Christos* was indistinguishable from *ē* in *Chrēstus*. One cannot help but wonder, then, whether Suetonius's Chrestus was not a garbled reference to Christian emissaries active in synagogues of Claudius's time.

But historians are rightly wary of neat solutions. Read without external constraints, the passage speaks unproblematically of an agitator named *Chrēstus*. The name was common ("useful," "reliable"), especially among slaves and freedmen—the status of much of the city's Jewish population. Dio (see above) saw the disturbances under Claudius as continuous with those of 19 CE under Tiberius (57.18.5), mentioning nothing of Christian involvement. Even Acts 18 mentions only an expulsion of Jews. There is no reason to doubt that a man named Chrestus was active in Rome's Jewish community under Claudius. To be sure, Chrestus does not appear among the hundreds of names on surviving *Jewish* funerary inscriptions, but those date from the second to fifth centuries. If the text should read *Christus*—a link made already in the fifth century by Paulus Orosius (*C. Pag.* 7.6)— delicate maneuvers would still be needed to make a Christ in Rome's synagogues (Christ is not Christianity) historically intelligible.

2.1.3. Pliny and Tacitus

P. Cornelius Tacitus (*consul suffectus* 97) and C. Caecilius Plinius (Pliny) Secundus (*consul* 100) were friends who belonged to the same senatorial elite that furnished so much of surviving Roman culture. Thoroughly trained in rhetoric for public life, they both served in the legions, climbed Rome's ladder of magistracies and priesthoods culminating in the consulship, governed choice Roman provinces, and enjoyed full engagement with the capital's literary culture.

Pliny's letter to the emperor Trajan, asking for guidance on dealing with Christians in his province of Bithynia-Pontus, and Trajan's reply (*Ep.* 10.96–97) are probably the most famous Roman sources on Christian origins. They say nothing directly about Jesus, however, only about Christian devotion to Christ.

Tacitus, by contrast, offers a clear statement about Jesus. As a writer of history, he tends to mention the origin of the nations, cities, or groups he is describing, as when he discusses Jerusalem's origins in preparation for his account of the city's destruction (*Hist.* 5.2–13). Tacitus's narration of Nero's reign includes the Great Fire of 64 (in annalistic format), the emperor's rebuilding of the city after the catastrophe, and his desperate effort to deflect blame by punishing Rome's Christians (*Ann.* 15.38–44). Tacitus pauses to elaborate: "The founder of the name [Christians], Christus, faced capital punishment when Tiberius was in power, at the hands of the procurator Pontius Pilatus. Although he [Pilate] curbed the deadly superstition for a time, it broke out again, not only in Judaea, source of the disease, but also here in the city [Rome] where all horrid or disgraceful things flow in from everywhere else and hold a festival."

For Jesus research, the first sentence is the gem. We do not know where Tacitus learned this information. It is unlikely that such a man read the Gospels. More likely, he heard reports at first or second hand from Christians facing trial, though he may have read whatever Josephus wrote about Jesus in *Antiquities* 18.63–64. Josephus was the source in Rome for things Judean, and there is reason to think that Tacitus used his *War* elsewhere (*Hist.* 5.1–13).

Tacitus's account of Nero and the Christians adds nothing material, again, to our information about Jesus. If he drew his statement about Jesus from Christian oral reports, that brief notice would have roughly the same evidentiary value as gospel statements, with the difference that a critical non-Christian finds it credible.

2.1.4. Lucian of Samosata

A final classical author deserves mention because he comes from the same broad date range as the others and likewise briefly mentions Jesus on the basis of, it seems, a Christian report. A migrant from Mara's city in Syrian Commagene, Lucian was not on the same social level as the Latin authors. He was a master of Greek rhetoric from the provinces who, partly through his brilliant Greek satirical essays, tried to make a reputation and a living in the fiercely competitive literary circles of Rome and the eastern Mediterranean. One satire attacked Peregrinus from Parium (western Asia Minor), a spiritual quester who ended his life in a blaze, in Lucian's presence, at Greek Olympia. Peregrinus is important for us because he spent some time among the Christians, before abandoning them. Lucian does not miss the opportunity to ridicule Peregrinus and the Christians together for this temporary association.

By Lucian's lights, Peregrinus was such a master *poseur* that he quickly duped the gullible Christians of Palestine into regarding him as a prophet, even eliciting their worship (*Peregr.* 11). Peregrinus allegedly even penned holy texts, thus making himself an object of veneration—"after, to be sure, that other fellow they still worship, that man who was impaled in Palestine because he brought this new form of initiation to life."

As we have come to expect with the other sources, Lucian offers no independent information, but only a typically sardonic take on information about Jesus taken from Christians.

Boman, Jobjorn. 2011. "Inpulsore Cherestro? Suetonius' *Divus Claudius* 25.4 in Sources and Manuscripts." *LASBF* 61: 355–76.

Cureton, William. 1855. *Spicilegium Syriacum: Containing Remains of Bardesan, Meliton, Ambrose, and Mara bar Serapion*. London.

Mara bar Sarapion, 2014. *Letter to His Son*. Edited and translated by Annette Merz, David Rensberger, and Teun Tieleman. Tübingen.

McVey, Kathleen E. 1990. "A Fresh Look at the Letter of Mara bar Serapion to His Son, V Symposium Syriacum." *OCA* 236: 257–72.

Schulthess, Friedrich. 1897. "Der Brief des Mara bar Sarapion: Ein Beitrag zur Geschichte der syrischen Literatur." *ZDMG* 51: 365–91.

Speidel, Michael A. 2012. "Making Use of History beyond the Euphrates: Political Views, Cultural Traditions, and Historical Contexts in the Letter of Mara bar Sarapion." In *The Letter of Mara bar Sarapion in Context*, edited by Annette Merz and Teun Tieleman, 11–42. Leiden.

Voorst, Robert E. van. 2000. *Jesus outside the New Testament: An Introduction to the Ancient Evidence*. Grand Rapids.

Steve Mason

2.2. Jewish Sources: Flavius Josephus

The thirty Greek volumes by Flavius Josephus (37–ca. 100 CE) were preserved more or less intact—a rare fate for classical texts—because Christians took a keen interest in them. Josephus had become famous from his connection with the Flavian imperial family, a connection that lent his work unparalleled prestige. But the knowledgeable priest from Jerusalem had described conditions in pre-70 Judea and Rome's destruction of Jerusalem with a fullness, clarity, and authority that no other source could match. From perhaps the fourth century, Christians began to take over from imperial scribes the task of copying Josephus's works, until the printing press facilitated mass dissemination. From the fifteenth to the early twentieth century, Josephus's works could be found in virtually every house that possessed a Protestant Bible as a historical companion. Western Christians bearing the name Josephus, sometimes even Flavius, were not hard to find as late as the early twentieth century.

This brief background already prompts two questions: Did the most important Jewish author, born in Jerusalem shortly after Jesus's crucifixion there, write about the founder of Christianity? If he did, during the long centuries of Christian copying, did scribes interfere with what Josephus wrote? We know that such scribes made thousands of adjustments, accidental and deliberate, to the New Testament texts. To what extent did they alter Josephus? He wrote a great deal that might have tempted Christian hands: elaborate narratives concerning Jesus's would-be murderer (according to Matthew), King Herod and his descendants, along with significant material on high priests such as Caiaphas or the governor Pontius Pilate, who reportedly colluded in Jesus's death, not to mention Pharisees, Sadducees, and assorted others. Surprisingly, however, scholars have found no clear evidence of Christian interference in all those passages. Josephus's compositions have survived more or less intact, granted thousands of small variants in the manuscripts.

Josephus's description of John the Baptist (*Ant.* 18.116–119) provides a clear example of restraint. The Gospels all declare, and historical-Jesus scholars agree, that John was somehow fundamental to Jesus's career: Jesus began his ministry with an immersion by John. According to the Gospels, but not the scholars, John's chief purpose was to introduce Jesus. Yet Josephus's portrayal of the Baptist, well after Josephus's passage on Jesus (below), shows no hint of Christian coloring. John appears as a uniquely popular teacher in his own right, executed by Herod Antipas because of his potentially subversive mass following, at Machaerus east of the Dead Sea (rather than in Galilee, as one would assume from the Gospels). There is no connection with Jesus. So, we cannot assume that Christian scribes freely altered Josephus's works as they copied them, to reflect their views. The overwhelming evidence is that they usually refrained from doing so.

The two passages crucial for Jesus research are, however, also the most likely candidates for any scribal adjustment that did occur. They come near the end of Josephus's second work, the *Judean Antiquities*, which he completed in 93/94 CE.

In the first passage, Josephus is describing Pontius Pilate's tenure as prefect for Judea within the province of Syria. After describing two incidents that led to great tumult and accusing Pilate of callous aggravation, Josephus continues (*Ant.* 18.63–64):

> Now about this time comes Jesus, a wise man, if indeed one should call him a man: he was a doer of remarkable deeds, a teacher of persons who welcome the true [things] with pleasure, and he won over both many Judaeans and also many of the Greek element. He was the Christ.
>
> On his indictment by the principal men among us, and having been condemned to the cross by Pilate, those who had loved him in the first place did not yield: he appeared to them after the third day living again, these and countless other amazing things having been spoken about him by the divine prophets. Even to now still, the breed [or tribe] of the "Christians"—named from this fellow—did not expire [perhaps: did not fail him].

Josephus then recounts "another cause of terrible troubles" at the time, among Judeans living in Rome (*Ant.* 18.65), before describing Pilate's removal from office.

The second passage appears to assume this one. It comes in a thematically charged narrative near the end of the work, detailing the malfeasance of Jerusalem's high priests as a cause of the coming war. *Antiquities* ends anticipating that war, which the earlier *Jewish War* has described in detail. To support his characterization of the high priest Ananus II (62 CE) as a venal and savage opportunist, in sharp contrast to the admiring portrait in *War*, Josephus mentions this high priest's execution of certain accused lawbreakers without competent authority. This occurred during the interval between the death of the Prefect/Procurator Festus and the arrival of his replacement, Albinus (20.200):

> Ananus convened a council of judges and hauled before it the brother of Jesus the one called Christ—a man by the name of Yakob [James]—and some others. He brought the charge that they had broken the law and thus handed them over to be stoned. But those in the *polis* who were reputed to be most careful when it came to the laws found this hard to bear. They send to the king [Agrippa II], urging him to write to Ananus not to do this kind of thing any more. [They also contact the new governor en route, who furiously reprimands Ananus before Agrippa obligingly deposes him.]

Considering these two "Jesus" passages together, most scholars have regarded only the first one, on Jesus himself, particularly suspect. Could Josephus have written that Jesus *was the Christ* and portrayed his resurrection as fulfilling prophetic predictions? The problem is not only that he elsewhere gives no hint of Christian allegiance, while devoting thirty volumes to the all-sufficient virtues of Moses, the laws, and Jerusalem. Simply as a literary matter, it is hard to imagine that he could have used the adjective *christos* in this way. Given that the word means "smeared," other Greek authors found few occasions to use it. Josephus himself uses it only once elsewhere, when speaking of a *plastered roof* (*Ant.* 8.137). So, what could he mean by calling this unusual *man* Jesus "the plastered/smeared one" without explaining his language? In Jewish and early Christian circles, of course, *Christos* had a technical meaning, as the Septuagint rendering of Hebrew *mashiach*: God's anointed (king or high priest). But Josephus is writing for Greek-speaking audiences, and is otherwise hostile toward charismatic leaders claiming biblical-prophetic authority (e.g., *J. W.* 2.259–263; 6.285). He is also careful otherwise to explain Hebrew concepts to his audiences, realizing that they will not understand traditional language. Although it is not impossible in principle that Josephus wrote carelessly here, without thinking to explain himself, the obvious agreement between this passage and the Christian beliefs held by his copyists makes some degree of Christian editing virtually certain.

Even more tellingly, Christian writers of the second and third centuries would surely have exploited Josephus's declaration of Jesus as "Christ" if it had been in what Josephus wrote. Yet Origen (mid-third century) knew Josephus's works, and he lamented repeatedly that the great Jewish author was no Christian (*Cels.* 1.47; *Comm. Matt.* 10.17). Only in the fourth century did Eusebius first quote the passage on Jesus as we have it, though in three somewhat different versions (*Hist. eccl.* 1.11; *Dem. ev.* 3.5; [Syriac] *Theophany* 5.44). Toward the end of that century, Jerome included Josephus in his *Lives of Outstanding Men* (13), largely on the strength of the Jesus passage, which he also quotes. But in his version, the crucial sentence reads "he was *believed to be* [the] Christ" rather than *he was Christ*. Such qualified versions would continue to appear in Christian texts through the Middle Ages. How should we explain them, if Josephus had written without qualification that Jesus was the Messiah?

Something is not right here, and sixteenth-century Protestant critics of church (Catholic) tradition already recognized that. In 1863, E. Gerlach conveyed an air of exhaustion as he summarized the various arguments that had already been made for and against the passage's authenticity, while he hoped to settle the question once and for all (in 1863!). He could have had no idea that the passage would continue to attract lively debate in the twenty-first century, as succeeding scholars try their hands at a definitive solution.

Of the three main options—Josephus wrote the whole passage, or none of it, or some but not all—majority opinion has settled on the diplomatic middle ground.

But some scholars still find a Jesus-free Josephus most compelling, and a recent study (K. Olson) argues for Eusebius's fabrication of the main Jesus passage.

The later passage, on James as Jesus's brother, which seems less complicated, may provide a useful side-door entry to the issues. That is because the men sentenced by Ananus are incidental to Josephus's narrative, which is mainly about conflicts among Jerusalem's priestly class (from 20.179ff., 189ff.), exacerbated by a standoff with King Agrippa II, his rapid removal and appointment of high priests, and the death of a Roman procurator in office. This is the moment chosen by a new high priest to flex his muscles against assorted enemies, perhaps posturing as "tough on crime," in a way that offended his enemies among the elite. It is characteristic of Josephus to name one ringleader or example of a large group ("X and those with him"), and not unusual for him to identify a person or place and then add a second name with *legomenos*: "called X" (*Ant.* 4.82; 8.100; *Life* 4; cf. *Ant.* 1.123; 2.6). So, his introduction of James looks normal. The order of his identifiers suggests that he chooses James as representative of the condemned group *because* he is "the brother of the one *called [or known as] Christos*," already known to the audience. James's name comes as an afterthought.

This formulation suggests, therefore, that Josephus has mentioned someone "known as *Christos*" recently enough that his audience might remember. The only plausible candidate is Jesus in book 18. Josephus also recalls *Antiquities* 13.288–298, when he notes that Ananus, as a Sadducee, was severe in judgment "as we have already explained" (20.199), a point alluded to again in 18.16–17 when Josephus recalls the Pharisees' popularity and therefore the constraints faced by Sadducees—abandoned here by Ananus II—who must yield to the Pharisees' legal principles when in office, because of popular pressure. Every part of the James passage makes decent sense, therefore, in the larger context of *Antiquities*, if Josephus has recently referred to a man known as *Christos*.

Were we to hypothesize that book 18 contained no reference to a Jesus known as Christ, we would have to suppose that whoever inserted that passage in book 18 was clever enough to work ahead and add this rather subtle connection with James, two volumes later. But then it would be hard to imagine what the later passage looked like without the insertion, for Jesus (unqualified) is a common name in Josephus. Why link James with an unclarified Jesus? As we have seen, the link with "the one called *Christos*" seems to be Josephus's reason for singling out this man Yakob among Ananus's victims.

An ingenious proposal by R. Carrier holds that Josephus wrote about a different but also important James, brother of a different Jesus. The high priest Ananus, that is, persecuted an otherwise unattested chief priest named James, brother *of the high priest Jesus son of Damnaeus*. That would explain why the new governor replaced Ananus with that Jesus (20.203), the dead man's brother. The appearance of this Jesus-James duo, however, inspired a fairly early Christian copyist to turn this James into the brother of Jesus Christ. Carrier's reconstruction, brilliant though it is, creates more problems than it solves. It would not explain the allegation of law observance (a live issue in early Christianity, in which James was reportedly implicated [Acts 21:17–26; cf. Gal. 2:12]), the men condemned along with James, the reported reaction from other members of the elite to this breach of due process, or the prospect of a high priest's exceeding his authority "in judgments/court cases"—not against elite rivals. The most economical explanation of the text in *Antiquities* 20 is that Josephus had written about a Jesus called *Christos* in book 18, which he could therefore use as a reference point to explain why he singled out this Yakob among Ananus's victims: he was the brother of that Jesus mentioned earlier.

Trying to figure out what Josephus wrote in the Jesus passage (book 18) is probably impossible now, given that all of our Greek manuscripts (from the tenth century and later) more or less agree on the passage we read in our texts. R. Eisler (1931), partly with an eye on the thirteenth-century Slavonic version, which he valued as a possible clue to Josephus's own writing, argued that much of the text could be seen as Josephus's writing *if* we understood the original diction in a more critical or sarcastic vein: Jesus was a wonder-worker who misled the gullible, sometimes broke the law, and was condemned. Not many have followed Eisler's lead in all respects, but it remains an appealing option that Josephus wrote something more detached or critical than our extant text indicates.

Some scholars have examined words and phrases in *Antiquities* 18.63–64 in relation to Josephus's usage elsewhere, and also in relation to the corpus of surviving Greek literature for comparison. Such examination shows that at least two phrases ("doer of deeds" and "even to now still") are strange to Josephus—and yet conspicuously at home in Eusebius. This strongly suggests, at least, that Eusebius's diction influenced the textual transmission of Josephus to some extent. The same thing may have happened with other phrases, leading one scholar to argue that Eusebius himself wrote the passage (Olson). But open-minded research in the same vein, not in the service of any particular hypothesis, turns up many phrases that are not only characteristic of Josephus but are particularly common in *Antiquities* 17–19, the stylistically distinctive section in which the Jesus passage falls. These phrases do not appear or take a different form in Eusebius. Examples are: "now comes," "about this time," "wise man," "if indeed," "remarkable deeds," "receiving X with pleasure" (usually in a sarcastic vein, eight times in *Ant.* 17–19), "the true (things)," "the Greek element," "on indictment," "the principal *men*," "among us," "condemn," "having the Xth day," "divine prophets," and "breed" (unflattering). It is easier to believe that Josephus himself wrote much of this, and that it was adjusted from the fourth century onward, than that a (Eusebian?) forger was diligent enough to search out Josephus's style and apply the traits of *Antiquities* 17–19, in particular, to this passage—while carelessly leaving a couple of telltale Eusebianisms in the passage.

In sum, it is most likely that Josephus mentioned Jesus, and even reported something about his life that may have been independent of Christian tradition, in the vein of his portrait of the Baptist (both in *Ant.* 18). Nothing in our extant text of Josephus helps us understand the historical Jesus, however, because of evident scribal tampering. The mere likelihood that Josephus mentioned John, Jesus, and James independently of Christian authors, among his hundreds of minor characters, is already a valuable reference point for historians. Although it is hazardous to speculate about what exactly Josephus wrote concerning Jesus, his brief accounts of the Baptist and Jesus's brother provide unique stimuli, outside the Christian orbit, for historical investigation.

Carrier, Richard. 2012. "Origen, Eusebius, and the Accidental Interpolation in Josephus, *Jewish Antiquities* 20.200." *JECS* 20: 489–514.

Eisler, Robert. 1931. *The Messiah Jesus and John the Baptist: According to Flavius Josephus' Recently Rediscovered "Capture of Jerusalem" and the Other Jewish and Christian Sources.* Translated by Alexander Haggerty Krappe. New York.

Gerlach, Ernst. 1863. *Die Weissagungen des Alten Testaments in den Schriften des Flavius Josephus und das angebliche Zeugniss von Christo.* Berlin.

Meier, John P. 1991. *A Marginal Jew: Rethinking the Historical Jesus.* Vol. 1, *The Roots of the Problem and the Person.* New York.

Olson, Ken. 2013. "A Eusebian Reading of the Testimonium Flavianum." In *Eusebius of Caesarea: Tradition and Innovations*, edited by Aaron P. Johnson and Jeremy M. Schott, 97–114. Hellenic Studies Series 60. Washington, DC.

Whealey, Alice. 2003. *Josephus on Jesus: The Testimonium Flavianum Controversy from Late Antiquity to Modern Times.* New York.

Steve Mason

III. Nonliterary Evidence

1. Archaeological Evidence

1.1. Statement of the Problem

Since neither Jesus nor his immediate adherents belonged to the culturally defined elite until into the second century CE (different from, for instance, Pilate;

see C.III.2) and left behind no recognizable material traces (buildings, inscriptions, objects), the search for direct archaeological evidence of the person of Jesus or his direct effect is viewed as dubious and has not led to any generally recognizable results. The task and the major potential of archaeology for research on Jesus lie, therefore, especially in the investigation of the regional fabric of life, which the sources connect with the person of the historical Jesus—especially in lower Galilee and Jerusalem. Excavations at locations such as Jerusalem, Capernaum, et-Tell (Bethsaida), or Magdala document multiple aspects of the daily material culture such as construction of houses and furnishings, burial practices, infrastructure or buildings and objects associated with religious practices (on what follows, see Zangenberg 2012a, 2013c; see D.III.4).

1.2. Elements of Material Culture

This can be clarified by means of various facts: the extensive excavations of several *insulae* in Capernaum inhabited between the late first century BCE and the sixth century CE convey good glimpses into the combination of urban planning of residential streets and quite traditional construction within residential neighborhoods (houses with courtyards). By contrast, the recently excavated urban residential area of Magdala of the first centuries BCE and CE exhibits clear Hellenistic influence and higher prosperity. In the Jewish section of Jerusalem, even larger distinctions in the construction before 70 CE showed up: on the one hand, a magnificent town house on the upper hillside; on the other, simple tenements in the area of the "burnt house." At the same time, it must be borne in mind that the current excavated areas of this location were not necessarily representative for the entire settlement (cf. the urban elements in the orthodox section of Capernaum).

The discovery of fragments of three fishing boats (one of which is very well preserved and is now known as the "Jesus boat") on the bank of the Sea of Gennesaret at the Kibbutz Ginosar provides significant knowledge about the high level of local construction of boats and fishing commerce from the time shortly after Jesus's activity in the region. The most well-preserved boat was assembled from various types of wood. A comparable type of boat is depicted in a mosaic of the first century CE at Magdala.

Excavations (among others) at Gamla (Golan), at Qirjat Sefer (Judea), and recently at Magdala have brought to light synagogue buildings from the time of Jesus. They permit not only important insights into architecture (rectangular construction with bench seats) and décor of the earliest stage of an entire tradition of construction (e.g., colored internal walls and mosaics in Magdala and partially sculptured pillars in Gamla). Further, in connection with pertinent texts

(Josephus, Mishnah, New Testament), they also make it possible to understand better the central social and religious function of these community centers.

From the beginning of archaeological investigations in Jerusalem, the Temple Mount stood at the center (see D.III.5). The systematic analysis of the Herodian part of the architecture in the rubble west and south of the platform makes it possible to surmise the splendor of the Jewish sanctuary and to understand better the literary tradition of Josephus, the Gospels, and the Mishnah. Especially many elements of pilgrimages associated with the temple have become established (shops along the street west of the platform, a monumental staircase from the south with a wastewater canal, the pool of Siloam [Shiloaḥ], large immersion baths for pilgrims, the Theodotus inscription). At the same time, numerous immersion baths and various types of stone jars document the large role of Jewish concepts of purity for large parts of Judea and Galilee. Other stone objects inspired by Hellenism (tables with a stone slab and lathed pedestal) as well as glass and fine ceramics document the openness of upscale Jewish social strata for international domestic and lifestyle culture (Magness 2011; Zangenberg 2013d).

In addition, the ongoing investigation of the texts from the caves at Qumran contributes enormously to the understanding of the variety in Judaism at the time of Jesus. The examination of the vicinity of the settlement shows how diverse Judea was economically. Excavations in Caesarea in the area of Herod's palace and the *praetorium* produced important evidence that makes it possible to portray the development of governing officials and administrative centers of the province *Iudaea*.

The Samaritan community also illustrates an important element of the cultural variety of *Iudaea*. Indeed, they recognized the Pentateuch as Holy Scripture and, like contemporary Judaism, were led by priests. But in competition with Jerusalem, they possessed their central sanctuary on Mount Gerizim. In the Jesus tradition, they are mentioned only on the margins (e.g., Matt. 10:5; Luke 9:51–56; 10:25–37; 17:11–19; John 4:4–42). Extensive excavations on this mountain brought to light remnants of the temple area destroyed by John Hyrcanus shortly before 100 BCE, as well as hundreds of fragments of inscriptions and an entire city of the second century BCE (Zangenberg 2012b).

Also, our knowledge of the contemporary burial culture is considerably enlarged thanks to archaeology. Elements of burial ritual (gathering at the grave, gifts for the deceased), the clear preference for the burial of the entire body, the gathering of the bones for a second burial for reasons of space, as well as the two popular types of graves (shaft grave, chamber grave, some with a large stone) are now well known, and they help in understanding the traditions that have to do with the burial of Jesus (Zangenberg 2009).

In 1968 several ossuaries were found in a chamber tomb in the Giv'at ha-Mivtar sector of Jerusalem. One of these ossuaries was inscribed with the name "Jehohanan, son of Hagkol (?)," and it contained the remains of several individuals, among which was the heel bone of a middle-aged man, through which a nail had been hammered. Remnants of wood between the nail and bone suggest that the man had been crucified. Evidently, after the execution he was then buried for the first time as usual in the chamber grave, before his mortal remains were collected by relatives, and a part of his skeleton together with bones of other members of the family were buried for the second time in the aforementioned ossuary. Hence, the "crucified man of Giv'at ha-Mivtar" is the only archaeological attestation up to now for execution by crucifixion from the time of Jesus. At the same time, the grave verifies that relatives evidently could ask a ruler for the return of the corpse of one who was crucified and in the context of the family bury it in a dignified way.

However, the so-called James ossuary that came from illegal excavations and the discovery possibly (!) contiguous to it of the chamber tomb Talpiot I in 1980, which has become known as Jesus's "family tomb," is highly disputed. Striking agreements of the names carved on the ossuaries from Talpiot I with Jesus's relatives mentioned in Mark 6:3, as well as the reference to a certain "Mariamne" (!), and the especially controversially debated reference to a certain "Yeshua bar-Yosef" pose questions about the statistical likelihood that this grave perhaps could have belonged to the family of Jesus. To be sure, the current state of research furthers the possibility that this is either an apology or sensationalism (Charlesworth 2013).

1.3. Relics of Jesus

Apart from these indeed contemporary but "indirect" sources, objects that are presumably directly associated with Jesus or the disciples constantly are quite significant in the history of Christianity. In this connection, especially objects from the context of Jesus's passion should be mentioned (spear, title on the cross, pieces of the cross), as well as pieces of clothing or cloth, that through contact with Jesus are supposed to have attained special virtues.

The list of significant relics of Jesus that in each case stands out because of closer regional context is not very long (Sörries 2012). So, for instance, the allegedly authentic *titulus* of the cross is treasured in the Basilica di Santa Croce di Gerusalemme (Roman Catholic) (cf. John 19:19 par.; the orthography, however, is from the time of the Crusades). In the Vienna Hofburg, the spear of the "centurion Longinus," on the blade of which a nail of the cross has been incorporated, is for veneration as part of the regalia of the Holy Roman Empire of the German Nation (John 19:34).

In 2012 the Holy Robe of Jesus was exhibited again in Turin, and in 2015 the so-called burial shroud was once more displayed in the Cathedral of Turin (Sacra/Santa Sindone Chapel). Especially since the 1950s, a very complex landscape of research has developed ("sindonology") that desires to establish the factual age of the cloth with methods of the natural sciences (at the time of Jesus or the Middle Ages?), but in addition endeavors to reconstruct how the shroud got from Palestine to Turin in upper Italy (for this also, analysis of pollen), as well as to attempt to explain the origin of the visible image of a male body. If, however, Mark 15:46 is taken into consideration (*one* cloth) along with John 19:40; 20:6–7 (cloths or *strips* of cloth, *plus* a face cloth), then it is dubious whether there ever was *one* single authentic "burial cloth" (Zangenberg 2008; Kollmann 2010).

Like the burial shroud of Turin, images of the face of Jesus are known from art and relics in the sphere of passion relics and are related either to the facecloth (*sudarion*) according to John 20:6–7 (unmentioned in the Synoptics) or to the veil of Veronica. Through popular scientific publications, something like the "Veil of Manoppello" (Santurario del Volto Santo) has become especially well known. A landscape of research comparable to that for the shroud of Turin does not (yet) exist here; the authenticity of the cloth is of course more than dubious and—like the shroud of Turin—it is also not claimed to be authentic by the magisterium of the Catholic Church.

Charlesworth, James H., ed. 2006. *Jesus and Archaeology*. Grand Rapids.

Kollmann, Bernd. 2010. *Das Grabtuch von Turin: Ein Porträt Jesu? Mythen und Fakten*. Freiburg.

Sörries, Reiner. 2012. *Was von Jesus übrig blieb: Die Geschichte seiner Reliquien*. Kevelaer, Germany.

Zangenberg, Jürgen K. 2013c. "Jesus der Galiläer und die Archäologie: Beobachtungen zur Bedeutung der Archäologie für die historische Jesusforschung." *MTZ* 64: 123–56.

Jürgen K. Zangenberg

2. Inscriptions and Coins

2.1. Inscriptions

2.1.1. General Remarks

Inscriptions in the ancient world were quite prominent in public and private spaces. Even though at the time of Jesus not all people could read or write, "perpetual" inscriptions and durable important news reports marked buildings, honored meritorious people such as rulers or benefactors, or referred to religious sentiments or practices. Inscriptions were chiseled, stamped, or carved into hard surfaces, written on wood (mostly not preserved); or applied on organic materials. Transitions from inscriptions to papyri were often smooth.

The oldest inscription that names Jesus is the *titulus* of the cross, the text of which the Gospels transmit in several versions (Greek in Mark 15:26; Matt. 27:37; Luke 23:38; three languages in John 19:19–22). The plaque itself is of course not preserved. Since neither Jesus nor his disciples belonged to the leading cultural social strata, they are not named in contemporary inscriptions outside the New Testament. In general, only a very few Greek, Aramaic, Hebrew, or (even fewer) Latin inscriptions from the immediate Palestinian vicinity of Jesus have been found. One of the few exceptions are ossuaries inscribed with about four hundred names, which are mostly short, from the late first century BCE into the early second century CE. They offer an interesting insight into Jewish practices of naming and at times give the occupation and provenance of the person who is buried. A further exception are severely fragmented dedication inscriptions from Hellenistic times found in secondary contexts on Mount Gerizim. In general, however, not until the fourth century CE did the volume of inscriptions increase perceptibly both in the countryside and in urban areas of Palestine, especially in Galilee.

2.1.2. Important Inscriptions from Jesus's Environment

In 1961 Italian archaeologists found an architectural fragment in the theater of Caesarea, which originally probably came from a large public building in the adjacent harbor area ("Tiberieum"). On it were engraved the name Pontius Pilate, who ruled between 26 and 36, and his title *praefectus Iudaeae* (W. Eck 2007, 34–37; Schröter and Zangenberg 2013, 67). The title *praefectus* indicates the rank of the ruler, who belonged to the equestrian class and up until the outbreak of the revolt in 66 was under the command of the Syrian legate. Not until after 70 did the governors of *Iudaea* come from the consular rank; after that a legion also was under their command.

During excavations south and west of the Temple Mount, numerous partially decorated fragments of architecture were found, which originally belonged to the portico of the sanctuary. Among these was a severely fragmented inscription (CIIP I/1, no. 3, pp. 45–47; Schröter and Zangenberg 2013, 469). It mentions a certain "[S]paris, son of Akeson, from Rhodes (?)," who had donated an unspecified sum of drachmas for "the pavement." This inscription is an important attestation of the fact that, like all other ancient holy places, the temple in Jerusalem also attracted private benefactors, alongside Herod and the priesthood, for its adornment.

In 1871 a complete specimen of an inscription that is known from Josephus (*J.W.* 5.193–197) was found, which warned non-Jews not to cross the barriers around the sanctuary on the punishment of death (CIIP I/1, no. 2, pp. 42–45; Schröter and Zangenberg 2013, 469). This inscription mentions the presumably only exception to the rule that local Jewish authorities were no longer allowed to administer the death penalty after the Roman takeover of *Iudaea*. Evidently the Romans were still aware of this old sacred law and respected it.

The construction inscription of a synagogue that was found in 1913/1914 on the Southeastern Hill of Jerusalem is of special significance (CIIP I/1, no. 9, pp. 53–56; Schröter and Zangenberg 2013, 483). It dates from the first century CE, and it commemorates a certain Theodotus, son of Vettenos, "Priest and leader of the Synagogue," of the third generation of synagogue leaders, who built the synagogue "for the reading of the law and the teaching of the commandments" and as a "hostel and rooms" for lodging needy strangers, and who also built a water installation. The inscription underscores the multiple functions of a Jewish synagogue as a house of prayer and teaching, but also as a hostel for pilgrims. That here a priest was the leader of the synagogue is doubtless partly due to the special situation in Jerusalem. The fact that the inscription is written in Greek and that Theodotus is a Greek name (translation for Matityahu or Yehonatan?), and that even his father has a Latin name, attests the cosmopolitan character of Jerusalem in the first century CE. Nevertheless, it is striking that, for example, not a single construction inscription from the numerous fortresses and palaces of Herod has been preserved.

2.2. Coins

2.2.1. The Use of Coins

Since their invention around the end of the seventh century BCE in western Asia Minor, coins, with their symbols, images of personalities, and legends, provide insight into the political, economic, and religious values and concepts of ancient people.

Therefore, coins are an important source also for the environment in which Jesus and early Christians lived, even though it would be centuries before Christians minted their first coins or until Christian motifs would appear on coins.

As in other regions of the ancient Mediterranean world, coins from various local, regional, and transregional systems circulated side by side. Since minted coins lacked designations of denominations, there was no fixed exchange rate between these systems nor a definite fixed value. The "value" of a coin in the first centuries BCE and CE was based first of all more or less on the type of metal (at the time of Jesus, gold, silver, bronze), then according to the size and the content of the metal, which of course could quite clearly fluctuate, especially with precious metals such as silver or gold. The imprint on the coin allowed the identification of the power that issued it and thereby helped with the assessment of the quality of the coin, that is, its precious metal content. As need be, one could also control this with scales or a simple scratch.

Although coins were produced in Palestine as early as the fourth century BCE, the high quantity of quite small bronze denominations issued since the late second century BCE marks the beginning of their use for such things as daily transactions at the market. In the course of the first century BCE, the deployment of coins in Palestine constantly increases ("monetization"). The intensified replacement of payment in kind by coins for payment of taxes and tolls or for wages or bonuses for soldiers pushes this process further. Nevertheless, it is assumed that at the time of Jesus, alongside business transactions based on coins, payment in kind and bartering were still widespread.

Differently than bronze coins, silver coins appear in archaeological material in Palestine of the first centuries BCE and CE only in quite small quantities (with a clearly increasing tendency at the time of the Jewish revolt). Gold coins remain extremely rare up until late antiquity. Silver coins served mostly, but not exclusively, for periodical payments of larger amounts (wages, debts; cf. Matt. 18:28, one-hundred δηνάρια; taxes, cf. Mark 12:15 par. δηνάριον) or for storing wealth or for transport of high values—in this regard, they were comparable to jewelry or vessels of precious metals, which could be smelted again. Up until the outbreak of the first revolt against Rome, local Palestinian authorities did not mint silver coins. Jews did, however, use Tyrian silver coins (tetradrachms, equalling two shekels) to pay the temple tax. Not until it was obligatory to exchange "foreign coins" with their objectional images of personalities or pagan symbols (for the silver shekel temple tax, see C.III.2.2.2.2) were some silver coins minted, no doubt for the temple treasury. Then simultaneously the demand for their own national identity appeared and a series of distinctly "Jewish" coins for monetary transactions came to fruition.

2.2.2. Coins in the World of the Jesus Tradition

Coins appear at various places in the Jesus tradition. The details of the texts are not always precise enough to put them unequivocally in a specific system or even in relationship to a specific coin. For example, what in Matt. 5:26 is called a κοδράν-της = *quadrans* is identified in Luke 12:59 as a λεπτόν. "Gold, silver, and copper" is also used according to common parlance as a collective term for "money" (Matt. 10:9; cf. Mark 6:8; Luke 9:3). The terms τάλαντον (Matt. 18:24; 25:14–30) and μνᾶ (only in Luke 19:13, a mina is equivalent to 100 δραχμαί and one sixtieth of a τάλαντον; cf. 4Q159) are encountered in the New Testament as units of measure for enormously large values (a τάλαντον of silver corresponds to six thousand δραχμαί/denarii, a weight of ca. seventy-five pounds) and for metal that had not been minted into coins. In reality this appears to have to do with bars, mostly of silver (cf. Matt. 25:27; Luke 19:15, interest earned in ἀγύρια = silver coins).

2.2.2.1. *Types of Coins in Galilee*

At the time of Jesus, Hasmonean bronze coins from the first century BCE were still widely distributed, and as a rule they display an inscription on the recto (title and name of the ruler) as well as Hellenistic symbols on the verso (quite often cornucopia, also a star, an anchor or a diadem), or less frequently Jewish symbols (palm fronds, lily; under Antigonus Mattathias also for the first time a menorah). Especially frequent, the bronze "anchor star" types of Alexander Janneus (r. 103–76 BCE) are encountered with the value of a prutah (ca. 2 grams) or a half prutah (ca. 1 gram), the smallest denomination. Very probably the Greek word λεπτόν in Mark 12:42 and Luke 12:59 and 21:2 indicates one of these two smallest bronze coins. Also, in later periods, some types of prutot were minted. Alongside the smallest bronze coins, pieces of the next highest unit of weight also circulated (Greek δίλεπτον), but these are not mentioned in the New Testament.

In the course of the new organization of the Orient under Pompey in 63 BCE, Judea fell gradually under Roman control. Following the Roman norm to decentralize power in local instances, also in Palestine the minting of bronze coins was left to the respective regional authorities. Silver and gold denominations, however, came from other regions and satisfied local needs, thereby continuing the large variety and the parallelism of different monetary systems from Hellenistic times. According to archaeological evidence, genuine *Roman* silver coins, like the denarius with Caesar's image in Mark 12:13–17 and parallels, remain quite rare until the arrival of Roman legionnaires during the Jewish war in Palestine (Ostermann 2009, 48–52). The fact that in the New Testament some Roman types of coins are named (*quadrans* = one-fourth of an *as*; *as*/ἀσσάριον = 1/16 of a denarius; the typical Roman *sestertius* is not mentioned) does not contradict this.

Like his Hasmonean predecessors, between 40/37 and 4 BCE, Herod the Great, who thanks to Rome was king over the previous Hasmonean regions and some more Hellenized territories, minted only bronze denominations (evidently at the whim of his own desire; cf. Hübner 2013; overall Ariel and Fontanille 2012, on silver coins, 29–42). Although Herod, like his predecessors, avoided images of himself or of the Caesars on his coins, he systematically utilized "semantically polyvalent" motifs like a Macedonian shield, tripod, diadem, Dioscurian helmet, anchor, or warship, in order to thereby emphasize his rank, his military power, as well as his loyalty to Rome without stressing Jewish sentiments too excessively (Hübner 2013, 108–12; D. Jacobson 2013, 132–41).

After Herod's death, his realm was divided among his sons. Up until 34 or 39 CE, his sons reigned as client rulers over, on the one hand, Galilee and Perea (Antipas), and on the other, Gaulanitis and Trachonitis (Philipp), and in 6 CE Roman rulers from the equestrian class took over from the hapless Archelaus. Neither the sons of Herod nor the rulers of the equestrian class produced silver or gold coinage. Overall, only six of eleven governors up to 66 CE struck any coins (Meshorer 2001, 168). With respect to iconography, the "Jewish" and "pagan" coinage drew closer and closer (Lichtenberger 2013 speaks of a real "motif transfer"). Thus did Jesus's local client ruler Herod Antipas, who had four different bronze denominations minted in negligible amounts in his capital Tiberias ("full" in value from one-eighth or one-twelfth denarius, "half," "one-fourth," and "one-eighth"), consistently avoid likenesses of Caesar or of himself. He nevertheless celebrated his great achievements as ruler (TIBERIAS with a laurel wreath) by inscriptions on his coins or illustrated his loyalty to his imperial Lord Caligula (Meshorer 2001, 82–83). Especially traditional symbols like palm trees and palm fronds as well as again oars of grain were frequent. Also, most coins of procurators depict traditional "Jewish" or generally innocuous symbols like ears of grain or palm trees (Coponious, 6–9 CE) or palm fronds (Festus, 59–62 CE), as well as lilies (Valerius Gratus, 15–26 CE). Only some coins of Pilate (26–36 CE) display decidedly pagan symbols (priestly instruments *simpulum*, *lituus*); others utilize "inoffensive" motifs. Only Felix (52–59 CE) depicted weapons (crossed "Germanic" or "Celtic" shields). The coins are normally dated by the year of the reign of the Caesar under whom the coins were struck. The coins minted likewise in four periods by Antipas's brother Philipp (4 BCE–34 CE) provide another image: they depict both the likenesses of Augustus and Livia and (less frequently) his own, and on the verso often the façade of the *Augusteum* in Philipp's capital city of Caesarea. In comparison with Galilee, Philipp's coinage reflects a much higher number of non-Jewish inhabitants in his territory.

During the first century BCE, free cities also began to disperse coins that displayed symbols that were mostly pagan, stylized buildings, inscriptions, and images of the emperor (mostly bronze, sometimes also silver). Especially Ptolemais, Tyre and Sidon, and Gadara and Hippos were important for the circulation of coins in Galilee.

From 37 to 44 CE, coins from King Herod Agrippa I, who ruled over large parts of Palestine, were clearly adapting to the "imagistic expression of the Roman imperial apparatus" (Lykke 2013b). Alongside some politically significant aniconic depictions (e.g., panoply), depictions of members of the family and a façade of a temple also appear. Exclusively Jewish motifs are absent; more prominent are references to the current members of the emperor's household. Agrippa's sudden death in Caesarea during a festival in honor of the emperor was thus viewed in pious circles as God's punishment (Josephus, *Ant.* 19.343–352; Acts 12:21–23).

2.2.2.2. Coins in the Gospels

Bronze coins are frequently found in the New Testament as the money of the "little people." So, Jesus watches how "the people" put χαλκόν (copper) in the treasury box at the entrance to the temple—appropriately the rich donate more (Mark 12:41). A poor widow passing by can give only two λεπτά with the value of a κοδράντης (*quadrans*; Mark 12:42: the readers of Mark are apparently familiar with Roman monetary standards; in the parallel in Luke 21:2, this equivalence is missing!), which causes Jesus to express great praise. According to Luke 12:6 par. and Matt. 10:29, a sparrow costs an ἀσσάριον (Greek for the Latin *as*), and in Luke 12:59, a vindictive person does not want to forgive his neighbor nor to consider forgiveness, but rather desires his debt to be repaid up to the very last tiny bronze (λεπτόν) (in the parallel in Matt. 5:26, κοδράντης appears again).

For silver coins, two conventional terms are encountered in the New Testament: the Greek δραχμή and the Hellenized Latin δηνάριον (from the Latin *denarius*), without any hint that a recognizable difference between the two monetary systems would be explicitly expressed. This common silver coin weighs about 3.5–4 grams. On the recto the δραχμή/*denarius* bears the ruler's image with an inscription; the verso is variously patterned. Δραχμαί with Greek inscriptions usually come from the eastern mints; *denarii* with Latin inscriptions come from the West and are quite rare in Palestine. According to the texts, *denarii*/δραχμαί were also used in everyday life for special transactions. Thus, according to Luke 10:35, the Good Samaritan pays two δηνάρια for the wounded man to be cared for in the inn. In Matt. 18:28, in a comparison with ten thousand talents (Matt. 18:24), a small debt is measured as one hundred δηνάρια (cf. Luke 7:41). According to Matt. 20:2, 9, 10, and 13, the value of a δηνάριον corresponds roughly to a day's labor for farm workers, with which, according to Rev. 6:6, in times of high prices one could buy only a χοῖνιξ ("volume" = somewhat more than one liter) of wheat. This makes it understandable why a poor homemaker searches so intensively for a lost δραχμή and rejoices extravagantly when she has found it (Luke 15:8–10). According to Mark 6:37 and John 6:7, the disciples desired to buy bread for five thousand hungry people for two hundred δηνάρια, which clearly is less than the three hundred δηνάρια that the expensive nard cost, with which, according to Mark 14:5, the unnamed woman in Bethany anointed Jesus's head (cf. John 12:5).

The two *denarii*/δίδραχμα (ca. 14 grams in weight), which were worth a silver shekel, and which every male Jew had to pay to the temple once each year, present a numismatic exception (Exod. 30:12–16; Neh. 10:32–33). The system of the temple tax meant a transaction of vast sums from all regions of the Mediterranean world to Jerusalem, and it made the temple a big powerful bank. The "Jewish prohibition of images" notwithstanding, apparently for the payment of this tax in the first centuries BCE and CE only silver pieces from the mint of the city of Tyre were used. On one side they show the image of Melqart, the city's patron deity; on the other side, an eagle. The reason for this perhaps is that the content of precious metal of these pieces was especially high or, alternatively, that two drachma pieces were notoriously rare (Meshorer 2001, 72–78; Ariel and Fontanille 2012, 29–42). Other coins, therefore, would have to be converted by money changers on site, which represented a further important factor of the economic system of the Jerusalem temple (Meshorer 2001, 77). However, much remains unclear.

On one occasion in the New Testament there appears to be a direct allusion to this silver shekel. According to Mark 14:11, Judas Iscariot received silver coins from the high priests in return for delivering up Jesus (par. Luke 22:5; according to Matt. 26:15, the amount was exactly thirty ἀγύρια). In view of the cultic and biblical connotations (Zech. 11:12–13 LXX), it is probable that at least Matt. 26:15 alludes to the temple shekel. According to Matt. 17:24, Peter is asked whether or not Jesus pays the two drachma (δίδραχμα). Peter answers in the affirmative, and in Matt. 17:27 he is able by means of a *stater* that is miraculously found in the mouth of a fish to pay the temple tax for himself and Jesus.

Alkier, Stefan. 2003. "'Geld' im Neuen Testament: Der Beitrag der Numismatik zu einer Enzyklopädie des Frühen Christentums." In *Zeichen aus Text und Stein: Studien auf dem Weg zu einer Archäologie des Neuen Testaments*, edited by Stefan Alkier and Jürgen Zangenberg, 308–35. TANZ 42. Tübingen.

Cotton, Hannah M., Leah Di Segni, Werner Eck, Benjamin Isaac, et al., eds. 2010. *Corpus Inscriptionum Iudaeae et Palaestinae*. Vol. 1, *Jerusalem*. Part 1, 1–704. Berlin and New York.

Eck, Werner. 2007. *Rom und Judäa: Fünf Vorträge zur römischen Herrschaft in Palästina*. Tria Corda 2. Tübingen.

Kreitzer, Larry J. 1996. *Striking New Images: Roman Imperial Coinage and the New Testament World*. JSNTSup 1134. Sheffield.

Lykke, Anne, ed. 2013a. *Macht des Geldes—Macht der Bilder: Kolloquium zur Ikonographie auf Münzen im ostmediterranen Raum in hellenistisch-römischer Zeit*. ADPV 42. Wiesbaden.

Schröter, Jens, and Jürgen K. Zangenberg, eds. 2013. *Texte zur Umwelt des Neuen Testaments*. UTB 3663. Tübingen.

Zangenberg, Jürgen K. 2012a. "Archaeology, Papyri, and Inscriptions." In *Early Judaism: A Comprehensive Overview*, edited by John J. Collins et al., 332–66. Winona Lake, IN.

Jürgen K. Zangenberg

D. The Life and Work of Jesus

I. Introduction

The third part of the handbook presents the contours of Jesus's life and work, as they can be reconstructed from the available sources. From the historical materials discussed in greater detail in part B, the political circumstances that are relevant for Jesus's activity will be surveyed. In a general sense, this applies to the structures of the Roman Empire that impacted the situation in Judea, Samaria, and Galilee from the time of the first century BCE. More specifically, it applies to the conditions that can be presupposed for the reign of Herod the Great and the subsequent reigns of his sons Archelaus, Antipas, and Philipp who succeeded him as rulers in Judea and Samaria, Galilee and Peraea as well as in the northeastern regions of the Gaulanitis and adjacent regions.

Concerning the religious circumstances, the developments in Second Temple Judaism, especially of the Maccabean or Hasmonean period, have to be taken into consideration. In this period, certain strands and parties originated in Judaism, which also existed in the time of Jesus, some of which are mentioned in the New Testament. In the historical context outlined in this way, biographical information about Jesus—his origin and his place in Judaism—are to be drawn.

In Jesus research of the twentieth century it has often been emphasized that it is not possible to write a "biography of Jesus," because the sources present Jesus's activity and fate on the basis of Easter faith, and therefore would not provide the information necessary for a historical biography. Even though this is true to a certain degree, nevertheless, aspects can be named that make it possible to place Jesus biographically into his time and the region of his provenance and activity. For this, it must be taken into account that the stories about Jesus's birth and childhood are in essence legendary, and can therefore hardly be used for a historical portrayal. Nevertheless, biographical features can be ascertained from observations on the cultural and religious milieu of Galilee and Judea, in particular, observations on Galilean Judaism for the period in question.

The approach to Jesus's public activity starts with observations on his social context, especially his relationship to John the Baptist and his place in the social and political circumstances of his time. This is followed by a treatment of the significant contents of Jesus's activity and teaching. The distinction between "activity" and "teaching" is of a heuristic and pragmatic character, since it goes without saying that there is a close connection between the two aspects since Jesus's teaching can also be understood as a form of his activity.

The aspects that are discussed bring into view the central contents of Jesus's public activity. Among these are the foundation of a community of followers within Israel, mighty deeds (as, e.g., healings) as well as Jesus's attitude toward groups in his environment such as the Samaritans and people at the margin of society such as tax collectors and sinners, but also toward groups within Israel such as the Pharisees and the Sadducees, and the people of Israel as a whole. Essential contents of Jesus's teaching are expressed in his designation of God as "Father," in the announcement of the dawning of God's kingdom in his own activity, in his attitude toward the Torah as well as his view of judgment and salvation. In this view, in Jesus's activity and teaching a specific self-understanding is revealed that points to his conviction that he himself is the very one who implements God's salvation on earth.

Jesus's ethos is closely connected with the two previously mentioned spheres. It can, however, be conceived of as an independent part of his teaching and his activity. In this ethos the conviction is expressed that a way of life corresponds to the beginning of the kingdom of God, which is oriented toward the radical demands to renounce earthly possessions and an uncompromising caring for the needy.

Finally, a special section is devoted to the passion events. These include both historical questions about the participation of the Sanhedrin in the trial and execution of Jesus and his crucifixion and burial, as well as a consideration of the course and meaning of Jesus's last supper with his disciples in Jerusalem.

In this way the third part of the handbook conveys an overview of the essential contents of Jesus's public activity in its historical context. What emerges is a multifaceted picture of the characteristic features of the activity, teaching, and ethos of the Galilean Jew, Jesus of Nazareth, including the circumstances that led to his execution.

Jens Schröter and Christine Jacobi

II. Political Conditions and Religious Context

1. Political Conditions: Roman Imperial Rule, Herod the Great, Antipas

Palestine in the days of Jesus was nearing the end of three political transitions: a very long-range transition from eastern rule of the Near East to western rule of the Near East; a middle-range transition from sovereign Jewish home rule to rule by a foreign power, Rome; and a very short-range transition from rule by a Roman vassal to direct imperial rule. In all three cases, which we shall consider in turn, it was the final establishment of direct Roman rule in all of Palestine, a mere decade and a half after the crucifixion, that completed the transition.

1.1. From Eastern to Western Domination in the Near East

Understanding the transition from an eastern orientation to a western one requires us only to remember that, for millennia until the fourth century BCE, eastern empires had ruled over the Near East. Whether they were (to confine ourselves to the first millennium BCE) Assyrians or Babylonians, or eventually Medes and Persians, it was always from the east that conquerors and rulers came. True, the fourth century BCE saw a major reorientation, with the conquest of the East by Alexander the Great; Daniel 11, and the first verses of 1 Maccabees, show how this was perceived, in ancient Palestine, as a watershed event. But with Alexander's death, chaos ensued, and when after the wars of his successors ("Diadochi") the smoke cleared and stability was achieved, to the extent that it was, Palestine was once again ruled by kingdoms based either in Egypt (the Ptolemies, until 200 BCE) or in Syria (the Seleucids). Although these were Hellenistic kingdoms, and the Greek culture that came with Alexander was here to stay in the region, they were nevertheless eastern kingdoms. Indeed, scholarship on the Hellenistic world insists more and more on the lasting importance, for the Hellenistic kingdoms, of the eastern cultures that subsisted despite the changes at the top.

Moreover, even through the second and first centuries BCE, and into the first century CE as well, the possibility of an eastern revanche was still quite real. In the second century BCE, the Parthian kingdom, expanding away from its ancestral homeland near the Caspian Sea, encroached more and more upon the Seleucid kingdom and thus contributed to shrinking it from one based in Mesopotamia to one based in Syria; north of the Seleucids other powerful kingdoms, such as Pergamum, Pontus, and Armenia, would raise their heads, also at times at the Seleucids' expense; and, to their south, and of most immediate relevance here, the Hasmonean dynasty rebelled against the Seleucids in Judea, around the same time that an Iturean state in Lebanon and an Arabian ("Nabatean") kingdom began to grow as well. Thus the East was still alive and well.

However, apart from those eastern powers that flourished in the second century BCE, that century also saw the powerful incursion into the east of a new western power, the Roman republic. After consolidating its control of Italy in the fourth and third centuries BCE, and crushing Carthage by the end of the third, Rome was now ready to move eastward: in the first decades of the second century, it put its power to work against the Seleucids, imposing military defeat and debilitating terms upon Antiochus III in 190 BCE, and high-handedly expelling his son, Antiochus IV, from Egypt in 168 BCE. This Roman involvement, although only sporadic at the beginning, worked at first to help the eastern powers who profited from the weakening of the Seleucid kingdom; the Hasmonean rulers of Judea even formalized this relationship with Rome in a series of treaties (see 1 Macc. 8; 12; and 15), and they were not the only ones. In the end, however, as the Seleucids weakened more and more, the other eastern states would come into direct confrontation with Rome, and they all fell to it one after another, one way or another. Attalus III of Pergamum bequeathed Pergamum to Rome upon his death in 133 BCE; in 85 BCE, after a long struggle, Sulla defeated Mithridates VI of Pontus; in 66 BCE Pompey defeated Tigranes the Great of Armenia, just a few years after Tigranes had ruled Syria for a decade and a half (83–69 BCE) and just a few years before Pompey himself went on to conquer Syria in 64 and Judea in 63 BCE; and Egypt too would fall, to Octavian (soon to be Augustus), in 30 BCE. Thus, the romantic death of Anthony and Cleopatra, three hundred years after the death of Alexander, seemingly reestablished western rule in the East.

That was so, but not totally, and at the time could not be taken for granted. First, and most importantly, Parthia remained beyond the reach of Rome. Alexander had conquered Mesopotamia (and well past it), but Rome never conquered the Parthian kingdom. Although the Euphrates basically came to serve as the border between the two superpowers, and thus between East and West, they went on fighting off and on for centuries, and no one could know how that would end; the Parthians successfully invaded the Roman East in 40 BCE and held onto it for three years, and the fear of that happening again remained alive and well. As we shall see, the ruler of the Galilee in Jesus's day, Herod Antipas ("the fox" of Luke 13:32), was removed from office, and expelled to Gaul, in 39 CE, because the emperor Tiberius became convinced that he was conspiring with the Parthians against Rome (Josephus, *Ant.* 18.250–252).

Secondly, although Rome conquered the region, and although in the major cases it established direct Roman rule (so, for example, Pergamum became the nucleus of the Province of Asia, Seleucid Syria became *Provincia Syria*, and Ptolemaic Egypt became an imperial province), in some cases, due to this or that circumstance or consideration, or simply due to lack of any pressing need to do anything, Rome allowed the continuation of home rule under conditions of vassalage. In such regions, this lack of finality could contribute, just as much as the lasting existence of the Parthian threat, to the hope for a local, eastern, comeback. Judea was one such small exception, and that brings us to the middle-range transition: from sovereign Jewish home rule to rule by a foreign power.

1.2. From Sovereign Jewish Rule to Foreign Roman Rule

As it happened, at the time that Pompey arrived in Syria and annexed it (64 BCE), in Judea two brothers, Aristobulus II and Hyrcanus II, the heirs of King Janneus Alexander (d. 76 BCE) and his widow and successor, Queen Salome Alexandra (d. 67 BCE), were fighting each other for the throne of the Hasmonean kingdom, which had been established after the Maccabean Revolt against the Seleucids a century earlier. Both brothers vied for Pompey's support, Hyrcanus received it, and so the Roman conquest of Jerusalem in the summer of 63 BCE amounted to a victory for Hyrcanus—and Pompey, for whatever reason, let it remain one. True, he did not allow Hyrcanus to be king of Judea. But neither did he annex Judea as a Roman province. Rather, he allowed Hyrcanus to continue as a vassal ruler with the title "high priest"; at some point, Hyrcanus also received an additional title, "ethnarch" (Josephus, *Ant.* 14.191).

True, the former title implies religious authority and the latter, if taken literally (and especially in light of the denial of "king"), applies to authority over the Jewish *ethnos* (people), not to the land itself (see Sharon 2010). And those meaningful formal moves to separate Hyrcanus from rule of the land were seconded by real measures as well: Pompey cut off, from Hyrcanus's realm of authority, numerous cities in Palestine that were populated by gentiles. Those cities had been conquered by the Hasmoneans but were now detached from Judea and put under the control of the Roman governor of the newly founded *Provincia Syria*. Thus, Hyrcanus did not rule all of Palestine, as his parents had. Paradoxically, however, that cutting-down-to-size of Hyrcanus's realm implied that he did rule what was left. That implication, together with a lack of Roman moves to make its hegemony apparent, meant that the Judeans could go on believing, for all practical purposes, that they were still living in the Hasmonean state. And the fact that Rome was involved in a long civil war during those middle decades of the first century BCE contributed, of course, to the lack of certainty about the finality of Rome's takeover of the East.

Indeed, apparently many Judeans did go on believing that the loss of independent Hasmonean rule was not a *fait accompli*. We read that Aristobulus II and his sons, although exiled by Pompey to Rome, continued time and again to escape and return to Judea, raise troops among their supporters, and attempt to retake power. This means that, in their eyes, the Hasmonean state still had a chance, and it was worthwhile to fight for rule of it. Similarly, it is no surprise that the most successful attempt of such a comeback, by one of Aristobulus's sons, came with Parthian help. In 40 BCE, in the early stages of the Parthian invasion of the Roman East, Aristobulus's son Mattathias Antigonus threw in his lot with the Parthians, exchanging his support for them for the royal title, which he was able to retain until, toward the end of their reconquest of the East at large, the Romans retook Judea in 37 BCE.

Even then, however, Rome did not annex Judea. It retained it as a vassal state, appointing a new Jewish ruler instead of Hyrcanus (who had been taken prisoner by the Parthians, and anyway was ineffective and getting old). That new ruler was Herod, the son of an influential and successful advisor and administrator, Antipater (d. 43 BCE), who had been Hyrcanus's right-hand man. Herod, who inherited his father's talents and had been entrusted with the governorship of the Galilee in the 40s, fled to Rome when Judea was taken over by the Parthians, and Octavian and Mark Anthony had the Senate appoint him Rome's client king of Judea, to oppose Parthia's client king there, Antigonus. Accordingly, much the same as in 63 BCE when Rome's victory had been Hyrcanus's, it was now to Herod that the spoils went when the Romans, after throwing the Parthians back across the Euphrates in 38, defeated and beheaded Antigonus for him in 37.

Herod, who was about thirty-five in 37 BCE, lived a long life, reigning until his death in 4 BCE. Here we have no need to survey his reign in general, but will underline two principles that were fundamental for his long survival. They will also allow us to understand what changed in the period of short-range transition in the decades after his death, which were the decades of Jesus's life. Those two principles encapsulate Herod's dealings with his overlords and with his subjects: total submission to Rome, on the one hand, and separation of religion from state, on the other. The former amounted to a recognition of the facts of life; the latter was meant to avoid clashes between Herod and his Jewish subjects.

1.2.1. Total Submission to Rome

As noted above, Herod was made king of Judea by the Roman Senate, at the behest of Octavian and Anthony, in 40 BCE. Two years earlier, however, that would not have been foreseen. That is because Herod, as governor of the Galilee, had proven himself a very efficient agent of law and order, and tax collection, in the service of Cassius Longinus, who was then ruling Roman Syria; since Cassius was then at war against Octavian and Anthony, and lost that war (being defeated at Philippi in 42 BCE), one might have expected the victors to punish Herod. Herod, however, still nominally working as an agent of Hyrcanus II's regime, went to meet Anthony in Bithynia and convinced him, despite opposition from other Judeans, to keep him on in his position (Josephus, *Ant.* 14.301–302). In doing so, Herod could depend not only on his charm and on his late father's connections with Julius Caesar and Anthony, but also on the argument that he had served Cassius not because he supported his side in the civil war. Rather, he had loyally served Cassius because he was the Roman ruler of the region, and Anthony (and his partner at the time, Octavian) could now expect the same from him. Whatever the arguments, Anthony bought them (and perhaps they were reinforced by an appropriate bribe—*Ant.* 14.303). So it happened that, when two years later the Parthians invaded Judea, Herod was Rome's man there. After he managed to flee to Rome, Octavian and Anthony confirmed him as their representative in Judea; they upgraded him to king so he could compete with Antigonus (whom the Parthians had enthroned as king), and eventually sent Roman forces to enforce their decision.

Similarly, a few years later, after Octavian and Anthony divided the Roman world between them, with Anthony ruling the East and Cleopatra ruling him, and Octavian ruling the West, when Octavian defeated Anthony and Cleopatra at Actium, in 31 BCE, Herod again found himself in the losing camp. Just as in the wake of Philippi, so too in the wake of Actium there was every reason to expect that his overlord's defeat would be Herod's downfall as well. However, Herod presented himself to Octavian at Rhodes, defended himself as having been loyal to Rome (this time the argument is explicit: *Ant.* 15.187–193), and this time too he came away confirmed in his position.

And Herod was as good as his word. Throughout his reign, he was careful to be demonstrative and even ostentatious about his loyalty to Octavian/Augustus, in a variety of ways, of which the most prominent were participation in Roman military campaigns as needed (*Ant.* 15.198–201, 317) and, especially, the founding of cities in honor of Augustus (Caesarea and Sebaste) and other prominent Romans; according to Josephus, who gives a long list of Herod's building projects in their honor (*J.W.* 1.401–416), "All in all, there is no respectable place to speak of in his kingdom that he allowed to remain without (a sign of) honor to Caesar" (§407). Whether or not we believe Josephus (*Ant.* 15.361), that Herod was Augustus's best friend apart from Marcus Vispanius Agrippa (Augustus's son-in-law and chief lieutenant), and Agrippa's best friend apart from Augustus, it is clear that Herod's loyalty to Augustus was the foundation upon which his throne rested.

1.2.2. Separation of Religion from State

Along with that positive foundation, however, there was another basic element of Herod's policy, a negative one meant to keep the Jewish population of his kingdom docile: a separation of religion from state. For several generations prior to the Roman takeover, and even during the generation of Hyrcanus II after that takeover, Judea had been ruled by Hasmonean high priests, who could—and did—rule with the help of the implicit or explicit claim that they were agents of the God of Israel, ruling God's land on behalf of God. Herod, in contrast, could not be a high priest. He was of Idumean descent, and there was no way that he could aspire to the priesthood; indeed, even apart from being a "commoner" (i.e., not a priest; *Ant.* 14.78, 489, etc.), some cast doubt on his being Jewish at all (see, inter alia, *Ant.* 14.403 ["half-Jew"] and 19.332 [even his grandson is not considered a "native"]). How, then, could he deal with the Jewish religion?

It seems that at the outset of his reign Herod thought he could co-opt the Hasmoneans: he married a Hasmonean princess, Mariamme, and installed her brother, Aristobulus III, as high priest. But if that was supposed to allow him to enhance his legitimacy as a Jewish ruler, and not just as a vassal of Rome, it did not work: the Jewish population evinced so much enthusiasm for Aristobulus, as opposed to Herod, that Herod was forced to organize the youth's death in a swimming accident, and Mariamme (and the rest of the survivors of her Hasmonean family) evinced such arrogance toward Herod that in short order he found he had to kill them all.

That, however, did not lead Herod simply to attempt to crush the Jewish religion as well. Rather, it led him to adopt a benevolent hands-off policy: he appointed high priests from families with no political aspirations (M. Stern 1982), while he himself ran the state without involving himself in affairs of the Jewish religion, apart from appointing and firing high priests (which made sure they stayed out of affairs of state) and from offering that religion his support, especially by his monumental renovation of the temple of Jerusalem.

By and large, that policy worked: Herod's illegitimacy as a Jewish ruler was neutralized by his abstention from asserting himself as a Jewish ruler. Rather, he was the ruler of the kingdom of Judea, who invested just as massively and successfully in Jerusalem as he did in building the pagan cities of his realm—as also he did in supporting projects around the Roman world (see Josephus, *J. W.* 1.401–428 and a detailed list: Richardson 1996, 197–202).

These two basic policies, of maintaining wonderful relations with Rome and a benevolent but hands-off relationship with Judaism, allowed Herod a basically peaceful and prosperous reign. The terrible stories with which his name is linked have to do with difficulties within his own family, mostly in the last decade of his life. The stories are nasty, as might be expected when an aging king has nine or ten wives and, therefore, too many potential heirs, who are increasingly impatient as he continues to age far beyond normal life expectancy in his day, but they do not have many implications for his regime as a whole.

A focus on Herod's two basic policies is also basic for an understanding of the third and final transition that this brief essay addresses, namely, the short-range transition from vassal rule to direct Roman rule.

1.3. Short-Range Transition from Vassal Rule to Direct Roman Rule

When Herod died, in 4 BCE, Augustus decided not to preserve Judea as a kingdom. Rather, adhering in the main to what is said to have been Herod's final will (Josephus, *Ant.* 17.188–189), the emperor divided the kingdom into three principalities, awarding one each to three of Herod's sons. Already this division of the realm was a fairly clear announcement of the intention eventually to annex the country. And that was seconded by Augustus's decision to deny the royal title to all three heirs, instead granting "ethnarch" to Archelaus (Matt. 2:22 wrongly refers to him as reigning as king), who received the Judean and Samarian heartland, and "tetrarch" to the other two: Herod Antipas, who received Jewish-occupied territories in the Galilee and Transjordan north of the Dead Sea, and Philip, who received further-flung and mostly gentile-inhabited territories in the north. Little principalities, ruled by second-rate rulers, were of course easy prey to be absorbed into the empire, and within half a century of Herod's death—the half century that was the stage for Jesus's career—that is in fact what happened.

Each stage of that story had, of course, its own circumstances. Augustus exiled Archelaus to Gaul in 6 CE, and his territory was made subject to direct Roman rule. It is uncertain whether this involved the establishment of a Roman province (*Provincia Iudaea*, as Josephus claims in *J.W.* 2.117) or only the annexation of Judea to *Provincia Syria*, as he claims in *Ant.* 17.355 and 18.2. It seems, however, that the difference between those alternatives is not much more than semantic. There is, on the one hand, plenty of evidence for involvement of the governors of Syria in Judea, especially when disorders had to be quelled, and it does not matter much if they did that only because they had legions at their disposal or, rather, because Judea was formally part of their province. On the other hand, there is plenty of evidence for Roman officials in Judea, charged with keeping Roman law and order, including military units and tax-collectors (such as the Gospels' "publicans"), and for Judeans the question how the province was defined will not have mattered much.

As for *why* Augustus exiled Archelaus: Josephus reports (*Ant.* 17.342) that he did so because Archelaus's Judean and Samaritan subjects complained that he was cruel and tyrannous. That might well be so, but the case of Herod shows well that cruelty on the part of a ruler, if claimed to be in the interest of preserving law and order (and subservience to the empire), need not be looked at askance in Rome; after all, "a widely publicized potential to wreak havoc was certainly a powerful political asset for the greatest state-builder of the time, Augustus" (S. Schwartz 2014, 59–60). Thus perhaps we should simply view this first annexation of Judea as what an empire that had set out on the "divide and conquer" course might be expected to do. Similarly, when Philip's territory was annexed to Syria after he died in 34 CE, his childlessness may have made that decision all the easier; but (as we shall see) when ten years later Agrippa I died and did leave an heir, that did not stop Claudius from annexing his kingdom. As for Herod Antipas—he was exiled to Gaul in 39 CE; as noted above, the charge was that he had been colluding with the Parthians.

That charge was bad enough. But there may have been more as well. Herod Antipas was tetrarch of the Galilee, and to the—unknown—extent that anyone in Rome had any specific information about regions of Judea, the Galilee must have stood out, in fact and in image, as a hotbed of anti-Roman rebelliousness (for a survey, cf. esp. Loftus, 1977–1978). It was the scene of rebellion against Rome already in Herod's day, and after his death, and again in 6 CE (when a Judean rebellion against the first Roman census in Judea was led by one Judas the Galilean—Acts 5:37), and then again in the days of Pontius Pilate, when we hear of "the Galileans whose blood Pilate mixed with their sacrifices" (Luke 13:1) and, of course, of Jesus of Nazareth and his followers, who too were rebels in Roman eyes and treated accordingly. So if, as Herod the Great knew well, the first obligation of a ruler in the Roman world was to preserve Roman rule, Herod Antipas was a failure. Moreover, to ice that cake: if Herod well understood that, as a vassal of Rome, he had to abstain from warfare (apart from supporting Roman efforts) and from all independent foreign policy, Herod Antipas broke those rules: he both meddled in international politics, thus arousing the resentment of powerful enemies in Rome (*Ant.* 18.104–105), and became embroiled in a war of his own, against the Nabateans, which would require the intervention of a Roman army (*Ant.* 18.109–115, 120–125).

So much for the afterlife of Herod's first principle: total subservience to Rome. It has been supposed that Archelaus too deviated from it, as is suggested by the fact that although he was active in building projects (*Ant.* 17.340), though on a smaller scale than his father before him, he built a town in his own honor (Archelaus) but none in honor of Augustus or any other Roman. Perhaps he resented the denial of the royal title (Bernett 2007, 182–83, 188). However that may be, it is certainly the case that Herod Antipas, whether due to lack of ability or lack of trying, did not manage to keep his subjects the way Rome would like them.

As for Herod's second principle, his hands-off policy vis-à-vis the Jewish religion, its role in the establishment of direct Roman rule is more indirect. To understand it, we should revert to the anomaly we have mentioned a few times and ask: Why did the Romans abstain, for such a long time, from annexing Judea? Why did seventy years have to go by, from Pompey's conquest of Judea to Augustus's decision, upon exiling Archelaus, to establish direct Roman rule? The answer would seem to be that Judea was anomalous from a Roman point of view. The Romans knew how to conquer kingdoms and how to appoint governors instead of native kings, and that was, in fact, the nature of their empire, as any empire: empires conquer and annex, as Rome had done in Pontus, Armenia, Asia, Syria, and Egypt, to mention only the main eastern examples cited above. But dealing with a state ruled by a high priest, and centered upon a temple, was another story. And the Jews' monotheism too posed a problem, sowing intolerance and sensitivities with which it was difficult for outsiders to deal (Bernett 2007, 182–83, 188; Momigliano 1986). Better to have some Jewish buffer, a vassal, between the Jews and the Romans. This explains why Hyrcanus II was allowed to stay on after the Roman conquest in 63 BCE, and is one important reason, among some others, why the Romans allowed Herod to rule after their reconquest of Judea in 37 BCE.

But Herod's long reign had demonstrated that it was possible to separate the Jewish religion from the state, and the state could then be a normal kingdom. Indeed, Herod strove to make this point to his Roman overlords; as an emblematic example of that, one need think only of the way he fitted out Herodium as his guesthouse for prominent Roman visitors, making every effort to make them feel at home in a Roman ambience (cf. now Porat, Chachy, and Kalman 2015). From the way he received Romans at Caesarea, welcoming them with statues of Rome and of the emperor (*Ant.* 15.339), to the way he hosted them at Herodium, Herod made it clear to the Romans that Judea was a regular part of the Roman world. But that left the rulers of the empire with no reason, neither Jewish nor monotheistic, to abstain from the basic nature of their empire (as of any other empire), which was to conquer and to annex. While the Jewish religion continued to exist and even to thrive in Judea, Rome had—or thought it had—no reason to think that its continued existence, and that of the temple, posed any more of a contradiction to Roman rule than did the existence of numerous synagogues in Rome itself (D. Schwartz 2009).

And what was true for Judea could certainly be true for the Galilee. So if in 6 CE Augustus did not hold back from annexing Judea, although it was centered around Jerusalem and that which made it such an eminently Jewish place, the temple, certainly he—or, as it happened, his successors: Tiberius, Gaius, and Claudius—would have no reason to hesitate about annexing the territories of Philip and Herod Antipas, which were far from Judea proper and had no such obvious link to the Jewish religion. In fact, they were separated from Judea by Samaria, where the Samaritans had had their own temple that competed with that of the Jews (cf. John 4:20; *Ant.* 13.256; 18.29–31; 20.118); as such, the Romans might well expect the Galileans to be willing to behave like Jews of the diaspora.

It would seem, therefore, that all should have been over within a decade of the crucifixion, by 39 CE, when Gaius Caesar exiled Herod Antipas; we would expect to hear that he then established direct Roman rule in Herod Antipas's territories, just as in those of Archelaus in 6 and of Philip in 34, thus completing the Roman annexation of Palestine. Indeed, that would have been quite logical, as I have attempted to explain, however summarily. However, things were not quite over in 39 CE; history does not run by logic alone, and now and then circumstances hold things up or even change their course. In this case, there was such a circumstance and it did hold things up. Just as Herod's own personal friendship with Octavian/Augustus played some role in preserving him in office, so too did Agrippa I, a grandson of Herod's, who had grown up in Rome and was well connected with the imperial family, manage to ingratiate himself to such an extent that when Gaius exiled Herod Antipas in 39 CE he gave his territories to Agrippa. Moreover, already in 37 CE Gaius had detached Philip's territories from Syria and given them to Agrippa, and in 41 CE Claudius, who succeeded Gaius, gave Agrippa Judea and Samaria as well. Thus, between 37 and 41 CE there was, due to Agrippa's personal connections (and perhaps some lack of satisfaction with the success of provincial rule, as demonstrated by troubles under Pilate and again under Gaius), a complete reversal of the short-range trend to annex Palestine into the Roman Empire.

Agrippa I's kingdom, however, although a striking example of the power of individuals to divert history from its course, was also quite short-lived, and ended up testifying to the basic power of historical trends, despite the occasional delay or detour engendered by this or that personal circumstance. Within three years of the restoration of all of Herod's kingdom under his grandson, Agrippa I, he died (43/44 CE; see Acts 12:21–23), whereupon Claudius annexed all of Judea and began sending Roman governors to govern the entire country. And he did that, as noted above, even though Agrippa left a sixteen-year-old son, Agrippa II, who could well have taken over in his stead. That is, Agrippa I's rule turns out to be ironic: it was the mechanism by which all three parts of Herod's kingdom were reunited, only to be subjugated, together, to direct Roman rule. And so would Palestine remain, despite two major revolts (in 66–73 and 132–136 CE) and various other ups and downs, until the Arab conquest of the country in the seventh century CE.

To summarize: the political context of Jesus's career was the final completion of the establishment of western rule in the Near East, of the move from Jewish home rule to indirect Roman imperial rule via Jewish vassals, and of the move from indirect Roman imperial rule via Jewish vassals to direct Roman rule via Roman governors. With regard to the Galilee in particular, the latter transition, which corresponded to the basic nature of empire, was perhaps catalyzed by the vassal ruler's (Herod Antipas's) lack of success in maintaining law and order for Rome, and it was certainly made possible by a Roman realization, facilitated by Herod's policy vis-à-vis the Jewish religion, that, despite the idiosyncrasies of Judaism and monotheism, it was possible to rule Palestine just like any other part of the Roman empire.

Looking back, *we* can see that all three processes culminated in the mid-40s, with the full establishment of direct Roman rule in Judea after the death of Agrippa I. And we also know that, only some two decades later, a major Judean revolt that aimed to turn history around failed miserably and, completing all three processes, brought about the destruction of the Jewish capital of the country and what made it what it was, namely, the temple of Jerusalem. But we can also understand that people who were living at the time could not know how things would end. Especially for Jews who were familiar with biblical and other promises of a messianic future, the realization that things were in flux could well have contributed to their readiness to believe that the time was ripe for the establishment of a new kingdom.

Bernett, Monika. 2007. *Der Kaiserkult in Judäa unter den Herodiern und Römern.* WUNT 203. Tübingen.

Loftus, Francis. 1977–1978. "The Anti-Roman Revolts of the Jews and the Galileans." *JQR* 68: 78–98.

Momigliano, Arnaldo. 1986. "The Disadvantages of Monotheism for a Universal State." *CP* 81: 285–97.

Porat, Roi, Rachel Chachy, and Yakov Kalman. 2015. *Herodium: Final Reports of the 1972–2010 Excavations Directed by Ehud Netzer.* Vol. 1, *Herod's Tomb Precinct.* Jerusalem.

Richardson, Peter. 1996. *Herod: King of the Jews and Friend of the Romans.* Columbia, SC.

Schwartz, Daniel R. 2009. "One Temple and Many Synagogues: On Religion and State in Herodian Judaea and Augustan Rome." In *Herod and Augustus*, edited by David M. Jacobson and Nikos Kokkinos, 385–98. Leiden.

Schwartz, Seth. 2014. *The Ancient Jews from Alexander to Muhammed.* Cambridge.

Sharon, Nadav. 2010. "The Title *Ethnarch* in Second Temple Period Judea." *JSJ* 41: 472–93.

Stern, Menahem. 1982. "Social and Political Realignments in Herodian Judaea." *Jerusalem Cathedra* 2: 40–62.

Daniel R. Schwartz

2. Religious Context

2.1. Historical, Cultural, and Religio-Political Background

In the wake of Alexander the Great's conquest expedition, contacts between Greeks and the Near Eastern world intensified and broadened. After the Hellenistic kingdoms had emerged from the Diadochi Wars, Palestine and southern Syria (as "Syria and Phoenicia") were subject to the rule of the Ptolemaic dynasty for virtually a century after 301 BCE. In this time, in various parts and social contexts of the empire, Greek became established in varying degrees as the common language. Whereas Greek became the administrative language and the Judeans living in Egypt (some of whom were taken there under Ptolemy I) began to write their documents in Greek, those in Judea, by contrast, continued to use Aramaic along with Greek, and for certain purposes also Hebrew. Ptolemy's realm was a well-organized, centralized state. It was administered by the king, who claimed divine honor. His διοικητής, the "economic and finance minister," stood at his side. The land itself "belonged" to the king, and others could merely lease it. The tightly organized tax system was in the hands of numerous tax farmers. Egypt's heartland was divided into "districts" (νομοί); the provinces were divided into "hyparchies." For the province of "Syria and Phoenicia," the following hyparchies are attested: Judea, Samaria, Galilee, Idumea, and Ashdod (the land of the Philistines), as well as Ammanitis in Transjordan. The hyparchy of Judea constitutes an exception in that it was not administered by a στρατηγός but by the high priests in Jerusalem, and thereby it retained a certain kind of limited autonomy.

At the battle of Paneas in 200 BCE (some date it in 198), the Seleucid king Antiochus III succeeded in conquering the province. From then until 143 BCE, the province, under the name of Coele-Syria, belonged to the Seleucid kingdom. It was subdivided into the following four "eparchies": Idumea, Paralia (the land on the coast), Samaria, and Gilead. Samaria in turn was divided into Samaria in the narrow sense and Judea. The Seleucid kingdom was less tightly administered than the Ptolemaic kingdom. Uprisings and military conflicts contributed to its destabilization. At the beginning of his reign, Antiochus III appears to have pledged in a decree to the inhabitants of Jerusalem and its surrounding region the exemption from taxes and other privileges, including permission to live according to their "ancestral laws" (Josephus, *Ant.* 12.138–144). The high priesthood was initially held by the family of the Oniads: the successor of the high priest Simon II, the luminary of Sirach (Sir. 50:1–21), was Onias III, whose actions were less felicitous. After high reparation payments had been imposed on the Seleucids in the Treaty of Apamea in 188 BCE, the office of high priest was dragged into competing tribute pledges. With such a pledge Onias's brother Jason, who was more strongly hellenized, gained the tenure of the office at Antiochus IV's accession to the throne. In exchange for a further monetary contribution, he attained permission from the king to construct an exercise and education center (γυμνάσιον) and a training ground for youth (ἐφηβεῖον), and further to enroll the population of Jerusalem "as citizens of Antioch" (2 Macc. 4:9–10). With this transformation of Jerusalem following the model of a Hellenistic city, the Torah as the constitution of the Judean ethnos was suspended, and the liberties granted by Antiochus III lost their validity for Jerusalem. After Jason had been forced out of the high priesthood by Menelaus, who was supported by the Tobiads, the situation grew worse. Jason attempted a revolt, but he failed, and he had to flee. Antiochus IV reacted with a punitive action, apparently backed and advised by Menelaus, who pushed for the Judeans to conform to Near Eastern cults. The king issued edicts that made it illegal for the inhabitants of Jerusalem to live according to their "ancestral laws." Under the threat of death, he coerced them to adopt pagan customs; to abandon sacrifices in the temple and to erect altars for the slaughtering of unclean animals as well as temples and images of the gods; and to do away with the Sabbath and the festivals. He also prohibited circumcision (so, according to 1 Macc. 1:44–50; cf. 2 Macc. 6:1–7). The "desolating abomination" was erected on the altar of burnt offerings (*shiqquṣ [me]shomem*— possibly an allusion to the Near Eastern god Baʻal shamin; Dan. 9:27; 11:31; 12:11), essentially a baetyl stone, in which the god was venerated.

When the command regarding pagan sacrifice was to be enforced in the vicinity of Jerusalem, the Maccabees revolted around the priest Mattathias and his sons, especially Judas, with the nickname "Makkabaios" (so the Greek form from the Hebrew *maqqebet*, "hammer"). Following a guerilla uprising, the insurgents achieved the revocation of the prohibition of the Torah and some of its practices (cf. 2 Macc. 11:16–33). Subsequently Judas and his people conquered Jerusalem, and on the twenty-fifth of Kislev 164 BCE (or 165) they reestablished temple worship with new equipment and a newly constructed altar of burnt offerings (cf. 1 Macc. 4:36–59; 2 Macc. 10:1–8). At the beginning of the Seleucid succession crisis in the following years, Demetrius I installed the high priest Alcimus, who was moderately hellenized, whereupon the fighting flared up again. After that, in 150 BCE Alexander Balas, who had usurped the throne, appointed Jonathan, the brother of Judas (who in the meantime had been killed in battle), as the "friend of the king" and high priest of the people. Subsequently, the dynasty, designated "Hasmonean," after an ancestor, consolidated its rule. In 142 BCE another brother, Simon, was authorized as "High Priest, Commander, and Ethnarch of the Judeans" (1 Macc. 13:42). Following him, John Hyrcanus I was in office from 134 to 104 BCE. Under him territorial expansion took place and the Idumeans were subdued and conformed to Judaism—he "permitted them to stay in that country, if they would circumcise their genitals, and make use of the laws of the Judeans" (Josephus, *Ant.* 13.257; on Hyrcanus's action against the Samaritans, see D.II.2.3 below). Hyrcanus's son Aristobulus I (104–103 BCE) was the first Hasmonean to adopt the title "king." He pushed the expansion toward the north, and he required the Itureans who lived on the northern edge of Galilee to be circumcised and to live according to the Torah if they wished to remain in the land (*Ant.* 13.318). In addition, his brother Alexander Jannaeus (103–76 BCE) gained Transjordan territories and important cities such as Gaza. Alexander's widow, Salome Alexandra (76–67 BCE), appointed Hyrcanus II high priest, whose conflict with his younger brother Aristobulus II (67–63 BCE) brought the Romans under Pompey into the arena.

2.2. Integration and Diversification in the Judaism of Hellenistic-Roman Times

Judaism in Hellenistic-Roman times is characterized by a dialectic relationship of integration and diversification. Integration comes about through a series of common, fundamental concepts and institutions. By contrast, diversification arises on the one hand by differences between local institutions and practices (especially between the temple in Jerusalem and places of residence in the land of Israel and the diaspora), and on the other hand on the basis of the different interpretations and appropriations of common concepts and institutions by the various groups within the Judaism of the era. In terms of the history of research, such a view of early Judaism can be viewed as developing and modifying the model of "common Judaism" advanced by E. P. Sanders (1992). His model emphasizes commonality, but thereby gives too little consideration to the profile of distinct groups. For reasons of space, the following account does not deal in any detail with the Judaism of the diaspora (on this, see Barclay 1996): the latter is discussed only to the extent that it is relevant for Judaism in the land of Israel.

2.2.1. Institutions of Judaism in Hellenistic-Roman Times

First to be mentioned here is the Jerusalem temple. According to Jewish understanding, it was the place on earth where God allowed the divine name to dwell. Only here could sacrifices be offered (the Oniad Temple in Leontopolis, Egypt, was a temporary and peripheral matter). The Second Temple was dedicated in the spring of 515 BCE (Ezra 6:16). After its desecration under Antiochus IV, it was dedicated anew in December 164 (or 165) BCE in the context of the Maccabean revolt (1 Macc. 4:52–59; 2 Macc. 10:5–8). After an inner court of the temple had already been set apart in pre-Maccabean times (Josephus, *Ant.* 12.141), Herod I extended the temple compound on a grand scale (Josephus, *J.W.* 5.184–227; Mishnah Middot contains relevant details, but on the whole is idealized). The work was not finished until 63 CE (*Ant.* 20.219). Herod had the temple enlarged to about twice its size (144,000 square meters) and added a wall enclosure, partially of giant stone blocks. Upon entering it, one arrived first in the Court of the Gentiles. It was bordered by a barrier three cubits high (1.5 meters) on which there were stone plaques that warned non-Jews upon pain of death not to enter the inner area. Jewish males and females were permitted to proceed farther over some steps, provided they were ritually clean when they came up to the inner wall with ten gates. From there Jewish women entered into the Court of Women, Jewish men into the Court of the Israelites. This was separated from the court of the priests by a low barrier only a cubit high. The altar of burnt offering, the slaughtering block, and the water basin were located there. This was the area where the sacrifices were brought. Twelve steps led from this court to the temple building. This was two stories tall; the elevated lower story was further subdivided into the longer front hall and the holy of holies. The priests entered the front hall first through an open entrance and then through a gate, before (?) which hung a colorful woven curtain. This symbolized the universe (Josephus, *J.W.* 5.212–213). The seven-armed candelabrum (*menorah*), the table of showbread, and the altar of incense were in the front hall itself. An additional curtain set off the space called the holy of holies: "In this there was nothing at all. No one was allowed to enter it, or touch it, or even to look into it" (*J.W.* 5.219). Only the high priest entered it once a year on the Day of Atonement. Unlike in other sanctuaries, there was no cult image. Colonnades were stretched along the inner walls of the temple, the largest of which, the "Royal Stoa," stood on the south side.

Sacrifices and associated activities were at the center of what took place at the temple. Along with this, prayers and the recitation of passages from the Torah by priests as well as the singing of hymns and the blowing of trumpets took place at designated times. The priests were divided into twenty-four classes, which were assigned to weeklong rotations to oversee sacrifices. The Levites assisted them as gatekeepers and temple singers. Communal and individual sacrifices were distinguished from each other. To the first classification belonged the daily burnt offering (*tamid*)—a lamb in the morning and again in the afternoon— the Sabbath burnt offering and the additional offerings for new moons, annual festivals, and the Day of Atonement, each of which consisted of several burnt offerings and a ram as a sin offering. Following biblical prescriptions (Josephus deviates from this in details), the offerings brought by individuals included sin offerings for certain unintentional offenses (Lev. 4) and those that lepers had to bring for their purification (Lev. 14); guilt offerings for offenses against property or what is consecrated (Lev. 5), a type also used as one of the sacrifices of a purifying leper; as well as *shelamim* sacrifices, at which the meat was consumed corporately (Lev. 3). In addition to cattle and small livestock, the offering of a pair of (turtle)doves was permitted for certain kinds of sacrifices (such as for the purification sacrifice of persons who had suffered from discharges, Lev. 15:14–15, 29–30). These could also take the place of other sacrificial animals for poor people (such as the purification sacrifice by women at the birth of a child, Lev. 12:8). Offerings of grain and drink accompanied the animal sacrifices. Thus, only some offerings served the purpose of expiation. Thanksgiving or a gift to God was at the forefront of others, and still others concluded the processes of purification. Although in continuation of prophetic critiques of the cult the temple worship was time and again perceived as inadequate, and among different Jewish groups at times there were sharp controversies about the practice of temple worship, it was an important integrating symbol. The cult observed in it was accepted in broad circles. To be sure, Jews who lived far from the temple came into direct contact with it only occasionally. Nevertheless, the temple half-shekel tax (cf. Exod. 30:13), for which all males over twenty years of age were liable, constituted a connection. These funds were also collected in cities of the diaspora and at appointed times were brought to the temple by emissaries (Philo, *Spec.* 1.77–78; *Legat.* 156; Josephus, *Ant.* 18.312). The significance of the temple is manifested also in that even when the Second Temple was criticized, it was frequently expected to be a sanctuary instituted by God for the eschaton (cf. 4Q174 iii 2–6; at the time of the new creation, 11QTᵃ xxix 8–10; Jub. 1:27–29; 4:26).

Another important institution was the festival calendar, which was practiced both in the temple and in homes. Male Israelites were supposed to "appear" before the Lord (Exod. 23:17) at the three pilgrimage festivals—Passover, the Festival of Weeks, and the Festival of Tabernacles—although the actual participation in pilgrimages fluctuated and also depended on one's distance from the temple. In the afternoon of the fourteenth of Nisan, the heads of dining groups of about ten to fifteen people slaughtered a Passover animal each (lamb or kid) in the Court of the Israelites, while the priests assisted in the disposal of the blood. During the seven days of the Passover/*maṣṣot* festival, only unleavened bread was to be consumed. After the conclusion of the Sabbath after Passover or the conclusion of the first day of Passover (this was controversial; see below), a sheaf (*omer*) of barley was harvested and "waved" in the temple. Fifty days were counted from this day until the Festival of Weeks, at which two loaves of wheat bread were taken to the temple. The Festival of Tabernacles was observed by dwelling in booths (*sukkot*), the taking and shaking of the festival bundle of four species (*lulav* of palm branches, willow and myrtle leaves, and *etrog* = citron fruit), nightly celebrations in the courts of the temple with music and dancing, the ceremony of the willows as well as a water libation by the (high?) priest indicating the beginning of the rainy season (the last two ceremonies were controversial; see below). The Day of Atonement was characterized by atonement and fasting. The high priest conducted a complex ritual in accordance with Lev. 16, which included the slaughtering of a ram as a sin offering, the entering of the holy of holies, the utterance of the name of God and the sprinkling of the blood of the sin offering in the holy of holies, the sending out of another ram into the wilderness for the sins of the community, and a concluding sacrifice.

Away from Jerusalem, Jewish congregations gathered in synagogues in their local communities. The institution of the "prayer house" (προσευχή) is attested in Egyptian Judaism in inscriptions from the third century BCE. From the second century BCE, assemblies of Jews in the diaspora of Asia Minor are mentioned, and the building identified as a synagogue (Jewish or Samaritan) in Delos was probably used as such already before 88 BCE. In the land of Israel, the previous archaeological record of early synagogues at Gamla (first century BCE), Herodeion, and Masada (both of them in secondary use: at Masada at the time of the first Jewish revolt, at Herodeion, possibly at the time of the second revolt), and inscriptional evidence by the Theodotus inscription mentioning a synagogue in Jerusalem (CIIP I, no. 9; before 70 CE), has been expanded by the discoveries of structures for which identification as a synagogue dating before 70 CE has been proposed. These structures are Kiryat Sefer and Khirbet Umm el-Umdan in the Judean Shephelah, potentially Khirbet Diab and Khirbet al-Tawani in the Judean mountains, and Magdala and possibly Khirbet Qana in Galilee (though the latter may have operated between 70 and 135 CE; on the other hand, Netzer's identification of a synagogue from Hasmonean times in Jericho is questionable for typological reasons).

Typical for these buildings is a rectangular space with one or more rows of stone benches along three or all four sides. A consistent orientation of these buildings cannot be determined; rather, the inner "orientation" toward the center of the room surrounded by benches is conspicuous. In Magdala a low stone table was found apparently *in situ* probably originally equipped with horns (front side: seven-branched candelabrum, two jugs and perhaps the incense altar; back side: possibly the chariot throne over tongues of fire, presumably representing the holy of holies; the explanation of the topside and the surface of the sides is disputed). The practical function of the stone is not clear; most likely scrolls were placed on it during assemblies. Thus, the Magdala stone suggests a certain reference to the temple. The assumption that behind the institutions of temple and synagogue there were two "Judaisms" independent of each other (so Flesher) has been rendered unlikely by this discovery. On the other hand, it cannot be substantiated that synagogues were fundamentally considered holy places and therefore extensions of the temple (so Binder; on the debate with both positions, L. Levine 2004). Also, the pictorial evocation of the temple in the Synagogue of Magdala was hardly used to transfer those present into the temple courts, as it were. Rather, it establishes a connection with the temple and the activities of a different kind that were carried out in the synagogue.

According to the overwhelming attestation of literary sources, Jewish women and men assembled in order to hear the reading and exposition of the Torah, especially on the Sabbath (Philo, *Legat.* 156; *Hypoth.* [= Eusebius, *Praep. ev.*] 7.12–13; Theodotus inscription; Josephus, *Ag. Ap.* 2.175; how widely a reading from the Prophets [Luke 4:16–21] was already disseminated is contested). At the same time, some benedictions would probably have been pronounced during these occasions. Further, the name προσευχή means that activities took place there that would be understood as "prayer." Nevertheless, it is striking that prayers are rarely explicitly mentioned in this context (Josephus, *Life* 295 refers to the special situation of a day of fasting; Matt. 6:5 is unclear in view of the regularity of prayers in synagogues). Hence, it is not completely clear in what way daily or Sabbath prayers are associated with the synagogue. Prayer took place at various times and occasions, but especially in the morning and evening (Josephus, *Ant.* 4.212 [recitation of the Shema Yisrael?]; Qumran texts: 1QS x 1–7; 1QH^a xx 7–12 [*olim* 12.4–9]). Pious individuals sometimes coordinated their prayer with the last incense offering in the temple in the afternoon (Jdt. 9:1); prayer three times a day (Ps. 55:17–18; Dan. 6:10, 13) became obligatory only in the rabbinic period, although even then the obligatory character of evening prayer initially remained contested (m. Berakhot 4:1; y. Berakhot 4:1, 7c–d; b. Berakhot 27b; on the three times, cf. Did. 8:3). Although some individuals prayed facing Jerusalem (Dan. 6:10; 3 Esd. 4:58), that may not yet have been mandatory at first. Also, the ritual baths (*miqwaʾot*), which are often found in the vicinity of synagogues in the land of Israel, probably did not function for preserving a holy space (in analogy to the temple) but served either the wider population as centrally located immersion pools or, more specifically, the purification of those who handled Holy Scriptures and read from them in the synagogue. Overall, the evidence suggests that the connection between the temple and the local synagogues was mediated by the relationship both institutions had, in different ways, with the Torah. In addition to synagogues that obviously served the wider population of a city or village (like the synagogue in Capernaum from the first century [Mark 1:21], which archaeology has not yet unambiguously identified as a synagogue), there were also spaces for the assembly of specific groups; thus in Acts 6:9 we hear about the "so-called Synagogue of the freedmen (Λιβερτίνων)," and Philo of Alexandria mentions the synagogues of the Essenes (*Prob.* 81).

2.2.2. Basic Theological Concepts

The vast majority of Jews in Hellenistic Roman times were adherents of a mono-theistic adoration of God. The Shema Yisrael (Deut. 6:4–9), the confession of the unity and uniqueness of God, was to be recited by every Jew in the morning and evening. It is also found in the majority of ancient specimens of *tefillin* (phylacteries). The first two commandments of the Decalogue (according to the enumeration of Philo and Josephus) pertain to the prohibition of other gods and images (Exod. 20:3–4; Deut. 5:7–8). At the time of the Second Temple, the Decalogue appears to have been more broadly anchored in liturgy than in later periods. So, it was supposed to be part of the morning liturgy in the temple (m. Tamid 5:1), and it is found in one type of *tefillin* discovered at Qumran (whereas it is not counted among the *tefillin* passages by the rabbis: m. San. 11:3; Sifre Deut. 35). According to Josephus, Greek philosophers had also come to sim-ilar concepts of God, but only Moses had made it obligatory for an entire people (*Ag. Ap.* 2.168–169). Unnoticed by Josephus, Jews could speak in exalted rhetoric about intermediate beings such as higher angels or exalted figures (e.g., Enoch, Moses). But it is disputed whether this can be considered cultic worship.

The one and only God is according to a unanimous conviction the Creator, Sustainer, and Finisher of the World (Josephus, *Ag. Ap.* 2.190: God is "the begin-ning, middle, and end/goal of all things"). Following the YHWH-king psalms, God's kingly reign is proclaimed; from the time of Second Isaiah (cf. Isa. 52:7–10) onward, this takes the shape of a universal rule, though with a special consider-ation for Israel. In this respect a "theocratic" and an "eschatological-apocalyptic" concept can be differentiated. According to the first, God is already king (e.g., mediated through the current political rulers; so Dan. 2:21–22; 4:3; 6:27). Accord-ing to the second, God will (again) accede to rule in the eschaton, either with the cooperation of a messianic king (e.g., 1QSb v 17–29; 4Q285; Pss. Sol. 17–18) or without one (cf. Jubilees). In the latter case, an eschatological intermediary could play a role (e.g., an anointed prophet [4Q521] or the son of man [Dan. 7]); at times the concepts of the son of man and the messiah are combined (1 En. 37–71; 4 Ezra). Different views exist about the inclusion of the gentile world in this eschatological rule. Whereas some texts focus exclusively on Israel's restitu-tion (e.g., Psalms of Solomon; only the "sons of light": 1QM), others speak of a communion between Israel and the gentile world (Isa. 56:1–7; 66:18–24), some even of an eschatological transformation (1 En. 90:32–38 [the Animal Apoc-alypse]; however, it is disputed whether the transformation of the peoples as "white cattle" aims at their complete unification with Israel, which continues to be presented as "white sheep"). Along with the view that the present world is imperishable (Philo, *Aet.* 19), there is also the more frequent expectation of its end, either by means of a catastrophe (e.g., Sib. Or. 3.657–808) or transformation (Jubilees), sometimes as the reversion of creation with a subsequent new creation (4 Ezra 7:30–32). A correspondence between the end time (*Endzeit*) and primeval time (*Urzeit*) is a frequent pattern for eschatological thought (Doering 2011).

These universal aspects notwithstanding, God chose the people of Israel and made a covenant with them. Membership in the covenant community is conferred by descent (in prerabbinic times predominantly patrilinear), and for male descendants was confirmed by circumcision on the eighth day. Whereas some texts do not acknowledge circumcision after the eighth day as in accord with terms of the covenant (Jub. 15:25–27), from the second century BCE "conversions" of adult males to Judaism are attested, which included circumcision (Jdt. 14:10; Josephus, *Ant.* 20.38–48), although the role and character of (forced?) incorporation of the Idumeans and Itureans under the Hasmoneans remain controversial (cf. Cohen 1999). God has given Israel the Torah so that Israel will stay in this covenant ("covenantal nomism"; cf. E. Sanders 1985b, 397–401). As recent discussion has shown, this common conviction does not exclude significant variations in the role of works in the different literatures of ancient Judaism (Carson, O'Brien, and Seifrid 2001). The Torah is perceived as a gift (*Gabe*) and a duty (*Aufgabe*), each in different ways.

2.2.3. To Know and Do God's Will: Torah and Halakah

The Torah expresses God's will, although its exact wording was not fixed, and neither was there a closed canon of Holy Scriptures in Hellenistic-Roman times. To be sure, the Pentateuch had attained an undisputed primacy; however, the concept "Torah" is broader than the Pentateuch because the books of the prophets and additional writings also contained legal rules (a good example is Isa. 58:13–14, a passage that proved stimulating for the prohibition of trade and travel and encouraged the role of "joy" on the Sabbath). Other texts revised parts of the Torah and thus promoted additional legal details without replacing the Torah (e.g., Jubilees; 11QT^a). At any rate, the Torah offered only a selection of rules, which needed to be concretized and supplemented: the Torah depended on halakah. The conceptual framework regarding Torah and halakah varied among the groups in ancient Judaism (on these, see below); so, for the Pharisees, "ancestral traditions" are attested, whereas the Qumran texts distinguish between what is "revealed" in the Torah and what is "concealed" and available only to members of the group by means of inspired study. The Torah was variously correlated with natural law. Thus, it could be identified with wisdom (Ps. 19; Sir. 19:20; 24:23; Bar. 4:1, along with the creative Logos; Wis. 9:1–2) or understood as the law that, while having been inscribed in creation, nevertheless aims only at Israel (Jub. 1–3); it could further be understood as a written copy of the law of nature (Philo, *Mos.* 2.14, 51–52) or—analogous to the all-pervasive activity of God—as the law that emanates to all humanity (Josephus, *Ag. Ap.* 2.284). The Torah encompasses both cultic-ritual and moral-ethical commandments. Repeatedly summaries of the law are encountered in ancient Jewish literature with a particular parenetic and instructive purpose (e.g., Philo, *Hypoth.* [= Eusebius, *Praep. ev.* 8] 7.1–9; Josephus, *Ag. Ap.* 2.190–219; Niebuhr 1987), in which a weighting of the commandments may be expressed (cf. the Golden Rule in Tob. 4:15; Let. Aris. 207; Philo, *Hypoth.* 7.6; b. Šabb. 31a [attributed to Hillel the Elder] or the two "principles" [κεφάλαια] of "philosophy" [= exposition of Torah] in Philo, *Spec.* 2.63: "The regulating of one's conduct towards God by the rules of piety and holiness, and of one's conduct towards men by the rules of humanity and justice").

Halakah is the normative concretion of the law. It can be divided into the following areas (cf. the later system of the Mishnah): agricultural regulations and tributes, Sabbath and festivals, marriage and divorce, civil and criminal law, sacrifices and profane slaughter, and purity and impurity. In Hellenistic-Roman times, there was no halakah that was binding for all Jews. Rather, there were distinctions among the different religious parties, which, however, originate from ancient roots. Thus, a characteristically "rigorous" halakah is found as early as Jubilees, which is older than the texts of the Qumran Yaḥad. The distinctions were in part considerable and are related to social, legal-hermeneutical, and theological differences.

2.2.4. The Formation of Religious Parties (Elite Groups) in the Judaism of the Land of Israel

It is likely that under the Hasmoneans such differences led to the formation of various voluntary elite groups, which are often referred to in English as "sects," while German-language scholarship often prefers the label "religious parties." We find forerunners in the "assembly of the pious" ('Ασιδαῖοι), who joined the Maccabean revolt and whose roots probably lie in scribal circles (1 Macc. 2:42; 7:12–13). It is unclear how much this group is related to the "schools" (αἱρέσεις) of Pharisees, Sadducees, and Essenes, first mentioned by Josephus for the time of Jonathan (*Ant.* 13.171). The following reasons are given for their origin in the Maccabean or Hasmonean era (Baumgarten 1997): the conflict with Hellenism, which might have weakened the shared identity of the nation; an increase in literacy; the urbanization of Judean society; and eschatological expectations, which were associated with the Maccabean uprising. Not until the time of John Hyrcanus I are we informed more specifically about Pharisees and Sadducees. Hyrcanus turned away from the Pharisees in favor of the Sadducees. Under Alexander Jannaeus the conflict with the Pharisees escalated (Josephus, *Ant.* 13.372–373), and only Salome Alexandra approached the Pharisees again (*Ant.* 13.400–406). Josephus makes the elite groups understandable for his readers by referring to Greek philosophical schools. He presents the Pharisees as analogous to the Stoics (*Life* 12); he compares the Essenes with the Pythagoreans (*Ant.* 15.371); and for the Sadducees he suggests a comparison with the Epicureans. The points of comparison for this are primarily the stances on fate (εἱμαρμένη) and free will, as well as on the question of the "immortality of the soul," or more precisely, the resurrection of the dead and rewards and punishments after death. Later Josephus names a fourth group, "the fourth philosophy." Both from the comparison with the philosophical schools and from the later addition of a fourth group, it follows that the threefold grouping is a simplification (e.g., it remains unclear whether and how the groups named in Qumran texts might be correlated). In addition, large parts of the population belonged to none of these groups. Therefore, when these groups are described in what follows, the broad population of the land of Israel, who reacted to and interacted with the elite groups, should constantly be kept in mind.

The Pharisees: According to Josephus, the Pharisees believe in both fate and the power of the human will (*J.W.* 2.162–163; *Ant.* 18.13). They affirmed the immortality of the soul, although they assumed a transition into another body only for the good, whereas the wicked would be chastised by an eternal punishment (*J.W.* 2.163). Belief in the resurrection is also attributed to the Pharisees in the New Testament (Acts 23:8). They distinguish themselves by the accuracy of their observance of the law (*J.W.* 1.110; *Ant.* 18.41; *Life* 191; Acts 22:3; 26:5; the name *perushim*, from *parash*, perhaps "to define precisely" rather than "to separate themselves"). An important characteristic is that in addition to the Torah they follow statutes from the tradition of the ancestors (*Ant.* 13:297, 408; Mark 7:3–8; cf. Gal. 1:14). They pay special attention to keeping the Sabbath (Mark 2:23–3:6 par.), the purity rules (Mark 7:3–6), and tithing (Luke 11:42 par.). At the same time, their halakah is characterized by adaptability to the exigencies of life. Thus the family of Gamaliel, who is known as a Pharisee from Acts 5:34, is credited with acknowledging the *eruv* (m. Eruvin 6:2), a legal fiction by which one is permitted to take an object from one house to a courtyard shared by several parties on the Sabbath. The position of the Pharisees is often the precursor of what is later found in rabbinic literature (in part in stylized controversies between *perushim* and *ṣeduqim*; on this, see below). At the same time, rabbinic literature should not be used uncritically for the reconstruction of positions of the Pharisees, since the rabbis also take up additional traditions and follow their own system. Occasionally we detect Pharisees as a mirror image of a position that is rejected in texts from Qumran (where Pharisees are polemically depicted as "seekers of smooth things". CD-A i 18–19; 4Q169). Frequently the Pharisaic view is shared by wider circles, such that it is difficult to state "specific Pharisaic" positions. An example is the interpretation of Lev. 23:11, *mi-moḥorat ha-shabbat*, as relating to the day after the (Passover) festival, not the day following the Sabbath, a view that is also attested in the Septuagint as well as in Philo of Alexandria and Josephus. If we are allowed to draw on Josephus's rounded, schematic figures for the relative size of the elite groups, Pharisees had priority over the other groups ("over six thousand" Pharisees [*Ant.* 17.42] in contrast to four thousand Essenes [*Ant.* 18.20; Philo, *Prob.* 75]). They did not represent a "normative Judaism," which did not exist at that time, but—given their everyday practical leanings—they did have greater influence on the people at large than other groups (Josephus, *Ant.* 13.298).

The Sadducees: The Sadducees included members and followers of the priestly dynasty that traced its origins back to Zadok the priest (2 Sam. 8:17; etc.). Anchored in the priestly aristocracy (Josephus, *Ant.* 18.17), they formed one part of the Zadokites (*bene ṣadoq*), which explains similarities especially in legal concepts with positions in the Qumran texts, in which the *bene ṣadoq* also play an important role. According to Josephus, the Sadducees would have turned only to the "written law" and rejected additional traditions (*Ant.* 13.297; 18.16; whether they followed only the Pentateuch [so Origen, *Cels.* 1.49] is, however, doubtful). Thus, they are less amenable to innovations in beliefs and halakah, and they represent materially "conservative" positions. Nevertheless, their trenchant recourse to the text signifies a reform and thus a methodical innovation. Hence the Sadducees deny the resurrection of the dead (Mark 12:18–27 par.; Acts 23:8 [probably with an appositional understanding: ". . . say that there is no resurrection, either as an angel or as a spirit"]), which is mentioned only in a few, late texts of the Hebrew Bible (Isa. 24–27; Dan. 12). Or, as Josephus expresses it for readers steeped in Greek education, they disavow the immortality of the soul as well as rewards and punishment after death (*J. W.* 2.165; *Ant.* 18.16). According to Josephus, the Sadducees do not accept divine predetermination either, ascribing everything to human will (*J. W.* 2.164–165; *Ant.* 13.173). Regarding Sadducean halakah, one needs to rely on prudent interpretation of the controversies attested in Tannaitic literature between *ṣeduqim* and *perushim*, in which, however, it must be kept in mind that the rabbis, who understood themselves to be successors of the Pharisees, stylized the "Sadducees" tendentiously. It is also debated to what extent the "Boethusians" mentioned in rabbinic texts (sometimes alternating with "Sadducees") can be identified with the Sadducees. After all, both seem to have held similar positions. Controversies are attested, among others, about matters of the Sabbath and the calendar, criminal and civil law, and purity halakah. Accordingly, the Sadducees rejected the *eruv* of the courtyards (m. Eruvin 6:2), whereas the Boethusians related *ha-shabbat* in Lev. 23:11 to the weekly Sabbath and therefore protested against the reaping of the *omer*-sheaf at the conclusion of the first day of the Passover festival (m. Menahot 10:3). Further, they rejected the supersession of the Sabbath by the (unbiblical) beating of the willows (t. Sukkah 3:1) as well as the libation of water at Sukkoth (t. Sukkah 3:16). Furthermore, according to the Sadducees, an owner is liable for damages inflicted by slaves (m. Yadayim 4:7), and according to the Boethusians, daughters have the right of inheritance (t. Yadayim 2:20; Vienna Manuscript: *bayit siyyan*). According to Josephus, the Sadducees were stricter in the use of punishments than the Pharisees (*Ant.* 13.294; 20.199). In questions of purity, they hold that a priest who is a *ṭevul yom*, that is, has immersed but not yet awaited sunset, is unfit to burn the red cow (m. Parah 3:7). And they have the view that the stream of a pure liquid poured into an impure one (*niṣoq*) becomes itself impure (m. Yadayim 4:7). Similar positions are attested in Qumran texts.

The Essenes, the "New Covenant," and the Yaḥad ("Community"): The third group that Josephus names is the Essenes, who are also mentioned by Philo of Alexandria (as "Essaioi," Philo, *Prob.* 75–91; *Hypoth.* [= Eusebius, *Praep. ev.* 8] 11.1–18) and Pliny the Elder (*Nat.* 5.73). They attribute everything to divine predetermination (Josephus, *Ant.* 13.172; 18.18), and they affirm, as Josephus, borrowing from Greek concepts, expresses it, the "immortality of the soul" (*J.W.* 2.154–158; *Ant.* 18.18; the parallel in Hippolytus, *Haer.* 9.27.1, speaks of resurrection and immortality of body and soul). They are said not to participate in the general sacrifices but to send gifts to the temple and offer sacrifices "for themselves" (Josephus, *Ant.* 18.19). The most detailed report about them is found in Josephus, *J.W.* 2.119–161. According to this passage, the Essenes are more closely attached to each other than are other Jews; they have little regard for marriage, hold their property in common, avoid contact with oil, wear white garments, and live in a considerable number of cities (namely, of Judea). They offer traditional prayers before sunrise, then devote themselves to their work, which is interrupted by common meals at noon and in the evening, before which they immerse in water. They reject oaths, except when they are accepted into the group; they apply themselves to the ancient Scriptures and study them with reference to healing roots and stones. After a three-year probationary period, applicants are accepted on account of their commitment, accompanied by an oath. Anyone guilty of major offenses is excluded. It is also forbidden to expectorate in the assembly. In addition, the Essenes distinguished themselves by a scrupulous judiciary and a particularly strict observance of the Sabbath. Thus, they avoided relieving themselves on the Sabbath, whereas on other days they relieved themselves at remote places, digging a hole with a hatchet and covering the excrement immediately. In accordance with the duration of their membership, they were said to be divided into four groups. There was allegedly an additional group of Essenes that was more amenable to marriage.

Soon after the discovery of the first texts from Qumran in 1947, scholars began to propose the identification of the group(s) named in these texts with the Essenes. The idealized depiction of the ancient reports of the Essenes notwithstanding, a number of similarities in lifestyle and group organization, especially with the Yaḥad as outlined in the Community Rule (1QS, 4QS), point to some kind of relationship. To be cited are especially a gradual process of admission (1QS vi 13–23), communal meals (vi 4–5), common ownership of goods (i 11–13; v 1–3; vi 17–20), temporary and permanent exclusion (vi 24–7.25), the prohibition of spitting in the assembly (vii 13), and the duty to remain silent about esoteric teachings (iv 6; ix 17). Also, dualistic propositions about divine predetermination can be mentioned (iii 13–4.1). However, some of the details do not agree exactly with each other and some remain ambiguous. Whereas for instance certain texts ascribe functions of the temple to the community (1QS v 4–7; ix 3–6; viii 4–11; xi 7–9; cf. 4Q174 [=4QFlor] iii 6–7), evidence for the praxis of gifts and sacrifices as specified by Josephus (see above) is absent. Further, no text at Qumran expressly prescribes celibacy, even though silence about women and children in 1QS would fit a completely male community. Unlike the Community Rule, the Damascus Document, also found in the Qumran caves, provides prescriptions for life in settlements organized around families, which on the basis of a desert typology are called "camps." The most important group name in the Damascus Document is the "New Covenant" in the Land of Damascus, apparently a precursor of Yaḥad, whereas "Yaḥad" only appears marginally here. The precise relationship between the two rule texts and the lifestyles in them is debated. However, also within the Community Rule a plurality of locally organized communities is perceptible. Hence, recent Dead Sea Scrolls scholarship has moved away from a one-sided focus on the location at Khirbet Qumran, which may have been but one of a number of settlements, and assumes several communities and groups affiliated with each other (J. Collins 2010). "Essene" could therefore be understood as either an umbrella term for a series of communities or a designation of one or two among several communities with a similar outlook. In recent Dead Sea Scrolls scholarship, the debate on the distinction and relationship between writings that originated inside and those that originated outside the Yaḥad plays an important role. Thus, the Yaḥad took over broader Jewish tradition as well, such as wisdom literature (like 4QInstruction), apocalyptic texts (like parts of 1 Enoch), or specimens of "rewritten Scripture" with programmatic character (like Jubilees). Statements about resurrection are found predominantly in texts for which the provenance from the Yaḥad is questionable or unlikely (among others, 4Q521; 4Q385 [= 4QpsEzek]; and 4Q245 [= 4QpsDanc ar]). The halakah of the Yaḥad is predominantly rigorous, accepts little legal innovation, and stands close to the Sadducees in approach. A 364-day calendar is well attested, which, on account of its structure based on the number seven, is conducive to distinguishing Sabbaths clearly from festivals, as compared with the lunisolar calendar that was widely distributed elsewhere in Judaism. However, the degree to which it was put into practice is debated.

2.2.5. Anti-Roman Rebel Groups, Messianic Pretenders, and Sign Prophets

After the death of Herod the Great in 4 BCE, disturbances broke out in several places, among which were some attempts to provide for the restitution of a popular Jewish monarchy following a Davidic model (however, not necessarily from the Davidic dynasty). The first to place the diadem on his head was Simon, a former slave of Herod (Josephus, *Ant.* 17.273–277), followed by the shepherd Anthronges (*Ant.* 17.278–284), both thereby clearly raising up messianic claims. Further, a certain Judas is said to have plundered the royal weapon depot in Sepphoris and "made attempts on those who were jealously vying for sovereign power" (Josephus, *J.W.* 2.56; trans. S. Mason); that is, perhaps, they vied with him for the leadership (so *Ant.* 17.271–272). Before Judas, his father, Hezekiah, already could have had rebellion in mind. Josephus typifies him as a "chief brigand" (ἀρχιληστής; *J.W.* 1.204; *Ant.* 14.159), whom the young Herod, having just been deployed as commander of Galilee by his father, Antipater, under Julius Caesar, captured and killed. To be sure, for Josephus the term "brigand" has strong political overtones.

It is debated whether the Judas named here is identical with Judas "the Galilean." The latter instituted a revolutionary movement with the Pharisee Zadok after the exile of Archelaus and the annexation of Judea to the Roman province of Syria in 6 CE, a movement that ignited because of the tax assessment instigated by Quirinius (*J.W.* 2.117; *Ant.* 18.4–10; Acts 5:37). Josephus names this movement the "fourth philosophy" of the Jews in *Ant.* 18.9, 23. Apart from their love of freedom grounded in the claim of God's rule, they agreed in all relevant matters with the Pharisees. Judas and his followers met a violent end (Acts 5:37), and two of his sons were crucified under the procurator Tiberius Julius Alexander (*Ant.* 20.102). Commonly the "fourth philosophy" is identified with the "Zealots." However, Josephus avoids the latter term before the war. Also, the meaning of individual passages is debated (thus, ζηλωταί in *J.W.* 2.444, 564 perhaps means "fanatic follower"; not until *J.W.* 2.651 is a group clearly named). Nevertheless, the reference to "Simon the Zealot" among Jesus's disciples (Luke 6:15) might suggest the existence of a group named "Zealots" as early as the first half of the first century CE. Generally, it is debated whether one can speak of an ideologically unified revolutionary movement in the first century CE, promoted, among others, by the descendants of Judas the Galilean (Hengel 1989), or whether or not social and conceptional differences are to be weighed more strongly (Horsley 1999). Inter alia, the historical essence and classification of the "Sicarii" are discussed. Named after the term for "dagger" (Latin *sica*), with which they committed murder (first against fellow Judeans), they emerged according to Josephus before the first explicit naming of the Zealots (*J.W.* 2.254–257: under Felix; *Ant.* 20.186: under Festus; the reference for the time of Judas the Galilean, *J.W.* 7.253–254, is probably schematic). The value of other sources is controversial (Acts 21:38, here associated with "the Egyptian" [see below]; m. Makshirin 1:6: *ha-siqrin* = "Sicarii"?; b. Gittin 56a: "Abba Siqra" as chief of the *baryone*, "bandits," of Jerusalem). A certain flexibility in the use of the appellation in Josephus that vacillates between the designation of a group and rhetorical disqualification has been suggested. The latter is clear in the appearance of "Sicarii" in Alexandria as well as in Cyrenaica after the war's end (*J.W.* 7.410–419, 437–450; Brighton 2009).

In any case, at the beginning of the first Jewish War, renewed messianic claims from another of the sons of Judas the Galilean, Menachem, became apparent. After the plundering of the weapons depot on Masada, he turned back toward Jerusalem "like a king" (*J.W.* 2.434). After initial successes, as he went up to prayer in the temple "in a pompous manner, and adorned with royal garments," he was killed by the priestly insurgents around the captain of the temple, Eleazar. A grandson of Judas, Eleazar ben Yair, fled to Masada (*J.W.* 2.444–448), where he led the resistance of the Sicarii. Distinct social-revolutionary and messianic aspects can also be perceived in Simon bar Giora, who gained entry to Jerusalem in 69 CE in order to liberate the city from the tyranny of the rebel leader John of Gischala. His adherents followed him "as their king" (*J.W.* 4.510). Before his capture by the Romans, he appeared in the temple precincts in a white garment and purple mantle (*J.W.* 7.26–31). The fact that at the end of the triumph of Vespasian and Titus, he—and not John—was killed in Rome (*J.W.* 6.434; 7.153–155) is indicative that the Romans saw him as the more important leader of the subjected people.

Political eschatology also motivated the activities of a series of "sign prophets." They enacted the crossing over the Jordan and with that a new conquest of the land (so Theudas [*Ant.* 20.97–99; Acts 5:36]; cf. John the Baptizer), also including a transfer of the miracle of the walls of Jericho to Jerusalem (so the "Egyptian," according to *Ant.* 20.169–172; cf. *J.W.* 2.261–263; Acts 21:38), or a new exodus in the wilderness (anonymous prophets under Felix [*J.W.* 2.258–260; *Ant.* 20.167–168] and Porcius Festus [*Ant.* 20.188]). Also, the prophet Jesus, son of Ananias, should be counted among these. At the Festival of Tabernacles he prophesied about the city, the temple, and the people, and the procurator Albinus declared him to be insane (*J. W.* 6.300–309).

2.3. Samaritans

The history of the Samaritans in antiquity is characterized by an increasing alienation from Judaism. However, both Jews and Samaritans traditionally belong to, and attach themselves to, "Israel." The Samaritans trace themselves back to the northern tribes Ephraim and Manasseh as well as the tribe of Levi. In a critical perspective there are several factors that led to the origin of the Samaritans (cf. Böhm 2010). Following tensions between Samaria and Jerusalem during the construction of the Jerusalem temple and, afterward, in connection with it, a sanctuary was built on Mount Gerizim apparently in the fifth century BCE. This construction was sponsored by the governor of Samaria, Sanballat the Horonite (cf. Neh. 13:28), and he used dissident Jerusalem priests for the practice of the cult. Magen (2007) confirms this dating of the first phase of the construction of the sanctuary on the basis of archaeological evidence with a high degree of probability. Josephus erroneously places this migration of Jerusalem priests in the time of Alexander (*Ant.* 11.302–311). However, the later influx of settlers, which Josephus presents as a reaction to the strict actions by the Jerusalem leaders on the questions of intermarriage, purity, and Sabbath observance (*Ant.* 11.312, 346), can be correlated with the enlargement of the sanctuary and the construction of a city in Hellenistic times, as Magen has established (Pummer 2009, 139–50). Probably the northern Israelite populace who remained in Samaria supported this sanctuary as well. To be sure, the Judean-Jewish tradition (2 Kings 17:24–41) knows about a settlement of foreign demographic groups ("Cuthites") and syncretic practices in Samaria after the conquest under Sargon II. However, to the extent this is described here, this is certainly polemical. In the further course of history, the tensions between Judeans and Samaritans increased, also in the diaspora, to which more and more Samaritans migrated. Josephus reports conflicts between the two in the middle of the second century BCE before Ptolemy VI in Alexandria about the legitimacy of their respective temples (*Ant.* 13.74–79). Nevertheless, the actual schism did not take place until around 110 BCE, when John Hyrcanus I destroyed the Samaritan sanctuary on Mount Gerizim and the city connected with it (on this revised date, see Pummer 2009, 200–210), and incorporated Samaria into his territory. On the one hand, in Roman times the relationship between Jews and Samaritans was characterized by tensions and provocations (cf. *Ant.* 18.29–30 [but textually corrupt]; 20.118–136). On the other hand, representatives of both groups could enter into alliances of convenience (see *Ant.* 17.342 on Archelaus's dismissal). Also, a passage like Luke 10:30–37 suggests that both could continue to relate to each other (under the implicit rubric "Israel").

According to their own self-understanding, the Samaritans have preserved Israelite tradition unaltered (*shomerim*, "guardians"). The most distinctive feature in comparison with the Jews aligned with Jerusalem is the location of the sanctuary on Mount Gerizim, to which the Samaritans remained attached even after its destruction. It remains (to this day) the destination of festival pilgrimages and the place of the Passover slaughtering. The Holy Scripture is the Pentateuch alone in a specific text recension, written in the Samaritan script, which is based on paleo-Hebrew. The basis of this text recension is in turn a "pre-Samaritan" recension also found among the Qumran manuscripts (e.g., 4QpaleoExod^m), which features harmonizations and expansions (e.g., already in 4Q158 [= 4QRP^a] and 4Q175 [=4QTest] the verses from Deut. 18:18–19 are inserted in Exod. 20:21). There is also an affinity with the (antecedent of the) Septuagint. With that said, specific Samaritan insertions into the text prove to be a slim stratum, which has to do especially with Gerizim as the location of the sanctuary. Notably, the "Gerizim Commandment" is the tenth commandment of the Decalogue with the addition of Exod. 13:11a; Deut. 11:29b; 27:2–7*; 11:30, and the change in enumeration of the other commandments, as well as the tense of the verbs, which designate the choice of the sanctuary (perfect, instead of MT imperfect). The focus on the Pentateuch corresponds to the special place of Moses for the Samaritans (cf. Deut. 34:11–12). The central figure of hope is the "prophet like Moses" (Deut. 18:15, 18), later called the "Taheb."

Barclay, John M. G. 1996. *Jews in the Mediterranean Diaspora: From Alexander to Trajan (323 BCE–117 CE)*. Edinburgh.

Collins, John J. 2010. *Beyond the Qumran Community: The Sectarian Movement of the Dead Sea Scrolls*. Grand Rapids.

Sanders, Ed P. 1992; ²1994. *Judaism: Practice and Belief, 63 BCE–66 CE*. London and Philadelphia.

Stemberger, Günter. 1991; ² 2013. *Pharisäer, Sadduzäer, Essener*. Stuttgart.

Lutz Doering

III. Biographical Aspects

1. Jesus: Descent, Birth, Childhood, Family

A number of New Testament writings (e.g., Matt. 1:1; Luke 1:32; Acts 2:29–32; 13:23; Rom. 1:3; 2 Tim. 2:8; Rev. 22:16; cf. Heb. 7:14) assign Davidic descent to Jesus. Affirmation of Davidic descent was important for the Christian claim that Jesus was the "Christ," the (Davidic) Messiah. That theological interest raises the question of the historical reliability of the claim that Jesus was from the line of David.

The ostensibly clearest evidence for Jesus's Davidic descent lies in the genealogies of Matthew (1:1–17) and Luke (3:23–38). However, the two genealogies differ in ways that cannot be easily reconciled, which raises questions about their authenticity. In this respect they are like other biblical genealogies. Already in the Old Testament one finds multiple genealogies for the same person, and it is evident that theological, political, social, or other interests often override concern for historical accuracy (Brown [2]1993, 57–95, 505). It is not implausible that at the time of Jesus Jewish families that claimed Davidic descent possessed family genealogies, whether written or oral. Yet the fact that Matthew's and Luke's genealogies differ already on the name of Jesus's paternal grandfather raises a question about their origin. It is unlikely that the genealogies come from a family source, although a minority of scholars today would claim that one of the genealogies, probably Luke's, preserves an authentic family genealogy, at least for the last few generations before Jesus (e.g., Bauckham 1990, 315–73). More likely, the genealogies were adapted from popular Davidic genealogies. In addition, they may have been composed to show Jesus to be the culmination of the history of salvation (for these issues, see M. Johnson 1969).

According to the Gospels, during his ministry Jesus was recognized as "Son of David." Most of the places where the title appears are redactional, particularly in Matthew, whose interest in the Davidic descent of Jesus is patent and who has a tendency to link Jesus's messiahship with his healing miracles (9:27; 11:2–6; 12:23; 15:22; 21:9, 14–15). There is, however, at least one instance of the title that has a strong claim to be based on old tradition (Mark 10:47–48 pars.). Furthermore, the apostle Paul, writing to the Roman Christians around 57 or 58 CE, affirms Jesus's Davidic descent, probably drawing on an existing Jewish-Christian tradition (Rom. 1:3), which suggests that Jesus's Davidic descent was already then a well-established belief.

An important pericope touching on the question is the dialogue about David's son in Mark 12:35–37. Jesus asks: How do the scribes say that the Messiah is the son of David? In (the messianically interpreted) Ps. 110, David, the alleged author of the psalm, calls the Messiah "Lord," who sits at God's right hand. So how can he be David's son? According to some interpreters, Jesus challenges the received view that the Messiah must be of Davidic descent and—by extension—implicitly denies his own Davidic descent. However, a more likely interpretation is that Jesus is simply suggesting that traditional Davidic conceptions of "Messiah" are inadequate. Indeed, Jewish sources from the time attest a variety of messianic conceptions (Brown 1993, 506–7). In any case, the pericope would seem to suggest that Jesus did not consider Davidic descent of central importance to whatever "messianic consciousness" he might have had, which makes it unlikely that the title "Son of David" in the gospel traditions comes from Jesus himself. That does not rule out that contemporaries who knew of his Davidic descent addressed him with that title, possibly in connection with his healing ministry. Even so, caution is required, as the title may have been used in connection more with Jesus's redemptive role than with his ancestry.

From a later period, Eusebius preserves accounts from Hegesippus (second century) according to which, during the emperor Domitian's attempts to eliminate members of the house of David, the grandsons of Jude, the brother of Jesus, were accused of being Davidic, while Simon the son of Clopas, a cousin of Jesus, suffered martyrdom as a Davidide (and as a Christian) under the emperor Trajan (*Hist. eccl.* 3.11.1; 3.20.1–7; 3.32.3, 5). All things considered, there is no compelling reason to deny Jesus's Davidic descent, even if some of the textual evidence that ostensibly supports it cannot withstand critical scrutiny.

The claim that Jesus was descended from David through Joseph appears to compete with the claim that Jesus was conceived by a virgin. Yet if Joseph had effectively "adopted" Jesus by claiming him to be his son, it is likely that legally Joseph's paternity would have been recognized as on the same level as if he were Jesus's biological father. Moreover, it is possible that the gospel tradition in its first decades preserved two different accounts of Jesus's origin side by side: that he was the "son of Joseph" (Luke 4:22; John 1:45; 6:42), and that he was conceived by the Holy Spirit from a virgin; for it was not unknown in antiquity for an important person to be given both a divine and a human father (Lincoln 2013).

Of greater interest is the question of the historical reliability of the tradition of the virginal conception of Jesus and the circumstances surrounding his birth. Matthew and Luke alone in the New Testament treat Jesus's conception and birth in detail. On the most widely accepted view of gospel origins, these two gospels were written after the year 70, and their accounts of Jesus's birth, infancy, and childhood are later additions to the main body of gospel tradition, which extended from Jesus's (adult) baptism to his death and resurrection (the basic framework in Mark, John, and the apostolic preaching in Acts, e.g., 10:34–43). That does not demand an extremely late date for the origin of the birth stories, but it does warn against granting them too great antiquity. Mark, the earliest gospel, shows no knowledge of the specific traditions transmitted by Matthew and Luke.

It is not possible to harmonize the details of Matthew's and Luke's birth and infancy narratives, which exclude a single source for them, let alone an origin in Jesus's family. That said, the independent sources behind Matthew and Luke agree on numerous details, which suggests that the evangelists' sources were themselves based on an older body of tradition with roots in Palestinian Jewish

Christianity (for a list of agreements between Matthew and Luke, see Brown 1993, 34–35; a more ambitious list is in Corley 2009, 200–201). From a historical perspective, the most important of these agreements are the virginal conception of Jesus through the Holy Spirit, the birth in Bethlehem, and the dating of events to the reign of King Herod.

Given the state of our sources, it is no longer possible to recover the origins of belief in Jesus's virginal conception. A historical point of departure may have been the memory of a "too early" birth of Jesus after Joseph and Mary began to live together (cf. Matt. 1:18). Such a memory, combined with the early confession that Jesus was (from his baptism or from the resurrection) "Son of God," may have coalesced into the tradition of a virginal conception. Jewish sources from the second century, perhaps having roots in the first century, alleged that Jesus was the illegitimate son of Mary. One cannot prove that the Jewish allegation goes back in time before the Gospels. The Jewish claim may have risen in response to the gospel accounts, although it is just possible that the Jewish allegation preserves an early, alternative account of an irregularity in connection with the conception of Jesus. The virginal conception of Jesus by the Holy Spirit is an article of Christian faith, neither provable nor disprovable by historical methods. But there is no reason to deny the possibility that the gospel stories preserve memories of a conception by a betrothed Mary under unusual circumstances.

As for the location of Jesus's birth, majority scholarly opinion is skeptical toward the claim that "Jesus of Nazareth" was born in Bethlehem and would generally locate the birth in Nazareth. The historical difficulties with Bethlehem include: (1) the fact that Matthew and Luke disagree on where Joseph and Mary resided immediately before Jesus's birth. Matthew presupposes that they resided in Bethlehem. Luke places them in Nazareth, and the birth happened in Bethlehem only because Joseph and Mary went to Bethlehem to be registered in a census. (2) Yet there are numerous historical problems pertaining to the worldwide census under Augustus alleged by Luke. (3) Finally, there is no independent evidence to confirm Herod's slaughter of infants in Bethlehem, even though the first-century Jewish historian Josephus otherwise records Herod's atrocities in detail. Together these difficulties suggest that the location of Jesus's birth in Bethlehem may not have a historical basis but may have a different origin, for example, in messianic exegesis of Scripture (Matt. 2:4–6) as part of an overall effort to defend the Davidic messiahship of a man known only to have come from Nazareth in Galilee (John 1:46; 7:41–42; see further Matt. 2:23). That said, a birth in Bethlehem cannot be ruled out, and a minority of scholars would still argue for the reliability of the tradition. That Jesus was born toward the end of the reign of King Herod, probably sometime between 7 BCE and his death in 4 BCE, is considered plausible by scholars.

Due to the gospel tradition's primarily kerygmatic orientation, Matthew and Luke have relatively little to offer about Jesus's infancy and childhood (compared to his adult ministry). Such stories as they do record betray highly theological interests, and the details of the stories present insuperable obstacles to harmonizing them into a composite account of Jesus's early years. Matthew's stories manifest a combination of messianic exegesis and Mosaic typology, which may have provided the structure for his infancy narratives. Luke's stories highlight the family's observance of the Mosaic law. In one place, however, the details do not agree with the requirements of the law (2:22–24), which raises the question of historical authenticity. Luke depicts the circumstances of Jesus's birth and infancy in terms reminiscent of the Old Testament figure Samuel, which corresponds to Luke's interest in presenting Jesus as a prophetic figure. Luke preserves the one canonical story of Jesus as a child, his visit to Jerusalem at the age of twelve with his parents (2:41–52). The story depicts Jesus as a boy endowed with unusual intelligence and conscious of an intimate relationship with God his "Father." It contains motifs common in legendary stories about the childhood of prominent figures (both within and outside of Judaism). The story once again underlines the family's obedience to the law (Passover pilgrimage) and Jesus's lawful obedience to his parents, even as it foreshadows Jesus's intimacy with his heavenly Father and his uncompromising commitment to God's will, also above family commitments, in his adult ministry. Later apocryphal stories (beginning, at least in written form, in the second century) carry forward the tradition's tendency to develop legendary accounts of Jesus's birth and childhood (Markschies and Schröter 2012, 1/1:280–342; 1/2:886–1029). The core gospel tradition seems to remember a rather unremarkable childhood and young adulthood (Mark 6:2–3), so that the later legends, including remarkable miracles performed by Jesus as a child that foreshadow his adult ministry, hardly have claim to authenticity.

The New Testament gives the following as members of the family of Jesus: his father, Joseph; his mother, Mary; four named brothers (James, Joses, Judas, and Simon; Mark 6:3); and some (unnamed) sisters. One finds a diversity of views in antiquity as to whether the brothers and sisters of Jesus were true, biological brothers and sisters by way of birth from Mary (the Helvidian view), stepbrothers and stepsisters (from an earlier marriage of Joseph; the Epiphanian view), or cousins (the Hieronymian view). That the "brothers" were actually cousins depends on the following: identifying the first two brothers mentioned in Mark 6:3 with the James and Joses referred to as sons of Mary in Mark 15:40; identifying that Mary with the sister (or sister-in-law) of Mary the mother of Jesus (John 19:25); and identifying Simon with Simon the son of Clopas. All of this, however, is speculative. Some evidence from the second century onward may be adduced in support of the Epiphanian view. But the view that Jesus's brothers (and sisters) were not born of Mary may have its roots in early ascetic tendencies that glorified virginity or in traditions that upheld the perpetual virginity of Mary as a way of bolstering the claim of the virginal conception and birth of Jesus. In addition to the sister (or sister-in-law) of Mary the mother of Jesus already mentioned, Elizabeth is said to have been a kinswoman of Mary (Luke 1:36), which would make John the Baptist and Jesus relatives of each other, but the proximity of their relationship is uncertain. There has been speculation that other persons named in the New Testament (including some of Jesus's disciples) were relatives of Jesus, but the claims remain mostly unprovable (on all this, see Bauckham 1990, 5–44).

The Gospels indicate that during the greater part of his ministry Jesus's relationship with his family was strained (Mark 3:20–21, 31–35; John 7:5). Both Jesus's teaching on discipleship (Matt. 8:21–22; 10:34–37; Mark 10:29–30) and the actual practice of discipleship as the Gospels represent it (Mark 1:16–20) suggest that Jesus viewed commitment to the kingdom of God as a calling that took priority over family relationships, and there is no reason to suppose that this view did not also shape Jesus's relationship to his family.

In the post-Easter period, however, the New Testament leaves no doubt that the brothers of Jesus took on significant roles in the Christian mission. James eventually advanced to the leadership of the Jerusalem church (Acts 15:13; 21:18; Gal. 2:9), while Paul mentions "brothers of the Lord" (1 Cor. 9:5; see also Acts 1:14) who were itinerant missionaries. Apart from James, we know little about their work. Later traditions indicate that relatives of Jesus worked in Palestine, especially in Galilee, and perhaps beyond (Bauckham 1990, 45–133). Also according to a later tradition, Simon, the son of Clopas and Jesus's cousin (Clopas being the brother of Joseph), succeeded James as head of the Jerusalem church. Two New Testament letters, James and Jude (= Judas), are traditionally attributed to Jesus's brothers, but their authorship remains a point of debate.

Bauckham, Richard J. 1990. *Jude and the Relatives of Jesus in the Early Church*. London.

Brown, Raymond E. ²1993. *The Birth of the Messiah: A Commentary on the Infancy Narratives in the Gospels of Matthew and Luke*. New York.

Corley, Jeremy, ed. 2009. *New Perspectives on the Nativity*. London.

Johnson, Marshall D. 1969. *The Purpose of the Biblical Genealogies: With Special Reference to the Setting of the Genealogies of Jesus*. SNTSMS 8. Cambridge.

Lincoln, Andrew T. 2013. *Born of a Virgin? Reconceiving Jesus in Bible, Tradition, and Theology*. London.

Markschies, Christoph, and Jens Schröter, eds. 2012. *Antike christliche Apokryphen in deutscher Übersetzung.* Vol. 1, *Evangelien und Verwandtes (Teilband 1 & Teilband 2).* Tübingen.

Stephen Hultgren

2. Jesus's Education and Language

2.1. Jesus's Education

We have little direct or indirect information pertaining to the nature and level of Jesus's education. Texts from the canonical Gospels to be considered include a story about Jesus reading Scripture in the synagogue (Luke 4:16–19); a story about Jesus writing on the ground (John 8:6, 8); a story about Jesus at twelve years engaged in conversation with the teachers in the Jerusalem temple, and the people's astonishment at his wisdom (Luke 2:46–47); other stories in which people express astonishment at the adult Jesus's teaching authority and wisdom (Mark 1:22; 6:2), or at his ability to teach and his knowledge of "letters," even though he has not "studied" (John 7:14–15); and the statement that Jesus was a carpenter (Mark 6:3), having learned this trade (presumably) from his father (Matt. 13:55). In addition, there is more general evidence to consider, such as Jesus's familiarity with scribal and Pharisaic teaching traditions (e.g., Mark 7:6–13) and conversations with opponents that include references to reading biblical texts (e.g., Matt. 12:3, 5; 21:16; Mark 12:10, 26; cf. Luke 10:26). Finally, a number of later, noncanonical texts touch on the question of Jesus's literacy (see Keith 2011, 156–63).

Given the paucity of evidence, it is difficult to rise above speculation and generalities about the education that Jesus received and the level to which he advanced in it. We are assisted to some degree by the evidence for Jewish education and literacy in first-century Palestine within the Greco-Roman context, from which we can by way of analogy make some modest deductions about Jesus's education, but even here the evidence is limited and open to divergent interpretations.

Traditionally in Judaism the locus of education was the home. The Torah imposes upon parents the duty of teaching the Torah to their children (Deut. 6:7; 11:19) and of explaining the commandments within the context of the nation's history (Exod. 10:2; 12:26–27; 13:8–10; Deut. 6:20–25). The wisdom tradition also points to the home as the main locus of education (e.g., Prov. 1:8 and passim). For most people, learning the Torah did not require reading but was a matter of hearing it read, reciting it, and memorizing it (Deut. 6:7). Priests and Levites were entrusted with the task of teaching the Torah to the people (Lev. 10:11; Deut. 33:10; 2 Kings 17:27–28; etc.), and provision was made for public reading and teaching of the law (Deut. 31:9–13). Didactic psalms give us further insight into the content of teaching, with a focus on the Torah and the nation's history (Pss. 1; 78; 119). The Torah requires writing in certain situations (Deut. 6:9; 11:20; 24:1–4), but professional scribes could write where others could not do so.

The foregoing provides the background for education in the Second Temple period. One finds a concern among the priests and Levites to teach the Torah to the people (Ezra 7:25; Neh. 8:8–9; Mal. 2:7; Sir. 45:17; on the evidence of the Dead Sea Scrolls and other noncanonical literature, see Carr 2005, 201–39). But there is also evidence for a broadening of the base of education. Ben Sira 51:23 (early second century BCE) is the first Palestinian Jewish text that refers to a formal school. Even in this book, though, sages and parents stand alongside each other as teachers (Sir. 8:8–9; 30:3). If schools were established at this time, they were probably encouraged both by Hellenistic educational ideals and by Jewish reactions to Hellenism (Hengel 1974, 1:78–83). It is also about this time that the Pharisees emerge, who would become popular, mostly lay teachers of the law (Josephus, *Ant.* 13.171–173; 18.15).

Rabbinic texts speak of the establishment of teachers or schools in the Second Temple period. A tradition in the Palestinian Talmud states that Simon ben Shetah (first half of the first century BCE) ordained that children should go to school (y. Ketubbot 8:11, 32c). The Babylonian Talmud preserves a tradition according to which Joshua ben Gamala (Jesus son of Gamaliel, high priest, 63–65 CE) ordained that teachers of young children be appointed in every town and that children should be brought to learn at age six or seven (b. Bava Batra 21a). The latter tradition presupposes that a system of education already existed, and Joshua reformed it. Another tradition claims that Jerusalem had 480 (or 460) synagogues with associated schools before the destruction of the city in the year 70 (y. Megillah 3:1, 73d; y. Ketubbot 13:1, 35c). The reliability of these traditions, however, is doubted by many scholars.

The archaeological evidence for the existence of schools is very slight, and late at that. An argument from silence is not decisive, since we cannot assume that all early "schools" must have been housed in their own buildings or rooms. But while later, Amoraic texts frequently mention synagogues and study houses as places of learning, Tannaitic texts are more restrained. They do occasionally speak of the school (e.g., m. Ketubbot 2:10) and of provision of education for children outside the home, but they also emphasize the father's responsibility for teaching his son (Hezser 2001, 48–52, 75). In the Dead Sea Scrolls, the Rule of the Congregation (1QSa i 6–8) foresees for the eschatological community that boys are educated, apparently for ten years or more, in the law and in the precepts of the community, which may give insight into the educational ideals of the community that produced the document. Josephus speaks of the law's command to teach children "letters" so that they should understand the laws of the nation and the deeds of their forefathers (*Ag. Ap.* 2.204; cf. 1.60). He also boasts that the Jewish people gather each week to hear and to learn the law, and that, if one were asked about the laws, he would be able to repeat them more easily than his own name (*Ag. Ap.* 2.175, 178). Josephus's statement is undoubtedly exaggerated for apologetic purposes.

It is difficult from the evidence to reach a judgment about the existence of schools or teachers outside the home in the first century. One relatively recent examination of the evidence concludes that in the Second Temple and Tannaitic periods education was still mostly a concern of the home, and that the spread of schools from the third century onward reflects the rabbis' desire to provide an alternative to Greco-Roman schools (Hezser 2001, 39, 59, 71, 103). At the same time, one cannot ignore the fact that also before 70 CE Jewish teachers were interested in educating the people in the law, especially in the face of foreign influences, and the possibility remains that attempts were made to provide basic education for children outside the home in Second Temple times. Who (besides fathers) would have been responsible for education is difficult to say, although priests, synagogue officers, and scribes are possibilities. Nor can we say with certainty where education (outside the home) took place. There is evidence that the synagogue served as a place for "teaching the commandments" in the first century (e.g., the famous Theodotus inscription in Jerusalem), but that does not necessarily imply formal methods of teaching. It is only in later centuries that the synagogue clearly emerges as a typical locus for more formal education (Hezser 2001, 51–54).

As for the content of education, rabbinic literature offers the following model. Children (that is, usually boys) began to attend elementary school (בית הספר) between the ages of five and seven. The written Torah stood at the center of education. The teacher (a סופר) taught children the alphabet and how to read the Torah. With reading the Torah at the heart of education, writing does not seem to have been central to basic education but was rather a specialized skill acquired by scribes and the upper class. Nonetheless, it is possible that some children learned to write. After learning the basics, some students might go on to learn oral Torah (Mishnah), perhaps in a secondary school (בית המדרש). Beyond that, a student might proceed to even more advanced study, including dialectics and the interpretation of Scripture and of the oral Torah, as well as jurisprudence.

We cannot retroject the rabbinic model into the first century. However, the model has parallels in ancient Greco-Roman education, where primary education (typically from age seven or earlier) consisted of learning the alphabet, reading (and writing), and reciting and memorizing classical texts, and higher education consisted of the interpretation of classical texts, progressing to rhetoric, philosophy, and law, among other things (Hezser 2001, 72–89). It is not implausible that the kind of primary education described in rabbinic literature had precedents in the first century. It is difficult to know, however, how widespread such education might have been. Recent estimates have tended to set literacy rates among Jews in Roman Palestine, as in the rest of the Roman world, very low (10 percent or less) (Keith 2011, 72–85), although it is possible that the importance of Torah tended to increase Jewish literacy above the average.

Given the evidence from the Gospels, as well as from Second Temple Judaism, it is hazardous to draw any firm conclusions about Jesus's education. It is plausible that Jesus received a basic education, at least learning to read Scripture in Hebrew. But Luke 4:16–19 is the only biblical text that attests this clearly, and it is possible that the portrayal of Jesus reading Scripture is a secondary development in the tradition (compare Mark 6:1–6). Since John 8:6, 8 does not tell us what Jesus wrote, it is difficult to draw conclusions from it. It is not implausible that Jesus could write some letters and words (if that is what John means), but that would not necessarily entail a high level of writing ability. Jesus became a carpenter under the tutelage of his father (Mark 6:3; Matt. 13:55), as it appears to have been customary for at least one of a man's sons to adopt his father's trade. That would also have been an occasion to learn some basic skills in reading, perhaps also in writing, and in arithmetic (cf. Keith 2011, 112–14). John 7:15 is not particularly helpful, since the text can be used to argue either for an educated or a noneducated Jesus. One cannot draw from it anything more than that Jesus did not have a *higher* Jewish education in Scripture interpretation, a point that is hardly in question (cf. Mark 1:22; 6:2–3). There is no reason to think that Jesus ever engaged in advanced studies. While Luke 2:46–47, which shows the twelve-year-old Jesus debating with the "teachers," might suggest otherwise, the story's legendary character renders it unsuitable as evidence. Jesus could have picked up his knowledge of scribal or Pharisaic traditions from what he heard as an outsider.

2.2. Jesus's Language(s)

The canonical Gospels are all written in Greek, and so they record the words of Jesus in that language. In a few places, however, the Gospels have transliterated words of Jesus into Greek from a Semitic language (usually Aramaic, less frequently Hebrew). Since literary and epigraphic evidence indicates that first-century Jewish Palestine was trilingual (with Aramaic, Greek, and Hebrew used in varying degrees), the question arises as to which language or languages Jesus spoke and understood (and possibly read and wrote).

The sayings of Jesus that have been transliterated from a Semitic language are few. In Mark 5:41 Jesus commands the daughter of Jairus ταλιθα κουμ, which represents the Aramaic טליתא קום and which Mark translates accurately into Greek as "little girl, arise." Mark (15:34) records Jesus's last words on the cross as ελωι ελωι λεμα σαβαχθανι, which represents in Greek transliteration an Aramaic translation of Ps. 22:2. Matthew (27:46) renders those words as ηλι ηλι λεμα σαβαχθανι. There has been a long debate—too complicated to review here—over whether Matthew's version represents Hebrew or Aramaic (or even a mix of the two) (see Buth and Notley 2014, 395–421), though one might have expected Matthew to make the words conform more closely to the biblical Hebrew text if that were the language intended. One may also wonder what Jesus's original words were (assuming the report is authentic), since Matthew's ηλι explains more easily than Mark's ελωι the crowd's mistaken view that Jesus was calling upon Elijah. Though it consists of only one word, we may also include here εφφαθα, which Mark accurately translates into Greek as "be opened," in the healing of the deaf man in Mark 7:34. This almost certainly represents Aramaic אתפתח, becoming אפתח under assimilation of ת to פ (although it has been argued that εφφαθα could represent the Hebrew niphʿal הפתח). These cases are the best evidence that Jesus spoke Aramaic.

In addition to these sayings, the Gospels preserve a number of individual words transliterated from Aramaic or Hebrew that suggest that Jesus regularly spoke in a Semitic language. There are too many such words to list here (for a convenient list, see Jeremias 1971, 5–7), but prominent among them are his use of *Abba* in address to God as "Father" and his distinctive use of the nonresponsorial *Amen* in the phrase "Amen [truly] I say to you." Of the Semitic words recorded of Jesus, most appear to be Aramaic, although some are Hebrew and some can be both. Finally, many sayings of Jesus in the Gospels recorded in Greek are thought to reflect underlying Aramaic vocabulary or syntax. In particular, cases of possible mistranslation from Aramaic into Greek, alternative translations of Aramaic into Greek represented by two Gospels, and plays on words discoverable when the Greek is translated back into Aramaic often make it possible to detect this Aramaic substratum (still important is M. Black [3]1967, despite recent criticism of this approach; e.g., Porter 2000, 89–99).

Given this evidence, it is not surprising that most scholars consider Aramaic to have been Jesus's mother tongue and his primary teaching language. Occasionally, however, scholars have asked whether Jesus may not have also taught in Greek or Hebrew, and the question has grown stronger in recent decades due to the increasing evidence for the use of Greek and Hebrew among Palestinian Jews at the time of Jesus. At this point, it is necessary to say something about the overall linguistic situation in first-century Palestine.

Our understanding of the language situation in Jewish Palestine has changed dramatically over the last century. The dominant view, starting as early as the sixteenth century and continuing to the mid-twentieth century, was that since the return from the Babylonian exile, the language of the general Jewish population in Palestine was almost exclusively Aramaic, with Hebrew the preserve of the educated elite, used mostly for literature, study, prayer, and liturgy. Some scholars viewed Mishnaic Hebrew as an artificial, scholastic language, a kind of amalgam of popular Aramaic and learned Hebrew. There were exceptions to this view, scholars who believed that Hebrew continued as a living language at the time of Jesus, but their views were not widely accepted. And while the evidence for the use of Greek among Jews in Palestine was acknowledged, that language too was thought to be the preserve of the upper class or the well educated. Accordingly it was assumed, almost without argument, that Jesus too spoke almost exclusively Aramaic. A classic example is Gustaf Dalman, who, after briefly presenting the evidence that Aramaic (not Hebrew) was the language of the people, proceeds to unearth the underlying Aramaic of the words of Jesus and explains their meaning on that basis, although he often adduces Hebrew parallels as well (Dalman 1902, originally published in German in 1898).

The late twentieth and early twenty-first centuries have witnessed a thoroughgoing revision of this picture. The great documentary discoveries in the Judean wilderness have revealed that Hebrew continued to be used, not only in elite and learned priestly and scribal circles but also among the general population—if not to the same degree as Aramaic, yet to such a degree that we can no longer discount its use in everyday communication. The evidence has also shown that Mishnaic Hebrew was not an artificial language but a genuine development within a living Hebrew language, influenced, to be sure, by Aramaic. Greek, the documentary discoveries have shown, was more widely used than previously thought. Biblical books and other Jewish writings from Palestine that were either first written in Greek or translated into Greek from Hebrew or Aramaic are further evidence for the widespread use of Greek. The Hellenists mentioned in Acts 6:1 and 9:29, probably Greek-speaking Jews in Jerusalem, some of whom became Christian, provide still more evidence. The ongoing discovery of inscriptions has confirmed what the literary evidence suggests: Aramaic was indeed prevalent, but not to the exclusion of Greek or Hebrew. Many Jews in Palestine in the first century must have spoken Greek or Hebrew in addition to or in place of Aramaic. A new picture of the first century has emerged in which Aramaic, Greek, and Hebrew were spoken and written side by side and in close contact with each other. Estimating the proportion of the population that used each language continues to be difficult (for a recent attempt at estimation, see Wise 2015). Although Latin was used by Roman officials in Palestine, its use among the indigenous population was negligible. (For recent overviews of the history and current state of scholarship, see esp. Buth and Notley 2014 and Wise 2015, 7–20; older but still useful is Fitzmyer 1970.)

Scholars recognize that one must make room for differences in the use of languages not only by time but also by location. The prevalence of Greek in various parts of Galilee, where Jesus grew up and conducted the bulk of his ministry, continues to be debated, largely because evidence for the linguistic situation in Galilee has not been as abundant as it has been for Judea. It is clear that in the larger, hellenized cities and towns in and around Galilee Greek was used widely. The degree to which Greek penetrated beyond those cities and towns is uncertain. Scholars generally regard it as likely that a good number of Galilean Jews would have spoken Greek, especially those who interacted with Greek-speaking gentiles as a matter of daily work, even if the main language of daily life was Aramaic (or Hebrew). It has been thought that Hebrew was less prevalent in first-century Galilee than in Judea (e.g., Emerton 1973, 16–17), but recently that view too has been challenged (Buth and Notley 2014, 110–81). It is difficult to move beyond generalities and speculation in these questions.

What does all this mean for the language(s) of Jesus? First of all, the evidence of the Gospels fits well into the new picture of the language situation in first-century Palestine. The evidence would seem to indicate that Jesus mostly spoke and taught in Aramaic. But if the story in Luke 4:16–30 is authentic, it shows that Jesus was able to read from the book of Isaiah in the synagogue of Nazareth (presumably in Hebrew). Moreover, since we know that in the Second Temple period Mishnaic Hebrew was used in halakic contexts, it is possible that Jesus debated with other teachers in Hebrew. A number of places where Jesus is depicted as interacting with gentiles (e.g., Matt. 8:5–13; Mark 7:25–30; 15:2–5) are considered likely occasions on which Jesus might have spoken Greek (see further John 12:20–22). (For other such possible situations, see Porter 2000, 144–54.) That Jesus *taught* in Greek is more difficult to prove. It has been proposed that some words of Jesus (e.g., "hypocrite") must have been spoken in Greek, but that has not been convincing to most scholars (see Fitzmyer 1992, 62–63). Even if one does not deny that in some particular situations Jesus probably spoke Greek, more work is needed to show that in particular *teaching* situations Jesus not only could have but must have spoken in Greek.

Black, Matthew. 1967. *An Aramaic Approach to the Gospels and Acts*. Third edition. Oxford.

Buth, Randall, and R. Steven Notley, eds. 2014. *The Language Environment of First Century Judaea*. Leiden.

Dalman, Gustaf. 1902. *The Words of Jesus. Considered in the Light of Post-Biblical Jewish Writings and the Aramaic Language*. Translated by D. M. Kay. Edinburgh.

Hengel, Martin. 1974. *Judaism and Hellenism: Studies in Their Encounter in Palestine during the Early Hellenistic Period*. Translated by John Bowden. 2 volumes. London.

Hezser, Catherine. 2001. *Jewish Literacy in Roman Palestine*. TSAJ 81. Tübingen.

Jeremias, Joachim. 1971. *New Testament Theology.* Translated by John Bowden. London.

Keith, Chris. 2011. *Jesus's Literacy: Scribal Culture and the Teacher from Galilee.* LNTS 413. New York and London.

Riesner, Rainer. [3]1988. *Jesus als Lehrer: Eine Untersuchung zum Ursprung der Evangelien-Überlieferung.* WUNT II 7. Tübingen.

Wise, Michael Owen. 2015. *Language and Literacy in Roman Judaea: A Study of the Bar Kokhba Documents.* New Haven.

Stephen Hultgren

3. Jesus in the Judaism of His Time (Jewish Influence on Jesus)

Jesus was born into a Jewish family. As "Joseph's son" (Luke 3:23; 4:22; John 1:45; cf. Matt. 1:16), he was regarded as a Jew by virtue of descent according to the prevailing kinship system at that time. According to Luke 2:21, he was circumcised on the eighth day (cf. Gen. 17:12–14). As an adult he participated at least once in the pilgrimage to Jerusalem for Passover. John's Gospel has him present in Jerusalem several times and during additional Jewish festivals. Whether his last supper was a Passover meal (as in the Synoptics) is disputed, but this is not decisive for our question. During his public activity in Galilee, Jesus went into local synagogues to teach (Matt. 4:23; 9:35; 13:54), especially on the Sabbath (Mark 1:21; Luke 4:15, 16; 13:10). Even if some of these notices are redactional, attendance in synagogues fits well with Jesus's healings on the Sabbath (Mark 3:1 par.), inasmuch as the Jewish populace of a locale assembled in synagogues on this day. It is more clearly perceived today than in earlier research that here "synagogue" designates a building (and not simply an "assembly" of people), as such buildings have often been discovered in villages and towns populated by Jews in the first century. Like in other accounts of assemblies in synagogues on the Sabbath, the focus in this context is on Jesus's teaching and reading of Scripture rather than his prayer (although a fixed reading from the books of the prophets cannot be generally proven for the period). Jesus's command to the man with the withered hand: "Come to the middle" (ἔγειρε εἰς τὸ μέσον; Mark 3:3), which places the man in the public view of the assembled community, thus fits the typical construction of a synagogue from the first century, the most important characteristic of which is a rectangular space in the middle of rows of benches (see D.II.2). In spite of the association of the healing in Mark 3:5 (and parallels) with a mere word, it can be assumed that such healing on the Sabbath was considered to be offensive (as for other healings on the Sabbath, Luke 13:13 ascribes to Jesus the laying on of hands, and according to 14:4 he touches the person). At the same time, Jesus tries to persuade by reasoning in that, according to Mark 3:4, he appeals to saving life. From the time of the Maccabees, this plays a role in Sabbath discourse (self-defense: 1 Macc. 2:39–41); in rabbinic sources it is referenced as *piqquaḥ nefesh*, such that for the sake of saving life the Sabbath might be "superseded" (t. Shabbat 9[10]:22, 15[16]:16–17; Mekilta *shabbata ki tissa* 1 [on Exod. 31:13; ed. Horovitz and Rabin 340–41]), even for suspected danger to life (*sfeq nefashot*: t. Shabbat 15[16]:11, 16–17; m. Yoma 8:6). Even in some texts from Qumran, concern for the life of an endangered person is a motive (CD-A xi 16–17; 4Q265 vi 6–7). Yet here it leads to a creative solution that remains *below* a violation of the Sabbath commandment (rescue, for example, by a helping hand, according to 4Q265, by offering an outer garment). Jesus suggests in his reasoning in Mark 3:4 that his opponents (according to Mark 2:24 and 3:6, at least in part "Pharisees") agreed, that on the Sabbath one ought to do good and save life. In this he is closer to the Pharisees than to the position of Qumran texts, though in his understanding of the healing as "lifesaving" he goes beyond them (Doering 2015).

Jesus cannot be identified as belonging to one of the elite groups (Pharisees, Sadducees, Essenes or Yaḥad, respectively). At the same time, as this example shows, on some issues he is nearer to the Pharisees than to the other groups. From a sociological point of view, it is possible to infer a competition of Jesus and his movement with the Pharisees in the same milieus. The frequency of debates with the Pharisees precisely concerning questions of the law suggests a certain affinity in approach; also, the Jesus tradition offers a partial recognition of "righteousness" influenced by Pharisees (Mark 2:17; Luke 5:31; 15:7, 29, 31; cf. Mark 12:34; Berger 1988). Nevertheless, Jesus apparently criticized legal traditions of Pharisees (or endorsed by Pharisees); so, washing hands is futile, since consumption of food cannot pollute a person (Mark 7:15–23; cf. Furstenberg 2008). A critique of legal traditions is found implicitly in the Sabbath saying in Mark 2:27, where reference is apparently made to the institution of the Sabbath in creation for the sake of human beings (διὰ τὸν ἄνθρωπον ἐγένετο). On divorce, Jesus even goes so far as to view the Mosaic concession of a divorce certificate in Deut. 24:1 as not covered by the original destiny and relation between husband and wife established in creation, which Jesus then validates anew (Mark 10:4–9). In this he partially joins up with the Damascus Document (citation of Gen. 1:27 in CD-A iv 21), which however also locates the principle of the joining of one male with one female outside of the creation story (citations from Gen. 7:9 in CD-A v 1–2; Deut. 17:17 in CD-A v 1–2), and in addition does not prohibit divorce (this is permitted according to 4Q266 9 iii 4–7; CD-A xiii 17), but rather prohibits polygyny (concomitant or serial) during the lifetime of the partner (Doering 2009). Jesus's weighting of the commandments (as in Matt. 23:23, τὰ βαρύτερα τοῦ νόμου, "the heavier [matters] of the Law") and their summary in the Golden

Rule (Matt. 7:12 par.) and in the double love commandment (Mark 12:28–31 par.) have partial antecedents in ancient Judaism (see D.II.2), although Jesus's formulations differ from them in detail.

The attestation in the Synoptics that Jesus taught "with authority" (ἐξουσία; Mark 1:22 par.; 1:27 par.) is readily understandable in the framework of Jewish culture and expectations. Several Qumran texts refer to spirit-endowed prophets, who were expected in the time of the end (4Q521 2 ii 1–2; 4Q558 51 ii 4: Elijah; 11Q13 ii 25–19; 4Q175 i–viii; 1QS ix 11: the "prophet like Moses"; CD-A vi 10–11: the one "who teaches righteousness at the end of days"; perhaps also CD-A vii 18; 4Q174 iii 11: the "interpreter of the Torah," which could be about the priestly messiah). To be sure, some of the plausibility structures argued by Jesus are thereby shifted toward the acceptance of this authority. In this respect, we need to pay constant attention to the horizon of Jesus's ministry, that is, the kingdom of God that has come near (Mark 1:14–15 par.), which is shown to be inaugurated in his exorcisms and healings as well as in his proclamation (Luke 11:20 par.; Matt. 11:4–6 par.). Thereby, Jesus draws on Jewish traditions of the kingdom of God understood eschatologically. Again, texts from Qumran are instructive for such an understanding of the time of the end and God's acts taking place in it (4Q521 2 ii 5–15 in comparison with Matt. 11:4–6 par.). It is striking that Jesus's activity as a whole fits quite well with that of a prophet, whereas the *titulus crucis*, "the King of the Jews," calls to mind the multiply attested expectations in first-century Judaism of a royal messiah as well as the embodiment of this expectation in concrete forms, but it is hardly indicative of Jesus's public activity. Solely with the entrance to Jerusalem (Mark 11:1–10 par.; John 12:12–19) does Jesus explicitly appear with royal-messianic accents, and he seems to have connected these with the largely prophetic signature of his other activity (cf. J. Collins [2]2010, 229–34).

Berger, Klaus. 1988. "Jesus als Pharisäer und frühe Christen als Pharisäer." *NovT* 30: 231–62.

Collins, John J. [2]2010. *The Scepter and the Star: Messianism in Light of the Dead Sea Scrolls*. Grand Rapids.

Doering, Lutz. 2009. "Marriage and Creation in Mark 10 and CD 4–5." In *Echoes from the Caves: Qumran and the New Testament*, edited by Florentino García Martínez, 133–64. STDJ 85. Leiden.

———. 2015. "Jesus und der Sabbat im Licht der Qumrantexte." In *Jesus, Paulus und die Texte von Qumran*, edited by Jörg Frey and Enno E. Popkes, 33–61. WUNT II 390. Tübingen.

Furstenberg, Yair. 2008. "Defilement Penetrating the Body: A New Understanding of Contamination in Mark 7:15." *NTS* 54: 176–200.

Lutz Doering

4. Galilee and Environs as the Sphere of Activity

4.1. Statement of the Problem and the State of Research

According to the evidence in the Synoptics, with the exception of his birth, an episode from his youth (Luke 2), and the last intensive week of his life in Jerusalem (Mark 11:1–16:8 par.), Galilee was Jesus's primary field of activity. The Gospel of John shares this point of view but has Jesus journey from Galilee to Jerusalem on several occasions in order to participate in festivals (John 2:13; 5:1; 7:2–10; 10:22–23; 11:55) and to teach with intensity in the temple (7:14–52). According to all four canonical Gospels, Jesus calls his disciples and encounters a wide variety of people (Pharisees, tax collectors, "sinners" of quite diverse sorts, fishermen, leaders of synagogues). In addition, Galilean local color pervades most of the gospel genres (conflict stories, miracle stories, especially parables in the Synoptics). Hence, with respect to the history of origin, places and events in Galilee are part of the oldest layers of the Jesus tradition.

With respect to *geographical outlines* of "Jesus's movement" in Galilee, however, the Synoptics differ from the Gospel of John. Whereas with the exception of Nazareth (Matt. 4:13; Luke 4:16–30) and the transfiguration on Mount Tabor (Mark 9:2–10 par.), the former locate Jesus's activity almost exclusively on the northern edge of the Sea of Gennesaret (Capernaum, Bethsaida, Gadara, indirectly Magdala), in addition to the lake region, the Gospel of John is also aware of locations of activity in the center of lower Galilee such as Cana and Nain. These conceptual distinctions impede attempts to reconstruct the actual course and the sphere of activity of the historical Jesus from the Gospels. Because the Johannine version is just as much the product of redactional activity as that of the Synoptics, no version can be assigned unmediated priority over another.

The insight into the incremental redactional formation of the Jesus tradition also brings into question the assumption propagated in research until not so long ago that the Gospels depict Galilee accurately, such that a close correspondence exists between "Jesus the Galilean" and "the Galilee of Jesus." But this applies only quite contingently. With reference to the *Galilean context* of Jesus's public presence, the Gospels do not offer any representative "cross section" of the Galilean milieu but rather only a snippet. Certain elements are thematic (villages, fishing, poverty), others are not (larger cities, cultural influences). In this sense the Jesus tradition creates "its" Galilee similarly, for instance, to how Josephus designs "his" Galilee in his autobiographical reports in his *Life* or the historical presentation in the *Jewish Wars* (Zangenberg 2007).

We now have a good four decades of intensive archaeological field research, paired with sociohistorical inquiries into such matters as the structure of settlements, the living conditions of farmers, the relationship of the urban dwellers to the inhabitants of the countryside, the social location of Galilean resistance movements, the composition of the Jewish upper class, and the role of religion (e.g., Freyne 1998; Zangenberg and Schröter 2012; Fiensy and Strange 2014–2015). Between the time of Herod the Great and the catastrophic first rebellion, Galilee emerged again and again as a thoroughfare between the urban centers on the coast and the Decapolis, the Jewish culture of which was subjected to a vigorous process of change, to which distinct regional groups of the population adapted in different ways. Especially southeastern Galilee, and hence Jesus's geographical environment in lower Galilee (so the Gospel of John) or on the north shore of the sea (so the Synoptics and John), was, according to the results of recent research, more urban and more "hellenized" than the picture of Galilee depicted by the Gospels as villages and small cities would allow. The question whether the concentration on rural Galilee depicts a conscious choice of the historical Jesus or is based on the emphases of the preliterary and early literary formation of tradition is disputed and awaits clarification.

4.2. Topography and History

Geographically, Galilee is somewhat clearly bounded only in the south by the rise of hill country along the Jezreel Valley and in the east by the Jordan Valley together with the Sea of Gennesaret. In the southwest the Galilean hill country gently descends into the coastal plain; in the northwest it reaches up to the Mediterranean Sea. In the north, only the Litani River, today located outside of Galilee, forms a genuine topographic border. However, none of these lines separated ancient Galilee from its surroundings in a stable way, and even the Mediterranean was accessible from Galilee by way of coastal cities such as Ptolemais, Tyre, and Sidon. Galilee was always impacted both by its physical topography *and* by its checkered history and connections with the surrounding region. Hence, one cannot understand Galilee's cultural history apart from the inclusion of the neighboring territories—particularly the Decapolis and the coastal strip. Especially many cultural impulses from outside often impacted Galilee.

Due to insufficient data, the history of the region before the Hasmonean conquest and colonization still remains rather shadowy; until now, neither the exact borders of the "district" (*galil*) nor the structure of its population can be determined with desirable clarity. The well-known passage from Isa. 9:1–2 quoted in Matt. 4:15–16 implies that, according to a Jewish perspective, at least at the time of the Isaianic tradition "gentiles" lived in the northern district of "Galilee." In the third and second centuries BCE, Galilee was populated by groups whose customary pottery was partly in the late iron age tradition ("Galilean coarse ware"), but these groups were also exposed to the cultural influence of the Phoenician Hellenism of the coastal cities. Apart from a palace (Tel Kedesh), some fortifications (Keren Naftalı, Beersheba ha-Galil), a trading post in the agrarian hinterland (Tel Anafa), and shrines such as Mitzpe Yamin, especially pottery discoveries in numerous later settlements show that Galilee was very well settled before 100 BCE.

However, in addition to this pagan, Phoenician Semitic population, at that time Jews already appear to have lived in the region or, more specifically, had infiltrated the southern area (1 Macc. 5:14–24). To be sure, here research is still under way; new findings can be expected at any time.

In the wake of the broad Hasmonean expansion to the north at the end of the rule of John Hyrcanus I (ca. 110 BCE), and shortly thereafter under the reign of his successor Aristobulus I (104–103 BCE), the cultural character of the region was fundamentally changed: the influence of the coast was replaced by a Jewish version of Hellenism inspired by the Jerusalem coterie. The new masters endeavored to integrate their growing realm as seamlessly as possible by government investments and infrastructure measures. The destruction of earlier settlements and their replacement by new villages and cities with material culture influenced from the south clearly show that Galilee was systematically colonized. Although this did not have to mean the physical end of the pre-Hasmonean populace, after the beginning of the first century BCE they are no longer conspicuous. Naturally the Hasmonean conquest also had consequences for determining the boundaries, which from that time on operated under the name "Galilee." From then on Galilee's border ran where the Hasmonean influence was not able to be established permanently: territories east of the Jordan and the Sea of Gennesaret, along the coastal plain, as well as in the north below the Litani River remained "outside" and retained their pre-Hasmonean traditions (cf. the geographical excursus in Josephus, *J. W.* 3.35–43). By the creation of a relatively homogeneous population and settlements in the interior and the definition of more clearly, culturally influenced borders toward the exterior, the Hasmoneans became the actual creators of "Galilee" in the sense of a territory inhabited by Jews confined to the hill and mountainous regions of north Palestine. Not until Augustus assigned territory around Mount Hermon and in the Decapolis to Herod the Great was it assured that territories not populated by a Jewish majority were taken into Galilee. On the other hand, Jews also lived outside of Galilee, for instance, in Gaulanitis beyond the Jordan (e.g., Gamla), in Trachonitis (Caearea Philippi), or as diaspora communities in neighboring cities of the Decapolis such as Hippos or Gadara. A strong communal spirit, grounded religiously and culturally among Jewish groups on both sides of the sea, made sure that the rapidly changeable political boundaries had little influence on their contacts and communication.

Thus the fact that according to Mark 5:1–20 par. (Decapolis) and 7:24–31 par. ("region of Tyre and Sidon") the disciples moved about between the territory of Philip and Antipas is, therefore, thoroughly plausible.

In the Hasmonean "vision" for Galilee, there is an immense amount of information about a building project, which has been made available through intensive excavations in recent times: the port and commercial center Magdala. Apparently with government funds and planning during the first half of the first century BCE, in Magdala a monumental, fortified harbor located approximately in the middle of the west bank of the Sea of Gennesaret was built in increments, with a wharf, pier, and towers. Magdala possessed urban structures such as a quadriporticus, a well house, thermal baths, and villas. Due to its location on the lake, the city was the decisive link in the apparently increasingly lucrative trade between Ptolemais in the west and the Decapolis on the east bank of the lake. For the Hasmoneans, the harbor promised the potential of tapping into this commerce through their newly won territory. Hence, the hometown of Mary Magdalene was anything but a sedate village (DeLuca and Lena 2015).

Two other significant urban centers at the time of Jesus were Sepphoris and Tiberias. As early as Persian and Hellenistic times, Sepphoris, because of its location, served as an important connection for commerce between the Mediterranean and the Sea of Gennesaret. At the beginning of the first century BCE, Alexander Jannaeus successfully defended Sepphoris against an attack by Ptolemy IX Lathyros (Josephus, *Ant.* 13.337–338). From then on the settlement served as a Hasmonean administrative center for Galilee. Herod the Great occupied the city in 37 BCE in a snowstorm and used it as a northern headquarters (*Ant.* 17.271). A rebellion after the death of Herod in 4 BCE was quelled by the Syrian legate Quinctilius Varus (*Ant.* 17.289; Josephus, *J. W.* 2.68). Antipas rebuilt it as a capital under the name αὐτοκρατορίς (*Ant.* 18.27); however, lack of archaeological evidence makes the scope of these activities difficult to comprehend. The term πρόσχημα used by Josephus in this context can allude to the fortification of the city as well as to its exceptional splendor. That Jesus of Nazareth, a village located near Sepphoris, like hundreds of other men, might have participated in these public construction projects is conceivable but cannot be verified. Sepphoris does not appear in the Jesus tradition. At any rate, the theater appears to date from the end of the first century CE. After the founding of Tiberias, Sepphoris took second place in Antipas's realm. The size and appearance of the settlement at the time of Jesus are by and large obscure. During the Jewish revolt, Sepphoris remained loyal, likely because the town feared commercial losses and did not anticipate a break from Rome. Apparently Sepphoris moved from a village to a more urban status only after the Second Revolt under the name Diocaesarea (Meyers and Meyers 2013).

Tiberias was founded in 19/20 CE by Herod Antipas in honor of Tiberius Caesar; it was located some seven kilometers south of the already vibrant port city Magdala. According to Josephus (*Ant.* 18.36–38), the city was erected on an abandoned cemetery and Antipas settled it with Jewish and gentile inhabitants of various origins and statuses. The fact that Antipas relocated his capital from Sepphoris to Tiberias underscores again the great importance that the west bank of the Sea of Gennesaret occupied between the interior of Galilee and the Decapolis.

In the New Testament, Tiberias plays a rather marginal role (John 6:1, 23; 21:1). When Jesus was active only a little north of Magdala and Tiberias, the city was certainly still to a great extent under construction. Not only the elaborately decorated palace with the royal treasury and archives (Josephus, *Life*, 37–39, 64–66, 68–69) but also institutions such as a city council with six hundred members, a council of "ten elders" (δέκα πρῶτοι), a market supervisor (ἀγορανόμος), and a ruling official (ἄρχων) attest the Hellenistic-Jewish character of the new capital (Josephus, *J. W.* 2.599, 639–640; *Life* 64–65; *Ant.* 18.149; Miller 2013). A large synagogue served the citizens for religious and political gatherings (*Life* 276–280). The city followed a clearly designed plan, and at the time of Antipas probably already had a cardo (remains found at the tower in the south of the city), a theater, and a stadium (*J. W.* 2.618–619; *Life* 90–96). In the middle of the first century, not only the large diversity of their origins but also competing religious, social, and economic interests fueled serious conflicts among the population. As in Sepphoris, the upper class of Tiberias was also against participation in the revolt against Rome. However, other inhabitants from the middle class supported the rebellion; yet others were openly set against the inhabitants of the neighboring Decapolis (*Life*, 33–42; Miller 2013).

In addition to tolls and fees from local intermediary and terminal trade and from craftsmanship associated with shipbuilding (see C.III.1), the ports of Magdala and Tiberias offered ample opportunities to exploit the abundance of fish in the lake (Hakola 2016). Ship owners and fishermen could unload their boats and sell their products there. Likewise, in the late first century BCE, fish hatcheries developed along the shore of Magdala to meet the strong demand for fish products; these hatcheries were known as far away as Spain and North Africa. Magdala was obviously known for this industry, since in addition to its Aramaic name *Migdal* (rendered Μαγδαλά in Greek = "tower"), the city was also known in Greek as Ταριχέα (τάροχος = salt/pickled fish) (DeLuca and Lena in Fiensy and Strange 2014–2015). Evidently, in the urbanely impacted region on the lake, Greek- and Aramaic-speaking groups lived side by side (cf. also Hippos [Susita]). This suggests that Jesus and his disciples in a limited way were bilingual. Neither the unusually large port facilities for an interior lake nor the "industrialized" methods of fish farming are conceivable without the continuation of the intensive opening of Galilee to the broader Mediterranean area under the Hasmoneans, and then in addition by Herod the Great and Antipas. All of this underscores that Galilee at the time of Jesus was not a remote, purely agricultural backcountry (Zangenberg 2013c).

4.3. Social and Religious Conditions

In view of the high level of government investments initially in Magdala, it may be supposed that with the conquest and annexation of Galilee the Hasmoneans began to install their own Jewish upper class from the south, who obviously profited to a great extent from the upsurge generated by the commercial tax and customs income of the region. The Galilean elite may have been present at the beginning, especially in Magdala and Sepphoris. Under Herod Antipas (regency 4 BCE–ca. 37 CE) this trend was reinforced. Not only did he expand Sepphoris as a second capital with a palace, archives, and wealthy houses in splendor (Josephus, *Ant.* 18.27), he was the first regent who was *directly* responsible for Galilee (and Perea) and who also lived there (*Ant.* 18.36–38). Hence, taxes no longer flowed, as with the Hasmoneans and Herod the Great, to Jerusalem from Galilee, which from 6 CE was under its own Roman prefect but remained under Antipas's control, who as a client ruler maintained his own tax administration in the service of Rome. Hence, it is not by chance that in the Jesus tradition again and again there is talk of tax collectors, who were detested by the local populace as collaborators and exploiters (Mark 2:13–17 par.).

From numerous discoveries in localities in the interior, it is possible to deduce that at the time of Jesus, local leaders (village and family patriarchs), alongside the elite associated with the ruling party, also profited from commerce and agriculture and desired to demonstrate their increasing wealth by buildings and accoutrements in a Hellenistic fashion. For example, the extensive use of blown glass or fine ceramics and murals on walls in the domus of Jotapata or Gamla is of interest. Generally rural settlements also were continually differentiated socially and economically. Villages evolve into rural towns (Jotapata, Gamla, Capernaum, Khirbet Qana), which, as a connection between the villages of their vicinity and cities such as Magdala, Sepphoris, or Tiberias, played an important role in the dynamization of the economic and social life in Galilee. Interestingly Matt. 9:1 mentions the Jewishly influenced small town of Capernaum as a "missionary base" of the Jesus movement. This rural town, located at an important transportation link not far from Magdala, clearly displayed urban elements and was classified as a customs and border station in the political and economic system of Antipas's territory

(Mark 2:14–15 par.). Even if Jesus may have avoided Tiberias and Sepphoris on account of their proximity to the court of Antipas, due to his base in Capernaum he could not have withdrawn from the Jewish-Hellenistic world on the lake.

At the end of the first century BCE and in the first half of the second century CE, the population of Galilee increased. People settled even the less arable fringes of the cultivated land, so that before the first Jewish revolt Galilee achieved its highest density of settlement ever (Leibner 2009). How much common people like farmers, craftsmen, and fishers were able to profit from this dynamic or whether or not further parts of the population were thrown into poverty because of it is disputed, depending on the underlying model in research. Unfortunately, very few authentic Galilean villages have been excavated. Et-Tell (Bethsaida) near the Jordan River on the northeast bank of the Sea of Gennesaret is a very good example both for the resilience of village settlements and for the structure of such a village. In the early first century CE, the settlement consisted of individual houses standing loosely beside each other. In addition, Et-Tell (Bethsaida) and Capernaum also show that in villages and small towns "objects of upscale daily use" such as fine ceramic ware and glass had been introduced. At the same time, recent sociohistorical-oriented investigations demonstrate how complex a village actually was: "farmers" (*peasants*) were not a homogenous group, always impoverished and oppressed *underdogs*. Even at the village level, differences in production and marketing of agricultural products already existed, which was reflected in the prosperity of the people. Subsistence agriculture and marketing complemented each other and closely linked city and countryside with each other.

Nevertheless, there certainly were losers from the social and cultural upheavals that intensified beginning in the first century BCE. The local resources such as available land and crop yield were inadequate to support the growth in population, so that people frequently fell into poverty, and possibly on account of adverse living conditions, excessively large families, or illness, fell into arrears in taxes, mortgaged their possessions, or even had to resort to indentured servitude.

Almost immediately at the death of Herod the Great in 4 BCE, an insurrection broke out. Its watchword of resistance to Roman domination and exclusive fidelity to God was heard even long after its suppression by the Syrian legate Publius Quinctilius (Josephus, *J.W.* 2.68; *Ant.* 17.289). Traditional biblical concepts of proprietorship of land used for agriculture, fidelity to ancestral laws, and the freedom of God's people could certainly be recalled in Jesus's time among some Galileans. Other groups, especially in the urban milieus of Sepphoris, Tiberias, or Magdala, profited from the good relationship with the authorities and rejected the revolt.

The Galilean populace of the first century CE, therefore, was not a homogeneous bloc but encompassed groups with different economic concerns, social identity, and corresponding loyalties (Fiensy and Strange 2014–2015). That the overwhelming portion of Galileans regardless of status and wealth was of the Jewish belief at the time of Jesus is established in today's research. In turn, this belief was not a monolithic bloc but rather was lived and construed diversely. Loyalty to the Jerusalem temple and its priesthood, and the observance of Jewish *essentials* such as circumcision, the Sabbath, and certain fundamental purity prescriptions, certainly were a part of the basic core advocated by all Galilean Jews. Not only the Jesus tradition but also later rabbinic literature shows that people could argue heartily about the correct exposition of God's will even in Galilee. Some of the religious legal positions advocated in Galilee can certainly have corresponded to what we know from Judea (cf. the frequent naming of Pharisees in the Jesus tradition). Substantial differences between "Galilean" and "Judean" halakah are indeed not discernible. As in Judea, so also in Galilee did Hellenistic influence prove to be a challenge for consideration of one's own identity and values, even if individual groups of the populace reacted differently to it. As in Judea, so also in Galilee did Hellenistic influence stimulate the formation of a quite different Jewish-Palestinian material culture by supplying new architectural and decorative options. Thus, the availability of waterproof mortar made the construction of mikvehs possible and thereby created new possibilities for the implementation of widely discussed purity regulations. The Greek city hall design (βουλευτήριον) was the godparent for the development of the earliest synagogue architecture (Gamla, Magdala).

In Jesus's time Galilee was a dynamic region whose development was put in motion by internal and external factors. The particular attention of the Jesus tradition to the *personae miserae* and the subversive tendentiousness of the proclamation of the kingdom of God do not result from the oppressive poverty of just this region but are due to the accent that Jesus himself evidently planted and that the Jesus tradition consequently passed on extensively.

Fiensy, David A., and James R. Strange, eds. 2014–2015. *Galilee in the Late Second Temple and Mishnaic Periods*. Vol. 1, *Life, Culture, and Society*. Vol. 2, *The Archaeological Record from Cities, Towns, and Villages*. Minneapolis.

Zangenberg, Jürgen K. 2013c. "Jesus der Galiläer und die Archäologie: Beobachtungen zur Bedeutung der Archäologie für die historische Jesusforschung." *MTZ* 64: 123–56.

Zangenberg, Jürgen K., and Jens Schröter, eds. 2012. *Bauern, Fischer und Propheten: Galiläa zur Zeit Jesu, Zaberns Bildbände zur Archäologie*. Darmstadt and Mainz.

Jürgen K. Zangenberg

5. Jerusalem and Judea as a Sphere of Activity

5.1. The Political Situation of Judea at the Time of Jesus

After the death of Herod the Great in 4 BCE, and after Judea and Samaria (the heartland of his kingdom) had been ruled for ten years by his inauspicious son Archelaus, these territories were allocated to the *Provincia Syria* in the year 6 CE. Aside from the intermezzo under the Jewish king Agrippa I in 37–44 CE, altogether thirteen *praefecti* from the equestrian class ruled *Iudaea* as an autonomous administrative unit. Doubtless the most famous of these governors was Pontius Pilate (term of office 26–36 CE).

A census was linked with the establishment of this new administrative unit, which was carried out under the leadership of the Syrian finance procurator (the background of Luke 2:1–2). The purpose of this action was to levy taxes that had to be paid to Rome. The capital of *Iudaea*, and thus the residence of the governor as well as the seat of administration, was the cosmopolitan port city Caesarea Maritima founded by Herod the Great, in which Jews, Greeks, Syrians, and probably also some Romans lived, not always without tension. Normally the governor came to Jerusalem only in extraordinary cases (such as major pilgrim festivals), to demonstrate his presence and to keep the situation under control. A garrison of auxiliary troops stood by him (perhaps five thousand, not a legion; W. Eck 2007, 105–55), who were charged with maintaining internal security, and because of their brutality and arrogance were anything but popular among the Jewish portion of the population. For example, from Acts 10:1 we know about a *Cohors Italica*. If the governor was in Jerusalem, presumably he resided in what was previously Herod's palace on the western edge of the present Old City; the troops were primarily quartered in the Antonia Fortress at the northern boundary of the temple precincts, so that in case of unrest they could immediately intervene. As the name indicates, the Antonia Fortress had been erected right at the beginning of Herod's rule. It consisted of a rectangular block of 120 by 45 meters, built along the north side of the sanctuary, with a turret 26 meters high (37 meters on the southeast corner, *tetrapyrgos*: "fortress with four corner towers"). Its purpose was to protect the vulnerable northern side of the sanctuary (Josephus, *J. W.* 1.387–390, 401; 5.238–246). The Romans were well aware of this function (Tacitus, *Hist.* 5.12.1, *templum in modum arcis propriique muri*). A luxurious palace was located inside, which Herod occupied until the completion of his new palace in the western part of the city. Only very little of it is preserved (Küchler 2007, 349–55).

In addition to the Antonia Fortress there were other, small military posts at strategically important points in the countryside, but also at crossroads, among which are especially the former fortresses of Herod.

Aside from the fertile coastal zone and the hilly country connected to it, in the west Judea consisted especially of mountainous country, to the north rising up to approximately eight hundred meters with Jerusalem at the center, as well as a semiarid to arid zone along the Jordan Valley. The synoptic tradition locates the advent of John the Baptizer in this "wilderness" (Mark 1:4, ἔρημος; Mark 1:4–11 par.; Matt. 3:1–12 par.; vaguely in John 1:19, according to 3:23 the Baptizer appeared in the Samaritan Aenon near Salim). Jesus also spent forty days in the wilderness (Mark 1:12–13 par.; Matt. 4:1–11 par.). For both accounts the region possesses theological significance as the place of a renewed conquest of the land (Joshua tradition) or of the encounter with God and solitude.

The population of *Iudaea* was anything but homogenous. Jewish inhabitants, who spoke Greek and Aramaic, lived especially in the Judean heartland and as a minority in the coastal cities. But in addition, religiously independent, Aramaic-speaking Samaritans lived in the area of Gerizim in Samaria, and there were non-Jewish groups (in the sources often designated as "Greeks" or "Syrians") in the hellenized cities along the coast. "Genuine," Latin-speaking Romans were quite rare. Religiously and culturally motivated tensions among all these groups, as well as internal tensions within each group (such as between "conservative" and "progressive" Jews of various shades), were a part of everyday life.

In general, the Romans allowed the native population to live according to their conventional traditions, provided that internal security was not endangered, which included not impeding collection of taxes and tribute. The usual practice was to allow villages, synagogue congregations, and clans to regulate their internal affairs as much as possible. So after Judea became a province, the priestly elite retained a large portion of their rights (especially over the temple and the religious and economical issues associated with it) and continued to exercise a large influence over the people. As elsewhere, in spite of all mutual aversion, the Roman administration and the native elite in *Iudaea* maintained a tolerable modus vivendi on the basis of pragmatic considerations. This is elucidated not least of all by the fateful synergy between the Sanhedrin and the governor in the execution of Jesus.

5.2. Judea and Jerusalem in the Gospels

According to the Synoptics, Jesus travels to Jerusalem from Galilee for the first time at the end of his life. This journey is only briefly recounted in Mark (10:1–51): Jesus's route takes him first to "the region of Judea and beyond the Jordan" (i.e., Perea; Mark 10:1) and then by way of Jericho (Mark 10:46; Zangenberg 2013a) from the east directly to the outskirts of Jerusalem (Mark 11:1). Hence, he goes around Samaria and travels through the Jordan Valley, which in view of the repeated attacks by Samaritans on Galilean pilgrims was a common route (Luke 9:52–53; Tacitus, *Ann.* 12:54; Josephus, *J.W.* 2.232–247, *Ant.* 20.118–136). Matthew 19:1–20:34 presumes the same route as Mark, only he fills it in with some additional accounts. Only Luke heavily expands Jesus's journey with material from Q and his special source, and combines the route taken over from Mark by way of Jericho with insertions of a separate Samaritan route. This combination is hardly plausible historically and geographically. According to the Gospel of John, Jesus visits Jerusalem several times.

In all four canonical Gospels, Jerusalem has special importance above all other localities in Judea, and Jerusalem is clearly theologically "loaded" as the pole opposite Galilee. The passion predictions (Mark 8:31–33; 9:30–32; 10:32–34 par.) already depict Jerusalem as the city of the betrayal and execution of the Messiah, but also as the place of his triumphal resurrection. At the same time, Galilee and Jerusalem are also the showplace of messianic teaching with authority. The decision to kill him is already conceived in Galilee (Mark 3:6 by Pharisees and Herodians), but then intensified and implemented under divine governance and with Jesus's consent (Mark 11:18 by high priests and scribes; Mark 14:32–42; δεῖ).

5.3. Jesus's Places and Routes in Jerusalem according to Mark

According to the Synoptics, Jesus approaches the city precincts of Jerusalem, thickly settled with many villages, from the east (Mark 11:1: Bethphage and Bethany). From the "Garden of Gethsemane" (= "Oil Press," presumably typical of a country estate for the region, which was covered with olive trees and farming installations: Mark 14:32; χωρίον), located on the Mount of Olives, he goes back and forth several times to the temple on the east side of the city.

After the triumphal entry into the city (Mark 11:1–10; see D.III.5.1), Jesus goes directly "into the temple" (ἱερόν; Mark 11:11). Coming from the Mount of Olives in the east, Jesus had to cross the Kidron Valley in order to enter the temple through the only gate located there, the immense "Shushan Gate." This certainly was not the most magnificent entry, but theologically probably the most significant one: The gate was located directly across from the altar and the entrance to the temple itself. On the Day of Atonement, the high priest led the scapegoat out through this gate into the wilderness to the east. The diction in Mark 11:11 means that Jesus entered the holy precinct but not the temple edifice in the narrower sense, which in any case would not have been allowed him because he was not a priest.

Like other large temples in the late republic and early empire (cf. the Caesareum in Cyrene or the Hercules Victor temple of Tibur in Latium), the temple consisted of a huge platform surrounded by porticos, in the center of which stood the actual temple (on the temple in general, cf. Josephus, *J.W.* 5.184–237; *Ant.* 15.391–402; Patrich 2009; Kollmann 2013, 42–53). Herod began the construction of the temple either in 23/22 BCE (*J.W.* 1.401) or in 20/19 BCE (*Ant.* 15.380), hence simultaneously with the equally ambitious construction of Caesarea as the residential and port city. The Jerusalem temple was one of the largest sanctuaries of its time (Tacitus, *Hist.* 5.8.1, *immensae opulentiae templum*; cf. Pliny, *Nat.* 5.15.70). According to Mark 13:1–2, even Jesus's disciples were full of admiration for its splendor and size. But Jesus sees all this as headed for complete destruction, which later is presented as a reason for his condemnation (Mark 14:57–59 par.). Sitting in a location opposite the temple, Jesus delivers his revelatory apocalyptic discourse (Mark 13:3 par.).

The sanctuary was the religious, spiritual, and social center of Judaism in Palestine, as it was for all Jews in the widely dispersed diaspora. Its cult was God's gift to his people, a cosmic event, and it gave people the opportunity to pray to God and worship him. The king made sure that the cult was not disrupted during the construction. Only qualified priests were permitted to work in the cultically sensitive areas. In the year 9 or 8 BCE, the temple proper was rededicated (Josephus, *Ant.* 15.423), but work on the sanctuary lasted until shortly before the outbreak of the Jewish revolt (John 2:20; Josephus, *Ant.* 20.219). The final completion of the complex meant mass layoffs and high unemployment, which additionally exacerbated the already strained situation in *Iudaea* and Jerusalem.

The sanctuary first of all consisted of a large platform, the *temenos*. In its last, Herodian form, the sacred precinct was almost double the size of its Hellenistic predecessor, with dimensions of 485 meters on the west side, 460 meters on the east side, 315 meters on the level north side, and 280 meters on the steep and especially immense south side. This trapezoid was hewed out of rock in the north and in the south, created by enormous substructures as high as 50 meters at the pinnacle in the southeast. It had a perimeter of 1,550 meters and a surface area of 146,000 square meters. The limestone blocks were quarried locally and so meticulously hewed that no mortar was necessary. Typically they were between 1 and 2 meters long and weighed between 5 and 6 metric tons; at structurally weighty places, however, much larger blocks, up to 12 meters long and weighing 70 metric tons, were installed. The largest building stone discovered up until now is 13.6 meters long, 3.5 meters high, 4.6 meters thick, and weighs 560 metric tons.

The southern end of the platform was dominated by the "royal portico" (Acts 5:20–42), the largest freestanding basilica of its time with a length of 185 meters and height of 15 meters. It not only embellished the beauty of the already dramatic southern façade but was used for assemblies, as a marketplace, or as a law court, and thus fulfilled the function of a *forum* that was lacking in Jerusalem until the establishment of Aelia Capitolina. The lower but hardly less immense porticos that enclosed the platform on the other three sides served a similar purpose. All these porticos opened toward the interior to the court and afforded shade in which visitors could sit, talk, listen, discuss, trade gifts for sacrifices, or exchange money. Here the prophetic driving out of the traders in the temple could have taken place (Mark 11:15–19 par.; see D.III.5.1). The constantly flowing income from the temple tax and streams of pilgrims made the temple an immense economic factor for the city (Goodman 1999). Further, the porticos were an ideal stage for the many teaching discourses that, according to Mark 11:27–13:2 par., Jesus conducted like a peripatetic philosopher (περιπατεῖν; cf. Mark 11:27) in the ἱερόν with high priests, scribes, and elders, then from Mark 12:13 with Pharisees and Herodians, and from Mark 12:18 also with Sadducees.

In common with the porticos in the area of the southern platform, the entrances in the north, east, and west offered a good opportunity to observe the multitude of people who streamed into the holy precinct to perform prayers, offer private sacrifices, or take vows. In addition to a poor woman, Jesus also sees members of the rich upper class. Differently from the humble woman, who because of compassion gives away all she has (Mark 12:41–44 par.), the scribes like to be greeted in public and wear long garments; they desire the best seats in the synagogue and places of honor at a banquet; and they devour widows' houses (Mark 12:37b–40 par.). So the compact scene of the sanctuary creates a stage for theological debates and vigorous social critique.

The vast temple platform was divided according to "degrees of holiness," into, in ascending degrees, the Court of the Gentiles (an innovation of Herod), the Court of the (Israelite) Women, and the Court of (Male) Israelites. A barrier with inscriptions warned non-Jews not to cross beyond the area allotted to them (see C.III.2).

Probably in the area of the present-day Dome of the Rock stood the actual temple with the great altar of burnt offerings, enclosed by a high wall with splendid gates and chambers for storage of temple offerings, tools, firewood, and other equipment. This area was accessible only to priests. None of this has been preserved; nevertheless, texts give us a quite precise concept of the appearance of this house of God. The temple was aligned toward the east. It belonged to the Syrian longhouse design and consisted of a broad and high entrance hall, followed by a lower and smaller main hall with two areas (the "holy place" and the "holy of holies," which only the high priest was permitted to enter on the Day of Atonement).

Year after year this temple was the destination of countless pilgrims, who streamed into the city especially for the celebration of the great pilgrimage festivals (Passover, Festival of Weeks, Festival of Booths). The pilgrims, who altogether could add up to around forty thousand people, stayed in private homes or inns or camped out on plots in the vicinity of the city. The association of all these festivals with Israel's traditions of freedom and holiness made the large multitude an almost uncontrollable security risk. According to Mark 14:1–2 par., two days before Passover the atmosphere was quite stirred up. Also, Pilate was in residence in the city. Like thousands of others, Jesus and his disciples celebrated their meal in a rented dining hall on the upper floor of a house in the city—reclining on cushions, corresponding to Hellenistic custom (location unknown, traditionally on Mount Zion; Küchler 2007, 617–18). Because of the strong shaping of the report owing to the Christian meal tradition and the absence of many elements that were a part of the Passover, the question is disputed whether and to what extent this was a Passover meal. After the meal, Jesus retired to the Mount of Olives.

After the betrayal and arrest, Jesus was brought into the house of the high priest Caiaphas (Mark 14:26–52 par.), where those belonging to the leading priestly families gathered to interrogate Jesus and deliberate how to execute the death penalty. The character and legitimacy of this trial before the Sanhedrin have constantly been disputed. Nevertheless, in view of the strong literary shape of the reports and the confused situation on the eve of the Passover festival, one should not set the standards too high regarding the formal correctness of the conduct of the trial as it is established somewhat later in the Mishnah. The report in Mark 14:53–72 par. implies a large house with an interior court in which individual companions of Jesus and domestic servants were able to gather around a fire. Indeed, various houses of this type in the Upper City, such as the "Palatial Mansion," the "House of Columns," or the "Herodian Mansion," and on the Southern Hill adjacent to Mount Zion (St. Peter in Gallicantu), have been investigated archaeologically. But none of these buildings could be identified as Caiaphas's house unequivocally. All the same excavations attest the numerous attempts of the priestly upper class of Jerusalem before 70 to bring their Jewish identity into line with the upscale luxury of the Hellenistic world. Mikvehs and mosaics, ornamental plaster and stoneware become fascinating evidence for an emerging Jewish-Hellenistic material culture in Palestine, the development of which was precipitously disrupted by the Jewish revolt (Küchler 2007, 608–13; Zangenberg 2013b).

In the course of the interrogation of Jesus, the Sanhedrin arrived at an unequivocal conclusion: according to Mark 14:62–64, Jesus was sentenced to death on account of βλασφημία (he threatened to destroy the temple and also identified himself with God's heavenly representative; cf. differences in the parallel accounts!). He was also abused by bystanders. However, apparently because the Jewish temple authorities could no longer execute anyone on their own authority or did not want to risk it because of the volatile situation in the city, they took

Jesus to Pilate (Mark 15:1). The setting of this trial is the courtyard (αὐλή) in the headquarters of the governor (πραιτώριον, Mark 15:16; cf. Acts 23:35). Traditionally this location is associated with the λιθόστρωτος in the area of the Antonia Fortress in the present-day convent of the Sisters of Zion on the northern border of the temple precinct. However, after the Hadrianic date of this paved area was unequivocally demonstrated, the place of the trial is presumed to be in the former palace of Herod on the western border of the city, which was better suited for Pilate's demands and, in view of the tense situation at Passover, was also more secure (Küchler 2007, 381–82, 500–501; Gibson 2012, 99–125).

The fortress-like, secured palace was first ready for occupancy in 23 BCE (Josephus, *J. W.* 5.156–183; *Ant.* 15.318). In luxury it excelled anything that Herod had heretofore constructed (*J. W.* 1.402); measured circa 100 meters by 300 meters; had huge halls decorated with mosaics; and had guest rooms with one hundred beds, interior courts with gardens, water installations, and columbaria for breeding pigeons. All this created a paradisaical atmosphere. Excavations under the present citadels and the Armenian patriarchate revealed remains of the massive substructures of the foundation. The structures resting on these foundations were demolished after the Roman conquest.

According to the Jesus tradition, at the beginning Pilate apparently showed little inclination to let himself be exploited for inner-Jewish affairs (Mark 15:1–20a), but then in view of the imponderable will of the people, he followed his instinct to avoid turmoil and not to inflame the upper class against himself. Instead of Jesus he granted freedom to Barabbas, a convicted terrorist (στασιαστής), and allowed Jesus to be led away to his execution. In spite of the tendency in the Jesus tradition to absolve Roman authorities from guilt for the execution and to encumber the Jewish leaders with it, this depiction of a Roman official who avoided conflict and embraced opportunity is not implausible. As governor, Pilate had all legal authority over an ordinary provincial inhabitant such as Jesus. That he came from Galilee, which was governed by Antipas, played no role in this. The reason for the execution is specified as Jesus's claim to be king of the Jews—thus, in the final analysis, insurrection, which Rome unfailingly punished with the ultimate penalty. For ordinary provincials, this meant dreaded crucifixion. Did Pilate (mis)understand Jesus's message of the kingdom of God in this fashion? The *titulus* makes the verdict conspicuous for anyone who encounters the doomed person on his final journey.

The execution consisted of several acts of abuse, mockery, and hortatory exhibition of the delinquent (Gibson 2012, 127–46). No limit was set for the sadism of the execution squad, which was selected from the auxiliary troops and led by a centurion. Again, elements that play on Jesus's "kingship" are striking, which certainly is not only a literary characteristic. In Mark 15:20b–41 Jesus was then led out of the city to Golgotha, the place of execution, most likely an abandoned stone quarry on a cliff in which some burial caves had already been hollowed out. Golgotha presumably lies north or northwest of the second wall (the third wall did not yet exist), roughly in the area of the present-day Church of the Holy Sepulcher (Küchler 2007, 416–18). Because of massive quarrying in Roman times, however, its precise location can no longer be identified.

Crucifixion was not only an especially gruesome form of execution (malefactors suffocated from the weight of their own body), it also was reserved in antiquity as a punishment for slaves and infamous villains. By means of the exhibition of the one who was dying, that is, of death on a cross, this kind of execution also served to intimidate potential untrustworthy provincialists and to demonstrate Rome's unlimited power over life and death.

Unlike many who were crucified and denied a burial, Jesus was interred in the chamber tomb of a rich council member named Joseph of Arimathea (see C.III.1; Mark 15:42–16:8 par.). After the release of the body and its removal from the cross, it was wrapped in cloths, brought to the tomb, and, because of the approaching Passover, quickly placed on a stone bench. A stone was rolled against the entrance of the tomb, as seems to have been the practice especially for the burial of elites ("Royal Tombs," "Herod's Tomb"). Since the nineteenth century, thousands of graves of various sizes have been discovered in the necropolis, especially to the south, to the east, and to the north of Jerusalem (Kloner and Zissu 2007). On the day after the Sabbath, women from among Jesus's followers came with spices and ointment to complete the funeral rites. Their purpose was not to mummify Jesus's body and preserve it for the hereafter, but rather to honor the deceased and restore at least some of his dignity, as is demonstrated by texts as well as archaeological discoveries (Zangenberg 2008; Gibson 2012, 147–67).

Gibson, Shimon. 2012. *Die sieben letzten Tage Jesu: Die archäologischen Tatsachen*. Munich.

Kollmann, Bernd. 2013. *Jerusalem: Geschichte der Heiligen Stadt im Zeitalter Jesu*. Darmstadt.

Küchler, Max. 2007. *Jerusalem: Ein Handbuch und Studienreiseführer zur Heiligen Stadt*. OLB IV/2. Göttingen.

Patrich, Joseph. 2009. "538 BCE–70 CE: The Temple (Beyt Ha-Miqdash) and Its Mount." In *Where Heaven and Earth Meet: Jerusalem's Sacred Esplanade*, edited by Oleg Grabar and Benjamin Z. Kedar, 36–71. Jerusalem and Austin, TX.

Zangenberg, Jürgen K. 2013b. "Jerusalem: Hellenistic and Roman." In *The Oxford Encyclopedia of the Bible and Archaeology*, edited by Daniel M. Master et al., 2:23–37. Oxford.

Jürgen K. Zangenberg

IV. Public Ministry

1. Jesus's Social Context

1.1. Jesus and John the Baptizer

John the Baptizer stands at the beginning of the history of Jesus. Jesus himself leaves no doubt about this point of origin (cf. Q 7:31–34; Mark 11:27–33). Early Christian sources from Mark to the Apocrypha clearly reflect John's initial position. The trajectory of the interpretation of John's role as an interpreter shows a clear trend. If at first he is the independent baptizer of Jesus (Mark), he then inquires—still in doubt—about Jesus's mission (Q); then he recognizes Jesus's superiority first at his baptism (Matthew), but already while still in his mother's womb (Luke), and he is a witness who has a vision of Jesus's preexistence (John). Even on the descent into hell, he prepares the way for Jesus (Gospel of Nicodemus), and finally he becomes no less than an ascetic saint who is defined solely by his relationship to Jesus Christ. His humble refusal to baptize Jesus (Matt. 3:14) can even be reversed into its opposite: Jesus baptizes John (cf. Opus imperfectum in Matthaeum 4.15; PG 56:658). So the reception history confirms his saying: "He must increase, and I must decrease" (John 3:30). The predecessor became the harbinger.

1.1.1. Sources and Methods for Research on the Baptizer

From the time of Reimarus, research on the Baptizer was in many ways the forerunner of the quest for Jesus. Here both bold theses and classical methods could be tested on widely distributed but manageable textual materials. All narrative writings of the New Testament serve as sources, including the sayings source, as well as early Christian literature, which is indeed mostly concise but occurs in surprising spans, from Jewish Christian gospels by way of the Protoevangelium of James and Justin Martyr to the Pseudo-Clementine and gnostic writings. The report of Josephus is historically relevant, which depicts the Baptizer as a respectable Hellenistic teacher of virtue, whose baptism ritual and eschatological message are expressly weakened to take into consideration his Roman readers (*Ant.* 18.116–119). Later sources hardly contribute to the historical issue. It is apparent that the Qur'an is especially fascinated with his devout father, Zechariah, and pictures John as a God-fearing prophet without a ritual of repentance or an eschatological message. In the first third of the twentieth century, excited interest in Mandean literature was prominent, with a portrayal of the Baptizer as a significant teacher and Jesus as his dark rival. In the meantime, such "Mandean fever" died down. Even if this gnostic religion likely goes back to the Syro-Palestinian milieu of the Baptizer, it "discovered" John, at least in the theologically loaded narrative form, rather under Muslim influence, as it needed a prophet of its own. Also, the *Slavonic Josephus* (supplements to the text of the *Jewish Wars*) aroused unnecessary excitement in the first half of the twentieth century: the Baptizer appears here in two fragments as an ascetic and political-rebellious wild man. The image belongs in the hagiography of Byzantine Middle Ages and has no value as a source for the first century.

Frequently research has speculated about sources from the "sect of the disciples of the Baptizer" (esp. Mark 6:17–29; Luke 1:46–55, 68–79; John 1:1–18; Sib. Or. 4.159–178), but the reconstructions are methodologically open to questions and the postulated groups behind the texts can hardly be historically useful. If one considers that early Christianity itself originated from the Baptizer movement, the prominent initial position of John in early Christian literature is just as comprehensible as his "apologetic" position. Only the history-of-tradition core of the Pseudo-Clementine literature refers to a prominent religious group that venerates John in the region of Syria, which also makes explicable the veritably conspicuous argument of the Fourth Gospel with the person of John (cf., e.g., John 1:6–8, 15, 19–28). In this group—temporally and geographically confined as far as we can see—John was revered supposedly as Elijah, who by means of baptism gathers God's people for the time of the end. Qumran writings do not mention John, although there are certain intersections with the milieu of the Baptizer.

So especially the Gospels, Acts, and Josephus remain the primary sources about John the Baptizer. In view of this finding, the dilemma of research has been compared with the challenge of distilling the historical person of Jesus from the Qur'an (Reumann 1972). But the quest is not so futile. Precisely because early Christianity developed as a continuation of the Baptizer movement, historically viable traditions are to be expected. If the course of the interpretation of the Baptizer's role stood under Christian auspices, this proves to be a propitious condition for the criterion of embarrassment: where John proves to be awkward or independent from the Jesus tradition, a historical reference can be assumed to be valid (e.g., the Messiah receives John's baptism for repentance). Also, the other proven criteria in Jesus research render helpful services: multiple attestation (e.g., the popularity of John and his baptism for repentance), coherence (e.g., embedding in the more comprehensive Baptizer movement and continuity with the practice of baptism in early Christianity), and casual unsuspicious details (e.g., topographical notices in John). Altogether we thus attain an admittedly fragmentary but plausible overall impression. To modify Albert Schweitzer's image, the historical John is set free from the block of christological dogma and returns to his time.

1.1.2. Impact, Baptism, Message

John the Baptizer unleashed a movement. Extended crowds were drawn by his baptism for repentance. His appearance and his significance engendered lively discussion in contemporary Judaism (cf. esp. Mark 1:4–5; Q 7:24–26; Matt. 21:32; Luke 3:15; 7:29–30; Acts 13:25). The Fourth Gospel confirms this impression indirectly in that it seeks to make adjustments for it (e.g., John 3:26–29; 4:1–3; 10:40–42). Although the synoptic notices may be biased in favor of a restoration of the people of God, it is beyond doubt that the striking preacher of repentance resonated in Judea, Galilee, and Samaria. Still decades after the execution of the Baptizer, religious boundary breakers appealed to him (cf. Acts 18:24–28; 19:1–7). His execution by the tetrarch Herod Antipas led to long-term reactions among the people (cf. Josephus, *Ant.* 18.116, 119).

John's broad impact is explained by the baptism for repentance, which was named after him and after which he was named. Cultic purifications that were already provided for in the Torah were expanded and popularized in Hellenistic times. Regarding the baptist movements that can be traced especially in the Syrian-Palestinian milieu, the urban cult center moved to the margin and sacred purity, often pursued in a secluded lifestyle, attained a central place without having to discard the concept of the official sacrificial cult. Qumran writings attest such a deviating piety of a dominating religious type much like the Fourth Sibyl in the first century or the Hermit Bannus, who lived off of products of the desert and who constantly subjected himself to cold ablutions. The fact that Josephus as a searching youth desires to be with him for three years (*Life* 11–12) attests the popularity of this style of piety.

John presupposed this style of piety but intensified it radically (Q 3:7–9, 16–17). He simplified the act of immersion, liberated it from elitist precincts, developed it into a *Realsymbol* of an all-inclusive decisive salvific conversion bestowed once for all, and, as an apparent gifted communicator, made it popular by his preaching. This performative act, especially in the water of the Jordan River, which is full of evocative associations, mediated exemption from the judgment of fire and gathered the baptized as a holy remnant for the eschatological reception of the spirit. Recent times have seen much speculation about the ritual of this baptism. It will have hardly been distinguished from the early Christian baptism by immersion, inasmuch as the Jesus movement—then under the banner of the expected parousia—carried forward what under Jesus's claim of fulfillment had been interrupted for only a few years. Unlike Christian baptism, John's baptism was certainly not an initiation ritual—those baptized went back to their environment, in which they were to produce "fruits," corresponding to their return to the God of Israel. This will have been expressed in a decisive change according to the

Torah, much of which perhaps anticipated something that in the future would determine the ethic of Jesus and Christianity (Q 3:8; cf. Luke 3:10–14). The temple cult in the capital city was not thereby fundamentally devalued, but it moved from the center of religion to the periphery. The "marginal cult" of John the Baptizer provided the center. To the extent that neither theological convention nor ethnic membership decided the reception of salvation, but rather the conscious decision of the willful conversion of the individual, the Baptizer stands for a momentous ethical individualization. His radical theo-centrism notwithstanding, the resoluteness with which he tied baptism as a soteriological experience to himself and his message and conducted himself virtually as an essential mediator of Israel's salvation is striking. Thus, he paved the way for the very connection between eschatological proclamation and his own activity, which—in another way—would become characteristic for Jesus's message about the kingdom of God.

Insofar as the sparse notices, especially the sayings source, permit, John's announcement of judgment comes across with apocalyptic urgency: Israel is judged only on their direct relationship with their God. The past does not guarantee salvation; the future does not guarantee any continuity; the present stands under the banner of the immediately impending fiery judgment of wrath: already the axe is lying at the root of the trees. For some, in addition to fire as an element of God's judgment, *pneuma* evoked the notion of the apocalyptic storm, but it appears more plausible to consider the *pneuma* in concert with the earliest Christian tradition of the eschatological gift of the Spirit of God, which of course is likewise overpowering. A message of punishment without an aspect of hope would leave the attractiveness of the Baptizer's message just as difficult to understand as its interpretive role in the Christian motif of baptism in the Spirit. The activity of the Baptizer aims at the assembling of the holy remnant of Israel. Thus, the salvific gift of the Spirit of God is promised to the baptized, who escape the judgment of fire.

Controversially, it is debated who the coming one is whom the Baptizer announces (Mark 1:7–8; Q 3:16–17). A series of eschatological mediator figures are discussed, especially the Son of Man. If we scrutinize all the figures to which the thematic and metaphoric characterization by the Baptizer can be applied, none other than YHWH is most likely to fulfill the anticipated heavenly fiery judgment. Actually, in the highly intense imminent expectation, no place remains for an additional *persona dramatis*. Isaiah 40:3 (cf. Mark 1:3) is something like a slogan of the Baptizer movement (cf. 1QS viii 12–14), as it is originally an announcement about the coming of God. If Malachi is the Baptizer's "scroll" (see D.III.1.1.3), then the "great and fearful day" of the fiery judgment is the day of none other than the divine judge. It would cost early Christianity a great deal of interpretive labor before this expectation could be interpreted christologically.

1.1.3. Fragments of a Biography

According to Luke 1:5–80, John was born in the time of Herod (r. 37–4 BCE) as the son of the priest Zechariah and his wife, Elizabeth, and he was a relative of Jesus. The possibility that oral tradition underlies this report should not be excluded, but here, in his characteristic picturesque style, Luke puts forth a salvation-historical interpretation, just as the infancy narrative as a whole connects the message about Christ with Israel's Scriptures. The son of a priest who is thoroughly portrayed in the style of the "Old Testament" locates the Messiah in the venerable fellowship of Israel's ancestors.

We step onto historically sound ground with the Baptizer's public activity. According to Luke 3:1–2, John comes on the stage around 28 CE. Since he died before Jesus, we have to reckon with a short but exciting period of activity, most likely in 28/29 CE. John moved along the banks in the lower Jordan Valley and was presumably active also in Samaria (cf. John 3:23). The wilderness and the Jordan as his stage as well as his nomadic clothing and food (cf. Mark 1:4–6) served as the symbolic embodiment of a life completely dependent on YHWH, which could be associated with the traditions of the exodus and Elijah (cf. 2 Kings 1:8). The self-perception that John claimed was that of a preaching prophet, and to be sure, the self-perception of an eschatological prophet as for instance Jesus expresses in his assessment of John as "more than a prophet" (cf. Q 7:24–28). The wilderness as especially the place of God's nearness, the message of repentance and judgment, the lifestyle with a group of disciples of the prophet, the critical distance from the Jerusalem establishment, and the conflict with the ruler are reminiscent of Israel's prophetic tradition. The prophetic typology defined how the Baptizer was perceived, from Mark's report of his martyrdom to the stylized biography of Luke's preface.

At the Jordan Elijah was taken up into heaven (cf. 2 Kings 2:1–14); in a certain sense, Elijah returned in John. Presumably this "coming again" was thought of less as a personal identity than as a functional embodiment of a biblical role pattern (cf. Luke 1:16–17). Just as (Deutero-)Isaiah was the context for understanding Jesus's message of the kingdom, so also the identity of the Baptizer was formed according to Malachi on the role model of *Elias redivivus*, who—by means of baptism as the vehicle of conversion—assembles the people before God's wrathful judgment (cf. Mark 1:2: Q 7:27; Mal. 3:1 with Exod. 23:20): Elijah prepares the way of YHWH (cf. esp. Mal. 3:1–3; 4:5–6; further Sir. 48:10; Luke 1:76–77). Only gradually was the perspective for Christian interpretations of the Baptizer opened to see in *Elias redivivus* the precursor of the Messiah (cf. Mark 9:11–13 par. Matt. 17:10–13; differently John 1:21).

The most certain individual historical fact in John's life is his execution. If conceptual differences are taken into consideration, the folk tradition of Mark

(Mark 6:17–29) is quite compatible with the political depiction of Josephus (*Ant.* 18.109–119): when Herod Antipas (r. 4 BCE–39 CE) married his relative Herodias, the spouse to whom he was already married fled to her father, the Nabatean king Aretas IV. The Baptizer's criticism, highlighted by Mark, of the tetrarch's marriage practice, especially in the borderland with the Nabatean kingdom, was thus a delicate political issue. This explains why the military defeat of Antipas by Aretas (about 36 CE) was still interpreted by the people as punishment for the execution of the influential popular preacher years after the event. John was executed at the Machaerus Palace in Perea, presumably by beheading. Mark presents a vivid palatial court scene of eros and intrigue, which may be traced back to folk rumors, but it is pervasively theological: John suffers a biblical fate and thereby likewise becomes the precursor of the Messiah.

1.1.4. John and Jesus

Jesus stood at the side of the Baptizer, but whether or not the Baptizer knew Jesus is questionable. It can be regarded as certain that before his own public activity Jesus was affiliated with the repentance movement and was baptized by John in the Jordan (Mark 1:9–11). It is likely that when Jesus entered this forceful and probably also impressive penitential movement of his contemporaries to the God of Israel, it influenced him considerably. Although later Jesus's solicitous lifestyle deviated from the Baptizer's strict preparation for judgment and instead was characterized by the motif of a wedding celebration (cf. esp. Mark 2:18–19; Q 7:31–35), Jesus was publicly perceived as a "disciple" of the prophet at the Jordan (e.g., Mark 6:14–16; 8:28; cf. 1:14–15). He recruited some of his own disciples in the milieu of the Baptizer (cf. John 1:35–51), and the early Jesus movement maintained continuity with the Baptizer's movement in the areas of baptism, prayer, and fasting (cf., e.g., Mark 2:20; Luke 11:1). The enigmatic saying of the Johannine Jesus that "others" had prepared the fields for the harvest (John 4:35–38) must refer to the Baptizer's mission in Samaria, which the Jesus movement was able to draw on later.

This continuity also has a theological side. John permanently inspired Jesus's view of God and humanity. The proclamation of the kingdom of God advanced the Baptizer's preaching of repentance: Jesus's *basileia* message *was* the Baptizer's message—with the claim of fulfillment and the priority of grace and in the dramatic shift to Jesus's salvific activity. Nevertheless, the relationship of the two prophets is not evenhanded, if, as is often the case, Jesus the messenger of joy is put into a black-and-white contrast with John the messenger of warning. One might rather speak of a soteriological shift: for John judgment is the first prospect and forgiveness is the exception that is granted; for Jesus what is granted first is salvation and judgment is the last prospect for those who refuse it.

Thus, if Jesus's proclamation of the kingdom of God presupposed John's message of judgment, at the same time his proclamation was not rooted in John's message but rather in Jesus's very own experience of the *Abba* who was coming near. The essential distinction from the Baptizer's announcement of the time of the end is the way in which Jesus presented himself in general: God had not come near as the fiery judge under the banner of wrath, but as the merciful Father under the banner of affection. The axe lying at the root of the tree no longer determined the perception of time, but the vegetation metaphor in the established rhythm of the yearly harvest. In other words, if Jesus's message cannot be logically derived from the Baptizer's message, it is nevertheless in the mode of a dramatic prophetic turnaround. Precisely because the people of Israel do not turn around, since justly so, there is nothing more for them to hope for, it is Israel's God who turns around, and instead of the wrath they deserve God lets the time of astonishing grace dawn (cf., e.g., Jer. 31:31–34). This dramatic turn in comparison with the Baptizer's message (which cannot be mistaken for a conceptual turning away) became tangible at the beginning of Jesus's activity in his proclamation of the *basileia*. At the end of his ministry, Jesus himself took it up again in the face of Jerusalem's refusal when at his last supper he once again announced God's unexpected loving care in spite of everything. Matthew perceived this connection with sensitivity when he transplanted John's definition of baptism "for the forgiveness of sins" into Jesus's saying interpreting his death (Matt. 26:28).

To the end, Jesus appealed to the "power" of the movement of the Baptizer, in alignment with which he himself urged Israel's repentance in the temple in Jerusalem (cf. Mark 11:27–33). A break between Jesus and John or a phase of Jesus as a disciple of the prophet or as an assistant in baptisms is nowhere directly apparent, and also nowhere in an early apologetic or polemic context. Whether hypotheses such as these make texts or facts that need explanation accessible or require their exclusion as inexpedient auxiliary assumptions is disputed. The only personal contact that is transmitted in early tradition and from time to time is assessed as historical memory is the scene—which admittedly gives the impression that it is apocryphal—of an indirect inquiry of Jesus by John's disciples: "Are you the one who is to come, or are we to wait for another?" (Q 7:18–19). Some futilely seek the presuppositions for this in the message of the Baptizer about the heavenly fiery judge, and Jesus's answer, which instead of demonic exorcisms refers to the raising of the dead (Q 7:22–23), seems saturated with Christology. Here a last word from the Baptizer is not to be sounded, but rather the first, still tentative attempt to integrate the figure of the Baptizer in the Jesus tradition—more precisely: to integrate the figure of Jesus in the Baptizer's message. John becomes the one who knows Jesus; declares his support for him; paves the way for him; becomes his witness, his first believer, and ecclesiastical saint, and this reflects the strategy of christological memory: the Jewish Baptizer serves the self-assurance of Christianity when faced with its origins. From a history-of-religions point of view, the theological imprint certainly appears to be coherent: John the Baptizer is the (quite dramatic) "beginning of the gospel."

Backhaus, Knut. 2011. "Echoes from the Wilderness: The Historical John the Baptist." In *Handbook for the Study of the Historical Jesus*, vol. 2, *The Study of Jesus*, edited by Tom Holmén and Stanley E. Porter, 1747–85. Leiden and Boston.

Becker, Jürgen. 1972. *Johannes der Täufer und Jesus von Nazareth*. Biblische Studien 63. Neukirchen-Vluyn.

Ernst, Josef. 1989. *Johannes der Täufer: Interpretation—Geschichte—Wirkungsgeschichte*. BZNW 53. Berlin.

Müller, Ulrich B. 2002. *Johannes der Täufer: Jüdischer Prophet und Wegbereiter Jesu*. Biblische Gestalten 6. Leipzig.

Webb, Robert L. 1991. *John the Baptizer and Prophet: A Socio-Historical Study*. JSNT-Sup 62. Sheffield.

Knut Backhaus

1.2. Jesus within the Political and Social Circumstances of His Time

Discussions of Jesus in his political and social contexts can take any number of forms. In analyses of both the ancient and modern worlds, categorizing what counts as "political" can range from the decision making of the ruling elite through understandings of race, class, or gender to whether taxes should be paid. The problem is that, in one sense, everything is political (and social), which in turn means any attempt to categorize will inevitably exclude what others might deem significant. What follows, then, can only be a general guide, though it will look at the developments of some of the main emphases in historical Jesus scholarship. Indeed, a common way of understanding such issues in scholarship has typically (but not exclusively) involved Jesus's attitude toward imperial power, revolution, and authority. Such ideas can be traced back to Reimarus and beyond, though one of the most prominent understandings of Jesus as having zealot-style revolutionary tendencies came from S. G. F. Brandon (1967) in the 1960s, which in turn provoked responses and counterarguments from major scholars (Cullmann 1970; Hengel 1970; Bammel and Moule 1984). With influences of Marxist and postcolonial scholarship, and as increasing work on the social, economic, and political settings of Jesus was carried out, the idea of Jesus in relation to Rome, the Herodian dynasty, or "imperialism" more generally would continue to have a strong presence in scholarship, though typically without Brandon's hard seditious angle (e.g., among many, Horsley 1987; Crossan 1991; Stegemann and Stegemann 1995; Herzog 2005). An interrelated feature of scholarship from the 1970s onward has been an increased interest in gender and "identity politics," which, in crude terms, has begun to shift from Jesus's attitude toward women to understandings of the constructions of gender in relation to localized issues in Galilee and imperial issues more widely (Moxnes 2003; Martin 2006, 94–98; LeDonne 2013; Crossley 2015, 134–62).

But while the idea of a more "pacifist" Jesus is a common assumption in contemporary scholarship, there has been a revival of ideas similar to the Brandon thesis by, in different ways, Fernando Bermejo-Rubio (2014) and Dale Martin (2014), the latter arguing that Jesus's following was armed and expected supernatural assistance to attack the Romans and their client rulers (cf. Oakman 2012). Assessing claims on all sides is problematic because they are tied up with difficulties of historicity and notions of consistency. It would not be difficult to imagine that the earliest "Christians" would want to suppress the idea of a violent revolutionary Jesus, but this does not mean they did. It is also possible that the historical Jesus could condone the carrying of a sword or expect divine retribution in the near future while also talking about turning the other cheek elsewhere. Many of these theses hang on the historicity of a small number of passages, which makes the ideas difficult to establish with any degree of certainty. Nevertheless, as long as we are aware of the difficulties of establishing specific positions to attribute to Jesus, we can make some broad statements about Jesus's attitude to some of the classic issues discussed in scholarship.

We know that Jesus was active when Herod Antipas was ruling Galilee, and the Gospels suggest a degree of hostility between the two (e.g., Mark 3:6; 8:15; 12:13; Luke 13:31–33; 23:11; cf. Luke 3:19–20). We know that, in Jerusalem, Caiaphas was high priest and Pilate was governor. Given the problems in establishing the historicity of Jesus's trial, it is not easy to establish the degree of interaction between Jesus and these two key figures of authority. However, the implication that Jesus was executed as a bandit (e.g., Mark 15) would suggest a potentially uncomfortable memory but one that is unsurprising when we think that Rome and its client rulers would execute leaders of movements (like John the Baptist), irrespective of whether they posed a violent threat (Josephus, *Ant.* 18.116–119; 20.97–99). What we can say is that Jesus was *perceived* to be an alternative "political" leader and that, as we will see, his death was tied up with such perceptions.

If we think more broadly about such issues in the gospel tradition, then it also worth thinking about broader sociopolitical trends from which these themes emerged. By the time the Jesus tradition was developing, Herodian Galilee had witnessed the building and rebuilding of the key urban centers, Tiberias and Sepphoris, with significant socioeconomic consequences. In Judea, the Jerusalem temple had likewise become an extensive building project. Such urbanization has been tied in with the reasons behind the relatively rare phenomenon of peasant unrest and the emergence of millenarian groups in agrarian empires, with calls for change ranging from the reactionary to the revolutionary (Crossley 2015, 23). The labor and materials had to come from somewhere, and people would have faced the possibility of dislocation, as we find in Josephus's description of Tiberias (*Ant.* 18.36–38). As well as a period that gave us prophetic and millenarian figures such as Theudas and John the Baptist, it may be of some significance that there was a full-scale revolt against Rome in 66–70 CE, accompanied by reports of great hatred leveled at Sepphoris and Tiberias (Josephus, *Life* 30, 39, 66–68, 99, 374–84). It is in this broad context of social upheaval that we can contextualize the emergence of the Jesus movement.

Some qualifications are necessary. The emphasis should be on the social impact of such urbanization projects, irrespective of whether historical actors attributed their changing circumstances to them, or even knew much about what was happening in the major towns. Another important point for understanding social change in Galilee is the notion of perception. Perception should be strongly stressed because Morten Hørning Jensen's (2006) important work on Galilean archaeology has challenged conflict-based approaches to Jesus's Galilean context, suggesting that there is more evidence for a prosperous Herodian economy. However, unrest and social upheaval do not simply have to be the reaction to or the result of an unambiguous decline in the general standard of living or a reaction to people being explicitly exploited—indeed, the situation would no doubt have been a more complex mix of reactions from different interested parties (cf. Josephus, *Ant.* 18.36–38). The way in which we should alternatively use a conflict-based model is to focus on localized change where at least some among the populace do not *perceive* that this is for the better (Crossley 2015, 23–27). We cannot make strong claims about standard of living, the extent of any agitations, uses of physical violence, or whether the populace was more or less "oppressed." But we can say that there were dramatic changes, including household relocations and displacements, as Jesus was growing up.

One of the most obvious connections between these social changes in Galilee and the historical Jesus involves millenarianism or, more conventionally, eschatology and the kingdom of God. The broad arguments associated with Schweitzer and Weiss, namely, that Jesus was an eschatological prophet, continue to be persuasive (Frey 2006; Casey 2010, 212–26; Allison 2010, 31–220). If there was the expectation of a coming kingdom and a coming reign of God on earth, then this would carry the implication that Rome would not be ruling forever, and certainly not in Israel. Josephus gives us some idea about how Daniel's understanding of power and kingship could have been understood and retold in the first century, including the implied end of Rome (*Ant.* 10.209–10, 268, 272–77). This concern for the future and the future of Rome would not have ruled out the importance of a "present" kingdom in the earliest tradition, nor the idea that such thinking is incompatible with millenarian thinking. Such presentist understandings of the kingdom may simply complement the future kingdom (e.g., Mark 4:26–32; cf. Dan. 4:34–37). The idea of a "present" kingdom would also have implications for understanding who was really deemed to be the overarching hegemony. Read from a first-century perspective, Daniel would seem to have clear implications for Rome (Dan. 2:44). Daniel did look to the future coming kingdom, but the basic assumption was that even Nebuchadnezzar could recognize that God was really in charge (Dan. 4:34).

However, this thinking about the new kingdom cannot escape imperial ideology. Less prominent in contemporary historical Jesus scholarship is the idea that theocratic imperialism is also part of the earliest Jesus tradition. Most obviously, the language of βασιλεία / מלכות typically denotes God's rule or kingship as well as a more spatial dimension, that is, God's territory and rule over all peoples, including the possibility of a Davidic king (cf. 1 Chron. 28:5). Language of God's kingdom on earth, or language associated with early kingdoms more generally, is imperial, theocratic, and territorial, all familiar ideas from the ancient world (cf. Obad. 19–21; Zech. 14:9; Ps. 47:2–3; Dan. 7:27). One of the most explicit gospel passages suggesting dominance in relation to the kingdom of God is found in Matt. 19:28 par. Luke 22:29–30. Luke and Matthew develop this in different ways, but the trope of followers sitting on thrones judging the twelve tribes of Israel is common to both, and a good case can be made that this reflects earlier ideas. For instance, the idea of judging the twelve tribes of Israel concerns only Israel in end times, which would suggest issues emerging from the earliest Palestinian tradition with little concern for gentiles (cf. Mark 11:10). Much of this imperial language in the gospel tradition replicates and reinscribes ideas of imperialism, domination, and authority, rather than advocating a world that does away with imperial power. This general way of thinking is found in the development of the kingdom sayings. For instance, in Matt. 16:19 (which presumably does not come directly from the historical Jesus), Jesus promises Peter "the keys of the kingdom of heaven." He adds, "Whatever you bind on earth will be bound in heaven, and whatever you loose on earth will be loosed in heaven." Similarly, Luke 22:29–30 provides a telling addition to the twelve tribes, in which Jesus says, "I confer on you, just as my Father has conferred on me, a kingdom, so that you may eat and drink at my table in my kingdom, and you will sit on thrones judging the twelve tribes of Israel." Again, a case can be made for this sort of human ownership or stewardship of the kingdom being a Lukan redaction, but such thinking is implicit in the gospel sayings about the present and growing kingdom (e.g., Mark 4:26–32; Luke 13:20–21 par. Matt. 13:33; Matt. 13:44; Luke 17:20–21; Gos. Thom. 113). The dispute about casting out demons (Mark 3:22–30), including the words "If a kingdom is divided against itself, that kingdom cannot stand," works with the assumption of connections with a powerful kingdom in the present, as seen also in Matt. 12:28 par. Luke 11:20 (cf. Mark 10:14–15; 12:34). While these sorts of sayings are not as obviously later developments like Matt. 16:19, this does not necessarily mean that they "go back" to the historical Jesus, though dealing with the problematic memory of Jesus being thought to be in league with the satanic (Mark 3:22–30) may imply an earlier tradition. But on the basis of the evidence we have and how it would have been understood, imperialistic ideas were most likely assumed in the earliest kingdom traditions.

Eschatological role reversal in relation to traditions about, and constructions of, "rich" and "poor" is similarly explicable in this context. Among the most explicit passages in this respect, and with direct eschatological implications, are Mark 10:17–31 and Luke 16:19–31. The idea that rich people are to be barred from eschatological reward stands in the tradition of equating wealth with wickedness (e.g., CD iv 15–19; 1QS xi 1–2; Pss. Sol. 5.16) and is likely to have been an attempt at explaining a rethinking of reward theology. While Luke has a clear interest in issues of rich and poor, this economic take on eschatological reversal of rich and poor is also likely to reflect views found in the earliest Palestinian tradition. Yet the hierarchical structure remains in place in cases such as Mark 10:17–31 and Luke 16:19–31. In Mark 10:17–31, replication of the system of reward being challenged is clearer still as material rewards come even in "this age" and not just "the age to come (Mark 10:28–31). Arguments concerning replication and mimicry of preexisting systems similarly apply in the case of reward theology where the reward gets pushed to the future or the afterlife (see, e.g., 1 En. 92–105; cf. Job 42:10–17).

This theme is likely to have been present in the earliest tradition. Such thinking about God and mammon is found across the synoptic tradition, including independent tradition (irrespective of whether we accept some form of Q or not) and different forms (e.g., Mark 10:17–31; Luke 6:20–26 par. Matt. 5:3–12; Matt. 6:24 par. Luke 16:13; Luke 14:12–24 par. Matt. 22:1–14; Luke 4:18; 12:13–21; cf. Gos. Thom. 64). We can also point to interrelated concerns across the synoptic tradition, such as the recurring theme of debt (e.g., Luke 12:57–59 par. Matt. 5:25; Luke 6:35; 16:1–8; Matt. 5:40–42; 6:12; 18:23–35); concern for those without food, clothing, drink, and community (Matt. 25:31–46; Luke 6:20–21); opposition to wealth, fine clothing, and eating well (e.g., Matt. 11:8 par. Luke 7:25; Matt. 6:25–34 par. Luke 12:22–31; Luke 6:24–25; cf. 1 En. 98:2; 102:9–11); and the theme of stark difference between rich and poor (Luke 6:20–26 par. Matt. 5:3–12; Luke 14:12–24 par. Matt. 22:1–14; cf. Gos. Thom. 64). The sheer amount and concentration of such themes in independent sources and forms strongly suggest that this was a theme inherited by the gospel writers and that such a concern is likely to have been partly generated by the perceptions of what was happening as a result of the social upheavals in Galilee with the rebuilding of Sepphoris and the building of Tiberias.

Domination, subjugation, imperialism, and theocracy are part of both the gospel tradition and the relevant contextualizing sources, and represent perhaps the only way people could realistically conceive an alternative to the present world powers. A similar phenomenon of mimicry-through-criticism can be found in the earliest "christological" traditions. In different ways, scholars have compared Jesus with figures associated with millenarian movements who provocatively challenge the status quo (Rowland 1986, 111–13; Allison 2010, 85–86, 221–304; cf. Theissen and Merz [4]2014, 175–80). Similarly, we can make cross-cultural comparisons with figures in agrarian contexts who mediate between humanity and the divine, particularly those outside privileged social strata and official lines of divine authority (Crossley 2015, 23–27). Such figures can—but do not necessarily—support a redistribution ethic and the needs of those at the lower end of the social structure. The idea of direct access to the divine from outside the "channels of salvation" of the ruling classes has historically posed conflict and tensions because authority that comes directly from the divine challenges the official channels of the ruling classes. This is a useful way of understanding the Jesus tradition, as his authority is presented as charismatic authority directly from God and questions of his authority are raised in the Gospels, notably in relation to healing and exorcism and John the Baptist (e.g., Mark 1:23–27; 2:10; 11:27–33).

Yet this approach also helps us appreciate the potential for making connections between social upheaval, exalted perceptions of individuals, mimicry of power, and christological development. We might add that other movements and leaders in times of social upheaval can also have agendas of power. Bandits could be remembered as a product of social upheaval (e.g., Josephus, *Ant.* 17.270–284; 18.269–275; *J. W.* 2.57–65; 2.585–588; *Life* 35, 66), attacking power, wealth, and Rome (*J. W.* 2.227–248; *Ant.* 18.269–275; *J. W.* 2.228–231; *Ant.* 20.113–117; *Life* 126–127), and mimicking the world of kings and kingship (*J. W.* 2.57–62; *Ant.* 17.273–278; Tacitus, *Hist.* 5.9). This is not to claim that Jesus was a bandit, but it helps us understand Jesus as a subversive figure who nevertheless replicated hegemonic ideas of authority and power. One of the more obvious possibilities of reflecting ideas present in the earliest Palestinian tradition is Matt. 12:28 par. Luke 11:20. The finger/spirit difference is not especially problematic for purposes of reconstruction, as both concern ideas about divine power. The combination of exorcism, possession, and Jesus's power is well attested across the gospel tradition in different sources, stories, and forms (e.g., Mark 1:23–27; 3:11–12, 14–15, 22–29; 7:24–30; 9:17–29; Matt. 4:23–25; 9:35; 15:30–31; Matt. 12:43–45 par. Luke 11:24–26; Luke 8:2; 13:10–11), and we should note the related issue of lack of power Mark claims that Jesus had in Nazareth (Mark 6:5–6), which is one of the less likely creations of the early church. This combination of exorcism, authority, and power is presumably a powerful memory from early tradition (and one that John's Gospel did not like). Something like the logic of Matt. 12:28 par. Luke 11:20 would no doubt have been assumed throughout healings and exorcisms. A comparison with the use of the "present" kingdom in Dan. 4 is again instructive, particularly Nebuchadnezzar's speech blessing the "Most High" and praising his "everlasting sovereignty" and his enduring kingdom (Dan. 4:31–32). The early gospel tradition has Jesus closely associated with, and possibly channeling, this sort of divine power.

While exorcisms are typically seen to be part of the earliest themes in the gospel tradition, one of the more difficult problems for historical Jesus research involves the chronological development of Christology, which appears to have developed rapidly after Jesus's death; this makes it difficult to establish what sorts of ideas might have been present while Jesus was active. Nevertheless, a good case can be made, as we saw above, that the earliest perceptions of Jesus involved, or even assumed, an understanding of some sort of enthronement. Matthew 19:28 par. Luke 22:28–30, for instance, envisages Jesus and the Twelve having a prominent role in the kingdom (e.g., judging Israel). Similarly, in Mark 10:35–45 the sons of Zebedee ask to sit at the right and left of Jesus in his glory. Mark 10:35–45 looks like it is tied in with Maccabean martyr theology of dying for Israel (e.g., 2 Macc. 7; 4 Macc. 17:20–22), which is tied in with ideas of glorification after death (Dan. 12:2–3). The "son of man" saying potentially works as a generic idiomatic Aramaic saying with reference to the speaker, and dying for "the many" may imply a limited group, perhaps Israel (cf. 1QS vi 1, 7–25; CD xiii 7; xiv 7). "Proving" historicity is never easy, but we can at least suggest that Mark 10:35–45 is compatible with ideas from the earliest Palestinian tradition. We can also make general claims that kingly and "messianic" traits were likely to have been present across the earliest tradition. A significant individual example is "king of the Jews" in Mark 15, which is also present as a mocking inscription on the cross (Mark 15:26). This title given by his executioners is not directly in line with early Christology and so may reflect an early memory of Jesus.

If these arguments are along the right lines, then texts discussing the role of royalty, kingship, and exaltation suggest what might be expected if Jesus and the Twelve were to rule and judge (e.g., Pss. Sol. 17; 4Q246 ii 1–9; 1QM vi 4–6; 4Q252 v 1–4; 4Q521 2 ii 1–13; 11Q13 ii 13; 2 Bar. 72:2–73:2). The recurrent themes in these texts show how promises of peace and prosperity are intertwined with power, force, and dominance, all themes found throughout the gospel tradition. Put another way, could not such claims equally be made of Rome? The common scholarly and popular arguments that the Jesus traditions entertain radical egalitarian ideas and challenges to wealth and privilege are only one side of the story. Even if the cliché that Constantine or Paul "betrayed" Jesus's teaching may have some truth to it, it is equally clear that ideas of king and judge, no matter how benign, are simultaneously present, and it should be no surprise that development of imperialistic Christology was happening rapidly after Jesus's death. Paul clearly envisaged Christ playing an extremely elevated role in this alternative imperial system (e.g., Phil. 2:10–11), and in a different, seemingly more benign way, in the removal of particular identities (Gal. 3:28). Echoing and expanding the gospel tradition of judging, Paul (1 Cor. 6:2) too is clear about eschatological change in power relations. It is difficult to remove Jesus from the history of such ideas.

Constructions of gender cannot easily be disassociated from broader sociopolitical developments, and we can make connections between social upheaval, imperialism, and such areas designated "political" in the history of scholarship. We can no longer work with the once near-certain assumption that Jesus was celibate, unmarried, of unambiguous sexuality, and (therefore) in some way countercultural in terms of masculinity. However, we do have one obvious gendered example from the earliest tradition: Jesus's death by crucifixion. Jesus could have been understood as another emasculated, passive victim at the hands of the empire. As Colleen Conway (2008) has shown, there are indications of this sort of understanding in Mark's Gospel (Mark 14–16), alongside more "masculinized" traditions of a strong man (Mark 1–8) and noble martyr (Mark 8–10). Of course, others were less prepared to keep Jesus so emasculated; Paul, for instance, already constructs Jesus in more "manly" and heroic terms. And we should not necessarily succumb to the old temptation of layering these interpretations, as if the emasculated construction came first, followed later by the masculinizing of Jesus's death. Different, perhaps contradictory, perceptions could coexist, and we should expect different people and audiences to react differently. However, the issue of Jesus's masculinity in relation to being crucified and penetrated with nails would have been present from the outset, and this would have been known to Jesus and his followers when it became clear that he would die in such a manner. Indeed, with John the Baptist killed, there is a good chance Jesus himself knew what would happen in Jerusalem. Difficult questions concerning masculinity were always going to be present from the beginning and would need answering.

We also get a different nuance in other traditions, where a contrast is established between two different forms of the family in terms of gender relations: Jesus's physical family and his alternative family (e.g., Mark 3:31–35). As Halvor Moxnes (2003, 101–5) suggests, this theme of alternative family queers standard assumptions of households, as the fictive household around Jesus is notably fatherless (at least on earth; cf. Matt. 23:9) and includes women such as a "mother" (and, presumably, widows) as it presumably mimics the adult Jesus's own family. Whether or not Jesus was married, unmarried, celibate, or sexually active, his alternative household shows no signs of performing certain expected roles. It may have been expected, of course, that, as head of the household, a man was supposed to procreate, and by doing so keep the family unit functioning socially and economically (cf. Gen. 22:17). Such roles may not have even been possible as Jesus's group moved around Galilee. It is probably not a surprise to find that the gospel presentation of Jesus and his alternative family can be framed in contexts of conflict. A good case can also be made for this theme being early. The fragmentation of households is clear enough in the gospel tradition (e.g., Mark 3:20–22, 31–35; 10:29–30; Matt. 8:22 par. Luke 9:60; Matt. 10:34–36 par. Luke 12:51–53 par. Gos. Thom. 16; Matt. 10:37 par. Luke 14:26), and it is presumably significant that Jesus moves around and is remembered in Mark as returning to Nazareth only once, where he was given a hostile reception (Mark 6:1–6).

Yet despite, or because of, tensions with received assumptions of gendered space and behavior, it seems clear in the gospel tradition that from the outset structural constraints were simultaneously present in that received assumptions of gender and power are reinscribed as they are mimicked. The concept of household may be queered in the gospel tradition, but the idea of a dominant male figure is hardly lost. Moreover, the fatherhood of God is, of course, a known theme in the gospel tradition (cf. Matt. 23:9). There is evidence of more complexity and contradiction as a masculinizing of Jesus is likewise taking place. Tat-siong Benny Liew (2003) has noted a strong tendency in Mark's Gospel to portray Jesus in "manly" and militarized terms, and some of his suggestions are important for understanding earlier perceptions. For instance, he has pointed out that a man active outside the home, as relentlessly presented in Mark and presumably an early construct of Jesus, conforms to a different Greco-Roman stereotype, with the reverse being the domestic space being the confines of women. Jesus likewise takes on traits of fatherhood in the language of fictive family in addressing others as "sons," "daughters," and "children" (Mark 5:34; 10:24); engages in conflicts of authority with opponents; and alone can take the severest of beatings on the way to the crucifixion. It is plausible enough to imagine that these sorts of ideas about gender were simultaneously present alongside the queering tendencies detected by Moxnes.

Another assessment of Jesus in his political and social context might have looked at any number of themes, such as his action in the temple, the Sermon on the Mount, his view of taxation, his specific views of Antipas, or his assessment of Samaritans and foreigners. All these ideas would be legitimate areas to cover. However, any assessment would probably have to acknowledge how such themes were affected by the sociopolitical situation in Galilee and broader issues of imperialism and the Roman Empire. As we have seen above, the earliest traditions are products of this time, both challenging and reinscribing accepted notions of power and authority. It is little wonder that receptions of Jesus's teachings can be found to support positions from across the political spectrum, as well as both "antiestablishment" and "proestablishment" positions. In broad terms, these seemingly contradictory notions are present in the earliest gospel memories and were ready to be taken in any number of directions by the Christian movement, in both imperial and anti-imperial directions (for two contrasting assessments of the implications of such teaching, see Feldmeier 2012 and Crossley 2015).

Bermejo-Rubio, Fernando. 2014. "Jesus and the Anti-Roman Resistance: A Reassessment of the Arguments." *JSHJ* 12: 1–105.

Crossley, James G. 2015. *Jesus and the Chaos of History: Redirecting the Quest for the Historical Jesus*. Oxford.

Oakman, Douglas E. 2012. *The Political Aims of Jesus*. Minneapolis.

Stegemann, Ekkehard W., and Wolfgang Stegemann. 1995. *Urchristliche Sozialgeschichte: Die Anfänge im Judentum und die Christusgemeinden in der mediterranen Welt*. Stuttgart.

Theissen, Gerd, and Annette Merz. [4]2011. *Der Historische Jesus: Ein Lehrbuch*. Göttingen.

James G. Crossley

2. Jesus's Activity

2.1. Jesus as an Itinerant Preacher

According to all four Gospels, Jesus preached and wandered around. At first sight, then, the label "itinerant preacher" seems to be quite appropriate to describe at least part of Jesus's ministry. Yet, such a qualification raises a number of questions and problems .

Three comments should be made with regard to Jesus's preaching that have a bearing on the wandering aspect as well. Preaching is no doubt an important aspect of Jesus's ministry as depicted in the Gospels. It is therefore all the more remarkable that the Gospels do not seem to have one particular verb to denote it. Apart from the plain and general λέγω or εἶπον, three verbs seem to describe in a more specific way most of what can be caught under the heading "preaching"—εὐαγγελίζομαι, κηρύσσω, and διδάσκω; only with the latter, the noun derived from it is also applied to Jesus. The first term (which is used in Matthew once, Mark never, Luke ten times, John never, Acts fifteen times, Paul twenty-three times, the Catholic Epistles three times, and Revelation twice), a clear favorite of Luke, is once used to refer to Jesus's ministry in an indirect way, through a citation from Scripture (Matt. 11:5 = Luke 7:22 and Luke 4:18), and then more often directly (Luke 4:43 as a self-reference, for Mark 1:38, κηρύξω; Luke 8:1, with κηρύσσων, for Mark 6:6b, διδάσκων, and Matt. 9:35, διδάσκων . . . καὶ κηρύσσων τὸ εὐαγγέλιον; Luke 20:1, in combination with διδάσκοντος, for Matt. 21:23, διδάσκοντι, and Mark 11:27, περιπατοῦντος), and once also for John the Baptist (Luke 3:18), for the disciples (Luke 9:6, for Mark 6:12 = Matt. 10:7 a form of κηρύσσω), and for what is perhaps best regarded as a self-reference of Jesus to his and his disciples' efforts (Luke 16:16 diff. Matt. 11:13).

The other two verbs are the more commonly used ones and somehow seem to vie for the reader's attention. Κηρύσσω (used in Matthew nine times, Mark twelve/fourteen times, Luke nine times, John never, Acts eight times, Paul nineteen times, the Catholic Epistles once, and Revelation once) is first found with reference to John the Baptist proclaiming his message of a baptism of repentance (Mark 1:4, 7 = Matt. 3:1 and Luke 3:3; cf. Acts 10:37). It is then smoothly transferred to Jesus immediately after (Mark 1:14 = Matt. 4:17, for Luke 4:15, ἐδίδασκεν, but see the quotation from Isa. 61:1–2 in 4:18–19; Mark 1:38, for Luke 4:43, εὐαγγελίσασθαι; Mark 1:39 = Matt. 4:23, in combination with διδάσκων, and Luke 4:44; Matt. 11:1, again in combination with a form of διδάσκω; Matt. 9:35 = Luke 8:1 as an addition to the secondary parallel in Mark 6:6b; cf. also 1 Pet. 3:19). Jesus himself uses it to describe one of the tasks the disciples have to perform when they are sent out (Mark 3:14 diff. Matt. 10:1 and Luke 6:13, but see 9:2; Mark 6:12 = Matt. 10:7, for Luke 9:6, διήρχοντο . . . εὐαγγελιζόμενοι, but see again 9:2; so also Mark 13:10 = Matt. 24:14, cf. Luke 24:47; Mark 14:9 = Matt. 26:13, diff. Luke 7:47; Matt. 10:27 = Luke 12:3; also Mark 16:15, 20), and it becomes a common feature in Acts and in Paul's letters to denote the preaching ministry of the apostles. Occasionally it is also applied to one who was healed by Jesus (Mark 1:45, with a different connotation, as illustrated by the accompanying διαφημίζειν, diff. Luke 5:15, διήρχετο; Mark 5:20 = Luke 8:39; Mark 7:36).

Διδάσκω is rather more common still than κηρύσσω (used in Matthew fourteen times, Mark seventeen times, Luke seventeen times, John nine or ten times, Acts sixteen times, Paul eighteen times, the Catholic Epistles three times, and Revelation twice). It is used more broadly throughout the Gospels, and there above all for Jesus. The exceptions are the very negative reference to the "hypocrites" in Mark 7:7 = Matt. 15:9, the summary of the first sending of the disciples in Mark 6:30 (ὅσα ἐποίησαν καὶ ὅσα ἐδίδαξαν, for Luke 9:10, ὅσα ἐποίησαν and diff. Matt. 14:12), the general warning in Matt. 5:19 twice (the second time in combination with ποιήσῃ), the isolated reference of Jesus's disciples to the Baptist teaching his disciples in Luke 11:1 and with reference to the Spirit in Luke 12:12 (from Q?) and in John 14:26 (identified as the Paraclete), the two instances in Matt. 28:15, 20, the first referring to the instructions given to the guard and the other to one of the tasks given by the risen Lord to his disciples, and finally the man born blind referring to Jesus in John 9:34, and Jesus himself referring to the teaching he received from the Father in 8:28. Mark has it twice in the first public appearance of Jesus as a preacher in a synagogue (Mark 1:21 = Luke 4:31; Mark 1:22 = Luke 4:32 and cf. Matt. 7:29) and shortly after for introducing the story of the call of Levi (Mark 2:13, omitted in Luke 5:27). A similar use as part of the framework is found in Mark 4:1–2 (diff. Matt. 13:3, ἐλάλησεν, and Luke 8:4, εἶπεν, but see 5:3), Mark 6:2 (= Matt. 13:54, for Luke 4:16, ἀναγνῶναι, but see 4:15), the more isolated Mark 6:6b (= Matt. 9:35, followed by κηρύσσων τὸ εὐαγγέλιον), Mark 6:34 (for Luke 9:11, ἐλάλει, and diff. Matt. 14:14), Mark 10:1 (diff. Matt. 19:2, ἐθεράπευσεν). Mark uses it twice for the passion prediction (8:31 diff. Matt. 16:21, δεικνύειν, and Luke 9:22, εἰπών, and 9:31 diff. Matt. 17:22 = Luke 9:43, εἶπεν, but see also οἷς ἐποίει in the latter) and occasionally also for introducing a saying of Jesus, as in 11:17 (omitted in Matt. 21:13 = Luke 19:46, but see v. 47), or to express how his opponents (12:14 = Matt. 22:16 and Luke 20:21 twice, and 12:35 omitted in Matt. 22:41 and Luke 20:41) and Jesus himself refer to his teaching and preaching activity (14:49 = Matt. 26:55, omitted in Luke 22:53). In addition to the cases mentioned with regard to Mark, Matthew adds it to Mark 1:39 in his version of the summary in 4:23 and uses it to introduce *and* to end the Sermon on the Mount (Matt. 5:2 diff. Luke 6:20, ἔλεγεν, and 7:29, above; the same function as the latter also in 11:1). He also changes Mark in this way at 21:23 (above). Like Mark, Luke seems to have a certain preference for the verb when introducing a scene, as in 4:15 (above), 5:17 (Mark 2:2, ἐλάλει), 6:6 (diff. Mark 3:1), 11:1 twice (the first as a request from the disciples, the second for the Baptist), 13:10, 22; 20:1 (above). Apart from the parallels with Mark cited above, the verb is also used as a self-reference in Jesus's rebuke in Luke 13:26 (assigned to Q, though not in Matthew), after a discourse of Jesus to evoke a summary scene (21:37), and as part of the criticism of Jesus's adversaries (23:5; see above on Mark 12:14, 35 and par.). In Acts 1:1 it combines with ποιεῖν for a most succinct but telling summary of Jesus's ministry. Like Matthew, John, too, uses the verb to conclude (6:59; 8:20) or to introduce a new discourse of Jesus (7:14, referring to a discourse that provokes a reaction and a reply, and then twice more in vv. 28 and 35). John 8:2 can be compared to Luke 21:37, Jesus's defense in John 18:20 to Mark 14:49 = Matthew.

The evidence is perhaps not univocal, and maybe not all the instances listed above are equally relevant for our purpose. One might exclude those in which

Jesus teaches the disciples, privately or publicly, because he is addressing "his own." Yet, on the other hand, a good deal of this teaching happens somewhere "on the way," and part of it is (inter)connected with public instruction or preaching. Hence it may be of some interest for getting "the full picture" of Jesus the preacher. These instances have therefore been included in the typology that follows on the assumption that it may be wise to keep as broad a perspective as possible, all while realizing that a "teacher" is not always identical with a "preacher."

The survey gives a first indication of the different connotations that can be evoked when speaking about Jesus's preaching. It can be described as "proclaiming" or "announcing," and more formally as "teaching." The three verbs may overlap and generally seem to refer to the same kind of activity, but semantically they are not fully identical in meaning. The survey also shows that these verbs are apparently combinable (Matt. 4:23; 9:35; 11:1; Luke 8:1; 20:1), interchangeable (Mark 1:14 and Luke 4:15; Mark 6:6b and Luke 8:1; Mark 6:12 and Luke 9:6; also by Jesus himself: Mark 1:38 and Luke 4:43), and not absolutely necessary (maybe the best example of the latter is the way Matthew and Luke introduce the Sermon on the Mount/Plain, the first using a formal phrase with διδάσκω, while the second has a mere ἔλεγεν; see also Mark 4:1–2 diff. Matthew/Luke). Moreover, Jesus also speaks on other occasions and related to other activities—when performing healings, or instructing his disciples in private, or entering into dispute with opponents.

2.1.1. Various Formats Dealing with Various Topics

Jesus's preaching can take quite variant formats and deal with quite different topics, even if the latter can be subsumed under larger headings. It not only makes for different types of preaching but also introduces a degree of variety in the typology of the preacher. If we focus on the three verbs surveyed above, we note that all gospel authors occasionally use them absolutely (or almost), merely mentioning that Jesus "preached" ("taught"/"proclaimed") but without giving any further information (cf. Mark 1:21 = Luke; 1:38 diff. Luke; 1:39 = Luke, but diff. Matthew; 2:13; 4:1, but see v. 2; 6:2 = Matthew; 6:6b diff. Matthew; 6:34 πολλά; 10:1; Matt. 11:1; 21:23 = Luke; Luke 4:15, but see vv. 16–27; 4:18 and 7:22 = Matt. 5:3, 17; 6:6; 13:10, 22; 19:47; 20:1; 21:37; John 7:14; [8:2]; as self-reference of Jesus in Mark 14:49 = Matthew and in John 18:20; also for the disciples in Mark 3:14; 6:30; [16:20]; Luke 9:6; twice by the opponents: Luke 13:26 and John 7:35; and once also for the Father and the Spirit: John 8:28; 14:26, πάντα). Of course, something of the contents can perhaps be derived from the context, or from comparison with similar passages, but in these cases the content clearly is deemed to be second-ary to the act itself, or is just an occasion for introducing another topic: Jesus's teaching/proclamation urges the audience/opponents to ponder/question his authority (Mark 1:21, 22 = Luke; Mark 6:2 = Matthew; Matt. 21:23 = Luke 20:1; and John 7:14); the opponents grasping the opportunity to question Jesus on other matters (Mark 10:1; Luke 13:22; [John 8:2]) or considering a murder plot (19:47); the Baptist wondering about Jesus's identity and receiving a response (Matt. 11:1); or Jesus calling disciples (Mark 2:13 and Luke 5:3) or performing a healing (Luke 5:17; 6:6; 13:10).

Not really informative are phrases such as ὅσα ἐδίδαξαν (Mark 6:30), ὃ εἰς τὸ οὖς ἀκούετε (Matt. 10:27 ~ Luke 12:3), ἃ δεῖ εἰπεῖν (Luke 12:12), or πάντα ὅσα ἐνετειλάμην (Matt. 28:20), all four with reference to the disciples, the contents of which can somehow and to different degrees be "reconstructed" on the basis of what had preceded. Perhaps only slightly more informative are those instances in which the message Jesus has to bring is presented in its core format, though the Gospels do not fully agree on what this core message consists of, and the reader is left speculating on how it was elaborated in some more detail and what precisely Jesus told his audience apart from the few words in which it is packed in such cases. But such phrases give at least a general idea of what the message was about. The promise of the nearness of the kingdom (of God/of heaven), which Mark defines as "the gospel of God" and combines with a call for repentance the first time he mentions it, represents its most pointed and complete form (Mark 1:14–15 par. Matthew, but without the defining element; cf. also Matt. 10:7 for the motif of "nearness"). Occasionally this can even be further summarized as merely "the gospel" (Mark 13:10; 14:9 = Matthew; Mark [16:15]) or a call for repentance only (Mark 6:12 and Luke 24:47). Matthew shows a preference for the phrases ἡ βασιλεία τῶν οὐρανῶν (10:7 par. Mark 6:12, and often throughout his gospel) and τὸ εὐαγγέλιον τῆς βασιλείας (4:23; 9:35; 24:14), which he uses as a sort of standard formula. Luke keeps to the equivalent ἡ βασιλεία τοῦ θεοῦ (4:43; 8:1; 9:2; 16:16), while occasionally also pointing to the social dimension of this message (4:18–19; 7:22).

But there are also a number of instances in which a direct link is made with a (more or less) substantial amount of Jesus's teaching. This is the case in Mark 8:31 and 9:31 (the passion predictions) and 11:17 and 12:36 (both interpreted citations from Scripture), and indirectly also in 4:1–2; in Matt. 5:2 and 7:29 (the Sermon on the Mount); in Luke 11:1 (the Lord's Prayer), and in a much more formal context in 4:15, with the synagogue homily; and in John 6:59 and 8:20 (both times referring back) and 7:28 (see vv. 28b–29).

Of some interest are also instances in which the opponents characterize Jesus's preaching, using terminology he himself did not use, as in Mark 12:14 (ἐπ᾽ ἀληθείας τὴν ὁδὸν τοῦ θεοῦ διδάσκεις = Luke), or putting an utterly negative take on it, as in Luke 23:5 (ἀνασείει τὸν λαόν); note also their aporia in John 7:35.

So, very general references, elaborate discourses, and isolated sayings can all contribute to create a picture of Jesus's preaching, and all add different elements and perspectives to the picture of the itinerant preacher. His message does not just consist of a series of bon mots or of stereotypical phraseology, but can develop into elaborate compositions, and even take the form of a formal synagogue homily on the Sabbath. Similarly, the audience can consist of the disciples, a positively minded crowd, and the ever-negative opponents. In addition, Jesus's preaching is not infrequently accompanied with other forms of proclamation, such as a feeding miracle (Mark 6:34), a call story (Mark 2:13; Luke 5:3), an intervention in the commerce in the temple (Mark 11:17), a controversy (Luke 13:22, 26), or more often, healings. The latter can be formulated in a concrete way (Mark 1:21 = Luke, cf. v. 23; Mark 1:39 = Matt. 4:23; Mark 6:12–13 par. Matt. 10:7 = Luke 9:2, 6; Matt. 9:35; Matt. 11:5–6 = Luke 7:22 and 4:18–19; Luke 6:6; 8:1; 13:10), but also more generally (Mark 6:30, ὅσα ἐποίησαν καὶ ὅσα ἐδίδαξαν, for the disciples; Acts, ποιεῖν τε καὶ διδάσκειν). In sum, then, Jesus preaches to all, and in all formats.

2.1.2. A Preacher/Teacher from the Beginning

The Gospels present Jesus as a preacher/teacher right from the beginning of his public ministry and up to the moment of his trial (Mark 14:49 par.), and exceptionally even after that, but then only for the disciples (Matt. 28:20). In Mark, it is the way the reader is introduced to this public ministry itself (1:14–15). In the Synoptic Gospels, there does not seem to be any dip in this part of Jesus's activity. The situation is perhaps slightly different in John, who first makes an explicit reference to Jesus's preaching only toward the end of chapter 6 and generally uses the motif more sporadically than the other evangelists, though he also brings it up at the trial (18:20, cf. Mark 14:49 par. Matthew/Luke).

2.1.3. Characteristics of a Preaching Ministry

During his ministry, Jesus is hardly ever pictured as being alone. And if every now and then he is apparently looking for some rest and solitude, this mostly seems to be in vain. From the outset, he is said to be accompanied by disciples he himself had called. Their number differs, and it is not always clear how many are present (see the use of "the Twelve" in the various gospels), though at times only a select company is allowed to stay with him. Fairly late in the Gospels, the reader is informed that the group also includes women (Mark 15:40-41 par. Matthew/Luke/John, though Luke had mentioned them earlier in 8:1-3). They are not explicitly called disciples, though they are given a rather eminent role in the last days of his life and after his death. Apart from his disciples, Jesus is also followed, at least when circulating in Galilee, by crowds of people who are as a rule depicted sympathetically and eager to hear his message (cf. Mark 2:2; 4:1-2), if perhaps also a bit hapless (see Mark 6:34 par.). Once he is also approached and questioned by John's disciples (Matt. 11:2-6 = Luke). In addition, he is apparently almost constantly met by representatives of his opponents and exceptionally also by members of his own family. If the first group shifts between hearing Jesus out (cf. Mark 3:22 par., and several other instances) and trying to silence him (Mark 3:6 par.), the second definitely is more intent on the latter (Mark 3:21 and 3:31-35 par.).

Jesus's preaching meets with differing success. The call stories and some of the healing stories seem to argue forcefully that Jesus made a great impact on individuals and crowds alike, who wonder at his teaching and decide to follow him—this is a major interest of the gospel authors (see Mark 1:18; 2:14-15; 3:7; 5:24; 6:1; 10:28, 32, 52; 11:9; 15:41, most of these with parallels in Matthew/Luke; a similar interest in John; see further also its negative foil in Mark 9:38), as well as of Jesus himself (Mark 8:34; 10:21 and par.; cf. the more symbolically loaded John 13:36-37). Yet his ministry never seems to have reached a 100-percent success rate, as there were also always dissenters or people who did not wish to be convinced. Ultimately, that will be the overall outcome, as described in the Gospels, when the preacher is left by all, with the exception of a few of his female followers, who fortunately bring the other disciples of the first hour back to the fold with the help of the risen Lord himself appearing to the latter. It makes for some impressive scenes, even if not all the Gospels are equally keen on developing this motif (see Mark 16:8, after the promise of v. 7) and some of this material is brought on in the form of an epilogue (John 21; see esp. vv. 19-22) or a later addition (Mark's longer ending).

Jesus preaches "everywhere." This word is used a couple of times in the Gospels in this general form (Luke 9:6, πανταχοῦ; also Mark 16:20), but more often the same notion is presented in more descriptive ways, though with the same intention (below). Of course, it is never to be taken at face value. The formulas are always somehow geographically restricted and hardly useful for reconstructing anything like a travel scenario. Jesus is repeatedly said to preach "all through the towns and villages of Galilee" (Mark 1:14a = Matthew/Luke/John, εἰς τὴν Γαλιλαίαν; Mark 1:38, ἀλλαχοῦ εἰς τὰς ἐχομένας κωμοπόλεις = Luke, ταῖς ἑτέραις πόλεσιν; Mark 1:39, εἰς ὅλην τὴν Γαλιλαίαν, cf. Matthew, for which Luke reads "in the synagogues of Judea"; Mark 6:6, περιῆγεν τὰς κώμας κύκλῳ = Matt. 9:35, τὰς πόλεις πάσας καὶ τὰς κώμας; Matt. 11:1, ἐν ταῖς πόλεσιν αὐτῶν; Luke 8:1, διώδευεν κατὰ πόλιν καὶ κώμην; Luke 9:6, κατὰ τὰς κώμας; Luke 13:22, διεπορεύετο κατὰ πόλεις καὶ κώμας). In some instances, the Gospels are slightly more specific, adding that he preached in his hometown (Mark 6:1–6 par. Matthew/Luke) or in neighboring Capernaum (Mark 1:21 par.; John 6:59), or in the synagogues (on the Sabbath: Mark 1:21 par.; 1:39 par.; 6:2* par. Matthew and Luke*; Luke 4:15; 6:6*; 13:10*; John 6:59; 18:20). Preaching in the synagogue gives a more formal character to his ministry, though it did not help to make him more acceptable to part of the audience and rather raised additional questions about his status and qualification to do so (the prime example here is Luke 4:16–30 and the parallels in Mark 6:1–6 = Matthew). But Jesus's field of ministry certainly was not limited to such gathering places and could as well be the town square (so his interlocutors in Luke 13:26, even if this is nowhere exemplified in the Gospels) as private houses (cf. Luke 7:36–50), the lakeside (Mark 2:13; 4:1–2 = Matthew; cf. Luke 5:3), an unspecified mountain (Mark 3:13 = Matthew/Luke; Matt. 5:1), a desert or lonely place (Mark 6:34 par.; Luke 4:42–43), or somewhere "on the road" (Mark 8:31; 9:31 par.; also Luke 5:17 diff. Mark/Matthew; Luke 11:1, ἐν τόπῳ τινί); that of his disciples is never clearly defined and seems to be just "anywhere" (cf. Mark 6:12 par.; 6:30). It is again interesting how the opponents look at it, accusing Jesus of preaching "all through Judea" (Luke 23:5), which is not really demonstrated by the evidence of the Gospels. At one point the traveling comes to an end and the location for preaching is fixed and limited to (the precincts of) the temple of Jerusalem (Mark 11:17; 12:35; 14:49 and par.; Matt. 21:23 par. Luke; Luke 19:47; 21:37; and often in John, who gives special attention to this: 7:14, 28; 8:2, 20; 18:20). Only late in the Gospels do these general notions seem to take a truly universal dimension when Jesus instructs the disciples about the mission to come (Mark 13:10, εἰς πάντα τὰ ἔθνη = Luke 24:47 and par. Matt. 24:14, ἐν ὅλῃ τῇ οἰκουμένῃ; Mark 14:9 = Matthew, εἰς ὅλον τὸν κόσμον; cf. [Mark 16:15]) and the risen Lord confirms the same once more in a different way (Matt. 28:20). But during his lifetime Jesus hardly ever left Palestine. Matthew even has him warn his disciples not to cross the boundaries of the land of Israel (10:5–6, 23; see also the healings at distance in Mark 7:24–30 = Matthew). And if he transgressed this rule, it was only reluctantly, as Luke seems to imply in sketching out the Jerusalem itinerary in 9:52–56 (but see Mark 10:1 par. Matthew, though the text is somewhat unclear). Quite remarkably, it is left for the opponents to ponder whether he maybe also plans to travel into the diaspora (John 7:35).

The Gospels use a multiplicity of verbs to describe Jesus's traveling. The picture is that of one who is constantly on the move, coming and going, entering and leaving (towns or houses, or the temple), traveling through (Luke 8:1, διοδεύω;

cf. Acts 17:1), and traveling around the lake and in the countryside (Mark 6:6 and Matt. 4:23; 9:35, περιάγω, which, by the way, is also what the Pharisees and scribes are said to do in Matt. 23:15). Occasionally, a rather plain verb can apparently also be given a more intense meaning (see πορεύομαι in Luke 9:52). One may also note the remarkable use of περιπατέω in Mark 11:27 (diff. Matthew/Luke) to describe his teaching in the temple (area), which gives it almost a philosophical touch.

Little is said about the circumstances in which Jesus and his company were traveling, but every now and then they were invited in by someone (Mark 14:3–9 par.; Luke 7:36–50; John 11), and that is also what is expected to happen when the disciples are sent out. Now and then Jesus is said to take some precautions or preparatory measures, as when traveling through Samaria (Luke 9:52–56), much to the distress of his disciples, and readying for Passover in Jerusalem (Mark 14:12–17). But times of harshness and destitution are evoked as well; these times both allow Jesus to accommodate his company and those who had come to him (the feeding narratives) and generate complaints from his disciples (Mark 10:28 = Matthew/Luke) and from Jesus himself (Matt. 8:20 = Luke 9:58). Jesus travels under quite frugal conditions, and expects this to be the fate of his disciples.

It is impossible to try to reconstruct a travel route beyond the general information on Jesus circulating in the neighborhood of Capernaum and the lakeside and his one (or repeated: John) pilgrimage travel(s) to Jerusalem, the itinerary of which also remains vague and evidently is not the prime interest of the evangelists. But that should not be a problem for describing the activities of an itinerant preacher, who, by definition, is not expected to follow a fixed pattern but goes "where the wind blows" and the Spirit takes him.

2.1.4. Models of Itinerancy

One does not necessarily have to travel to teach or proclaim a message. It is possible to settle somewhere and make that place one's "center" or "headquarters," as Socrates did when basing himself in Athens, and as others did who followed his model. This is probably easier to realize when operating from a city, which has a larger potential for drawing an audience, than from a village in a corner of a province, but in principle it is not impossible; Epictetus opened his school in Nicopolis, a hub for travelers to the east and the west, but all in all a provincial town. Jesus chose the provincial option, even if he finally ended up in Jerusalem to meet his destiny. So, what kind of preacher is this then, and which models are there to describe him? Four models in particular have been put forward to picture this aspect of Jesus's ministry. All four are open to criticism.

One option is to look at Jewish social and religious tradition. The first connotation that comes to mind is that of the prophet of Jewish tradition. The various pictures of Jesus in the Gospels show affinities with that tradition. Yet all the evangelists also point out that Jesus is "more than a prophet." Moreover, if the prophets repeatedly took a critical stance in social matters and could be very outspoken in their theological interpretation of political events, which adds another element for comparison, they are hardly a prime model for the motif of itinerancy. A second possible parallel from the same tradition is also helpful only to a certain degree. The final part of Jesus's traveling invites comparing him with Jewish pilgrims on the way to Jerusalem (see the passage on how to arrive on the Temple Mount in the rabbinic tractate m. Berakhot 9:5). This parallel has been cited to illustrate the harsh conditions Jesus puts on his disciples when sending them out on their mission. The problem with this is twofold: first, Jewish pilgrims may have had a hard time, but they were allowed some of the basic accommodation and equipment that Mark's Jesus wishes to abandon. Second, and more important, pilgrims travel and pray, but they do not, as a rule, preach.

In recent years, a number of scholars have looked to Q and the Didache for possible parallels. The problem here is that the first source speaks about the mission of the disciples but hardly refers to Jesus's travels (the exceptions are Q 9:57–60 and the saying about following in Q 14:27). It is of course quite plausible that the modalities of the former were copied on the latter, but this is not really developed in any detail in Q, and it remains disputed whether Q can be reduced to a preaching aid for traveling missionaries. The Didache knows of traveling teachers/apostles/prophets visiting communities but is critical of them and (on purpose?) avoids comparing their behavior in any way with Jesus's (Did. 11). So again, not much can be found here to illustrate Jesus's ministry in this respect. The text comes from a different age and addresses a different situation.

Even more debated is the suggestion that Jesus was, or was perceived to be, a (kind of) Cynic philosopher. If a number of similarities can be cited in this regard, some even quite appealing (many of these from Q material, though not exclusively), overall the parallel has been widely felt to be unconvincing, because of the differences in the message and specific claims made about and by Jesus as presented in the Gospels, but that may in part miss the mark. The point of comparison is not so much content as behavior. But also, itinerancy was not an unconditional key aspect of a Cynic life, and displaying an attitude of absolute indifference toward settling does not automatically translate into constantly being on the move. So maybe something can be found here, but probably on condition that it is broadened to include similar lifestyles by otherwise very different figures from Greek philosophical tradition. Philostratus's life of the first-century philosopher Apollonius of Tyana (written in the first decades of the third century) presents the protagonist as an indefatigable traveler, eager to bring his message to every city of the ancient world and to instruct his disciples or whatever audience he meets. The problem here is that not much is known about the historical Apollonius, apart from what can be read in Philostratus, and there is a good chance that his story was partly modeled after the Gospels in an attempt to create a pagan counterpart for their protagonist.

A fourth option, which has perhaps not yet received the attention it may deserve, is to look at Jesus's opponents in the Gospels. First among these are the scribes and Pharisees, who seem to show a keen interest in checking on what Jesus is saying and doing while circulating in Galilee. Unfortunately, far too little is known about their agenda and activities in the province and how these were structured and organized, but they are present where Jesus goes, they are concerned about his status as a teacher and about the effect of his preaching on the crowds, and they are criticized by Jesus for how they try to "educate" their people. It was most probably not true that each place had its "village Pharisee," but they were prominently present and did care about what was going on. Matthew's rant against their missionary zeal in 23:15 may greatly exaggerate the horizon of their activities, but it had to have some basis if it was meant to be effective. So, in the end, the two "enemies" are perhaps closer to each other than one might suspect, which would help explain the tensions between them that the Gospels have recorded.

We conclude with two observations. First, Jesus's traveling ministry of proclamation, and of healing, is depicted in much detail in the Gospels, using a variety of motifs and vocabulary that reflects its complexity as a phenomenon. Traveling is an integral ingredient of his ministry, and one that Jesus is said to have promoted also among his disciples, but it is limited in its geographical scope and apparently can be divided into two parts: one that focuses on the vicinity of his hometown and one that is set for Jerusalem. Second, this aspect of Jesus's ministry shows affinities with several models from Jewish and Greek tradition, though none of these can claim priority or exclusivity as a parallel. Integral to the ministry and unique in scope and message are perhaps the key themes in defining this part of Jesus's activity as presented in the Gospels.

Downing, Francis Gerald. 1988. *Christ and the Cynics: Jesus and Other Radical Preachers in First-Century Tradition*. JSOTSup 4. Sheffield.

Schmeller, Thomas. 1989. *Brechungen: Urchristliche Wandercharismatiker im Prisma soziologischorientierter Exegese*. SBS 136. Stuttgart.

Theissen, Gerd. 1979; ³1989. *Studien zur Soziologie des Urchristentums*. WUNT 19. Tübingen.

Tiwald, Markus. 2002. *Wanderradikalismus: Jesu erste Jünger—ein Anfang und was davon bleibt*. ÖBS 20. Frankfurt.

Joseph Verheyden

2.2. *Founding a Community*

2.2.1. Call to Discipleship

Jesus's call to become a disciple is a motif that runs all through the Gospels. It is thematized in three rather distinct forms that together should yield a more or less complete picture of what is intended by it, what is required, and what are its privileges and duties. These aspects will be discussed in turn.

2.2.1.1. The Call

To be called, and to respond to the call, is a motif that is known from Hebrew Scripture (especially in relation to prophets) and that is also employed in the infancy narratives for various characters. Calling upon people to become disciples is one of the first things Jesus is said to have done when he started his public ministry. Mark's and Matthew's versions of their first call story are almost identical and are found at the same place in their gospels (Mark 1:16–20 = Matt. 4:18–22). Luke brings in a more elaborate form of the same story (5:1–11), which he places later in his account, after he has already told the reader quite extensively about Jesus's teaching and healing activities. But this difference should perhaps not be overemphasized, for also in Mark and Matthew Jesus had already begun his preaching (Mark 1:14–15 = Matt. 4:13–17); Luke is simply a bit more concrete about it. John offers a rather more complicated story, but he puts it at the beginning, as in Mark and Matthew, though no other activity of Jesus is mentioned before he extends his call (John 1:35–51). Yet, even in John, Jesus does not come out of nowhere. He had been announced and spoken about by the Baptist in the presence of large crowds, though unlike in the Synoptic Gospels, it is not said that he is actually also baptized by him.

Jesus is, then, not a complete stranger when he appears at the shore of the Sea of Galilee (so Mark = Matthew; Luke: the Sea of Gennesaret). This could explain why he does not seem to need any introduction in Mark's and Matthew's version and does not introduce himself when approaching the fishermen, and why they do not ask any questions about his identity, unless, of course, one rather wishes to opt for a more theological explanation and read the call stories as a kind of revelation to the disciples. This absence of any hint at Jesus's person is indeed a striking element, though it is difficult to be certain about its meaning, as those called in no way indicate whether or how they knew who Jesus was. Luke deviates from this and has Peter address Jesus as "Master" (ἐπιστάτης) and refer to himself as a "sinner" (Luke 5:5, 8). The title is a favorite of Luke, who is the only evangelist to use it—although outcasts who address Jesus also use it (the lepers in Luke 17:13)—but no explanation is given why this would be an appropriate way for addressing Jesus in this context. Peter's reference to himself will show up again later for other people in the context of calling upon individuals (see below). In addition, Jesus shows his power or knowledge when successfully ordering Peter to launch out into the lake again, and Peter shows his confidence in this man when he blindly executes the command. Luke explains what was left unaddressed in Mark and Matthew, but even in his presentation some mystery remains, with regard both to this man and to Peter's reaction.

The synoptic versions of the call story contain three other remarkable features. Only a few people are called (four in Mark and Matthew, three of these also in Luke), and they belong to the lowest social classes. The number is not explained; the social location does not seem to pose a problem, and no reason whatsoever is given for it, which leaves the reader wondering where this will go. Further, Jesus does not use the word "disciple" when addressing the fishermen and hardly gives any information on what they are expected to do, beyond the invitation—or more probably, the command—to follow him and become "fishers of men," which looks like a quite appropriate, though mysterious, formulation. This in turn makes the reaction of the men all the more remarkable. They abandon everything (including their closest family and their father, that is, those they are supposed to take responsibility for) and follow immediately. These two motifs will be taken up again later in the Gospels, and there they will illustrate that the disciples' on-the-spot decision was a final one and not just a tryout. Together these features make the synoptic call stories prototypes in the genre: no questions are asked, hardly any answers are given. All is open and the suspense is maintained.

John takes a rather different path in telling his version of the story. There is no lake scene and no mention of fishermen, hence there is no reason to keep to the key word of the synoptic call stories. Instead, the reader is almost overwhelmed with information about Jesus and about the way those who are called inquire about this and react to it. John agrees with the synoptic accounts in telling about a double call of two pairs each, but otherwise goes very much his own way. It starts right with the first two. They are already disciples of John the Baptist, and they are introduced to Jesus by their master with the same mysterious formula he had used before in announcing Jesus that opens up a divine dimension ("behold, the Lamb of God," John 1:29, 35–36). The disciples heed and follow, but when spoken to by Jesus, they refrain from addressing him in the same way as their master and keep to the more mundane "Rabbi" (John 1:38). Equally mundane is the question they have for Jesus: they want to know where he is staying. The courageous decision of the disciples in the synoptic stories seems far away. They stay for a day and are instructed. No direct account of this is given, but its outcome seems to have convinced at least one of the two (the other disappears from the scene, though it is not said that he left). Andrew goes looking for his brother Simon, reveals to him the identity of his new master (the Messiah!), and just as he had been introduced, now in turn brings his brother to Jesus, who immediately gives him another name. If the same name occurs also in the synoptic accounts, though only later, here it adds a motif that is well known in initiation rites and is in that sense not completely out of context after the "initiation," which Andrew himself had received. If one might be tempted to question if this first part can actually be regarded as a call story when compared with the synoptic accounts, John seems to make up for this by introducing the second part in a way that comes close to these when he has Jesus approach Philip and directly require him to follow (John 1:43). Philip responds, most remarkably, by telling yet another person in a more indirect way than Andrew had that he has met the Messiah, without it being said that he had received any such instruction, unless the information that he hailed from the same village (John 1:44) as Andrew and Peter should be regarded as revealing his source, which would in a sense weaken Jesus's firm call to follow him. The last one to be called proves to be the toughest to convince (John 1:46–48). However, once he is brought so far, his confession surpasses anything the others had proclaimed about Jesus, for he reverts to the Baptist's witness in John 1:34 and calls Jesus the Son of God and the King of Israel (1:49), thus combining a previous confession with his own interpretation of what this Messiah represents. Jesus does not deny or affirm his outcry, but his reply in turn reverts to a motif the Baptist had used for him, though he formulates it in a different way while introducing a phrase as a self-reference that is commonly used in all the Gospels ("Son of Man," John 1:51).

When compared with the synoptic accounts, it looks as if John gives everything away right from the start and, moreover, as if he wishes to diminish Jesus's role in this first calling by elaborating on that of those called. But even in John some things remain unexplained—from the identity of that other disciple of the Baptist to what is now to be expected from those who have decided to follow Jesus. And even in John's version Jesus remains very much in command. If in the Synoptic Gospels the initiative is solely with Jesus, John presents a more complex account in which the interplay between the two parties is put into the picture, but in the end, it is Jesus who instructs the disciples in such a way that they come to follow him, and he has the last word when it comes to identifying himself. So in the end, there is no reason to suggest that John's version should be completely set apart from the synoptic accounts. His certainly is an elaborate and more complex version, but it brings out the same core message: Jesus calls, and the disciples follow unconditionally.

Shortly after this first call story, Mark tells another one (2:13–17). He is closely followed by Luke and Matthew; they do not take it over until later in their Gospels (Luke 5:27–32 = Matt. 9:9–13). The story is only in part a repetition of the first one. This time a "real" outcast is called—the man is a tax collector. It happens in the same succinct way: Jesus calls upon him to follow (now with the more "technical" ἀκολουθέω), and the man consents to it without muttering a word. But then the story takes a different turn in two respects. Jesus uses the tax collector to introduce himself to other representatives of his class, who are now designated as "sinners," just as Peter referred to himself at his call (the phrase "tax collectors and sinners" can be read as a reference to two distinct groups, or perhaps more probably, as a synonymous expression). Mark alone adds a short puzzling phrase about the many who followed Jesus. It is unclear whether it refers to the tax collectors or, again more probably (that the tax collectors were numerous had been mentioned just before), to his disciples, who are also present and are now for the first time in Mark called by that name (see also Luke 5:30). Clearly, Jesus's calls were successful beyond the few examples that had been described so far, but it is not said how these many others were called—in person, as those of the first story and as Levi-Matthew, or as a result of his preaching to the multitudes. To this a twofold second element is added: the calls and the success are looked upon critically by representatives of the established order and lead to a second confrontation (but the first with the Pharisees in Mark) after the first one, at the healing of the paralytic just before. In turn, the resulting dispute gives Jesus an opportunity to emphasize the salvific character of his action. People ("sinners") are being called in order to be saved (Mark 2:17 par.).

Then there is what one might label a call story "in the second degree," when Jesus picks out a selected number of disciples from among the many who are following him, for that is how Mark and Luke present the election of the Twelve, who are assigned the task of proclaiming the message and exorcising the possessed (Mark 3:13–15 par. Luke 6:13; Matt. 10:1–4 by contrast describes this as an assignment for a group that had already been constituted). Mark speaks of Jesus summoning to him those he wished to come and appointing twelve (καὶ προσκαλεῖται οὓς ἤθελεν αὐτός, . . . καὶ ἐποίησεν δώδεκα, Mark 3:13). Luke 6:13 has something similar (προσεφώνησεν τοὺς μαθητὰς αὐτοῦ, καὶ ἐκλεξάμενος ἀπ' αὐτῶν δώδεκα). A select group is chosen to perform a precisely described task (so in Mark, but cf. also Luke 9:1–2); more details will follow in Jesus's Mission Discourse. Upon their return, those who are sent out are then called "apostles" (Mark 6:30 = Luke 9:10). There is no reason to suppose that these are a different body, but it should also be noted that neither "disciples" or "apostles" is then used consistently when referring to the missionary activity of the disciples (see the failed exorcism of "the disciples" in Mark 9:18 = Matthew/Luke).

In addition to these "formal" call stories, a number of other accounts could perhaps in some respect also be qualified in this way. A good candidate is the story of the rich young man (Mark 10:17–31 par.), which ends in a call by Jesus that unfortunately is not answered by the one who is addressed (Mark 10:21–22 = Matthew/Luke). Maybe the little scene in John 11:28–29 in which Jesus calls (φωνέω) Mary, who immediately goes to him, should also be included. Others present themselves as would-be disciples, as does the scribe in Matt. 8:19–20 (cf. par. Luke 9:57–58, where the would-be disciple remains anonymous). Matthew gives him a counterpart in the person of a disciple who asks permission to bury his father, only to be denied and to be confronted with a stern "follow me" (Matt. 8:21–22). Luke has expanded the same into a triple scene in which the second and the third interlocutor are still only candidates for discipleship (Luke 9:59–62). The motif of following Jesus is central to all these scenes, and the focus is on the hardships of joining, to which Luke then also adds a soteriological component as well as a brief reference to the task of a disciple (see Luke 9:62 and 60). The same can be said of blind Bartimaeus, whose call is heard and is himself "called" by Jesus (note φωνέω in Mark 10:49 and Matt. 20:32), which results in his healing and his following Jesus (Mark 10:52 par. Matthew/Luke). Matthew omits this last element in his doublet in 9:27–31, and instead has the two who are healed proclaim Jesus, which is a motif that is also found in other passages and can be regarded as a variant on the motif of following, or perhaps, better, a "light version" of discipleship (see also in Mark 1:45, with the same verb, διαφημίζω, as in Matthew). Maybe one should also put into this category the story in Luke 10:38–42 about Martha and Mary, in which the latter chooses "the better part" and wishes to be instructed by the Lord, even if it is not said that she follows him.

From this last passage it is but a small step to such stories that tell about people who follow Jesus without any reference to their being called. These "implicit call stories," if that is how they can be labeled, are perhaps more difficult to assess, as it is not always clear whether the protagonists wished to be with Jesus on a permanent basis, as is obviously implied in the "real" call stories. But for some of them at least, this is what they had been doing. Repeatedly it is said in the Gospels that a crowd is with Jesus or following after him apparently for some time (Mark 3:7 = Matthew/Luke; Mark 5:24 = Luke, but the latter without the verb ἀκολουθέω; Mark 6:33 = Matthew/Luke, but both with ἀκολουθέω for Mark's συνέδραμον; Mark 10:1, συμπορεύονται, par. Matt. 19:2, ἠκολούθησαν; Matt. 8:1; 8:10 = Luke; Matt. 20:29 par. Mark 10:46, but without ἀκολουθέω; Luke 23:27, in the rather precarious context of the road to Golgotha; John 6:2). In the same way, almost in passing, the reader also receives information about female followers of Jesus, though only very late in the story in Mark and Matthew (Mark 15:41 = Matthew/Luke; cf. also John 19:25), but already much earlier in Luke (8:1–3).

There are two more comments to conclude this section. Taking into account the interest the gospel writers show for this motif, it is quite surprising that in a few cases Jesus seems to avoid attracting people to his person, as in Mark 2:12 par., where the paralytic is merely told "to go home" (see Mark 8:26); also Mark 5:34 = Matthew/Luke, where a woman is sent off with a blessing, or the two healings-at-distance (Mark 7:24–30 = Matthew, and Matt. 8:1–10 = Luke), where both suppliants are sent home to find out about the hoped-for result. More pointed still are passages such as Mark 1:38 = Luke, where Jesus tries to escape attention from the crowds; Mark 5:19 = Luke, where the healed demoniac is also told to go home in reply to his request to stay with Jesus; or Matt. 12:16, where those healed are simply forbidden to speak about Jesus (it is less clear who is meant in Mark). The evangelists probably did not want to say that these people did not become disciples, but that they in any case do not follow Jesus on his itinerary as others do. Finally, there is the strange reply of the disciples to Jesus in Mark 9:38 = Luke when objecting to an exorcist using his name on the basis that he is not one of them (οὐκ ἀκολούθει ἡμῖν/μεθ᾽ ἡμῶν). Following Jesus becomes the norm for judging others, at least for his own disciples.

2.2.1.2. Being Called Is a Process

To be called to become a disciple and to follow Jesus, or to make the decision to respond to such a call, is no doubt a crucial moment, but this is not enough. The call goes on. As presented in the Gospels, becoming a disciple is a process that never really ends and always is in danger of falling apart. Both aspects are given due attention all through the Gospels. The disciples-followers, both the crowds and the "in crowd," are constantly being taught by Jesus. The larger part of this teaching deals with Jesus's message and with his person and role in it, but more than once Jesus is also said to instruct his followers about what it means to be his disciple. He informs them about their relation to the Master (Matt. 10:24–25 = Luke; Mark 6:34 and 14:27 = Matthew; also in his own vivid way, John 10:4–5), their task as apostles of the gospel (the Mission Discourse), and the hardships of discipleship (Mark 6:8–9, 11 = Matthew/Luke; 8:34–9:1 = Matthew/Luke; 13:9, 11 = Matthew/Luke; Matt. 5:11–12; 10:23; 23:37 = Luke; John 15:20). He does so in word and deed, by warning and praising them, by instructing them on the kingdom and his person, but also by sending them on a mission on which they are expected to report back (Mark 6:30 = Matthew/Luke), by acting out what true discipleship is about (the foot washing in John 13:1–20), and even by showing them how to resist opponents (cf. the controversies in Mark 11–12 par. Matthew/Luke, where the disciples are assumed to be part of the audience, and more directly already long before, when Jesus steps up for them in the Sabbath controversy in Mark 2:18–22 = Matthew/Luke). He is keen on making a distinction between his closest followers and other sympathizers by pointing out the former's privileged status as those who are granted private instruction (Mark 4:10–12, 13–20 = Matthew/Luke), and within this narrower group some occasionally are singled out for assisting in an even more private encounter (see the transfiguration story in Mark 9:2–10, 11–13 = Matthew/Luke). But the "education" of the disciples is a long, difficult, and indeed frustrating process, as the gospel writers do not grow tired of repeating. The disciples are slow to understand, or do not understand at all (cf. Mark 6:52 and 8:14–21 = Matt. 16:5–12, with Matthew's typical ὀλιγόπιστοι; Luke 18:34), though every now and then they see the light (Matt. 16:12; 17:13). They can cause shame and trouble for others (preventing people from approaching Jesus: Mark 10:13 = Matthew/Luke; Matt. 15:23; ready to pick a fight, as at his arrest: Mark 14:47 = Matthew/Luke/John), and for themselves (their panic in Mark 4:38 and 6:49 = Matthew/Luke; falling asleep in Gethsemane: Mark 14:32–42 = Matthew/Luke), and among themselves (Mark 9:33–37 = Matthew/Luke; Mark 10:35–45 = Matthew, and par. Luke). At times Jesus has to face what appears to be a real crisis, as when Peter, speaking for all, confronts him with the fact that they have left everything for him (Mark 10:28 = Matthew/Luke), or when he has to denounce the traitor among them (Mark 14:18–21 = Matthew/Luke/John). He reacts in different ways to these failures, rebuking them (Mark 8:30 = Luke), foretelling their defection (Mark 14:27 = Matthew, and Mark 14:30 = Matthew/Luke), patiently repeating or explaining once again what he had said or done (Mark 4:13–20 = Matthew/Luke), damning the traitor (Mark 14:21 = Matthew), or promising (heavenly) rewards to those who remain faithful (Mark 10:29–30 = Matthew, to which the latter also adds a different type of reward in 19:28 = Luke 22:28–30; Luke 12:37; and the parables about masters and servants). At times, one may also have the impression that Jesus made it difficult on himself, as when he first praises and then rebukes Peter for his glorious confession (Mark 8:29, 33 = Matthew), about which the reader might ask what was wrong with it. The entire long time in Galilee and the entire long way to Jerusalem Jesus is busy training the disciples to become *his* disciples. But then, in the end, all seems to fall apart, for he is abandoned by almost all of them (except for the women) and denied by his closest followers (Mark 14:50 = Matthew; Mark 14:66–72 = Matthew/Luke/John). The crisis is complete, but it is not the end of the story.

2.2.1.3. *Called Again, for a New Task*

Indeed, in a sense, the training resumes after the drama of Jesus's death and resurrection. The old disciples are called once again, now by the risen Lord, and they are called to become new and true disciples, ready to continue the work Jesus wants them to perform. The appearance stories can be read as new call stories, in which Jesus the Lord urges the group to take courage, to discover their faith again, and then also to ready themselves for the huge task that is awaiting them. Matthew ends his gospel in this way (the Lord's commandment in 28:19–20), and so does Luke, where Jesus urges them to stand ready for what is to come (24:49). And it is most probably no coincidence that the appearance story in John 21:1–11 resembles the call story in Luke 5:1–11 and that the verb ἀκολουθέω is a key word in the second part of that chapter (see John 21:19.20, 22), or that a later author thought it useful to expand upon the original ending of Mark with the somewhat chaotic description of the heroic deeds of the "newborn" disciples, which gives content to what is expected to follow from the promise that disciples would meet Jesus in Galilee (Mark 16:7). Perhaps most striking in all of this is that no hint is made and no word is spoken about their previous failure. The risen Lord acts as if nothing had happened. His disciples may have failed, but they are quietly brought back into the fold and given the final instructions to start their mission for good (emphatically so in the finale of Matthew and John).

2.2.1.4. Expectations of the Call

The disciples are an inherent part of Jesus's life as presented in the Gospels. They are to be instructed, even initiated into the message, so that they can continue his work. Some are said to have been "called" by Jesus, which can be expressed rather plainly by a mere εἶπεν (Mark 1:17 par. Matthew/Luke), but also by the perhaps more forceful καλέω (Mark 1:20 = Matthew; cf. Mark 2:17 = Matthew/Luke). They are most commonly referred to as "disciples" (μαθηταί), though occasionally other words appear (the Twelve, apostles, "those with Jesus"), which opens possibilities for presenting Jesus as the "master" or "teacher" (ἐπιστάτης, διδάσκαλος, but also rabbi) and for pondering the relation between both. They are above all described as "following" Jesus, the verb that will soon replace the perhaps rather plainer δεῦτε ὀπίσω μου of the first call story in Mark and Matthew, though occasionally also other verbs can be used to express that they are accompanying or traveling with Jesus. It allows for assuming that ἀκολουθέω in this case probably also carries a symbolic meaning. The disciples follow Jesus not only literally but also in deed and in spirit.

They are given instructions and they receive "knowledge" about their master and his message. They have to learn in order to be able to teach others. They come to realize that there are privileges to their status, but even more, duties. They are expected to be courageous and to have and keep faith (see the motif of "those of little faith" in Matthew), and to endure the troubles and hardships they incur. They are repeatedly reminded that they are not like, and cannot be like, their master, who is of divine origin. Yet at times their master himself also poses as the ideal disciple, showing such virtues as patience, empathy with those in need, humility, and love for every human being, and inviting the disciples to imitate him in this. They are faced with a huge task that will consume their whole life, but they will come to learn and understand that only after their encounter with the earthly Jesus had been transformed into something higher—the experience and conviction of being called to discipleship by the Lord. Such a perspective makes discipleship a key motif of the Gospels.

2.2.2. The Formation of the Circle of the Twelve

Paul, the four Gospels, Acts, and the author of Revelation all know that Jesus was accompanied by a selected body of disciples that was referred to as "the Twelve (disciples)." The label and motif (for it is more than just a label) pose some intriguing questions with regard to its origin, its precise meaning, and its use in the Gospels and other early Christian writings.

2.2.2.1. The Number Twelve in Jewish Scripture

Among the many numbers that receive a special (symbolic) meaning in Jewish Scripture, the number twelve takes a place of its own (all references in the following are according to the LXX). There are twelve "minor" prophets (note also Sir. 49:10); twelve springs (and seventy palm trees) in Elim (Exod. 15:27 and Num. 33:9, two passages that have been linked to Luke's seventy or seventy-two disciples in Luke 10:1); twelve loaves for food offerings (Lev. 24:5); twelve royal enemies of Joshua (Josh. 24:12); twelve oxen carrying the bronze Sea in Solomon's Temple (2 Chron. 4:4, 15; cf. Jer. 52:20). The size of the two pillars stolen by the Chaldeans from Solomon's Temple is twelve cubits (Jer. 52:21–22). Solomon (1 Kgs. 2:12) and Manasseh are crowned king at the age of twelve (2 Kgs. 21:1). Twelve years constitute the reigns of Omri (1 Kgs. 16:23), Jehoram (2 Kgs. 3:1), Amon (2 Kgs. 21:19 v.l.), and Alexander the Great (1 Macc. 1:7). Twelve lions guard Solomon's throne (1 Kgs. 10:20 = 2 Chron. 9:19). Women are required to undergo twelve months of preparation to meet Artaxerxes (Esther 2:12). Ishmael has twelve escorts (Jer. 48:1–2, v.l.). Twelve sons are born to Ishmael (Gen. 17:20; 25:16) and to Jacob (Gen. 35:22). Israel comprises twelve tribes (Gen. 49:28; Ezek. 47:13), from which representatives are chosen (twelve chiefs of Israel: Num. 1:44; twelve spies: Deut. 1:23; twelve carriers of stones: Josh. 3:12; 4:3–5; twelve fighters for Benjamin and David's servants: 2 Sam. 2:15; twelve governors: 1 Kgs. 4:7; twelve chosen for temple service in 1 Chron. 25:9–31; twelve from the leaders of the priests in 2 Esd. 8:24). Israel is sometimes symbolized by twelve objects (stones in Exod. 24:4; 28:21; Josh. 4:2, 8–9, 20; 1 Kgs. 18:31; oxen in Num. 7:3, and a whole series of other objects for sacrifice in Num. 7:84–87; staffs in Num. 17:2, 6; calves or bulls in Num. 29:17; 2 Esd. 8:35; pieces of a cloak in 1 Kgs. 11:30; and male goats in 1 Esd. 7:8 and 2 Esd. 6:17). In a number of instances also a multiplier is used (12,000: Num. 31:5; Josh. 8:25; Judg. 21:10; 2 Sam. 10:6 and 17:1; 1 Kgs. 4:26; 10:26 = 2 Chron. 1:14 and 9:25; Jdt. 2:15; Jon. 4:11; 1 Macc. 11:45 and 15:13; and 2 Macc. 8:20 and 12:20); also, twelve is used in combination with 100, as in Tob. 14:1 (dying at 112 years of age). There are hardly any instances that do not carry a symbolic meaning—possible exceptions are the numbers of cities in Josh. 21 and of kinsmen elected for service of the ark in 1 Chron. 15:10; vessels for the temple service in 1 Esd. 8:56; the size of the vestibule and the dimensions of the hearth of the altar in Ezek. 40:49 and 43:16; the offerings to Bel in Bel. 3, because the number twelve occurs here together with other numbers; maybe Elisha's twelve pair of oxen in 1 Kgs. 19:19; and perhaps also the twelve parts of the dismembered body in Judg. 19:29, though these last two are less certain. As can be seen from this brief survey, the number twelve can carry various meanings and can be used in various ways. No wonder the motif has impressed later authors.

2.2.2.2. The Number Twelve in the New Testament

The twelve tribes of Israel are referred to in Matt. 19:28 (= Luke; in Matthew in combination with "twelve thrones"), James 1:1, Rev. 21:12, and most emphatically in Rev. 7:4–9; it is also used for the sons of Jacob in Acts 7:8 (referred to as "patriarchs"). The number twelve can carry the connotation of innumerableness (a twelve-year illness in Mark 5:25 = Matthew/Luke; twelve legions in Matt. 26:53), and more often, of abundance (the twelve baskets in Mark 6:43 = Matthew/Luke/John; Mark 8:19 par. Matthew, though here only indirectly; John 11:9: twelve hours in a day) and completeness and perfection (repeatedly in Revelation: the twelve stars in a crown in Rev. 12:1; the twelve foundations, inscribed with the names of the twelve apostles, and the twelve gates, likened to twelve pearls, while each is made of one pearl, inscribed with the names of the twelve tribes and guarded by twelve angels, in Rev. 21:12, 14, 21, and its exponent in Rev. 21:16; and the twelve fruits of the tree of life in Rev. 22:2, possibly combining abundance with perfection). Occasionally the number does not seem to have any symbolic meaning (see Mark 5:42 = Luke: the girl's age; Luke 2:42: Jesus's age; Acts 19:7: "about twelve men," and 24:11: "not more than twelve days"; in these two last instances the Textus Receptus instead reads δεκαδύο, in contradistinction to "the Twelve"); but even in these cases one could argue that sometimes perhaps something more is in play than mere counting (an allusion to maturity in Luke 2:42, and then maybe also in Mark 5:42; the "about" twelve in Acts 19:7 were already disciples; see 19:1).

2.2.2.3. Analysis of "the Twelve"

"The Twelve," οἱ δώδεκα, are referred to in this way by Mark, Luke, and John, but rather more systematically as οἱ δώδεκα μαθηταί by Matthew (10:1; 11:1; [20:17]; as a variant in 26:20; see also Mark 11:11 v.l.). Matthew also once writes οἱ δώδεκα ἀπόστολοι (10:2), as does the author of Revelation, though with a twist that is peculiar and typical (οἱ δώδεκα ἀπόστολοι τοῦ ἀρνίου, "the twelve apostles of the lamb," Rev. 21:14), and also Mark in his own way (Mark 3:14). They are by definition regarded as a group, though once they are also identified and on a number of occasions only one member of it can be singled out (see below).

The expression "the Twelve" is also known to Paul, who mentions it once in 1 Cor. 15:5, in a passage that is generally considered to reflect an ancient confessional tradition. He seems to assume that his readers know what he is talking about, but his use of the phrase poses some problems when compared with the information found in the Gospels (see below). In the Gospels "the Twelve" are introduced in various ways and at various moments. In Mark the label first shows up in a passage that is textually shaky, but that is quite informative (Mark 3:13–16):

> [13] And he [i.e., Jesus] went up the mountain and called to him those whom he wanted, and they came to him. [14] And he appointed twelve [whom he named apostles] to be with him, and to be sent out to preach [15] and to have authority to cast out demons. [16] [And he appointed the twelve] . . .

> [13] καὶ ἀναβαίνει εἰς τὸ ὄρος καὶ προσκαλεῖται οὓς ἤθελεν αὐτός, καὶ ἀπῆλθον πρὸς αὐτόν. [14] καὶ ἐποίησεν δώδεκα [οὓς καὶ ἀποστόλους ὠνόμασεν] ἵνα ὦσιν μετ᾽ αὐτοῦ καὶ ἵνα ἀποστέλλῃ αὐτοὺς κηρύσσειν [15] καὶ ἔχειν ἐξουσίαν ἐκβάλλειν τὰ δαιμόνια. [16] [καὶ ἐποίησεν τοὺς δώδεκα,] . . .

The first passage between brackets (v. 14) has an identical parallel in Luke and can therefore be suspected to have been inserted into Mark, on purpose or by mistake. The second one is suspect, as it looks like a repetition of the same phrase at the beginning of v. 14. They are not the only variants in a passage that seems to have suffered heavily in the textual tradition, but they are the two that have made it into the text of the standard edition of the New Testament (*Novum Testamentum Graece*), albeit with some reservation. The passage fits well into the style of Mark (note the extensive parataxis). It evokes a formal scene, in which Jesus is said to have called twelve people to join him and to send them out on mission to proclaim the message equipped with special powers to face evil forces. The two elements of their task reflect Jesus's ministry. The reader already knows that Jesus was accompanied by disciples (Mark 2:15–16, 18, 23). As a consequence, even though this is not explicitly said, the reader is entitled to assume that these twelve are apparently chosen from this group, whose composition and extent are not further detailed. Its members are not called disciples, but that is no doubt how we have to imagine them, and neither are the Twelve, who are rather called "apostles," which is quite fitting in light of the task they are given and which is the term Mark will use when reporting on their return from their first mission (Mark 6:30 = Luke, omitted in Matthew). Mark does not give either reasons or criteria for the choice of the Twelve. The choice is Jesus's and his alone. It obviously is effective: all those called follow him, without uttering a word. "The Twelve" is a creation of Jesus. In this respect, one is probably entitled to give some force to the slight but maybe significant difference between the two phrases at the beginning of vv. 14 and 16. The second has the article, which could mean that the first one is to be understood as "he picked twelve" and the latter as "he made them 'the Twelve.'" They are the result of Jesus's decision to select a restricted number from an apparently larger group for a special double task, the second leg of which is further detailed (preaching and healing), whereas the first one ("to be with him") remains rather vague but characterizes the members as something like close, or privileged, disciples. Mark goes on to list their names. The first four to be mentioned are known to the reader from the call story in Mark 1:16–20. Simon and Andrew are no longer identified as brothers, whereas James and John are presented as at the beginning of the gospel as the sons of Zebedee. Simon and the two sons of Zebedee are formally given new names, as if being initiated in a secret association. The remaining eight names follow in an order that is not explained. All these names are new to the reader, and nothing is said about their history or how they came to join Jesus. One in the list is identified as "the son of Alphaeus" in the same way as was the tax collector Levi, the only other disciple whose call is told (Mark 2:13–14), but this one has another name (James), and the identification is added to distinguish him from one of the two brothers. The list concludes with Judas Iscariot, who is immediately discredited as the betrayer. Mark will repeat part of this story in partially identical wording in Mark 6:6b–7, where Jesus, while on his mission, is said to call "the Twelve" to him to send them out, in pairs, on their first missionary ministry:

⁶ᵇ and he [i.e., Jesus] went among the surrounding villages teaching. ⁷ He called the twelve and began to send them out two by two and gave them authority over the unclean spirits.

⁶ᵇ καὶ περιῆγεν τὰς κώμας κύκλῳ διδάσκων. ⁷ καὶ προσκαλεῖται τοὺς δώδεκα καὶ ἤρξατο αὐτοὺς ἀποστέλλειν δύο δύο καὶ ἐδίδου αὐτοῖς ἐξουσίαν τῶν πνευμάτων τῶν ἀκαθάρτων.

Again the statement is well in the style of Mark and corresponds in form to the previous one, so that the reader should have no difficulty linking the two. This second passage strengthens the special character of this body and the task it is given. They are geared up for missionary work.

Matthew avoids the doublet and merges the two stories into one, which he locates at the same place as Mark 6:6b-7, but not without also saving the introductory scene of Mark 3:13a. He uses the latter for locating the Sermon on the Mount, which is spoken in the presence of and for the disciples (Matt. 5:1-2). This says a lot about the importance Matthew gives to this Markan parallel and also informs the reader about how he sees the composition of this group. The operation is not really successful in all its aspects. Matthew has simplified Mark's account, but has thereby also created some confusion. If Mark first said that Jesus chose twelve people from among his followers, and later added that they are now effectively sent out, Matthew basically omits telling about their selection and apparently considers this to be known when merely writing in Matt. 10:1, καὶ προσκαλεσάμενος τοὺς δώδεκα μαθητὰς αὐτοῦ ("Then summoning his twelve disciples"), unless this statement actually would signify that these twelve are the complete body of Jesus's disciples. It does not really help that he calls them "his" twelve disciples or that he has Jesus complain to his disciples about the huge missionary task that is awaiting and the lack of missionaries to take it on (Matt. 9:36-37, added to his parallel of Mark 6:6b in v. 35), for so far the reader has never heard about these "twelve" and only knows about an indistinct group and number of disciples, and so the confusion remains. In this respect, Mark's somewhat laborious presentation is clearer. The Twelve are given the same task of proclaiming and healing as in Mark, they are also called "apostles," and their names are given in a list that is identical to Mark's, except that Simon Peter and Andrew are put together again at the beginning, the sons of Zebedee are not granted any special name, Matthew and Thomas switch places, and the former is identified as the tax collector (Matt. 10:2-4).

Luke follows Mark in telling about their selection, but then goes his own way when speaking of their mission. He retains the mountain scene from Mark, adding to it his favored topic of Jesus praying there in solitude, which brings some extra solemnity to the next scene. Now Luke says explicitly that they are chosen "from the disciples" (Luke 6:13, προσεφώνησεν τοὺς μαθητὰς αὐτοῦ, καὶ ἐκλεξάμενος ἀπ᾽ αὐτῶν δώδεκα). They are likewise called "apostles," even though at this stage their task has not been mentioned; their names are listed, as in Mark and Matthew, but with some slight changes. Luke agrees with the latter in putting the first couple together, but then also fails to identify the second pair as brothers, and agrees with Mark in the order of Matthew and Thomas but replaces Thaddaeus with one Judas son of James, who takes the next-to-last position right before that other Judas (Luke 6:14–16). In Acts, Luke will return to Mark's order for the two pairs of brothers but move Thomas before Bartholomew and Matthew, and obviously drop the traitor's name, all while scaling down the identification to the mere names, except for the second James, the second Simon, and the second Judas (Acts 1:13–14). Luke also follows Mark in mentioning the Twelve, as a group, in introducing his first Mission Discourse (Luke 9:1), only leaving out (as did Matthew) the detail about sending them out in pairs, which, however, is picked up in the introduction to his second version of the Mission Discourse (Luke 10:1). But now the Twelve have company, for this time not twelve (they are not mentioned at all) but seventy(-two) are sent out, in pairs, in a phrase that clearly plays on yet another number symbolism known from the Old Testament. The task remains the same, and so does the formal character of the scene, which is even enhanced compared to Mark by the addition of Luke 10:2, which has a parallel in Matt. 9:36–37 mentioned above and is likely to be attributed to Q. For Luke the missionary task obviously is not the privileged task solely of "the Twelve."

John takes yet a different path. The Twelve are first introduced much later in the story, and in truly dramatic circumstances, namely, in John's parallel to the story of Peter's confession (John 6:67–71). No names are given, but they are addressed by Jesus right after he had confessed to his disciples (in reply to their objection that they cannot bear what he had been saying about eating his flesh and blood) that he knew in advance that some would not believe in him (6:64). As a consequence, many went away (6:66). In this moment of crisis, he turns to the Twelve, asking whether they too plan to leave him, which provokes Peter, speaking for all and using the first-person plural, to reply that this is not going to happen and to confess Jesus as the Holy One of God (6:69). Apparently unimpressed, Jesus adds oil to the fire, by recalling that he had chosen them, a scene John did not report, in the knowledge that one would betray him (6:70–71). John thus picks up on the information readers of the Synoptic Gospels had received when reading the list, but adds to it, not once but three times, that Jesus evidently knew this would happen (see 6:64, 70, 71). Far from being invited, or ordered, to join Jesus in his missionary task, the Twelve are challenged in a very different and far more dramatic way, which hardly leaves room for some compliment on Jesus's side for Peter's profound confession. Of course, in light of what will follow, Peter will prove to be hardly better than the one who is here called a traitor, for he too in a sense will betray Jesus. So maybe the lack of approval has a meaning that would fit very well in John's idea of an all-knowing Jesus.

After the initial scene of the (s)election of the Twelve, the evangelists part ways and also use this motif each in his own way. Mark does so shortly after he had introduced them, making the Twelve the privileged audience of private instruction by Jesus. The disciples are mentioned only indirectly and in passing in Jesus's disputes with the scribes and with his own family (see Mark 3:20) and are not singled out when he addresses the crowd in Mark 4:1-9. But the Twelve reappear in a somewhat odd phrase, as part of a larger group (Mark 4:10), to receive private instruction on the meaning of the parable. Matthew and Luke agree in rephrasing Mark's οἱ περὶ αὐτὸν σὺν τοῖς δώδεκα as οἱ μαθηταί (αὐτοῦ) (Matt. 13:10 par. Luke 8:9). Mark himself seems to have forgotten about them at the end of the parable discourse (Mark 4:34) and now merely speaks of οἱ ἴδιοι μαθηταί in reference to the inner circle (κατ᾽ ἰδίαν), while Matthew stays with the general "his disciples" (and Luke has left Mark by then). So the Twelve are mentioned in explaining Jesus's tactic for instructing his own, but they are not particularly singled out from the rest. No wonder then that some scribes have replaced Mark's expression by a mere "his disciples."

Matthew uses the label once more right after the Twelve are introduced (Matt. 10:1-2), but the reference in v. 5 is merely a slightly relocated copy of an element from Mark 6:7. However, at the end of his long version of the Mission Discourse, in which he has integrated a couple of very explicit instructions on the status of a disciple (see Matt. 10:24-25, 37-39), he emphasizes that all this was spoken to "the twelve disciples" (Matt. 11:1). Such an observation is missing from Mark and Luke, who instead speak about "the apostles," the label they had used (deviating from Matthew) when first introducing the Twelve. Luke, for his part, makes a passing reference to the Twelve (Luke 8:1-3) in a section that is peculiar to him and is in part built on the model of Mark 6:6b and, one might add, Mark 3:13-19: The Twelve are not the only ones to follow Jesus on his preaching mission. Also a number of women follow who are mentioned by name, as if a foil to that other list. Not much is done with this information at this stage, but it will prove to be of some importance as it anticipates what will be said about these women much later at the crucifixion, and it gives the reader a perspective on this much later event. There follows another such isolated mention of the Twelve right after the first Mission Discourse, when the Twelve are said to have suggested to Jesus that he dismiss the crowd to go and look for food and lodging in the surrounding villages (Luke 9:12, deviating from Mark/Matthew, "the disciples"), but Luke does not continue in this fashion, and at the end of the feeding narrative speaks again about "the disciples," as in his model (Luke 9:16 = Mark/Matthew).

It takes a while after the Mission Discourse before the Twelve are mentioned again in Mark, and when they are, it is in a rather negative context (Mark 9:33–36). In Mark 9:35 they are rebuked for disputing which one of them would be the greatest and shown humility by the example of a child whom Jesus puts among them. The final part of the rebuke echoes a similar warning by Jesus at the end of the Q version of the Mission Discourse (see Mark 9:37, and compare Matt. 10:40–42 par. Luke 10:16). Matthew and Luke copy the scene, but without mentioning the Twelve, keeping instead to the more common "his disciples" (Matt. 18:1) or the even more general "them" (Luke 9:46). But for all three evangelists, this is a crucial topic, to which they will return later (see Mark 10:43–44 = Matthew/Luke, and Matt. 23:11–12 par. Luke 14:11; 18:14; cf. also John 13:1–20). In the first of these parallels, the dispute is explicitly said to have been initiated by two members of the Twelve (Mark 10:35 = Matthew, the sons of Zebedee); the same group is at least implied also in Luke and John, who both agree on locating this dispute in the context of the Last Supper.

The Twelve do not fare much better the next time they are mentioned in Mark 10:32–34, who is now copied by Matthew and Luke. Mark is the only one who says the disciples are gradually becoming more afraid of what is to come (Mark 10:32), but the three agree that Jesus takes the Twelve apart (that is probably the best way to understand παραλαμβάνω, which occurs in all three) to instruct them once more (Mark: πάλιν) and for the third time to make his fate thematic. His first attempt, spoken to "the disciples" (Mark 8:31 = Matthew, and see Luke 9:18), had failed miserably with Peter replying boastfully, which forces Jesus to a harsh rebuke (Mark 8:33 = Matthew) and a firm statement on what it means to be his follower (Mark 8:34–9:1 = Matthew/Luke). The second attempt, also addressed to "the disciples" (Mark 9:31 = Luke, Matthew "them"), was equally not understood (Mark 9:32 = Luke, omitted by Matthew) and answered by the disciples with their request about rank and honor (Mark 9:33–37 = Luke, and Matthew, with a short intermezzo). The third attempt is a repetition of the second one, as Luke makes explicit (Luke 18:34), as the repeated dispute about honor in Mark 10:35–45 = Matthew shows. The disciples fail to understand the essence of Jesus's pilgrimage to Jerusalem and instead are occupied by issues he firmly rejects as unworthy of his disciples; and the Twelve are not different in this from the larger group (if a larger group was in view).

The Twelve come up once again at another crucial moment. Jesus enters Jerusalem in the company of his disciples, two of whom had been sent ahead to prepare for his arrival (Mark 11:1 = Matthew/Luke; cf. John 12:16). Luke alone adds that these are not only the Twelve (Luke 19:37, ἅπαν τὸ πλῆθος τῶν μαθητῶν). All three Synoptics say that Jesus stayed in Bethany overnight, but Mark alone adds that he was accompanied there only by the Twelve (Mark 11:11). The detail has consequences for how one has to imagine what follows. It is assumed that only the Twelve have witnessed the withering of the fig tree on the next day (Mark 11:12-14); and it is Peter, their usual spokesman, who asks Jesus about it (Mark 11:21). Luke had already introduced the story much earlier, but Matthew keeps to Mark's order, though he continues to speak of "the disciples" as its witnesses (Matt. 21:20). It is possible to maintain the distinction on who is with Jesus for the controversy scenes, which are located in Jerusalem, and for the great eschatological discourse that is spoken outside of the temple area in the presence of "the disciples," and maybe also for the anointing, about which it is not said who of the disciples is present (Mark 14:4, τινες). But right after that, Mark seems to have made a *lapsus*, when Jesus is said to speak to "his disciples," sending two of them ahead to prepare for Passover (Mark 14:12 = Matthew), μετὰ τῶν μαθητῶν μου (14:14 = Matthew/Luke), which actually turns out to be "the Twelve" (Mark 14:17 = Matthew; Luke, ἀπόστολοι, but there is a variant with δώδεκα). Matthew and Luke in a sense make the same mistake, but now because they had never introduced any such distinction. Matthew follows Mark for the preparation scene, hence continues to speak of "the disciples" (Matt. 26:17), as he had done before, but in the end they are only the Twelve (Matt. 26:20). Deviating from Mark, Luke picks out two from the Twelve to be sent ahead and names them, though without mentioning that they belong to this select group (Luke 22:8). When he then says that "the apostles" are joining Jesus for Passover (22:14), he avoids Matthew's problem but creates a similar one, as these had been identified with the Twelve before. All three synoptic accounts thus somehow suffer from a lack of precision, because they do not, or insufficiently (wish to), distinguish between the two groups. This leaves John as the only consistent one, but only because he does not specify how many ate with Jesus.

At this late stage in the synoptic accounts, a formula is introduced, which John had already used when he first mentioned the Twelve: εἷς τῶν δώδεκα—"one of the Twelve." The formula seems to have a distinctively negative connotation, as it is almost exclusively used for referring to Judas as the traitor (John 6:71; Mark 14:10 = Matthew, par. Luke 22:3, ὄντα ἐκ τοῦ ἀριθμοῦ τῶν δώδεκα; Mark 14:20; 14:43 = Matthew/Luke). The one exception is John 20:24, which applies it to Thomas (as εἷς ἐκ τῶν δώδεκα) in circumstances that are not really flattering for him. Judas's betrayal also (temporarily) signifies the end of "the Twelve" as a body, but in a sense, all of its members followed Judas in leaving Jesus, including their leader and spokesman, who is the only other one to be mentioned by name as a coward, and thereby takes his place as one more εἷς τῶν δώδεκα along with Judas. But unlike him, Peter repents, just as the other members find each other again and reconstitute the group, which is now referred to as "the Eleven (disciples)" (οἱ ἕνδεκα [μαθηταί], Matt. 28:16; Luke 24:9, deviating from Matt. 28:8: "his disciples," and Luke 24:33, in the presence of others; also in the secondary ending of Mark 16:14).

Paul knows that "the Eleven" were the recipients of appearances by the risen Lord, but somewhat confusingly writes that this occurred to "the Twelve" (1 Cor. 15:5). The Gospels give a more complex and diversified picture. Only Matthew (and the longer ending of Mark) tells about such an appearance to the remaining eleven disciples, which causes a disturbance and unbelief (Matt. 28:16–17; also Mark 16:14, with an even more negative comment), but not before some women (Mark 16:1–8 = Matthew/Luke; John: one woman) had first witnessed the empty tomb. In Luke and John they are joined by one or two members of the group (Luke: Peter; John: Peter and "the other disciple"). These same women (Matt. 28:9; John 20:14–18; also Mark 16:9) and two other disciples, one of which is identified by name (Luke 24:13–35), are also the first to meet the risen Lord. The report of the empty tomb and the encounters with the risen One is communicated variously to "the disciples" (Mark 16:7 = Matthew), "the Eleven" (Luke 24:9), or two of them (John 20:2). The promise of a future encounter with the risen One in Galilee, which the women received from the angel at the empty tomb, is addressed to Peter and the disciples (Mark 16:7) or to the disciples (Matt. 28:7) or even "the brothers" (Matt. 28:10), but no longer specifically to the Twelve/ Eleven. The same is true for the appearance scene in John 21: Peter, Thomas, and the sons of Zebedee are present, and also Nathanael "and two others" (John 21:2), one of which must be the Beloved Disciple, who is also mentioned later in the story (John 21:20).

Somewhat later the group will once more be made complete by voting by lot (Acts 1:26). But it seems that the label had lost its appeal, for "the Twelve" are mentioned as such only two more times in Acts, once as the mere background for Peter's Pentecost speech (Acts 2:14) and once, more forcefully, as those who broker a compromise in the conflict between the Hellenists and the Hebrews (Acts 6:2). However, their role cannot be pinned down to the sole mention of the label. Acts is the prime witness of a "transformation" that seems to have taken place rather early on: "the Twelve" are "the apostles." The development is already indirectly attested by Paul (see, e.g., 1 Cor. 9:5, and the many self-references using this title in his letters), had in a sense been announced right from the beginning by Mark (Mark 3:14 and 6:30 = Luke), but without further exploring this avenue, and was picked up by Luke in his gospel and continued in Acts (see Luke 17:5 par. Mark/Matthew, "the disciples"; Luke 22:14 par. Mark/Matthew, "the Twelve"; Luke 24:10 par. Mark/Matthew, "the disciples"; somewhat less clear in Luke 11:49 deviating from Matthew; and repeatedly in Acts, where the apostles become the cornerstone of the Jerusalem church). The same transformation can be witnessed in the passing reference in Rev. 21:14, with its idiosyncratic phrase, and also in the Didache, which bears the title Διδαχὴ κυρίου διὰ τῶν δώδεκα ἀποστόλων τοῖς ἔθνεσιν ("The Teaching of the Lord through the Twelve Apostles to the Gentiles/Nations"), even if this text hardly left a trace in later tradition and, just as this is the case in Acts, turns "the twelve (apostles)" into missionaries of a very different sort than the wandering travelers Jesus wanted them to be in the Gospels. But this original aspect was not completely forgotten, and later tradition has preserved the story of how they were sent out all over the world, each of them having been given a region, or even a continent, to missionize (see Eusebius, *Hist. eccl.* 3.1.1, with reference to Origen). "The Twelve" seem to have developed in two directions, becoming the central authority in the constitutive years of the church and alternatively the prime models for all future traveling missionaries all over the earth. These are the two modes in which they, "the apostles," went down in Christian memory.

2.2.2.4. The Twelve and Disciples in General

The Twelve, introduced as a small but symbolically significant body selected from those set to follow Jesus and with the explicit task to be sent out on mission, are not always clearly distinguished and at times seem to get mixed up with the disciples in general, who are not limited to their number. The first aspect is especially made evident by Luke when he says they are selected from the disciples (Luke 6:13), but this is no doubt also the way they are looked upon by the other evangelists, even if this is not always said so clearly. Matthew's distinction between "the twelve disciples" and "his disciples" may point in the same direction. The second aspect, the lack of differentiation, makes it hazardous to speculate whether those following Jesus on his way to Jerusalem are only the Twelve, even though a couple of them are sometimes singled out for a special experience (as in the transfiguration story). It is also hazardous to conclude that the labels "the Twelve" and "the disciples" would be merely interchangeable, even if that may be the impression that is sometimes created (see Mark 14:10, where the author is probably just imprecise). If initially they may look like a sort of elite group, selected for a special task, it soon turns out that they are considered to be equally imperfect as any other of the disciples (their lack of understanding and their general behavior in Mark 9:31–32, 33–37 and 10:32–34, 35–45 par.). In addition, Luke points out that also others were sent out on a mission (Luke 10:1). The privileges they are granted by Mark in terms of receiving instruction (Mark 4:10; 11:11) are of little help to raise or keep up their status, for in the end they prove to be as weak and vulnerable as all the others (except the women). They are not particularly singled out as a specific group after Jesus's resurrection (also not in 1 Cor. 15, for five hundred others are also named as witnesses of the resurrection). But they did not disappear; they merely changed the label and, as "the apostles," take a prominent role in the early church as presented by Luke (and Paul). In short, in the Gospels they are presented as a body that played a certain role in Jesus's life but failed to live up to the expectations. But then, as depicted by Luke and as referred to by Paul, they managed to transform themselves and, as "the apostles," would become the ruling body in the earliest decades of the church and the heroes of a large number of (apocryphal) stories on Christian mission (see E.V.).

Betz, Hans Dieter. 1967. *Nachfolge und Nachahmung Jesu Christi im Neuen Testament.* BHT 37. Tübingen.

Dunn, James D. G. 1992. *Jesus' Call to Discipleship.* Cambridge.

Freyne, Seán. 1968. *The Twelve: Disciples and Apostles; A Study in the Theology of the First Three Gospels.* London.

Hengel, Martin. 1968. *Nachfolge und Charisma: Eine exegetisch-religionsgeschichtliche Studie zu Mt 8,21 f. und Jesu Ruf in die Nachfolge.* BZNW 34. Berlin.

Klein, Günter. 1961. *Die zwölf Apostel: Ursprung und Gestalt einer Idee.* FRLANT 77. Göttingen.

Meier, John P. 2001. *A Marginal Jew: Rethinking the Historical Jesus.* Vol. 3, *Companions and Competitors.* New York. Pages 40–124, 125–285.

Roloff, Jürgen. 1965. *Apostolat—Verkündigung—Kirche.* Gütersloh.

Schille, Gottfried. 1967. *Die urchristliche Kollegialmission.* ATANT 48. Zürich.

Schulz, Anselm. 1964. *Nachfolgen und Nachahmen: Studien über das Verhältnis der neutestamentlichen Jüngerschaft zur urchristlichen Vorbildethik.* SANT 6. Munich.

Joseph Verheyden

2.3. Jesus's Communal Meals

The earliest Jesus tradition recounts or mentions Jesus's meals with other people in various contexts. What the texts have in common is that they do not refer to or illustrate Jesus's everyday practice but portray or emphasize significant incidents. On the one hand, the concept of communal meals expresses the fact that the discourse is never about one meal of Jesus alone; on the other hand, it indicates that the aspect of social relationships is of particular importance for the attribution of meaning to the meal practice of Jesus in the sources. The tradition about the last supper of Jesus with his disciples (see D.IV.5.2) and the image field of meals in Jesus's narrative parables (see D.IV.3.3) are to be considered separately.

2.3.1. Overview of the Constituent Texts

The relevant texts can be differentiated further according to their respective plots:

- Jesus's communal meals with "tax collectors" (Mark 2:13–17 par.; cf. Luke 19:1–10)
- Other meal scenes (Mark 14:3–9 par.; Luke 14:1–24)
- Food miracles (Mark 6:31–44 par. John 6:1–13; Mark 8:1–8 par. Matt. 15:32–39; John 2:1–11)
- Meal scenes after Jesus's passion and resurrection (Luke 24:13–35; 24:36–43; John 21:9–13; cf. Gos. Heb. frag. 6 [Jerome, *Vir. ill.* 2, ed. Bernoulli, 8])
- Sayings about the meal practices of Jesus and his disciples (Mark 2:18–22 par.; 7:1–23 par.; Matt. 11:19 par. Luke 7:34–35; 15:2)
- Further sayings of Jesus about eating (Luke 12:35–38; 13:29 par. Matt. 8:11; see Gos. Eb. frag. 7 [Epiphanius, *Pan.* 30.22.4, ed. Holl, GCS 25:363])

In the expanded narratives, it is only exceptionally stated that Jesus himself eats (Luke 24:43; cf. Gos. Thom. 61). This indicates that the texts intend to bring out different accents, but that in all of them a special role falls on Jesus. Likewise, it is an exception in the early Christian meal tradition that Jesus—as in the gospel accounts of the last supper with his disciples—takes on the functions of the host; usually he is presented as a special guest, whose sayings and actions at meals add importance and significance to the event, which is thus worthy of being remembered. Jesus being depicted as a servant at the meal (Luke 22:25–27; John 13:4–5, 12–17) is a christological declaration.

2.3.2. Eating with "Tax Collectors and Sinners"

Jesus's communal meals explicitly come into focus in the short narrative in Mark 2:13–17 par., which connects the calling of a disciple (Levi; Matt. 9:9 = Matthew) with a conflict scene confronting Jesus with the Pharisees (Luke 5:30 adds "the scribes") during a meal (Luke 5:29 speaks of a "banquet" [δοχή]) (on the possible history of its origins, see D.-A. Koch 1989). The issue is Jesus's eating together with "tax collectors and sinners" (Mark 2:15 par. Matt. 9:10; Mark 2:16 par.; Luke 7:34 par. Matt. 11:19; Luke 15:1–2; 19:2–7). Jesus's response interprets the entire scene in terms of his own sending and ties it back to the initial calling. The term "sinner" used both in the question and in the answer implies a moral and theological qualification, and thus interprets and amplifies the term "tax collector" (meaning tax farmers as well as tax collectors; cf. Herrenbrück 1990). The explicit reference to Jesus's disciples (Mark 2:15 par. Matt. 9:10; Mark 2:16 par.) presumably looks beyond the frame of the narrative and gives the scene an orienting function for early Christian readers. The social relationship depicted here is nevertheless not to be interpreted in the sense of a respectful tolerance, but as an expression and example of Jesus's mission and his turning also to social and religious outcasts—and thereby as a fundamental recognition not of this ostracism but of the value system underlying it. In Luke 5:32 this is further stressed by the key word "repentance" (μετάνοια), which identifies the goal of turning to these values. The debate in Mark 2:16 par. is also found in similar words in P. Oxy. 1224 (frag. 2 *verso* = p. 175; Lührmann 2000, 175).

Luke 19:1–10, a text that does not explicitly speak of a communal meal, can be read as an exemplary illustration of this aspect of the mission of Jesus (and his disciples). Here Jesus encounters not only a "chief tax collector" but at the same time also a rich man (v. 2). The piece is situated at an important point of the overall composition of the gospel and exhibits close relationships especially to chapter 15 (Wolter 2008, 611). The mention of the name Zacchaeus makes the piece a personal legend (Dibelius ⁶1971, 114–15).

Understood as symbolic action, these scenes do represent a turn to social outsiders more generally. However, in Jesus's environment and time, hospitality and communal meals were important as tangible forms of social relationships and integration. In the texts in focus, they thus do not stand for something completely or overwhelmingly different, but as *pars pro toto*.

2.3.3. Additional Meal Scenes

The Markan and Johannine versions of the anointing at Bethany (Mark 14:3–9 par. Matt. 26:6–13 par. John 12:1–11)—somewhat less clearly so in Matthew—are foreshadowing Jesus's passion. The meal sets the framework (necessary for the narrative of the anointing) for the action of the woman upon which Jesus comments, but the meal itself is not discussed. Mark 14:9 par. Matt. 26:13, one of the so-called "Amen" sayings pronounced by Jesus, explicitly alludes to the memory of this event in the earliest communities (in the world of the narrative, a prolepsis), a prediction, which anticipates working out the validity of the tradition of the entire account of the passion (cf. Mark 13:9–10, differently Matt. 10:18), but not merely the credibility of this specific episode (Lührmann 1987, 233). The Lukan version detaches the scene from connections with the passion contextually and thematically, transfers it to the house of a Pharisee named Simon (Luke 7:36, 40–41; cf. Mark 14:3), and makes the anonymous woman of the Markan version a "sinner" (γυνὴ ἁμαρτωλός; vv. 37, 47–49; in the Gospel of John, she is identified as Mary, Martha's sister). These elaborations help transform the episode into an example of the forgiveness of sin. In this way it is an expression of the older concept of Jesus's closeness to sinners also attested elsewhere.

In Luke 14:1–24, a Sabbath meal in the house of a leading Pharisee forms the framework for a healing connected with a conflict scene (vv. 2–9). The passage comprises metaphorical sayings about ranks at a marriage celebration and invitations to a midday or evening meal (v. 12: ἄριστον ἢ δεῖπνον), but also a parable, at the center of which is a festive meal (vv. 15–24 par. Matt. 22:1–14). Especially in these texts the invitation to a meal becomes the central motif and the point of contact for the interpretation. The narrative introduction of the Lukan composition clearly prepares for the sayings that follow; the meal scene itself is possibly neutral, but possibly also designed for contrast (cf. vv. 1b, 4). The literary character of the composition is evident, so that there is no question of a possible historical reminiscence of a particular event. However, it should be pondered whether Jesus's personal proximity to the Pharisees mentioned here and elsewhere in Luke (cf., e.g., 7:36; 11:37) expresses an otherwise irreducible memory of the pre-Easter Jesus.

2.3.4. Feeding Miracles

The imposing narratives in the Gospels about Jesus's feeding miracles (or: miracles of provision) do not have their point in Jesus's meal *fellowship* with other people.

On the one hand, in the story of the feeding of the five thousand or the four thousand, it is clear that Jesus mandates his disciples to feed others (Mark 6:37 par.; cf. John 6:5–9; Mark 6:41 par. and Mark 8:6–7 par. Matt. 15:36). On the other hand, the crowd of people mentioned in the passage is hardly specified (but see Matt. 14:21). To be sure, Jesus participates in the *meal* (Mark 6:41 par.; differently John 6:11), but it is nevertheless questionable whether Jesus participates in the communal *consumption of the food*. The prayer of praise and the breaking of bread are reminiscent of the scene at the Last Supper (on the motif of breaking bread in Luke's two volumes, see Löhr 2012, 71). The instruction for the disciples in Mark 8:17–21 par. Matt. 16:7–10 provides the readers with an interpretation of both feeding miracles, which by means of an allegorical explanation tied to the numerical data, refers to the mission of Jesus and his followers. This functions only on the level of the narrative of the Gospels as a whole. In this respect, it is hardly plausible to infer a historical reminiscence.

The bread of life discourse in John 6:22–59 interprets the element of bread from the foregoing feeding miracle as "the bread from heaven" and "the bread of life" (vv. 33–35, 48–50), in contrast to the manna of the sojourn in the desert. The bread is Jesus himself, and thus in a last step of the discourse, bread and wine—a clear allusion to the eucharistic elements—are identified with the flesh and blood of the Son of God (vv. 52–58). However, the combination of the tradition of feeding miracles and the theological-sacramental interpretation of the celebration of the eucharistic meal that becomes tangible here cannot be traced back to earlier Jesus tradition; this discourse stops short of attesting a Jesus tradition that stands behind it.

The Johannine account of the wine miracle in Cana is comparable with the synoptic feeding miracles: Jesus provides the essential instructions that bring about the miracle (2:7–8). However, a collective consumption of the wine is not mentioned. If one does not simply assume that the account is incomplete, this feature is best explained by the intention to portray Jesus as the person at the center of the episode. By contrast, a specifically eucharistic overtone (so, among others, Cullmann ²1950, 70–71) cannot be identified. The text is a pithy example of the narrative Christology of the Fourth Gospel, which perhaps takes up and transforms an older image of Jesus such as the reference to Jesus's family and the consumption of wine, but also foreshadows the passion (cf. John 12:23). Cana in Galilee is also mentioned in 4:46 and 21:1 (but nowhere else in the New Testament).

2.3.5. Post-Easter Meals

The accounts of encounters with the risen One in the context of a meal are found among the canonical Gospels only in Luke and John. The presentations appear to prompt or define several distinct aspects: emphasis on (in everyday categories of perception: surprising) identifying the one who appears with the one who a few days earlier was executed is achieved by the stock motif of recognition (Luke 24:30–31; John 21:12–13; cf. 21:4–8, and see John 6:1–21 par. as well as Luke 5:1–11). The intention of the note in Luke 24:42–43 seems to be to emphasize the corporeality of the risen One; however, a corporate meal does not take place here. Individual features of the account may also serve to establish the eucharistic celebration of early congregations in a meal of the risen One, or else to forge a bridge between pre-Easter table fellowship and the community's sacramental celebration (cf. Luke 24:30; Gos. Heb. frag. 7 [Jerome, *Vir. ill.* 2, ed. Bernoulli, 8]; this is less likely for John 21). Insofar as the methodologically established historical criticism is interested exclusively in the (re)construction of earthly, this-worldly processes capable of analogy, and insofar as it is only able to judge on testimonies about paranormal phenomena to a very limited extent, these texts are excluded in standard scholarly exegesis from a methodologically controlled quest for the historical Jesus and his meal practice.

2.3.6. Sayings about the Meal Practices of Jesus and His Followers

In the debate in Mark 2:18–22 par. (cf. Gos. Thom. 104), the motif of table fellowship plays no explicit role; however, the preceding rebuke of Jesus's nonascetic life is taken up positively and treated in the image of a wedding and a bridegroom. At the same time, the image alludes to the concept of the salvific end time.

In the Markan introduction to Jesus's sayings about what is clean and unclean (Mark 7:1–23 par.), a question from Pharisees and scribes about purity commands in connection with eating provides the starting point for what follows. Jesus's followers are reproached for disregarding Jewish halakah (the "tradition of the elders," v. 5). The preceding explanation in vv. 3–4 points to the fact that the intended readers are not familiar with such regulations, and that they do not represent an issue for them. From this it is plausible to conclude that possibly not the precise verbatim account of the discussion but perhaps its theme can be explained as a memory of a conflict (arguably occurring repeatedly) of Jesus and his followers with other groups in Palestinian Judaism (arguably occurring not only once). Thus, the text could provide insight into a striking feature for the environment in the everyday life of groups around Jesus.

In the framework of the statements about John the Baptist (Luke 7:24–25 par. Matt. 11:7–19, perhaps originating with an older source Q), Jesus cites the opinion (perhaps of Pharisaic and scribal opponents) that he is "a glutton and drunkard, a friend of tax collectors and sinners." The coupling of the two motifs could be a reflection of an older portrait of Jesus that had been passed down and was secondarily developed into narratives about eating with tax collectors.

One piece of evidence for the Lukan reception of this tradition might be the redactional (Jeremias 1971b) introduction to the scene in Luke 15:2: the opponents, Pharisees and scribes, reproach Jesus for his meal fellowship with "sinners"; it is not certain whether the verb προσδέχεσθαι (to receive) used here carries soteriological connotations. The sentence is clearly framed in reference to the following parable composition.

2.3.7. Additional Sayings of Jesus about Eating

The vision of dining in the kingdom of God, to which participants from the four corners of heaven will stream, is clearly formulated in Jesus's mouth in

Luke 13:29 par. Matt. 8:11–12 (on the possible composition of the saying in Q, cf. Fleddermann 2005, 686–88).

Visions of Israel's gathering at the end of days are Jewish biblical prototypes of and parallels to this declaration (Ps. 107:2–3; Isa. 27:13; 49:12; Zech. 10:9–10; Bar. 4:37; 5:5; Pss. Sol. 11:2; 1 En. 57:1; Wolter 2008, 493), but also to an eschatological meal with the participation of the anointed one (or those who are anointed) or of the Son of Man (1QSa ii 11–22; 1 En. 62:13–16; Pitre 2009, 136–38), as well as the eschatological pilgrimage to Zion (Zeller 1971–1972; associated with Israel's gathering: Isa. 43:5–9; Zech. 8:7–8, 20–23; associated with a [sacrificial] meal: Isa. 25:6–9). The combination of vv. 28 and 29 in Luke 13 implies the presence of the patriarchs and prophets in the kingdom of God, a vision that likewise originates in Jewish tradition (Pitre 2009, 143–45). Along with the participation of the Messiah (or a similar redeemer figure), important elements of the motif are thus attested in Jewish sources before or at the time of Jesus and the emergence of Christian tradition. By contrast, the *explicit* reference to the terminology (which is not attested earlier in connection with the motif) of the "kingdom of God" in this context could be an innovation of the Jesus tradition. Both features rather speak in favor of the assumption that this view was actually part of Jesus's self-interpretation.

The prospect of dining in the kingdom of God also occurs in Jesus's renunciation of eating in the Last Supper tradition (Mark 14:25 par. Matt. 26:29). The same motif is also found in Jesus's saying in Luke 22:28–30 (differently, Matt. 19:28), which is stressed further by its combination with a saying of the eschatological rule over the twelve tribes (on Jewish parallels, cf. Pitre 2009, 144). The parable in Luke 14:16–24 par. Matt. 22:1–14 (see D.IV.5.2) is influenced by the complex of motifs of an eschatological meal (cf. the macarism in Luke 14:15).

Such an impact is unlikely for the synoptic feeding miracles, whereas John 2:1–11 (cf. esp. v. 4) evidently takes up the motif and reshapes it in a narrative fashion. The beatitude in Luke 6:21 par. Matt. 5:6 and the instruction about fasting in Matt. 6:16–18 do not belong in the same context of motifs.

To be sure, the saying in Luke 12:35–38 figuratively foreshadows an eschatological event; however, there is no mention of the kingdom of God here. Pragmatically, the emphasis is on the warning to be vigilant in the face of uncertainty about the time of the end.

2.3.8. Summary

The tradition of sayings and narrative materials of earliest Christianity discussed here assigns an important role to the motif of eating and table fellowship in

Jesus's sayings and deeds. The concern of the sources is not to add color to the everyday life of Jesus and his followers but to give the readers theological and moral direction. In these significant narratives and sayings, historical research does not discover reliable reports in detail about individual incidents, but rather exemplary visualizations of characteristic features of a portrait of Jesus, which can be regarded as historically plausible. Especially the evidently striking non-ascetic lifestyle of Jesus and his followers in the Palestinian-Jewish context of the time, the turning to social and religious outcasts designed to bring about transformation, and the inclusion of the figurative world of dining and feasting in view of the expected end of time belong to these features.

Heil, John Paul. 1999. *The Meal Scenes in Luke-Acts: An Audience-Oriented Approach.* SBLMS 52. Atlanta.

Kollmann, Bernd. 1990. *Ursprung und Gestalten der frühchristlichen Mahlfeier.* GTA 43. Göttingen.

Pitre, Brant. 2009. "Jesus, the Messianic Banquet, and the Kingdom of God." *Letter and Spirit* 5: 133–62.

Hermut Löhr

2.4. Jesus's Healings

2.4.1. Jesus's Healings of the Sick in Distinct Genres and Levels of Tradition

Jesus's healings of the sick are a threshold phenomenon. Jesus encounters sickness and death from every point of view (Feldmeier and Spieckermann 2011, 394). Various genres (narrative traditions, summaries, apothegms, and sayings) and, likewise, various levels of tradition (Q, special material, and Gospel of Thomas) have preserved indications of Jesus's healing activity. Like all ancient stories of healing, New Testament *healing narratives* have a consistent repertoire of personages who appear: the healer, the sick person (male or female), the crowd, helpers of the sick person, opponents. Typical structures can be identified for narrative traditions, which, however, do not all have to materialize, such as the arrival of a miracle worker, the sick person, or someone who intercedes for the one who is ill in the introduction; the characterization of the sickness in the exposition, and the healing by touching, a healing medium, a saying about faith, or prayer as the center of the story; and finally, the demonstration of the healing as the last motif of the healing story, which can be accompanied by astonishment, fear, consternation, acclamation, or hostile reactions (Theissen [5]1987, 47–80).

New Testament texts along with their history-of-religions parallels conform with these structural elements.

Narrative traditions present healings of the blind (Mark 8:22–26; John 9:1–7, and elsewhere), the lame (Mark 2:1–12 par.; John 5:2–9b, and elsewhere), the cultically unclean such as lepers (Mark 1:40–45 par.; Luke 17:11–19), or the woman with a flow of blood (Mark 5:25–34 par.), but also healings on the Sabbath such as the man with the withered hand (Mark 3:1–6 par.) and healings from a distance of non-Jews such as the son of a centurion (Matt. 8:5–13 par.). In addition, there are resuscitations, such as Jairus's daughter (Mark 5:22–24, 35–43 par.). Healing stories were passed down as isolated traditions, which makes it possible to observe embellishments of the miraculous, such as (1) introducing two sick persons (Matt. 8:28–34; 20:29–34) instead of one (Mark 5:1–20; 10:46–54) or (2) developing variants of a basic form (such as the healing of the lame man in Mark 2:1–12 and John 9:1–7).

In addition to Mark, other levels of tradition also contain healings. In the sayings source Q, the healing of the slave of a centurion (Matt. 8:5–13) is found along with the sayings tradition, and the Special Material (Special L) in Luke contains three healings (Luke 13:10–13; 14:1–6; 17:11–19) and one resuscitation (Luke 7:11–17); the Special Material (Special M) in Matthew contains the healing of two blind men (Matt. 9:27–31). Exorcisms do not appear either in Special L or Special M, and are completely missing in John. Rather, Jesus has an altercation with Satan about the cross and resurrection (John 16:11, and elsewhere). In the Gospel of Thomas the disciples are similarly commissioned for healing but not for driving out demons (Gos. Thom. 14).

The narratives emphasize the need of the sick person in various ways. Designations of time accentuate the duration and thereby the hopelessness of the disease (Mark 5:25 par.: flow of blood for twelve years; Luke 13:11: bent over for eighteen years; John 5:5: afflicted for thirty-eight years; John 9:1: blind from birth; see in detail Weissenrieder 2003). In addition, it is emphasized that help that is humanly possible has been utilized: the woman with the flow of blood, who had spent all she had on physicians (Mark 5:26 par.); the maniac who cannot be subdued by any human power (Mark 5:3 par.); the disciples who are unable to heal the epileptic boy (Mark 9:18 par.). Further, the locations where Jesus encounters the sick reflect the adversity of the sick, their social marginalization, and helplessness (e.g., Luke 17:12; John 5:7). Only in a few stories is an active sick person encountered (the blind man in Mark 10:46–52; the woman with the flow of blood, who, however, approaches Jesus "from behind" and touches his cloak in secret in Mark 5:27 par.). Moreover, some of the designations of illness and explicit wording indicate the severity of the malady (i.e., a high fever, πυρετῷ μεγάλῳ, in Luke 4:38; the man with dropsy, ἄνθρωπός τις ἦν ὑδρωπικός, in Luke 14:2;

the lame man, παραλυτικός [the unusual adjective in Mark 2:3 and Matt. 9:2]; the perfect participle παραλελυμένος in Luke 5:18). The reactions to the healings are described as fear (Mark 5:15 par.), terror (e.g., Mark 1:27 par.), and even astonishment (Mark 5:42). Some texts attest that healings by the power of God were not expected until the messianic time of salvation (Matt. 11:5; Luke 7:22). Accordingly, Jesus's healings of the sick are interpreted as indications of the glory of God in the present (Luke 9:43).

In research a distinction is made between healing (illness as a bodily weakness) and exorcisms of demons (illness as possession by an external power). While Mark and Matthew more strongly differentiate healings from expulsion of demons, Luke associates the two phenomena by describing both with verbs that imply the carrying out of a healing rather than an expulsion. If the descriptions in the Gospels of symptoms of sickness and possession are taken into consideration from the perspective of ancient medicine, distinctions between the two can hardly be made (Weissenrieder 2003). The indicators of illness, as for instance, "moon struck (lunatic)" (Aretaeus, *Sign. diut.* 1.4.2; Galen, *Di. dec.* 3.2 [9.902–903 Kühn]; *De loc. aff.* [8.175–177, 233]; Matt. 17:15), "fever" (Hippocrates, *Progn.* 17.2; *Iudic.* 11.4), "gnashing of teeth" (Hippocrates, *Morb. sacr.* 7.1–39; Weissenrieder and Dolle 2019, 640; Caelius, *Acut.* 1.65; Mark 9:18), or "falling in fire or water" (Celsus, *Med.* 3.23; Mark 9:22), are used similarly both in the New Testament and in ancient writings on medicine. Similarly, expressions that indicate healing are found in medical tractates, as for instance the expression "the fever left her" (ἀφῆκεν αὐτὴν ὁ πυρετός; Bendemann 2014, 300). In Roman medicine numerous sources are characterized by speaking metaphorically about "attacking" or "departing" from a person, and for this they use terminology that also is used in Old Latin manuscripts of the Gospels, such as *eicere, dimittere, remittere* (Langslow 2000, 178–202). The medical sociological perspective is capable of enlarging even more on this aspect: numerous religious interpretations of maladies are also preserved by ancient physicians. The tractate *De morbo sacro* of the Corpus Hippocraticum attests, in a passage that admittedly is grammatically controversial, that social deviance on the part of healthy people can be designated as demonic (Eijk 2005, 89–116); this applies especially when illnesses are classified as incurable, such as epilepsy or "massive" fever. Perhaps it would be possible to assert a comparable interpretation for cases of raising the dead, as some sources suggest (see Diogenes Laertius 8.61; Empedocles B17.9–13 = 26.8–12; see also Aristotle, *Resp.* 7.473a15–474a24; so-called "those without breath"; Weissenrieder and Dolle 2019, 583). In antiquity the border between supernatural and natural explanations appears to run according to other parameters (Tieleman 2013; Staden 2003).

In addition, disease as a biological malady is differentiated from "illness" as a social (and ritual) experience (Kleinman 1995; Pilch 2000; for a critique,

Weissenrieder 2003). This distinction assumes a clear separation between the physical and the sociocultural phenomena of a disease. Thus, "leprosy" is interpreted as a harmless skin disease, which supposedly merely has social and ritual consequences (Wohlers 1999). Against this way of thinking, a gloss in manuscript M of the medical writing of the Corpus Hippocraticum, *De alimento*, points out Galen's explanation on this position as well (Hippocrates, *Alim.* 20.1; Galen, *Differ. morb.* [6.863 Kühn]): the disease "leprosy" is always dangerous for the sick person, both when it is visible only on the surface but also as it acts inside the body and arrests the "flow of blood" in the body. This interpretation is found likewise in ancient medicine and in Jewish writings (4Q269 viii; Sepfer-ha-Rephu'ot, and elsewhere; see Weissenrieder 2013). In this view Galen identifies "leprosy" as a disease that turns "against human nature." Jewish and medical texts attest a temporally limited exclusion from social relationships (Caelius, *Acut.* 4.1.13). A separation between physical and sociocultural dimensions of illness is therefore questionable.

Further, recently in disability studies some differentiate between illness and disability, between recuperation and the demand for a standardized body. Thereby, because, depending on the type of story, the focus in the interpretation of healings supposedly falls on the recovery, the healthy body is elevated to normality (Moss and Schipper 2011; on the hermeneutical aspects of illness, see Bendemann 2014; Weissenrieder 2003). Healing stories are declared to be "texts of terror" (Betcher 2013). In fact, the historical Jesus embraced the petitions for healing that came to him, but at the same time, the narratives report the failure of the disciples (Mark 9:14–29 par.) to become masters over illnesses, and the resulting despair of people. Theologically, this accordingly poses the question not only about the cruelty of the social environment but also about creation. In New Testament research this question has up until now been virtually ignored. The question regarding the concept of "disability" is posed with respect to history. Ancient literature is concerned with the condition of being sick rather than the sickness itself. For example, in Galen's writings the designations νόσον, νόσημα, and νοσεῖν are noticeably diminished. What is named is in fact the affected part of the body. Perhaps behind this stands a concept of nature that reckons with the divinely interpreted artisanship of nature (Galen, *Inaequ. intemp.* 5 [7.743 Kühn]; *Meth. med.* 10.41, 50–51, 59, 71 Kühn; Weissenrieder and Dolle 2019, chap. 7).

Along with the narrative tradition, healings are mentioned together with the casting out of demons in *summaries* (Mark 1:32–34 and elsewhere; in the last summary in Mark 6:53–56 the casting out of demons is absent). In *discussions* (Matt. 11:2–6 and elsewhere) the doubt of Jesus's contemporaries is manifest ("Is he the one who is to come?"); Jesus points to the healing of the blind, the lame, lepers, the deaf, and the resuscitation of the dead as indications of the fulfillment of prophetic promises (exorcisms are not mentioned). In *sayings traditions* (Luke 7:18–23 and elsewhere) healings are associated with the central content of his message: with the kingdom of God (esp. in the sending in Luke 10:9), with the challenge to repent (Matt. 11:20–24), and with the turning to the poor (Luke 7:18–23). At least on the evidence of the tradition it is regarded as uncontested: the historical Jesus performed healings.

2.4.2. Jesus's Techniques of Healing

Whereas healing stories employ references to illnesses sparingly, they portray healing techniques or formulaic expressions on healing in more detail. Thus, one can assume that these serve as instructions for Christian healers. The most important technique for healing is the laying on of hands, an act of a special power (δύναμις) and so-called dirty remedies (*Drecksapotheke*).

The New Testament Jesus tradition reports the touching of a leper (ἄπτομαι; Mark 1:41 par.) and touching the eyes of a blind man (Mark 8:23, 25). In addition, the sources are acquainted with the lifting up of Peter's mother-in-law (Mark 1:31 par.) and the epileptic boy (Mark 9:27). Luke enlarges the specifications in that he associates the laying on of hands directly with the assurance of healing ("he laid his hands on them," Luke 4:40; 13:13) or Jesus touches the severed ear (Luke 22:51) or the bier of the young man in Nain (Luke 7:14). In addition, the Gospels give numerous reports of sick people whom Jesus touched (Mark 3:10 par.; 5:27–28; 5:30–31 par.; and elsewhere). Some New Testament passages document sick persons touching (ἄπτομαι) Jesus, also touching his garments, which could link Jesus with impurity (see Mark 5:27, 28, 30; differently Luke 8:44). It is disputed whether laying on of hands can be traced back to Jewish texts, where, however, they appear quite seldom (Flusser 1957, 107–8). As a possible case, 2 Kings 5:11 can be adduced, where the Hebrew text provides the unique usage והניף ידו אל־המקום ("to swing the hand over the spot"), which is translated with ἐπιθήσει τὴν χεῖρα αὐτου ("he will lay his hand on"), as this also is multiply attested in the Jesus tradition (Mark 5:23; 6:5; 7:32; and elsewhere.). The Genesis Apocryphon provides another instance, where Abraham's laying on of hands that heals the ailing pharaoh is mentioned. The text uses for this סמך, which the Septuagint normally translates with ἐπιτίθημι.

Touching with the hand is frequently associated with Jesus's δύναμις, his powerful or mighty deeds (e.g., Mark 5:30 par.; 6:14; Matt. 11:5 par.; Luke 4:18–21, cf. Isa. 61:1–2; not in John; see also 4Q521 2 ii 12). The translation of δύναμις in Old Latin manuscripts of Luke, however, is noteworthy: it is translated with *virtus*, which is comparable with *qualitas*, and which in Roman medicine denotes the quality of a medication (Soranus, *Gyn.* 17.13; 73.22; Anonymus Parisinus, *De mor-*

bis acutis et chroniis 24.V, 3; Caelius, *Acut.* 3.17). This is distinct from a further possible translation of δύναμις as *vires*, which expresses bodily strength (Soranus, *Gyn.* 96.29; Caelius, *Acut.* 1.86). Accordingly, the early Latin translation from the second century CE construes Jesus's touch as "medicine."

It is not Jesus's touch alone that is interpreted as power or medicine. Mark and John are acquainted with spittle as a medium of healing, which can also be referred to as "dirty pharmacology." In Mark 7:32–37 Jesus heals a man who is blind and deaf by putting his fingers into his ears, touching his tongue with saliva, sighing as he looks into heaven, and uttering an Aramaic appeal for help. In Mark 8:22–26 he heals a blind man by rubbing spittle on his eyes, laying on his hands (8:22), and touching his eyes with his hands (8:25; Yarbro Collins 2007, 369). Further, in John 9:1–11 Jesus heals a man who was "blind from birth" by treating his eyes with a mixture of saliva and soil, and finally sending him to the pool of Siloam for him to wash himself in it. As early as Aristotle, human saliva is avowed to make snakes flee (Aristotle, *Hist. an.* 8.206–209; see Pliny, *Nat.* 7.2.13–15; Aelian, *Nat. an.* 9.4). Pliny also identifies saliva in a list not only as a guard against epilepsy but also as a medium (*precatio*) against blindness (*Nat.* 27.7: *lippitudines*; 26.60; 28.22: *cruentatis oculis, epiphoras*). But it is Galen who intensifies the significance of saliva, especially in his writing *On the Usefulness of the Parts—De usu partium*: food, which in the mouth is mixed with saliva, changes its substance notably quickly and becomes a part of a person's body. This process takes place by assimilation as well as by contamination. Galen explains in addition that in the mouth, along with food and fluids, also "the residue of the brain through the palate (ἐξ ἐγκεφάλου δι' ὑπερῴας περίττωμα)" is taken up "through the palate" and "saliva from the glands at the base of the tongue (καὶ τῶν παρὰ τῇ ῥίζῃ τῆς γλώσσης ἀδένων τὸ σίελον)," which are then intermingled (Galen, *UP* 3.7.161–165; *SMT* 10.16; 12.289 Kühn; Alex. Trall. *Therap.* 11.1; 2.473–475.13 refers to Galen's medical efficacy of saliva: ἐπί τε γὰρ τῶν ὑπὸ σκορπίου πληγέντων ἐπειράθην ὠφελείας). From this it is plausible that a greater power of healing is attributed to the saliva of an important person, as examples of Vespasian attest. The evidence cautions us to beware of assigning magical practices to saliva on the one hand and healing by means of saliva as a phenomenon among lower classes on the other. In Mark 7:32–33 an argument from a theology of creation is articulated based on the will of the creator, "who has made everything good" (perfect; cf. Gen. 1:31 LXX aorist). This is also like much in Galen's teleological physiology. When Matthew and Luke pass over this aspect of healing, they perhaps do so to avoid labeling spitting as a disrespectful gesture and spittle as a polluting substance, as they are often identified in the Septuagint (1 Sam. 21:14; Isa. 40:15 LXX), or to emphasize Jesus's power of healing, or to guard against comparison with other miracle workers of antiquity (see D.IV.2.4.4).

2.4.3. History-of-Religions Context of New Testament Healing Stories

To be sure, illness and healing are mentioned in texts of the Second Temple, but the texts often do not follow the classical schema of healing stories. In wisdom literature, healing miracles are signs of salvation (Wis. 16:5–14; 18:20–25: σύμβολον ... σωτηρίαν). By means of God's word and medications, they unfold their effect likewise only by God's assistance (Sir. 38:1–15; vv. 9–11, prayers and sacrifices). References to sicknesses in the so-called Enoch literature, like the eschatological hope for healing in Jub. 23:14–31, point to a Satan-free time with days of "blessing and healing" (Jub. 23:29), although the healing of disease can be construed metaphorically just as well for the restoration of the covenant between God and the people. The Jewish historian Flavius Josephus refers multiple times to the Essenes' special interest in the healing of illnesses (*J.W.* 2.136 and elsewhere), which in research has led to the tendency to translate "Essenes" with "healers" (Vermes 1975, 8–36). Josephus refers infrequently to biblical healing miracles, such as Elijah's healing of the son of the widow (1 Kings 17:17–24 MT; Josephus, *Ant.* 8.325; cf. y. Sukkah 5.1, 55a and Midrash Bereshit Rabbah 98.11) or the miraculous healing of King Hezekiah by Isaiah (Isa. 38:9, here, however, without a miraculous character; Josephus, *Ant.* 10.27–31). Healings are interpreted as a part of God's providence, and it is certainly no accident that here Josephus has recourse to the concept of Stoicism, πρόνοια ("providence"; Attridge 1976, 154–65 and passim), in order to demonstrate that the healings are authentic providence (Josephus, *Ant.* 2.286), which is antithetical to human evaluation of miraculous events (*Ant.* 2.330–337). The *Testimonium Flavianum* (*Ant.* 18.63), in which Jesus is characterized as doer of "wonderful works" (παράδοξα ἔργα), is controversial. Philo of Alexandria discusses healing the sick especially in the context of the Therapeutae and, along with the healing of bodily illness (Philo, *Spec.* 1.77; *Sacr.* 70.123; and elsewhere), is acquainted with the healing of the soul, which can only be cured spiritually (*Contempl.* 2; *Opif.* 155; *Spec.* 1.179; and elsewhere).

Parallels to New Testament healings are found in Greco-Roman literature in reports about miraculous healings by emperors. So, Plutarch gives reports about King Pyrrhus of Epirus, by whose touch someone who was suffering from a disease of the spleen was able to recuperate (Plutarch, *Pyrrh.* 3.7–9); about Alexander the Great, who in a dream received instructions for the healing of Craterus with hellebore (Plutarch, *Alex.* 41.6; see on this Cicero, *Div.* 2.66.135); and about Pericles, who healed an artisan injured in the construction of Propylaea, after Athena Hygieia appeared to him in a dream (Plutarch, *Per.* 13.12–13; Pliny, *Nat.* 22.20.44). Of special importance especially for the upper class might have been the anecdotes about Vespasian's healings, which are attested by Suetonius (*Vesp.* 7.2.12), Tacitus (*Hist.* 4.81–82), and in Greek by Dio Cassius (68.1.1).

Tacitus and Suetonius give reports about a blind man from Alexandria who was sent by the god Serapis to plead with Vespasian for healing (*"Qua re tibi auxilium feram"*— "How am I supposed to help you?"), which Vespasian accomplished by spreading spittle on his eyes; about a man with a paralyzed leg (see also Plutarch, *Pyrrh.* 3); and about a man with a paralyzed hand (Tacitus, *Hist.* 4.81–82), who also experienced healing by Vespasian when he touched the affected body part (Leppin 2013; Engster 2010). In addition, Tacitus reports that Vespasian was worried about his *fama vanitatis* ("rumor of failure"), especially about a possible "denial of supernatural powers." As a result, before he performs the healing, he first seeks the confirmation by physicians (*medicis*). Miraculous healings by touching are also attributed to Hadrian in the *vita Hadriani* (*Historia Augusta, Vit. Hadriani*, 25.1–4) and Trajan in Pliny's panegyric texts, which report about sick people who were healed by the presence of the emperor (Pliny, *Pan.* 22.3). Apollonius of Tyana, who was active as a wandering neo-Pythagorean philosopher around 96–97 CE, could also be named as another prominent example of a miracle worker (related by Philostratus, third century CE). Apollonius performed healings of a man from Assyria with edema, whom he cured with dietary teaching (*Vit. Apoll.* 6.43), and of a young man suffering from mania by gazing at him (*Vit. Apoll.* 4.20). References to divine powers of healing are also known in medical writings, such as the Hippocratic tractate *Decorum* from the first century CE shows, where it reads that deeds of power of the gods are "intertwined with medical knowledge and thought." "Medicine is held in honor by the gods. And physicians have turned to the gods. Because in medicine the ruling power [δύναμις] is not unimportant. Although physicians consider and are responsible for many issues, some [illnesses] are cured spontaneously for them" (Hippocrates, *Decent.* 6). Accordingly, spontaneous healing was attributed to the gods. In addition, numerous sources report that Galen took a critical look at early Christian healing stories. The corresponding tractates are missing; however, the tradition can be found in Syriac, Arabic, and Latin transliterations (cf., e.g., Bar Hebraeus, who in his *Chronicon Syriacum* alludes to the "miracles" of the Nazarene, or Casiri's Latin translation: *Christiani nuncupantur religionem suam in parabolis et miraculis constituisse*).

2.4.4. New Testament Concepts of Healing in a History-of-Religions Context

The New Testament is familiar with numerous terms that express healing, among which θεραπεύω is at the center. In medical writings such as the Corpus Hippocraticum (*Vet. med.* 15.1; *Aph.* 6.38; *Vict.* 4.2.59; and more often) or also in Galen (*Nat. fac.* 1.13; 2.9; 2.126; Kühn; Weissenrieder and Dolle 2019, 730), the verb means "to serve," "to take care of," "treat, as by a physician," or an expeditiously produced result of a physician's effort for the healing of the sick and their infirmities. As a rule, this also goes along with continuity of the conditions of healing, such as the alteration of lifestyle by the sick person (usually in the present or imperfect tense; Wells 1998). Θεραπεία means service in vulnerable times of life, as the Hippocratic oath makes clear. In addition, numerous authors of antiquity are acquainted with the "word," the λόγος, as a healing force that points to a communication that demands a corresponding response from hearers (as, for instance, in Marcus Aurelius 5.28; see also Porphyry, *Marc.* 31.34), an intention, like what is also found in a comparable way in the New Testament. In the Septuagint, the verb θεραπεύω describes a human effort to heal (exception: Wis. 16:12). In the New Testament, the verb in the gnomic aorist is found in Matt. 4:24, 8:16, and elsewhere (parallel to "teaching," διδάσκειν, and "proclamation," κηρύσσειν, in Matt. 4:23; 9:35), whereas in Mark it is used primarily in the present or imperfect and thereby connotes an enduring action. Luke alone adduces the verb in the present or imperfect passive, and associates it with the active hearing of the word, which also brings with it a change (μετάνοιαν, 5:32). The objects of healing can be maladies (Luke 6:18 par.) as well as sick persons. Only Luke uses θεραπεύω for the action ("physician, heal yourself") and the inability of physicians to heal (Luke 8:43). Θεραπεύω appears surprisingly often in healings on the Sabbath, and in these cases it means the activity of healing, which has a result of a change in lifestyle (Luke 13:10–17). This association is intensified in the summaries: Θεραπεύω stands right beside the preaching of the coming kingdom of God. This aspect of an actively changing situation with respect to healing associates New Testament assertions with such situations from their environment.

In some passages the Gospels use the verb ἰάομαι, as the Septuagint does (Tob. 12:14; Pss. 6:3; 29:3; 40:4–5; Wis. 16:10; Sir. 38:9; Mark 5:29; Matt. 8:8; 13:15; 15:28), but especially Luke (Luke 5:17; 6:18; and elsewhere; John 4:47; 5:13; 12:40). Particularly impressive is the phraseology of Exod. 15:26 LXX; "For I am the Lord who heals you." Healing and prayer are correlated to each other. From a history-of-religions perspective, the verb and its derivatives are amplified in the so-called ἰάματα or accounts of healing that are dedicated to Asclepius, the god of healing (e.g., *IG* IV² 1.121–122), and accrue the function of a kind of advertisement for miraculous healing. The name goes back to the collection of στῆλαι (stone tablets), the majority of which are found in the Asclepeions in Epidaurus, Kos, and Pergamum, and which reflect the methods of healing. These are described as dreams of the sick, which then appear in the ἰάματα in a formula ("he/she saw in a dream; and it appeared to him/her"). Along with the god-patient consultation, these ἰάματα attest arrays and methods of the gods such as touching or prescription of medicinal remedies (*IG* IV² 1.126 and elsewhere). In research often an affinity of the healing gods with ancient medicine is presumed, especially of Hippocratic or Galenic provenance. The terms encountered in the ἰάματα are primarily ὑγιής ("the person is healed") and ἰάομαι ("to heal"; *IG* II² 4475a, 4514: here it is the healing power of Asclepius in his manifestation as a snake; Dillon 1994). The period of residence in an Asclepius sanctuary often includes the payment of a fee (see *Die Altertümer von Pergamon* VIII 3.161.8; *Lois sacrées des cités grecques* 69.20–24) as well as compliance with dietary prescriptions, abstinence from sexual activity (*Die Altertümer von Pergamon* VIII 3.161.11–14), ritual baths, sacrifices, a period of residence in a dormitory (*Lois sacrées des cités grecques* 69.43–47), faith and prayer, and healing and thanksgiving. Here the verb ἰάομαι means healing by a divine power and the restoration of the condition before the illness.

Along with this, the verb ὑγιαίνειν is especially attested in Luke (5:31, where ἰσχύοντες is changed to ὑγιαίοντες; 7:10; 15:27). The derivatives of the term ὑγίεια are used in the Asclepius cult and in ancient medicine, and they refer to divinity of human nature. Only in Mark 5:34 in the healing story of the "woman with the flow of blood" do we find the expression "be healed from your plague" (see Ps. 37[38]:18 LXX). The term "plague" in biblical texts denotes an exclusion from the cult and the cult community. The state of being healthy, therefore, goes along with reinstatement in the community of believers. Accordingly, the woman who was healed is called "daughter" (Mark 5:34 par.).

The medical anthropologist Arthur Kleinman (1995, 307–10) has made it clear that healing is not indicated only by means of the terminology that has been mentioned, like θεραπεύω, but equally by the descriptions that suggest a transformation or also a "therapeutic alteration" and hence a recovery. In New Testament texts, suffering is complemented by a verb that indicates recuperation: so the fever abandons Peter's mother-in-law (Matt. 8:15), the leper is *made clean*, or the blind man can *see*.

2.4.5. The Theological Relevance of Jesus's Healings

Generally speaking, New Testament research has reflected on three matters. First, it is debatable whether in the New Testament stories of healing the healing of disease and the forgiveness of sin belong together. In John 9:2–3 this connection is clearly denied; Mark 2:1–12 par., where Ps. 103 functions as a precursor text, is the only example. In Ps. 102:3 LXX complete forgiveness of sin and healing of diseases are placed together in a *parallelismus membrorum*, and God's compassion is compared with that of a father who is devoted to his children (Mark 2:5c). This connection between sickness and sin is redeployed narratively in Mark 2:1–12.

The malady is a visible expression of sin. Anyone who is so afflicted is evidently a sinner (v. 9). Jesus does not ask either about the origin of the malady or about who was the cause of it. What is decisive is that in Jesus's presence and action sin and sickness lose their power. Also, the forgiveness of sin and healing do not stand in a temporal sequence. For the sick man, sins do not have to be forgiven *first*, and afterward he is healed. But this means that the association of sickness and sin is thus broken. To be sure, in antiquity healing a malady was not commonplace, but it was definitely counted among possible experiences. By contrast, forgiveness of sin is God's prerogative (Exod. 34:7; Isa. 43:25; 44:22). By forgiving sin Jesus arrogates divine authority.

A second matter is related to Jesus's healings on the Sabbath (as, e.g., in Mark 3:1–6 par.; John 5:1–18). The Damascus Document describes the assistance that could be rendered on the Sabbath within quite narrow limits, which do not permit help in giving birth or the rescue of a person from a cistern (CD-A x 14–11.18; see also 4Q265 vi 5–6). However, the document is silent about healings. The rabbis argue differently; they definitely permit medical help when life is at risk (m. Yoma 8:6; Doering 1999, 448–49); however, this does not make Jesus's healings as such understandable. Jubilees provides the most decisive statements on the observance of the Sabbath in the time of Jesus, indicating that violating the Sabbath is designated as a transgression (see Jub. 2:25, 27; 50:8, 12). This is because the Sabbath can be read as evidence of eschatological salvation and the restoration of creation (Jub. 50:9; Dietzfelbinger 1978, 295–98). This interpretation is now read anew in light of the experience of the kingdom of God in the healings: in the blessed work of creation in healings (and also in exorcisms), the nearness of God's rule can be experienced corporeally. In this sense the verb ἀποκαθίστημι (restore) in Mark 3:5 points equally to a medical and an eschatological blessing (with respect to an association with Elijah's activity, cf. Mal. 3:1–3; Mark 9:12; Doering 2008, 236–39).

Finally, healing is based on faith (Mark 5:34; 10:52; Matt. 9:22; Luke 7:50; 17:19), the direct object of which is not always mentioned; thus that to which faith is directed is unclear. In this respect, the story of the slave of the centurion in Capernaum is instructive, in that here trust in Israel's God, who is manifested through Jesus's salvific action, is explicitly expressed. This trust is especially enunciated by persons who as "non-Jews" first recognize Israel's primacy for Jesus's efficacious power. This is based on the hope of "non-Jews" that in the history of salvation this efficacious power is extended, as this is expressed in Isa. 56:1–8. Whereas, however, the Syro-Phoenician woman argues that non-Jews in the end belong to the house of Israel (Matt. 15:21–28), the faith of the centurion points to Jesus's word transcending even this boundary—for a long-serving soldier of the Herodians.

2.4.6. Jesus, the Healer

Research reflects on various titles for Jesus's ministry (physician, divine man, miraculous charismatic, magician; see D.IV.2.5). The only ascription that we find in the New Testament is "physician." At that time, medical tractates demonstrate a proximity to religious interpretations of disease and the role of the physician, especially in Galen, who can subordinate his medical practice to the power to interpret Asclepius. The religious interpretation of illness as divine punishment lost its relevance in the Jesus tradition, so that space is opened for a positive elaboration of the relationship of religion and medicine: in Luke 5:31 "those who are well" (ὑγιαίνω; the verb appears exclusively in Luke) are contrasted with "those who are badly off" (κακῶς ἔχοντες). Jesus the physician did not come to call the righteous but sinners. This commitment to sinful human beings is associated with Jesus acting like a physician healing the sick. The physician metaphor, which takes hold in Irenaeus and Origen (Irenaeus, *Haer.* 2.5.2; Origen, *Cels.* 2.67; Kollmann 1996, 364), points to an intersection that medical and religious concepts evoke (and interprets Jesus as a "physician," ἰατρός), as they are known, for instance, in the Hippocratic oath, which in antiquity was sworn to Asclepius. Furthermore, there are additional aspects that suggest a comparable dimension between medicine and religion. Some introductory medical textbooks begin their treatises with a list of virtues (e.g., Hippocrates, *Decent.* 3; *Medic.* 1), such as the conduct of the physician on the basis of trust (Hippocrates, *Flat.* 1; Eusebius, *Hist. eccl.* 10.4.11; Temkin 1991, 141–44), but also the virtues of moderation, self-control, fair behavior (Rosen and Horstmanshoff 2003), and treating the sick equally without respect of person (Stamatu 2005). Visiting the sick also belongs among the virtues of a physician (often by pupils; see Hippocrates, *Decent.* 17; cf. Matt. 25:36). By declaring the body to be the place of health, the author of Luke makes clear that he knows about this traditional image of a physician. To be sure, he intensifies the image theologically: as early as the inaugural sermon based on Isa. 61:1, Luke refers to God's acceptance of those who are sick and poor. That this occurs in the context of a meal, which for Lukan theology is so significant, shows that the image of a physician is theologically central.

Hints of Asclepius, the god of healing, which some believe are found in John 5:1–9 (the healing of the afflicted man at the pool of Bethesda), could possibly indicate an intersection between a religious and a medical interpretation (Steger 2004). This can be verified especially since the excavation in 1956 of a large bath in Jerusalem, the northern pool of which was located outside the city up until the time of Herod Agrippa (41–44 CE) (Rengstorf 1953; Küchler 1992). At the end of the first century CE, this complex was then developed as an Asclepeion, as statues of Asclepius in the *abaton* of the grounds suggest. In addition, a votive sacrifice was found, the marble votive sacrifice of a woman named "Pompeia Licilia" (CIIP 1.2.709). Thus, one can assume in all probability that there was an Asclepeion in Jerusalem (Weissenrieder and Etzelmüller 2015). Of course, it is not substantiated with certainty that John 5:1–9 is related to this. However, the use of the adjective ὑγιής is striking, because it can refer to Hygieia the daughter of Asclepius, the god of healing, and in John 5 it appears frequently (vv. 6, 9, 11, 14–15; elsewhere only in John 7:23). In antiquity miraculous power is ascribed to the figure of the divine man, θεῖος ἀνήρ. For Asclepius, this ascription is indisputable, but it is more frequently attested for philosophers or historical founding figures without miraculous power (Bieler 1967, 2:105–9; Dormeyer ²2002, 222–25). The adjective θεῖος belongs to the semantic field of εὐσεβής or θεοσεβής, and it denotes a tradition of perception that is also detectable in Judaism (Toit 1997, 109–10 and elsewhere). In addition, researchers make reference to Jewish charismatic miracle workers, especially Hanina ben Dosa. However, these references are quite vague, inasmuch as only one healing of an illness by Hanina is recorded (see b. Berakhot 34b; John 4:46–53; Vermes 1973, 55–64; skeptical: M. Becker 2002, 343–44).

Jesus's healings of the sick are attested in distinct genres and transmissions of tradition, which bring together a wide variety of themes and motifs, such as bodily manifestations of the kingdom of God, the preaching of repentance, and Jesus's message for the poor and sinners. Jesus's healings of the sick point to God's interventions as the onset of a messianic time of salvation; God's power, however, is relatively seldom mentioned (Matt. 11:5 and elsewhere). Jesus himself is the bearer of a "numinous power" that overcomes a situation of deficiency. In Jesus the physician, God's beneficent power becomes efficacious (Kahl 1994, 230–33: "bearer of numinous power").

Bendemann, Reinhard von. 2014. "Die Heilungen Jesu und die antike Medizin." *Early Christianity* 5: 273–312.

Bieler, Ludwig. 1967. *Theios Anēr: Das Bild des Göttlichen Menschen in spätantike und Frühchristentum.* Vol. 2. Darmstadt.

Dillon, Matthew P. J. 1994. "The Didactic Nature of the Epidaurean Iamata." *ZPE* 101: 239–60.

Kollmann, Bernd. 1996. *Jesus und die Christen als Wundertäter: Studien zu Magie, Medizin und Schamanismus in Antike und Christentum.* FRLANT 170. Göttingen.

Tieleman, Teun. 2016. "Religion and Therapy in Galen." In *Religion and Illness*, edited by Gregor Etzelmüller and Annette Weissenrieder, 15–31. Eugene, OR.

Weissenrieder, Annette. 2003. *Images of Illness in the Gospel of Luke: Insights of Ancient Medical Texts.* WUNT II 164. Tübingen.

Weissenrieder, Annette, and Katrin Dolle. 2019. *Körper und Verkörperung: Biblische Anthropologie im Kontext antiker Medizin und Philosophie; Ein Quellenbuch für die Septuaginta und das Neue Testament.* Fontes et Subsidia ad Bibliam Pertinentes 8. Berlin.

Annette Weissenrieder

2.5. Exorcisms

Exorcisms belong to the most widely attested deeds of Jesus (Annen 1976; Kollmann 1996, 174–215), and they are closely associated with his message of the kingdom of God. In exorcisms (actually conjurations), what is at stake is the ritual expulsion of evil spirits that have taken possession of a human body. The exorcism ritual is characterized by a vehement power struggle, in which the exorcist attempts to induce the demon to abandon the possessed person by threatening gestures, massive intimidation, and commands to leave.

Jesus puts exorcisms together with healings at the center of his activity (Luke 13:32). In the Beelzebul controversy (Mark 3:22–27), they are a topic of dispute with opponents. The latter recognize Jesus's exorcisms as indisputable facts; however, they accuse him of an alliance with Beelzebul, one of many designations for Satan, who in Jewish demonology is regarded as the chief of evil spirits. Jesus invalidates the reproach by employing the concept of a kingdom divided against itself. It would be preposterous if Satan were to proceed against the realm of his own dominion. The power that stands behind Jesus is in reality none other than God. While God effects the expulsion of the demons, Jesus thinks of himself as God's instrument and medium, through which the power of the kingdom becomes operative (Luke 11:20). In this dynamic process the disciples are also included and trained for exorcisms (Matt. 10:8).

In the narrative tradition of the Gospels, some of Jesus's exorcisms are extensively depicted (Mark 1:21–28; 5:1–20 par.; 7:24–30 par.; 9:14–29 par.). The reports are influenced by christological interests and aligned with formal patterns of exorcism stories, but they have preserved a reliable historical memory of Jesus's activity (Meier 1994, 646–77; Dunn 2003b, 673–77). Even if unique contours of Jesus become indistinct, they convey an impression of how Jesus must have acted in his exorcisms and what effect they had on his contemporaries. The report of the driving out of seven evil spirits from Mary Magdalene transmitted only by Luke (8:2) is perhaps also based on a historical memory. In the largely redactional summaries of the Gospels (Mark 1:34–39 par.; 3:10–12 par.), Jesus's actions depicted in the individual traditions are generalized and enhanced.

2.5.1. Demonic Possession

Demonic possession (cf. Trunk 1994, 10–21; Keener 2011, 776–79, 788–809) expresses a culturally-specific threshold phenomenon. In the Mediterranean world of antiquity and comparable cultures today, it may have positive connotations, but it is usually encountered in a pathological form. The concept of possession serves in a milieu that believes in demons as a way of explaining an abnormal pattern of human behavior, and helps persons who are affected to a form of expressing needs or their identity. Hence it assigns or offers a role in society to people who demonstrate an appearance that sharply deviates from a normal personality. Typical manifestations of possession are a distorted facial expression, an altered pitch of voice, speaking in a strange language, and uncontrolled or aggressive behaviors that mostly occur quite impetuously. It gives the impression that the affected person is completely handed over to the demonic power and has lost all control over his or her own body.

Possession can be conceived of from a cultural anthropological perspective as a socially acquired *performance* (C. Strecker 2002, 54–59). Presumably persons possessed by demons act out in dramatic form behaviors that are taken to be evidence for possession in a society that is shaped by mythical thinking. In this way possessed persons create a demonic reality, which in the exorcist's action as a public performance undergoes a bursting open in which the identity of the possessed person is constituted anew and the person's place in society is defined anew. Demonic possession as a dramatic performance does not automatically represent an illness. However, it does not do justice to Jesus's exorcisms simply to assume from the ludic performance that possessed persons are behaving conspicuously to gain heightened attention.

The possessed Gerasene (Mark 5:1–20) demonstrates with his relentless howling, his dwelling among the tombs, his wandering around without clothes, and his drive toward self-destruction all the ways of behaving that in ancient sources are regarded as traits of mania. Evidently he suffers from a dissociative personality disorder, which because of its severe accompanying features is interpreted as possession. The fact that an entire legion of demons has taken hold of him alludes not only to the severity of his suffering but also to political conditions. In Jesus's environment, the situation of Roman foreign rule with its demonic imperialism; the impoverishment of the rural population, which is characteristic of many agrarian societies; as well as the inner conflict of people between admiration and condemnation of the Hellenistic-Roman culture must be taken into account when assessing the frequent occurrence of psychopathic phenomena of possession (Crossan [2]1995, 402–68; Witmer 2012, 61–96). In societies that are in inner turmoil because of political, social, and cultural antagonisms, more mental disorders than usual emerge, which are expressed in a cry for help by the shattered people as domination by demons. When Mary Magdalene is possessed by seven evil spirits (Luke 8:2), this also depicts evidence of a severe personality disorder.

On the other hand, the gnashing of teeth, foaming at the mouth, and sudden collapsing of the possessed boy in Mark 9:14–29 all point to behavior that, according to Hippocratic medicine (Hippocrates, *Morb. sacr.* 1.7), is typical of epileptic seizures. Consequently, Matthew speaks of his being "moonstruck" (lunatic) (Matt. 17:15), a widespread designation for epilepsy in antiquity, because the interval between the seizures was viewed as controlled by the moon. Along with severe personality disorders and epilepsy, crippling (Luke 13:11), blindness (Matt. 12:22), and the inability to speak (Luke 11:14) are experienced or interpreted as a result of demonic possession. When a society accepts that desperate people interpret their psychological or physical problems as loss of control over their own bodies as a result of the activity of demonic powers, possibilities are opened for the resolution of their problems by means of ritual exorcisms.

2.5.2. The Eschatological Context of Jesus's Exorcisms

Jesus's exorcisms are manifestations of God's eschatological action. The belief in demons of ancient Judaism stands in the background, as it occurs in intertestamental writings (Jubilees, Testaments of the Twelve Patriarchs, Qumran texts). Satan, who sits in heaven as the prosecutor of human beings (Job 1:6–12), is considered to be lord over a host of demons, a host that is responsible for evil deeds on the earth (Jub. 10:8). In the setting of apocalyptic hopes, it was expected that at the end of days God would bind or overthrow Satan in an annihilating judgment in order thereafter to exercise unrestricted sovereignty over creation again as in paradisaic times (T. Levi 18:10–13; T. Dan. 5:10–12). The hope of an end of sickness and suffering was associated with the annihilation of the devil and the restoration of God's universal kingly sovereignty, since evil was eliminated once and for all (As. Mos. 10:1; 2 Bar. 73:1–3).

Jesus shared the demonistic worldview and the apocalyptic patterns of ancient Judaism. In contradistinction to his contemporaries, he was certainly convinced that Satan is already disempowered and that God has already begun the restoration of divine sovereignty. Jesus said this had been revealed to him in a visionary experience in which he saw Satan fall from heaven like a flash of lightning (Luke 10:18). The parable of the strong man whose house cannot be invaded until he is first bound (Mark 3:27) describes the disempowerment of Satan that has already been consummated as the presupposition for Jesus's successful exorcisms. Because Beelzebul has been bound by God, the evil spirits under him are without a lord and can be fought against. With every exorcism evil loses space and the sphere of God's power on earth increases. In the decline of demons, God's new world takes shape step by step, which commonly was not expected until the end of days (Luke 11:20). Much speaks for the assumption that on the basis of the vision of the fall of Satan, Jesus carried out his separation from John the Baptizer in order to play a part in the implementation of the kingdom of God (U. Müller 1977, 427–29; Hollenbach 1982, 207–17). This eschatological perspective of Jesus's exorcisms is unprecedented, and it makes them unmistakable.

2.5.3. History-of-Religions Context

The New Testament already recognizes that Jesus was by no means the only Jewish exorcist of his time (Matt. 12:27; Mark 9:38; Acts 19:13). Ritual exorcism in ancient Judaism is first attested in Tob. 8:1–3, where the driving out of evil spirits known from Egypt by the smoking of fish entrails is regarded as a gift of God, who revealed it through God's angel Raphael (Kollmann 1994; Stuckenbruck 2002). In the Genesis Apocryphon from Qumran, Abraham is stylized as an exorcist invested with power, who by prayer, laying on of hands, and threats heals the pharaoh, who has been afflicted with plagues (Gen. 12:17; 1Q20 xx 28–29). In Jesus's time exorcisms in the magic tradition that went back to David and Solomon were dominant. The demonic incantations carried out in Qumran with the Psalms of David (11Q11; cf. LAB 60:1–3) and other songs (4Q510, 511, 560) belong in this context (J. Sanders 1997; Naveh 1998; Eshel 2003, 396–415). This also applies to the activity of the exorcist Eleazar known by Josephus's eyewitness report (*Ant.* 8.44–49) in the time of the Jewish war (Duling 1985; Deines 2003). Eleazar used a signet ring with a root with healing power hidden underneath it, in order to pull the demon out of the nostrils of a possessed person. With this he made use of an instrument that is widely attested in antiquity especially for the healing of epilepsy. In addition, he recited Solomon's incantation formulas, which according to Josephus's depiction also were used by other Jewish magicians. Probably Eleazar had a magic compendium at his disposal, comparable to the "Book of Remedies" mentioned in rabbinic tradition and considered the work of Solomon. Also, the Jewish-influenced exorcism formula *PGM* 4.3019–3078, adjuring demons by the "Seal of Solomon" and the magic rites in the Testament of Solomon, reflects this art of healing.

In Hellenistic literature the most direct parallels to Jesus's driving out demons are found in Lucian of Samosata and Philostratus. Lucian (second century), in his work *Philopseudes*, in which he ridicules ancient belief in miracles, describes the appearance of two exorcists. The Syrian from Palestine, who is unnamed (Lucian,

Philops. 16), specialized in the healing of lunatics (epileptics) in the manner of the magicians who were already fought by the Hippocratic tradition (Hippocrates, *Morb. sacr.* 1.10), and he thereby provides his livelihood. To this end he approaches the possessed person and inquires where the demon came from and in what way he gained entrance into the sick person. After the demon disclosed both things in his mother tongue, he is expelled by the exorcist by incantation formulas and intimidation. Lucian also recounts how in Corinth a Pythagorean philosopher, Arignotus, who must be a fictional character, drove out a spirit of death by gruesome magic words in the Egyptian language and thereby made a house, which had been commandeered by him, habitable again (*Philops.* 16).

Philostratus (third century) mentions Indian sages that drive out evil spirits by means of letters (Philostratus, *Vit. Apoll.* 3.38), and depicts an exorcism of the Pythagorean philosopher Apollonius of Tyana (first century), who in Athens healed a possessed boy by massive intimidation of the demon (*Vit. Apoll.* 4.20). This boy suffered from a personality disorder that expressed itself by abrupt laughter or crying and incessant talking to himself. The demon is overwhelmed with fear by means of a mere glare and is made willing to be driven out. Then Apollonius addresses it in furious agitation and commands it to escape visibly. Thereupon the demon flees and, in so doing, destroys a pillar. An occasionally presumed dependence of Philostratus on the New Testament is unlikely. At the core the episode may reproduce a local tradition from Athens and go back to the historical activity of Apollonius. The *Papyri Graecae Magicae* from Egypt offer descriptive insights into the practice of exorcism, as it was taught by specialists in esoteric circles. This body of papyri is a complex compilation of magical prescriptions and ritual instructions, among which are also instructions on the healing of persons possessed by demons (*PGM* 4.1227–1264; 4.3019–3078; 5.96–171; 13.242–244). These texts compiled in the fourth century recount magical practices that must have already been largely in use in New Testament times.

2.5.4. Jesus's Exorcism Techniques

In the explanatory sayings accompanying his exorcistic activity, Jesus comments that he drives out demons by the finger or spirit of God and sees himself thereby as God's tool in the battle against evil (Luke 11:20 par. Matt. 12:28). For the rituals of expulsion depicted in the narrative reports (cf. Poplutz 2013, 101–6), it cannot be said with certainty whether at all points they match Jesus's actual procedures or were described according to the prototype of other ancient exorcists.

At the center of techniques ascribed to Jesus stand the interrogation and threatening of demons, imperatives to come out, prohibition of returning, and the command to enter into other objects. The threatening or intimidation of the spirit of illness (Mark 1:25; 9:25: ἐπετίμησεν) is among the typical practices of ancient exorcists. The Gospels leave open the concrete form in which Jesus threatened demons. In the battle against evil, the exorcist is directed to strong allies. Frequently in an exorcism ritual a divinity is invoked, in order to adopt a superior threatening posture against unclean spirits. Perhaps Jesus intimidated the demons by reciting Zech. 3:2, "YHWH rebuke [LXX: ἐπιτιμήσαι] you, Satan," which served as a magical formula against the devil or demons (L.A.E. 39; b. Berakhot 51a; cf. Jude 9). This would fit in with the fact that he considered God as the true author of his expulsion of demons and that he implicitly presumed this for other Jewish exorcists as well.

On the other hand, direct parallels for Jesus's imperatives to evil spirits to come out (Mark 1:25; 5:8; 9:25) are found in the magical papyri from Egypt. There, in three exorcism instructions, an exorcism order to the demons is documented, formulated exactly as in the New Testament reports with "Come out of him" (ἔξελθε), but supplemented by accompanying actions, magic words, incantations, and accelerating formulas such as "now, now, quickly, quickly" (PGM 4.1242, 3007; 5.158). When the command to come out in Mark 9:25 is complemented with a prohibition against returning, the apprehension that the expelled spirit of illness can take possession of the body anew stands in the background. Also, in another passage (Matt. 12:43–45 par.), after driving out the demons Jesus addresses the necessity of precautionary measures in order to guard against falling back into the condition of being possessed. Further techniques ascribed to Jesus are asking the name of the demon (Mark 5:9), the knowledge of which confers upon the exorcist power over it, and sending the evil spirits into another object (Mark 5:13), as was also practiced by Eleazar (Josephus, Ant. 8.48) and Apollonius of Tyana (Philostratus, Vit. Apoll. 4.20). The purpose of these manipulative accompanying actions is to express the annihilation of the demonic power and to demonstrate to the healed persons the actual expulsion of the spirits from their body. When Jesus drives a legion of demons out of the Gerasene who was possessed, sends them into a herd of swine, and lets them drown in the Sea of Gennesaret, this also acquires symbolic revolutionary significance against the background of the foreign Roman domination.

According to the portrayal of the Gospels on the whole, Jesus accomplished his exorcisms exclusively through an awe-inspiring presence and power of the word, whereas other ancient exorcists such as Eleazar or the magicians of the Egyptian papyri also worked with supplementary amulets, signet rings, music, smoke, palm fronds, or curative roots. Incantation formulas to spirits or divinities, as they characterize exorcism in the narrower sense, are also not attested for Jesus's expulsion of demons.

2.5.5. Jesus's Exorcisms in the Light of Magic and Shamanism

Jesus is not a representative of rational arts of healing but is to be located in the scope of diagnostics of illnesses influenced by magic concepts. Jesus assumed that personality disorders, epilepsy, and other maladies were caused by demonic possession and battled them with exorcisms. Hence, according to the presentation of the Gospels, practices were employed that came from the realm of magic. The degree to which this effectively makes Jesus a magician is controversial, and debated (Kollmann 2011, 3057–61). That he was a powerful as well as a shady magician is plainly represented in the ancient non-Christian perception of his person (Stanton 2004, 129–44; Gemeinhardt 2010, 471–76). The most influential modern concepts of Jesus as a magician come from Morton Smith (1978), who attempts to reconstruct from the Gospels and non-Christian sources such as the Talmud or the "True doctrine" of the Platonist Celsus a coherent magical career of Jesus, and John Dominic Crossan (²1995, 402–68), according to whom Jesus had a social program of magic and meal as part of his vision of a better society. Since the term "magician" is often used in a negative sense, Jesus is alternatively considered a shaman, who exercised control over spirits and mediated wisdom from the divine world (Craffert 2008, 245–308; cf. Drewermann ³1992, 43–309). On the other hand, in spite of his seemingly magical practices of exorcism, some seek to dissociate Jesus more sharply from ancient magic. They call him a charismatic who heals through personal presence rather than mechanical technique (Meier 1994, 537–52; Twelftree 2007, 81–86), or a Hasid who acts unmediated in the power of God (Vermes 1993a, 45–68), or a messianic prophet (Aune 1980, 1523–39), or a folk healer sharing a significant element of his worldview and concepts of illness with his followers (W. Stegemann 2004, 84–88).

The controversial discussion about Jesus as a magician is clearly mitigated by a paradigm change in the evaluation of magic. The view of magic as a primitive antecedent or a degenerate aberration of religion proves to be a cliché. Where the line between a repudiated magical miracle and an approved charismatic miracle is drawn is subjective and involves consideration of social power (Segal 1981; Aubin 2001). Preferentially, phenomena that do not conform to the socially prevalent understanding of religion and science are disqualified and discredited as magic. Magic meets needs that religion does not cover and presents a subversive form of social protest. Without doubt this applies to Jesus's exorcisms. With this he shares the destiny of virtually all prominent magicians or shamans of antiquity, venerated by their followers as superhuman because of the miracles while discredited by opponents as sorcerers.

However, qualifications to these fundamental understandings of the activities of a magician or a shaman are necessary. Jesus's deeds of power cover only a rather meager segment of the sphere of activity of an ancient magician. In contrast to professional magicians, Jesus does not allow his ministrations to be remunerated. Aspects that make magic a problematic form of the practice of religion, especially the coerced manipulation of divinities, the implementation of questionable desires, and the employment of harmful spells, prove to be irrelevant for Jesus's activity. The transmigration of souls, which is a constitutive teaching for healings by shamans, is not attested for Jesus, nor does he appear to have undertaken ecstatic otherworldly journeys in order to give last respects to the souls of the deceased or to provide the souls of the living relevant information for healing from their earlier incarnation. He does not dovetail with any kind of magical or shamanic grid of his time. The initiation period for a magician or shaman was lengthy and required a comprehensive introduction to esoteric teaching. John the Baptizer, the only known teacher of Jesus, does not come into consideration for this, since he did not perform any miracles (John 10:41). According to the Talmud (b. Shabbat 104b) and Celsus (Origen, *Cels.* 1.28, 38), Jesus received schooling in magic in Egypt, which to be sure is questionable, since it appears to be linked with the legend of the Egyptian sojourn of the holy family (Matt. 2:13–15). Also, Jesus manifests no direct lines of association with the dominant streams of contemporary Jewish magic. The fact that Jesus is not related in any recognizable way with the magical art of healing associated with David and Solomon is striking. In contrast to the Qumran community and Eleazar, in his exorcisms he made no use of either David's psalms or Solomon's incantation formulas. The evidence as a whole indicates that Jesus became aware of his special powers in something of a call-vision (Luke 10:18) devoid of magic or shamanic knowledge and saw himself commissioned to expel demons in the context of the in-breaking kingdom of God.

Ebner, Martin. 2013. "Die Exorzismen Jesu als Testfall für die historische Rückfrage." In *Jesus—Gestalt und Gestaltungen: FS Gerd Theißen*, edited by Petra von Gemünden et al., 477–98. NTOA 100. Göttingen.

Kollmann, Bernd. 2011. "Jesus and Magic: The Question of the Miracles." In *Handbook for the Study of the Historical Jesus*, vol. 4, *Individual Studies*, edited by Tom Holmén and Stanley E. Porter, 3057–85. Leiden and Boston.

Strecker, Christian. 2002. "Jesus und die Besessenen." In *Jesus in neuen Kontexten*, edited by Wolfgang Stegemann, 53–63. Stuttgart.

Twelftree, Graham H. 1993. *Jesus the Exorcist: A Contribution to the Study of the Historical Jesus*. WUNT II 54. Tübingen.

Witmer, Amanda. 2012. *Jesus, the Galilean Exorcist*. LNTS 459. London and New York.

Bernd Kollmann

2.6. Resuscitations of the Dead and Nature Miracles

2.6.1. Controversies over the Historical Background

In addition to exorcisms and healings, resuscitations of the dead and nature miracles are attributed to Jesus. With respect to nature miracles, distinctions are made among gift miracles, deliverance miracles, punishment miracles, and epiphanies. Whereas exorcisms and healings stand incontestably in the center of Jesus's historical activity, it is difficult to shed light on the historical background of resuscitations of the dead and nature miracles. In the quest for the actual events, there are completely contradictory appraisals (cf. Kollmann 2014, 3–25). Supernatural expositions take the documentary reports as their starting point and reckon thereby that by circumventing the laws of nature Jesus could effect resuscitations of the dead and natural events. Rationalistic interpretations attempt to bring the reports of Jesus's resuscitations and nature miracles in line with critical reason, by which what is miraculous is interpreted by speculation about the actual attendant circumstances. By contrast, for mythological treatments of miracles, fictitious events are imputed to Jesus by recourse to Old Testament tradition to demonstrate his messianism. Kerygmatic, history-of-religions explanations draw on this but see in Hellenistic parallels the prevailing model for the New Testament reports that have to do with symbolic stories of faith to illustrate the divine power of the exalted Christ over death and creation. Depth psychological illuminations of selected resuscitations of the dead and nature wonders of Jesus give rise to theories on the reality standing in the background, which are not all that far from rationalism. From ethnological perspectives, contemporary eyewitness reports of resuscitations of the dead and nature miracles in Africa, Asia, and Latin America are regarded as evidence for the fact that corresponding New Testament reports are to be taken seriously and could reflect events that are not rationally explicable (Keener 2011, 536–600).

2.6.2. Resuscitations of the Dead

In the New Testament, three cases are reported in which Jesus called the dead back to life. The story of Jairus's daughter (Mark 5:21–24, 35–43) recounts how Jairus, the leader of a synagogue, asks Jesus to come to his house to heal his dying daughter by laying on his hands. At just this time messengers arrive to report the death of the twelve-year-old girl. The statement of her age heightens the drama, because she has died just before becoming eligible for marriage. Jesus proceeds to the synagogue leader's house, where the death lamentation is already being intoned. He dismisses the crowd and resuscitates the girl by taking her hand and uttering the words "little girl, arise" (*talitha cum*). The girl arises, walks about, and demonstrates the renewal of her life by eating something.

As to what could have actually taken place, Christian rationalism that set in after the Enlightenment assumed an apparent death. In antiquity a false diagnosis of death is not uncommon, and the assured signs for the actual occurrence of death were intensively discussed in the medical tradition (cf. Kollmann 1996, 93–94). Empedocles was renowned for resuscitating an apparently dead woman who lay in a coma for seven days and had been declared dead by physicians (Heracleides Ponticus, *Frag.* 76–89). According to Mark 5:39, Jairus's daughter was "not dead but sleeping"; to be sure, death was euphemistically referred to as sleep; however, there is some suspense as to whether the girl has actually died. Rationalistic explanatory models still occur today. So some consider the girl comatose because of low blood glucose, and the food she eats brings her back around (Wilcox 1982, 476), or from a depth psychology perspective, some think the girl rejected the onset of adulthood with a tonic immobility reflex, and Jesus liberated her from her anxiety (Drewermann [3]1992, 295–301). By contrast, under the influence of a mythological hermeneutic of miracles, the story is considered to be an unhistorical product of early Christian messianic belief. It was developed from the resuscitations performed by Elijah and Elisha in order to portray Jesus as an eschatological prophet who overtakes and surpasses the activity of all prophets (Gnilka 1978–1979, 212, 219). In fact, echoes of Elisha's miracle in 2 Kings 4:8–38 are apparent. Both accounts belong to a stock type of resuscitations of the dead, where the miracle worker proceeds to the house of the dead person. In addition, in both accounts people are excluded. To be sure, the parallels do not go so far as to suggest a transfer of Elisha's miracle to Jesus. The concrete data that the father of the girl is named Jairus, that he occupies the office of leader of the synagogue, and that Jesus employs the Aramaic words *talitha cum* speak against a purely fictitious story (Meier 1994, 784–88). Conceivably, Jesus's healing of Jairus's daughter stands in the background, which was later envisioned as a resuscitation of a dead person (Fischbach 1992, 178–81).

In the revivification of the young man in Nain (Luke 7:11–17), Jesus encounters the procession bearing the body to its final resting place and accomplishes the miracle in public. From the city gate of Nain, a dead person is being taken to the place of burial outside the walls. The fact that this has to do with the only son of a widow heightens the tragedy of the death, since the widow's provider and legal representative has died. In this case, Jesus steps in without being asked. He reassures the mourning mother, approaches the bier, and touches it. As soon as he has thus brought the procession to a halt, he turns to the person who has died with the command, "Young man, I say to you, rise!" The dead man awakens immediately and begins to speak. The report summons memories of the prophet Elijah's revivification miracle (1 Kings 17:17–24). Both cases have to do with the death of the son of a widow, and like Elijah, Jesus demonstrates by his miracle that he is a great prophet. The description of Luke 7:12 directly follows 1 Kings 17:10 ("and when he came to the gate of the city"). The phrase from the Old Testament story "and he gave him to his mother" (17:23) recurs verbatim. In addition, in both accounts the resumption of speaking serves to verify the miracle. These correspondences have led to the assumption that Luke's miracle story replicates 1 Kings 17:17–24 (Brodie 1986).

Multiple literary features that have no model in Elijah's miracle stand in the way, but they are attested in the Hellenistic typology of revivification of the dead, where the miracle worker directly encounters the procession of mourners and spontaneously offers his help. Because of his scholarly curiosity, the physician Asclepiades of Prusa (first century BCE) drew near to a funeral procession, diagnosed the dead person, who had already been anointed for cremation on a pyre, by feeling latent traces of life in the body, and reanimated him by employing medications (Apuleius, *Flor.* 19.92–96).

Parallels between Jesus's miracle and the revivification of a girl by Apollonius of Tyana (Philostratus, *Vit. Apoll.* 4.45) are even closer. The girl had died in Rome immediately after her wedding. Philostratus implies the possibility that this was a case of tonic immobility. Both Jesus and Apollonius meet the respective funeral processions accompanied by a large crowd of people, take the initiative without being solicited, and bring about the resuscitation by touching the dead person or the coffin and by directing miraculously efficacious words to them. Both resuscitated persons speak to demonstrate the restoration of life. Presumably Luke 7:11–17 originated in a milieu in which both the Old Testament and the Hellenistic typology of resuscitation of the dead could have influenced the picture of Jesus (Bovon 1989–2001, 357–60). The intent of Luke 7:11–17 entails presenting Jesus as the powerful Lord over death, who with respect to the restoration of life is in no way inferior to Israel's great prophets or to Hellenistic miracle workers. Whether the story has historical points of contact is questionable (Meier 1994, 797–98).

The most impressive resuscitation of the dead in the New Testament is the case of Lazarus in John 11:1–44. This consists of a multiply layered text, the final form of which is due to the disruption and arrangement of an original orally transmitted miracle story by a series of dialogue scenes (Theobald 2009, 714–18; cf. Wagner 1988, 42–87). As in the story of Jairus, Jesus is called to a sick person, who by the time of his arrival has already died, and brings about the revitalization by a command. To be sure, this miracle is massively enhanced. On the fourth day Lazarus lies in a tomb, which is a cave sealed with a stone, and has already begun to emit the stench of death. With this information, it should be excluded that Lazarus only suffered tonic immobility, and in addition according to rabbinic tradition, the soul hovered over the sepulcher only for up to three days in the hope of being able to return to the dead person (Midrash Bereshit Rabbah 100.7). The end of the story is especially dramatic, where the resuscitated Lazarus steps out of the cave still wrapped in the burial cloths. For John the evangelist, the miracle foreshadows the resurrection of Jesus and demonstrates his unfettered dominion over the power of death. Hence, features are established in the narration between the resuscitation of Lazarus and the resurrection of Jesus by presenting, in both cases, a stone tomb as the final resting place, the corpse wrapped in linen cloths, and the head covered with a face cloth.

The purpose of the account is to demonstrate Jesus's preeminent salvific significance by ascribing a case of resuscitating someone from the dead to him. Frequently the Lazarus miracle is seen as a narrative elaboration of the parable of the rich man and the poor man Lazarus of Luke 16:30 ("But if someone goes to them from the dead, they will repent"). In Luke's parable, the return of Lazarus to the earth after his death is requested, so it is now told by John as an actual case by Lazarus becoming the hero of a resurrection scene (Ernst 1977, 477). This assumption might suggest that the historical memory of a healing of Jesus underlies the Lazarus miracle, which later was heightened to a resuscitation of the dead (Kremer 1985, 105–8; Theobald 2009, 719–20).

2.6.3. Gift Miracles

Gift miracles entail a surprising allocation of material goods. This can be motivated by a situation of need, but most of them take place spontaneously in order to demonstrate the power of the miracle worker (Theissen [5]1987, 111–14). As the best-known gift miracle, the account of the miraculous feeding is about how at the Sea of Gennesaret Jesus satiated a gigantic crowd of people with a few loaves and a few fish, and even then bread was left over. In the course of the history of tradition, the original account was split into two versions, the feeding of the four thousand (Mark 8:1–10 par.) and the feeding of the five thousand (Mark 6:30–44 par.). In ancient Jewish tradition there are multiple comparable texts, among which are the feedings with manna and quail in the wilderness wandering, the miraculous multiplication of meal by Elijah (1 Kings 17:7–16), and the oil miracle of Elisha (2 Kings 4:1–7). It is said about Hanina ben Dosa that he filled an empty oven with bread in a miraculous way (b. Ta'anit 24b–25a). The most direct parallel, however, is the bread miracle of Elisha (2 Kings 4:42–44), which exhibits extensive agreement with the New Testament feeding account. The ability to miraculously provide food is also attributed to Egyptian magicians (Origen, *Cels.* 1.68; *PGM* 1.103–104) and to the Roman king Numa (Plutarch, *Num.* 15.2–3).

Rationalism conjectured that there was a secret cave full of food, which was surreptitiously brought out, or assumed that Jesus motivated the rich to share bread and fish that they had in their bags (cf. Schweitzer [9]1984, 82, 92). These explanations are hardly viable. The origin of the story of the miraculous feeding is due to the cumulative effect of multiple factors. In ancient Jewish tradition, future salvation was described with the image of sumptuous food and drink (Isa. 25:6). Jesus brought these future hopes into the present by portraying the kingdom of God in shining colors of a great feast (Luke 14:16–24) and brought about its in-breaking symbolically by table fellowship with tax collectors and sinners. The account of the miraculous multiplication of bread has its roots in the present time of salvation proclaimed by Jesus and exemplified by his table fellowship, in which material hardships are overcome and all the hungry are satiated. The historical point of contact might well be Jesus's meal fellowship at the Sea of Gennesaret. For the elaboration of it as a miracle, the example of Elisha, who was able to feed 100 persons with twenty loaves and still have leftovers, was the guiding force. Jesus is proclaimed as a miraculous prophet and an eschatological redeemer who surpasses Elisha's feat. From the perspective of faith, the feeding miracle tells the story of satisfying hunger and becoming satiated in God's new world brought about by Jesus.

For the history-of-religions school, the wine miracle at Cana in John 2:1–12 was a prime example of the penetration of Hellenistic miracle traditions into the Jesus tradition (Bousset [5]1965, 270–74). The provision of huge amounts of wine is characteristic of Dionysus, the wine god. In the Dionysus sanctuary of Elis, the priests locked away three empty vessels in a sealed building on the evening before the annual Dionysus festival and presented them on the next day full of wine (Pausanias, *Descr.* 6.26.1–2). Often in connection with Dionysus the concept is attested that at certain times wine bubbles from springs. With this a transformation of water that otherwise flowed from the springs might have been imagined (Broer 1999). In ancient Jewish tradition, an immeasurable abundance of wine is a symbol for the joy of the time of salvation (Gen. 49:11–12; 1 En. 10:19; 2 Bar. 29:5). With the establishment of the Dionysian cult in Palestine from the second century BCE, a mutual interpenetration of the two circles of tradition occurred (Hengel 1987). In the time of Jesus, a center of the Dionysian cult was located not very far from Cana in Nysa-Scythopolis. Beyond doubt, in John 2:1–12 a competition between Jesus and Dionysus is reflected (Eisele 2009; Theobald 2009, 203–8). The arrival of Jesus with his mother and the consequent effected wine miracle can be understood as the antithesis to the myths of the wine god Dionysus and his nursemaid Nysa. So to speak, right at his own doorstep a competitor Dionysus grows up with Jesus, and Jesus breaks into his domain by creating especially delectable wine in abundance (Eisele 2009, 24). A historical point of contact for John 2:1–12 might be Jesus's participation in a wedding feast in Cana, from which the account of a wine miracle that took place there developed. As a counterpart to the Dionysus legend, the Cana miracle proclaims the power of Jesus and aims as well at winning adherents of Dionysus to the Christian faith.

As the parallel in John 21:1–14 suggests, the miraculous catch of fish in Luke 5:1–11 is arguably about a resurrection story first associated with the calling of the disciples by Luke and thus backdated into Jesus's earthly life (Meier 1994, 899–904). The miracle is limited to Jesus's extraordinary prescience about an occasion of casting nets crowned with success. The story of the coin in the mouth of a fish (Matt. 17:24–27) is finally a post-Easter miracle for regulating the question of whether Jewish Christians should still pay the temple tax. On that point, a widespread motif of finding a coin or a piece of jewelry inside a fish (Herodotus, *Hist.* 3.42; Strabo, *Geogr.* 14.1.16) is appropriated and transferred to Jesus.

2.6.4. Deliverance Miracles, Epiphanies, and Punishment Miracles

The most significant deliverance miracle is the stilling of the storm (Mark 4:35–41), which is about preservation from hostile forces of nature, which ancient people thought were controlled by angels or demons. Hence, inasmuch as wind and waves are thought of as personified violence, the stilling of the storm bears features of driving out demons with threats and commands to silence.

In antiquity, the coerced manipulation of wind and waves belonged firmly to the sphere of activity of magicians, shamans, and conjurors (cf. Kratz 1979, 95–106). Persian magicians rescued the flotilla of Xerxes from a dangerous storm at sea by getting the wind to die down by magic incantations and the water to calm down by animal sacrifices (Herodotus, *Hist.* 7.191). Also, Pythagoras (*Vit. Pyth.* 28.135), Sophocles (Philostratus, *Vit. Apoll.* 8.7.8), and magicians from Cleonai (Clement of Alexandria, *Strom.* 6.31.1–2) are said to have had the ability to calm the powers behind the forces of nature with magic incantations, songs, or sacrifices. Empedocles was even tagged with the nickname "Wind Charmer" because of his stilling the storm in Agrigent (Clement of Alexandria, *Strom.* 6.30.1). By contrast, in Jewish traditions of stilling storms (Jon. 1; Ps. 107:23–32; T. Naph. 6:1–10; b. Bava Metzi'a 59b; y. Berakhot 9:1, 12c–13c), the appeasement of the forces of nature is accomplished as the work of God alone, who responds to the supplication of those who encounter distress at sea. The formative notion in Mark 4:35–41 that evil spirits lie behind the wind and waves, which can be hushed in a special way by qualified persons by threats and coerced manipulations, thus turns out to be genuinely Hellenistic. Rationalism explained Jesus's miracle fancifully by saying that the boat came into a cove where there was no wind or that Jesus anticipated the sudden subsiding of the storm. Along a similar line runs the conjecture that Jesus as a shaman lived in harmony with nature, had extraspecial meteorological knowledge at his disposal, and thus knew precisely when the storm would calm down (Drewermann [3]1992, 165–69). A historical origin of the story inspired by ancient traditions of stilling a storm (Mark 4:35–41) could be the transformation of boating excursions of Jesus and the disciples on the Sea of Gennesaret and the downdraft on hot days directly on a menacing body of water with lashing waves. In all other points, doubtless "poetic fantasy has usurped historical memory" (Theissen and Merz [4]2011, 268). The account responds to the question aroused by fear of the essence of Christ by reporting the epiphany of the Son of God as Lord over wind and waves. At the same time, the ability to still the storm transfers a central attribute of God's salvific activity to Jesus.

In Jesus's walking on the water, which plays out likewise on the Sea of Gennesaret (Mark 6:45–52 par. John 6:16–21), wind and waves again put the disciples in a menacing situation before the storm is calmed by the unexpected appearance of Jesus. This deliverance miracle, however, is completely suppressed by the epiphany of seeing Jesus walking on the water and possibly is only brought in later secondarily (Bultmann [9]1979, 231). The epiphany exhibits a surprising affinity to the Easter story in Luke 24:36–43, where the disciples also take Jesus's sudden appearance for a ghost, before he makes himself known with the formula "it is I." Therefore, it is frequently conjectured that a resurrection story was back-dated into the earthly life of Jesus (Madden 1997, 116–39), but this is doubtful. For the quest for the historical background, rationalistic theology envisaged a floating piece of timber on which Jesus walked, or an optical illusion for the disciples sitting in the boat, which in the fog led them to imagine Jesus walking on the water when in reality he walked along the shore (cf. Schweitzer [9]1984, 82, 91). In 2006, North American and Israeli scholars postulated the bizarre theory that Jesus did not walk on the water but on ice floes. They claimed that Palestine had at least two extended cold periods in ancient times, which would have made it possible for water to freeze near the shore. From a cultural anthropological perspective, the attempt is ventured to comprehend the report as a historically reliable tradition against the background of an altered state of consciousness of the participating eyewitnesses. The vision of Jesus walking on the water is said to be a classic example of an experience, as it could easily have been made by 80 percent of the Mediterranean population of that time without exercising any kind of stimulant (Pilch 2002, 38; cf. Malina 1999).

These explanations hardly do justice to the intention of the text. The motif of walking on water is widely attested in both Jewish and Greco-Roman tradition (Yarbro Collins 1994, 211–25). The Old Testament speaks about God's walking on the water (Job 9:8) and about God's power over the sea (Ps. 77:17). Dio Chrysostom writes programmatically that "of all men under the sun that man is most powerful and in might no whit inferior to the gods themselves who is able to accomplish the seemingly impossible—if it should be his will, to have men walk dryshod over the sea" (*3 Regn.* [*Or.* 3.30]). Rulers like Xerxes (Dio Chrysostom, *3 Regn.* [*Or.* 3.31]), Alexander the Great (Menander, *Frag.* 924K), and Antiochus IV (2 Macc. 5:21) are said to have walked across the sea to prove their divinity, or at least to have attempted to do so. Also, magicians like the Hyperboreans mocked by Lucian (*Philops.* 13) and "Corkfeeters" (*Ver. hist.* 2.4) allegedly were able to run on water without going under. Likely the ability of God or divine humans to master walking on water is attributed to Jesus without any historical points of reference (Meier 1994, 919–24) in order to demonstrate his messianism and divinity.

Finally, the account of the withered fig tree (Mark 11:12–14, 20–21) as Jesus's only punishment miracle falls beyond the pale. In the prophets the fig tree symbolizes the people of Israel. Against the background of Old Testament prophecies of judgment (Jer. 8:13; Jon. 1:7, 14), an account of a punishment miracle originated dealing with a withered fig tree that is aimed at Israel. Perhaps the parable of the fig tree in Luke 13:6–9 also influenced the formation of the tradition. By contrast, the curse of the tree likely represents a prophetic symbolic action that goes back to Jesus, with which he expressed disappointment over the rejection of his message. Later it was said that the tree had in fact withered.

2.6.5. Conclusion

Under critical analysis of resuscitations and nature miracles ascribed to Jesus, a sobering conclusion emerges. The relevant reports of miracles are substantially influenced by the faith of the church, have little that in themselves is distinctive in comparison with their ancient parallels, and with respect to their historicity are subject to quite formidable doubt. On account of their absence in the oldest level of tradition in the Gospels alone (sayings tradition, logia source), the nature miracles are met with skepticism. To be sure, individual reports of deliverance and gift miracles have historical points of contact, such as Jesus's symbolically loaded meal fellowship, his participation in a wedding, or the customary boating excursions with the disciples on the Sea of Gennesaret, but they hardly reflect historical events. In the case of resuscitations of the dead, the starting point presents itself somewhat differently, in that they are transmitted not only in the narrative tradition but also in the mouth of Jesus (Luke 7:22 par.). The reliable diagnosis of the actual incidence of death was an intensively discussed theme in antiquity, and not infrequently were persons who were unconscious or in a coma declared dead. Against this background, it lies within the realm of possibility that in particular cases Jesus called people back to life who were mistakenly taken to be dead. Of course, some go a step further and think that as a bearer of God's creative power Jesus performed resuscitations of the dead and nature miracles that cannot be explained scientifically, with which in divine freedom God put unexpected signs in the world (Reiser 2011, 158–97; cf. Keener 2011, 742–43).

Fischbach, Stefanie M. 1992. *Totenerweckungen: Zur Geschichte einer Gattung.* FB 69. Würzburg.

Kollmann, Bernd. 2005. "Totenerweckungen in der Bibel—Ausdruck von Protest und Zeichen der Hoffnung." In *Leben trotz Tod*, edited by Martin Ebner and Erich Zenger, 121–41. JBT 19. Neukirchen-Vluyn.

Labahn, Michael. 2014. "Wunder verändern die Welt: Überlegungen zum sinnkonstruierenden Charakter von Wundererzählungen am Beispiel der sogenannten 'Geschenkwunder.'" In *Hermeneutik der frühchristlichen Wundererzählungen: Geschichtliche, literarische und rezeptionsorientierte Perspektiven*, edited by Bernd Kollmann and Ruben Zimmermann, 369–93. WUNT 339. Tübingen.

Meier, John P. 1994. *A Marginal Jew: Rethinking the Historical Jesus.* Vol. 2, *Mentor, Message, and Miracles.* New York. Pages 773–1038.

Twelftree, Graham H., ed. 2017. *The Nature Miracles of Jesus: Problems, Perspectives, and Prospects.* Eugene, OR.

Bernd Kollmann

2.7. Women in Jesus's Entourage

It was not until the second half of the twentieth century that feminist theology intensively started bringing the question of the depiction of women's role in Jesus's entourage (as in New Testament writings in general) into focus. Feminist exegetes have made it clear that modern portrayals of women mentioned in the New Testament were mostly molded from the perspective of male exegetes toward women in their own environment. Simultaneously, feminist theology questioned to what extent the authors of the Gospels themselves shaped their presentations of women subjectively on the basis of the situation in their communities at the time. For instance, this holds for the language conventions in the evangelists' way of speaking, which, in antiquity, were based on androcentrism (Schüssler Fiorenza 1988, 63, 76–77 and passim; V. Phillips 2000, 24–26); for the limitation of the circle of the Twelve to men (Bieberstein 1998); as well as for the depiction of women's behavior. In this debate the so-called historical deterioration model was justly criticized (Petersen 1999, 6–9); this model postulated the increasing disintegration of the equality of men and women that had prevailed in Jesus's time. Similarly, the thesis that Jesus liberated (Jewish) women from oppression was revised (A.-J. Levine 1994), and the importance of knowledge on the role and depiction of women in contemporary Judaism was emphasized (Bauckham 2002, xvi–xvii).

In the structure of the canonical Gospels, women appear first of all as members of Jesus's family (see D.III.1) or of the families of the first disciples (Mark 1:30). From the beginning of Jesus's public appearance in Galilee, they are addressees of Jesus's message, being part of the people (see D.IV.2.8) and recipients of his powerful action in healings and exorcisms (see D.IV.2.4–5). Women follow Jesus and become his disciples (so, for instance, Mary the sister of Martha in Luke 10:38–42 and Mary Magdalene in John 20:16), although explicit accounts of their calling are absent. According to the presentation of all canonical Gospels, no women are found in the circle of the Twelve. All the Gospels assign a special role to Mary Magdalene.

According to the accounts in Mark, Jesus first comes in direct contact with women in the context of healings, which are, however, less numerous than the healings of men. According to the plot of Mark's narrative, after the first expulsion of a demon, Jesus heals Peter's mother-in-law (Mark 1:30–31). The healing power of the kingdom of God dawning in Jesus is underscored by the combination of the narrative of the resuscitation of Jairus's daughter with the healing of the woman with the chronic flow of blood (Mark 5:21–43). Women are participants in the power of the kingdom of God that encompasses the entirety of life and death; they participate in the power of God that is efficacious in Jesus. The narrative of the Syro-Phoenician woman in the border region of Tyre and Galilee, whose daughter is also healed (Mark 7:24–30), highlights that the healing power of the kingdom of God also reaches a pagan woman. By the dialogue between the Syro-Phoenician woman and Jesus, which makes reference to the universality of salvation, Mark ascribes a major function to the non-Jewish woman by referencing the reception of Jesus's message in the pagan populace. By categorically being part of the people, women are always also recipients of Jesus's message, which contains images of the environment of men and women in equal measure. In its radicality, the new constitution of the concept of family dispensing with the physical family and emphasizing the creation of the *familia Dei* instead, is valid for men just as it is for women (Mark 3:33–35), whose gender will be suspended in the eschatological kingdom of God (Mark 12:18–27). However, this new constitution is not meant to lead to a complete recension of earthly family structures; thus, the Markan Jesus radicalizes the Jewish law of divorce by forbidding it (Mark 10:2–12). Women also serve to elucidate appropriate action in the kingdom of God. The account of the poor widow, who in exemplary fashion contributes all she had to live on to the temple (Mark 12:41–44), contrasts with the pericope about the hesitant behavior of a rich man who finds Jesus's demand for him to abandon his possessions onerous (Mark 10.17–31). Moreover, the anointing of Jesus in Simon's house in Bethany by an anonymous woman, which was criticized by some of those present, is portrayed as exemplary: Jesus interprets the anointing as anticipating the anointing at his burial. Further, he emphasizes that wherever the gospel is proclaimed in the entire world, this woman will be remembered (Mark 14:3–9). By means of the literary juxtaposition of this story with the following account of Judas's betrayal, Mark underscores the exemplary behavior toward Jesus of the woman who anoints him. The account of the proleptic anointing for burial together with the action of three women who go to the empty tomb to anoint Jesus frames the passion narrative. Even though by means of the Syro-Phoenician woman and the anointing woman Mark demonstrates Jesus's significance beyond Israel, it is not until the passion narrative that the women disciples who had already followed him from Galilee and served him are identified by name (Mark 15:40–41). Standing out from the group are Mary Magdalene, Mary the "mother of James the younger and Joses" (presumably the same as Mary the mother "of Joses" in Mark 15:47 and Mary the mother "of James" in Mark 16:1; Reiprich 2008, 162–64, identifies her with Mary the mother of Jesus), and Salome (possibly Jesus's sister; cf. Bauckham 2002, 225–56). They watch the crucifixion from a distance with other women. All three women are Jewish, their family situation permitting them to affiliate with Jesus—either because their husbands followed Jesus (cf. also Mark 10:29) or because they are unmarried. In the literary construct of characters, this group of three parallels the three most prominent disciples (Mark 5:37; 9:2; 14:33). Even though these named women do not belong to the exclusively male circle of the Twelve, they are prominent disciples of Jesus in that they believe Jesus's teaching, follow him all the way to the cross, and serve him after the crucifixion (Melzer-Keller 1997, 54–55; cf. earlier the feminine figuration for Jesus's disciples in Mark 3:33–35 and the call to follow in Mark 8:34–35). In distinction from the male disciples and the circle of the Eleven, the women are witnesses of Jesus's death, his burial, and the message about his resurrection (cf. 1 Cor. 15:3b–5). The two women named Mary in Mark 15:40–41 observe the place of the burial (Mark 15:47); all three women take aromatic ointments to the tomb (Mark 16:1). The three women are ultimately the first recipients of the message of the resurrection, and they are commissioned by the angel in the empty tomb to report to Peter and the other disciples about the reunion with Jesus that is expected in Galilee (Mark 16:7; cf. 14:28). The women's fright at the tomb is to be understood as a reaction to the appearance of the angel and the encounter with divine power (cf. Mark 2:12; 4:41; Melzer-Keller 1997, 64–65, by contrast, sees in the fear of the women an analogy to the misunderstanding of the [male] disciples). The women's silence about what they experienced (Mark 16:8), however, stands in contrast with those who were healed in the gospel repeatedly violating the command to silence. Together with the women's fear, this presents a dramatic climax, giving utmost importance to the message of the resurrection and hermeneutical potential to the scene. In the secondary ending of the gospel, Jesus appears first to Mary Magdalene, who reports her vision to the disciples, and only thereafter Jesus appears to the disciples (Mark 16:9–20). This text indicates the special role of Mary Magdalene in one part of the Jesus tradition, which is also described by the Gospel of John and the Gospels according to Mary and Philip.

In Matthew, women are found in Jesus's genealogy and, from the very beginning, take a central role in the narrative—predominantly through the role of Mary in the birth story (see D.III.1). In addition, almost all texts from Mark centering on women are found in Matthew; but Matthew dispenses with the exemplary magnanimous widow and transmits the healing story of the woman with the chronic flow of blood and her exemplary faith and the resuscitation of the synagogue leader's daughter in a distinctly shorter form. On the other hand, the Canaanite (Syro-Phoenician) woman is now praised for her "great faith" (Matt. 15:28). Matthew takes into account the integration of pagan and sinful women into the company of Jesus's followers. References to women among the μαθηταί and the circle of the Twelve, however, are missing; since Matthew obviously understands the disciples and the Twelve to be identical, he thereby appears to reflect the situation of male domination in the Matthean community (Melzer-Keller 1997, 182–85; the metaphorical talk in 12:49 can hardly be a reference to women among the μαθηταί). In the preaching of the Matthean Jesus, women are explicit addressees (cf. Matt. 10:34–36 par. Luke 12:49–53), especially in the context of his depictions of the eschaton (Matt. 24:40–41; 25:1–13), which will pertain to women as well as to men. Members of socially marginal groups (tax collectors and prostitutes) will also be part of the eschatological kingdom of God (Matt. 21:31), which will be shaped by the ideal of abstinence (Matt. 19:12). The directives of the Matthean Jesus for conduct in life on earth are addressed in equal measure to men and women. In Matthew, marriage is also the target of special regulations (Matt. 5:27–32), which are nonetheless relativized in view of the focus on circumstances in the coming kingdom of God (Matt. 19:12; 22:23–33 par.). In the passion narrative, the mother of the sons of Zebedee is mentioned as the third woman at the cross (27:55–56), who is perhaps identical with Salome in Mark. More generally, in Matthew, the sons of Zebedee are given an especially prominent role among the disciples (Matt. 20:20; 26:37). However, only the two Marys are witnesses at the tomb, where they not only react to the message of the angel about the resurrection with fear—as in Mark—but also with joy

(Matt. 28:8). The two women are also the ones to whom the risen One appears first; he also gives them the mandate to send the disciples to Galilee, where they would see him. In contradistinction to the disciples (Matt. 28:17), the two women entertain no doubt during this encounter. In their joy over the message and their belief in the truth of the vision and audition of the risen One, Mary Magdalene and the "other" Mary are exemplary believers, the first witnesses of the resurrection, and recipients of a mandate. Contrasting with Mark's presentation, the women in Matthew pass on the summons to the disciples to see Jesus in Galilee. In doing so, Matthew assigns them a significant communicative role in what follows. Matthew 28:16–20 then gives a report about this vision and the audition of the circle of the eleven disciples.

Separately from the prologue (Luke 1–2; see D.III.1), which focuses on women from Jesus's family and the prophet Anna, the Gospel of Luke also contains the greatest number of texts that place women into the events as actors, wherein they often are paralleled with male actors. Therefore, women appear in Luke in the accounts of the birth, passion, and resurrection at central places in the gospel. Luke depicts an additional story of the healing of a woman (Luke 13:10–17; cf. 14:1–6) and portrays Jesus as the one who, in accordance with his proclamation, turns especially to the outcasts and the poor. This becomes clear, for instance, in the story about the sinful woman who anoints Jesus (Luke 7:36–50; cf. Mark 14:3–9), but also in his compassion for the widow in Nain (Luke 7:13), or by means of the metaphorical stories in Luke 18:1–8 and 21:1–4. In these stories, not only suffering women in need are at the center of attention, but also socially marginalized groups more broadly speaking (Luke 5:27–32; 15:1). The group of the three women initially highlighted by Mark and Matthew in the context of the passion narratives is complemented by Luke's stories of the prologue around the triad of Elizabeth, Mary, and Anna, who already recognize the conception and birth of Jesus as a divine revelatory event. Quite early in the narrative, Luke introduces women disciples of Jesus who in Mark and Matthew do not come into focus until the accounts of the passion: in addition to the Twelve, many women who in part support Jesus financially are already named in the Galilean cycle (Luke 8:1–3), where Mary Magdalene; Joanna, the wife of Chuza, a steward of Herod Antipas; and Susanna (as persons healed by Jesus) are noted by name. With the introduction of Joanna, Luke emphasizes the importance of Jesus's activity in Galilee and the success of his proclamation in the social upper class (Bauckham 2002, 109–61). In addition, Luke introduces Jesus's encounter with the sisters Mary and Martha (Luke 10:38–42), in which Mary becomes an exemplary believer by listening to Jesus's message. By sitting at Jesus's feet, she is depicted as his pupil (cf. Acts 22:3), whose action Jesus evaluates as "good" in comparison to Martha's serving. From this as well as other passages, Bieberstein (1998, 281) concludes that Luke uses the concept of μαθηταί inclusively. Just as in Mark and Matthew, women are again witnesses of the crucifixion (Luke 23:49), but now Jesus's "acquaintances" also stand in the vicinity of the cross. Lamenting women, who contrast with the people who favor Jesus's death, accompany Jesus to the cross (Luke 23:27–31) and then also accompany his body to the tomb (Luke 23:55–56). In the resurrection account, Mary Magdalene—as in Mark and Matthew—Mary (the mother of James; cf. Mark 15:40), and Joanna are highlighted as witnesses (Luke 24:10; cf. 8:3). Luke interprets the angel's message of the resurrection by means of the prediction of the passion and resurrection (Luke 9:22), which was also addressed to the women (Luke 24:7–8). Thereafter, together with the two Marys and Joanna, other women also (cf. Luke 8:1–3) bring the message of the resurrection to the Twelve and the disciples, whereas Peter alone reacts to the message. Luke's concept of portraying women explicitly as addressees and patrons of the propagation of the message of Christ is continued in Acts (Acts 9:36–43; 16:11–15).

In comparison with the Synoptics, the compiler of the Gospel of John mentions women less, does not call any women disciples by name, does not report any healings of women, yet assigns key hermeneutical positions to various female figures over the course of the narrative. This applies to Jesus's mother, who is assigned an important role as early as the first miracle (John 2:1–12), who accompanies Jesus (John 2:12), and together with her sister also stands at the cross (John 19:25); moreover, this also applies to the Samaritan woman at Jacob's well (John 4:1–30), who poses the question about Jesus's messianic identity (John 4:29). In addition, John, like Luke, gives a report of Jesus's encounter with Mary and Martha in Bethany (John 12:1–11; 11:2), assigning these two women an even more important role than persons whom Jesus "loved"—such as their brother Lazarus (John 11:5). Martha identifies Jesus as Messiah, the Son of God (11:27; cf. Peter in Mark 8:27–30 par.). In addition, John 11:2 seems to identify Mary with the anonymous woman who anoints Jesus (Mark 14:3–9 par.). The resuscitation of Lazarus and Jesus's conversation with Mary about raising the dead anticipate Jesus's resurrection and indicate its theological dimension (John 11:1–45). By contrast, the pericope of Jesus's encounter with the sinful woman is secondary (John 7:53–8:11). To what extent women's special function in John can be explained on the grounds of the situation in the Johannine community is subject to debate (Hartenstein 2012, 432–33). Just as in the Synoptic Gospels, Mary Magdalene plays a special role, yet as in Mark and Matthew, she first appears as an observer of the crucifixion (John 19:25). Although in the Synoptic Gospels she was not among the witnesses of the crucifixion, here she is named together with the mother of Jesus and her sister, (and with) Mary Cleopas's wife (on this, see Bauckham 2002, 203–23). John moves the mother of Jesus (and the favorite disciple) to the center as attendees of the crucifixion, but Mary Magdalene is also assigned a central role in the discovery of the empty tomb (John 20:1–18; Taschl-Erber 2007). In contrast to Peter and the disciple whom Jesus loved, Mary ponders the absence of the dead body; she is granted the first appearance of Christ, in which John characterizes her as his obedient disciple by her way of addressing Jesus ("*rabbouni*"), and which she reports to the disciples according to Jesus's instruction with the words "I have seen the Lord" (John 20:18). The first vision of Christ by Mary is of great importance for the narrative and gains special significance against the background of Paul's self-understanding as an apostle on the basis of his vision of Christ (1 Cor. 9:1).

Mary (Hebrew Miriam) from Magdala (presumably the present-day el-Meğdel on the West Bank of the Sea of Gennesaret) is portrayed as an apparently unmarried disciple of Jesus who, according to statements in all the Gospels, witnesses Jesus's crucifixion and resurrection. According to the Synoptic Gospels, Mary also observes the entombment (namely, in Mark 15:47 and Matt. 27:61; as part of the "women" in Luke 23:55). Since Mary is a witness of the resurrection and the first one to receive a vision of Christ, she also has central significance after the resurrection (Matt. 28:9–10; John 20:11–18; secondarily Mark 16:9–11). Although in 1 Cor. 15:5–8 Paul does not mention Mary among the witnesses of the resurrection, from a historical perspective, these narratives point toward her discipleship early in Galilee and possibly a leading position in the oldest community (Taschl-Erber 2007, 477). In addition, they put Mary in competition with Peter, which also explains the later tradition about her: in apocryphal writings she is depicted as Jesus's favorite disciple, who receives special revelations from him, passes these on to the disciples, and is impugned by Peter (Gospel of Mary; Gospel of Philip; Petersen 1999).

Due to various hermeneutical problems, the question of how the Gospels represent women in detail remains unresolved (see on this Bauckham 2002, xv–xvi); nevertheless, we can summarize—also in view of historical probabilities: the Gospels consistently report the presence of women already in Jesus's Galilean environment, and these women are impressed by Jesus's proclamation and by his powerful healings. Therefore, the Gospels' thoroughly positive characterization of female figures toward Jesus is remarkable (Pellegrini 2012, 410–12). It is equally clear that women had a place in Jesus's entourage (which makes the Jesus movement like other Jewish groups at the time; Ilan 2000, 125–28); among them were presumably both married and single women, poor and wealthy women. The mentioned names probably reflect the historical names of female followers of Jesus (Ilan 2000, 121–23; Bauckham 2002). Equally clear is women's special function in the context of the events of the crucifixion and resurrection, Mary Magdalene being consistently presented as a particularly prominent female disciple of Jesus.

Bauckham, Richard J. 2002. *Gospel Women: Studies of the Named Women in the Gospels*. Grand Rapids.

Kitzberger, Ingrid Rosa, ed. 2000. *Transformative Encounters: Jesus and Women Re-Viewed*. BibInt 43. Leiden.

Melzer-Keller, Helga 1997. *Jesus und die Frauen*. Freiburg.

Petersen, Silke. 2011. *Maria aus Magdala: Die Jüngerin, die Jesus liebte*. Biblische Gestalten 23. Leipzig.

Standhartinger, Angela. 2004. "Geschlechterperspektiven auf die Jesusbewegung." *Zeitschrift für Pädagogik und Theologie* 4: 308–18.

Christiane Zimmermann

2.8. Jesus and the People

With his proclamation as well as his mighty actions, Jesus primarily addressed the Jewish people, who, especially in Mark, but also in Matthew and Luke, seldom in John, are designated with the lexeme ὄχλος (multitude of people). In this context, ὄχλος evokes a large number of people without further differentiation, representing the "ordinary" people functioning as Jesus's addressees, although a part of these people is also of pagan origin. Alongside the group of Jewish leaders and the group of the Twelve emerging from the people, as an ongoing audience of Jesus, the people constitute a central body responding to Jesus's teaching and activity. The frequent pejorative connotation of ὄχλος (rabble) found in contemporaneous pagan literature is not implied in the Gospels; this rather fits the lexeme γενεὰ αὕτη, the generation of people of Jesus's time, which nevertheless can also refer to targeted adversarial characters (see, for instance, Q 7:31–35; 11:14–52; Mark 9:19). In addition to the lexeme ὄχλος, the numerical lexemes πολλοί, πάντες, and πλῆθος also appear as designations of the large number of people. Frequently, however, the people as a literary character are concealed in the predicate of a sentence ("them"), in personal pronouns, or in local descriptions ("the whole Judean countryside and all the inhabitants of Jerusalem," Mark 1:5; "the whole city," Mark 1:33). The people are not an invariably consistent entity, which also explains the distinctive reactions of the people to Jesus's activity in Galilee and on the occasion of the Passover amnesty in Jerusalem. Although the primary addressees of Jesus's message are initially identical with the people of God, the lexeme λαός seldom appears in Mark, by contrast more frequently in Matthew and Luke, and is restricted to the chosen people of Israel based on the language of the Septuagint (but cf. Luke 2:31). As a rule, the ὄχλος—also including pagan female and male auditors—is the part of the λαός confronted with

Jesus's proclamation over the course of the narrative. The extent to which ὄχλος and λαός refer to the same group, however, has to be determined on a case-by-case basis—translating both lexemes with "people" would blur the nuances. The thematic inclusion of λαός raises the historical question about hope for a final salvation of the members of the people as λαὸς Ἰσραήλ who hitherto have not turned to believing in Christ. This question is increasingly answered positively (Konradt 2007, 89–91 for Matthew; Schröter 2007a, 261, 263 for Luke). The lexeme ἔθνος refers either to a people in the sense of "nation," which can also mean the Jewish people (Luke 23:2; John 18:35), or to the religious status of non-Jewish people ("non-Jews"). Hence the ἔθνη appear especially as a contrasting entity or group, who will increasingly come into contact with the message of salvation after Jesus's death and resurrection (Matt. 28:19).

In the Gospels the people serve as literary characters who directly encounter Jesus's teaching and salvific activity on behalf of God (cf. Luke 24:19: "Jesus of Nazareth, who was a prophet mighty in deed and word before God and all the people"). They elucidate the broad, positive response to Jesus, yet also help to highlight a nuanced account of Jesus's identity. In doing so, the evangelists suggest the representation of historical processes, but at the same time, the view of the people is strongly shaped by a post-Easter perspective. From the latter perspective the people serve both as a depiction of the distinct ways of receiving Jesus's deeds and teaching and as a parenetic foil aimed at the communities addressed by the evangelists. Depending on the evaluation of the people, they are considered the primary character with which readers identify (Minear 1972, 89), or take second place behind the disciples (Meiser 1998, 212).

For Jesus's relationship with the people, the metaphor of "sheep without a shepherd" (Num. 27:17; Mark 6:34; Matt. 9:36; John 10:7, 9) is pivotal; on the one hand, it depicts the deficient situation of the people, but on the other hand, it illustrates Jesus's function of safeguarding and leading—he can save the people by teaching and healing them as well as by feeding them. Whereas repeatedly Jesus's teaching of the people is simply stated, at times it is also described as a teaching considered "astonishing" (Mark 1:22; 6:2; 11:18). In connection with healings, most of which focus on specific individuals from the people, his teaching sparks various reactions such as admiration and acclamations of the people. Admiring reactions such as wonder, astonishment, and fear (θαυμάζειν, ἐκπλήσσεσθαι, φοβεῖσθαι) demonstrate—especially in the conclusions to miracle stories—how divine power is perceived and results in commitment to Jesus. Reactions of acclamation (δοξάζειν) confirm this perception and indicate thereby the continuity of divine fidelity to the people (of Israel), which is powerfully shown again in Jesus (Meiser 1998, 74–108, 369–70). The people illustrate the growing success of Jesus's proclamation and salvific power, inasmuch as the number of those wanting to come close to Jesus grows constantly and in part even hinders Jesus's action (Mark 2:4); yet Jesus's success among the people contrasts with the critical attitude of the religious leaders. In the passion narrative, the people of Jerusalem, by speaking up for the release of Barabbas under the influence of Jewish leaders in the context of the Passover amnesty, contribute to Jesus's crucifixion.

To date, the investigation of this collective literary character has not attracted significant attention, especially not in regards to its individual characterization in the respective gospels (cf. Meiser 1998, 2–30; Cousland 2002, 3–21). Moreover, the particular significance of this literary figure is assessed differently. Within the Gospels, one can identify the following distinct emphases in the portrayal of the people.

Mark sparsely employs the lexeme λαός and describes the ὄχλος as Jesus's primary and continuous audience, from which the disciples and the Twelve originate. Jesus teaches the people repeatedly, he challenges them to listen and to understand (Mark 7:14); the people can possibly be understood as part of the group gaining access to the secret of the kingdom of God (Mark 4:10–11; Minear 1972, 82). The people, together with the circle of disciples, are subject to the call to follow (Mark 8:34). However, in distinction from the disciples, the people do not identify Jesus as the anointed one but as John the Baptizer, as Elijah, and as one of the prophets (Mark 8:27–29). Nevertheless, the people are the recipients not only of Jesus's teaching and salvific power but also of his affective devotion: Jesus has compassion for the starving people (Mark 6:34; 8:2) and tasks the disciples with taking care of them after Easter (Mark 6:37; 8:4–6). Healings and feeding miracles lead the people to perceive the divine power at work in Jesus (Mark 9:15), and they react in the ways mentioned above. The people in Judea also react positively to Jesus (Mark 10:1). In Jerusalem, the Jewish leaders fear the people not only because they comprise a large number of adherents but also because of their response to Jesus's teaching (Mark 11:18), and they decide to arrest Jesus. The last four instances of ὄχλος in Mark (14:43; 15:8, 11, 15) refer to a group of the people of Jerusalem joining the upheaval against Jesus and contributing to his crucifixion. By contrast, in the passion narrative, the ὄχλος preceding Jesus and rejoicing at him as he enters Jerusalem (Mark 11:7–9) is only represented by the women at the cross who came from Galilee (Mark 15:40–41), who function as their own group of characters.

Among the evangelists, Matthew characterizes the people most clearly (Cousland 2002). From the outset, he emphasizes Jesus's function as savior of his people (Matt. 1:21). His people include the non-Jewish peoples through the history of salvation (Matt. 1:1, on this see Konradt 2007, 286–88; Matt. 4:15; 5:16; 12:21; and explicitly 28:19). Matthew employs the lexeme λαός instead of ὄχλος far more frequently than does Mark, whereas ὄχλος refers to people who are present (Poplutz

2008, 105–6). However, the extent to which the two lexemes consistently have the same referent is a matter of discussion, especially in view of Matt. 27:24–25 (Konradt 2007, 169). Matthew gives his portrayal of the people a clear Israel-theological character (Meier 1998, 247–57). He reinforces the positive relations of the ὄχλος with Jesus and ascribes some critical comments of the people in a passage taken from Q to the Pharisees (Matt. 9:32–34; 12:22–24). In addition, he contrasts the reactions of the people more strongly with those of the religious leaders (Matt. 9:32–34). In the Sermon on the Mount, the people are corecipients of Jesus's extensive admonitions (Matt. 5:1), they recognize his power, and they react to it with astonishment (Matt. 7:28–29; on the meaning of ἐξεπλήσσοντο, see Konradt 2007, 98). In Jesus, the people recognize God's compassionate devotion to Israel (Matt. 9:33), and Jesus himself as the promised Davidic Messiah (Konradt 2007, 96–108). Matthew replaces the πολλοί who rejoice at the Markan Jesus as he enters Jerusalem explicitly with ὁ πλεῖστος ὄχλος (Matt. 21:8). In the passion accounts in Matthew, the crowd of people acting against Jesus (Matt. 27:24–25) are differentiated from the other ὄχλοι as a local group in Jerusalem.

Like Mark and Matthew, Luke uses the people as respondents to Jesus's activity and shares a view of the people as the people of Israel with Matthew (Meiser 1998, 270–78). The lexeme λαός appears in Luke almost as frequently as ὄχλος and is already employed in the Lukan prologue to describe the meaning of the birth of Jesus for the people of Israel (Luke 2:10). Whereas the lexeme ὄχλος in Luke especially serves to portray the reactions of the people to Jesus's teaching and healings, with the lexeme λαός Luke usually zeros in on the destiny of the people of Israel. In comparison to Mark and Matthew, in various passages he replaces ὄχλος or πλῆθος with λαός or amplifies it (e.g., Luke 6:17; 7:1; 8:47; 9:13). And yet, Luke already stresses Jesus's significance beyond Israel in Simeon's prophecy: Jesus is the salvation πάντων τῶν λαῶν, which split between the ἔθνη and the λαός σου Ἰσραήλ (2:31–32). At the same time, from the outset, the failure to accept this salvation is taken into account (2:34). In the passion narrative, alongside a critical evaluation of the λαός, we find Jesus's sorrow over his rejection by the people. Luke gives expression to this sorrow by supplementing the lament from Q (Luke 13:34–35 par.) with Jesus's weeping over Jerusalem (Luke 19:41–44). In the passion narrative, Luke depicts more strongly than Mark or Matthew how Jesus turns to the people in Jerusalem whom he gathers in the temple (Luke 19:47 par.; 21:37–38). In Luke 19:47–21:38 he designates the people exclusively as λαός in order to highlight the concentration of events on the Jewish people (Meiser 1998, 316). In the scene with Pilate, he reduces the role of the people (Luke 23:13–25), places the leaders in the foreground (Luke 24:19–20), and introduces the women of Jerusalem, who lament Jesus's death, and the man crucified along with Jesus who declares him innocent (Luke 23:27; 23:41). The rejection of the glad tidings by parts of the people of Israel is criticized and lamented at the same time; in addition, as in Matthew, the hope of the salvation of all of Israel prevails (Luke 24:21; Schröter 2007a, 261, 263). From a post-Easter perspective, Jesus's actions and admonitions to the people serve as the basis for faith and as didactic pareneses for the present of the Lukan community (Meiser 1998, 336–50, 359; cf., for instance, Luke 11:27–28; 12:4–21).

John has Jesus act as the incarnate Logos not in front of the people but in front of the world (κόσμος). In doing so, John generalizes Jesus's addressees from the beginning; his appearance pertains to everybody (John 1:7; cf. also 11:51–52), not a local or religiously defined group. Only in John 6, 7, and 12 do the people appear more prominently, whereas John paints a picture of the people partially resembling opponents from the group of Ἰουδαῖοι (Bennema 2013; cf. for a diversified assessment of the Ἰουδαῖοι, Kierspel 2006), or he identifies the people with the κόσμος (John 12:17–19); and yet, the people and the Ἰουδαῖοι are again characters responding positively to Jesus's teaching and activity (cf. John 7:31–32 and 12:9–11). Thus, the questions of the people, like those of the Ἰουδαῖοι, spur the plot and facilitate theological reflection.

Especially in the Synoptic Gospels, the people are the decisive characters encountering Jesus's actions and teaching and exhibit varying degrees of readiness for acceptance. Whereas the response to Jesus's proclamation in Galilee is described with the growing size of the people following him, the people of Jerusalem play a significant negative role in Jesus's trial. Deliberately using a post-Easter perspective and under the influence of Q, Matthew and Luke depict the people as the people of Israel to a greater extent than does Mark. The hope for Israel's complete salvation prevails for these two evangelists. Thus, in all the Gospels, the people as a literary character (constituted by Jews and non-Jews) demonstrate the universal possibilities and consequences of accepting or rejecting the message of Christ.

Bennema, Cornelis. 2013. "The Crowd: A Faceless, Divided Mass." In *Character Studies in the Fourth Gospel: Narrative Approaches to 70 Figures in John*, edited by Steven A. Hunt et al., 347–55. WUNT 314. Tübingen.

Cousland, J. R. C. 2002. *The Crowds in the Gospel of Matthew*. NovTSup 102. Leiden.

Malbon, Elizabeth Struthers. 2000. *In the Company of Jesus: Characters in Mark's Gospel*. Louisville.

Meiser, Martin. 1998. *Die Reaktion des Volkes auf Jesus: Eine redaktionskritische Untersuchung zu den synoptischen Evangelien*. BZNW 96. Berlin and New York.

Siegert, Folker. 2000. "Jesus und sein Volk in der Quelle Q." In *Israel als Gegenüber: Vom alten Orient bis in die Gegenwart; Studien zur Geschichte eines wechselvollen Zusammenlebens*, edited by Folker Siegert, 90–124. Göttingen.

Christiane Zimmermann

2.9. Jesus's Perspective on Israel

Among the most important characteristics of recent research on Jesus is the insight that first and foremost Jesus's activity was aimed at Israel. Hence, God's chosen people, the people with whom he established his covenant and to whom he gave his directive, the Torah, come to the fore as the addressees of Jesus's teaching, his healings, and his call to follow. By contrast, non-Israelites occur only sporadically in the Jesus tradition. This becomes apparent already in the geographical concentration of Jesus's presence in the regions under Jewish influence, namely, Galilee and Judea. The traditions about Jesus's excursions in the Decapolis (Mark 5:1–20 par.; Mark 7:31–37), in the Phoenician coastal region around Tyre (and Sidon; Mark 7:24–30 par. Matt. 15:21–28), as well as in the villages of Caesarea Philippi (Mark 8:27–30 par. Matt. 16:13–20) report incidental "detours" in the neighboring regions of Galilee; they do not alter the picture of Jesus's activity directed toward Israel but rather confirm it in their own way. In addition, these accounts are concentrated in Mark and therefore present a specific feature of Mark's portrayal of Jesus. By contrast, the question about the relationship of Israel and the gentiles in Matthew and Luke is worked out in its own way. Finally, in John "Greeks" (John 7:35; 12:20) or non-Jews (10:16: "other sheep"; 11:52: the "dispersed children of God") are occasionally mentioned, but these references also make clear that Jesus's activity is primarily oriented toward Israel.

Accordingly, Jesus's activity is only comprehensible when it is apprehended in its Jewish environment and in its rootedness in Israel's Scriptures and traditions. Thereby it becomes transparent that Jesus understood himself to be endowed with the mandate to bring God's dominion over his people to fruition. Hence, his appearance came about at a time when Israel stood under Roman sovereignty and their expectations were turned to the hope that God's action promised to his people in Israel's Scriptures might soon come about. These expectations could be directed toward the coming of a deliverer sent by God or anointed by God, who would liberate the people from foreign domination, raise up the sovereignty of the house of David, and govern Israel in justice. Such hopes were coupled with Jesus's person and his ministry by his disciples and sympathizers, which is perceptible in texts like Mark 11:1–10 (at the entrance into Jerusalem, Jesus is received with the cry, "Blessed is the coming kingdom of our father David") and Luke 1:32–33 (at the annunciation of the birth of Jesus, it is stated, "He will be great and will be called Son of the Most High, and the Lord God will give him the throne of his father David. And he will rule over the house of Jacob forever"). Thus, the hope was linked with Jesus to the effect that he would put an end to Roman domination over Israel and raise up the Davidic rule.

To be sure, Jesus's ministry is not only and also not in the first place to be explained by the social and political circumstances in Galilee and Judea, even though by all means these played a role. Jesus's activity and teaching are not primarily a reaction to foreign domination and social oppression, because in the time of Jesus there were no profound political and social tensions in Galilee. Antipas, the ruler of Galilee in Jesus's time, pursued a politics of economic upswing and largely respected the Jewish character of the territory he ruled. Moreover, the situation between Romans and Jews was not strained in the same way as in Judea and Jerusalem, because at the time of Jesus and Antipas, no Roman military were stationed in Galilee. The general conditions for the appearance of Jesus are therefore not to be explained in the first place from the politico-social situation. His activity aimed rather at Israel's restitution on the basis of its Scriptures and traditions, which form the decisive foundation.

First and foremost, Jesus wanted to mediate God's kingdom and salvation and to bring God's will to fruition in Israel. Hence his call to join the kingdom of God breaking in through his activity stood at the center. The political and social implications are to be understood against this background. Thus, the designations "Anointed One" (Messiah, Christ), "Son of God," "Son of David," and also "Son of Man" are defined anew and in this way are adopted into Christian faith (see E.IV).

To put into concrete terms the context of Jesus's activity, his self-understanding, and his perspective toward Israel, the region of his activity and the Jewish groups of Jesus's time are considered in detail in the context of relevant traditions for his ministry. Following this, features of Jesus's ministry that characterize his view toward Israel are investigated.

2.9.1. The Geographical Perspective of Jesus's Activity

The center of Jesus's activity was located in Galilee (see D.III.4). According to the Synoptic Gospels, the region around the Sea of Gennesaret, in particular the village of Capernaum, constitutes the center. Among the other Galilean locations, which are mentioned in the Gospels, are Nazareth (Mark 1:9; Matt. 2:23; Luke 1:26; 4:16; John 1:45–46; and passim), Cana (John 2:1), and Nain (Luke 7:11). By contrast, the Galilean cities Sepphoris and Tiberias do not come into view. Tiberias is mentioned only in John 6:1, 23 and 21:1, but not as a location of Jesus's activity; Sepphoris is never named. Magdala, another important Galilean place, comes into view only as Mary's hometown. According to Mark 6:45, Jesus goes to Bethsaida with his disciples in the territory of Herod's son Philip, in Mark 8:22, where the healing of a blind man takes place; in John 1:44 and 12:21 Bethsaida is also mentioned as the hometown of Jesus's disciples; in Matt. 11:21 par. Luke 10:13 Bethsaida is addressed together with Chorazin in Jesus's announcement of woes.

From this it follows that Jesus's activity concentrated essentially on the villages of Galilee, whereas there is no evidence that Jesus also went to Sepphoris and Tiberias or to Magdala, which were under urban influence. Therefore, the Galilean villages, especially the region around the Sea of Gennesaret, evidently constituted the primary social and religious context of his activity.

Together with Samaria, Galilee was part of the Northern Kingdom, which, as a result of the Assyrian conquest in the eighth century BCE, took on its own development over against Judea. Unlike Samaria, apparently no foreign population was located in Galilee. After a phase of presumably sparse settlement in the Persian and early Hellenistic periods, in the course of the Maccabean, or Hasmonean, conquests in the second and first centuries BCE, the Jewish population of Galilee clearly increased. Especially under the Hasmonean Aristobulus I (104–103 BCE), Galilee was settled from Judea and integrated religiously and culturally into the region under Jewish rule (apparently also by coercive measures to which Flavius Josephus refers, *Ant.* 13.318–319). Accordingly, the earlier, occasionally asserted cultural tension between Galilee and Judea does not apply to the time of Jesus, which Jesus's visits to Jerusalem indicate (according to the Gospel of John, there were several such excursions, especially in connection with Jewish feasts, which is quite plausible). It is to be assumed that non-Jews also lived in Galilee, to which the characterization "Galilee of the Gentiles" in Isa. 9:1 could refer. Nevertheless, in no way does this lead to the conclusion that Galilee was under gentile influence at the time of Jesus's activity (cf. Chancey 2002). The citation of Isa. 9:1 in Matt. 4:15–16 cannot be adduced for this. Rather, this citation expresses programmatically that Jesus's activity goes beyond Israel and is also aimed at gentiles—which at the end of Matthew, with the risen One's commission to teach and make disciples of *all nations*, then also takes place.

The Jewish influence on Galilee in the Hasmonean or Roman period is confirmed by recent archaeological research, which attests a lively Jewish religious praxis (Reed 2000; Fiensy and Strange 2014–2015). The Jewish character of locations such as Sepphoris (Zippori), Magdala (Migdal), Capernaum (Kfar Nahum), and Jotapata (Yodefat) is attested by synagogues; stone vessels, which indicated the observance of ritual purity prescriptions; the absence of swine bones; and dwellings with mikvehs. These make it clear that Jewish piety defined the cultural and everyday life in Galilee at the time of Jesus, irrespective of regional differences in Judea and Jerusalem. This is to be presupposed as the cultural milieu for Jesus, his followers, and his addressees.

At the same time, there were presumably rivalries between the predominantly agrarian Galilee and the religious elites as well as the urban population in Judea and Jerusalem, who considered Galilee to be an insignificant province with an uneducated rural population (cf., for instance, Matt. 26:73; John 7:49–52; Acts

2:7). Also, tensions between the Pharisees and the Sadducees, the latter belonging to the Jerusalem temple aristocracy (cf. Mark 12:18; Acts 23:6–9), fit in here. But a fundamental conflict between Galilee and Judea is not to be concluded from this. Rather, it is to be assumed that from the time of the Hasmonean expansion close relationships existed between Judea/Jerusalem and Galilee, which were grounded in the emphatic significance of Jerusalem and the temple as the center of Jewish religion (Freyne 2001). The appearance of Jesus in Jerusalem is to be understood not least of all against this background.

Jesus's sojourn in the Decapolis on the east bank of the Sea of Gennesaret reported in the Synoptic Gospels makes it clear that he enters a non-Jewish area. The existence of a herd of swine (Mark 5:11 par.) would be unthinkable in a Jewish region such as Galilee. In the story of the encounter of Jesus with a Syro-Phoenician woman reported in Mark and Matthew (Matthew: Canaanite), it is emphasized that the healing of her daughter presents an exception, which takes place only after Jesus made her aware of the distinction between Jews and gentiles (in the figuration of "children" and "dogs"; in Matthew, supplemented by Jesus's indication that he was sent only to the "lost sheep of the house of Israel"). It is the persistence or the faith of the woman, however, that finally leads to the healing of her daughter (Mark 7:29; Matt. 15:28). The healing of a centurion's son reported in Matt. 8 and Luke 7 can be put beside this. In the Matthean version of the story, the orientation of Jesus's ministry to Israel is emphasized again (Matt. 8:7 is presumably to be understood as a rhetorical question: "Should *I* come and heal him?"). Accordingly, all three episodes indicate that Jesus's activity extended to the bordering areas of Galilee, without being construed as an active turning to gentiles. Rather, Jesus might have gone to these areas because he envisaged them to be part of the land to which God's promises for the restoration of Israel applied and therefore wanted to extend his activity to them.

The geographical profile of Jesus's appearance also becomes clear in the summaries, which present his activity as oriented toward "all Galilee" (Mark 1:39 par. Matt. 4:23; cf. Luke 4:14; Acts 10:37) or enumerate those areas from which the sick were brought so that he might heal them (Mark 3:7–8; Luke 6:17). The last-mentioned places show that the news about Jesus also reached regions outside of Galilee: Jerusalem and Judea, the land east of the Jordan, the Syro-Phoenician coastal region, and Idumea. With this, that region is approximately delineated to which especially from Hasmonean times the hopes for the establishment of God's dominion in the promised land were directed (cf. Freyne 2004).

Jesus's appearance in Jerusalem, which led to the confrontation with the Jewish authorities (see D.III.5), belongs in this context, since it is an expression of his ministry to all Israel. Jerusalem as the location of the temple, seat of the Sanhedrin and the high priest, was the religious and political center of Judaism. The political conditions in Judea and Jerusalem are thereby distinguished from those in Galilee. Judea was under the control of a Roman prefect, and a Roman cohort was stationed in Jerusalem. By contrast, Galilee was farmed out to Antipas, who was responsible for tribute to the Romans.

Jesus's call to repentance and discipleship in view of the dawning kingdom of God through his activity was accordingly a program for Israel's renewal as the people chosen by God. With this he came into conflict with the Jewish authorities in Jerusalem, but also with Jewish groups of his time, such as the Pharisees, Sadducees, and scribes mentioned in the Gospels.

2.9.2. Jesus's Stance toward Jewish Traditions

Needless to say, Jesus shared with his Jewish contemporaries belief in the God of Israel as the one and only God (Mark 10:18 par. Matt. 19:17; Luke 18:19; Mark 12:29), the conviction of the significance of the Torah and the Prophets as Israel's fundamental writings (cf. Matt. 5:17; 7:12; 11:13; Luke 24:44; John 1:45), as well as the temple as the religious center of the people. From Jesus's perspective, the central content of Torah is encapsulated in the so-called double love command (Mark 12:29–31; Matt. 22:37–40; Luke 10:27): the commandment to love one's neighbor (Lev. 19:18) is put side by side with the commandment to love God (Deut. 6:5). Jesus's stance toward Jewish traditions as well as his own role in God's history with his people are to be described in this context.

With his table fellowship (see D.IV.2.3), his speaking in figurations and parables (see D.IV.3.3), as well as his authoritative exposition of Jewish Torah (see D.IV.3.6), Jesus's conviction came to expression that the kingdom of God comes into being through his own activity. With his interpretation of Torah as God's authoritative instruction, he did not leave or even contradict Jewish ways of understanding and practicing the Torah but established his own accents. In doing so, he came into conflict especially with the Pharisees, who had concentrated on the application of the Torah to daily life and wanted to cultivate purity prescriptions for everyday praxis. The controversy was so intense because the Pharisees' intent was quite comparable with that of Jesus. Both wanted to interpret Torah in such a way that it effectively defined the life of people in Jewish territory. Thus, they strove for an interpretation that was as far as possible faithful-to-life and feasible. Jesus's critique was therefore directed less against the Pharisees' teaching than against their desire to go beyond the fixed, written Torah by means of additional regulations and interpretive practices in the form of oral directives (cf. Mark 7:8, 13). By contrast, Jesus's stance toward the Torah moved the inner attitude toward God into the foreground, which should guide the interpretation of Torah precepts. This becomes clear in the so-called antitheses of the Sermon on the Mount (Matt. 5:21–48), a series of Jesus's statements on the Torah compiled by the writer of the Gospel of Matthew. There Jesus does not merely denounce murder, but even anger against others; adultery begins even in the lustful look of a man at a woman; not only is swearing of false oaths forbidden, but swearing altogether; even love of enemies is demanded. With this attitude, Jesus confronted the "oral Torah" of the Pharisees critically and opposed it with the fundamental orientation toward the intention of God's precepts. This is expressed paradigmatically in the interpretation of the prohibition of divorce oriented toward the command at creation, which Jesus opposes to the regulation of a certificate of divorce from Deut. 24:1–3 (Mark 10:2–9). Thereby Jesus behaves as a teacher and interpreter of Torah, by means of which God deals with his people.

Also, with his attitude toward the Sabbath, Jesus moved into a spectrum of interpretations of the Sabbath commandment, which reached as far as regulations that under special conditions allowed for particular activities on the Sabbath (cf., for instance, CD-A x 14–11, 18). In the Sabbath controversies in Luke 13:10–17 and 14:1–6, it becomes clear that Jesus interprets the Sabbath commandment programmatically with regard to the meaning of the day, in which the relationship between God and human beings stands at the center (cf., for instance, Jub. 2:17–18). Therefore, actions that are in the service of the life of human beings such as healings should be permitted. This is expressed programmatically in the formulation that the Sabbath exists for human beings and not human beings for the Sabbath (Mark 2:27).

Accordingly, it is not by chance that controversies reported in the Gospels between Jesus and the Pharisees take place often. The common, sometimes sharp condemnations of the Pharisees in the reports (for example, in the woes in Luke 11:39–52 par. Matt. 23:13–33) are polemical intensifications, not historical descriptions of the Pharisees' view of the Torah. In addition, they were formulated after Jerusalem and the temple had been destroyed, during which time rabbinic Judaism developed (which, to be sure, was significantly rooted in the Pharisees).

By contrast, Jesus might have come into conflict with the Sadducees on the basis of their attitude to the temple and their teaching that denied the resurrection of the dead. Like the Pharisees, Jesus advocated belief in the resurrection of the dead and saw in it a demonstration of the power of God over death (cf. Mark 12:18–27). Jesus's action in the court of the temple shows that his attitude toward the temple was fundamentally different from that of the Sadducees. Whereas the Sadducees considered it to be the central Jewish holy place, Jesus's action and also the saying about the destruction and rebuilding of the temple express his view that the kingdom of God, which was proclaimed by him and was breaking in through him, was not tied to the temple. Rather, he considered the temple a provisional, human institution unlike the kingdom of God. This might have been a reason for the Jewish authorities to proceed against him and to deliver him to the Roman administration.

Accordingly, Jesus's call to repentance and his announcement of the dawning kingdom of God were firmly anchored in the traditions of Israel and Judaism. At the same time, on the basis of the authority that he claimed for his person and work, he called for the decision between acceptance and rejection.

2.9.3. Israel in the Jesus Tradition

When the Gospels mention Israel, they frequently do so to define more closely Jesus's mission or that of his disciples: they are sent only to the "lost sheep of the house of Israel" (Matt. 10:6; 15:24); the disciples will not have fulfilled their mission in Israel's cities and towns before the "Son of Man comes" (Matt. 10:23); Jesus promises the disciples that they will judge the twelve tribes of Israel (Matt. 19:28; Luke 22:30); Jesus can also be designated the "King of Israel" (Mark 15:32 par. Matt. 27:42; John 1:49; 12:13). According to Luke 24:21, the hope for the redemption of Israel is bound up with him. The expectations of the coming of the deliverer or the anointed one also occur in connection with Jesus's birth (Matt. 2:6, 20–21; Luke 1:68; 2:25, 32).

Other statements emphasize the extraordinary nature of Jesus's teaching and activity: Jesus's teaching is a "new teaching with authority" (Mark 1:27); Jesus accomplishes healings, which heretofore were not seen in Israel (Matt. 9:33), and are the occasion for people to praise the God of Israel (Matt. 15:31); he heals people whose maladies were virtually incurable and from which they had already suffered for many years, and even brings the dead back to life (Mark 5:21–43 par.; Luke 7:11–17; John 11:1–44). Jesus's activity is, therefore, interpreted as fulfillment of God's salvific action announced in the prophetic writings: the blind see, the lame walk, lepers become clean, the deaf hear, the dead are raised, the gospel is proclaimed to the poor (Luke 7:22 par. Matt. 11:4–5; cf. Mark 7:37; Matt. 15:30). Hence, in the Gospel of Luke Jesus's appearance is interpreted by the citation from Isaiah about the prophet anointed by God who brings the good news to the poor and proclaims liberty to the imprisoned and recovery of sight to the blind (Luke 4:18–19).

Accordingly, the texts that explicitly mention Israel build a close relationship between Jesus's activity and the promises for Israel, especially with the establishment of the kingdom of God through the work of the anointed one. This is reinforced by additional aspects of Jesus's ministry.

The concept of the kingdom of God that Jesus put at center stage (see D.IV.3.2) takes up the idea of God's kingship (cf., for instance, Pss. 47; 147; Tob. 13:1–6;

2 Macc. 1:24–29) and correspondingly of God's sovereignty to be established in the future (cf., e.g., 1QM vii 6; As. Mos. 10:1–10) and brings both aspects—the present and future of God's rule—into a dynamic relationship: in Jesus's ministry God's kingdom is dawning hidden and inconspicuously but will be consummated in the future (cf., e.g., Mark 4:30–32: the parable of the mustard seed).

Further, the symbolic actions of Jesus related to Israel's renewal are important. Among these are, for instance, the choosing of the Twelve (Mark 3:14–19 par.), Jesus's entrance into Jerusalem, the action in the court of the temple, as well as the Last Supper with his disciples in Jerusalem. In these acts Jesus's perspective toward Israel is clearly noticeable: he challenges the Jewish people to return to God and to join the community of his followers, in order to participate in the kingdom of God mediated through him.

Thereby, a striking difference from John the Baptist can be observed. Whereas the latter had announced the immediately approaching judgment of God, and in view of this had called for repentance and the washing away of sins by the symbolic act of immersion in the Jordan River carried out by him (Mark 1:4; Matt. 3:7–10 par. Luke 3:7–9), Jesus invites his addressees to enter into the kingdom of God by joining the community founded by him. To be sure, the time for this is limited by the coming judgment of God; therefore, for John and Jesus, each in his own way, salvation and judgment stand in a close connection with each other (see D.IV.3.4). In the Jesus tradition, for example, the parables in Matt. 24:43–25:30, but also the woes in Matt. 11:20–24 par. Luke 10:13–15, point to this.

A specific facet of Jesus's ministry is his compassionate turning to the marginalized: tax collectors, sinners, the poor, the sick, lepers (see D.IV.2.10). Manifestly he saw in these people the primary addressees of the invitation to the kingdom of God. Texts in which this is programmatically expressed are the Beatitudes (Luke 6:20–23, followed by the woes to the rich in 6:24–26; Matt. 5:3–12), the call of a tax collector (Mark 2:13–17 par.), Jesus's healings, and the parables narrated in the programmatic meal scene in Luke 15 about God's compassionate turning to sinners and the lost.

A consequence of the establishment of the kingdom of God in Jesus's own work is the separation between those who will participate in it by accepting his message and those who are lost (cf., for instance, Matt. 8:11–12 par. Luke 13:28–29). Thereby, belonging to Jesus's community is even placed above belonging to Israel by birth (Mark 5:34 par.; 10:52; 11:22 par.; Matt. 8:10; 15:28). Here a tendency becomes evident that post-Easter Christianity took up, when the Christian message was directed also at non-Jews.

Jesus's activity in Israel led to a division between the Jews of Galilee and those in Judea. One group saw in him the very one through whom God deals with Israel salvifically; they accepted his claim to be God's earthly representative. Within this group a distinction can be made between those who entered into Jesus's entourage and shared his itinerant lifestyle (such as the Twelve) and those who were positive about his message and supported him and his immediate followers but continued their life in the villages of Galilee. The other group rejected Jesus, perceived his appearance as a provocation, and saw in it a contradiction to the Scriptures and traditions of Israel and Judaism. This conflict around the legitimacy of the authority that Jesus claimed is reflected, for example, in the controversy about the origin of Jesus's power over demons and unclean spirits in Mark 3:22–30 par. There arose from this the community of those who held fast to their conviction that he was the one sent by God even in view of his death on a cross. In this the Easter experiences played a constitutive role, because they mediated the assurance to Jesus's adherents that his execution was the end only of his earthly way.

The Gospels portray Jesus's activity from a post-Easter perspective; the turning of the Christian mission to the gentiles is already presupposed. The Synoptic Gospels, therefore, each in its own way, place Jesus's ministry in relationship with the post-Easter universal orientation of the gospel. In Mark the extension by way of Galilee into non-Jewish areas is recounted, without the transition to the gentile mission explicitly becoming a theme. By contrast, in Matthew Jesus's mission to Israel is expressly emphasized, and the commission to teach and baptize all nations is formulated only at the very end of the gospel by the risen One (Matt. 28:19–20). In Luke, Jesus's mission is completely focused on Israel and the extension to the gentiles is not recounted until Acts. Thus it becomes evident that in early Christianity the relationship of Jesus's activity in Israel and the post-Easter orientation of Christian proclamation to Jews and gentiles needed to be clarified. This is still the case in contemporary Jesus research.

2.9.4. Jesus and Israel—Continuity or New Perspective?

These characteristics of Jesus have led to two different views. The first position emphasizes that Jesus belongs in the context of Judaism; accordingly, his ministry is to be interpreted within Jewish culture and Jewish traditions. Jesus's call to repentance, like his appearance as a whole, does not go beyond Israel's traditions. Rather, it moves within the Judaism of his time. Neither with his interpretation of Torah nor with his announcement of the dawning kingdom of God did he exceed the framework of Jewish discourse of his time. This view is advocated, with different accents, for example, by Ed Parish Sanders, John Meier, Tom Wright, Martin Hengel, James Dunn, and Wolfgang Stegemann.

The second position, by contrast, claims that Jesus acted within Judaism and cannot be reconciled with Jewish positions of his time. His stance toward Torah and temple, his claim to be God's decisive and final envoy, as well as the conviction of God's immediate acting through his own deeds would instead have been perceived as an offense by his Jewish contemporaries and would have provoked his rejection and eventually his handing over for trial and execution. Such a view is advocated, for example, by Jürgen Becker, John Dominic Crossan, Ben Meyer, and Steven Bryan.

Nevertheless, it is possible to mediate between these two positions. Jesus's activity in the Judaism of his time stands in continuity with the Law and the Prophets, which Matt. 5:17–20 expresses programmatically. At the same time, Jesus established a community of those who saw in him the one whom God had sent for the redemption of God's people and who expounds God's directive for Israel with authority. Of central importance thereby is his self-understanding to be the one through whom God establishes his kingdom in Israel. This conviction, sometimes designated his "messianic claim" (Hengel), of the significance of his own work is expressed in the designation "Son of Man," which Jesus presumably used for himself. It is also apparent in his parables and healings as well as in his symbolic actions mentioned above. Continuity and discontinuity, therefore, stand not in conflict with each other but rather in a tension-filled dynamic. A turning to the gentiles did certainly not take place in Jesus's ministry, but it can be understood as the consequence of his view that belonging to the community founded by him is the decisive presupposition for attaining God's salvation.

2.9.5. Conclusion

Jesus's activity in Israel is concentrated in his call to repentance and the invitation to enter into the kingdom of God mediated through him. This message, which became concretely tangible in Jesus's healings and table fellowships, is grounded on the promises of God's salvific action as they are attested in Israel's Scriptures. These promises are interpreted by Jesus in a new way. They are coupled with his own work that mediates God's salvation. This is not proclaimed as a political program for the elimination of Roman domination but as the mediation of God's salvific proximity, especially for the poor, sick, and marginalized. Jesus's appearance, his exposition of the Jewish law, and his critique of the temple, however, provoked rejection and enmity in Judaism, which finally led to his being delivered to the Romans and to his execution. His followers nevertheless held fast to their conviction that he was the decisive representative of God, even in view of his death. After Easter they passed on the proclamation of Jesus as the risen and exalted One in Israel. In the history of Christianity, the programmatic turning to non-Jews was an important step based on this.

Bryan, Steven M. 2002. *Jesus and Israel's Traditions of Judgment and Restoration.* SNTSMS 177. Cambridge.

Chancey, Mark A. 2002. *The Myth of a Gentile Galilee.* SNTSMS 118. Cambridge.

Freyne, Seán. 2004. *Jesus, a Jewish Galilean: A New Reading of the Jesus Story.* London.

Hengel, Martin, and Anna Maria Schwemer, eds. 2001. *Der messianische Anspruch Jesu und die Anfänge der Christologie.* WUNT 138. Tübingen.

Meyer, Ben. 1979. *The Aims of Jesus.* London.

Reed, Jonathan L. 2000. *Archaeology and the Galilean Jesus: A Re-examination of the Evidence.* Harrisburg, PA.

Darrell L. Bock and Jens Schröter

2.10. Tax Collectors and Sinners as Addressees of Jesus's Activity

2.10.1. Table Fellowship with Tax Collectors and Sinners

According to the tradition shared by all sources of the Synoptic Gospels (in two versions: [1] Mark 2:15-17 par. Matt. 9:10-13; Luke 5:29-32; [2] Matt. 11:18-19 par. Luke 7:33-35 [Q 7:33-34]), Jesus was accused of associating freely with "tax collectors and sinners" (τελῶναι καὶ ἁμαρτωλοί), in contrast to the manner of his predecessor John the Baptist. Notwithstanding some doubts concerning the credibility of this tradition (Walker 1978), it is generally presumed to reflect a genuine habit of Jesus. At the same time, each of the Gospels (excluding John, who makes no mention of this issue) understands the significance of this accusation differently. In the basic form of this controversy narrative, Jesus's opponents, feeling discomforted with his spectacular success among the Galilean population, blame him for indiscriminately hosting all followers, contrary to what was generally considered a respectable practice. His miracles attracted many who sought proximity to his powers, and he was willing to host and dine with anyone, irrespective of his or her background or occupation. To the amazement of the Pharisee bystanders, Jesus did not refrain from sharing his table with disreputable persons, such as tax collectors, providing a double justification: "Those who are well have no need of a physician, but those who are sick; I have come to call not the righteous but sinners" (Mark 2:16-17).

In attempting to locate the tension between Jesus and the Pharisees within a concrete social setting, scholars have suggested various identifications of the sinners and their social standing. Alongside the tax collectors (or preferably toll collectors), the sinners may specifically denote those engaged in despised trades. Rabbinic literature has preserved lists of occupations, including tax collectors and usurers, who were deemed wicked, רשעים, and untrustworthy (Jeremias 1931, 296). Scholars, however, have tended to include in this category all who would have been considered sinners by Jesus's opponents. Some have identified the sinners in general as *am ha-'ares*, literally people of the land, that is, the common people (Jeremias 1971a, 112). According to rabbinic literature, the Pharisees considered this group impure and would not host them nor dine with them (m. Hagigah 2:7; m. Demai 2:3). Presumably, the Pharisees also believed that the ignorance of the *am ha-'ares* in matters of the law marked them as sinners and prevented their access to salvation; therefore the Pharisees opposed both Jesus's association with them and his promise of salvation. Jesus, however, believed that even if others considered his followers "little" and "simple," these "lost sheep" and "poor" were no less entitled to hear the good news (Mark 9:42; Matt. 10:6, 42; Luke 6:20). This reconstruction is hard to accept, since the Pharisees, despite their deep concern for purity, express no enmity toward *am ha-'ares* and refrain from identifying the impure non-Pharisees as sinners (a notion that appears only in later Talmudic sources, b. Pesahim 49a). The Pharisees did not share with other sects, such as the members of the Yahad, the notion that nonmembers were excluded from the inheritance of Israel. Indeed, Second Temple sources employ the title sinner in a factional context to denote those outside the boundaries of one's group, to the degree that "sinners" are occasionally synonymous with gentiles (Dunn 2005, 478–82). However, this standpoint is barely compatible with Pharisaic presumptions. They established their self-image as religious leaders by their scrupulous observation of the law, particularly in purity matters, but it prevented them from flatly identifying *am ha-'ares* as sinners (Furstenberg 2015). They may have been critical of others, but they would be careful not to associate them with the infamous tax collectors and participants in other disreputable occupations.

Alternatively, some have identified the sinners as apostates who renounced the covenant and were not willing to repent. These people were generally acknowledged to have excluded themselves from the people of Israel. They practically made themselves into gentiles (Perrin 1967, 103) and therefore were not entitled to inherit the world to come (m. Sanhedrin 10:1; t. Sanhedrin 13:4–5; Sifre Numbers 112). Jesus offended the Pharisees and popular notions of salvation by eating with these wicked outlaws, showing them the way to repentance and forgiveness or even accepting them unconditionally into the kingdom (E. Sanders 1985a, 200–208). However, as the examination of the term "sinners" in the relevant passages indicates, it is doubtful whether it should be associated with a strict social category (in contrast to the rabbinic "heretic" or "apostate"). This term never appears within a narrative context (except in relation to Jesus's table fellowship, Mark 2:15, where it follows the formulation in the Pharisees' accusation), but exclusively in admonitions, either accusing the addressees (Mark 8:38) or warning them to dissimilate themselves from sinners (Luke 5:30–32). "Sinners" is therefore a fluid category, whose scope and meaning depend on the specific context in which it is applied.

Concerning the accusation of associating with sinners, this issue does not imply a broad disagreement on the boundaries of the community and the inclusion of those cut off from the people. In his image of the kingdom, Jesus may have indeed upset the hierarchy within the community, but he did not upset the community's boundaries. The issue at stake here is much more limited. The accusation against Jesus makes perfect sense within the prevalent conventions of table fellowship. A common notion of sapiential wisdom warns against associating and sharing one's table with untrustworthy evildoers. Ben Sira advises to hold back the bread of the ungodly and not to give it to them (12:5). No one, he adds, pities one who has associated with a sinner, for he is untrustworthy, and, when the opportunity comes, he will never have enough of his blood (12:13–18). Finally, "What does a wolf have in common with a lamb? No more has the sinner with the devout" (13:17; compare m. Avot 1:7). This common wisdom was observed particularly with respect to the notorious tax collectors, who were considered the exemplars of untrustworthiness. These characters were banned from the rabbinic purity association (t. Demai 3:4) and from testifying in court (b. Sanhedrin 25b); nor was this sentiment unique to Judean resentment of Roman direct and indirect rule (Donahue 1971), for Greek writers expressed the very same feeling toward this trade. Thus Lucian may excuse people who, bound by necessity, chose the shameful trade of tax collecting, but nonetheless, "it is not decent to ask people who so act to the same table, to share a cup with them and to partake of the same food" (Lucian, *Pseudol.* 30–31). It would seem then that the complete disregard of this elementary moral standard and the willingness to associate freely with tax collectors undermined Jesus's own moral standing in the eyes of his opponents and threw into question the integrity of his intentions. Moreover, such behavior gave the Pharisees another reason to suspect Jesus for failing to observe the laws properly.

2.10.2. Sinners in the Synoptic Gospels

In Mark's account, the accusation and response "I have come to call not the righteous but sinners" does not resonate beyond this one incident. The proclamation of God's kingdom through healing and calling for repentance (Mark 1:15) necessarily involved a threateningly close contact with the sick and impure as well as the sinful, more than accepted in a typical social setting. Jesus called all Jews to join him in preparation for the kingdom, including Levi the tax collector, among others (Mark 2:14), but there is no indication of his involvement in a particular mission to the lawless margins of Jewish Galilean society. Beyond the circle of his disciples, Jesus did not develop a distinct connection with any specific group, including the sinners, as he pictured the whole people of Israel as straying sheep in need of a shepherd (6:34).

The accusation of Jesus in the Q version of the tradition is quite similar to that of Mark, but it sets the ground for an exclusive relationship and more elaborate message concerning the sinners. In this tradition (Matt. 11:16–19 par. Luke 7:31–35), Jesus is accused by the people of the generation for being a glutton and a drunkard, a friend of sinners and tax collectors. As in the parallel tradition, the accusation is enhanced by contrasting Jesus to John (see Mark 2:18 par. Matt. 9:14; Luke 5:33). The distinction between them is twofold: John fasted but Jesus feasts, and John promoted repentance while Jesus enjoys the company of sinners. The overtly polemical tone conceals the actual reality the accusation is referring to—can one imagine that Jesus was really a friend of sinners and tax collectors? And it may plausibly reflect the very discomfort with Jesus's association with sinners described in the previous section. At the same time, this Q tradition has generated in both Luke and Matthew a more elaborate consideration of Jesus's position toward those in the sinful margins and their path for salvation.

In the Lukan rendering of the tradition, the complaint against Jesus serves as a starting point for depicting the exclusive relationship Jesus held with the sinners as a defined social group. First, according to Luke's revision of Mark, Jesus did not host tax collectors and sinners but rather chose to dine at the house of Levi together with his colleagues, the other tax collectors (5:29). Luke then adds other incidents, unique to this gospel, which demonstrate the habit of Jesus to actively seek the company of such sinners. When passing through Jericho, Jesus commands Zacchaeus, the rich chief tax collector, to host him (19:1–10). Regardless of the sincerity of Zacchaeus's motivations, Jesus proclaims that the Son of Man has come to seek out and save the lost. This mission produced an inherent tension between two distinct groups, who according to Luke were pursuing the company of Jesus, the Pharisees and the sinners. Jesus indeed accepted the invitations of the Pharisees but preferred the company of the sinners. While dining with a Pharisee, Jesus praises the hospitality of a sinful woman who washed and anointed his feet (7:36–50), and after dining with esteemed Pharisees, they protest his eating in the company of sinners (15:1–2). In his threefold parables on the joy of finding the lost sheep, the lost coin, and the lost son, unique to Luke, Jesus justifies the special interest he takes in the lost ones who have returned in repentance. The contrast embodied in Jesus's original statement, "I have come to call not the righteous but the sinners," is transformed in the Lukan rendering into a full-fledged rivalry between the two groups.

This reconstructed social setting further allows Luke to develop his criticism toward the privileged religious elite, such as the Pharisees, whose confidence in their conduct and social standing renders them unprepared for the radical change required with the coming of the kingdom, whereas the sinful are in a receptive state, and therefore the first to follow Jesus and to enter the kingdom. The parable on the prayers of the Pharisee and the tax collector demonstrates this claim on the personal level. On the public level, Jesus reproaches (according to Luke) the Pharisees and law experts for their self-assured refusal to be baptized by John, in contrast to the tax collectors (7:29–30; compare Matt. 3:7; 21:23–32). The oppositional positions of the Pharisees and the sinners in Luke create the impression that Jesus headed a social movement of the disreputable and uneducated standing up against the Pharisaic elite (Jeremias 1971a, 112). However, more than the social context of Jesus's activity, this structure represents Luke's understanding of the radical nature of Jesus's proclamation of the kingdom.

In contrast to Luke, Matthew does not add to Mark's single account of association with sinners. At the same time, he too is sensitive to implications of the Q tradition, where Jesus is accused of being "a friend of the tax collectors and sinners." On the one hand, Matthew singles out sinners and tax collectors as the only guests in his meal (Matt. 9:10). On the other hand, Jesus in the Matthean account, in stark contrast to Luke, makes a special effort to disassociate his addressees from the tax collectors and sinners. In the Sermon on the Mount, he instructs them not to act like tax collectors and gentiles (Matt. 5:46–47), whereas Luke's version only refers to sinners in general (Luke 6:32–33). And again, in his instructions concerning reproof, Jesus concludes that if a fellow member is unwilling to accept reproof from the community, "let such one be to you as a Gentile and tax collector" (Matt. 18:17). Luke, in contrast, calls for an infinite measure of forgiveness (Luke 17:3–4). Finally, whereas Luke understands the parable of the lost sheep as referring to the joy with the return of the sinner, Matthew diverts it to a different issue, the care for the humble "little ones" (Matt. 18:1–14). Like children, these may not be the most impressive of members, but they are in no way declared sinners. In the Matthean account then, Jesus seeks to disassociate his followers both from the Pharisees and from the professional sinners. His message of repentance is addressed to the needs of a specific community, and it offers them an alternative path away from the sinful.

2.10.3. Jesus, Repentance, and Atonement

The comparison between Jesus and John in all versions of the tradition concerning Jesus and sinners raises the obvious question: What was the nature of Jesus's call to sinners, and what path for repentance did he offer them? John demanded confession and admonished the baptized to bear fruit worthy of repentance. How did Jesus prepare the people for the coming of the kingdom? Did he diverge from John's message and proclaim the inclusion of all? How did following him serve to elevate the moral standard of his associates? Scholars hold to a wide range of positions concerning the relationship between Jesus's call for repentance and his own power and authority. These in turn determine the degree of continuity between Jesus's own message and the atonement following his crucifixion. Arguably, the answer to these questions depends on the way we view the nature of his relationship with the sinners and their role in his mission. Thus, our understanding of Jesus's conception of repentance and forgiveness and its degree of novelty varies in accordance to the different accounts of his association with sinners in the Synoptic Gospels.

Some scholars have viewed Jesus as a faithful disciple of John, who extended the period for repentance (as in the parable of the fig tree, Luke 13:6–9) and carried this message further to his own disciples. Both called for repentance and warned against the impending judgment. The differences between the two did not extend beyond the accepted notions and practices among Jewish groups of the time. The widespread expectation for ultimate purification in current eschatological discourse shaped John's baptism, and there was nothing exceptionally unique in the comforting notion, highlighted by Jesus, that God loves his children and expects their reintegration into the covenant. John and Jesus were unique only in the urgency they prophetically ascribed to the issue, due to the imminent coming of the kingdom. In contrast to later notions, which followed the death of Jesus, he himself did not offer any new conception of repentance and atonement (Fredriksen 2012; Choi 2000). Other scholars contend that Jesus promoted revolutionary views through his table fellowship with sinners, which undermined the accepted covenantal framework and challenged prevalent values. According to one version, Jesus expanded the boundaries of forgiveness and atonement to include the worst of sinners who had excluded themselves from the covenant (Perrin 1967, 93–103). Alternatively, assuming that no one would object if Jesus had caused these people to repent and return to the covenant, Sanders proposed that Jesus promised sinners admittance into the kingdom without any expression of repentance (E. Sanders 1985a). Furthermore, he even waived the scriptural commands of restitution and sacrifice. In contrast to John, Jesus did not call the people to repent (and Sanders questions the authenticity of sayings that indicate otherwise), holding that all people of Israel have a place in the kingdom (compare m. Sanhedrin 10:1).

Intermediate positions attempt to explain the unique transformative process Jesus offered his followers through their proximity to him. The question therefore is not whether Jesus called for repentance, but rather how his personality brought about the change of heart he himself called for. One possibility is that Jesus's messianic image served to redefine salvation exclusively with relation to him. Accepting the kingship of Jesus displaced earlier notions of law, and it was a prerequisite for entering the kingdom. Salvation of both righteous and sinners was not dependent anymore on covenant, but solely on the commitment to Jesus as a savior. According to this view, Jesus did not offer a lifeline to sinners but rather redefined the conditions for salvation around his figure. In so doing, he laid the foundations to the post-Easter conceptions of salvation, which assume there is no salvation outside of faith in Jesus (Allison 1987, 68–74). More in line with current views of repentance is the possibility that Jesus's exclusive status was derived not from his authority to admit people into the kingdom but rather from his power to restore the world through healing and purification. The Qumran sectarians acknowledge that due to their enslavement to their bodily qualities they are not free to repent. Within the demonological world order, the basic condition for restoration is not the autonomous decision of the individual but the appearance of a purifying spirit to emancipate the person from enslavement to sin. Thus we read in the Thanksgiving Psalm: "And I chose to purify according to your will . . . knowing no one is justified without you and I seek your presence with the spirit you have given me, to make complete your graces among your slaves for eternity, to purify me with your holy spirit" (1QH viii 28–30). While in Qumran the admission into the sect brought about the desired transforming spirit, Jesus saw himself as an embodiment of that purifying force. He identified his exorcism with the annulment of sin and offered his followers a new creation.

2.10.4. Forms of Repentance in the Gospels

The array of scholarly interpretations of Jesus's call for repentance reflects to some degree the diversity within the Synoptic Gospels. Mark shows no concern for the dynamics of repentance, the conditions that enable the change of heart (μετάνοια) and the ways to accomplish it. He does mention that both Jesus and his disciples called for repentance (Mark 1:15; 6:12), but his activity is not governed by this interest. It suffices that the healing powers of Jesus embody his authority to forgive sins (2:1–12). His teachings and parables do not instruct the principles for proper behavior under the Torah, but rather faith in Jesus himself and the renunciation of all worldly goods in favor of following him (10:21).

In contrast, the Q material presents Jesus as a teacher of Torah to a wide circle of addressees, and this position inherently involves his expectation that they repent and adhere to his instructions. Similar to John the Baptist, who according to

Matthew and Luke demanded confession and specific ways of repentance, Jesus's mission involves moral instructions. Having set a high standard of moral obligations, Jesus expected his hearers to follow his sermons, and not only to have heard him or call him "Lord, Lord" (Matt. 7:21–24; Luke 6:46–49; 8:21). The urgency of repentance unfolds in the following teachings. Jesus laments the cities who have not accepted his call for repentance (Matt. 11:20–24; Luke 10:13–15). He compares himself to Jonah, and warns that the people of Nineveh will rise up at the judgment with this generation, who refuse to repent (Matt. 12:41–42; Luke 11:30–32). The message intensifies, as Jesus proclaims that only repentance will save his listeners from perishing. Association with Jesus is not enough, and one must bear the fruit of repentance before the gate is finally shut (Luke 13:1–9, 24–30; Matt. 7:13–20). Significantly, the reluctance of the addressees to accept his teachings resonates in the Q parable of the great banquet. Since the leadership was not worthy and unwilling to adequately prepare for the kingdom, the Lord was compelled to elect others, even of a sinful background, to constitute his alternative group of associates and participate in his son's wedding (compare Matt. 22:1–14 and Luke 14:16–24).

Allison, Dale C. 1987. "Jesus and the Covenant: A Response to Sanders." *JSNT* 29: 57–78.

Donahue, John R. 1971. "Tax Collectors and Sinners: An Attempt at Identification." *CBQ* 33: 39–61.

Dunn, James D. G. 2005. "Pharisees, Sinners and Jesus." In *The Historical Jesus in Recent Research*, by James D. G. Dunn and Scot McKnight, 463–88. SBTS 10. Winona Lake, IN.

Fredriksen, Paula. 2012. *Sin: The Early History of an Idea*. Princeton.

Furstenberg, Yair. 2015. "Outsider Impurity: Trajectories of Second Temple Separation Traditions in Tannaitic Literature." In *Tradition, Transmission, and Transformation from Second Temple Literature through Judaism and Christianity in Late Antiquity*, edited by Menahem Kister et al., 40–68. Leiden.

Jeremias, Joachim. 1931. "Zöllner und Sünder." *ZAW* 30: 293–300.

———. 1971a. *New Testament Theology*. Part 1, *The Proclamation of Jesus*. London.

Sanders, Ed P. 1985a. *Jesus and Judaism*. London.

Walker, William O. 1978. "Jesus and the Tax Collectors." *JBL* 97: 221–38.

Yair Furstenberg

2.11. Jesus's Relationship to the Samaritans

For the question about Jesus's relationship to the Samaritans, the following come into consideration as sources:

- three texts in Luke (Luke 9:51–56: the rejection of Jesus in a Samaritan village; Luke 10:25–37: an example story of the Good Samaritan; Luke 17:11–19: the healing of ten lepers); in addition, texts about the post-Easter Samaritan mission in Acts 1:8; 8:1, 4–25; 9:31; and 15:3 are consulted;
- a detailed account and a note in John (John 4:4–42: Jesus's encounter with a Samaritan woman; John 8:48: an accusation of opponents that Jesus is a Samaritan); and
- a logion in Matthew (Matt. 10:5–6: command for the disciples not to go to the gentiles and not to enter any Samaritan city, but rather to go to the "lost sheep of the house of Israel").

The context in each case shows that this is not a question only about inhabitants of Samaria in geographical-political terms but about those persons designated Σαμαρίτης, Σαμαρῖτις, and Σαμαρῖται who are understood to be Samaritans in a religious sense. Each one of the three Gospels that are strongly influenced by Jewish Christianity demonstrates its own perspective on Jesus's relationship with the Samaritans by its Christology and understanding of Israel. Luke, John, and Matthew represent distinct positions, which are also found in contemporaneous Judaism with respect to the Samaritans. According to their theological view of history and their understanding of Israel, Samaritans could be classified either as an integral part of the people of God or as non-Israelites.

All the Samaritan texts have to do with respective special material. Mark and presumably also Q (cf. Matt. 10:5–6) do not mention either Samaria or the Samaritans. Because parallel material is absent, it cannot be said whether and to what extent texts in the special material go back to older traditions. This also makes the quest for the historical Jesus virtually impossible. In the spectrum of inner-Jewish classifications of relationships with Samaritans, what position Jesus took from the mandate for his mission can no longer be reconstructed. Rather, only cautious, reasonable considerations remain, with reservations—if at all.

In what follows, the texts of the individual gospels are considered in themselves and interrogated with respect to their literarily constructed view of Jesus's relationship with the Samaritans. Reflections on the purpose of the text and on possible historical backgrounds are incorporated into this.

2.11.1. Matthew (Matt. 10:5-6)

This command might originate from pre-Matthean tradition; however, it is likely that Matthew himself composed the logion and placed it at the beginning of his mission discourse. The Σαμαρῖται come into view here in the same way the gentiles do, as neighboring populations of Galilee. Whether Matthew identifies them (in synonymous parallelism) with the gentiles or whether he sees them located in a position between gentiles and the lost sheep of the house of Israel can hardly be decided. In any case, they do not belong to the people of God. On the level of the narrative, the sending of the disciples stands in analogy to Jesus's ministry as it has been developed in the narrative up until Matt. 10. Also up to this point, Jesus has not entered any Samaritan city, but has focused his activity entirely on Galilee as the place, according to Scripture, of turning to Israel. However, Matthew understands the Samaritans to be non-Israelites that must be included in the universal, post-Easter commission of Matt. 28:19 (πάντα τὰ ἔθνη), even if they are not explicitly mentioned there.

Especially two possibilities exist for why Matthew categorized the neighbors to the south as non-Israelites. Because Matthew refers only to the cities of the Samaritans, he could have been influenced by the historical concept of 2 Kings 17:24–41 and could have shared a view of the cities in the neighboring southern region that was broadly disseminated in contemporaneous Judaism and communicated literarily. According to 2 Kings 17:24–41, descendants of foreign colonial people who lived in the Samaritan cities were in fact instructed in the YHWH cult but nevertheless practiced syncretism—and indeed, practiced it "to this day" (v. 41).

The other possibility is connected with Matthew's special emphasis on Jesus's Davidic messianism and the fulfillment of the prophetic promises connected with it. Matthew underscores basic christological statements, which could hardly have found points of contact among the Samaritans. The Samaritans had no theological reference to Jewish prophets and to traditions about Zion and David but were grounded only on Mosaic writings in the particular form of the Samaritan Pentateuch. It established for them not only the cultic priority of Gerizim but also an eschatology focused on Moses. At the end of the first century CE, these theological differences became more and more clear because of the canonization processes in Judaism. For Matthew, this might also have been the reason for categorizing the Samaritans who were oriented only to the Pentateuch (and even then to their own version) as non-Jews and thus for him also non-Israelites.

2.11.2. Luke (Luke 9:51–56; 10:25–37; 17:11–19)

By contrast, the entirely positive relationship between Jesus and the Samaritans in Luke is astonishing; Luke's Christology is committed to Jewish messianic promises just as strongly as Matthew's Christology. Luke's Samaritan texts also have to do with traditions from special material, the origin of which is no longer available. To be sure, Luke had access to Jesus traditions that are otherwise no longer accessible (cf. Acts 20:35). All three texts make it possible to discover detailed information about the Samaritans and their relationship with Jews in the first century CE. Luke's perspective on the Samaritans is not influenced by the literary perspective of 2 Kings 17:24–41, but it demonstrates—in insinuations—that they are a Torah-observant part of God's people Israel who reject the Jerusalem temple cult. For Luke they are foreign/ἀλλογενεῖς (Luke 17:18) and a separate nation/ἔθνος (Acts 8:9) because, viewed from the inner-Jewish perspective, they do not belong to their own "group."

In Luke, Jesus first takes a route that includes a stop in a Samaritan village on his journey to Jerusalem (Luke 9:51–52). This first, redactionally placed stop shows that for Luke the Samaritans belong in Jesus's messianic mission mandate to gather and restore the people of God. The disciples' preparations not only involve lodging but also are related to Jesus's arrival and proclamation. However, the plan fails. Jerusalem as the goal of the journey—in the larger context, it is more precisely the Passover festival—explains the cultically motivated rejection of Jesus by the Samaritans, who consider him and his disciples to be Jewish festival pilgrims. Here, as also in the reaction of the disciples (v. 54), the tensions become obvious, which in historical terms were latently present between Jews and Samaritans and which were caused by the destruction of the Samaritan sanctuary on Mount Gerizim by the Jerusalem high priest John Hyrcanus at the end of the second century BCE. These tensions were vented in the first century CE in the context of festival pilgrimages and activities (Josephus, *Ant.* 18.29–30; 20.118–136). The request to take lodging with Samaritans shows, quite apart from the primary theological significance of this stop for Luke, that in spite of the difficult common history a neighborly collective purpose existed between Jews and Samaritans, and Galilean pilgrims could take the route to Jerusalem through Samaria (cf. Josephus, *Life* 268–270). Thus, the short account mirrors at least a factual possibility for the historical Jesus, and it might be the reflection of a memory that he, with his message and his understanding of his own commission, was unable to gain a foothold with the Samaritans. The consummation of his mission aimed at Jerusalem lets a failure of Jesus in Samaria appear quite plausible.

In Luke's view, success among the Samaritans was modest until the post-Easter proclamation of Christ. In Acts 1:8 the promise and mandate of the risen One to the disciples for the Samaritan mission are found, and then the Samaritans also demonstrate an open posture toward the message of Christ (Acts 8:4–25; cf. 9:31; 15:3). The texts presume, as does John 4:4–42, the existence of an early Samaritan Christianity. Whether it is possible here to reckon with historical memory or whether it is a literary strategy to demonstrate the comprehensive restitution of the people of God, or only a paradigm on overcoming religious limitations in emulation of Jesus, cannot be decided with certainty. Still, with Acts 8 and John 4 there are two traditions independent from each other about an early Christianity in Samaria. It could have been an accommodation to emerging Samaritan Christianity that in parts of early Christian proclamation the Jerusalem temple, as in general every construction made by hand, as the place of worshiping God could be critically assessed and relativized as a cultic location (cf. Acts 6:13; 7:48–50).

Also, the fictional short story of the Good Samaritan (Luke 10:30–35) again takes up the difference on cult locations between Jews and Samaritans but uses this in a very subtle way. The Samaritan is a representative of the other part of Israel and is an antitype to the priest and Levite. He demonstrates in exemplary fashion that in the people of God the location of the cult does not matter, but rather what is essential is the love of God and the compassionate turning to people in need on the street and in everyday life (Jews and Samaritans hold in common the Torah commandment introduced into the context of the narrative in v. 27). In the context of Luke, the example story indicates the wider established attitude of Jesus to the non-Jewish part of the people of God—even after his rejection in a Samaritan village (Luke 9:51–56). In a countermove in Luke 17:11–19, a Samaritan demonstrates, differently from the Jewish members of the group of healed lepers, the appropriate attitude toward Jesus, since he recognizes in Jesus's person the right place of thanksgiving and praising God. This account also relativizes the significance of the two different cult locations of Jews and Samaritans; still, it points to a new, eschatological, location for worshiping God in common for both parts of God's people Israel: Jesus Christ.

2.11.3. John (John 4:4–42; 8:48)

The alternative eschatological concept of worshiping God, founded in Christ, that integrates both groups is also found in John 4:4–42. Also in John, whose author possesses precise and intimate knowledge about the Samaritans, Jesus makes his way to Samaria. At Jacob's well in the vicinity of the village of Sychar, a theological discussion takes place between Jesus as a representative of Jewish tradition and a Samaritan woman. The Samaritan woman, who is keenly aware of her religious identity, designates Jesus a prophet (v. 19) and conjectures that he is the Χριστός (v. 29). The form of hope upon which Samaritan eschatology is focused is in fact the promised prophet like Moses in Deut. 18:18; when the woman, nevertheless, designates Jesus as the Christ, the author lets her speak the language of Jewish messianology, which also early Christianity spoke and understood.

In John 4:20, the theological criterion of the difference between Jews and Samaritans—the respective place that each esteemed as the central location of worshiping God—is called up. Here Jesus himself represents the Jewish self-understanding (ἡ σωτηρία ἐκ τῶν Ἰουδαίων ἐστίν) and also takes up the traditional

Jewish-Samaritan polemic (v. 22); then, however, he introduces a new concept of worshiping God (ἐν πνεύματι καὶ ἀληθείᾳ) that will relativize the heretofore established different cult locations (v. 24). In the further development of the discussion, Jesus turns out in the context of his self-revelation to be the one who fulfills not only the Jewish but also the Samaritan eschatological expectations. At the end, in the course of a messianic courtship, he won many Samaritans for the offer of salvation associated with him; they confess him to be "Savior of the world" (v. 42).

On the one hand, the text, which is substantially shaped by Johannine Christology and amplified with Old Testament motifs, attempts to demonstrate that the Samaritan Christianity existing in the time of John was founded by none other than Jesus. On the other hand, the text shows that Jesus himself overcame the theological disputes between the two parts of the people of God and that the eschatological hopes of both parties are fulfilled in faith in him. In addition, here the author of John implies the soteriological perspective that already reaches beyond Israel: οὗτός ἐστιν ἀληθῶς ὁ σωτὴρ τοῦ κόσμου (v. 42).

In the second text, John 8:48, Jesus's Jewish opponents and others accuse him of being a Samaritan because he calls into question their claim to Old Testament traditions of salvation and thereby their relationship with God. By this they meant to indicate that an affinity in theological positions exists between Jesus and the Samaritans. Here the dissent between Jews and Samaritans characterized by polemics with reference to ancestral traditions appears. As in John 4:4–42, in the Johannine way of seeing things the dissent is overcome by Jesus's claim about himself.

Böhm, Martina. 1999. *Samarien und die Samaritai bei Lukas: Eine Studie zum religionsgeschichtlichen und traditionsgeschichtlichen Hintergrund der lukanischen Samarientexte und zu deren topographischer Verhaftung.* WUNT II 111. Tübingen.

Frey, Jörg. 2012. "'Gute' Samaritaner? Das neutestamentliche Bild der Samaritaner zwischen Juden, Christen und Paganen." In *Die Samaritaner und die Bibel/The Samaritans and the Bible,* edited by Jörg Frey, Ursula Schattner-Rieser, and Konrad Schmid, 203–33. SJ 70/StSam 70. Berlin and Boston.

Konradt, Matthias. 2007. *Israel, Kirche und die Völker im Matthäusevangelium.* WUNT 215. Tübingen.

Lindemann, Andreas. 1993. "Samaria und Samaritaner im Neuen Testament." *WD* 22: 51–76.

Zangenberg, Jürgen K. 1998. *Frühes Christentum in Samarien: Topographische und traditionsgeschichtliche Studien zu den Samarientexten im Johannesevangelium.* TANZ 27. Tübingen and Basel.

Martina Böhm

3. Jesus's Discourses/Jesus's Teaching

3.1. Jesus's Concept of God and the Meaning of the Father Metaphor

As our tradition shows, the one God of Israel stands at the center of the proclamation of Jesus of Nazareth. However, it was not concerned with a teaching about the essence of God in itself, but with unfolding what God, in particular, what the imminent "kingdom of God" (see D.IV.3.2), means for human beings.

Jesus's demands for repentance to behavior in keeping with God's demands and God's example, as also his words and his own conduct, imply comprehensive knowledge of God and trust in God by the hearers of his message. Thus, the following presentation cannot simply describe "Jesus's concept of God" but must reconstruct it from Jesus's sayings from traditions passed on to us, which were spoken in particular situations. The criteria of the plausibility of historical effects and the plausibility of historical context (Theissen and Merz [4]2011, 116–20) are foundational for this without being able to perform it.

In Jesus research, it is disputed whether, in spite of continuity with Jewish discourse about God, Jesus's own views can be labeled as innovations (so, for instance, Schnelle 2007: "a new but in no way un-Jewish concept of God," "in tension with the dominant concepts of God in Judaism" [70]; but especially older Jesus research before the third quest), or alternatively, as a profile of talk of God within the possibilities of the multiple voices in Jewish theology (cf. Thompson 2011 as well as the work done by Jewish researchers, esp. Vermes 1993b; see B.X). In the last analysis, the answer depends on how one evaluates the theologoumena and *argumenta e silentio* in the reconstruction as well as on how one interprets the central metaphor of God as father in the Jesus tradition. Here the vote goes to interpreting Jesus's concept of God in continuity with Jewish conceptions of God. This assumption is substantiated by the content as well as by the fact that nowhere is a "renewal" of the proclamation of God asserted, and as is demonstrated in the Jesus tradition, God's essence and activity were not at all controversial: the in-breaking kingdom of God, God's power, and "fatherly" turning are the bases for arguments, for demands and assurance, without having to be justified. What is debatable is what this means for people and their standing before God.

The fact that according to accounts in the Gospels Jesus did not make Israel's *Heilsgeschichte* a topic (Sinai covenant, exodus, occupation of the land, etc.; emphasized, for instance, by Schnelle 2007, 70) can be explained by the selection of Jesus tradition, since that was formed by the later interest, that is, the expansion of the mission beyond Israel. Also, God's being as creator, the fundamental ability to know God (cf. Rom. 1:18–20), and warnings against worshiping other gods (cf. Exod. 20:3; 1 Cor. 10:21; and passim) are barely topics in the Jesus tradition, or not at all, without inferring that they were irrelevant for the earthly Jesus.

The following presentation assumes that the implicitly recognizable concept of God derived from Jesus's sayings and activities (see D.IV) complies with Old Testament–Jewish tradition, and this very aspect is expressed pointedly; also, in the supra-individual metaphorical figuration of the kingdom of God, Jesus put *the relationship of God with individuals, and vice versa, the relationship of individuals with God*, in the foreground in that he proclaimed what God demands (see D.IV.3.4), but especially God's loving care.

What follows will outline in a nutshell (1) how according to our tradition Jesus refers to God, (2) which concept of God involving Old Testament–Jewish tradition this assumes, (3) and, more precisely, what is mediated by means of the metaphorical figuration of God as father.

3.1.1. Terms and Metaphors for Speaking about God

Because of our tradition, which is reshaped and present only in Greek, how Jesus originally referred to God can no longer be reconstructed. According to the New Testament tradition (cf. overall Schlosser 1987, 21–51), he speaks about God occasionally using the Septuagint rendering of the divine name YHWH as κύριος ("Lord"; Luke 10:21; Mark 13:20; especially in taking up Old Testament citations, e.g., Mark 12:29–30 par.). More often he uses θεός ("God"; Matt. 12:28; 22:37 par.; Mark 10:27; and passim). God's transcendence is represented in the association of God with heaven as the sphere apart from humanity (cf., for instance, Luke 12:33–34 par., cf. only Deut. 30:12).

In order to make it possible to talk about the transcendent God in human experiences of reality, as elsewhere in religious discourse, God is spoken of in metaphors. According to the Synoptic Gospels, at the center of the theology of the historical Jesus stands his talk about the βασιλεία τοῦ θεοῦ, "the rule of God" or "the kingdom of God" (see D.IV.3.2), which indirectly visualizes God as a king (cf. Matt. 18:23; 22:2; 25:34), and his talk about God as father (πατήρ, Aramaic *abba*; see D.IV.3.1.3). Both metaphors are at times encountered side by side (Luke 11:2 par.; 12:32), but the concepts of "king" and "father" are not linked to each other.

In addition, there are other metaphors and parables (see D.IV.3.3), which are created from different source domains in everyday experience in Palestine. God appears in figurations as a slaveholder (cf. Luke 16:13 par.) and as an owner of a vineyard and an employer (Matt. 20:1–15; cf. Isa. 5:1–7). God is compared to a judge who is open to persuasion (Luke 18:1–8). Never is this a matter of characterizing God's essence but rather various aspects of God's relation to individual persons, which are described as a hierarchical gradient of authority. These images respectively adduce a male figure for God with (in some cases absolute) power. However, God is also envisioned as a person who gives an invitation to a feast

(Luke 14:6–14), as a friend who turns to another (Luke 11:5–8), as a shepherd who searches for a lost sheep (Luke 15:3–7 par.), and as a poor woman who searches for a lost drachma with great vigor and shares her joy over finding the coin with her women friends (Luke 15:8–10; cf. Schottroff 1994, 138–51).

3.1.2. Main Features of Jesus's Concept of God

The concept of God underlying Jesus's discourse and activity conforms with the generally shared Jewish convictions of his time (see D.I.2; cf. in greater detail Thompson 2011). The following basic convictions about God are implied, even if only a few references are found.

There is only one God (Mark 12:29, 32, with Deut. 6:4; Mark 10:18; Matt. 23:9). This God is to be loved with the whole heart (Mark 12:30 par., with Deut. 6:5). He created heaven and earth (cf. Mark 10:6), and also sustains them: he bestows sunshine and rain (Matt. 5:45). The thought of *creatio continua* underlies vegetation metaphors when these make the growth of seed or fruit signs of the expansion of the kingdom of God (Mark 4:26–29, 30–32), as they also are the grounds for the exhortation not to worry: from the fact that God so cares for small things like flowers of the field and sparrows, one can deduce God's provision for the things that are necessary (Matt. 6:26, 28–30; Luke 12:24, 27–28). God is thus perceptible from the creation. (The "Johannine logion" from Q, according to which no one knows the Father except the Son and anyone to whom he wishes to reveal him, Matt. 11:27 par., is a post-Easter formulation, which presumes the Christology of the Son [with Luz 1990, 200; cf. Rau 2011 on Q 10:21–11:13 as a Q composition about God as Jesus's Father for the legitimization of Jesus's mission].)

The universalism following from this monotheism is expressed in Jesus's talk about the kingdom of God: This is all-encompassing.

God is not reproduced in figurations, but revealed. Even if not every Old Testament citation attributed to Jesus is "historical," nevertheless in the multiple references to the Old Testament in the mouth of Jesus the certainty will have been reflected that this one God is attested in the Scriptures of Israel (cf. esp. Matt. 5:17; Mark 11:17 par.; 12:24 par.; Luke 10:26–28). From this the faith underlying the Old Testament is likewise to be taken for granted, namely, that God chose Israel, made a covenant with them, and shaped their history even if this is not made explicit (with Frankemölle 2006, 231–32). Thus, Jesus's activity itself is oriented toward Israel (cf. Mark 7:27; cf. Matt. 15:24). Sharp criticism of groups in Israel (see above) is also part of the prophetic tradition, without meaning that God had rejected Israel (Thompson 2011, 2591–92).

God's will, especially his law, is binding for human beings (Mark 3:35 par.; Matt. 5:18–19). In Jesus's discussions and interpretations of the law, it is not controversial that the law reflects God's will, but rather in what way the practice of life accords with God's will (see D.IV.3.7). This is shown in the exposition of the commandments (Matt. 5:21–48), in the critique of the cult (Mark 11:15–17 par.; cf. John 2:14–16; see D.IV.5.1), or in discourses about observing the Sabbath (e.g., Mark 2:27; 3:4 par.; cf. Matt. 12:11–12; Luke 13:15–16). God's action even becomes the model for humans: the high demand to love even enemies is founded in the example of none other than God, who gives sunshine and rain even to the unrighteous and evil (Matt. 5:45; cf. Luke 6:35–36; 11:42).

Whether among the Jewish theologies of his time Jesus follows an apocalyptic or sapiential conception is debated among researchers (cf. Toit 2002a, 120–24). His talk of God in relation to experience can derive from wisdom theology; an eschatological interpretation in the sense that Jesus reckoned with God's imminent and ultimate activity, however, appears to me compelling (Luke 11:2 par.; further see D.IV.3.2). In this sense Jesus shared with the majority of Jewish currents the expectation of a resurrection of the dead, which was rejected by the Sadducees—it is finally an expression of God's power and abiding fidelity to individual human beings as the "God of the living" (Mark 12:18–27 par.).

Belief in God's omnipotence is the basis of the praxis of prayer, since for God all things are possible (Mark 11:22–24 par.; 14:36; cf. 10:27 par.). Evil is consequently subjected to God, for which reason Jesus can expel demons "with the finger of God" (Luke 11:20) or, respectively, "with the spirit of God" (Matt. 12:28). It is, however, also a part of God's power and sovereignty that he is free to decide to whom he reveals knowledge, from whom he conceals it (Luke 10:21 par.), and to whom he turns (Luke 4:25–27). God is likewise free to bestow benevolence on people independently from what individuals have accomplished (Matt. 20:15).

God's power in history, however, is also demonstrated in the threats of the punishment of God, who sees what is concealed (Matt. 6:4, 6, 18). To be sure, God's judgment (see D.IV.3.4) is sovereign but not arbitrary, since the woes against Jewish cities (Luke 10:13–15 par.), against authorities (Pharisees and scribes: Luke 11:39–52; 20:45–47; Matt. 23; Mark 12:38–40), also as formulated in general fashion (Luke 12:4–5; 13:1–5; Matt. 10:28), are grounded in the behavior of those who in each case are accused.

However, the image of God perceptible in the Jesus tradition does not put threats of judgment in the forefront, but rather God's positive compassionate turning to human beings. As in Jesus's practice, what counts in God's turning to those in need such as the marginalized and sinners (female and male) is the individual person. So also, at the center of the theology implicit in this practice and teaching of Jesus stands God's relationship to individual persons and individual persons' relationship to God. Jesus stresses that God turns to the poor, the hungry, and those who mourn (Luke 6:20–23; cf. Matt. 5:3–12). Children and those who make themselves humble like them will obtain a portion in the kingdom of God (Mark 10:14–15 par.). Precisely those who humble themselves are exalted (Matt. 23:12 par.), and God forgives those who seek forgiveness (Luke 11:4 par.). Even this is not an innovation in the image of God in comparison with Old Testament–Jewish belief, but rather an individualized elucidation of reliance on God's grace along the line of the Old Testament. Compassionate turning to the needy is correlated with the social situation of the Jesus movement and with the people encountering Jesus and his disciples. And it goes along with the theological point that the approaching kingdom of God invites everyone to repentance (Mark 1:14–15 par.) but is also connected with the metaphor of God as father.

3.1.3. The Significance of Jesus's Metaphorical Speech about God as Father

In accordance with the plausibility of historical effects, the large number of Jesus sayings in the Gospels that use the metaphor of God as "father" (ca. 167 times; cf. C. Zimmermann 2007a, 41, 74–76; on the numbers and as a basic principle, Schlosser 1987, 103–209; Vermes 1993b, 152–83) must be reminiscent of the manner of speaking of the earthly Jesus. For it is striking that in the Gospels talk of God as father is encountered only on the lips of Jesus. Just this can reflect that Jesus himself used this metaphor frequently. The unusual transmission of the Aramaic *abba* as a loanword transcribed in Greek in Jesus's address of prayer in Mark 14:36 (cf. Rom. 8:15; Gal. 4:6 on the lips of believers, in each case translated with ὁ πατήρ) speaks in favor of the fact that this pertains especially to *abba* as the address of prayer ("Father" as an address, and "my father").

With sizable repercussions, Joachim Jeremias ([4]1988, 67–73) popularized the thesis that *abba* is "child talk, everyday language, polite expression" and therefore was "disrespectful for the sensitivity of Jesus's contemporaries [in Palestinian Judaism], indeed as unthinkable to address God with this familiar word" (72). Hence it is the "ipsissima vox of Jesus" and expresses "the heart of Jesus's relationship with God," his "consciousness of sonship," and knowledge of his authority (73).

This thesis has been accepted up until recently (references in Schelbert 2011, 23–34). It rests, however, on a fragile *argumentum e silentio*, because hardly any literary evidence from agrarian or Galilean Judaism at the time of Jesus is preserved, likewise no oral prayers. Further, the critical examination of the instances of *abba* by Schelbert 2011 shows that the word is not only vocative, that in the first place it means "my father" (also in Hebrew for *abbi*), and that this address to a father has no connotations of the language of children (191–92; cf. aptly Vermes 1993b: "Abba isn't daddy" [180]). Thus, from the (contingent?) observation that there are no parallels for *abba* as an address in prayer, no specifics of theological content of Jesus's concept of God can be derived.

This holds all the more as in recent years it has been verified that the metaphor of God as father, including the address of God as "father" in prayer, was common in Judaism at the time of Jesus (and also in pagan religiosity; cf. C. Zimmermann 2007, 64–70). After a few references in the Old Testament, the metaphor of God as father clearly increased in early Judaism (cf. the detailed examination by C. Zimmermann 2007, 41–79, in particular; on the Old Testament, Böckler 2000; on early Judaism, Strotmann 1991; on the oldest rabbinic texts, Tönges 2003).

In the New Testament, once again the metaphorical talk of God as "father" increases but also shows development. In New Testament epistles, it is now a stock metaphor (cf., for instance, the epistolary greeting formulas in 1 Cor. 1:3 and passim), and the correlative metaphor of Jesus as the only "Son of God" flows into the significance of the concept of God as father (so esp. in the Gospel of John, cf., e.g., 20:31; 3:35). For the question of how the historical Jesus did conceptualize God, of course only the oldest synoptic texts are informative, which do not show a deepening Christology. Statements that correlate the father and son (Mark 13:32; Luke 10:22 par.), and ones in which Jesus speaks of "*my* father (in heaven)" (overview in Schneider 1992), cannot be held valid as authentic Jesus material. They are nearly absent in Mark, appear seldom in Luke (2:49; 10:22; 22:29; 24:49), and are frequent only in Matthew. Where synoptic comparison is possible (cf. Matt. 10:32–33 with Luke 12:8–9; Matt. 12:50 with Mark 3:35; Matt. 20:23 with Mark 10:40), they are recognizably Matthean redaction, and the expression ὁ πατήρ μου ἐν τοῖς οὐρανοῖς ("my father in heaven," e.g., also in Matt. 18:10, 19, 35) is already formulaic.

Therefore, there are not very many statements from which the meaning of the metaphor of God as father in Jesus's speech can be read. In addition to statements about God as father (Mark 8:38 as father of the son of man; 11:25; Matt. 5:16, 45, 48; 6:4, 6, 8, 14–15, 32; 7:21; 10:20, 29; Luke 6:36; 12:30, 32) is the aforementioned address to God in prayer as *abba* or πατήρ. Indisputably "authentic" among the prayers is the Lord's Prayer (D.IV.3.5) in the version in Luke 11:2–4 (cf. Matt. 6:9). But also, even though the appeal to God as father in Jesus's prayer in Gethsemane (Mark 14:36 par.) and Jesus's prayers according to Luke 10:22 par. and 23:34 (but text critically uncertain) are post-Easter formulations, they can carry on the memory of Jesus's praxis of prayer.

In order to determine the contribution of talk about God as father to Jesus's concept of God and its pragmatic functions, it is necessary to follow a methodologically guided exposition, which takes note of the metaphorical character of the individual statements. Each one has to be interpreted in itself in view of what from the *ancient concept of father is concretely transferred to God* (cf. on the methodology, Gerber 2008). The picture then is more nuanced than in the research that is often limited in seeing in the predication of God as father the expression of God's "nearness," but thereby only to substitute one metaphor (a kinship metaphor) for another (spatial metaphorical) (cf. accordingly, Schlosser 1987, 203–9).

For interpretation it is necessary to proceed from the source vehicle of the metaphor, the ancient concept of father. "Father" is a relational term, since it always implies the relationship of a man with one or more children. This relationship is determined by a lifelong duration and asymmetrical exclusivity: a child has only one father but a father can have many children. Thus, talk of God as father always has one or more "children" in mind, whether explicitly or not. So the metaphor can qualify the relationship of God to human beings in that it particularly expresses the oneness of this God and the *exclusive* relationship with him. At the same time, it can be *inclusive* in that it leaves open who belongs to God as "father."

Being the "child" of a father in antiquity is, however, not simply a biological given, but rather a statement about recognition as the father's legitimate child by the father. Roman law gave prominence to the authority and freedom of the *paterfamilias* to decide whether to let a newborn babe die or to adopt unnatural children as fully valid (Schiemann 2006).

Thus, "son of God" or "child of God" can describe a status bestowed by God, such as in the metaphor of the Jewish people as "children of God" (Mark 7:27 par.). Differently, according to Luke 6:35 and Matt. 5:44–45, 48 (cf. 5:9), God will promise this status to those who follow God's example or make peace (cf. also John 1:12; Gal. 4:1–7). Simultaneously, in these sayings another aspect of the paternal role is implied: the ideal father is an example by which ideal children can be guided. So the injunction to imitate God is not haphazardly linked with the paternal metaphor (cf. also Eph. 5:1; John 5:19–23).

The other metaphors of God as father from the presumably oldest Jesus tradition revolve around specific themes: prayer to God and the assurance that God hears prayer, God's parental care, and his readiness to forgive. Already the Old Testament and Jewish tradition linked this with the metaphor of God as father (Böckler 2000, 377–94; Strotmann 1991, 360–79; Tönges 2003, 247–51, 257–62). The authority, which in antiquity was especially assigned to a father, is not emphasized here (but cf. Mark 13:32 par.; Matt. 7:21; cf. 12:50). Also, "fatherly love," with which, in modern appropriation of the metaphor, God as father is often associated, is not the issue (only indirectly; cf. Luke 6:36; 15:11–32). Authority and loving attention are, however, presumed in these ascriptions to God.

These motifs of a caring parent, hearing prayer, and forgiveness are found bundled together in the Our Father (see D.IV.3.5) in Luke 11:2–4 par., but they are also developed in parables and figurations: the sayings about worry in Matt. 6:25–32 par. refer to the "heavenly father" as creator and provider. A deduction by analogy of the parable in Matt. 7:7–11 is that God hears prayers (Matt. 6:6): if even evil earthly parents or fathers grant the requests of their children, how much more will "the father in heaven" (Luke 11:13 par.)? Further, the metaphor of God as father emphasizes that God already knows the needs of human beings (Matt. 6:6, 32 par.; 10:29 par.). Thus, prayer to God as to a father expresses the trust that God knows the requests of humans and is able to fulfill them (cf. also Mark 14:36).

Also, God's readiness to forgive is especially linked with the concept of father (Mark 11:25; Matt. 6:14-15; cf. 18:35; Luke 23:34). The parable of the father of two sons in Luke 15:11-32 develops this motif in a narrative. It is based on the notion that the father as a person with sovereign authority can mete out punishment for his children or remit it.

These aspects in the concept of God that are formed by the metaphor of God as father relate to characteristics and functions that in our culture are also associated with a "motherly" attitude (care, forbearance, etc.). However, in the context of the ancient concept of the patriarchal family, in which the mother is subservient to the father, only the role of father can be put in the figuration of the omnipotent God who is over all (cf. Gerber 2008). But even if the metaphor of God as father takes up the patriarchal structures as the source vehicle of the imagery, it can simultaneously mediate a critique of power relations. The omission of the father in the new family (Mark 3:34-35 par.; 10:29-30) demonstrates this. In addition, if Jesus supposedly demanded that no one be called "father" but God, as it is transmitted in Matt. 23:9, he derived from this metaphorical figuration of God as father a critique of ascribing humans' paternal authority. This critique could also have been turned against the Roman imperial metaphorical paternal figuration, such as the veneration of Caesar as *pater patriae* (D'Angelo 2006).

3.1.4. Conclusion

Within the possibilities of Jewish talk about God, God is addressed by Jesus especially in diverse metaphors, which are created from everyday life and make different things perceptible. The metaphors of God's kingship and God as father are central. They move God's oneness, authority, and relationship with individual persons to the foreground in various pointed statements. This is not about describing God's essence anew and differently than previously, but rather about inviting people into trust in God and a life in conformity with God's will.

Schelbert, Georg 2011. *Abba Vater: Der literarische Befund vom Altaramäischen bis zu den späten Midrasch- und Haggada-Werken in Auseinandersetzung mit den Thesen von Joachim Jeremias.* NTOA 81/SUNT 81. Göttingen.

Schlosser, Jacques. 1987. *Le Dieu de Jésus: Étude exégétique.* LD 129. Paris.

Thompson, Marianne Meye. 2011. "Jesus and God." In *Handbook for the Study of the Historical Jesus,* vol. 3, *The Historical Jesus,* edited by Tom Holmén and Stanley E. Porter, 2575–95. Leiden.

Zimmermann, Christiane. 2007. *Die Namen des Vaters: Studien zu ausgewählten neutestamentlichen Gottesbezeichnungen vor ihrem frühjüdischen und paganen Sprachhorizont.* AJEC 69. Leiden.

Christine Gerber

3.2. The Kingdom of God

The "kingdom of God" concept is rooted in Israel's ancient Scriptures and stands at the center of the preaching of Jesus (G. Klein 1970).

3.2.1. The Kingdom of God in the Old Testament and Related Literature

The concept of the kingdom of God is founded on the conviction that Yahweh (the Lord), the God of Israel, is king. It is he who reigns over Israel, over the nations, and over the whole earth. The kingdom, kingship, or reign of God is expressed in a variety of ways, sometimes explicitly; often it is implied (Beasley-Murray 1986; Patrick 1987).

3.2.1.1. God as Judge and Redeemer

God's role as king is implied in his actions as judge, redeemer, warrior, and savior, attributes and actions associated with kings in the ancient Near East. Many of these elements come together in an important testimony in Isaiah: "For the Lord is our judge, the Lord is our ruler, the Lord is our king; he will save us" (Isa. 33:22).

God's role as redeemer finds frequent expression in the Prophets and the book of Psalms. In Second Isaiah Yahweh is many times called redeemer and holy one, sometimes in contexts of endearment and intimacy: "Thus says the Lord, your Redeemer, who formed you from the womb" (Isa. 44:24; 54:5: "your Maker is your husband"; 54:8: "with everlasting love I will have compassion on you"; 63:16: "thou, O Lord, art our Father, our Redeemer"). God has "comforted his people" and "redeemed Jerusalem" (52:9). God is "Redeemer" and the "Holy One of Israel" (41:14; 43:14; 48:17; 49:7; 54:5), the "Lord of hosts" (47:4), who is "the first and . . . the last," the only God (44:6), the "Mighty One of Jacob" (49:26). God "will come to Zion as Redeemer, to those in Jacob who turn from transgression"

(59:20). The day will come when Israel will know that the Lord is her "Savior" and "Redeemer, the Mighty One of Jacob" (60:16). Echoing the Isaianic tradition, Jeremiah confesses, "'Their Redeemer is strong; the Lord of hosts is his name" (Jer. 50:34). The psalmist addresses God as his rock and redeemer (Ps. 19:14; cf. 78:35), a God who "redeems the life of his servants" (34:22).

3.2.1.2. God as King

God as king is explicitly affirmed in several places in Israel's Scriptures. In what is probably the earliest tradition, Yahweh consoles Samuel the prophet and priest when Israel demands to have a king, that the people may be like other nations (1 Sam. 8:5-6): "Hearken to the voice of the people in all that they say to you; for they have not rejected you, but they have rejected me from being king over them" (8:7).

This breach is in part healed in the kingship of David, the man whose character is after God's heart (1 Sam. 13:14). David is adopted as God's son: "You are my son, today I have begotten you" (Ps. 2:7; cf. 2 Sam. 7:14; Ps. 89:26). If Israel's kings are God's sons, it is implied, then God is himself Israel's great king. In a sense, David's kingdom is an adumbration of God's kingdom (which becomes explicit in the later Chronicles).

Isaiah and his tradition explicitly speak of God as king: "In the year that King Uzziah died I saw the Lord sitting upon a throne, high and lifted up; and his train filled the temple. . . . And I said: 'Woe is me! For I am lost; for I am a man of unclean lips, and I dwell in the midst of a people of unclean lips; for my eyes have seen the King, the Lord of hosts!'" (Isa. 6:1, 5; cf. 33:22). In Second Isaiah the Lord identifies himself as "the King of Jacob" (41:21) and "the King of Israel" (44:6).

Similarly the prophet Jeremiah refers to Israel's God as "King" (Jer. 10:10; 51:57), the "Lord of hosts" (48:15), who resides in Zion (8:19). God is Israel's everlasting king (10:10). Israel's God is the "King of the nations" (10:7). This language is echoed in Zephaniah, who calls God "the King of Israel" (Zeph. 3:15), and in Zechariah, "the king, the Lord of hosts" (14:16), and "King over all the earth" (14:9). God, the "Lord of hosts," says of himself in Malachi, "I am a great King" (Mal. 1:14).

The Psalter frequently speaks of God as king (Ps. 5:2; cf. Pss. 44:4; 47:6; 68:24). The Lord loves justice, establishes equity, and executes justice and righteousness in Israel (99:4).

3.2.1.3. The Kingdom of the Lord

The expression "kingdom of Yahweh" occurs twice in Israel's ancient Scriptures, both times in Chronicles and both times in close association with David's royal house (1 Chron. 28:5; 2 Chron. 13:8).

The idea of God sitting on a throne is ancient, reaching back at least to the time of the prophet Micaiah: "Therefore hear the word of the Lord: I saw the Lord sitting on his throne, and all the host of heaven standing beside him on his right hand and on his left" (1 Kings 22:19; 2 Chron. 18:18), which recalls Isaiah's vision (Isa. 6:1).

When all the relevant data are assembled, it becomes clear that the concept of Yahweh as king of Israel and king of the whole earth runs throughout Israel's ancient Scriptures, even if the precise phrase "kingdom of the Lord" only occurs twice and the phrase "kingdom of God" never occurs.

3.2.2. Kingdom of God Language and Expectation in Intertestamental Literature

Kingdom of God language and expectation become more explicit and variegated in intertestamental literature (J. Collins 1987; Lattke 1984). Some of this developing tradition becomes foundational for Jesus and early Christian theology.

3.2.2.1. Daniel

The Aramaic-Hebrew book of Daniel is an important witness to kingdom ideas in the intertestamental period of time (Chilton 1994; Evans 2009b). The book envisions a succession of four human kingdoms or empires. These human kingdoms will be destroyed by the kingdom that "the God of heaven will set up." This will be the final kingdom, "which shall never be destroyed" (Dan. 2:44; cf. 4:34; 6:26). The Babylonian king later confesses: "How great are his [God's] signs, how mighty his wonders! His kingdom is an everlasting kingdom, and his dominion is from generation to generation" (4:3; cf. 4:17, 25, 31, 34, 37; 5:21). In his night vision Daniel learns that "the kingdom and the dominion and the greatness of the kingdoms under the whole heaven shall be given to the people of the saints of the Most High; their kingdom shall be an everlasting kingdom, and all dominions shall serve and obey them" (7:27; cf. 7:14).

3.2.2.2. Dead Sea Scrolls

Although the precise phrase "kingdom of God" does not appear in the scrolls, the concept nevertheless occurs many times (Viviano 1987). In the eschatological blessings of the second appendix to the Rule of the Community, the congregation is instructed to say of the priest: "May you serve in the temple of the kingdom" (1QSb iv 25–26). Given the context, it is almost certain the kingdom referred to is the kingdom of God. A later blessing speaks of the renewal of the covenant and the establishment of "the kingdom of his (God's) people forever" (v 21).

Elsewhere we read: "Your (God's) kingdom is exalted among the peoples . . . the council of the pure divine beings with all those who know how to praise eternally, and to bless your (God's) glorious name through all the times of eternity. Amen. Amen" (4Q286 7 i 5–7; see the parallel 4Q287 v 10–11). Another wisdom text refers to God's kingdom: "As for God, His dwelling is in heaven, and [His king]dom embraces the lands, the sea" (4Q302 3 ii 9–10). The author of the Hodayot ("hymns") speaks of God's kingdom, but the text is fragmented (1QHª iii 27: ". . . His kingdom. Who has done all of these things?").

Most of the references to the kingdom of God in the Dead Sea Scrolls occur in texts known as the Songs of the Sabbath Sacrifice (4Q400–4Q405). In these texts, one finds some twenty references to God's kingdom (though almost always using the personal pronoun). Only a small portion of these songs has survived. If these scrolls had survived in full, we would have dozens of additional references to God's kingdom.

The men of the Qumran community anticipated the coming of this kingdom in its fullness, at which time the community's enemies would be vanquished and a righteous priesthood would be reestablished in Jerusalem. "So the kingdom shall belong to the God of Israel, and by the holy ones of his people he shall act powerfully" (1QM vi 6). The righteous of Israel will reign forever (1QM xii 15–16). The men of Qumran praise God: "You, O God, are awe[some] in the glory of your kingdom" (1QM xii 7). With the restoration of the kingdom and the high priesthood, a "great temple of the [ki]n[g]dom will be built in majestic splendor to endure for eternal generations" (4Q212 1 iv 18).

3.2.2.3. *Other Literature*

Other writings from the intertestamental period speak of the kingdom of God or of God as King (Jub. 1:28; T. Dan 5:13). The author of the Testament of Moses predicts the appearance of God's kingdom after Israel endures a period of wrath: "Then his (God's) kingdom will appear. . . . For the Heavenly One will arise from his kingly throne" (T. Mos. 10:1, 3). Because of Israel's sin, "the kingdom of the Lord" will be taken away (T. Benj. 9:1). Elsewhere we are told that God's "kingdom is an everlasting kingdom, which will not pass away" (T. Jos. 19:12). In 1 Enoch God is exalted as "King of the Universe" (12:3) and "God of the whole creation" (84:2).

3.2.3. Kingdom of God in the Proclamation and Actions of Jesus

At the very center of Jesus's proclamation is the kingdom of God. Indeed, the kingdom of God is itself the gospel or good news, for which Israel has waited:

"The time is fulfilled, and the kingdom of God is at hand; repent, and believe in the gospel" (Mark 1:15). This proclamation of the kingdom is explicitly said to be the "gospel" or "good news" (1:14). The evangelist Mark rightly understands the proclamation of the kingdom of God to lie at the very heart of Jesus's message.

Jesus's understanding of the good news of the kingdom of God reflects the good news proclaimed in the book of Isaiah. The good news (or good tidings) is the appearance of God (Isa. 40:9), the announcement of his reign (52:7), and his saving, redemptive work (61:1–2). Some of these texts are quoted or alluded to in Jesus's preaching (e.g., Isa. 61:1–2 in Matt. 11:5 par. Luke 7:22 and in Luke 4:18–19). Jesus's wording and interpretation reflect how Isaiah was paraphrased and interpreted in Aramaic.

3.2.3.1. Proclamation

The theme of the kingdom of God is the subject of many of Jesus's parables. Response to the kingdom is likened to seed that is sown (Mark 4:3–20 [that it is the *kingdom* is made explicit in the parallel at Matt. 13:19]; 4:26–29, 30–32). Petitioning God that his kingdom come is the basic theme of one's prayer (Matt. 6:10; Luke 11:2: "May your kingdom come!"). Seeking the kingdom is one's first priority (Matt. 6:33); it is valuable above all else (13:44, 45–46, 47–48). Those who are blessed are those who will enter the kingdom of God (5:3, 10), no matter what the cost (Mark 9:42–50).

Wealth, greed, hypocrisy, unwillingness to forgive, and indifference toward the poor and hungry may prevent people from entering the kingdom of God (Matt. 18:23–35; 23:13; Mark 10:17–31). Divided loyalties, folly, and lack of preparation may also shut a person out of the kingdom (Matt. 25:1–13; Luke 9:61–62).

The kingdom of God is a central feature in the Words of Institution at the Last Supper: "Truly, I say to you, I shall not drink again of the fruit of the vine until that day when I drink it new in the kingdom of God" (Mark 14:25). The coming kingdom is certain (Mark 9:1); it involves struggle (Matt. 11:12); but the time of its coming is not known (Matt. 24:14; 25:13; Mark 13:8, 32; Luke 17:20–21). The crucifixion of Jesus for claiming to be the "king of the Jews" (Matt. 27:37; Mark 15:26; Luke 23:38; John 19:19) serves as a grim reference to the earlier proclamation of the kingdom of God.

3.2.3.2. Healings and Exorcisms

A striking feature in Jesus's preaching is his linking of the kingdom of God with healing and exorcism. Healing and exorcism are not incidental to Jesus's proclamation; they are illustrative and demonstrative.

Jesus appoints twelve apostles to "preach and have authority to cast out demons" (Mark 3:14–15; 6:7–13). In Luke the linkage between proclaiming the gospel of the kingdom of God and healing and exorcism is made explicit: "And he called the twelve together and gave them power and authority over all demons and to cure diseases, and he sent them out to preach the kingdom of God" (Luke 9:1–2).

The linkage between the kingdom of God and exorcism is clarified when Jesus is accused of being in league with Beelzebul (or Satan). To this charge Jesus retorts: "And if I cast out demons by Beelzebul, by whom do your sons cast them out? Therefore they shall be your judges. But if it is by the finger of God that I cast out demons, then the kingdom of God has come upon you" (Luke 11:19–20 par. Matt. 12:27–28). The expression "finger of God" harks back to the confession of Pharaoh's magicians (Exod. 8:19). According to Jewish interpretation, Pharaoh's magicians were in league with Satan. Jesus's allusion to the confession of the magicians is rhetorically effective. Jesus has affirmed that his exorcisms are not the result of magic or Satan's assistance; they are the result of God's kingly power (Chilton 1994).

Jesus reasons further: "If a kingdom is divided against itself, that kingdom cannot stand. And if a house is divided against itself, that house will not be able to stand. And if Satan has risen up against himself and is divided, he cannot stand, but is coming to an end" (Mark 3:24–26). The reference to the divided kingdom implies that Jesus thinks of Satan's sphere of power as a kingdom, a kingdom at war with the kingdom of God. The last part of the quotation, "is coming to an end" (τέλος ἔχει; lit. "has an end"), finds a significant parallel in the Testament of Moses, where, after a season of persecution and suffering, God's people are assured: "Then his (God's) kingdom will appear throughout his whole creation. Then the devil will have an end. . . . For the heavenly One will arise from his kingly throne" (T. Mos. 10:1, 3). The Latin "will have an end" (*finem habebit*), apart from the tense itself, is an exact parallel to Mark's "is coming to an end" (Evans 2009a). The opposition of the kingdoms of God and Satan is made explicit. The progress of the kingdom of God requires the retreat and eventual destruction of the kingdom of Satan.

3.2.3.3. Jewish Background

Jesus's proclamation of the kingdom of God as having come probably reflects the Aramaic tradition in which texts like Isa. 40:9 and 52:7 are paraphrased to read, "the kingdom of your God is revealed" (Chilton 1994). The hope for the coming of the kingdom of God was expressed in the Kaddish, a very old Aramaic prayer (Elbogen 1993), a version of which seems to lie behind the Lord's Prayer.

3.2.4. Distinctive Elements in Jesus's Understanding of the Kingdom of God

We learn from Josephus that from the time of Herod the Great (r. 37–4 BCE) until the destruction of the temple in 70 CE there were a number of would-be messiahs and prophets who offered signs of coming redemption. It is in this general context that we should understand the request put to Jesus: "Teacher, we wish to see a sign from you" (Matt. 12:38; cf. 16: 1–4; Mark 8:11; Luke 17:20). In contrast to many of his contemporaries, Jesus refuses to offer a sign. Provocatively, Jesus declares: "The kingdom of God is not coming with signs to be observed; nor will they say, 'Lo, here it is!' or 'There!' for behold, the kingdom of God is in the midst of you" (Luke 17:20–21).

The kingdom runs throughout Jesus's ministry, from his public preaching to his private teaching, especially on the eve of Passover and his passion. The very Words of Institution (Matt. 26:26–29; Mark 14:22–25; Luke 22:15–20) are linked to the kingdom of God. Jesus has desired to eat the Passover with his disciples before his passion (Luke 22:15)—perhaps implying that the Last Supper was not the Passover meal but a meal the night before (which, if so, would be in agreement with the chronology of the Gospel of John). But he shall not eat it "until it is fulfilled in the kingdom of God" (Luke 22:16).

Mark and Luke regularly speak of the "kingdom of God" (ἡ βασιλεία τοῦ θεοῦ). The expression occurs some fourteen times in Mark and thirty-two times in Luke, while in Matthew the kingdom (usually "of heaven," ἡ βασιλεία τῶν οὐρανῶν) is referenced some thirty-six times. Distinctive elements in Jesus's proclamation of the kingdom of God can be observed in the four Gospels.

3.2.4.1. *Jesus and the Kingdom according to Mark*

In the Gospel of Mark, probably the first of the four Gospels to have been written and circulated, the kingdom of God is mysterious, or secret, whose true meaning has only been disclosed to the disciples of Jesus; by way of contrast, outsiders receive riddles (Mark 4:11, 24–25; cf. 4:33–34). Not all respond in faith to the proclamation of the kingdom (4:3–9). How the kingdom of God grows is also mysterious (4:26–29, 30–32).

No price is too high to enter the kingdom of God. No one should allow anything to prevent entry into the kingdom. Jesus admonishes his disciples to pluck out an eye or cut off a hand rather than be drawn into sin and be cast into hell (9:42–48). Indeed, wealth often prevents people from embracing the message of the kingdom (10:17–22). Against widely held assumptions, wealth was no sure indication of one's fitness for entry into the kingdom of God. On the contrary, says Jesus, "It is easier for a camel to go through the eye of a needle than for a rich man to enter the kingdom of God" (10:25).

Jesus teaches that the weak and the poor are more likely to be received into the kingdom of God than the wealthy and powerful. Accordingly, children are to be received and blessed, "for to such belongs the kingdom of God" (10:14). Indeed, says Jesus, "Whoever does not receive the kingdom of God like a child shall not enter it" (10:15).

3.2.4.2. Jesus and the Kingdom according to Matthew

Although "kingdom of God" occurs in Matthew four times, the evangelist's preferred language is "kingdom of heaven," which occurs some thirty-two times. The difference is purely formal and reflects Matthew's tendency, probably observed in the synagogue of his day, to avoid pronouncing the name of God. Often in Matthew "kingdom" appears without further qualification. These appearances also refer to the kingdom of God. In all, there are some fifty-four references to the kingdom (of God/heaven) in the Gospel of Matthew.

Matthew also uniquely speaks of the "sons of the kingdom" (8:12; 13:38). The second reference is positive: the good seed of the parable of the wheat and tares is the sons of the kingdom. However, the first passage, which is embedded in the story of the healing of the centurion's servant (Matt. 8:5–13 par. Luke 7:1–10), warns that the sons of the kingdom "will be thrown into outer darkness." Here the sons of the kingdom are Israelites, who by heritage and ancient promises expect to enter the kingdom of heaven and sit at table with the patriarchs. But because of unbelief and refusal to repent, they will be excluded. Other, less likely candidates, such as those who "come from east and west," will be included. The parables of Jesus in Matthew that distinguish between the good and the bad should be understood in the same way. Some seed is good; some seed is bad (13:24–30). Some fish are good; some fish are bad (13:47–50). Some maidens are wise; some maidens are foolish (25:1–13). The Matthean parables seem to serve as warnings to ethnic Israel: failure to repent and embrace Jesus's proclamation will result in being excluded from the kingdom.

3.2.4.3. Jesus and the Kingdom according to Luke

The implications for election seen in some of Jesus's teaching on the kingdom in Mark are more forcefully expressed in the Gospel of Luke. The evangelist Luke seems to have been especially interested in the question of election, that is to say, who are qualified for entry into the kingdom and on what basis.

In response to a man who pronounces a blessing on all "who shall eat bread in the kingdom of God" (Luke 14:15), an allusion to Isaiah's prophecy of the great eschatological banquet (Isa. 25:6), Jesus utters his parable of the great banquet (Luke 14:16–24), in which, contrary to popular expectations, "the poor and maimed and blind and lame" enjoy the feast, while the affluent, that is, those who outwardly appear to have enjoyed God's blessing, will not participate. Jesus's parable would have startled his contemporaries, for the parable understands election in a way that seemingly stands in tension with the Torah itself, as it touches on cultic purity (Lev. 21:17–23), and especially with contemporary interpretation, as seen in 1QSa ii 5–22, where on the occasion of the appearance of the Messiah, to celebrate the eschatological banquet, the "lame, blind, deaf, dumb, or possessed of a visible blemish in his flesh" will not be allowed to sit at table with the great ones of Israel.

Jesus surprises his hearers with additional parables that run counter to assumptions about the kingdom of God. In the parable of the rich man and the poor man (Luke 16:19–30), it is Lazarus the poor man who is received into Paradise, not the wealthy man. In the parable of the Pharisee and the tax collector (Luke 18:9–14), it is the repentant tax collector, not the self-righteous Pharisee, who is justified in the sight of God.

3.2.4.4. Jesus and the Kingdom according to John

The function of "kingdom of God" in the Gospel of John is quite distinctive. The expression only occurs twice, both times in John 3 (at vv. 3 and 5), in the well-known conversation with Nicodemus. Jesus tells the teacher that he must be born from above (or *anew*), and he must be "born of water and the Spirit," if he is to see or enter the kingdom of God. In Johannine theology, the kingdom of God is part of the evangelist's theology of salvation and mystical union with Christ (as seen esp. in John 14–16). The distinctive language and style are Johannine, to be sure, but the themes and content may well derive from Jesus (on this possibility, see Bartholomä 2012).

3.2.5. Kingdom of God Language in Acts

Given the prominence of the kingdom of God in the preaching of Jesus, it is surprising that this language plays so small a role elsewhere in the New Testament.

The expressions "kingdom" and "kingdom of God" occur eight times in the book of Acts. During the forty days the risen Jesus was with his disciples, he was "speaking of the kingdom of God" (1:3). This leads to the disciples' question:

"Lord, will you at this time restore the kingdom to Israel?" (1:6). The disciples are told only that the "times or seasons" are known only to God (1:7). They are to wait for the Holy Spirit and then bear witness to Jesus (1:8). This occurs on the Day of Pentecost (Acts 2).

Philip preaches the "good news about the kingdom of God and the name of Jesus Christ" (8:12). Paul teaches his converts, "Through many tribulations we must enter the kingdom of God" (14:22). Paul enters a synagogue "and for three months [speaks] boldly, arguing and pleading about the kingdom of God" (19:8). The apostle reminds the Ephesian elders that he had preached the kingdom (20:25). Under arrest in Rome, Paul continues to speak to the Jews concerning "the kingdom of God" (28:23). The book of Acts concludes on a positive note, saying that Paul "welcomed all who came to him, preaching the kingdom of God and teaching about the Lord Jesus Christ" (28:30–31).

What is interesting in the book of Acts is not only the few occurrences of "kingdom" or "kingdom of God," but how reference to the kingdom is expanded to include something about Jesus. The message is no longer simply the message of Jesus, namely, the in-breaking of the kingdom of God; the message is just as much about Jesus himself, his suffering and death and, more importantly, his resurrection.

Beasley-Murray, George Raymond. 1986. *Jesus and the Kingdom of God.* Grand Rapids.

Hengel, Martin, and Anna Maria Schwemer, eds. 1991. *Königsherrschaft Gottes und himmlischer Kult im Judentum, Urchristentum und in der hellenistischen Welt.* WUNT 55. Tübingen.

Vanoni, Gottfried, and Bernhard Heininger. 2002. *Das Reich Gottes.* NEchtB.Themen 4. Würzburg.

Willis, Wendall, ed. 1987b. *The Kingdom of God in 20th-Century Interpretation.* Peabody, MA.

Craig Evans and Jeremiah J. Johnston

3.3. Similitudes and Parables

Jesus told parables. Parables are short, pithy stories that use everyday experiences in order to convey a theological message. This way of speaking is so characteristic for Jesus that the evangelists can even summarize his entire teaching as "speaking in parables" (Mark 4:34: "He did not speak to them except in parables"; cf. John 16:25). Some of these texts, such as the parable of the Good Samaritan

(Luke 10:30–35) or the parable of the prodigal son (Luke 15:11–32), are numbered among the most powerfully efficacious texts of the New Testament in general (cf. on the reception history, Gowler 2017). What makes them so captivating? Why are they so central for Jesus's teaching?

3.3.1. Did the Historical Jesus Speak of the "Kingdom of God" in Parables?

Metaphorical discourse on God was popular in Judaism, because whereas a material representation of God had been disallowed (see the prohibition of images in Exod. 20:4), people dared to enter into the boundary areas of what could be predicated by figurative speech. Jesus did not merely draw on these traditions of metaphors but composed "metaphorical stories" in order to speak about God and God's reality. This way of speaking and its pointed emphasis in content on the βασιλεία τοῦ θεοῦ (God's realm/the kingdom of God; see D.IV.3.2) are closely related to each other. It is no surprise, therefore, that research on the historical Jesus has adhered with great unanimity to the affirmation that Jesus proclaimed the "kingdom of God in parables" (e.g., Hengel and Schwemer 1998, 398; Hultgren 2000, 384). But is the evidence in the sources really so unequivocal?

According to the two-source hypothesis accepted by the majority, in the oldest sources only a few isolated instances of "parables of the kingdom of God" are found. Amid an abundance of parable texts in the sayings source Q (twenty-eight texts; see R. Zimmermann ²2015, 59–60), the kingdom of God as a field of reference is introduced only two times: in the parables of the mustard seed and the yeast we read: "To what shall I compare the kingdom of God?" (Q 13:18, 20). A similar picture is apparent in Mark. Here also, among seventeen parables (cf. R. Zimmermann ²2015, 262–63), explicit language about the kingdom of God occurs only twice (Mark 4:26, 30–31), one instance of which is the parallel in Q on the parable of the mustard seed. Hence, out of forty-five parables transmitted in the two oldest sources, only three refer to the kingdom of God. Not until the later tradition of the Gospels, especially the Gospel of Matthew, can we document a more unambiguous picture in that here the kingdom of God as the field of reference for the parables is mentioned ten times (Matt. 13:24–30; 13:44, 45–46, 47–50, 52; 18:23–35; 20:1–16; 21:28–32; 22:1–14; 25:1–13); not infrequently this has to do with special material of the first evangelist (cf. also John 3:3–5; Gos. Thom. 22, 64, 97, 98).

When we evaluate this evidence rigorously in accordance with an origin-oriented research on the historical Jesus, we see that only infrequently did Jesus speak of the kingdom of God in parables. Doubtless, the actual originator of this idea was Matthew. By contrast, research on Jesus following the so-called memory approach sees in Matthew the conflation of two streams of the memory of Jesus: the memory that Jesus spoke in parables and the memory of the constitutive significance of the kingdom of God in his proclamation. Consequently, Matthew does not stand against the tradition, which has to be freed from his redaction, but in the midst of the stream of tradition, and he weaves together what is substantiated in the subject matter itself: speaking in parables is considered to be constitutive for Jesus's teaching of God's reality. It is the concrete life of human beings, by which Jesus expresses his theological message. Accordingly, James D. G. Dunn (2003b, 385) can summarize comprehensively: "Jesus was evidently remembered as using parables to illustrate or illumine what he had in mind when he spoke of the kingdom." The example shows how closely research on Jesus and research on parables are intertwined.

3.3.2. The Quest for the Historical Proclaimer of Parables— a Foray into the History of Research

Historical research on the parables is distinguished by two fundamental affirmations: One, throughout all phases of research the authenticity of the parables as Jesus's original discourse has been held onto. Two, this discourse of Jesus has been viewed as altered, manipulated, and often enough corrupted by the gospel tradition.

A prominent example of such an evaluation exists in the magnum opus of Adolf Jülicher, *Die Gleichnisreden Jesu* (vol. 1, 1886; vol. 2, 1899), whose work became formative in several respects. Jülicher ([2]1910, 1:24) held the conviction that the parables "went back to Jesus himself," indeed, "that they belonged to the most assured and best transmitted of Jesus's sayings that we now possess." However, he saw striking differences between Jesus's simple parables and the tendency of the tradition of the evangelists to allegorize (1:2, 8, 202). Joachim Jeremias ([11]1998, 18–19) picked up these convictions and accordingly drew methodological consequences: it was necessary to recognize "laws of transformation" in order to be able to go back "from the early church to Jesus," all the way to Jesus's "*ipsissima vox.*"

What held for the form of individual parables could also be applied to the parables as a whole. Especially in American research the criterion of dissimilarity was taken over into parable research in the early work of John Dominic Crossan under the title *In Parables: The Challenge of the Historical Jesus* (1973): "Those narrative parables seemed to be most surely his own characteristic pedagogic genre as distinct from the usage of the primitive church and also contemporary Judaism" (Crossan 2002, 248, with reference to his earlier work).

In the "Jesus Seminar" of the Westar Institute, with such criteria a list of twenty-two parables were designated "authentic" (Funk 2006). Quite typical for the "third quest" of Jesus research was the inclusion of extracanonical sources such as the Gospel of Thomas, from which two parables from special material were included (Gos. Thom. 97, 98; see B.X). Recently J. P. Meier (2016) has postulated a stupendous reduction of the textual base to only four authentic parables of Jesus (Mark 4:30–32; 12:1–11; Matt. 22:2–14: 25:14–30 with parallels). Notwithstanding such extreme outcomes, historical Jesus research applied to parables has continued until the most recent publications. However, mostly circular hermeneutical-methodological reasoning underlies the determination of "authentic" parables of Jesus.

On the one hand, the "classics" such as the parable of the lost sheep (Luke 15:1–7) are not permitted to go missing, whereas shocking texts such as the parable of the brutal slave, whom the returning head of the house "cuts into pieces" (Luke 12:42–46), are frequently disregarded. On the other hand, as an underlying pattern one can observe the attempt to isolate an original message of Jesus from the later tradition preserved in the New Testament. Recent examples include the interpretations of parables by Schottroff and Levine. In her "nondualistic" interpretation, Luise Schottroff (2005) wanted to separate Jesus's eschatological message from an ecclesiastical allegorical interpretation, which not infrequently led to the conviction that Jesus formulated antiparables. A king who carried out imperial feasts and military campaigns (e.g., Matt. 22:1–14) could only portray a caricature of the kingdom of God (on this, see also Crüsemann 2014). Also, the Jewish exegete Amy-Jill Levine (2014, 14, 278) sees in the tradition of the parables a serious shift in meaning: "The evangelists wanted to domesticate the parable by turning it into a lesson." According to Levine, the task of exposition is to rediscover Jesus as a Jewish proclaimer of parables, the "initial context" (9) and the "original provocation" (10) of the voice of Jesus as a Jewish contemporary would have heard it.

3.3.3. Jesus as the "Inventor" of the Parables? On the Religious- and Literary-Historical Background

The question of Jewish Jesus's parable discourse has occupied research for a long time. First, in the exuberance of parable research of the early twentieth century, a sharp distinction was emphasized: "The contrast between Jesus's method of teaching and that of his contemporary authors in Israel is enormous. . . . Jesus . . . as a parabler stands above Jewish haggadah. His originality in comparison with them is demonstrated by his mastery. Emulators never achieve something that is great, immortal" (Jülicher [2]1910, 1:165, 172; similarly Jeremias [11]1998, 8).

Early on Paul Fiebig (1912, 119–22), a contemporary of Jülicher, had criticized such a virtually anti-Jewish assessment. Then, especially at the end of the twentieth century, parallels and analogies between New Testament and rabbinic parables were advanced (Flusser 1981; Dschulnigg 1988; Young 1989, 1998; F. Stern 2006). By now it is hardly contested that the form of Jesus's parables can quite correctly be located in the environment of Jewish narrative style (Kollmann 2004). Also, we find a certain terminological background in the Hebrew lexeme מָשָׁל, which the Septuagint often renders with the Greek παραβολή. According to Schöpflin (2002, 22–23), מָשָׁל can be translated as "analogy/similitude." However, the concrete instances of מָשָׁל are multifaceted: in most cases proverbs are called מָשָׁל (e.g., summarily, Prov. 1:1). Only a small number of narrative parables appear in the Hebrew Bible, such as the Song of the Vineyard (Isa. 5:1–7), the parable of the sheep owner in Nathan's judgment to David (2 Sam. 12:1–15), the plant fables of Jotham (Judg. 9:7–15) and Jehoash (2 Kings 14:8–14), or the fable of the two eagles and the vine in Ezek. 17:3–10. However, this also raises the question whether animal or plant fables can be named "parables" or are a genre *sui generis* (R. Zimmermann 2014a).

Whereas later rabbinic literature records an abundance of parables (Thoma and Lauer [1986, 12] mention from 500 to 1,400 parables, depending on the method of counting; Pesiqta of Rab Kahana, fifth century CE), the term מָשָׁל is used only three times in the Mishnah (m. Sukkah 2:9; m. Niddah 2:5; 5:7; on this, Neusner 2006). In early Tannaitic texts, only a few texts can be designated parables (cf. Notley and Safrai 2011). It is therefore just as one-sided as it is questionable in the history of tradition, when Jesus is located in a broad stream of Jewish parabolic poetry, as A.-J. Levine (2014) would recently have it, to intentionally dissociate Jesus as a Jewish parable teller from the one of Christian memory.

A similar picture emerges if we wish to locate the parables of the New Testament in the context of the Greco-Hellenistic history of literature and ancient rhetoric (see Berger 1984, 1110–24; Dormeyer 1993, 140–58). There are close similarities between ancient fables and New Testament parables. Furthermore, Jesus's parables perform an argumentative function of persuasion, which moves into the proximity of ancient teaching on rhetoric. Under the main category of examples (παράδειγμα), both Aristotle (*Rhet.* 1393a28–31) and Quintilian (*Inst.* 5.11) had put forth παραβολή as an artistic and persuasive means of speaking. Certainly, here also a more precise comparison shows that simple analogies or genealogical linear derivations go astray (R. Zimmermann 2007) and further research will be required. Indeed, in their own way, Jesus's parables remain special, though not isolated, in the history of literature. Further inquiry into an antecedent and environmental field ought not to overlook the creative and innovative dealing with available forms.

3.3.4. Diversity in the Tradition

Nevertheless, even if the original and efficacious narrative style of the historical Jesus makes for an indisputable postulate, it remains difficult to access, and all attempts of historical Jesus research to reconstruct authentic parables of Jesus by means of criteria (on this, Keith and Le Donne 2012) were hypothetical and ideological. Therefore, an approach based on memory chooses to analyze the four or five forms of the gospel tradition (Matthew, Mark, Luke, John, Gospel of Thomas) as a starting point. In this the sayings source Q remains a borderline case, because whereas some exegetes doubt its existence (Goodacre and Perrin 2004; Kahl 2012), for others it presents a second-order tradition, since the parallelism of the double tradition of Matthew and Luke suggests a fixed written source (Fleddermann 2005; Roth 2018). This holds all the more when one assesses the existence of the parables in Q not on the basis of verbatim wording but by means of narratological criteria such as plot and constellations of figures of speech as well as the fields of figurations (R. Zimmermann 2014b; on this in general, Foster 2014).

In the sayings source Q, "classics" are found such as the parable of the mustard seed–yeast (Q 13:18–22) or the lost sheep" (Q 15:1–7). In addition to some multilevel parables (Q 12:42–46: parable of the slaves; Q 19:12–26: parable of the entrusted pounds), short parables dominate, which meet in the full sense the criteria of the genre (see below). In the structure of the sayings source, for instance, according to Hoffmann and Heil ([4]2013, 14–15), parables are prominently represented in all seven parts and hence can be seen as the framework of the sayings source (Kern [2]2015, 54–55; Roth 2018). As in Q overall, the eschatological perspective plays a central role, whereby the image of the near end impacts behavior in the present (Q 6:34–45; 10:2; 13:24–27; 17:34–35). In this a striking principle of composition of parables is antithesis, in which for a given situation a good and right behavior is juxtaposed with a wicked and reprehensible one (Q 6:47–49; 12:42–46; 17:34–35; 19:12–13, 15–24, 26). Negative patterns of behavior are painted in plain view (Q 7:31–35; 11:24–26; 12:39–40; 12:58–59; 13:24–27), or even "impossible possibilities" are acted out in the narration (Q 6:41–42; 11:34–35; 14:34–35; 16:13), in order to usher the recipients of Q into the story of catastrophe not only mentally but also affectively. In this way they should be provoked to decide for or against Jesus's message.

Parable discourse in Mark is appraised as a central form of speaking right from the beginning of Jesus's activity (Mark 4) and at the same time enables a meta-discussion (so-called parable theory; Mark 4:10–12) about the (in)comprehensibility of this figurative way of speaking. The polarization of the recipients (outside-inside) and the correlation with the motif of hardening (Isa. 6) might present a historical reflex to the early rejection of Jesus's message; possibly, however, it might create a pragmatic literary stimulation for the mission.

The Gospel of Matthew demonstrates its own specificity in the creation of its own "parable discourse" (Matt. 13) in its five blocks of discourse, which are also permeated with parables (so, e.g., thirteen parables in the Sermon on the Mount, eight in the eschatological discourse). The eschatological orientation is linked with a sharp dualism, in which violent scenarios are directly contrasted with motifs of the joy of a wedding feast (Matt. 22; 25). Finally, this structure also serves the ethical dimension of the texts, which in Matthew is especially intensified by introductions and conclusions (Münch 2004; R. Zimmermann 2009).

The memory of Jesus in Luke moves Jesus's compassionate turning to those who are marginalized to the center. So characters on the margin of society, whether slaves (Luke 7:31–35), women (15:8–10; 13:20–21; 18:1–7), or children (7:31–35; 11:11–13; 18:17), become leading characters in the parables. The familiarity with the urban milieu is striking and shines through in many places (πόλις in 14:21; 18:2; 19:17). Especially clear is the turning to the poor (4:18) and sinners (15:1) in the combination of three parables on the lost (sheep, coin, son) in chapter 15, in which God's compassionate preference is emphasized.

By means of the course set by Jülicher, the Gospel of John had been excluded from research on parables. Just recently considerations regarding source material in John (Theobald 2002, 334–423) as well as literary studies (Stare 2011; R. Zimmermann 2012a) have shown that the Fourth Gospel also remembers Jesus's parables. Fictional miniature narratives about the shepherd who leads his sheep from the sheepfold (John 10:1–5), the grain of wheat that is sown and bears fruit (12:24), and the woman in childbirth (16:21; on this, R. Zimmermann 2015b) positively present their own memory of Jesus's parables, which occasionally overlaps with the synoptic tradition (John 5:19–23: Q 10:22; Matt. 11:27; John 13:16: Matt. 10:24–26).

Forty-one of the 109 sayings in the Gospel of Thomas can be classified as parables. The diachronic-historically oriented American research has identified more original versions (e.g., the version of the parable of the feast in Gos. Thom. 64); it has even seen special material in Gos. Thom. 97 (parable of the jar of meal; on this, R. Zimmermann 2015a) or 98 (parable of the assassin) as authentic parables of Jesus, which are absent from the canonical tradition. Despite the numerous parallel traditions, however, striking gnostic colorings of the memory are recognizable, in which, for instance, the sheep that was lost was the largest one (Gos. Thom. 107). Recent research on the Gospel of Thomas allows more room for the lack of homogeneity of the text transmitted to us, so that presumably both early versions and later traditions are found in the same manuscript (Schwarz 2020).

Accordingly, it is difficult to determine a unified tendency, literary characteristics, or one theological line of the parables in the Gospel of Thomas.

3.3.5. Questions of Genre and Methodology: Interpreting and Understanding "Parables"

Following the memory approach, the actual number of parables Jesus might have told cannot and must not be determined. The individual sources vary from seventeen in Mark to fifty-four in Luke. If the entire memory is added up, there are over one hundred parables. However, such a high number, in comparison with other numbers in many books on parables, is also connected with the determination of the genre. Which passages are to be called parables?

The New Testament knows two terms with which Jesus's figurative speech is comprehensively designated and which also appear in the introduction to individual texts. The Synoptics speak of παραβολή, the Gospel of John of παροιμία (John 10:6; 16:25, 29). Although with παραβολή the synoptic sources provide an overarching concept of genre, research on parables has repeatedly made distinctions. For German exegesis, the best known was the classification of Adolf Jülicher ([2]1910, 1:25–184) in the subgenres "similitude in the narrower sense," "parable," and "example stories." Further, Bultmann ([10]1995, 181–84) had also added the genre "figurative saying" (*Bildwort*). For a long time the genre of example story as *sui generis* has been criticized, because all parables—as also their rhetorical tradition (see above) shows—have an exemplary character and possess a persuasively appealing plot (cf. Harnisch [4]2001, 84–97; Baasland 1986; in detail Tucker 1998). Also, the concept "figuration/figurative speech" (*Bildwort/Bildrede*) is inept as terminology for genre, because this can serve best as a collective concept for all forms of figurative speech (cf. R. Zimmermann 2012b). Finally, on the evidence of sources, the criteria for the differentiation of "parable" and "similitude in the narrower sense" repeatedly reach their limits: so, in many texts, mixtures in time are found ("thief in the night," Matt. 24:43–44; "slaves who are awake," Luke 12:35–38; "on the way to the judge," Luke 12:58–59; bread for dogs, Mark 7:27–28; etc.), and, further, the temporal forms in the synoptic tradition change (Mark 4:30–32: present tense; Luke 13:18–19 par. Matt. 13:31–32: aorist). The evaluation of what is commonplace or out of the ordinary stands on the fragmentary and constantly variable thin reconstructions of our knowledge of the ancient world (e.g., the practice of sowing seed in Mark 4:1–9; the arrival of the bridegroom in Matt. 25:1–13). Events that appear to be commonplace, such as the process of leavening bread dough, on closer examination (amount of leaven; omission of the kneading process) turn out to be downright uncommon (on Q 13:20–21).

One is therefore well advised, if one follows the genre consciousness of early Christian authors and searches for criteria, to combine all texts identified by παραβολή. Following the discussion on genre in literary studies as well as Anglophone research, the term "parable" serves as the superordinate concept of genre: in the compendium of Jesus's parables, a team of authors has agreed on six criteria, among which, according to recent genre theory, four hard and two soft criteria can be differentiated: "A parable is a short narratival (1) fictional (2) text that is related in the narrated world to known reality (3), but by way of implicit or explicit transfer signals, denotes a metaphorical shift in meaning into another semantic field" (R. Zimmermann 2015a, 137). Parables are miniature narratives, which, considered from the point of view of literary studies, are differentiated from short stories (in contrast to A.-J. Levine 2014, "short stories"), novellas, or novels. Whether they span one verse or twenty makes no difference as long as they (1) satisfy the minimal conditions of a narrative, report at least a change in status, and do more than give a description of a condition (e.g., Matt. 5:14: You are the light of the world). The narrative is (2) invented (fictional) and not meant to reproduce a historical event (factual). At the same time, the narrative content remains (3) related to the tangibly perceived world (realistic). In contrast to many fables or myths in which animals and divine forms appear anthropomorphically, parables remain realistic. It could happen the way it is narrated. To be sure, transfer signals are given by means of immanent notes (e.g., benevolence of the owner of the vineyard in Matt. 20:1–16), by means of framing verses (e.g., "the kingdom of God is like . . .), as well as by means of contexts (discussion in the house of Simon the Pharisee in Luke 7:36–50), by which the narrative content is (4) carried over (metaphorically) to a different semantic field, to, as a rule, religious or ethical spheres. Thus, one field of perception is "put beside another," or literally "thrown," as the etymology of "parable" from παρα-βάλλειν shows ("to throw beside one another"). Frequently, comparison formulas make this correlation explicit (e.g., οὕτως . . . ὡς, Mark 4:26, 31; cf. John 15:6). (5) A hearer or reader should then discern a profound religious meaning in what is narrated. This is expressed, for instance, by direct address in questions like "Which of you . . . ?" (Q 11:11; 12:25; Luke 11:5; 14:28; 17:7) or imperatives (Q 11:9; "Ask! Seek! Knock!"; 12:40: "Be ready!"; 13:24: "Enter!"), which address any reader (an active appeal). (6) Unlike proverbs, parables are usually located in larger contexts of the narrative and the line of thought (related to the context). Although in the Gospel of Thomas such contexts in view of the macrotext are not easy to ascertain, nevertheless they repeatedly shine through (so Popkes [2]2015, in view of Gos. Thom. 83).

At the same time, a special method of interpretation arises from the specific criteria of genre (cf. R. Zimmermann 2017). First, it is vital to embrace the narrative style with the aid of narratological methods as precisely as possible. Many parables consist of only one sentence (e.g., Q 13:21: yeast) or a rhetorical question (e.g., Q 6:39: blind leading the blind; Matt. 18:12–14: on the lost sheep). But frequently the narration is about various characters in more complex configurations of relationships and multilevel strands of plot. Wolfgang Harnisch ([4]2001, 80–81) has observed the setup of three characters as the prevailing principle of design of many parables (cf. Funk 1974); Dan O. Via (1970) distinguishes two types of a dramatic sequence of episodes: (a) action-crisis-solution; (b) crisis-action-solution, as well as between ascending (comic) or descending (tragic) plot movements. Further, dialogue (e.g., Matt. 20:1–16: vineyard owner) or "internal monologue" (e.g., Luke 12:17: grain farmer; 15:17–19: lost son) is characteristic (cf. Heininger 1991, 14).

To be able to understand the transfer process in parables, it is vital to comprehend the fields of reality, which serve as donor fields for the parables, as precisely as possible by means of sociohistorical and factual-historical analyses. In this connection Jesus's parables demonstrate a large variety: virtually all spheres of *private and public life* are included, beginning with elementary life situations such as birth, sickness, and death, continuing through assuaging basic needs such as sleeping (Q 17:34), eating, and drinking (Q 11:11–13), all the way to spatial conditions of life such as building a house (Matt. 7:24–27). Frequently, however, a parable has to do less with the condition of something than with the social relationships associated with it. So, for example, the division of a household is of interest (Q 17:34–35; Mark 3:25; Gos. Thom. 61). Precisely the complex and ambiguous *relationships among people* become the object of perception such as the relationship between parents and children, between siblings and friends or slaves and masters. *Work and service relationships* in the wider sense also play a role—for example, the wages of day laborers (Matt. 20:1–16) or the dismissal of a manager (Luke 16:1–8). Regarding the field of work and employment, the referential background of the farming milieu of a Galilean village (fishing, agriculture, etc.) can be observed. Here especially the living conditions of women are featured, as are, for instance, elementary human experiences such as the birth of a child in John 16:21 (on this, R. Zimmermann 2015a; in general Beavis 2002); likewise, how the servant or slave parables configure a conspicuous group (Q 12:42–46; Mark 13:33–37; Luke 17:7–10; Matt. 18:23–35). However, the narrative world of the parables is not restricted to a particular social class, as parable exposition of liberation theology wanted to show (Herzog 1994; E. Eck 2016). So we read about rich owners of herds (Luke 15:1–7) and land (Mark 12:1–12; Luke 12:16–20), and in an entire series of parables, the realms of commerce (Matt. 13:45–46; Gos. Thom. 76, 109), finance (Luke 7:41–42; 16:1–8; Q 19:12–26), and the legal system (Q 12:58–59; Luke 18:1–8) come into view. Finally, the *nonhuman sphere* can also be moved to the center, in that plants, for example, a fig tree (Mark 13:28–29; Luke 13:6–9), lilies (Q 12:27), or individual mustard seeds (Mark 4:30–32) and wheat (John

12:24; 1 Apoc. Jas. NHC dI.8.10–27, cf. Mark 4:1–9, a sower), indeed, even "weeds" (darnel in Matt. 13:24–40), can be used as the fields of perception to transport the theological message. Here, once again, the functions and movement of the plants are the point of reference, as can be demonstrated within the parables of growth (e.g., Mark 4:26–29; Matt. 13:24–30; John 12:24) or harvest (Q 6:43–45; 10:2; 12:24; John 4:35–38; Gos. Thom. 63). But Jesus also had a heart, or at least an eye, for animals, since we read about swine (Matt. 7:6; agraphon 165), dogs (Mark 7:27–28; Gos. Thom. 102; cf. Luke 16:21), and horses (Gos. Thom. 47), as well as nesting birds (Mark 4:32), fish (Matt. 13:47–50; Gos. Thom. 8), ravens (Q 12:24), wolves (John 10:12), and vultures (Q 17:37), without their becoming characters being anthropomorphized in the same way as in fables.

Finally, the metaphorical nature and appeal structure are an invitation to active interpretation, for which reason parables became a popular field of learning and appropriation for reader response methods (Schulte 2008) as well as for teaching the Bible (P. Müller ²2008; R. Zimmermann 2013). The specific style of speaking of the parables also requires a multifaceted scholarly analysis, which includes both historical aspects and narrative and reader-response aspects. The texts that in their figurative style are basically left open should not be restricted by unilinear explanations. Only in the opening up of horizons of understanding does parable discourse remain God's word, which in the act of reading and applying again and again imbues new meaning and even awakens faith.

Crüsemann, Marlene, et al., eds. 2014. *Gott ist anders: Gleichnisse neu gelesen auf der Basis der Auslegung von Luise Schottroff*. Gütersloh.

Roth, Dieter T. 2018. *The Parables in Q*. LNTS 582. London.

Schulte, Stefanie. 2008. *Gleichnisse erleben: Entwurf einer wirkungsästhetischen Hermeneutik und Didaktik*. PTHe 91. Stuttgart.

Schwarz, Konrad. 2020. *Gleichnisse und Parabeln Jesu im Thomasevangelium: Untersuchungen zu ihrer Form, Funktion und Bedeutung*. BZNW 236. Berlin and Boston.

Snodgrass, Klyne. ²2018. *Stories with Intent: A Comprehensive Guide to the Parables of Jesus*. Grand Rapids.

Zimmermann, Ruben. 2008. *Hermeneutik der Gleichnisse Jesu: Methodische Neuansätze zum Verstehen urchristlicher Parabeltexte*. WUNT 231. Tübingen (Studienausgabe 2011).

———, ed. ²2015. *Kompendium der Gleichnisse Jesu*. Gütersloh.

———. 2015a. *Puzzling the Parables of Jesus: Methods and Interpretation*. Minneapolis.

———. Forthcoming. *Parabeln der Bibel. Die Sinnwelten der Gleichnisse Jesu entdecken*. Gütersloh.

Ruben Zimmerman

3.4. Jesus's Concepts of Judgment

3.4.1. Introduction

The concepts of judgment of Jesus of Nazareth move entirely within the context of eschatological *expectations of judgment of the Judaism of his time*. They were directed toward an end-time intervention of God that takes place with the goal of restoring the salvific order in the world installed by him and of establishing his universal sovereignty over everything opposing it, even by force if necessary. This intervention of God was expected as an action by which God annihilates everything that opposes his sovereignty and punishes all who have not lived according to his world order but rather have acted contrary to it. As to the form of God's intervention, two concepts of judgment can be distinguished. While the execution of these two appears to be incompatible with each other, both concepts can exist alongside each other without any problem. Frequently they do so even in one and the same document.

On the one hand, God's judgment was expected as a so-called *judgment of destruction*. This concept is linked to the old traditions of a divine war of YHWH, which God wages against his enemies and the enemies of his people: God comes (with his angelic hosts if need be) from heaven to earth and destroys everything that opposes his divine will. Descriptions of this type of judgment are found, for example, in Zech. 14; Sib. Or. 3:51–60, 556–561; As. Mos. 10:1–10; 12:3–16. This act of judgment is always directed only against the adversaries of God and his people. The devout and just experience it as liberation from their enemies and oppressors. So with this type of judgment, it is always a foregone conclusion who stands on the side of salvation and who has no expectation of disaster.

Alongside this there is the expectation of a *forensic proceeding before the throne of the judge*, as it, for example, is portrayed in 1 En. 62 (but cf. also 1 En. 47:3–4; 90:20–27; Dan. 7:9–10; and passim). Also, in Matt. 25:31–46 this type of judgment is described, even if this story of the last judgment probably does not go back to Jesus. It is characteristic of this view of the judgment that it is not a trial in which the truth must first be discovered. The proceedings before the throne of the end-time judge do not reach a judgment nor have an open outcome. Rather, what is at stake is only the allocation of salvation and perdition, and it is established beforehand by the judge who is allocated salvation and who receives perdition. Moreover, this type of judgment does not focus on individuals but on groups: frequently only sinners must appear before the judge to be assigned to perdition. Even if the just come before the throne of the judge, they appear there also only as a group and so that the judge can award them salvation.

In its theological substance, God's end-time act of judgment, as it has been expected from early Judaism, always *also*—correctly understood—is essentially salvific action. It is *judgment* in the sense that in it God sets *right* his salvific world order anew. "Judgment" and "salvation" are therefore always connected to each other, because if God defeats his enemies and the enemies of his people and also assigns perdition to sinners and salvation to the just, as a judge God always acts also as a redeemer, and his act of judging is always also an act of salvation.

Of these two types of judgment, the first type, the so-called judgment of destruction, is exclusively attested in the tradition of John the Baptizer (Luke 3:7–9, 16–17): John heralds the judge of fire, who will cover all Israel with his "wrath," whereby only those who have submitted to the "baptism of repentance for the forgiveness of sins" preached by him (Mark 1:4; Luke 3:3; cf. also Matt. 3:11; Acts 13:24; 19:4) escape destruction by "unquenchable fire" (Luke 3:17 par.). Also for John, judgment has no other purpose than to *assign* salvation and perdition. How it is allocated is a foregone conclusion.

By contrast, within the Jesus tradition both types of judgment are represented: the expectation of a judgment of destruction is recognizable in Luke 13:1–5 and 17:26–30, 34–35, whereas in Luke 11:31–32 par. and 12:8–9 par. (cf. also Mark 8:38) the concept of a forensic proceeding before the throne of the judge shines through.

3.4.2. Criteria of Judgment

The theological profile that the distinctiveness of Jesus's appropriation of this basic knowledge of end-time judgment constitutes is determined by the *criteria* by which in his judgment God orients the distribution of salvation and perdition.

In Jewish tradition in the broadest sense it was the Torah, with which God instituted his salvific world order, that functioned as the critical standard for guiding the allocation of salvation and perdition in the judgment. For John the Baptizer, "baptism of repentance for the forgiveness of sins" (see references above) entered into this function: all who believed his prophetic message and were "baptized" by him stand on the side of salvation in the allocation of salvation and perdition at the end: they are not burned as the straw but are like wheat that is gathered into the storehouse (Luke 3:17 par.; cf. also Mark 1:8: they will be "immersed in the Holy Spirit").

On the other hand, for Jesus of Nazareth the concepts of judgment and salvation are incorporated into the context of his interpretation of himself, as he preaches it as an element of his proclamation of the kingdom of God. For this, two elements that stand in close connection with each other are constitutive.

For one, Jesus appears on the scene with the claim that in his activity, that is, when he expels demons, heals the sick, or eats and drinks with people, the end-time salvation of the kingdom of God is already present and tangible (cf. esp. Luke 11:20 par.; 17:20–21 par. as well as Luke 7:22 par. Matt. 11:5 with the allusion to Isa. 26:19; 29:18; 35:5–6; 61:1; Luke 16:16 par.; cf. also Mark 2:18–19a). It corresponds to this that the forgiveness of sins that appertains to God alone takes place in Jesus's compassionate turning to people (cf. Mark 2:5, 7) or that he interprets the turning of sinners to *him* as turning back to *God* (Luke 7:36–50; 15:1–32).

Second, a theologically profiled expectation for the future goes hand in hand with this, because, even though the salvific reality of the kingdom of God comes about *selectively* in Jesus's activity already in the present, something else is yet to come: its *universal* establishment over the entire globe. Consequently, this comes about in that none other than God comes, and starting from Jerusalem will establish his sovereignty over the entire world (cf. Luke 11:2 par. Matt. 6:10; Mark 1:15; 14:25). For Jesus, this establishment of God's universal kingdom was approaching immediately. Moreover, he expected that it would be accompanied by God's act of judging, which will be focused on nothing other than the allocation of salvation and perdition on the basis of how people have reacted to the claim expressed in Jesus's interpretation of himself: everyone who accepts this claim receives the allocation of salvation in the judgment accompanying God's accession to sovereignty; everyone who rejects it collapses into perdition.

3.4.3. Jesus and Judgment

This configuration provides the context in which the texts that furnish information about Jesus's concepts of judgment and salvation can be classified.

3.4.3.1. *Lex Talionis*

In the most general form, the connection of the attitude toward Jesus in the present with what is pronounced in the future judgment is described in the talion type of formulation in Luke 12:8–9 (par. Matt. 10:32–33; cf. also Mark 8:38): everyone who "confesses" Jesus before others, the Son of Man will also "confess" in the end-time judgment, and all who "deny" Jesus before others will also be denied in the end-time judgment. Here the opposition of "confess" and "deny" reproduces first the opposition between acceptance and denial of Jesus's claim and then the opposition between the ascription of salvation and perdition in the end-time judgment. In Mark 8:38, only the perdition side becomes a topic: those who are "ashamed" of Jesus and his words, of them will the Son of Man also be "ashamed," that is, they receive perdition. The complementary correspondence to this on the side of salvation is transmitted in Luke 7:23 par.: "Blessed is anyone who takes no offense at me." Just as "takes no offense at me" is tantamount to "confesses me" (Luke 12:8 par.) and is the opposite of "is ashamed of me and my words" (Mark 8:38), so the preceding "blessed is" promises not to repudiate end-time salvation to all who claim to be agents of God's salvation among human beings. With recourse to another metaphorical figuration but with an identical focus, Jesus also produces the same connection in Luke 14:15–24 and 13:23–29 (both texts have variations and parallels in Matt. 22:1–10 and 7:13–14, 22–23; 8:11–12; 25:10–12): here the invitation to the feast stands for the summons to celebrate with Jesus the advent of the end-time time of salvation experienced in him and his activity (cf. also Mark 2:18–19a; Luke 19:9). Those who reject this invitation because they do not recognize him and therefore continue their everyday activities (cf. Luke 14:18–20) are punished with exclusion from the end-time feast, which is celebrated in the kingdom of God with all those who have already achieved the outcome of Jesus's invitation in the present. The same opposition turned into ethics is also carried further with other imagery in the parable of the two houses in Luke 6:46–49 par. The exclusive alignment of the assignment of salvation and perdition in the end-time judgment involves a radical individualization of them. It depends always and exclusively on how each individual person has reacted to Jesus's claim. This depends on whether he or she experiences salvation or perdition. This principle is expressed in Luke 17:34–35 par.: according to this, in the implementation of God's judgment, two persons, as close to each other as two men lying in one and the same bed (Luke 17:34) or working in the same field (Matt. 24:40), or as two women who at the same moment are working at the same grinder (Luke 17:35 par.), might each receive a different judgment: one receives salvation, and in fact is preserved from the destructive judgment because he or she is "taken away," whereas the other is "left behind," and so perishes with everyone else. In all instances a case-by-case trial takes place, and it is based on nothing other than the stance each took toward Jesus's claim.

3.4.3.2. *Call to Repentance*

The consequent alignment of Jesus's expectations of judgment and salvation by the reaction to his interpretation of himself finds its counterpart in that Jesus's proclamation is accompanied by a call to repentance, and human beings who refuse to repent are threatened with end-time perdition (cf. esp. Luke 13:1–5, but also Matt. 18:3 and Mark 1:15). In this context "repentance" means leaving behind the conventional orientation to existence and expectations of salvation and accepting Jesus as the one in whose advent the salvation of God's kingdom is accessible. The call to repentance is not based on the threat of perdition but rather on the promise of salvation: according to Matt. 13:44, 45–46, the parables of the treasure in the field and the pearl of great price, the repentance that the encounter with Jesus requires is equated to the conduct of people, who give up their entire possessions to be able to buy a field with a hidden treasure in it or a precious pearl. The salvation of God's kingdom available in Jesus has a value that is worth giving up everything that up until this point was important. The parable of the prudent manager (Luke 16:1–8) is not far removed from this, because here also a successful response to Jesus's proclamation is recounted. Jesus himself appears in vv. 1–3: his advent strips away the foundation of the familiar orientation to the existence and salvation of the people and demands that they align themselves anew in a way that stands in radical discontinuity from what up to that point in their lives had given stability and certainty. Just this is what the manager does, and he is commended for his prudence (v. 8a). His conduct is presented to the hearers of the parable as a positive example for the repentance demanded by Jesus. In Luke 13:24 par., Jesus clothes the demand for repentance in the metaphor of "going in through the narrow gate."

3.4.3.3. Imminent Arrival

Moreover, an essential element of Jesus's concepts of judgment and salvation was the assurance that the universal implementation of God's kingdom was imminent. This imminent expectation imparted a special urgency to his demand for repentance. It is also an element of Jesus's interpretation of himself; it attains its particularity in that Jesus challenges people to recognize in his advent the final opportunity to align the orientation of their existence with the advancing judgment. In this sense in Luke 12:54–59 he characterizes the situation in which his activity located people as "this kairos" (v. 56b) of decision: he portrays them as debtors who find themselves on the way to court and the very last opportunity is afforded them to escape a verdict and its disastrous outcome, by "repenting" in the sense of Luke 13:3, 5 and accepting his interpretation of himself. For those who fail to recognize this character of the situation because they refuse to accept the eschatological significance of Jesus's presence, things turn out the way they did for the grain farmer in Luke 12:15–20 (originally the theme of this parable was not the distinction between genuine and false wealth but the proper discernment of the time): he is a "fool" (v. 20), because he still counts on "many years" (v. 19) and does not consider that he must leave his life "in this very night" (v. 20).

3.4.3.4. Rejection by Others

Accordingly, a part of the context for this concept is also a series of statements whose common denominator is that they are to be interpreted as responses of Jesus to the rejection of his claim. He interprets them as a refusal of the requisite repentance (see D.IV.3.4.3.2), and he responds to them that the imminent judgment is no longer merely conditional as in Luke 12:58–59 par. and 13:1–5 but rather will bring definitive and unavoidable destruction upon them. This expectation becomes obvious in the woes against Chorazin and Bethsaida (Luke 10:13–14 par.), in the saying against Capernaum (Luke 10:15 par.), and in the double saying about the rising up of the "queen of the South" and the Ninevites in the judgment day as witnesses against "this generation" (Luke 11:31–32 par.). In these sayings the announcement of the unavoidable destruction is repeatedly accounted for by the refusal of the repentance that the encounter with Jesus had called for.

3.4.3.5. Role of Judgment in the Teaching of Jesus

However, it also comes out from the texts just mentioned that it is not sufficient simply to ask about Jesus's *concepts* of judgment and salvation. It is essential rather to discuss the pragmatic *use* Jesus makes of the concepts. The woes against Chorazin and Bethsaida as well as the saying against Capernaum are recounted in Luke 10:13–14, 15 as part of a speech that Jesus directs to the disciples. Similarly, one would also presuppose from the other announcements of destruction that Jesus's disciples at least heard the announcements, if indeed they were not their intended audience. After all, it was not Jesus's opponents but always only his disciples who transmitted his sayings. In that case, these announcements are not sayings *to* those named in them but rather sayings *about* them. The actual addressees of these judgment sayings are the disciples, who have made a decision for Jesus. The announcement of destruction for those who declined this decision thereby takes on a comforting and stabilizing function for Jesus's disciples. Jesus's conceptions of judgment and salvation have this pragmatic purpose in common not only with Jewish apocalyptic but also with John the Baptizer's preaching of judgment, as it is transmitted in Luke 3:17 par.

Moreover, this is also expressed in Luke 17:26–30 par., a passage from Jesus's saying about the coming of the Son of Man, which likewise is directed to the disciples. Here Jesus constructs an analogy between the present on the one hand and the times of Noah and Lot on the other. For the disciples, two aspects especially ought to be comparable to each other: first, the fact that in both cases the deliverance of a few goes along with the annihilation of everyone else, and second, the striking description of Noah's people and the inhabitants of Sodom in vv. 27a and 28b. Jesus does not describe their sinfulness but precisely what the disciples see in their own environment—that the people do not pay attention to Jesus but rather continue with their everyday life. The similarity with the behavior depicted in Luke 12:19 and 14:18–20 (see D.IV.3.4.3.1) should not be overlooked. To immunize his disciples against the doubt emanating from this situation about their own decision for Jesus, for which they have renounced their entire previous life, he announces that those whose daily activities are not disturbed by his proclamation will suffer the same fate as did the generation of the flood and the inhabitants of Sodom. This announcement of destruction has no other function than to assure the disciples of the validity of their decision for Jesus.

3.4.3.6. Fear

Finally, additional judgment and salvation announcements belonging to a separate group are elements of parenetic speeches, which have the purpose of impressing on Jesus's disciples that their decision for Jesus results in particular behavior. They mobilize for this the rhetorical affection of fear, in that they reinforce the ethical demand with a threat of judgment. For one thing, the object of such admonitions can be a caution concerning the task of the newly achieved orientation of existence and against turning away from Jesus. Doubtless related to this are the sayings transmitted in Mark 9:43–48, which perhaps have an independent correspondence in Matt. 5:29–30. Luke 12:4–5 also makes good sense in this connection, and also, the saying already discussed about "confessing" and "denying" in Luke 12:8–9 par. (cf. also Mark 8:38; see D.IV.3.4.3.1) is not implausible in this context.

In other texts, threats of judgment and destruction are deployed in order to make certain behaviors obligatory among Jesus's disciples in social relationships with others. In this sense the parable of the unmerciful slave in Matt. 18:23–35 threatens with destruction all who receive forgiveness from God and do not pass it on to others. Quite analogously, the demand to refrain from mutual judging/condemning (Luke 6:37 par.) is grounded on a view of one's own deeds with a type of talion prospect in judgment.

3.4.4. Conclusion

Seen as a whole, Jesus's concepts of judgment and salvation move entirely within the context of the common expectation in ancient Judaism, which John the Baptizer also shared: when God comes in judgment, its outcome is no longer open, because the function of judgment is limited to the *allocation* to human beings of salvation and perdition. This can happen in the form of a judgment of destruction or in the form of a forensic court proceeding. The decision about which people receive salvation and which receive destruction is made in the present, and it is unchangeably fixed at the beginning of judgment. Like everyone who conceived of scenarios of judgment in early Judaism, Jesus also knows in the present how the allocation of salvation and perdition is assigned.

What constitutes the distinctiveness of Jesus's own expectation of judgment can be described in two steps: On the one hand, he expects the in-breaking of this judgment to be immediately imminent. Possibly, Jesus adopted this imminent expectation from the Baptizer. On the other hand—and here one would have seen the unique characteristic of Jesus's expectation of judgment—for him the allocation of salvation and perdition focuses exclusively on the criterion whether people have accepted his claim or have refused it: namely, that in his own activity God's salvation can be experienced already in the present. This aspect, therefore, separates Jesus's expectation of judgment from that of John the Baptizer, so that it is possible to say: the only significant distinction between the concepts of judgment and salvation of Jesus of Nazareth and John the Baptizer is Jesus.

Reiser, Marius. 1990. *Die Gerichtspredigt Jesu: Eine Untersuchung zur eschatologischen Verkündigung Jesu und ihrem frühjüdischen Hintergrund.* NTAbh, n.s., 23. Münster.

Riniker, Christian. 1999. *Die Gerichtsverkündigung Jesu.* EHS 653. Bern.

Wolter, Michael. 2009. "'Gericht' und 'Heil' bei Jesus von Nazareth und Johannes dem Täufer: Semantische und pragmatische Beobachtungen." In *Der historische Jesus: Tendenzen und Perspektiven der gegenwärtigen Forschung,* edited by Jens Schröter and Ralph Brucker, 355–92. BZNW 114. Berlin.

Zager, Werner. 1996a. *Gottesherrschaft und Endgericht in der Verkündigung Jesu: Eine Untersuchung zur markinischen Jesusüberlieferung einschließlich der Q-Parallelen.* BZNW 82. Berlin and New York.

Michael Wolter

3.5. Jesus's Prayer, the Lord's Prayer

3.5.1. Premises

Jesus's prayer life—like that of all who pray—is determined by the image of God (see D.IV.3.1), the image of himself (see D.IV.3.8), and the content of the prayers. These distinct factors stand in a reciprocal relationship. From the type of praying and the content of the prayers, one can conclude the relationship in which the people praying see themselves to the addressee of the prayer, and it becomes clear who and what God is for them.

At the same time, any image of God or of oneself implies specific forms of prayer and excludes other forms. Thus, on the one hand, a praying person who sees himself exclusively as the Son of God does not correspond to a repentant confession of sin. On the other hand, by contrast, a heartfelt, personal prayer would be unsuitable for an aloof and abstract God. Any change of one of the three main components (image of God, self-image, content of prayer) has an effect directly on the overall structure and the manifestation of each of the other factors.

Every statement about the prayer of Jesus reflects the image of Jesus held by those who look at it. That means, whoever describes or assesses Jesus's praying has to be aware of the reciprocity mentioned above and has to inquire about the extent to which one's own ideas and wishes influence individual aspects and thereby the overall pattern.

The presentation of Jesus's praying offered here describes central aspects of his prayer life. However, New Testament testimonies differ in their interpretation of Jesus's prayer life, and each of the New Testament authors was bound to the interdependence described at the beginning.

There is hardly any other figure of antiquity about whom there is so much source material on his prayer life and his prayer environment as Jesus of Nazareth. Also, the time gap between Jesus's death and the first records of his life and message is remarkably short compared to that of other historical figures. Hence, it is likely that impressions of contemporary witnesses and people who had knowledge of their direct reports have been incorporated into the accounts, thereby lending a high degree of authenticity to the transmitted texts.

It is a consensus among biographers that Jesus of Nazareth is substantially characterized by his praying. Thus, the evangelist Luke provides prayers at decisive points of his gospel: only he mentions that Jesus prayed at his baptism (Luke 3:21–22) and before his transfiguration (9:29). Luke does not specify the content of the prayers. Even if no material about the existence of these prayers had been available to Luke, it would have been self-evident to him that Jesus was praying when there was a voice from heaven, which others had failed to note.

The high significance of Jesus's prayer in Gethsemane is expressed not only in the Gospels but also by the reference to it in Hebrews (Heb. 5:7).

The traditional prayer of Jesus is usually a nonliturgical, personal prayer. However, to infer from this that Jesus "invented" this way of praying and that *he* alone prayed in this manner would be methodically problematic, as would the conclusion that Jesus did not participate in worship prayers (see below).

The account of Hannah in the sanctuary (1 Sam. 1:10–13, 15–17), the mention of Zechariah's prayer (Luke 1:13), and the parable of the tax collector and the Pharisee in the temple (Luke 18:10–14) indicate that very personal prayer was quite common before Jesus as well as in his environment. The special nature of Jesus's praying was less in its privacy and more in the exclusivity of his self-image and his image of God—this becomes clear, for example, in his distinction between "my Father" and "your Father" (e.g., John 8:38; 20:17; cf. Matt. 18:35; Luke 22:29).

3.5.2. Jesus's Prayer Life and the Jewish Prayer of His Environment

Jesus was a Jew from Galilee in an epoch that was characterized by the question of living right before God and the appropriate form of communication with him. The temple cult in Jerusalem and the observance of rites and practices (festival days, questions of purity, circumcision, etc.) shaped life. In this context, a person who was to be marked as something special had to have his individual relationship to God expressed. He had to be described as a praying person who was communing with God in a unique and intense way.

In the time before his trial in Jerusalem, the criticism of Jesus, his message, and his ministry, which has been transmitted, is essentially confined to inner-Jewish questions of detail.

Jesus's membership in Jewish society is unquestioned. His way of praying did not go beyond the acceptable. None of the critical queries about Jesus touch on the content, quantity, or form of his praying. Only this inner-Jewish consensus and the acceptance of Jesus as a learned dialogue partner (cf. Matt. 22:16, 24, 36 par.) make controversial, sometimes polemical, discussions possible. If Jesus had been outside the religious-social framework, no conversation about theological questions would have been thinkable.

Luke reports that Jesus attended the synagogue "as was his custom" (Luke 4:16). Here it is presupposed that he participated in congregational prayers. According to the New Testament reports, Jesus prayed with or for the people surrounding him at meals—at the feedings (Mark 6:41 par.; 8:6-7 par.) and at his last supper (Mark 14:22-23 par.).

With his kind of prayer Jesus stands for the successful balancing act between participation in the Jewish prayer life of his time and elements that set his praying off from the customary praying of the congregation.

It can be assumed that Jesus did not question the customary *times* of prayer of his environment. The numerous mentions of his praying indicate that praying three times a day was a minimum for Jesus, and for him to fall short of this was not an option. Whether Jesus recited the Jewish Creed (the Shema Yisrael) in the morning and evening, and whether its recitation in the form known today was already common practice in Galilee at the beginning of the first century, is beyond our knowledge. According to the synoptic tradition, Jesus assumed regarding the question about the greatest commandment that the wording of the Shema Yisrael was known (Mark 12:29-30 par.).

Jesus understood the temple in Jerusalem primarily as a place of prayer (Mark 11:17 par.; cf. Isa. 56:7). Three groups of people were involved in the temple cult: priests as sacrificers, Levites as temple servants, and nonpriestly representatives of the people. The latter formed the *standing team* (*maamadot*), who accompanied the sacrificial ritual with prayers (Ostmeyer 2006, 217-18). The priesthood was divided into twenty-four divisions, dispersed in the regions of Judea and Galilee. They practiced their service for one week at a time at the temple. That means each division of priests traveled to Jerusalem at least twice a year. While the priesthood of one place was in Jerusalem, the nonpriestly inhabitants, who stayed at home, gathered for prayer and readings. This is a foundation for the development of temple-independent services and the establishment of worship in synagogues. It is likely that Jesus also participated in the public worship of his hometown (Luke 4:16). For Jesus, prayer would have been performed while standing, as it also would have been in temple worship. The Synoptics mention different postures for Jesus's prayer in Gethsemane (prostration: Matt. 26:39; Mark 14:35; kneeling: Luke 22:41).

Jesus's action in the temple (Mark 11:15-17 par.) was directed against disturbances of prayer and thus of the relationship between God and those praying. He himself will have used the temple as a place of personal prayer.

An external characteristic of Jesus's prayer was his retreat into solitude for prayer (Mark 1:35 par.; 6:46 par.; Luke 5:16; 6:12; 9:18, 28-29; 11:1). Personal prayer usually has no witnesses, and only rarely do we find people who record the wording of such prayers for posterity. Even in cases where it is reported that Jesus took along a small group of companions (Luke 9:28; Mark 14:33 par.), they remain at a distance or are asleep (Mark 14:35, 37, 40-41 par.). It seems to be a deliberate tension that the lack of ear-witnesses speaks for Jesus's personal prayers, but at the same time the contents of his prayers are passed down.

3.5.3. Jesus's Prayers and His Understanding of Prayer

The Gospels portray Jesus, among other things, as a teacher, a miracle worker, a storyteller, and a praying man. The evangelists deem it worth reporting that Jesus prayed extensively and regularly himself and encouraged his followers to do so as well (Matt. 7:7-11 par.).

Jesus is encountered as praying for others (Peter; Luke 22:31-32), as praising (Jesus's shout of joy; Matt. 11:25-27 par.), as giving thanks (Mark 14:22-23 par.), as blessing (Mark 10:16; Luke 24:50-51), and as suffering (in Gethsemane and on the cross: Mark 14:32-41; 15:34; cf. Ps. 22:1). Jesus's life is a life before and with God. If every form of communication with God is understood as prayer (cf. Ostmeyer 2006, 32), then the New Testament tradition depicts Jesus as one whose nature it is to pray.

For the evangelists, the life, works, and words of Jesus are the fulfillment of what was proclaimed in "the scriptures" (e.g., Matt. 1:22; Mark 14:49; Luke 24:44; John 19:24, 28, 36). Consequently, it corresponds to Jesus's self-understanding that he refers to every detail of the tradition and makes it his own. The God to whom Jesus prays as his Father is the one attested in the Jewish Scriptures. The kingdom of God proclaimed by Jesus is nothing other than the one promised from eternity and expected in Jesus's environment.

As a consequence of this hermeneutical premise, Jesus recognizes in the two Lords named by the psalmist David in Ps. 110:1 God and Christ (Mark 12:36–37 par.; Acts 2:34), that is, himself. With his dying cry on the cross from Ps. 22:1 (Matt. 27:46 par.), he reveals himself as the one prefigured by this psalm. The words of the psalm are thereby contextualized in the life of Jesus and obtain with him their true *Sitz im Leben*. From the perspective of the evangelists Matthew and Mark, the words of Ps. 22 are reserved for none other than the crucified Christ. Those who pray recite Ps. 22:1 as the words of the dying Jesus.

The same basic hermeneutical understanding comes into play in the interpretation of Jesus's praise by the minors after his cleansing of the temple (Matt. 21:16) as a fulfillment of Ps. 8:2. Also, Jesus's praise of the Father (Matt. 11:25–26) for hiding his wisdom from the wise and prudent as the fulfillment of Isa. 29:14 follows this line of thought.

Jesus's thinking was shaped by the expectation of the kingdom of God and the crises accompanying it. Thus, according to Luke, he prays for Peter to stand firm in faith (Luke 22:32) and announces that Satan will "sift" the disciples (Luke 22:31).

People repeatedly expect Jesus to pray for them. Regarding the distribution of seats in the kingdom of God, Jesus declares himself not responsible (Mark 10:35–40 par.). He answers the request to pray for the children in Matt. 19:13 with their acceptance (he lets them come to him) without saying a separate prayer (Ostmeyer, 2004b, 8–10).

Prayer in the Gospel of John is often an expression of the mutual glorification of Jesus and his Father (cf. John 11:4b). At the raising of Lazarus, Jesus thanks his Father for hearing him (John 11:41–42) without the actual prayer being mentioned previously.

Between the Last Supper and his arrest, Jesus prays in the Garden of Gethsemane. In Luke 22:28, he speaks of strengthening in his tribulations. He admonishes his companions repeatedly to watch and pray with him, so that they do not fall into temptation (Mark 14:37–38, 40–41 par.; cf. Luke 8:13). According to Mark 14:17–42 par., Jesus knows about his impending death. He calls upon God as *abba* and pleads that the cup may pass him by (Mark 14:36), but he submits everything to the will of his Father, and dies, according to Luke 23:46, with a verse from Ps. 31 as his last word: "Father, into your hands I commend my spirit" (Ps. 31:5).

3.5.4. Prayer Instructions

Jesus prays for his disciples (Luke 22:31–32) and instructs them what they should pray (the "Lord's Prayer": Matt. 6:9–13; Luke 11:2–4) and how they should pray

(Matt. 6:6). The praying of Jesus's followers should be different from the "jabber of the Gentiles" (Matt. 6:7) by focusing on what is substantial (6:9–13). Like Jesus himself, the disciples should withdraw when they pray (6:6). Personal prayer is done in private (6:5–6). The decisive factor about praying is the Father-child relationship between the individual prayers and God as the addressee of prayer.

The transmitted contents of prayer usually refer to the dawning of the kingdom of God: Jesus urges his disciples to ask the Father for more laborers for the harvest (Matt. 9:37–38 par.) and that the "messianic woes" may not take place in winter (Mark 13:18–20).

The filial relationship to God of those who pray differs—according to essential voices in the New Testament—from the filiation of Jesus to God (John 8:38; 20:17; cf. Matt. 18:35; Luke 22:29). According to Rom. 8:29, his followers owe their inclusion in the Father-child relationship to their relationship to Jesus as their elder brother (cf. Heb. 2:11–12, 17). In the Pauline correspondence, the filiation of Jesus's followers to God is mediated through him. Only in his name do they call God *abba* (Rom. 8:15; Gal. 4:6).

An individual filial relationship (Matt. 6:5–6) does not exclude communal prayer. Jesus himself participates in Jewish religious life (Luke 4:16), and the plural address to God as Father recommended in Matt. 6:9 implies a prayer in worship communities.

Just as the Father-child relationship does not tolerate any disruption, so should the communication between the praying person and the addressee of the prayer not stop. Verbal communication is only *one* possible expression of the relationship (cf. Ehrlich 2004). Calls to constant prayer are found in both the New Testament epistles (1 Thess. 5:17; Eph. 6:18; Heb. 13:15; and passim) and the Gospels (Luke 18:1; 21:36).

If prayer is understood as existing in the filial relationship to God, then individual words of prayer and requests do not play a crucial role. The question whether the prayer will be heard is already decided: God knows the needs of those who pray before they are specified (Matt. 6:8; cf. v. 32) and has accepted them in the best interest of believers. God hears their requests, regardless of whether each individual prayer request comes true.

3.5.5. The Lord's Prayer (Matt. 6:9–13; Luke 11:2–4; Did. 8:3)

Most exegetes assume that Jesus phrased an early form of the Lord's Prayer in Aramaic, which he passed on to his circle of disciples. The identical wording of the beginning of the petition for bread in Matt. 6:11 and Luke 11:3, especially in the use of the rare term ἐπιούσιον, suggests that there was a basic common form in Greek. H. Klein (2009, 92–93) assumes a written original form (Q), which contained the first four petitions following the Gospel of Luke and was linguistically oriented toward Matthew. Jesus's original prayer probably included the invocation of God with *abba*, the petition for the coming of the kingdom of God, the petition for bread, and, in the light of the Gethsemane pericope (cf. Mark 14:36 par.), also the petition for God's will to be done. The parallel between the beginning petition of the Lord's Prayer and the Jewish Kaddish is remarkable (Schwier 2005, 894).

In the history of research, a shift in focus of interpretation can be traced. From the middle of the previous century, a more historical exegesis has been dominant. Jesus's expression of the Father-child relationship (*abba* as "babble word" of small children), the presumed unprecedented invocation, and the concise wording were considered evidence—to be sure, controversial—for the uniqueness of the Lord's Prayer (cf. Jeremias 1966, 63–64).

The address to God as "Father" transmitted in Luke 11:2—without further immediate addition—suggests that the invocation originally chosen by Jesus was the Aramaic *abba* ("my Father" or "dear Father"). The fact that the word *abba* is also used by children toward their biological father is irrelevant (Barr 1988, 28–47). Rather, it is about the filiation to God mediated by Jesus, irrespective of age. The phrase "our Father" (Matt. 6:9) is not to be understood as if the Father were the property of the believers, but it is God to whom the believers are assigned as his children through Christ.

Since the end of the last century, research tends toward a stronger eschatological understanding (the soon coming of the kingdom of God; explanation of the bread as "bread of the time of salvation"; cf. Philonenko 2002, 84–86; Schwier 2005, 894). Recent studies set more functional accents: Hurtado (2014, 51–53) draws attention to the singular role of Jesus in the history of religions. Holmås (2014, 91–111) focuses on the boundary function of the Lord's Prayer: whoever recites the characteristic prayer of a group thereby professes to belong to that group. The Lord's Prayer was the specific prayer of those who believed in Christ. Such a prayer functions as an indication of belonging (cf. Sandnes 2014, 209–30; Ostmeyer 2004a, 332–34). K. Müller (2003, 196) calls the Lord's Prayer an "identity marker," and Kvalbein (2014b, 233–63) refers to the community-creating function of the prayer.

In Luke 11:1, the disciples ask Jesus for a prayer analogous to the one John the Baptist taught his disciples. The wording of the Lord's Prayer contains nothing to which his Jewish environment could have taken offense, and its comparatively fixed text marks those who pray as followers of Jesus of Nazareth.

From a christological-soteriological perspective, the mediation of filiation through Jesus *the* Son and through his salvation is central; through him the believers join in the *abba* cry (cf. Rom. 8:15; Gal. 4:6). Only in this function as well as through Jesus's understanding of himself and his image of God tied to it does the Lord's Prayer become *the Christian prayer* per se.

While the question of whether Jesus himself prayed the Lord's Prayer is answered in the affirmative for the "You" petitions (cf. Philonenko 2002, 3, 109–10), the Lord's Prayer petition for the forgiveness of one's own guilt, for example, cannot be reconciled with Jesus's image of himself as handed down through the New Testament writings (John 8:46; 2 Cor. 5:21; Heb. 4:15; 7:26; 1 Pet. 2:22; cf. H. Klein 2009, 94).

In the invocation of God as *abba*, (dear) Father, Jesus's understanding of himself, of prayer, and of God is combined (Mark 14:36). Accordingly, Jesus understands himself exclusively as *the* Son of God and presupposes that no one else stands in a comparable relationship with God.

Believers who recite this name (*Father*) in prayer commit themselves to Jesus as *the* Son of God, through whom they know themselves to be redeemed. Understood in this way, recitation of the Lord's Prayer is at the same time a confession of faith.

The Lord's Prayer presents Jesus's message in a compact form (cf. Jeremias 1966, 161): those who pray ask that the kingdom of the Father proclaimed by Jesus may come (soon), and they ask that they will be ready and prepared for entering this kingdom.

Dalman, Gustaf. 1898; ²1930. *Die Worte Jesu: Mit Berücksichtigung des nachkanonischen Schrifttums und der aramäischen Sprache*. Vol. 1, *Einleitung und wichtige Begriffe*. Leipzig.

Jeremias, Joachim. 1966. *Abba: Studien zur neutestamentlichen Theologie und Zeitgeschichte*. Göttingen.

Ostmeyer, Karl-Heinrich. 2004a. "Das Vaterunser: Gründe für seine Durchsetzung als 'Urgebet' der Christenheit." *NTS* 50: 320–36.

———. 2004b. "Jesu Annahme der Kinder in Mt 19,13–15." *NovT* 46: 1–11.

———. 2006. *Kommunikation mit Gott und Christus: Sprache und Theologie des Gebetes im Neuen Testament*. WUNT 197. Tübingen.

Philonenko, Marc. 2002. *Das Vaterunser: Vom Gebet Jesu zum Gebet der Jünger*. UTB 2312. Tübingen.

Stemm, Sönke von. 1999. *Der betende Sünder vor Gott: Studien zu Vergebungsvorstellungen in urchristlichen und frühjüdischen Texten*. Leiden.

Karl-Heinrich Ostmeyer

3.6. Jesus's Interpretation of the Torah

3.6.1. Jesus and the Law in Scholarship

How did Jesus relate to the Torah and to the variety of halakic interpretations flourishing toward the end of the Second Temple period? These are questions that have troubled New Testament research for centuries, quite naturally, since most scholars had their roots in the Christian or Jewish tradition and tried to negotiate the relationship between the church and the synagogue. The differences between the two, which soon (but only gradually) evolved during the first centuries CE, came to be justified by the church as a distinction between ethics and ritual, which is quite arbitrary and hardly possible to uphold today. In past scholarship, as in the church, Jesus was often understood to have somehow "fulfilled" not only the prophecies but also those ritual parts of the law that Christians no longer observed, at least not in the same ways as Jews did.

Few scholars today wish to be associated with the explicit or implicit supersessionist and anti-Jewish sentiments often expressed in past research on Jesus and the law. Many nineteenth-century "lives of Jesus" portray him as a liberal, in contrast to legalistic Pharisees and enthusiastic apocalypticists. With Albert Schweitzer in 1906, apocalypticism was allowed to return. However, various attempts to understand Jesus's teaching from a Jewish perspective during the first half of the twentieth century (Montefiore, Klausner, Branscomb), as more or less in line with the mainstream of Jewish religion, did not win the day. For scholars of the so-called new quest from the 1950s and onward, headed by people like Käsemann and Bornkamm and governed by criteria of authenticity among which dissimilarity was the foremost, Jesus was different from Judaism, in particular in his understanding of law. He did not ground his ethics in law but in the immediate will of God, which he knew by experience or revelation, and against which every biblical command should be tested. Such views have proved to be less historical than theological, but nevertheless continue to attract and influence, in part because of their implicit Christology, but also because of their appeal to the cultural myth of the "great man" or "individual hero." While almost every scholar today will affirm Jesus's "Jewishness," this can mean close to anything.

In a situation like this there is always a risk that in reaction the pendulum will swing too far in the other direction, which has its own problems, although these might not be obvious at first. As the picture of Jesus as teacher and rabbi has become commonplace, and as the diversity of Second Temple Judaism has become visible through the publication of the Dead Sea Scrolls, it is now possible to position Jesus in a continuum of legal interpretation and halakic development from the beginning of the Second Temple period, through Qumran and the Pharisees, to rabbinic Judaism. Comparison between the Jesus tradition and rabbinic material, once popular and then discredited, is again becoming more common, as the evidence from the Dead Sea Scrolls can now be used for triangulation. This enterprise is, however, fraught with difficulties, as the level of argument and distinction in rabbinic texts is too often assumed for the time of the temple. This easily leads to new and treacherous types of anachronism, of which a few examples will be provided below. To avoid such traps, we need a precise understanding of halakic development and the level of argument toward the end of the Second Temple period.

3.6.2. Jesus and the Law in the Sources

The Jesus tradition repeatedly relates Jesus's teaching to the law. The Q narrative is often seen to portray Jesus as upholding the law (cf. Q 16:17). Mark, on the other hand, pictures Jesus in a manner that confirms his gentile audience's partly "unobservant" practices, either as in line with the law if interpreted in Jesus's way or as weightier matters having priority over certain points of law (Mark 2:15–17, 18–22; 2:23–3:6; 7:1–23). Matthew does his best to correct this picture by tweaking Mark's narrative of Jesus's teachings and conflicts on legal matters and combining them with Q in a more responsible and rabbinic direction, fitting them into the state of halakic discussion known to his audience in the late first century CE (Matt. 12:5–7, 11–12; 5:32/19:9; change of order in 19:4–8; omission of Mark 7:19). In doing this, he also modifies Q's criticisms of the teachers of law by emphasizing their lack of righteousness and further elaborating on accusations of hypocrisy found in his source (Matt. 23:13–36). Although Luke combines the same or similar sources, he rather presents Jesus's relationship to the law within a context that is characterized by piety and faithfulness to the commandments of Jewish law understood as religious custom, *ethos* (Luke 1:9; 2:22–24, 27, 41–42; 4:16; 22:39; 23:56). In Luke there is no real break with the law until Acts, and even there only as a result of non-Jews joining the Jesus movement (Acts 10–11; 15). Although the Lukan (Q) Jesus criticizes religious leaders (Luke 11:37–54), accusations of hypocrisy are not as vehement as in Matthew. The Markan conflict narratives on hand washing and divorce are omitted. Extant extracanonical fragments are not sufficient for a coherent picture, and the Gospel of Thomas (see below) is ambiguous, too. In spite of their different emphases, the synoptic sources all display similar ambiguities in their diverging portrayals of Jesus's attitude to the law. Although Jesus is understood to have been in conflict with leaders and teachers of law about various matters, he is not thought to break or invalidate the Torah. It is only in John that the Jesus tradition turns clearly antinomistic, by casting Jesus in constant opposition to the "Jews" and "their law" (John 1:17; 7:19; 8:17; 10:34; 15:25). As part of John's christological argument, "the law and the prophets" witness to Jesus (1:45), but in the symbolic world of the Gospel of John, Jesus not only fulfills but also replaces the function of the Jewish law. It should be quite evident that John's programmatic theological refraction says little or nothing about the historical Jesus's stance toward Israelite tradition; hence John will not be dealt with any further here. While the Synoptics are similarly programmatic and theological, the way they wrestle with their sources makes it very unlikely that Jesus would have opposed the Torah (cf. Loader).

3.6.3. Jesus's Relationship to the Pentateuch

The Torah in the form of pentateuchal tradition would have been a natural and authoritative guide for any Israelite in the late Second Temple period. During the Hellenistic era in particular, a gradual shift in the Torah's status and function from formative to normative begins, which is part of the background to the long and protracted process of "canonization." There is, however, no reason to believe that this recharacterization of the law was complete, or became unanimously accepted, during the time of the temple. Through this period the Torah, as practical instruction, was subject to rewriting, redaction, and reinterpretation. As the text of the Pentateuch became more or less fixed and as the status of the Torah took on more judicial proportions, legal interpretation evolved in particular along halakic lines. But to the extent that groups and teachers held on to earlier and more flexible attitudes to Torah as instruction and guidance, discussions of law and its application would not need to employ the new types of arguments that were developed.

We must not assume that in his discussions with Sadducees and Pharisees over Torah interpretation Jesus necessarily followed those forms and displayed those judicial characteristics of argument that we find in later rabbinic literature. The same caveat applies to our reading of "halakic" texts from Qumran. We need to acknowledge that the gospel authors of the late first century often shape their narratives of Jesus's conflicts and discussions in the light of similar conflicts and discussions of their own times, thereby imbuing the Jesus tradition with the characteristics of legal thinking and argument from a slightly later period.

Nor must we think that in his references to the law Jesus was assuming canonical authority, in any developed sense, as if the canon were already a clear concept. In Q, Jesus refers to "the prophets and the law" (Matt. 11:13) or "the law and the prophets" (Luke 16:16). In Luke this is part of what is arguably an earlier Q collection of sayings, which juxtaposes a saying about the kingdom in relation to the law and the prophets with a saying about the validity of the law in order to prevent the first saying from being misunderstood (Luke 16:17), and then exemplifies this with a saying on divorce (16:18). Matthew integrated the last two in his Sermon on the Mount (Matt. 5:18, 32) but kept (the main part of) the first saying for explaining the role of John the Baptizer (11:12). Luke's version is more in line with his characteristic *heilsgeschichtliche* thinking. In both cases, "the law and the prophets" refers to the narrative and historical backdrop to the in-breaking kingdom. If Jesus used this expression, there is little to suggest that he thereby intended to demarcate two normative sections of the canon. Most other occurrences of this phrase seem to depend on this Q saying. Matthew's related saying about abolition or fulfillment (Matt. 5:17) and his addition to the "golden rule" ("this is the law and the prophets"; 7:12) are both secondary and depending on the Q saying, as is his conclusion to Jesus's reply to the lawyer, quoting the Shema ("on these two commandments the whole of the law and the prophets depend"; 22:40). Luke's references to Moses and the prophets (Luke 16:29; 24:27, 44) are from the late first or possibly even the early second century CE and cannot claim to originate with the historical Jesus. For Jesus's own attitude we are left with Q (Luke) 16:16, which originally seems to explain Jesus's kingdom in relation to previous prophets rather than issues of scriptural authority. Mark never uses the expression "the law and the prophets"; in fact, he never uses *nomos* at all.

3.6.4. The Shema, the Holiness Code (HC), and the Sermon
on the Mount/Plain

Although Mark's Jesus never talks about *nomos*, he does talk about commandment (*entolē*) and refers to the Decalogue as well as to the central Israelite confession, the Shema (Deut. 6:4–9), and to the Holiness Code (HC; Lev. 17–27), both of which are combined in the so-called double love commandment. There are two distinct traditions in which Jesus replies to questions about law: one about requirements for eternal life (Mark 10:17–22 par. Matt. 19:16–22 par. Luke 18:18–23) and another about the greatest commandment (Mark 12:28–34 par. Matt. 22:34–40 par. Luke 10:25–28). According to the first of these, adherence to the commandments (the choice of which seems influenced by the HC) leads to eternal life but needs to be complemented (or perhaps proved?) by social action (sale of property for the sake of the poor). According to the second, the greatest commandments are to love God (Deut. 6:5) and one's neighbor (Lev. 19:18). Luke has reworked the second tradition and employs the question about eternal life in the discussion about the greatest commandment, too, so that the double love commandment is presented even more clearly as the law's means of salvation. In Mark, adherence to the law leads to the kingdom (Mark 10:23; 12:34), to which Matthew adds perfection (Matt. 19:21). In spite of the different uses the synoptic authors make of these two traditions, they give us all reason to think that Jesus did relate his kingdom vision to the Torah and that adherence to pentateuchal tradition, and to its prosocial instructions in particular, was important to him.

A similar picture is provided by the ethical teaching in Matthew's Sermon on the Mount and Luke's Sermon on the Plain, much of which is usually assigned to the Q source. Similar to the Markan tradition, according to which mere obedience to the Torah's commandments is not deemed enough, Matthew has Jesus require a righteousness surpassing that of the religious elite (Matt. 5:20). Matthew has further developed and transformed Q's criticism of the leaders' hypocrisy (cf. Luke 11:37–52) to the point of slander and vilification (Matt. 23:1–36), and in the Sermon on the Mount he frames these accusations to reflect conflicts between his own communities and the evolving rabbinic Judaism of his own time. Although Matthew's rendering is highly exaggerated and partly anachronistic, the underlying critique of the elite for only nominally practicing the law while disregarding social justice and showing more concern for honor than for the poor is consistent with Markan tradition and is likely to have originated with the historical Jesus.

One of the most conspicuous strands in the Q material underlying Matthew's and Luke's versions of the Sermon is found in the prosocial instructions about nonretaliation and enemy love (Matt. 5:38–42, 43–48; Luke 6:27–36; the fifth and sixth of the Matthean "antitheses"). Their clash with a general sense of justice and proportionality has often been observed, and the sayings must be understood as hyperbolic to a degree (cf. Kazen 2021). Although Matthew separates the difficult nonretaliatory actions (5:38–42) from the more manageable mental attitudes (5:43–48), they must have belonged together in Q, as they do in Luke. Interestingly, this material runs almost like a commentary to parts of the HC (Lev. 19), which played a central role in several strands of the early Christ movement and was frequently referred to. In the Sermon on the Mount, Jesus's teaching is contrasted to talion law (Exod. 21:23–24; Deut. 19:21; Lev. 24:19–20), which clearly results from Matthean redaction. Q, however, does not polemize, but interprets the HC, which negotiates the Covenant Code and Deuteronomic law and advocates a broadened concept of neighbor, including resident foreigners; both neighbors and immigrants are to be loved as oneself (Lev. 19:18, 33–34). The Q sayings on nonretaliation and enemy love are thus of one piece with the love commandment and do not stand in contrast to the Torah but interpret the HC. Only in Matthew's redaction do these sayings contrast with the teaching and behavior of the late-first-century opponents of the Matthean community. Without this overlay, the Q sayings could reasonably have been triggered by Jesus's teachings, as they reflect attitudes consistent with what we have observed so far in other strands of the Jesus tradition and could represent a strategy for extended kinship and intragroup conflict resolution within a context of covenant renewal.

3.6.5. Conflicts over Torah and Halakah

If Jesus did not oppose the law but based his teaching and ethics on the Torah, how do we explain and interpret those traditions that suggest tension and conflict over religious and cultural practices with regard to Sabbath observance, divorce and remarriage, ritual purity, food laws, tithes, oaths, and fasting? Numerous scholars of Jesus and the law have tried to reconcile this dilemma by suggesting that Jesus based his views on a unique authority, an indifference to certain aspects of biblical law, and a different understanding of, or pipeline access to, God's will (cf. Westerholm 1978; Meier 2009, 5–8, 415). As an alternative to such implicitly theological explanations, or complementing them, some have suggested that Jesus defended biblical law against oral tradition and recent expansion. Close but not identical are views of Jesus and his adversaries as defending competing interpretations, or representing conflicting halakic standpoints.

An in-depth understanding of halakic development and argumentation toward the end of the Second Temple period is necessary for evaluating historical traces in the synoptic conflict narratives. Legal interpretation in the first century CE is situated between Qumran and the rabbis. Authority in Qumran was based on concepts of revelation and divinely inspired interpretation of the Torah, while the later rabbis emphasized the role of human activity and exegesis. Halakic argument in Qumran does not always represent ancient tradition. Close reading frequently gave rise to halakic innovations, opposing earlier custom, which in turn could trigger traditionalists to invent strained exegetical arguments to defend traditional practice (cf. Shemesh 2009). The beginnings of such developments can be traced in the Jesus tradition, but the full results are only seen in rabbinic texts, which frequently also display clear examples of "nominalism" (legal formalism)—an understanding of divine law as a more or less arbitrary basis for morality, in need of human interpretation. The predominant attitude in Qumran was rather "realistic" (legal essentialist) and sees the Torah as a reflection of the divine intent and order of creation; hence halakic expansion and innovation become possible through analogy. These observations should not be exaggerated to indicate an absolute dichotomy, but close attention to historical and ideological principles of halakic development facilitates more qualified analyses of the Jesus tradition (cf. Kazen 2013). Elaborate interpretation and complicated exegesis are more likely to represent the gospel authors than the historical Jesus, while simple arguments based on close reading of the Torah rather suggest early origins. Arguments based on creation and divine intent are more likely to originate with Jesus than discussions reflecting "nominalist" tendencies; examples of the latter can be seen in Matthew's versions of Markan narratives, which often reflect interpretative conflicts between the Matthean communities and the evolving rabbinic movement.

3.6.6. Jesus and the Sabbath

A good example of this is provided by the Sabbath conflict stories. The cornfield incident (Mark 2:23–28; Matt. 12:1–8; Luke 6:1–5) has often been regarded as unhistorical. Some of the exegetical arguments, particularly in Matthew, are of a late date: customary behavior is justified by textual interpretation (Matt. 12:5–7) against those who wish to introduce stricter practices based on a close reading of Scripture. This strategy is known both from early Christian polemics and from rabbinic discussion, but it is less likely to represent the historical Jesus. According to Tannaitic texts, serious hunger outweighs the Sabbath (m. Yoma 8:6), but this is not the case here. The story is more likely to reflect a conflict regarding a recent expansion of the command to prepare food in advance (cf. Exod. 16:23–29; 35:2–3) into a prohibition against the earlier custom to eat things found in nature (CD x 22–23)—an interpretation not generally accepted. Nothing prevents such a core from being historical, even if Matthew's christological interpretation and developed exegetical arguments, turning Jesus into a halakic authority, reflect a later date.

The synoptic Sabbath healing story is found in several versions (Matt. 12:9–14; Mark 3:1–6; Luke 6:6–11; 13:10–17; 14:1–6). Most scholars refer to the rabbinic principle that danger of life outweighs Sabbath restrictions (*piquach nefesh*). This principle is clearly established in Tannaitic texts (t. Shabbat 9[10]:22; 15[16]:17; m. Yoma 8:6) and applied so liberally that no conflict would be conceivable had it been generally accepted during Jesus's time. In rabbinic texts the *piquach nefesh* principle is defended by quite advanced exegetical arguments, suggesting a lengthy process of development and a need to defend a previous practice from expansionist restrictions based on close reading. Such strict interpretations of the Sabbath command can be found in Jubilees (2:29–30; 50:6–13) as well as in the Damascus Document (CD x 14–xi 18).

The animal in the pit (Matt. 12:11–12; Luke 14:5; cf. Luke 13:15) is a classical school example used to probe the limits for Sabbath observance (cf. t. Shabbat 14[15]:3; m. Betzah 3). Scholars often assert that the Pharisees were more liberal than the Essenes (Qumran) in balancing emergencies against the Sabbath commandment, but the question arises why the subsequent rabbis then needed elaborate justifications for their lenient halakah. The answer is probably that the need to defend the obvious only appeared when customary behavior was questioned. The Damascus Document only allows humans to be lifted out of a pit on the Sabbath with the help of clothes (i.e., without tools) and makes no concession for animals (CD xi 13–17; 4Q265 vi 4–8). This is not because one commandment overrules another (as with the *piquach nefesh* principle), but reflects an absolute interpretation of the Torah's prohibition against work to include the use of tools even in an emergency, which goes against customary behavior. As a result, the Pharisees were forced to discuss limits of interpretation, and subsequent rabbis eventually formulated the principle of lifesaving and defended it exegetically. Jesus probably interacted with the Pharisees, but not at the argumentative level of the rabbis.

When Matthew and Luke combine the animal-in-the-pit-tradition from Q with the Markan Sabbath healing narrative or motif (Matt. 12:9–14; Luke 13:10–17;

407

14:1–6), they may already be aware of an evolving lifesaving principle and thus relate Jesus to the level of rabbinic discussion current in their own days. The Sabbath healing motif, however, relates to a different issue: the healing of chronic disease. According to an ancient tradition, Shammaites prohibited prayer for the sick on the Sabbath while Hillelites allowed it (t. Shabbat 16[17]:22). Here is a possible background to Jesus's Sabbath healings. Such healings have a strong position in the Jesus tradition and are provided with a variety of theological interpretations. Historically, the Sabbath healing motif likely reflects Jesus's stance in relation to an ongoing debate between Shammaites and Hillelites, in a situation when some defend pragmatic custom against others who advocate stricter interpretations based on close reading, at a time when a clear *piquach nefesh* principle had not yet been defined.

3.6.7. Jesus and Divorce

It was common in the past to interpret the Markan conflict narrative about the question of the Pharisees concerning divorce (Mark 10:1–12) as evidence for Jesus's restrictive attitude, in line with the Essenes (Qumran) and the Shammaites, but in contrast to the "liberal" view of the Hillelites. The male prerogative to divorce was assumed throughout the ancient Near East. Attempts have been made to argue that Jewish women were able to initiate divorce, but the evidence is weak and exceptional (e.g., Elephantine marriage contracts; Josephus on Herodian divorces in *Ant.* 15:259–260; 18:136; 20:141–143; and Murabba'at 19). Hence Mark's concluding prohibition (Mark 10:11–12) against men divorcing their wives and wives divorcing their husbands should be read as a modification in view of the author's Greco-Roman environment.

The idea that divorce was prohibited in Qumran has been abandoned in view of evidence to the contrary (4Q12ᵃ Mal 4:16; CD xiii 17; 11QT lxvi 11, liv 4; 4Q159 ii–iv+8:10). The texts previously appealed to rather refer to polygyny (CD iv 20–21; 11QT lvii 15–19). However, the Damascus Document bases its argument against polygyny on divine intent (creation story) and partly appeals to the same Scripture as does Mark, displaying a similar type of interpretative legal essentialism or "realism." The Shammaite-Hillelite controversy, on the other hand, betrays conspicuously late traits. In rabbinic texts, this debate is usually associated with advanced exegesis and a high degree of legal formalism or "nominalism" (Sifra on Lev. 21:7; Sifre on Deut. 24:1; b. Gittin 90a). Not even Matthew's halakic reworking of the narrative, which reinforces Jesus's rabbinic authority (Matt. 19:1–9), comes close to the level of argument in the corresponding rabbinic texts. While Matthew's "excepting clause" (19:9), included also in the Sermon on the Mount (5:32) and allowing divorce in cases of adultery, does suggest some knowledge of the Shammaite-Hillelite controversy, it only represents an intermediary stage in the development of the rabbinic halakic discussion on the issue.

The core of the Markan conflict narrative, with its simple "realism" appealing to creation order, probably originates with the historical Jesus. This view is strengthened by the fact that the strict stance on divorce soon became problematic for the early church. However, if the Shammaite-Hillelite controversy did not occasion Jesus's stance, we need to look further for a plausible explanation. Although hypothetical, an explanation based on Jesus's criticism of the elite is appealing. Like his mentor, the Baptizer, who criticized Antipas for his marital affairs (Mark 6:17–19; Matt. 14:3–5; Luke 3:19), Jesus was opposed to, and hunted by, the tetrarch (Luke 13:31–32). When the Lukan (Q) divorce saying (Luke 16:18), which lacks a narrative framework, is taken into account, the possibility opens up that the Markan narrative either elaborates an original saying against Antipas or represents a discussion occasioned by Jesus's critique.

Given the cultural context, the blend of customs and groups in the region, and the increasing trend to regard divorcees as intrinsically immoral regardless of the reason for divorce, a clear prohibition against men putting aside their wives could be understood as a protective measure in favor of the women. Such a stance would be reasonable to ascribe to the historical Jesus in view of the evidence for his general attitudes, his criticisms of power abuse, and a "realist" understanding of the divine will.

3.6.8. Purity and Food

The story about hand washing (Mark 7:1–13; Matt. 15:1–20) has become a virtual battleground for conflicting interpretations. Today most interpreters consider the statement that Jesus declared all foods clean (Mark 7:19; not in Matthew) as a Markan comment, by which the author applies the hand-washing narrative to quite different issues of commensality and purity of food, relevant to his predominantly gentile context. The narrative tradition on which Mark builds (Mark 7:1, 5, 15), however, concerns ritual impurity (contact contagion) in its capacity to spread via food and liquid. There is no evidence that the historical Jesus questioned or discussed food laws.

It has become fairly common to suggest that Jesus opposed extrabiblical traditions in favor of Scripture and that the custom of hand washing before meals only evolved after the time of Jesus as a rabbinic innovation, or at least did not become general practice until later (cf. m. Berakhot 8:2). The saying that nothing from the outside, going into a human being, can defile, but only that which goes out from a human being can defile (Mark 7:15) has often been understood as a hyperbole or a dialectic negation, and interpreted in a relative sense (nothing from the outside defiles *as much as* things from the inside).

Recently, some scholars have suggested an absolute interpretation in the sense that food cannot defile human beings at all; only human beings can act as contaminants. This is based on an understanding of ritual hand washing as a security measure, at the time of Jesus only practiced by a few, to prevent the spread of impurity via ordinary food to priestly rations (through which it could affect the temple and the cult). Again, Jesus would have defended Scripture against extrabiblical innovations.

This view is problematic for several reasons. First and foremost, the contrast between Scripture and tradition (here not in the sense of custom, but in the sense of Pharisaic halakah) is entirely a result of Markan literary activity and redaction of his traditions. This contrast occasions both the references to Isaiah (Mark 7:6–7) and the insertion of the *korban* example (7:10–13). The point is to demonstrate that the (Markan!) adversaries do not follow the Torah's intention (7:8–9, 13). This opposition between Scripture and Jewish halakah is typical for early Christ believers in their polemical defense of their own behavior as more observant than that of the evolving rabbinic movement (Col. 2:8, 22; Titus 1:14; cf. Eph. 2:15). The arguments and critique against the legal formalism or "nominalism" of the opponents suggest the context of the gospel authors rather than the time of Jesus.

Furthermore, the view that Jesus defended Scripture against extrabiblical traditions depends on severe anachronism, since we then need to accept later rabbinic interpretations of purity as valid descriptions for the late Second Temple period. Rabbinic texts assume that purity rules were completely focused on the cult and supply complicated and exegetically strained explanations for the relationship between liquids, foodstuffs, and vessels (b. Pesahim 14b, 17b–20b; Sifra Shemini 8), assuming a complete system for the transmission of impurity through a number of "removes" (m. Teharot). This results in a view of ritual hand washing as a rabbinic innovation, possibly practiced by a small group of extremists only at the time of Jesus. Ordinary food would then not have (been generally considered to) become contaminated by contact with impure people.

In reality, however, views on how impurity was transmitted were less developed and more diverse during the Second Temple period than many rabbinic texts suggest. Even the Mishnah preserves traces of diverging views, including an early understanding of the eater sharing the same degree of impurity as the food (m. Teharot 2:2; cf. m. Zavim 5:12). Hand washing evolved as one of several means to handle the transmission of various forms of impurity during the late Second Temple period, when views on how impurity spread were expanding.

As a ritual practice, hand washing has roots both in Scripture (Lev. 15:11) and in custom, and like some other water rites, it gradually came to be practiced in new contexts. By contrast, rabbinic discussions about liquids, food, and vessels display so many traits of advanced interpretation and legal formalist or "nominalist" argument that they cannot be taken to represent early views.

Although Mark exaggerates about "all Jews" practicing hand washing before meals (Mark 7:3), it is reasonable that some did, including groups of Pharisees, and that the practice was on the increase as an alternative to immersion in certain cases. Mark's almost desperate use of the hand-washing tradition for quite a different purpose suggests a prehistory and the probable presence of a historical core: Jesus defended his disciples against accusations from expansionists for insufficiently observing purity halakah. His defense, however, did not concern biblical commandments against rabbinic law, but the relative weight of the heart or the insides of a human being (Mark 7:15, 18–19) compared to bodily impurity. This suggests neither a break with nor a general critique of purity law and purity halakah, but rather reflects a prophetic tradition of emphasizing social and economic justice, along the lines suggested by Q (Luke 11:39–42; cf. Matt. 23:25–26; P. Oxy. 840).

3.6.9. Other Texts and Topics

Prophetic critique also suggests a plausible paradigm for understanding other areas of conflict between Jesus and his opponents, which are suggested by parts of the Jesus tradition: tithes, fasting, and oaths. Tithing provides perhaps the clearest example of a criticism that does not object to the practice itself but contrasts meticulous observance in one area with less concern about prosocial and humanitarian behavior (Luke 11:42; Matt. 23:23). The material comes from Q and fits the general tendency of Jesus's teaching.

Oaths are explicitly prohibited in an argument about truthfulness (Matt. 5:34–37), but in a manner that suggests hyperbole for the sake of emphasis—a method well known in prophetic tradition. A similar saying does not prohibit swearing altogether, but only the misuse of oaths with specific formulas to avoid their binding effect (Matt. 23:16–22). Both of these are uniquely Matthean and suggest acquaintance with evolving rabbinic discussions; the latter in particular seems to polemicize against a legal formalist strategy to handle rash oaths, of which the subsequent stages and more elaborate examples can be found in the Mishnah (e.g., m. Nedarim 2:5; 6:9–7:5). It is thus very uncertain whether these traditions may be traced back to the historical Jesus. Stronger claims can be made for the core of the Markan tradition about the *korban* vow (Mark 7:10–12; Matt. 15:5–6), which could be read as an objection to the rash use of vows in view of their negative consequences, but again, the Markan implication that this vow was being deliberatively used at the time of Jesus to deprive parents of support must not be taken at face value. Such extreme formulations rather constitute a backdrop to evolving legal formalist interpretations that aim at lessening the binding force of rash oaths.

According to Markan tradition (Mark 2:18-20; Matt. 9:14-15; Luke 5:33-35), Jesus and his disciples were criticized for not fasting. Since fasting was practiced generally as part of popular piety, and finds its natural continuation in the early Christ movement, there is good reason to consider a historical background for the core of this tradition. The concluding comment that disciples will fast when the bridegroom is taken away (Mark 2:20) might even be understood as an addition, negotiating an uncomfortable piece of tradition with actual practice. In uniquely Matthean tradition, fasting is assumed, although criticized when practiced as a display of piety (Matt. 6:16-18; cf. Did. 8:1). Fasting is, however, never commanded in the Torah, and Jesus's negligence of this practice might be better understood within the framework of his open commensality. By itself, a deviant fasting practice would hardly indicate lack of Torah observance, but criticism against fasting when contrasted with social justice is rather an intrinsic part of prophetic tradition (cf. Isa. 58).

Other texts that relate to Jesus's interpretation of the law include P. Oxy. 840 and the Gospel of Thomas. In P. Oxy. 840 Jesus and his disciples are criticized by a temple priest for walking in the holy precincts without having washed or bathed their feet. Jesus retorts by contrasting purification by immersion in ordinary water with the waters of eternal life. Although the text is late and the interpretation of the fragment is much contested, the relative importance of the interior in contrast to the exterior is reminiscent of other Jesus traditions as well as Israelite prophetic discourse.

The Gospel of Thomas is more ambiguous. Sayings address fasting (6, 14, 27, 104), prayer and almsgiving (6, 14), purity (14, 89), Sabbath (27), and circumcision (53). Fasting, prayer, and almsgiving are all considered negative (14)—prayer even causes condemnation. The interpretation is contested, and the statement cannot be taken entirely literally. A saying about defilement through that which comes out rather than that which goes into the mouth (14) is rendered in the Matthean version (Matt. 15:11) and juxtaposed to a Lukan saying about commensality and healing (Luke 10:8), which suggests a disregard for purity or food laws as part of itinerant missionary activity. The Sabbath saying is notoriously difficult to interpret, while circumcision seems to be rejected. These sayings might reflect later negotiations of Jewish traditions by non-Jews. This might also be the case with one of the agrapha, Luke 6:4 D, about the man working on the Sabbath. None of these sayings can be used to argue about the historical Jesus's interpretation of the law.

3.6.10. Conclusions

There is no evidence that Jesus opposed the Torah. Jesus's interpretation of Israel's legal tradition displays traits of legal essentialism or "realism," asking for divine intent. His stance often suggests prophetic priorities of human need or well-being, as well as popular common sense.

The synoptic authors occasionally portray Jesus as a defender of Scripture against rabbinic innovations, and in Matthew especially, as a superior rabbi, mastering scribal arguments and interpretations. Contemporary interpreters sometimes have an interest in a Jesus who abolishes or modifies Jewish law by virtue of his (divine) authority. Others prefer to put him in dialogue with the Tannaitic rabbis. The historical Jesus is easily curtailed by such anachronistic construals.

Suggestions that Jesus relativized the role of Torah because of eschatological haste or that his inherent authority licensed him to proclaim God's will irrespective of the law, probably tell more about the interpreter's eschatology and Christology than about Jesus. The material reviewed here does not support such speculations.

As a judicial understanding of the Torah evolved only gradually, the need to outweigh one commandment with another and motivate humanitarian exceptions by advanced exegesis and strained arguments is a fairly late phenomenon. Jesus appears as a legal interpreter but does not display full-blown halakic interpretative techniques. Jesus's stance displays a traditional attitude to the law, for which there is no real conflict between the guidance and instruction of the Torah and its pragmatic application, governed by a prophetic concern for human welfare and social justice. Hence Jesus's kingdom vision is built on the law and its humanitarian concerns in particular.

Kazen, Thomas. 2013. *Scripture, Interpretation, or Authority? Motives and Arguments in Jesus' Halakic Conflicts.* WUNT 320. Tübingen.

———. 2021. "Emotional Repression and Physical Mutilation? The Cognitive and Behavioural Impact of Exaggeration in the Sermon on the Mount." In *Social and Cognitive Perspectives on the Sermon on the Mount,* edited by Rikard Roitto, Colleen Shantz, and Petri Luomanen. Sheffield.

Loader, William. 2011. "Jesus and the Law." In *Handbook for the Study of the Historical Jesus,* vol. 3, *The Historical Jesus,* edited by Tom Holmén and Stanley E. Porter, 2745–72. Leiden.

Meier, John P. 2009. *A Marginal Jew: Rethinking the Historical Jesus.* Vol. 4, *Law and Love.* New Haven and London.

Shemesh, Aharon. 2009. *Halakhah in the Making: The Development of Jewish Law from Qumran to the Rabbis.* Taubman Lectures in Jewish Studies 6. Berkeley, CA.

Thomas Kazen

3.7. Jesus as a Teacher of Wisdom

3.7.1. The Career of Jesus's Wisdom Teachings

If one takes the degree of familiarity of Jesus's sayings as a measure, then Jesus appears to be a teacher of wisdom from whose mouth sapiential insights into life simply gush out: "No one can serve two masters" (Matt. 6:24; Luke 16:13); "Are grapes gathered from thorns or figs from thistles?" (Matt. 7:16; cf. Luke 6:44); "Can wedding guests fast . . . ?" (Mark 2:19). There are such proverbial sayings as well as short stories in which everyday experiences are condensed (e.g., a lost sheep: Q 15:4–7; talents/*mna*: Matt. 25:14–30; Luke 19:12–27; cf. the list in Lips 1990, 198–203, 228–32) that have made their mark in the reception history and have developed into "sayings with wings" (cf. Theissen 2008). In the New Testament they are found in great numbers in the sayings source Q, that is, in the sayings material of Matthew and Luke, as well as in concluding points of many conflict stories in Mark. Much less known are the sayings of the apocalyptic Jesus, which are found especially in the eschatological speeches of the Gospels. It is no different with the sayings of Jesus the scribe, who argues with citations of Scripture and beats his discussion partners with their own weapons (cf. Mark 2:25–26; 7:6–13), or even with the philosophical Jesus in his discourses in the Gospel of John. Indeed, here also sapiential sayings are found such as "the wind blows where it chooses" (John 3:8), but they are micro elements woven into the sprawling course of the argument (cf. John 4:37; 10:12; 16:21; on this, R. Collins 1990; Poplutz 2006). From a point of view of sources, with the sapiential sayings of the sayings source and the punch lines of the apothegms in Mark, we strike the bedrock of the Jesus tradition.

3.7.2. Seed and Sheep, Wedding and Sabbath (Inventory of Motifs)

The inventory of motifs of the sapiential logia and stories encompasses the agrarian and domestic domains (cf. Mark 4:3–8, 26–29, 30–32; Q 15:3–7; Mark 3:24–25; 4:21, cf. Q 11:33; Mark 4:24, cf. Q 6:38; Mark 9:50, cf. Q 14:34–35; Q 6:48–49; Luke 15:8–10), similarly the ways of communicating and modes of conduct (cf. Q 6:37–42; Mark 2:19; 3:27; 6:4; Matt. 26:52; Mark 9:40, cf. Q 11:23; Luke 11:5–8; 15:11–32), from time to time also religious domains such as the Sabbath (Matt. 12:11; Luke 13:15–16; 14:5) or purity (Mark 7:15). In short, the world of the little person stands in the context.

3.7.3. Everyday Logic and the Function of Sapiential Sayings (Paremiology)

Sapiential sayings and stories are readily and easily remembered for simple reasons: They are short and normally concentrate solely on one idea. They seize on experiences, which are familiar from banal everyday life. Thereby they culminate in one specific point, for which usually a wholehearted agreement of the addressees is expected. Taken in themselves, sapiential sayings thus first of all reflect everyday experiences condensed into concise wording. However, if they stand in the context of a particular set of problems with which these experiences have nothing to do, they can become arguments inasmuch as the recipients draw the intended analogical conclusion: on an issue under discussion, the sapiential saying casts a new perspective, which puts the problem in a distinct light. Normally the conclusion resulting from it is drawn by the addressees themselves, but at the same time, the addressees themselves come to a decisive insight or are guided to it. The speaker simply triggers this process of recognition.

Precisely this should be the reason that proverbs and sapiential short stories are so popular: they are not only easy to perceive because they are so close to everyday reality, but they also leave the sovereignty of application to the addressee. Further, they can be employed without any problem as a commentary or aid in making a decision for other cases.

In this process the speaker who chooses a familiar sapiential saying or even contrives a new one nevertheless in no way has a passive role. By focusing on a particular aspect of everyday life, the speaker is already probing—and therefore has a particular option for the problematic case in view. If the addressees agree with the surprising proposition brought in from an apparently completely different field, the dialogue partners are already hooked. Because as soon as they draw the analogies to the problem under negotiation or discussion, they have taken over—as a perceived autonomous awareness—the option of the dialogue partner (Ebner 1998, 35–43). The paremiology speaks of "out of context statements" and defines proverbs as "strategies for dealing with situations" (Burke ³1973, 296; cf. Seitel 1981; A. Jacobson 1990).

If this "out of the context" use of a sapiential utterance is present, then—expressed specifically in terms of genre—a sapiential experiential saying becomes a figuration, and a sapiential short story becomes a similitude or a parable or an example story (see D.IV.3.7.4.3). If the intended instruction is directly expressed as an imperative, it is an admonition, to which for its part a rational justification can follow, although not necessarily (cf. Mark 4:24–25; Matt. 6:34; 7:6). Finally, if another sapiential saying is appended, the last one functions additionally for the rational justification as normal support for the admonition. But at the same time, this shows that the sapiential saying is in no way definitively tied to the admonition at hand; from it other conclusions can be drawn or it might also be applicable for other admonitions; therefore, an independent origin is likely (cf. Q 11:9–13: "Ask, and it will be given to you. . . . For everyone who asks receives. . . . Is there anyone among you who if your child asks for bread will give him a stone?"). Vice versa, there are also isolated admonitions, which go without any justification (cf. Matt. 5:39–42; cf. Luke 6:29–30; cf. the list and analysis, Zeller 1977).

In view of the pragmatics, the communication situation must be taken into account. In an admonition, the speaker makes use of authority with respect to his or her audience. Formulating an admonition is a matter of a teacher addressing his or her pupils. On these grounds alone, the argumentation can also fall away, because in a communication situation intended to be continuous a specific learning context stands in the background. By contrast, sapiential proverbs and short stories about everyday life are communicated on an equal footing and put the decision for a specific course of action in the hands of the addressee. In this respect, in admonitions Jesus's inside group of followers (both historically and also in the individual congregations in which the Gospels are read) is reflected as the audience, whereas sapiential proverbs and short stories about everyday life can apply to a larger circle of addressees.

3.7.4. Problematic Areas and the Impact of Content (Pragmatics)

If the processes of transmitting tradition correctly present the original circumstances only to some degree, in the textual units in the Gospels in their present configurations, not only the *form* of argumentation is reflected in apothegms with figurations as the punch line (cf. Mark 2:15–17, 18–22; 3:20–30; Q 11:14–20), or with sapiential short stories as parables or similitudes (cf. Luke 15:1–32), as well as in groups of proverbs oriented toward problems (cf. Q 12:22–31), but also reflected are the *problematic areas* as well as the dialogue partners. Three distinct areas of impact can be stipulated.

3.7.4.1. Reactions to Outside Animosity

According to the razor-sharp criterion of the Enlightenment theologian Hermann Samuel Reimarus (1694–1768), we stand on historically certain ground if fans pass on negative traditions about their idol (Reimarus 1979, 20). These are obviously matters of fact that even with the best intentions cannot be eliminated or kept under wraps. This phenomenon is found in the Jesus tradition in two cases. Both of the oldest traditions, Mark and the sayings source Q, record rebukes against Jesus from outsiders in almost the same phrasing. They concern the evaluation of Jesus's demon exorcisms that are obviously accepted as successful as well as his meal practices. In both cases Jesus's sapiential sayings, in what is now the narrative context of the Gospels, are transmitted as refutations.

"He drives out demons by Beelzebul, the ruler of demons" (Q 11:15; cf. Mark 3:22). With this reproach Jesus is openly denounced. Behind this stands a dangerous report: Jesus did not expel demons by the power of the God of Israel but rather by the help of a foreign, dark power, even the "ruler of demons," so to speak, as an intermediary on the opposite side. In this context several sapiential sayings are transmitted as Jesus's reaction. Jesus puts up a defense in which he poses a question: "If I cast out demons by Beelzebul, by whom do your sons cast them (demons) out?" (Q 11:19). With this Jesus demands the same right for everyone: if his exorcisms are scrutinized in bad faith because of the power by which he accomplishes them, then the same suspicion also holds for other exorcists in Galilee; alternatively, the acceptance claimed as a matter of course for one's own people also applies to both sides, and the God of Israel is the one who is at work in his exorcisms. In Mark 3:24–25 Jesus floats the sapiential insight that a kingly rule, just like a household, that is divided against itself cannot survive. Hearers who are ready and willing to draw the corresponding analogies to the negotiated issue will immediately see through the absurdity of the Beelzebul charge. Finally, in the saying about "binding the strong man" (Mark 3:27), Jesus resorts to the experience of plundering: no one can rob the strong man's house without first tying up the strong man—and he obviously intends thereby to arouse analogies to the apocalyptic expectation of the eschatological battle between the powers faithful to God and adversaries hostile to God. That battle begins in heaven and is also decided there, thus it not only precedes the corresponding earthly struggle chronologically but also determines its outcome. In short, for Jesus the expulsion of demons can be successful only because the heavenly power struggle is already definitively decided. Only in Q 11:20 ("But if I cast our demons by the finger of God, the kingdom of God has already come [ἔφθασεν] upon you") does Jesus hold on in a declamatory form what he otherwise indicates in words of wisdom, using the metonymy the "finger of God" (cf. Exod. 8:19) as the pivotal power (cf. overall Ebner [2]2012, 104–17).

With the reproach "See, a glutton and winebibber, a friend of tax collectors and sinners" (Q 7:34) or, alternatively, "he eats with tax collectors and sinners" (Mark 2:16), Jesus's meal practice is denounced: he sits down at the table with the "wrong" people, who are classified as "sinners" by the opposing group. Whereas in this case the tradition of the sayings source—in the context of wisdom theology—presents Jesus's alternative lifestyle as an experiment of wisdom, that nevertheless can be found only in the recognition among those who prove to be wisdom's true children (Ebner 2016). The Gospel of Mark again puts a sapiential rejoinder in Jesus's mouth: "Those who are well have no need of a physician, but those who are sick" (Mark 2:17)—in the tradition, however, this is combined with a programmatic mission mandate ("I have not come to call the righteous but sinners").

The slur "glutton and winebibber" likely takes up from the Old Testament background precisely those key words among which the condemnation of a "stubborn and rebellious son" should take place before the court of elders, because he continuously and in spite of punishment "does not listen to the voice of his father and mother" (cf. Deut. 21:18–21); thus he obtrusively contravenes conventionally expected conduct.

For Jesus, his so-called "a-familial ethos" (Klauck 1995) likely stands in the background, the practice of which is dealt with under the rubric "discipleship" and "forsaking parents" but which concretely means that Jesus abandoned his hometown Nazareth, did not provide for his parents—and expected the same from his disciples (cf. Q 9:59–60; Mark 1:16–20). Thereby he broke a taboo against the commandment to provide for parents (Exod. 20:12; Deut. 5:16; cf. Jungbauer 2002), the imitation of which the originators of the reproach "glutton and winebibber" wished to nip in the bud.

Finally, Jesus does not follow in the footsteps of convention. He moves through the countryside as an itinerant preacher, works as a day laborer if he needs to (Mark 6:3: τέκτων), and thus does not gather provisions according to the model of the diligent ant (cf. Prov. 6:6–11). He runs the risk of becoming impoverished (cf. Prov. 23:19–21), of becoming a beggar, and eventually of being a burden on the community. Jesus wisely puts these facts into a different light, too. As addressees, however, he then has his closest circle of followers before his eyes.

3.7.4.2. Anxiety and Needs in the Circle of Disciples

The challenge to learn from the ravens and lilies (cf. Q 12:22–31) bathes in new light his unwillingness to provide for himself à la the industrious ant of Jewish tradition. He directs the challenge to the circle of disciples: the apparently idyllic picture of ravens, which neither sow nor reap, and do not gather into barns, as well as lilies, which neither weave nor spin, consciously oscillates between the world of animals or plants and the world of human beings. In the (relinquished) activities, Jesus reflects the situation of men and women who have abandoned the sedentary life in the villages and move through the countryside with him as itinerant preachers. What they can actually observe in birds and lilies is that God takes good care of them. And they should learn that as human beings they are worth much more to God than animals or plants. With these sayings, not only are concerns about nourishment and clothing of women and men in the circle of followers placed in new light, but also their behavior, which appears to be "lazy." On the contrary, their behavior manifests a carelessness that completely relies on God. Jesus attempts to arouse this reliance with a further double saying, which takes up the conventional activities of women and men anew and appeals to the maternal and paternal instinct of his people—as an analogy for God's benevolence: "Who among you is a person, who if your son asks for bread, would give him a stone? Or if he asks for a fish, would give him a snake?" (Q 11:11–12). Other sapiential sayings, transmitted in part in combination with corresponding admonitions, attempt to bring into question disputes or prejudices (cf. the saying about the splinter in the eye of another: Q 6:41–42, or about the tree, which is known by its fruit: Q 6:43–45).

3.7.4.3. Protreptic Stories "for Beginners within the Old World"

Finally, a series of example stories are found, which recount the exemplary behavior of a particular character, that should stimulate emulation, although it is quite unexpected and unusual. Thus, the behavior of the "compassionate Samaritan" (Luke 10:30–35): he practices exactly what one would expect from the Jewish priest and Levite, who, however, remain completely apathetic to the man who fell among brigands, although they are returning from the temple and cannot use the excuse of possibly incurring impurity. The story insinuates: perhaps the Samaritans are quite different from what Jews usually think.

Also, the story of the mina belongs in this series. Matthew develops it into the parable of the talents (Matt. 25:14–30), while Luke has provided it with historical associations with Archelaus, who in Rome wishes to be vested as king over Palestine (Luke 19:12–27). At the core, the example story actually presents the third slave as the hero: he balks at the test of his economic aptitude, thereby forfeiting the possibilities of his advancement, and ridicules the Roman taxation system as outright thievery (Luke 19:21; Matt. 25:24). Also, Luke 16:1–7 tells the story of a "dropout" who, on account of his luxurious lifestyle as a manager, comes to his downfall and "links up" with the creditors of his master. The importunate widow of Luke 18:2–5, in no way corresponding to the expected, submissive behavior of a widow, pounds relentlessly for her rights and brings the judge around—as Israelite divine law prescribes (Exod. 22:21–22; Deut. 24:17)—to take her side (for analysis, cf. Ebner 2010).

All these stories have in view the concrete sociopolitical situation in Palestine at the time of Jesus. They tell about people who are "different," behave "differently," and thereby—in the middle of the "old world"—allow something new to come to light. It is based on how God imagines Israel to be: free from foreign sovereignty, free from exploitation of one another, caring for those on the margin, and enacting familial relationships among the twelve tribes (to which also the Samaritans belong). In the judge, in the manager, and in the third slave, figures of the lower or middle administrative levels are presented as examples. The specific addressees of these stories can be situated in this sociological field. Altogether, these stories thus have a protreptic character.

3.7.5. Wisdom and Apocalyptic (Theology)

According to a wide consensus in scholarship, Jesus's fundamental conviction consisted in viewing the kingdom of God as having already "arrived" (Q 11:20; Mark 1:15). Thereby he differentiated himself from apocalypticists such as John the Baptizer, who expected the coming of God's kingdom in the future—in close proximity, to be sure, but beyond the history for which human beings are responsible, preceded by a universal end-time judgment (cf. Q 3:7–9). This is distinct from the kingdom of God theology in Qumran, which assumes—like Jesus—for instance, in the Songs of the Sabbath Sacrifice, the present kingdom of God, experienced, however, only in the cult on the basis of following the sun calendar that was traditionally valid in the temple, which guaranteed synchrony with the heavenly rhythm of weeks. By contrast, for Jesus the kingdom of God in the present is shown in quite normal everyday life, everywhere demons are driven out (Q 11:20), as well as in Jesus's open table fellowship, in which for him God's expected end-time marriage with his people is reflected (cf. Mark 2:19 and Isa. 49:18; 61:10; 62:5), which conventionally must begin with a celebratory feast (Gen. 29:22; Judg. 14:10, 12, 17; Matt. 22:2–5). In short, the eschatological newness of the kingdom of God can be experienced in the middle of the old world, although only in fragmentary form, but accessible to real experience—provided it is interpreted in Jesuanic terms.

In this theological context, Jesus's sapiential logia and short stories can be understood as aids to regulate the everyday world of the kingdom of God, especially in the broad field of communication between Jesus's very different table companions, beginning with the women and men who have left all, then including the sick who had been healed, all the way to tax collectors, who even diminish the small profit for the fishermen and farmers but offer the Jesus people tables with sumptuous food (cf. Q 7:34). Here also belong the explications about the gradual but unstoppable growth of the kingdom of God (cf. Q 13:18–21: mustard seed and yeast), the recruitment for an impartial proclamation with the promise of manifold fruit of that seed "that falls on good earth" (Mark 4:3–8), as well as the illumination of rejection on the side of the Galilean populace at the feast celebrated by Jesus and his people as a missed opportunity (cf. Matt. 22:1–10; Luke 14:16–23).

Alternative solutions assume that the so-called future declarations of the eschatologically expected kingdom of God are a fixed point and attempt to correlate the sapiential sayings accordingly: as folkloric material "that first was taken up by the communities in the Christian tradition and were marked as Jesus's sayings" (Bultmann [10]1995, 106); as *argumenta ad hominem* (Merklein [3]1984, 181, 232); as special admonitions that spell out the consequences of the message of the kingdom of God to those who have already decided for Jesus (Zeller 1977); as an expression of the reflection of creation theology (Lips 1990; cf. the recent evaluation of Grandy 2012, 31–44). Nevertheless, queries remain: (1) Does what is distinctive in Jesus's message of the kingdom of God, namely, the assertion of its presence in the everyday reality of the old world (Weder 1993), really receive the corresponding central theological place in the evaluation of the undisputed future declarations that expect a definitive implementation of the kingdom of God at the turn of the aeons (cf. only Mark 14:25)? (2) Is the general flexibility of Jewish eschatology taken seriously, which simply has a motivational character and intends to move to the doing of the Torah but never builds the foundation from which everyday Jewish life is structured (cf. K. Müller 1999)?

3.7.6. A Teacher of Wisdom or a Sage (Categorization)?

Judaism links the designation "teacher of wisdom" with people like Jesus Sirach or the anonymous compiler of Proverbs or the other books of wisdom literature. A teacher of wisdom gathers up pieces of folk wisdom, reflects on them, and correlates them with themes of the Torah, intended for the behavioral training of the elite. Jesus, on the other hand, in the line of many wise women and men of Israel, seems to have brought everyday experiences for specific problems or disputed situations to a point, or to have clothed them in a story, in order to ignite a thought process, which scrutinizes one's own (preconceived) opinion and ideally should lead to a revision (cf. 2 Sam. 12:1–4; 14:5–7; cf. Ebner 2001). Initially, early Christian tradents assembled Jesus's logia in clusters of sayings thematically (Piper 1989) or linked them to currents of tradition of the actualization of Torah (Matt. 5–7).

What is striking in this process is that both complexes of material, which in later communities and in the history of theology in general acquire utmost importance, namely, the Lord's Supper (who ought to eat with whom?) and Christology (what power is at work in Jesus?), stand at the focal point of the historically assured debate about his person and his practices contested on these two points. But, for his defense, the historical Jesus does not make use of a heavenly revelation or a divine directive or a divinely legitimated right. Rather, he adduces prudent arguments derived from everyday life, which should justify his behavior—for everyone who is willing to decipher his wisdom sayings.

Ebner, Martin. 2001. "'Weisheitslehrer'—eine Kategorie für Jesus? Eine Spurensuche bei Jesus Sirach." In *Der neue Mensch in Christus: Hellenistische Anthropologie und Ethik im Neuen Testament*, edited by Johannes Beutler, 99–119. QD 190. Freiburg.

———. 2010. "Face to Face—Widerstand im Sinn der Gottesherrschaft: Jesu Wahrnehmung seines sozialen Umfeldes im Spiegel seiner Beispielgeschichten." *Early Christianity* 1: 406–40.

———. ²2012. *Jesus von Nazaret: Was wir von ihm wissen können*. Stuttgart. Sonderausgabe 2016.

Grandy, Andreas. 2012. *Die Weisheit der Gottesherrschaft: Eine Untersuchung zur jesuanischen Synthese von traditioneller und apokalyptischer Weisheit*. NTOA/SUNT 96. Göttingen.

Müller, Karlheinz. 1999. "Gibt es ein Judentum hinter den Juden? Ein Nachtrag zu Ed Parish Sanders' Theorie vom 'Covenantal Nomism.'" In *Das Urchristentum in seiner literarischen Geschichte, FS Jürgen Becker*, edited by Ulrich Mell and Ulrich B. Müller, 473–86. BZNW 100. Berlin.

Martin Ebner

3.8. Jesus's Understanding of Himself

3.8.1. The Representative of God's Kingdom

The depiction of Jesus's understanding of himself can proceed from his proclamation of the kingdom of God (see D.IV.3.2). Here it is a matter of an eschatological concept that in the early Judaism of his time was prevalent and invested with clearly recognizable contours. Jesus takes up this expectation of salvation but provides it with an independent profile: according to a Jewish expectation, the inbreaking of the kingdom of God on the earth was understood in the way that *none other than God* comes and establishes his sovereignty already existing in heaven now also on the earth. Accordingly, the implementation of God's sovereignty was understood as an event that would attain a universal scope encompassing the entire creation. It was *God's own doing*, which he does not share with anyone else. Rather, it remains reserved for him alone. This eschatological expectation concentrating on the coming of none other than God is, therefore, about hopes of salvation that are carefully distinguished from those that have the activity of human mediators of salvation as their subject. Israel as God's own people had to expect from God's sovereignty only salvation: the hope of God's people was directed toward God's liberation from oppression by foreign nations and their rulers.

The semantic innovation that characterizes Jesus's adoption of this eschatological expectation of salvation is that he does not simply announce the imminent proximity of the in-breaking of God's sovereignty like a prophet but raises a much more far-reaching claim: that specifically in his own work God's sovereignty and the salvation that they expected are present and tangible. With this Jesus did not abandon the expectation of a universal implementation of the kingdom of God, which God will bring to pass. One can explain the relationship between the present and future of God's kingdom by saying that the salvation of God's kingdom is present *selectively*, that is, wherever Jesus appears. By way of contrast, the *universal* implementation of God's sovereignty remains reserved for the future, which God will bring to pass by his own appearance in Zion-Jerusalem (see D.IV.3.8.4). This is explicitly expressed in Luke 11:20 par. ("If it is by the finger/spirit of God that I cast out demons, then the kingdom of God has come upon you"). With this saying Jesus makes the claim that in his exorcisms the heavenly reality of the kingdom of God attains earthly and thereby tangible reality that can be experienced by human beings. In connection with Luke 10:18 ("I saw Satan fall from heaven like a flash of lightning") and Mark 3:27 par. ("No one can enter the house of a strong man . . . without first tying up the strong man"; this involves a double tradition in Mark and Q, of very high antiquity), Jesus's exorcisms attain a distinctive significance: the vision of Satan's fall led Jesus to the awareness that God is present to set up his sovereignty over the entire creation (for the history of traditions background of this concept, cf. As. Mos. 10:1–3; Rev. 12:7–10). Jesus would have then understood his expulsion of demons as an integral element of the creation-wide implementation of God's victory over Satan.

Luke 17:20–21 is also not far removed from Luke 11:20 par.: it is not needful to calculate the coming of the kingdom of God by portents, because it is already present among human beings, and indeed in Jesus's activity. In the tradition, which is taken up in Luke 16:16 par., an element of this self-understanding is also present.

3.8.2. Jesus Brings What Israel Expected from God

Jesus's claim that in his activity God's eschatic salvation among human beings has become a reality is also perceptible in Luke 7:22 par.: "The blind see, the lame walk, lepers are cleansed, the deaf hear, the dead are resuscitated, the poor have good news proclaimed to them." This saying contains allusions to a series of texts in Isaiah (26:19; 29:18; 35:5–6; 61:1). These texts describe God's eschatic saving action for his people or function as metaphors for the reversal of Israel's damnation to salvation brought about *by God*. The theological point of this saying is that Jesus applies the promises passed down through Isaiah to his own work in Israel: in this way he interprets his own activity as the fulfillment of these promises focused on *God's* action, and thereby he raises no small claim that he himself acts in the place of God. What Israel expects from *God* is fulfilled through Jesus. Something analogous is perceptible in Luke 19:10 ("For the son of man came to seek out and save the lost"). Here Ezek. 34:16 stands in the background, where God promises his people: "I will seek the lost, and I will bring back the scattered, and I will bind up the injured, and I will strengthen the sick." This assessment of himself also left behind traces in Jesus's macarism to the disciples passed down in Luke 10:23–24: it is the disciples who, as eyewitnesses and hearers of Jesus's works, experience what "many prophets and kings" hoped for in vain—the eschatic fulfillment of God's promises of salvation for his people. The specific outline of this text for Jesus's understanding of himself is also illustrated in Pss. Sol. 17:44, where those are blessed "who live in those days to see Israel's salvation . . . , which God will accomplish." Also in accord with this text, Jesus fulfills the expectations of salvation focused on God.

3.8.3. Fellowship with "Tax Collectors and Sinners"

Jesus's interpretation of himself, which is expressed in these sayings about his activity as a charismatic healer and exorcist, also has a coherent equivalent in content in those parts of the Jesus tradition that express his turning to the so-called tax collectors and sinners as well as the fellowship that he practiced with them. This likewise has to do with a typical element of Jesus's demeanor (see D.IV.2.10), and the reproach that he was a "friend of tax collectors and sinners" (Luke 7:34 par.; cf. also Mark 2:16; Luke 15:2) is due to this. This turning is condensed in the assertion of forgiveness of sin (Mark 2:5; Luke 7:48), with which Jesus makes a claim for himself; the forgiveness of sin that is exclusively reserved for God (cf. Mark 2:7: "Who can forgive sins but God alone?") is assigned directly and validly to people. In this respect also, Jesus makes a claim for himself that he acts in place of God. Considered from another perspective, this interpretation Jesus gives to his activity is expressed in that Jesus interprets the turning of "tax collectors and sinners" to *him* as their turning to *God* (Luke 7:36–50; 15:1–32): turning to Jesus makes the relationship with God right.

3.8.4. Jesus's Parables

An important source for Jesus's understanding of himself is also his *parables*. When Jesus speaks metaphorically in them about God and God's approaching challenge, about his listeners' reaction to it, and about the consequences arising from this reaction, he always speaks about himself and characterizes the theological meaning of his action. In this sense it emerges from Mark 2:19b, Luke 14:16 par., and 15:24c that he understands his activity as the in-breaking of the eschatic time of salvation, which he therefore wanted to celebrate as a feast. This aspect of Jesus's self-understanding is expressed in that he quite obviously gladly ate and drank with people (cf. Mark 2:15–17; 6:34–44; Luke 7:36; 14:1; 15:1–2; 19:5–6), which garnered from his opponents the accusation that he was "a glutton and winebibber" (Luke 7:34 par.; see D.IV.4.4).

An integral element of Jesus's eschatological interpretation of himself sketched up to this point is the awareness that it stands in discontinuity with the traditional expectations of salvation of the Jewish people of his time. The attachment of God's salvation to his person and his presence therefore requires people to separate themselves from their familiar concepts of salvation and reorient themselves. For them to deny this new orientation is like sewing a "new patch" on an "old garment" or pouring "new wine" in "old wine skins" (Mark 2:21–22), or putting a hand to a plow and looking back (Luke 9:62). In all these texts a self-understanding is reflected that excludes every compromise between the salvation that has become reality in Jesus's presence and the previous orientation to salvation and existence held to be valid. The situation Jesus brings about for people is therefore like the situation of the manager described in Luke 16:1–3, who loses his previous basis for existence and is then praised for completely changing his orientation to salvation (Luke 16:8a). The parables recounted in Matt. 13:44–46 communicate something analogous about Jesus's self-understanding: the people's encounter with Jesus is like finding a treasure or a valuable pearl, and they react correctly if, after finding it, they separate themselves from everything that has been important to them up to that point.

The theme of forgiveness of sin (see D.IV.3.8.3) is brought up in Matt. 18:23–35. This parable also provides information about Jesus's self-understanding in that in vv. 23–27 it speaks about God, in the way he encounters people through *Jesus*: Jesus does not simply proclaim the mercy of God, who forgives people their sins. Rather, he *is* God's mercy or—to speak more explicitly—in his presence God's mercy becomes a reality.

In the parable of the mustard seed (Mark 4:30–32 par.) and the yeast (Luke 13:20–21 par.), as well as partly in the parable of the growing seed (Mark 4:26–29), Jesus speaks about the relationship of his own action to the still-pending implementation of the kingdom of God on the universal scale of creation (see D.IV.3.8.1). These parables in which the contrasts of small and large or of a few and many are connected with each other by natural processes (growth and fermentation) bring the *selective* presence of the kingdom of God in Jesus's activity (the mustard seed, the yeast) into a conceptual connection with the still-pending *universal* implementation of God's sovereignty.

3.8.5. "Blessed Is Anyone Who Takes No Offense at Me" (Luke 7:23 par.)

An additional element of Jesus's eschatological self-understanding is perceptible in texts that speak about the allocation of salvation and damnation in the
judgment, which will accompany the implementation of God's universal sovereignty and will be guided solely by whether people have agreed with or rejected
Jesus's interpretation of himself (on this in detail, see D.IV.3.4). The facticity of
Jesus's healings and exorcisms was not controversially evaluated but rather the
question of how they were to be interpreted: Neither the inhabitants of Nazareth (Mark 6:1–6a) nor Jesus's opponents in Mark 3:22–27 disputed *that* Jesus
expelled demons or accomplished mighty deeds and was a teacher of wisdom.
What they did not recognize or accept is the *interpretation* that Jesus attached to
them—that in them God's eschatic salvation among human beings is experienced
(see D.IV.3.8.1–2). In contrast, the accusation that Jesus casts out the demons "by
Beelzebul the ruler of demons" views Jesus simply as a magician, who therefore
is successful only because he is in control of certain exorcism techniques. Conversely, the acceptance of Jesus's interpretation of his healings and exorcisms is referred to as "taking no offense in me" (μὴ σκανδαλίζεσθαι ἐν ἐμοί) (Luke 7:23 par.;
cf. Mark 6:3). In this regard, talk in the synoptic tradition about "believing" and
"faith" is also infrequent (Mark 2:5; 5:34, 36; 10:52; Luke 7:9 par.; 7:50; 17:19; Matt.
8:13; 9:28; 15:28; cf. also Mark 6:6a: here "offense taken" [v. 3] at Jesus is designated
as "unbelief" [ἀπιστία]); indeed, in most cases this probably has to do with early
Christian language, which was secondarily entered into the Jesus tradition.

3.8.6. Ethical Teaching

Jesus's challenge to accept his self-understanding, because at the judgment this will
determine the assignment of salvation and damnation, also extends to his *ethical
instruction*. The parable of building a house placed at the end of the Sermon on the
Mount and the Sermon on the Plain (Luke 6:47–49 par.), which on good grounds
is held to be authentic, is a clear instance of this connection. "To take no offense
at me" (Luke 7:23 par.) expresses that one not only "hears" what Jesus says but also
"does what he says." Only someone who observes this basic tenet receives the allocation of salvation in the judgment; anyone who does not "do" Jesus's words even
after hearing them awaits damnation. Jesus thereby claims for his ethical instruction a status that early Judaism ascribed to the Torah (cf. also Luke 16:16 par.).

Nevertheless, one cannot say that Jesus pitted his authority against the authority
of the Torah, and that he took it upon himself to override the legal requirements of
the Torah by his own instructions. Especially the Sabbath conflicts (Mark 2:23–28;

3:1–5; Luke 13:10–16; 14:1–6; cf. also Matt. 12:11–12), the discussion about clean and unclean (Mark 7:14–23), and Jesus's directives, as they can be reconstructed from the so-called antitheses of the Sermon on the Mount (Matt. 5.21–48), make it possible to recognize that Jesus did not position himself in opposition to the Torah. Rather, his directives related to the Torah make it possible to recognize that the antitheses are directed at bringing about the bestowal of a new Torah. It speaks in favor of this that Jesus understood himself as one authorized by God to administer the Torah, who interprets the Torah anew in the context of the salvific presence of the kingdom of God as it is experienced in his activity. In this he comes on the scene with the claim to be that one who, in an exclusive way, orients behavior to God's will as it is demanded in the eschatic situation of the advancing kingdom of God already present in Jesus's presence. This claim to authority is also expressed in the so-called nonresponsorial "amen," followed by the phrase "I say to you," which in ancient Jewish and Christian literature is found only on the lips of Jesus (cf., e.g., Matt. 5:18; 10:15; 17:20; 18:3; Mark 3:28; 9:1, 41; 10:15, 29; 13:30; 14:25; Luke 4:24). It is, therefore, correctly held to be a manner of speaking typical of Jesus, with which he asserts his exclusive authority.

3.8.7. The Appointment of the Twelve

An essential element of Jesus's self-understanding is also perceptible in the *appointment of the Twelve* (see D.IV.2.2) (Mark 3:14). The number twelve stands in continuity with Israel's eschatological hopes for salvation, which point to the end-time restoration of the people of God. But it also stands in discontinuity with these hopes because Jesus does not undertake a restoration of the "old" covenant people, which is simply a matter of prolonging the past into the future, but rather in a certain sense he establishes Israel anew: the Twelve, chosen from the circle of his followers, are the core or the "patriarchs" of the new Israel, and by choosing them and enthroning them as regents (Luke 22:30 par.), he makes himself creator of the eschatic renewed Israel. Such a self-understanding converges with what is said above on the interpretation of Jesus's healings and exorcisms, because with the creation of Israel anew, Jesus ascribes to himself an action that is on a level with the action of God, who chose Israel to be his own people.

3.8.8. How Did Jesus Understand His Death?

It is difficult to answer the question about the way in which Jesus made his *death* an element of his understanding of himself. It certainly holds that Jesus did not expect his violent death, at the start, to be a consequential or even necessary element of his activity. But it is to be assumed that at a later point—perhaps not until his entry into Jerusalem—he did expect that he would die a violent death. This circumstance makes it possible to ask whether a specific model can be identified by the help of which Jesus could also integrate his death in the interpretation of his advent.

With relatively ample certainty one can rule out that Jesus interpreted his death according to the fourth Servant Song in Isa. 52:13–53:12 and understood himself as God's suffering servant, through whose suffering and death people would be liberated from their sins. Against such a correlation the references to these texts in the Jesus tradition are not only much too scanty (they are only in Matt. 8:17 and Luke 22:37) but they also originate from redaction. In addition, the reference to Isa. 53:4 in Matt. 8:17 is neither cited as a saying of Jesus nor does it refer to Jesus's death.

With this, however, the possibility is not excluded that without reference to Isa. 53 Jesus understood his death as a death that he suffers vicariously for human beings and thereby liberates them from their sins. The following texts count as evidence for such an interpretation: Mark 10:45 ("For the Son of Man came not to be served but to serve and to give his life as a ransom for many") and the saying over the cup from Mark 14:24 ("This is my blood of the covenant, which is poured out for many"). The authenticity of these two texts in the Jesus tradition is debated (pro, e.g., Stuhlmacher 1981; Hampel 1990, 302–42; contra, e.g., Zager 1996b, 170–79). Although the question of originality cannot be decided with obligatory certainty, it is more likely that both texts do not go back to the historical Jesus but presuppose a post-Easter interpretation of Jesus's death as a salvific death. It became not only essential but, in the first place, possible as early Christianity reflected theologically on Jesus's death in light of the Easter event.

It is, therefore, likely that Jesus interpreted his death in the framework of the Deuteronomic "tradition of the death of the prophets," according to which Israel persecuted and killed God's messengers (cf. 1 Kings 19:10, 14; 2 Chron. 36:15–16; Neh. 9:26; Jer. 2:30). Traces of this interpretation can be identified especially in Luke 13:34 par. and Mark 12:5 par. Moreover, this tradition is also attested in Luke 6:23 par., 11:47–51 par., Acts 7:52, Rom. 11:3, and 1 Thess. 2:15 (cf. Steck 1967, 60–77; Weihs 2003, 15–69). Characteristically, this tradition is always about the demonstration of Israel's guilt. With this interpretation of his death, Jesus does not indirectly make himself a prophet, but by means of it he desires to demonstrate Israel's guilt: as Israel at one time persecuted and killed the prophets, just so does Israel now deal with Jesus. By placing his death in the light of this tradition, he ascribes to it not a salvific meaning but to a certain degree a meaning of doom. The so-called abstention saying of Mark 14:25 ("Amen, I say to you:

I will not drink again from the fruit of the vine, until the day when I drink it anew in the kingdom of God") signifies that Jesus indeed interpreted his death as the rejection of his proclamation by Israel, not, however, as a rebuttal of its content. In this saying Jesus expresses his assurance that God consummates the universal implementation of his sovereignty, which Jesus began with his advent, and thereby will undertake the assignment of salvation and damnation, as it was proclaimed by him (see D.IV.3.8.5).

3.8.9. The Issue of a Title

To what extent Jesus's self-understanding was also expressed in a *title* is difficult to say. There is nothing to rely on, and from Jewish tradition there is also no titular designation, which would represent the aspects of Jesus's self-understanding sketched above in a corresponding way. Here it becomes evident again that in this respect Jesus's self-understanding stood in discontinuity with the eschatological expectations of ancient Judaism. From the inventory of individual salvific figures whose coming was expected in the eschatologies of early Judaism, none would have functioned as a model for Jesus's self-understanding.

Hampel, Volker. 1990. *Menschensohn und historischer Jesus: Ein Rätselwort als Schlüssel zum messianischen Selbstverständnis Jesu.* Neukirchen-Vluyn.

Hengel, Martin, and Anna Maria Schwemer. 2007. *Geschichte des frühen Christentums.* Vol. 1, *Jesus und das Judentum.* Tübingen.

Konradt, Matthias. 2010. "Stellt der Vollmachtsanspruch des historischen Jesus eine Gestalt 'vorösterlicher Christologie' dar?" *ZTK* 107: 139–66.

Kreplin, Matthias. 2001. *Das Selbstverständnis Jesu: Hermeneutische und christologische Reflexion; Historisch-kritische Analyse.* WUNT II 141. Tübingen.

Wolter, Michael. 2019. *Jesus von Nazaret*, Göttingen. Pp. 253–71.

Michael Wolter

4. The Ethics of Jesus

4.1. Love of Neighbor and Love of Enemies

The concept of love is often employed in a general sense for different forms of Jesus's turning to the socially needy, the poor, the marginalized, and those in need of help (widows, the sick, tax collectors, beggars, children, prostitutes, foreigners, Samaritans, and others). However, from its origin in the context of a Torah commandment (Lev. 19:18), it is defined differently and more narrowly in that the primary object of the love command is the Jewish community in the land of Israel. When the Jewish exegetical tradition speaks of universal love, it does not refer to Lev. 19:18 (Luz 1997, 283). However, both the Hebrew רע and the Greek πλησίον do not refer exclusively to ethnically Jewish people (Söding 1995, 47–49; Wolter 2008, 394). In Jesus's saying in the synoptic tradition, for the first time the commandment to love God (Deut. 6:5) is combined with the commandment to love the neighbor (Lev. 19:18), so that a first/greatest commandment and a second commandment (Mark 12:28–31; Matt. 22:36–39) or even one single commandment (Luke 10:27), the double love commandment, is spoken about. This focus on and combination of the entire Torah on two commandments (Mark 12:28–34; Matt. 22:35–40; Luke 10:25–28) doubtless have a background in Hellenistic Judaism to the extent that people asked about the main points of the Torah and found them especially in devotion and righteousness. To be sure, this focus is brought up only as a matter of concern without going into these two Torah commandments. In addition, the love command as a citation of Lev. 19:18 in the sixth antithesis of the Sermon on the Mount (Matt. 5:43) is surpassed by Jesus's command to love enemies (see below). Along with the synoptic texts, the double love command is also attested in Did. 1:2, Justin, *Dial.* 93.2, and Polycarp, *Phil.* 3.3, which indicates a quite limited response (J. Becker 1996, 391). Gospel of Thomas 25 speaks about brotherly love but does not provide the double command. In Gal. 5:14 and Rom. 13:8–10, Paul interprets one single command, namely, the command to love the neighbor (Lev. 19:18), as recapitulating the entire Torah, and he dissolves the boundaries of the command for all believers independent of their origin. James 2:8 understands the love of neighbor (Lev. 19:18) as the royal law.

In research, the question regarding the relationship of different versions of the double command to each other was the focal point, combined with the question of whether this should be attributed to the theology of early Christian community. In any case, wide-ranging decisions with a view to the relationship of Jesus or the community to the Torah are tied to the answer to these questions.

A synoptic overview (Niederwimmer 1989, 90) of Deut. 6:5, Lev. 19:18 LXX, Mark 12:28–34, Matt. 22:35–40, Luke 10:25–28, and Did. 1:2 provides the following substantial observations.

- Mark and Matthew present the double command in a controversy story with a scribe or teacher of the law in Jerusalem in which he takes the initiative. Luke follows this pattern, but his report about a didactic dialogue with a teacher of the law occurs at the beginning of the so-called travel narrative, and he links this with the parable of the compassionate Samaritan (10:29–37). In the Didache, the double command occurs not in the framework of a narrative and also not explicitly as a saying of Jesus, but as the basic teaching of the two ways in the introduction to this writing.

- The two commands are taken up following the Septuagint, but especially with regard to Deut. 6:5, in wording that diverges from one other. Matthew and Luke (also Did. 1.2), differently from Mark, do not cite the introductory *schema yisrael* (Deut. 6:4). As opposed to the Septuagint in Matthew, Mark, and Luke, after "heart" (καρδία) and "soul" (ψυχή), "mind" (διάνοια) is also inserted as a third or fourth item as the case may be, and in the place of "power" (δύναμις), "strength" (ἰσχύς) is specified in Matthew, Mark, and Luke. The Didache, by contrast, first presents only the command to love God; however, without reference to the adverbial modifiers with heart, soul, and strength but going beyond Deut. 6:5, it refers to God's creative activity.
- Mark, Matthew, and the Didache speak about the two commands as an enumeration and not as a hierarchy of a first and second command, whereas Matthew emphasizes that the second command is on equal standing with the first. In Luke, by contrast, the didactic dialogue is no longer oriented to the question of the greatest commandment in the Torah but rather to the question regarding what the teacher of the law must do to inherit eternal life (cf. similarly the question of the rich young man in Mark 10:17 par.). To be sure, in the answer both commands are cited, but they are no longer designated as such but joined into a single didactic answer. Justin likewise combines both commands, but in introducing them speaks of two commands.
- The command to love the neighbor is cited in close dependence on Lev. 19:18 LXX, although Luke and the Didache do not repeat the initial imperative "you shall love."

Research has advanced quite different theses for a source-critical and history-of-traditions explanation and for the mutual dependence of the texts on each other; these theses, however, do not entirely convince everyone. A consensus is not in view. Against the simple assumption that Matthew and Luke draw directly from Mark stands the occurrence of many significant *minor agreements* (common agreements of Matthew and Luke against Mark) (Wolter 2008, 392). The common variations are partially explained by redaction history (Kilunen 1989; Meier 2009, 523). It is conceivable that these common agreements against Mark are based on the influence of Q (although, in my opinion, improbable) or on the influence of a further tradition on Matthew and Luke (Theissen and Merz 1996, 340). Also, the hypothesis of a common dependence on a revised Markan prototype (deutero-Mark) has a certain plausibility while lacking the ability to explain all the evidence. Even if Luke omits this text at the passage between 20:40 and 20:41, at which he must in fact have read it in Mark, and moves forward, the existence of a doublet or rather the avoidance of it cannot be deduced from this (but so Luz 1997, 270). G. Bornkamm (1968, 45) even asks whether Luke 10:25–28 did not preserve the relatively oldest form of the tradition; Luz (1997, 271) recognizes in this text a special tradition. Burchard (1970, 50–51) sees in Mark 12:28b–34b the most original tradition. Does Did. 1:2 present an independent version of the double love command? The enumeration of first and second is reminiscent of the version in Mark and Matthew, but both commands are considerably shortened, and also do not issue from the mouth of Jesus but rather as a community regulation.

No argument has been advanced that the combination of these two commands as the greatest/most important in the law (Matthew), or as the first of all the commandments (Luke) explicitly in this form, was formulated already in Jewish literature or Jewish theology (Meier 2009, 499–522). To be sure, the attempt can be recognized (Nissen 1974, 230–44; Theissen and Merz 1996, 340–43) to summarize the requirements of the entire Torah in its main points (κεφάλια), which apply to God and fellow human beings (Philo, *Spec.* 2.63). Without citing Old Testament commands, texts in the Testaments of the Twelve Patriarchs speak about the love for God and neighbor (T. Iss. 5:2), for every person (7:6), and for one another (T. Dan 5:3). This multiply attested focus of the requirements of the law on εὐσέβεια and δικαιοσύνη presents an important parallel to the Hellenistic canon of the two virtues. Without question they also served in the apologetics of the diaspora synagogue, which had been opened to Hellenistic teaching of virtue and connected this with the Torah. However, what is new is the declaration that this double command reproduces the entire law and the prophets (Matt. 22:40), or that no other commandment is greater than this (Mark 12:31) and it exceeds all burnt offerings and sacrifices (Mark 12:32–34). Accordingly, in the synoptic debates on the double command, fundamental convictions of the Jewish synagogue were taken up, sharpened, and fixed in Jesus's saying. Hence, Mark 12:32–34 can verify definitively a wide-ranging agreement of the Jewish scribe with Jesus. The combination of the two commands into a double command will most likely be found in a sphere of early Christianity, which on the one hand was influenced by Hellenistic Judaism and its focus on the two virtues (G. Bornkamm 1968, 37; Burchard 1970, 57), but which on the other hand was engaged in the question of the binding character of the entire Torah and was partially engaged in a critique of the law (so clearly Mark 12:33). One can at best question whether the double command was already combined in the realm of Hellenistic Judaism (or even in the preaching of virtues of John the Baptizer; so Theissen 2003a, 70–72), without this being deposited in the sources. In the texts an arrangement in a hierarchy is expressed, which explains the double love command to be what the essence of Torah is and, for instance, as in Mark 12:33, devalues the sacrificial cult, without intending thereby to abrogate the Torah in its binding character altogether. While this dispute and the decisive answer are anchored in Jesus's saying, simultaneously the community distinguishes Jesus as that authority who stands for this decision to summarize the Torah in the double love command (G. Bornkamm 1968, 42; Berger 1972, 256). That the double command intentionally fits into Jesus's proclamation is at the same time put on record (Söding 1995, 37; Theissen and Merz 1996, 345). A return back to the historical Jesus is also entertained (Theissen 2003a, 61; Meier 2009, 522). The question of who belongs to the group of neighbors, or who is unconditionally excluded from it, is not discussed further in the debate, and it is also not of special interest. Already in Judaism and also under the influence of Stoic thought, an extension had been provided in an inclusive sense in terms of creation or natural rights.

From its Old Testament historical background, love of neighbor means comportment related to community and solidarity (Luz 1997, 283). In comparison with the Jewish background, the unreserved extension of the concept of neighbor beyond fellow members of the nation is new. For the Christian understanding of love of neighbor, the connection of the double command with the parable of the compassionate Samaritan became dominant. In this parable, on the one hand, the question of the object of love of neighbor (Luke 10:29: Who is my neighbor?) changes into the question of the subject of love of neighbor (10:36: Who became neighbor to the man who fell among brigands?), whereby love of neighbor is defined as active conduct. The acquired identity (to become a neighbor) supplants the ascribed identity (to be a neighbor), and the ethical paradigm supplants the cultic paradigm (Wolter 2008, 398). This is because, on the other hand, it does not introduce a priest and Levite, who as those who serve in the temple stand in a special way for all the purity issues of the Torah, as examples of such charitable behavior (10:37, ἔλεος ποιεῖν), but rather a Samaritan, who in a Jewish perspective does not belong to their communal cult (on this, Böhm 1999, 254–55).

In the sixth antithesis (Matt. 5:43–48) of the Sermon on the Mount in Matthew, the love of neighbor is cited as part of Moses's discourse on Sinai ("you have heard that it was said"), but then in the form of an antithesis Jesus's command is counterposed to it: love your enemy. Immediately after this, further demands and rationales are connected. The Sermon on the Plain in Luke 6:27, 35 provides the closest and verbatim parallel to the command to love enemies and also to the further demands and rationales even if the command to love enemies is not incorporated in an antithetical form. In addition, both texts, Matt. 5:43–48 and Luke 6:27–36, exhibit a series of further agreements in wording and sequence, but also each has its own noticeable particularities. Matthew 5:38–42 has assimilated the admonition to renounce retaliation (Luke 6:29–30) into the fifth antithesis.

It is not possible to reconstruct a convincing common basic text. Even so, it is indisputable that at the core both versions go back to the sayings source, and in the case of the command to love enemies, reach further back to Jesus's preaching (Lührmann 1972, 412). First, both texts should be briefly presented.

The command to love the neighbor in Matt. 5:43 is complemented by the command to hate one's enemy. The latter is not part of the Torah, although here in the thesis it is displayed as a citation. 1QS i 3–4 is considered a close parallel to hate of the enemy: God has commanded "to love all God has chosen and hate all that he has rejected." But Jesus's antithesis refers to the supplement, which limits the scope of the command to love the neighbor ahead of the enemy; indeed, the supplement presents virtually a desired bridge. Two demands are mentioned: the love of "your enemy" and prayer for the "one who persecutes you." Immediately after this the promise follows, that this is the way to become children of God who, so runs the first rationale, act impartially toward all people. A second rationale adds that limiting love exclusively to those "who love me" is unacceptable, since such behavior is not different from that of tax collectors and gentiles, and also does not correspond to the required "more" or the better righteousness in the Sermon on the Mount.

In the version in Luke's Sermon on the Plain, the antithetical structure is absent. The command to love enemies is accomplished by three further concrete specifications: to do good to those "who hate you"; to bless those "who curse you"; and to pray for those "who abuse you" (Luke 6:27–28). It includes the example of robbery in which one should let the aggressor go free (Luke 6:29–30; presented as the fifth antithesis by Matthew in 5:38–42). In a comparison in Luke 6:32–34, the question is posed about the thanks one can expect if love, doing good, and lending money are exclusively related to those from whom reciprocity can be expected. The episode ends with a renewed demand to love enemies, do good, and to lend, and flows into the promise that this is the way to become children of God. The concluding admonition makes believers imitators of God when they conform to his mercy.

The two versions have expanded in different directions. Matthew asks about the relationship to the Torah and extends the Old Testament command with respect to enemies. Luke gives tangible enmity (hate, cursing, abuse) clear contours, but adjusts the command to love enemies verbally (do good, receive thanks) and functionally (the Golden Rule in Luke 6:31) to the ideal Hellenistic friendship ethic. Both versions have in common (a) the demand to love enemies and to pray for persecutors; (b) the demand to set aside behavior that is mindful of reciprocity; (c) instruction on the way to become children of God; (d) the grounding of love of enemies in God's impartiality; and (e) the demand to conform to God (imitation ethic).

Which enemies are in view? Both versions speak about concrete opponents, "your" enemies. Matthew 5:44 thematizes their hate and persecution; Luke 6:27–28 thematizes hate and verbal injuries such as cursing and abusive speech (cf. on the matter, 1 Pet. 3:16), which can imply religious marginalization. Such experiences are also commented on in the concluding macarism in Matt. 5:11–12 par. Luke 6:22–23, in which it is clear that these marginalizing measures come from Israel and lead to exclusion from synagogues. The tradents of the sayings source have allowed the experiences to be incorporated into the texts. Persecution of Jesus's followers in the first half of the first century can have various causes and jurisdictions: (a) Pharisaic zeal for the purity of Jewish belief encountered Christ-believing Jews in Jerusalem and in diaspora synagogues (Gal. 1:13; Acts 6:8–15; 9:1–2); (b) the Sanhedrin or part of it perpetrated punitive and disciplinary measures against Jesus's disciples (Acts 4:1–3; 5:17–18; cf. also 1 Thess. 2:15); and (c) the Jewish king Herod Agrippa abused the community and executed James (Acts 12:1–2). In addition, there are also sporadic attacks on Christians on the part of pagan society, initially mostly on the basis of their unsettled place in the diaspora synagogue (Acts 14:4; 16:21; 18:12–17; and others). Part of the Jewish populace counts as enemies, as do all who exercise power in the Roman provincial system by such means as taxation, tolls, land holdings and tenancy, service, and customs; also counted as enemies are participants by way of cooperation (large land holders, tax collectors, Herodians, high priestly families, Sadducees). The zealot measures that escalated from the year 6 CE, which in 67 CE flowed into the Jewish-Roman war, found enemies in the occupation and in the Jewish parties allied with it. A delimitation of enemies cannot be accomplished on the basis of synoptic texts. Both religious and political opponents are conceivable; however, a reduction to personal enmity does not reside in the train of thought of the text.

The demand to love enemies in both texts is linked to Jesus's authority and to his teaching. In the sphere of the history of religions, it is without a direct parallel (Wolter 2008, 256; Meier 2009, 532–51), and therefore it is considered to be a specifically Christian ethic. As a heightening and intensification of the love command in Lev. 19:18, the scope of the love for neighbor or foreigner (Lev. 19:34) is again expanded further. The primary form of the love of enemies is in religious actions (prayer, blessing), but also in performances oriented toward friendship (do good, lend money). The rationale aims at a critique of the Hellenistic ethic of reciprocity, which orients one's own conduct toward the calculated reaction of the other. On the other hand, in keeping with wisdom theology, it is reminiscent of God's behavior in his creation, who in his care by means of sun and rain does not discriminate between good and evil, unjust and just. Hence the command to love enemies stands in the context of an *imitatio Dei* ethic. In contrast to the contemporaneous ethical instruction, this certainly is no longer expected as virtue predominantly of rulers, but of Jesus's followers, many of whom are counted as coming from the lower classes (Schottroff 1975, 208–11).

In addition to scriptural support of the anchoring of the love of neighbor in the double love command, other texts have promoted the understanding of the love of neighbor in Jesus's sayings and deeds in a general sense, even if no reference to Lev. 19:18 is present. These show that to a high degree Jesus was committed to the Jewish ethic of benevolence. First, all those terms are to be mentioned that speak of ἔλεος, ἐλεημοσύνη, ἐλεεῖν ("compassion," "alms," "to be merciful": Matt. 5:7; Luke 11:41; 12:33; and others). In addition are οἰκτίμων ("merciful": Luke 6:36), ἀγαθοποιεῖν ("do good": Luke 6:35), σπλαγχνίζεσθαι ("to have compassion": Matt. 9:36; 14:14; 15:32; and others). Also, the image of Jesus as a shepherd (Matt. 9:36; John 10:11) or as the one who has come to seek and find the lost (Matt. 10:6; Luke 19:10; cf. also 5:31 and elsewhere) belongs in this context, and likewise the characterization of Jesus as a friend of tax collectors and sinners (Matt. 11:19 par.; Luke 15:1). The synoptic tradition offers multiple stories in which Jesus emphasizes those who stand on the margins of society, often in opposition to religious leaders. In this connection the calling of disciples (Mark 2:13–17; Luke 8:1–3; 19:1–10) and table fellowship (Mark 2:16 par.; Luke 19:5) occur, and revaluations take place (Luke 6:20–21) to the extent that prostitutes (Matt. 21:31), the poor (Luke 6:20; 16:19–31), sinners (Matt. 9:13 par.; Luke 18:14), and tax collectors (Matt. 21:31) are promised an eschatological priority over the scribes and spiritual leaders of the people. Also, healings and exorcisms reclaim the sick or demon-possessed to Jewish society. Thus, what is at stake in these texts is primarily the sending of Jesus to all Israel, and in fact, predominantly to those who on the basis of halakah or their social location live on the margin of society.

Berger, Klaus. 1972. *Die Gesetzesauslegung Jesu: Ihr historischer Hintergrund im Judentum und im Alten Testament.* Vol. 1, *Markus und Parallelen.* WMANT 40. Neukirchen-Vluyn.

Burchard, Christoph. 1970. "Das doppelte Liebesgebot in der frühen christlichen Überlieferung." In *Der Ruf Jesu und die Antwort der Gemeinde, FS Joachim Jeremias,* edited by Eduard Lohse, 39–61. Göttingen.

Lührmann, Dieter. 1972. "Liebet eure Feinde." *ZTK* 69: 412–38.

Meier, John P. 2009. *A Marginal Jew: Rethinking the Historical Jesus.* Vol. 4, *Law and Love.* New Haven and London.

Theissen, Gerd. ³1989c. "Gewaltverzicht und Feindesliebe (Mt 5,38–48/Lk 6,27–38) und deren sozialgeschichtlicher Hintergrund." In *Studien zur Soziologie des Urchristentums,* by Gerd Theissen, 160–97. WUNT 19. Tübingen.

Friedrich Wilhelm Horn

4.2. Possessions and Wealth

The theme of possessions/wealth is present in the Jesus tradition in all levels of the sources and in many textual genres with quite distinct *Sitze im Leben*, and it will have made up a pervasive theme of Jesus's proclamation and of the early Jesus movement. Since the nineteenth century, it has presented a convenient platform for updating portraits of Jesus, which occasionally are reactivated in recent scholarship on Jesus. Jesus is considered to be an advocate of class warfare, a social reformer, an advocate of the poor, and a spokesperson for the underclasses, as a social "dropout," and so forth. Sociohistorical exegesis and Palestinian archaeology have introduced an objectifying contextualization confronting the prevailing direct access to Jesus's sayings and behavior. Jesus's talk about and attitude on possessions and wealth are now considered in the context of the social history of Galilee and the formative Hellenistic-Jewish culture. Research vacillates over whether the theme in Jesus's proclamation is to be assigned rather to the ethics of material goods (critique of possessions and wealth, at the same time advocating voluntary poverty), to social ethics (critique of the propertied, rich), or to a protest ethic ("cynic" itinerant radicalism), and it asks how dominant the influence of the Old Testament–Jewish and Hellenistic tradition is to be ranked with respect to this. The theme of possessions/wealth is often dealt with in connection with the renunciation of possessions, poverty, and benefaction (alms) (cf. on this D.IV.4.3).

As vocabulary for possessions/wealth (in addition to the various designations of coins), especially the following occur: πλούσιος (a rich person), πλουτεῖν (to be rich), πλοῦτος (wealth), κτῆμα (possessions), κτᾶσθαι (to possess), χρῆμα (assets, money), ἀργύριον, ἄργυρος (money), φιλάργυρος (greedy for money, avaricious), χρυσός (gold), τὰ ὑπάρχοντα (assets, possessions), θησαυρός (treasure), θησαυρίζειν (to collect treasure), τὰ ἴδια (property), χαλκός (money), πλεονεξία (greed), ἀγαθά (goods), κληρονομία (inheritance), and μαμωνᾶς (mammon). The use of "mammon," borrowed from Aramaic מָמוֹן, has contributed to the fundamentally negative quality of all possession in Jesus's understanding (on this, Rüger 1973). On the one hand, in Q 16:13 "mammon" is anarthrous, like a person as an antagonist in opposition to God, and this implies that a decision for God and against mammon must take place. On the other hand, in Luke 16:9 "mammon" is qualified by injustice (genitive attribute instead of an adjective), and in 16:11 it is unjust. Not only does a wrong use make money unjust mammon, but money in itself is characterized as unjust. Notably, however, this unjust mammon should now be deployed positively and used benevolently (on this Konradt 2006, 120–22).

It is worthwhile first to acquire an overview about the essential inventory of texts that is directly linked with the theme. Some texts are listed multiple times.

- Parables, figurative sayings: Q 12:33–34; Luke 12:16–21; 16:1–9, 19–31; Gos. Thom. 63.
- Calling and following sayings: Mark 1:18 par.; 6:8–9 par.; 10:17–27 par.; 10:28–31 par.; Matt. 9:9–10 par.; Luke 5:28; 10:4.
- Social critique sayings or evaluations: Mark 4:19 par.; 11:15–19 par.; 12:38–40 par.; 12:41–44 par.; Luke 16:14.
- Wisdom sayings: Q 12:33–34; Gos. Thom. 30, 63, 81.
- Prophetic sayings: Q 16:13; Luke 6:24–26; 12:15; Gos. Thom. 110.
- Individual ethics and group ethics: Mark 10:29; Q 6:34; 12:33–34; Luke 14:33; 19:8; Gos. Thom. 95.
- Critique of Pharisees and scribes regarding wealth: Q 11:39; 16:14; Mark 12:38–40.
- Appreciation of wealth or a neutral assessment: Mark 14:3–5; 15:42–46; Luke 10:35.

These texts convey diverse voices: Jesus's sayings as they have been preserved in Christian memory; transitions into writing in the Gospels in which the hand of the evangelists becomes clearly discernible; texts that are ascribed to Jesus, the original locus of which cannot be determined unambiguously. Jesus's attitude on possessions and wealth must be differentiated from attitudes linked to his person in the later Gospels, especially in Luke. The context of Jesus's critique of wealth in Galilee at the beginning of the first century varies from the critique of wealth that Luke the evangelist writes in the name of Jesus in the Mediterranean region for Christian communities a scant century later and was the subject of many investigations (recently Konradt 2006; Breytenbach 2007). Possessions and wealth occasionally play a role in parables, but there they occur entirely in the figurative half and without any assessment of wealth as such (Mark 12:1–12 par.; Gos. Thom. 65; Luke 19:11–27 par.; agraphon 31). Also, in miracle stories the highlighted social location of those who are healed or their family (Mark 5:21–43 par.; Luke 7:1–10 par.) is not evaluated. How is the life of the rich described in the Gospels? I gather up some aspects:

1. Clothing (Q 7:25; 12:22; Luke 15:22; 16:19; Gos. Thom. 36). In contrast to the Baptizer, who wore a garment of camel's hair (Mark 1:6), in palaces there are soft clothes and luxury (Q 7:25) as well as unimaginable luxury (Luke 16:19). On the other hand, for many people clothing is not self-evident (Matt. 25:36; Q 12:22).
2. Food (Luke 6:21, 25; 15:23). The opposition of hunger and satiation is pronounced (Luke 16:21). Opulent feasts belong to the everyday world of the rich and to the hopes of the poor (also Mark 6:32–44 par; 8:1–10 par.; John 2:1–11).

3. A permanent dwelling and a beggar's existence form a contrast (Luke 16:20).
4. Lifestyle and luxury (Q 7:38; Mark 4:19 par.; Luke 12:16; 15:13; 17:8).
5. Social location: absolute contrast to the poor (Luke 6:24–26; 16:19–31); a rich man has a manager (Luke 16:1), slaves (Luke 12:43; 15:26; 17:7; 19:13), tenants (Luke 20:9), but also debtors (Luke 16:5).

Mostly here traditional and stereotypical depictions of the propertied and rich have been taken up, which do not directly lead to Jesus's attitude on possessions and wealth. The contours become clearer in three areas in which possessions and wealth are thematic: (a) on various occasions there occurs a critique of rich Jewish authorities, Pharisees, and scribes, who are hostile to Jesus's followers. (b) By contrast, the life of Jesus's followers is depicted as determined by absolute renunciation of possessions. (c) Finally, a critique of wealth and possessions occurs in parables and figurative sayings, which are in close proximity to Jewish texts and take up their critique of possessions and wealth. In the synoptic tradition there existed in part an intensification, in part a moderation, of statements critical of possessions. These tendencies are considered in the following account.

a. The Pharisees and scribes are accused of being full of greed and wickedness (Q 11:39). Pharisees are portrayed as greedy for money (Luke 16:14). They have transformed the temple into a den of thieves (Mark 11:17 par.; also John 2:16–17). Scribes devour widows' houses, hence they enrich themselves illegitimately (Mark 12:40 par.). These reproaches are flanked by further accusations in the social realm (Matt. 23:6; Luke 11:42). In the woes of the Sermon on the Plain, which follow the macarisms (Luke 6:20–26), the contrast to Israel's authorities in apocalyptic language is overlaid by the contrast of the poor to the rich. On one side stand the rich, who at the present time are satiated, laugh, and are spoken well of among the people. They stand in a line with the false prophets of Israel, of whom the people also spoke well. On the other side stand the poor, Jesus's disciples, and his followers, who on account of their commitment to the Son of Man experience hate, persecution, and exclusion. But in this respect they stand in line with the true prophets of Israel, who were treated in the same way by the people of Israel. The opposition of the poor and rich experienced in the present is thus part of the overarching conflict in Jewish society on account of the commitment to Christ or the Son of Man, and this conflict is interpreted in the context of a well-known historical pattern (Blomberg 1999, 145; Wolter 2008, 253).

b. With Jesus's disciples in mind in both call narratives and the discourses about following and sending on a mission, and in all levels of the sources, a radical distance between possessions and wealth is described and in part demanded in Jesus's saying. The first disciples who are called leave behind the nets of the boat (Mark 1:18 par.), their father (Mark 1:20), and, according to Luke

5:11, everything. Likewise, in Luke 5:28 Levi, the tax collector who was called, leaves everything behind. According to Mark 10:28 par., Peter, speaking for the disciples, says they have left behind everything (Luke 18:28; what belongs to us) in discipleship. They have abandoned their material existence, including occupation and family.

Among the discipleship sayings, what stands out is the demand to the young man who had many possessions (Mark 10:22) or was very rich (Luke 18:23) and who, according to Mark 10:21, should sell what he has (Luke 18:22: everything he has) and give to the poor and follow Jesus. Origen provides an apocryphal variant as a citation from the Gospel of the Nazarenes (Schneemelcher 1990, 135). In this text this demand appears as an indispensable condition for eternal life, even surpassing the observance of all commandments. Similarly, Luke 14:33 and 16:9 explain the leaving behind of one's possessions as a condition of discipleship. If we ask about a rationale for this renunciation of possessions, Q 12:33 gives an explanation on the basis of a wisdom point of view. True wealth does not consist in earthly possessions, which are exposed to multiple threats, but in a heavenly treasure bought about by benevolence (Q 12:33–34). The concluding sentence on true wealth, "where your treasure is, there will your heart be also" (Q 12:34), excludes compromises (similarly Q 16:13). In a follow-up conversation with the disciples about the failed call of the young man, Jesus includes various observations about whether the rich can enter the kingdom of God. Although the verdict for entering is that this way seems "hard" for the rich (Mark 10:23), a possibility not yet completely excluded, the rhetorical hyperbole of the camel and the eye of the needle (Mark 10:25) emphasizes the improbability. In conclusion, however, Jesus says that the salvation of a person, even if it is impossible for this person, depends entirely on God, and for God "all things" are possible (Mark 10:27). In his version Luke deleted this "everything" (Luke 18:27). In any case, a manifold recompense is promised to the disciples, who in their following have intentionally left everything (Mark 10:28).

The synoptic mission discourses (Mark 6:6b–13 par.; Q 10:1–12) prohibit in addition to other provisions such as a staff (differently Mark 6:8), a purse, shoes/sandals (differently Mark 6:9), bread, a bag, two garments, even money (Mark 6:8). Matthew 10:9 even introduces three terms for money: χρυσός, ἄρ-γυρος, χαλκός. We should interpret this renunciation of money in the context of the sweeping renunciation of provisions of any kind (see below).

c. The parables of the rich fool (Luke 12:15–21; Gos. Thom. 63; as the introduction to this also Luke 12:13–15 par. Gos. Thom. 72) and the rich man and Lazarus (Luke 16:19–31) make a theme of possessions and wealth per se, but hardly of the false, antisocial behavior arising from possessions of the rich people encountered in them.

A discussion precedes the first parable, which describes the theme, which is in turn illustrated in the concluding parable: "because the life of a man does not consist of the abundance of his possessions" (Luke 12:15c; on the translation, see Wolter 2008, 446). The warning pronounced from this is about πλεονεξία (greed as striving for more and more), the danger of which in the parable is not described in terms of social strife but rather in an individual miscalculation about life. A rich person, not actually a farmer but rather a large landholder, stands at the center of the parable. He stocks up a good harvest; enlarges his buildings, in which he stores the harvest and his possessions; and in view of the large reserves organizes a resplendent life in the coming years, which would be earmarked by eating, drinking, and being merry (so also Eccles. 8:15; Jos. Asen. 20:8; among others). The rich man's mistake is not located either in the stockpiling or in the delightful life that is described, but rather in bad chronological planning. If he prepares for many years, then death sent by God "in this night" thwarts all the plans arranged for years to come (so also Gos. Thom. 63). Hence, the parable warns about false security in the example of the rich man. Only in the application of the parable in Luke 12:21, which is absent in Gos. Thom. 63, is an alternative specified, which is critical of accumulating possessions for himself—being rich with respect to God. Now the death of the rich man appears to be punishment for wealth. By contrast, true wealth consists of wealth with respect to God, which is acquired by benevolence (alms) (Luke 11:41; 12:33; 16:9).

In the parable of the rich man and Lazarus (Luke 16:19–31), the vast wealth of one person (purple and linen) and the destitute need of the other are described at the beginning. After the death of both, an abrupt inversion takes place. Whereas the poor man arrives in Abraham's bosom, the rich man suffers agonies in the underworld. Abraham explains the postmortem inversion by saying that the rich man in his lifetime had received what is good and the poor man what is bad and that now a reprisal takes place, which is irrevocable, which the image of a great chasm between the underworld and Abraham illustrates. Contrast this with the Egyptian story of the burial of a rich man and a poor man, which is often considered a direct parallel (on this, see Wolter 2008, 557–58). There is a crucial difference between the parable and the Egyptian story, in that in the parable there is no question of guilt or wrongdoing on the part of the rich man, which would be responsible for this inversion in the other world. Rather, this inversion, as similarly in Luke 1:46–55 and 6:20–26, is described as an equalizer determined by God in the other world. Only in the concluding dialogue is reference made to "repentance in the lifetime" of the brothers of the rich man and to the instruction of the law and the prophets. This indicates a prudent social responsibility. In the literary context of the Gospel of Luke, which addressed pecuniary, greedy Pharisees and the worthlessness of their superiority (16:14–15), the parable becomes an example story, which warns about the results of wealth and the wrong dealings with possessions.

The majority of recent interpretations of the present textual evidence are oriented toward research on the sociological history and archaeology of Galilee (W. Stegemann 2010, 250–57), but they arrive at varying conclusions. It appears as if a simple model of social classes in Galilee has been superseded by a quite differentiated description of economics, which is energized by new archaeological evidence (Zwickel 2013). The thesis of an antagonism between urban and rural populations, to which the Jesus movement belonged, has been abandoned again (Schröter 2006b, 95). The extent to which Jesus's proclamation mirrors the actual relationships is disputed. In addition to ethical statements critical of possessions, many texts speak of Jesus's fellowship with the wealthy and propertied (Hengel 1973, 34–36, speaks therefore about a radically critical and a simultaneously free attitude of Jesus on possessions). The entire Jesus tradition knows of no criticism of the extreme wealth of the Herodians and the leading high priestly families who collaborated with the Roman prefect (Hengel 1973, 31). Also, we do not find any explicit criticism of the two cities Sepphoris and Tiberias and the prosperity spread out in them (differently Reed 2000).

Since 1973 Gerd Theissen (1977; 1979; [3]1989b) has propounded a sociological interpretation of the Jesus movement that also makes possessions and wealth a theme. The Jesus movement, as a movement of the poor in a comprehensive social crisis, abandons the norms of the environment (unstable and deviant behavior) and becomes a radical itinerant movement. "The horrible end of the rich and the blessedness of the poor in the other world was painted in fantasies saturated with aggression (Luke 16:19–31)" (1977, 18). The disciples' renunciation of possessions is a form of the "mendicancy of a higher order, charismatic mendicancy" (19). The poverty of the disciples must be understood in the context of the fundamental renunciation of provisions as a symbolic act. It stands with respect to the external appearance in proximity to Cynic wandering preachers, but it contains intentional distinctions (Theissen and Merz 1996, 200). Primarily, poverty is interpreted as a reference to the messengers' view of God, according to which God takes care of human beings (Q 11:2–4; 12:22–34). Thus, poverty does not attest the autarchy of the messengers as with the Cynics, but rather has a function of referring to the nearness of the kingdom of God.

John D. Crossan propounded a variant of this thesis, which portrays Jesus's disciples explicitly as Jewish Cynics (or Cynic Jews), whose resistance is directed against all constraints of Mediterranean culture. Richard A. Horsley (1989) objected to both the thesis of wandering radicalism and the Cynic interpretation. According to his view, Jesus gives instructions for the organization of village life in Galilee, which completely renounce hierarchy and domination. Suggestions to understand the critique of wealth with the expected total inversion of relationships by the kingdom of God (Hengel 1973, 32; Merz 2001; Riches 2004, 232) interpret things in this direction. Zeller (2004, 198–99) emphasizes that Jesus expected the kingdom of God as an inversion, and, in an apocalyptic perspective similar to 1 En. 94:8, attacked complacent rich people.

In addition to such interpretations, the plausibility of which arises only from the social and political contextualization, still other, more existential interpretations are propounded, which largely renounce a sociohistorical classification. Thus, Meier emphasizes that Jesus especially repudiated the trust in money and possessions as "a spiritual danger": "Jesus saw wealth as a danger to total commitment to God and acceptance of his proclamation of the kingdom" (Meier 2001, 515; similarly, Berges and Hoppe 2009, 76–77; Giesen 2011). Reiser (1998, 461) locates the theme of wealth in Jesus's proclamation in the theory of goods and not in social theory. The critique of wealth implies the option for poverty. By contrast, for Rau (2006, 267), Jesus's distance from the rich arises exclusively from his proximity to the poor whom he seeks, who in turn come into view only "because the Isaianic expectation of salvation opens Jesus's eyes for the uniqueness of their standing before God."

Most of the themes and texts touched on here can be interpreted such that the coming kingdom of God calls into question possessions and wealth and reorganizes present relationships. The Synoptic Gospels, especially Luke, have taken up this point of view, but in the process have disarmed the irreconcilable opposition of possessions and the sovereignty of God and have deferred it in the sense of an ethic of benevolence.

Berges, Ulrich, and Rudolf Hoppe. 2009. *Arm und Reich*. NEchtB 10. Würzburg.

Giesen, Heinz. 2011. "Poverty and Wealth in Jesus and the Jesus Tradition." In *Handbook for the Study of the Historical Jesus*, vol. 4, *Individual Studies*, edited by Tom Holmén and Stanley E. Porter, 3269–3303. Leiden and Boston.

Merz, Annette. 2001. "Mammon als schärfster Konkurrent Gottes—Jesu Vision vom Reich Gottes und das Geld." In *Gott oder Mammon: Christliche Ethik und die Religion des Geldes*, edited by Severin J. Lederhilger, 34–90. Linzer philosophisch-theologische Beiträge 3. Frankfurt.

Rau, Eckhard. 2006. "Arm und Reich im Spiegel des Wirkens Jesu." In *Eschatologie und Ethik im frühen Christentum, FS Günter Haufe*, edited by Christfried Böttrich, 249–68. Greifswalder Theologische Forschungen 11. Frankfurt.

Theissen, Gerd. [3]1989b. "Wir haben alles verlassen (Mc. X,28): Nachfolge und soziale Entwurzelung in der jüdisch-palästinischen Gesellschaft des 1. Jahrhunderts n.Chr." In *Studien zur Soziologie des Urchristentums*, by Gerd Theissen, 106–41. WUNT 19. Tübingen.

Friedrich Wilhelm Horn

4.3. Discipleship, Radical Renunciation, "A-familial" Ethic

In distinction from the Baptizer's threatening radical call to repentance in face of the judgment, the message of the in-breaking kingdom of God, which in Jesus's proclamation and action already creates a new reality in "fragment" (Weder 1993, 26–34, esp. 33), puts the invitation into the community of salvation in the foreground. This invitation aims at unconditional acceptance. Refusal and rejection are penalized by God in the end-time judgment. The proclamation of the kingdom of God is consequently also the end-time locus of the decision. New patterns of behavior follow from the acceptance of the invitation. These patterns are determined by the coming kingdom and anticipate its regulations. In this special situation, directives for living are issued by Jesus as the proclaimer of the kingdom of God, which is determined by the coming and the nearness of God.

Even though the proclamation of the kingdom of God is an obligatory ethical directive for a particularly qualified time, it is to be interpreted as related less to time and more to the matter at hand; it has the character of a system of thought, albeit admittedly restricted, without establishing an in-depth reflexive discourse. God's claim as a caring father and creator (e.g., Schnelle 2007, 94–97), who loves those who are addressed and has the objective of a response of unconditional love, becomes word and deed in Jesus's ministry. This dimension is of fundamental hermeneutical importance for Jesus's demands of radical discipleship and its partly "a-social" character. In spite of christological overcoating, the provocative, shocking, radical demands in view of the approaching kingdom of God are indicative of the original Jesus tradition.

4.3.1. Discipleship

4.3.1.1. Calls to Discipleship

The calls of Jesus's closest coworkers are calls to discipleship: Mark 1:16–20 (see also Mark 2:14; John 1:35–51). Independently from the successive shaping of discipling scenes up to their literary incorporation, the memory of Jesus's call to follow him as the proclaimer of the kingdom of God is reflected in them. The call is issued in everyday life, and it leads to a direct following after him (behind me—ὀπίσω μου), with renunciation of relationships and possessions (cf. Mark 10:28–31 par.), in dedication to the coming kingdom of God and its proclamation.

Jens Schröter (2006b, 214–15) draws attention to the fact that in Jesus's demands distinctions are to be made among the respective addressees. The calls to discipleship put them in a new construct of roles, which is determined by the proclamation of the kingdom itself. Like Jesus himself, the disciples issue an invitation into the kingdom of God (Q 10:2–16; Mark 6:6b–13). This special profile is to be noticed, even though the fundamental demand of focusing on God and his coming kingdom is by no means restricted by it. "Accordingly, a unique ethos pertains also for the entire movement, that holds for the reign of God, for which like a treasure in a field or a particularly valuable pearl everything else is to be set aside and relativized (cf. Matt. 13:44, 45–46). How the abundant value of the reign of God is concretely noticed, depends on the concrete circumstances" (Schmeller 1989, 69).

In individual cases a differentiation is difficult, especially in the demands that do not lead directly to collaboration; they depict the urgency of the decision for the kingdom of God, which is assigned to all the addressees of the proclamation.

4.3.1.2. General Calls to Discipleship

"Discipleship" is essentially a complete focus on the basis of Jesus's call that subordinates everything to the kingdom of God: Q 9:57–60, 61–62 (Matt. 8:19–22 par.; see also Gos. Thom. 86). Independent from the question whether Luke 9:61–62 was already in Q (on the discussion, see Labahn 2010, 148–50; against, e.g., Schröter 1997, 161–62), the three sayings exhibit traces of later editing. At the core, however, they must reflect the sharpness of Jesus's call of invitation into the kingdom of God, which grates against social and religious norms. Especially the priority of discipleship before the burial of a father (Q 9:59–60; see below) presents an unparalleled violation of norms. As to content, the directive and demand of the God who has come near are indisputably placed in the center. The central point of the saying in the context of the sayings source is "the inculcation of the conditions for following Jesus without compromises or false illusions" (Ebner 2004, 85); this corresponds to the original intention of the calls to discipleship in Jesus's proclamation.

4.3.1.3. Summary

Jesus's call to discipleship subordinates the addressees and their social context to his call and integrates them into the kingdom of God and its norms. Discipleship does not primarily produce devotees of a teacher but rather an inter-pretation of reality, which is brought about by the proclamation and action of the teacher (Labahn 2019, 56–65). In this respect, from the start, discipleship was connected with Jesus and his ministry, but not until the development of Christology does it become following Christ, as it attains central importance in the Gospel of Mark.

4.3.2. Renunciation as Profit in the Context of the In-Breaking Kingdom of God

4.3.2.1. Renunciation of Rights and Judging

The demand to renounce rights (Q 6:29, 30; Matt. 5:38–42 par.) is contained in a small collection of sayings, which serves the following themes: no retaliation, waiver of juridical controversies regarding an undergarment, acceptance of mil-itary compulsory labor, readiness to help, and unselfish loans. According to the reconstruction of Hoffman and Heil, the text of Q runs: "To the one who strikes you on the cheek, hold out the other to him also, and to the one who takes you to court and wants to take away your undergarment, give him your outer garment also. And when one forces you to perform one mile of military compulsory labor, go two. To the one who asks, give; and from the one who borrows, do not demand what is yours back."

If the blow to the face referenced above is committed against a slave (Valan-tasis 2005, 59), then the saying would be an exception that strengthens social stratification. Debtor laws come into play in the dispute over the garment, which laws were of significance in rural Palestine at the time of Jesus. Outstanding debt could be demanded in court, and renouncing one's rights could threaten one's existence. The acceptance of compulsory military labor refers to the situation in Palestine under Roman occupation, but the doubling of the required service is politically and socially shocking. Further, the admonition to be willing to help and to make a loan without thinking about reimbursement (see also Gos. Thom. 95) also involves a renunciation that could endanger one's existence.

In these sayings the issue is not only the renunciation of judicial rights but also the renunciation of the right of one's personal integrity. Because of their offensiveness, the sayings likely go back to Jesus's proclamation of the kingdom of God, and they imply the sociopolitical situation in which Jesus and his early followers carry out their proclamation. These sayings are initially not meant to anticipate the organization of the in-breaking kingdom of God but to transform its order of life that is influenced by love of neighbor (double love command:

Mark 12:28–34 par.); they challenge hearers to interact productively with injustice and coercion without destroying themselves through retribution and hatred.

The challenges are fundamentally shaped by love as the center of Jesus's ethical thought, and the danger to the social safeguards of life has its counterpoint in trust in the God of love (e.g., J. Becker 1996, 322–37). In renunciation, the good action of the God who comes near is experienced by the members of God's kingdom as an alternative design for social reality.

That the concept of love by God and love for God presents the hermeneutical key for understanding the sayings about renunciation has already been recognized in the sayings source; here the exhortation to love enemies was placed in front of the sayings about renunciation of rights: "Love your enemies" (Q 6:27; Matt. 5:44a par.).

In Q the saying about love of enemies responds to the macarism about victims of persecution (Q 6:22) and thereby serves the formation of identity of the devotees of the Q community—in the literary context, the "enemy" is a character who has the objective of destroying the life of the addressees; the love of God confronts this character (Q 6:35c). In the secondary literary context, both are rightly singled out. At the same time, in Q the ability to communicate with outsiders is retained by means of the exhortation to love (6:27) (Labahn 2010, 446–48). Q's literary design supplements in exemplary fashion intercession for the enemy (6:28) and points to God's action to preserve creation (6:35).

Even if the challenge of absolute love of enemies may be limited by the interpretation in Q, it still holds fundamentally that love as a creative form of the relationship with an "enemy" is anchored in God's love and care, who comes near in his in-breaking kingdom. "God's radical unlimited love forces its way into the everyday life of a person, who is expected to participate in God's love by loving enemies. A rationale for love of enemies cannot be derived from the present reality, but such unusual behavior can obtain its meaning and commitment only from God's action" (Schnelle 2007, 99).

Even if the future kingdom of God will know no enemies, love is the essential element of the organization of life. The concept of love of enemies anticipates the new organization of life in the kingdom of peace without any enmity (J. Becker 1996, 323) and thereby thwarts a social system built on power and the use of force, as is normal (not only) in the ancient world. Love of enemies shows that the present world is the provisional world, as opposed to the salvific reality of the kingdom of God, which has arrived in "fragment."

In addition, the exhortation to "serve" should be brought to mind, in which following Jesus's own model (cf. in essence Mark 10:45), the right to dominate in the social practices of the community of the addressees is denied (Mark 10:42b–44; behind the Markan composition stands a process of memory that will have preserved impulses of Jesus's proclamation; see also Luke 12:37; 22:27; John 13:3–16). This order of life is less a general critique of domination—which it, of course, also includes—than a new structure of interaction for the kingdom of God. With the renunciation of domination, which structured the social pyramid at that time, social hierarchies are deconstructed by the new paradigm of "serving." Pertinently the model of love as the central motif of ethics of the kingdom of God that has come near corresponds to mutual service. The behavior of the addressees anticipates the organization of the kingdom of God and declares the orientation of status in the contemporaneous society to be absurd and superseded.

Along with the sayings about renunciation (of rights) directed at the organization of life of the kingdom the prohibition of judging is to be recalled (Q 6:37–38; Matt. 7:1–2 par.), which is motivated differently. Here what is at stake is every act of judging over fellow human beings, which can lead to social marginalization and possibly to the destruction of the other. Included are the condemnation of injustice and the renunciation of criticizing that which is not motivated by love but rather by God's end-time judgment. Every compensation of injustice resides with the God who comes near in his kingdom; functionally renunciation makes it possible to appropriate the exhortation to love enemies.

4.3.2.2. Abandoning Possessions

Jesus's call to discipleship includes the disciples' renunciation of their original possessions and modest economic well-being; this pertains to a special degree to those called by Jesus to preach, but also basically as anticipation of the coming kingdom of God for every person who is invited into the kingdom. In radical trust in the God who comes near and his activity to preserve creation (cf. Q 12:6–7; Matt. 5:45), the disciple receives from God what he or she actually needs for life.

One who is invited will utilize all "assets" for the "treasure in the field" or the "pearl of great price" of the kingdom of God: Matt. 13:44–46. In these two parables, the radical focus on the kingdom of God is expressed, for which the renunciation of possessions becomes an illustration. Whether it is found by the addressee or actively sought, the kingdom of God leads to a new orientation of life, which is not focused on the receipt of possessions or striving for possessions but rather on the kingdom itself. In the motif of selling all belongings in order to get hold of the kingdom ("and in his joy he goes and sells everything he has and buys the field/pearl"), the claim of the short stories oriented to behavior in Matthew becomes clear. In comparison with the "claim of possession" of the approaching kingdom of God, all belongings (πάντα ὅσα ἔχει) are to be abandoned.

448

So, according to Q 12:33–34 (Matt. 6:19–21 par.), Jesus gives advice, "do not store up for yourselves treasures on earth," but rather store them up in heaven; in the Gospel of Luke this challenge, which is critical of possessions and moves God and the kingdom of God into the foreground, is concretized in abandoning possessions and giving alms (Luke 12:33a).

The renunciation of possessions is reflected in the negative assessment of wealth:

"It is easier for a camel to go through the eye of a needle than for someone who is rich to enter the kingdom of God." (Mark 10:25 par.)

"No slave can serve two masters; for a slave will either hate the one and love the other, or be devoted to one and despise the other. You cannot serve God and mammon." (Q 16:13; Matt. 6:24 par.; on Q 16:13a: Gos. Thom. 47:2)

In both sayings wealth stands in opposition to the kingdom of God as a matter of principle, which without doubt was offensive for later generations of the Jesus movement. Q 16:13 provides a rationale, which is in line with Yahweh's commandment of exclusivity. In the term "mammon" money becomes a divinity (e.g., Labahn [2]2015, 223). The addressees are faced with the decision to choose "between serving the true God and serving a pseudo-deity—Mammon" (H. Betz 1995, 454). Possessions and wealth not only stand in danger of being deified, but they also stand in opposition to the undivided devotion to God as the giver and preserver of life and all goods. To be sure, Q 16:13 does not comment about economic ethics (Horsley 1999, 293); nevertheless, economic consequences arise, since service to God includes care for others (cf. Labahn 2008, 278–79). The trust demanded by Jesus and the complete focus on the coming kingdom of God form the theological context.

In this context, Q 16:16 is also significant, even if historical inquiry and the interpretation present difficult problems: "Since then the kingdom of God suffers violence [the kingdom of God is established by force] and violent people take it by force [ἡ βασιλεία τῶν οὐρανῶν βιάζεται καὶ βιασταὶ ἁρπάζουσιν αὐτήν]."

If one prefers the first variant of the translation of the reconstruction of Hoffman and Heil (on this, C. Heil 2003, 127), the addressees become perpetrators of violence, who appropriate the kingdom of God by violence (cf., e.g., Theissen 2003b, 162). The present aimed at by the indication of time in Q 16:16b (ἀπὸ τότε) is a time of unconditional focus on the kingdom of God, since it is to be seized by the addressees with force. The addressees should not only renounce possessions, but in this scene portrayed with morally disreputable language, they are encouraged to appropriate the kingdom of God with force.

4.3.2.3. Renunciation of Life

The most radical form of renunciation is the renunciation of one's own life. The saying about the willingness to lose one's life ("The one who finds his/her life, will lose it, and the one who loses his/her life for my sake, will find it" [Q 17:33]; see also Mark 8:35) makes a challenge to radical discipleship that can go as far as death, in order thereby to attain the life that God gives in the kingdom of God (on historical questions and interpretation, C. Heil 2014b, 77–83).

This notion is further intensified when the loss of life itself is associated with the complete exposure and total loss of honor. This takes place in the saying about taking up the cross, which does not necessarily reflect Jesus's death but rather formulates the thought of surrendering life in such an unsettling intensification as a condition of discipleship that it is compatible and likewise plausible as a memory of Jesus (cf. Schnackenburg 1986, 62–63): "Anyone who does not take up his/her cross, cannot be my disciple" (Q 14:27; Mark 8:34b; Gos. Thom. 55.2). Q 14:27 defines discipleship and willingness to follow as readiness to surrender life and honor. The gift of life (Mark 8:35) corresponds to such readiness. Renunciation thereby becomes an acquisition as a gift vouchsafed by God.

4.3.2.4. Summary

The challenges to renunciation have their context in the invitation to radical trust in God, as in the saying about not worrying (Q 12:22–31; in my opinion, the sequence is not aimed at the closest disciples of Jesus, but at those who orient their existence to the presence of the coming kingdom of God; on this, Schröter 2006b, 218) and in the background of trust encountered in the petition for bread in the Lord's Prayer (Q 11:3; see also Q 11:9–10). As creator of the world, God is also its sustainer, to whom the creatures are to respond with radical trust. Trusting in God, faith, is the positive response to the invitation into the kingdom of God. It is in essence about freedom for the active and uncompromising acceptance of God's will (cf. Mark 3:35). The challenges to renunciation obtain their plausibility in the nearness of the caring God; especially in their extreme seriousness, they might have had their point of contact in the closest circle of Jesus's followers.

4.3.3. "A-social" and "A-familial" Ethos

In Jesus's proclamation, the kingdom of God that is being established deconstructs social norms and obligations in that it redefines its addressees (e.g., in the Beatitudes: Q 6:20–21; Matt. 5:1–6 par.) and simultaneously dismantles hierarchies and standards, such as in the wages in the parable of the workers in the vineyard (Matt. 20:1–16), in which salvation is vouchsafed beyond social norms. At the same time, Jesus's ethos of discipleship provokes the violation of socially and religiously recognized norms. Here the end-time will of God can come into conflict with the traditional understanding of God's will, or it may even be reset (cf. on the eschatological interpretation of Torah, Maier 2013). This is especially clear in Jesus's sayings in which family relationships and obligations are called into question or are dissolved (on the compatibility of Q 9:58–60 with Torah, see C. Heil 2014a).

4.3.3.1 Jesus's Sayings Annulling Social Norms and Obligations

In the parable of the great banquet (Q 14:16–24; Matt. 22:1–14 par.), the originally invited notables of society of that time reject the invitation. Against social practice, Jesus says all those persons "who normally are not invited to such a banquet" (Schottroff 1987, 198) are now to be solicited by slaves sent as messengers. With this the parable substantiates the adaptation of the message of the kingdom of God to the religiously and socially marginalized (C. Heil 2003, 92).

More than the reassessment of the ancient canons of honor, the violation of norms by Q 9:59–60 stands out. The honoring, and with it especially also the piety in relation to parents, belongs to fundamental ancient ethical norms, and likewise is an essential foundation of biblical-Jewish ethics (cf., e.g., Balla 2003, 5–110; Jungbauer 2002, 7–253). A part of this is the preeminent obligation for the burial of parents: "But another said to him, 'Lord, first let me go and bury my father.' But he said to him, 'Follow me, and let the dead bury their dead'" (Q 9:59–60; Matt. 8:21–22, par.). With this saying Jesus puts "his disciples in provocative opposition to the expectation, which the environment had with respect to family cohesion and the duties in the family" (Jungbauer 2002, 296). The urgency that comes with the proclamation of the kingdom of God to completely turn and accept God's kingdom cannot be stated more shockingly and trenchantly. This urgency holds for all addressees, even if not all of Jesus's coworkers disband their social relationships.

4.3.3.2. Annulment of Family Relationships and New Family Relationships

Those sayings in which the proclamation of the kingdom of God results in internal domestic and intrafamilial conflict are also scandalous: Q 12:51, 53, and 14:26. These sayings likewise present a violation of taboos. They have probably been preserved solely because Jesus said them (in fact, the family relationships of the early disciples of Jesus may have also been dissolved because of their new relationship to the remembered Jesus):

> "Do you think that I have come to bring peace to the earth? I have not come to bring peace but a sword. For I have come to divide: a son against a father and a daughter against her mother and a daughter-in-law against her mother-in-law." (Q 12:51, 53; Matt. 10:34–36 par.)

> "Anyone who does not hate father and mother, cannot be my disciple; and anyone who does not hate his son and his daughter cannot be my disciple." (Q 14:26; Matt. 10:37 par.; Gos. Thom. 55.1; 101.1–2)

In Q, both sayings are closely joined and form a close interpretive connection because of the family semantics of father and son as well as of mother and daughter. With the coming of the kingdom of God, the pressure for a decision is built up, which causes even the closest relationships of a family to become something secondary; what is at stake is the decision concerning discipleship in the kingdom of God. The presence of the kingdom of God aims at a focus that includes the dissolution of basic social structures.

According to the feminist hermeneutic of Luise Schottroff (1991, 339), Jesus calls "the patriarchal order into question." "Thus alongside of the wandering male and female messengers of Jesus there is no longer a 'normal' family structure and no love [of] patriarchalism as a form of organization of the community." According to Arland Jacobson (2000, 201), programmatically the necessity exists "of breaking free from enmeshed family structures in order to pursue an alternative vision and/or lifestyle, and . . . the need to adopt lifestyle features that would mark the new group off from their neighbors and yield group self-definition and solidarity." In contrast, the dissolution of social and familial relationships in the proclamation of the in-breaking kingdom of God generated a new fellowship shaped by the orientation of the kingdom of God as Jesus's "family"—here, Jesus still uses family metaphors in a positive way: "He answered them and said, 'Who are my mother and my brothers?' And looking at those who sat around him in the circle he said: 'Look, my mother and my brothers. Whoever does the will of God is my brother and my sister and my mother'" (Mark 3:33–35 par.; cf. Gos. Thom. 99).

The complete focus on the kingdom of God creates a fellowship of people who are shaped by the love of God and are related to each other in this love beyond traditional gender roles. Still, the motif of "family" (mother and siblings) stands as a metaphor for this community, because it obviously has an abiding positive figurative value and so can appropriately designate the eschatological community in the love of God.

4.3.3.3. Summary

By means of targeted provocations and violations of norms, a relativizing revaluation of social obligations in relation to the kingdom of God is already on its way in "fragment." The proximity of the kingdom presses for a complete orientation to the kingdom, deconstructs social rules in the light of the God who is coming, and demands the willingness of people to get involved with this kingdom. Simultaneously Jesus's proclamation creates a new association of the new people of God, which transforms traditional social structures in their provisional nature in comparison with the kingdom of God.

4.3.4. Prospects

The message of God's kingdom present in "fragment" in Jesus's activity develops radical ethical instructions, which, with calls to discipleship, basic challenges to renunciation, and violations of social taboos, exhort believers to enact a way of life corresponding to the coming of the kingdom. Jesus's production of ethical instructions calls for extraordinary decisions on the part of the addressees so that they let themselves be determined completely by the kingdom of God, which is becoming present. This leads to new social relationships on the one hand and to responsibility for social standards and upright requirements on the other hand. God's offer of salvation presents an obligation that does not tolerate either alternatives or delay, but rather targets immediate and complete acceptance. Any possibility of directing the engagement toward something other than this kingdom of God is mistaken, since insufficient focusing as rejection of the offer of salvation leads into judgment.

Jesus's production of ethical instructions has its conceptual core in his image of God, which moves God's love and care into the center. This focus is closely bound to the proclaimed nearness of the coming kingdom. Nevertheless, the radical demands are not an ethical blueprint for a temporally limited transition into the kingdom of God (Schweitzer [1901] ²1973a, 229, "interim ethic"), but rather form an opposing outline to structures of the present world and anticipate the orientation of the kingdom of God. The deconstruction of present social structures is thereby part of the extensive interpretation of reality in Jesus's proclamation of the kingdom of God, but is in no way primarily contextual and unsystematic (differently W. Stegemann 2002, 167).

In view of the provocative and at times unsettling character of Jesus's ethical radicalism, it cannot be surprising that the narratives about Jesus in the New Testament undergo further systematization in changing times. Jesus's provocative challenges are adapted and christologically redefined according to the social and economic needs of the developing Christian communities.

Labahn, Michael. 2019. "'Enthüllte' Wirklichkeit: Neutestamentliche Spielarten, wie Wahrheit und Glaube in der Erschließung und Wahrnehmung neuer Wirklichkeit zur Geltung gebracht werden." In *Wahrheit—Glaube—Deutung: Theologische und philosophische Konkretionen*, edited by Christof Landmesser and Doris Hiller, 51–78. Veröffentlichungen der Rudolf-Bultmann-Gesellschaft für Hermeneutische Theologie e.V. Leipzig.

Schnackenburg, Rudolf. 1986. *Die sittliche Botschaft des Neuen Testaments 1: Von Jesus zur Urkirche*, 58–67. HThKNTSup 1. Freiburg.

Schnelle, Udo. 2007. *Theologie des Neuen Testaments*, 94–104. UTB 2917. Göttingen.

Schröter, Jens. 2006b; ⁵2012. *Jesus von Nazareth: Jude aus Galiläa—Retter der Welt*, 213–30. Biblische Gestalten 15. Leipzig.

Michael Labahn

4.4. Jesus as a Glutton and Winebibber

4.4.1. Introduction

The interpretation of Jesus's advent does not begin only with the post-Easter memory nor take place exclusively with positive christological assessments. The process of interpretation starts with the perception of Jesus's proclamation and actions by his contemporaries, which provoked diverse reactions. The memory of controversies and rejection is not only preserved in Jesus's debates shaped after Easter or in the reports of his passion and crucifixion, but also in the polemic directed against Jesus. These polemic assessments are of value for external interpretations of Jesus's advent not only for the understanding of Jesus's activities but also as memories of Jesus only secondarily influenced by Christianity. In addition to the accusations of being possessed (Mark 3:22, 30; John 7:20; 8:48, 52; 10:20) and of being in league with demons (Q 11:15 par.; Mark 3:22 par.), Jesus is also charged with being a glutton and winebibber.

4.4.2. Textual Evidence

The accusation of being a glutton and winebibber is preserved in Q 7:34 combined with the charge that Jesus is a friend of tax collectors and sinners. In what follows, the textual evidence is presented on the basis of the reconstruction of the text published in Hoffmann and Heil:

Q 7:34

The son of man came, he ate and drank and you say: "This man there—a glutton and winebibber, a friend of tax collectors and sinners."	ἦλθεν ὁ υἱὸς τοῦ ἀνθρώπου ἐσθίων καὶ πίνων, καὶ λέγετε• ἰδοὺ ἄνθρωπος, φάγος καὶ οἰνοπότης, τελωνῶν φίλος καὶ ἁμαρτωλῶν.

The designation of Jesus as a glutton and winebibber is found in the concluding passage of the first main part of Q (3:3a–7:35). After John the preacher of judgment (3:7–9) announced one who comes (3:16b–17), Jesus is shown to be the coming one whom the Baptizer announced and God legitimates throughout the narrative by a voice from heaven (3:21–22), temptations (4:1–13), instruction (6:22–49), and healings (7:1–10). On the basis of the introduction of the Baptizer as the proclaimer of the one who comes before the appearance of Jesus as the leading character in the text of Q, and on the basis of the absence of direct identification of the one who comes with the one who is proclaimed, the relationship of John and Jesus requires an explanation (7:18–35). At the same time, both protagonists are placed in a relationship with Jesus's followers (7:28) and with his opponents (7:31–35). The authority of the Baptizer as a voice for the one who comes is sanctioned by Jesus (7:24–27) but also subordinated to the one who comes.

After his discourse about the Baptizer (7:24–28), Jesus compares his opponents, who are characterized with Deuteronomistic motifs of "this generation," with children sitting in the marketplace (7:31–32). Their judgment is arbitrary, but by means of the citation of their polemic against the Baptizer and against the one who comes formulated in an essentially parallel passage (7:33–34; both judgments are introduced by the perfect ἐλήλυθεν, introduced in each case with two circumstantial participles in the present, ἐσθίων and πίνων), they are characterized as incapable of understanding: "In the immediate context it contrasts Jesus' ministry with that of John thus exposing the capriciousness of the people of 'this generation' who fail to respond to either" (Fleddermann 2005, 385). Differently, Jesus's disciples (according to Luz [3]1999, 185, the "Q community . . . as 'children of wisdom'") follow God's wisdom and vindicate it:

Q 7:33 For John came, he did not eat, he did not drink, and you said: he has a demon.	Q 7:34 The son of man came, he ate and drank, and you said: "This man there—a glutton and winebibber, a friend of tax collectors and sinners."	Q 7:35 And wisdom is vindicated by her children

The polemic taken up in Jesus's discourse is in principle not contradicted, but rather it takes its starting point in an overall picture of Jesus's ministry. The double saying is an expression of the misunderstanding of "this generation," which in spite of their familiarity with Jesus's story do not recognize him, but distinguish themselves from him. The entire activity of the two protagonists is focused on the selective experience of their having come, which is depicted as asceticism or as joyful and festive table fellowship. The misunderstanding resides in their assessment of the Baptizer as possessed and of Jesus as a glutton, winebibber, and sinner.

At the beginning of Q, the document portrays Jesus as fasting (4:2; cf. however 13:26). The Jesus missionaries in Q 10:7 are definitively required to eat and drink in houses as a symbol of a fellowship of peace (Schröter 1997, 182, "symbolic[.] Action in view of the future basileia"—however, the reconstruction is disputed). Q anticipates the motif of the eschatological joyful feast (cf. 13:29; see also 14:16–23). Jesus's table gatherings with tax collectors, sinners, or prostitutes are not narrated, but they are incorporated in Q 7:34 as a "gap" in the external knowledge of the addressees about Jesus's meal practices. In this context of understanding, Q interprets Jesus's eating and drinking with tax collectors and sinners as a symbolic prefiguration of the coming meal of salvation. Eating and enjoying wine are an expression of paradisiac-eschatological salvation, which demolishes religio-social frameworks, in which tax collectors and sinners can attain participation by means of God's forgiveness. Even if Q makes use of knowledge external to the addressees of the text, much speaks in favor of the inclusion of traditional material.

4.4.3. Tradition and Historical Issues

In the context of the document, Q 7:33–34 does not constitute an isolated group of sayings (Kloppenborg 1999, 111) but comments on (see also Wanke 1981, 35–40) the traditional parable of the children in the marketplace. Both passages can already form an ancient unity as an "antecedent- and commentary saying" (e.g., Luz [3]1999, 186–87, which could go back to Jesus), although in view of the meager interrelation attested only in Q, this assumption appears doubtful (e.g., Sevenich-Bax 1993, 229–30, with substantiation).

The substantiation for this is that, in addition to the polemic characteristic of Jesus, the polemic of the Baptizer also has a plausible *Sitz im Leben* in the ongoing tradition in Q, for instance, in the discussion between the Baptizer's group and Jesus's group (reflections in Ebner 1998, 197–98). But this resists being conclusive. The discussion with the Baptizer belongs rather in the argument of the Q context, because the statements developing the double polemic saying are scripted for the Baptizer, who was presented in opposition to those who dwell in palaces and as a prophet (7:25–26).

It is possible that Q took up a short assessment against Jesus circulating among opponents of Jesus's adherents. What is difficult to explain is the literary form of this tradition. If already there was talk of the coming of the son of man, which to be sure fits into the context of sayings and the line of thought of Q, then a christologically shaped tradition would already be present (Bultmann [9]1979, 166, considers that the term "son of man" was used with the meaning "human being"), the historical point of contact of which can be doubted.

The rhetorical strategy of marking boundaries has its point of contact in the discussion about the historical Jesus. A post-Easter, Christian formation is unlikely, because in this context the degradation of the religious hero for the purpose of the polemic of opponents would not be comprehensible, but also elements of post-Easter reflections are not conceivable. What needs to be asked is whether a saying of Jesus lies behind this, in which Jesus designates himself as the son of man and turns the polemic against his opponents (Pokorný 2009, 173), or whether a polemic of opponents because of its continuing use found its way into the memory of Jesus. The perpetration of the transmission of the polemic is already drawn against its speakers in Q by the reference to the historical activities of Jesus, who in the behavior that is criticized undertakes a revaluation of the religious values of his contemporaries and breaks through the drawing of social boundaries. The parallel polemic against the Baptizer is a secondary development (differently, e.g., Ernst 1989, 74; Pokorný 2009, 173, in which an argument for the authenticity appears in the undifferentiated rejection of both figures, the Baptizer and Jesus), which belongs in the polemic of Q against "this generation."

4.4.4. Contextualization of the Accusation in the Contemporary Encyclopedia

Jesus's activity in the judgment of the opponents is reduced to the accusation of gluttony and intemperate enjoyment of alcohol. This reproach can be understood especially on the basis of a wisdom background: gorging food and guzzling alcohol are defined as foolish ways of conduct, which can destroy a person's social location and possessions (Sir. 18:32–33; see also Prov. 28:7). Fellowship with a person who is characterized as a glutton and winebibber is deemed to be something to avoid (Prov. 23:20–21). Gorging food (and intemperate enjoyment of alcohol) is a mode of behavior that excludes participants from wisdom (Prov. 28:7). Such a person keeps company with sinners, which also explains the second part of the polemic in Q 7:34. The accusation links economic observations with social and religious components, which are pivotal in the polemic. A person labeled as such cannot be acknowledged as a teacher and prophet, because this person has no access to God's wisdom. Any devout person has to avoid association with this kind of person.

The reproach can be read somewhat differently in the context of Greco-Roman moral concepts. Exaggerated and showy luxury is subjected to the mockery of the satirists (cf. *Cena Trimalchionis* of Titius Petronius) and philosophical critique (cf. Seneca, *Ep.* 95.15–16, 23). The Cynic movement regards auspiciousness and luxury as contradictions to it, which can be expressed in clothing, jewelry, but also binge drinking. The Cynic ideal aims at life without needs. That Jesus the preacher of the kingdom of God or his early followers offered critiques of such luxury is unlikely; nevertheless, it points to a broad negative range of resonance to such a polemic.

Based on Dionysos Scythopolis's explanation of the veneration of god, Seán Freyne (2000b) generates another context. Freyne notices points of contact between Q 7:31–35 and motifs of veneration in Dionysos. With a view to Q 7:34, the term οἰνοπότης (winebibber, guzzler) points to the celebration of the cult of Dionysos. "Tax collectors and sinners" points to "foreign powers and prostitutes," with whom Jesus had companionship. Hence, "ultraconservative opponents" label Jesus a "Dionysiac" (Freyne 2014, 43). As fascinating as this inference is because of the local color, it imposes too much argumentative weight on the term οἰνοπότης, which also occurs in Prov. 23:20.

4.4.5. Contextualization of the Reproach in Jesus's Ministry

If memory of a polemic against Jesus lies behind Q 7:34, then its historical point of contact must lie in the table fellowship, which Jesus enters into with social and especially religious fringe groups or outsiders (in the sense of marginalized groups). If in the texts of the Gospels men and women sinners and tax collectors are spoken about, then a provocative breach of norms becomes perceptible, if measured by religious values. At the same time, a double theological program becomes apparent, which consists in the concept of the kingdom of God that has already dawned in a "fragment" (Weder 1993, esp. 33) and continues being established. The sinners and unclean are also invited into the kingdom of God that has arrived, because they are absolved from their guilt (Luke 7:48; see also Mark 2:10 par.; 2:15–17). At the same time, in table fellowship the eschatological celebratory feast is a reality in a "fragment" (cf., e.g., Luke 19:9a). Jesus's proclamation in parables tells about the kingdom of God as a banquet with abundantly supplied tables (e.g., cf. Q 13:29 par.; see also 14:16–23 par.). The expectation of a paradisiac abundance, including the enjoyment of wine, is an essential part of this eschatological feast (e.g., Sib. Or. 3:741–748; see also Amos 9:13–14; Hos. 2:22; 14:7; Joel 3:18 [MT 4:18]; Zech. 8:12; and many others). Even if in Jesus's table fellowship only a faint copy of this feast will have taken place, the accusation of a glutton and winebibber here can be a plausible indicator of it (e.g., Holmén 2001, 506; D.-A. Koch 1989, 64; Labahn 2010, 279).

This anticipation of the reality of the kingdom of God with the forgiveness of sin and celebration of the eschatological future met with opposition. Labeling Jesus a glutton and winebibber serves as a commentary on Jesus's actions, as the disavowal of his preaching as well as of the preacher himself, and finally as the dissociation from him on the basis of his social and religious behavior. With the labeling of their assessment, the speakers assure themselves of their higher moral quality. Especially they dispute the religious quality and reliability of the other's message. It is also possible that the different behavior is understood as an act of "rebellion and sedition" (with Deut. 21:20 as the postulated primary background of Q 7:34: Kee 1999, 329; Ebner 1998, 156; Modica 2008, 73).

4.4.6. Conclusion

The accusation that Jesus is a glutton and winebibber and a friend of tax collectors and sinners is a remembrance of a contemporaneous polemic against Jesus. The two reproaches form a unity, which comprehends Jesus's preaching and works as a whole. The reproach is a negative picture of Jesus's table fellowship. From the negative, a picture of Jesus's proclamation can be developed that depicts him as an eschatological messenger of the kingdom of God. In his table fellowship, the community committed to and vouchsafed by God celebrates in a joyful feast as a "fragment" of the kingdom that is already a reality. The enjoyment of wine is related to the abundance of wine, which is reflected in numerous eschatological concepts of the end-time feast.

The polemic serves the purpose of discrediting Jesus and his followers and of warning against fellowship with them. The derogatory warning against the glutton and winebibber is primarily a wisdom argument, by which cultic elements lead to the religiously motivated, social exclusion of the polluting association with tax collectors and sinners.

Kee, Howard Clark. 1999. "Jesus: A Glutton and Drunkard." In *Authenticating the Words of Jesus*, edited by Bruce Chilton and Craig A. Evans, 311–32. NTTS 28/1. Leiden, Boston, and Cologne.

Labahn, Michael. 2010. *Der Gekommene als Wiederkommender: Die Logienquelle als erzählte Geschichte*, 221–26, 279–80. Arbeiten zur Bibel und ihrer Geschichte 32. Leipzig.

Modica, Joseph B. 2008. "Jesus as Glutton and Drunkard: The 'Excesses' of Jesus." In *Who Do My Opponents Say That I Am? An Investigation of the Accusations against the Historical Jesus*, edited by Scot McKnight and Joseph B. Modica, 50–73. London.

Pokorný, Petr. 2009. "Demoniac and Drunkard: John the Baptist and Jesus according to Q 7:33–34." In *Jesus Research: An International Perspective*, edited by James H. Charlesworth and Petr Pokorný, 170–81. Princeton-Prague Symposia Series on the Historical Jesus 1. Grand Rapids and Cambridge.

Witetschek, Stephan. 2007. "The Stigma of a Glutton and Drunkard: Q 7,34 in Historical and Sociological Perspective." *ETL* 83: 135–54.

Michael Labahn

5. The Passion Events

5.1. The Entrance into Jerusalem, the Cleansing of the Temple (Jesus's Attitude toward the Temple)

5.1.1. Jesus, Jerusalem, and the Temple as Attested by the Canonical Gospels

The narrative plot of the oldest gospel might lead one to believe that Jesus visited the temple in Jerusalem only at the end of his life, that is, as the destination of his programmatic journey from Galilee to Jerusalem (cf. Mark 10:33; 11:11) in order to carry out the "cleansing of the temple" (Mark 11:15–18) as the prelude to his arrest and execution soon thereafter. At least for Jesus's public ministry, this plot is also adopted by the other two synoptic authors; although the infancy gospels (see Matt. 2:1, 11, e.g.) situate the hometown of Jesus's family in Bethlehem near Jerusalem, in Luke's infancy narrative, as also in the first chapters of Acts, one can even speak of a pronounced centrality of the temple (Luke 1:9–23; 2:22–39; 2:41; 2:42–51; Acts 2:46; 3:1–10; 5:20–21, 25, 42). But the Gospel of John paints us a different picture. The Fourth Gospel suggests that during his public ministry Jesus did not only go to Jerusalem one time programmatically at the end of his life but was present repeatedly at the festivals in Jerusalem, where he also preached: John 2:13, 5:1, 7:2–10, 10:22–23, and 11:55. Even if we assume that the Johannine depiction is theologically reshaped, it nevertheless essentially merits the higher credibility in this case. It was Jesus's decisive aspiration to reach *all Israel* with his message. He clears the way for the restitution of all Israel, for instance, in the symbolic installation of the Twelve, which prefigures the expected eschatological restitution of the twelve tribes of Israel (cf. Isa. 60:4). But the gathering of *all Israel* is also made plain in Jesus's special turning to sinners, the poor, the sick, and the marginalized, which especially includes the "lost sheep of the house of Israel" (Matt. 10:6). However, this objective would have been impossible if Jesus had carried out his mission solely in Galilee, and Jerusalem had gone unnoticed. Indeed, it can be expected that Jesus made use of the pilgrim festivals, for which Galilean pilgrims regularly traveled to Jerusalem, in order to proclaim his message also at the center of his religion.

The reference to only one journey of Jesus to Jerusalem throughout his public ministry is due to the narrative plot of the Synoptics. To start with, it was to the credit of the earliest evangelist Mark to assemble the multiple individual narrative episodes about Jesus into a chronological and regional order. The shift from Galilee to Judea begins in Mark 10:1 and takes Jesus by way of Jericho (10:46) finally to Bethphage, Bethany, and Jerusalem (11:1). In this narratological outline the three predictions of the passion (8:31; 9:31; 10:32–34) assume a central position; these are counteracted by the misunderstanding of the disciples (8:32; 9:32–34; 10:35–41). In the course of this, the blind Bartimaeus is a figure with a positive identity and a contrast against the ignorant disciples. In spite of his blindness, Bartimaeus sees more clearly than Jesus's disciples, who see but do not yet believe: he "followed Jesus on the way" (10:52). No later than here it becomes clear that Mark has depicted Jesus's programmatic journey to Jerusalem as an example for each person who wishes to follow Jesus through cross and suffering. Luke took up this concept and developed it independently and in accordance with his Jerusalem-centricity. For Luke it is clear: "A prophet cannot perish anywhere outside of Jerusalem" (Luke 13:33). Accordingly, Jesus's journey to Jerusalem is introduced in a celebratory way with the resonant saying: "When the days drew near for him to be taken up, he set his face to go to Jerusalem." The so-called Lukan travel narrative then stretches over ten long chapters from Luke 9:51 to the arrival in Jerusalem in 19:28.

In addition to the Johannine report, we also have multiple positive references to the temple in the Synoptics (cf. Mark 1:40–44; 11:11; 12:35, 41–44; 14:49; cf. also the parallels in Matthew and Luke; further: John 5:14; 7:14, 28; 8:2, 20; 10:23; 18:20; cf. Ådna 2000, 130–31, 434–40). These positive reminiscences suggest that throughout his life, Jesus never called the temple into question in a fundamental way. This being the case, passages critical of the temple—especially Jesus's prophetic action, which is not entirely accurately designated the "cleansing of the temple" (see below)—must be interpreted against a different background. This can be found without difficulty in basic theological currents of early Judaism.

5.1.2. Early Jewish Positions on the Temple

In early Judaism we can find a widespread assumption of a cultic insufficiency of the temple—which of course does not categorically call the temple cult into question (cf. Paesler 1999, 40–89 and 150–66; Evans 1992, 236–41; Ådna 2000, 122–27). In broad circles the dominant notion was that in the eschaton the earthly temple in Jerusalem would be replaced by a new temple not made by humans but by God himself. This applies most prominently to the community behind the Qumran writings, who considered the current temple to be desecrated. According to 4Q174 iii 7, the Qumran community replaces the temple with a מקדש אדם, a temple of living people, who offer it works of praise, מעשי התודה, instead of animal sacrifices (cf. Ådna 2000, 105). Yet in spite of this severe critique, the Qumran community still sends consecrated gifts to the temple, as Josephus (*Ant.* 18.19) and Philo (*Prob.* 75) report in agreement. Therefore it is clear: even if the current temple is desecrated in the eyes of the Qumran community because of unworthy cultic personnel and fallacious rites, the fundamental claim that this is the house of God remains valid in spite of all criticism. Similarly, T. Mos. 5:5 and 6:1 criticize the impurity of temple priests, and likewise Pss. Sol. 2:3–5, 2 Bar. 10:18, Jub. 23:21b, and Josephus, *J.W.* 4.323. Hence, Jub. 1:29 also expects the construction of a new temple in the eschaton. Also, 4 Ezra 10:46–55 and 1 En. 90:28–29 envisage a new, eschatological temple. However, there were also similar tendencies outside of Palestine in nonapocalyptic Judaism, for instance, in Philo. He states in *Spec.* 1.66–67 that God has made the entire world (σύμπαντα κόσμον) his temple; the temple made with human hands (χειρόκμητον) in Jerusalem is only a concession to human notions. All these examples show that in the Judaism of that period the temple could obviously be criticized without categorically calling the validity of the temple cult into question. Such tendencies can be seen as a continuation of the prophetic critiques of the temple in the Old Testament (cf. Isa. 1:10–17; 66:1–2; Jer. 7:3–7; 26:18/Mic. 3:12; Hos. 4:4–6; Amos 5:21–24). Indeed, the position of John the Baptist is situated entirely in line with this. Although he is a son of a temple priest (if one may believe Luke 1:5 on this), vis-à-vis the temple cult he nevertheless proclaims an alternative possibility for the forgiveness of sins by means of his baptism. On the basis of the plausibility of context (*Kontextplausibilität*), one may also assume for Jesus that he neither categorically called the temple into question nor declared the temple cult obsolete. Rather, Jesus's critique of the temple is to be located quite in line with prophetic symbolic actions, as we will see in what follows.

5.1.3. The Entrance into Jerusalem

Even if in the course of his public ministry Jesus repeatedly visited Jerusalem (see above), a special significance can nevertheless be assigned to his final visit. During this last journey, he quite intentionally seeks to bring about a decision of either belief or rejection on the part of his hearers. Against Mark's *ex eventu* depiction, we can assume that Jesus does not go to Jerusalem to die but rather in a final, ultimate attempt to confront the people with his message. In doing this he intentionally aims at the heart of Jewish life: the temple. In the light of the kingdom of God, the dawning of which Jesus indeed expected as immediately imminent, he sees himself as empowered for such a prophetic escalation. His entrance into Jerusalem is already programmatic for this: Jesus's disciples also expect the immediately imminent dawning of the kingdom of God. In the crying of "hosanna," clear messianic expectations resonate; in the hope of the "kingdom of our father David" (Mark 11:10) and in the acclamation "king of Israel" (John 12:13), one can even detect political hopes (see Acts 1:6 as well). Even though Jesus had repudiated being misunderstood as a political revolutionary throughout his life (Matt. 5:5–9; Matt. 5:39 par. Luke 6:29; Matt. 10:16 par. Luke 10:3), nevertheless, his talk about the "kingdom of God" could arouse such misunderstandings. Most probably, Jesus never used the title "king of the Jews" for himself. Nevertheless, the inscription on the cross in all four Gospels mentions as the basis for Jesus's execution the title "king of the Jews" (Mark 15:26 par.; John 19:19)—a misunderstanding due to Jesus's announcing his expectation of the "kingdom of God." To be sure, in his claim Jesus was by no means *apolitical*—the kingdom of God proclaimed by him would sweep away and turn all earthly systems of injustice inside out. Yet this claim is not enforced by human beings with the force of arms, but rather by God himself. Therefore, one could rather call Jesus's claim *prepolitical* (Stegemann and Stegemann ²1997, 183). Jesus's objective is primarily religious, which then certainly indirectly disrupts political realities.

5.1.4. Jesus's Temple Prophecy: Temple Action and Temple Saying

Just as Jesus's entrance into Jerusalem can be understood as a prophetic sign for the immediately imminent dawning of the kingdom of God, his temple prophecy should be interpreted in the same way. For Old Testament prophets, prophetic symbolic action and interpretive prophetic sayings were often interlinked (cf. Jer. 27; Ezek. 4:12–13; Hos. 1–2). Perhaps Jesus's contemporaries rejected his urgent call to repentance with reference to the salvific presence of the temple. Then

Jesus's response could have sounded like Jer. 7:4–7: "Do not trust in these deceptive words: The temple of the Lord, the temple of the Lord, the temple of the Lord is here! For only if you reform your ways and your deeds from the ground up . . . then will I dwell with you." But perhaps Jesus's claim to the temple simply represented a fundamental characteristic of his message: entirely within the context of the temple critique of early Judaism (see above), Jesus also expected a new temple at the end of time. As the messenger of the kingdom of God, it was consequently his obligation to reclaim this temple in terms of his message. For Jesus, not the abrogation of the temple but rather the claim to the temple comes to light here. Jesus's action in the temple (Mark 11:15–19 par.) was a spectacular symbolic activity, probably in the Court of the Gentiles, presumably at Solomon's Portico (cf. Söding 1992, 50). One should preferably describe this "action in the temple" not as a "cleansing of the temple," because for Jesus this was neither a *cultic* cleansing nor a cleansing of *despicable marketers*, but a prophetic symbolic action. This becomes clear especially in Jesus's temple saying (Mark 14:58; John 2:19); both—temple action and temple saying—belong together (cf. Theissen and Merz ²1997, 381; Ebner 2003, 183), although the two are reported in the same text only in the Gospel of John (2:13–22). Even though in Mark 14:58 the saying occurs only in the mouth of "false witnesses," the parallel testimony in John 2:19, the high accuracy of which fits with the action in the temple, as well as similar traditions in Q 13:34–35 and Mark 13:2, leads to the conclusion that this is an authentic saying of Jesus (cf. Theissen and Merz ²1997, 381). Apparently the early Christians had a hard time with Jesus's temple critique, as the reference to "false witnesses" in Mark 14:58, the additional spiritualized statement with reference to Jesus's body in John 2:19, and the rendering in the subjunctive in Matt. 26:61 attest. Luke took the saying completely out of the mouth of Jesus and ascribed it to Stephen (Acts 6:14). Recently, Dieter-Alex Koch (2013, 175–76) argued against the historicity of the temple action, but Gerd Theissen and Annette Merz (²1997, 381) correctly judge: "A prophecy that created so much embarrassment and difficulty was not put in the mouth of Jesus only retrospectively" (in this same sense also Ebner 2003, 183).

In the temple action and the temple saying Jesus claims in a prophetic manner his message of the coming kingdom of God as the ultimately binding interpretation of the eschatological saving will of God. The temple cult also has to be subordinated to this message. With this, however, no *abrogation* of the temple cult is intended, but rather an *integration* of the institution of the temple in Jesus's concept of the presently dawning kingdom of God.

Jesus must have been aware of the consequences of this action. In this prophetic escalation he knowingly and deliberately cuts to the nerve center of the religious elites of that time. This symbolic action is not a rejection of the temple independently of any context, but rather a reinterpretation of the temple rooted within the context of early Judaism (see above the early Jewish critique of the temple). For Jesus, with his symbolic entrance into Jerusalem and with his prophetic provocation in the temple area, the final phase of the proclamation of the kingdom of God is initiated and the final stage of prophetic escalation is reached. He himself is now prepared to avow for his message with his entire existence. Even if his struggle on the Mount of Olives (Mark 14:26, 32–41) is dramatically and theologically embellished, it demonstrates historically correctly that Jesus was aware of the implications of his action. From the Garden of Gethsemane Jesus would only have had to flee over the Mount of Olives into the Jewish wilderness in order to withdraw from the grasp of his opponents. However, here too Jesus seeks a prophetic confrontation. In spite of consciously accepting his failure to convince the Jerusalemites, he still counts on the dawning of the kingdom of God, as the proposition in Mark 14:25 shows, which in essence is doubtless authentic: "I will never again drink of the fruit of the vine until that day when I drink it anew in the kingdom of God." In spite of accepting his violent death ("never again drink"), he expects the kingdom of God to come ("drink it anew in the kingdom of God"). Here one has to agree with Martin Hengel (1978, 170): "That Jesus would have been caught unsuspectingly unaware of his arrest and conviction is completely implausible." The temple was a religious (for the Sadducees) and political (for the Romans) nerve center; disruptive actions were immediately punished—Jesus must have been aware of this. After Jesus's previous provocations (entrance into Jerusalem and the temple action), the high priests doubtless worried that Jesus could incite a popular uprising at Passover: "If we let him go on like this . . . the Romans will come and will take away our holy place and our nation" (John 11:48). Consequently they wanted to get Jesus quickly out of the way before Passover, as Mark 14:2 suggests: "not during the festival, so that there may be no riot among the people" (thus John [18:28; 19:31] has the better chronology, because there, against the Synoptics, the death of Jesus is expected before Passover evening; cf. Theissen and Merz [2]1997, 152). Jesus was intentionally willing to risk all these consequences of his temple action—not to seek death, but to usher the people by prophetic escalation into a situation of decision making.

John 2:12–22 situates Jesus's temple action already at the beginning of his public ministry. This is historically improbable and the result of the narrative intention of the Fourth Gospel: right at the beginning of his public ministry, Jesus claims the temple for himself. Other than in the Synoptics, the trigger for Jesus's conviction according to John 11 is the stylized resuscitation of Lazarus as the last of the seven "signs," rather than his action in the temple.

5.1.5. The New Temple in the Kingdom of God

From what has been said, it becomes clear that Jesus neither "abrogated" the temple nor wanted to found a new cult against the temple (against Theissen and Merz [2]1997, 382–83, who see the temple action and the Last Supper as a "foundational cultic symbolic action"). The question of the fundamental validity of the temple was no more up for debate for Jesus than it was for other groups within early Judaism (see above). In accordance with this, the early church upheld the continuing validity of the temple cult, as the texts from Acts cited above point out (albeit in the stylizing narrative pragmatics of Luke). Jesus's action in the temple—interpreted by his temple saying—was thus simply a prophetic symbolic action in order to underscore the urgency of belief in the kingdom of God.

Yet at the same time, the question of how Jesus conceived of the eschatological destiny of the temple remains unanswered. The expectation of a new temple not made with human hands but by God was widespread in the Judaism of the period (see above). However, did Jesus share such concepts, as Mark 14:58 could suggest, or are early Jewish Hellenistic expectations, which later Christians adopted, reflected in this saying (cf. Philo, *Spec.* 1.66–67)? How did Jesus perceive the kingdom of God in relation to the temple? The Qumran Sabbath Hymns create a strong connection between the kingdom of God and the temple cult (cf. Schwemer 1991, 116–18). Participation in the Sabbath liturgy signifies participating in the heavenly temple cult; this heavenly temple will supersede the defiled earthly temple in the end times. The presently occurring participation of the members of Qumran already in the heavenly temple cult through the Sabbath liturgy becomes a prolepsis of the reign of God, which indeed is already realized in heaven (cf. Schwemer 1991, 76, 81–84, 94–103; cf. on this the especially well preserved second and third Sabbath Hymns of Qumran). For Jesus, too, the kingdom of God in heaven is already realized ("your kingdom come, your will be done on earth as it is in heaven," Matt. 6:10). Sabbath worship, however, does not serve as a prolepsis of the kingdom of God, but rather Jesus's miracles of healing and his forgiveness of sins do. Precisely in the restitution of prelapsarian holiness and sanctity, the eschatological event is taking shape: according to the *analogy of primordial time and end time*, one expects that in *eschatological* time the *protological* integrity of human beings would be restored (cf. Tiwald 2011, 371, 379). Perhaps one should take these expectations to apply not only to Jesus's miraculous healings and forgiveness of sins but also to his understanding of the temple. The assumption that in the eschaton the protological divine immediacy is restored, is found as early as Joel 3:1–5 (MT, LXX), to which Acts 2:17–21 also refers. Similar concepts are also featured in Rev. 21:22, where the heavenly Jerusalem is entirely without a temple, because the immediate presence of God replaces the temple in the eschatological Jerusalem, whereby the entire city becomes a single temple. The analogy to the expected eschatological immediacy of the Spirit in the book of Joel could then well lead to the fact that for Jesus — as it is stated in John 4:20-24—any place where the Spirit of God is can be a temple. Even if Jesus's detailed notions about the eschatological temple can no longer be reconstructed with precision, concepts that the believing community equated with the temple were carried on further in early Christianity (1 Cor. 3:16-17; 6:19-20; 2 Cor. 6:16; 1 Pet. 2:5). Whether such concepts go back as far as Jesus himself or represent an early Christian adaptation of early Jewish patterns of interpretation can no longer be decided definitively. But in any case, for the historical Jesus, no "abrogation" or rejection of the temple per se can be found. What we find instead is a new interpretation of the temple under the auspices of the dawning kingdom of God.

Ådna, Jostein. 2000. *Jesu Stellung zum Tempel: Die Tempelaktion und das Tempelwort als Ausdruck seiner messianischen Sendung.* WUNT II 119. Tübingen.

Evans, Craig A. 1992. "Opposition to the Temple: Jesus and the Dead Sea Scrolls." In *Jesus and the Dead Sea Scrolls*, edited by James Charlesworth, 235-53. New York.

Paesler, Kurt. 1999. *Das Tempelwort Jesu: Die Tradition von Tempelzerstörung und Tempelerneuerung im Neuen Testament.* FRLANT 184. Göttingen.

Söding, Thomas. 1992. "Die Tempelaktion Jesu." *TTZ* 101: 36-64.

Tiwald, Markus. 2011. "ΑΠΟ ΔΕ ΑΡΧΗΣ ΚΤΙΣΕΩΣ . . . (Mk 10,6): Die Entsprechung von Protologie und Eschatologie als Schlüssel für das Tora-Verständnis Jesu." In *Die Memoria Jesu: Kontinuität und Diskontinuität der Überlieferung*, edited by Ulrich Busse, Michael Reichardt, and Michael Theobald, 367-80. BBB 166. Bonn.

Markus Tiwald

5.2. Jesus's Last Supper

All four canonical Gospels (but not the hypothetical sayings source Q, additional references to the passion scattered in New Testament writings, or early extracanonical writings such as the Gospel of Thomas or the Gospel of Peter) tell us about Jesus's last meal together with his disciples before his arrest in Jerusalem (Matt. 26:20-30; Mark 14:17-26; Luke 22:14-38; John 13:1-18:1). In 1 Cor. 11:23-25, Paul also speaks about a meal of the "Lord" (κύριος), Jesus, on the night of his betrayal. It is disputable to what extent this evidence presents a multiple independent attestation for the assessment of the historicity of the event: perhaps an older account of the passion underlies the presentation of the passion event in Mark. The Gospels of Matthew and Luke are supposedly literarily dependent on the Gospel of Mark; and the Gospel of John probably exhibits references to the Synoptics, such that similarities of the accounts of the Last Supper could be explained by literary relationships. The words of institution (1 Cor. 11:24–25—an indication of a preliterary stage of tradition?) could also have their own history; their beginning is hardly to be found in early Christian worship, but rather in catechesis. So perhaps only very few sources constitute the origin of the tradition.

However, this does not determine the historical reliability of these witnesses. If one does not wish to assume that Jesus of Nazareth went to meet his arrest in Jerusalem completely unaware—nothing speaks in favor of this surmise—one ought to assume that a final meal of a farewell character took place. Based on this consideration, important elements of the earliest tradition about the Last Supper can be tested for their historical plausibility. In addition to a general interest in the history of the event, such an examination is suggested by the sources: they depict a unique event of the past at a particular time in a particular location that carries time-transcending significance and serves as the starting point of a practice to be emulated.

The time of the meal according to Mark 14:12, 17 par. was the night after the "first day of the feast of Unleavened Bread, when the Passover lamb is sacrificed"— a somewhat inexact phrase (E. Sanders [2]1994, 132–33), which means the night of the Passover meal. Thus this account leaves no room for doubt that Jesus's meal would have been a Passover meal, even if all typically assumed elements of the Passover meal at the time of Jesus are not present (although in reality we know extremely little about that; cf. Stemberger 1990; Leonhard 2006, esp. 73–118). By contrast, the meal scene in John 13:1–2 is explicitly dated *before* the Passover feast. The motivated (admittedly only vague and implicit; critically Pitre 2015, 325–30) synchronization of Jesus's death—not his crucifixion—with the slaughter of the Passover lamb may have theological origins (additional motifs of Passover are found in John 19:31–37; cf. Exod. 12:9, 46; Ps. 34:20; see further Zech. 12:10; Jeremias [4]1967, 75–76). Such theological motivation nevertheless does not exclude the possibility that, by this redating, John also wanted to correct the well-known synoptic tradition with regard to the facts. Chronologically both the synoptic and the Johannine datings are possible; nevertheless, they lead back to different years for the time of Jesus's execution (at least if one takes as historically accurate the note about the Sabbath in Mark 15:42 par. Matt. 27:62 par. Luke 23:54 par. John 19:31, 42 or Mark 16:1; Matt. 28:1; Luke 24:1; John 20:1). If one compares the theological motifs associated with the Passover meal in contemporaneous Judaism, which are connected with Jesus's Last Supper in the earliest Christian tradition, then the convergence is of a rather general kind (Löhr 2008, 112–16). Hence, the assumption that Jesus's meal that was not originally connected with the Passover was then designed as a Passover meal for theological reasons in the early Christian tradition is hardly plausible. In 1 Cor. 11:23–25 the Passover meal is not mentioned; there is no consensus on whether this means that Paul did not know of the coincidence or that he presumed it (so Hengel 2006a, 462–65, 483–84). Christ himself is referred to as the Passover lamb in 1 Cor. 5:7; also, compare the *mazzot* motif in context; however, these observations do not settle the question of dating. Incidentally, it is also conceivable that the circle around Jesus gathered together before the beginning of the festival to observe a meal commemorating Passover.

The location of the event is Jerusalem according to the unanimous testimony of the Gospels. The comparatively detailed account of the location of the room for the supper (Mark 14:12–16 par. Luke 22:7–13; abridged in Matt. 26:17–19) could allude to a memory of a concrete location that was still being passed on (on the later tradition of the location of the "upper room" in the early church according to Mark 14:15 par. or Acts 1:13 on the Southwestern Hill of Jerusalem, see Küchler 2007, 605–6).

The participants in the meal are identified in Mark 14:17 and Matt. 26:20 as the Twelve. Luke 22:14 speaks of the apostles, which likewise means the Twelve. Earlier Luke had mentioned that Peter and John prepared for the meal; in all the Synoptics the prediction of Peter's denial is linked to the scene of the meal. The focus on the closest circle of Jesus's disciples is a necessity for the sake of the narrative because of the prediction of the betrayal by Judas integrated into the meal scene. But is the report also historically plausible if one assumes that the Last Supper was intentionally celebrated by Jesus as a farewell meal and the Twelve had in fact already originated in Jesus's lifetime? According to John 13:5, 22, and elsewhere, the meal takes place in the circle of the disciples (v. 1 speaks of "his own"; according to v. 33, Jesus addresses them as "children"; according to 15:12–15, explicitly as "friends"), individual disciples such as Peter (13:24, 36–37), Thomas (14:5), Philip (14:8), and Judas (14:22) are also mentioned, as well as the anonymous disciple "whom Jesus loved" (13:23). 1 Cor. 11 presumes the presence of several people without mentioning them.

Whereas later reports about practices in ancient Judaism identify the Passover festival as a family meal, the earliest tradition of Jesus's Last Supper depicts a strikingly different picture: supposedly only a small circle exclusively of men (qualified to participate in the temple cult?) participated. The historical assessment of this report depends on that of the existence and significance of the Twelve in Jesus's lifetime.

The course of the meal is only hinted at in the sources that have been mentioned. Mark's report (and that of Matthew, who follows him) refers to the following elements:

14:18: lying at the table and eating together;

14:20: dipping the bread into the bowl (τρύβλιον);

14:22: bread;

14:23: cup, it follows from v. 25 that a cup with wine is in view;

14:26: concluding hymn.

The Lukan account (on the text-critical problem, cf. Rese 1975–1976) deviates more clearly: in the context of the meal, the Passover lamb (or Passover food in general) is mentioned (22:15), the cup is mentioned twice (vv. 17, 20—here the cup "after supper"; see also 1 Cor. 11:25). By contrast (and as in Paul) the bowl is not mentioned (cf. v. 21). Not only the words of institution but also additional statements of Jesus and the responses of his disciples (vv. 24–28) are part of the Lukan meal scene. The concluding hymn is not mentioned.

The Johannine meal scene reports that Jesus washes the feet of his disciples (13:4–5, 12). In addition, lying at the table is worked out as a motif (v. 23), and the dipping of a morsel (of bread?) is mentioned (vv. 26–27). Moreover, the scene contains some dialogues and, above all, extensive speeches of Jesus. The introduction in 17:1 and the address of Jesus's speech to God make the following words a long intercessory prayer. Whether the hymn (ὑμνεῖν) in the tradition in Mark and Matthew points to a specific Jewish meal ritual is just as uncertain as its more specific determination as a recitation of the Hallel (Pss. 113–118); the association of this practice with the Passover meal for the time of Jesus is unverified (Stemberger 1990, 369–70).

The indication or Jesus's *designation of the betrayer* by name (Mark 14:17–21; Matt. 26:21–25; Luke 22:21–22; John 13:21–30) is also part of the portrayal of the Gospels. At the level of the narrative, naming or not naming Judas Iscariot makes no difference; also, in Mark (3:19) and in Luke (6:16) the betrayer is already known to the readers from a literary prolepsis. At the same time, it is possible to determine that the oldest available account of the Last Supper does not explicitly refer to Judas Iscariot, whose name in early Christian tradition as a whole is firmly connected to the betrayal. The passage from John 13 could be interpreted as an attempt to reconcile the two specified traditions with each other.

The parts of the Last Supper tradition referred to as *the words of institution* (Mark 14:22–25 par. Matt. 26:26–29 par. Luke 22:[14–18] 19–20; 1 Cor. 11:23–25) are small pieces of the narrative that place two sayings of Jesus at the center for the interpretation of what happens in the meal with the bread and wine. The reference to "memory" (ἀνάμνησις) in 1 Cor. 11:24 par. Luke 22:19 as well as especially the command for repetition in 1 Cor. 11:25 point beyond the narration of the original situation, probably in the early Christian ritual praxis (cf. also 1 Cor. 11:17–18, 20, 33), while the so-called abstinence saying in Mark 14:25 par.

Matt. 26:29 looks ahead to Jesus's eschatic continued existence without explicitly using the catchword "resurrection." Jesus's action over the bread (ἄρτος; the situational context, not the lexeme itself, makes it possible to think of unleavened bread) according to 1 Cor. 11 involves taking the bread, giving thanks (i.e., a prayer; the synoptic tradition mentions a hymn of praise), breaking the bread, and offering an interpretive saying. The reference to the cup is narrated more tersely; however, a prayer of thanksgiving and the passing of the cup (as in the synoptic texts) could also be meant. Two insights are noteworthy here: (1) In the context of a Jewish (celebratory) meal, aside from the interpretive sayings, nothing is striking beyond a specific celebratory rite (D. Smith 2003, 133–72). In this scene Jesus takes on the role of the head of the house or the host. (2) The words of institution obviously do not aim at a complete depiction of the event, but rather at the interpretation of bread and wine. Thus, this interpretation is in fact rendered verbatim, but not Jesus's preceding prayer. Therefore, the absence of specific details can by no means be adduced for the assessment of the historicity of the account. At the same time, it is nevertheless clear that the words of institution provide an intentionally shaped and focused tradition about Jesus, but not a neutral report.

Jesus's sayings identify the bread shared among the disciples with Jesus's body (σῶμα) (1 Cor. 11:24: "for you"; Luke 22:19 appends: "given"), and the single cup passed around (with wine and perhaps water) with the "new covenant in my blood" (1 Cor. 11:25; Luke 22:20 adds: "that is poured out for you") or with "my blood of the covenant that is poured out for many" (Mark 14:24; Matt. 26:28 appends: "for the forgiveness of sins"). These formulations point with distinct clarity to Jesus's death, which is understood as salvific for others. The word over the bread can be understood from the word over the cup in the context of the concept of the salvific sacrifice; however, in itself this interpretation is not compelling. Also, the talk about the body can be interpreted in the sense of the entire embodied existence up until death. With the talk of the shed blood, the cup saying refers to Jesus's violent death that is efficacious "on behalf of" (ὑπέρ) others. An allusion to the fourth Servant Song in Isa. 52–53 (esp. 53:12) is possible (Wolff ²1950, 64–66), but it is not clearly elaborated. If these formulations alone do not compel an interpretation in the context of cultic sacrifice at all, then the talk of the "blood of the covenant" in Mark 14:24 points to the ritual of ratification of the covenant in Exod. 24, especially v. 8. The Pauline interpretive saying in 1 Cor. 11:25 alludes to the concept of the new covenant (Jer. 31:31). However, this intertextual reference is not a sufficient explanation, because Jeremiah does not talk about a covenant made with blood like the blood or death of a human being. Hence the version transmitted in Paul might also take up Exod. 24 indirectly. However, to determine such a common thread does not mean tracing it directly back to Jesus.

That the concept of the atoning blood of the Passover lamb in some way impinged on the words of institution is improbable because the premise—the existence of such a concept at the time of Jesus—is far from certain (Schlund 2005, 225).

On various occasions attempts have been made to reconstruct an *original version of the words of institution* or the very words of Jesus contained in them. But the verbatim reduction of the Markan and Pauline versions, which with their meager but significant differences stand at the beginning of the development, can hardly be achieved. In a historical perspective, this evidence in the sphere of ancient tradition is not surprising. The attempt to rediscover elements of the characteristic voice of Jesus in the Greek text (Jeremias ⁴1967, 194–95) has been extensively discussed; the introductory "Amen, I say to you" in Mark 14:25, the *passivum divinum* in Luke 22:16, as well as Jesus's (doutbtless too) general "preference for parables, comparisons, and parabolic actions" (195) are mentioned.

It is contested whether the essential common characteristics developed in the tradition—the interpretation of bread and wine, reference to the anticipation of death, and its soteriological meaning—are due to a reliable memory of the historical Last Supper. This holds also, when one investigates the connection of the tradition of the Last Supper with Jesus's other activities. However, from such a comparison there are no compelling arguments against an essentially reliable tradition of Jesus's Last Supper.

The following aspects should be addressed in particular.

1. In the Gospels, Jesus's Last Supper is only one (in Mark: the last) of several community meals of Jesus that are recounted. Like other meal scenes, this account is especially shaped by Jesus's sayings and actions that are theologically highly significant. In distinction from some other meals, in the presentation of the Last Supper no accent is placed on fellowship with social outsiders.

2. The significance of the Twelve for the portrayal of Jesus's pre-Easter appearance is assured from texts such as Mark 3:13–19 par., 6:7–13 par., and John 6:66–71 (cf. 1 Cor. 15:5). There are good reasons to hold the existence of this group as historically probable, until the last days before Jesus's death in Jerusalem.

3. Among the Synoptics, only Luke mentions beforehand a Passover festival to which Jesus travels to Jerusalem (2:41–42). This is not so in the Gospel of John: John 2:13 and 6:4 mention earlier Passover festivals at which Jesus was present. The difference is explained (and determined) by the differently estimated total duration of Jesus's public appearance. This evidence allows the conclusion that an observance of one of the main Jewish festivals by the Jesus movement by all means corresponded to the contemporaneous practice, even if we cannot assume for sure that this became the occasion for a repeated pilgrimage to Jerusalem.

4. The concept of the covenant, which shapes the words of institution, is alien to the rest of the Jesus tradition; it is also not identifiable with the announcement

of God's kingdom (Vogel 1996, 88–92). Just this surprising finding speaks against rather than for the assumption that only the post-Easter taking up and revision of the tradition of the Last Supper brought in this motif.

5. The tradition of the Last Supper is not the only passage of the canonical Jesus tradition that points to the fourth Servant Song in Isa. 52–53. Even more than the voice of the narrator in Matt. 8:17, references to the prophetic text in John 12:38, and the saying of the Baptist in John 1:29, the self-referential statements in Mark 9:12b and 10:45, as well as (in the context of the passion narrative) Luke 22:37, indicate the meaning the passage must have had for understanding Jesus's ministry. The texts referred to in Mark associate the concept of the Servant of God with that of the Son of Man, which has a parallel in the Book of Similitudes in 1 Enoch. This would surely be exceptional but nevertheless conceivable not only as a motif of the portrayal but also as a factual claim of Jesus for himself in the context of the Judaism of that time (Boyarin 2012). On the other hand, anyone who takes superhuman claims of a human being to be in principle excluded as historical will also come to a negative judgment here.

6. With their reference to suffering, death, and resurrection, the predictions about the future destiny of the Son of Man in Mark 8:31–33 par., 9:30–32 par., and 10:32–34 par. stand especially close to Jesus's statements about himself in the words of institution, but without being completely identical in substance. They provide structure and the orientation toward the passion for the narratives of the gospel; this holds especially for the third passage. The assumption that these pieces—at least in their redactional form—are formulated *ex eventu* (or *ex narratione*) and are integral parts of the redaction and composition of the Gospels is obvious. In addition, the Gospels attribute to Jesus further statements about these announcements that express directly or indirectly the expectation of a violent end without direct reference to the resurrection hope (Mark 11:27–33 par.; 12:1–9 par.; Luke 11:49–51 par.; 13:34–35 par.). Clearly the biblical-Jewish motif of the violent destiny of the prophets (Steck 1967) had an impact. Especially the differences between such sayings and the portrayal of the passion can be evaluated as evidence for their (partial) authenticity. Nevertheless, an exact reconstruction of the sayings of the historical Jesus, in the same way as an introspection into his thinking and feelings, lies beyond what historical work is able to ascertain from the extant sources.

Jeremias, Joachim. ⁴1967. *Die Abendmahlsworte Jesu*. Göttingen.
Pitre, Brant. 2015. *Jesus and the Last Supper*. Grand Rapids and Cambridge.

Hermut Löhr

473

5.3. The Trials of Jesus

5.3.1. A Jewish and a Roman Trial?

The Roman trial and execution of Jesus are mentioned by Tacitus in his *Annales* (ca. 115 CE) and by Josephus in his *Antiquitates* (ca. 93 CE). Tacitus, having mentioned that the emperor Nero blamed and punished Christians for the devastating fire in Rome in 64, goes on to explain what kind of people the Christians were, why they were called by that name, and who the founder of this new movement was: "Christus, the founder of the name, had undergone the death penalty in the reign of Tiberius, by sentence of the procurator Pontius Pilatus, and the pernicious superstition was checked for a moment" (Tacitus, *Ann.* 15.44).

Josephus mentions the trial of Jesus in connection with various disturbances in the province of Judea during the governorship of Pontius Pilate (26–36 CE). There are three Christian interpolations in the received text; when they are removed, the text reads as follows: "At this time there appeared Jesus, a wise man. For he was a doer of startling deeds, a teacher of people who receive the truth with pleasure. And he gained a following both among many Jews and among many of Greek origin. And when Pilate, because of an accusation made by the leading men among us, condemned him to the cross, those who had loved him previously did not cease to do so. And up until this very day the tribe of Christians (named after him) has not died out" (Josephus, *Ant.* 18.63–64; for a thorough discussion, see Meier 1991, 56–88; for a history of scholarship, see Whealey 2003). Here we observe that Josephus introduces a piece of information that Tacitus was either unaware of or did not care about, namely, that Jewish leaders brought an accusation (ἔνδειξις) against Jesus: they accused their fellow Jew, and Pilate condemned him.

The Gospel of Mark is the oldest writing dealing with the trial—or trials—of Jesus. It was probably written around 69 CE, and quite possibly in the same place as the works of Tacitus and Josephus quoted above, that is, Rome (Hengel 1984). Mark relates that Jesus was betrayed by Judas Iscariot, arrested in the Gethsemane garden, and deserted by all his disciples (Mark 14:43–52); he was brought to the palace of the high priest, denied by Peter, and found guilty of blasphemy by the Sanhedrin (14:53–72); then he was delivered to Pilate, accused of setting himself up as a king, and found guilty (15:1–15); finally, he was crucified, died, and was buried by Joseph of Arimathea (15:16–47). These are the main scenes of the Markan passion narrative.

Mark wrote about forty years after the events; Jesus was probably crucified on the fourteenth of Nisan, 30 CE (see, e.g., Meier 1991, 386–402; Riesner 1994, 43–52; cf., however, the skepticism of Bond 2013). Yet it is probable that Mark made use of an older passion narrative containing more or less the same scenes as those indicated above. This pre-Markan narrative may be considerably older than the gospel and may thus bring us comparatively close in time to the events (Pesch 1977, 1–27; Theissen 1989a, 177–211). It must be pointed out, however, that both the precise reconstruction and the dating of the pre-Markan passion narrative remain controversial (cf. the discussion by M. L. Soards in R. Brown 1994b, 1492–1524).

Mark, his precursor(s) who authored the pre-Markan passion story, and his followers Matthew, Luke, and John did not write as reporters who were just interested in the facts. Above all, they were theological teachers who wanted to instruct their audiences, and they wrote as Christian believers: "The fact *that* they tell, *what* they tell and *how* they tell it—all this is determined by their faith in the Crucified One as the resurrected Christ" (Dahl ²1961, 154). The Markan passion narrative shows how everything happened just as Jesus had predicted (Mark 8:31; 9:31; 10:33–34), as the Scriptures had foretold (Mark 14:27, 49), and hence according to the will of God. In the light of the Psalms, Jesus may be seen as a suffering righteous person (e.g., Mark 15:24, 34), but above all he is the Messiah, the king of Israel/the Jews (Mark 14:61–62; 15:2, 26; etc.), and the Son of God (Mark 14:61–62; 15:39), whose sacrifice brings salvation to "the many" (Mark 14:24; cf. 10:45). Since Mark's intention is to offer instruction regarding the identity and saving work of Jesus rather than historical facts as such, we should not expect him to be overtly interested in, for example, the technical aspects of Jewish and Roman trials. On the other hand, as Nils A. Dahl (²1961, 156) states, "even if the historical interest is never an end in itself, it is still there."

Since there are no weighty reasons to doubt that Jesus, on one hand, was sentenced and executed as a self-proclaimed "king of the Jews" (Mark 15:2, 9, 12, 18, 26), and since Jesus, on the other hand, was no political revolutionary (see, e.g., Hengel 2007; cf. Bermejo-Rubio 2014: Jesus portrayed as an anti-Roman seditionist), it seems reasonable to argue that the accusation against him was based on his claim to be the Messiah of Israel, just as the Markan passion narrative has it (Mark 14:61–62; see, e.g., Dahl ²1961, 166; Dunn 2000, 21–22; Hengel 2001, 45–63). Josephus and Mark may well be right, then, in suggesting that Jesus was condemned by Pilate on the basis of an accusation made by "the leading men" of the Jews (Josephus), that is, the Sanhedrin (Mark).

5.3.2. The Jewish Trial

However, the historicity of the Markan account of the Jewish trial of Jesus (Mark 14:53, 55–65) has been called into question. In a classic article originally published in 1931, Hans Lietzmann (1958, 257–60) argued that the Sanhedrin did have the authority to have Jesus executed; but since Jesus was not stoned to death, as he would have been had he been found guilty of blasphemy (cf. Lev. 24.14), he cannot have been condemned by the Sanhedrin; hence, Mark's account of the Jewish trial is unhistorical.

Further, early Christians could not have had any knowledge of the events at the Sanhedrin trial, since none of them was present at the occasion: "For the historian, the story stands freely in the air" (Lietzmann 1958, 254). In addition, the Markan account contains several elements that in themselves are unrealistic or anachronistic: the accusation regarding Jesus's intention to destroy the temple (Mark 14:58) is surprising; the question of the high priest whether Jesus is the Messiah, "the Son of the Blessed One" (14:61), contains Christian rather than Jewish terminology; the characterization of Jesus's answer as blasphemy (14:64) is not plausible, nor is the maltreatment of Jesus by the Sanhedrinists (14:65) (254–57).

Other scholars have repeated and refined these arguments (e.g., E. Sanders 1985a, 297–98), as well as added some new ones: for example, it has been claimed that a formal court could hardly have convened on the night of Passover (thus the Markan chronology), nor would an additional, second meeting have been held the next morning (cf. Mark 15:1); and the account of the Jewish trial of Jesus is to be understood as a reflection of an early Christian wish to incriminate the Jews and excuse the Romans (E. Sanders 1985a, 298). It has even been suggested that Mark intended to portray the Jewish trial as a parody of justice (Bond 2004, 105); hence, his account is a piece of polemic rather than a historically reliable report of what really happened.

Lietzmann's main argument—involving the competence of the Sanhedrin— has been extensively discussed (see R. Brown 1994a, 315–22, 364, for references). It has to be noted, however, that even if the Sanhedrin had had the authority to carry out the death penalty, it does not follow that it must have done so in a particular instance; it may well have deemed it prudent to submit the case to the governor (Bickermann 1935, 233–34).

Be that as it may, the Sanhedrin did in fact not have the legal authority to put people to death. It is true that Rome allowed native courts to function in the provinces and that these courts had competence also in criminal matters. But their competence did not include the right to impose capital punishment; this right remained in the hands of the Roman governor (R. Brown 1994a, 337–38, 363–72). Judging from the limited evidence at hand (cf. Bickermann 1935, 188–190; K. Müller 1988; R. Brown 1994a, 337–38, 363–72), the Sanhedrin seems to have had several legal options in the case of Jesus: it could have chosen just to investigate the case and prepare an accusation (thus, e.g., Bickermann 1935, 190–93, 199); or it could first try the case itself and then—since it lacked the competence to carry out a death penalty—refer the matter to the governor (thus, e.g., Thür and Pieler 1977, 386–87).

Several scholars have maintained that the Markan account of the Jewish trial of Jesus is plausible from a historical point of view. The initial charge against Jesus (Mark 14:58), the high priest's question (14:61), Jesus's reply (14:62), the verdict of blasphemy (14:63–64)—all this, it is argued, may well have happened more or less in the way Mark describes (see, e.g., O. Betz 1982, 625–37; Dunn 2000; Schwemer 2001, 144–54; Schwemer argues in particular against the view that the Markan account is anti-Jewish).

One of the reasons—or the main reason—why Jesus was brought before the Sanhedrin was probably his provocative temple act (see Mark 11:15–18) and temple sayings (Ådna 2000, 324–28); one of his alleged sayings was accordingly quoted against him during the trial: "I will destroy this temple that is made with hands, and in three days I will build another, not made with hands" (Mark 14:58; cf. 13:2). Without entering into the problems related to this *Tempelwort* (cf. esp. Ådna 2000, 25–153; for a [re]translation of the entire saying into Aramaic, see 127–28), we may observe that there is an inner connection between the *Tempelwort* and the ensuing question about Jesus's messianic claim: at least in certain circles, the building of a new temple was understood as a messianic task (for a discussion of the evidence, see esp. Ådna 2000, 50–89).

Hence, Caiaphas's question does not introduce a new line of interrogation but is a natural follow-up to the temple saying: "Are you the Messiah, the Son of the Blessed One?" (Mark 14:61; see O. Betz 1982, 625–28; Dunn 2000, 7–10; on Caiaphas, see Bond 2004; his name is never mentioned by Mark). In addition, Caiaphas may also have been guided by his awareness of messianic expectations surrounding Jesus. That a Jewish high priest would use the phrase "the Son of the Blessed One" of the Messiah is plausible; there is no need to suppose that a typically early Christian way of speaking about Christ has been put into the mouth of the high priest. (For the Messiah as "Son of God" in ancient Jewish literature, including the Qumran document 4Q246, see, e.g., J. Collins 1995, 154–72; for a discussion of "the Blessed One" as a reference to God, see Dunn 2000, 9–10.)

According to the Markan account, Jesus answered the high priest's question in the affirmative and, in addition—by way of reference to Ps. 110:1 and Dan. 7:13—pointed to his future vindication: "I am; and you will see the Son of Man seated at the right hand of the Power, and coming with the clouds of heaven" (Mark 14:62). This answer was deemed blasphemous, and Jesus was condemned to death (14:63–64).

If Jesus did affirm the question regarding his messianic claim ("I am"), this would explain why he was accused and condemned as "the king of the Jews" in the Roman trial, which was to follow. However, it is not necessary to assume that Jesus claimed, or admitted, to be the Messiah in exactly the same sense as Caiaphas understood it; he may well have wanted to modify the concept. (The possibility of Jesus modifying the Messiah concept was debated already in the eighteenth and nineteenth centuries; for references, see Back 2011, 1025–26.) Matthew's version of the answer, "You said it" (Matt. 26:64), could perhaps be paraphrased as "It depends what you mean by the term" (Dunn 2000, 12) (cf. below on Mark 15:2). This version is secondary but could nevertheless be a correct interpretation of what Jesus intended.

Maintaining that one is a "king" without the emperor's approval was a serious matter from a Roman perspective. In a Jewish context, however, a messianic claim was not considered blasphemous, as far as we know (E. Sanders 1985a, 298; R. Brown 1994a, 534–35; Evans 1995, 407). Hence, Jesus's affirmation as such would hardly have been a reason for the Sanhedrin to condemn him and "hand him over to the Gentiles" (Mark 10:33). Instead, the blasphemous element in Jesus's answer, as reported by Mark (Mark 14:62), probably lies in the way he refers to his future vindication. Alluding to Ps. 110:1 and Dan. 7:13, Jesus made a self-claim that was far too high; he portrayed himself as being too close to God. In addition, his answer could be construed as a threat against the high priest of God: "He makes claims as a judge who one day will render a verdict . . . against the very leadership that sees itself as appointed by God" (Bock 1998, 231; see further Evans 1995, 409–23).

The authenticity of Jesus's answer in Mark 14:62 remains controversial. According to many scholars, it should be seen as an early Christian creation put into Jesus's mouth. Some scholars, however, defend at least the basic authenticity of the answer (e.g., O. Betz 1982, 635; Dunn 2000, 12–17; cf. also Schwemer 2001, 150–51). If Jesus was indeed sentenced for blasphemy, Caiaphas and the other members of the Sanhedrin would not have had any reason to conceal the matter. On the contrary, it would have been in their interest to inform the public about what had taken place during the trial.

In sum, the chain of events leading up to what Josephus terms "an accusation made by the leading men among us" (*Ant.* 18.64) may have been as follows: Jesus was arrested and brought to trial in particular because of his temple act and temple sayings; as a consequence of the interrogation regarding the temple, the messianic question was raised; Jesus answered in the affirmative; in addition, he spoke in high terms of his future exaltation and vindication, and this in turn led to his condemnation for blasphemy.

5.3.3. The Roman Trial

The earliest text describing the Roman trial of Jesus is Mark 15:1–15. The text begins with the Sanhedrin delivering Jesus to Pilate (v. 1) and ends with Pilate delivering Jesus to be crucified (v. 15). In between, there is an interrogation by

Pilate (with Jesus's short answer, v. 2), accusations by the high priests (to which Jesus does not respond, vv. 3–5), and the Barabbas story (vv. 6–14). Mark may have made some minor additions to the text, which was part of the pre-Markan passion story (Gnilka 1978–1979, 296–98). The Barabbas story hardly ever existed as a separate item, but only as an integral part of the story of the Roman trial (297).

The account is rather meager, and a curious present-day reader will see that there are several things Mark does not care to explain: Did Pilate use an interpreter when interrogating Jesus? Did he discuss the case with advisors? How did he define Jesus's "crime"? Why is there no formal verdict? And so on. There are at least two ways to explain the scantiness of the Markan account. First, Mark's main purpose is to show who Jesus is, that is, the "king of the Jews" in the deepest sense of the term; hence, the technicalities of the trial are insignificant. Secondly, Mark expects the readers/listeners to know certain things by themselves; they are self-evident and in need of no explanation.

Mark 15:1 implies that the Sanhedrin trial went on until the early morning, and then at last a decision was made (συμβούλιον ποιήσαντες) to take Jesus to Pilate (Sherwin-White 1963, 44; Gnilka 1978–1979, 298–99), who was present in Jerusalem for the Passover. Mark does not feel the need to explain that Pilate was the governor (*praefectus*) of the Roman province of Judea, and that, in this capacity, he was the supreme judge and in addition responsible for public order, and that he would be at his official duties early in the morning. Mark also expects the reader to understand that the high priests, who appeared as Jesus's accusers (v. 3), presented Jesus's messianic confession as a political statement: Here is a man who aspires to be a Jewish king; hence Pilate's first question: "Are you the king of the Jews?" (v. 2).

Jesus's answer, "You say it" (v. 2), is not crystal clear. No exact parallel from antiquity seems to have been discovered (Hartman 2005, 536). Probably it is to be understood as a guarded affirmation, with the implication that Jesus would put things differently (V. Taylor 1955, 579; cf. Gnilka 1978–1979, 300: "keine glatte Bejahung . . . aber auch keine Zurückweisung"). Jesus speaks no more during the trial; he ignores the further accusations of the high priests (vv. 3–5). The words "You say it" seem to have been a sufficient reason for a death sentence to follow. At least this is what the Markan account implies.

It is difficult to assess the historicity of the Barabbas story; the reference to the "paschal amnesty" in v. 6 cannot be corroborated by other sources (for discussion, see, e.g., Winter 1961, 131–34; R. Brown 1994a, 814–20; Hengel 2001, 55–56). Leaving this problem aside for the moment, we may maintain that the Markan account of the Roman trial of Jesus has a historical kernel (see, e.g., Lietzmann 1958, 260). Jesus was crucified as the "king of the Jews," and hence his alleged claim to kingship must have been an important issue in the trial, just as Mark has it (15:2). Pilate would have focused on this issue, and Jesus's response made it impossible for Pilate to dismiss the case. Jesus at least did not deny that he was a "king," and setting oneself up as a king without the consent of the emperor was a most serious matter. Quite possibly Pilate considered it as a case of high treason (*maiestas*). (This is the usual assessment among scholars; cf., however, Sherwin-White 1963, 46, and Cook 2011, 199–203: Jesus was condemned for sedition; according to R. Brown [1994a, 717–19; 1994b, 1206], it is "debatable" whether Jesus was condemned for *maiestas*.)

No matter how Jesus's alleged claim should be classified in legal terms—as *maiestas* or otherwise—Pilate was not likely to ignore it. From an incident related by Philo, we can understand how uneasy he must have been about a case like this. In his Jerusalem residence—thus the story told by Philo—Pilate had set up some gilded shields, which carried inscriptions deemed to be offensive by many Jews. Pilate refused to remove the shields, for he had set up them in honor of Tiberius and, as Philo remarks, "did not have the courage" to take them down (Philo, *Legat.* 299–305). The underlying reason for this was probably that Pilate was aware of the frequent trials of *maiestas* under Tiberius and was unwilling to risk being seen as disloyal toward the emperor (Bond 1998, 43–44; for the trials involving *maiestas* under Tiberius, see Klostermann 1955; Saeger [2]2005, 125–38). Following the same logic, Pilate could not risk letting a self-proclaimed Jewish king go unpunished, especially if he was accused by leading men in Jerusalem.

On the other hand, however, Pilate would probably not have wanted to create any upheaval among the people during Passover. (Both Philo and Josephus ascribe bad anti-Jewish intentions to Pilate, but their assessments are not to be taken at face value; cf. Bond 1998, 25–93, for an analysis of Philo's and Josephus's depictions of Pilate.) He may have deemed it reasonable to test public opinion in order to see what support, if any, there was for Jesus. On one hand, if there was no support to be seen, the matter would be clear. On the other hand, if there was strong support among the crowds, he would have to take this into account. If the Barabbas story has a historical kernel, it may point to Pilate's attempt to find out if Jesus had any supporters. Pilate, as Mark describes him, is not a weakling, but a clever politician who knows how to manipulate the crowd to avoid a potentially difficult situation (Bond 1998, 117).

Bond, Helen K. 1998. *Pontius Pilate in History and Interpretation*. SNTSMS 100. Cambridge.

Brown, Raymond E. 2008. *The Death of the Messiah*. Vol. 1. ABRL. New Haven. (Orig. 1994).

Dunn, James D. G. 2000. "'Are You the Messiah?' Is the Crux of Mark 14,61–62 Resolvable?" In *Christology, Controversy, and Community: New Testament Essays in Honour of David R. Catchpole*, edited by David G. Horrell and Christopher M. Tuckett, 1–22. NovTSup 99. Leiden.

Schwemer, Anna Maria. 2001. "Die Passion des Messias nach Markus und der Vorwurf des Antijudaismus." In *Der messianische Anspruch Jesu und die Anfänge der Christologie*, edited by Martin Hengel and Anna Maria Schwemer, 133–63. WUNT 138. Tübingen.

Theissen, Gerd, and Annette Merz. ²1997. *Der Historische Jesus: Ein Lehrbuch*, 387–410. Göttingen.

Sven-Olav Back

5.4. The Crucifixion and Burial of Jesus

5.4.1. The Crucifixion

Dying on a cross was considered a shame in antiquity (cf. Heb. 12:2: σταυρὸς αἰσχύνης), and preaching a crucified Messiah was regarded as utter foolishness. "We preach Christ crucified: a stumbling block (σκάνδαλον) to the Jews and foolishness (μωρία) to Gentiles," Paul says in 1 Corinthians (1:23). About one hundred years later Justin Martyr, in his *Apology on Behalf of the Christians*, feels the need to address the popular view that the Christians are simply mad in their commitment to Jesus: "For it is there they [the critics] declare our madness (μανία) to be manifest, saying that we give second place after the unchangeable and eternal God . . . to a crucified man" (*1 Apol.* 13.4). Justin goes on to defend the Christian devotion to Jesus by pointing to his teaching, partly to its power to change people's lives (14.2–3), partly to its noble contents (14.4–17.4).

The letters of Paul contain the earliest references to the crucifixion of Jesus, but the earliest depiction of the event is found in Mark 15 (vv. 20b–41). Here, after having been flogged (15:15) and mocked (15:16–20a), Jesus is led out of the palace of Pilate and out of the city, then brought to Golgotha and crucified there together with two robbers (15:20b–27). Hanging on the cross, he is again mocked and insulted (15:29–32). Darkness descends upon the whole earth (or perhaps "the whole land") for three hours; then Jesus dies, his last words being, "My God, my God, why have you forsaken me?" (15:33–37). The scene is concluded by the tearing of the veil of the temple (15:38), the confession of the centurion (15:39), and the observation of the whole drama, from a distance, by a group of women (15:40–41). In addition to them (on their names, cf. below), the Markan account

481

also introduces one more person by name: Simon from Cyrene, who was forced to carry Jesus's "cross" (σταυρός) (15:21).

In the Markan story, it is remarkable that the portrayal of the crucifixion itself consists of just one clause: καὶ σταυροῦσιν αὐτόν ("and they crucified him," Mark 15:24); similarly, the flogging, which was a usual part of the punishment, is mentioned with one single word: φραγελλώσας ("having flogged [him]," Mark 15:15). Clearly, Mark (and the pre-Markan tradition) had no interest in describing repulsive things like these in detail. (For a comprehensive study on crucifixion in the Mediterranean world, see especially Cook 2014; cf. Hengel 2008; H.-W. Kuhn 1982; D. Chapman 2008; Samuelsson ²2013). Instead, other themes and motifs are underlined. First, Jesus is depicted as the suffering righteous one; note the echoes and the quotation of Ps. 22:18, 7, and 1, respectively, in Mark 15:24, 29, and 34, and the echo of Ps. 69:21 in Mark 15:36. Second, Jesus is repeatedly mocked as "the king of the Jews/Israel" (15:26, 32; also v. 18); that is, he is mocked as "the one who he is" (Hartman 2005, 566). Third, everything that happens follows the divine plan in detail: in the third hour, Jesus is crucified (15:25); in the sixth hour, darkness comes upon the earth/land (15:33); and in the ninth hour, Jesus breathes his last (15:34, 37). Fourth, he is recognized as "God's son" (15:39), the centurion's confession being deeper than he himself understands (cf. 1:1, 11; 3:11; 5:7; 9:7; 14:61).

According to one plausible analysis (Gnilka 1978–1979, 310–14), the first and second of the aforementioned motifs (the suffering righteous one, the king of the Jews/Israel) were present already in the earliest layer of the pre-Markan crucifixion account (vv. 20b–22a, 24, 26–27, 29a, 31–32ac, 34, 36a, 37, 40), and the third motif was introduced at a secondary, apocalyptically colored stage (addition of vv. 22b, 25, 29b–30, 33, 38), whereas it was Mark himself who, in the final redaction (vv. 23, 32b, 35, 36b, 39), added the centurion's confession.

Apart from the fact of the crucifixion itself, several particulars in the earliest layer of the pre-Markan account can be reasonably regarded as being rooted in memories of the actual event, as they have parallels in crucifixion accounts and depictions from the ancient Mediterranean world. (Regarding the following points, see Cook 2014, 423–30, for detailed references.) Such particulars include: (1) the carrying of the *patibulum*, that is, the horizontal bar of the cross (Mark 15:21) (on the Latin term, see Cook 2014, 15–26; there was no exact Greek term corresponding to *patibulum*, but it is clear that σταυρός could be used for the same object; Cook 2014, 28–32); (2) the nudity of the crucified one (Mark 15:24); (3) the *titulus crucis* explaining the reason for the punishment (15:26); (4) the location of the crucifixion outside of the city walls (15:20, 22); and (5) people passing by on the nearby road (15:29). (On the site of Jesus's crucifixion, see J. Taylor 1998, 182–93.)

5.4.2. The Burial

In Mark 15:42 47 a new person is introduced: Joseph of Arimathea, a prominent "member of the council" (βουλευτής), that is, the Jerusalem Sanhedrin (R. Brown 1994b, 1213–14; Myllykoski 2002, 55). Late on Friday afternoon, he went to Pilate and asked for Jesus's body (vv. 42–43). The governor was surprised to hear that Jesus was already dead, but having received confirmation of the matter, he "gave the corpse to Joseph" (vv. 44–45). Joseph took it down (or rather, had it taken down) from the cross, wrapped it in linen cloth, placed it in a tomb, and had the entrance sealed with a stone (v. 46). Mary Magdalene and Mary the mother of Joses saw where this took place (v. 47).

The burial story was hardly ever passed on as a separate item but was probably always an integral part of the pre-Markan passion narrative (Blinzler 1974, 75; Pesch 1977, 509–10; Gnilka 1978–1979, 332; Aejmelaeus 1993, 85), where it serves as a link between the crucifixion scene and the story about the empty tomb (Mark 16:1–8). Mark may have made some additions to the story: the remark on the late hour in 15:42a (ἤδη ὀψίας γενομένης) and the verses 15:44–45 are often suggested as Markan redactions, but at least the mention of Pilate's giving the body to Joseph (v. 45b) must have been part of the traditional account (thus, e.g., Gnilka 1978–1979, 331).

The mention of the women in Mark 15:47 constitutes a special problem that has to be considered in conjunction with the lists in 15:40 and 16:1. The simplest solution may be to regard all these lists as original parts of the pre-Markan passion narrative. Mark 15:40 seems to mention not three but four different women ("the mother of Joses" being distinct from "Mary of James the younger") as observers of the crucifixion; 15:47 names two of them as witnessing the burial; and 16:1 has three of them going to the tomb on Sunday morning (Pesch 1977, 505–8; cf. Theissen 1989a, 188–89, on the ambiguous language of 15:40: the circles where the pre-Markan passion narrative was transmitted and received were familiar with the women and had no difficulties in understanding an expression that may seem unclear to later readers). However, there are several other possible ways to solve the problem of the lists in Mark 15:40, 47, and 16.1.

Commentators often observe that the Markan burial account leaves many questions unanswered. Some of them may seem rather immaterial (e.g., "Why did Joseph of Arimathea not care about the bodies of the two robbers?"), but even so, the account contains "many holes and obscure points" (Hartman 2005, 574). Some points are likely to remain obscure, but some may probably be clarified with the help of more or less learned guesses.

The main reason behind Joseph of Arimathea's request of Jesus's body may of course be the stipulation of the Torah, according to which the body of a man "hung on a tree" must not be left hanging there overnight but has to be buried "that same day" (Deut. 21:22–23). "The Jews are so careful about funeral rites that even malefactors who have been sentenced to crucifixion are taken down and buried before sunset" (Josephus, *J. W.* 4.317). The fact that it was the day before the Sabbath (παρασκευή) made the matter all the more urgent: on other days, the burial might be completed during "night" (Josephus, *Ant.* 4.264), but on the Sabbath the burial cannot be done. The rather unclear phrase "because it was Preparation Day" (ἐπεὶ ἦν παρασκευή, Mark 15:42) implicitly refers to the aforementioned requirements of the law.

Joseph may have acted on his own initiative, as a law-abiding Jew. However, if he was a member of the Sanhedrin, it is possible that he acted on its behalf, or at least with the consent and support of the high priest Caiaphas, who probably was on reasonably good terms with Pilate (Bond 2004, 50–55). Be that as it may, first-century readers of Mark's Gospel were hardly surprised to learn that a "prominent member of the council" was allowed into the residence of the governor to present his request.

Confronted with Joseph's petition, Pilate had a choice: when faced with the disposal of corpses of executed persons, "prefects and procurators were able to do as they pleased" (Cook 2011, 213). On the one hand, Pilate could have insisted on the normal Roman rule, according to which the bodies of executed criminals were to be left unburied as an additional punishment—no matter the nature of the crime or the manner of execution (Mommsen 1899, 987–89; Cook 2011, 195–96, 206–9). This practice is referred to, for example, in Plautus's *Miles Gloriosus* (372–73), where a slave cynically affirms that "the cross will be my future sepulchre: there my ancestors have been buried." On the other hand, the governor was free to show clemency and allow the corpse to be taken down from the cross and buried (Mommsen 1899, 989; Cook 2011, 209–13). According to the jurist Ulpian, writing around 200 CE, "the corpses of those who were sentenced to die are not to be withheld from their relatives," and "the corpses of executed persons are buried as if permission had been asked for and granted." Sometimes (*nonnumquam*), however, permission for burial was not granted, and this was especially the case "when the charge was high treason" (*maxime maiestatis causa*) (*Dig.* 48.24.1, quoted by Cook 2011, 195). Even in the case of *maiestas*, then, clemency with regard to burial was possible (even if not certain), according to Ulpian.

According to Mark 15:45, Pilate granted Joseph's request: ἐδωρήσατο τὸ πτῶμα τῷ Ἰωσήφ. This piece of information is plausible. First, as mentioned above, Pilate was under no constraints to act otherwise. Second, he would not have wanted to cause any trouble by preventing Jews from obeying their law; his actions in other situations betray no wish to deliberately provoke his Jewish subjects (cf. Bond 1998, 25–93). Third, he was presumably on good terms with Caiaphas (see above) and hence would have had no reason to look unfavorably on a request by a member of the Sanhedrin, especially if the member had the support of the high priest. R. Brown (1998, 235–36, 241; 1994b, 1208–9) supposes that Pilate would hardly have given Jesus's followers the right to bury their master if he were condemned for *maiestas* (which is "debatable," according to Brown), but since Joseph of Arimathea was not among Jesus's followers, the difficulty did not arise.

With Pilate's consent, then, Joseph had Jesus's body taken down from the cross. (A literalistic reading of Mark would suggest that Joseph himself took down the body, but since this was a most difficult thing to do, the reader is certainly supposed to understand that Joseph was assisted by his servants; Hartman 2005, 575.) In principle he could now have brought the body to the graveyard reserved for executed criminals (cf. R. Brown 1994b, 1209–10)—if such a one existed outside of Jerusalem at this time. According to the Mishnah, "There were two graveyards made ready for the use of the court, one for those who were beheaded or strangled, and one for those who were stoned or burned" (m. Sanhedrin 6:5, transl. Neusner). Josephus's mention of a "burial without honor" (ταφὴ ἄτιμος, *Ant.* 5.44; cf. 4.202) may reflect knowledge of burials in the criminals' graveyard (cf. Blinzler 1974, 94).

In any case, according to the Markan account, Joseph did not take the body of Jesus there—was it far outside of the city (Blinzler 1974, 94–95)?—but instead "placed it in a tomb cut out of rock" and "rolled a stone against the entrance of the tomb" (Mark 15:46). (On ancient Jewish burial customs, see Hachlili 1992.) Probably Joseph had no time to take the body elsewhere and had to make use of a tomb nearby (Blinzler 1974, 96–98, with reference to John 19:42). (Mark may very well be right, then, in stating that Joseph of Arimathea entered the stage late in the afternoon.) There is no need to suppose that the primitive Christian community, for apologetic reasons, would have wanted to suppress the notion of Jesus being buried elsewhere: "For the earliest Christians, it would by no means have been impossible to relate an dishonorable burial, just as it related a dishonorable death on the cross" (Blinzler 1974, 75; see also Aejmelaeus 1993, 122).

The Markan account of the burial may be regarded as plausible from a historical point of view. On one hand, there is nothing improbable about it. On the other hand, that the figure of Joseph of Arimathea would have been made up and assigned an imaginary role in the burial of Jesus is a far-fetched idea indeed. As R. Brown (1994b, 1240) remarks, "A Christian fictional creation from nothing of a Jewish Sanhedrist who does what is right is almost inexplicable." In the early church, there was rather a need to explain his "positive" attitude: he was "waiting for the kingdom of God" (Mark 15:43), he had become "a disciple of Jesus"

(Matt. 27:57), or he was "a good and upright man, who had not consented to their [the Sanhedrin's] decision and action" (Luke 23:50–51). Among the witnesses to Joseph's deed, the pre-Markan passion narrative mentions Mary Magdalene and Mary the mother of Joses (Mark 15:47; cf. above).

Blinzler, Josef. 1974. "Die Grablegung Jesu in historischer Sicht." In *Resurrexit: Actes du symposium international sur la résurrection de Jésus, Rome 1970*, edited by Édouard Dhanis, 56–107. Rome.

Brown, Raymond E. 2010. *The Death of the Messiah*. Vol. 2. ABRL. New Haven. Orig. 1994.

Cook, John Granger. 2014. *Crucifixion in the Mediterranean World*. WUNT 327. Tübingen.

Hengel, Martin. 2008. "Mors turpissima crucis: Die Kreuzigung in der antiken Welt und die 'Torheit' des 'Wortes vom Kreuz.'" In *Studien zum Urchristentum: Kleine Schriften VI*, by Martin Hengel, edited by Claus-Jürgen Thornton, 594–652. WUNT 234. Tübingen.

Taylor, Joan E. 1998. "Golgotha: A Reconsideration of the Evidence for the Sites of Jesus' Crucifixion and Burial." *NTS* 44: 180–203.

Sven-Olav Back

E. Early Traces of the *Wirkungen* (Effects) and Reception of Jesus

I. Introduction

The effects of Jesus in the history of Christianity (and beyond) are an essential part of the study of his activity and fate. By "effects" we mean the impulses that can be traced back to Jesus's activity and that continued into the post-Easter period. These include the establishment of a circle of twelve disciples as a symbolic representation of the twelve tribes of Israel, which is recounted in the Synoptic Gospels (cf. esp. Matt. 19:28 par. Luke 22:30). In early post-Easter times, the Twelve apparently served as leaders of the Jerusalem congregation (cf. 1 Cor. 15:5; Acts 1:16–26; 6:2). Another symbolic action of Jesus is the last supper with his disciples in Jerusalem on the eve of his death. In all historical probability, Jesus himself gave this meal a significance that extends beyond the meal itself. As a consequence, a common meal as a symbolic representation of Jesus Christ and the communion between him and the community was already celebrated in the earliest congregations (cf. esp. 1 Cor. 10:16; 11:24–25; Luke 22:19). Another example is the requirements of consistent discipleship, which were mainly compiled in the Sermon on the Mount and related texts (for instance, the first chapters of the Didache) and served from early on as an ethical orientation for Christians. The term "receptions," by contrast, denotes interpretations of the activity and fate of Jesus Christ in the history of Christianity, as, for example, the development of early Christology, visual presentations of episodes from Jesus's life as well as legendary elaborations of his birth, his earthly activities, and his resurrection, primarily in apocryphal texts. The distinction between "effects" and "receptions" is thus not to be understood in an absolute way, but rather as a heuristic instrument for describing the relationship between events of Jesus's activity and its various interpretations in the history of Christianity.

The relationship between event and interpretation has been discussed at several places in this handbook. The perspective of this final part, which examines examples of the effects and receptions of the person of Jesus in post-Easter times, takes up recent hermeneutical approaches, which have drawn attention to the wide range of interpretations of historical traditions. Hans-Georg Gadamer's concept of *Wirkungsgeschichte* (history of effects) provides a helpful approach for this. This model, put forward by Gadamer in his study *Wahrheit und Methode* (*Truth and Method*), which first appeared in 1960, is based on the premise that historical understanding is not to be taken as the interface of a subject who is interpreting and an object that is being interpreted. Instead, understanding is a constant process that takes place in a hermeneutical situation that is likewise impacted by the historical phenomenon and the situation of the interpreter. In the interpretation of historical events by way of a fusion of the two horizons, the tradition has an effect on the present of the interpreter. Gadamer's reflections thus aim at overcoming the antithesis of history and its appropriation, in that they call attention to the fact that interpreters and the historical object do not encounter each other in a neutral fashion but are constantly connected with each other in a "nexus of interactions." For the Jesus tradition, this means that today's understanding of the multiple interpretations of the activity and fate of Jesus Christ in the history of Christianity and beyond cannot be disregarded. In fact, these interpretations of events and historical data as potential meanings influence and determine later understandings. They enhance the historical event by proposals for understanding and integrate it into the history of those effects, which it has evoked and can evoke anew again and again. A hermeneutically oriented approach to Jesus's activity and fate will therefore not proceed from a strict separation of event and interpretation, but will rather consider the close relationship between them.

The effects and receptions of Jesus dealt with in this handbook are intended to highlight some prominent aspects of his *Wirkungsgeschichte* and reception history. In particular, interpretations will be considered that illumine the relationship between Jesus's activities and the formation of early Christian creeds, but also the emergence of early Christian social formations and ethical convictions. The conviction of the resurrection of Jesus from the dead thereby serves as the pivotal starting point. Already in early times this conviction was connected with traditions about appearances of the risen One, including instructions given by him. These traditions aim at the connection of the pre-Easter activity of Jesus with the history of the post-Easter communities. They are accordingly directed toward the bestowal of the Spirit, the renewal of table fellowship, and the instruction for mission. In apocryphal gospels they could also contain new teachings of Jesus that go beyond his pre-Easter instructions. Early Christian confessions formulate the unique significance of Jesus Christ and his belonging to God in summary statements. These formulations are therefore fundamental for the further development of Christology, in which they are interpreted in multiple ways and elaborated into comprehensive creeds. The so-called christological titles, which were attributed to Jesus to express his exclusive relationship to God and his divine majesty, are closely associated with this. Finally, the interpretations of his person in extracanonical texts and visual representations also belong to the early receptions of Jesus. They draw attention to the fact that receptions of Jesus from early times on were not confined to the gospels that became canonical, but were also expressed in texts and visual representations that place the authoritative texts of the Christian tradition in a broader context and form important witnesses of Christian piety.

Jens Schröter and Christine Jacobi

II. Resurrection, Appearances, Instructions of the Risen One

Jesus's appearances after his death on a cross and the affirmation of his being raised by God are often understood in a historical perspective as the decisive turning point that sets the activities of the earthly Jesus off from the history of early Christianity. Portrayals of the historical Jesus arising from the eighteenth century have been guided by this turning point. They distinguished the resurrection of Jesus as a secondary interpretation from the historical facts.

Rationalists such as Hermann Samuel Reimarus counted the empty tomb among the "historical facts" that in the age of the Enlightenment became the starting point for belief in the resurrection. They did this in different ways, but always in agreement with natural laws: thus, Joseph of Arimathea first buried Jesus's body in his family tomb, which the women could no longer find, or Jesus was reburied (Lake 1907; cf. also Bostock 1994). Early on Tertullian attests a comparable explanation, according to which the rumor circulated about a gardener who removed Jesus's body so that visitors would not step on his lettuce (*Spect.* 30).

Also the hypothesis of suspended animation was prevalent among Enlightenment theologians such as Heinrich Eberhard Gottlob Paulus, Karl von Hase, and Friedrich Schleiermacher, which simultaneously supposedly explained the empty tomb *and* Jesus's appearances. In the coolness of the tomb Jesus regained consciousness and left the tomb on his own accord.

According to the rationalistic pattern of interpretation, the discovery of the empty tomb produced visions of the risen One. By contrast, other interpretations reckon with the priority of the appearances, from which legends of the empty tomb were then generated. But what was the nature of these appearances? The conjecture that the risen Jesus was an *illusion* or even a *hallucination* of the disciples was repeatedly advocated. As early as the second century, the Epistle

489

to Rheginos (NHC I 4 48), which is included in the Christian Apocrypha, opposes this conjecture. Under a modern perception of reality shaped by the natural sciences, this so-called subjective vision hypothesis, which assumes internal, psychic causes of the disciples' experiences of appearances, was once again introduced into the discussion by David Friedrich Strauss (1835–1836). Liberal theologians of the nineteenth century interpreted the concept of resurrection in the context of the subjective vision hypothesis as compensation for the disciples' pre-Easter faith in Jesus as the Messiah that was shaken by the crucifixion.

In the more recent past, the German Protestant theologian Gerd Lüdemann (1994, 2002) drew on the subjective vision hypothesis and described Jesus's tomb as "full." This position can be considered a minority opinion. At present, however, the assumption that Jesus's tomb was indeed empty and that his disciples were convinced that they had seen the resurrected Jesus finds wide support among New Testament scholars (cf. Wright 2003 and the overview of scholarship in Habermas 2005). In addition, an alternative to the subjective or objective character of the visions, which has long determined the discussion of the appearances, has recently been critiqued from the perspective of cognitive theory (Wolter 2012).

Actually, anyone who seeks the historical Jesus beyond the belief in the resurrection is confronted with the problem that none of the Gospels offers a description of Jesus's earthly journey free of the conviction of his being raised. Only because of the belief in the resurrection, which put Jesus's ignominious death in new light, does primitive Christianity turn back to the events of Jesus's activities lying in the past. In this respect, the confession of Jesus's resurrection is present throughout all the Gospels that became canonical. On the grounds of this conviction and transmitted early Jewish apocalyptic motifs, early Christianity interpreted the course of events concerning the pre-Easter Jesus. From this, it developed its self-understanding and a new interpretation of history. In a theological-historical respect, the experiences of appearances and belief in the resurrection should be understood not as a turning point but as a center point: in the concept of Jesus's resurrection, interpretations of Jesus's proclamation and his destiny converge, and from this conceptualization the post-Easter interpretation of the present time of early Christianity eventuates. The message of the resurrection sets in motion the activity of early Christian proclamation and ensures—from then on under a new signature—the continuing significance of Jesus's earthly ministry, which can become the new standard for the judgment that is to come (cf. Luke 12:8–9). And conversely, it changes traditional concepts of the resurrection of the dead in the eschaton and expands the Israelite–early Jewish confession of God.

In the New Testament, the raising of Jesus, although not directly described anywhere, becomes thematic in various ways. In the oldest tradition it stands at the center of formulaic confessional statements (see E.III). In the Gospels, which arise later, the message that Jesus was raised was communicated by one or two figures dressed in radiant garments, who thereby explain the empty tomb (Mark 16:5–7; Matt. 28:2–7; Luke 24:4–8, 23; cf. also John 20:12–13). The primitive Christian veneration of Jesus as Lord (cf. Rom. 10:9) and the conviction obtained by taking over the statement of exaltation in Ps. 110 (109 LXX) that Jesus sits at the right hand of God or is taken up into God's glory are tied to the resurrection, but the exaltation can also occur without a statement of the resurrection.

Moreover, the Gospels report Jesus's appearances. It is disputed in research whether the appearance narratives, which are literarily more recent than the formulas, nevertheless transmit the historical starting point of the Christian confession of the resurrection of Jesus. It would also be conceivable that no historical incidents stood at the beginning of the belief in the resurrection, but rather theological ways of thinking stood at the outset: Jesus's disciples could have further developed his proclamation seamlessly beyond his death to the concept of his resurrection/exaltation and position of power. Rudolf Pesch (1973) argues in a similar direction, according to which a pre-Christian tradition of dying and rising prophets stands behind Mark 6:14–16 and Rev. 11:7–12, which could have served the disciples as the prototype of their belief in the resurrection.

However, the Gospels present Jesus's death as a decisive turning point that unsettles Jesus's followers. From this it is plausible that the early Christian affirmation of the raising of Jesus arose from the overwhelming experiences of appearances of some of Jesus's followers after his death. The experiences of appearances could be interpreted by means of traditional models of interpretation as well as in association with aspects of Jesus's earthly activity. New Testament exegesis can reconstruct these processes. Historical-critical work can trace how under the influence of the Easter confession not only the experiences of Easter were verbalized in New Testament texts but also how Jesus's activities and passion were narrated. The confession formed in early Christianity that Jesus was raised from the dead can be understood only if its tradition-historical background and possible starting points in the activities of the earthly Jesus are ascertained. Which parts of the early Christian interpretation of the apparitions, on the other hand, go back to real experiences of the disciples can hardly be answered. This is because already the kinds of experiences of appearances themselves can have been codetermined by known traditions of heavenly appearances and corresponding expectations (cf. the similar case of an expected resurrection of John the Baptist according to Mark 6:14). On this basis a purely historical-event dimension of appearances cannot finally be reconstructed.

1. Early Christian Talk about the God Who Raised Jesus from the Dead, and Its Traditio-Historical Background

The oldest traditions about the raising of Jesus are theo-centric formulations, which present a new predication of God as a statement (1 Cor. 6:14; 15:15; Rom. 10:9) or participial expressions (2 Cor. 4:14; Gal. 1:1; Rom. 4:24; 8:11).

Linguistic and semantic analogies to Israel's fundamental confession of God as the one who led Israel out of Egypt (Exod. 16:6; Deut. 8:14) and made heaven and earth (Pss. 115:15; 121:2), but especially as the one who makes the dead alive (the second of the Eighteen Benedictions; cf. also 2 Cor. 1:9; Rom. 4:17), show that early Christianity with its confession of the God who makes alive acting anew in the raising of Jesus describes a unique mighty deed in a fundamental way similar to the way the Israelite–early Jewish predications of God express it. These form the basis for a saving and justifying belief in the raising of Jesus. The primitive Christian confession thus affirms that God is Lord over life and death.

Likewise, the primitive Christian formulaic traditions raise the not insignificant claim that God has revealed himself anew in the raising of this one man who was crucified. In 1 Cor. 15:15 Paul focuses attention on the dimension of a new way of speaking about God: Christians would be guilty of worshiping God invalidly if the talk about Christ's resurrection were false.

Early on Paul employs the fundamental primitive Christian confession about the raising of Jesus as the demonstration of God's power over death in a christological statement, which launches a further development: according to Rom. 14:9, Christ died and was made alive for the purpose of ruling over the dead and the living. As a result, a sphere of power reserved for God in Israelite-Jewish tradition is transferred to Christ and a connection is drawn between God's action in Christ and the destiny of Christ believers.

This corresponds to formulas with two or more members in which Jesus (Christ) is the subject and the proposition of the resurrection is connected to a statement about his sacrifice or his death: 1 Thess. 4:14, 1 Cor. 15:3, and 2 Cor. 5:15. This also shows that in the Pauline sphere of tradition, the salvific significance of Jesus's death for Christ believers is attached to the concept of resurrection. Thus the raising of Jesus unfolds a salvific effect that is relevant for believers.

Although the appearances may have formed the historical origin of belief in the resurrection, up until 1 Cor. 15:3b–5 a reference to them and also to the empty tomb is missing in the formulaic tradition of the Epistles. Thus, the formulaic expressions are not about a legitimating validation of the resurrection. Also, a justification of the possibility in principle that someone who is dead is resurrected lies beyond the context of the Epistles. In Corinth the bodily resurrection of the dead was contested; thus, to be sure, Paul was able to adduce the formulaic tradition in 1 Cor. 15:3b–5 as a basis for argumentation; nevertheless, its inferences had to go beyond that.

2. The Accounts of Appearances in the Gospels

2.1. Tradition-Historical Presuppositions

2.1.1. ὤφθη

The Gospels present statements comparable to the formulaic tradition. On the one hand, among these are the passion summaries in which Jesus, who speaks about himself as the Son of Man, predicts the resurrection and gives it a time frame ("after three days," Mark 8:31; 9:31; 10:33–34); on the other hand, among these the concise message of the specially robed figures at the empty tomb can also be adduced: ἠγέρθη, a *passivum divinum* (Mark 16:6; Matt. 28:6; Luke 24:6).

The accounts of the appearances provide more information about the notions that were associated with the raising of Jesus than these short formulas. The reprocessing of the accounts of the appearances in the Gospels gives altogether diverse answers as to what preunderstanding could have affected Jesus's appearances to the disciples and the categories by which they were interpreted.

The two oldest references to appearances of Jesus, namely, the pre-Pauline formula in 1 Cor. 15:3b–5 and the formulaic notice of an appearance to Peter in Luke 24:34 with ὤφθη, employ the aorist passive of ὁράω, a particularly qualified term in the Septuagint. Although ὤφθη is not encountered elsewhere in the detailed accounts of the appearances in the Gospels, the expression is the oldest available verbalization for interpretations of the appearances in early Christianity. However, ὤφθη is a translation of a standard *terminus technicus* for the appearance of God in the Greek translation of the Old Testament. In the passages in Paul and Luke, however, it does not necessarily have to have been used terminologically and to have designated Jesus's divine status. The Septuagint is acquainted with a profane use of ὤφθη, and also in Luke 1:11 the appearance of an angel and in Mark 9:4 the appearance of Elijah and Moses are depicted with ὤφθη. Pivotal for the earliest conveyance of the Easter experiences with ὤφθη, however, is that as a rule in Israelite-Jewish tradition it is never about a dead person who comes from the underworld. Rather, the expression ὤφθη puts emphasis on the heavenly revelatory character of the event. The appearance of a dead person, as described in 1 Sam. 28:13, for instance, would in any case be differentiated once again from an appearance interpreted by ὤφθη. In this sense Jesus's appearances are not interpreted as the appearance of a dead person or ghost. With the emphasis on the corporeality of the risen One in the more recent narrative elaborations of the reports of appearances, this essential characteristic is further intensified (cf., for instance, Luke 24:37–40, where the interpretation of Jesus's appearance as that of a ghost is corrected).

The ambiguous meaning of ὤφθη between the active "to show oneself" and the passive "to be seen," which is relevant in the discussion about the objectivity and reality of the event, should be added. Although with ὤφθη the active role in the event is attributed to the one who "shows him/herself," numerous instances in Josephus indicate that ὤφθη is not a technical term for a revelation but rather can describe an ordinary sense perception (*J.W.* 3.239; 4.190; 6.118; *Ant.* 7.256; 11.232; 12.205; 18.239; cf. Haacker 2018).

The detailed accounts in Luke 24 and John 20–21 exhibit typical elements for the genre of appearances: the sudden presence of the risen One and his likewise sudden disappearance, the alarm and fear of the witnesses, the admonition from the one who appears, as well as his subsequent speech (Luke 24:36–51; cf. also Luke 24:31; John 20:19–29; Mark 16:9–19). The more detailed accounts of the appearances in the Gospels throw light on the tradition of the short, formulaic experience of an appearance to Peter: in any case, the experience designated by ὤφθη possessed a visual character and entailed Jesus's visible, unusual presence (cf. also 1 Cor. 9:1).

On the other hand, what is extraordinary about the appearances is that, differently from the theophanies described in numerous psalms (cf. Pss. 29; 68; Nah. 1; Hab. 3), they are not accompanied by demonstrations of power. The older descriptions of the post-Easter situation and Jesus's appearance are characterized by a tendential reticence. External signs and demonstrations of power are not expected until Jesus's parousia (1 Thess. 4:16; Mark 13:24–27).

Embellished portents and supernatural apocalyptic phenomena come up only in the detailed narrative of Matthew (Matt. 27:52–53: the opening of the graves and the raising of many saints; 28:2: the earthquake) and in the appended last chapter of John (the miraculous catch of fish). The signs are also spectacular, which, according to the later ending to canonical Mark, are supposed to authenticate the disciples' proclamation. Even more clearly, in the second century essentially more eye-catching narratives of the resurrection and appearances arise, which deviate from the reticent narrative version. In the Gospel of Peter, for instance, the readers themselves become witnesses of the resurrection from the tomb, and the risen One appears in supernatural form (see E.VI).

Such embellished elaboration stands in stark contrast to the oldest report of Easter in Mark 16:1–8, which is restricted to the discovery of the empty tomb and gives only the prediction of an appearance without a commission to a worldwide proclamation, but rather concludes with the silence of the women. Also, according to Luke 24:13–35 and John 20:15, the risen One, who shows himself to his disciples, is not recognized at first and his appearance is misinterpreted. The knowledge of the significance of the event is not produced by either the empty tomb or Jesus's appearance, but according to the first reports of appearances, it is rather in need of an interpretive act by the Easter witnesses. Only from this do faith and public proclamation eventuate. The Gospels capture this process of interpretation in addition to the events in the categories of nonrecognition/doubt/fear and recognition/faith (cf. Matt. 28:17; Mark 16:11–14; Luke 24:16, 31, 37–43; John 20:24–29). Finally, thereby the Gospels themselves point to the fact that an access directed purely to the event would be insufficient for explaining belief in the resurrection.

2.1.2. The Empty Tomb

In the history of research, as described above, a controversy developed around the empty tomb and its possible rational or legendary interpretations about the triggering of Easter faith. Whereas rationalists took the empty tomb to be a historical fact and negotiated it by means of a scientific worldview, history-of-traditions interpretations fit the tradition of the discovery of the empty tomb into ancient parallels from the environment of early Christianity. If the ὤφθη terminology points to the appearance of a heavenly personality or a figure who is taken up into heavenly spheres, then occasionally the motif of the empty tomb is also interpreted as an early Christian legend, which is based on the concept of Jesus's being taken up (cf. the presentation of this position and ancient examples in Allison 2005b). The search in vain for the body and the discovery of the empty tomb transmitted in Mark 16:6 possess certain, although not unambiguous, analogies in Israelite-Jewish and pagan reports of being taken up into heaven (cf. Gen. 5:24 par. Sir. 44:16; 2 Kings 2:1–18 par. Sir. 48:9 par. 1 Macc. 2:58, as well as Josephus, *Ant.* 4.326; in Greco-Roman tradition the ascent of Heracles, Diodorus Siculus 4.38.5). In the parallels just mentioned, however, the protagonists are not transferred into heaven *after* but rather *instead of* (a violent) death.

Indeed, T. Job 39:8–40:3, a text dated between the first century BCE and the second century CE, attests the motif of an undiscoverable, raptured *body*. Job's children who are struck dead in a house that collapses cannot be found under the rubble. They were taken up by God into heaven, as a vision further confirms. The objective of the story is to reinterpret the conventional interpretation of violent death as God's punishment. In a comparable sense, the accounts of Jesus's empty tomb perhaps serve the function of understanding his bodily ascent or resurrection as vindication by God. But whether these accounts are to be understood as illustrations of the resurrection message in the context of ancient rapture legends (so Hoffmann 1979) remains uncertain.

495

Although Paul takes up an old tradition of Jesus's burial (1 Cor. 15:4; see D.IV.5.4), he appears not to know the tradition of the discovery of the empty tomb. It is transmitted for the first time in Mark 16:1–8. As a result, it is frequently assumed that it was actually unknown before Mark and that the curious silence of the women at the conclusion of the Gospel of Mark provides the Markan rationale for the late emergence of the tradition (Wolter 2012). From the Gospel of Mark the tradition of the women, who visit the tomb on the first day of the week, enters into the synoptic parallels and eventually also into the Gospel of John.

However, with this the historicity of the empty tomb is still not determined. Perhaps an empty tomb, which was taken to be Jesus's burial place, was later discovered and was interpreted with the belief of the resurrection that was already formed. One argument for the historicity is that in ancient Judaism women were incompetent to bear witness and therefore the tradition of the empty tomb, which is primarily associated with female figures such as Mary Magdalene, cannot be the result of apologetic tendencies. However, female incompetence as witnesses is particularly related to juridical contexts (Vahrenhorst 1998). According to the narrative proclivity, the fact that according to Luke 24:9–11 the women with their news collided with the disciples' unbelief has to do with the extraordinary message and not with their lack of competence as witnesses.

The question about the historicity of the empty tomb, therefore, cannot be answered. Nevertheless, it is decisive that no significance is ascribed to it according to the witness of the New Testament. In the Gospels, the empty tomb in itself does not produce faith. Its function on the level of the narrative, however, consists in linking the experience of the crucifixion and burial with the appearances. To this extent it is a part of the narrative implementation of the Easter traditions in the framework of the story of Jesus in the Gospels.

2.1.3. Martyr Traditions

In the Testament of Job the concept of rapture responds to the question of theodicy. Such a pattern of argument was already prominent in early Jewish martyr traditions and also became significant for the early Christian understanding of Jesus's death. According to 2 Maccabees, the destiny of the law-observant Jews, who experienced violent death during the crisis of Antiochus in the second century BCE, raised the question of God's justice in a particularly striking way. Second Maccabees developed the concept of an individual, decisive raising of the body as compensation for experiences of martyrdom, as recompense for fidelity to God unto death and as a guarantee of divine justice (2 Macc. 7:29). The assurance that martyrs are raised (cf. 2 Macc. 7:11) aimed at their complete vindication in view of their gruesome death and the divine confirmation of their interpretation of the true will of God in the face of competing, stronger assimilated manifestations of Judaism.

In their interpretation of the experiences of appearances as a vision of a righteous one taken up bodily from the dead, the first Christians picked up a topic that was also well known in martyr theology. In this line of interpretation, the appearances to the disciples led to the conviction that God had vindicated Jesus's pre-Easter activity, which was experienced as controversial.

2.2. Characteristic Features of Appearances according to Matthew, Luke, and John

2.2.1. The Emphasis on the Bodily Resurrection and the Belief of the Disciples

The interest in emphasizing the identity of the risen One with the earthly Jesus is common to all literary receptions of the motifs of the discovery of the empty tomb, the message of the resurrection, and Jesus's appearances. Whereas Matthew realizes this identity especially by means of a retrospective link to the proclamation of the earthly Jesus and depicts an image of the risen One as pantocrator, who from Matt. 1:23 is at the same time "Emmanuel," in the accounts of appearances of Luke and John the *corporeality* of the risen One in accordance with Israelite-Jewish anthropology plays a central role. Already in the older tradition cited by Paul in 1 Cor. 15:3b–5, the affirmation of the raising of Jesus and the reference to his appearances first say that Jesus was *buried*, and it is this Jesus whom God raised.

In Luke and John, particular actions of the risen One establish the connection to his pre-Easter existence and at the same time elicit the memory and belief of the disciples, which flow into the primitive Christian proclamation. Here Jesus himself is the one who draws the connection to his activities in that he reveals his identity by his greeting of peace, interpretation of Scripture, celebration of a meal, or showing his wounds (John 20:20) and his hands and feet (Luke 24:39; the wounds are implicit here also). Precisely the showing of the marks of the wounds, the invitation to touch him, but also eating broiled fish (Luke 24:38–43) strive for a tactile assurance that the crucified Jesus appears to the disciples tangibly, bodily.

This recognition of Jesus aims at the transformation of the disciples from unknowing and nonbelieving to those who know and believe—and, to be sure, not on hearing the message of the resurrection alone but also on the proclamation of the pre-Easter Jesus in a new way. In Luke this metamorphosis is depicted in the Emmaus disciples, who first take Jesus for a stranger before the Scripture is opened up to them and Jesus reveals himself in a corporate meal, and then in the circle of the remaining Eleven who first take Jesus to for a ghost. Jesus does not appear in a strange form, as it is reported about gods disguised as humans in some Greco-Roman sagas, but as the one who he was and is. The reason that he was not recognized, therefore, lies with the *disciples*, whose "eyes" are hindered from recognizing (cf. the literary framing in Luke 24:16 and 24:31). They realize only in the moment in which Jesus as the risen One breaks bread in a customary way, that is, in the pre-Easter way, and thereby establishes the pre-Easter celebration of a meal anew after his death. From this act new light falls not only on the pre-Easter celebration of meals of the past, but also on Jesus's entire pre-Easter way of life. The christological recognition of the disciples, therefore, portrays the kind of hermeneutic under which the Gospels are intended to be read.

2.2.2. Authentication of Pre-Easter Teaching and Commissioning

Along with the recognition and understanding of the disciples in Luke, a second crucial motif for the accounts of appearances is set up: the commissioning of the disciples for mission. In its own way this motif produces, in common with the emphasis on the corporeality of the risen One, a connection with the pre-Easter Jesus. This becomes clear first of all in the speech of the figure(s) at the tomb in Mark 16:7 and Luke 24:6–8, in which sayings of the earthly Jesus are brought to mind and thus his message of resurrection is brought into conformity with his statements about himself in order to support belief in the resurrection.

Moreover, in the commissioning appearances, Matthew and Luke have recourse back to Jesus's teaching, in order to safeguard it for the time after Easter. With their commissioning for proclamation, baptism, and testimony among all people, the risen One legitimates the post-Easter missionary activity, for which the disciples are endowed with the Spirit in John 20:22. At this point the Gospels look ahead to a future that should be shaped by the commission of the risen One himself.

Especially in Matthew's Easter narrative, the putting into action of the teaching of the earthly Jesus, which from then on is invested with enhanced authority by the exalted status of the risen One, and the carrying on of its transmission to disciples form the critical point (cf. Matt. 28:16–20). Whereas according to Luke 24:44–48 the *salvific event* (Jesus's suffering and resurrection), foretold by Scripture, and the call to repentance should be the content of the future mission (cf. Luke 18:31), according to Matt. 28:20, the risen One commissions the disciples from Galilee outward with the worldwide teaching of his pre-Easter *precepts* (cf. v. 20: διδάσκοντες αὐτοὺς τηρεῖν πάντα ὅσα ἐνετειλάμην ὑμῖν).

Thus Jesus's appearances also make the activity of the pre-Easter Jesus accessible to a worldwide circle of recipients and preserve it under an altered sign (cf.

John 20:19–23; 21:15–22). The risen One mediates no new teaching, but the old is reinforced by his appearance. What is "new" is that Jesus himself first enables the understanding of the resurrection event and thereby provides the hermeneutical key for the "correct" understanding of the pre-Easter proclamation and of Scripture. Although both Jesus's pre-Easter predictions of his fate and Scripture already prefigured the resurrection (cf. also the double reference to Scripture in 1 Cor. 15:3–4), according to the portrayal of the accounts of appearances, the moment in which the risen One *himself* enables the disciples to recognize him is required. Only in this way are they enabled to act as witnesses in the world.

In spite of the sovereignty of the risen One and the perceptible dependence of the disciples, the accounts of appearances are also tied up with the aspect of legitimation of early Christian leaders. This is suggested by the order of priority of the list of witnesses in 1 Cor. 15:5–8, in which ὤφθη is the term chosen likewise for all of Jesus's appearances, and the interlaced fashion of the narrative in Luke 24:13–35. The arrangement of the accounts of appearances is such that the experience of an appearance provides the witnesses direct and privileged access to the new hermeneutic of pre-Easter Jesus tradition and the traditional Scriptures. With the taking up of Jesus into heaven and his placement at God's right hand (cf. Mark 16:19; Luke 24:50–51 and Acts 1:9), the appearances become chronologically limited, the authorization of witnesses is closed, and other Christ believers are rendered dependent on the witnesses to the appearances.

The traditions of appearances thus control the reception of the Jesus tradition in early Christian proclamation. In this regard they occupy a central place in the history of the development of theology in early Christianity. The consequences of this perhaps can be perceived in Gal. 1, where Paul derives his gospel from a revelation received *independently*. But then they become recognizable above all from the second century, when a narrative of the tradition of apparitions to individual disciples began to develop and completely new revelation reports were produced, which broke with the conception of Easter narratives that had become canonical.

Within the New Testament, it is the proto-epiphany to Peter that both Luke and Paul attest and that reflects its elevated historical position in the primitive community. In the Johannine supplemental chapter, the leadership of the church is even conferred upon Peter by the risen One (John 21:15–23). According to Matt. 28:9 and John 20:14–18, however, the women at the empty tomb (especially Mary Magdalene) become the first witnesses in a certain rivalry with him. In addition, in John 20:3–10 the beloved disciple, who in John already possessed a special pre-Easter role, is profiled in comparison with Peter by winning the race to the tomb, but, most notably differently from Peter, in view of the empty tomb he already "believes." The accounts of appearances in the Gospel of John thus already demonstrate initial efforts to situate a valid authority in the prominent post-Easter revelation tradition in each one's own community.

3. An Innovative Concept of Resurrection in Primitive Christianity: The Connection of One Individual Resurrection with the Dawning of the End Time and the Expectation of a General Resurrection of the Dead

According to the detailed accounts of the Gospels, the true significance of their visions was opened up to Jesus's followers when they interpreted them in the light of Scripture and especially in the light of Jesus's proclamation. It is possible that in this the accounts of appearances reflect the belief in the resurrection. However, the *earliest*, very brief verbalizations of the Easter experience—the affirmation of Jesus being raised by God—go substantially further with respect to content: the raising of Jesus is placed in a series with God's demonstrations of power in creation and in Israel; it is characterized as an eschatological event relevant for all people. Designations of Jesus such as "*the first fruit* of those who sleep" (1 Cor. 15:20; cf. also 6:14) lie in the line of interpretation of this affirmation. How this could come to such an extension of the conviction of the resurrection is debated in scholarship. There are no history-of-religions parallels of figures who have been raised and raptured, whose resurrection was at the same time understood as the beginning of the eschatological raising of the dead. The concept of an immediate resurrection of individual martyrs and the end-time raising of the righteous to life are not linked to each other in Israelite-Jewish literature. In this regard, the early Christian belief in the proleptic resurrection of the dead in Jesus is innovative.

The fact that the first Christians combined two distinct conceptual spheres about Jesus's person can go back to appropriating the interpretation of the earthly Jesus's proclamation: according to apocalyptic tradition, the imminent kingdom of God, the dawning of a new aeon, which Jesus saw manifested in particular points in parables, deeds of power, and corporate meals (see D.IV.3.3; D.IV.2.3–6), implied a resurrection of the dead (cf. Dan. 12:1–3; 1 En. 22). Indeed, the raising of the righteous who had died ought to make it possible for them to be able to participate in the beginning of the time of salvation. As shown in the Jesus tradition, admittedly the resurrection of the dead did not belong to the emphatic content of Jesus's proclamation, but it nevertheless did belong to his convictions, which can be discerned in the debate with the Sadducees transmitted in Mark 12. Moreover, it was presumably also anchored in popular religion (cf. the rumor about the resurrection of the Baptizer in Mark 6:14) and part of the content of the belief of Pharisaic Judaism in the first century (cf. Josephus, *J.W.* 2.163; Acts 23:6–8), to which Paul also belonged. If the first Christians understood Jesus's appearances as confirmation of his teaching of the imminent kingdom of God, whose representative Jesus was, then accordingly the hope for a *comprehensive* resurrection of the dead could also find entry into early Christian thinking. The conviction that the entirety is already shown proleptically in an individual, that in the raising of Jesus the eschatological resurrection of the dead was prefigured, could have evolved in a way analogous to the episodic appearance of the presence of the βασιλεία in Jesus's parables, deeds of power, and corporate meals.

In Jesus's proclamation and actions, it is also shown that Jesus attributed a central significance to his own role in the growth of the kingdom of God and presumably held the acceptance of his invitation to the kingdom of God as decisive for salvation (cf. Matt. 8:11–12; Luke 13:28–30, see D.IV.3.8; D.IV.3.4). Those who accepted Jesus's message and professed him expected fellowship with the patriarchs in the βασιλεία, as did the martyrs according to 4 Macc. 13:17 and 16:25. In the Jesus tradition the eschatological enactment and the allotment of salvation and perdition are thus connected to the stance toward Jesus, and thereby, in its own way, a connection between deeds and consequences is created (cf. also Mark 8:38; Matt. 10:32–33; Luke 12:8–9). Here the disciples' prominent relationship with Jesus indeed belonged first to the eschatological expectation of Jesus's return as judge without presupposing his death and resurrection.

Initiated by the Easter experience and combined with the common hope in the raising of the dead in early Jewish apocalyptic, the restoration of the connection between deeds and consequences could now also be employed in a concept of resurrection in which Jesus's followers viewed the hoped-for recompense in their resurrection to everlasting fellowship with the Lord.

By means of the post-Easter memory of the characteristics of the pre-Easter proclamation, the fundamental, unrivaled quality of the risen One was produced in comparison with the return from the realm of death of those who had died or martyrs who were raptured to God. With the appearance of the risen Jesus, his message of the imminent kingdom of God and the in-breaking of the end time were simultaneously confirmed.

4. Further Developments in the Second and Third Centuries

The Easter message of those extraordinary figure(s) at the empty tomb primarily provided strategies for *Jesus's* mastery over death, because the perspective of the Gospels was directed from the activities of the earthly Jesus and his death on a cross to the Easter experiences. The earliest proclamation of the raising of Jesus does not yet contain the belief in the general resurrection of the dead. There-fore, in the four Gospels the message of Easter is not linked to such a concept of resurrection, although in the Jesus tradition a relationship between him and the successor community going beyond Jesus's absence is laid out. The apocalyptic context of Jesus's proclamation described above and the participation Christol-ogy developed by Paul, however, led to a soteriological "enrichment" of belief in the raising of Jesus. Literary reflections in 1 Cor. 15 and Acts 17:18, 32 already attest this and simultaneously also transmit the controversial potential of this concept in the environment of Christianity influenced by paganism. Apologetic and apocryphal writings originating later sought to answer the problem of the mortality *of all* human beings with the aid of the raising of Jesus. Consequently, Jesus's resurrection had to be conveyed with anthropological concepts. Espe-cially in the contact with pagan religious belief and the contemporaneous Middle Platonic doctrine of the soul, quite different concepts of redemption arose, and also in the sphere of Christology the increasing soteriological significance of the resurrection triggered far-reaching developments.

Thereby a culture of philosophical thought influenced the biblical theological design of apologists such as Justin and Irenaeus as well as the gnostic doctrines of redemption against which they fought. A central challenge of Christians of the second century was to negotiate the early Christian concept in agreement with the Israelite-Jewish tradition of the unified and created nature of human beings, to which also the flesh or the body (σάρξ, σῶμα) belongs, with a Middle Platonic dualistic body-soul anthropology and with the concept of redemption as liberation from matter of an originally divine element in human beings.

Thus the question concerning the corporeality of the resurrection and the capacity of the flesh for redemption provided a subject for controversies. The spectrum of devised solutions included on the one hand christological reasons for the bodily resurrection of the dead, according to which Jesus's incarnation as "assuming flesh" led to the redemption of human flesh (Epistle to Rheginos 44–49; Epistle to the Apostles). Also, new light fell on the Eucharist; it could now be understood as the life-giving offering of Jesus's flesh, which vouchsafes the par-ticipation in immortality (Gos. Phil. 23b; Justin, *1 Apol.* 66; Irenaeus, *Haer.* 5).

On the other hand, especially the genre "appearance stories" was taken up anew, in order to provide the figure of Jesus as a redeemer with aspects that are foreign to the picture of Jesus depicted in the canonical Gospels. Newly accented accounts of appearances arose; these report a wide range of dialogues and, instead of the resurrection of the body, speak of the ascent of the soul (Gospel of Mary). In such writings Jesus's earthly journey, and with it also his full humanity and his death on a cross, no longer played any role, since according to these new concepts Jesus's pre-Easter teaching did not need to be legitimized and his death did not need to be interpreted, but rather his function as redeemer of the parts in human beings that were capable of being redeemed needed to be highlighted. The way to the redemption of humanity could not be conveyed at all until after Easter by means of the revelation of his role in a mythological event. According to such writings, the way to the redemption of humanity does not consist in faith in the salvific event in Jesus and in the Eucharist, but rather in the knowledge that Jesus discloses.

5. Conclusion

The uniqueness of early Christian talk about the resurrection is that the first Christians ascribed to one man from their past a tangible position of power already in the present and the decisive role in the apocalyptic scheme of history. Differently from the patriarchs and characters of Israel's past who were endowed with special authority, such as Enoch, Abraham, Moses, and Elijah, who in early Jewish apocalyptic were portrayed as raptured to become recipients of revelation and thus could legitimate transcendent interpretations of history, and also differently from those who because of their fidelity to the law were held to be exemplary risen martyrs, in Jesus's case a Galilean Jew who shortly before was violently executed became the center of apocalyptic expectations and of an eschatologically attuned movement. This particularity is strongly interrelated with the activity of the earthly Jesus. The Easter narratives of the four Gospels demonstrate this implicitly and explicitly. Jesus's proclamation, combined with the disciples' Israelite-Jewish conviction of the power of God over life and death and of the implementation of his justice beyond the boundaries of death, finally made space for the assumption such that Jesus's disciples confessed Jesus as raised from the dead; conversely, the conviction that Jesus had been raised by God confirmed his pre-Easter message. The four Gospels detect no break between Jesus and the risen One, but rather, with the resurrection, allow Jesus to be confirmed as the one who he essentially is from the beginning (Luz 2002a). The changes caused by the resurrection lie on the part of the disciples and Jesus's followers, who go undergo a cognitive process. On this point, namely, on the close connection to the efficacy of the pre-Easter Jesus, later receptions of heavenly revelations of Jesus deviate.

Allison, Dale C. 2005b. *Resurrecting Jesus: The Earliest Christian Tradition and Its Interpreters.* London and New York.

Avemarie, Friedrich, and Hermann Lichtenberger, eds. 2001. *Auferstehung—Resurrection: The Fourth Durham-Tübingen Research Symposium; Resurrection, Transfiguration, and Exaltation in Old Testament, Ancient Judaism, and Early Christianity.* WUNT 135. Tübingen.

Becker, Jürgen. 2007. *Die Auferstehung Jesu Christi nach dem Neuen Testament: Os-tererfahrung und Osterverständnis im Urchristentum.* Tübingen.

Lethipuu, Outi. 2015. *Debates over the Resurrection of the Dead: Constructing Early Christian Identity.* Oxford.

Mainville, Odette. 2001. *Résurrection: L'après-mort dans le monde ancien et le Noveau testament.* Geneva.

Müller, Ulrich B. 1998. *Die Entstehung des Glaubens an die Auferstehung Jesu: His-torische Aspekte und Bedingungen.* SBS 172. Stuttgart.

Vinzent, Markus. 2011. *Christ's Resurrection in Early Christianity and the Making of the New Testament.* Farnham, UK.

Wolter, Michael. 2012. "Die Auferstehung der Toten und die Auferstehung Jesu." In *Auferstehung*, edited by Elisabeth Gräb-Schmidt and Reiner Preul, 13–54. MJT 24. Leipzig.

Wright, Nicholas Thomas. 2003. *The Resurrection of the Son of God.* Minneapolis.

Christine Jacobi

III. Early Confessions of Faith

Quite early after Jesus's death, his followers attempted to put into words their faith in him and their self-understanding that was connected with it. They expressed their new identity by, on one hand, boundaries directed toward the outside, and on the other hand, inwardly by explicatory processes. Early Christian literature often documents traces of these processes of self-definition in which Christians affirm that they *belong to Jesus*. Characteristic for this are particularly defined formulations that distinguish themselves by a certain stereotype and that make basic, foundational facts thematic. In these, scholarship has identified firmly shaped units of tradition, which, as preliterary forms, go back to the oldest primitive oral tradition (in summary Vielhauer [2]1978, 9–57). Especially this has to do with foundational data regarding the status of Jesus Christ, which are constitutive for the self-understanding of early Christians: regarding the relevance of Jesus's death and resurrection for salvation. The germinative cells of later confessions of faith can be apprehended in formulations of this type, which attain normative status for their representatives and by means of which they present themselves in public. But the variability of the old formulations itself shows that in the first century the spectrum of possible confessional statements is perceived as still extensively open and undefined. There was no "original confession." Also, one can speak of "formulas" in a fixed sense or even inflexible phrases only with considerable hesitation; in what follows, the more open category *traditional formulations* is given preference.

Confessional statements are found in most early Christian literary genres. In the Gospels, however, they are often so strongly embedded in the dynamics of the narrative that inferences to older preshaped material are hardly possible (example: Peter's confession in Mark 8:29 or that of Thomas in John 20:28). Things are different in the Epistles. Because confessional formulations often function there as the starting point or the foundation for specific lines of argument, they express to a certain extent general, consensual material that is unconditionally capable of assent. In addition, since epistles constitute the oldest texts of early Christian literature, research has especially found there traditional statements that "with a certain probability present the starting point (not of Christian faith, but) of Christian theology" (Conzelmann and Lindemann [14]2004, 133). Occasionally an author of an epistle ascribes such statements expressly to older tradition shared in common (1 Cor. 15:3).

1. Criteria

Some indicators for the identification of older confessional formulas have been suggested (Vielhauer [2]1978, 12–13; Staudt 2012, 10–11), which for given situations are capable of bearing weight to a greater or lesser degree. Especially in more recent research they are again extensively rendered problematic.

One such indicator is a citation formula, which unequivocally ensures that we are dealing with preexisting, verbally compressed tradition (1 Cor. 15:3; cf. 1 Thess. 2:13; Phil. 4:9; 2 Thess. 3:6). Another indicator is change in style, which serves as a sign for the implementation of preexisting older tradition. However, this can be utilized only conditionally, because especially with epistolary authors we can count on their ability to vary styles and use language creatively. It must be made plausible *in each individual case*, whether "the emergence of a text from its environment by means of stereotype form or poetic elements of style such as rhythmic structure, strophic construction, relative or participial style" (Vielhauer [2]1978, 12) permits recourse to preexisting tradition. Especially stylistic shifts and special vocabulary can also be intended by the author. Something analogous holds for formulas that are used with relative autonomy with respect to the literary context.

Differently from magic incantations and hieratic texts, strict invariability is not a characteristic of early Christian confessions of faith; rather, indistinct borders and variable fixed central statements are taken into account. Assurance can be verified only by multiple attestation.

The presence of special theological material is actually not a reliable indicator, since modern criteria of systematic coherence and consistency are often not applicable to ancient texts, especially to functional literature.

Correlating preliterary tradition with a precise, identifiable *Sitz im Leben* as an indication of older confessional formulas has suffered markedly in recent times. Whereas the location of faith formulas in a catechetical setting can still claim a certain measure of plausibility, the postulate of liturgical traditions comes about by extremely fabricated procedures. Statements such as *maranatha* (1 Cor. 16:22) or eucharistic cultic formulas (1 Cor. 11:23–25; Mark 14:22–25) present rather the exception. "Baptismal confessions," by contrast, remain completely hypothetical; such are identifiable only in the late second century (cf. also the reading in Acts 8:37). But if the function of confessions of faith in worship is uncertain, reticence is also recommended in the face of the popular exegetical characterization of theological and christological predications as "acclamations," since these presuppose God or Christ as direct addressees of the exclamation.

2. Typologies

Self-evidently, the complex textual reality can only be limitedly depicted by means of the categories suggested in exegesis. Instead of a sophisticated constructive model, as was standard in the era of form criticism, in what follows a modest descriptive procedure is chosen.

The image of two concentric circles is suggested. Its center forms the foundational conviction of "christological monotheism," according to which, by his relationship with Jesus, the one God defines and reveals himself anew. In the inner circle stand so-called *pistis formulas* (introduced by Kramer 1963), readily associated with "faith" as a verb or noun (πιστεύειν/πίστις). Scholarship has placed another type in comparison with these *pistis* formulas, so-called *homologies* (Conzelmann 1974b), also associated with technical vocabulary (ὁμολογεῖν/ὁμολογία). The basis for this distinction is the statement from Rom. 10:9, where both types are combined:

> If you confess with your mouth that Jesus is Lord,
> and believe in your heart that God has raised him from the dead,
> you will be saved.

> ἐὰν ὁμολογήσῃς ἐν τῷ στόματί σου κύριον Ἰησοῦν
> καὶ πιστεύσῃς ἐν τῇ καρδίᾳ σου ὅτι ὁ θεὸς αὐτὸν ἤγειρεν ἐκ νεκρῶν,
> σωθήσῃ.

Much speaks in favor of the thesis of more or less fixed *pistis* formulas. By contrast, the hypothesis of fixed homologies, which for their part can be subdivided into *kyrios* acclamations and statements of identification as Son of God (Vielhauer ²1978), is hardly reliable because variability and dependence on the context in all attestations are to be appraised as formidable. In what follows, statements of christological predications with other formulations that exhibit a kerygmatic or soteriological profile are located in an outer circle. Especially monotheistic formulas, and christological formulas associated with them, are to be taken into account; special traditions such as Rom. 3:24–25 are to be added to them. Also, confessional-like statements contained in the Gospels are grouped here. Statements that retain worship language, especially doxologies and benedictions, form a special complex outside of the concentric circles. "Songs" and "hymns" represent, again, a separate field that is only to a limited extent part of the topic of early confessions of faith.

3. *Traditional* Pistis *Formulations*

Pistis formulations are statements found in epistolary literature about the death or resurrection of Jesus, which are distinguished by means of succinct content and linguistic stereotype. They are readily connected with a technical use of "faith." This is a matter of traditional material (cf. 1 Cor. 15:3: παρέδωκα/παρ-έλαβον). The formulations look back into the substratum of faith in the (not distant!) past with its decisive salvific events that define the present. Three types are found: one-member formulations deal with (1) Jesus's resurrection or (2) his death; (3) multiple-member formulations combine the two, thus Jesus's death and resurrection are correlated with each other. The widely scattered data do not permit reconstructions of a history of development (according to which, for instance, the one-member formulas are older, and those about the resurrection are earlier than those about his death). Also, specific historical locations (for instance, in "Hellenistic Jewish Christianity" for the formulas about death in distinction from Palestinian Christianity) or the specification in a particular *Sitz im Leben* (for instance, in the catechumenate) can hardly be made plausibly.

At the center stands the theological statement that God *raised* Jesus from the dead (mostly in the aorist). The one-member formulation with God as the subject and with a finite verb is found in Rom. 10:9b, 1 Cor. 6:14, 15:15, and 1 Thess. 1:10; with a participial verb form in Rom. 4:24, 8:11, and 2 Cor. 4:14. A variant (with a quite thorough christological profile) presents the statement with Christ (!) as the subject, with a participial verb form in Rom. 6:9 and 8:34 or with a finite verb in Rom. 6:4; in this the passive form points in like manner to God as the agent. The formulations also occur in epistles of a later time (cf. Col. 2:12; Eph. 1:20; 1 Pet. 1:21). The fundamental metaphor of the succinct statements compares being dead with sleep, the resurrection with being awakened (ἐγείρεσθαι). The focus rests entirely on the action of being awakened, that is, on God. In addition to the metaphoric figuration of sleeping and waking, the figuration of rising occurs, that is, of standing up (ἀνιστάναι). Although it may more strongly express a nuance of the initiative of the one concerned (1 Thess. 4:14; Mark 8:31), the weight rests mostly on the "raising" (Acts 2:24; 10:40–41). The considerable reciprocal interactions between the two figurations is to be noted.

The statement of faith "God raised Jesus from the dead" or "Christ has been raised from the dead" appears to be extremely compact. If one wishes to make it alive hermeneutically, three broad perspectives are to be considered. First, it points out *retrospectively* that Jesus did not fail: God himself confirms Jesus's earthly life and teachings, which for its part comprehensively includes the Old Testament and Jewish belief and hope in itself. Second, it signals *prospectively* an anticipation of the eschatological resurrection of the dead: Jesus's resurrection stands in an apocalyptical context and initiates the eschatological events. Third, and this is the most crucial point, the statement brings into play a *theo-logical* dimension: God himself is defined anew by means of his action with respect to the dead Jesus. Obviously the formulation rests on the Old Testament–Jewish *predications about God*—his self-revelation in the exodus of Israel out of Egypt (Exod. 6:7; 20:2; Deut. 5:6; 6:12; Lev. 19:36) and in his creation of the world (Gen. 14:19; Ps. 115:15). Moreover, presumably it is also a mutation of Israel's affirmation of God as the one who makes the dead alive (Eighteen Benedictions 2; Jos. Asen. 20:7; 4Q521 vii 6; Rom. 4:17; 2 Cor. 1:9) into the affirmation of God as the one who raised the dead Jesus (differently J. Becker 2007, 96).

Formulations about *Jesus's death* are clearly more bountiful in variations than those about his being raised. It is in individual cases hardly possible to extricate a fixed formula from statements bound to the line of argument in an epistle. But here, too, we are undoubtedly confronted with very old convictions among Christ believers, which have been compressed and guide, for instance, Paul's wording: Jesus's death denotes a final, teleological dimension, which is expressed through prepositions: Jesus died "for," "on behalf of," "for the sake of," etc. (ὑπέρ, ἀντί, περί, διά). Two types are accessible: a *"death formula"* (Wengst 1972) with Christ as the subject and the verb in the aorist (ἀποθανεῖν; 1 Cor. 15:3b; Rom. 5:6, 8; 14:15; 1 Cor. 8:11; 1 Thess. 5:10; cf. 1 Pet. 3:18), and a *handing over formula* with God or Christ as the subject and a finite or participial verb form (παραδοῦναι, δοῦναι; Rom. 8:32; Gal. 1:4; 2:20; Eph. 5:2, 25; cf. John 3:16; 1 John 3:16). These statements are also extremely compressed; Old Testament–early Jewish concepts of atonement and vicarious substitution are received by Christ followers and transferred over to Jesus's death. Their specific location in Judaism (cultic atonement? death of martyrs? originally Greek tradition of "dying for"?) is the subject of debates, as is the status of the reception of Isa. 53:12 LXX ("that his soul was given over to death . . . he took the sins of many upon himself, and for the sake of their sins he was handed over").

Finally, *combined formulations* with the two poles of death and resurrection occur. They are by no means later than the simple statements. A prime example is the statement in 1 Cor. 15:3–5, which Paul himself explicitly ascribes to tradition that has been handed down. The traditional formulation probably spans vv. 3b–5. The amplifications are interesting: Jesus's dying and resurrection, here on the third day, are qualified by "according to the Scriptures"; the burial comes on the side of dying, the Easter manifestations are on the side of the resurrection. Precisely this statement, often understood as a "primordial confession," readily shows how the "formulas" call up a virtual pool of figures, conceptions, and intertextual relationships. They can be actualized or adjusted respectively by the particular author. Especially in Rom. 4:25 the question arises to what degree the double high points of the formulation are traced back to Paul (at least the recourse in v. 25a to Isa. 53:12 speaks against this). Combined formulations occur also in 2 Cor. 5:15, 1 Thess. 4:14, and Rom. 14:9; cf. Ignatius, *Rom.* 6.1.

4. Homological Predication Statements

In the statements customarily identified as *homologies*, a predicate, that is, the personal designation "Jesus" or "Jesus Christ," is associated with a high christological title, usually "Kyrios" ("Lord"), as the subject (Rom. 10:9–10; 1 Cor. 12:3; Phil. 2:11). In distinction from the *pistis* formulas, this is not a matter of a past event relevant for salvation but of a current rank of dignity, the godlike status of Jesus. At the same time, the terminology ὁμολογεῖν/ἐξομολογεῖσθαι expresses a juridical aspect: the "ideal scene" for this would be an earthly or, alternatively, heavenly court of justice; more widely, it is reminiscent of the *public manifestation of a binding belonging*. By predications of this type, their advocates set themselves off from other religio-political programs (for instance, imperial programs) and define their own identity. This act of "confessing for" interprets itself in the self-designation of Christ followers as those who "call on" "the name of the Lord" (Joel 3:5 MT and LXX; 2:32 NRSV), namely, Jesus Christ (1 Cor. 1:2; Rom. 10:13; Acts 9:14, 21). It speaks to the public character of the confession that the predication can attain the character of calling out, of an acclamation; thus, it goes along with a performatively consummated acknowledgment and submission (so esp. Phil. 2:11). Thereby the "confession" is a mutation of "extol" in the alignment of Septuagint language (cf. Rom. 14:11; 15:9; Hengel 2010, 316–17). In spite of this, it is in no way certain that divine worship can be postulated as the *Sitz im Leben* for the "confession."

Identifying confessional statements, in some cases with technical "homology" semantics, also occurs apart from specific Kyrios predications. In this it becomes detectable how the development of confessions is associated with the concern to *preserve* tradition deemed to be authentic. Thus the author of 1 John takes a stand against a division of the Johannine community with the confession of Christ. In its discussion with the opponents, 1 John is guided by the "confession" of Jesus Christ as "God's Son" (4:15; 5:5), and indeed specifically as the incarnate One (4:2–3; 2 John 7). Accordingly, the internal debate in the community about the appropriate interpretation of the Johannine tradition eventuates in succinct, formula-like statements, which intend to safeguard the Johannine heritage.

Especially Hebrews makes the confession of Jesus Christ as the Son of God (ὁμολογία: 3:1; 4:14; 10:23) a way of sustaining believers, who respond to the faithfulness of God and his promises with steadfastness and endurance. Even though the content of this confession is clearly shaped, it does not have to exist as a fixed catalogic formula. That its setting is situated in baptism (G. Bornkamm 1959) cannot be made certain.

At this point a glance at the confession in Q 12:8–9 suggests itself (for Campenhausen 1972, 213–14, the "starting point for the entire development" for creedal formation): "Everyone who confesses me before others, the Son of Man will confess before the angels. Everyone who denies me before others, will be denied before the angels."

This logion, probably going back to Jesus, which experiences a wide-ranging reception and reinterpretation (Matt. 10:32–33 par.; Mark 8:38 par.; Rev. 3:5; 2 Tim. 2:13; 1 John 2:23?; 4:15?; 2 Clem. 3:2), correlates the conduct toward the earthly Jesus with the conduct of the heavenly Son of Man; it places the circumstances of persecution (cf. Mark 13:9 par.) in opposition to the final judgment. Mark 8:38 embeds the saying in the ethics of discipleship. In striking distinction to the primary line of the homological traditions, "confessing" (ὁμολογεῖν) and "denying" are not related to grandeur in a majestic position (Son of Man), but precisely the other way around in contrast to a person of low estate (the "I" of Jesus).

5. Other Traditional Formulations with a Kerygmatic or Soteriological Profile

In their mission among Jews and gentiles, the first Christians went back to shaped topoi and sharply defined theological figures in order to proclaim God's new work and thereby also to present themselves as Christ believers. So, for example 1 Thess. 1:9b, 10 provides a form of missionary kerygma addressed to gentiles. But it is in no way like a fixed formula. Rather, it is better to speak of such only where (1) "God/Lord" formulations or (2) key soteriological phrases occur, which are to be appealed to as striking condensations of wide-ranging theological concepts.

Traditional formulations that are *monotheistically* contoured and to some extent associated with *christological* statements take on an especially important significance in early Christian literature. On the one hand, *unitarian formulas* (Staudt 2012) allude to the ancient Jewish *šəma* (Deut. 6:4) and, on the other hand, resort back to the Greco-Hellenistic εἷς θεός formula. Alongside statements on "the one God" themselves (Mark 2:7 par.; Rom. 3:30; Gal. 3:20; James 2:19; and esp. Eph. 4:6), "one Lord" formulations (εἷς κύριος) play a role that can hardly be overestimated. In this they reflect the Septuagint translation of Deut. 6:4 (κύριος ὁ θεὸς ἡμῶν κύριος εἷς ἐστιν; cf. Mark 12:29 par.). Eminently instructive is the passage in 1 Cor. 8:4–6, where Paul surpasses the "enlightened" thesis of the Corinthians, that there is but one God (v. 4), with a confessional statement (with the dative *iudicantis* [Hofius 2002, 173–74]) that functions with predications and all-statements combined with prepositions:

> For us there is only *one* God, the Father,
> from whom are all things and for whom we exist,
> and *one* Lord, Jesus Christ,
> through whom are all things, and through whom we exist.

It is the oneness that God shares with the Kyrios Jesus that ranks as an exclusively divine characteristic. God and Christ move extremely close together and nevertheless are distinguished from each other in a subordinate way. The program of "christological monotheism," claimed "for us," allows Paul to balance knowledge and love in the debate about eating sacrificial meat (cf. vv. 2–3). It is doubtful whether the confessional statement had a function in worship (therefore its designation as a doubled acclamation is also not without problems). The "binitarian" divine sphere outlined here is already occasionally differentiated in a triadic fashion (2 Cor. 13:13; Matt. 28:19).

Ephesians 4:4–6 presents a sevenfold declaration of oneness, introduced thematically by the "oneness of the Spirit," which is embodied in the *one* church, in the body of Christ (the rhetoric of "one" also occurs especially in 2:14–18). A doxology—here as a formulation about "all," modified by prepositions—concludes the series. Everything speaks in favor of the formulation by none other than the author of Ephesians, and we do not have before us a portion of a handed-down tradition. Even though the solemn evocation of oneness attains the character of a confessional statement, it is nevertheless embedded in the entire passage 4:1–16 with its programmatic correlation of the doctrine of God (Christ and the

Spirit included), ecclesiology, and ethic. The content of the "one faith" of v. 5 is developed, as v. 13 indicates, in vv. 7–16.

In the context of instruction about prayer, 1 Tim. 2:5–6 provides a statement about unicity that combines the "*one* God" with the "*one* mediator between God and humankind." Differently from 1 Cor. 8:6, Christ's achievement is not emphasized cosmologically but rather soteriologically. Patently the author of 1 Timothy reverts to the "ransom" saying in Mark 10:45. Once again it must remain open whether the literary context of the key kergymatic-soteriological statement also indicates its *Sitz im Leben*, that is, divine worship (1 Tim. 2:1–15).

6. Further Christological Confessions

Brief, pithy statements about who Jesus of Nazareth was and is attain the status of confessions for his followers when they are situated in public milieus (cf. E.III.4 above). Moreover, Christian men and women express their belonging to Jesus, which simultaneously obligates and distinguishes them in multiple ways. For this, "*Messiah*" or "*Christ*" and "*Son of God*" are the two eminent titles that are appealed to primarily as christological centers of gravity.

Paul works with confession-like formulations specifically where he deliberately comes to an understanding with his addressees about a common foundation (cf. Gal. 1:1b, 4a). He thus locates a christological statement at the beginning of Romans (1:3–4), in order to establish a platform capable of consensus in the discussion with a congregation that does not know him personally. With the distinction of Son of David and Son of God as well as of flesh and spirit, he provides a prelude to extensive argumentative nexuses (so the beginning of chaps. 9–11, namely, 9:4–5, transparently refers back to 1:3). Thus, confessional statements serve not only the self-presentation toward outsiders but also the self-clarification toward insiders. Once again, it is methodologically virtually impossible to separate "tradition" and "redaction" from each other.

The *synoptic accounts of Jesus* often make a topic of the question of Jesus's identity—"Who is this . . . ?" (Mark 4:41 par.). Peter's confession of "Christ" in Mark 8:27–33 introduces programmatically the section 8:27–10:52, which is about following in the shadow of the cross, condensed in the three passion predictions and the respective scenes following that, which develop in an exemplary fashion the disciples' failure to understand. The narration concerns verifying those who belong to Christ, the one who undergoes the passion. Christian life thus becomes a "confession." Contrapuntally, the three accounts aimed at the predication of God's Son (Mark 1:11; 9:7; 15:39) point to Jesus's unique union with God. But this high christological title together with the "Anointed One," like the "Son of Man," also attains confession-like status in a prominent public scene, namely, in Jesus's appearance before the Sanhedrin (14:61–62).

More pronounced, the *Gospel of John* moves Jesus's unique nature into the foreground by means of high christological predications, partly associated explicitly with "confessional" terminology (1:20; 9:22; 12:42). Apart from Jesus's prominent self-affirmations together with the "I am" sayings, the confessions of disciples and followers should be especially noted, which appeal directly to the capacity of readers to become mentally prepared. The confessions of the Samaritan woman (4:25–26), Peter (6:68–69), Martha (11:27), Mary (20:16–17), and, as a climax, Thomas (20:28) constitute key scenes. First John documents how the confession-like predications of the Gospel of John launch debates and processes of self-clarification in the Johannine circle (see E.III.4.2).

Differently from the narrative texts presented above, where the confessional statements are completely fitted into the narrative setting, *summarizing compilations* of Jesus's activities have given occasion to inquire about the preshaped traditional material. This applies not only to the three passion predictions (Mark 8:31; 9:31; 10:32–34, each with parallels), which offer a brief outline of the story of the passion and Easter, but especially also to the speeches of Acts, where miniature stories of Jesus occur (10:37–43; 13:28–31; cf. 2:31–33; 3:13–15, 20–21; 4:10; 5:30–31). Luke's exceptional ability to summarize with variation and simultaneously archaize, that is, to produce an antiquated patina, however, makes it almost impossible to penetrate behind the surface of the Lukan text and to isolate older fragments of tradition.

7. Liturgical Forms

In distinction from strong trends in exegesis of the twentieth century, liturgical forms can be moved more to the margin in a discussion of early confessions of faith. They are either too hypothetical (cultic forms, hymns) or too unproductive (doxologies) to be very informative on the question.

Verified *cultic formulas* (on this, see E.III.1.5 above) are preserved only sparsely. For the subject of confessions, they are marginally productive.

Doxologies and *benedictions* occur sporadically in early Christian literature, especially as the conclusion of prayers as well as epistles (Rom. 16:25–27; Jude 24–25) and epistolary sections (Rom. 11:36; Gal. 1:5; Eph. 3:21; 1 Tim. 1:17; 6:16), in the case of benedictions at the beginning of epistles (2 Corinthians, Ephesians, 1 Peter). They document beginnings of a "high" Christology, especially where Christ together with God (Rev. 5:13–14; 7:10) or independently becomes the recipient of the doxology (2 Tim. 4:18; 2 Pet. 3:18; Rev. 1:6; perhaps Heb. 13:21;

1 Pet. 4:11). Like cultic formulas, doxologies are marginally informative for the subject of confessions.

The existence of *songs*, more specifically hymns or psalms, in primitive Christian literature has been advocated in the twentieth century frequently and with considerable effort (so, for instance, for John 1:1–18; Phil. 2:6–11; Col. 1:15–20; 1 Tim. 3:16; 1 Pet. 2:21–24; Revelation). The methodological problems for their reconstruction, which were indicated above (E.III.3.1), are so formidable that a minimalist thesis is more advisable: obviously New Testament authors draw on traditional linguistic forms, figures, and conceptions in them. But their linguistic competence is generally so highly esteemed that it is hardly possible to dissect preexisting fragments. They provide no reliable basis for wider-reaching hypotheses like a liturgical *Sitz im Leben* (cf. Brucker 2013). Of course, apart from their postulated hymnic profile, the texts in question also have enormous significance for primitive Christian theology and devotion. But they go far beyond the narrower question pursued here regarding confessions.

8. Conclusion

Although the New Testament is not acquainted with any fixed confessional texts, it does have a series of traditional formulations in which Christ followers publicly testify that they belong to Jesus. On the one hand, with their "confession" they dissociate themselves from their environment, critically in the situation of persecution; on the other hand, they communicate on the inside about their fundamental convictions. In the late first century a concentration of confessional traditions can be observed. The "good confession" provides protection in face of external pressure (1 Tim. 6:12–13) and guidance in the way of faith under the threat of weariness (Hebrews). But especially confessions safeguard the normative Christian tradition in internal clarification processes, especially in disputes with dissidents (1 John, Acts, Pastoral Epistles). Thereby they pave the way for developments of the second and third centuries.

Campenhausen, Hans von. 1972. "Das Bekenntnis im Urchristentum." *ZNW* 63: 210–53.

Conzelmann, Hans. 1974b. "Was glaubte die frühe Christenheit?" (1955). In *Theologie als Schriftauslegung: Aufsätze zum Neuen Testament*, by Hans Conzelmann, 106–19. BEvT 65. Munich.

Hahn, Ferdinand. 2006. "Bekenntnisformeln im Neuen Testament." In *Studien zum Neuen Testament*, vol. 2, *Bekenntnisbildung und Theologie in urchristlicher Zeit*, by Ferdinand Hahn, 45–60. WUNT 192. Tübingen.

Hengel, Martin. 2010. "Bekennen und Bekenntnis." In *Theologische, historische und biographische Skizzen: Kleine Schriften VII*, by Martin Hengel, 313–47. WUNT 253. Tübingen. ET: "Confessing and Confession." In *Earliest Christian History: History, Literature, and Theology*, by Michael F. Bird and Jason Maston, 589–623. WUNT II 320. Tübingen, 2012.

Hoffmann, Paul. 1994. "Der Glaube an die Auferweckung Jesu in der neutestament-lichen Überlieferung." In *Studien zur Frühgeschichte der Jesus-Bewegung*, by Paul Hoffmann, 188–256. SBAB 17. Stuttgart.

Kinzig, Wolfram. 2017. *Faith in Formulae: A Collection of Early Christian Creeds and Creed-Related Texts*. Vol. 1, 35–60. OECT. Oxford.

Longenecker, Richard N. 2005. "Christological Materials in the Early Christian Communities." In *Contours of Christology in the New Testament*, by Richard N. Longenecker, 47–76. MMNTS 7. Grand Rapids.

Neufeld, Vernon H. 1963. *The Earliest Christian Confessions*. NTTS 5. Leiden.

Vielhauer, Philipp. ²1978. *Geschichte der urchristlichen Literatur: Einleitung in das Neue Testament, die Apokryphen und die Apostolischen Väter*. Berlin and New York.

Wengst, Klaus. 1984. "Glaubensbekenntnis(se) IV. Neues Testament." *TRE* 13: 392–99.

Samuel Vollenweider

IV. Christological Titles

Usually the term "christological titles" designates predications, that is, "stable linguistic attributes" (Karrer 1998, 18), which served in early Christianity to express Jesus's significance and grandeur (*Hoheit*) succinctly. These are primarily the designations "Anointed One"/"Messiah"/"Christ" (χριστός), "Lord" (κύριος) and "the Son of God" (ὁ υἱὸς τοῦ θεοῦ) or alternatively "the Son" (ὁ υἱός), further "the Son of Man" (ὁ υἱὸς τοῦ ἀνθρώπου and ὁ υἱὸς [τοῦ] Δαυίδ), as well as some terms occurring only occasionally, for example, "Savior"/"Redeemer" (σωτήρ: Phil. 3:20; Luke 2:11; Acts 5:31; 2 Tim. 1:10), "the Word" (ὁ λόγος: John 1:1, 14), "the Prophet" (ὁ προφήτης: John 6:14; 7:40), and "Wisdom" (ἡ σοφία: Matt. 11:19 par. Luke 7:35).

In this article the designations "Lord," "the Anointed One," and "Son of God" will be taken into consideration, since they are attested in almost all New Testament writings and therefore present ancient, traditional christological predications. In addition, the Son of Man title (which is broadly anchored in the New Testament narrative traditions) as well as the Son of David title (which—although present only in a narrow strain of tradition—played a large role in christological research as a presumed abbreviation for an ancient Christology) will also be considered. The task will be to relate the origin of the so-called christological titles with Jesus's ministry, that is, to inquire about the extent to which the christological titles reflect the relationship between Jesus's ministry and use of the titles in post-Easter Christianity. The origin of these designations, however, has been highly contested from the time of Wilhelm Bousset's pioneer work *Kyrios Christos* (1913) because precisely at this point the question of continuity or discontinuity of the earthly Jesus and Jesus's post-Easter christological significance is raised at its sharpest. To this day, several large-scale investigations (e.g., Cullmann 1957; Hahn 1963 [⁵1995]; Kramer 1963; Dunn 1980 [²1992]; Karrer 1998; Hurtado 2003) as well as special investigations (e.g., Berger 1971, 1973; Hengel 1975; Fitzmyer 1979; Hurtado 1988; Karrer 1990; Jung 2002; Casey 2007) have not led to any consensus on the issue.

Methodologically speaking, it is essential to consider first the semantic, history-of-religions and history-of-traditions backgrounds as well as the use of the christological titles within earliest Christianity independently from the question about a possible origin in the ministry/preaching of Jesus. Only in a second stage can hypotheses about a possible origin in Jesus's ministry be formulated.

1. Lord

The noun κύριος in Greek is a designation for persons of authority, who exercise power or rule (frequently in conjunction with the power to make decisions) over other persons in a particular social context. The word derives originally from household terminology and from time immemorial has designated the father of the family as lord of the household, especially in his status as owner and authoritative master of household slaves. By metaphorical application it expanded gradually to other social contexts, first in early Hellenism to political contexts as a designation for rulers, thereafter to the context of religion as a designation for gods and other supernatural powers and figures, and finally as a respectful designation for all sorts of people of higher social standing (overview in C. Zimmermann 2007, 187–93).

The earliest confession of nascent Christianity discernible by us was "*Jesus* is Lord" (1 Cor. 12:3; Rom. 10:9; Phil. 2:11; see E.IV.3). With this, early Christians acknowledged Jesus as an authority endowed with discretionary power over them ("*our* Lord"; cf., e.g., 1 Cor. 1:7) and accordingly acclaimed him as "Lord!" (Acts 1:6; 7:59–60; 9:10, 13; cf. also Matt. 7:21 par. Luke 6:46; Matt. 25:31–46). The resurrection (Rom. 10:9; Phil. 2:9–11; Luke 24:3, 34; Acts 2:36), the status attained by means of it, and the power associated with it (1 Cor. 8:6; 2 Cor. 4:5–6; Phil. 2:9–11; Acts 2:34–36) constituted the foundation for this. The call μαραναθά (Aramaic:

māranā' tā' or *māran 'ātā'* = "our Lord, come!") in 1 Cor. 16:22 indicates that the address of Jesus as Lord hails back to the earliest Aramaic-speaking Christians (cf. Hahn [5]1995, 100–109).

As for continuities with Jesus's ministry, on the one hand the Jesus tradition does not remain untouched by this post-Easter titular usage, as, for example, the rather frequent use of ὁ κύριος for Jesus in the Gospel of Luke demonstrates (cf. 7:13, 19; 10:1, 39, 41, and passim; cf. also Mark 11:3 par.). On the other hand, reference is also made outside the Gospels to the earthly Jesus with the designation κύριος, so, for instance, when referring to sayings of the earthly Jesus (1 Cor. 7:10; 9:14; 11:23; cf. further, οἱ ἀδελφοί or ὁ ἀδελφὸς τοῦ κυρίου: 1 Cor. 9:5; Gal. 1:19). In the Jesus tradition, Jesus is addressed as "Lord" (κύριε) both by outsiders (cf., e.g., Mark 7:28; Matt. 9:28; 20:30–33; Luke 7:6; 19:8; John 4:11, 15, 19, 49) and by his disciples (Matt. 8:25; 26:22; Luke 9:57–61; John 11:3, 34; and passim). It can be assumed that κύριος/κύριε reflects the usage of the Aramaic *mār/mārêh* as a designation for persons of authority, which probably was occasioned by Jesus's teaching, proclaiming, and acting with authority. Within the circle of his disciples, the designation surely reflected the difference in authority between a teacher and his disciples (Matt. 10:24–25). This also is indicated in Jesus's authority over his disciples, when he, for example, commissions or sends them out (cf., for instance, Mark 11:2–3; 14:13–14; further Mark 6:7–13 par. and Luke 10:1, there also ὁ κύριος).

It must be considered quite probable that Jesus's disciples still referred to him as "Lord" after they had come to the conviction that he is alive although he had been crucified. To be sure, the referential context of the term was radically changed by the conviction of Jesus's resurrection and exaltation: he was now no longer the teacher with authority but rather the one exalted to God who thereby possesses heavenly power and status (with the result that the benchmarks change; cf. only 1 Cor. 8:6). One can thus speak of continuity and simultaneously discontinuity in the pre- and post-Easter use of the term "Lord" for Jesus.

2. The Anointed One (Christ/Messiah)

The christological title used most often in the New Testament is "Christ"/"Messiah," that is, "the Anointed One" (χριστός). In the earliest attestations in Paul, χριστός occurs primarily in the form Ἰησοῦς χριστός or χριστὸς Ἰησοῦς, further in the absolute form (ὁ) χριστός as well as in various syntagms with *kyrios* (κύριος Ἰησοῦς χριστός, etc.). In all probability, the syntagms Ἰησοῦς χριστός or χριστὸς Ἰησοῦς are abbreviations of early Christian confessions (see E.IV.3), which revered Jesus as the "Anointed One" or "Christ" (cf., e.g., Mark 8:29; John 7:26, 41; 1 John 5:1). Χριστός is a verbal adjective of the verb χρίειν with the meaning of "to anoint (with oil/ointment)." In Greek the word is used with respect to humans *only* in the Septuagint, the New Testament, and in writings dependent on them. In this personal usage it translates the Hebrew *māšîaḥ* or Aramaic *məšîḥāʾ* (as a loanword: μεσσίας; cf. John 1:41; 4:25). For the semantic valence this means that the term must have been considered unusual in non-Jewish contexts and was therefore recognizable as a term hailing from ancient Judaism.

The anointing of the king in Israel (2 Sam. 19:22, etc., which, however, came to an end with the exile and was not revived afterward), the anointing of the high priest (which was discontinued after the crisis under Antiochus Epiphanes), as well as the (metaphorical) reference to the anointing of prophets in Israel's Scriptures (for instance, 1 Kings 19:16; further, Isa. 61:1) provided the history-of-religions and history-of-traditions roots. At the time of Jesus and the origin of Christianity, there was therefore no anointing of either kings or priests. It is to be noted in particular that the terminology of anointing was not associated at any time since the exile with the political restitution of kingly rule in Israel, neither by the Hasmoneans and Herodians nor by post-Herodian pretenders to the throne; especially the ideal of a political restoration of Davidic rule was not associated with the concept of a messiah (Karrer 1998, 135–36).

At the time of Jesus and of the origin of Christianity, the personal predication "messiah" or "christ" was reserved in contemporaneous Judaism (under the influence of 1 Kings 19:16?) for great *prophetic* figures from Israel's *past* (the patriarchs[!], Moses, and other prophets; however, *not for kings, not even for David!*). However, it also referred to end-time figures, who will appear variously as ruling figures (e.g., Pss. Sol. 17–18; 4Q252; 1 En. 52:4; 4 Ezra 11–13; 2 Bar. 29–30; 39–40; 70–73), priestly figures (e.g., 11Q13 ii 18; T. Reu. 6:8), or prophetic figures (4Q521) (cf. Karrer 1990, 95–376). Thus, at the time of Jesus and the origin of Christianity, the messiah predication referred to ideal representatives of God in the past and future, who—as ones "anointed (by God)"!—are designated as especially authorized and sanctified by God and therefore are in a unique way close to God.

The fact that the predication "Christ" occurs conspicuously frequently in (in part, ancient formulaic) statements that deal with Jesus's death or resurrection (cf. 1 Thess. 5:9–10; 1 Cor. 8:11; 15:1–3; Gal. 1:4; 2:21; Rom. 5:6, 8; 6:3–4, 9; 8:34; 10:6–7; 14:15; and passim) and crucifixion (1 Cor. 1:23; 2:2; Gal. 3:1, 13) (cf. esp. Kramer 1963) indicates that the confession that Jesus is (God's) Anointed One or Christ was formulated in view of the death on the cross and on the basis of the resurrection. The predication signifies that Jesus who died and arose is precisely the one who was anointed (by God), and who therefore stands uniquely close to God (Acts 2:36; 2 Cor. 4:4). Thus the result is that God's presence is realized in him (cf. 2 Cor. 4:4, 6; 5:19) and God's beneficent, that is, saving, activity is therefore channeled through him. In accordance with the history-of-tradition (cf. above), the exalted Jesus fulfills as God's Anointed One a central eschatological role (e.g., 1 Cor. 15:20–24; 1 Thess. 5:9–10; Luke 3:15–16; cf. Acts 2:32; 17:31).

To what extent did the post-Easter concept of Jesus as the "Anointed One" or "Christ" relate to Jesus's ministry? We note that when "Christ"-terminology occurs in the Jesus tradition, the influence of the post-Easter confessional tradition is usually obvious (cf. Mark 8:29 par.; John 9:22; 11:27; 20:31; cf. further Mark 1:1; 14:61 par.; Matt. 16:20; Luke 22:67; John 1:41; 4:29; 7:41); or at least a post-Easter perspective is clearly recognizable (Matt. 1:18; 16:20; 23:10; 27:17; Luke 24:26, 46; John 9:22). Since Jesus nowhere in the Jesus tradition uses the predication "Messiah" or "Christ" for himself, one can confidently assume that Jesus had not made any explicit "messianic" claim that led to the post-Easter usage of the title. If we ask whether Jesus's ministry prepared for or prefigured his predication in early Christianity with the christological title "Messiah" or "Christ," his proclamation of the coming kingdom of God should primarily be taken into consideration. First, it conveyed to his followers the eschatological context in which they interpreted their Easter experiences. Further, since Jesus linked the coming kingdom of God intimately with his own ministry and conceived of this as the turning point of salvation, so that the eschatological and ultimate breaking in of God's rule was at some points in his work already realized (Luke 11:20 par. Matt. 12:28; further Luke 17:20–21; Luke 7:22–23 par. Matt. 11:5–6), he ascribed to himself a central role in the realization of eschatological salvation. At the same time, this implies a unique proximity to God, who realizes his ultimate rule through Jesus. Since the early Christian concept of the Anointed One (Christ/Messiah) implies unique proximity to God on the one hand and a central eschatological function on the other, the predication of the risen One with the title of Messiah or Christ not only served to indicate the status of the risen Jesus as well as his future eschatological function (see above), but also simultaneously succinctly expressed central aspects of Jesus's earthly ministry and his self-perception. Although the use of the designation "Anointed One" can hardly be made plausible with respect to the historical Jesus, the post-Easter predication stands in some continuity with the ministry and proclamation of the earthly Jesus that is not to be underestimated.

A further aspect should be considered: the use of χριστός for a human person unambiguously indicates the provenance from ancient Judaism and has the effect that the predication "Christ" makes it clear that salvation through Jesus as God's Anointed is irrevocably bound to Israel and their God (cf. Rom. 9:4–5). This accords with the fact that Jesus's ministry took place in Israel and his proclamation was intended for Israel.

3. Son of God

The predication "Son of God" (ὁ υἱὸς τοῦ θεοῦ κτλ) is quite broadly dispersed in the New Testament in the confessional tradition (cf. 1 John 4:15; 5:5; John 11:27;

20:31; Matt. 16:16; further Heb. 4:14) and—although only rarely used by Paul for Jesus—"the Son of God Jesus Christ" was, according to 2 Cor. 1:19, the content of Paul's proclamation (thus also Rom. 1:1–4:9; Gal. 1:16), so that one can assume the use of this christological title in early Christianity from a very early stage on. The quite frequent combination with the predication "Christ" is striking (cf. only Mark 14:61 par.; Matt. 16:16; John 20:31; 1 John 4:15; 5:5).

To define more precisely the meaning of this predication, we need to inquire about the motif background and the history-of-religions background. The origins of this designation as applied to Jesus in early Christianity are intensely debated (cf. Hahn [5]1995, 474–84 [appendix]). There is currently a relative consensus that it is explained from ancient Jewish presuppositions. If one looks at the attestations of "son of God" in the Old Testament and early Jewish literature in particular, one sees that the term refers at one time or another to angels or heavenly beings (Gen. 6:2, 4; Job 1:6; 2:1; 38:7; Pss. 29:1; 82:6; 89:7; Dan. 3:25; Wis. 5:5), to Israel (Exod. 4:22; Hos. 11:1) or the Israelites (Deut. 14:1; 32:5, 18–19; Isa. 43:6; 45:11; 63:8; Jer. 4:22; further as an eschatological promise: Jub. 1:24–25; Pss. Sol. 17:27; T. Jud. 24:3; 1 En. 62:11), to the king of Israel (2 Sam. 7:14; Pss. 2:7; 89:27–28), to a righteous person (Wis. 2:13, 16, 18) or an individual such as Joseph (Jos. Asen. 6:3, 5; 13:13; 18:11; 21:4; 23:10), and so forth—all attestations denoting a unique intimate relationship or closeness to God of the one so designated. The "son of God" belongs in a special way to God or stands especially close to God. This should be considered the semantic content of the expression (the striking semantic affinity with the Christ predication also has an effect on the confession tradition, cf., for instance, 1 John 4:15; 5:5; John 11:27; 20:31; Matt. 16:16; etc.). However, the foundation for this unique proximity to God varies from context to context (e.g., physical closeness, spirit possession, faithfulness to the Torah, faithfulness to God, etc.).

In Jesus's case, this unique proximity to God is, according to Rom. 1:3–4, grounded in Jesus's resurrection and exaltation to God (cf. also Heb. 1:3–8; 4:14). Correspondingly, the risen Jesus who is revealed by God is called "the Son of God" in Gal. 1:16. Similarly, his exaltation is presupposed in 1 Thess. 1:10 and Gal. 4:6, where Paul likewise speaks of the Son of God: Jesus stands as the risen One and therefore as God's Son in the heavenly court, thus in direct proximity to God, like the angels (cf. in this regard esp. Heb. 1:3–8; cf. also Mark 13:32)—such angelomorphic christological concepts also appear to constitute the background of the so-called transfiguration of God's beloved Son in Mark 9:2–9 par. (cf. also 1 Cor. 4:4–6, where, however, it is not combined with the designation "Son of God" but with "Christ" and "Kyrios").

Regarding a possible prefiguration in Jesus's ministry, we note that in Paul Jesus's status as the heavenly Son of God is repeatedly linked with the possession of the Spirit; see, for example, Gal. 4:6, according to which God endowed the believing children (υἱοί) of God with the Spirit of the exalted Son of God (cf. further Rom. 1:4). This corresponds in a striking way to the synoptic tradition, where Son of God terminology is primarily linked with the endowment of the Spirit (Mark 1:9–11 par.; Mark 15:39 par. Matt. 27:54); against the background of Isa. 52:7 and 61:1, this person is understood as God's Spirit-anointed last messenger or eschatological prophet (cf. Toit 2006, 344–58): as bearer of the Spirit, Jesus is "God's Son," who thus stands in a singular intimate relationship with God. Since Jesus's possession of the Spirit or, alternatively, his activity by means of the Spirit belongs to the oldest stock of the Jesus tradition (Q and Mark; cf. esp. Mark 3:28–30 par. Matt. 12:31–32 par. Luke 12:10, as well as Matt. 12:28 par. Luke 11:20), a claim by Jesus to a unique relationship with God might be justifiable. Thus, through the use of the christological title "Son of God" in the Jesus tradition—the title that in earliest Christianity designated the exalted and risen Jesus—a certain continuity was established between the post-Easter status of the exalted Jesus and the ministry of the earthly Jesus or his claim to a special relationship with God. This, however, does not allow us to conclude with certainty that the use of the title reached back to Jesus's lifetime (cf., however, Casey 2010, 388–91).

In this connection a further aspect of the Jesus tradition should be pointed out: in the Gospel of John Jesus's unique relationship with God, which is reflected in the revelatory unity of both will and action, is primarily expressed with the aid of the Father-Son imagery (John 3:35–36; 5:19–23; and passim; cf. also the address of God as πάτερ in 17:1; cf. 3:16–18, etc., for Son of God terminology). In Q (Matt. 11:25–27 par. Luke 10:21–22) the case is similar. Because the unity of the will of Jesus and God is also linked in Mark 14:36 to the address of God as Father ("*Abba*"), we seem to have here a motif that is attested broadly in the Jesus tradition and perhaps reflects an aspect of Jesus's self-perception according to which he stood in an especially close relationship with God, which, among other ways, was expressed in his conformity to the will of God, his Father (cf. also Mark 3:25 par. Matt. 12:25; cf. Matt. 7:21; 18:14). There therefore seems to exist a certain link to the predication of Jesus as "Son of God" in early Christianity. However, no attempt should be made to explain the titular use in early Christianity solely on this basis.

4. Son of Man

In Greek, the unusual expression "the Son of Man" (ὁ υἱὸς τοῦ ἀνθρώπου), which in the Jesus tradition (with the exception of John 5:27) appears only in the form of doubled definite articles ("*the* Son *of the* Man"), is linguistically a Semitism, which goes back to an equivalent Aramaic expression (*bar-('æ)nāš/bar-('æ) nāša'*). In the Aramaic of the time, the expression means "(the) human being," "someone," or "every human/person," that is, "everybody" or "everyman." It was thus used with a generic and generalizing meaning, in order to make generalizing statements (so M. Casey, J. Fitzmyer; on the research, cf. the clear presentations in Schröter 1997, 451–55; Hurtado 2003, 299–304; Dunn 2003b, 724–37). In such generalizing statements the speaker can relate the term (similar to the use of "*man*" in German or of "one" in English) especially to herself/himself, if applicable in the sense of "someone like me," "someone in my situation" (B. Lindars). However, it cannot be used simply as an exclusive reference to oneself in the sense of "I" (so the hypothesis of G. Vermes, refuted by Fitzmyer and Casey).

The expression appears in the Gospels and Acts 7:56 as a designation for Jesus, and indeed (with the exception of John 9:35 and Acts 7:56) always in the mouth of Jesus. This is usually interpreted to the effect that Jesus spoke in some form about the "Son of Man." If one examines the instances where "Son of Man" is used, it becomes clear that its use in the Gospel of John is deeply integrated into the Johannine preexistent and incarnational Christology, and therefore can be utilized only with extreme care in the quest for the historical Jesus. The examination of instances in the synoptic tradition shows that the expression occurs in three distinct, but typical, contexts.

1. One part of the "Son of Man" sayings is related to Jesus's earthly and authoritative ministry (Mark 2:10 par.; 2:28 par.; Q Luke 7:33–34 par. Matt. 11:18–19; Q Luke 9:58 par. Matt. 8:20; Q Luke 12:10 par. Matt. 12:32; Luke 19:10).

2. Other "Son of Man" sayings refer to the eschatological coming or Jesus as judge or as an eschatological figure (Mark 8:38 par.; 13:26 par.; 14:62 par.; Q Luke 17:24, 26–27, 30 par. Matt. 24:27, 37–38, 39; Matt. 10:23; 13:41; 16:27; 19:28; 25:31–46; Luke 6:22; 12:8–9; 17:22).

3. A third group concerns the suffering (and the resurrection) of the Son of Man (Mark 8:31 par.; 9:31 par.; 10:33–34 par.; 14:21, 41 par.; 9:9; 10:45 par.; Matt. 17:9; 20:28; 12:40).

This state of affairs is even more complicated by the fact that in some parallel statements "Son of Man" is rendered instead with "I" (cf., e.g., Luke 6:22; 12:8–9 par.; Matt. 5:11; 10:32–33; Mark 8:27 par. Matt. 16:13; Mark 10:45 par. Matt. 20:28 par.; Luke 22:27).

The "Son of Man" statements in the third group can be excluded from the question about the origin of the use of the title in early Christianity or in Jesus's ministry, since it is a matter of a Markan innovation and its reception by Matthew/Luke.

Another aspect of the tradition is that the use with the definite article ("*the* Son of Man") can be understood anaphorically in the sense of "the well-known, specific Son of Man." The Jesus tradition has this characteristic in common with the definite use of the expression in the Book of Similitudes in 1 En. 37–71 (cf., for instance, 46:3–4; 62:5, 7, 14), where the term is also related (similarly as in Mark 8:38 par.; 13:28 par.; 14:62 par.) to an eschatological figure of judgment (cf., e.g., 1 En. 62; 70–71; cf. on this J. Becker 1996, 112–16). For both cases, the expression "one like a son of man" in Dan. 7:13–14 constitutes an intertextual background, where the "one like a human" serves as a metaphor for "the people of the holy ones of the Most High" or Israel (Dan 7:27; this comparative expression [= "one like a son of man"] also occurs in the first century in 4 Ezra 13:2 for an eschatological, salvific figure of judgment). For the issue at hand, this history-of-traditions context is of decisive significance: in current research a consensus exists (in contrast to older research) that, firstly, for the time of Jesus and the origin of Christianity, no firmly outlined concept of an eschatological Son of Man figure in Judaism can be substantiated, and that, secondly, a history-of-traditions dependence of Jesus or early Christianity on the Book of Similitudes, that is, 1 En. 37–71 (which was probably written only in the second half of the first century), most probably can be excluded. This means that the manner of speaking about "*the* son of man" with the definite article with recourse to Dan. 7 as an eschatological heavenly figure of judgment in the Jesus tradition and in the Book of Similitudes in 1 Enoch constitutes analogous history-of-religions phenomena in the first century, without our being able to discover any mediating traditions.

If one poses against this background the question about the possible origin of the post-Easter titular usage of the expression "the Son of Man" in early Christianity (e.g., John 3:14–15; 9:35), one gets involved in one of the most complicated questions—if not *the* most complicated question—of Jesus scholarship: not only must the multifaceted evidence of the Gospels be coordinated with the linguistic and history-of-traditions evidence, but it must also be correlated with a plausible historical development, which ranges from the Baptizer's discourse about "one who is coming" through Jesus's proclamation of the kingdom of God to the origin of early Christianity and early Christian high Christologies. I do not intend here to present my own personal approach to this issue; rather, the approaches that are advocated in scholarship are to be briefly presented.

One of the most influential solutions of the problem in the history of research goes back to Rudolf Bultmann; it was propagated especially by Ferdinand Hahn ([5]1995, 13–53; 1983, 927–35), and in more recent Jesus research, for example, Jürgen Becker (1996, 249–67) championed it. The basis for this is the observation that in Luke 12:8–9 and Mark 8:38 the first-person singular and the designation "Son of Man" are used such that the former points toward Jesus at that time but the expression "Son of Man" refers to the future recompense of this conduct in the eschatological judgment. This is interpreted such that Jesus used the expression "Son of Man" to refer to someone other than himself, namely, a coming figure upon whom the responsibility of eschatological judgment will lie. After Easter, Jesus was—in view of the Easter experiences and the conviction that he was risen and exalted to God—identified in early Christianity with the eschatological Son of Man expected by Jesus. The concept was expanded with reference to Dan. 7, Ps. 110, and Zech. 12, and then projected back into the tradition about the earthly Jesus, so that statements about Jesus's earthly ministry and his suffering (and resurrection) were combined with the term "Son of Man."

One part of Jesus scholarship opted for a solution that explains the formation of the "Son of Man" Christology in analogy to the post-Easter formation of other christological titles. It goes back to Philipp Vielhauer, and through Norman Perrin became very popular in Anglophone scholarship of the so-called second quest for the historical Jesus. According to this hypothesis, the concept of an eschatological "Son of Man" stands in conflict with Jesus's proclamation of the kingdom of God, so that the "Son of Man" logia must have developed completely independently from the historical Jesus in post-Easter early Christianity as a creation of the Christian community under the influence of the Enochian Book of Similitudes (Vielhauer) or of early Christian *pesher* traditions (Perrin). Today this model of explanation has hardly any proponents.

Especially in Anglophone scholarship, an approach has been established since the 1970s under the substantial influence of Geza Vermes to explain the development only against the background of the Aramaic linguistic evidence. The approach was further developed—with differences in detail—by Joseph A. Fitzmyer, Carsten Colpe, Barnabas Lindars, Maurice Casey, and Mogens Müller, and has been extremely popular in the noneschatological branch of the so-called third quest (cf., for instance, Crossan 1994a, 238–61). The root of the entire development is seen in the supposedly generalizing statements Jesus made about humanity per se. Especially Mark 2:10, 28 par. as well as Q Luke 9:58 par. Matt. 8:20 serve as the key evidence. According to this hypothesis, Jesus spoke about the general rootlessness of human beings and also said every human may forgive sins and exercise power over the Sabbath (cf., for instance, Crossan 1994a, 255–59). Only in early Christianity was this striking way of speaking of Jesus at first transformed into individualizing references to Jesus himself (Q Luke 7:33–34 par. Matt. 11:18–19; Q Luke 12:10 par. Matt. 12:32; Luke 22:48), in which "Son of Man" serves instead of "I" or next to "I" as a reference to himself. Thereafter a process of eschatologizing took place, in which the designation "Son of Man" became a christological title referring to the risen and exalted Jesus and was linked to Jesus's parousia and his function as eschatological judge. In a later stage, it was also linked to the suffering and resurrection of the earthly Jesus (cf., e.g., the presentation in Casey 2010, 369–88).

524

A fourth model is related to this approach, the proponents of which (for instance, J. D. G. Dunn, M. Casey) also see the point of departure for the development in Jesus's use of Aramaic. However, from the beginning they detect in the Son of Man sayings mentioned above an intentional reference by Jesus to himself ("in a general and self-referential way best indicated by a translation 'a man like me' equivalent to the English 'one'" [Dunn 2003b, 761]; "used in an idiomatic way in a general statement which refers particularly to the speaker with or without other people" [Casey 2010, 361]). Dunn and Casey consider Mark 2:10, 28 par.; Q Luke 12:10 par. Matt. 12:32 par. Mark 3:28–29; Q Luke 9:58 par. Matt. 8:20; Q Luke 7:33–34 par. Matt. 11:18–19 as authentic sayings of Jesus (Casey also considers the following authentic: Mark 9:12; 14:21; Luke 22:48). Both also hold Q Luke 12:8–9 par. Matt. 10:32–33 par. Mark 8:38 to be authentic, but in these they see no reference to an eschatological figure but simply Jesus's claim that he is to appear in the final judgment as an important witness (Casey) or Jesus's expectation of restitution ("vindication") in the final judgment (cf. Dunn 2003b, 737–62, esp. 760–61; Casey 2010, 358–68, esp. 368).

Related to this last approach is one that discerns in the Son of Man expression a striking self-designation of Jesus, with which he highlighted or emphasized his unique claim to be the authorized preacher of the kingdom of God (Berger 1994, 615–22, esp. 618–19; Schröter 1997, 451–57; 2006b, 244–54; similarly also Hurtado 2003, 304–6). This unique authoritative claim lent itself eminently as the starting point for a further development in early Christianity: the fact that statements in the Jesus tradition about the blessing of the persecuted for the sake of the Son of Man (Q Luke 6:22), or about Jesus's earthly authority or about his coming again as the eschatological judge, were linked precisely with the Son of Man terminology constitutes an appropriate early Christian unfolding of Jesus's striking claim to be God's authorized messenger as expressed in his use of the "Son of Man" terminology (Schröter 1997, 457).

5. Son of David

The designation "Son of David" (ὁ υἱὸς [τοῦ] Δαυίδ) differs from the other christological titles in that it is not used for the risen and exalted Jesus but only for the earthly Jesus. Moreover, it occurs only in the Synoptic Gospels (Mark 10:47 par.; 12:35–37 par.), and there especially in the Gospel of Matthew (1:1; 9:27; 12:23; 15:22; 20:30–31; 21:9). Two aspects are to be discerned in this context (cf. in general on the theme, Karrer 1998, 187–90).

1. Most instances occur in the context of Jesus's activity of healing or exorcism (Mark 10:47 par.; Matt. 9:27; 12:22–23; 15:22; 20:30–31, cf. the connection of 20:29–

34 with 21:1–11, esp. v. 9!). The Jewish concept of Solomon as the ideal and wise offspring of David constitutes the history-of-traditions background: according to the tradition, Solomon had at his disposal knowledge over demons or the power to heal with herbs (Wis. 7:20) and especially was considered to be a conqueror of demons (T. Sol. 1–2; 20; there with the title "son of David," cf. 1:7; 20:1; LAB 60:3; Josephus, *Ant.* 8.45–49; 11Q11 i). As a healer and exorcist Jesus therefore appears as a kind of new Solomon. The tradition, however, relativizes this by recording that he is more than Solomon (Matt. 12:42–43; cf. the connection with 12:43–45 and 12:22–30). That Jesus in his lifetime was so designated on the basis of his reputation as an exorcist must be considered possible in principle; however, the quite meager attestation in the Jesus tradition probably speaks against it.

2. In Mark 12:35–37 objections against a non-Davidic origin of the Christ (cf. also John 7:41–42) are discounted with reference to Ps. 110, and thus are judged to be irrelevant for the issue of Jesus's messiahship. The dispute thus presupposes the early Christian conviction of Jesus as the Anointed One or Christ/Messiah (see above). In other circles of early Christianity, Davidic ancestry was ascribed to Jesus in response to this problem, but aside from Matt. 1:1, it was not combined with the designation "Son of David" (cf. Rom. 1:3; Matt. 1–2, esp. 1:1[!], 6, 17, 20; Luke 1–3, esp. 1:27, 31–33; 2:3–4; 3:31; 2 Tim. 2:8).

Berger, Klaus. 1971. "Zum traditionsgeschichtlichen Hintergrund christologischer Hoheitstitel." *NTS* 17: 391–425.

Casey, Maurice. 2010. *Jesus of Nazareth: An Independent Historian's Account of His Life and Teaching*, 353–400. London.

Hahn, Ferdinand. ⁵1995. *Christologische Hoheitstitel: Ihre Geschichte im frühen Christentum.* FRLANT 83. Göttingen. Original 1963.

Karrer, Martin. 1990. *Der Gesalbte: Die Grundlagen des Christustitels.* FRLANT 151. Göttingen.

———. 1998. *Jesus Christus im Neuen Testament.* GNT 11. Göttingen.

David du Toit

V. The Formation of Structures: The Twelve, Wandering Charismatics, the Primitive Jerusalem Community, and Apostles

The history of groups that emerged after Jesus's death and reports about his resurrection can be viewed from the perspectives of continuity, adaptation, and innovation, which distinctly come to light in each sphere of early Christian development. The first perspective assumes that under transformed conditions the Jesus movement continued more or less in the same form ("the Twelve," "wandering charismatics"). For the second, the social structures from the lifetime of Jesus of Nazareth became adjusted such that essential elements of Jesus's activity and proclamation became viable in an altered form ("Jerusalem primitive community"). For the third, the new orientation of the proclamation in view of the kingdom of God and the resurrection warranted developments that advanced the origin of new groups and functions ("apostles"). Processes of the construct of identity, which also were represented by structures, are also connected with these various developments.

1. The Twelve

According to the predominant view, the pre-Easter Jesus movement was composed of two groups: the fellowship of those who moved through Palestine with Jesus and those who remained in their hometowns (sympathizers). Standing out from the itinerant movement was the group of the Twelve whom Jesus himself evidently had chosen and had promised a special position in the kingdom of God (Q 22:30; list of disciples in Mark 3:16–19; Matt. 10:1–4; Luke 6:12–16; Acts 1:13). In the pre-Pauline tradition about appearances (1 Cor. 15:5), as in the proclamations of meeting with the risen One in Galilee (Mark 16:7 with 14:28), the post-Easter role of the Twelve as a prominent group is detectable. Both in Matthew (Matt. 28:10, 16) and in Luke (Luke 24:33; Acts 1:2–13), this group is held to be a fixed unit (cf. also John 20:24–29), for which the terminology "apostle" is coterminous (Mark 6:30; Matt. 10:2; Luke 6:13; and passim).

First, the high importance of the Twelve certainly did not change after Easter; indeed, the number stands for the twelve tribes of the people of Israel and their renewal by means of and in the kingdom of God. Accordingly, the identification of one of the twelve apostles named Matthias after the death of the betrayer Judas Iscariot is in principle very likely historical (Acts 1:15–26), although the Lukan adaptation as a transition story to the Pentecost incident leaves no room for concrete conclusions. For Luke, especially the connection of this with the pre-Easter Jesus is decisive (Acts 1:21–22) for Matthias to take up the office of apostle (ἀποστολή). Hence, in Acts the Twelve/the apostles constitute that group that stands at the forefront of the primitive Jerusalem community and directs the development of Christianity up until the Apostolic Council. The fact that after the death of James the son of Zebedee (41 CE; Acts 12:1–2) a further election does not occur also shows that, for Luke, the Twelve/the apostles are the formative group of the earliest times of the church that cannot be continued. Hence, for Luke, Paul (like Barnabas) cannot be an apostle (in Acts 14:4, 14, the word means to be sent by the community).

By contrast, the Pauline evidence enables the discovery of something else: for Jerusalem, Paul names as the decisive persons not the Twelve but primarily the apostles Peter and James, the brother of the Lord (Gal. 1:18–19), but then especially the three "pillars," James the brother of the Lord, Peter, and John (Gal. 2:9). This group probably had developed informally, but then, evidently shortly after the Apostolic Council, it was replaced by the sole leadership of James, together with elders (cf. Acts 21:18). Nothing more is known about the other members of the Twelve. The ancient ecclesiastical legendary creations have them appear as preachers who went into all the world. Thus, as early as the Epistula Apostolorum (mid-second century), it is recorded that the Twelve proclaimed the gospel in all the cardinal directions (Ep. Apos. 30). Moreover, the Twelve served as sources for numerous apocryphal texts (Gospel of the Twelve; Didache of the Twelve Apostles).

The significance of the Twelve as bearers of the Jesus tradition is quite probably historical, although that certainly does not permit restricting the transmission of Jesus's words and deeds to the circle of the Twelve. To be sure, the Twelve were not the only group that supposedly preserved a personal continuity with pre-Easter Jesus tradition, but they were an essential component (Schürmann [2]1961). This is already reflected in the early ascription of the Gospels to disciples (Matthew or John) or an interpreter (Mark for Peter). Their role in proclamation (cf. Mark 3:14; 6:12–13; Luke 9:1–2) would not have been the same for each one; after all, some of the Twelve (esp. Peter and the sons of Zebedee, James and John) would have been of special importance.

2. Wandering Charismatics/Wandering Radicals

The thesis of radical wandering charismatics has been known since Adolf von Harnack's (1902) pioneering work on the history of missions in early Christianity. With Gerd Theissen's elaboration by means of sociological models, the thesis became established, according to which a part of early Christianity was made up of radical wandering charismatics who were of decisive importance for establishing and transmitting the Jesus tradition, especially the sayings source (Theissen 1989a, 2004; Tiwald 2002). The "vagabond charismatic movement" (Theissen 2004) carried on Jesus's lifestyle after Easter.

The relevant textual references for this are found in the Didache, a manual for community order originating in Syria around 100 CE. In Did. 11–13 there is talk about the arrival of various persons who should receive hospitality under diverse conditions (Niederwimmer 1998): teachers (11:1; 13:1), apostles (11:3–6), prophets (11:7–12; 13:6), as well as people in general who come in the name of the Kyrios

(12:1–5). For the question of continuity with the pre-Easter Jesus movement, which also remains of high significance for scholarship on Jesus, the observation is important that these wandering persons should possess the "Lord's way of life" (τρόποι κυρίου, 11:8). According to this view, this generally held regulation points to Jesus's itinerant existence, which was characterized by the lack of home, family, possessions, and protection (Theissen 2004).

If we follow the trail blazed by the Didache, then New Testament texts can also be read as evidence of the post-Easter movement of radical itinerants. These include, among others, the Pauline note about the livelihood for preachers commanded by Jesus himself (1 Cor. 9:14), the reports about the sending out of the Twelve (Mark 3:13–15; Luke 9:1–6), the texts about following (among others, Mark 10:28–29; Q 9:57–60; 14:26), but especially the speeches about sending on a mission (Q 10:2–16; Mark 6:7–13). These include specifications regarding lack of possessions (Q 10:4; Mark 6:8–9) and itinerancy (Q 10:5–12; Mark 6:10b-11), and also indicate that one who is sent represents the Lord himself (Q 10:16; Mark 9:37b). In addition to the Twelve and the apostles, Theissen's (2004) interpretation includes the circle of the seven Hellenists with Philip (Acts 6:1–6; 8:4–13), the five prophets and teachers from Antioch (Acts 13:1), and the prophet Agabus (Acts 11:27–28; 21:10) among the wandering charismatics (cf. also Eusebius, *Hist. eccl.* 3.37.2). Also, texts from non-Christians (Lucian, *The Passing of Peregrinus*; Celsus in Origen, *Cels.* 7.8–9) can be interpreted with respect to this group.

An essential component of the thesis about "wandering charismatics" is the assumption that there was also a stable local group of sympathizers that hosted and provided for the itinerants. These communities, whom Theissen called "tertiary charismatics," sent out the preachers of the gospel and simultaneously are responsible for the written form of the tradition, which Theissen (2004) refers to with the ill-fitting terminology "preventative editorial control." Whether women were also among the wandering charismatics cannot be determined with certainty (Tiwald 2002).

The critique of the thesis of wandering/radical charismatics is multifaceted. For one thing the reception of the Didache is contested: the text neither infers that apostles and prophets wandered from place to place nor that they carried on Jesus's ascetic lifestyle, nor that they functioned as bearers of the oral tradition about Jesus (Draper 1998). In addition, taking into account the historical circumstances in Galilee, the instructions in the speeches about sending on a mission in Mark 6 and Q 10 can hardly be assessed as radical: the places are so close to each other that the renunciation of a bread bag, money, clothing, and so forth is explicable and does not have to refer to a radical wandering existence (Kloppenborg Verbin 2000). Numerous texts point to a village and domestic context, so that a metaphorical understanding of the pre-Easter texts about discipleship and sending on a mission is also quite possible. In line with this, the language in the sayings source could reflect the terminology of Hellenistic administration (Bazzana 2015). Moreover, the extension of the thesis of wandering charismatics to further circles of early Christianity, according to which in some way once or repeatedly they would have changed location (see above), is understood as a hasty generalization that does not sufficiently take into view specific rationales. Also, questions arise concerning the concept of charismatics taken over from Max Weber. So the thesis of post-Easter wandering charismatics/radicals who operate as bearers of the Jesus tradition, especially the sayings source, comes under multifaceted criticism (Horsley 1989, 1996; Draper 1998; Kloppenborg Verbin 2000; Arnal 2001; Rollens 2014). Indeed, the hypothesis according to which the early Christians' itinerant movement was formed from the example of Hellenistic Cynics (Crossan ²1995; Downing 1988) has not proved to be successful (cf. Tiwald 2002).

As alternatives to the wandering charismatic thesis coined by Theissen, two other models are being discussed at the present time. One posits that this could have been a prophetic movement, which in an economical and cultural situation carried on the (also political) renewal of Israel that Jesus initiated (Horsley 1989). At this time, with respect to the sayings source, an alternative explicatory model appears preferable, according to which a group of local scribes ("village scribes") construed under the impact of Jesus's proclamation a new identity of the kingdom of God (Kloppenborg Verbin 2000; Arnal 2001; Rollens 2014; Bazzana 2015). Models that posit that there was indeed no fundamental existence of wandering radicals, but one that was temporary, could perhaps mediate between these different reconstructions (Schmeller 2008).

3. The Jerusalem Community

To be sure, research is nearly exclusively reliant on the Lukan account in Acts 1–6 (Schnelle 2015). Nevertheless, in combination with the Pauline information, it is possible to understand to some extent how the Jerusalem community first attempted to interpret Jesus's message about the kingdom of God as impacted by the experiences of appearances and to translate this into an appropriate way of life. What is more, it is especially significant that the developing structures were construed in expectation of the imminent fulfillment of God's sovereignty and judgment. Both the further development of the baptism of John the Baptizer into baptism in the name of Jesus and the experience of ecstatic enthusiasm, understood as the pouring out of the Spirit, show that new forms of religious experience were joined to the pre-Easter foundations. At the same time, Jesus's actions and proclamation were interpreted in a way that preserved them; the renunciation of possessions, for example, could have been adapted by forming the so-called community of goods, at least according to Luke's portrayal (Acts 2:44; 4:32–35).

In addition to the Twelve (Luke moves Peter especially into the center [Acts 1–12]), other male and female followers of Jesus who had affiliated with him in Galilee or in Judea and Jerusalem also played a decisive role. Among them with some probability were women such as Mary Magdalene, or Mary and Martha of Bethany, as well as numerous men who likewise belonged to the movement of disciples. Members of Jesus's family are newly added, among whom his brother James is prominent as one of the pillars. According to Gal. 1:19 and 2:9, early on he had a leading role in the Jerusalem congregation (cf. also Acts 12:17; 15:13–21; 21:18–26).

Within the Jerusalem community a division into two groups appears relatively soon, which Luke refers to as "Hebrews" and "Hellenists" (Acts 6:1). Whereas members of the first group operated under post-Easter conditions relatively unchanged and were impacted by the Twelve and Jesus's family, for the Hellenists new traditions shaped more strongly by Hellenistic-Jewish culture of the diaspora became part of early Christian identity. In addition to the Greek language and culture, there were also the relationship to the Septuagint, the critique of the significance of the temple cult, the institution of the synagogue as an assembly of Jews of a certain region, and perhaps also less anxiety of contact with non-Jews. To be sure, the Lukan report about the installation of the seven Hellenists for serving tables is clearly schematized in the sense of subordination under the twelve apostles (Acts 6:1–7), but likely in the persons of Stephen and Philip, at least two from this team emerged as preachers of the kingdom of God (Acts 6:8–7:60 and 8:5–40; 21:8–9). Following the death of Stephen, the expulsion of the Hellenistic part of Christ believers by the temple aristocracy in Jerusalem (Acts 8:1–4; 11:18–20) led subsequently to the spreading of the gospel in Phoenicia, Syria, and Cyprus and was a final impetus for the inclusion of non-Jews into the community. These refugees, albeit in dire straits, did not constitute a "group of wandering charismatics" (Schmeller 1989). Thus, for example, in Acts 21:8–9, after his preaching activity, Philip took up residence in Caesarea Maritima (and later in Hierapolis in Asia Minor; Eusebius, *Hist. eccl.* 3.39.8), and he also had prophetically gifted daughters. With the violent death of the Lord's brother James (62 CE) and the Jewish War (66–70 CE), however, the traces of the Jerusalem community disappear.

4. Apostles

To understand what an apostle is, we must distinguish between Pauline and Lukan perspectives: Luke takes as apostles (almost) exclusively those chosen by Jesus and, after Easter, the Eleven supplemented by Matthias (Luke 6:13; 24:10; Acts 1:2; and elsewhere; cf. also Mark 6:30; Matt. 10:2). Only in Acts 14:4, 14 does Luke show that he also can take persons sent out by communities to preach to be apostles.

By contrast, Paul differentiates (although not always sharply) three types of apostles (Frey 2004): those who were sent for specific, temporally limited functions (2 Cor. 8:23: messages; Phil 2:25: conveying money); those who received apostleship by means of the Spirit (1 Cor. 12:28–29) but evidently are active in the community itself; and finally, those—like Paul himself—who in connection with an appearance of the risen One received a commission for proclamation (1 Cor. 9:1; 15:7–9; Gal. 1). The last were also expressly associated with deeds of power (2 Cor. 12:12) and included, for example, Barnabas (1 Cor. 9:1–6), Apollos (1 Cor. 4:6–9), as well as Andronicus and Junia (Rom. 16:7). Quite solely on account of the reference to Easter appearances, this form of more or less mobile preachers of the gospel constituted an innovation, which of course carried on particular aspects of Jesus's pre-Easter itinerant movement such as being sustained by communities (1 Cor. 9:14) and suffering austerities (2 Cor. 11:23b–28; Gal. 6:17).

In the Didache apostles who come into the community from outside are also mentioned. But whereas in 2 Cor. 11:5, 13; 12:11; and Rev. 2:2 these are characterized as false apostles, the author of the Didache is more positively engaged (Did. 11:4–6): basically, apostles should be received. But there are two restrictions: a stay longer than two days and a request for financial support make the apostle a "false prophet." Of course, it is uncertain what kind of apostle is meant here: Do these apostles correspond to wandering charismatics/radicals (Theissen 1989a, 2004; Niederwimmer 1998; Tiwald 2002)? Among other things, the affinity to the sending speech in Matt. 10 and the inclusion of "as the Lord" (Did. 11:2, 4 par. Matt. 10:40), the provision with food (Did. 13:1 par. Matt. 10:10), and the renunciation of money (Did. 11:6, 12 par. Matt. 10:9) speak in favor of this. Or is the Didache concerned with a specific, temporally limited task that does not point to a general wandering activity (Draper 1998)? Among other things, the fact that the mission is not one of proclamation by the apostle speaks in favor of this, although in 11:1–2, teaching of outsiders in general is thematic. Aside from this, such a form of wandering radicalism is absent (differently Schmeller 1989; Niederwimmer 1998).

If one assumes the first, then the wandering apostles stand together with the prophets (Did. 11:7–12; 13:1), apparently in a tensive relationship with local bishops and deacons (15:1–2). It would then become clear from the Didache how the wandering charismatics were pushed back in favor of institutionalized congregational structures—often termed "early Catholicism." This factor would then be illustrated, for instance, in 3 John, because there the brothers sent out by the elder were not received by the leader of the community (3 John 9–10).

If one follows the thesis of only a limited sending of apostles, then no extension of the concept of wandering missionaries influenced by Paul is to be seen here, let alone a reconstruction of wandering charismatics from the sayings source. Conflicts between teachers coming from outside and local functionaries would then be an accompanying effect of the social structure of early Christianity, but not part of the transformation to the great church of the second century.

Horsley, Richard A. 1989. *Sociology and the Jesus Movement.* New York.

Kloppenborg Verbin, John S. 2000. *Excavating Q: The History and Setting of the Sayings Gospel.* Edinburgh.

Schmeller, Thomas. 1989. *Brechungen: Urchristliche Wandercharismatiker im Prisma soziologischorientierter Exegese.* SBS 136. Stuttgart.

Theissen, Gerd. 2004. *Die Jesusbewegung: Sozialgeschichte einer Revolution der Werte.* Gütersloh.

Tiwald, Markus. 2002. *Wanderradikalismus: Jesu erste Jünger—ein Anfang und was davon bleibt.* ÖBS 20. Frankfurt.

Markus Öhler

VI. Jesus in Noncanonical Texts of the Second and Third Centuries

The following passage is found among the fragments of Papias cited by Eusebius in his *Church History*:

> If . . . anyone came who had followed the presbyters, I inquired about the sayings of the presbyters: What did Andrew or Peter say, or what Philipp or Thomas or James, or what John, or Matthew, or any other disciple of the Lord, what indeed Aristion and John the Elder (both) disciples of the Lord say? For I did not think that things from books would profit me as much as things from the living and abiding voice (τὰ παρὰ ζώσης φωνῆς καὶ μενούσης). (Papias of Hierapolis according to Eusebius, *Hist. eccl.* 3.39.4)

Writing sometime around the year 110, thus approximately four generations after the death of Jesus, Papias stands on an important threshold for the Jesus tradition: even if indirect, access to the "living voice" of oral tradition from reports about Jesus is still open. However, now the reports from books—undoubtedly this means the first gospels—play a progressively important role. This does not mean in any way that at the time of Papias we should already speak of a four-gospel canon, and it especially does not mean that the Gospels found in the

New Testament were accessible to every congregation, let alone to every Christ follower. Even where tradition of Jesus material was already available in written form, this was further accompanied by a living oral tradition, which increasingly was influenced by written texts and in some cases was transcribed anew. Some of the texts about Jesus of the second century, whose relationship of literary dependence on the canonical Gospels was contested for a long time, perhaps can best be explained in this way.

The "Unknown Gospel" of Egerton Papyrus 2 (and the Cologne Papyrus 255) is preserved in a single, and also severely fragmentary, textual witness, probably from the turn of the second to the third century. In spite of this, some scenes about Jesus can be rather reliably reconstructed; in addition to passages strongly reminiscent of the Gospel of John, the text presents an account, among others, of the healing of a leper that displays strong echoes of Mark 1:40–45 par. The literary relationship this "apocryphal" account has to the New Testament parallels is difficult to ascertain and pushes conventional methods of literary criticism, but also of form criticism, to their limits. The brief scene exhibits relationships to all three synoptic parallels, which, however, are not so specific that they have to be explained by literary dependence. There are parallels to this in John 5:14 (or alternatively John 8:11) and perhaps to the healing of the ten lepers (Luke 17:11–19). That the author of this writing had all these passages in front of him as literary texts and purposefully wove them into a new account appears highly unlikely. However, form-critical problems also arise: the leper accompanies his request with such a detailed (and peculiar) explanation of his malady that one would expect it to be a later version; however, the account as a whole is briefer than that of the canonical Gospels. The most probable explanation of this fact may be that the author of the "apocryphal" account knew one or more of the accounts in the Synoptic Gospels, perhaps had also read or heard them. Thus, he could have drawn on the memory of the basic structure of the available written texts and substituted his own narrative emphases, which nevertheless are not to be conceived of in terms of classical redaction criticism in the narrow sense: Jesus is designated as a "teacher," any bodily contact between Jesus and the sick person is avoided, and the text demonstrates a surprising interest in the sinfulness of the leper, which is associated with the injunction for him thereafter to sin no more. Are these indications that the text depicts a Jesus (possibly) as a teacher of Torah who regards Jewish concepts of "clean" and "unclean" as more important than perhaps the Markan Jesus does? The passage is certainly too brief—and the Egerton Papyrus 2 as a whole too fragmentary—to work out a reliable profile; nevertheless, the trend could run in this direction.

Similar examples could be added to this—many noncanonical traditions of the second and third centuries are so fragmentary that any answers to large questions about the circumstances of their origin such as the christological profile can only be hypothetical. Thus on P. Oxy. 840, a small parchment leaf of only 8.5 × 7 centimeters of a miniature codex presumably from the fourth or fifth century, a conflict between Jesus and a Pharisaic high priest about the issue of purity turns on whether washing with water can really liberate human beings from their inner impurity. Repeated attempts have been made to fit this text into an early Christianity influenced by Judaism that still preserved memories of the local conditions of the Jerusalem temple and halakic debates of the earthly Jesus. But on the basis of linguistic observations, the tendency today is rather to classify the preserved passage as a mirror of controversies on baptismal theology of the third century of our era (or even later).

Doubtless with less than ultimate certainty, the question is asked whether the lone manuscript first discovered by Morton Smith in 1958, shortly thereafter lost, of an alleged letter of Clement of Alexandria in which passages of a "secret Gospel of Mark" are cited presents a (skillful) forgery or an authentic witness of Alexandrian Christianity. In fragment 1, for example, Jesus brings back to life a young man who has died and subsequently teaches him the secret of the kingdom of God. Should the text be authentic, this could be interpreted as a witness of a Christianity influenced by ancient mystery cults—however, only the rediscovery of the manuscript could provide a final answer to this question.

In spite of many further cases in which crucial questions must remain open, such an abundance of Jesus material is available that in the following only some important lines of the development can be presented.

1. "Jewish Christian" Gospels

The remnants of so-called Jewish Christian gospels are transmitted only in some citations of ancient church authors, that is to say, gospel writings of Christ followers who appealed to their Jewish origin or distinguished themselves by their Torah observance and thereby marked themselves off from the emerging main church, especially from communities influenced by Paul, in a partly polemical manner. The state of transmission of the few preserved text fragments is, however, so problematic that it is still debated how many such "Jewish Christian" gospels actually circulated and to what extent the various designated texts should be classified as gospels. Perhaps for the period that is of interest here, we can presume three gospels, the Gospel of the Hebrews, the Gospel of the Ebionites, and the Gospel of the Nazarenes, among which the last is especially debated. It is quite possible to depict the development of the image of Jesus in the Gospel of the Ebionites (that is, the "Poor"). The preserved citations from this text, differently from what Epiphanius of Salamis says in *Pan.* 30.3.7 and 30.13.2, can be adumbrated arguably not simply as the issuing of a redacted Gospel of Matthew but as a writing that especially edited synoptic material for the special claims of the Ebionites. The Jesus of this text, which evidently contained no childhood stories with their concepts of Jesus's birth from the Virgin Mary, is designated first as a "man" (and thereby emphatically only as a "human being"). Not until in his baptism does he become the "Son of God," as is made clear by the emphatic "*today* I have begotten you" from Ps. 2:7, which in the synoptic parallels is absent (with the exception of Luke 3:22 D and some Western witnesses), as well as a directly subsequent appearance of a light (cf. also Justin, *Dial.* 88.3, and the supposedly corresponding scene in Tatian's *Diatessaron*). At Passover the Jesus of this gospel eats no meat (Epiphanius, *Pan.* 30.22.4), which is parallel to the testimony about the Baptizer, who instead of locusts consumes honey cake (*Pan.* 30.13.5). Although in the judgment of accounts of ancient church heresiology the greatest caution is necessary, this could be explained by a statement preserved in (pseudo-)Hippolytus of Rome, according to which the Jesus of the Ebionites, because they are not in their purely Jewish homeland in Transjordan (cf. the evidence of Eusebius, *Hist. eccl.* 1.7.14; *Onom.* 14.15 and Jerome, *De nominibus hebraicis*), had to be especially careful with the purity of foods, primarily as the halakic model held to be valid (Epiphanius, *Pan.* 7.34.2).

Although it is not part of a "Jewish Christian gospel" but a noncanonical dominical saying at the location of Luke 6:5 in Codex Bezae Cantabrigiensis (D), the "saying of the Sabbath worker," to whom Jesus calls out, "Man, if you know what you are doing, blessed are you; but if not you are accursed and a transgressor of the Law," can also be brought into line with the debate with Jewish (or Judaizing) followers of Jesus about the observance of the Sabbath. For this brief text, the Sabbath commandment appears not simply to be abrogated in principle or even that the Sabbath is replaced by the Lord's Day; rather, a discussion is going on about situations that permit working on the Sabbath, but that every transgression of the Sabbath commandment is to be justified according to halakah so as not to transgress against the Torah.

2. The Gospel of Peter

The Gospel of Peter, a text mentioned by Serapion of Antioch (according to Eusebius, *Hist. eccl.* 6.12.1–6), Origen (*Comm. Matt.* 10:17), and some other ancient church authors, was discovered at the end of the nineteenth century in a grave close to Akhmim, Upper Egypt, during the time other possible textual witnesses were being discussed. The preserved text provides remnants of an account of the passion and Easter probably from the middle of the second century. Jesus—the name does not appear in the fragment at all—is depicted as "Lord" and "Son of God," who is tortured and crucified by the "Jews." Similar to the already mentioned "unknown Gospel" on the Egerton Papyrus 2, many features of the Gospel of Peter likely can be explained by the author knowing the canonical Gospels, but they might not have been accessible in written form. The portrayal of Jesus in the text has been disputed for a long time: except for the sentence "my power, power, you have forsaken me" (Gos. Pet. 19), reminiscent of Jesus's last words in Mark and Matthew, the preserved text does not transmit any sayings of Jesus. The text's surprising interest in the corporeality of the maltreated and crucified Lord even after his death, which moves the text close to descriptions of the martyrs, speaks against a docetic interpretation of this sentence and also some other passages as suggested by Serapion's reference. At the same time, the Gospel of Peter seeks to overwhelm its readers by a spectacular scene of the resurrection. Before the eyes of the guards at the tomb, namely, of the elders and the scribes, two enormous angels raise the Lord, whose head now towers above the heavens, and fetch him out of the tomb (vv. 39–40); the cross follows him, from which to the question resounding from heaven, "Have you preached to those who have died?" a "yes" can be heard (vv. 41–42). This presentation itself exceeds the quite drastic Matthean Easter narrative in that it basically makes the event of the raising of "the Lord" "objectively" visible for his opponents. A precise interpretation of the gigantic form of the risen One is not possible—but perhaps here he himself is also presented as an exceedingly large angel, an image that is reminiscent of similar visions from the Book of Elchasai (likewise dated in the second century), transmitted only in citations, as well as possibly from the Revelation of John (Rev. 10:1–3, in case this angel should represent Christ).

3. God and the Question of Death

The question how it is possible that the Son of God was put to death on the cross and as a heavenly or even divine essence—always to be interpreted more precisely—had participated in the materiality of the created world and thereby in human suffering concerned the church from earliest times. A "divinity" who suffers appears inconceivable. An extreme solution to this problem that radically separates the cross or suffering from God or the divine logos is found in writings with a docetic Christology. In this connection the term "docetism" is understood in a broad sense as the teaching according to which God or the divine logos took on only the appearance of human form and therefore also did not suffer on the cross. A good example of the narrative transformation of such a teaching is preserved in the so-called Acts of John. In chapters 94–102 of this writing, whose precise dating is debated (between the first half of the second century and the beginning of the third century?), is a passion narrative that can be assessed as testimony for this disposition. After chapters 94–96 give an account of a danced Christ hymn, in chapters 97–102 the mystery of the cross is revealed to John. As he flees and weeps before the sight of the one who is crucified, the Lord appears to him in a cave on the Mount of Olives and instructs him (97:7–12), a cross of light is revealed to him (98:1–60), and subsequently an admonition by the heavenly voice of the Lord follows (98:7–101:16). Especially important is the differentiation between this cross of light and the "wooden cross" that no longer has anything to do with the "Lord"; furthermore, at the top of the Mount of Olives John receives a revelation of the truth, while the crowd below observes the false Jesus on the cross. In addition, it is striking that the "Lord" in this text is simultaneously observed in several forms—in this connection one speaks of "polymorphism": whereas he no longer has anything to do with the one who was crucified on the wooden cross, he simultaneously appears amorphous over the cross of light and as the cross of light itself, which connects the upper and lower world together. This is an example of a text designated "docetic." Similarly, the Coptic Apocalypse of Peter (difficult to date) from Nag Hammadi (NHC VII,3) differentiates between the crucified body and the "living Christ," which Peter sees "cheerful and laughing beside the wood," whereas, for instance, Basilides (d. ca. 145 CE) probably assumed that the divine nous was in fact united with the human Jesus, but, instead of Jesus, Simon of Cyrene had been crucified in the form of Jesus.

4. The Gospel of Thomas

With the most well-known noncanonical "Jesus text" of the second century, the Gospel of Thomas, we have an example of a "sayings gospel," that is, a collection of (partly) sapiential Jesus sayings, which however are not, or are hardly ever, embedded in a narrative context. The text, which is preserved completely only in the Coptic language as well as three Greek fragments from Oxyrhynchus, is arranged in 114 logia of Jesus. For a long time its interpretation was dominated by two questions: Is this gospel literarily dependent on the canonical Gospels, especially the Synoptics, or does it present a special ancient collection that brings us closer to the historical Jesus than do the Synoptics? The second question is at least indirectly related to this: Is the Gospel of Thomas to be classified as a writing with a "gnostic" or, more likely, sapiential character? The fact that the sayings of Jesus transmitted in the Gospel of Thomas lack a narrative framework shows that the text has *no* interest in embedding the logia in concrete historical contexts. Rather, in the incipit Jesus is already described as the "living one"—this is not simply synonymous with "the risen One"—who reveals "hidden sayings" to Didymus Judas Thomas: "Whoever finds the interpretation of these sayings will not taste death." However, among the sayings of Jesus collected in the text, much is familiar to the reader of the canonical Gospels: the parables of the sower (Gos. Thom. 9; cf. Mark 4:3–9 par.) and of the mustard seed (Gos. Thom. 20; cf. Mark 4:30–32), but also parallels to the sayings about peace and fire (Gos. Thom. 16; cf. Q 12:51–53) or of the splinter in the eye of a brother (Gos. Thom. 26; cf. Q 6:41–42). Other passages appear to presuppose synoptic scenes and develop them further—so, for instance, Jesus's question to his disciples asking who he is like, with a series of responses in which Peter's confession amounts to only the first step (Gos. Thom. 13). Other passages, such as the mysterious logion 42—"Become passers-by"—or the woe about the flesh that depends on the soul (Gos. Thom. 112; cf. similarly 87), are unknown from canonical parallels. Thus the Gospel of Thomas by all means contains quite old Jesus material, most of which doubtless is transmitted by way of the Synoptics, seldom by way of John. However, it arranges this in a new way or connects it with new material, by which new interpretations arise. Thus the text demonstrates sparse interest in the story of Jesus: the passion narrative falls out almost entirely; most christological titles, which we know from the canonical Gospels, are missing—instead of this, Jesus is the possessor of the revealed wisdom that is decisive for redemption. Henceforth he is to be seen as the one who lives and who also speaks to us now. To follow his words, to immerse oneself into them, means to become more like the "true human being" and to enter the "kingdom of the Father." Therefore, characteristics of wisdom obviously befit the text; a decidedly "gnostic" redemption myth is lacking, but the recognizable tendency toward withdrawal from the world enabled the compilers of the Nag Hammadi Codex II to have comprehensibly placed the Gospel of Thomas in the context of clearly "gnostic" writings like the Apocryphon of John.

The Gospel of Philip, whose only preserved textual witness is transmitted immediately after the Gospel of Thomas in the Nag Hammadi Codex II (NHC II,3), could also be described as a "sayings gospel." The difficult-to-date text (third century?), the background of which is found in the Valentinian movement, understands Christ as the redeemer, who is described as the bridegroom of the lower Sophia, who is named Achamoth. The quite cumbersome text eludes a simple summary; among other things, it is interesting on the basis of its sacramental theology and its interpretation of the passion.

5. *Gospel of Mary and Gospel of Judas*

The New Testament already differentiates between Jesus's teachings for everyone and teachings that are available for only a smaller circle. In this connection Mark 4:11 par. speaks about the "mystery of the kingdom of God." Also, the farewell discourses, which are decisive for the understanding of the Gospel of John (John 13–17), are directed only to the inner circle of the disciples. An entire series of writings, best designated "dialogue gospels," follows this line or carries it further. Frequently they place at the center a disciple as a chosen recipient of special revelations often of a (so-called) "gnostic" character—they are about complex cosmologies as well as possibilities of the ascent of the soul, or about the fallen components of light in the person from the world ruled by a demiurge. In the most well-known of these texts, the Gospel of Mary, (probably) Mary Magdalene, here called only Mary, assumes the role of this beloved female disciple. The text, which is transmitted in two Greek fragments (P. Oxy. 3525; P. Ryl. 463) as well as in an incomplete Coptic manuscript (Cod. BG) and must have originated at the end of the second century at the latest, is interested in the origin and goal of creation, discusses the sin of the world, and makes a theme of the ascent of the soul. It has been quite intensively discussed on account of the key role assigned to Mary (Magdalene) as the female disciple "whom the Redeemer loved more than all women" (Cod. BG 1, p. 10), precisely as the counterpart to Peter. It is obvious that here the concept is suggested that a community already influenced by "gnostic" thought makes a theme of its relationship to a "proto-orthodoxy" represented in the text especially by Peter. However, here also the fragmentary state of preservation of the writing should caution against conclusions that go too far.

Whereas the revelation scenes of most dialogue gospels are either post-Easter or cannot be located chronologically, in the Gospel of Judas, which first became known in 2006, Jesus's dialogues with Judas Iscariot and his other disciples occur prior to the passion. Memories of Jesus's earthly life diminish almost completely—only scantily is there talk of Jesus's "signs and wonders"; in broad strokes, knowledge of the story of the passion is presupposed. Whereas the Eleven quite unambiguously are understood as representatives of a "church," probably the developing early Christian majority church, (according to the Gospel of Judas) lapsing into the satanic, material world of dominant demiurges and misunderstanding Jesus as the Son of a false divinity, Judas arrives at a knowledge about Jesus's true essence. Whether he for this reason is characterized as the beloved disciple or as an especially demonic figure (connected to the satanic creator-demiurge) is not easy to decide (partly because of the bad state of preservation of the only manuscript); some arguments speak for the second possibility.

6. *Protevangelium of James and Infancy Gospel of Thomas*

The Jesus tradition of the second and third centuries, however, demonstrated not only increasing interest in new, "secret revelations" of the Lord, often accessible for only a small group of the elite, but also interest in his origins. The childhood accounts in Matthew and Luke project perceptions of Christology acquired after Easter into Jesus's origins and hence speak, for example, of the virginal conception of Jesus, whose divine sonship is thereby already manifested in his procreation. Although this concept, as the report of the Ebionites already cited shows, was by no means generally recognized in early Christianity, and the exposition of Isa. 7:14 associated with it encountered opposition on the part of Jews (cf. Justin, *Dial.* 43; 66–67), quite early there was talk not only about Jesus's conception in a virgin but also about a virgin birth. Perhaps the Ascension of Isaiah provides the earliest witness for this. This is an apocalypse of the early second century that concisely reports the life of Jesus. In Ascen. Isa. 11:14 we read: "She has not borne a child, and a midwife has not gone [up to] her, and we have not heard the cries of pain." Especially because of the danger of docetic misinterpretations accompanying the emphasis on Jesus's miraculous virgin birth, this concept prevailed only with difficulty and against resistance (e.g., Tertullian, *Carn. Chr.* 4 and 20).

The so-called Protevangelium of James might have played an important role in this. This late second-century writing is normally classified as an "infancy gospel," although it is actually interested especially in Mary, as the undoubtedly more original title "The Birth of Mary" shows. Here not only is the virgin birth of Jesus attested in that nature came to a standstill, but it is also attested by the midwife and subsequently by a doubtful woman named Salome (comparable to Thomas in John 20:25–27).

Differently from what is in the Protoevangelium of James, Jesus's childhood plays a role in the *Paidika*, better known as the Infancy Gospel of Thomas. The picture of Jesus that this text outlines today seems to be disturbing. We read about a young Jesus who in playing forms birds out of mud and brings them to life, causes children who disrupt his play to die, strikes those who blame him for this with blindness, and puts his teachers to shame. Some have reflected on how serious all these stories are intended to be, and also have imagined that the text could be thought of as an ancient children's book. However, perhaps the theological impulse behind these stories consists in imagining what it means that God, the creator of this world, whose wrath ought not to be provoked, became a human being and therefore as a tangible human child grows up in a village like Nazareth. In addition, the report from late antiquity about pilgrims from Piacenza (ca. 570 CE) makes clear that the stories about the child Jesus finally took on a concrete significance for the village of Nazareth: pilgrims were shown Jesus's (alleged) school notebook and a beam on which Jesus sat with other children (*Antonini Placentini Itinerarium*).

7. Conclusion

We have treated only a few topics. Hardly anything has been said about the profusion of noncanonical sayings of the Lord, frequently a bit unfortunately designated "agrapha." I did not write about such important writings as Tatian's *Diatessaron*, possibly a witness of encratic tendencies; the Gospel of Marcion; the Epistula Apostolorum; or the rich literature about Pilate, which in its origins also falls in our time period. At the same time, we did not take up most writings from Nag Hammadi and said almost nothing about the portrayal of Jesus in apocryphal acts or apocalypses of the apostles. For example, the narrative framework of the Greek or Ethiopic Apocalypse of Peter would be especially interesting, as would be Christian passages of the Sibylline Oracles. But it is already becoming clear that the multiplicity of noncanonical Jesus tradition that at one time was disqualified as historically worthless is highly significant for our understanding of the history of the early Christian movement. Perhaps these writings might tell us just a bit about the historical Jesus; simultaneously, however, they are appropriately investigated for the reflection of the multiplicity of spiritual and (more narrowly) theological challenges and the developments resulting from them within the different groups of ancient men and women followers of Christ, who are described by the highly inadequate expression "early church."

Frey, Jörg, and Jens Schröter, eds. 2010. *Jesus in apokryphen Evangelienüberlieferungen*. WUNT 254. Tübingen.

Markschies, Christoph, and Jens Schröter, eds. 2012. *Antike christliche Apokryphen in deutscher Übersetzung*. Vol. 1, *Evangelien und Verwandtes (Teilband 1 & Teilband 2)*. Tübingen.

Schneemelcher, Wilhelm, ed. ⁶1997. *Neutestamentliche Apokryphen II: Apostolisches, Apokalypsen und Verwandtes*. Tübingen.

Schröter, Jens, ed. 2013. *The Apocryphal Gospels within the Context of Early Christian Theology*. BETL 260. Leuven.

Tobias Nicklas

VII. Visual Representations of Jesus up until ca. 500 CE

New Testament writings provide no information about Jesus's physical appearance. But we can reconstruct a discourse, going back to Christian sources as early as the second century, about how Jesus might have looked (cf. Acts John 87–90). Whereas in some acts of the apostles he is described as a beautiful young man (Acts Andr. 33; Acts Petr. 2.5), on the basis of a christological interpretation of Isa. 53:2–3, according to which the servant of God "had no form or beauty," many theologians argued against the approximation of images of Jesus to the ancient ideal of beauty (Justin, *Dial.* 14.8; Clement of Alexandria, *Paed.* 3.3.3; Tertullian, *Carn. Chr.* 9). While on the basis of Jesus's saying in John 14:9 ("whoever has seen me has seen the Father") pictorial portrayals of Jesus might seem legitimate, they stand in tension with the fundamental repudiation of cultic images in early Christianity.

The iconographic evidence for the first centuries is likewise ambivalent. The oldest "depictions" of Jesus are impersonal symbols such as an anchor, a vine, a cross, a fish, a lamb, a phoenix, or a chi rho. In part, these symbols were also known in non-Christian iconographic tradition and then interpreted in a Christian fashion. This holds also for personal symbols, which are attested from the second half of the third century: figures from mythology (Orpheus, Helios [plate 1]) or from the popular idyllic pastoral (bucolic) images in antiquity. So, for instance, the shepherd carrying a sheep (plate 2) was a popular pagan pictorial motif for a peaceful life in the hereafter, which on the basis of Ps. 23 could be related to Jesus through the parable of the lost sheep (Matt. 18:12–14) or the Good Shepherd discourse in John 10:1–30. Whether these portrayals are symbols for Jesus Christ can therefore frequently be decided only from the context, and is frequently debated in scholarship in detail.

The iconography of early Christian art, which shows Jesus as a beardless young man with locks of hair down to his neck, was decisively shaped by these depictions. This indicates that artist studios in the Roman Empire did not devise their own forms of expression for Christian pictorial motifs but rather drew on the existing stylistic repertoire. Thus the specific Christian evidence did not arise as a result of their own forms of expression, but by choosing and combining motifs (see pictorial motifs, pictorial cycles below) as well as by positioning them in a new context. Corresponding to the symbolic character of early Christian art, Jesus is not portrayed in terms of his personal identity but in his function as redeemer of humanity. Nevertheless, in the course of the first five centuries, a specific type was developed (see typology below), which has influenced the iconography of Jesus up until modern times.

1. Pictorial Motifs

Early Christian art is essentially symbolic art. It did not aim to depict persons, but substance and salvific declarations. Since most of the preserved works of art were produced for burial contexts (catacombs, sarcophagi), the symbolism is over-whelmingly related to the afterlife and the Christian message of redemption. In-dividual motifs cannot always be attributed completely unambiguously to specific gospel pericopes. So, for instance, in the portrayal of Jesus with a kneeling woman, three stories coincide: that of the Canaanite woman, that of the bleeding woman, and that of Jesus's conversation with Mary, the sister of Lazarus (plate 3).

Since the dating of early Christian works of art is often difficult and remains uncertain, it is not possible to construct a detailed and exact chronology of pic-torial motifs. But individual works of art can be arranged in at least a roughly determined spectrum of motifs, which represent the various aspects of Jesus's activity. From the third century onward, a number of episodes recur in visual depictions: the multiplication scenes (bread miracle, wine miracle in Cana) and healings (healing the blind, healing the lame, healing a woman, the resuscitation of Lazarus and further raising of the dead), teaching conversations (with the Sa-maritan woman at the well, Jesus in the circle of apostles), and Jesus's baptism. In the fourth century we find depictions of his birth (esp. frequently the adoration of the Magi, but also manger scenes) and the passion (entrance to Jerusalem; the scene of Peter, Christ, the cock; Judas's kiss; Jesus before Pilate; depictions of Christ on the cross [initially absent]), resurrection and ascension into heaven, as well as representative depictions of the exalted Christ as teacher and judge (handing over of instructions to Peter, Christ in the circle of apostles).

2. Typology of Depictions of Jesus

It accords with the symbolic character of early Christian art that the depictions of Jesus are not portraits in the sense of the reproduction of his appearance or of the character of the individual person. Rather, they represent Christ's function in the respective pictorial motifs as healer, teacher, conqueror of death, judge, and so forth.

Three basic types can be distinguished in the early Christian evidence, which appear with distinctive frequency and can be arranged at least partially in the spectrum of motifs mentioned above.

The oldest and, in the first four centuries, by far the most frequent type shows Jesus without a beard and with locks of hair down to his neck, wearing a tunic and robe as well as sandals. The proximity to pagan depictions of shepherds, but also to mythological figures such as Apollo, Orpheus, or Helios, likely indicates the iconographic origin of this type in Roman pagan art and makes it clear that this is not a specific iconography of Jesus. Not until the embedding of the individual motifs in a specific iconographic and real-world context (e.g., catacombs or churches) does an identification become possible. The beardless type occurs primarily in healing and multiplication scenes, but also in depictions of the passion (plate 5).

From the fourth century onward, depictions of the adoration of the Magi appear quite frequently, with Jesus as a baby, sometimes wrapped in swaddling clothes, sitting on Mary's lap. Jesus is depicted in the same beardless type and distinguished only by his size and sitting posture (plate 4). In early depictions of his baptism, Jesus is portrayed as beardless and with locks of hair down to his neck, but unclothed and in turn considerably smaller than John the Baptizer (plate 2). In this case, the small size no doubt symbolizes not a younger age but rather the act of self-abasement of the Son of God during incarnation and baptism.

In some portrayals Jesus is represented with locks of hair down to his neck and a beard. This second type is oriented toward ancient portrayals of philosophers, which also served as models for the iconography of the apostles Peter and Paul. This type is rather rare and cannot be assigned to any concrete scene or spectrum of scenes (plate 6). The distinctive hairstyle and also the short beard conceivably reflect the fashion of the times in which they originated.

The third basic type of Jesus iconography, which surfaces for the first time in the fourth century and perhaps is a further development of the type with a beard and locks of hair down to the neck, shows a man again wearing a tunic, robe, and sandals but with long hair. This appears primarily in the depictions of the handing over of instructions to Peter. In this scene he can also appear on one and the same monument alongside one that is beardless with locks of hair down to the neck (plate 7). With the emergence of representative depictions of Jesus Christ as teacher, judge, and potentate, and with the influence of the iconography of rulers, this type becomes predominant in Christian art from the fourth century on (plate 8). And it dominates the portrayals of Jesus up until modern times. It is most probably this type from which the idea of a specific iconography of Jesus emerges.

3. Overview

Type	Characteristics	Pictorial Motifs	Time Period
Beardless with short or medium length hair	Beardless short/medium length hair with locks down to the neck Tunic, robe, and sandals	Scenes of multiplication Scenes of healing Teaching discussions Passion	3rd–5th c.

Type	Characteristics	Pictorial Motifs	Time Period
	Small, naked infant/an infant wrapped in a cloth A naked small-medium-sized body	Mother and child, with or without the adoration of the Magi	From the beginning of the 4th c.
		Manger scenes Jesus's baptism	From the 3rd c.
Bearded with short or medium-length hair	Beard Short/medium-length hair with locks down to the neck Tunic, robe, and sandals	Teaching discussions Passion Scenes of healing Scenes of multiplication	4th/5th c.
Bearded with long hair	Beard Long hair Tunic, robe, and sandals Frequently enthroned Mostly with nimbus	Representative depictions as teacher, judge, and potentate	From the 4th c. predominant from the 6th c.

4. Pictorial Cycles/Sequences of Figures

Iconographic contexts are of great relevance for the interpretation of depictions of Jesus. From the third century, Old Testament figures (e.g., Adam, Moses, Jonah, Abraham) are typologically juxtaposed to Jesus (cf. figs. 1, 2, and 5). From the fourth century, complete pictorial cycles emerge, which represent biblical salvation history typologically (plate 5) or put Jesus's historical life into a narrative tableau. One such cycle from the second half of the fifth century is well preserved in the Roman Basilica of Santa Maria Maggiore, whose apse features the oldest childhood cycle with the annunciation, presentation in the temple, adoration of the Magi, flight to Egypt, and Herod's slaughter of the innocents. In the later fourth century we find individual scenes of the account of the passion lined up in order on the so-called passion sarcophagi. The wooden door of the Church of Saint Sabina in Rome displays the first depiction of Christ on the cross (plate 9).

The oldest preserved Jesus cycle on a monument is found in the Basilica of Sant'Apollinare Nuovo in Ravenna. It originated around 500 and features twenty-six scenes from Jesus's life. Striking is the juxtaposition of the beardless type in the healing, multiplication, and teaching scenes on the south wall with the bearded type in the passion scenes on the north wall of the church (figs. 10 and 11).

5. Developments

Overall, we can identify several lines of development in the history of early Christian Jesus iconography: one leads from impersonal to personal portrayals of Christ; a second, from coded compositions to narrativized and representative presentations; and a third, from a beardless type to a type with a beard and long hair. The variety of types of Jesus and pictorial motifs was at its greatest in the fourth century.

6. Plates with Explanatory Notes

Plate 1. *Helios Christ* (?), mosaic in the Mausoleum of Julier; Rome, ca. 300
COURTESY OF FABBRICA DI SAN PIETRO, VATICAN

This mosaic in a burial chamber shows the youthful Helios the Son of God in his chariot, with a nimbus corona and surrounded by vine tendrils. The prophet Jonah is depicted on the opposite wall. Is this a rather coincidental collocation of the pagan divinity and the Old Testament prophet? Or is it an antitypical juxtaposition of Jonah and Helios Christ? In any case, this depiction is an example of the participation of Jewish Christian iconography in pagan pictorial expression and motifs.

Plate 2. Sarcophagus from the Church of Santa Maria Antiqua; Rome, ca. 245

D-DAI-ROME 1542

From the left: scenes of Jonah's shipwreck, praying woman (prayer posture), philosopher with a book, shepherd carrying a sheep, Jesus's baptism. The three motifs in the middle are taken from pagan sarcophagus art. It is only on the basis of the baptism scene that this sarcophagus can be identified as Christian. The shepherd carrying a sheep can also, therefore, be interpreted as a symbol of Christ. It is easy to recognize the typology of Jesus carrying the sheep and Jesus being baptized: both cases have to do with the type of the beardless Jesus with locks of medium-length hair.

Plate 3. Arcosolium in the Catacombs of Marcellinus and Peter; detail: Jesus with a kneeling woman; Rome, 1st half 4th c.

PONTIFICAL COMMISSION OF SACRED ARCHAEOLOGY, POS. 1 /2 / 2212—PROT. 224 / 16

Christian motifs adorn the interior of the arch over the burial place, whereas the wall is decorated with winged attendant spirits. Jesus is portrayed in the type of the beardless young man with locks, as in most of the healing and miracle depictions of the third and fourth centuries. The encounter with the kneeling woman cannot be unambiguously assigned to any gospel pericope (see above).

Plate 4. Sarcophagus relief from Museum Pio Cristiano; Rome, 2nd third of 4th c.
D-DAI-ROME 4305

The adoration of the Magi is a favored pictorial motif from the fourth century at the latest. Jesus appears here as the beardless type with locks of hair down to his neck, as he appears especially in healing, multiplication, and resuscitation scenes (cf. plates 2, 3, 5). The child in the manger in swaddling clothes cannot be assigned to any specific type. The figure to the right side of the crèche depicts a praying man.

Plate 5. Sarcophagus relief from Museum Pio Cristiano; Rome, 4th c.

This is a fine example for the dominant beardless type with locks down to the neck, which predominated up until the fifth century. In the background, bearded youths as "assistants" of the salvific event form the second row. In the foreground, the following scenes are located from the left to the right: Adam and Eve, the healing of a lame man, a multiplication miracle, Jesus's entrance into Jerusalem, the healing of a blind person, the healing of a (naked) child, the resuscitation of Lazarus with his sister, who is praying.

Plate 6. Sarcophagus relief from the Metropolitan Museum, New York; Rome, 4th c.

BPK—BILDAGENTUR FÜR KUNST, KULTUR UND GESCHICHTE

The scenes depicted on this Roman sarcophagus frieze are partially the same as on the previous sarcophagus (plate 5): On the left Jesus is in a crowd, in the middle he enters Jerusalem, on the right he performs a multiplication miracle and the resuscitation of Lazarus. But here we find the rare type with a beard and medium-length hair, reminiscent of the depiction of philosophers (plate 2) and apostles (plates 5–8), and which most notably is common for Jesus in the middle of the fourth century.

Plate 7. Sarcophagus relief from the Museum of Antiquity, Arles, France; end of the 4th c.

N°INV.FAN.92.00.2487, MDAA, M. LACANAUD RÉFÉRENCE AUTORISATION: 2016–14

On this column sarcophagus, both dominant types of Jesus are found in specific pictorial motifs: in the outer side panels, Jesus is depicted in the foot-washing scene as beardless, and with locks of hair down to his neck (left) and before Pilate (right); in the middle, beardless and with long hair as a teacher in the handing over of instructions to Peter with Paul and two other apostles. The sheep at Jesus's feet are reminiscent of the motif of the good shepherd (cf. plate 2).

Plate 8. Apse mosaic in the Santa Pudenziana Church; Rome, beginning of the 5th c.
PHOTO BY KATHARINA HEYDEN

This oldest-preserved monumental Christian mosaic displays Jesus in a golden garment upon a bejeweled throne as a kingly teacher and judge in the circle of the apostles. In the representative depictions, he is portrayed in the characteristic bearded fashion with long hair and marked as divine by a nimbus (cf. plate 1). The assemblage is surrounded by city architecture; at the same time, the red clouds denote an apocalyptic setting. A mountain with a golden bejeweled cross that protrudes into heaven soars over Jesus Christ. Here the four symbols of the evangelists are depicted, an angel (for Matthew), a lion (for Mark), a bull (for Luke), and an eagle (for John).

Plate 9. Plaque on the wooden door of Santa Sabina Church; Rome, ca. 430
D-DAI-ROM 61.2535

This is the oldest-preserved depiction of the crucifixion. Jesus is portrayed with long hair and beard, clearly contrasted with the malefactors by size and hairstyle.

551

Plates 10 and 11. Mosaics from S. Apollinare nuovo; top: healing of a lame man; bottom: Jesus before Pilate; Ravenna, ca. 500 PHOTO BY KATHARINA HEYDEN

These two mosaic panels from the Jesus series in S. Apollinare Nuovo in Ravenna are good depictions of the juxtaposition of the beardless and bearded type. Above is the healing of a lame man on the south wall of the church. Here Jesus is beardless and accompanied by a disciple. In the scene before Pilate on the north wall, Jesus is depicted in the same clothing, but in the type with a beard and long hair.

Baudry, Gérard-Henry. 2010. *Handbuch der frühchristlichen Ikonographie. 1. bis 7. Jahrhundert.* Freiburg, Basel, and Vienna.

Dietz, Karlheinz, Christian Hannick, Carolina Lutzka, Elisabeth Maier, eds. 2016. *Das Christusbild: Zu Herkunft und Entwicklung in Ost und West.* Das Östliche Christentum, n.s., 62. Würzburg.

Dresken-Weiland, Jutta. 2010. *Bild, Grab und Wort: Untersuchungen zu Jenseitsvorstellungen von Christen des 3. und 4. Jahrhunderts.* Regensburg.

Kollwitz, Johannes. 2012. "Das Christusbild der frühchristlichen Kunst." In *Lexikon der christlichen Ikonographie,* edited by Engelbert Kirschbaum et al., 356–71. Darmstadt.

Krischel, Roland, et al., eds. 2005. *Ansichten Christi: Christusbilder von der Antike bis zum 20. Jahrhundert.* Cologne.

Schiller, Gertrud. 1966. *Ikonographie der christlichen Kunst.* Vol. 1, *Inkarnation, Kindheit, Taufe, Versuchung, Verklärung, Wirken und Wunder Christi.* Gütersloh.

———. 1968. *Ikonographie der christlichen Kunst.* Vol. 2, *Die Passion Jesu Christi.* Gütersloh.

———. 1971. *Ikonographie der christlichen Kunst.* Vol. 3, *Die Auferstehung und Erhöhung Christi.* Gütersloh.

Katharina Heyden and Rachel Schär

VIII. Ethics (Sermon on the Mount)

1. Ancient Ethical Tradition

Adolf von Harnack's ([⁴1909] 2015, 1:20) renowned dictum, which is still controversial today, that Trinitarian theological dogma was in its "conception and development a work of the Greek spirit on the soil of the gospel," could certainly also have been correlated with ancient Christian ethics. Ethics is understood "on the soil of the gospel" and especially of the Sermon on the Mount. However, the concepts and structures of ancient Christian ethics cannot be understood without taking into account the ancient philosophical-ethical tradition. In the second and third centuries, that is, before the establishment of a comprehensive synodical system that formulated declarative confessions of faith, the one central theological concern was constituted by the struggle with the ethical heritage of Jesus's preaching, namely, the Sermon on the Mount and other ethically oriented sayings of Jesus. The formulation of a pertinent confession of God the Creator (Acts 17:24–28a; on this, cf. Volp 2013) and the Son of God Jesus Christ was of course closely connected with Christian ethics (cf. as early as 2 Clem. 4:1–3). The debate with biblical ethics did not take place by any means in a spiritual world in which ethical reflections were something new, but quite the opposite. At all levels of ethical development, Greek and Latin thought played out virtually all conceivable ways of thinking: there were an explicit canon of ethical virtues (on this, cf. fundamentally Aristotle, *Eth. eud.* 2–6) and instructions as well as extensive descriptions of human behavior (cf. Aristotle, *Ethica nicomachea*), that is, what can be expressed as "prescriptive" and "descriptive" ethics. Moreover, for centuries Greek philosophy had reflected at the highest level on the realization of descriptive and prescriptive propositions, on ethical norms, such as the (highest) good or virtue. It had agreed critically on ways of substantiating ethics, and thus had already developed something like a reflective "metaethics." Augustine (354–430) made the centrality of ethics explicit in his famous definition of philosophy, which stresses the constraints and limitations of philosophy: "Philosophers have expressed a great variety of diverse opinions regarding the ends of goods and of evils, and this question they have eagerly canvassed, that they might, if possible, discover what makes a man happy" (Augustine, *Civ.* 19.1). The section following this passage makes it likely that the fathers were well acquainted with the philosophical-ethical discourse of their time. At the same time, when, according to their own understanding, they stood "on the soil of the gospel," this does not mean that these two traditions could be easily reconciled without inconsistencies or conflicts. The history of ethics in the ancient church could be written quite essentially as the history of conflict of biblical and philosophical ethics, of biblical and philosophical anthropology and cosmology (on this, see Volp 2006). On one side there were differences in material ethics, which (pre-scriptive) ethical directives always had to deal with. If one takes the Sermon on the Mount as a paradigm, then the sayings handed down from Jesus about killing (Matt. 5:21–26), about swearing (Matt. 5:33–37), or about loving enemies (Matt. 5:43–48; see D.IV.4.1) turned into quite immediate problems: for instance, for Roman soldiers who turned to Christianity (cf. also, e.g., Matt. 27:54; of course, in the pre-Constantine era especially the connection of military service with the cult had to be considered; cf., e.g., Tertullian, *Idol.* 19). Also, the reframing of the ancient understanding of justice (Matt. 5:39) encountered massive criticism, for example, in the second century by Celsus, the critic of Christianity who was strongly devoted to Platonism, who referred to contradictions with the Mosaic law (according to Origen, *Cels.* 7.18).

On the other hand, there were many overlaps in this area, such as the rela-tionship with earthly wealth (see D.IV.2). So, at another place, Celsus claimed that Christian moral teaching was not an especially new or sublime teaching, which Origen the theologian, who was Celsus's opponent, did not contest either (Origen, *Cels.* 1.4). All in all, differences from Jewish concepts were even smaller (see D.IV.4.1), for which reason conflicts often became virulent and conspicuous in sources only outside the environment of Jewish communities. But at least fundamental differences in ethical reflection were just as weighty. For one thing, they are of a philosophical-theological nature and are based on an anthropology and cosmology that are clearly different from pagan philosophy. For another, the forms of biblical ethical reflection did not correspond to what was customary in antiquity: neither the narrative ethical reflection of the Gospels and Jesus's preaching, as it is suggested in the parable of the Good Samaritan (Luke 10:25–37) or the story of the rich young man (Matt. 19:16–26 par. Luke 18:18–26), nor the ethical plausibility generated by Christian worship, found strong analogies in the Greek or Roman traditions (cf. Volp, Horn, and Zimmermann 2016). Cor-responding complaints from non-Christian quarters, which acknowledged the success of the narrative and doxological establishment of ethics, make this clear (cf., e.g., Julian, *Ep.* 89b, addressed to a priest with the request to incorporate ethics in the pagan cult—as the Christians did).

2. Early Christian Communal Ethics

Early Christian communal ethics of the second century, with its concrete ethical directives as recorded in virtue and vice catalogues, could initially be connected rather naïvely to traditional sayings of Jesus, especially to the love command (cf., e.g., as early as 1 Thess. 4:6–7 or the concretization of love as νόμος Χριστοῦ in Gal. 5–6; the double love command is found rather infrequently, as in Did. 1:2; Polycarp, *Phil.* 3.3; Justin, *Dial.* 93.2). Thus in 2 Clement, composed perhaps around the middle of the second century, the promise of the Sermon on the Mount that those who "do the will of the Father" "enter into the kingdom of heaven" (εἰσέρχεται εἰς τὴν βασιλείαν τῶν οὐρανῶν) is extended solely to those who practice justice and therefore are saved (σώζεσθαι, 2 Clem. 4:1). There were constant appeals to the directives of the Lord Jesus Christ, who was understood to have closely connected ethical behavior and promised redemption with each other. This example shows that Jesus's preaching was constitutive for communal ethics, even though evidently quite early on the necessity and the latitude for interpretation were recognized. In spite of modifications in detail of the escha- tological context, common characteristics of Jesus's preaching and communal ethics include a fundamentally positive but not uncritical connection with the Old Testament "law" (cf. Matt. 5:17–20—along with simultaneous objections to the danger of its perversion; cf. Luke 18:9–14), as well as emphasis on the love of neighbor (Luke 10:25–37; Matt. 20:28; cf. Lev. 19:18). The imitation of Jesus be- came the highest ethical goal (cf. Matt. 16:24; Mark 2:14; Matt. 11:28; see D.IV.3). At the same time, one could nevertheless formulate concrete directives, which, in spite of their similarity to the Ten Commandments, might have been regarded as open collections and not as of equal rank with the Torah or dominical sayings (1 Tim. 3:1–13). The Didache, for example, stipulates this in a not unusual way: "You shall not kill; you shall not commit adultery; you shall not desecrate boys; you shall not be sexually promiscuous; you shall not steal; you shall not practice magic; you shall not mix poison; you shall not murder a child by abortion nor kill a child at birth" (Did. 2:1).

Moreover, the conviction was also constitutive that in Jesus Christ, in his death on a cross and his resurrection, the salvation proclaimed in the Sermon on the Mount had been made available, but also that in him the judgment is in view (Gal. 3:26–28; Acts 17:31; Matt. 25:31–46; on the reception of these passages, e.g., Brändle 1979). In older German New Testament scholarship (Bultmann 1924; cf., more recently, Wolter 2011, 310–38), this has been described as the "indicative" of the reconciliation event, which in a sense brought with it the "imperative" for Christian moral behavior (but cf. critically Horn and Zimmermann 2009). With Paul's thinking in mind, the Christ event would exclude a legalistic exis- tence. The structure of the Christ event—Jesus's sacrifice of love for his own, the sacrifice of the Son of God for his people ("for God so loved the world," John 3:16)—had to have consequences for the Christian life, which would also explain the strikingly strong place of the love command quite simply as the criterion for Christian behavior. An aristocratic life lived in self-chosen leisure, extensively isolated from the harder side of human life, as the presumed setting of ethical manuals like Cicero's *De officiis* or Aristotelian friendship ethics, obtained no paradigmatic character for Christian communities. Against this background, it becomes comprehensible why as early as in the second century a special Christian ethic could develop, which in detail deviated considerably from the moral manuals of Greek and Latin literature. The portfolio of moral requirements and values that could appeal to Jesus's preaching, and that differed from Torah and ancient popular philosophy, included the command to love enemies (Matt. 5:44), the evaluation of deed and thought as equivalent (Matt. 5:28), but especially what was now perceived as specifically Christian humility (Matt. 5:3; 20:25–28). A contradiction also existed between Luke 15:7 ("There will be more joy in heaven over one sinner who repents than over ninety-nine righteous persons") and the prevailing ethical concepts of the world surrounding Christianity, of both philosophical ethics and also of Judaism. All of this was augmented by quite concrete regulations regarding addiction to alcohol, bribery, flattery (toward sinners), and exhortations to obedience, forbearance, mercy, and compassion for the poor. This occurred repeatedly with reference to the discourse of Jesus, who promised a redeemed transcendent existence as a reward for a life conforming to the law (as, for instance, in the Epistula Apostolorum from the second century; but on this passage, cf. Köhler 1987, 476–81). In the rules for admission to Christian congregations, which in their basic inventory are perhaps still preserved in the *Traditio apostolica* originating in the early third century, a list of sixteen occupations is found that without further ado are not compatible with a Christian lifestyle: gladiators, soldiers, coin counterfeiters, brothel operators, and so forth, could become Christians only under special conditions. Perhaps the Sermon on the Mount originally did not have all of this in view, but the substantial claim on individuals promoted by it led historically to rules taken quite seriously for admission into Christian congregations.

3. Challenges for Christian Ethics in the Second Century

Things did not continue in this way of prescriptive communal ethics in connection with Jesus's preaching and modification of Jewish traditions. The basis for this was several crucial challenges that changed Christianity in the second century theologically and led to a much more extensive ethical reflection. The inventory for Christian ethics was thus laid down, but it also paved the way for the special features of later Christian monasticism. Challenges "from the outside," that is, from the dominant pagan society, Judaism, and (popular) philosophical ethics, are to be differentiated from challenges "from within," that is, from internal Christian reform movements, such as Marcionism (see below). In addition to this was the intellectual challenge from Gnosticism, which—in part on biblical foundations—advocated alternative concepts in anthropology and cosmology. The prescriptive Christian communal ethic connected with Jesus's preaching could not cope with any of these challenges: only to a certain extent could the challenges to orthodoxy posed by internal Christian heresies be countered by community discipline. Heretics were condemned not least of all on the basis of ethics, because they not only "suffered shipwreck in faith" (1 Tim. 1:19; note the analogy to 1 Tim. 6:10) but also seduced their own brothers and sisters to fall away and thereby to transgress the commandment of mutual "edification" (e.g., Jude 20).

Emerging Christianity had to establish itself outwardly over against Judaism in the diaspora, with which it shared the foremost theological traditions. It can hardly be established whether the so-called Testament of the Twelve Patriarchs or parts of the Sibylline Oracles, for example, are Jewish or early Christian writings. On the level of piety, as early as the time of Paul, many Christian congregations consisted in part of gentile Christians who from the beginning did not participate in Jewish life. However, even quite later there were some mixed forms such as "God-fearing" gentiles, with lively participation in the life of synagogue communities. John Chrysostom (344/49–407) still complains about such mixed constituents. The first intellectual apologetic discussion with Judaism is found in the eminent apologist Justin (100–165). Both Justin's apology (e.g., *Dial.* 8.3) and Chrysostom's later polemic (see, e.g., the reference to Matt. 25:35–36 in *Jud. gent.* 2.5) employ ethical arguments. Institutionally, Christian and Jewish communities were probably separated quite early, which one might also infer from the charitable activities of the two groups.

Over against the pagan majority in society, Christian apologetics emphasized even more strongly the superior morality of members of the Christian communities, especially since rumors were afloat that, for instance, Christians ritually murdered children and arranged "Thyestes banquets" as well as "Oedipal relations," that is, they engaged in "incestuous" relationships between "brothers" and "sisters" (cf., e.g., Tertullian, *Apol.* 7–9). Against such charges, the apologists illustrated a Christian morality molded by reason, which they differentiated from that of the most prominent proponents of Roman society only in its theological foundation. Appropriate to the apologetic genre, these texts avoid biblical formulations as far as possible, because they indeed emphasized precisely the agreement with the norms and values of the non-Christian majority in society. Bridge building with philosophy was also attempted, especially by Justin, who aligned the form of his *Dialogue with Trypho* with Platonic models and sought connections in content with the Stoa and Middle Platonism.

The approach against Gnosticism was shaped somewhat differently. Christian Gnosticism presumably presented the first genuinely dangerous internal Christian challenge, although its precise beginnings lie in obscurity. To be sure, the term *gnosis* (knowledge) is found in the sources, but as a descriptive term it is obviously imposed by outsiders, if not considered a complete "typological construct" (Williams ²1999), both by modern scholarship and by the fathers who early on opposed it. It designates a syncretistic mixture of elitist and esoteric teachings, which especially in the second and third centuries CE found broad distribution and fed on elements of philosophy, pagan religions, and cults, which were adopted into Christianity and perhaps also into Judaism. These teachings attempted to explain the origin and essence of the world, and thereby especially the question of the origin of evil, and to develop strategies for the ultimate conquest of it. Only a few chosen people obtained access to these veiled strategies, which were often embedded in individual myths and divine dramas but not openly proclaimed, and they could be correctly understood only by the initiated. For example, the Pronoia Hymn of the Apocryphon of John speaks of the "prison of the body" (Ap. John 2.26), a well-known topos of Platonic anthropology (from Plato, *Phaed.* 62b up to Porphyry, *Vit. Plot.* 1; cf. Courcelle 1976), which is problematic not only for the Christian doctrine of the bodily resurrection but also for Christian ethics, especially since Matt. 5:25–26 par. Luke 12:58–59 was also understood in this figurative sense (Irenaeus, *Haer.* 1.25.4). In the final analysis, the postulated detachment from matter and the total spiritualization of human beings do not allow for any materially effective action for the benefit of other people in need (see on this—at least also—the rejoinder of Clement of Alexandria, *Quis dives salvetur*, which can be understood as antignostic). This example makes clear how gnostics living ascetically must have appeared to oppose this world and its affairs, human history, and everyday life, at least in the eyes of their Christian opponents.

The ancient philosophical theory of virtue presented a further challenge that was not merely intellectual. In many respects, it could not be brought into seamless agreement with biblical precepts or with Jesus's preaching in particular. Platonic or Stoic thinkers would have been able without further ado to express agreement with the disparagement of material goods in Matt. 6:24. Nevertheless, with the reference to God the Creator, to whom one ought confidently to entrust care for the body (Matt. 6:26–32), they would have objected that the reference to the "gentiles" (τὰ ἔθνη) probably presupposed them (6:32). Likewise, the tenet of the bodily resurrection (1 Thess. 4:13–18) must have been abhorrent to Platonists and gnostics. For the most part, both simply held the human soul or the faculty of reason or, in any case, a purely spiritual part of humans to be divine, transcendent, and supratemporal, whereas the body, or at least the physical substance of humans, was material, earthly, and temporal. It was connected with the spiritual parts of humans for a certain period of time but was actually foreign and repulsive for them. Traditional ascetic prescriptions directed against human corporeality such as the prohibition of eating meat or abstinence from sex sounded similar to Gnosticism and Neoplatonism, a similarity that many contemporaries will have noticed above the dissimilarity between the two groups. Against this background, the Christian defense of the bodily resurrection (cf., e.g., Tertullian, *De resurrectione carnis*; Pseudo-Athanagoras, *De resurrectione*; Pseudo-Justin, *De resurrectione*) and material aspects of Christian ethics such as care for the poor often applied to both tendencies in equal measure. However, the defense mainly appeared more forcefully as polemics against Gnosticism, which indeed was perceived as an internal Christian heresy. And only Gnosticism assumed in its cosmological myths an intrinsically autonomous evil power opposing the intelligible one. What is more, the rational forms of gnostic anthropology came forcefully into direct opposition with the predominant narrative foundation of Christian ethics of New Testament stories and Jesus's discourses. To understand fully why Gnosticism was considered the more dangerous challenge, the consequences of this way of thinking for ethics need to be taken into account: Gnosticism assumed the existence of different classes of people, such as "somatics," "psychics," and "pneumatics" (according to the "Valentinian" system; on this, cf. Markschies 2002). Their essence determined whether they were attracted to the earthly bodily-material or to the otherworldly spiritual-immaterial; human freedom of choice appeared not to be presumed by most gnostic groups. But such an understanding meant at least indifference to, if not the end of, every ethic taken seriously.

In terms of content related in some way to Gnosticism, the shipowner and Christian reformer Marcion also positioned himself against the mainstream Christian church in a way that was perceived to be dangerous. Differently from Gnosticism and above all from non-Christian intellectual currents, he relied on a biblical canon that presented the foundation for Marcionite communal theology. It likely contained his own introduction, a gospel, and the *Apostolikon*. Presumably the last two consisted of parts of the Gospel of Luke (according to another opinion, he himself substantially wrote this part on the basis of oral tradition) and Paul's letters. This was explosive because the gospels that later became canonical were still not authoritative in Christian congregations of the early second century; at any rate, almost no traces of their reception have been preserved from this period. Marcion's theology does not assume, like Gnosticism, a good immaterial principle and an evil material one, but more specifically the existence of two Gods, which above all are distinguished by their view on ethics. The "old God" was responsible for the creation of the world, and this God's deeds of justice and retribution are to be read in the Old Testament; by contrast, the newer, heretofore unknown God is a God of mercy, forgiveness of sins (Luke 5:18–26), and love of enemies (Luke 6:27–31), who stands diametrically opposed to the old one (Luke 5:36–38; 10:9) and who had revealed his ethical regulations and directives not in the form of laws or ethical discourses but in narrative form, in parables, and in Jesus's conversation with his disciples. The law of the old God had the character of a cosmic coercive power, from which Christ redeems human beings (cf. Rom. 7). In contrast to Gnosticism, this redemption accordingly stands open for the entirety of humanity, who were willing to subject themselves at the outset to rigorous regulations of congregational life and who led to the propagation of Marcionism from Pontus and Rome to southern Galatia, North Africa, Egypt, Crete, Asia Minor, Syria, and Mesopotamia. In no other Christian movement did the *lex caritatis* of the Sermon on the Mount have a similar centrality, especially because there was no threat of relativizing the ethical imperative by means of an imminent eschatological expectation: Marcion's purpose was to make a decision in this world in the battle between the old God and the new God and to establish a kingdom of love; no member of the community was allowed to withdraw from this.

In the second half of the second century especially, the so-called anti-Gnostic fathers—Irenaeus of Lyon (ca. 135–200), Hippolytus of Rome (ca. 170–235), Tertullian of Carthage (ca. 150–200), and Clement of Alexandria (ca. 150–215)—responded to this twofold internal Christian challenge to Christian ethics and communal theology. The most consequential was the biblically oriented (*heils*)*geschichtliche* approach of Irenaeus of Lyon, with his fundamental concept resorting back to the Pauline Adam-Christ typology (Rom. 5–7, esp. 5:18 and 6:23). The perfection of the image of God in humanity (Gen. 1:26), which was partially lost in the Fall, took place in the incarnation of the "Word of God" as the final "recapitulation" (*recapitulatio*) of the human being; the incarnate one becomes the beginning of a new humanity, which in the Platonic *Philosophumena* of image/copy/likeness/replica can be expressed comprehensibly as an interpretation of the image terminology of Gen. 1:26. But this especially propagated the concept of a progressively advancing history. Human beings and their ethical possibilities and duties were now no longer seen as timeless as in philosophy, but embedded in the progression of history. Irenaeus stands for a christological ethical concept on the basis of Jesus's declaration about himself from Matt. 5:17, that the Old Testament law is not abrogated by him but rather amplified and fulfilled (*non dissolvit, sed extendit et implevit* [Irenaeus, *Haer.* 4.13.1]). The fall into sin was the cause of death; since the Christ event, the power of death is abolished—and in fact by righteousness/justice (Rom. 3–6; Matt. 5:20). When Irenaeus described Jesus Christ from his New Testament preaching as a man according to God's will on the basis of his obedience to God and his love of neighbor, he made him the foundation stone of ethics, the fulcrum and pivot of his model of progress. Thus, in Christ the nature of creation actually appeared, whereby Christian ethical behavior is defined as acting in accord with creation or, that is to say, in accord with nature. One can see here the origin of later approaches to Christian ethics based on natural law, for which the central place of the revelation of Christ should not be overlooked (cf. Martin Luther's understanding of the *lex naturalis*), which in many concepts of natural law is later sometimes confined to the back benches (Augustine, Thomas Aquinas).

4. Outlook: The Ethic of the Sermon on the Mount in Alexandrian Theology and Monastic Ethics

Clement of Alexandria (ca. 150–215) is the first Alexandrian theologian from whom extensive theological writings have been preserved. He is also sometimes still counted among the anti-Gnostic fathers. However, ever stronger than they, he engaged in an academic theology on equal footing with pagan philosophy and philosophical ethics and theories of virtue, like his successor Origen (185–ca. 254), who was then to bring this to an initial culmination. Both assumed the concept of an incremental knowledge of God, which in principle was accessible to everyone. Human freedom of choice granted access to the μυστηρίοι, that is, to baptism and the Lord's Supper, which are sufficient for participation in the glory of God (Clement, *Protr.* 12.118.4). Also, Jesus's simple ethical instructions allowed a beginning of Christian existence in faith. There is of course some distance from there to a perfect Christian existence and to that of the "genuine gnostic." Clement describes this way in his second work, *Paedagogos* ("Tutor"), which aims at the ethical maturation process of those who have come to faith. It ends in a portrait of the genuine gnostic, which is developed unsystematically in his third main work, *Stromateis* ("Patchwork"). Such a "perfect" Christian (Matt. 5:48), which he, for example, visualizes in those who "are persecuted for righteousness' sake" (Matt. 5:9–10, cited by Clement, *Strom.* 4.41.1; cf. Matt. 5:48, cited in *Strom.* 7.84.5), possesses all virtues, but especially the love of neighbor and the love of God, and prays not only on certain days and at certain hours but is in perpetual communication (ὁμιλία) with God (Clement, *Strom.* 7.39.6). This person sees God "face-to-face" and therefore becomes like God, and thus attains the ὁμοίωσις τῷ θεῷ, which corresponds to the original creation (Gen. 1:26; cf. Plato, *Theaet.* 17a–b). With this the *heilsgeschichtliche* maturation process is broken down into individual advances; the ethical directives of the Sermon on the Mount (e.g., the blessedness understood as the injunction to humility of the poor in spirit; cf. Gregory of Nazianus, *Or. Bas.* 1 on Matt. 5:3) receive a fixed role in this process, which of course had to be supported by other practices, such as the metriopathy (moderation of the passions). In Eastern monasticism, such processes of perfection became the central goal of Christian existence (here, e.g., Matt. 5:8 was understood as an injunction to a *vita contemplativa* in chastity; cf. in this sense the Acts of Paul and Thecla 5–6), which was to impact Christianity in the West and East for centuries.

Brennecke, Hanns Christof, and Johannes van Oort, eds. 2011. *Ethik im antiken Christentum.* SPA 9. Leuven.

Dihle, Albrecht. 1966. "Ethik." In *RAC* 6:646–796.

Mühlenberg, Ekkehard. 2006. *Altchristliche Lebensführung zwischen Bibel und Tugendlehre: Ethik bei den griechischen Philosophen und den frühen Christen.* AAWGPH 3.272. Göttingen.

Osborn, Eric. 1976. *Ethical Patterns in Early Christian Thought.* Cambridge.

Volp, Ulrich. 2006. *Die Würde des Menschen: Ein Beitrag zur Anthropologie in der Alten Kirche.* SVigChr 81. Leiden and Boston.

Ulrich Volp

Bibliography

Achtemeier, Paul J. 1996. *1 Peter: A Commentary on First Peter*. Minneapolis.

Ådna, Jostein. 2000. *Jesu Stellung zum Tempel: Die Tempelaktion und das Tempelwort als Ausdruck seiner messianischen Sendung*. WUNT II 119. Tübingen.

Aejmelaeus, Lars. 1993. *Jeesuksen ylösnousemus, osa I: Tausta ja Paavalin todistus*. SESJ 57. Helsinki.

Akker-Savelsbergh, Yvonne van den. 2004. *Het onzevader—een meerstemmig gebed? Een tekstsemantisch en redactiekritisch onderzoek naar het onzevader in de versie van Matteüs (Mt 6,9b–13)*. Zoetermeer.

Alkier, Stefan. 1993. *Urchristentum: Zur Geschichte und Theologie einer exegetischen Disziplin*. BHT 83. Tübingen.

———. 2003. "'Geld' im Neuen Testament: Der Beitrag der Numismatik zu einer Enzyklopädie des Frühen Christentums." In *Zeichen aus Text und Stein: Studien auf dem Weg zu einer Archäologie des Neuen Testaments*, edited by Stefan Alkier and Jürgen Zangenberg, 308–35. TANZ 42. Tübingen.

Allison, Dale C. 1982. "The Pauline Epistles and the Synoptic Gospels: The Pattern of Parallels." *NTS* 28: 1–32.

———. 1985. "Paul and the Missionary Discourse." *ETL* 61: 369–75.

———. 1987. "Jesus and the Covenant: A Response to Sanders." *JSNT* 29: 57–78.

———. 1994. "A Plea for Thoroughgoing Eschatology." *JBL* 113: 651–68.

———. 1997. *The Jesus Tradition in Q*. Harrisburg, PA.

———. 1998. *Jesus of Nazareth: Millenarian Prophet*. Minneapolis.

———. 2005a. "Explaining the Resurrection: Conflicting Convictions." *JSHJ* 3 (2): 117–33.

———. 2005b. *Resurrecting Jesus: The Earliest Christian Tradition and Its Interpreters*. London and New York.

———. 2010. *Constructing Jesus: Memory, Imagination, and History*. Grand Rapids.

———. 2011. "How to Marginalize the Traditional Criteria of Authenticity." In *Handbook for the Study of the Historical Jesus*, vol. 1, *How to Study the Historical Jesus*, edited by Tom Holmén and Stanley E. Porter, 3–30. Leiden.

Alt, Albrecht. 1953. "Die Stätten des Wirkens Jesu in Galiläa territorialgeschichtlich betrachtet." In *Kleine Schriften zur Geschichte des Volkes Israels*, vol. 2, edited by Albrecht Alt, 436–55. Munich.

Alt, Peter-André. 2007. *Aufklärung, Lehrbuch Germanistik*. Stuttgart and Weimar.

Anderson, Paul N. 2006. *The Fourth Gospel and the Quest for Jesus: Modern Foundations Reconsidered*. London and New York.

Anderson, Paul N., Felix Just, SJ, and Tom Thatcher, eds. 2007. *John, Jesus, and History I: Critical Appraisals of Critical Views*. SBLSS 44. Atlanta.

———, eds. 2009. *John, Jesus, and History II: Aspects of Historicity in the Fourth Gospel*. SBLSS 44. Atlanta.

———, eds. 2016. *John, Jesus, and History III: Glimpses of Jesus through the Johannine Lens*. SBLSS 44. Atlanta.

Andreau, Jean. 1999. *Banking and Business in the Roman World*. Cambridge.

Angenendt, Arnold. 1997. *Geschichte der Religiosität im Mittelalter*. Darmstadt.

Annen, Franz. 1976. "Die Dämonenaustreibungen Jesu in den synoptischen Evangelien." *TBer* 5: 107–46.

Argyle, Aubrey W. 1974. "Greek among the Jews of Palestine in New Testament Times." *NTS* 20: 87–89.

Ariel, Donald T. 2011. "Identifying the Mints, Minters and Meanings of the First Jewish Revolt Coins." In *The Jewish Revolt against Rome: Interdisciplinary Perspectives*, edited by Mladen Popović, 373–97. JSJS 154. Leiden and Boston.

Ariel, Donald T., and Jean-Philippe Fontanille. 2012. *The Coins of Herod: A Modern Analysis and Die Classification*. AJEC 79. Leiden and Boston.

Arnal, William E. 2001. *Jesus and the Village Scribes: Galilean Conflicts and the Setting of Q*. Minneapolis.

———. 2005. *The Symbolic Jesus: Historical Scholarship, Judaism, and the Construction of Contemporary Identity*. London.

———. 2011. "The Synoptic Problem and the Historical Jesus." In *New Studies in the Synoptic Problem: Oxford Conference, April 2008; Essays in Honour of Christopher M. Tuckett*, edited by Paul Foster, Andrew F. Gregory, John S. Kloppenborg, and Jozef Verheyden, 371–432. BETL 239. Leuven.

Assmann, Aleida. 1999. *Erinnerungsräume: Formen und Wandlungen des kulturellen Gedächtnisses*. Munich.

Assmann, Jan. 1992. *Das kulturelle Gedächtnis: Schrift, Erinnerung und politische Identität in frühen Hochkulturen*. Munich.

Attridge, Harold W. 1976. *The Interpretation of Biblical History in the Antiquitates Judaicae of Flavius Josephus*. Missoula, MT.

Aubin, Melissa. 2001. "Beobachtungen zur Magie im Neuen Testament." *ZNT* 4: 16–24.

Aune, David E. 1980. "Magic in Early Christianity." *ANRW* II.23.2: 1507–57.

Aurenhammer, Hans. 1959. *Lexikon der christlichen Ikonographie*. Vienna.

Avemarie, Friedrich, and Hermann Lichtenberger, eds. 2001. *Auferstehung—Resurrection: The Fourth Durham-Tübingen Research Symposium; Resurrection,*

Transfiguration, and Exaltation in Old Testament, Ancient Judaism, and Early Christianity. WUNT 135. Tübingen.

Baasland, Ernst. 1986. "Zum Beispiel der Beispielerzählungen." *NovT* 28: 193–219.

Bäbler, Balbina, and Ulrich Rehm. 2001. "Jesus Christus in künstlerischer Darstellung." In *RGG* 4:485–95.

Back, Sven-Olav. 2011. "Jesus of Nazareth and the Christ of Faith: Approaches to the Question in Historical Jesus Research." In *Handbook for the Study of the Historical Jesus,* vol. 2, *The Study of Jesus,* edited by Tom Holmén and Stanley E. Porter, 1021–54. Leiden and Boston.

Backhaus, Knut. 1991. *Die "Jüngerkreise" des Täufers Johannes: Eine Studie zu den religionsgeschichtlichen Ursprüngen des Christentums.* PaThSt 19. Paderborn.

———. 2011. "Echoes from the Wilderness: The Historical John the Baptist." In *Handbook for the Study of the Historical Jesus,* vol. 2, *The Study of Jesus,* edited by Tom Holmén and Stanley E. Porter, 1747–85. Leiden and Boston.

Bailey, Kenneth E. 1995. "Informal Controlled Oral Tradition and the Synoptic Gospels." *Themelios* 20 (2): 4–11.

Baird, William. 1992. *History of New Testament Research.* Vol. 1, *From Deism to Tübingen.* Minneapolis.

Balla, Peter. 2003. *The Child-Parent Relationship in the New Testament and Its Environment.* WUNT 155. Tübingen.

Baltzer, Eduard. 1860. *Das Leben Jesu.* Nordhausen, Germany.

Bammel, Ernst. 1971–1972. "The Baptist in Early Christian Tradition." *NTS* 18: 95–128.

Bammel, Ernst, and C. F. D. Moule, eds. 1984. *Jesus and the Politics of His Day.* Cambridge.

Banks, Robert. 1975. *Jesus and the Law in the Synoptic Tradition.* Cambridge.

Bar-Asher, Moshe. 2006. "Mishnaic Hebrew: An Introductory Survey." In *The Cambridge History of Judaism,* vol. 4, *The Late Roman-Rabbinic Period,* edited by Steven T. Katz, 369–403. Cambridge.

Barclay, John M. G. 1996. *Jews in the Mediterranean Diaspora: From Alexander to Trajan (323 BCE–117 CE).* Edinburgh.

Barr, James. 1988. "ABBA Isn't Daddy!" *JTS* 39: 28–47.

Barrett, Charles Kingsley. 1956; ²1978. *The Gospel according to St. John.* London.

———. 1985. "Sayings of Jesus in the Acts of the Apostles." In *À cause de l'Évangile: Études sur les Synoptiques et les Actes offertes au P. Jacques Dupont, O. S. B à l'occasion de son 70e anniversaire,* 681–708. Paris.

Barth, Karl. 1919; ²1922. *Der Römerbrief.* Munich.

Barth, Ulrich. 2010. "Hermeneutik der Evangelien als Prolegomena zur Christologie." In *Zwischen historischem Jesus und dogmatischem Christus: Zum Stand der Christologie im 21. Jahrhundert,* edited by Christian Danz and Michael Murrmann-Kahl, 275–305. Tübingen.

Bartholomä, Philipp F. 2012. *The Johannine Discourses and the Teaching of Jesus in the Synoptics: A Contribution to the Discussion concerning the Authenticity of Jesus' Words in the Fourth Gospel.* TANZ 57. Tübingen.

Barton, Stephen C. 1994. *Discipleship and Family Ties in Mark and Matthew.* SNTSMS 80. Cambridge.

Bassler, Moritz, et al., eds. 1996. *Historismus und literarische Moderne.* Tübingen.

Bauckham, Richard J. 1990. *Jude and the Relatives of Jesus in the Early Church.* London.

———. 2002. *Gospel Women: Studies of the Named Women in the Gospels.* Grand Rapids.

———. 2006a. *Jesus and the Eyewitnesses: The Gospels as Eyewitness Testimony.* Grand Rapids.

———. 2006b. "Messianism according to the Gospel of John." In *Challenging Perspectives on the Gospel of John,* edited by John Lierman, 34–68. WUNT II 219. Tübingen.

———. 2007. "Historiographical Characteristics of the Gospel of John." *NTS* 53: 17–36.

Baudry, Gérard-Henry. 2010. *Handbuch der frühchristlichen Ikonographie. 1. bis 7. Jahrhundert.* Freiburg, Basel, and Vienna.

Bauer, Bruno. 1841–1842. *Kritik der evangelischen Geschichte der Synoptiker.* 3 vols. Leipzig.

Baumgardt, David. 1991. "Kaddish and Lord's Prayer." *JBQ* 19: 164–69.

Baumgarten, Albert I. 1997. *The Flourishing of Sects in the Maccabean Period: An Interpretation.* JSJS 55. Leiden.

Baumotte, Manfred, and Stephan Wehowsky, eds. 1984. *Die Frage nach dem historischen Jesus: Texte aus drei Jahrhunderten, Reader Theologie. Basiswissen— Querschnitte—Perspektiven.* Gütersloh.

Baur, Ferdinand Christian. 1847. *Kritische Untersuchungen über die kanonischen Evangelien, ihr Verhältnis zueinander, ihren Charakter und Ursprung.* Tübingen.

———. 1853. *Geschichte der christlichen Kirche.* Vol. 1, *Das Christentum und die christliche Kirche der drei ersten Jahrhunderte.* Tübingen. ET: 1878–1879. *The Church History of the First Three Centuries.* London.

———. 1864. *Vorlesungen über neutestamentliche Theologie.* Edited by Ferdinand Friedrich Baur. Leipzig.

Baur, Jörg. 1993. *Luther und seine klassischen Erben: Theologische Aufsätze und Forschungen.* Tübingen.

Bauspiess, Martin, et al., eds. 2014. *Ferdinand Christian Baur und die Geschichte des frühen Christentums.* WUNT 333. Tübingen.

Bazzana, Giovanni B. 2015. *Kingdom of Bureaucracy: The Political Theology of Village Scribes in the Sayings Gospel Q.* Leuven.

Beasley-Murray, George Raymond. 1986. *Jesus and the Kingdom of God.* Grand Rapids.

Beavis, Mary Ann, ed. 2002. *The Lost Coin: Parables of Women, Work, and Wisdom.* Biblical Seminar 86. London, New York, and Sheffield.

Beck, David R. 1997. *The Discipleship Paradigm: Readers and Anonymous Characters in the Fourth Gospel*. BibInt 27. Leiden.

Becker, Jürgen. 1972. *Johannes der Täufer und Jesus von Nazareth*. Biblische Studien 63. Neukirchen-Vluyn.

———. 1995. "Feindesliebe—Nächstenliebe—Bruderliebe: Exegetische Beobachtungen als Anfrage an ein ethisches Problemfeld." In *Annäherungen: Ausgewählte Aufsätze*, edited by Jürgen Becker and Ulrich Mell, 382–94. BZNW 76. Berlin.

———. 1996. *Jesus von Nazaret*. Berlin.

———. 2001. "Das vierte Evangelium und die Frage nach seinen externen und internen Quellen." In *Fair Play: Diversity and Conflicts in Early Christianity; Essays in Honour of Heikki Räisänen*, edited by Ismo Dunderberg, Christopher Tuckett, and Kari Syreeni, 203–41. NovTSup 103. Leiden.

———. 2007. *Die Auferstehung Jesu Christi nach dem Neuen Testament: Ostererfahrung und Osterverständnis im Urchristentum*. Tübingen.

Becker, Michael. 2002. *Wunder und Wundertäter im frührabbinischen Judentum*. With collaboration of Jörg von Frey, Martin Hengel, and Otfried Hofius. WUNT II 144. Tübingen.

Beirne, Margaret M. 2004. *Women and Men in the Fourth Gospel*. London.

Belle, Gilbert van. 1994. *The Signs Source in the Fourth Gospel: Historical Survey and Critical Evaluation of the Semeia Hypothesis*. BETL 116. Leuven.

Bendemann, Reinhard von. 2014. "Die Heilungen Jesu und die antike Medizin." *Early Christianity* 5: 273–312.

Bennema, Cornelis. 2013. "The Crowd: A Faceless, Divided Mass." In *Character Studies in the Fourth Gospel: Narrative Approaches to 70 Figures in John*, edited by Steven A. Hunt et al., 347–55. WUNT 314. Tübingen.

Berger, Klaus. 1971. "Zum traditionsgeschichtlichen Hintergrund christologischer Hoheitstitel." *NTS* 17: 391–425.

———. 1972. *Die Gesetzesauslegung Jesu: Ihr historischer Hintergrund im Judentum und im Alten Testament*. Vol. 1, *Markus und Parallelen*. WMANT 40. Neukirchen-Vluyn.

———. 1973. "Die königlichen Messiastraditionen des Neuen Testaments." *NTS* 20: 1–44.

———. 1984. *Hellenistische Gattungen im Neuen Testament*, 1031–1432. ANRW II.25.2.

———. 1988. "Jesus als Pharisäer und frühe Christen als Pharisäer." *NovT* 30: 231–62.

———. 1994. *Theologiegeschichte des Urchristentums: Theologie des Neuen Testaments*. Tübingen and Basel.

Berges, Ulrich, and Rudolf Hoppe. 2009. *Arm und Reich*. NEchtB 10. Würzburg.

Bermejo-Rubio, Fernando. 2014. "Jesus and the Anti-Roman Resistance: A Reassessment of the Arguments." *JSHJ* 12: 1–105.

Bernett, Monika. 2007. *Der Kaiserkult in Judäa unter den Herodiern und Römern*. WUNT 203. Tübingen.

Best, Ernest. 1970. "I Peter and the Gospel Tradition." *NTS* 16 (2): 95–113.

———. 1978. "Mark's Use of the Twelve." *ZNW* 69: 11–35.

———. 1981. *Following Jesus: Discipleship in the Gospel of Mark*. JSNTSup 4. Sheffield.

Betcher, Sharon. 2013. "Disability and the Terror of the Miracle Tradition." In *Miracles Revisited: New Testament Miracle Stories and Their Concepts of Reality*, edited by Stefan Alkier and Annette Weissenrieder, 161–80. Studies on the Bible and Its Reception. Berlin.

Betz, Hans Dieter. 1967. *Nachfolge und Nachahmung Jesu Christi im Neuen Testament*. BHT 37. Tübingen.

———. 1994. "Jesus and the Cynics: Survey and Analysis of a Hypothesis." *JR* 74: 453–75.

———. 1995. *The Sermon on the Mount. A Commentary on the Sermon on the Mount Including the Sermon on the Plain (Matthew 5:3–7:27 and Luke 6:20–49)*. Hermeneia. Minneapolis.

Betz, Otto. 1982. "Probleme des Prozesses Jesu." *ANRW* II.25.1: 565–647.

Beutel, Albrecht. [2]2009. *Kirchengeschichte im Zeitalter der Aufklärung: Ein Kompendium*. UTB 3180. Göttingen.

———. 2013. "Frömmigkeit als 'die Empfindung unserer gänzlichen Abhängigkeit von Gott.' Die Fixierung einer religionstheologischen Leitformel in Spaldings Gedächtnispredigt auf Friedrich II. von Preußen." In *Spurensicherung: Studien zur Identitätsgeschichte des Protestantismus*, by Albrecht Beutel, 165–87. Tübingen.

———. 2017. "Die reformatorischen Wurzeln der Aufklärung: Beobachtungen zur frühneuzeitlichen Transformationsgeschichte des Protestantismus." *ZTK* special issue.

Beyschlag, Karlmann. [2/1]1988–2000. *Grundriß der Dogmengeschichte*. 2 vols in 3. Darmstadt.

Bickermann, Elias. 1935. "Utilitas crucis: Observations sur les récits du procès de Jésus dans les Évangiles canoniques." *RHR* 112: 169–241.

Bieberstein, Sabine. 1998. *Verschwiegene Jüngerinnen—vergessene Zeuginnen: Gebrochene Konzepte im Lukasevangelium*. Freiburg, Switzerland, and Göttingen.

Bieler, Ludwig. 1967. *Theios Anēr: Das Bild des "Göttlichen Menschen" in Spätantike und Frühchristentum*. Vol. 2. Darmstadt.

Black, C. Clifton. 1989. *The Disciples according to Mark: Markan Redaction in Current Debate*. JSNTSup 27. Sheffield.

Black, Matthew. [3]1967. *An Aramaic Approach to the Gospels and Acts*. Oxford.

Blanke, Horst-Walter. 1984. *Von der Aufklärung zum Historismus: Zum Strukturwandel des historischen Denkens*. Historisch-politische Diskurse 1. Paderborn.

———. 1990. "Die Wiederentdeckung der deutschen Aufklärungshistorie und die Begründung der Historischen Sozialwissenschaft." In *Die sog: Geisteswissenschaften; Innenansichten*, edited by Wolfgang Prinz and Peter Weingart, 105–33. STW 854. Frankfurt.

———. 1991. *Historiographiegeschichte als Historik, Fundamenta Historica*. Texte und Forschungen 3. Stuttgart–Bad Cannstatt.

Blanke, Horst-Walter, and Dirk Fleischer, eds. 1990. *Theoretiker der deutschen Aufklärungshistorie.* Vol. 1, *Die theoretische Begründung der Geschichte als Fachwissenschaft.* Vol. 2, *Elemente der Aufklärungshistorik, Fundamenta Historica.* Texte und Forschungen 1.1/2. Stuttgart–Bad Cannstatt.

Blinzler, Josef. 1974. "Die Grablegung Jesu in historischer Sicht." In *Resurrexit: Actes du symposium international sur la résurrection de Jésus, Rome 1970,* edited by Édouard Dhanis, 56–107. Rome.

Blomberg, Craig L. 1999. *Neither Poverty nor Riches: A Biblical Theology of Material Possessions.* New Studies in Biblical Theology 7. Leicester.

———. 2001. *The Historical Reliability of St. John's Gospel: Issues and Commentary.* Downers Grove, IL.

Bock, Darrell L. 1998. *Blasphemy and Exaltation in Judaism and the Final Examination of Jesus: A Philological-Historical Study of the Key Jewish Themes Impacting Mark 14:61–64.* WUNT II 106. Tübingen.

Bock, Darrell L., and Robert Webb, eds. 2009. *Key Events in the Life of the Historical Jesus: A Collaborative Exploration of Context and Coherence.* WUNT 247. Tübingen.

Böckler, Annette. 2000. *Gott als Vater im Alten Testament: Traditionsgeschichtliche Untersuchungen zur Entstehung und Entwicklung eines Gottesbildes.* Gütersloh.

Boehmer, Heinrich. 1914. *Studien zur Geschichte der Gesellschaft Jesu.* Vol. 1. Bonn.

Böhm, Martina. 1999. *Samarien und die Samaritai bei Lukas: Eine Studie zum religionsgeschichtlichen und traditionsgeschichtlichen Hintergrund der lukanischen Samarientexte und zu deren topographischer Verhaftung.* WUNT II 111. Tübingen.

———. 2002. "'Und sie nahmen ihn nicht auf, weil sein Gesicht nach Jerusalem zu ging' (Lk 9,53): Samaritaner und Juden zwischen dem 4. Jh. v. und 1. Jh. n.Chr." In *Regionale Systeme koexistierender Religionsgemeinschaften,* edited by Walter Beltz and Jürgen Tubach, 113–27. HBO 34. Halle.

———. 2010. "Samaritaner." WiBiLex. www.bibelwissenschaft.de/stichwort/25967/.

———. 2012. "Wer gehörte in hellenistisch-römischer Zeit zu 'Israel'? Historische Voraussetzungen für eine veränderte Perspektive auf neutestamentliche Texte." In *Die Samaritaner und die Bibel / The Samaritans and the Bible,* edited by Jörg Frey, Ursula Schattner-Rieser, and Konrad Schmid, 181–202. SJ 70 / StSam 70. Berlin and Boston.

Bolyki, János. 1998. *Jesu Tischgemeinschaften.* WUNT II 96. Tübingen.

Boman, Jobjorn. 2011. "Inpulsore Cherestro? Suetonius' *Divus Claudius* 25.4 in Sources and Manuscripts." *LASBF* 61: 355–76.

Bond, Helen K. 1998. *Pontius Pilate in History and Interpretation.* SNTSMS 100. Cambridge.

———. 2004. *Caiaphas: Friend of Rome and Judge of Jesus?* Louisville.

———. 2013. "Dating the Death of Jesus: Memory and the Religious Imagination." *NTS* 59: 461–75.

Borg, Marcus J. 1983. *Conflict, Holiness, and Politics in the Teachings of Jesus.* New York and Toronto.

———. 1986. "A Temperate Case for a Non-Eschatological Jesus." *SBLSP* 25: 521–35.

———. 1987. *Jesus: A New Vision.* San Francisco.

———. 1994. *Jesus in Contemporary Scholarship.* Valley Forge, PA.

Bornkamm, Günther. 1956; [3]1959; [15]1995. *Jesus von Nazareth.* Urban-Taschenbücher 19. Stuttgart.

———. 1959. "Das Bekenntnis im Hebräerbrief." In *Studien zu Antike und Urchristentum: Gesammelte Aufsätze II,* by Günther Bornkamm, 188–203. BEvT 28. Munich.

———. 1960. *Jesus of Nazareth.* Translated by Irene and Fraser McLuskey with James M. Robinson from [3]1959. New York.

———. 1962; [2]1966. "Die Bedeutung des historischen Jesus für den Glauben." In *Die Frage nach dem historischen Jesus,* edited by Ferdinand Hahn, Wenzel Lohff, and Günther Bornkamm, 57–71. Evangelisches Forum 2. Göttingen.

———. 1968. "Das Doppelgebot der Liebe." In *Geschichte und Glaube,* vol. 1, *Gesammelte Aufsätze Band III,* by Günther Bornkamm, 37–45. BEvT 48. Munich.

———. 1969. "The Significance of the Historical Jesus for Faith." In *What Can We Know about Jesus? Essays on the New Quest,* by Ferdinand Hahn, Wenzel Lohff, and Günther Bornkamm, translated by Grover Foley, 69–86. Edinburgh.

Bornkamm, Karin. 1998. *Christus—König und Priester: Das Amt Christi bei Luther im Verhältnis zur Vor- und Nachgeschichte.* BHT 106. Tübingen.

Bostock, Gerald. 1994. "Do We Need an Empty Tomb?" *ExpTim* 105: 201–5.

Botha, Pieter J. 1993. "The Social Dynamics of the Early Transmission of the Jesus Tradition." *Neot* 27: 205–32.

Bousset, William. 1913; [2]1921; [5]1965; [6]1967. *Kyrios Christos: Geschichte des Christusglaubens von den Anfängen des Christentums bis Irenäus.* FRLANT 21. Göttingen.

Bovon, François. 1989–2001. *Das Evangelium nach Lukas.* EKKNT III/1–3. Zürich and Neukirchen-Vluyn.

Boyarin, Daniel. 2012. *The Jewish Gospels: The Story of the Jewish Christ.* New York.

Brandenburg, Hugo. 2004. *Die frühchristlichen Kirchen in Rom vom 4. bis zum 7. Jahrhundert.* Regensburg and Milan.

Brändle, Rudolf. 1979. *Matth. 25,31–46 im Werk des Johannes Chrysostomus: Ein Beitrag zur Auslegungsgeschichte und zur Erforschung der Ethik der griechischen Kirche um die Wende vom 4. zum 5. Jahrhundert.* BGBE 22. Tübingen.

Brandon, Samuel G. F. 1967. *Jesus and the Zealots: A Study of the Political Factor in Primitive Christianity.* Manchester.

Branscomb, Bennett Harvie. 1930. *Jesus and the Law of Moses.* London.

Braund, David. 1984. *Rome and the Friendly King: The Character of the Client Kingship.* New York.

Breckman, Warren. 1999. *Marx, the Young Hegelians, and the Origins of Radical Social Theory: Dethroning the Self.* Cambridge.

Brennecke, Hanns Christof, and Johannes van Oort, eds. 2011. *Ethik im antiken Christentum*. SPA 9. Leuven.

Breuer, Yochanan. 2006. "Aramaic in Late Antiquity." In *The Cambridge History of Judaism*, vol. 4, *The Late Roman-Rabbinic Period*, edited by Steven T. Katz, 457–91. Cambridge.

Breytenbach, Cilliers. 1984. *Nachfolge und Zukunftserwartung nach Markus: Eine methodenkritische Studie*. ATANT 71. Zürich.

———. 1985. "Das Markusevangelium als episodische Erzählung: Mit Überlegungen zum Aufbau des zweiten Evangeliums." In *Der Erzähler des Evangeliums: Methodische Neuansätze in der Markusforschung*, edited by Ferdinand Hahn, 137–69. SBS 118/119. Stuttgart.

———. 1997. "Das Markusevangelium, Psalm 110,1 und 118,22 f. Folgetext und Prätext." In *The Scriptures in the Gospels*, edited by Christopher Tuckett, 197–222. BETL 131. Leuven.

———. 1999. "Mark and Galilee: Text World and Historical World." In *Galilee through the Centuries: Confluence of Cultures; The Proceedings of the 2nd International Conference on Galilee*, edited by Eric M. Meyers, 75–85. Winona Lake, IN.

———. 2007. "Was die Menschen für großartig halten: Das ist in den Augen Gottes ein Greuel (Lk 16,15c)." In *Gott und Geld*, edited by Martin Ebner, 131–44. JBT 21. Neukirchen-Vluyn.

———. 2013. "From Mark's Son of God to Jesus of Nazareth—Un cul-de-sac?" In *The Quest for the Real Jesus: Radboud Prestige Lectures by Prof. Dr. Michael Wolter*, edited by Jan van der Watt, 19–56. BibInt 120. Leiden.

Brighton, Mark. 2009. *The Sicarii in Josephus's "Judean War": Rhetorical Analysis and Historical Observations*. SBLEJL 27. Atlanta.

Brin, Gershon. 1995/1997. "Divorce at Qumran." In *Legal Texts and Legal Issues: Proceedings of the Second Meeting of the International Organization for Qumran Studies*, edited by Moshe Bernstein et al., 231–44. Cambridge and Leiden.

Brodie, Thomas Louis. 1986. "Towards Unravelling Luke's Use of the Old Testament: Luke 7.11–17 as an Imitatio of 1 Kings 17.17–24." *NTS* 32: 247–67.

Broer, Ingo. 1999. "Das Weinwunder zu Kana (Joh 2,1–11) und die Weinwunder der Antike." In *Das Urchristentum in seiner literarischen Geschichte: Festschrift für Jürgen Becker zum 65. Geburtstag*, edited by U. Mell and Ulrich B. Müller, 291–308. BZNW 100. Berlin.

———. 2004. "Jesus und die Tora." In *Jesus von Nazareth—Spuren und Konturen*, edited by Ludger Schenke et al., 216–54. Stuttgart.

Brooten, Bernadette. 1982. "Konnten Frauen im alten Judentum die Scheidung betreiben?" *EvT* 42: 65–80.

Browe, Peter. 1938. *Die eucharistischen Wunder des Mittelalters*. Breslauer Studien zur historischen Theologie, n.s., 4. Breslau.

Brown, Colin. 1985. *Jesus in European Protestant Thought, 1778–1860.* SHT 1. Durham, NC.

Brown, Raymond E. ²1993. *The Birth of the Messiah: A Commentary on the Infancy Narratives in the Gospels of Matthew and Luke.* New York.

———. 1994a. *The Death of the Messiah: From Gethsemane to the Grave; A Commentary on the Passion Narratives in the Four Gospels (2008–2010).* Vol. 1. ABRL. New Haven.

———. 1994b. *The Death of the Messiah: From Gethsemane to the Grave; A Commentary on the Passion Narratives in the Four Gospels (2008–2010).* Vol. 2. ABRL. New Haven.

———. 1998. "The Burial of Jesus (Mark 15:42–47)." *CBQ* 50: 233–45.

———. 2008. *The Death of the Messiah.* Vol. 1. ABRL. New Haven. Orig. 1994.

———. 2010. *The Death of the Messiah.* Vol. 2. ABRL. New Haven. Orig. 1994.

Brucker, Ralph. 2013. "'Hymnen' im Neuen Testament?" *VF* 58: 53–62.

Bryan, Steven M. 2002. *Jesus and Israel's Traditions of Judgment and Restoration.* SNTSMS 177. Cambridge.

Bucher, Jordan. 1859. *Das Leben Jesu Christi und der Apostel: Geschichtlich-pragmatisch dargestellt.* Vol. 1, *Das Leben Jesu Christi.* Stuttgart.

Buchinger, Harald, and Elisabeth Hernitscheck. 2014. "P. Oxy. 840 and the Rites of Christian Initiation: Dating a Piece of Alleged Anti-Sacramentalistic Polemic." *Early Christianity* 5: 117–24.

Buller, Andreas. 2002. *Die Geschichtstheorien des 19. Jahrhunderts: Das Verhältnis zwischen historischer Wirklichkeit und historischer Erkenntnis bei Karl Marx und Johann Gustav Droysen.* Berlin.

Bultmann, Rudolf K. (1913) 1994. "Was lässt die Spruchquelle über die Urgemeinde erkennen?" *Oldenburgisches Kirchenblatt* 19: 35–37, 41–44.

———. 1924. "Das Problem der Ethik bei Paulus." *ZNW* 23: 123–40.

———. 1948; ²¹1984. *Das Evangelium des Johannes.* KEK II. Göttingen.

———. 1967a. "Der religionsgeschichtliche Hintergrund des Prologs zum Johannes-evangelium" (1923). In *Exegetica*, edited by Erich Dinkler, 10–35. Tübingen.

———. 1967b. "Das Verhältnis der urchristlichen Christusbotschaft zum historischen Jesus." In *Exegetica*, edited by Erich Dinkler, 445–69. Tübingen.

———. 1967c. "Bekenntnis- und Liedfragmente im ersten Petrusbrief" (1947). In *Exegetica*, edited by Erich Dinkler, 285–97. Tübingen.

———. ⁹1979; ¹⁰1995. *Die Geschichte der synoptischen Tradition* (1921). With a postscript by Gerd Theißen. FRLANT 29. Göttingen.

———. ⁸1980a. "Die liberale Theologie und die jüngste theologische Bewegung." In *Glauben und Verstehen I*, by Rudolf K. Bultmann, 1–25. Tübingen.

———. ⁸1980b. "Zur Frage der Christologie" (1927). In *Glauben und Verstehen I*, by Rudolf K. Bultmann, 85–113. Tübingen.

———. [8]1980c. "Die Bedeutung des geschichtlichen Jesus für die Theologie des Paulus" (1929). In *Glauben und Verstehen I*, by Rudolf K. Bultmann, 188–213. Tübingen.

———. [9]1984. *Theologie des Neuen Testaments*. Tübingen.

———. 1988. *Jesus*. UTB 1272. Tübingen. First published 1926.

Burchard, Christoph. 1970. "Das doppelte Liebesgebot in der frühen christlichen Überlieferung." In *Der Ruf Jesu und die Antwort der Gemeinde, FS Joachim Jeremias*, edited by Eduard Lohse, 39–61. Göttingen.

———. 2000. *Der Jakobusbrief*. HNT XV/1. Tübingen.

Burke, Kenneth. [3]1973. *The Philosophy of Literary Form: Studies in Symbolic Action*. Berkeley, CA.

Buth, Randall, and R. Steven Notley, eds. 2014. *The Language Environment of First Century Judaea*. Leiden.

Byrskog, Samuel. 1994. *Jesus the Only Teacher: Didactic Authority and Transmission in Ancient Israel, Ancient Judaism, and Matthean Community*. Stockholm.

———. 2000. *Story as History—History as Story: The Gospel Tradition in the Context of Ancient Oral History*. WUNT 123. Tübingen.

———. 2011. "The Transmission of the Jesus Tradition." In *Handbook for the Study of the Historical Jesus*, vol. 2, *The Study of Jesus*, edited by Tom Holmén and Stanley E. Porter, 1465–94. Leiden.

Campenhausen, Hans von. 1972. "Das Bekenntnis im Urchristentum." *ZNW* 63: 210–53.

Carleton Paget, James. 2014. "Albert Schweitzer and the Jews." *HTR* 103: 363–98.

Carr, David M. 2005. *Writing on the Tablet of the Heart: Origins of Scripture and Literature*. Oxford.

Carrier, Richard. 2012. "Origen, Eusebius, and the Accidental Interpolation in Josephus, *Jewish Antiquities* 20.200." *JECS* 20: 489–514.

Carson, Don A. 1981. "Historical Tradition in the Fourth Gospel: After Dodd, What?" In *Gospel Perspectives II*, edited by R. T. France and David Wenham, 84–145. Sheffield.

Carson, Don A., Peter T. O'Brien, and Mark A. Seifrid, eds. 2001. *Justification and Variegated Nomism*. Vol. 1, *The Complexities of Second Temple Judaism*. WUNT II 140. Tübingen.

Carter, Warren. 1993. "The Crowds in Matthew's Gospel." *CBQ* 55: 54–67.

Casey, Maurice. 2007. *The Solution to the "Son of Man" Problem*. LNTS 343. London.

———. 2010. *Jesus of Nazareth: An Independent Historian's Account of His Life and Teaching*. London.

Chamberlain, Houston Stewart. 1899. *Die Grundlagen des neunzehnten Jahrhunderts*. 2 vols. Munich.

Chancey, Mark A. 2002. *The Myth of a Gentile Galilee*. SNTSMS 118. Cambridge.

———. 2005. *Greco-Roman Culture and the Galilee of Jesus*. SNTSMS 134. Cambridge.

————. 2007. "The Epigraphic Habit of Hellenistic and Roman Galilee." In *Religion, Ethnicity, and Identity in Ancient Galilee: A Region in Transition*, edited by Jürgen Zangenberg et al., 83–98. WUNT 210. Tübingen.

Chapman, David W. 2008. *Ancient Jewish and Christian Perceptions of Crucifixion.* WUNT II 244. Tübingen.

Chapman, Mark. 2001. *The Coming Crisis: The Impact of Eschatology on Theology in Edwardian Britain.* Sheffield.

Charlesworth, James H. 1988. *Jesus within Judaism: New Light from Exciting Archaeological Discoveries.* ABRL. New York.

————. 1994. *The Lord's Prayer and Other Prayer Texts from the Greco-Roman Era.* Valley Forge, PA.

————, ed. 2006. *Jesus and Archaeology.* Grand Rapids.

————. 2013. *The Tomb of Jesus and His Family? Exploring Ancient Jewish Tombs Near Jerusalem's Walls; The Fourth Princeton Symposium on Judaism and Christian Origins, Sponsored by the Foundation on Judaism and Christian Origins.* Winona Lake, IN.

————. 2015. "An Unknown Dead Sea Scroll and Speculations Focused on the *Vorlage* of Deuteronomy 27:4." In *Jesus, Paulus und die Texte von Qumran*, edited by Jörg Frey and Enno E. Popkes, 393–414. WUNT II 390. Tübingen.

Chilton, Bruce. 1988. "Jesus and the Repentance of Sanders." *TynBul* 39: 1–18.

————. 1994. "The Kingdom of God in Recent Discussion." In *Studying the Historical Jesus: Evaluations of the State of Current Research*, edited by Bruce Chilton and Craig A. Evans, 255–80. NTTS 19. Leiden.

————. 2000. *Rabbi Jesus: An Intimate Biography.* New York.

Chilton, Bruce, and Craig A. Evans, eds. 1994. *Studying the Historical Jesus: Evaluations of the State of Current Research.* NTTS 19. Leiden.

Chladenius, Johann Martin. (1742) 1969. *Einleitung zur richtigen Auslegung vernünftiger Reden und Schriften, Instrumenta philosophica.* Series hermeneutica 5. Düsseldorf.

————. (1752) 1985. *Allgemeine Geschichtswissenschaft, Klassische Studien zur sozialwissenschaftlichen Theorie.* Weltanschauungslehre und Wissenschaftsforschung 3. Vienna.

Choi, J. D. 2000. *Jesus' Teaching on Repentance.* International Studies in Formative Christianity and Judaism. Binghamton, NY.

Clivaz, Claire, et al., eds. 2011. *Infancy Gospels: Stories and Identities.* WUNT 281. Tübingen.

Cohen, Shaye J. D. 1999. *The Beginnings of Jewishness: Boundaries, Varieties, Uncertainties.* Berkeley, CA.

Collins, John J. 1987. "The Kingdom of God in the Apocrypha and Pseudepigrapha." In *The Kingdom of God in 20th-Century Interpretation*, edited by Wendall Willis, 81–95. Peabody, MA.

———. 1995. *The Scepter and the Star: The Messiahs of the Dead Sea Scrolls and Other Ancient Literature*. ABRL. Grand Rapids and New York.

———. 2010. *Beyond the Qumran Community: The Sectarian Movement of the Dead Sea Scrolls*. Grand Rapids.

———. [2]2010. *The Scepter and the Star: Messianism in Light of the Dead Sea Scrolls*. Grand Rapids.

Collins, Raymond F. 1990. "Proverbial Sayings in St. John's Gospel." In *These Things Have Been Written: Studies on the Fourth Gospel*, by Raymond F. Collins, 128–57. Louvain Theological and Pastoral Monographs 2. Leuven.

Conway, Colleen M. 2008. *Behold the Man: Jesus and Greco-Roman Masculinity*. Oxford.

Conzelmann, Hans. 1974a. "Geschichte und Eschaton nach Mk 13 (1959)." In *Theologie als Schriftauslegung: Aufsätze zum Neuen Testament*, by Hans Conzelmann, 62–73. BEvT 65. Munich.

———. 1974b. "Was glaubte die frühe Christenheit?" (1955). In *Theologie als Schriftauslegung: Aufsätze zum Neuen Testament*, by Hans Conzelmann, 106–19. BEvT 65. Munich.

Conzelmann, Hans, and Andreas Lindemann. [14]2004. *Arbeitsbuch zum Neuen Testament*. UTB 52. Tübingen.

Cook, John Granger. 2000. *The Interpretation of the New Testament in Greco-Roman Paganism*. STAC 3. Tübingen.

———. 2011. "Crucifixion and Burial." *NTS* 57: 193–213.

———. 2014. *Crucifixion in the Mediterranean World*. WUNT 327. Tübingen.

Corley, Jeremy, ed. 2009. *New Perspectives on the Nativity*. London.

Cotton, Hannah M., Leah Di Segni, Werner Eck, Benjamin Isaac, et al., eds. 2010. *Corpus Inscriptionum Iudaeae et Palaestinae*. Vol. 1, *Jerusalem*. Part 1, 1–704. Berlin and New York.

Coulot, Claude. 1987. *Jésus et le disciple: Étude sur l'autorité messianique de Jésus*. Paris.

Courcelle, Pierre. 1976. "Gefängnis der Seele." In *RAC* 9:294–318.

Cousland, J. R. C. 2002. *The Crowds in the Gospel of Matthew*. NovTSup 102. Leiden.

Craffert, Pieter F. 2008. *The Life of a Galilean Shaman: Jesus of Nazareth in Anthropological-Historical Perspective*. Eugene, OR.

Crook, Zeba A. 2013. "Collective Memory Distortion and the Quest for the Historical Jesus." *JSHJ* 11: 53–76, 98–105.

Crossan, John Dominic. 1973. *In Parables: The Challenge of the Historical Jesus*. San Francisco.

———. 1985. *Four Other Gospels: Shadows on the Contours of Canon*. Minneapolis.

———. 1988. *The Cross That Spoke: The Origins of the Passion Narrative*. San Francisco.

———. 1991; [2]1995. *The Historical Jesus: The Life of a Mediterranean Peasant*. San Francisco.

———. 1994a. *Der historische Jesus*. Munich.

———. 1994b. *Jesus: A Revolutionary Biography*. San Francisco.

———. 1998. *The Essential Jesus: Original Sayings and Earliest Images*. San Francisco.

———. 2002. "The Parables of Jesus." *Int* 56: 247–59.

Crossan, John Dominic, Luke T. Johnson, and Werner H. Kelber. 1999. *The Jesus Controversy: Perspectives in Conflict*. Harrisburg, PA.

Crossley, James G. 2015. *Jesus and the Chaos of History: Redirecting the Quest for the Historical Jesus*. Oxford.

Crüsemann, Marlene, et al., eds. 2014. *Gott ist anders: Gleichnisse neu gelesen auf der Basis der Auslegung von Luise Schottroff*. Gütersloh.

Cullmann, Oscar. ²1950. *Urchristentum und Gottesdienst*. ATANT 3. Zürich.

———. 1957. *Die Christologie des Neuen Testaments*. Tübingen.

———. 1970. *Jesus und die Revolutionären seiner Zeit: Gottesdienst, Gesellschaft, Politik*. Tübingen.

Culpepper, Robert Alan. 2000. *John the Son of Zebedee: The Life of a Legend*. Edinburgh.

Cureton, William. 1855. *Spicilegium Syriacum: Containing Remains of Bardesan, Meliton, Ambrose, and Mara bar Serapion*. London.

Dahl, Nils Alstrup. ²1961. "Der gekreuzigte Messias." In *Der historische Jesus und der kerygmatische Christus*, edited by Helmut Ristow and Karl Matthiae, 149–69. Beiträge zum Christusverständnis in Forschung und Verkündigung. Berlin.

Dalman, Gustaf. 1898; ²1930. *Die Worte Jesu: Mit Berücksichtigung des nachkanonischen Schrifttums und der aramäischen Sprache*. Vol. 1, *Einleitung und wichtige Begriffe*. Leipzig.

———. 1922. *Jesus-Jeschua: Die drei Sprachen Jesu; Jesus in der Synagoge, auf dem Berge, beim Passahmahl, am Kreuz*. Leipzig.

D'Angelo, Mary Rose. 2006. "Abba and Father: Imperial Theology in the Contexts of Jesus and the Gospels." In *The Historical Jesus in Context*, edited by Amy-Jill Levine, Dale C. Allison Jr., and John Dominic Crossan, 64–78. Princeton Readings in Religions. Princeton.

Danto, Arthur C. 1968. *Analytical Philosophy of History*. Cambridge.

Davids, Peter J. 1982. *The Epistle of James: A Commentary on the Greek Text*. Exeter.

Davies, Stephen J. 2014. *Christ Child: Cultural Memories of a Young Jesus*. New Haven and London.

Davies, Stevan L. 2005. *The Gospel of Thomas and Christian Wisdom*. Oregon House, CA.

Deichmann, Friedrich Wilhelm. 1967. *Repertorium der christlich-antiken Sarkophage*. Vol. 1, *Rom und Ostia*. Wiesbaden.

Deines, Roland. 1993. *Jüdische Steingefäße und pharisäische Frömmigkeit: Ein archäologisch-historischer Beitrag zum Verständnis von Joh 2,6 und der Jüdischen Reinheitshalaka zur Zeit Jesu.* WUNT II 52. Tübingen.

———. 1997. *Die Pharisäer. Ihr Verständnis im Spiegel der christlichen und jüdischen Forschung seit Wellhausen und Graetz.* WUNT 101. Tübingen.

———. 2003. "Josephus, Salomo und die von Gott verliehene τέχνη gegen die Dämonen." In *Die Dämonen: Die Dämonologie der israelitisch-jüdischen und frühchristlichen Literatur im Kontext ihrer Umwelt,* edited by Armin Lange et al., 365–94. Tübingen.

———. 2004. *Die Gerechtigkeit der Tora im Reich des Messias: Mt 5,13–20 als Schlüsseltext der matthäischen Theologie.* WUNT 177. Tübingen.

———. 2013. "God or Mammon: The Danger of Wealth in the Jesus Tradition and in the Epistle of James." In *Anthropologie und Ethik im Frühjudentum und im Neuen Testament: Wechselseitige Wahrnehmungen,* edited by Matthias Konradt and Esther Schläpfer, 327–85. WUNT 322. Tübingen.

DeLuca, Stefano, and Anna Lena. 2015. "Magdala/Taricheae." In *Galilee in the Late Second Temple and Mishnaic Periods,* vol. 2, *The Archaeological Record from Cities, Towns, and Villages,* edited by David A. Fiensy and James R. Strange, 280–342. Minneapolis.

Denzey Lewis, Nicola. 2014. "A New Gnosticism: Why Simon Gathercole and Mark Goodacre on the Gospel of Thomas Change the Field." *JSNT* 36: 240–50.

Deppe, Dean B. 1989. *The Sayings of Jesus in the Epistle of James.* Chelsea.

Dibelius, Martin. 1919; 6⁄1971. *Formgeschichte des Evangeliums.* Tübingen.

Dietz, Karlheinz, Christian Hannick, Carolina Lutzka, Elisabeth Maier, eds. 2016. *Das Christusbild: Zu Herkunft und Entwicklung in Ost und West.* Das Östliche Christentum, n.s., 62. Würzburg.

Dietzfelbinger, Christian. 1978. "Vom Sinn der Sabbatheilungen Jesu." *EvT* 38: 281–98.

Dihle, Albrecht. 1957. "Demut." In *RAC* 3:735–78.

———. 1966. "Ethik." In *RAC* 6:646–796.

Dillon, Matthew P. J. 1994. "The Didactic Nature of the Epidaurean Iamata." *ZPE* 101: 239–60.

Dippel, Johann Konrad. 1729. *Vera Demonstratio Evangelica, Das ist, ein in der Natur und dem Wesen der Sachen selbst so wohl, als in heiliger Schrift gegründeter Beweiß der Lehre und des Mittler-Amts Jesu Christi.* Frankfurt.

Dodd, Charles Harold. 1953. *The Interpretation of the Fourth Gospel.* Cambridge.

———. 1963. *Historical Tradition in the Fourth Gospel.* Cambridge.

Doering, Lutz. 1999. *Schabbat: Sabbathalacha und -praxis im antiken Judentum und Urchristentum.* TSAJ 78. Tübingen.

———. 2008. "Much Ado about Nothing? Jesus' Sabbath Healings and Their Halakhic Implications Revisited." In *Judaistik und neutestamentliche Wissenschaft: Stand-*

orte—Grenzen—Beziehungen, edited by Lutz Doering, Hans-Günther Waubke, and Florian Wilk. FRLANT 226. Göttingen.

———. 2009. "Marriage and Creation in Mark 10 and CD 4–5." In *Echoes from the Caves: Qumran and the New Testament*, edited by Florentino García Martínez, 133–64. STDJ 85. Leiden.

———. 2010. "Sabbath Laws in the New Testament Gospels." In *The New Testament and Rabbinic Literature*, edited by Reimund Bieringer et al., 207–53. JSJS 136. Leiden and Boston.

———. 2011. "Urzeit-Endzeit Correlation in the Dead Sea Scrolls and Pseudepigrapha." In *Eschatologie-Eschatology: The Sixth Durham-Tübingen Research Symposium; Eschatology in Old Testament, Ancient Judaism, and Early Christianity, Tübingen, September 2009*, edited by Christof Landmesser, Heinz-Joachim Eckstein, and Hermann Lichtenberger, 19–58. WUNT 272. Tübingen.

———. 2015. "Jesus und der Sabbat im Licht der Qumrantexte." In *Jesus, Paulus und die Texte von Qumran*, edited by Jörg Frey and Enno E. Popkes, 33–61. WUNT II 390. Tübingen.

Donahue, John R. 1971. "Tax Collectors and Sinners: An Attempt at Identification." *CBQ* 33: 39–61.

———. 1983. *The Theology and Setting of Discipleship in the Gospel of Mark*. Milwaukee.

Dormeyer, Detlev. 1993. *Das Neue Testament im Rahmen der antiken Literaturgeschichte*. Darmstadt.

———. ²2002: *Das Markusevangelium als Idealbiographie von Jesus Christus, dem Nazarener*. SBB 43. Stuttgart.

Downing, Francis Gerald. 1984. "Cynics and Christians." *NTS* 30: 584–93.

———. 1988. *Christ and the Cynics: Jesus and Other Radical Preachers in First-Century Tradition*. JSOTSup 4. Sheffield.

Draper, Jonathan A. 1998. "Weber, Theissen, and 'Wandering Charismatics' in the Didache." *JECS* 6: 541–76.

Dresken-Weiland, Jutta. 1998. *Repertorium der christlich-antiken Sarkophage*. Vol. 2, *Italien mit einem Nachtrag Rom und Ostia, Dalmatien, Museen der Welt*. Mainz.

———. 2010. *Bild, Grab und Wort: Untersuchungen zu Jenseitsvorstellungen von Christen des 3. und 4. Jahrhunderts*. Regensburg.

Drewermann, Eugen. ³1992. *Tiefenpsychologie und Exegese*. Vol. 2, *Wunder, Vision, Weissagung, Apokalypse, Geschichte, Gleichnis*. Olten, Switzerland.

Drijvers, Jan Willem. 1992. *Helena Augusta, the Mother of Constantine the Great and the Legend of Her Finding of the True Cross*. Leiden.

Droysen, Johann Gustav. ⁸1977. *Historik: Vorlesungen über Enzyklopädie und Methodologie der Geschichte*. Edited by Rudolf Hübner. Munich.

Dschulnigg, Peter. 1988. *Rabbinische Gleichnisse und das Neue Testament: Die Gleich-*

nisse der PesK im Vergleich mit den Gleichnissen Jesu und dem Neuen Testament. JudChr 12. Bern.

Duling, Dennis C. 1985. "The Eleazar Miracle and Solomon's Magical Wisdom in Flavius Josephus's *Antiquitates Judaicae* 8.42–49." *HTR* 78: 1–25.

Dunn, James D. G. 1980; ²1992. *Christology in the Making: A New Testament Inquiry into the Doctrine of the Incarnation.* London.

———. 1990. "Paul's Knowledge of the Jesus Tradition: The Evidence of Romans." In *Christus bezeugen: FS Wolfgang Trilling,* edited by Karl Kertelge, Traugott Holtz, and Claus-Peter März, 193–207. Freiburg, Basel, and Vienna.

———. 1992. *Jesus' Call to Discipleship.* Cambridge.

———. 2000. "'Are You the Messiah?' Is the Crux of Mark 14,61–62 Resolvable?" In *Christology, Controversy, and Community: New Testament Essays in Honour of David R. Catchpole,* edited by David G. Horrell and Christopher M. Tuckett, 1–22. NovTSup 99. Leiden.

———. 2003a. "Altering the Default Setting: Re-envisaging the Early Transmission of the Jesus Tradition." *NTS* 49: 139–75.

———. 2003b. *Jesus Remembered: Christianity in the Making.* Vol. 1. Grand Rapids.

———. 2005. "Pharisees, Sinners and Jesus." In *The Historical Jesus in Recent Research,* by James D. G. Dunn and Scot McKnight, 463–88. SBTS 10. Winona Lake, IN.

———. 2009. "Reflections." In *Das Gebet im Neuen Testament: Vierte europäische orthodox-westliche Exegetenkonferenz in Sâmbăta de Sus. 4.–8. August 2007,* edited by Hans Klein, Vasile Mihoc, and Karl-Wilhelm Niebuhr, 185–201. WUNT 249. Tübingen.

Early Christianity 6 (3). 2015. *Jesus and Memory: The Memory Approach in Current Jesus Research* (with contributions by Alan Kirk, Eric Eve, David du Toit, and Chris Keith).

Ebeling, Gerhard. ³1967. "Die Bedeutung der historisch-kritischen Methode für die protestantische Theologie und Kirche" (1950). In *Wort und Glaube,* by Gerhard Ebeling, 1:1–49. Tübingen.

Ebersohn, Michael. 1993. *Das Nächstenliebegebot in der synoptischen Tradition.* MThSt 37. Marburg.

Ebner, Martin. 1998. *Jesus—ein Weisheitslehrer? Synoptische Weisheitslogien im Traditionsprozess.* HBS 15. Freiburg (CH).

———. 2001. "'Weisheitslehrer'—eine Kategorie für Jesus? Eine Spurensuche bei Jesus Sirach." In *Der neue Mensch in Christus: Hellenistische Anthropologie und Ethik im Neuen Testament,* edited by Johannes Beutler, 99–119. QD 190. Freiburg.

———. 2003. *Jesus von Nazaret in seiner Zeit: Sozialgeschichtliche Zugänge.* SBS 196. Stuttgart.

———. 2004. *Überwindung eines "tödlichen Lebens": Paradoxien zu Leben und Tod in den Jesusüberlieferungen,* 79–100. JBT 19. Neukirchen-Vluyn.

———. 2009. "Die Auferweckung Jesu—oder: Woran glauben Christen? Die urchristliche Osterbotschaft im Kontext zeitgenössischer Vorstellungen." *BK* 64: 78–86.

———. 2010. "Face to Face—Widerstand im Sinn der Gottesherrschaft: Jesu Wahrnehmung seines sozialen Umfeldes im Spiegel seiner Beispielgeschichten." *Early Christianity* 1: 406–40.

———. ²2012. *Jesus von Nazaret: Was wir von ihm wissen können.* Stuttgart. Sonderausgabe 2016.

———. 2013. "Die Exorzismen Jesu als Testfall für die historische Rückfrage." In *Jesus—Gestalt und Gestaltungen: FS Gerd Theißen,* edited by Petra von Gemünden et al., 477–98. NTOA 100. Göttingen.

———. 2016. "Abgebrochene Karriere? Überlegungen zur Funktion der jüdischen Weisheitsspekulation bei der Entwicklung der neutestamentlichen Christologien in den synoptischen Evangelien." In *Vermittelte Gegenwart: Konzeptionen der Gottespräsenz von der Zeit des Zweiten Tempels bis Anfang 2. Jh. n.Chr.,* edited by Irmtraud Fischer and Andrea Taschl-Erber. Tübingen.

Eck, Ernest van. 2016. *The Parables of Jesus the Galilean: Stories of a Social Prophet.* Eugene, OR.

Eck, Werner. 2007. *Rom und Judäa: Fünf Vorträge zur römischen Herrschaft in Palästina.* Tria Corda 2. Tübingen.

Eckey, Wilfried. ²2006. *Das Lukasevangelium unter Berücksichtigung seiner Parallelen.* 2 vols. Neukirchen-Vluyn.

Eckstein, Evelyn. 2001. *Fußnoten: Anmerkungen zu Poesie und Wissenschaft.* Anmerkungen: Beiträge zur wissenschaftlichen Marginalistik 1. Münster.

Ehrlich, Uri. 2004. *The Nonverbal Language of Prayer: A New Approach to Jewish Liturgy.* TSAJ 105. Tübingen.

Eichhorn, Johann Gottfried. 1780–1783. *Einleitung ins Alte Testament.* 3 vols. Leipzig.

———. 1790. *Versuch über die Engels-Erscheinungen in der Apostelgeschichte: Allgemeine Bibliothek der biblischen Literatur,* 3:381–408. Leipzig.

———. 1794. *Ueber die drey ersten Evangelien: Einige Beyträge zu ihrer künftigen kritischen Behandlung; Allgemeine Bibliothek der biblischen Literatur,* 5:759–996. Leipzig.

———. 1804–1827. *Einleitung in das Neue Testament.* 3 vols. (vol. 3 in two parts; 2nd ed. supplemented by a fourth and fifth volume). Leipzig.

Eijk, Philip J. van der. 2005. "The 'Theology' of the Author of the Hippocratic Treatise *On the Sacred Disease.*" In *Medicine and Philosophy in Classical Antiquity: Doctors and Philosophers on Nature, Soul, Health, and Disease,* edited by Philip J. van der Eijk, 45–74. Cambridge. Reprinted in *Apeiron* 23 (1990): 87–119.

Eisele, Wilfried. 2009. "Jesus und Dionysos: Göttliche Konkurrenz bei der Hochzeit zu Kana (Joh 2,1–11)." *ZNW* 100: 1–28.

———. 2013. *Gott bitten? Theologische Zugänge zum Bittgebet.* Freiburg.

Eisler, Robert. 1931. *The Messiah Jesus and John the Baptist: According to Flavius Josephus' Recently Rediscovered "Capture of Jerusalem" and the Other Jewish and Christian Sources*. Translated by Alexander Haggerty Krappe. New York.

Elbogen, Ismar. 1993. *Jewish Liturgy: A Comprehensive History*. Philadelphia, New York, and Jerusalem.

Elert, Werner. 1957. *Der Ausgang der altkirchlichen Christologie*. Edited by Wilhelm Maurer and Elisabeth Bergsträsser. Berlin.

Emerton, John Adney. 1961. "Did Jesus Speak Hebrew?" *JTS* 12: 189–202.

———. 1967. "Maranatha and Ephphatha." *JTS* 18: 427–31.

———. 1973. "The Problem of Vernacular Hebrew in the First Century A.D. and the Language of Jesus." *JTS* 24: 1–23.

Encyclopédie ou dictionnaire raisonné. (1782) 1993. Organized by Jean Le Rond d'Alembert and Denis Diderot. Edited by Fortuné Barthélemy de Félice. Paris.

Engemann, Josef. 2014. *Römische Kunst in Spätantike und frühem Christentum bis Justinian*. Darmstadt.

Engster, Dorit. 2010. "Der Kaiser als Wundertäter-Kaiserheil als neue Form der Legitimation." In *Tradition und Erneuerung: Mediale Strategien in der Zeit der Flavier*, edited by Norbert Kramer and Christiane Reiz. BzA 285. Berlin and New York.

Ernesti, Johann August. 1761. *Institutio interpretis Novi Testamenti ad usum lectionum*. Leipzig.

Ernst, Josef. 1977. *Das Evangelium nach Lukas*. RNT. Regensburg.

———. 1989. *Johannes der Täufer: Interpretation—Geschichte—Wirkungsgeschichte*. BZNW 53. Berlin.

Eshel, Esther. 2003. "Genres of Magical Texts in the Dead Sea Scrolls." In *Die Dämonen: Die Dämonologie der israelitisch-jüdischen und frühchristlichen Literatur im Kontext ihrer Umwelt*, edited by Armin Lange et al., 395–415. Tübingen.

Evans, Craig A. 1992. "Opposition to the Temple: Jesus and the Dead Sea Scrolls." In *Jesus and the Dead Sea Scrolls*, edited by James Charlesworth, 235–53. New York.

———. 1995. "In What Sense 'Blasphemy'? Jesus before Caiaphas in Mark 14:61–64." In *Jesus and His Contemporaries*, by Craig A. Evans, 407–34. AGJU 25. Leiden.

———. 1996. *Life of Jesus Research: An Annotated Bibliography*. NTTS 24. Leiden.

———. 2009a. "Exorcisms and the Kingdom: Inaugurating the Kingdom of God and Defeating the Kingdom of Satan." In *Key Events in the Life of the Historical Jesus: A Collaborative Exploration of Context and Coherence*, edited by Darrell L. Bock and Robert Webb, 151–79. WUNT 247. Tübingen.

———. 2009b. *Der Sieg über Satan und die Befreiung Israels: Jesus und die Visionen Daniels*. SNTSU 34, 147–158. Tübingen.

Eve, Eric. 2013. *Behind the Gospels: Understanding the Oral Tradition*. London.

Fassberg, Steven E. 2012. "Which Semitic Language Did Jesus and Other Contemporary Jews Speak?" *CBQ* 74: 263–80.

Feldkämper, Ludger. 1978. *Der betende Jesus als Heilsmittler nach Lukas*. Sankt Augustin, Germany.

Feldmeier, Reinhard. 1987. *Die Krisis des Gottessohnes: Die Gethsemaneerzählung als Schlüssel der Markuspassion*. WUNT II 21. Tübingen.

———. 2012. *Macht-Dienst-Demut: Ein neutestamentlicher Beitrag zur Ethik*. Tübingen.

Feldmeier, Rainer, and Hermann Spieckermann. 2011. *Der Gott der Lebendigen: Eine biblische Gotteslehre*. Topoi biblischer Theologie 1. Tübingen.

Feuerbach, Ludwig. 1841. *Das Wesen des Christentums*. Leipzig.

Fiebig, Paul. 1912. *Die Gleichnisreden Jesu im Lichte der rabbinischen Gleichnisse des neutestamentlichen Zeitalters: Ein Beitrag zum Streit um die "Christusmythe" und eine Widerlegung der Gleichnistheorie Jülichers*. Tübingen.

Fiensy, David A., and Ralph K. Hawkins. 2013. *The Galilean Economy in the Time of Jesus*. Atlanta.

Fiensy, David A., and James R. Strange, eds. 2014–2015. *Galilee in the Late Second Temple and Mishnaic Periods*. Vol. 1, *Life, Culture, and Society*. Vol. 2, *The Archaeological Record from Cities, Towns, and Villages*. Minneapolis.

Filtvedt, Ole Jacob. 2014. "With Our Eyes Fixed on Jesus: The Prayers of Jesus and His Followers in Hebrews." In *Early Christian Prayer and Identity Formation*, edited by Reidar Hvalvik and Karl Olav Sandnes, 161–82. Tübingen.

Finze-Michaelsen, Holger. 2004. *Vater unser—unser Vater: Entdeckungen im Gebet Jesu*. Göttingen.

Fiocchi Nicolai, Vincenzo, Fabrizio Bisconti, and Danilo Mazzoleni. 1998. *Roms christliche Katakomben. Geschichte—Bilderwelt—Inschriften*. Regensburg.

Fischbach, Stefanie M. 1992. *Totenweckungen: Zur Geschichte einer Gattung*. FB 69. Würzburg.

Fitzmyer, Joseph A. 1970. "The Languages of Palestine in the First Century A.D." *CBQ* 32: 501–31.

———. 1979. "The New Testament Title 'Son of Man' Philologically Considered." In *A Wandering Aramean: Collected Aramaic Essays*, by Joseph A. Fitzmyer, 143–60. SBLMS 25. Missoula, MT.

———. 1992. "Did Jesus Speak Greek?" *BAR* 18 (5).

Fleddermann, Harry T. 2005. *Q: A Reconstruction and Commentary*. Biblical Tools and Studies 1. Leuven.

Flusser, David. 1957. "Healing through the Laying-On of Hands in a Dead Sea Scroll." *IEJ* 7: 107–8.

———. 1981. *Die rabbinischen Gleichnisse und der Gleichniserzähler Jesus*. JudChr 4. Bern.

Fortna, Robert T. 1970. *The Gospel of Signs: A Reconstruction of the Narrative Source Underlying the Fourth Gospel*. SNTSMS 11. Cambridge.

———. 1988. *The Fourth Gospel and Its Predecessor*. Edinburgh.

Foster, Paul. 2006. "Educating Jesus: The Search for a Plausible Context." *JSHJ* 4: 7–33.

——. 2014. "The Q Parables: Their Extent and Function." In *Metaphor, Narrative, und Parables in Q*, edited by Dieter T. Roth, Ruben Zimmermann, and Michael Labahn, 255–85. WUNT 315. Tübingen.

France, Richard T. 2011. "The Birth of Jesus." In *Handbook for the Study of the Historical Jesus*, vol. 3, *The Historical Jesus*, edited by Tom Holmén and Stanley E. Porter, 2361–82. Leiden.

Frankemölle, Hubert. 2006. *Frühjudentum und Urchristentum: Vorgeschichte, Verlauf, Auswirkungen (4. Jahrhundert v.Chr.—4. Jahrhundert n.Chr.)*. KStTh 5. Stuttgart.

Fredriksen, Paula. 2012. *Sin: The Early History of an Idea*. Princeton.

Frey, Jörg. 1997. *Die johanneische Eschatologie: Ihre Probleme im Spiegel der Forschung seit Reimarus*. WUNT 96. Tübingen.

——. 2004. "Apostelbegriff, Apostelamt und Apostolizität." In *Das kirchliche Amt in apostolischer Nachfolge*, edited by Theodor Schneider and Gunther Wenz, 91–188. DiKi 12. Freiburg and Göttingen.

——. 2006. "Die Apokalyptik als Herausforderung der neutestamentlichen Wissenschaft: Zum Problem; Jesus und die Apokalyptik." In *Apokalyptik als Herausforderung neutestamentlicher Theologie*, edited by Michael Becker and Markus Öhler, 23–94. Tübingen.

——. 2012. "'Gute' Samaritaner? Das neutestamentliche Bild der Samaritaner zwischen Juden, Christen und Paganen." In *Die Samaritaner und die Bibel/The Samaritans and the Bible*, edited by Jörg Frey, Ursula Schattner-Rieser, and Konrad Schmid, 203–33. SJ 70/StSam 70. Berlin and Boston.

——. 2013a. "Wege und Perspektiven der Interpretation des Johannesevangeliums." In *Die Herrlichkeit des Gekreuzigten: Studien zu den Johanneischen Schriften I*, edited by Juliane Schlegel, 3–41. WUNT 307. Tübingen.

——. 2013b. "Das vierte Evangelium auf dem Hintergrund der älteren Evangelientradition: Zum Problem; Johannes und die Synoptiker." In *Die Herrlichkeit des Gekreuzigten: Studien zu den Johanneischen Schriften I*, edited by Juliane Schlegel, 239–94. WUNT 307. Tübingen.

——. 2013c. "'Die Juden' im Johannesevangelium und die Frage nach der 'Trennung der Wege' zwischen der johanneischen Gemeinde und der Synagoge." In *Die Herrlichkeit des Gekreuzigten: Studien zu den Johanneischen Schriften I*, edited by Juliane Schlegel, 339–77. WUNT 307. Tübingen.

——. 2014. "Ferdinand Christian Baur und die Johannesauslegung." In *Ferdinand Christian Baur und die Geschichte des frühen Christentums*, edited by Martin Bauspiess, Christof Landmesser, and David Lincicum, 227–58. WUNT 333. Tübingen.

——. 2015. "Das Corpus Johanneum und die Apokalypse des Johannes." In *Poetik und Intertextualität der Johannesapokalypse*, edited by Stefan Alier, Thomas Hieke, and Tobias Nicklas, 71–133. WUNT 346. Tübingen.

———. 2016. "From the 'Kingdom of God' to 'Eternal Life': The Transformation of Theological Language in the Fourth Gospel." In *John, Jesus, and History*, vol. 3, *Glimpses of Jesus through the Johannine Lens*, edited by Paul N. Anderson, Felix Just, SJ, and Tom Thatcher. SBLSS 44. Atlanta.

———. 2018. *Theology and History in the Fourth Gospel: Narration and Interpretation.* Waco, TX.

———. 2019. "Baptism in the Fourth Gospel, and Jesus and John as Baptizers: Historical and Theological Reflections on John 3:22–30." In *Expressions of the Johannine Kerygma in John 2:23–5:18*, edited by R. Alan Culpepper and Jörg Frey, 87–115. Historical, Literary, and Theological Readings from the Colloquium Ioanneum 2017 in Jerusalem. WUNT 423. Tübingen.

Frey, Jörg, and Jens Schröter, eds. 2010. *Jesus in apokryphen Evangelienüberlieferungen.* WUNT 254. Tübingen.

Freyne, Seán. 1968. *The Twelve: Disciples and Apostles; A Study in the Theology of the First Three Gospels.* London.

———. 1988. *Galilee, Jesus, and the Gospels: Literary Approaches and Historical Investigations.* Dublin.

———. 1998. *Galilee from Alexander the Great to Hadrian, 323 BCE to 135 CE: A Study of Second Temple Judaism.* Edinburgh.

———. 2000a. *Galilee and Gospel.* WUNT 125. Tübingen.

———. 2000b. "Jesus the Wine-Drinker: A Friend of Women." In *Transformative Encounters: Jesus and Women Re-Viewed*, edited by Ingrid Rosa Kitzberger, 162–80. BibInt 43. Leiden.

———. 2001. "The Geography of Restoration: Galilee-Jerusalem Relations in Early Jewish and Christian Experience." *NTS* 47: 289–311.

———. 2004. *Jesus, a Jewish Galilean: A New Reading of the Jesus Story.* London.

———. 2014. *The Jesus Movement and Its Expansion: Meaning and Mission.* Grand Rapids and Cambridge.

Frossard, André. 2004. *Il Vangelo secondo Ravenna.* Castel Bolognese, Italy.

Fuchs, Eckhardt. 1994. *Henry Thomas Buckle: Geschichtsschreibung und Positivismus in England und Deutschland.* Leipzig.

Fulda, Daniel. 1996. *Wissenschaft aus Kunst: Die Entstehung der modernen deutschen Geschichtsschreibung 1760–1860.* European Cultures. Studies in Literature and the Arts 7. Berlin and New York.

———. 2013. "Wann begann die 'offene Zukunft'? Ein Versuch, die Koselleck'sche Fixierung auf die 'Sattelzeit' zu lösen." In *Geschichtsbewusstsein und Zukunftserwartung in Pietismus und Erweckungsbewegung*, edited by Wolfgang Breul and Jan Carsten Schnurr, 141–72. Göttingen.

Funk, Robert W. 1974. "Structure in the Narrative Parables of Jesus." *Semeia* 2: 51–81.

———, ed. 1997. *The Five Gospels: What Did Jesus Really Say?* San Francisco.

————, ed. 1998. *The Acts of Jesus: What Did Jesus Really Do?* San Francisco.

————. 2006. "Jesus: The Silent Sage." In *Funk on Parables: Collected Essays*, 165–69. Santa Rosa, CA.

Furnish, Victor P. 1972. *The Love Command in the New Testament.* Nashville and New York.

Furstenberg, Yair. 2008. "Defilement Penetrating the Body: A New Understanding of Contamination in Mark 7.15." *NTS* 54: 176–200.

————. 2015. "Outsider Impurity: Trajectories of Second Temple Separation Traditions in Tannaitic Literature." In *Tradition, Transmission, and Transformation from Second Temple Literature through Judaism and Christianity in Late Antiquity,* edited by Menahem Kister et al., 40–68. Leiden.

Gabler, Johann Philipp. 1975. "Von der richtigen Unterscheidung der biblischen und der dogmatischen Theologie und der rechten Bestimmung ihrer beider Ziele." In *Das Problem der Theologie des Neuen Testaments,* edited by Georg Strecker, 32–44. WdF 367. Darmstadt.

Gadebusch Bondio, Mariacarla. 2010. "Warum eine Medizin- und Kulturgeschichte der Hand? Einleitende Gedanken." In *Die Hand: Elemente einer Medizin- und Kulturgeschichte,* edited by Mariacarla Gadebusch Bondio, 9–18. Berlin.

Gall, Lothar. 1992. "Ranke und das Objektivitätsproblem." In *Liberalitas, FS Erich Angermann,* edited by Norbert Finzsch and Hermann Wellenreuther, 37–44. Stuttgart.

Galor, Katharina, and Gideon Avni, eds. 2011. *Unearthing Jerusalem: 150 Years of Archaeological Research in the Holy City.* Winona Lake, IN.

Gamm, Gerhard. 2012. *Der Deutsche Idealismus: Eine Einführung in die Philosophie von Fichte, Hegel und Schelling.* Universal-Bibliothek 9655. Stuttgart.

Gardner-Smith, Percival. 1938. *Saint John and the Synoptic Gospels.* Cambridge.

Gathercole, Simon. 2012. *The Composition of the Gospel of Thomas: Original Language and Influences.* Cambridge.

Gatterer, Johann Christoph. 1765. *Abriß der Universalhistorie nach ihrem gesamten Umfange von Erschaffung der Welt bis auf unsere Zeiten erste Hälfte nebst einer vorläufigen Einleitung von der Historie überhaupt und der Universalhistorie.* Göttingen.

Gemeinhardt, Peter. 2010. "Magier, Weiser, Gott: Das Bild Jesu bei paganen antiken Autoren." In *Jesus in apokryphen Evangelienüberlieferungen: Beiträge zu außerkanonischen Jesusüberlieferungen aus verschiedenen Sprach- und Kulturtraditionen,* edited by Jörg Frey and Jens Schröter, 467–92. WUNT 254. Tübingen.

Georgi, Dieter. 1992. "The Interest in Life of Jesus Theology as a Paradigm for the Social History of Biblical Criticism." *HTR* 85: 51–83.

Gerber, Christine. 2008. "'Gott Vater' und die abwesenden Väter: Zur Übersetzung von Metaphern am Beispiel der Familienmetaphorik." In *Gott heißt nicht nur Vater: Zur Rede über Gott in den Übersetzungen der "Bibel in gerechter Sprache,"* edited by Christine Gerber and Benita Joswig, 145–61. BTSP 32. Göttingen.

Gerhard, Johann. 1863–1875. *Loci Theologici (1610–1622)*. Edited by E. Preuß. Berlin.

Gerhardsson, Birger. 1961; ³1998. *Memory and Manuscript: Oral Tradition and Written Transmission in Rabbinic Judaism and Early Christianity*. ASNU 22. Lund, Copenhagen, and Grand Rapids.

―――. 1979. *The Origins of the Gospel Traditions*. London.

Gerlach, Ernst. 1863. *Die Weissagungen des Alten Testaments in den Schriften des Flavius Josephus und das angebliche Zeugniss von Christo*. Berlin.

Gibson, Shimon. 2012. *Die sieben letzten Tage Jesu: Die archäologischen Tatsachen*. Munich.

Gielen, Marlis. 1998. "Und führe uns nicht in Versuchung: Die 6. Vater-Unser-Bitte— eine Anfechtung für das biblische Gottesbild." *ZNW* 89: 201–16.

Gierl, Martin. 2012. *Geschichte als präzisierte Wissenschaft: Johann Christoph Gatterer und die Historiographie des 18. Jahrhunderts im ganzen Umfang*. Fundamenta historica 4. Stuttgart–Bad Cannstatt.

Giesen, Heinz. 2004. "Eigentum im Urteil Jesu und der Jesustradition." In *Jesu Heilsbotschaft und die Kirche*, by Heinz Giesen, 231–44. BETL 179. Leuven.

―――. 2011. "Poverty and Wealth in Jesus and the Jesus Tradition." In *Handbook for the Study of the Historical Jesus*, vol. 4, *Individual Studies*, edited by Tom Holmén and Stanley E. Porter, 3269–3303. Leiden and Boston.

Gitler, Haim. 2010. "Coins." In *The Eerdmans Dictionary of Early Judaism*, edited by John J. Collins and Daniel C. Harlow, 479–82. Grand Rapids.

Gnilka, Joachim. 1978–1979. *Das Evangelium nach Markus*. 2 vols. EKKNT II/1/2. Zürich.

―――. 1990. *Jesus von Nazaret: Botschaft und Geschichte*, 166–93. HThKNTSup 3. Freiburg.

Gogarten, Friedrich. 1977. *Die Christliche Welt* 34 (1920): 374–78. Reprint in Jürgen Moltmann, ed. *Anfänge der dialektischen Theologie*, part 2, "Rudolf Bultmann— Friedrich Gogarten—Eduard Thurneysen," 95–101. Munich.

Gonnet, Giovanni. 1958. *Enchiridion Valdensium: Recueil critique concernant les Vaudois au moyen âge, du IIIe Concile de Latran au Synode de Chanforan*. Torre Pellice, Italy.

Goodacre, Mark S. 2012. *Thomas and the Gospels: The Case for Thomas's Familiarity with the Synoptics*. Grand Rapids.

Goodacre, Mark S., and Nicholas Perrin, eds. 2004. *Questioning Q*. London.

Goodman, Martin. 1999. "The Pilgrimage Economy of Jerusalem in the Second Temple Period." In *Jerusalem: Its Sanctity and Centrality to Judaism, Christianity, and Islam*, edited by Lee I. Levine, 69–76. New York.

―――. 2005. "Coinage and Identity: The Jewish Evidence." In *Coinage and Identity in the Roman Provinces*, edited by Christopher Howgego et al. New York and Oxford.

Goppelt, Leonhard. 1977. *Theologie des Neuen Testaments*. Vol. 1, *Jesu Wirken in seiner theologischen Bedeutung*. Berlin.

Gottsched, Johann Christoph. 1730; ²1737; ³1742; 1982. Facsimile reprint ⁴1751. *Versuch einer Critischen Dichtkunst für die Deutschen.* Leipzig and Darmstadt.

Gowler, David B. 2017. *The Parables after Jesus: Their Imaginative Receptions across Two Millennia.* Grand Rapids.

Grandy, Andreas. 2012. *Die Weisheit der Gottesherrschaft: Eine Untersuchung zur jesuanischen Synthese von traditioneller und apokalyptischer Weisheit.* NTOA/SUNT 96. Göttingen.

Graves, Michael. ²2013. "Languages of Palestine." In *Dictionary of Jesus and the Gospels*, edited by Joel B. Green et al., 484–92. Downers Grove, IL.

Green, Peter. 1993. *From Alexander to Actium: The Historical Evolution of the Hellenistic Age.* Berkeley, CA.

Greschat, Katharina. 2005. *Die Moralia in Job Gregors des Großen: Ein christologischer Kommentar.* STAC 31. Tübingen.

Griesbach, Johann Jakob. 1776. *Synopsis Evangeliorum Matthaei, Marci et Lucae: Textum Graecum ad fidem codicum versionum et patrum emendavit et lectionis varietatem.* Halle.

———. 1789–1790. *Commentatio qua Marci Evangelium totum e Matthaei et Lucae commentariis decerptum esse monstratur.* Jena.

Grimm, Werner. 1972. "Zum Hintergrund von Mt 8,11 f./Lk 13,28f." *BZ*, n.s., 16: 255f.

Grintz, Jehoshua M. 1960. "Hebrew as the Spoken and Written Language in the Last Days of the Second Temple." *JBL* 79: 32–47.

Grondin, Jean. ³2012. *Einführung in die philosophische Hermeneutik.* Darmstadt.

Gruber, Margarete. 2015. "Annäherungen an den Gebetsglauben Jesu: Lesespuren im Markusevangelium." *IKaZ* 44: 52–64.

Guelich, Robert A. 1982. *The Sermon on the Mount.* Waco, TX.

Haacker, Klaus. 2018. *Kommentar zur Apostelgeschichte.* THKNT 5. Leipzig.

Haakonssen, Knud, ed. 1996. *Enlightenment and Religion: Rational Dissent in Eighteenth-Century Britain.* Cambridge.

Habermas, Gary R. 2005. "Resurrection Research from 1975 to the Present: What Are Critical Scholars Saying?" *JSHJ* 3 (2): 135–53.

Hachlili, Rachel. 1992. "Burials, Ancient Jewish." In *ABD* 1:789–94.

Häfner, Gerd, ed. 2013. "Die historische Rückfrage nach Jesus." *MTZ* 64 (2).

Hagenmeyer, Heinrich. 1879. *Peter der Eremite: Ein kritischer Beitrag zur Geschichte des ersten Kreuzzuges.* Leipzig.

Hahn, Ferdinand. 1962; ²1966. "Die Frage nach dem historischen Jesus und die Eigenart der uns zur Verfügungstehenden Quellen." In *Die Frage nach dem historischen Jesus*, edited by Ferdinand Hahn, Wenzel Lohff, and Günther Bornkamm, 7–40. Evangelisches Forum 2. Göttingen.

———. 1963; ⁵1995. *Christologische Hoheitstitel: Ihre Geschichte im frühen Christentum.* FRLANT 83. Göttingen.

———. 1967. "Die Nachfolge Jesu in vorösterlicher Zeit." In *Die Anfänge der Kirche im Neuen Testament*, edited by Ferdinand Hahn, August Strobel, and Eduard Schweizer, 7–36. Göttingen.

———. 1969a. *The Titles of Jesus in Christology: Their History in Early Christianity*. Translated by Harold Knight and George Ogg. Cambridge.

———. 1969b. "The Quest of the Historical Jesus and the Special Character of the Sources Available to Us." In *What Can We Know about Jesus? Essays on the New Quest*, by Ferdinand Hahn, Wenzel Lohff, and Günther Bornkamm, translated by Grover Foley, 9–48. Edinburgh.

———. 1983. "υἱός." In *Exegetisches Wörterbuch zum Neuen Testament*, 3:912–37.

———. 2006. "Bekenntnisformeln im Neuen Testament." In *Studien zum Neuen Testament*, vol. 2, *Bekenntnisbildung und Theologie in urchristlicher Zeit*, by Ferdinand Hahn, 45–60. WUNT 192. Tübingen.

Hakola, Raimo. 2016. "Fishermen and the Production and Marketing of Fish in First-Century Galilee." In *Gender, Social Roles, and Occupations in Early Christian World*, edited by Antti Marjanen. Leiden.

Haliburton, Gordon MacKay. 1973. *The Prophet Harris: A Study of an African Prophet and His Mass-Movement in the Ivory Coast and the Gold Coast, 1913–1915*. Oxford.

Hampel, Volker. 1990. *Menschensohn und historischer Jesus: Ein Rätselwort als Schlüssel zum messianischen Selbstverständnis Jesu*. Neukirchen-Vluyn.

Hanson, Kenneth C., and Douglas E. Oakman. 1998. *Palestine in the Time of Jesus: Social Structures and Social Conflicts*. Minneapolis.

Harnack, Adolf von. 1900. *Das Wesen des Christentums*. Leipzig.

———. 1902. *Die Mission und Ausbreitung des Christentums in den ersten drei Jahrhunderten*. Leipzig.

———. 1907. *Sprüche und Reden Jesu: Die zweite Quelle des Matthäus und Lukas*. Beiträge zur Einleitung in das Neue Testament 2. Leipzig. ET 1908.

———. ([4]1909) 2015. *Lehrbuch der Dogmengeschichte I–III*. Tübingen.

Harnisch, Wolfgang. [4]2001. *Die Gleichniserzählungen Jesu*. Göttingen.

Harris, Horton. 1973. *David Friedrich Strauss and His Theology*. Monograph Supplements to the Scottish Journal of Theology. Cambridge.

———. 1975. *The Tübingen School*. Oxford.

Hartenstein, Judith. 2012. "Männliche und weibliche Erzählfiguren im Johannesevangelium." In *Die Bibel und die Frauen: Eine exegetisch-kulturgeschichtliche Enzyklopädie*, vol. 2.1, *Neues Testament: Evangelien; Erzählungen und Geschichte*, edited by Mercedes Navarro Puerto and Irmtraud Fischer, 421–33. Stuttgart.

Hartin, Patrick J. 1991. *James and the Q Sayings of Jesus*. JSNTSup 47. Sheffield.

Hartman, Lars. 2005. *Markusevangeliet 8:27–16:20*. Stockholm.

Harvey, Anthony E. 1982. *Jesus and the Constraints of History*. Philadelphia.

Hase, Karl von. 1829; ²1835. *Das Leben Jesu: Lehrbuch zunächst für akademische Vor-lesungen.* Leipzig.

Hauck, Albert. ⁶1952. *Kirchengeschichte Deutschlands.* 5 vols. in 6. Leipzig.

Haufe, Günter. 1985. "Reich Gottes bei Paulus und in der Jesus Tradition." *NTS* 31: 467–72.

Hedrick, Charles W. 1988. *The Historical Jesus and the Rejected Gospels.* Semeia 44. Atlanta.

Heil, Christoph. 2003. *Lukas und Q: Studien zur lukanischen Redaktion des Spruch-evangeliums Q.* BZNW 111. Berlin and New York.

———. 2014a. "Nachfolge und Tora in Q 9,57–60." In *Das Spruchevangelium Q und der historische Jesus,* by Christoph Heil, 87–117. SBAB 58. Stuttgart.

———. 2014b. "Was ist 'Nachfolge Jesu'? Antworten von Q, Matthäus, Lukas—und Jesus." In *Das Spruchevangelium Q und der historische Jesus,* by Christoph Heil, 77–85. SBAB 58. Stuttgart.

Heil, John Paul. 1999. *The Meal Scenes in Luke-Acts: An Audience-Oriented Approach.* SBLMS 52. Atlanta.

Heininger, Bernhard. 1991. *Metaphorik, Erzählstruktur und szenisch-dramatische Ge-staltung in den Sondergutgleichnissen bei Lukas.* NTAbh, n.s., 24. Münster.

———. 2002. "Apokalyptische Wende Jesu? Ein Beitrag zur Vor- und Frühgeschichte des Vaterunsers." In *Brückenschläge: Akademische Theologie der Akademien, FS Fritz Hofmann,* edited by Erich Garhammer and Wolfgang Weiss, 183–206. Würz-burg.

———. 2005. "Tischsitten." In *Neues Testament und Antike Kultur,* vol. 2, *Familie— Gesellschaft—Wirtschaft,* edited by Klaus Scherberich, 34–37. Neukirchen-Vluyn.

Hengel, Martin. 1968. *Nachfolge und Charisma: Eine exegetisch-religionsgeschichtliche Studie zu Mt 8,21 f. und Jesu Ruf in die Nachfolge.* BZNW 34. Berlin.

———. 1970. *War Jesus Revolutionär?* Stuttgart.

———. 1973. *Eigentum und Reichtum in der frühen Kirche: Aspekte einer frühchristli-chen Sozialgeschichte.* Stuttgart.

———. ²1973. *Judentum und Hellenismus: Studien zu ihrer Begegnung unter besonderer Berücksichtigung Palästinas bis zur Mitte des 2. Jh.s v.Chr.* WUNT 10. Tübingen.

———. 1975. *Der Sohn Gottes: Die Entstehung der Christologie und die jüdisch-hellenistische Religionsgeschichte.* Tübingen.

———. 1978. "Jesus und die Tora." *TBei* 9: 152–72.

———. 1984. "Entstehungszeit und Situation des Markusevangeliums." In *Markus-Philologie: Historische, literargeschichtliche und stilistische Untersuchungen zum zweiten Evangelium,* by Hubert Cancik, 1–45. WUNT 33. Tübingen.

———. 1987. "The Interpretation of the Wine Miracle at Cana: John 2:1–11." In *The Glory of Christ in the New Testament: Studies in Christology in Memory of George*

Bradford Caird, edited by Lincoln D. Hurst and Nicholas T. Wright, 83–112. Oxford.

———. 1989. *The Zealots: Investigations into the Jewish Freedom Movements from Herod I until 70 A.D.* Translated by D. Smith. Edinburgh: T&T Clark.

———. 1993. *Die johanneische Frage: Ein Lösungsversuch, mit einem Beitrag zur Apokalypse von Jörg Frey.* WUNT 67. Tübingen.

———. 1999. "Das Johannesevangelium als Quelle für die Geschichte des antiken Judentums." In *Judaica, Hellenistica et Christiana: Kleine Schriften II*, by Martin Hengel, with collaboration of Jörg von Frey and others, 293–334. WUNT 109. Tübingen.

———. 2001. "Jesus der Messias Israels." In *Der messianische Anspruch Jesu und die Anfänge der Christologie*, by Martin Hengel and Anna Maria Schwemer, 1–80. WUNT 138. Tübingen.

———. 2006a. "Das Mahl in der Nacht, 'in der Jesus ausgeliefert wurde' (1 Kor 11,23)." In *Studien zur Christologie: Kleine Schriften IV*, by Martin Hengel, edited by Claus-Jürgen Thornton, 451–95. WUNT 201. Tübingen.

———. 2006b. "ABBA, Maranatha, Hosanna und die Anfänge der Christologie." In *Studien zur Christologie: Kleine Schriften IV*, by Martin Hengel, edited by Claus-Jürgen Thornton, 496–534. WUNT 201. Tübingen.

———. 2007. "War Jesus revolutionär?" In *Jesus und die Evangelien: Kleine Schriften V*, by Martin Hengel, edited by Claus-Jürgen Thornton, 217–43. WUNT 211. Tübingen.

———. 2008. "Mors turpissima crucis: Die Kreuzigung in der antiken Welt und die 'Torheit' des 'Wortes vom Kreuz.'" In *Studien zum Urchristentum: Kleine Schriften VI*, by Martin Hengel, edited by Claus-Jürgen Thornton, 594–652. WUNT 234. Tübingen.

———. 2010. "Bekennen und Bekenntnis." In *Theologische, historische und biographische Skizzen: Kleine Schriften VII*, by Martin Hengel, 313–47. WUNT 253. Tübingen. ET: "Confessing and Confession." In *Earliest Christian History: History, Literature, and Theology*, by Michael F. Bird and Jason Maston, 589–623. WUNT II 320. Tübingen, 2012.

———. ³2012. *Die Zeloten: Untersuchungen zur jüdischen Freiheitsbewegung in der Zeit von Herodes I. bis 70 n. Chr.* Edited by Roland Deines and Claus-Jürgen Thornton. WUNT 283. Tübingen.

Hengel, Martin, and Anna Maria Schwemer, eds. 1991. *Königsherrschaft Gottes und himmlischer Kult im Judentum, Urchristentum und in der hellenistischen Welt.* WUNT 55. Tübingen.

———. 1998. *Paulus zwischen Damaskus und Antiochien: Die unbekannten Jahre des Apostels.* WUNT 108. Tübingen.

———. 2001. *Der messianische Anspruch Jesu und die Anfänge der Christologie.* WUNT 138. Tübingen.

———. 2007. *Geschichte des frühen Christentums*. Vol. 1, *Jesus und das Judentum*. Tübingen.

Hentschel, Anni. 2007. *Diakonia im Neuen Testament*. WUNT II 226. Tübingen.

Herder, Johann Gottfried von. 1880. *Von Gottes Sohn, der Welt Heiland* (1797). In *Sämtliche Werke*, edited by Bernhard Suphan, 19:1–424. Berlin.

———. 1985–2000. *Werke in zehn Bänden: Bibliothek deutscher Klassiker*. Frankfurt.

Herrenbrück, Fritz. 1990. *Jesus und die Zöllner: Historische und neutestamentlich-exegetische Untersuchungen*. WUNT II 41. Tübingen.

Herzog, William R., II. 1994. *Parables as Subversive Speech: Jesus as Pedagogue of the Oppressed*. Louisville.

———. 2005. *Prophet and Teacher: An Introduction to the Historical Jesus*. Louisville.

Hezser, Catherine. 2001. *Jewish Literacy in Roman Palestine*. TSAJ 81. Tübingen.

———. 2010. "Private and Public Education." In *The Oxford Handbook of Jewish Daily Life in Roman Palestine*, edited by Catherine Hezser, 465–81. Oxford.

Hoehner, Harold W. 1972. *Herod Antipas*. Cambridge.

Hoffmann, Paul. 1979. "Auferstehung II: Auferstehung Jesu Christi II/1, Neues Testament." In *TRE* 4:478–513.

———. 1994. "Der Glaube an die Auferweckung Jesu in der neutestamentlichen Überlieferung." In *Studien zur Frühgeschichte der Jesus-Bewegung*, by Paul Hoffmann, 188–256. SBAB 17. Stuttgart.

Hoffmann, Paul, and Christoph Heil, eds. ⁴2013. *Die Spruchquelle Q: Studienausgabe Griechisch und Deutsch*. Darmstadt and Leuven.

Hofius, Otfried. 2002. "'Einer ist Gott—Einer ist Herr': Erwägungen zu Struktur und Aussage des Bekenntnisses 1Kor 8,6." In *Paulusstudien II*, by Otfried Hofius, 167–80. WUNT 143. Tübingen.

Holl, Karl. 1904. *Amphilochius von Ikonium in seinem Verhältnis zu den großen Kappadoziern*. Tübingen and Leipzig.

Hollenbach, Paul. 1982. "The Conversion of Jesus: From Jesus the Baptizer to Jesus the Healer." *ANRW* II.25.1, 196–219.

Holmås, Geir Otto. 2014. "Prayer, 'Othering' and the Construction of Early Christian Identity in the Gospels of Matthew and Luke." In *Early Christian Prayer and Identity Formation*, edited by Reidar Hvalvik and Karl Olav Sandnes, 91–113. Tübingen.

Holmén, Tom. 2001. "Knowing about Q and Knowing about Jesus: Mutually Exclusive Undertakings?" In *The Sayings Source Q and the Historical Jesus*, edited by Andreas Lindemann, 497–514. BETL 158. Leuven.

Holmén, Tom, and Stanley E. Porter, eds. 2011. *Handbook for the Study of the Historical Jesus*. Vols. 1–4. Leiden and Boston.

Holtzmann, Heinrich Julius. 1863. *Die synoptischen Evangelien: Ihr Ursprung und geschichtlicher Charakter*. Leipzig.

————. 1885. *Lehrbuch der historisch-kritischen Einleitung in das Neue Testament*. Sammlung theologischer Lehrbücher 1. Freiburg.

————. 1897. *Lehrbuch der neutestamentlichen Theologie*. 2 vols. Sammlung theologischer Lehrbücher 12/1.2. Freiburg and Leipzig.

————. 1907. *Das messianische Bewußtsein Jesu: Ein Beitrag zur Leben-Jesu-Forschung*. Tübingen.

Hoppe, Rudolf. 1977. *Der theologische Hintergrund des Jakobusbriefes*. FB 28. Würzburg.

Horbury, William. 1986. "The Twelve and the Phylarchs." *NTS* 32: 503–27.

Horn, Friedrich Wilhelm, and Ruben Zimmermann, eds. 2009. *Jenseits von Indikativ und Imperativ*. WUNT 238. Tübingen.

Horn, Friedrich Wilhelm, Ulrich Volp, and Ruben Zimmermann, eds. 2013. *Ethische Normen des frühen Christentums: Gut—Leben—Leib—Tugend, Kontexte und Normen neutestamentlicher Ethik 4*. WUNT 313. Tübingen.

Horrell, David. 1997. "'The Lord Commanded . . . but I Have Not Used . . .': Exegetical and Hermeneutical Reflections on 1 Cor 9,14–15." *NTS* 43: 587–603.

Horsley, Richard A. 1987. *Jesus and the Spiral of Violence: Popular Jewish Resistance in Roman Palestine*. San Francisco.

————. 1989. *Sociology and the Jesus Movement*. New York.

————. 1991. "Q and Jesus: Assumptions, Approaches and Analyses." *Semeia* 55: 175–209.

————. 1994. "The Death of Jesus." In *Studying the Historical Jesus: Evaluations of the State of Current Research*, edited by Bruce Chilton and Craig A. Evans, 395–422. NTTS 19. Leiden.

————. 1996. *Archaeology, History, and Society in Galilee: The Social Context of Jesus and the Rabbis*. Valley Forge, PA.

————. 1999. *Bandits, Prophets, and Messiahs: Popular Movements in the Time of Jesus*. Harrisburg, PA.

Horsley, Richard A., and Jonathan A. Draper. 1999. *Whoever Hears You, Hears Me: Prophets, Performance, and Tradition in Q*. Harrisburg, PA.

Horsley, Richard A., and John S. Hanson. 1985. *Bandits, Prophets, and Messiahs: Popular Movements at the Time of Jesus*. Minneapolis.

Howgego, Christopher. 1995. *Ancient History from Coins*. London and New York.

Hübner, Ulrich. 2013. "Die Münzprägungen Herodes' des Großen (40/37—4 v.Chr.): Selbstdarstellung und politische Realität." In *Macht des Geldes—Macht der Bilder: Kolloquium zur Ikonographie auf Münzen im ostmediterranen Raum in hellenistisch-römischer Zeit*, edited by Anne Lykke, 93–122. ADPV 42. Wiesbaden.

Hughes, John H. 1972. "John the Baptist: The Forerunner of God Himself." *NovT* 14: 191–218.

Hultgren, Arland J. 1979. *Jesus and His Adversaries: The Form and Function of the Conflict Stories in the Synoptic Tradition*. Minneapolis.

———. 2000. *The Parables of Jesus: A Commentary*. Grand Rapids and Cambridge.

Hurtado, Larry. 1988. *One God, One Lord: Early Christian Devotion and Ancient Jewish Monotheism*. London.

———. 2003. *Lord Jesus Christ: Devotion to Jesus in Earliest Christianity*. Grand Rapids and Cambridge.

———. 2014. "The Place of Jesus in Earliest Christian Prayer and Its Import for Early Christian Identity." In *Early Christian Prayer and Identity Formation*, edited by Reidar Hvalvik and Karl Olav Sandnes, 35–56. Tübingen.

Ilan, Tan. 1995. *Jewish Women in Greco-Roman Palestine*. TSAJ 44. Tübingen.

———. 2000. "In the Footsteps of Jesus." In *Transformative Encounters: Jesus and Women Re-Viewed*, edited by Ingrid Rosa Kitzberger, 115–36. BibInt 43. Leiden.

Ingraham, Joseph Holt. 1855. *The Prince of the House of David; or, Three Years in the Holy City*. London.

———. 1858. *Das Leben Jesu: Der Fürst aus David's Hause oder drei Jahre in der heiligen Stadt*. Philadelphia.

Instone-Brewer, David. 1992. *Techniques and Assumptions in Jewish Exegesis before 70 CE*. TSAJ 30. Tübingen.

Isaac, Benjamin. 2010. "Jerusalem—an Introduction." In *Corpus Inscriptionum Iudaeae et Palaestinae*, vol. 1, *Jerusalem*, part 1, 1–37. Berlin and New York.

Ittel, Gerhard Wolfgang. 1970. *Jesus und die Jünger*. Gütersloh.

Jacobi, Christine. 2015. *Jesusüberlieferung bei Paulus? Analogien zwischen den echten Paulusbriefen und den synoptischen Evangelien*. BZNW 213. Berlin.

Jacobson, Arland D. 1982. "The Literary Unity of Q." *JBL* 101: 365–89.

———. 1990. "Proverbs and Social Control: A New Paradigm for Wisdom Studies." In *Gnosticism and the Early Christian World, FS James M. Robinson*, edited by Hans Dieter Betz et al., 76–88. Forum Fascicles 2. Sonoma, CA.

———. 2000. "Jesus against the Family: The Dissolution of Family Ties in the Gospel Tradition." In *From Quest to Q, FS James M. Robinson*, edited by Jon Ma Asgeirsson, Kristin de Troyer, and Marvin W. Meyer, 189–218. BETL 146. Leuven.

Jacobson, David M. 2013. "Understanding Herod the Great through His Coins." In *Macht des Geldes—Macht der Bilder: Kolloquium zur Ikonographie auf Münzen im ostmediterranen Raum in hellenistisch-römischer Zeit*, edited by Anne Lykke, 123–50. ADPV 42. Wiesbaden.

Jäger, Friedrich, and Jörn Rüsen. 1992. *Geschichte des Historismus: Eine Einführung*. Munich.

Jaubert, Annie. 1957. *La Date de la Cène*. Paris.

Jensen, Morten Hørning. 2006. *Herod Antipas in Galilee*. WUNT II 215. Tübingen.

Jeremias, Joachim. 1931. "Zöllner und Sünder." *ZAW* 30: 293–300.

———. ³1963. *Unbekannte Jesusworte*. Gütersloh.

———. 1966. *Abba: Studien zur neutestamentlichen Theologie und Zeitgeschichte*. Göttingen.

———. ⁴1967. *Die Abendmahlsworte Jesu*. Göttingen.

———. 1969. *Jerusalem in the Time of Jesus: An Investigation into Economic and Social Conditions during the New Testament Period*. London.

———. 1971a; ⁴1988. *Neutestamentliche Theologie*. Part 1, *Die Verkündigung Jesu*. Gütersloh. ET: *New Testament Theology*. Part 1, *The Proclamation of Jesus*. London.

———. 1971b. "Tradition und Redaktion in Lukas 15." *ZNW* 62: 172–89.

———. ¹¹1998. *Die Gleichnisse Jesu*. Göttingen.

Johnson, Luke Timothy. 1996. *The Real Jesus: The Misguided Quest for the Historical Jesus and the Truth of the Traditional Gospels*. San Francisco.

Johnson, Marshall D. 1969. *The Purpose of the Biblical Genealogies: With Special Reference to the Setting of the Genealogies of Jesus*. SNTSMS 8. Cambridge.

Jordan, Stefan, ed. 1999a. *Schwellenzeittexte: Quellen zur deutschsprachigen Geschichtstheorie in der ersten Hälfte des 19. Jahrhunderts*. Waltrop, Germany.

———. 1999b. *Geschichtstheorie in der ersten Hälfte des 19. Jahrhunderts: Die Schwellenzeit zwischen Pragmatismus und Klassischem Historismus*. Frankfurt and New York.

———. 2001. "Zwischen Aufklärung und Historismus: Deutschsprachige Geschichtstheorie in der ersten Hälfte des 19. Jahrhunderts." *Sitzungsberichte der Leibniz-Sozietät* 48 (5): 5–20.

———, ed. 2002. *Lexikon Geschichtswissenschaft*. Stuttgart.

———. 2009. *Theorien und Methoden der Geschichtswissenschaft: Orientierung Geschichte*. UTB 3104. Paderborn.

Jülicher, Adolf. ²1910. *Die Gleichnisreden Jesu* (1976). 2 parts in 1 vol. Tübingen.

Jung, Franz. 2002. *ΣΩTHP: Studien zur Rezeption eines hellenistischen Ehrentitels im Neuen Testament*. NTAbh, n.s., 39. Münster.

Jungbauer, Harry. 2002. *"Ehre Vater und Mutter": Der Weg des Elterngebots in der biblischen Tradition*. WUNT II 146. Tübingen.

Kahl, Werner. 1994. *New Testament Miracle Stories in Their Religious-Historical Setting: A Religionsgeschichtliche Comparison from Structural Perspective*. FRLANT 163. Göttingen.

———. 2012. "Erhebliche matthäisch-lukanische Übereinstimmungen gegen das Markusevangelium in der Triple-Tradition: Ein Beitrag zur Klärung der synoptischen Abhängigkeitsverhältnisse." *ZNW* 103: 20–46.

Kähler, Martin. ³1961. *Der sogenannte historische Jesus und der geschichtliche, biblische Christus*. Edited by Ernst Wolf. TB 2. Munich.

Kant, Immanuel. 1956. "Religion innerhalb der Grenzen der bloßen Vernunft." In *Werke in sechs Bänden*, edited by Wilhelm Weischedel, 4:645–879. Wiesbaden.

———. 1958. "Was heißt: Sich im Denken orientieren?" In *Werke in sechs Bänden*, edited by Wilhelm Weischedel, 3:265–83. Wiesbaden.

———. 1976. *Kritik der reinen Vernunft*. Edited by Raymund Schmidt. S. 7 (= A XI). Hamburg.

Karrer, Martin. 1990. *Der Gesalbte: Die Grundlagen des Christustitels*. FRLANT 151. Göttingen.

———. 1998. *Jesus Christus im Neuen Testament*. GNT 11. Göttingen.

Käsemann, Ernst. 1954. "Das Problem des historischen Jesus." *ZTK* 51 (2): 125–53.

———. 1960; ⁷1970. *Exegetische Versuche und Besinnungen*. Vol. 1. Göttingen.

———. 1964a. "The Problem of the Historical Jesus." In *Essays on New Testament Themes*, translated by W. J. Montague from ²1960, 15–47. SBT 41. London.

———. 1964b. "Sackgassen im Streit um den historischen Jesus." In *Exegetische Versuche und Besinnungen*, by Ernst Käsemann, 2:31–68. Göttingen.

Kauhaus, Hanna. 2011. *Vielfältiges Verstehen: Wege der Bibelauslegung im 18. Jahrhundert*. AKThG 35. Leipzig.

Kawan, Christine Shojaei. 2005. "Legend and Life: Examples from the Biographies of ʿĀʾishah Bint Abī Bakr, Mary Carleton, and Friedrich Salomo Krauss." *Folklore* 116: 140–54.

Kaylor, Robert D. 1994. *Jesus the Prophet: His Vision of the Kingdom on Earth*. Louisville.

Kazen, Thomas. 2010a. *Issues of Impurity in Early Judaism*. Winona Lake, IN.

———. 2010b. *Jesus and Purity Halakhah: Was Jesus Indifferent to Impurity?* Winona Lake, IN.

———. 2013. *Scripture, Interpretation, or Authority? Motives and Arguments in Jesus' Halakic Conflicts*. WUNT 320. Tübingen.

———. 2015. "Theology: New Testament." In *The Oxford Encyclopedia of Bible and Law*, edited by Brent Strawn et al., 2:384–400. New York.

———. 2021. "Emotional Repression and Physical Mutilation? The Cognitive and Behavioural Impact of Exaggeration in the Sermon on the Mount." In *Social and Cognitive Perspectives on the Sermon on the Mount*, edited by Rikard Roitto, Colleen Shantz, and Petri Luomanen. Sheffield.

Kee, Howard Clark. 1999. "Jesus: A Glutton and Drunkard." In *Authenticating the Words of Jesus*, edited by Bruce Chilton and Craig A. Evans, 311–32. NTTS 28/1. Leiden, Boston, and Cologne.

Keener, Craig S. 2011. *Miracles: The Credibility of the New Testament Accounts*. Vols. 1–2. Grand Rapids.

Keim, Theodor. 1861. *Die menschliche Entwicklung Jesu Christi: Akademische Antrittsrede am 17. Dezember 1860*. Zürich.

Keith, Chris. 2011. *Jesus' Literacy: Scribal Culture and the Teacher from Galilee*. LNTS 413. New York and London.

———. 2014. *Jesus against the Scribal Elite*. Grand Rapids.

Keith, Chris, and Anthony Le Donne, eds. 2012. *Jesus, Criteria, and the Demise of Authenticity*. London and New York.

Kelber, Werner H. 1995. "Jesus and Tradition: Words in Time, Words in Space." *Semeia* 65: 139–67.

Kelber, Werner H., and Samuel Byrskog, eds. 2009. *Jesus in Memory: Traditions in Oral and Scribal Perspectives*. Waco, TX.

Keppler, Angela. 2002. "Soziale Formen individuellen Erinnerns: Die kommunikative Tradierung von (Familien-)Geschichte." In *Das soziale Gedächtnis: Geschichte, Erinnerung, Tradierung*, edited by Harald Welzer, 137–59. Hamburg.

Kern, Gabi. ²2015. "Parabeln in der Logienquelle: Einleitung." In *Kompendium der Gleichnisse Jesu*, edited by Ruben Zimmermann et al., 49–60. Gütersloh.

Kierspel, Lars. 2006. *The Jews and the World in the Fourth Gospel: Parallelism, Function, and Context*. WUNT II 220. Tübingen.

Kilunen, Jarmo. 1989. *Das Doppelgebot der Liebe in synoptischer Sicht: Ein redaktionskritischer Versuch über Mk 12,28–34 und die Parallelen*. Helsinki.

Kingsbury, Jack D. 1969. *The Parables of Jesus in Matthew 13: A Study in Redaction Criticism*. London.

Kinzig, Wolfram. 2017. *Faith in Formulae: A Collection of Early Christian Creeds and Creed-Related Texts*. Vol. 1, 35–60. OECT. Oxford.

Kirk, Alan. 2003. "'Love Your Enemies,' the Golden Rule, and Ancient Reciprocity (Luke 6:27–35)." *JBL* 122: 667–86.

Kirk, Alan, and Tom Thatcher, eds. 2005. *Memory, Tradition, and Text: Uses of the Past in Early Christianity*. SemeiaSt 52. Atlanta.

Kirn, Hans-Martin. 2001. "Contemptus mundi—contemptus Judaei? Nachfolgeideale und Antijudaismus in der spätmittelalterlichen Predigtliteratur." In *Spätmittelalterliche Frömmigkeit zwischen Ideal und Praxis*, edited by Berndt Hamm and Thomas Lentes, 146–87. SuR, n.s., 15. Tübingen.

Kitzberger, Ingrid Rosa, ed. 2000. *Transformative Encounters: Jesus and Women Re-Viewed*. BibInt 43. Leiden.

Klauck, Hans-Josef. 1982. "Die erzählerische Rolle der Jünger im Markusevangelium: Eine narrative Analyse." *NovT* 24: 1–26.

———. 1995. "Die Familie im Neuen Testament: Grenzen und Chancen." In *Familie leben: Herausforderungen für kirchliche Lehre und Praxis*, edited by Gottfried Bachl, 9–36. Düsseldorf.

Klausner, Joseph. 1925. *Jesus of Nazareth: His Life, Times, and Teaching*. London.

Klein, Dietrich. 2009. *Hermann Samuel Reimarus (1694–1768): Das theologische Werk*. BHT 145. Tübingen.

Klein, Günter. 1961. *Die zwölf Apostel: Ursprung und Gestalt einer Idee*. FRLANT 77. Göttingen.

———. 1970. "'Reich Gottes' als biblischer Zentralbegriff." *EvT* 30: 642–70.

Klein, Hans. [10]2006. *Das Lukasevangelium*. KEK I/3. Göttingen.

———. 2009. "Das Vaterunser: Seine Geschichte und sein Verständnis bei Jesus und im frühen Christentum." In *Das Gebet im Neuen Testament: Vierte europäische orthodox-westliche Exegetenkonferenz in Sâmbăta de Sus. 4.-8. August 2007*, edited by Hans Klein, Vasile Mihoc, and Karl-Wilhelm Niebuhr, 77–114. WUNT 249. Tübingen.

Kleinman, Arthur. 1995. *Patients and Healers in the Context of Culture: An Exploration of the Borderland between Anthropology, Medicine, and Psychiatry*. Berkeley, CA.

Kloner, Amos, and Boas Zissu. 2007. *The Necropolis of Jerusalem in the Second Temple Period*. ISACR 8. Leuven and Dudley, UK.

Kloppenborg, John S. 1987; 1999. *The Formation of Q: Trajectories in Ancient Wisdom Collections, Studies in Antiquity and Christianity*. Harrisburg, PA.

———. 1995. "Jesus and the Parables of Jesus in Q." In *The Gospel behind the Gospels: Current Studies on Q*, edited by Ronald A. Piper, 275–319. NovTSup 75. Leiden.

———. 1996. "The Sayings Gospel Q and the Quest of the Historical Jesus." *HTR* 89: 307–44.

———. 2001. "Discursive Practices in the Sayings Gospel Q and the Quest of the Historical Jesus." In *The Sayings Source Q and the Historical Jesus*, edited by Andreas Lindemann, 149–90. BETL 158. Leuven.

———. 2006. "H. J. Holtzmann's Life of Jesus according to the 'A' Source." *JSHJ* 4: 75–108, 203–23.

———. 2010. "Agrarian Discourse in the Sayings of Jesus." In *Engaging Economics: New Testament Scenarios and Early Christian Interpretation*, edited by Bruce Longenecker and Kelly Liebengood, 104–28. Grand Rapids.

———. 2012. "Memory, Performance and the Sayings of Jesus." *JSHJ* 10 (2): 97–132.

Kloppenborg Verbin, John S. 2000. *Excavating Q: The History and Setting of the Sayings Gospel*. Edinburgh.

Klostermann, Erich. 1955. "Die Majestätsprozesse unter Tiberius." *Historia* 4: 72–106.

Klumbies, Paul-Gerhard. 2015. *Herkunft und Horizont der Theologie des Neuen Testaments*. Tübingen.

Knoch, Otto Bernhard. 1966. *Einer ist euer Meister: Jüngerschaft und Nachfolge*. Stuttgart.

Koch, Dietrich-Alex. 1989. "Jesu Tischgemeinschaft mit Zöllnern und Sündern: Erwägungen zur Entstehung von Mk 2,13–17." In *Jesu Rede von Gott und ihre Nachgeschichte im frühen Christentum: Beiträge zur Verkündigung Jesu und zum Kerygma der Kirche, FS für Willi Marxsen*, edited by Dietrich-Alex Koch, Gerhard Sellin, and Andreas Lindemann, 57–73. Gütersloh.

———. 2005. "The Origin, Function and Disappearance of the 'Twelve': Continuity from Jesus to the Post-Easter Community?" *HTS* 61: 211–29.

———. 2013. *Geschichte des Urchristentums*. Göttingen.

Koch, Klaus. 1978. "Offenbaren wird sich das Reich Gottes." *NTS* 25: 158–65.

Koester, Craig R. [2]2003. *Symbolism in the Fourth Gospel: Meaning, Mystery, Community*. Minneapolis.

Koester, Helmut. 1990; [2]1992. *Ancient Christian Gospels: Their History and Their Development*. London.

———. 1992. "Jesus the Victim." *JBL* 111: 3–15.

Köhler, Wolf-Dietrich. 1987. *Die Rezeption des Matthäusevangeliums in der Zeit vor Irenäus*. WUNT II 24. Tübingen.

Kollmann, Bernd. 1990. *Ursprung und Gestalten der frühchristlichen Mahlfeier*. GTA 43. Göttingen.

———. 1994. "Göttliche Offenbarung magisch-pharmakologischer Heilkunst im Buch Tobit." *ZAW* 106: 289–99.

———. 1996. *Jesus und die Christen als Wundertäter: Studien zu Magie, Medizin und Schamanismus in Antike und Christentum*. FRLANT 170. Göttingen.

———. 2004. "Jesus als jüdischer Gleichnisdichter." *NTS* 50: 457–75.

———. 2005. "Totenerweckungen in der Bibel—Ausdruck von Protest und Zeichen der Hoffnung." In *Leben trotz Tod*, edited by Martin Ebner and Erich Zenger, 121–41. JBT 19. Neukirchen-Vluyn.

———. 2010. *Das Grabtuch von Turin: Ein Porträt Jesu? Mythen und Fakten*. Freiburg.

———. 2011. "Jesus and Magic: The Question of the Miracles." In *Handbook for the Study of the Historical Jesus*, vol. 4, *Individual Studies*, edited by Tom Holmén and Stanley E. Porter, 3057–85. Leiden and Boston.

———. 2013. *Jerusalem: Geschichte der Heiligen Stadt im Zeitalter Jesu*. Darmstadt.

———. 2014. "Von der Rehabilitierung mythischen Denkens und der Wiederentdeckung Jesu als Wundertäter: Meilensteine der Wunderdebatte von der Aufklärung bis zur Gegenwart." In *Hermeneutik der frühchristlichen Wundererzählungen: Geschichtliche, literarische und rezeptionsorientierte Perspektiven*, edited by Bernd Kollmann and Ruben Zimmermann, 3–26. WUNT 339. Tübingen.

Kollwitz, Johannes. 1957. "Christusbild." In *RAC* 3:2–24.

———. 2012. "Das Christusbild der frühchristlichen Kunst." In *Lexikon der christlichen Ikonographie*, edited by Engelbert Kirschbaum et al., 356–71. Darmstadt.

Konradt, Matthias. 1998. *Christliche Existenz nach dem Jakobusbrief: Eine Studie zu seiner soteriologischen und ethischen Konzeption*. SUNT 22. Göttingen.

———. 2004. "Der Jakobusbrief im frühchristlichen Kontext." In *The Catholic Epistles and the Tradition*, edited by Jacques Schlosser. BETL 176. Leuven.

———. 2006. "Gott oder Mammon: Besitzethos und Diakonie im frühen Christentum." In *Diakonie und Ökonomie*, edited by Christof Sigrist, 107–54. Zürich.

———. 2007. *Israel, Kirche und die Völker im Matthäusevangelium*. WUNT 215. Tübingen.

———. 2010. "Stellt der Vollmachtsanspruch des historischen Jesus eine Gestalt 'vorösterlicher Christologie' dar?" *ZTK* 107: 139–66.

———. 2013. "Die Ausrichtung der Mission im Matthäusevangelium und die Entwicklung zur universalen Kirche: Überlegungen zum Standort des Matthäus-evangeliums in der Entwicklung des Christentums." In *The Rise and Expansion of Christianity in the First Three Centuries of the Common Era*, edited by Clare K. Rothschild and Jens Schröter, 143–64. WUNT 301. Tübingen. .

———. 2015. *Das Evangelium nach Matthäus*. NTD 1. Göttingen.

Körtner, Ulrich H. J., ed. 2002. *Jesus im 21. Jahrhundert, Bultmanns Jesusbuch und die heutige Jesusforschung*. Neukirchen-Vluyn.

Koselleck, Reinhart. 1975. "Geschichte, Historie V: Die Herausbildung des modernen Geschichtsbegriffs. VI. 'Geschichte' als moderner Leitbegriff. VII. Ausblick." In *Geschichtliche Grundbegriffe. Historisches Lexikon zur politisch-sozialen Sprache in Deutschland* 2: 647–717.

———. 1979a. "Einleitung." In *Geschichtliche Grundbegriffe: Historisches Lexikon zur politisch-sozialen Sprache in Deutschland*, vol. I A–D, edited by Otto Brunner, Werner Conze, and Reinhart Koselleck, xiii–xxvii. Stuttgart.

———. 1979b. *Vergangene Zukunft: Zur Semantik geschichtlicher Zeiten*. Frankfurt.

Kramer, Werner. 1963. *Christos Kyrios Gottessohn: Untersuchungen zu Gebrauch und Bedeutung der christologischen Bezeichnungen bei Paulus und der vorpaulinischen Gemeinde*. ATANT 44. Zürich.

Kratz, Reinhard. 1979. *Rettungswunder: Motiv-, traditions- und formkritische Aufarbeitung einer biblischen Gattung*. EHS XXIII.123. Frankfurt.

Kraus, Thomas J., and Tobias Nicklas, eds. 2004. *Das Petrusevangelium und die Petrusapokalypse: Die griechischen Fragmente mit deutscher und englischer Übersetzung*. GCS, n.s., 11. Berlin and New York.

Kraus, Thomas J., Michael J. Kruger, and Tobias Nicklas. 2009. *Gospel Fragments*. Oxford Early Christian Gospel Texts. Oxford.

Kreitzer, Larry J. 1996. *Striking New Images: Roman Imperial Coinage and the New Testament World*. JSNTSup 1134. Sheffield.

Kremer, Detlef. [3]2007. *Romantik: Lehrbuch Germanistik*. Stuttgart and Weimar.

Kremer, Jakob. 1985. *Lazarus: Die Geschichte einer Auferstehung*. Stuttgart.

Kreplin, Matthias. 2001. *Das Selbstverständnis Jesu: Hermeneutische und christologische Reflexion; Historisch-kritische Analyse*. WUNT II 141. Tübingen.

Krischel, Roland, et al., eds. 2005. *Ansichten Christi: Christusbilder von der Antike bis zum 20. Jahrhundert*. Cologne.

Kruger, Michael J. 2005. *The Gospel of the Savior: An Analysis of P. Oxy. 840 and Its Place in the Gospel Traditions of Early Christianity*. Leiden.

Kruse, Heinz. 1954. "Die 'dialektische Negation' als Semitisches Idiom." *VT* 4: 385–400.

Küchler, Max. 1992. "Die 'Probatische' und Betesda mit den fünf Stoas." In *Peregrina Curiositas*, 127–54. NTOA 27. Freiburg (CH).

———. 2007. *Jerusalem: Ein Handbuch und Studienreiseführer zur Heiligen Stadt*. Göttingen.

Kühl, Ernst. 1907. *Das Selbstbewußtsein Jesu*. Berlin.

Kuhn, Hans-Jürgen. 1988. *Christologie und Wunder: Untersuchungen zu Joh 1,35–51*. BU 18. Regensburg.

Kuhn, Heinz-Wolfgang. 1982. "Die Kreuzesstrafe während der frühen Kaiserzeit." *ANRW* II.25.1: 648–793.

Kuhn, Johannes. 1838. *Das Leben Jesu, wissenschaftlich bearbeitet*. Mainz.

Kühne-Bertram, Gudrun. 1983. "Aspekte der Geschichte und der Bedeutung des Begriffs 'pragmatisch' in den philosophischen Wissenschaften des ausgehenden 18. und des 19. Jahrhunderts." *Archiv für Begriffsgeschichte* 27: 158–86.

Kümmel, Werner Georg. 1958. *Das Neue Testament: Geschichte der Erforschung seiner Probleme*. Freiburg and Munich.

———. 1963; [21]1983. *Einleitung in das Neue Testament*. Heidelberg.

Kvalbein, Hans. 2014a. "Jesus as Preacher of the Kingdom of God." In *The Identity of Jesus: Nordic Voices*, edited by Samuel Byrskog, Tom Holmén, and Matti Kankaanniemi, 87–98. WUNT II 373. Tübingen.

———. 2014b. "The Lord's Prayer and the Eucharist Prayers in the Didache." In *Early Christian Prayer and Identity Formation*, edited by Reidar Hvalvik and Karl Olav Sandnes, 233–66. Tübingen.

Labahn, Michael. 1999. *Jesus als Lebensspender: Untersuchungen zu einer Geschichte der johanneischen Traditionanhand ihrer Wundergeschichten*. BZNW 98. Berlin.

———. 2008. "Das Reich Gottes und seine performativen Abbildungen: Gleichnisse, Parabeln und Bilder als Handlungsmodelle im Dokument Q." In *Hermeneutik der Gleichnisse Jesu: Methodische Neuansätze zum Verstehen urchristlicher Parabeltexte*, edited by Ruben Zimmermann, 259–82. WUNT 231. Tübingen.

———. 2010. *Der Gekommene als Wiederkommender: Die Logienquelle als erzählte Geschichte*. Arbeiten zur Bibel und ihrer Geschichte 32. Leipzig.

———. 2011. "The Non-Synoptic Jesus." In *Handbook for the Study of the Historical Jesus*, vol. 3, *The Historical Jesus*, edited by Tom Holmén and Stanley E. Porter, 1933–96. Leiden and Boston.

———. 2014. "Wunder verändern die Welt: Überlegungen zum sinnkonstruierenden Charakter von Wundererzählungen am Beispiel der sogenannten 'Geschenkwunder.'" In *Hermeneutik der frühchristlichen Wundererzählungen: Geschichtliche, literarische und rezeptionsorientierte Perspektiven*, edited by Bernd Kollmann and Ruben Zimmermann, 369–93. WUNT 339. Tübingen.

———. [2]2015. "Über die Notwendigkeit ungeteilter Leidenschaft (Vom Doppeldienst)—Q 16,13." In *Kompendium der Gleichnisse Jesu*, edited by Ruben Zimmermann et al., 220–26. Gütersloh.

———. 2019. "'Enthüllte' Wirklichkeit: Neutestamentliche Spielarten, wie Wahrheit und Glaube in der Erschließung und Wahrnehmung neuer Wirklichkeit zur Geltung gebracht werden." In *Wahrheit—Glaube—Deutung: Theologische und phil-*

osophische Konkretionen, edited by Christof Landmesser and Doris Hiller, 51–78. Veröffentlichungen der Rudolf-Bultmann-Gesellschaft für Hermeneutische Theologie e.V. Leipzig.

Lake, Kirsopp. 1907. *The Historical Evidence for the Resurrection of Jesus Christ*. London.

———. 1979. "The Twelve and the Apostles." In *The Beginnings of Christianity*, part 1, *The Acts of the Apostles* (1933), edited by Frederick John Foakes-Jackson and Kirsopp Lake, 37–59. Grand Rapids.

Lambrecht, Jan. 1995. "The Great Commandment Pericope and Q." In *The Gospel behind the Gospels: Current Studies on Q*, edited by Ronald A. Piper, 73–96. NovTSup 75. Leiden.

Lang, Bernhard. 2000. "The 'Our Father' as John the Baptist's Political Prayer." In *Shall Not the Judge of All the Earth Do What Is Right? Studies on the Nature of God in Tribute to James L. Crenshaw*, edited by David Penchansky and Paul L. Redditt, 239–53. Winona Lake, IN.

Lang, Manfred. 1999. *Johannes und die Synoptiker*. FRLANT 182. Göttingen.

Langslow, David R. 2000. *Medical Latin in the Roman Empire*. Oxford.

Lannert, Berthold. 1989. *Die Wiederentdeckung der neutestamentlichen Eschatologie durch Johannes Weiss*. Tübingen.

Lategan, Bernard C. 1984. "Reference: Reception, Redescription and Reality." In *Text and Reality*, by Bernard C. Lategan and Willem S. Vorster, 67–93. Philadelphia.

———. 2004. "History and Reality in the Interpretation of Biblical Texts." In *Konstruktion von Wirklichkeit: Beiträge aus geschichtstheoretischer, philosophischer und theologischer Perspektive*, edited by Jens Schröter and Antje Eddelbüttel, 135–52. Berlin and New York.

Lattke, Michael. 1984. "On the Jewish Background of the Concept 'Kingdom of God.'" In *The Kingdom of God in the Teaching of Jesus*, edited by Bruce Chilton, 72–91. IRT 5. London and Philadelphia.

Lau, Viktor. 1999. *Erzählen und Verstehen: Historische Perspektiven der Hermeneutik*. Würzburg.

Lauster, Jörg. 2004. *Prinzip und Methode: Die Transformation des protestantischen Schrift- prinzips durch die historisch-kritische Methode von Schleiermacher bis zur Gegenwart*. HUT 46. Tübingen.

LeDonne, Anthony. 2013. *The Wife of Jesus: Ancient Texts and Modern Scandals*. New York.

LeFebvre, Michael. 2006. *Collections, Codes, and Torah: The Re-characterization of Israel's Written Law*. OTS 451. New York.

Leibner, Uzi. 2009. *Settlement and History in Hellenistic, Roman, and Byzantine Galilee: An Archaeological Survey of the Eastern Galilee*. TSAJ 127. Tübingen.

Leonhard, Clemens. 2002. "Vaterunser II: Judentum." In *TRE* 34:512–15.

———. 2006. *The Jewish Pascha and the Origins of the Christian Easter: Open Questions in Current Research*. SJ 35. Berlin and New York.

Leppin, Hartmut. 2013. "Imperial Miracles and Elitist Discourses." In *Miracles Revisited: New Testament Miracle Stories and Their Concepts of Reality*, edited by Stefan Alkier and Annette Weissenrieder, 233–49. Studies on the Bible and Its Reception. Berlin.

Lessing, Gotthold Ephraim. 1784. "Neue Hypothese über die Evangelisten als bloss menschliche Geschichtsschreiber betrachtet" (1778). In *Theologischer Nachlass*, by Gotthold Ephraim Lessing, 45–72. Berlin.

Lethipuu, Outi. 2015. *Debates over the Resurrection of the Dead: Constructing Early Christian Identity*. Oxford.

Leutzsch, Martin. 2013. "Karl Heinrich Venturinis Natürliche Geschichte des großen Propheten von Nazareth (1800/02): Der einflussreichste Jesusroman bis heute." In *Der historische Roman zwischen Kunst, Ideologie und Wissenschaft*, edited by Ina Ulrike Paul and Richard Faber, 445–63. Würzburg.

Levine, Amy-Jill. 1994. "Second-Temple Judaism, Jesus and Women: Yeast of Eden." *BibInt* 2: 8–33.

———. 2012. "Das Matthäusevangelium: Zwischen Bruch und Kontinuität." In *Die Bibel und die Frauen: Eine exegetisch-kulturgeschichtliche Enzyklopädie*, vol. 2.1, *Neues Testament: Evangelien; Erzählungen und Geschichte*, edited by Mercedes Navarro Puerto and Imtraud Fischer, 118–39. Stuttgart.

———. 2014. *Short Stories by Jesus: The Enigmatic Parables of a Controversial Rabbi*. New York.

Levine, Lee I. 1999. "Second Temple Jerusalem: A Jewish City in the Greco-Roman Orbit." In *Jerusalem: Its Sanctity and Centrality to Judaism, Christianity, and Islam*, edited by Lee I. Levine 53–68. New York.

———. 2002. *Jerusalem: Portrait of a City in the Second Temple Period (538 B.C.E.–70 C.E.)*. Philadelphia.

———. 2004. "The First Century Synagogue: Critical Reassessments and Assessments of the Critical." In *Religion and Society in Roman Palestine: Old Questions, New Approaches*, edited by Douglas R. Edwards, 70–102. New York.

Lichtenberger, Achim. 2013. "Anker, Füllhorn, Palmzweig: Motivbeziehungen zwischen 'jüdischen' und 'paganen' Münzen." In *Macht des Geldes—Macht der Bilder: Kolloquium zur Ikonographie auf Münzen im ostmediterranen Raum in hellenistisch-römischer Zeit*, edited by Anne Lykke, 69–91. ADPV 42. Wiesbaden.

Lieberman, Saul. 1942. *Greek in Jewish Palestine: Studies in the Life and Manners of Jewish Palestine in the II–IV Centuries C.E.* New York.

———. 1962. *Hellenism in Jewish Palestine: Studies in the Literary Transmission, Beliefs, and Manners of Palestine in the I Century B.C.E.–IV Century C.E.* New York.

Lietzmann, Hans. 1958. "Der Prozeß Jesu." In *Kleine Schriften. II: Studien zum Neuen Testament*, 251–63. TU 68. Berlin.

Liew, Tat-siong Benny. 2003. "Re-Mark-able Masculinities: Jesus, the Son of Man, and the (Sad) Sum of Manhood?" In *New Testament Masculinities*, edited by S. D. Moore and J. C. Anderson, 93–135. Society of Biblical Literature Semeia Studies. Atlanta.

Lincoln, Andrew T. 2013. *Born of a Virgin? Reconceiving Jesus in Bible, Tradition, and Theology*. London.

Lindars, Barnabas. 1983. *Jesus Son of Man: A Fresh Examination of the Son of Man Sayings in the Gospels in the Light of Recent Research*. London.

Lindemann, Andreas. 1993. "Samaria und Samaritaner im Neuen Testament." *WD* 22: 51–76.

Link, Hans-Georg. 1975. *Geschichte Jesu und Bild Christi: Die Entwicklung der Christologie Martin Kählers in Auseinandersetzung mit der Leben-Jesu-Theologie und der Ritschl- Schule*. Neukirchen-Vluyn.

Lips, Hermann von. 1990. *Weisheitliche Traditionen im Neuen Testament*. WMANT 64. Neukirchen-Vluyn.

Litt, Stefan. 2009. *Geschichte der Juden Mitteleuropas 1500–1800, Geschichte kompakt*. Darmstadt.

Loader, William. 2002. *Jesus' Attitude towards the Law*. WUNT II 97. Tübingen (1997) and Grand Rapids.

———. 2011. "Jesus and the Law." In *Handbook for the Study of the Historical Jesus*, vol. 3, *The Historical Jesus*, edited by Tom Holmén and Stanley E. Porter, 2745–72. Leiden.

Loftus, Francis. 1977–1978. "The Anti-Roman Revolts of the Jews and the Galileans." *JQR* 68: 78–98.

Lohfink, Gerhard. ²2013. *Das Vaterunser neu ausgelegt*. Stuttgart.

Lohmeyer, Ernst. 1936. *Galiläa und Jerusalem*. FRLANT 52. Göttingen.

———. ⁵1962. *Das Vater-Unser*. Göttingen.

Löhr, Hermut. 2008. "Das Abendmahl als Pesach-Mahl: Überlegungen aus exegetischer Sicht aufgrund der synoptischen Tradition und des frühjüdischen Quellenbefunds." *BTZ* 25: 99–116.

———. 2009. "Formen und Traditionen des Gebets bei Paulus." In *Das Gebet im Neuen Testament: Vierte europäische orthodoxwestliche Exegetenkonferenz in Sâmbăta de Sus. 4.–8. August 2007*, edited by Hans Klein, Vasile Mihoc, and Karl-Wilhelm Niebuhr, 115–32. WUNT 249 Tübingen.

———. 2012. "Entstehung und Bedeutung des Abendmahls im frühesten Christentum." In *Abendmahl*, edited by Hermut Löhr, 51–94. TdT 3. Tübingen.

Lohse, Eduard. 2009. *Vater unser: Das Gebet der Christen*. Darmstadt.

Longenecker, Richard N. 2005. "Christological Materials in the Early Christian Communities." In *Contours of Christology in the New Testament*, by Richard N. Longenecker, 47–76. MMNTS 7. Grand Rapids.

Lüdemann, Gerd. 1994. *Die Auferstehung Jesu: Historie, Erfahrung, Theologie*. Göttingen.

————. 2002. *Die Auferweckung Jesu von den Toten: Ursprung und Geschichte einer Selbsttäuschung.* Lüneburg.

Lührmann, Dieter. 1972. "Liebet eure Feinde." *ZTK* 69: 412–38.

————. 1987. *Das Markusevangelium.* HNT 3. Tübingen.

————. 2000. *Fragmente apokryph gewordener Evangelien in griechischer und lateinischer Sprache.* MThSt 59. Marburg.

Lundström, Gösta. 1963. *The Kingdom of God in the Teaching of Jesus.* Richmond, VA.

Lupieri, Edmondo. 1988. *Giovanni Battista fra storia e leggenda.* Brescia.

Luz, Ulrich. 1971. "Die Jünger im Matthäusevangelium." *ZNW* 62: 141–71.

————. 1985. *Das Evangelium nach Matthäus (Mt 1–7).* EKKNT I/1. Zürich.

————. 1990; ³1999. *Das Evangelium nach Matthäus (Mt 8–17).* EKKNT I/2. Zürich.

————. 1997. *Das Evangelium nach Matthäus (Mt 18–25).* EKKNT I/3. Zürich.

————. 2002a. *Das Evangelium nach Matthäus (Mt 26–28).* EKKNT I/4. Zürich.

————. 2002b. "Vaterunser I. Neues Testament." In *TRE* 34:504–12.

Luzarraga, Jesús. 2008. *El "Padrenuestro" desde el arameo.* Rome.

Lykke, Anne, ed. 2013a. *Macht des Geldes—Macht der Bilder: Kolloquium zur Ikonographie auf Münzen im ostmediterranen Raum in hellenistisch-römischer Zeit.* ADPV 42. Wiesbaden.

————. 2013b. "Die Münzikonographie von Herodes Agrippa I. und ihre Beziehung zur römischen Bildsprache." In *Macht des Geldes—Macht der Bilder: Kolloquium zur Ikonographie auf Münzen im ostmediterranen Raum in hellenistisch-römischer Zeit,* edited by Anne Lykke, 151–69. ADPV 42. Wiesbaden.

Mack, Burton L. 1988. *A Myth of Innocence: Mark and Christian Origins.* Philadelphia.

Madden, Patrick J. 1997. *Jesus' Walking on the Sea: An Investigation of the Origin of the Narrative Account.* BZNW 81. Berlin and New York.

Magen, Yitzhak. 2007. "The Dating of the First Phase of the Samaritan Temple on Mount Gerizim in Light of the Archaeological Evidence." In *Judah and the Judeans in the Fourth Century B.C.E.,* edited by Oded Lipshits, Gary N. Knoppers, and Rainer Albertz, 157–212. Winona Lake, IN.

Magness, Jodi. 2011. *Stone and Dung, Oil and Spit: Jewish Daily Life in the Time of Jesus.* Grand Rapids and Cambridge.

Maier, Johann. 2013. "Torah und Normen systeme in den Qumranschriften." In *Kein Jota wird vergehen: Das Gesetzesverständnis der Logienquelle vor dem Hintergrund frühjüdischer Theologie,* edited by Markus Tiwald, 35–59. BWANT 200. Stuttgart.

Mainville, Odette. 2001. *Résurrection: L'après-mort dans le monde ancien et le Noveau testament.* Geneva.

Malbon, Elizabeth Struthers. 2000. *In the Company of Jesus: Characters in Mark's Gospel.* Louisville.

Malina, Bruce J. 1999. "Assessing the Historicity of Jesus' Walking on the Sea: Insights from Cross-Cultural Social-Psychology." In *Authenticating the Activities of Jesus,* edited by Bruce Chilton and Craig A. Evans, 351–71. Leiden.

———. 2001. *The Social Gospel of Jesus: The Kingdom of God in Mediterranean Perspective*. Minneapolis.

———. 2011. "Social-Scientific Approaches in Jesus Research." In *Handbook for the Study of the Historical Jesus*, vol. 1, *How to Study the Historical Jesus*, edited by Tom Holmén and Stanley E. Porter, 743–75. Leiden.

Manson, Thomas Walter. 1967. *The Teaching of Jesus: Studies in Its Form and Content*. Cambridge.

Mara bar Sarapion. 2014. *Letter to His Son*. Edited and translated by Annette Merz, David Rensberger, and Teun Tieleman. Tübingen.

Markschies, Christoph. 2002. "Valentinian." In *TRE* 34:495–500.

Markschies, Christoph, and Jens Schröter, eds. 2012. *Antike christliche Apokryphen in deutscher Übersetzung*. Vol. 1, *Evangelien und Verwandtes (Teilband 1 & Teilband 2)*. Tübingen.

Marshall, Ian Howard. 1978. *The Gospel of Luke: A Commentary on the Greek Text*. NIGTC 3. Grand Rapids.

———. 2009. "The Last Supper." In *Key Events in the Life of the Historical Jesus: A Collaborative Exploration of Context and Coherence*, edited by Darrell L. Bock and Robert Webb, 481–588. WUNT 247. Tübingen.

Marshall, Mary J. 2005. "Jesus: Glutton and Drunkard?" *JSHJ* 3: 47–60.

Martin, Dale B. 2006. *Sex and the Single Savior: Gender and Sexuality in Biblical Interpretation*. Louisville.

———. 2014. "Jesus in Jerusalem: Armed and Not Dangerous." *JSNT* 37: 3–24.

Martyn, James Louis. 1968; ²1979. *History and Theology in the Fourth Gospel*. Nashville.

Marx, Karl, and Friedrich Engels. 1844. "Zur Kritik der Hegelschen Rechts-Philosophie." *Deutsch-Französische Jahrbücher* 1, 7–10 (February 1844): 71–85.

Marxsen, Willi. ²1959. *Der Evangelist Markus: Studien zur Redaktionsgeschichte des Evangeliums*. FRLANT 67, n.s., 49. Göttingen.

McIver, Robert K. 2011. *Memory, Jesus, and the Synoptic Gospels*. SBL Resources for Biblical Study. Atlanta.

McKnight, Scot. 2005. *Jesus and His Death: Historiography, the Historical Jesus, and Atonement Theory*. Waco, TX.

McVey, Kathleen E. 1990. "A Fresh Look at the Letter of Mara bar Serapion to His Son, V Symposium Syriacum." *OCA* 236: 257–72.

Meier, John P. 1991. *A Marginal Jew: Rethinking the Historical Jesus*. Vol. 1, *The Roots of the Problem and the Person*. New York.

———. 1994. *A Marginal Jew: Rethinking the Historical Jesus*. Vol. 2, *Mentor, Message, and Miracles*. New York.

———. 2001. *A Marginal Jew: Rethinking the Historical Jesus*. Vol. 3, *Companions and Competitors*. New York.

———. 2009. *A Marginal Jew: Rethinking the Historical Jesus.* Vol. 4, *Law and Love.* New Haven and London.

———. 2016. *A Marginal Jew: Rethinking the Historical Jesus.* Vol. 5, *Probing the Authenticity of the Parables.* New Haven.

Meinecke, Friedrich. 1936; [4]1965. *Die Entstehung des Historismus.* Edited and with an introduction by Carl Hinrichs. *Friedrich-Meinecke-Werke,* vol. 3. Munich.

Meiser, Martin. 1998. *Die Reaktion des Volkes auf Jesus: Eine redaktionskritische Untersuchung zu den synoptischen Evangelien.* BZNW 96. Berlin and New York.

Meisinger, Hubert. 1996. *Liebesgebot und Altruismusforschung: Ein exegetischer Beitrag zum Dialog zwischen Theologie und Naturwissenschaft.* NTOA 33. Freiburg (CH) and Göttingen.

Melzer-Keller, Helga. 1997. *Jesus und die Frauen.* Freiburg.

Merkel, Helmut. 1971. *Die Widersprüche zwischen den Evangelien: Ihre polemische und apologetische Behandlung bis Augustin.* WUNT 13. Tübingen.

Merklein, Helmut. [3]1984. *Die Gottesherrschaft als Handlungsprinzip: Untersuchung zur Ethik Jesu.* FB 34. Würzburg.

Merz, Annette. 2001. "Mammon als schärfster Konkurrent Gottes—Jesu Vision vom Reich Gottes und das Geld." In *Gott oder Mammon: Christliche Ethik und die Religion des Geldes,* edited by Severin J. Lederhilger, 34–90. Linzer philosophisch-theologische Beiträge 3. Frankfurt.

Meshorer, Ya'aqov. 2001. *A Treasury of Jewish Coins: From the Persian Period to Bar Kokhba.* Jerusalem and New York.

Metternich, Ulrike. 2000. *Sie sagte ihm die ganze Wahrheit: Die Erzählung von der "Blutflüssigen"—feministisch gedeutet.* Mainz.

Metzger, Franziska. 2011. *Geschichtsschreibung und Geschichtsdenken im 19. und 20. Jahrhundert.* UTB 3555. Bern, Stuttgart, and Vienna.

Metzner, Rainer. 1995. *Die Rezeption des Matthäusevangeliums im 1. Petrusbrief: Studien zum traditionsgeschichtlichen und theologischen Einfluss des 1. Evangeliums auf den 1. Petrusbrief.* Tübingen.

Meye, Robert P. 1968. *Jesus and the Twelve: Discipleship and Revelation in Mark's Gospel.* Grand Rapids.

Meyer, Ben. 1979. *The Aims of Jesus.* London.

Meyers, Eric M., ed. 1999. *Galilee through the Centuries.* Confluence of Cultures. Winona Lake, IN.

Meyers, Eric M., and Carol Meyers. 2013. "Sepphoris." In *The Oxford Encyclopedia of the Bible and Archaeology,* edited by Daniel M. Master et al., 2:336–48. Oxford.

Michaelis, Johann David. 1750; [4]1788. *Einleitung in die göttlichen Schriften des neuen Bundes.* Göttingen.

Miethke, Jürgen. 1999. "Paradiesischer Zustand—Apostolisches Zeitalter— Franziskanische Armut: Religiöses Selbstverständnis, Zeitkritik und Gesellschaftstheorie im 14. Jahrhundert." In *Vita Religiosa im Mittelalter, FS Kasper Elm*, edited by Franz J. Felten and Nikolas Jaspert, 503–32. Berlin.

———. 2000. *De potestate Papae*. SuR, n.s., 16. Tübingen.

Milavec, Aaron. 2003. *The Didache: Faith, Hope, and Life of the Earliest Christian Communities, 50–70 C.E.* New York.

Millard, Alan. 2000. *Reading and Writing in the Time of Jesus*. Sheffield.

Miller, Shulamit. 2013. "Tiberias." In *The Oxford Encyclopedia of the Bible and Archaeology*, edited by M. Daniel et al., 2:429–37. Oxford.

Minear, Paul S. 1972. "Audience Criticism and Marcan Ecclesiology." In *Neues Testament und Geschichte: Historisches Geschehen und Deutung im Neuen Testament, FS Oscar Cullmann*, edited by Bo Reicke and Heinrich Baltensweiler, 79–90. Zürich and Tübingen.

———. 1974a. "Jesus' Audiences, according to Luke." *NovT* 16: 81–109.

———. 1974b. "The Disciples and the Crowds in the Gospel of Matthew." ATR Supplement Series 3, 28–44.

———. 2004. "When Jesus Saw the Crowds." *ExpTim* 116: 73–78.

Minns, Denis, and Paul Parvis, eds. 2009. *Justin, Philosopher and Martyr: Apologies*. Edited with an introduction, translation, and commentary on the text. OECT. Oxford.

Modica, Joseph B. 2008. "Jesus as Glutton and Drunkard: The 'Excesses' of Jesus." In *Who Do My Opponents Say That I Am? An Investigation of the Accusations against the Historical Jesus*, edited by Scot McKnight and Joseph B. Modica, 50–73. London.

Momigliano, Arnaldo. 1986. "The Disadvantages of Monotheism for a Universal State." *CP* 81: 285–97.

Mommsen, Theodor. 1899. *Römisches Strafrecht*. Leipzig.

Montefiore, Claude G. ²1927. *The Synoptic Gospels*. London.

Morag, Shlomo. 1972. "Εφφαθά (Mark VII. 34): Certainly Hebrew, Not Aramaic?" *JSS* 17: 198–202.

Morgan, Robert. 1989. "From Reimarus to Sanders: The Kingdom of God, Jesus, and the Judaisms of His Day." In *The Kingdom of God and Human Society*, edited by Robin Barbour, 80–139. Edinburgh.

Moss, Candida R., and Jeremy Schipper. 2011. *Disability Studies and Biblical Literature*. New York.

Moxnes, Halvor. 2003. *Putting Jesus in His Place: A Radical Vision of Household and Kingdom*. Louisville.

———. 2012. *Jesus and the Rise of Nationalism: A New Quest for the Nineteenth-Century Historical Jesus*. London.

Mühlenberg, Ekkehard. 2006. *Altchristliche Lebensführung zwischen Bibel und Tugendlehre: Ethik bei den griechischen Philosophen und den frühen Christen*. AAWGPH 3.272. Göttingen.

Müller, Karlheinz. 1988. "Möglichkeit und Vollzug jüdischer Kapitalgerichtsbarkeit im Prozeß gegen Jesus von Nazaret." In *Der Prozeß gegen Jesus: Historische Rück-frage und theologische Deutung,* edited by Karl Kertelge, 41–83. QD 112. Freiburg.

———. 1999: "Gibt es ein Judentum hinter den Juden? Ein Nachtrag zu Ed Parish Sanders' Theorie vom 'Covenantal Nomism.'" In *Das Urchristentum in seiner literarischen Geschichte, FS Jürgen Becker,* edited by Ulrich Mell and Ulrich B. Müller, 473–86. BZNW 100. Berlin.

———. 2003. "Das Vaterunser als jüdisches Gebet." In *Identität durch Gebet: Zur gemeinschaftsbildenden Funktion institutionalisierten Betens in Judentum und Christentum,* edited by Albert Gerhards, Andrea Doeker, and Peter Ebenbauer, 159–204. Studien zu Judentum und Christentum. Paderborn.

Müller, Peter, et al., eds. ²2008. *Die Gleichnisse Jesu: Ein Studien- und Arbeitsbuch für den Unterricht.* Stuttgart.

Müller, Ulrich B. 1977. "Vision und Botschaft: Erwägungen zur prophetischen Struktur der Verkündigung Jesu." *ZTK* 74: 416–48.

———. 1998. *Die Entstehung des Glaubens an die Auferstehung Jesu: Historische Aspekte und Bedingungen.* SBS 172. Stuttgart.

———. 2002. *Johannes der Täufer: Jüdischer Prophet und Wegbereiter Jesu.* Biblische Gestalten 6. Leipzig.

Münch, Christian. 2004. *Die Gleichnisse Jesu im Matthäusevangelium: Eine Studie zu ihrer Form und Funktion.* WMANT 104. Neukirchen-Vluyn.

Myllykoski, Matti. 2002. "What Happened to the Body of Jesus?" In *Fair Play: Diversity and Conflicts in Early Christianity; Essays in Honour of Heikki Räisänen,* edited by Ismo Dunderberg, Christopher Tuckett, and Kari Syreeni, 43–82. Leiden, Boston, and Cologne.

Naveh, Joseph. 1998. "Fragments of an Aramaic Magic Book from Qumran." *IEJ* 48: 252–61.

Neander, August. 1837. *Das Leben Jesu Christi in seinem geschichtlichen Zusammenhange und seiner geschichtlichen Entwicklung.* Hamburg.

Neirynck, Frans. 1977. "John and the Synoptics." In *L'Évangile de Jean,* edited by Marinus de Jonge, 73–106. BETL 44. Leuven.

———. 1979. "The Miracle Stories in the Acts of the Apostles: An Introduction." In *Les Actes des Apôtres: Tradition, Rédaction, Théologie,* edited by Jacob Kremer, 169–213. BETL 28. Leuven.

———. 1991. "Luke 14,1–6: Lukan Composition and Q Saying." In *Der Treue Gottes trauen: Beiträge zum Werk des Lukas; Für Gerhard Schneider,* edited by Claus Bussmann and Walter Radl, 243–63. Freiburg.

Neufeld, Vernon H. 1963. *The Earliest Christian Confessions.* NTTS 5. Leiden.

Neugebauer, Fritz. 2008. *Das Vaterunser: Eine theologische Deutung.* Leipzig.

Neusner, Jacob. 1988. *The Mishnah: A New Translation.* New Haven.

———. 2006. "The Parable ('Mashal')." In *Ancient Israel, Judaism, and Christianity in Contemporary Perspective: FS Karl-Johan Illman*, edited by Jacob Neusner, 259–83. Lanham, MD.

Nicklas, Tobias. 2011. "Traditions about Jesus in Apocryphal Gospels (with the Exception of the Gospel of Thomas)." In *Handbook for the Study of the Historical Jesus*, vol. 3, *The Historical Jesus*, edited by Tom Holmén and Stanley E. Porter, 2081–2118. Leiden.

———. 2014. *Jews and Christians? Second Century "Christian" Perspectives on the "Parting of the Ways."* Tübingen.

Nicolaus, Georg. 2005. *Die pragmatische Theologie des Vaterunsers und ihre Rekonstruktion durch Martin Luther.* Leipzig.

Niebuhr, Karl-Wilhelm. 1987. *Gesetz und Paränese: Katechismusartige Weisungsreihen in der frühjüdischen Literatur.* WUNT II 28. Tübingen.

———. 1998. "Der Jakobusbrief im Licht frühjüdischer Diasporabriefe." *NTS* 44: 420–43.

Niederwimmer, Kurt. 1989. *Die Didache.* KAV 1. Göttingen.

———. 1998. "Zur Entwicklungsgeschichte des Wanderradikalismus im Traditionsbereich der Didache." In *Quaestiones theologicae: Gesammlte Aufsätze*, edited by Wilhelm Pratscher and Markus Öhler. BZNW 90. Berlin and New York.

Nissen, Andreas. 1974. *Gott und der Nächste im antiken Judentum: Untersuchungen zum Doppelgebot der Liebe.* WUNT 15. Tübingen.

Noack, Bengt. 1954. *Zur johanneischen Tradition.* Copenhagen.

Noam, Vered. 2005. "Divorce in Qumran in Light of Early Halakhah." *JJS* 41: 206–23.

———. 2006. "Traces of Sectarian Halakhah in the Rabbinic World." In *Rabbinic Perspectives: Rabbinic Literature and the Dead Sea Scrolls; Proceedings of the Eighth International Symposium of the Orion Center for the Study of the Dead Sea Scrolls and Associated Literature, 7–9 January 2003*, edited by Steven D. Fraade et al., 67–85. STDJ 62. Leiden.

———. 2009. "Stringency in Qumran: A Reassessment." *JSJ* 40: 342–55.

Notley, Steven, and Ze'ev Safrai. 2011. *Parables of the Sages: Jewish Wisdom from Jesus to Rav Ashi.* Jerusalem.

Oakman, Douglas E. 1986. *Jesus and the Economic Questions of His Day.* SBEC 8. Lewiston, NY.

———. 2012. *The Political Aims of Jesus.* Minneapolis.

Oexle, Otto Gerhard. 1996. *Geschichtswissenschaft im Zeichen des Historismus.* Göttingen.

———. 1997. "Aufklärung und Historismus: Zur Geschichtswissenschaft in Göttingen um 1800." In *Johann Dominicus Fiorillo: Kunstgeschichte und die romantische Bewegung um 1800, Akten des Kolloquiums "Johann Dominicus Fiorillo und die Anfänge der Kunstgeschichte in Göttingen" am Kunstgeschichtlichen Seminar und der Kunstsammlung der Universität Göttingen vom 11.–13.11.1994*, edited by Antje Middeldorf Kosegarten, 28–56.

Öhler, Markus. 1997. *Elia im Neuen Testament: Untersuchungen zur Bedeutung des alttestamentlichen Propheten im frühen Christentum.* BZNW 88. Berlin.

Ohst, Martin. 2010. "Luthers 'Schrift prinzip.'" In *Luther als Schriftausleger*, edited by Hans Christian Knuth, 21–39. LASR 7. Erlangen.

————. 2012. "Gottes Nähe und Gottes Ferne in der Theologie Martin Luthers." In *Medialität, Unmittelbarkeit, Präsenz*, edited by Johanna Haberer and Berndt Hamm, 359–76. SMHR 70. Tübingen.

————. 2014. "Urheber und Zielbild wahren Menschseins: Jesus Christus in der Kirchengeschichte." In *Jesus Christus*, edited by Jens Schröter, 119–79. TdT 9. Tübingen.

O'Loughlin, Thomas. 2010. *The Didache: A Window on the Earliest Christians.* London.

Olson, Ken. 2013. "A Eusebian Reading of the Testimonium Flavianum." In *Eusebius of Caesarea: Tradition and Innovations*, edited by Aaron P. Johnson and Jeremy M. Schott, 97–114. Hellenic Studies Series 60. Washington, DC.

Osborn, Eric. 1976. *Ethical Patterns in Early Christian Thought.* Cambridge.

Osiek, Carolyn. 2009. "When You Pray, Go into Your ταμεῖον (Matthew 6:6)." *CBQ* 71: 723–40.

Osterhammel, Jürgen. ⁵2010. *Die Verwandlung der Welt: Eine Geschichte des 19. Jahrhunderts.* Munich.

Ostermann, Siegfried. 2009. "Lepton, Quadrans und Denar: Drei Münzen im Jerusalemer Tempel zur Zeit Jesu." In *Jerusalem und die Länder: Ikonographie—Topographie—Theologie*, edited by Gerd Theissen et al., 39–56. NTOA 70. Göttingen.

Osthövener, Claus-Dieter. 2004. *Erlösung: Transformationen einer Idee im 19. Jahrhundert.* BHT 128 Tübingen.

Ostmeyer, Karl-Heinrich. 2002. "Das immerwährende Gebet bei Paulus." *TBei* 33: 274–89.

————. 2003. "Die identitätsstiftende Funktion der Gebetsterminologie im Johannesevangelium." In *Identität durch Gebet: Zur gemeinschaftsbildenden Funktion institutionalisierten Betens in Judentum und Christentum, Studien zu Judentum und Christentum*, edited by Albert Gerhards, Andrea Doeker, and Peter Ebenbauer, 205–22. Paderborn.

————. 2004a. "Das Vaterunser: Gründe für seine Durchsetzung als 'Urgebet' der Christenheit." *NTS* 50: 320–36.

————. 2004b. "Jesu Annahme der Kinder in Mt 19,13–15." *NovT* 46: 1–11.

————. 2005. "Armenhaus und Räuberhöhle? Galiläa zur Zeit Jesu." *ZNW* 96: 147–70.

————. 2006. *Kommunikation mit Gott und Christus: Sprache und Theologie des Gebetes im Neuen Testament.* WUNT 197. Tübingen.

————. 2009. "Prayer as Demarcation: The Function of Prayer in the Gospel of John."

In *Das Gebet im Neuen Testament: Vierte europäische orthodox-westliche Exegetenkonferenz in Sâmbăta de Sus. 4.–8. August 2007*, edited by Hans Klein, Vasile Mihoc, and Karl-Wilhelm Niebuhr, 233–47. WUNT 249. Tübingen.

Overbeck, Bernhard. 1993. *Das Heilige Land: Antike Münzen und Siegel aus einem Jahrtausend jüdischer Geschichte.* Munich.

Paesler, Kurt. 1999. *Das Tempelwort Jesu: Die Tradition von Tempelzerstörung und Tempelerneuerung im Neuen Testament.* FRLANT 184. Göttingen.

Parker, Pierson. 1962. "John the Son of Zebedee and the Fourth Gospel." *JBL* 81: 35–43.

Patrich, Joseph. 2009. "538 BCE–70 CE: The Temple (Beyt Ha-Miqdash) and Its Mount." In *Where Heaven and Earth Meet: Jerusalem's Sacred Esplanade*, edited by Oleg Grabar and Benjamin Z. Kedar, 36–71. Jerusalem and Austin, TX.

Patrick, Dale. 1987. "The Kingdom of God in the Old Testament." In *The Kingdom of God in 20th-Century Interpretation*, edited by Wendall Willis, 67–79. Peabody, MA.

Patterson, Stephen J. 1990. *The Gospel of Thomas and Jesus: Retrospectus and Prospectus. SBLSP* 29: 614–36.

———. 1993. *The Gospel of Thomas and Jesus.* Sonoma, CA.

Paulus, Heinrich Eberhard Gottlob. 1800–1802. *Philologisch-kritischer und historischer Kommentar über die drey ersten Evangelien.* 3 vols. Lübeck.

———. 1828. *Das Leben Jesu, als Grundlage einer reinen Geschichte des Urchristentums.* 2 vols. Heidelberg.

———. 1830–1833. *Exegetisches Handbuch über die drei ersten Evangelien.* 3 Theile (parts 1 and 2 each in two vols.). Heidelberg.

Pellegrini, Silvia. 2012. "Frauen ohne Namen in den kanonischen Evangelien." In *Die Bibel und die Frauen: Eine exegetisch-kulturgeschichtliche Enzyklopädie*, vol. 2.1, *Neues Testament: Evangelien; Erzählungen und Geschichte*, edited by Mercedes Navarro Puerto and Irmtraud Fischer, 383–421. Stuttgart.

Perrin, Norman. 1963. *The Kingdom of God in the Teaching of Jesus.* London.

———. 1966. "The Wredestrasse Becomes the Hauptstrasse: Reflections on the Reprinting of the Dodd Festschrift; A Review Article." *JR* 46 (2): 296–300.

———. 1967. *Rediscovering the Teaching of Jesus.* London.

———. 1971. "The Christology of Mark: A Study in Methodology." *JR* 51 (3): 173–87.

———. 1972. "The Evangelist as Author: Reflections on Method in the Study and Interpretation of the Synoptic Gospels and Acts." *BR* 17: 5–18.

———. 1976a. *Jesus and the Language of the Kingdom.* London and Philadelphia.

———. 1976b. "The Interpretation of the Gospel of Mark." *Int* 30 (2): 115–24.

Pesch, Rudolf. 1973. "Zur Entstehung des Glaubens an die Auferstehung Jesu." *TQ* 153: 201–28.

———. 1977. *Das Markusevangelium, Kommentar zu Kap. 8,27–16,20.* HThKNT II/2. Freiburg.

Petersen, Silke. 1999. *"Zerstört die Werke der Weiblichkeit!" Maria Magdalena, Salome und andere Jüngerinnen Jesu in christlich-gnostischen Schriften.* NHMS 48. Leiden.

———. 2011. *Maria aus Magdala: Die Jüngerin, die Jesus liebte.* Biblische Gestalten 23. Leipzig.

Pfannmüller, Gustav. [2]1939. *Jesus im Urteil der Jahrhunderte.* Berlin.

Phillips, Victoria. 2000. "Full Disclosure: Towards a Complete Characterization of the Women Who Followed Jesus in the Gospel according to Mark." In *Transformative Encounters: Jesus and Women Re-Viewed,* edited by Ingrid Rosa Kitzberger, 13–32. BibInt 43. Leiden.

Phillips, Thomas E. 2008. "'Will the Wise Person Get Drunk?' The Background of the Human Wisdom in Luke 7:35 and Matthew 11:19." *JBL* 127: 385–96.

Philonenko, Marc. 2002. *Das Vaterunser: Vom Gebet Jesu zum Gebet der Jünger.* UTB 2312. Tübingen.

Pilch, John J. 2000. *Healing in the New Testament: Insights from Medical and Mediterranean Anthropology.* Minneapolis.

———. 2002. "Ereignisse eines veränderten Bewusstseinzustandes bei den Synoptikern." In *Jesus in neuen Kontexten,* edited by Wolfgang Stegemann, Bruce J. Malina, and Gerd Theissen, 33–42. Stuttgart.

Piper, Ronald A. 1989. *Wisdom in the Q-Tradition: The Aphoristic Teaching of Jesus.* SNTSMS 61. Cambridge.

Pitre, Brant. 2009. "Jesus, the Messianic Banquet, and the Kingdom of God." *Letter and Spirit* 5: 133–62.

———. 2015. *Jesus and the Last Supper.* Grand Rapids and Cambridge.

Poeschke, Joachim. 2009. *Mosaiken in Italien 300–1300.* Munich.

Poirier, John C. 1996. "Why Did the Pharisees Wash Their Hands?" *JJS* 47: 217–33.

———. 2003. "Purity beyond the Temple in the Second Temple Era." *JBL* 122: 247–65.

Pokorný, Petr. 2009. "Demoniac and Drunkard: John the Baptist and Jesus according to Q 7:33–34." In *Jesus Research: An International Perspective,* edited by James H. Charlesworth and Petr Pokorný, 170–81. Princeton-Prague Symposia Series on the Historical Jesus 1. Grand Rapids and Cambridge.

Pokorný, Petr, and Ulrich Heckel. 2007. *Einleitung in das Neue Testament: Seine Literatur und Theologie im Überblick.* UTB 2798. Tübingen.

Poorthuis, Marcel. 2013. *Awinu—das Vaterunser: Über die jüdischen Hintergründe des Vaterunsers.* Uelzen, Germany.

Popkes, Enno E. [2]2015. "Das Licht in den Bildern—EvThom 83." In *Kompendium der Gleichnisse Jesu,* edited by Ruben Zimmermann et al., 909–15. Gütersloh.

Popkes, Wiard. 1986. *Adressaten, Situation und Form des Jakobusbriefes.* Stuttgart.

Poplutz, Uta. 2006. "Paroimia und Parabole: Gleichniskonzepte bei Johannes und Markus." In *Imagery in the Gospel of John: Terms, Forms, Themes, and Theology of*

Johannine Figurative Language, edited by Jörg Frey, J. G. van der Watt, and Ruben Zimmermann, 103–20. WUNT 200. Tübingen.

———. 2008. *Erzählte Welt: Narratologische Studien zum Matthäusevangelium*. BThS 100. Neukirchen-Vluyn.

———. 2013. "Dämonen—Besessenheit—Austreibungsrituale." In *Kompendium der frühchristlichen Wundererzählungen*, vol. 1, *Die Wunder Jesu*, edited by Ruben Zimmermann et al., 94–107. Gütersloh.

Porat, Roi, Rachel Chachy, and Yakov Kalman. 2015. *Herodium: Final Reports of the 1972–2010 Excavations Directed by Ehud Netzer. Vol. 1, Herod's Tomb Precinct, Jerusalem*. Jerusalem.

Porter, Stanley E. 1993. "Did Jesus Ever Teach in Greek?" *TynBul* 44: 199–235.

———. 2000. *The Criteria for Authenticity in Historical-Jesus Research: Previous Discussion and New Proposals*. JSNTSup 191. Sheffield.

———. 2011. "The Language(s) Jesus Spoke." In *Handbook for the Study of the Historical Jesus*, vol. 3, *The Historical Jesus*, edited by Tom Holmén and Stanley E. Porter, 2455–71. Leiden.

Preuss, Hans. 1915. *Das Bild Christi im Wandel der Zeiten*. Leipzig.

Price, Jonathan J. 2011. "The Jewish Population of Jerusalem from the First Century B.C.E. to the Early Second Century C.E.: The Epigraphic Record." In *The Jewish Revolt against Rome: Interdisciplinary Perspectives*, edited by Mladen Popović, 399–417. JSJS 154. Leiden and Boston.

Prüfer, Thomas. 2002. *Die Bildung der Geschichte: Friedrich Schiller und die Anfänge der modernen Geschichtswissenschaft*. Cologne.

Puigitàrrech, Armand. 2011. "Why Was Jesus Not Born in Nazareth?" In *Handbook for the Study of the Historical Jesus*, vol. 4, *Individual Studies*, edited by Tom Holmén and Stanley E. Porter, 3409–36. Leiden and Boston,.

Pummer, Reinhard. 2009. *The Samaritans in Flavius Josephus*. TSAJ 129. Tübingen.

Rabinowitz, Isaac. 1967. "'Be Opened' = Ἐφφαθά (Mark 7 34): Did Jesus Speak Hebrew?" *ZNW* 53: 229–38.

———. 1971. "Ἐφφαθά (Mark VII. 34): Certainly Hebrew, Not Aramaic." *JSS* 16: 151–56.

Ranke, Leopold. 1824. *Geschichten der romanischen und germanischen Völker von 1494 bis 1535*. Vol. 1. Leipzig and Berlin.

Ratzinger, Joseph (Benedict XVI). 2007. *Jesus von Nazareth*. Vol. 1, *Von der Taufe im Jordan bis zur Verklärung*. Freiburg (CH).

Rau, Eckhard. 2006. "Arm und Reich im Spiegel des Wirkens Jesu." In *Eschatologie und Ethik im frühen Christentum, FS Günter Haufe*, edited by Christfried Böttrich, 249–68. Greifswalder Theologische Forschungen 11. Frankfurt.

———. 2011. "Unser Vater im Himmel: Eine These zur Metaphorik der Rede von Gott in der Logienquelle." *NovT* 53 (3): 222–43.

Reed, Jonathan L. 2000. *Archaeology and the Galilean Jesus: A Re-examination of the Evidence*. Harrisburg, PA.

Regev, Eyal. 2000. "Pure Individualism: The Idea of Non-Priestly Purity in Ancient Judaism." *JSJ* 31: 176–202.

Reicke, Bo I. 1987. "From Strauss to Holtzmann and Meijboom: Synoptic Theories Advanced during the Consolidation of Germany, 1830–1870." *NovT* 29: 1–21.

Reimarus, Hermann Samuel. 1778. "Von dem Zwecke Jesu und seiner Jünger." In *Fragmente des Wolfenbüttelschen Ungenannten*, edited by Gotthold Ephraim Lessing, 3–174. Brunswick, Germany.

———. 1972. *Apologie oder Schutzschrift für die vernünftigen Verehrer Gottes, im Auftrag der Joachim Jungius-Gesellschaft der Wissenschaften Hamburg*. Edited by Gerhard Alexander. 2 vols. Frankfurt.

———. 1979. "Die Vernunft lehre, als eine Anweisung zum richtigen Gebrauche der Vernunft in dem Erkenntniß der Wahrheit, aus zwoen ganz natürlichen Regeln der Einstimmung und des Widerspruchs" (1756). In *Hermann Samuel Reimarus: Gesammelte Schriften*, edited by Frieder Lötzsch, vol. 2. Munich.

Reinke, Andreas. 2007. *Geschichte der Juden in Deutschland 1781–1933, Geschichte kompakt*. Darmstadt.

Reinmuth, Eckhard. 1995. "Narratio und argumentation—zur Auslegung der Jesus-Christus-Geschichte im ersten Korintherbrief: Ein Beitrag zur mimetischen Kompetenz des Paulus." *ZTK* 92: 13–27.

Reiprich, Torsten. 2008. *Das Mariageheimnis: Maria von Nazareth und die Bedeutung familiärer Beziehungen im Markusevangelium*. FRLANT 223. Göttingen.

Reiser, Marius. 1990. *Die Gerichtspredigt Jesu: Eine Untersuchung zur eschatologischen Verkündigung Jesu und ihrem frühjüdischen Hintergrund*. NTAbh, n.s., 23. Münster.

———. 1998. "'Selig die Reichen!'—'Selig die Armen!'" *EuA* 74: 451–66.

———. 2000. "Numismatik und Neues Testament." *Bib* 81: 457–88.

———. 2011. *Der unbequeme Jesus*. BThS 122. Neukirchen-Vluyn.

Renan, Ernest. 1863. *Vie de Jésus/Das Leben Jesu*. Paris and Berlin.

Rengstorf, Karl Heinrich. 1953. *Die Anfänge der Auseinandersetzung zwischen Christusglaube und Asklepiosfrömmigkeit*. Münster.

Resch, Alfred. [2]1906. *Agrapha: Aussercanonische Schrift fragmente*. TU, n.s., 15/3–4. Leipzig.

Rese, Martin. 1975–1976. "Zur Problematik von Kurz- und Langtext in Luk. XII.17ff." *NTS* 22: 15–31.

Reumann, John. 1972. "The Quest for the Historical Baptist." In *Understanding the Sacred Text: FS Morton S. Enslin*, edited by John Reumann, 181–99. Valley Forge, PA.

Reventlow, Henning Graf. 2001. *Epochen der Bibelauslegung*. Vol. 4, *Von der Aufklärung bis zum 20. Jahrhundert*. Munich.

Reventlow, Henning Graf, Walter Sparn, and John Woodbridge, eds. 1988. *Historische Kritik und biblischer Kanon in der deutschen Aufklärung*. Wiesbaden.

Richardson, Peter. 1996. *Herod: King of the Jews and Friend of the Romans*. Columbia, SC.

Riches, John K. 1980. *Jesus and the Transformation of Judaism*. London.

———. 2004. "Reichtum. III. Neues Testament." In *RGG* 7:232–33.

Richstaetter, Carl. 1949. *Christusfrömmigkeit in ihrer historischen Entwicklung*. Cologne.

Richter, Georg. 1977. *Studien zum Johannesevangelium*. Edited by Josef Hainz. BU 13. Regensburg.

Ricoeur, Paul. 1998. *Das Rätsel der Vergangenheit: Erinnern—Vergessen—Verzeihen*. Essen.

Riesner, Rainer. 1981; ³1988. *Jesus als Lehrer: Eine Untersuchung zum Ursprung der Evangelien-Überlieferung*. WUNT II 7. Tübingen.

———. 1990. "Bethesda." *Das große Bibellexikon* 1:194–95.

———. 1994. *Die Frühzeit des Apostel Paulus: Studien zur Chronologie, Missionsstragegie und Theologie*. WUNT 71. Tübingen.

———. 2011. "From the Messianic Teacher to the Gospels of Jesus Christ." In *Handbook for the Study of the Historical Jesus*, vol. 2, *The Study of Jesus*, edited by Tom Holmén and Stanley E. Porter, 405–46. Leiden and Boston.

Rigaux, Béda. ²1961. "Die 'Zwölf' in Geschichte und Kerygma." In *Der historische Jesus und der kerygmatische Christus: Beiträge zum Christusverständnis in Forschung und Verkündigung*, edited by Helmut Ristow and Karl Matthiae, 468–86. Berlin.

Riniker, Christian. 1999. *Die Gerichtsverkündigung Jesu*. EHS 653. Bern.

Ristow, Helmut, and Karl Matthiae, eds. ²1961. *Der historische Jesus und der kerygmatische Christus: Beiträge zum Christusverständnis in Forschung und Verkündigung*. Berlin.

Ritschl, Albrecht. (1880–1886) 1966. *Geschichte des Pietismus*. 3 vols. Bonn.

Robinson, James M., Paul Hoffmann, and John S. Kloppenborg, eds. 2000. *The Critical Edition of Q: A Synopsis, Including the Gospels of Matthew and Luke, Mark and Thomas*. Hermeneia Supplements. Leuven and Minneapolis.

Rollens, Sarah E. 2014. *Framing Social Criticism in the Jesus Movement: The Ideological Project in the Sayings Gospel Q*. Tübingen.

Roloff, Jürgen. 1965. *Apostolat—Verkündigung—Kirche*. Gütersloh.

———. 1969. "Das Markusevangelium als Geschichtserzählung." *EvT* 29: 73–93.

Rosen, Ralph M., and Manfred Horstmanshoff. 2003. "The Andreia of the Hippocratic Physician and the Problem of the Incurables." In *Andreia: Studies in Manliness and Courage in Classical Antiquity*, edited by Ralph M. Rosen et al., 95–114. Leiden.

Rosenzweig, Franz. 1984. "Atheistische Theologie." In *Der Mensch und sein Werk:*

Gesammelte Schriften, vol. 3, *Zweistromland: Kleinere Schriften zu Glauben und Denken*, edited by Reinhold Maier and Annemarie Maier, 687–97. The Hague.

———. 2000. "Atheistic Theology (1914)." In *Philosophical and Theological Writings*, edited by Paul W. Franks and Michael L. Morgan, 10–24. Indianapolis.

Roth, Dieter T. 2018. *The Parables in Q*. LNTS 582. London.

Rowland, Christopher. 1986. *Christian Origins: The Setting and Character of the Most Important Messianic Sect of Judaism*. London.

———. 1989. "Reflections on the Politics of the Gospels." In *The Kingdom of God and Human Society*, edited by Robin Barbour, 224–41. Edinburgh.

Rubenstein, Jeffrey L. 1999. "Nominalism and Realism in Qumranic and Rabbinic Law: A Reassessment." *DSD* 6: 157–83.

Rüger, Hans Peter. 1973. "Μαμωνᾶς." *ZNW* 64: 127–31.

Ruh, Kurt. 1990–1999. *Geschichte der abendländischen Mystik*. 4 vols. Munich.

Saeger, Robin. ²2005. *Tiberius*. Oxford.

Safrai, Shemuel, and Menahem Stern, eds. 1976. *The Jewish People in the First Century: Historical Geography, Political History, Social, Cultural, and Religious Life and Institutions*. 2 vols. CRINT 1. Assen.

Saldarini, Anthony J. 1988. *Pharisees, Scribes, and Sadducees in Palestinian Society: A Sociological Approach*. Wilmington, DE.

Samuelsson, Gunnar. ²2013. *Crucifixion in Antiquity*. WUNT II 310. Tübingen.

Sanders, Ed P. 1985a. *Jesus and Judaism*. London.

———. 1985b. *Paulus und das palästinische Judentum: Ein Vergleich zweier Religionsstrukturen*. SUNT 17. Göttingen.

———. 1992; ²1994. *Judaism: Practice and Belief, 63 BCE–66 CE*. London and Philadelphia.

———. 1993. *The Historical Figure of Jesus*. London.

Sanders, James A. 1997. "A Liturgy for Healing the Stricken (11 QPsApa = 11Q11)." In *The Dead Sea Scrolls*, vol. 4A, *Pseudepigraphic and Non-Masoretic Psalms and Prayers*, edited by James H. Charlesworth, 216–33. Tübingen.

Sandnes, Karl Olav. 2014. "'The First Prayer': Pater Noster in the Early Church." In *Early Christian Prayer and Identity Formation*, edited by Reidar Hvalvik and Karl Sandnes, 209–32. Tübingen.

Sandt, Huub van de, and Jürgen Zangenberg, eds. 2008. *Matthew, James, and Didache: Three Related Documents in Their Jewish and Christian Settings*. SBLSS. Atlanta.

Sauer, Jürgen. 1991. *Rückkehr und Vollendung des Heils: Eine Untersuchung zu den ethischen Radikalismen Jesu*. Theorie und Forschung 133. Philosophie und Theologie 9. Regensburg.

Schacter, Daniel L., ed. 1995. *Memory Distortion: How Minds, Brains, and Societies Reconstruct the Past*. Cambridge.

Schalit, Abraham. ²2000. *König Herodes: Der Mann und sein Werk*. Berlin.

Scheel, Otto. 1901. *Die Anschauung Augustins über Christi Person und Werk*. Tübingen.

Schelbert, Georg. 2011. *Abba Vater: Der literarische Befund vom Altaramäischen bis zu den späten Midrasch- und Haggada-Werken in Auseinandersetzung mit den Thesen von Joachim Jeremias*. NTOA 81/SUNT 81. Göttingen.

Schenke, Ludger. 2004. "Jesus und Johannes der Täufer." In *Jesus von Nazaret—Spuren und Konturen*, by Ludger Schenke, 84–105. Stuttgart.

Schiemann, Gottfried. 2006. "Pater familias." In *DNP* 9:394–95.

Schiffer, Werner. 1980. *Theorien der Geschichtsschreibung und ihre erzähltheoretische Relevanz*. Studien zur allgemeinen und vergleichenden Literaturwissenschaft, vol. 19. Stuttgart.

Schille, Gottfried. 1967. *Die urchristliche Kollegialmission*. ATANT 48. Zürich.

Schiller, Friedrich von. 1788. *Geschichte des Abfalls der vereinigten Niederlande von der Spanischen Regierung*. Part 1. Leipzig.

Schiller, Gertrud. 1966. *Ikonographie der christlichen Kunst*. Vol. 1, *Inkarnation, Kindheit, Taufe, Versuchung, Verklärung, Wirken und Wunder Christi*. Gütersloh.

———. 1968. *Ikonographie der christlichen Kunst*. Vol. 2, *Die Passion Jesu Christi*. Gütersloh.

———. 1971. *Ikonographie der christlichen Kunst*. Vol. 3, *Die Auferstehung und Erhöhung Christi*. Gütersloh.

Schlatter, Adolf. 1905. *Atheistische Methoden in der Theologie*. BFCT 9, no. 5. Gütersloh.

Schleiermacher, Friedrich. 1832. "Über die Zeugnisse des Papias von unsern beiden ersten Evangelien." *TSK* 5: 735–68.

Schlosser, Jacques. 1980. *Le Règne de Dieu dans les dits de Jésus*. 2 vols. Paris.

———. 1987. *Le Dieu de Jésus: Étude exégétique*. LD 129. Paris.

Schlund, Christine. 2005. *"Kein Knochen soll gebrochen warden": Studien zur Bedeutung und Funktion des Pesachfest in Texten des frühen Judentums und im Johannesevangelium*. WMANT 107. Neukirchen-Vluyn.

Schmahl, Günther. 1974. *Die Zwölf im Markusevangelium: Eine redaktionsgeschichtliche Untersuchung*. TThSt 30. Trier.

Schmeller, Thomas. 1989. *Brechungen: Urchristliche Wandercharismatiker im Prisma soziologischorientierter Exegese*. SBS 136. Stuttgart.

———. 2008. "Réflexions socio-historiques sur les porteurs de la tradition et les destinataires de Q." In *La source des paroles de Jésus (Q): Aux origines du christianisme*, edited by Andreas Dettwiler and Daniel Marguerat, 149–71. Geneva.

Schmidt, Eckart David. 2014. "David Friedrich Strauß (1808–1874): Mythos im Zeitalter des romantischen Idealismus." In *Studienbuch Hermeneutik: Bibelauslegung durch die Jahrhunderte als Lernfeld der Textinterpretation; Porträts—Modelle—Quellentexte*, edited by Susanne Luther and Ruben Zimmermann, 259–66, 374–75. Gütersloh.

———. 2015. "Ein aufgeklärter Jesus in der Neuen Welt: Methode und Intention in den Bibelkompilationen Thomas Jeffersons; Historische Faktualität als Paradigma der Aufklärungsexegese?" In *Wie Geschichten Geschichteschreiben: Frühchristliche Literatur zwischen Faktualität und Fiktionalität*, edited by Susanne Luther, Jörg Röder, and Eckart David Schmidt, 391–423. WUNT II 395. Tübingen.

———. 2016. "Eine alte, heimliche Ehe: Eine Skizze zum 'historischen Jesus' und dem 'literarischen Jesus' im Geschichtspragmatismus der Spätaufklärung." In *Religion und Aufklärung: Akten des Ersten Internationalen Kongresses zur Erforschung der Aufklärungstheologie (Münster, 30. März bis 2. April 2014)*, edited by Albrecht Beutel and Martha Nooke. Tübingen.

Schmidt, Karl Ludwig. (1919) 1969. *Der Rahmen der Geschichte Jesu: Literarkritische Untersuchung zur ältesten Jesusüberlieferung*. Berlin; reprint published in Darmstadt.

———. 1923. "Die Stellung der Evangelien in der allgemeinen Literaturgeschichte." In *Eucharistērion, FS Hermann Gunkel*, 51–134. Göttingen.

Schnackenburg, Rudolf. 1986. *Die sittliche Botschaft des Neuen Testaments 1: Von Jesus zur Urkirche*, 58–67. HThKNTSup 1. Freiburg.

Schneemelcher, Wilhelm, ed. 1990. *Neutestamentliche Apokryphen I: Evangelien*. Tübingen.

———, ed. ⁶1997. *Neutestamentliche Apokryphen II: Apostolisches, Apokalypsen und Verwandtes*. Tübingen.

Schneider, Gerhard. 1992. "Gott, der Vater Jesu Christi, in der Verkündigung Jesu und im urchristlichen Bekenntnis." In *Jesusüberlieferung und Christologie: Neutestamentliche Aufsätze 1970–1990*, by Gerhard Schneider, 3–38. NovTSup 67. Leiden.

Schnelle, Udo. 1992. "Johannes und die Synoptiker." In *The Four Gospels 1992: FS Frans Neirynck*, vol. 3, edited by Frans van Segbroeck et al., 1799–1814. BETL 100/3. Leuven.

———. ²2000; ⁴2008; ⁵2016. *Das Evangelium nach Johannes*. THKNT 4. Leipzig.

———. 2007. *Theologie des Neuen Testaments*. UTB 2917. Göttingen.

———. ⁸2013. *Einleitung in das Neue Testament*. Göttingen.

———. 2015. *Die ersten 100 Jahre des Christentums 30–130 n.Chr. Die Entstehungsgeschichte einer Weltreligion*. UTB 4411. Göttingen.

———. ⁹2017. *Einleitung in das Neue Testament*. UTB 1830. Göttingen.

Schniewind, Julius. 1930. "Zur Synoptiker-Exegese." *TRu*, n.s., 2: 129–89.

———. 1952. *Nachgelassene Reden und Aufsätze*. Edited by Ernst Kähler, 169, 171. Berlin.

Scholder, Klaus. 1966. *Ursprünge und Probleme der Bibelkritik im 17. Jahrhundert: Ein Beitrag zur Entstehung der historisch-kritischen Theologie*. FGLP 10.33. Munich.

Scholtissek, Klaus. 2000. "'Geboren aus einer Frau, geboren unter das Gesetz' (Gal 4,4): Die christologisch-soteriologische Bedeutung des irdischen Jesus bei

Paulus." In *Paulinische Christologie: Exegetische Beiträge, Hans Hübner zum 70. Geburtstag*, edited by Udo Schnelle and Thomas Söding, 194–219. Göttingen.

Schöpflin, Karin. 2002. "מֹשָׁל—ein eigentümlicher Begriff der hebräischen Literatur." *BZ* 46: 1–24.

Schottroff, Luise. 1975. "Gewaltverzicht und Feindesliebe in der urchristlichen Jesustradition (Mt 5,38–48; Lk 6,27–36)." In *Jesus Christus in Historie und Theologie, FS Hans Conzelmann*, edited by Georg Strecker, 197–221. Tübingen.

———. 1987. "Das Gleichnis vom großen Gastmahl in der Logienquelle." *EvT* 47: 192–211.

———. 1991. "Wanderprophetinnen: Eine feministische Analyse der Logienquelle." *EvT* 51: 332–44.

———. 1994. *Lydias ungeduldige Schwestern: Feministische Sozialgeschichte des frühen Christentums*. Gütersloh.

———. 2005. *Die Gleichnisse Jesu*. Gütersloh.

Schremer, Adiel. 2001. "'[T]he[y] Did Not Read in the Sealed Book': Qumran Halakhic Revolution and the Emergence of Torah Study in Second Temple Judaism." In *Historical Perspectives: From the Hasmoneans to Bar Kokhba in Light of the Dead Sea Scrolls; Proceedings of the Fourth International Symposium of the Orion Center for the Study of the Dead Sea Scrolls and Associated Literature, 27–31 January 1999*, edited by David Goodblatt et al., 105–26. STDJ 37. Leiden.

Schröter, Jens. 1996. "The Historical Jesus and the Sayings Tradition: Comments on Current Research." *Neot* 30: 151–68.

———. 1997. *Erinnerung an Jesu Worte: Studien zur Rezeption der Logienüberlieferung in Markus, Q und Thomas*. WMANT 76. Neukirchen-Vluyn.

———. 1998. "Markus, Q und der historische Jesus: Methodologische und exegetische Erwägungen zu den Anfängen der Rezeption der Verkündigung Jesu." *ZNW* 89: 173–200.

———. 2003. "Die Bedeutung der Q-Überlieferungen für die Interpretation der frühen Jesustradition." *ZNW* 94: 38–67.

———. 2006a. *Das Abendmahl: Frühchristliche Deutungen und Impulse für die Gegenwart*. SBB 210. Stuttgart.

———. 2006b; ⁵2012. *Jesus von Nazareth: Jude aus Galiläa—Retter der Welt*. Biblische Gestalten 15. Leipzig.

———. 2007a. "Heil für die Heiden und Israel: Zum Zusammenhang von Christologie und Volk Gottes bei Lukas." In *Von Jesus zum Neuen Testament: Studien zur urchristlichen Theologiegeschichte und zur Entstehung des neutestamentlichen Kanons*, by Jens Schröter, 247–67. WUNT 204. Tübingen.

———. 2007b. *Von Jesus zum Neuen Testament: Studien zur urchristlichen Theologiegeschichte und zur Entstehung des neutestamentlichen Kanons*. WUNT 204. Tübingen.

———, ed. 2013. *The Apocryphal Gospels within the Context of Early Christian Theology*. BETL 260. Leuven.

Schröter, Jens, and Ralph Brucker, eds. 2002. *Der historische Jesus: Tendenzen und Perspektiven der gegenwärtigen Forschung.* BZNW 114. Berlin.

Schröter, Jens, and Jürgen K. Zangenberg, eds. 2013. *Texte zur Umwelt des Neuen Testaments.* UTB 3663. Tübingen.

Schulte, Stefanie. 2008. *Gleichnisse erleben: Entwurf einer wirkungsästhetischen Hermeneutik und Didaktik.* PTHe 91. Stuttgart.

Schulthess, Friedrich. 1897. "Der Brief des Mara bar Sarapion: Ein Beitrag zur Geschichte der syrischen Literatur." *ZDMG* 51: 365–91.

Schulz, Anselm. 1964. *Nachfolgen und Nachahmen: Studien über das Verhältnis der neutestamentlichen Jüngerschaft zur urchristlichen Vorbildethik.* SANT 6. Munich.

Schürer, Emil. 1973–1987. *The History of the Jewish People in the Age of Jesus Christ (175 B.C.–A.D. 135).* Edited by Geza Vermes et al. 3 vols. Edinburgh.

Schürmann, Heinz. ²1961. "Die vorösterlichen Anfänge der Logienquelle: Versuch eines formgeschichtlichen Zugangs zum Leben Jesu." In *Der historische Jesus und der kerygmatische Christus*, edited by Helmut Ristow and Karl Matthiae. Berlin.

———. 1968. "Die vorösterlichen Anfänge der Logiertradition: Versuch eines formgeschichtlichen Zugangs zum Leben Jesu." In *Traditionsgeschichtliche Untersuchungen zu den synoptischen Evangelien*, by Heinz Schürmann, 39–65. KBANT. Düsseldorf.

———. 1994. *Jesus—Gestalt und Geheimnis: Gesammelte Beiträge.* Edited by Klaus Scholtissek. Paderborn.

Schüssler Fiorenza, Elisabeth. 1988. *Zu ihrem Gedächtnis . . . Eine theologische Rekonstruktion der christlichen Ursprünge.* Munich.

———. 1994. *Jesus: Miriam's Child, Sophia's Prophet.* New York.

Schwartz, Barry. 2005. "Christian Origins: Historical Truth and Social Memory." In *Memory, Tradition, and Text: Uses of the Past in Early Christianity*, edited by Alan Kirk and Tom Thatcher, 43–56. SemeiaSt 52. Atlanta.

———. 2009. "Collective Forgetting and the Symbolic Power of Oneness: The Strange Apotheosis of Rosa Parks." *Social Psychology Quarterly* 72: 123–42.

Schwartz, Daniel R. 1990. *Agrippa I: The Last King of Judaea.* TSAJ 23. Tübingen.

———. 1992. "Law and Truth: On Qumran-Sadducean and Rabbinic Views of Law." In *The Dead Sea Scrolls: Forty Years of Research*, edited by Devorah Dimant and Uriel Rappaport, 229–40. STDJ 10. Leiden.

———. 2009. "One Temple and Many Synagogues: On Religion and State in Herodian Judaea and Augustan Rome." In *Herod and Augustus*, edited by David M. Jacobson and Nikos Kokkinos, 385–98. Leiden.

Schwartz, Seth. 2014. *The Ancient Jews from Alexander to Muhammed.* Cambridge.

Schwarz, Konrad. 2020. *Gleichnisse und Parabeln Jesu im Thomasevangelium: Untersuchungen zu ihrer Form, Funktion und Bedeutung.* BZNW 236. Berlin and Boston.

Schweitzer, Albert. (1901) ²1973a. "Das Messianitäts- und Leidensgeheimnis: Eine

Skizze des Lebens Jesu." In *Ausgewählte Werke in fünf Bänden*, edited by Rudolf Grabs, 5:195–340. Berlin.

———. 1906. *Von Reimarus zu Wrede: Eine Geschichte der Leben-Jesu-Forschung.* Tübingen.

———. (1913) ²1973b. "Geschichte der Leben-Jesu-Forschung." In *Ausgewählte Werke in fünf Bänden*, edited by Rudolf Grabs, vol. 3. Berlin.

———. 1925. *The Mystery of the Kingdom of God.* London. ET of the second half of 1913. *Das Abendmahl im Zusammenhang mit dem Leben Jesu und der Geschichte des Urchristentums.* Originally entitled *Das Messianitäts- und Leidensgeheimnis.* Tübingen. 1901.

———. (1931) ²1973c. "Aus meinem Leben und Denken." In *Ausgewählte Werke in fünf Bänden*, edited by Rudolf Grabs, 1:19–252. Berlin.

———. 1949. *Out of My Life and Thought.* London.

———. ⁹1984. *Geschichte der Leben-Jesu-Forschung.* UTB 1302. Tübingen. ET: 2001. *The Quest of the Historical Jesus.* Edited by John Bowden. Minneapolis.

———. 1995. *Reich Gottes und Christentum.* Munich.

———. 2000. *The Quest of the Historical Jesus.* London. ET of the 2nd ed. of 1913. *Die Leben-Jesus-Forschung.* Tübingen.

Schweizer, Eduard. 1982. "Scheidungsrecht der jüdischen Frau? Weibliche Jünger Jesu?" *EvT* 42: 294–300.

Schwemer, Anna Maria. 1991. "Gott als König und seine Königsherrschaft in den Sabbatliedern aus Qumran." In *Königsherrschaft Gottes und himmlischer Kult im Judentum, Urchristentum und in der hellenistischen Welt*, edited by Martin Hengel and Anna Maria Schwemer, 45–118. Tübingen.

———. 2001. "Die Passion des Messias nach Markus und der Vorwurf des Antijudaismus." In *Der messianische Anspruch Jesu und die Anfänge der Christologie*, edited by Martin Hengel and Anna Maria Schwemer, 133–63. WUNT 138. Tübingen.

Schwier, Helmut. 2005. "Vaterunser." In *RGG* 8:893–96.

Scott, Bernard B. 1989. *Hear Then the Parable: A Commentary on the Parables of Jesus.* Minneapolis.

Segal, Alan F. 1981. "Hellenistic Magic: Some Questions of Definition." In *Studies in Gnosticism and Hellenistic Religions*, edited by Roelof van den Broek and Maaten Jozef Vermaseren, 349–75. EPRO 91. Leiden.

Segovia, Fernando G., ed. 1985. *Discipleship in the New Testament.* Philadelphia.

Seitel, Peter. 1981. "Proverbs: A Social Use of Metaphor." In *The Wisdom of Many: Essays on the Proverb*, edited by Wolfgang Mieder and Alan Dundes, 122–39. New York.

Selge, Kurt-Victor. 1966. "Rechtsgestalt und Idee der frühen Gemeinschaft des Franz von Assisi." In *Erneuerung der Einen Kirche, FS Heinrich Bornkamm*, edited by J. Lell, 1–31. Göttingen.

———. 1970. "Franz von Assisi und die römische Kurie." *ZTK* 67: 129–61.

Sevenich-Bax, Elisabeth. 1993. *Israels Konfrontation mit den letzten Boten der Weisheit: Form, Funktion und Interdependenz der Weisheitselemente in der Logienquelle.* MThA 21. Altenberge.

Sevenster, Jan Nicolaas. 1968. *Do You Know Greek?* NovTSup 19. Leiden.

Sharon, Nadav. 2010. "The Title 'Ethnarch' in Second Temple Period Judea." *JSJ* 41: 472–93.

Shemesh, Aharon. 2009. *Halakhah in the Making: The Development of Jewish Law from Qumran to the Rabbis.* Taubman Lectures in Jewish Studies 6. Berkeley, CA.

———. 2013. "Shabbat, Circumcision, and Circumcision on Shabbat in Jubilees and the Dead Sea Scrolls." In *Rewriting and Interpreting the Hebrew Bible: The Biblical Patriarchs in the Light of the Dead Sea Scrolls*, edited by Devorah Dimant and Reinhard G. Kratz, 263–87. BZAW 439. Berlin.

Sherwin-White, Adrian Nicholas. 1963. *Roman Society and Roman Law in the New Testament.* Oxford.

Siegert, Folker. 2000. "Jesus und sein Volk in der Quelle Q." In *Israel als Gegenüber: Vom alten Orient bis in die Gegenwart; Studien zur Geschichte eines wechselvollen Zusammenlebens*, edited by Folker Siegert, 90–124. Göttingen.

———. 2007. *Das Evangelium des Johannes in seiner ursprünglichen Gestalt: Wiederherstellung und Kommentar.* SIJD 6. Münster.

Simmonds, Andrew. 2012. "Mark's and Matthew's Sub Rosa Message in the Scene of Pilate and the Crowd." *JBL* 131: 733–54.

Smallwood, E. Mary. 1981. *The Jews under Roman Rule: From Pompey to Diocletian.* Leiden.

Smith, D. Moody. ²2001. *John among the Gospels.* Columbia, SC.

Smith, Dennis E. 1987. "Table Fellowship as a Literary Motif in the Gospel of Luke." *JBL* 106: 613–38.

———. 1992. "Messianic Banquet." In *ABD* 4:788–91.

———. 2003. *From Symposium to Eucharist: The Banquet in the Early Christian World.* Minneapolis.

Smith, Morton. 1973. *Clement of Alexandria and a Secret Gospel of Mark.* Cambridge.

———. 1978. *Jesus the Magician.* San Francisco.

Smith, Morton, and Elias Joseph Bickerman. 1976. *The Ancient History of Western Civilization.* New York.

Snodgrass, Klyne. 2008; ²2018. *Stories with Intent: A Comprehensive Guide to the Parables of Jesus.* Grand Rapids.

Söding, Thomas. 1992. "Die Tempelaktion Jesu." *TTZ* 101: 36–64.

———. 1995. *Das Liebesgebot bei Paulus: Die Mahnung zur Agape im Rahmen der paulinischen Ethik.* NTAbh 26. Münster.

Sörries, Reiner. 2012. *Was von Jesus übrig blieb: Die Geschichte seiner Reliquien.* Kevelaer, Germany.

Spalding, Johann Joachim. 2002. *Ueber die Nutzbarkeit des Predigtamtes und deren Beförderung* (1772). Edited by Tobias Jersak. SpKA I/3. Tübingen.

Speidel, Michael A. 2012. "Making Use of History beyond the Euphrates: Political Views, Cultural Traditions, and Historical Contexts in the Letter of Mara bar Sarapion." In *The Letter of Mara bar Sarapion in Context*, edited by Annette Merz and Teun Tieleman, 11–42. Leiden.

Staden, Heinrich von. 2003. "Galen's Daimon: Reflections on 'Irrational' and 'Rational." In *Rationnel et irrationel dans la médicine ancienne et médiévale: Aspects historiques, scientifiques et culturels, Centre Jean Palerne Mémoires XXVI*, edited by Nicoletta Palimieri, 15–44. Saint-Etienne.

Stamatu, Marion. 2005. "Nächstenliebe." In *Antike Medizin: Ein Lexikon*, edited by Karl-Heinz Leven, 638–41. Munich.

Standhartinger, Angela. 2004. "Geschlechterperspektiven auf die Jesusbewegung." *Zeitschrift für Pädagogik und Theologie* 4: 308–18.

Stanton, Graham N. 2004. "Jesus of Nazareth: A Magician and a False Prophet Who Deceived God's People?" In *Jesus and Gospel*, by Graham N. Stanton, 127–47. Cambridge.

Stare, Mira. 2011. "Gibt es Gleichnisse im Johannesevangelium?" In *Hermeneutik der Gleichnisse Jesu: Methodische Neuansätze zum Verstehen urchristlicher Parabeltexte*, edited by Ruben Zimmermann, 321–64. WUNT 231, Studienausgabe. Tübingen.

Staudt, Darina. 2012. *Der eine und einzige Gott: Monotheistische Formeln im Urchristentum und ihre Vorgeschichte bei Griechen und Juden*. NTOA 80. Göttingen.

Steck, Odil Hannes. 1967. *Israel und das gewaltsame Geschick der Propheten*. WMANT 23. Neukirchen-Vluyn.

Stegemann, Ekkehard W., and Wolfgang Stegemann. 1995; [2]1997. *Urchristliche Sozialgeschichte: Die Anfänge im Judentum und die Christusgemeinden in der mediterranen Welt*. Stuttgart.

Stegemann, Hartmut. [4]1994. *Die Essener, Qumran, Johannes der Täufer und Jesus*. Freiburg.

Stegemann, Wolfgang. 2002. "Kontingenz und Kontextualität der moralischen Aussagen Jesu: Plädoyer für eine Neubesinnung auf die sogenannte Ethik Jesu." In *Jesus in neuen Kontexten*, edited by Wolfgang Stegemann and Bruce J. Malina, 167–84. Stuttgart.

———. 2004. "Dekonstruktion des rationalistischen Wunderbegriffs." In *Dem Tod nicht glauben, FS Luise Schottroff*, edited by Frank Crüsemann et al., 67–90. Gütersloh.

———. 2010. *Jesus und seine Zeit*. BE 10. Stuttgart.

Steger, Florian. 2004. *Asklepiosmedizin: Medizinischer Alltag in der römischen Kaiserzeit, Medizin*. Gesellschaft und Geschichte-Beihefte 22. Stuttgart.

Stemberger, Günter. 1990. "Pesachhaggada und Abendmahlsberichte des Neuen Testaments." In *Studien zum rabbinischen Judentum*, by Günter Stemberger, 357–74. SBAB 10. Stuttgart.

———. 1991; ²2013. *Pharisäer, Sadduzäer, Essener*. Stuttgart.

Stemm, Sönke von. 1999. *Der betende Sünder vor Gott: Studien zu Vergebungsvorstellungen in urchristlichen und frühjüdischen Texten*. Leiden.

Stemmer, Peter. 1983. *Weissagung und Kritik: Eine Studie zur Hermeneutik bei Hermann Samuel Reimarus*. Veröffentlichung der Joachim Jungius-Gesellschaft der Wissenschaften Hamburg 48. Göttingen.

Stern, Frank. 2006. *A Rabbi Looks at Jesus' Parables*. Lanham, MD.

Stern, Menahem. 1982. "Social and Political Realignments in Herodian Judaea." *Jerusalem Cathedra* 2: 40–62.

Stock, Alex. 1999."Christusbilder. II.1. Alte Kirche." In *RGG* 2:327–29.

Stock, Klemens. 1975. *Boten aus dem Mit-Ihm-Sein: Das Verhältnis zwischen Jesus und den Zwölf nach Markus*. AnBib 70. Rome.

Strange, William A. 2000. "The Jesus-Tradition in Acts." *NTS* 46: 59–74.

Strauss, David Friedrich. 2012 [1835–1836; ³1838]. *Das Leben Jesu: Kritisch bearbeitet*. 2 vols. Darmstadt. ET: 1972. *The Life of Jesus, Critically Examined*. Philadelphia.

Strecker, Christian. 2002. "Jesus und die Besessenen." In *Jesus in neuen Kontexten*, edited by Wolfgang Stegemann, 53–63. Stuttgart.

Strecker, Georg. 1978. "Die Antithesen der Bergpredigt (Mt 5,21–48)." *ZNW* 69: 36–72.

———. ²1985. *Die Bergpredigt: Ein exegetischer Kommentar*. Göttingen.

Stroker, William D. 1989. *Extracanonical Sayings of Jesus*. Atlanta.

Strotmann, Angelika. 1991. *"Mein Vater bist du!" (Sir 51,10): Zur Bedeutung der Vaterschaft Gottes in kanonischen und nichtkanonischen frühjüdischen Schriften*. FTS 39. Frankfurt.

Stuckenbruck, Loren T. 2002. "The Book of Tobit and the Problem of 'Magic.'" In *Jüdische Schriften in ihrem antik-jüdischen und urchristlichen Kontext*, edited by Hermann Lichtenberger and Gerbern S. Oegema, 258–69. Gütersloh.

Stuckenbruck, Loren T., Stephen C. Barton, and Benjamin G. Wold, eds. 2007. *Memory in the Bible and Antiquity*. WUNT 212. Tübingen.

Stuhlmacher, Peter. 1981. "Existenzstellvertretung für die Vielen: Mk 10,45 (Mt 20,28)." In *Versöhnung, Gesetz und Gerechtigkeit*, by Peter Stuhlmacher, 27–42. Göttingen.

Süssmann, Johannes. 2000. *Geschichtsschreibung oder Roman? Zur Konstitutionslogik von Geschichtserzählungen zwischen Schiller und Ranke (1780–1824)*. Frankfurter historische Abhandlungen 41. Stuttgart.

Szondi, Peter. 1975. *Einführung in die literarische Hermeneutik*. STW 124. Frankfurt.

Tal, Oren. 2012. "Greek Coinages of Palestine." In *The Oxford Handbook of Greek and Roman Coinage*, edited by William E. Metcalf. Oxford.

Tan, Kim Huat. 2011. "Jesus and the Shema." In *Handbook for the Study of the His-*

torical Jesus, vol. 3, *The Historical Jesus*, edited by Tom Holmén and Stanley E. Porter, 2677–2707. Leiden.

Taschl-Erber, Andrea. 2007. *Maria von Magdala—Erste Apostolin? Joh 20,1–18: Tradition und Relecture.* Freiburg.

Taylor, Joan E. 1997. *The Immerser: John the Baptist within Second Temple Judaism.* Grand Rapids.

———. 1998. "Golgotha: A Reconsideration of the Evidence for the Sites of Jesus' Crucifixion and Burial." *NTS* 44: 180–203.

Taylor, Vincent. 1955. *The Gospel according to St. Mark.* London.

Tellenbach, Gerd. 1988. *Die westliche Kirche vom 10. bis zum frühen 12. Jahrhundert.* KIG 2, ser. 1. Göttingen.

Temkin, Owsei. 1991. *Hippocrates in a World of Pagans and Christians.* Baltimore and London.

Theissen, Gerd. 1974; ⁵1987. *Urchristliche Wundergeschichten: Ein Beitrag zur formgeschichtlichen Erforschung der synoptischen Evangelien.* SNT 8. Gütersloh.

———. 1977. *Soziologie der Jesusbewegung: Ein Beitrag zur Entstehungsgeschichte des Urchristentums.* TEH, n.s., 194. Munich.

———. 1979; ³1989. *Studien zur Soziologie des Urchristentums.* WUNT 19. Tübingen.

———. 1989a. *Lokalkolorit und Zeitgeschichte in den Evangelien.* NTOA 8. Göttingen.

———. ³1989b. "Wir haben alles verlassen (Mc. X,28): Nachfolge und soziale Entwurzelung in der jüdisch-palästinischen Gesellschaft des 1. Jahrhunderts n.Chr." In *Studien zur Soziologie des Urchristentums*, by Gerd Theissen, 106–41. WUNT 19. Tübingen.

———. ³1989c. "Gewaltverzicht und Feindesliebe (Mt 5,38–48/Lk 6,27–38) und deren sozialgeschichtlicher Hintergrund." In *Studien zur Soziologie des Urchristentums*, by Gerd Theissen, 160–97. WUNT 19. Tübingen.

———. 2003a. "Das Doppelgebot der Liebe: Jüdische Ethik bei Jesus." In *Jesus als historische Gestalt: Beiträge zur Jesusforschung. Zum 60. Geburtstag*, edited by Annette Merz. FRLANT 202. Göttingen.

———. 2003b. "Jünger als Gewalttäter (Mt 11,12 f; Lk 16,16): Der Stürmerspruch als Selbststigmatisierung einer Minorität." In *Jesus als historische Gestalt: Beiträge zur Jesusforschung. Zum 60. Geburtstag*, edited by Annette Merz, 153–68. FRLANT 202. Göttingen.

———. 2004. *Die Jesusbewegung: Sozialgeschichte einer Revolution der Werte.* Gütersloh.

———. 2008. *Die Weisheit des Urchristentums.* Munich.

Theissen, Gerd, and Annette Merz. 1996; ²1997; ⁴2011. *Der Historische Jesus: Ein Lehrbuch.* Göttingen.

———. 1998. *The Historical Jesus: A Comprehensive Guide.* London.

Theissen, Gerd, and Dagmar Winter. 1997. *Die Kriterienfrage in der Jesusforschung: Vom Differenzkriterium zum Plausibilitätskriterium.* NTOA 34. Göttingen.

———. 2002. *The Quest of the Plausible Jesus: The Question of Criteria.* Louisville.

Theobald, Michael. 2002. *Herrenworte im Johannesevangelium.* HBS 34. Freiburg (CH).

———. 2009. *Das Evangelium nach Johannes, Kapitel 1–12.* RNT. Regensburg.

Thoma, Clemens, and Ernst Lauer. 1986. *Die Gleichnisse der Rabbinen.* Vol. 1, *Pesiqta deRav Kahana (PesK), Einleitung, Übersetzung, Parallelen, Kommentar, Texte.* JudChr 10. Bern.

Thompson, Marianne Meye. 2011. "Jesus and God." In *Handbook for the Study of the Historical Jesus,* vol. 3, *The Historical Jesus,* edited by Tom Holmén and Stanley E. Porter, 2575–95. Leiden.

Thür, Gerhard, and Peter E. Pieler. 1978. "Gerichtsbarkeit." In *RAC* 10:360–492.

Thyen, Hartwig. 2005. *Das Johannesevangelium.* HNT 6. Tübingen.

Tieleman, Teun. 2010. "Religion und Therapie in Galen." In *Religion und Krankheit,* edited by Gregor Etzelmüller and Annette Weissenrieder, 83–95. Darmstadt.

———. 2013. "Miracle and Natural Cause in Galen." In *Miracles Revisited: New Testament Miracle Stories and Their Concepts of Reality,* edited by Stefan Alkier and Annette Weissenrieder, 101–15. Studies on the Bible and Its Reception. Berlin.

———. 2016. "Religion and Therapy in Galen." In *Religion and Illness,* edited by Gregor Etzelmüller and Annette Weissenrieder, 15–31. Eugene, OR.

Tilly, Michael. 1994. *Johannes der Täufer und die Biographie der Propheten: Die synoptische Täuferüberlieferung und das jüdische Prophetenbild zur Zeit des Täufers.* BWA(N)T 137. Stuttgart.

Tiwald, Markus. 2002. *Wanderradikalismus: Jesu erste Jünger—ein Anfang und was davon bleibt.* ÖBS 20. Frankfurt.

———. 2011. "ΑΠΟ ΔΕ ΑΡΧΗΣ ΚΤΙΣΕΩΣ . . . (Mk 10,6): Die Entsprechung von Protologie und Eschatologie als Schlüssel für das Tora-Verständnis Jesu." In *Die Memoria Jesu: Kontinuität und Diskontinuität der Überlieferung,* edited by Ulrich Busse, Michael Reichardt, and Michael Theobald, 367–80. BBB 166. Bonn.

Toit, David S. du. 1997. *Theios Anthrōpos: Zur Verwendung von "Theios Anthrōpos" und sinnverwandten Ausdrücken in der Literatur der Kaiserzeit.* Tübingen.

———. 2001. "The Teaching of Jesus and Its Earliest Records." In *Redefining Jesus: Current Trends in Jesus Research; Jesus, Mark, and Q,* edited by Michael Labahn and Andreas Schmidt, 82–124. JSNTSup 214. Sheffield.

———. 2002a. "Erneut auf der Suche nach Jesus: Eine kritische Bestandsaufnahme der Jesusforschung am Anfang des 21. Jahrhunderts." In *Jesus im 21. Jahrhundert: Bultmanns Jesusbuch und die heutige Jesusforschung,* edited by Ulrich H. J. Körtner, 91–134. Neukirchen-Vluyn.

———. 2002b. "Der unähnliche Jesus: Eine kritische Evaluierung der Entstehung des Differenzkriteriums und dessen geschichts- und erkenntnistheoretischen Voraussetzungen." In *Der historische Jesus: Tendenzen und Perspektiven der gegen-*

wärtigen Forschung, edited by Jens Schröter and Ralph Brucker, 89–129. BZNW 114. Berlin.

———. 2006. *Der abwesende Herr: Strategien im Markusevangelium zur Bewältigung der Abwesenheit des Auferstandenen*. WMANT 111. Neukirchen-Vluyn.

———. 2013. "Die methodischen Grundlagen der Jesusforschung: Entstehung, Struktur, Wandlungen, Perspektiven." *MTZ* 64: 98–123.

Tomson, Peter J. 2010. "Divorce Halakhah in Paul and the Jesus Tradition." In *The New Testament and Rabbinic Literature*, edited by Reimund Bieringer et al., 289–332. JSJS 136. Leiden.

Tönges, Elke. 2003. *"Unser Vater im Himmel": Die Bezeichnung Gottes als Vater in der tannaitischen Literatur*. BWA(N)T 147. Stuttgart.

Townsend, John T. 1992. "Education (Greco-Roman)." In *ABD* 2:312–17.

Trilling, Wolfgang. 1977. "Zur Entstehung des Zwölferkreises: Eine geschichtskritische Überlegung." In *Die Kirche des Anfangs: FS Heinz Schürmann*, edited by Rudolf Schnackenburg et al., 201–22. Leipzig.

Troeltsch, Ernst. 1977. *Der Historismus und seine Probleme* (1922). *Gesammelte Schriften*, vol. 3. Aalen.

Trumbower, Jeffrey A. 1993. "The Historical Jesus and the Speech of Gamaliel (Acts 5.35–9)." *NTS* 39: 500–517.

———. 1994. "The Role of Malachi in the Career of John the Baptist." In *The Gospels and the Scriptures of Israel*, edited by Craig A. Evans and W. Richard Stegner, 28–41. JSNTSup 104. Sheffield.

Trunk, Dieter. 1994. *Der messianische Heiler: Eine redaktions- und religionsgeschichtliche Studie zu den Exorzismen im Matthäusevangelium*. HBS 3. Freiburg.

Tucker, Jeffrey T. 1998. *Example Stories: Perspectives on Four Parables in the Gospel of Luke*. JSNTSup 162. Sheffield.

Tuckett, Christopher M. 1979. "The Griesbach Hypothesis in the 19th Century." *JSNT* 3: 29–60.

———. 1988. "Q, the Law and Judaism." In *Law and Religion: Essays on the Place of the Law in Israel and Early Christianity*, edited by Barnabas Lindars, 90–101. Cambridge.

———. 1989. "A Cynic Q?" *Bib* 70: 349–76.

———. 2002. "Q and the Historical Jesus." In *Der historische Jesus: Tendenzen und Perspektiven der gegenwärtigen Forschung*, edited by Jens Schröter and Ralph Brucker, 213–41. BZNW 114. Berlin.

———. 2007. *The Gospel of Mary*. Oxford Early Christian Gospel Texts. Oxford.

Twelftree, Graham H. 1993. *Jesus the Exorcist: A Contribution to the Study of the Historical Jesus*. WUNT II 54. Tübingen.

———. 2007. "Jesus the Exorcist and Ancient Magic." In *A Kind of Magic: Understanding Magic in the New Testament and Its Religious Environment*, edited by Michael Labahn and Bert Jan Lietaert Peerbolte, 57–86. London and New York.

———, ed. 2017. *The Nature Miracles of Jesus: Problems, Perspectives, and Prospects.* Eugene, OR.

Tyson, Joseph B. 1961. "The Blindness of the Disciples in Mark." *JBL* 80: 261–68.

Ulbert, Thilo, ed. 1998/2003. *Repertorium der christlich-antiken Sarkophage.* Vol. 2, *Italien mit einem Nachtrag Rom und Ostia, Dalmatien, Museen der Welt,* revised by Jutta Dresken-Weiland. Vol. 3, *Frankreich, Algerien, Tunesien,* revised by Brigitte Christern-Briesenick. Mainz.

Vahrenhorst, Martin. 1998. "'Se non è vero, è ben trovato': Die Frauen und das leere Grab." *ZNW* 89: 282–88.

Valantasis, Richard. 2005. *The New Q: A Fresh Translation with Commentary.* New York.

Vanoni, Gottfried, and Bernhard Heininger. 2002. *Das Reich Gottes.* NEchtB. Themen 4. Würzburg.

Van Voorst, Robert E. 2000. *Jesus outside the New Testament: An Introduction to the Ancient Evidence.* Grand Rapids.

Venturini, Karl Heinrich Georg. 1800–1802; ²1806. *Natürliche Geschichte des großen Propheten von Nazareth.* Vol. 4, *Als Anhang zur natürlichen Geschichte des großen Propheten von Nazareth, Jesus der Auferstandene.* Bethlehem and Copenhagen.

Verheyden, Joseph. 1992. "P. Gardner Smith and 'the Turn of the Tide.'" In *John and the Synoptics,* edited by Adelbert Denaux, 423–52. BETL 101. Leuven.

Vermes, Geza. ³1967. "The Use of Bar Nasha/Bar Nash in Jewish Aramaic." In *An Aramaic Approach to the Gospels and Acts,* edited by Matthew Black, 310–30. Oxford.

———. 1973. *Jesus the Jew: A Historian's Reading of the Gospels.* London.

———. 1975. *Post-Biblical Jewish Studies.* SJLA 5. Leiden.

———. 1993a. *Jesus der Jude: Ein Historiker liest die Evangelien.* Neukirchen-Vluyn.

———. 1993b. *The Religion of Jesus the Jew.* London.

Verweyen, Hansjürgen. 2005. *Philosophie und Theologie: Vom Mythos zum Logos zum Mythos.* Darmstadt.

Via, Dan O. 1970. *Die Gleichnisse Jesu: Ihre literarische und existentiale Dimension.* BEvT 57. Munich.

Vielhauer, Philipp. ²1978. *Geschichte der urchristlichen Literatur: Einleitung in das Neue Testament, die Apokryphen und die Apostolischen Väter.* Berlin and New York.

Vincent, John James. 1976. *Disciple and Lord: The Historical and Theological Significance of Discipleship in the Synoptic Gospels.* Sheffield.

Vinzent, Markus. 2011. *Christ's Resurrection in Early Christianity and the Making of the New Testament.* Farnham, UK.

Viviano, Benedict Thomas. 1987. "The Kingdom of God in the Qumran Literature." In *The Kingdom of God in 20th-Century Interpretation,* edited by Wendall Willis, 97–107. Peabody, MA.

———. 1988. *The Kingdom of God in History*. GNS 27. Wilmington, DE.

Vogel, Manuel. 1996. *Das Heil des Bundes: Bundestheologie im Frühjudentum und im frühen Christentum*. TANZ 18. Tübingen and Basel.

Volp, Ulrich. 2006. *Die Würde des Menschen: Ein Beitrag zur Anthropologie in der Alten Kirche*. SVigChr 81. Leiden and Boston.

———. 2013. "Der Schöpfergott und die Ambivalenzen seiner Welt: Das Bild vom Schöpfergott als ethisches Leitbild im frühen Christentum in seiner Auseinandersetzung mit der philosophischen Kritik." In *Gut und Böse in Mensch und Welt: Philosophische und religiöse Konzeptionen vom Alten Orient bis zum frühen Islam*, edited by Heinz-Günther Nesselrath and Florian Wilk, 143–59. ORA 10. Tübingen.

Volp, Ulrich, Friedrich Wilhelm Horn, and Ruben Zimmermann, eds. 2016. *Metapher—Narratio—Mimesis—Doxologie: Begründungsformen frühchristlicher und antiker Ethik*. Kontexte und Normen neutestamentlicher Ethik 6. WUNT 356. Tübingen.

Vorster, Willem S. 1983. "Kerygma, History and the Gospel Genre." *NTS* 29: 87–95.

Vos, Louis A. 1965. *The Synoptic Traditions in the Apocalypse*. Kampen.

Wachob, Wesley Hiram, and Luke Timothy Johnson. 1999. "The Sayings of Jesus in the Letter of James." In *Authenticating the Words of Jesus*, edited by Bruce Chilton and Craig A. Evans, 431–50. NTTS 28/1. Leiden, Boston, and Cologne.

Wagner, Josef. 1988. *Auferstehung und Leben: Joh 11,1–12,19 als Spiegel johanneischer Redaktions- und Theologiegeschichte*. BU 19. Regensburg.

Wahlde, Urban C. von. 2010. *The Gospel and Letters of John*. 3 vols. ECC. Grand Rapids.

Walker, William O. 1978. "Jesus and the Tax Collectors." *JBL* 97: 221–38.

Walter, Johannes von. 1903–1906. *Die ersten Wanderprediger Frankreichs: Studien zur Geschichte des Mönchtums*. SGTK IX/3, 2 Teile. Leipzig.

Wanke, Joachim. 1981. *"Bezugs- und Kommentarworte" in den synoptischen Evangelien*. EThSt 44. Leipzig.

Watson, Francis. 2011. "Eschatology and the Twentieth Century: On the Reception of Schweitzer in English." In *Eschatologie-Eschatology: The Sixth Durham-Tübingen Research Symposium*, edited by Hans-Joachim Eckstein and Hermann Lichtenberger, 331–47. Tübingen.

Watts Henderson, Suzanne. 2006. *Christology and Discipleship in the Gospel of Mark*. SNTSMS 135. Cambridge.

Webb, Robert L. 1991. *John the Baptizer and Prophet: A Socio-Historical Study*. JSNTSup 62. Sheffield.

———. 1994; ²1998. "John the Baptist and His Relationship to Jesus." In *Studying the Historical Jesus: Evaluations of the State of Current Research*, edited by Bruce Chilton and Craig A. Evans, 179–229. NTTS 19. Leiden.

Wedderburn, Alexander J. M. 1989. "Paul and the Story of Jesus." In *Paul and Jesus*, by Alexander J. M. Wedderburn, 161–89. JSNTSup 37. Sheffield.

Weder, Hans. 1993. *Gegenwart und Gottesherrschaft: Überlegungen zum Zeitverständnis bei Jesus und im frühen Christentum*. BThS 20. Neukirchen-Vluyn.

Weeden, Theodore J. 2009. "Kenneth Bailey's Theory of Oral Tradition: A Theory Contested by Its Evidence." *JSHJ* 7: 3–43.

Weihs, Alexander. 2003. *Jesus und das Schicksal der Propheten*. BThS 61. Neukirchen-Vluyn.

Weiss, Bernhard. 1861. "Zur Entstehungsgeschichte der drei synoptischen Evangelien." *TSK* 34: 29–100, 646–713.

Weiss, Johannes. 1888. *Der Barnabasbrief, kritisch untersucht*. Berlin.

———. 1892; [2]1900; [3]1964. *Die Predigt Jesu vom Reiche Gottes*. Göttingen.

———. 1901. *Idee des Reiches Gottes in der Theologie*. Giessen.

———. 1985. *The Preaching of Jesus about the Kingdom of God*. Translated by Richard Hiers and David Holland. Atlanta. ET of 1892. *Die Predigt Jesus vom Reiche Gottes*. 1st ed. Göttingen.

Weisse, Christian H. 1838. *Die evangelische Geschichte: Kritisch und philosophisch bearbeitet*. 2 vols. Leipzig.

———. 1856. *Die Evangelienfrage in ihrem gegenwärtigen Stadium*. Leipzig.

Weissenrieder, Annette. 2003. *Images of Illness in the Gospel of Luke: Insights of Ancient Medical Texts*. WUNT II 164. Tübingen.

———. 2013. "Stories Just under the Skin: Lepra in the Gospel of Luke." In *Miracles Revisited: New Testament Miracle Stories and Their Concepts of Reality*, edited by Stefan Alkier and Annette Weissenrieder, 73–100. Studies on the Bible and Its Reception. Berlin.

Weissenrieder, Annette, and Katrin Dolle. 2019. *Körper und Verkörperung: Biblische Anthropologie im Kontext antiker Medizin und Philosophie; Ein Quellenbuch für die Septuaginta und das Neue Testament*. Fontes et Subsidia ad Bibliam Pertinentes 8. Berlin.

Weissenrieder, Annette, and Gregor Etzelmüller. 2010. "Christentum und Medizin: Welche Kopplungen sind lebensförderlich?" In *Religion und Krankheit*, edited by Gregor Etzelmüller and Annette Weissenrieder, 1–34. Darmstadt.

———. 2015. "Christus Medicus: Die Krankenheilungen Jesu um Dialog zwischen Exegese und Dogmatik." *ZDT* 31: 1–21.

Wellhausen, Julius. 1905. *Einleitung in die drei ersten Evangelien*. Berlin.

———. 1908. *Das Evangelium Johannis*. Berlin.

Wells, Louise. 1998. *The Greek Language of Healing from Homer to New Testament Times*. Berlin.

Wendland, Paul. [2,3]1912. *Die urchristlichen Literaturformen*. HNT I/3. Tübingen.

Wengst, Klaus. 1972. *Christologische Formeln und Lieder des Urchristentums.* SNT 7. Gütersloh.

———. 1981. *Bedrängte Gemeinde und verherrlichter Christus: Der historische Ort des Johannesevangeliums als Schlüssel zu seiner Interpretation.* BThS 5. Neukirchen-Vluyn.

———. 1984. "Glaubensbekenntnis(se) IV. Neues Testament." *TRE* 13: 392–99.

———. 2013. *Der wirkliche Jesus? Eine Streitschrift über die historisch wenig ergiebige und theologisch sinnlose Suche nach dem "historischen" Jesus.* Stuttgart.

Wenham, David, ed. 1985. *The Jesus Tradition outside the Gospels.* Gospel Perspectives 5. Sheffield.

———. 1994. *Paul—Follower of Jesus or Founder of Christianity?* Grand Rapids.

Wenham, John W. 1975. "The Relatives of Jesus." *EvQ* 47: 6–15.

Wernle, Paul. 1899. *Die synoptische Frage.* Leipzig, Freiburg, and Tübingen.

Westerholm, Stephen. 1978. *Jesus and Scribal Authority.* ConBNT 10. Lund.

Wette, Wilhelm Martin Leberecht de. 1817/1826. *Lehrbuch der historisch kritischen Einleitung in die kanonischen und apokryphischen Bücher des Alten Testaments (= Lehrbuch der historisch kritischen Einleitung in die Bibel Alten und Neuen Testaments, Erster Theil: Die Einleitung in das A.T. enthaltend / Zweyter Theil: Die Einleitung in das N.T. enthaltend).* Berlin.

Whealey, Alice. 2003. *Josephus on Jesus: The Testimonium Flavianum Controversy from Late Antiquity to Modern Times.* New York.

Wick, Peter. 1998. "Der historische Ort von Mt 6,1–18." *RB* 105: 332–58.

Wiersing, Erhard. 2007. *Geschichte des historischen Denkens: Zugleich eine Einführung in die Theorie der Geschichte.* Paderborn.

Wilcox, Max. 1982. "taliqa koum(i) in Mk 5,41." In *Logia: Les paroles de Jesus—The Sayings of Jesus,* edited by Joel Delobel, 469–76. BETL 59. Leuven.

Wilker, Julia. 2007. *Für Rom und Jerusalem: Die herodianische Dynastie im 1. Jahrhundert n. Chr.* Studien zur Alten Geschichte 5. Frankfurt.

Wilkins, Michael J. 1988. *The Concept of Disciple in Matthew's Gospel as Reflected in His Use of the Term Mathētēs.* NovTSup 59. Leiden.

———. 1992. *Following the Master: Discipleship in the Steps of Jesus.* Grand Rapids.

Willems, Gottfried. 2012–2013. *Geschichte der deutschen Literatur.* Vol. 2, *Aufklärung.* UTB 3654. Vol. 3, *Goethezeit.* UTB 3734. Vienna, Cologne, and Weimar.

Williams, Michael Allen. ²1999. *"Rethinking Gnosticism": An Argument for Dismantling a Dubious Category.* Princeton.

Willis, Wendall. 1987a. "The Discovery of the Eschatological Kingdom: Johannes Weiss and Albert Schweitzer." In *The Kingdom of God in 20th-Century Interpretation,* edited by Wendall Willis, 1–14. Peabody, MA.

———, ed. 1987b. *The Kingdom of God in 20th-Century Interpretation.* Peabody, MA.

Windisch, Hans. 1926. *Johannes und die Synoptiker: Wollte der vierte Evangelist die älteren Evangelien ergänzen oder ersetzen?* UNT 12. Leipzig.

Wink, Walter. 1968. *John the Baptist in the Gospel Tradition.* SNTSMS 7. Cambridge.

Winter, Paul. 1961. *On the Trial of Jesus.* Berlin.

Wise, Michael Owen. 1992. "Languages of Palestine." In *Dictionary of Jesus and the Gospels*, edited by Joel B. Green et al., 434–44. Downers Grove, IL.

———. 2015. *Language and Literacy in Roman Judaea: A Study of the Bar Kokhba Documents.* New Haven.

Witetschek, Stephan. 2007. "The Stigma of a Glutton and Drunkard: Q 7,34 in Historical and Sociological Perspective." *ETL* 83: 135–54.

Witherington, Ben, III. 1984. *Women in the Ministry of Jesus: A Study of Jesus' Attitude to Women and Their Roles as Reflected in His Earthly Life.* SNTSMS 51. Cambridge.

———. 1995. *The Jesus Quest: The Third Search for the Jew of Nazareth.* Downers Grove, IL.

———. 1999. *Jesus the Seer: The Progress of Prophecy.* Peabody, MA.

Witmer, Amanda. 2012. *Jesus, the Galilean Exorcist.* LNTS 459. London and New York.

Wohlers, Michael. 1999. "'Aussätzige reinigt' (Mt 10,8). Aussatz in antiker Medizin, Judentum und frühem Christentum." In *Text und Geschichte: FS Dieter Lührmann*, edited by Stefan Maser and Egbert Schlarb, 294–304. Marburg.

Wolff, Hans Walter. ²1950. *Jesaja 53 im Urchristentum.* Berlin.

Wolter, Michael. 2002. "'Gericht' und 'Heil' bei Jesus von Nazareth und Johannes dem Täufer: Semantische und pragmatische Beobachtungen." In *Der historische Jesus: Tendenzen und Perspektiven der gegenwärtigen Forschung*, edited by Jens Schröter and Ralph Brucker, 355–92. BZNW 114. Berlin.

———. 2008. *Das Lukasevangelium.* HNT 5. Tübingen.

———. 2009. "'Gericht' und 'Heil' bei Jesus von Nazareth und Johannes dem Täufer." In *Theologie und Ethos im Neuen Testament: Studien zu Jesus, Paulus und Lukas*, by Michael Wolter, 31–63. WUNT 236. Tübingen.

———. 2011. *Paulus: Ein Grundriss seiner Theologie.* Neukirchen-Vluyn.

———. 2012. "Die Auferstehung der Toten und die Auferstehung Jesu." In *Auferstehung*, edited by Elisabeth Gräb-Schmidt and Reiner Preul, 13–54. MJT 24. Leipzig.

———. 2013. "Jesus bei Paulus." In *The Rise and Expansion of Christianity in the First Three Centuries of the Common Era*, edited by Clare K. Rothschild and Jens Schröter, 205–32. WUNT 301. Tübingen.

———. 2019. *Jesus von Nazaret*, 253–71. Göttingen.

Wrede, William. 1901; ⁴1969. *Das Messiasgeheimnis in den Evangelien: Zugleich ein Beitrag zum Verständnis des Markusevangeliums.* Göttingen. ET 1971.

Wright, Nicholas Thomas. 1996. *Jesus and the Victory of God.* London.

———. 2001. "The Lord's Prayer as a Paradigm of Christian Prayer." In *Into God's*

Presence: Prayer in the New Testament, edited by Richard N. Longenecker, 132–54. Grand Rapids.

——. 2003. *The Resurrection of the Son of God*. Minneapolis.

Yarbro Collins, Adela. 1994. "Rulers, Divine Men, and Walking on the Water (Mark 6:45–52)." In *Religious Propaganda and Missionary Competition in the New Testament World, FS Dieter Georgi*, edited by Lukas Bormann et al., 207–27. NovTSup. Leiden.

——. 2007: *Mark: A Commentary*. Hermeneia. Minneapolis.

Young, Brad H. 1989. *Jesus and His Jewish Parables: Rediscovering the Roots of Jewish Teaching*. Mahwah, NJ, and New York.

——. 1998. *The Parables: Jewish Tradition and Christian Interpretation*. Peabody, MA.

Zager, Werner. 1996a. *Gottesherrschaft und Endgericht in der Verkündigung Jesu: Eine Untersuchung zur markinischen Jesusüberlieferung einschließlich der Q-Parallelen*. BZNW 82. Berlin and New York.

——. 1996b. "Wie kames im Urchristentum zur Deutung des Todes Jesu als Sühnegeschehen?" *ZNW* 87: 165–86.

——, ed. 2014. *Jesusforschung in vier Jahrhunderten: Texte von den Anfängen historischer Kritik bis zur "dritten Frage" nach dem historischen Jesus*. de Gruyter Texte. Berlin and Boston.

Zangenberg, Jürgen K. 1998. *Frühes Christentum in Samarien: Topographische und traditionsgeschichtliche Studien zu den Samarientexten im Johannesevangelium*. TANZ 27. Tübingen and Basel.

——. 2007. "Das Galiläa des Josephus und das Galiläa der Archäologie: Tendenzen und Probleme der neueren Forschung." In *Josephus und das Neue Testament: Wechselseitige Wahrnehmungen. II. Internationales Symposium zum Corpus-Judaeo-Hellenisticum 25.–28. Mai 2006*, edited by Christof Böttrich and Jens Herzer, 265–94. WUNT 209. Greifswald and Tübingen.

——. 2008. "Buried according to the Customs of the Jews: John 19,40 in Its Material and Literary Context." In *The Death of Jesus in the Fourth Gospel: Colloquium Biblicum Lovaniense LIV*, edited by Gilbert Van Belle, 873–94. BETL 200. Leuven.

——. 2009: "Trockene Knochen, himmlische Seligkeit. Todes- und Jenseitsvorstellungen in Qumran und im Alten Judentum." In *Tod und Jenseits im Alten Israel und in seiner Umwelt: Theologische, religionsgeschichtliche, archäologische und ikonographische Aspekte*, edited by Angelika Berlejung and Bernd Janowski, 655–89. FAT 64. Tübingen.

——. 2012a. "Archaeology, Papyri, and Inscriptions." In *Early Judaism: A Comprehensive Overview*, edited by John J. Collins et al., 332–66. Winona Lake, IN.

——. 2012b. "The Sanctuary on Mount Gerizim: Observations on the Results of 20 Years of Excavation." In *Temple Building and Temple Cult: Architecture and*

Cultic Paraphernalia of Temples in the Levant (2.-1. Mill. B.C.E.); Proceedings of a Conference on the Occasion of the 50th Anniversary of the Institute of Biblical Archaeology at the University of Tübingen (28th-30th of May 2010), edited by Jens Kamlah et al., 399–418. ADPV 41. Wiesbaden.

———. 2013a. "Herodian Jericho." In *The Oxford Encyclopedia of the Bible and Archaeology*, edited by Daniel M. Master et al., 1:490–99. Oxford.

———. 2013b. "Jerusalem: Hellenistic and Roman." In *The Oxford Encyclopedia of the Bible and Archaeology*, edited by Daniel M. Master et al., 2:23–37. Oxford.

———. 2013c. "Jesus der Galiläer und die Archäologie: Beobachtungen zur Bedeutung der Archäologie für die historische Jesusforschung." *MTZ* 64: 123–56.

———. 2013d. "Pure Stone: Archaeological Evidence for Jewish Purity Practices in Late Second Temple Judaism (Miqwaʾot, Stone Vessels)." In *Purity and the Forming of Religious Traditions in the Ancient Mediterranean World and Ancient Judaism*, edited by Christian Frevel and Christophe Nihan, 537–72. Leiden.

Zangenberg, Jürgen K., and Jens Schröter, eds. 2012. *Bauern, Fischer und Propheten: Galiläa zur Zeit Jesu, Zaberns Bildbände zur Archäologie.* Darmstadt and Mainz.

Zeller, Dieter. 1971–1972. "Das Logion Mt 8,11 f/Lk 13,28 f und das Motiv der 'Völkerwallfahrt.'" *BZ*, n.s., 15: 222–37; 16: 84–93.

———. 1977. *Die weisheitlichen Mahnsprüche bei den Synoptikern.* FB 17. Würzburg.

———. 2004. "Jesu weisheitliche Ethik." In *Jesus von Nazareth—Spuren und Konturen*, edited by Ludger Schenke et al., 193–215. Stuttgart.

Ziegler, Ruprecht. 2004. "Münzen, Münzsysteme und Münzumlauf im Palästina der frühen römischen Kaiserzeit." In *Neues Testament und Antike Kultur*, vol. 1, *Prolegomena, Quellen, Geschichte*, edited by Kurt Erlemann et al., 130–36. Neukirchen-Vluyn.

Ziegler, Theobald. 1908. *David Friedrich Strauß.* Straßburg.

Zimmermann, Christiane. 2007. *Die Namen des Vaters: Studien zu ausgewählten neutestamentlichen Gottesbezeichnungen vor ihrem frühjüdischen und paganen Sprachhorizont.* AJEC 69. Leiden.

Zimmermann, Ruben, ed. 2007. "Formen und Gattungen als Medien der Jesus-Erinnerung: Zur Rückgewinnung der Diachronie in der Formgeschichte des Neuen Testaments." In *Die Macht der Erinnerung*, edited by Ottmar Fuchs and Bernd Janowski, 131–67. JBT 22. Neukirchen-Vluyn.

———. 2008. *Hermeneutik der Gleichnisse Jesu: Methodische Neuansätze zum Verstehen urchristlicher Parabeltexte.* WUNT 231. Tübingen (Studienausgabe 2011).

———. 2009. "Die Ethico-Ästhetik der Gleichnisse Jesu: Ethik durch literarische Ästhetik am Beispiel der Parabeln im Matthäus-Evangelium." In *Jenseits von Indikativ und Imperativ*, edited by Friedrich Wilhelm Horn and Ruben Zimmermann, 235–65. WUNT 238. Tübingen.

———. 2012a. "Are There Parables in John? It Is Time to Revisit the Question." *JSHJ* 9: 243–76.

———. 2012b. "Bildworte/Bildreden/Bildersprache." WiBiLex. http://www.bibelwis senschaft.de/stichwort/50003/.

———. 2013. "Gleichnisse/Parabeln Jesu." In *Handbuch Bibeldidaktik,* edited by Mirjam Zimmermann and Ruben Zimmermann, 196–201. Tübingen.

———. 2014a. "Fable III. NT." In *EBR* 8:650–51.

———. 2014b. "Metaphorology and Narratology in Q Exegesis: Literary Methodology as an Aid to Understanding the Q Text." In *Metaphor, Narrative, and Parables in Q,* edited by Dieter T. Roth, Ruben Zimmermann, and Michael Labahn, 3–30. WUNT 315. Tübingen.

———, ed. ²2015. *Kompendium der Gleichnisse Jesu.* Gütersloh.

———. 2015a. *Puzzling the Parables of Jesus: Methods and Interpretation.* Minneapolis.

———. 2015b. "The Woman in Labor (John 16:21) and the Parables in the Fourth Gospel." In *The Gospel of John as Genre Mosaic,* edited by Kasper B. Larsen. SANT 3. Göttingen.

———. 2017. *Parabeln in der Bibel: Die Sinnwelten der Gleichnisse Jesu entdecken.* Gütersloh.

———. Forthcoming. *Parabeln der Bibel: Die Sinnwelten der Gleichnisse Jesu entdecken.* Gütersloh.

Zwickel, Wolfgang. 2013. "Der See Gennesaret in hellenistischer und frührömischer Zeit." *ZNW* 104: 153–76.

Contributors

Sven-Olav Back, adjunct professor of New Testament exegesis and lecturer in biblical languages and exegesis, Åbo Akademi University, Finland.

Knut Backhaus, professor of New Testament exegesis and biblical hermeneutics, Department of Catholic Theology, Ludwig Maximillians University of Munich, Germany.

Reinhard von Bendemann, professor of New Testament, Department of Protestant Theology, Ruhr University Bochum, Germany.

Albrecht Beutel, professor of church history, Department of Protestant Theology, University of Münster, Germany.

Darrell L. Bock, senior research professor of New Testament studies, Dallas Theological Seminary, USA.

Martina Böhm, professor of biblical exegesis and early Jewish religious history, Department of Protestant Theology, University of Hamburg, Germany.

Cilliers Breytenbach, emeritus professor of New Testament with a focus on the religion, literature, and history of early Christianity, Department of Theology, Humboldt University of Berlin, Germany; extraordinary professor of New Testament and ancient studies, Stellenbosch University, South Africa.

James Carleton Paget, senior lecturer in New Testament studies, University of Cambridge; fellow and tutor of Peterhouse, UK.

James G. Crossley, professor of Bible, society, and politics, Centre for the Social-Scientific Study of the Bible, St. Mary's University, Twickenham, London, UK.

Lutz Doering, professor of New Testament and ancient Judaism and director for the Institutum Judaicum Delitzschianum, Department of Protestant Theology, University of Münster, Germany.

Martin Ebner, emeritus professor of New Testament exegesis, Department of Catholic Theology, Rhenish Friedrich Wilhelm University of Bonn, Germany.

Craig A. Evans, John Bisagno Distinguished Professor for Christian Origins and dean of the School of Christian Thought, Houston Baptist University, USA.

Jörg Frey, professor of New Testament studies with a focus on ancient Judaism and hermeneutics, Department of Theology, University of Zurich, Switzerland; research associate, Department of Theology, North-West University, Potchefstroom, South Africa.

Yair Furstenberg, associate professor of rabbinic literature, Jewish History Department, Ben Gurion University of the Negev, Beer Sheva, Israel.

Simon Gathercole, reader in New Testament studies, University of Cambridge, UK.

Christine Gerber, professor of New Testament, Department of Theology, Humboldt University of Berlin, Germany.

Katharina Heyden, professor of the ancient history of Christianity and interreligious encounters, Department of Theology, University of Bern, Switzerland.

Friedrich W. Horn, emeritus professor of New Testament, Department of Protestant Theology, Johannes Gutenberg University of Mainz, Germany.

Stephen Hultgren, lecturer in New Testament, Australian Lutheran College, University of Divinity, Adelaide, Australia.

Christine Jacobi, lecturer in New Testament, Department of Theology, Humboldt University of Berlin, Germany.

Jeremiah J. Johnston, associate professor of Christian origins, Houston Baptist University, USA.

Thomas Kazen, professor of biblical studies, Stockholm School of Theology, Sweden.

Chris Keith, research professor of theology, University of Notre Dame Australia; research professor of New Testament and early Christianity, St. Mary's University, Twickenham, London, UK.

John S. Kloppenborg, professor and chair, Department for the Study of Religion, University of Toronto, Canada.

Bernd Kollmann, professor of New Testament exegesis and theology, Department of Philosophy, University of Siegen, Germany.

Michael Labahn, assistant professor, Protestant Theology University, Amsterdam, Netherlands; extraordinary associate professor, Department of Theology, North-West University, Potchefstroom, South Africa.

Hermut Löhr, professor of New Testament, Department of Protestant Theology, Rheinische Rhenish Friedrich Wilhelm University of Bonn, Germany.

Steve Mason, distinguished professor of ancient Mediterranean religions and cultures, Qumran Institute and Faculty of Theology and Religious Studies, University of Groningen, Netherlands.

Tobias Nicklas, professor of New Testament exegesis and hermeneutics, Department of Catholic Theology, University of Regensburg, Germany.

Markus Öhler, professor of New Testament studies, Department of Protestant Theology, University of Vienna, Austria.

Martin Ohst, professor of historical and systematic theology, Department of Humanities and Cultural Studies (Protestant Theology), University of Wuppertal, Germany.

Karl-Heinrich Ostmeyer, professor of New Testament, Institute of Protestant Theology, Technical University of Dortmund, Germany.

Rachel Schär, research assistant, division of ancient history of Christianity and interreligious encounters, Department of Theology, University of Bern, Switzerland.

Eckart David Schmidt, lecturer in New Testament, Department of Theology, Ruprecht Karl University of Heidelberg, Germany.

Jens Schröter, professor of New Testament exegesis and theology and ancient Christian apocrypha, Department of Theology, Humboldt University of Berlin, Germany.

Daniel R. Schwartz, professor of Jewish history, Hebrew University of Jerusalem, Israel.

Markus Tiwald, professor of New Testament, Department of Catholic Theology, University of Vienna, Austria.

David du Toit, professor of New Testament, Department of Protestant Theology, Friedrich Alexander University of Erlangen, Germany.

Joseph Verheyden, professor of New Testament, Catholic University of Leuven, Belgium.

Samuel Vollenweider, emeritus professor of New Testament, Department of Theology, University of Zurich, Switzerland.

Ulrich Volp, professor of church and dogmatic history with a focus on ancient church history, Department of Protestant Theology, Johannes Gutenberg University of Mainz, Germany.

Annette Weissenrieder, professor of New Testament, Department of Theology, Martin Luther University of Halle-Wittenberg, Germany.

Michael Wolter, emeritus professor of New Testament, Department of Protestant Theology, Rhenish Friedrich Wilhelm University of Bonn, Germany.

Jürgen K. Zangenberg, professor of the history and culture of ancient Judaism and early Christianity, University of Leiden, Netherlands.

Christiane Zimmermann, professor of New Testament theology and literature, Christian Albrechts University of Kiel, Germany.

Ruben Zimmermann, professor of New Testament, Department of Protestant Theology, Johannes Gutenberg University of Mainz, Germany; research associate, Faculty of Theology, University of the Free State, Bloemfontein, South Africa.

Index of Authors

Index of Subjects

abba, 144, 219, 247, 359, 362–63, 397–400, 521
Abraham, 298, 310, 441, 503, 546
acclamation, 129, 294, 331, 463, 509, 511
Acts of the Apostles, 141, 155, 214, 242, 262, 281, 285–86, 374–75, 402, 513
Adam, 21, 546, 549, 561
admonition, 415–16, 419, 421
Aenon near Salim, 138, 234
Agabus, 529
agrapha, 125, 131, 153–54, 412, 542
Agrigent, 320
Akhmim, 536
Albinus, 162, 208
Alcimus, 193
Alexander Balas, 193
Alexander Jannaeus, 174, 183, 194, 202, 228
Alexander the Great, 181–82, 192, 208, 276, 300, 322
alms, 412, 436–37, 441, 449
Ammanitis, 192
Amon, 276
Ananus II, 162–64
Andrew, 82, 139, 270, 279–80, 533
Andronicus, 532
angel, 203, 277, 285, 310, 320, 325–26, 386, 493, 510, 520, 537
Anna, 110, 327
Annas, 138
Anointed One. *See* messianism/Messiah (Anointed One)
anointing/ointment, 163, 177, 199, 240, 284, 289, 293, 317, 325, 327, 332, 335–36, 341, 348, 512, 515–19, 521, 526. *See also* messianism/Messiah (Anointed One)
Anthronges, 206

anthropology, anthropological, 95, 100, 105, 308, 321, 497, 502, 555–58
Antigonus Mattathias, 174, 184–85
anti-Judaism, anti-Jewish, 379, 401
Antiochus III, 182, 192–93
Antiochus IV/Epiphanes, 182, 186, 193–94, 322, 496, 518
Antipater, 184, 206
antitheses, 86, 340, 405, 427, 430, 433–34
aphorism, 107, 126, 131
apocalyptic, 46, 88, 98–99, 100, 101, 103, 107, 126, 129, 130, 199, 205, 236, 244, 309, 361, 391, 401, 414, 417, 420, 439, 443, 462, 482, 490, 494, 500–503, 508, 541–42, 551
apocrypha, apocryphal, 24, 49, 69, 122–23, 152–54, 213, 241, 247, 287, 329, 440, 487–88, 490, 502, 528, 534, 542
Apollo, 544
Apollos, 532
apostle, 18–19, 21, 23, 31, 132–34, 141, 148–49, 152, 210, 258, 266, 271–75, 277–79, 281–82, 284–87, 329, 371, 375, 469, 502, 526–29, 531–33, 542–44, 545–51; apostolic council, 527–28; the twelve apostles, 57, 99, 110, 271, 276–87, 371, 526–28, 531
appearances of the Risen One, 10, 126, 131, 135, 141, 263, 275, 285, 488–502, 527, 530. *See also* resurrection/raising
archaeology, archaeological, 6, 8, 82, 94, 101, 105, 121, 152, 166–69, 171, 173–74, 197–98, 208, 216, 225, 228, 238, 240, 250, 337, 437, 442
Archelaus, 175, 179, 187–90, 206, 208, 233, 419
Aretas IV, 246
Aristobulus I, 194, 227, 337

Index of Scripture and Other Ancient Sources

667

ANCIENT JEWISH WRITERS